# International Directory of
# COMPANY HISTORIES

# International Directory of
# COMPANY HISTORIES

## VOLUME 115

*Editors*

**Derek Jacques and Paula Kepos**

**ST. JAMES PRESS**
*A part of Gale, Cengage Learning*

GALE
CENGAGE Learning™

Detroit • New York • San Francisco • New Haven, Conn • Waterville, Maine • London

**International Directory of Company Histories, Volume 115**

**Derek Jacques and Paula Kepos, Editors**

Project Editor: Miranda H. Ferrara

Editorial: Virgil Burton, Donna Craft, Louise Gagné, Peggy Geeseman, Julie Gough, Sonya Hill, Keith Jones, Matthew Miskelly, Lynn Pearce, Laura Peterson, Holly Selden

Production Technology Specialist: Mike Weaver

Imaging and Multimedia: John Watkins

Composition and Electronic Prepress: Gary Leach, Evi Seoud

Manufacturing: Rhonda Dover

Product Manager: Jenai Drouillard

Cover Photograph: Alvin Ailey American Dance Theater, New York. ©Thaddeus Jacques.

For product information and technology assistance, contact us at **Gale Customer Support, 1-800-877-4253.** For permission to use material from this text or product, submit all requests online at **www.cengage.com/permissions.** Further permissions questions can be emailed to **permissionrequest@cengage.com**

Gale
27500 Drake Rd.
Farmington Hills, MI, 48331-3535

LIBRARY OF CONGRESS CATALOG NUMBER 89-190943
ISBN-13: 978-1-4144-4726-1
ISBN-10: 1-4144-4726-4

This title is also available as an e-book
ISBN-13: 978-1-55862-778-9  ISBN-10: 1-55862-778-2
Contact your Gale, a part of Cengage Learning sales representative for ordering information.

BRITISH LIBRARY CATALOGUING IN PUBLICATION DATA
International directory of company histories, Vol. 115
Derek Jacques and Paula Kepos
33.87409

Printed in the United States of America
1 2 3 4 5 6 7 14 13 12 11 10

# Contents

# *Preface*

The St. James Press series *The International Directory of Company Histories* (*IDCH*) is intended for reference use by students, business people, librarians, historians, economists, investors, job candidates, and others who seek to learn more about the historical development of the world's most important companies. To date, *IDCH* has profiled more than 10,985 companies in 115 volumes.

## INCLUSION CRITERIA

Most companies chosen for inclusion in *IDCH* have achieved a minimum of US$25 million in annual sales and are leading influences in their industries or geographical locations. Companies may be publicly held, private, or nonprofit. State-owned companies that are important in their industries and that may operate much like public or private companies also are included. Wholly owned subsidiaries and divisions are profiled if they meet the requirements for inclusion. Entries on companies that have had major changes since they were last profiled may be selected for updating.

The *IDCH* series highlights 25% private and nonprofit companies, and features updated entries on approximately 35 companies per volume.

## ENTRY FORMAT

Each entry begins with the company's legal name; the address of its headquarters; its telephone, toll-free, and fax numbers; and its web site. A statement of public, private, state, or parent ownership follows. A company with a legal name in both English and the language of its headquarters country is listed by the English name, with the native-language name in parentheses.

The company's founding or earliest incorporation date, the number of employees, and the most recent available sales figures follow. Sales figures are given in local currencies with equivalents in U.S. dollars. For some private companies, sales figures are estimates and indicated by the abbreviation *est*. The entry lists the exchanges on which the company's stock is traded and its ticker symbol, as well as the company's NAICS codes.

Entries generally contain a *Company Perspectives* box which provides a short summary of the company's mission, goals, and ideals; a *Key Dates* box highlighting milestones in the company's history; lists of *Principal Subsidiaries, Principal Divisions, Principal Operating Units, Principal Competitors*; and articles for *Further Reading*.

American spelling is used throughout *IDCH*, and the word "billion" is used in its U.S. sense of one thousand million.

## SOURCES

Entries have been compiled from publicly accessible sources both in print and on the Internet such as general and academic periodicals, books, and annual reports, as well as material supplied by the companies themselves.

## CUMULATIVE INDEXES

*IDCH* contains three indexes: the **Cumulative Index to Companies**, which provides an alphabetical index to companies profiled in the *IDCH* series, the **Index to Industries**, which allows researchers to locate companies by their principal industry, and the **Geographic Index**, which lists companies alphabetically by the country of their headquarters. The indexes are cumulative and specific instructions for using them are found immediately preceding each index.

## SPECIAL TO THIS VOLUME

This volume of *IDCH* contains entries on the Blue Note Label Group, the venerable jazz label which produced albums for such artisits as Miles Davis, John Coltrane, and Thelonius Monk, and Millicom International Cellular S.A., a pager and cell phone service pioneer based in Luxembourg.

## SUGGESTIONS WELCOME

Comments and suggestions from users of *IDCH* on any aspect of the product as well as suggestions for companies to be included or updated are cordially invited. Please write:

The Editor
*International Directory of Company Histories*
St. James Press
Gale, Cengage Learning
27500 Drake Rd.
Farmington Hills, Michigan 48331-3535

St. James Press does not endorse any of the companies or products mentioned in this series. Companies appearing in the *International Directory of Company Histories* were selected without reference to their wishes and have in no way endorsed their entries.

# Notes on Contributors

**Stephen V. Beitel**
Writer and copyeditor based in East Amherst, New York.

**Joyce Helena Brusin**
Writer and essayist; contributor to the *Encyclopedia of World Governments*.

**Ed Dinger**
Writer and editor based in Bronx, New York.

**Melissa Doak**
Writer and editor based in Ithaca, New York.

**Louise B. Ketz**
Author, editor, book producer, and literary agent based in New York City; contributor to *Scribner Encyclopedia of American Lives*.

**Eric Laursen**
Writer and editor based in Buckland, Massachusetts.

**Michael L. Levine**
Writer and editor based in New York City.

**Mary C. Lewis**
Chicago–based editorial services professional specializing in reference books, educational publishing, copyediting, and developmental editing.

**Judson MacLaury**
Retired historian of the U.S. Department of Labor; author of *To Advance Their Opportunities* (2008) and of numerous articles, reviews, and encyclopedia entries.

**Stephen Meyer**
Writer and editor based in Missoula, Montana.

**Margaret L. Moser**
Writer based in New York City; licensed attorney, former COO of boutique financial consulting firm, and onetime actor and director.

**Grace Murphy**
Writer based in upstate New York with specialties in health care, business, and reference.

**Marie O'Sullivan**
Researcher, writer, and editor based in Ireland; expertise includes international education, student mobility, and globalization; editor and writer for the IIEPassport Study Abroad Directories.

**Roger Rouland**
Writer and scholar specializing in company histories, literary criticism, literary essays, and poetry; freelance photographer specializing in nature photography.

**Helga Schier**
Writer, editor, and translator (German/English) based in Los Angeles.

**Hanna Schonthal**
Massachusetts-based writer and editor.

**Roger K. Smith**
Writer and writing instructor in Ithaca, New York; contributor to the *Gale Encyclopedia of World History: Governments*, CQ Press's *Political Handbook of the World*, and other reference titles.

# List of Abbreviations

€ European euro
¥ Japanese yen
£ United Kingdom pound
$ United States dollar

**A**

**AB** Aktiebolag (Finland, Sweden)
**AB Oy** Aktiebolag Osakeyhtiot (Finland)
**A.E.** Anonimos Eteria (Greece)
**AED** Emirati dirham
**AG** Aktiengesellschaft (Austria, Germany, Switzerland, Liechtenstein)
**aG** auf Gegenseitigkeit (Austria, Germany)
**A.m.b.a.** Andelsselskab med begraenset ansvar (Denmark)
**A.O.** Anonim Ortaklari/Ortakligi (Turkey)
**ApS** Amparteselskab (Denmark)
**ARS** Argentine peso
**A.S.** Anonim Sirketi (Turkey)
**A/S** Aksjeselskap (Norway)
**A/S** Aktieselskab (Denmark, Sweden)
**Ay** Avoinyhtio (Finland)
**ATS** Austrian shilling
**AUD** Australian dollar
**Ay** Avoinyhtio (Finland)

**B**

**B.A.** Buttengewone Aansprakeiijkheid (Netherlands)
**BEF** Belgian franc

**BHD** Bahraini dinar
**Bhd.** Berhad (Malaysia, Brunei)
**BND** Brunei dollar
**BRL** Brazilian real
**B.V.** Besloten Vennootschap (Belgium, Netherlands)

**C**

**C. de R.L.** Compania de Responsabilidad Limitada (Spain)
**C. por A.** Compania por Acciones (Dominican Republic)
**C.A.** Compania Anonima (Ecuador, Venezuela)
**C.V.** Commanditaire Vennootschap (Netherlands, Belgium)
**CAD** Canadian dollar
**CEO** Chief Executive Officer
**CFO** Chief Financial Officer
**CHF** Swiss franc
**Cia.** Compagnia (Italy)
**Cia.** Companhia (Brazil, Portugal)
**Cia.** Compania (Latin America [except Brazil], Spain)
**Cie.** Compagnie (Belgium, France, Luxembourg, Netherlands)
**CIO** Chief Information Officer
**CLP** Chilean peso
**CNY** Chinese yuan
**Co.** Company
**COO** Chief Operating Officer
**Coop.** Cooperative
**COP** Colombian peso

**Corp.** Corporation
**CPT** Cuideachta Phoibi Theoranta (Republic of Ireland)
**CRL** Companhia a Responsabilidao Limitida (Portugal, Spain)
**CZK** Czech koruna

**D**

**D&B** Dunn & Bradstreet
**DEM** German deutsche mark (W. Germany to 1990; unified Germany to 2002)
**Div.** Division (United States)
**DKK** Danish krone
**DZD** Algerian dinar

**E**

**E.P.E.** Etema Pemorismenis Evthynis (Greece)
**EC** Exempt Company (Arab countries)
**Edms. Bpk.** Eiendoms Beperk (South Africa)
**EEK** Estonian Kroon
**eG** eingetragene Genossenschaft (Germany)
**EGMBH** Eingetragene Genossenschaft mit beschraenkter Haftung (Austria, Germany)
**EGP** Egyptian pound
**Ek For** Ekonomisk Forening (Sweden)
**EP** Empresa Portuguesa (Portugal)

**ESOP** Employee Stock Options and Ownership
**ESP** Spanish peseta
**Et(s).** Etablissement(s) (Belgium, France, Luxembourg)
**eV** eingetragener Verein (Germany)
**EUR** European euro

**F**
**FIM** Finnish markka
**FRF** French franc

**G**
**G.I.E.** Groupement d'Interet Economique (France)
**gGmbH** gemeinnutzige Gesellschaft mit beschraenkter Haftung (Austria, Germany, Switzerland)
**GmbH** Gesellschaft mit beschraenkter Haftung (Austria, Germany, Switzerland)
**GRD** Greek drachma
**GWA** Gewerbte Amt (Austria, Germany)

**H**
**HB** Handelsbolag (Sweden)
**HF** Hlutafelag (Iceland)
**HKD** Hong Kong dollar
**HUF** Hungarian forint

**I**
**IDR** Indonesian rupiah
**IEP** Irish pound
**ILS** Israeli shekel (new)
**Inc.** Incorporated (United States, Canada)
**INR** Indian rupee
**IPO** Initial Public Offering
**I/S** Interesentselskap (Norway)
**I/S** Interessentselskab (Denmark)
**ISK** Icelandic krona
**ITL** Italian lira

**J**
**JMD** Jamaican dollar
**JOD** Jordanian dinar

**K**
**KB** Kommanditbolag (Sweden)
**KES** Kenyan schilling
**Kft** Korlatolt Felelossegu Tarsasag (Hungary)
**KG** Kommanditgesellschaft (Austria, Germany, Switzerland)
**KGaA** Kommanditgesellschaft auf Aktien (Austria, Germany, Switzerland)
**KK** Kabushiki Kaisha (Japan)
**KPW** North Korean won
**KRW** South Korean won
**K/S** Kommanditselskab (Denmark)
**K/S** Kommandittselskap (Norway)
**KWD** Kuwaiti dinar
**Ky** Kommandiitiyhtio (Finland)

**L**
**L.L.C.** Limited Liability Company (Arab countries, Egypt, Greece, United States)
**L.L.P.** Limited Liability Partnership (United States)
**L.P.** Limited Partnership (Canada, South Africa, United Kingdom, United States)
**LBO** Leveraged Buyout
**Lda.** Limitada (Spain)
**Ltd.** Limited
**Ltda.** Limitada (Brazil, Portugal)
**Ltee.** Limitee (Canada, France)
**LUF** Luxembourg franc

**M**
**mbH** mit beschraenkter Haftung (Austria, Germany)
**Mij.** Maatschappij (Netherlands)
**MUR** Mauritian rupee
**MXN** Mexican peso
**MYR** Malaysian ringgit

**N**
**N.A.** National Association (United States)
**N.V.** Naamloze Vennootschap (Belgium, Netherlands)
**NGN** Nigerian naira
**NLG** Netherlands guilder
**NOK** Norwegian krone
**NZD** New Zealand dollar

**O**
**OAO** Otkrytoe Aktsionernoe Obshchestve (Russia)
**OHG** Offene Handelsgesellschaft (Austria, Germany, Switzerland)
**OMR** Omani rial
**OOO** Obschestvo s Ogranichennoi Otvetstvennostiu (Russia)

**OOUR** Osnova Organizacija Udruzenog Rada (Yugoslavia)
**Oy** Osakeyhtiö (Finland)

**P**
**P.C.** Private Corp. (United States)
**P.L.L.C.** Professional Limited Liability Corporation (United States)
**P.T.** Perusahaan/Perseroan Terbatas (Indonesia)
**PEN** Peruvian Nuevo Sol
**PHP** Philippine peso
**PKR** Pakistani rupee
**P/L** Part Lag (Norway)
**PLC** Public Limited Co. (United Kingdom, Ireland)
**PLN** Polish zloty
**PTE** Portuguese escudo
**Pte.** Private (Singapore)
**Pty.** Proprietary (Australia, South Africa, United Kingdom)
**Pvt.** Private (India, Zimbabwe)
**PVBA** Personen Vennootschap met Beperkte Aansprakelijkheid (Belgium)
**PYG** Paraguay guarani

**Q**
**QAR** Qatar riyal

**R**
**REIT** Real Estate Investment Trust
**RMB** Chinese renminbi
**Rt** Reszvenytarsasag (Hungary)
**RUB** Russian ruble

**S**
**S.A.** Sociedad Anónima (Latin America [except Brazil], Spain, Mexico)
**S.A.** Sociedades Anônimas (Brazil, Portugal)
**S.A.** Société Anonyme (Arab countries, Belgium, France, Jordan, Luxembourg, Switzerland)
**S.A. de C.V.** Sociedad Anonima de Capital Variable (Mexico)
**S.A.B. de C.V.** Sociedad Anónima Bursátil de Capital Variable (Mexico)
**S.A.C.** Sociedad Anonima Comercial (Latin America [except Brazil])
**S.A.C.I.** Sociedad Anonima Comercial e Industrial (Latin America [except Brazil])

**S.A.C.I.y.F.** Sociedad Anonima Comercial e Industrial y Financiera (Latin America [except Brazil])

**S.A.R.L.** Sociedade Anonima de Responsabilidade Limitada (Brazil, Portugal)

**S.A.R.L.** Société à Responsabilité Limitée (France, Belgium, Luxembourg)

**S.A.S.** Societe Anonyme Syrienne (Arab countries)

**S.A.S.** Societá in Accomandita Semplice (Italy)

**S.C.** Societe en Commandite (Belgium, France, Luxembourg)

**S.C.A.** Societe Cooperativa Agricole (France, Italy, Luxembourg)

**S.C.I.** Sociedad Cooperativa Ilimitada (Spain)

**S.C.L.** Sociedad Cooperativa Limitada (Spain)

**S.C.R.L.** Societe Cooperative a Responsabilite Limitee (Belgium)

**S.E.** Societas Europaea (European Union Member states

**S.L.** Sociedad Limitada (Latin America [except Brazil], Portugal, Spain)

**S.N.C.** Société en Nom Collectif (France)

**S.p.A.** Società per Azioni (Italy)

**S.R.L.** Sociedad de Responsabilidad Limitada (Spain, Mexico, Latin America [except Brazil])

**S.R.L.** Società a Responsabilità Limitata (Italy)

**S.R.O.** Spolecnost s Rucenim Omezenym (Czechoslovakia

**S.S.K.** Sherkate Sahami Khass (Iran)

**S.V.** Samemwerkende Vennootschap (Belgium)

**S.Z.R.L.** Societe Zairoise a Responsabilite Limitee (Zaire)

**SAA** Societe Anonyme Arabienne (Arab countries)

**SAK** Societe Anonyme Kuweitienne (Arab countries)

**SAL** Societe Anonyme Libanaise (Arab countries)

**SAO** Societe Anonyme Omanienne (Arab countries)

**SAQ** Societe Anonyme Qatarienne (Arab countries)

**SAR** Saudi riyal

**Sdn. Bhd.** Sendirian Berhad (Malaysia)

**SEK** Swedish krona

**SGD** Singapore dollar

**S/L** Salgslag (Norway)

**Soc.** Sociedad (Latin America [except Brazil], Spain)

**Soc.** Sociedade (Brazil, Portugal)

**Soc.** Societa (Italy)

**Sp. z.o.o.** Spólka z ograniczona odpowiedzialnoscia (Poland)

**Ste.** Societe (France, Belgium, Luxembourg, Switzerland)

**Ste. Cve.** Societe Cooperative (Belgium)

**T**

**THB** Thai baht

**TND** Tunisian dinar

**TRL** Turkish lira

**TTD** Trinidad and Tobago dollar

**TWD** Taiwan dollar (new)

**U**

**U.A.** Uitgesloten Aansporakeiijkheid (Netherlands)

**u.p.a.** utan personligt ansvar (Sweden)

**V**

**V.O.f.** Vennootschap onder firma (Netherlands)

**VAG** Verein der Arbeitgeber (Austria, Germany)

**VEB** Venezuelan bolivar

**VERTR** Vertriebs (Austria, Germany)

**VND** Vietnamese dong

**VVAG** Versicherungsverein auf Gegenseitigkeit (Austria, Germany)

**W–Z**

**WA** Wettelika Aansprakalikhaed (Netherlands)

**WLL** With Limited Liability (Bahrain, Kuwait, Qatar, Saudi Arabia)

**YK** Yugen Kaisha (Japan)

**ZAO** Zakrytoe Aktsionernoe Obshchestve (Russia)

**ZAR** South African rand

**ZMK** Zambian kwacha

**ZWD** Zimbabwean dollar

# A.G. Spanos Companies

**10100 Trinity Parkway, Fifth Floor**
**Stockton, California 95219**
**U.S.A.**
**Telephone: (209) 478-7954**
**Fax: (209) 473-3703**
**Web site: http://www.agspanos.com/**

*Private Company*
*Founded:* 1951 as A.G. Spanos Agricultural Catering
*Incorporated:* 1956 as A.G. Spanos Catering, Inc.
*Employees:* 600
*Sales:* $1.13 billion (2009)
*NAICS:* 236220 Commercial and Institutional Building
Construction

■ ■ ■

Based in Stockton, California, A.G. Spanos Companies is a family-owned developer and builder of commercial buildings, multifamily properties, and master-planned communities. Spanos also pursues mixed-use development and offers property management services. Regional division offices are located in Arizona, Colorado, Florida, Georgia, Kansas, Nevada, South Carolina, Texas, and northern and southern California. By 2010, after a half-century in operation, Spanos had constructed more than 120,000 apartments, 400 developments, and some 2 million square feet of office space. The company was founded by Alexander Gus Spanos, a self-made billionaire who is better known as the owner of the San Diego Chargers of the National Football League and a major contributor to the Republican Party. The team and Spanos Companies are run by his sons, Dean and Michael Spanos.

## FOUNDER BORN IN 1923

Alex Spanos was born in Stockton, California, the eldest son of Greek immigrants. Starting at the age of eight he began working at the family restaurant and bakery, awaking at 4:00 a.m. in order to put in several hours of work before attending school, a routine he and his brothers would follow through high school. His father was a man bound by Greek tradition, a taskmaster who had a lasting influence on Spanos, despite their sometimes strained relationship. In 1942 Alex Spanos quit college, the California Polytechnic State University, where he was to become an engineer to satisfy his father's desires, in order to serve in the Army Air Force during World War II. His father expressed his disappointment by transferring his affection to the next oldest son.

Following his discharge from the service in 1946, Spanos returned home to attend the College of the Pacific and resumed working in his father's bakery. He also married and began raising a family. Frustrated by his father's refusal to give him a raise in pay, Spanos quit in 1951. His father did not speak to him for the next two years. Desperate to find a way to support his growing family, Spanos decided to sell sandwiches from a truck to the many agricultural workers that filled the area during harvest season each year. He sought a bank loan of $1,500 to launch his business but was only able to secure $800.

## CATERING BUSINESS LAUNCHED: 1951

On a shoestring budget, Spanos launched A.G. Spanos Agricultural Catering in the summer of 1951, acquiring a used panel truck, slicing machine, meat cleaver, bread, bologna, and condiments. He and his wife made the sandwiches at home and then sold them to area farmers who were happy to feed them to their workers, deducting the cost from their wages. Thus, Spanos easily sold the 250 sandwiches he prepared each day. Not only did the farmers buy his sandwiches, they asked him if he knew where they could find more Mexican laborers, *braceros*, who at the time could legally work in the United States provided they returned home after the harvest.

Sensing a business opportunity, Spanos took a bus to Mexico where by chance he met a man who was recruiting braceros for many of the farmers on Spanos's sandwich route. Spanos then obtained a contract to house and feed 350 workers who were to be bused into the Stockton area. Spanos hurried home, and without any money at his disposal, he quickly arranged to rent the massive exhibition hall of the San Joaquin County Fair and install beds, kitchen equipment, and tables. For bed and board, Spanos was paid $1.75 per worker per day, which provided him with a $1 profit per man per day. When the harvest season came to an end, Spanos had banked $35,000.

The following year, Spanos expanded his business, taking advantage of an old army barracks at the Stockton Metropolitan Airport that included a mess hall. He also hired Mexican cooks and purchased a tortilla machine to provide traditional dishes to the braceros. He was now able to house and feed 1,500 workers, a number that would grow to 7,000 in a matter of five years, resulting in net income of $700,000 per year. It was so lucrative a business, in fact, that Spanos was paying an increasing amount of taxes, prompting his accountant in 1956 to advise that he invest in real estate to take advantage of available tax shelters.

## REAL ESTATE INVESTMENT BEGINS: 1956

Spanos began dabbling in real estate, spending $530,000 on three properties in 1956. He also began buying and selling land at a profit. Spanos next turned his attention to construction. Working with a friend of a friend, he became involved in apartment buildings and motels. Also in 1956, Spanos incorporated his catering business as A.G. Spanos Catering, Inc.

Spanos began to change his focus in 1960 as favorable conditions for the catering business began to erode. Not only was the bracero program coming under fire from unions objecting to the loss of American jobs, but harvesting was becoming increasingly mechanized. Moreover, Spanos found that the catering business created a high tax liability, despite his real estate tax shelters. In order to lower his taxes further, Spanos realized he would have to construct his own buildings in order to take advantage of depreciation provisions in the tax code. As a result, Spanos exited the catering business, and his company changed its name to A.G. Spanos Construction. To compensate for a lack of knowledge, he hired an experienced Stockton building contractor, Al Toccoli, to handle the construction of his initial project.

With California's population increasing at a rapid pace, resulting in a housing shortage, it was an excellent time to be an apartment builder. The first project for Spanos Construction was a 24-unit apartment building that cost $200,000 to complete. It also served as a classroom for Spanos, who observed every step of the nine-month construction process. Called the Bali Hai, the South Pacific–themed property was an instant success. Taking advantage of this experience, Spanos took complete charge of his second project, a sister property to the Bali Hai called the Outrigger, which cost $350,000 to complete.

With another success to his credit, Spanos now built his first office building, located in downtown Stockton. He also entered the retail market, completing his first shopping center in Tracy, California, called the McKinley Village Center. Although in time the area would become a popular San Francisco Bay area bedroom community, Tracy was not yet large enough to adequately support McKinley Village, which never reached an occupancy rate above 50 percent, and Spanos finally sold the property at a loss in 1973.

## PROPERTY PORTFOLIO LIQUIDATED: 1968

Spanos enjoyed continued success with his multifamily projects. Taking on 50-50 partners, he acquired land north of Stockton and a year later completed a mixed-use project on Robinson Drive that included an office

## KEY DATES

**1951:** Alex Spanos launches a catering business serving agricultural workers.
**1960:** After evolving into real estate and development, the company is renamed A.G. Spanos Construction.
**1977:** Spanos is the leading apartment builder in the United States.
**1984:** Alex Spanos acquires the San Diego Chargers professional football team.
**2008:** Alex Spanos retires due to declining health; his sons Dean and Michael Spanos assume control of the company.

building that became the Spanos corporate headquarters. From that point forward, Spanos no longer took on equal partners, although he would accept limited partners and percentage partners on some projects. He soon had high-end projects spread across northern California, but the flush times came to an abrupt end in 1968 when a recession hit.

Spanos found that although he possessed considerable real estate holdings, he was cash poor. He put his properties on the block and sold them for $10 million cash. It was more than enough to finance his retirement, but Spanos instead plotted how to put that money to use in pursuing a new phase in his construction career. This time, however, he vowed not to fall in love with his properties and hold onto them, recognizing that selling buildings as quickly as possible was the key to amassing profits. In addition, Spanos decided to no longer cater to the top 10 percent of the market, but to serve the masses. Rather than skimp on quality, he simply built smaller apartments within larger complexes.

During the early 1970s Spanos branched out beyond northern California, first to Reno, Nevada, where he hoped to build a casino, and then to Las Vegas, where he built a number of successful office buildings and apartment complexes. Spanos was joined in 1972 by his oldest son, Dean, after his graduation from the University of the Pacific. The younger Spanos headed up a new division in Florida, where the family had a home in Tampa. Nevertheless, it was the first time the Spanos operation would be doing business so far from its base in California and Nevada, and Dean Spanos, despite working summers for his father's construction company, was inexperienced. A seasoned area contractor was hired to take charge and serve as a men-

tor to the young Spanos on the construction of an office project in Clearwater, Florida.

Through the Clearwater project Alex Spanos met Jerry Reinsdorf, who introduced him to real estate syndication. The two men began doing business together, with Reinsdorf's Balcor real estate syndication company acquiring many of Spanos's properties. Over the years they would do more than $1 billion in business together. Success in Florida also led to the opening of divisions in Atlanta and Houston, and by the mid-1970s Spanos had in place a national expansion program, with the exception of the Northeast, which because of its winter weather he believed was not an ideal market for construction. By 1977 the company was the largest apartment builder in the United States.

## OWNERSHIP OF SAN DIEGO CHARGERS: 1984

A second son, Michael Spanos, joined the family business in 1981 after college graduation. By mid-decade, after 25 years involved in construction, the Spanos companies had built more than 2.5 million square feet of commercial property and 46,000 residential units. There were also division offices in 15 states. Major changes in the tax code were in the offing, however, ones that would eliminate long-used tax shelters. Spanos was quick to recognize the changing conditions and swiftly divested all of his unsold properties as well as $40 million worth of land on which the company planned to build apartments. It proved to be a wise decision.

Cashing out also allowed Spanos to pursue a childhood dream of owning a professional sports team. After failing in bids to purchase the San Francisco 49ers and Tampa Bay Buccaneers of the National Football League in the late 1970s and then passing up on a chance to buy Major League Baseball's Oakland Athletics, Spanos finally acquired the NFL's San Diego Chargers in 1984, paying $40.3 million for a 56-percent controlling interest as well as an additional $8 million to make up for a deficit. In 1994 he appointed his son Dean to run the Chargers' organization.

## CONTROL TRANSFERRED TO YOUNGER GENERATION: 2008

Although the Chargers became a preoccupation, construction remained the core business for the Spanos family. In 1990 a recession adversely impacted the building business. For the next three years the Spanos Companies did not build a single project yet did not lay off any personnel. Salaries were cut and then restored when the economy improved. Construction projects resumed, and Spanos moved into new markets, such as the Carolinas. By the end of the 1990s, Spanos was building as many as 15,000 apartment units per year and generating annual profits of more than $235 million. As the market retreated in the early part of the new century due to a downturn in the economy, Spanos was quicker than most to cut back.

Entering his eighties, Spanos turned over increasing control of the family enterprises to his sons and essentially retired. Dean Spanos served as president of A.G. Spanos Companies and the Chargers, while Michael served as executive vice president of both operations. With more than $1 billion to his name, Alex Spanos was among those listed by *Forbes* as the country's wealthiest people. Money could not, however, preserve his health. In late 2008 the 85-year-old Spanos made public a letter that revealed he was suffering from the deteriorating effects of dementia, and he expressed his love to his wife and children while his faculties still permitted. As for the Spanos Companies, they were in the experienced hands of his two sons and well positioned for ongoing growth.

*Ed Dinger*

## PRINCIPAL DIVISIONS

Arizona; Colorado; Florida; Georgia; Kansas/Missouri; Nevada; New York & North Carolina; Northern & Central California; Texas.

## PRINCIPAL COMPETITORS

Castle & Cooke, Inc.; The Irvine Company; SunCor Development Company.

## FURTHER READING

"Alex Spanos," *Greek America Magazine*, March–April 2008.

Beard, Alison, "Real Estate Tycoon Constructs a Platform for Long-term Success," *Financial Times*, April 16, 2002, p. 29.

Highfill, Bob, "Spanos' Revealing Letter," *Record (Stockton, California)*, December 29, 2008.

Lambrou, Evan C., "Dean Spanos: Stepping out of His Father's Shadow," *National Herald*, June 14, 2008, p. 1.

Sontakay, Arati, "Spanos Enters Market with 610 Apartments," *Charlotte Business Journal*, February 14, 1997.

Spanos, Alex, *Sharing the Wealth: My Story*, Washington, D.C.: Regnery Publishing, Inc., 2002, 254 p.

# ACEA S.p.A.

**Piazzale Ostiense 2**
**Rome, 00154**
**Italy**
**Telephone: (+39 06) 06 5799 1**
**Fax: (+39 06) 5758 095**
**Web site: http://www.aceaspa.it/**

*Public Company*
*Founded:* 1909 as Azienda Elettrica Municipale
*Employees:* 511
*Revenues:* €2.89 billion ($3.53 billion) (2009)
*Stock Exchanges:* Milan
*Ticker Symbol:* ACE
*NAICS:* 221122 Electric Power Distribution; 221210 Natural Gas Distribution; 221310 Water Supply and Irrigation Systems

■■■

Based in Rome, ACEA S.p.A. is Italy's largest municipal utility company and is involved in both energy and water. Besides generating, selling, and distributing power to more than 2.7 million homes and businesses in the Rome area, ACEA develops renewable sources of energy, distributes natural gas, and owns a district heating facility powered by a cogeneration plant. The company also designs and manages public and artistic lighting for roads, museums, monuments, and archaeological sites in Rome, Naples, and other parts of the country. As a provider of drinking water to more than 7 million people, ACEA is Italy's largest water utility. It manages water services in Rome as well as in Frosinone, Pisa,

Siena, Grosseto, Florence, and Sarnese Vesuviano. The company also provides laboratory, research, and consulting services related to water and is involved in aqueducts, sewage, purification, and other integrated water services. Moreover, it holds basic waterworks concessions in Colombia, Peru, Honduras, and the Dominican Republic.

## COMPANY FOUNDED: 1909

ACEA dates its founding to 1909, when the Rome City Council formed Azienda Elettrica Municipale (AEM) to municipalize control of the generation and distribution of electricity for public street and private household lighting. A private power plant had first been constructed in Rome in 1886 to provide electricity, but soon new technology that made the long-distance delivery of power possible led to the opening of a hydroelectric power station at Tivoli, the largest plant of its type in Europe at the time. The electricity it generated was transported 17 miles to Rome, where it powered public street and private household lighting and tramways.

In 1907 Ernesto Nathan, a progressive and controversial figure, was chosen as the new mayor of Rome. During his six years in office he took many steps to modernize Rome. Under his leadership the sanitation system was vastly improved and the city's death rate became one of the lowest in Europe. He also took on private monopolies. He assumed control of the tramways for the city and spearheaded the creation of AEM to seize control of the generation and distribution of electricity. At the same time he and the city council laid plans for a new power station in the city. In 1912 AEM opened the Montemartini Power Station, the first publicly funded power generation plant in the city. In 1917 a 3,000-kilowatt steam turbine was installed, and in 1924, 6,000-kilowatt turbine was set in place.

## SURVIVING THE WAR AND AFTER: 1937–85

AEM became involved in water in 1937, when the governor of Rome charged the company with the responsibility of building and managing the city's aqueducts and water distribution system. Because of the change in its mandate, the company was renamed Azienda Governatoriale Elettricità e Acque (AGEA; Gubernatorial Enterprise for Electricity and Water). That same year the company began work on the Peschiera aqueduct, which would become one of the largest water facilities in all of Europe. In 1938 the responsibility for the Vergine, Felice, and Paolo aqueducts was also transferred to AGEA. A fourth aqueduct, Acqua Marcia, remained under private control through a 99-year concession issued by the pope in 1865 to the British company Società Acqua Pia Antica Marcia (SAPAM; Anglo Roman Water Company), which renovated and operated the ancient aqueduct.

By the time AGEA took shape, Italy had long been under the control of Italian fascists led by the prime minister turned dictator Benito Mussolini. He launched massive public works projects, but he also made the misstep of siding with Nazi Germany during World War II. Italy was devastated by the conflict, and Mussolini was deposed and eventually executed. When the war came to an end in 1945, Rome could only rely on the Montemartini Power Station for electricity. By sheer chance, it was the only power plant in the city to emerge undamaged from the war, and it played a key role in Rome's recovery. Also in 1945 AGEA became Azienda

Comunale Elettricità e Acque (ACEA; Municipal Enterprise for Electricity and Water).

ACEA expanded its operations to keep pace as Rome grew during the postwar years. Besides new power stations and an expanded distribution network, ACEA added the Acqua Marcia aqueduct in 1964 after SAPAM's concession expired. As a result, ACEA controlled all four aqueducts supplying water to Rome and became the city's lone operator. In 1985 ACEA assumed control of the city water treatment operations, which served more than 3 million people.

## COMPANY EVOLUTION AND POLITICS: 1989–96

ACEA changed its name to Azienda Comunale Energia e Ambiente (Municipal Enterprise for Energy and Environment) in 1989, and three years later it made the conversion from a Municipal Company to a Special Status Company. As was the case when the company was founded at the start of the century, there was a change in the way utilities were viewed. What was once an attractive alternative to private monopolies was now seen as operations that lacked an entrepreneurial spirit. A new mayor of Rome appointed Francesco Rutelli to head ACEA and gave him the mandate to pursue a partial privatization of the utility in an effort to improve finances and make a greater financial contribution to the city's treasury.

ACEA's transformation continued in August 1996, when the governing executive of the Rome City Council approved converting ACEA into a Società per Azioni (S. p.A.; joint stock corporation). With this change, ACEA could take advantage of opportunities in some types water services outside of Rome that were being liberalized. The conversion of a stock corporation was not the same thing as privatization, however. There were politicians on both the left and the right of the political spectrum who opposed selling even a portion of the company. As a result, the transformation of ACEA took place at a measured pace. Studies were commissioned and recommendations were made. Most of the consultants suggested that Rome pursue partial privatization, with the city selling part of ACEA. This idea was met with approval. By contrast, a smaller number of consultants recommended that Rome split the energy and water assets, forming two separate enterprises to unlock the value and potential of ACEA's operations. This idea was rejected.

## EXPANDING BEYOND THE CITY OF ROME: 1998–2002

The Rome City Council approved ACEA's switch to a joint stock corporation in March 1997, and the change

## KEY DATES

**1909:** Azienda Elettrica Municipale is established in Rome.
**1937:** The company takes over Rome's aqueducts and water distribution system.
**1964:** ACEA assumes control of the Acqua Marcia aqueduct.
**1998:** ACEA becomes a joint-stock company.
**1999:** ACEA becomes a publicly traded company.

became official on January 1, 1998. The partial privatization plan also called for the sale of 49 percent of ACEA, a move that provided a $1 billion windfall to the city without ceding control of the company. Thus, a public stock offering was completed in July 1999 and afterward ACEA's shares were listed on the Milan Stock Exchange. Private shareholders were allowed to own no more than 3 percent of the company. In 2004 this was increased to 10 percent.

With greater flexibility, ACEA was able to grow on a number of fronts as the new century dawned. The company bought into local water companies to expand within Italy. It also forged an alliance with GDF Suez, a large energy and water company that was partially owned by the French government. Italy was an attractive market for foreign companies because it had insufficient power capacity, which made Italian electricity the most expensive power in western Europe. To avoid political problems, outside companies looked for Italian partners, and ACEA was an ideal candidate for a major player such as Suez.

In 2002 ACEA and the Suez subsidiary Electrabel established a joint venture to seek out opportunities in the Italian electricity and gas markets. All of ACEA's power generation assets were transferred to a new power generation company. The joint venture also resulted in the creation of a sales and trading company and a holding company. That same year Electrabel and ACEA took over the management of the entire sewage system in Rome. They were also selected by META S.p.A., Modena's municipally owned multiutility, to serve as a minority partner in joint ventures in energy, water, and waste management. Furthermore, ACEA teamed up with the U.S.-based National Fuel Gas Co. to build a new gas-fired power plant in Montenero di Bisaccias in the Italian region of Molise.

## CHANGE IN A NEW CENTURY: 2003–10

ACEA decided to venture beyond power and water into telecommunications. In light of the liberalization of the Italian telecommunications market, ACEA forged a joint venture with Spain's Telefonica called Atlanet to pursue opportunities in Italy and elsewhere. The worldwide telecommunications sector soon experienced a severe slump, however. In 2003 ACEA decided to exit the field and wrote off its entire investment in Atlanet, with losses totaling €108 million. The move into the telecommunications sector had been well received by investors, who bid up the price of ACEA's stock, but when the sector collapsed the company's stock price plummeted. Its share price did not begin to rebound and enjoy a steady rise until late 2003.

Returning all of its focus to energy and water, ACEA launched in 2004 a 10-year, €750 million program to upgrade Rome's electricity distribution network. A year later a 10-year, €100 million plan to upgrade Rome's public lighting system was begun. In 2006 the company entered the waste-to-energy business by acquiring Tad Energia e Ambiente. ACEA also began installing electronic meters to replace outdated electromechanical meters in Rome. In 2008 the company implemented a €2 billion investment plan that would support all of ACEA's growth strategies during the next four years.

In 2009 ACEA celebrated its centenary. In light of the global economic recession that began in late 2007, the company reconsidered its four-year business plan and made changes to the 2010–12 period. Nevertheless, its board of directors reiterated a desire to grow all aspects of the business. In late 2009 ACEA and Suez entered talks regarding the reorganization of their Italian operations. When the year came to a close, ACEA reported revenues of €2.9 billion, compared with €3.1 billion the year before. The company also posted a loss of €52.5 million in 2009 after netting €186.3 million in 2008. With its future relationship with Suez under review and market conditions that remained challenging, ACEA's short-term prospects were uncertain.

*Ed Dinger*

## PRINCIPAL OPERATING UNITS

Energy; Water.

## PRINCIPAL COMPETITORS

A2A S.p.A.; Edison S.p.A.; Società Italiana per il Gas pA.

## FURTHER READING

"ACEA to Launch against Rosy Italian Backdrop," *Euroweek*, May 7, 1999, p. 16.

"ACEA Sale Shows Depth of Demand for Italian Assets," *Euroweek*, July 16, 1999, p. 17.

"Confidential Report Analyses ACEA's Future," *Privatisation International*, October 1996, p. 17.

"Electrabel and Acea Move Closer," *Modern Power Systems*, June 2002, p. 12.

"Ex-mayor Nathan Dies in Rome at 75," *New York Times*, April 11, 1921, p. 10.

"Italian Power Supply Still Short of Demand," *Asia Africa Intelligence Wire*, September 29, 2004.

Lobina, Emanuele, and Daniele Iacovitti, "Watertime Case Study—Rome, Italy," European Commission, January 1, 2005, http://www.docstoc.com/docs/18389959/Rome-Case-Study---WaterTime.

"Rome Utility Ready for the Market," *Privatisation International*, September 1996, p. 20.

# Altera Corporation

—■—

**101 Innovation Drive**
**San Jose, California 95134**
**U.S.A.**
**Telephone: (408) 544-7000**
**Toll Free: (800) 767-3753**
**Fax: (408) 544-6403**
**Web site: http://www.altera.com**

*Public Company*
*Founded:* 1983
*Incorporated:* 1984
*Employees:* 2,600
*Sales:* $1.2 billion (2009)
*Stock Exchanges:* NASDAQ
*Ticker Symbol:* ALTR
*NAICS:* 334413 Semiconductor and Related Device
Manufacturing; 334515 Instrument Manufacturing
for Measuring and Testing Electricity and Electrical
Signals; 511210 Software Publishers

■ ■ ■

Altera Corporation is a leading developer of high-density programmable logic devices (PLDs) and field-programmable gate arrays (FPGAs) based on metal-oxide semiconductor technology (CMOS). These logic chips are circuits used in a variety of devices to produce electrical signals. The technology associated with programmable logic chips requires less power than that associated with other chips, and the programmable logic chips are more efficient than custom logic chips, reduc-

ing development time and time-to-market. In addition to PLDs and FPGAs, Altera also creates software that enables its customers to program standard integrated circuits (ICs). Altera's products are sold to makers of communications, computer, and industrial equipment. In addition to its extensive network of North American operations, the company has distributors in all European and major Asian markets.

## THE BIRTH OF THE ERASABLE, REPROGRAMMABLE CHIP: 1983–88

Altera began in 1983 under the guidance of Rodney Smith, a British applications engineer and then a manager for Fairchild Semiconductor. Joining Smith as founding members were four others with considerable semiconductor industry experience: Robert Hartmann, James Sansbury, Paul Newhagen, and Michael Magranet. The name "Altera" was introduced in 1984, standing for the word "alterable." That year the company introduced its first generation of chips.

Altera's sales strategy from the beginning has been to offer a range of standard, programmable parts for the IBM PC AT, IBM's second-generation personal computer, with inexpensive development tools, allowing customers to self-design and program custom logic circuits that meet their specific needs. This strategy was formulated to meet the industry need created by the delay associated with custom chips, due to the high percentage of silicon designs that require revision toward the end of the design cycle. With erasable, reprogrammable chips, revision can proceed immediately and repeatedly until all design bugs have been eliminated. A relationship with Intel Corp. began in August 1984, when the companies agreed to swap certain designs. In 1985 Intel began to market a group of Altera's logic microchips.

## ALTERA GOES PUBLIC

In 1988 Altera went public, and calendar sales for the year reached $38 million. The company also purchased a minority interest in Cypress Semiconductor's wafer fabrication facility (fab) and introduced a new generation of chips. The company launched the industry's first erasable programmable logic device (EPLD), which provided a complete interface to the PS2's Micro Channel Bus. This new device allowed vendors to save time and board space. New EPLD programming software, which was usable on IBM PC AT and compatible computers, accompanied the device. Later that year, Altera came forth with another innovation, MAX (multiple-array matrix), new architecture for ultraviolet erasable programmable logic devices that doubled the timing and quadrupled the density of previous EPLD arrays that used what is known as "and/or" architecture. The new devices presented up to 5,000 gates, system speeds of up to 40 MHz, and over 200,000 unique programmable elements. Because the structure of the new PLDs differed so much from previous PLD devices, which used the "and/or" architecture, Altera offered a tool-kit addition to speed up the learning curve for designers. The package, which was workable on IBM PC ATs and compatibles, contained a graphics-design editor, a design-processing engine, a timing simulator, and programming software modules, all controlled by a supervisor task-control module.

Altera's key competitor, Xilinx, introduced similar technology in 1988. Altera was no longer alone in its market niche of programmable logic. Altera's relationship with Xilinx would be a heated rivalry over the coming years.

## ALTERA EXPANDS INTO JAPAN: LATE EIGHTIES TO EARLY NINETIES

The U.S. semiconductor market during the 1980s was dominated by five large companies: Advanced Micro Devices, Inc., Intel Corp., Motorola, Inc., National Semiconductor Corp., and Texas Instruments, Inc. However, companies such as Altera and Xilinx were seen as formidable upstarts. Altera consistently ranked among the top five public semiconductor companies in the categories of net profits and gross margins, which reached an impressive 60 percent. The company had been able to carve a niche by specializing in the top-notch design of PLDs and spending its research-and-design budget on new product development. In 1989 sales rose 55 percent to $59 million, with $11 million net.

Looking primarily to Japan, Altera stepped up its overseas sales techniques in 1989. Lacking a Japanese office or distributor, the company hired two distributors with unique entrepreneurial approaches to aggressively promote Altera's product line to the Japanese market. The majority of Japanese sales were handled by JMC, a nine-year-old company led by Haruki Kamiyama. Kamiyama, the youngest member of a Japanese trade delegation that visited the United States around this time, was an entrepreneur committed to selling U.S. technology in Japan. Altera's other Japanese distributor, Paltek, focused primarily on market development. Because almost all semiconductor business in Japan is conducted through distributors (unlike in the United States, where 75 percent of business is done directly with customers), these two distributors were key to Altera's 1989 growth in Japanese business. By 1990, 15 percent of the company's business came from sales in Japan.

Sales in 1990 were $78.3 million, a 33 percent increase, with net income of $13.4 million. In June of that year, Altera made its first cash investment in a fabrication facility. The company invested $7.4 million in Cypress Semiconductor's plant in Round Rock, Texas. In exchange they received guaranteed IC production capability, a portion of the fab's CMOS capacity, access to next-generation products as they come on line, and the right to purchase up to 20 percent of the fab over time. Altera was already producing Cypress's line of programmable logic devices, SRAMs, and other products, and Cypress received the rights to Altera's next generation of MAX products. Rodney Smith, president of Altera, told *Computer Design* that the production purchasing option with Cypress would save Altera approximately $30 million in construction costs over sharing production with another vendor. Although

## KEY DATES

**1983:** Altera is founded by Robert Hartmann, Michael Magranet, Paul Newhagen, and Jim Sansbury; British applications engineer Rodney Smith joins later in 1983 as chairman, president, and CEO.

**1988:** Altera goes public; sales for the year reach $38 million.

**1989:** Altera establishes a Japanese market for its products, which helps to push sales up 55 percent over the previous year.

**1992:** A class-action lawsuit is filed against Altera, alleging violations of federal security laws.

**1994:** The class-action lawsuit is settled out of court; Altera purchases Intel's programmable logic device (PLD) business.

**1996:** Altera brings to market the industry's largest-capacity chip, the 10K 100, which has 10 million transistors.

**2000:** Altera acquires Northwest Logic, a privately held company that provides system-design services; John Daane replaces Rodney Smith as Altera's CEO; the company rolls out the Excalibur family of embedded-processor solutions.

**2001:** Altera forges a partnership with Nuvation Labs Corporation, a leading engineering-design firm.

**2006:** Altera comes under investigation by the Securities and Exchange Commission (SEC) on charges of irregular stock-option practices.

**2009:** Altera unveils the Stratix IV field-programmable gate array (FPGA), designed to assist with high-bandwidth technologies.

Altera had never before entered into this type of relationship with a fab, the company already had exchange and foundry agreements with Intel, Texas Instruments, and Sharp. These arrangements enabled the company to continue producing state-of-the-art chips with no production facilities.

Altera's partners also benefit from these relationships. For example, Texas Instruments used Altera's erasable programmable logic chip to design a compact, high-resolution video camera that was flexible enough to be used under different lighting systems. Its uses included closed-circuit security, industrial inspection,

and monitoring systems. The chip proved a low-cost, high-yield option.

In 1991 another new chip generation was introduced. The Max 7000 family of ultraviolet-erasable programmable logic devices provided between 4,000 and 40,000 gates, increasing up to five times the capacity of previous high-density programmable chips. Sales surpassed the $100 million mark, reaching $106.9 million, with net income of $17.8 million.

### CHALLENGES DURING THE EARLY NINETIES

The year 1992 included the development of another new chip generation as well as a series of challenges for Altera. The slowdown of Japanese business caused by overseas economic conditions, as well as competitive pricing by rival companies, led Altera to drop its chip prices. A drop in sales brought the company down to $101.5 million, with net income of only $11.5 million. The crisis was short-lived, however, as sales in Japan increased by 87 percent in 1993. Altera's Japanese sales accounted for about 20 percent of business. NEC was the company's largest customer, and Matsushita, Sony, Mitsubishi Electric, and Toshiba were among the company's biggest clients. Altera's Japanese-bound chips primarily serviced two types of products: telecommunications equipment, including digital telephone exchanges and cellular telephone base stations, and professional audio-visual equipment, such as portable camcorders. Also in 1992 a class-action lawsuit was filed against Altera. It included some current and former officers and directors. The suit alleged violations of federal security laws and was settled out of court in July 1994.

Overall 1993 revenues surged to $140.3 million, with an 84 percent increase in net income to $21.2 million. That year the company invented a system to protect delicate leads from ruin during burn-in and test processes and after customer purchase. The device also reduced time to market by facilitating programming and prototyping. The company developed two compatible sockets as well, one for use on PC boards and the other for programming EPLDs in carriers.

As new products aged, manufacturing costs went down, and Altera was able to drop prices on its products over time. In 1993 such a discount was passed on to Altera's customers, with 30 percent price cuts on the volume-driven FLEX 8000 family of PLDs. At the end of 1993 both Altera and Xilinx introduced Pentium-compatible products, seeking to migrate programmable array logic (PAL) markets toward programmable logic device solutions. Altera's product targeted the high-density macrocell portion of the PLD business, while

Xilinx's product was aimed at the low-density segment. Altera also released the MAX 7000E family of complex PLDs, which featured architectural improvements of circuit performance of complex PLDs and enhanced routability and usability features. At this time, Altera was the number-three volume manufacturer of programmable CMOS logic devices, with a 15 percent market share. Ahead of Altera was Advanced Micro Devices, and in the number-one position was competitor Xilinx, with a 24 percent share.

For Altera, 1994 was a year characterized by new product innovations and an ongoing effort to beat the competition with presence in new market segments. Seeking to gain a lead, Altera increased its market share to 20 percent in 1994 with the purchase of Intel's PLD business, for about $50 million in cash and stock. In addition, the Intel acquisition delivered new customers and 15 new products to Altera. Altera established itself as a programmable logic vendor, supporting Microsoft's Windows NT operating system by releasing MAX PLUS II version 4.0, representing a shift to the fully 32-bit software environment. MAX PLUS II incorporates VHDL, a very-high-speed integrated circuit hardware description language synthesis. This VHDL standard was promoted when eleven companies joined to form Analog VHDL International (AVI), an industry group that helped develop the IEEE 1076.1 standard (the analog extension of VHDL).

## ALTERA BATTLES XILINX: 1994–95

Altera also made a first step into the reconfigurable hardware products market in 1994. The company introduced a high-capacity programmable logic add-in board for PCs, called the Re-configurable Interconnect Peripheral Processor (RIPP 10). This ISA bus board supported up to 100,000 gates of reconfigurable logic, allowing up to eight Altera FLEX 8188 devices. The company also put forth the industry's highest-density single-die device, the 16,000-gate EPF51500 PLD, which was immediately followed by Xilinx's introduction of a 25,000-gate device. In April the company introduced the largest-capacity PLD on the market and the first off-the-shelf PLD/MCM, the 50,000-gate PLD multichip module PEF8050M, to support ASIC prototyping, imaging applications, and reconfigurable hardware products (RHPs).

In June 1994 both Altera and Xilinx brought forth products moving their devices to an unprecedented five-nanosecond pin-to-pin delay time range. Xilinx targeted new markets with faster devices, while Altera's EPM7032 was aimed at applications requiring logic integration in systems with next-generation microprocessors. In July Altera made its first overtures to the military market, offering four PLDs compliant with military standards. Although defense spending was decreasing, a new emphasis on upgrading existing programs made design engineers receptive to off-the-shelf solutions to integrate system features into smaller board space while keeping design costs low. As add-in card designers began to look toward PCI-compliant PLDs, both Xilinx and Altera claimed to introduce the industry's first programmable logic devices that were fully compliant with the peripheral component interconnect (PCI) specification.

In August 1994 competitor Advanced Micro Devices (AMD) filed a lawsuit against Altera. AMD charged Altera with violating six of AMD's programmable logic device technology patents. Altera followed with a countersuit, stating that AMD infringed upon at least two, and perhaps as many as six, of Altera's PLD patents. The case would be decided against AMD in 1996. Another suit had been initiated against Altera by Xilinx in June 1993, also regarding patent infringement. Altera filed a separate suit against Xilinx, and the case continued to boomerang with multiple countersuits probing the company patents over the next couple of years. In 1994 Xilinx continued to lead the CMOS PLD market with a 29 percent share, while Altera retained 18 percent, followed by AMD with 16 percent.

Another innovation in the MAX family, the MAX 9000 architecture, was introduced in October 1994. The 9000 family more than doubled the density of currently available EPLDs, reaching system speeds of up to 80 MHz and increasing cell utilization. Sales in 1994 neared $200,000, with almost 50 percent of revenues derived from foreign sales. Data communications and telecom customers made up about 44 percent of sales. The $58 million increase in sales over 1993 represented the largest one-year increase in Altera's history. International semiconductor shipments reached $100 billion, along with sales of CMOS PLDs (the newly preferred method for implementing logic design).

In 1995 Altera came out with its MAX 9000 family of erasable PLDs. After a 30 percent drop in the price of the MAX 7000 family of erasable PLDs, the company's sales burst to more than twice the previous year's, reaching an incredible $401.6 million, with $86.9 million in net income. By this time Altera had 881 employees, as compared with 370 just five years earlier. Also in 1995 Altera and Xilinx announced that their chips could service the lucrative $3 billion DSP semiconductor market, competing with dedicated and general-purpose DSP chips. Altera introduced flexible logic element matrix (FLEX) 10,000, a programmable logic architecture that sent the market over the 100,000-gate barrier. The device was created with an architecture that

Altera called a "sea of programmable bits," using the embedded/standard logic block combination.

The company put a new face on an old model in 1995, augmenting the three-year-old MAX 7000 line with the MAX 7000S family. This new line of CPLDs was based on a new 0.5 micron, triple-layer metal process developed with Altera's foundry partners. Since its introduction in 1992 when it generated $5 million in sales, the MAX 7000 had grown to an $80 million sales product by 1994, making it Altera's most successful CPLD line. Also in 1995, while industry reports bemoaned longer lead times in the field programmable gate array (FPGA) market, Altera announced that it had reduced lead times for two devices, the 12,000-gate EPF81188A and 16,000-gate EPF81500A, from 20 weeks to 10 weeks.

Altera and Xilinx once again were neck-and-neck in their announcements of industry landmark products, with Xilinx's introduction of the industry's fastest FPGA and Altera's announcement of the highest gate count FPGA shipped in volume.

## PARTNERSHIPS IN THE MID-NINETIES

Joining six intellectual property providers, Altera launched the Altera Megafunctions Partners Program (AMPP) in August 1995. Megafunctions are hardware description language (HDL)-based designs of system-level functions that may be compiled in MAX-PLUS II software and targeted to Altera's device architectures. This new alliance was charged with the development of synthesizable function blocks for Altera's PLDs. The five other partners in AMPP (Eureka Technology, CAST Inc., RAVIcad, Silicon Engineering, and Advacel) were provided with access to Altera's 21,000 design seats.

In another partnership development, Altera entered into a U.S. joint venture wafer fabrication site with foundry partner Taiwan Semiconductor Manufacturing Corp. (TSMC). The site was located in Camas, Washington. The agreement caused TSMC to displace Sharp as Altera's biggest wafer supplier. Later, the companies were joined by Analog Devices and Integrated Silicon Solutions, Inc., forming a joint venture company named WaferTech.

The industry's largest capacity chip was introduced by Altera in 1996. The 10K, 100-capacity chip contained 10 million transistors. Also that year, the company unveiled MegaCore and OpenCore, software programs that allowed engineers to evaluate MegaCore functions prior to licensing them. A major industry slowdown in computers led companies to downsize, and Altera was no exception. An oversupply of inventory

and reduction of chip demand led to revenue decline during the year's first quarter, and the company cut its workforce by 11 percent in June, eliminating about 100 positions. At the same time, the company authorized the repurchase of up to two million company shares.

Forging a new union, Altera joined Synopsis in a five-year agreement to jointly develop and sell designer tools to support complex programmable logic devices (CPLDs). The partnership targeted two market segments: second-wave designers changing to HDL-based designs for CPLDs and FPGAs, and gate-array designers migrating to programmable logic for designs with gate densities of 100,000 or less.

## ON THE VERGE OF A BRIGHT FUTURE: ENTERING THE TWENTY-FIRST CENTURY

In 1983 Altera brought a new idea to the market, introducing the reprogrammable logic device. That innovation became a billion-dollar industry, bustling with competition. By the latter half of the 1990s the PLD market had swelled to more than $2 billion in sales, and Altera was one of the industry's leaders due to the complexity of its chips. The company's success was fueled by its longtime emphasis on research and development over production and by its close customer relationships. At the end of 1998 Altera employed a staff of 1,208 and had $154 million in net income and $654 million in net revenue. Still, the competition was always knocking on Altera's door. In 1998 Altera held a wafer-thin edge over its archrival, Xilinx—31.5 percent vs. 30.3 percent—in the market for programmable logic chips.

Altera and Xilinx have been in a turf war for years, and while their products may seem similar, the inner workings of the two companies are reported to be vastly different. Altera is known in the industry as having a traditional, top-down management style, whereas Xilinx claims to operate by consensus, in which decision making is decentralized and delegated to the workers as much as possible to encourage employee innovation. Altera's CEO, Rodney Smith, describes his management style as demanding but fair. "We ask a lot of people, but we give a lot in return," Smith said in a 1999 article for the trade journal *Electronic Business*. He pointed out that Altera offers a profit sharing and bonus plan, which is unique from others in that it is distributed equally among employees regardless of position.

As the 1990s came to a close, a new competitor emerged from the pack to chase after Altera and Xilinx's dominance of the PLD marketplace. Lattice Semiconductor of Hillsboro, Oregon, became a third-place vendor with 20 percent of an estimated $2.5-billion PLD market by acquiring Vantis Corp. in April 1999. The three companies now accounted for 80 percent of all sales of PLDs.

The year 2000 was marked by Altera's record profits and rapid-fire product-introduction pace. Most significantly, Altera launched the Excalibur family of embedded-processor solutions, which included a range of high-density programmable logic devices with embedded processors. Altera extolled this new product line as creating true system-on-a-programmable-chip (SOPC) solutions for its customers and giving the company a foundation for future growth.

Also in 2000 John Daane took over Rodney Smith's role as Altera's CEO and president. Smith stayed on as the chairman of the board. In a letter to shareholders published in Altera's 2000 annual report, Daane regarded the year as a milestone for the company's long-term goal of capturing the SOPC market. He commented, "Our real competition in this area includes other types of devices, particularly application-specific integrated circuits (ASICs) and application-specific standard products (ASSPs). With the products introduced during 2000, we can now offer a broader range of PLD-based solutions that were previously only possible with ASICs and ASSPs, while adding the benefits of programmability—increased flexibility, the ability to easily differentiate a design, and faster time-to-market." Profits and revenues continued to reach new heights in 2000. Revenue grew 65 percent to $1.38 billion, while income from continuing operations increased 76 percent to $394 million.

As the PLD industry grew and reshaped itself with each new technological advancement, Altera continued to look for ways to stay on top. In September 2000 Altera acquired Northwest Logic, a privately held company specializing in telecommunications, data communications, and embedded processor systems design. Terms of the agreement were not disclosed, but the acquisition was heralded by Altera as its latest strategy to "invest in leading-edge capabilities that enhance its ability to provide solutions to customers." Continuing with that formula the following year, the company forged a partnership with Nuvation Labs Corporation. Altera was banking on Novation's reputation as a leading Silicon Valley engineering design firm to give it an advantage over its competitors in offering faster time-to-market delivery of complex PLDs.

Early in the new century, the Semiconductor Industry Association predicted that the market for programmable logic devices would reach $4.5 billion by 2002. The competitive atmosphere for PLD market share had become fierce. Established companies like Al-tera were forced to remain mindful of innovative upstarts that could bump them from their status as a top-tier semiconductor company. At the same time, Altera continued to battle with old foes like Xilinx, which had recently initiated another legal confrontation with Altera when it asked the U.S. International Trade Commission for an injunction that had the potential to jeopardize the U.S. sales of several major Altera products. Altera dismissed this latest round of legal maneuvering as "saber rattling." To be successful in the long term, Altera's goal was to create even more robust devices while continuing its long-standing business practice of not owning fabrication facilities and of serving three primary segments: communications, electronic data processing, and industrial applications.

## FORGING AHEAD WITH INNOVATION: 2001–10

In the wake of the economic downturn of 2001, growth in the global market for semiconductors slowed dramatically. In forecasting the industry's prospects for 2002, estimates were generally low. Some analysts predicted growth of only 1 percent, while others foresaw a decline of 3 to 4 percent. Throughout the downturn, Altera continued to dominate the global market for PLDs. Along with longtime rival Xilinx, Altera accounted for roughly 80 percent of PLD sales worldwide in 2001.

To maintain its competitive edge, the company continued to devote significant capital to product innovation during the early part of the new century, spending roughly 20 percent of its total sales revenues to research and development in 2001. In April 2002 the company launched a groundbreaking new PLD. Dubbed the Stratix, the new device was designed to perform at faster speeds than any of Altera's earlier PLDs and to make integration between different systems simpler and more efficient. In a press release quoted in the April 22, 2002, issue of *Electronic Engineering Design*, Altera representatives claimed that the company was "redefining programmable logic" with its new Stratix line.

Even as it was placing greater emphasis on product development as the cornerstone of future expansion, Altera continued to seek new ways to expand its global reach. In October 2002 the company established a branch office in Singapore to capitalize on the brisk growth of the semiconductor business in Asia. The company estimated that, by mid-decade, the Southeast Asia region would account for one-fifth of its total revenues, compared with only 13 percent in 2002. By this time, global sales of PLDs had grown to approximately $3.5 billion.

During the first half of 2003 Altera enjoyed strong earnings as sales of its new products, notably the Cyclone and Stratix PLDs, increased by nearly 75 percent. For the year 2003 Altera posted revenues of $827 million and had an international customer base of 14,000. Much of the company's growth was driven by the rapidly expanding Asian market, which by 2003 accounted for roughly 37 percent of the world's semiconductor business. Altera also posted strong sales in Europe during this period, where its regional offices generated approximately a quarter of the company's total revenues. To capitalize on the proven strength of its European operations, the company established a new service center in Cork, Ireland, in August 2004.

During the middle of the decade, however, the company suddenly found itself embroiled in a series of minor scandals. In the first half of 2005 Altera terminated communications with two industry analysts, Chris Danely of J.P. Morgan and Tad LaFountain of Wells Fargo, after they had published reports questioning some of the company's share-buyback practices. After LaFountain publicly announced that he would cease to provide coverage of Altera in his reports, the Securities and Exchange Commission (SEC) launched an investigation to determine whether the company had used intimidation to influence financial reporting. By May 2006 the SEC had also begun investigating the company's stock option policies. In the wake of the inquiry, Altera announced that it would conduct a thorough review of its financial statements during the previous ten-year period.

In spite of these challenges, the company was able to remain focused on improving its product line during the latter part of the decade. In 2006 the company released the Stratix III, a new device designed to offer 20 percent better performance than previous Stratix models. The Stratix IV, a high-speed field-programmable gate array (FPGA) designed for use with high-bandwidth technologies, followed in October 2009. By decade's end, industry studies revealed that bandwidth capability was becoming more vital to future growth than traditional, processor-based technologies. This trend was driven largely by the increased importance of the Internet, as more computing applications, notably gaming and media sharing, shifted to online platforms. With the introduction of the Stratix IV, Altera clearly

demonstrated that it had its hand on the pulse of future technological innovation.

*Heidi Feldman*
*Updated, Suzanne L. Rowe; Stephen Meyer*

## PRINCIPAL SUBSIDIARIES

Altera European Trading Company Limited (Ireland); Altera International, Inc. (Cayman Islands); Altera International Limited (Hong Kong).

## PRINCIPAL COMPETITORS

Actel Corporation; Lattice Semiconductor Corporation; Xilinx, Inc.

## FURTHER READING

"Altera Buys Northwest Logic," *Electronic Engineering Times*, October 2, 2000, p. 81.

"Altera's New CEO Approaches Difficult Position with Optimism," *Electronic Buyer's News*, December 11, 2000, p. 18.

Arnold, Laurence, "SEC Probes Blacklisting of Critical Analysts," *Philadelphia Inquirer*, September 26, 2005, p. D10.

DeTar, Jim, "Altera, Partners Launch PLD Program," *Electronic News*, August 14, 1995, p. 49.

Lammers, David, "Next-gen Architecture Aims to Take PLDs to System Level: Altera Plants Stake in ASIC Turf with Raphael," *Electronic Engineering Times*, August 31, 1998, p. 18.

Lineback, J. Robert, "Altera's Speedy Way to Tailor Add-ons to IBM's PS2," *Electronics*, February 18, 1988, pp. 99–102.

Matsumoto, Craig, "Xilinx Asks ITC to Ban Some Altera Products," *Electronic Engineering Times*, December 11, 2000, p. 4.

Mayer, John H., "Altera Buys into Cypress Fab Capability," *Computer Design*, June 18, 1990, p. 34.

Morgenson, Gretchen, "You'll Never Do Research in This Town Again," *International Herald Tribune*, September 24, 2005, p. 15.

Souza, Crista, "Chip Makers Tout Customizable Socs: Altera Rolls Out Mercury, a PLD Hybrid That Leaves Room for Integration," *Electronic Buyer's News*, February 19, 2001, p. 28.

"Xilinx, Altera Tout Faster, Larger Programmable Devices," *Electronic News*, October 16, 1995, pp. 52–53.

# Alvin Ailey Dance
# Foundation, Inc.

**The Joan Weill Center for Dance**
**405 West 55th Street**
**New York, New York 10019**
**U.S.A.**
**Telephone: (212) 405-9000**
**Fax: (212) 405-9001**
**Web site: http://www.alvinailey.org**

*Nonprofit Company*
*Founded:* 1958
*Incorporated:* 1967 as the Dance Theater Foundation
*Employees:* 130
*Sales:* $20.77 million (2009 est.)
*NAICS:* 711120 Dance Companies

∎ ∎ ∎

Alvin Ailey Dance Foundation, Inc., is the umbrella organization for the Alvin Ailey American Dance Theater, one of the best-known modern dance companies in the United States. Founded by African-American dancer and choreographer Alvin Ailey in 1958, the company was one of the few showcases for black dancers anywhere in the United States. Headquartered in New York, the Alvin Ailey company began touring internationally in 1962. The group has found a devoted following worldwide with its innovative dances, which often explore African-American culture in ways never previously seen. The Alvin Ailey American Dance Theater tours extensively abroad and in the United States. In addition, its junior company, known as Ailey II, tours and performs widely. The Ailey School

teaches dance to thousands of students from the age of three through adults. The school's curriculum is based on the dance techniques of Lester Horton and Martha Graham, and includes ballet, West African dance, and other dance techniques. The Alvin Ailey Dance Foundation also runs an extensive arts in education program, bringing dance to schools through performances, workshops, and artist-in-residence programs. The foundation runs Ailey Camps as well, which teach dance and other skills to underserved children.

## A CAREER SHAPED BY
## HAPPENSTANCE: 1931–53

Alvin Ailey Jr. was born on January 5, 1931, in a wooden cabin in the small southeastern Texas town of Rogers. His mother, Lula Cliff Ailey, and his father, Alvin Ailey Sr., separated when Alvin Jr. was just six months old. For years afterward, Lula Ailey subsisted by taking in washing, picking cotton, and doing cooking and cleaning for white families. Ailey and his mother moved frequently, and the child was often left alone while his mother worked. Alvin spent much of his childhood in Navasota, Texas, and then moved with his mother to Los Angeles in 1942. Young Ailey attended Thomas Jefferson High School, a neighborhood public school that served a mostly African-American, Mexican, Chinese, and Japanese population. The school made a point of introducing its students to the arts, taking them on field trips to see performances in downtown Los Angeles. Ailey first saw a professional ballet troupe in 1945 while on a school trip to a performance by the touring Ballet Russes. Ailey began attending other dance performances, and soon after he met the charismatic

## COMPANY PERSPECTIVES

AADF's mission is to further the pioneering work of Alvin Ailey by establishing an extended cultural community which provides dance performances, training and community programs for all people. This performing arts community plays a crucial social role using the beauty and humanity of the African American heritage and other cultures to unite people of all races, ages and backgrounds.

Katherine Dunham, an African-American woman who starred in an eclectic dance performance called the *Tropical Revue.*

Ailey had friends who were as interested in dance as he was, including Ted Crumb, who was later a member of the Negro Ballet Company, and Carmen de Lavallade, a fellow student at Thomas Jefferson who became a big star on her own and danced with Ailey on Broadway and as a guest with his company. Crumb and de Lavallade steered Ailey to the Lester Horton studios. Lester Horton was a white man who had studied various forms of modern and ethnic dance. He eventually began choreographing his own works, which often dealt with difficult social issues such as police brutality. Horton's works were performed side by side with works of the best-known modern dance companies of the time, including those of Martha Graham and Lincoln Kirstein. Headquartered in Los Angeles, however, Horton was out of the main current, which flowed from New York. He ran a racially diverse studio at a time when the dance world was extremely segregated. Horton's students learned the gamut of putting on a performance, not only dancing but making sets and costumes and writing publicity. Ailey began taking dance classes only reluctantly, first watching his friends dance for about six months. His teachers immediately noticed his talent, but Ailey was shy and unsure whether dance was really for him.

After graduating from high school, Ailey attended the University of California at Los Angeles, intending to major in romance languages. He did not do particularly well in college, but he was not sure he was committed to dance, either. He moved briefly to San Francisco, going to San Francisco State College, and then in 1953 he found a job as a dancer in a Los Angeles nightclub. He continued to study and perform with Lester Horton. Horton's company seemed to be achieving a new level of success. The company was invited to perform in New

York in 1953, and then was invited to the annual summer Jacob's Pillow dance festival in Massachusetts. The company had work lined up when Horton died of a massive heart attack in November 1953. Although Ailey had been ambivalent about his career in dance, with Horton's death he was thrust into a demanding role. He became the group's choreographer, as well as a teacher and one of its star dancers. Within months of Horton's death, Ailey was presenting a show of Horton classics, plus two full-length works of his own. If not for Horton's sudden demise, Ailey might never have realized his own gift for choreography.

### BEGINNING A COMPANY OF HIS OWN IN 1958

In 1954 Ailey went to New York with his friend Carmen de Lavallade to dance in the Broadway show *House of Flowers,* starring Pearl Bailey. Ailey and de Lavallade were featured in a duet, and Ailey had a show-stopping solo. After *House of Flowers* closed, however, there was little work for Ailey, or for other African-American dancers, no matter how talented. An all-African-American show like *House of Flowers* came around only once every five years or so, and many opportunities for white performers were closed to nonwhite dancers. Ailey taught dance classes and worked sporadically, living hand to mouth. In 1958 he decided to put on a performance at the 92nd Street Y, a popular venue for small theater and dance. The idea, in part, was to show off Ailey's choreography, which had not had much outlet since he left Los Angeles, and also to give underemployed African-American dancers something to do. The show was meant as a one-time performance, and Ailey and 13 other dancers approached it casually, rehearsing where they could in various studios between other jobs.

The show premiered Ailey's *Blues Suite,* a dance set in a tawdry bar, showing the kind of people the young Ailey had seen in the small Texas towns where he had lived with his mother. This dance in particular got a huge response from the audience and an ecstatic write-up in the major dance journal *Dance Magazine.* Nine months later Ailey put on another show at the 92nd Street Y, this time to a packed house. Other invitations to perform followed, and Ailey and his dancers began to work together as a company. In 1960 Ailey brought out a new dance, *Revelations,* set to spirituals and depicting moments of religious joy. The work stunned the audience at the Y, the first to see what would become one of the most-performed dance works in the U.S. repertory.

The Ailey company became a recognized force on the U.S. dance scene with the success of *Revelations.* The

## KEY DATES

**1953:** Alvin Ailey Jr. premieres his choreography with the Lester Horton group.

**1954:** Ailey moves to New York for a professional dance career.

**1958:** The company is founded after the first successful performance of Ailey's original works at the 92nd Street Y.

**1962:** The company makes its first international tour.

**1967:** The company incorporates as a nonprofit corporation, the Dance Theater Foundation.

**1978:** At its 20th anniversary, the company has doubled in size and runs the leading dance school in New York.

**1989:** Ailey dies; Judith Jamison takes over as artistic director.

**1993:** The company receives a stabilization grant to straighten out finances.

**2005:** The company opens the Joan Weill Center for Dance, its new home and the largest dance facility in the United States.

**2010:** Robert Battle is appointed new artistic director, to replace retiring Judith Jamison in 2011.

company became a little more organized when it incorporated as a nonprofit corporation, the Dance Theater Foundation. This way, the group became eligible for government and foundation grants. The dance foundation's first office was in Ailey's small apartment.

### GROWTH IN THE SEVENTIES

Alvin Ailey American Dance Theater toured abroad so much in the 1960s that it was better known in Europe than in its own country. In 1968 the group began an extended U.S. tour. Ailey continued to produce works that reflected African-American U.S. culture, at a time of great racial strife. His company featured mainly African-American dancers, although he used white and Asian dancers as well. The group's shows brought rave reviews, and the company got support from grants from the National Endowment for the Arts and from the Rockefeller Foundation. The company completed another domestic tour in 1970, and Ailey collaborated with jazz great Duke Ellington on a ballet for American Ballet Theater. Despite the group's growing fame and the influx of grant money, the company was still barely solvent. At the close of the 1970 season Ailey announced that financial problems would force him to disband the dance company. The company recently had moved to new quarters in the Brooklyn Academy of Music, which proved unsatisfactory, and a promised State Department–sponsored tour of the Soviet Union had been canceled.

The group had many supporters, however, and ultimately it moved back to Manhattan and the Soviet tour was reinstated. The company embarked on another long tour of the United States the next year. The year 1971 also saw the premiere of another Ailey classic, *Cry*, which featured the extraordinary, six-foot-tall dancer Judith Jamison. In new quarters at the American Dance Center on East 59th Street, the company worked relatively comfortably for the next nine years. Ailey established a popular school, and he added two student companies. The company reigned over modern dance in the United States in the 1970s and was lauded on its international tours. By 1978, when the company celebrated its 20th anniversary, the company included 29 dancers, more than twice its original number, and enrollment at the Ailey school was almost 5,000 students. The company's budget had grown to about $3 million annually, and Ailey himself was making a substantial income from choreography commissions and royalties, television appearances, and his salary for directing the company.

group, however, had little money and relied on the charity and volunteer work of friends and well-wishers. The Ailey company's first headquarters was in a donated space at the YWCA on Eighth Avenue and 53rd Street. The company rehearsed, taught classes, and performed in the small space at the Y, known as the Clark Center for the Arts. Ailey's reputation grew in New York, and in 1962 the State Department invited the company to tour Asia. The group spent three months abroad, performing in Australia, Korea, Japan, South Vietnam, the Philippines, Indonesia, Hong Kong, and elsewhere. Afterward, the company performed new dances in New York and traveled through the Midwest and South.

In 1964 Alvin Ailey American Dance Theater toured Europe for the first time. The slew of engagements was handled by a booking agent, while the finances of the company were taken care of by a husband-and-wife team of devoted volunteers. Ailey stopped dancing himself during the mid-1960s and spent all his time on choreography and directing his troupe. He repeatedly announced that he would disband the company, even as its fame grew. In 1967 the

## UPS AND DOWNS IN THE EIGHTIES

Alvin Ailey American Dance Theater gave a command performance for President Jimmy Carter at the White House in 1979, and then flew to Morocco for a New Year's performance at the behest of that country's king. Nevertheless, the company was still running a deficit. When its headquarters building was demolished, it could not afford to build a studio and school to its specifications. Instead it moved into three floors of a midtown building owned by one of its board members. Ailey's health was beginning to fail, and the 1980s were a slower decade for the group than the 1960s and 1970s had been. Ailey was arrested in 1980 for creating a disturbance, apparently while having a mental breakdown. He was released without charge, only to set off a similar incident a few months later. Ailey was apparently increasingly frustrated that his company still had to scrounge for funds and that he was seemingly treated better in Europe than in New York.

Ailey was beset by both mental and physical problems from 1980 on. He was under treatment for manic depression, and he was in pain from arthritis. He continued to choreograph in the 1980s, producing another of his best-loved works in 1984, *For Bird—With Love*. Ailey and his company were feted and honored repeatedly in the 1980s, and they toured both abroad and domestically. Ailey was made Distinguished Professor of Choreography at City University of New York in 1985. In 1986 Philip Morris Companies awarded Ailey's troupe a $300,000 grant to cover two years of touring. In 1987 Ailey was diagnosed with AIDS. Although he continued to travel and undertake new projects, by that time he was clearly very ill. In 1988 the Ailey company's lease expired on the midtown building it had rented, and yet again the group had to scramble to find a suitable space. Ailey died on December 1, 1989.

## FINDING STABILITY IN THE NINETIES

Leadership of the company fell to Judith Jamison, the dancer who had made her mark with Ailey's signature piece, *Cry*. She had left the company in 1980 to pursue her own choreography, but she returned after Ailey's death. She became the company's artistic director, dedicated to keeping the vision of Ailey alive. Alvin Ailey American Dance Theater had always made a point of performing work of other choreographers, and during the 1980s it put on far more non-Ailey works than Ailey originals. It therefore was not necessarily the loss of its chief choreographer that hurt the company most.

Furthermore, despite the Alvin Ailey group's long prominence, the company was still not on a sound financial footing. The company had amassed a deficit of roughly $1 million during the 1980s, and in the early 1990s government funding for dance began to dry up. The company could not continue without some restructuring and a plan for future fundraising. Jamison brought in a new director of development and recruited new trustees (essentially, corporate CEOs) who could contribute $10,000 and take a seat on the foundation's board of directors. In 1993 the company received a grant from the Lila Wallace-Reader's Digest Fund as part of its Art Stabilization Initiative. The grant gave money to the group not for performing or touring but to let it pay off debts. The grant allowed the company to build capital reserves so that its finances would no longer be so unstable.

By the mid-1990s the company was in much better shape. It had paid off its debts, increased its revenue from performances, and found other ways to bring in cash. In 1996 the group brought in $3 million through fundraising, about twice the figure from 1992. The Ailey company also got corporations to underwrite some of its domestic shows, while Philip Morris continued to give money for domestic and international touring. The group also increased its marketing efforts, finding new ways to spread the Ailey name, particularly through outreach programs in schools. The company began unusual co-marketing agreements in 1998, trading its name to corporations for major donations. For example Jaguar became the "official car of Alvin Ailey" (Ailey had long dreamed of owning a Jaguar), and a chain of sports medicine clinics used the Ailey name in its advertising, while giving free physical therapy to Ailey dancers. These various stratagems paid off. By 1998 the company had an operating budget of $12 million, and it managed a $1 million surplus. Jamison said in a December 1991 interview with *Black Enterprise* that for years she had "listened as Alvin struggled with prospective donors on one telephone line and bill collectors on the other." She was determined to ask for and get appropriate funding for her group to avoid that struggle, and she was extremely successful.

In the late 1990s Jamison began to plan for something the company had never been able to afford: a home of its own. Its rented space on West 61st Street was filled to overflowing, and the company was growing weary of having to move suddenly when leases expired. Jamison began working on funding to build a school, studio, and performance space. In 2001 plans were cemented to build a new dance center on 55th Street and Ninth Avenue in Manhattan. New York Mayor Rudolph Giuliani approved a $7.5 million matching grant from the city to the company, surprising many with his generosity. The company broke ground on the center in

2002. Named the Joan Weill Center for Dance, in honor of a generous benefactor, the gleaming, $56 million edifice was dedicated and opened its doors to the public in 2005. It was both the first permanent home for Alvin Ailey and the largest facility devoted exclusively to dance in the United States.

## GLIDING INTO THE TWENTY-FIRST CENTURY

The dance company that moved into the new Weill Center was proving itself more than worthy of the glitzy hall. By 2005 Alvin Ailey was being seen by 21 million fans across the United States and in 68 countries on every inhabited continent. One of the highlights of the early 2000s came when director Jamison carried an Olympic torch for the 2002 games in Salt Lake City, Utah. Jamison had been commissioned to create a new ballet, which the company performed at the Olympic Arts Festival. In 2003, after performing at a White House state dinner, the company embarked on tours of Russia and the United Kingdom. At home, the company's school was annually training 3,000 students from 21 countries, in addition to providing classes for the domestic public, maintaining Ailey II, the long-standing junior troupe, and establishing a bachelor of fine arts program for dancers at Fordham University. Launched in 2005, the Ailey Extension was an innovative new dance and fitness program for the general public that offered dance classes ranging from ballroom to hip-hop.

As the company approached its 50th anniversary, honors and accolades were coming one after the other. In 2001 President George W. Bush awarded Judith Jamison and the Alvin Ailey Dance Foundation each with a National Medal of Arts. This was the first time a dance organization had ever received this prestigious honor. In recognition of Jamison's success in partnering with corporations, she and members of the company opened a 2002 session of the NASDAQ. In 2003 *Worth* magazine recognized the Foundation as one of the top arts organizations and best charities in the United States. In 2004 the U.S. Postal Service issued a first class postage stamp honoring Alvin Ailey. Judith Jamison was elected to the 225th Class of the American Academy of Arts and Sciences. In 2006 the company gave something back to the nation, honoring the Library of Congress with the gift of the Alvin Ailey American Dance Theater Archives.

## AN ANNIVERSARY AND A NEW LEADER

The 50th anniversary of the company was celebrated in 2008 at length and in high style. Highlighted by star African-American performers and entertainers Jessye Norman, Oprah Winfrey, and Wynton Marsalis, the celebratory season at the Weill Center included a world premiere ballet by Mauro Bigonzetti and new productions of landmark Ailey pieces, including the signature work *Revelations*. Following the Weill Center season, the company embarked on a 26-city U.S. tour in honor of the company's first New York performance at the 92nd Street Y on March 30, 1958. A Congressional resolution termed the company a "vital American Cultural Ambassador to the World." As an unplanned grand climax to the celebration, longtime benefactor of American dance Glorya Kaufman pledged $6 million to support the Ailey School and the AileyCamp program for inner-city kids.

Perhaps the biggest surprise of the Golden Anniversary season, however, was Jameson's announcement in February 2008 that she would retire in 2011 and assume the position of Artistic Director Emerita. Now the organization that under her leadership had become probably the world's most successful modern-dance troupe was truly entering a crossroads in its storied history. Its well-established repertory of inspirational works celebrating and showcasing black creativity had impressed the world with the realization that, as critic Patricia Zohn wrote in the *Huffington Post* on February 27, 2009, "dance wasn't just beautiful, it could be an agent for change." At the same time, dance critics were becoming somewhat impatient, not with the quality of the dancing, but with the quality of the material the dancers were given to work with. Alistair Macauley, chief dance critic for the *New York Times*, writing on January 6, 2009, noted that the company had successfully shared aspects of the African-American heritage with a diverse audience. However, he lamented that "a large part of the Ailey experience has also to do with watching the dancers transcend choreography that is at best minor." The critics seemed to be ready for better choreography and a new approach, and patrons like Joan Weill agreed that the company needed to be more edgy.

On April 28, 2010, the company announced that Robert Battle, an innovative 37-year-old choreographer who had a long association with the company, would become the new artistic director and would begin his transition to the post in July 2010 in tandem with Jamison. Battle grew up in Miami, started dancing in high school there, attended the Juilliard School, and joined the Parsons Dance Company in New York City in 1994. Those looking for change at Ailey were probably heartened that Battle seemed poised to breathe new life into the company's dancing. He was quoted in the

*New York Times* on April 29, 2010, as saying, "I like things that sometimes challenge an audience." He announced that he planned to bring in top choreographers from Europe and elsewhere and produce works from other companies. *New York Times* critic Macaulay praised Battle for the excitement in his works and for his ability to show contrasts and multiple things happening on stage simultaneously. Only time would tell whether Battle would display the managerial agility to artistically reinvigorate the smooth-running dance machine that was the Ailey company, while simultaneously maintaining its solid financial footing through the Alvin Ailey Dance Foundation in difficult economic times.

*A. Woodward*
*Updated, Judson MacLaury*

## PRINCIPAL OPERATING UNITS

Alvin Ailey American Dance Theater; Ailey II; The Ailey School; The Ailey Arts in Education and Community Programs; The Ailey Extension.

## FURTHER READING

Barbieri, Kelly, "Alvin Ailey Tour Greeted with Increase in Advanced Ticket Sales," *Amusement Business*, February 14, 2000, p. 5.

DeNitto, Emily, "New Steps Bring Alvin Ailey into the Business of Art," *Crain's New York Business*, December 7, 1998, p. 4.

Dunning, Jennifer, "Ailey Troupe Goes in Search of Big Money," *New York Times*, November 27, 2001, p. E3.

———, *Alvin Ailey: A Life in Dance*. Reading, MA: Addison-Wesley, 1996.

Hruby, Laura, "$15-Million Promised to Dance Group; Other Gifts," *Chronicle of Philanthropy*, December 13, 2001, p. 16.

Macaulay, Alastair, "Ailey Wraps Up Season with Sampler of Classics and Newcomers," *New York Times*, January 6, 2009, p. C1.

Moran, Kate Mattingly, "Giuliani Helps Ailey Get a Home of Its Own," *Dance Magazine*, August 2001, p. 30.

Reiss, Alvin H., "Foundation Support, Board Upgrading Help Top Dance Troupe Achieve Stability," *Fund Raising Management*, January 1997, p. 34.

Ross, B., "Choreographing the Money Dance," *Black Enterprise*, December 1991, p. 82.

Wakin, Daniel J., "Alvin Ailey Company Names a New Leader," *New York Times*, April 29, 2010, p. C1.

# ANSYS

# ANSYS, Inc.

---

275 Technology Drive
Canonsburg, Pennsylvania 15317
U.S.A.
Telephone: (724) 746-3304
Toll Free: (866) 267-9724
Fax: (724) 514-9494
Web site: http://www.ansys.com

*Public Company*
*Founded:* 1970
*Incorporated:* 1970
*Employees:* 1,600
*Sales:* $516.9 million
*Stock Exchanges:* NASDAQ
*Ticker Symbol:* ANSS
*NAICS:* 511210 Software Publishers; 541511 Custom Computer Programming Services; 611420 Computer Training

■ ■ ■

ANSYS, Inc., develops and markets engineering simulation software and technology used by engineers and designers in a wide variety of industries, including aerospace, automotive, biomedical, defense, electronics, energy, and manufacturing. The goal of engineering simulation software is to decrease dramatically the amount of time needed to design and test products. Computer-aided design allows engineers to determine whether a design or an element of it will function as needed without having to build a true working model.

Saving time during the design process saves companies money. The ANSYS software framework "Workbench" provides the foundation upon which the rest of the company's engineering technology is built. The Workbench suite of products provides desktop accessibility beginning with concept design through to final testing. ANSYS distributes its products and provides sales and training support for its customers through a global network of partnerships spread throughout some forty countries, primarily in the United States, Canada, Japan, Germany, and other European countries. ANSYS distributes its software through a licensing program that entitles commercial and educational customers to the latest version of ANSYS in return for an annual fee.

## ANSYS BEGINS AS SASI

ANSYS had its start in 1970 when John Swanson founded Swanson Analysis Systems, Inc., known as SASI, to develop and support ANSYS simulation software. SASI released its first ANSYS software, ANSYS 2.0, in 1971. It was intended for use by engineers to test the strength and durability of a wide variety of products, ranging from golf clubs to airplanes, while they were still in the design phase. Westinghouse Electric Corporation became the new company's first customer.

Evaluation of product durability had important implications for manufacturing companies seeking to minimize product liability issues. ANSYS simulation software allowed designers to examine the strength, elasticity, and other behavior of proposed materials and determine how likely they would be to hold or change

## COMPANY PERSPECTIVES

■

ANSYS is passionate about pushing the limits of its world-class technology, so our customers can turn their design concepts into successful, innovative products.... . ANSYS develops, markets, and supports engineering simulation software used to predict how product designs will operate and how manufacturing processes will behave in real-world environments. The Company continually advances simulation solutions by, first, developing or acquiring the very best technology; then integrating it into a unified and customizable simulation platform that allows engineers to efficiently perform complex simulations involving the interaction of multiple physics; and, finally, providing system services to manage simulation processes and data—all so engineers and product developers can spend more time designing and improving products and less time using software and searching for data.

their shape. It also simulated a material's or a design's likely reaction to heat and cold, electric current, and stress or fatigue. The design evaluation made possible by ANSYS software was known as finite element analysis or FEA.

### A DECADE OF FIRSTS

The 1980s ushered in a period of innovation and growth at SASI. In 1981 the company became the first vendor of FEA software to adapt its software for individual workstations in addition to mainframe computers. In 1983 ANSYS software acquired the capability to examine the electromagnetic capabilities of a material or design. In 1985 SASI became the first commercial vendor of FEA software to offer online customer assistance. In 1987 SASI became the first commercial vendor of FEA software to support color graphics and run on a personal computer.

In 1990 the total revenue generated by the FEA software industry nationally was $287 million. In 1991 SASI employed approximately 153 people and generated some $28 million in annual revenue. By these estimates, 20 years after its founding, SASI controlled about 10 percent of the market for its product and was one of the two oldest FEA software companies in the United States.

### CHANGES IN THE NINETIES

Anticipating additional years of growth, SASI, between 1991 and 1992, introduced the first major revisions to its ANSYS software in a decade. In response to customer feedback, the company enhanced graphics capabilities and improved how ANSYS interfaced with similar software. This latest version, the fifth since the introduction of ANSYS in 1971, cost an estimated $12 million to $15 million to develop. Also in 1992 SASI added 30,000 square feet of office space to its Houston, Pennsylvania, headquarters.

In 1993 SASI announced that its president and founder John Swanson would sell his majority share in the company to the Boston-based venture capitalist firm TA Associates. Financial terms of the agreement were not disclosed, but Swanson also agreed to step down as company president, take a seat on the company's board of directors, and assume the role of SASI chief technologist. The move was expected to return Swanson to his preferred role in research and development and away from the increasingly pressing demands of running the company and overseeing its growth.

In 1994 SASI was renamed ANSYS, Inc., in recognition of its leading software product. On June 20, 1996, ANSYS became a publicly traded company listed on the NASDAQ with an initial public offering of more than 3.5 million shares at $13 each. Later that summer, building began on a new 110,000-square-foot corporate headquarters 15 miles south of Pittsburgh, Pennsylvania. The new building would house 300 personnel from three previous locations and offer room for a planned 20 percent increase in the ANSYS workforce.

Also in 1996, the company launched its DesignSpace software. The new product was intended to make FEA more useable for design engineers working on more mainstream engineering tasks. Given the potential for increased sales in a broader market, ANSYS expected that the new product would allow the company to grow more rapidly and profitably.

### RECOGNITION AND ACQUISITIONS

In 1999 *BusinessWeek* magazine named ANSYS one of its Top 100 "Hot Growth Companies" for the first time. The award evaluated companies based on their performance over the previous three years, with particular attention to indications of rapid growth such as earnings growth, sales growth, and return on investment. The magazine noted that ANSYS had experienced a three-year average of 16.1 percent return on capital, 12.1 percent sales growth, and a 162.5 percent increase in profits.

## KEY DATES

**1970:** John Swanson founds Swanson Analysis Systems, Inc. (SASI).

**1971:** SASI releases its first ANSYS software, AN-SYS 2.0.

**1985:** SASI becomes the first commercial vendor of finite element analysis (FEA) software to offer online customer assistance.

**1991:** SASI reports approximately $28 million in annual revenue.

**1994:** SASI renamed ANSYS, Inc.

**1996:** ANSYS, Inc., becomes a public company.

**2000:** ANSYS is recognized by *Forbes* as one of the 200 Best Small Companies.

**2006:** ANSYS acquires competitor Fluent, Inc., and its industry-leading fluid dynamics capabilities.

**2010:** ANSYS celebrates its 40th anniversary.

In 1999 ANSYS acquired Centric Engineering Systems, Inc., a California-based private company. The acquisition provided ANSYS with leading edge technology and multi-physics analysis software that could simultaneously examine a design's interacting fluid, structural, and temperature considerations.

In 2000 ANSYS was recognized as one of the 200 Best Small Companies by *Forbes* magazine for the first time. Earlier that year, ANSYS had acquired ICEM CFD Engineering for $12.4 million in cash and stock. The privately held California company developed engineering software for use in the aerospace, automotive, and electronics industries. Its 1999 revenue had totaled $6.8 million.

In 2001 ANSYS acquired CADOE, S.A., an independent French software vendor specializing in the computer-aided engineering (CAE) and computer-aided design (CAD) market. CADOE clients included Michelin, Renault, Airbus, Peugot Citroen, and French Telecom.

In 2003 CNN selected ANSYS for inclusion in its CNN Money's "Fabulous 40." The show tracked the trading price of shares from the NASDAQ peak reached at close of trading on March 10, 2000, and recognized those companies whose stock traded at a higher price on May 27, 2003.

In February 2003 ANSYS acquired CFX, a leading provider of fluid dynamics simulation software and services. The acquisition broadened the scope of physics

and engineering solutions ANSYS could offer. In 2003 fluid dynamics constituted the second-largest segment of the computer-aided engineering market, just behind solid mechanics, a field in which ANSYS already enjoyed market leadership.

In 2004 Swanson received the John Fritz Medal from the American Association of Engineering Societies. The highest award in the engineering profession, it recognized industrial or scientific achievement in any field of pure or applied science. John Swanson was recognized for his contributions in the field of finite element analysis.

In 2004 ANSYS appeared on *Fortune* magazine's list of the "100 Fastest Growing Small Companies in America." Ranked at number 55, ANSYS was only 1 of 10 technology firms listed. Companies were ranked on earnings growth, revenue growth, and stock performance over the previous three years.

## CAPABILITIES CONTINUE TO EXPAND

In 2005 and 2006 ANSYS continued its pattern of significant acquisitions. In January 2005 it acquired Century Dynamics, Inc., for an upfront purchase price of $5 million with the possibility of future payments contingent on certain performance criteria. Century Dynamics, a leading provider of simulation software for solving linear, nonlinear, explicit, and multi-body hydrodynamics problems increased the variety of specialty engineering simulation tools ANSYS could make available. The acquisition of thermal modeling company Harvard Thermal, Inc., also in 2005, provided ANSYS with new tools for analyzing electronic cooling. Terms of the transaction with Harvard Thermal were not disclosed.

In 2006 ANSYS acquired Fluent, Inc., and its industry-leading fluid dynamics capabilities for $299 million in cash and six million shares of ANSYS stock. Prior to the acquisition ANSYS had held third place in the world market for computational fluid dynamics software, just behind its new subsidiary, second-place Fluent, Inc.

## DECADE CLOSES WITH ACQUISITIONS AND ADDITIONAL RECOGNITION

ANSYS received multiple recognitions in 2007. The *Wall Street Journal* named the company to its Shareholder Scoreboard. *Baseline* magazine ranked AN-SYS second on its list of top software vendors, where it was the only computer-aided engineering software company.

In 2008 ANSYS acquired Ansoft Corporation for approximately $387 million in cash and 12.2 million shares of ANSYS stock. Ansoft was a leading manufacturer of software to simulate high-performance electronics designs found in mobile communication and Internet devices, broadband networking components, and other high-performance electronics and electro-mechanical systems.

In 2008 ANSYS was named to Standard & Poor's annual Global Challengers List, a roster of medium-sized companies around the world that exhibited high-growth potential. It was 1 of 13 U.S. information technology providers named to the list of 300 companies expected to emerge as global challengers to the world's current leading companies.

In 2008 ANSYS was also the only engineering software company selected for the first-ever *Forbes* magazine Fast 15. To compile the list, researchers examined analyst reports and other news sources to identify the strongest performers among public technology companies in the United States and those likeliest to attain higher growth in the future. *Forbes* editors selected and ranked companies according to revenue, profit growth, and total return over the last three years.

In August 2009 ANSYS was named one of *Fortune* magazine's Fastest Growing Companies for the first time. Ranked number 33 overall, ANSYS was the only engineering simulation provider listed. It ranked 8th among the list's 24t technology companies. *Fortune*'s Fastest Growing Companies included public companies with at least $50 million in annual revenue and a market capitalization of at least $250 million. *Fortune* editors ranked each according to revenue, profit growth, and total return over the previous three years.

On June 2, 2010, ANSYS celebrated its 40th anniversary. Its Workbench of products included Multiphysics, a product that combined technology for various physics disciplines; Structural Mechanics, which offered simulation tools for product design and optimization; Fluid Dynamics, a program that modeled fluid flow and related phenomena; and Explicit Dynamics, which simulated large-scale physical events that could result in material damage or failure.

Other ANSYS Workbench products available in 2010 included Electromagnetics, which provided electromagnetic field simulation for engineers designing and testing high-performance electronic and electromechanical products, such as mobile communication devices, Internet access devices, broadband networking components and systems, and automotive components. Another product was System and Circuit Simulation, which offered layout and design manage-ment to help engineers simulate high-power and high-speed electronic circuits. Engineering Knowledge Manager was another product, providing solutions for data management, including back-up and archival issues. Academic, another ANSYS offering, provided a portfolio of research, academic, and teaching products. High-Performance Computing (HPC) supported a single solution for structural, fluids, thermal, and electromagnetic simulations. Its capabilities were particularly useful for engineers considering multiple design ideas and helped them make the right design early in the design process. Geometry Interfaces provided geometry handling solutions capable of interfacing with all ANSYS computer assisted design systems.

*Joyce Helena Brusin*

## PRINCIPAL SUBSIDIARIES

Centric Engineering Systems, Inc.; Century Dynamics, Inc.; Fluent, Inc.; Ansoft Corp.; ICEM CFD Engineering; CADOE, S.A.; Harvard Thermal, Inc.

## PRINCIPAL COMPETITORS

Dassault Systèmes; MSC Software Corporation; Parametric Technology Corporation.

## FURTHER READING

"ANSYS, Inc.," *Venture Capital Journal*, August 1996.

"ANSYS, INC. Canonsburg, Pennsylvania; It Finds Genuine Success in Simulated Tests," *Investor's Business Daily*, January 4, 2005.

"ANSYS, Inc. Recognized as 'Hot Growth Company' by Busi-nessWeek," PR Newswire, June 21, 1999.

Bates, Daniel, "Swanson Owner to Divest Stake, Relinquish Presidency," *Pittsburgh Business Times*, October 25, 1993.

Bonasia, J. "ANSYS Simulation Software Spares Firms from Costly Real Life Tests," *Investor's Business Daily*, October 7, 2003.

"Canonsburg, Pa. Software Company Builds a Business in Computer-Aided Design," *Knight Ridder/Tribune Business News*, May 31, 2001.

Potter, Karen D. "FEA to the Core: New Visualization Techniques Give Engineers a Glimpse at the Internal Behavior of Their Finite-Element Analysis Models," *Computer Graphics World*, May 1993.

Tara, Roopindir, "Bringing FEA out of the Dark Ages," *Cadence*, June 1997.

Tascarella, Patty, "Technology Veteran Takes Over Swanson Analysis," *Pittsburgh Business Times*, June 13, 1994.

"200 Best Small Companies in America," *Pittsburgh Business Times*, October 27, 2000.

# Ashland Inc.

—■—

**50 East RiverCenter Boulevard**
**Covington, Kentucky 41012-0391**
**U.S.A.**
**Telephone: (859) 815-3333**
**Fax: (859) 815-5053**
**Web site: http://www.ashland.com/**

■ ■ ■

*Public Company*
*Incorporated:* 1924 as Ashland Refining Company
*Employees:* 14,700
*Sales:* $8.11 billion (2009)
*Stock Exchanges:* New York
*Ticker Symbol:* ASH
*NAICS:* 221310 Water Treatment and Distribution;
    324199 All Other Petroleum and Coal Products
    Manufacturing; 325199 All Other Basic Organic
    Chemical Manufacturing; 325211 Plastics Material
    and Resin Manufacturing; 325520 Adhesive
    Manufacturing; 325998 All Other Miscellaneous
    Chemical Product and Preparation Manufacturing

■ ■ ■

With nearly 15,000 employees and annual sales and operating revenues exceeding $8 billion, Ashland Inc. is a leading provider of chemical and petroleum products to the automotive, pharmaceutical, food, and other major industries. In addition to manufacturing a wide range of resins, additives, and polymers, Ashland is a major distributor of chemical products, while also producing and marketing the motor oil Valvoline. In the 21st century Ashland took steps toward transforming itself into a diversified specialty chemicals business, selling its oil refining and road construction operations and expanding into the water treatment sector. In 2008 the company purchased Hercules Inc., a leading specialty-chemical manufacturer.

## COMPANY ORIGINS: 1910–25

The history of Ashland Inc. begins with J. Fred Miles and the founding in 1910 of the Swiss Drilling Company in Oklahoma. Miles had been raised in Oklahoma and worked in the oil business from his youth. After gathering a store of capital, he created Swiss Drilling with two other men to explore and operate new wells.

During this period, Standard Oil had an overwhelming presence in the industry, and, as a result, the U.S. government ordered a breakup of the company in 1911. In the years immediately following the breakup, Standard Oil's near-monopoly was challenging the oil business, and Miles found that he could not survive on the low prices offered for Oklahoma crude. In 1916 he moved his operations to the new fields then opening in eastern Kentucky, where, with the help of some powerful financiers in Chicago and in Cleveland, Ohio, he obtained control of nearly 200,000 acres of oil land. Two years later the energetic Miles incorporated Swiss Oil Company in Lexington, Kentucky, with a group of backers that included the Insulls and the Armours of Chicago, with Miles serving as general manager and J. I. Lamprecht of Cleveland as president. Swiss Oil was soon one of the leading oil concerns in the state of Kentucky.

## COMPANY PERSPECTIVES

We satisfy our customers by delivering results through quality chemical products and services. Our desire to grow drives our passion to win in the marketplace. With a unified, low-cost operating structure, we'll remain competitive across every business and in every geographical region.

By the early 1920s, a postwar depression and the early exhaustion of key oil wells had thrust Swiss Oil into a precarious financial condition. Despite the company's difficulties, Fred Miles was eager to expand its operations into refining. In 1923 he hired the services of Paul Blazer to select, buy, and operate the most advantageously located and outfitted refinery obtainable in the area. Blazer had gone into the oil-trading business after college and then picked up valuable experience as a partner in a Lexington refinery, from which he had just resigned when Miles made him the head of Swiss Oil's new division, Ashland Refining Company, in 1924. Blazer selected for his refinery an existing facility at Cattletsburg, Kentucky, on the Ohio River near the West Virginia border and just upstream from Ashland, where Blazer set up his modest offices. The Cattletsburg refinery had a capacity of 1,000 barrels per day and, after a program of extensive repairs, was soon operating profitably.

Blazer's choice of Cattletsburg was excellent because of several factors that would prove critical to the company's long-term success. In general, a refining operation that had access to its own local crude-oil supplies would do well in the eastern Kentucky region. Swiss Oil, though not a terribly successful company, did own a substantial amount of the region's crude and could therefore supply its new subsidiary with most of its needs. Ashland was thus able to sell regionally refined petroleum products, such as gasoline and motor oil, more cheaply than competitors who were forced to transport their crude or finished products from the Atlantic seaboard, the Mississippi River, or the Gulf of Mexico. The Cattletsburg site promised ready access to hundreds of miles of navigable rivers, by means of which Ashland could both receive crude and deliver product to the greater Ohio River basin. Until the introduction of pipelines, river freight was unmatched as an economic carrier of oil, and Ashland remained dependent on its river barges and terminals for the delivery of much of its refined product. These factors gave Ashland an early advantage over its much larger rivals and allowed the company to achieve a firm and lasting position as a regional leader.

## SUCCESS DURING THE DEPRESSION AND WORLD WAR II

By 1926 Ashland's gross sales were $3 million per year, and Paul Blazer had confirmed his reputation as an outstanding refinery manager. Miles had been eased out of Swiss Oil when the company required a bailout by one of its investors, and it was not long before the Ashland subsidiary was outperforming its parent company. Blazer steadily improved the refinery's operation and expanded sales of its products, and in 1929 he convinced Swiss Oil's board of directors to authorize Ashland to spend $400,000 to acquire marketing companies in the area. Despite the onset of the Great Depression, this was followed by the 1930 acquisition of Tri-State Refining Company over the West Virginia border. Tri-State had a sizable refinery and its own team of gas stations and trucks, giving Ashland the makings of an integrated refining and marketing organization in the eastern Kentucky region. While inexpensive, river transport was continually threatened with the imposition of federal tolls that would largely negate its economy. Thus, in 1931 Ashland took the first in a long series of steps intended to lessen its dependence on river transportation of its crude supplies. When Ashland bought the Cumberland Pipeline Company for $420,000 in 1931, it facilitated shipment of crude from the Atlantic seaboard, as well as from its Kentucky fields. This opening to the sea would become vital when Ashland grew dependent upon Middle Eastern oil arriving by tanker.

So skilled an operator was Blazer that Ashland continued to turn a profit in the worst Depression years. Ashland was now the staff upon which leaned the ailing Swiss Oil, and in 1936, when it became apparent that the latter could not sustain the two companies, they were merged and Blazer elected president and chief executive officer of the new Ashland Oil & Refining Company. The combined companies showed a 1936 net profit of $677,583 on sales of $4.8 million, good results at any time but remarkable in the Depression era. Blazer forged ahead with new investments, joining Standard Oil Company (Ohio) in a pipeline from fields in southern Illinois and adding a costly new unit to the Cattletsburg refinery. By the time the United States entered World War II in 1941, Ashland had nearly doubled its sales to $8 million.

During World War II (1939–45) the petroleum industry came under fairly tight government control. Like all the other oil companies, big and small, Ashland

## KEY DATES

**1910:** Swiss Drilling Company is founded by J. Fred Miles.

**1923:** Paul Blazer is hired as head of Ashland Refining Company.

**1936:** Swiss Oil and Ashland Refining Company merge to create Ashland Oil and Refining Company.

**1948:** Ashland merges with Cleveland-based Allied Oil Company, while acquiring Aetna Oil Company, Frontier Oil Company, and Freedom-Valvoline Oil Company.

**1970:** Shareholders approve changing the company's name to Ashland Oil, Inc.

**1981:** CEO Orin Atkins is forced out after making illegal payments to Middle Eastern governments including Oman.

**1995:** Company changes its name to Ashland Inc.

**1998:** Ashland Inc. merges its refining and marketing operations with Marathon Oil Company, creating Marathon Ashland Petroleum LLC.

**2005:** Ashland sells its 38 percent stake in Marathon Ashland Petroleum LLC to the Marathon Oil Corporation for $3.7 billion.

**2008:** Ashland acquires specialty-chemical firm Hercules Inc.

benefited mightily from the rapid increase in demand for the entire spectrum of petroleum products, which were needed for everything from gasoline to rubber boots to explosives. With government assistance Ashland built a new facility at Cattletsburg for the refining of 100-octane aviation fuel, and within four years it had doubled and redoubled company revenues to $35 million in 1945. The following years saw an inevitable recession as the war machine was dismantled, but it soon became apparent that postwar America was about to indulge its love affair with the automobile as never before. From the remote mountain towns of West Virginia to the streets of Cincinnati, Ohio, the postwar economy moved on wheels powered by oil, and Ashland remained the region's most economical supplier of that commodity.

## GROWTH IN THE MID-20TH CENTURY

In 1948 Ashland took a major step when it merged with the Cleveland-based Allied Oil Company, a fuel-oil broker with sales slightly in excess of Ashland's. Allied had been started in 1925 by Floyd R. Newman and W. W. Vandeveer with the support of Blazer. The combined companies had revenue in that year of $100 million. Ashland's new Allied division was directed by Rex Blazer, nephew of Ashland's president and a former marketing executive at Allied. The merger extended Ashland's marketing area to Cleveland and as far west as Chicago, and, to make use of its new sales opportunities, Ashland soon added a trio of other acquisitions: Aetna Oil Company, a Louisville, Kentucky, refiner and distributor; Frontier Oil Company of Buffalo, New York; and Freedom-Valvoline Oil Company, the Pennsylvania maker of Valvoline motor oil. The latter was already a well-known brand name and under Ashland's ownership became one of the most widely distributed motor oils in the world. By the time these purchases were completed in 1950, Ashland was the 19th-largest oil company in the United States and for the first time was listed on the New York Stock Exchange.

Sales in 1955 topped $250 million, although net income was only $10 million. In contrast to its early years, Ashland as a mature company tended to earn rather low levels of net income, which Blazer attributed to two basic factors. First, the company had far outstripped its limited sources of crude oil and never had much success as a prospector. This meant that it would never enjoy the extraordinary profits brought in by big oil strikes and that its crude-oil expense would always be somewhat higher than for a fully integrated oil concern. Second, Ashland also sold more refined products than it made, supplementing its own production with purchases of refined goods for resale, which necessarily resulted in a diminished margin. Such a policy also meant that Ashland's refineries were kept running at or near capacity, a clear gain in efficiency over plants forced to cut back or work on shorter, more costly runs. Added to its advantageous system of waterway transport and freedom from the advertising expense associated with operation of a high-profile, branded chain of gas stations, Ashland's refining efficiency offset its lack of crude and enabled the company to earn a steady if unspectacular return on investment.

In 1957, after heading Ashland Oil for 22 years, Blazer retired as the chief executive. His nephew Rex Blazer took over the top management spot, while Everett Wells, a longtime associate of the senior Blazer, became the new president. The year before these changes, Ashland entered a new field with the purchase of the R.J. Brown Company of St. Louis, Missouri, a diversified manufacturer of petrochemicals. A great number of useful chemicals are derived from petroleum, and the oil industry as a whole was expanding rapidly into this new and largely unexplored area. Ashland steadily increased its petrochemical holdings, in 1962 buying United Carbon Company of Houston, Texas, makers of carbon black, and in 1966 adding Archer Daniels Midland Chemicals Company for $65 million. At that point Ashland formed a new operating subsidiary, Ashland Chemical Company, to oversee the workings of its manifold chemical interests.

The early 1960s were also notable for Ashland's 1962 purchase of the Central Louisiana pipeline system from Humble Oil & Refining. Central Louisiana was a major pipeline, gathering most of the oil produced in greater Louisiana and the Gulf of Mexico fields, and its acquisition by Ashland largely relieved the company of its worries about a steady supply of crude oil, made worse by the intermittent threat of new user tolls on the waterways. The net effect of these acquisitions was to boost Ashland's sales sharply, from $490 million in 1963 to $723 million three years later, elevating the company from the status of an independent to what might be called a "mini-major" oil firm. The robust U.S. economy had much to do with Ashland's prosperity, of course, as more citizens relied on the automobile.

## CHANGES AND CONSOLIDATION: 1970–75

In 1969 Ashland had entered the coal business and soon became one of the top-ten coal producers in the country. It also took advantage of its refineries' asphalt by-products to gain a leading place among the nation's road-construction firms. The result of such diversification was a gradual lessening of Ashland's dependence on oil refining for its sales dollar. By 1971 refining and marketing of oil accounted for only 57 percent of Ashland's $1.4 billion in revenue, with Ashland Chemical providing another 25 percent and its other holdings contributing the remainder. This apparent balance was somewhat misleading, however. Ashland continued to rely on its refining and marketing divisions for the bulk of its net income, as the growing chemical business proved to be a sluggish moneymaker. Refining capacity reached 350,000 barrels per day in 1973, and, as always, Ashland's crude production was less than 20 percent of that figure, forcing the company to join the mounting number of U.S. oil refiners dependent upon Middle Eastern crude for their survival.

In 1970 shareholders approved changing the company's name from Ashland Oil & Refining to Ashland Oil, Inc. That same year Ashland consolidated most of its Canadian interests with those of Canadian Gridoil Limited to form Ashland Oil Canada Limited. Domestically, Ashland acquired Union Carbide

Petroleum Company and Empire State Petroleum, and these were consolidated with other exploration and production activities into Ashland Exploration, Inc.

## LEGAL ISSUES EMERGE IN 1975

During the mid-1970s Ashland became entangled in the first of a series of legal controversies. In 1976 chief executive officer Orin Atkins, a lawyer who had served in that position since 1965, agreed in response to a shareholder suit to repay Ashland some $175,000 in funds he was said to have spent improperly. The previous year, 1975, Ashland had been fined by the Securities and Exchange Commission for illegally contributing more than $700,000 to several political campaigns.

Ashland's problems with meeting its own needs for crude oil became increasingly pronounced as the company continued to expand its refining and marketing operations. The 1973 embargo by the Organization of the Petroleum Exporting Countries (OPEC) and the ensuing energy crisis had effectively raised the stakes in the oil-exploration game. After the early 1970s, only those companies willing and able to mount massive drilling campaigns would be likely to reap the benefits of crude-oil supplies. Ashland was simply not big enough to join the majors in their exorbitant outlays, and Ashland therefore got out of the production business entirely. Sale of most of its oil leases, equipment, and reserves netted Ashland about $1.5 billion by 1980, but it also left the company wholly dependent on outside sources of crude, primarily in the Middle East. In 1975 all construction activities were consolidated, and Ashland Coal, Inc., was formed in anticipation of the increasing potential of coal in the national energy market. Ashland took a comprehensive review of all segments of its operations to determine necessary changes. As an initial step in this strategy to maximize return on existing assets, the company sold its 79 percent interest in Ashland Oil Canada.

In 1981 Atkins was forced out as chairman and chief executive officer by a group of executives who brought to light illegal payments Atkins had made to government officials in Middle Eastern countries, most notably Oman. He was replaced in both positions by John R. Hall. In 1988 two former Ashland employees won a wrongful-discharge suit against the company. The employees, a former vice president for oil supply and a former vice president for government relations, had accused Ashland of firing them in 1983 for refusing to cover up the illegal payments. The jury awarded the plaintiffs $70.85 million, $1.25 million of which was to be paid by Hall personally. The plaintiffs ultimately settled out of court for $25 million.

On July 13, 1988, Atkins was arrested by customs agents at John F. Kennedy International Airport in New York and accused with selling company documents to the National Iranian Oil Company (NIOC). Atkins denied the charges. The papers Atkins allegedly peddled related to an ongoing, $283 million billing dispute between Ashland and NIOC. In 1989 Ashland settled the case with a $325 million payment to NIOC. The company's public image was not helped by a 1988 spill of four million gallons of diesel fuel into the Ohio River, although Ashland was credited with a prompt, candid response.

## NAVIGATING ECONOMIC HIGHS AND LOWS: 1981–94

In the meantime, Ashland sales skyrocketed along with the price of oil. Hall watched revenue hit an all-time peak of $9.5 billion in 1981, but Ashland found itself squeezed by the high cost of crude, and net income actually dropped into a net loss during the first part of 1982, when a spreading recession only made matters worse. Atkins had also saddled Ashland with an unusually high debt ratio when, in 1981, he used the receipts from the oil-drilling asset sale to buy United States Filter Corporation and Integon Corporation for $661 million. Integon, an insurance holding company, hardly matched the range of Ashland's other interests and in due time was sold to reduce debt. Once the recession had eased by 1983, Ashland's earnings again picked up, and the company's future brightened.

Scurlock Oil Company, a crude-oil gathering, transporting, and marketing firm, was acquired in 1982, thereby aiding Ashland in a shift from foreign to domestic crude-oil sources. In 1982 more than 20 corporate staff departments were brought together to form Ashland Services Company, a division that would cut overhead and also provide cost-effective services to the corporation and to its divisions and subsidiaries.

Ashland began the 1990s with a strong financial position. In 1992 Ashland surpassed $10 billion in sales for the first time, and it also established itself as the leading distributor of chemicals and solvents in North America by acquiring the majority of Unocal's chemical distribution business. Although refining profits were largely disappointing during the early 1990s, Ashland's chemical profits remained a boon for the company. Operating income from chemicals increased to $47 million in the last three months of 1994 compared with $28 million the year before.

Several important developments occurred in 1994. Ashland's Valvoline division purchased Zerex, the nation's number two antifreeze manufacturer. Ashland also acquired Eurobase (Italy) and ACT Inc. (Pennsylvania), both companies that produced chemicals used in the creation of semiconductors. Also that year, Ashland began a new multi-well oil exploration in Nigeria and made a promising discovery in the first well sunk.

## REPOSITIONING AT THE CENTURY'S END

In an effort to have the name of the company reflect Ashland's increasingly diversified business, shareholders approved the name change from Ashland Oil, Inc., to Ashland Inc. in 1995. At the same time, the company began to shore up its nonrefining business segments to minimize the effect of its weak refining margins. According to Paul W. Chellgren, the company's president and chief operating officer, Ashland's strategy was to become an "integrated, but diversified company" by adding value to its petroleum products rather than by increasing volume. In 1996 Ashland chairman and chief executive officer John Hall announced his retirement, and Chellgren succeeded him in both positions.

In early 1997 Ashland announced plans to consolidate operations of Arch Mineral and Ashland Coal, thus creating the fifth-largest coal producer in the United States. Also in early 1997 Ashland was the first to be granted foreign trade subzone status at Akron-Canton Regional Airport in Ohio (known as "Foreign Trade Zone 181"). This status allowed Ashland to import crude oil to its Canton refinery and Lima storage facility without paying duties and tariffs. The subzone status was designed to protect those companies who imported oil not in its finished state (such as crude oil) and that diminished in volume once the oil had been processed into products such as asphalt, diesel fuel, or home heating oil. Tariffs on foreign crude were 2.5 cents a barrel in 1997. Not having to pay the fee saved Ashland more than $250,000 a year at its Canton facility. To further enhance efficiency and increase profitability, Ashland Inc. and Marathon Oil Co. announced in May 1997 a plan to merge their refining and marketing operations, with Marathon holding 62 percent of ownership and Ashland 38 percent. Ashland Chemical was expected to be the largest customer of the joint venture. On January 1, 1998, the merger was completed, and Marathon Ashland Petroleum LLC (MAP) was formed, combining the major elements of the refining, marketing, and transportation operations of the two companies.

During the late 1990s Ashland was a highly diversified energy company, with extensive coal and petrochemical holdings to complement its core of oil refining and marketing. It was the nation's leading designer and builder of roadways through its APAC subsidiaries, which laid more than 13 million tons of asphalt in fiscal 1996. Oil remained the centerpiece of Ashland's corporate structure, however. Still relying on cheap river transport for much of its outgoing freight, Ashland delivered gasoline and related petroleum products to a large network of wholesalers and Ashland-affiliated gas stations. Ashland itself operated 742 Super-America retail gasoline-grocery outlets in 1996 (Super-America Group's 1996 sales were $1.9 billion). Added to these was the $1.2 billion in sales generated by the Valvoline, Inc., subsidiary, Ashland's nationally recognized brand name. Combined oil activities thus still provided well over half of the company's revenue and earnings, as Ashland continued to fill a narrow niche between international oil giant and regional independent.

In 1998 Ashland purchased 20 companies, including Eagle One Industries, a maker of car-care products, and Masters-Jackson, a group of highway construction companies. Ashland exited the coal mining business by spinning off Arch Coal, resulting in a reduction of its company holdings from 58 percent to 12 percent. Ashland would later sell its remaining holdings. In 2000 Ashland acquired Copenhagen-based Superfos, the principal assets of which included a U.S. road construction business serving the Ashland operating area. The company was later sold, except for its road construction operations. Other acquisitions included Winyah Concrete & Block, a South Carolina–based full-service concrete and masonry supply organization, and Oklahoma's Vinita Rock Company. The purchase of Micro-Clean Inc., a semiconductor process parts-cleaning operation, enhanced Ashland's position as a leading provider to the microelectronics industry through its Specialty Chemical's division. In the area of e-commerce, Ashland and e-Chemicals, Inc., the leading online chemical marketplace, created the chemical industry's first e-commerce alliance, enabling customers to purchase an array of 2,500 Ashland-distributed products through the Web site e-chemicals.com.

CEO Chellgren reported an "outstanding year" in 2000: "We dramatically improved our financial performance, continued to narrow our business focus while expanding key businesses, and adopted a new identity that boldly declares who we are and how we work." Operating income, net income, and earnings per share all reached record highs. MAP continued to be the company's most important cash generator and was described by Chellgren as "one of the best performing refining and marketing operations in the United States."

## A CHANGE IN IMAGE: 2001

For 34 years the Ashland logo represented a gas station sign. To better portray the new image of a "can-do" company for the 21st century, Ashland adopted a new logo and tag line, "The Who in How Things Work." Through this new identity, Ashland hoped to project the diversity and innovative mentality that define Ashland and its people, the people who know how to ask the right questions and deliver the right answers.

Chellgren reported another successful year for Ashland in 2001. Records were set in earnings per share, net income, and operating income. He described 2001 as "the year of MAP." Ashland's 38 percent interest in Marathon Ashland Petroleum LLC yielded operating income from refining and marketing that was nearly double that of any prior year in the company's history. As a result, operating profit from refining and marketing accounted for 76 percent of the operating income before corporate expenses. The Valvoline division also produced near-record results, with sales of premium motor oils climbing 27 percent.

Other divisions performed less than remarkably. Ashland's chemical operations reported significant reductions in sales. Operating income fell in the APAC highway construction businesses due to compressed construction margins, a severe winter in APAC's market area, and special charges associated with improper recognition of construction contract earnings in the Manassas, Virginia, unit.

## EXPANSION AND CONTINUED SUCCESS IN 2002

Chellgren's vision for the future of Ashland was to provide solutions for customers, opportunity for employees, and value for shareholders. The company was optimistic for another successful year in 2002. This confidence was based on the strength of the MAP refining and marketing operations. In 2001 MAP launched or completed several initiatives that would add considerably to its future operating income, including retail expansion in the Midwest, a new nationwide network of travel centers, and the startup of a heavy crude oil conversion unit at the Garyville, Louisiana, refinery. In an attempt to consolidate operations, Ashland closed nine distribution facilities and conducted a "quality of business" review to focus on its most profitable accounts.

Ashland Specialty Chemical remained a worldwide market and technology leader supplying high-performance products and services. A leading European producer of gelcoats and polyester resins was acquired, which more than doubled the size of Ashland's unsaturated polyester resins business in Europe. Research and development efforts focused on new products and aggressively seeking new geographic markets and applications for existing product lines. Valvoline continued to develop new products, including MaxLife motor oil, the first oil specifically formulated for higher mileage engines, and MaxLife transmission fluids and antifreeze.

## REORGANIZATION AND DIVERSIFICATION: 2003–10

In November 2002 Paul Chellgren stepped down as CEO and chairman of Ashland. He was replaced by James J. O'Brien. Under O'Brien's leadership, the company embarked on an exhaustive restructuring program, aimed at both diversifying its chemical business and shedding several of its non-core operations. In July 2003 Ashland sold its electronic chemicals business to the Pennsylvania-based Air Products & Chemicals Inc. for $300 million. The divestment of the division, which specialized in the production of chemicals for use in the manufacture of semiconductors and generated sales of $200 million per year, signaled Ashland's intention to devote greater attention to expanding its specialty chemicals segments.

A more significant indicator of Ashland's future course followed in April 2004, when the company announced that it would sell its 38 percent stake in Marathon Ashland Petroleum LLC to the Marathon Oil Corporation, in a deal worth approximately $3.7 billion. Under the terms of the agreement, Ashland also sold Marathon a portion of its Valvoline subsidiary, as well as its maleic anhydride manufacturing division. With the sale, Ashland was able to devote more than $2.5 billion to paying down its sizable debt. Perhaps more noteworthy, the deal represented the end of Ashland's longtime involvement in the petroleum refining industry. The sale was finalized in June 2005.

In the ensuing months, Ashland began to seek ways to expand into new business areas. One area the company identified as having huge potential for growth was the water treatment sector. In March 2006 Ashland acquired Nanjing Clear Environment Protection, a Chinese water treatment concern, for an undisclosed price. That same month, the company purchased Stockhausen, the water management division of German-based Degussa AG, for $144 million. With the Stockhausen acquisition, Ashland obtained five water treatment plants on four continents. As the company shifted into this new business line, it continued to divest several of its existing business operations. In August 2006 Ashland agreed to sell its Ashland Paving and Construction subsidiary to the Irish firm CRH plc, in a deal valued at $1.3 billion.

During this period Ashland continued to develop its specialty chemical operations. In May 2007 the company's distribution unit entered into new agreements with ExxonMobil Chemical, BASF, and Sunoco Chemicals to distribute a wide range of resins and other chemical products. In November 2008 Ashland acquired Hercules Inc., a major producer of specialty chemicals for the water management and paper sectors, in a deal worth an estimated $3.3 billion.

As Ashland continued to reinvent itself, its revenues began to rise. Annual sales grew steadily during the latter part of the decade, from $6.73 billion in 2005 to $8.38 billion in 2008. Much of this growth was driven by the company's aggressive streamlining measures. By decade's end, Ashland had slashed its total workforce to fewer than 15,000 employees, a reduction of nearly 10,000 since September 2002. Although the global economic downturn caused the company's 2009 sales to dip slightly to $8.11 billion, as it entered the second decade of the new century Ashland remained confident that its reorganization efforts would pay dividends over the long term.

*Jonathan Martin*
*Updated, Terry Bain; Carol D. Beavers; Stephen Meyer*

## PRINCIPAL SUBSIDIARIES

Ashland International Holdings, Inc.; Ashmont Insurance Company, Inc.; AshThree LLC; CVG Capital II LLC; Hercules Incorporated.

## PRINCIPAL OPERATING UNITS

Ashland Aqualon Functional Ingredients; Ashland Consumer Markets (Valvoline); Ashland Distribution; Ashland Hercules Water Technologies; Ashland Performance Materials.

## PRINCIPAL COMPETITORS

Arkema (France); Brenntag Holding GmbH & Co. KG (Germany); Granite Construction Incorporated; Honeywell International Inc.

## FURTHER READING

"Ashland Considers Selling Its Big Stake in Arch Coal," *New York Times*, June 23, 1999, p. 4.

Block, Donna, "Ashland to Buy Hercules," *Daily Deal*, July 14, 2008.

Butters, Jamie, "Kentucky Merger Threatens to Subordinate One Company to the Other," *Knight-Ridder/Tribune Busi-*

*ness News*, May 19, 1997, p. 519B1012.

Fan, Aliza, "Ashland to Stay True to Solid Reputation," *Oil Daily*, January 30, 1995, p. 1.

Hamerman, Joshua, "Ashland Nets More than $1 Billion in Cash," *Mergers & Acquisitions Report*, July 11, 2005.

Kovski, Alan, "Ashland, Lyondell Gain on Chemicals, Slip Back on Poor Results in Refining," *Oil Daily*, January 24, 1995, p. 3.

———, "Marathon, Ashland Put Proposal in Writing to Combine Refining, Marketing Operations," *Oil Daily*, May 16, 1997, p. 1.

Sachdev, Ameet, "Ashland Inc. to Sell Shares in Exploration Unit," *Knight-Ridder/Tribune Business News*, January 31, 1997, p. 131B1290.

———, "Ashland Oil to Seek a Partner for Refinery Business," *Knight-Ridder/Tribune Business News*, December 10, 1996, p. 1210B0939.

Scott, Otto, *The Exception: The Story of Ashland Oil & Refining Company*, New York: McGraw-Hill Book Company, 1968.

# ASX Limited

---

**20 Bridge Street**
**Sydney, New South Wales 2000**
**Australia**
**Telephone: (61 (2)) 9338-0000**
**Fax: (61 (2)) 9227-0885**
**Web site: http://www.asx.com.au**

*Public Company*
*Founded:* 1987
*Incorporated:* 1987 as The Australian Stock Exchange Limited
*Employees:* 423
*Sales:* AUD $538.40 million ($448.89) (2009)
*Stock Exchanges:* Australian
*Ticker Symbol:* ASX
*NAICS:* 523210 Securities and Commodity Exchanges; 517110 On-line Access Service Providers, Using Own Operated Wired Telecommunications Infrastructure

■ ■ ■

ASX Limited is the principal stock exchange in Australia and one of the top 10 exchange groups in the world as measured by market capitalization. Operating under the name Australian Securities Exchange, ASX lists more than 2,000 stocks, including its own. ASX provides a platform for trading equities, derivatives, and fixed-income securities and facilitates the raising of capital by companies. Along with providing listing and trading services, ASX serves as a clearinghouse and payment-systems facilitator and provides market information.

ASX's customer base comprises members of the international and domestic professional financial community, including brokers and funds-managers, as well as retail investors. As of early 2010, ASX effectively operated a monopoly and served as supervisor of its own market, although the Australian Securities and Investments Commission (ASIC) held government oversight of ASX and supervised ASX's compliance as a listed company on its own exchange. Beginning in the fourth quarter of 2010, ASIC was expected to take over real-time trading supervision. While ASX was to continue supervision of listed entities, the greater role of ASIC was perhaps a first step towards ending the ASX monopoly.

## EARLY ROOTS IN THE 19TH CENTURY

ASX Limited traces its deep roots to the development of the Australian stock exchange industry beginning in the 19th century, the growth of the Australian Stock Exchange and the Sydney Futures Exchange (SFE) in the late 20th century, and the merger of those two exchanges in the 21st century. The history of the Australian stock market in general stems from the formation of six separate state exchanges at a time when Australia was still part of the British Empire. The first of these exchanges was an early Melbourne forerunner established in 1861. Other exchange formations followed, including those in Sydney in 1871, Hobart in 1882, Melbourne and Brisbane in 1884, Adelaide in 1887, and Perth in 1889. In 1896, following a land and mining boom and the subsequent failure of several companies seeking to capitalize on the boom, governments mandated company audits and annual presentations of fiscal statements. The mining bust of the 1890s also brought an end to smaller provincial exchanges that were formed to raise capital for mining companies.

In 1901 the Commonwealth of Australia was formed, setting the stage for increased communication and cooperation between state exchanges. The first interstate stock exchange conference was held in 1903. Representatives from Adelaide, Brisbane, Melbourne, and Sydney attended. State exchange representatives continued to meet on an informal basis through 1936, when Sydney encouraged the others to formalize their association. The result was the 1937 formation of the Australian Associated Stock Exchanges (AASE). Initially, the AASE had little real power, but it gradually adopted company listing requirements, uniform brokerage rules, and commission fee guidelines.

## THE SYDNEY FUTURES
## EXCHANGE: 1960

The Sydney Greasy Wool Futures Exchange, a direct forerunner to the SFE, was formed in 1960. As its name suggested, the exchange initially focused on wool futures, and by 1964 it was the world's premier futures market for wool. Soon, the exchange diversified into a broader range of commodities such as beef, live cattle, and gold, leading to the adoption in 1972 of the new name, Sydney Futures Exchange, to better reflect the widened scope of its activities.

Just as the mining bust of the1890s helped shape the growing exchange industry at the turn of the 20th century, a similar event did the same in 1969: the so-called "Poseidon bubble." The bubble occurred after the mining company Poseidon NL discovered a promising location for the mining of nickel, which was in short supply because of the Vietnam War and nickel's use in military applications. When the discovery was initially announced in September 1969, Poseidon NL stock sold for AUD 0.80 a share. As the nickel and mining bubble began to expand, the stock climbed to as high as AUD

280. Once Poseidon NL became too expensive for most investors, other nickel stocks, and then other mining company stocks, began to attract investor interest and gain value, including equity in start-up companies with little potential for nickel discovery. Some investors suffered significant losses on such stocks, and the resulting negative press cast a long shadow on the entire mining industry. By January 1970, mining stocks had peaked and then quickly fell.

The bursting of the mining bubble in 1970 had regulatory reverberations, leading to numerous changes in Australian stock market governance. In 1972 legislation requiring the national listing of all securities became effective, allowing a company to register in any state and automatically be registered nationally and in all states. Previously, a company had to register in each state in which it wished to do business. In 1974 the Interstate Corporate Affairs Commission was formed as the first national independent agency responsible for overseeing a uniform body of corporate regulations. The first national legislation of futures became active in 1976.

As market regulation grew, so did SFE's product line during the late 1970s. SFE launched the first gold futures contract in Australia in 1978 and the first financial futures market outside of the United States, the 90-Day Bank Accepted Bill Futures, in 1979. Five years later, SFE launched a two-year Commonwealth Treasury Bond Futures contract, the first bond futures outside the United States.

## FORMATION OF THE
## AUSTRALIAN STOCK EXCHANGE:
## 1987

Reflecting a growing trend towards nationalization of stock exchange activities, the Australian Stock Indices for national pricing replaced the separate Melbourne and Sydney Indices in 1980. After the Commonwealth and states agreed to cooperate in regulating company and securities activities in 1982, the first national legislation governing companies became effective. In 1984 stock exchange membership was deregulated, fixed commission rates were abolished, and negotiated rates became commonplace as commission fees gradually were lowered. Many brokerage houses merged with others, while some became affiliated with foreign companies, leaving the country with only a small number of independent brokers.

Representatives of all six state exchanges met in 1985 to discuss the creation of a single national exchange. All the representatives agreed to the proposal, viewed as a means to end interstate disputes and

```
┌─────────────────────────────────────────┐
│                                           │
│            KEY DATES                      │
│               ■                           │
│                                           │
│  1861:  The first Australian stock exchange is formed   │
│         in Melbourne.                     │
│  1987:  The Australian Stock Exchange (ASX) is cre-    │
│         ated from the union of six independent state  │
│         stock exchanges.                  │
│  1998:  ASX demutualizes and becomes a publicly  │
│         listed company on its own stock exchange. │
│  2002:  After demutualizing, the Sydney Futures  │
│         Exchange goes public and lists on ASX, mak-  │
│         ing ASX the only exchange in the world list-  │
│         ing two exchanges.                │
│  2006:  The Australian Stock Exchange and the Syd-   │
│         ney Futures Exchange merge, creating ASX    │
│         Limited.                          │
│                                           │
└─────────────────────────────────────────┘
```

modernize the market. As a result, through incorporation under legislation of the Australian Parliament in 1987, the six independent state exchanges merged to create one national exchange, the Australian Stock Exchange (ASX) Limited, based in Sydney.

In 1987 the newly incorporated ASX launched a computer-based trading system, the Stock Exchange Automated Trading System (SEATS), for a few selected stocks. Unfortunately for the exchange, the debut of SEATS corresponded with the first day of a major international stock crash, starting in Hong Kong and rippling around the world. Known as Black Monday (October 19) in the United States and Black Tuesday (October 20) in Australia, the period represented the largest one-day percentage drop in global stock market history: Hong Kong fell more than 45 percent, the United States more than 22 percent, and Australia more than 41 percent. At the time of the October 1987 crash, Australia had one of the more deregulated markets around the globe. While Australian markets experienced greater short-term losses than most world markets besides those in Hong Kong and New Zealand, both ASX and SFE, unlike other major markets, remained open throughout the crash.

## DEVELOPMENT OF PRODUCTS AND INFRASTRUCTURE: 1988–97

During the late 1980s, after initiating new products a decade earlier, SFE pioneered market changes in Australia, beginning after-hours trading sessions in 1988 and launching an electronic system for trading futures contracts and options in 1989. A year later, the new

national exchange, ASX, closed its trading floor when its electronic SEATS became the sole means of enacting trades there. ASX also launched its warrants market in 1990.

During the early 1990s SFE further developed its infrastructure and product line. In 1991 SFE established the subsidiary SFE Clearing House as a financial facility for settling, clearing, and maintaining a record of futures trades, and the following year, the New Zealand Futures and Options Exchange became a wholly owned subsidiary of SFE. In 1993 SFE debuted its overnight options on futures, the first such product of its type in the world, and during the mid-1990s SFE began developing trading links with other exchanges, like the New York Mercantile, allowing investors at one exchange to trade certain stocks listed on another.

In 1994 ASX introduced its broker-sponsored system of handling shares for a client, Clearing House Electronic Sub-register System (CHESS), which provided the exchange with its central register for share-ownership transfer. In efforts to bolster its image as an international trading center in the burgeoning Asia-Pacific trading arena, and to re-attract traders that had transferred to overseas exchanges, ASX in the mid-1990s made several improvements: it extended trading hours, reduced to three days its settlement period, established a trading link with the New Zealand Stock Exchange, and created the Australian Depository Receipt system. ASX closed the year with a market capitalization of AUD 385 billion, making it the world's 10th largest stock exchange. To further its growth, ASE broker-members voted to demutualize in order to enhance its transparency through public ownership.

## EARLY YEARS AS A PUBLIC COMPANY: 1998

ASX became a public company in 1998 and was listed on its own exchange. That same year, the exchange trading floor was officially closed. Individual investors thereafter accessed the exchange via brokers making electronic trades on their behalf. In 1999 ASX acquired a 13-percent stake in Austraclear Limited, the only Central Securities Depository (CSD) in Australia for debt securities, and joined with NASDAQ to develop a co-listing of stocks from the NASDAQ-100 Index of its largest non-financial securities and ASX's major index stocks.

SFE, meanwhile, had grown into one of the largest and most active regional markets of its kind, with annual trading volume of about 30 million traded futures contracts by 1997. The following year, SFE formed a partnership with Dow Jones Indexes and overtook the

Tokyo Stock Exchange to become the largest futures exchange in the Asia-Pacific region, based on the value of futures contracts traded. In 1999 SFE closed its trading floor and became exclusively an electronic exchange. SFE also launched a carbon emissions trading program and options and futures contracts in the Asia Pacific Extra Liquid Series (AP/ELS), a new set of indices developed in conjunction with Dow Jones.

In 1999 ASX attempted to merge with SFE through an offer of AUD 210 million. Initially, ASX managing director Richard Humphry and SFE chief executive Lee Hosking both seemed to support the deal. However, the Australian firm Computershare made a counter bid of AUD 240 million for SFE, and the Australian Competition & Consumer Commission (ACCC) objected to the ASX proposal, citing concerns that a merger could diminish competition. SFE board members, though, voted to block a merger with Computershare.

## A NEW CENTURY: GLOBAL LINKS, RELATIONS WITH SFE

ASX opened the 21st century by launching a two-way link with the Singapore Exchange and a one-way link to New York's NASDAQ and AMEX exchanges. In 2000 ASX also acquired a 15 percent interest in Bridge DFS (later renamed IRESS Market Technology), a supplier of wealth-management systems for stock market participants. ASX also established ASX Supervisory Review Pty Limited to monitor and oversee ASX's supervisory activity.

In late 2001 SFE voted to demutualize and also made known it was interested in a merger with ASX. ACCC's commissioner publicly stated, too, that the review of ASX's 1999 merger proposal was not fully vetted, conditions could have changed since that proposal, and that the ACCC would treat any new proposal as a fresh application to be reviewed. However, while SFE had gained an interest in a merger, and regulatory conditions seemed favorable, ASX's interest in such a merger had waned, given its establishment of a Singapore trading link and its pursuit of other such global links.

To help facilitate its future growth and foreign access to its exchange, ASX in 2002 launched its World Link, allowing brokers to easily trade on U.S. exchanges through ASX. The company also formed Australian Clearing House and debuted two new products in its resumption of selling share futures, something it abandoned shortly after ASX Limited was formed. One of its new futures, the Mini200, competed directly with an SFE product, suggesting ASX was no longer interested in a merger with SFE. About the same time, SFE acquired Austraclear Limited, a company in which, just three years earlier, ASX had purchased a minority stake.

## COMPETITORS ON THE SAME EXCHANGE: 2002

In the spring of 2002, SFE went public and was listed on ASX, which became the only exchange in the world to list two publicly traded exchanges. At the time of SFE's listing, Robert Elstone, head of SFE, indicated that his exchange was interested in a merger. He also claimed that ASX's reentrance into futures trading was "cannibalising" the activities of both exchanges.

While ASX's primary business of equity trades and capital raisings burgeoned with a restoration of share-market interest in 2002, its sales of futures sputtered. The company responded by introducing a property trust futures contract and by offering lower fees and rebates to derivative traders who also dealt in ASX futures. Meanwhile, SFE also struggled in the short term. After just two months of being listed on ASX, SFE shares had lost more than 12 percent of their value.

## SCRUTINY OF ASX AND SFE MERGER: 2004–06

During the summer of 2002, criticism as to how ASX governed its exchange began to mount, as the Australian Securities & Investments Commission (ASIC) called for ASX to adopt stricter standards in governing corporations, suggesting ASX's need to produce profits hampered its regulation of its market. In 2004 ASX formed a Market Integrity Division to review and modify exchange practices used to supervise the market.

After seven years of on-again, off-again courting of each other, in March 2006 the Australian Stock Exchange Limited acquired for AUD 2.2 billion SFE Corp. Ltd. and its Sydney Futures Exchange, both of which became subsidiaries of ASX. The merger, approved by the ACCC, represented the first time two listed exchanges in the world sealed such a pact. Elstone became chief executive and managing director of the combined exchange, which at the time comprised the ninth largest in the world, which was renamed ASX Limited later that year.

Soon after the merger the company created ASX Markets Supervision to carry out its exchange-supervisory role and introduced real-time indices for gold and for metals and mining. ASX also supplanted the SEATS trading system with the new CLICK XT, an integrated platform for cash-equity and equity-derivative product trades. In 2007 ASX and Standard & Poor's (S&P) together launched new indices, the S&P/ASX All Australian 50 and S&P/ASX All Australian 200, the latter which was Australia's portion of the Global 1200 index. That same year, ASX debuted its Contracts for Difference (CFDs), the world's first-ever such exchange-traded contracts.

## CHALLENGES IN 2007–09

The monopoly ASX held on trade processing in Australia was challenged in mid-2007 when two companies applied for an Australian Markets License, which would allow them to establish alternative platforms for trading ASX-listed entities. The applicants were Liquidnet Australia, a subsidiary of a leading U.S.-based institutional broker, and AXE ECN, an electronic trading network half-owned by the New Zealand Stock Exchange. Both firms specialized in crossings, off-market orders in which the buying and selling broker were the same, with that broker facilitating a matching order between its buyer and seller. While it awaited word on a license to establish a rival platform, Liquidnet in November 2007 was granted an Australian Financial Services License, allowing it to execute crossings through block trades worth at least $200,000 in assets. The license allowed Liquidnet to facilitate institutional investor trades that utilized an ASX member-broker for final execution. In February 2008 Liquidnet opened for business in Australia, and during the next four months alone, Liquidnet executed AUD 1 billion in trading of ASX-listed securities, with the firm's average trade size worth AUD 1.8 million, 100 times greater than that of the average trade on ASX. In May 2008 a third firm, Chi-X Australia, applied for a license to establish an exchange.

ASX addressed trading capacity, speed of trades, and market supervision issues late in the decade. In 2009 ASX invested in its equity market technology platforms in order to quadruple its trading capacity. The company also expanded its ASX Markets Supervision staff and upgraded its real-time trading surveillance system. Nonetheless, in August 2009 the federal government announced that ASIC would, by the fourth quarter of 2010, assume supervision of market participants in Australia while ASX would retain regulatory control over companies listed on its exchange. The announcement represented the first move to separate ASX from any potential conflict of interest between earning a profit and supervising the market by preparing to place in government agency hands the function of supervising market participants.

For its 2009 fiscal year ending in June, ASX recorded a net profit of AUD 313.6 million, a decline of 14 percent from 2008, on falling revenues of nearly the same percentage. The company, though, believed that given the global economic climate, ASX compared positively against its peer exchanges. Moreover, ASX profits were generated in a year when companies postponed initial public offerings and traders stayed away from equities because of an international credit crisis. ASX revenues had also increased 20 percent since the merger with SFE.

ASX in late 2009 established a co-location hosting service to enlarge its trader data center and accommodate traders that wanted to place their computers closer to exchange servers. Such a co-location system had recently been launched by the London Stock Exchange to allow traders to cut microseconds off trade-execution time. Drawing from the utilities/transport market sector of the S&P/ASX 300 Index, in November 2009 a new infrastructure index was launched on ASX that followed the performance of utilities and transportation stocks. The index was customized for the Australian market, targeted the growing interest in infrastructure holdings, and replicated the S&P Global Infrastructure Index.

As the decade neared a close, ASX launched its Western Australian Wheat (WAW) contract, similar to a wheat contract at the Chicago Stock Exchange. The WAW was one example of ASX increasingly competing with banks that charged customers a significant price for pooled-investment management services. While potential competition loomed from firms seeking to establish alternative trading platforms, ASX had begun competing directly with banks in the managed fund industry. In addition to its property trusts and listed investment management companies (LICs), ASX had developed a portfolio of exchange-traded funds (ETFs) and exchange-traded commodities (ETCs), offering a less costly type of pooled investment than banks.

## ENDING THE MONOPOLY: 2010

In February 2010 ASX announced the planned launch of its next generation of trading systems, ASX Trade, which utilized NASDAQ OMX's trading platform. The new platform was expected to allow for more than five million trades per day, offering trading speeds as fast as anywhere in the world. As ASX moved into the second decade of the 21st century, Elstone believed the company would grow closer to its competitors. He told the *Financial Times* in 2009 that the evolution "could take a number of forms; it could be product distribution co-operation, clearing and settlement co-operation to full-blown merger. Any of those are on that spectrum of possible outcomes.... I think you'll see us becoming even more international over the next five years." At the same time, under current law, ASX remained invulnerable to ownership takeover as no one shareholder was legally able to own more than 15 percent of ASX stock. Elstone, though, was more concerned about ASX's new competitors that could end the company's monopoly than ownership of ASX.

In March 2010 the Australian government gave preliminary approval to Chi-X to operate an alternative trading platform in direct competition with ASX. The government's nod to Chi-X represented its initial approval of financial market competition. AXE and Liquidnet also had pending license applications, but as of April 2010, neither appeared to be pushing the government, perhaps since final clearance for the Chi-X license was not expected to be granted until the fourth quarter of 2010, when ASIC began formally considering new market entrants. In the meantime, Chi-X was in talks with ASX about handling Chi-X clearing and settlement needs, since ASX continued to own the only Australian clearinghouse.

In 2010 ASX was the eighth largest listed exchange in the world, based on market capitalization, and the third largest exchange in the Asia-Pacific region. It also boasted the world's fourth largest equity-generating market, and it had trading hubs in London, New York, Singapore, Hong Kong, and Chicago and a diversified range of products expected to generate future growth. However, that growth in many respects was dependent upon, not only the global economy, but on how the Australian government modified its role as a national stock exchange.

*Roger Rouland*

## PRINCIPAL SUBSIDIARIES

ASX Clearing Corporation Limited; ASX Futures Exchange Pty Limited; ASX Markets Supervision Pty Limited; ASX Settlement and Transfer Corporation Pty Limited; Austraclear Limited; Australian Clearing House Pty Limited; Australian Securities Exchange (U.S.); Australian Stock Exchange Pty Limited; New Zealand Futures and Options Exchange Limited; SFE Clearing Corporation Pty Limited; SFE Corporation Limited; Sydney Futures Exchange Limited.

## PRINCIPAL DIVISIONS

Business Development; Markets Supervision; Operations; Technology.

## PRINCIPAL COMPETITORS

AXA Asia Pacific Holdings Limited; AXE ECN Pty Ltd.; Bendigo and Adelaide Bank Limited; Chi-X Australia Pty Ltd.; IntercontinentalExchange, Inc.; International Securities Exchange Holdings, Inc.; London Stock Exchange Group plc; NYSE Euronext; Perpetual Limited; Singapore Exchange Limited; Liquidnet Australia Pty Ltd.

## FURTHER READING

Adamson, Graeme, *Miners and Millionaires: The First One Hundred Years of the People, Markets and Companies of the Stock Exchange in Perth, 1889–1989.* Perth, Australia: Australian Stock Exchange Limited, 1989.

"ASX Joins NASDAQ in Strategic Alliance," *AsiaPulse News,* June 17, 1999.

"Aussie Regulation May End ASX Monopoly," *Compliance Reporter,* February 5, 2010.

Carew, Edna, *Fast Forward: The History of the Sydney Futures Exchange.* St. Leonards, Australia: Allen & Unwin, 1993.

———, *National Market, National Interest: The Drive to Unify Australia's Securities Markets.* Crows Nest, Australia: ASX Operations Pty Ltd, 2007.

Lowenstein, Jack, "Sydney Shook but Never Closed," *Euromoney,* December 1987, p. 59.

"SFE Launches Merger Broadside," *Australasian Business Intelligence,* April 14, 2002, p.1008104i9696.

"Sydney Futures Exchange Considered Merging with ASX," *AsiaPulse News,* October 30, 2001.

"Transcript: Robert Elstone, CEO of ASX," *Financial Times,* September 17, 2009.

Uribe, Alice, "Chi-X Gets Trading Green Light: More Players Could Lower Fees," *Investor Daily Online,* April 1, 2010, http://www.investordaily.com.au/cps/rde/xchg/id/style/8892.htm?rdeCOQ=SID-0A3D9633-157992A6.

# Augusta National Inc.

—————————■—————————

**2604 Washington Road**
**Augusta, Georgia 30904**
**U.S.A.**
**Telephone: (706) 667-6000**
**Fax: (706) 736-2321**
**Web site: http://www.masters.com/**

*Private Company*
*Incorporated:* 1935
*Employees:* 200
*Sales:* $10.60 million (2009)
*NAICS:* 711219 Other Spectator Sports

■ ■ ■

Augusta National Inc. is the corporation that owns and operates the Augusta National golf course and country club, home of the prestigious annual Masters tournament, which is one of the game's four major tournaments. The country club is highly exclusive, limited to about 300 members. Membership is strictly invitation only, and the ranks of the club include titans of finance and industry as well as politicians and well-known golfers, but no women. Members are not allowed to reveal the inner workings of the club or to exploit Augusta National financially. An unwritten rule even forbids them from discussing business at the club. Additionally, the Masters is tightly run by the corporation and is far less of a commercial vehicle than other golf tournaments. Television coverage is also limited, the number of commercials are prescribed, and announcers are forbidden from mentioning prize money.

## AUGUSTA NATIONAL'S FOUNDING

Augusta National's beginnings can be traced to 1930, when the famed golfer Bobby Jones announced his retirement from championship golf, a year in which he won golf's so-called Grand Slam. Born in Atlanta, Georgia, in 1902, Jones was the quintessential amateur golfer. He dominated the 1920s, winning 13 of the 21 major championships he played from 1923 to 1930. For years Jones had dreamed of building a golf course, and a friend, Clifford Roberts, suggested that because Jones had retired from championship play he now had the time to make that dream a reality.

Born Charles de Clifford Roberts Jr. on an Iowa farm in 1894, Roberts made his way to Wall Street to become an investment banker despite an education that never went beyond the eighth grade. He became a golf enthusiast and joined the Knollwood Country Club in New York's Westchester County, where he met Jones, who played an exhibition at the club in the mid-1920s. Both men also played winter golf in Augusta, which was located 150 miles east of Atlanta and offered a mild enough climate to permit the game to be played year-round. When Roberts suggested that Jones should build a golf course and offered to secure the financing, it was in Augusta that they searched for a suitable property.

In 1931 Jones and Roberts turned to a mutual friend who lived in Augusta, Thomas Barrett Jr., and he suggested Fruitland Nurseries, a 365-acre property that had been out of operation for the past dozen years but left behind the magnolias and azaleas that would become signature features of the Augusta National golf course. Upon seeing Fruitland Nurseries, Jones declared the property to be a perfect site, and Roberts went to work on securing an option on the property for $70,000.

## COURSE OPEN TO MEMBERS: 1933

Jones chose Alister Mackenzie to serve as the course architect. In February 1931 construction began on Augusta National, so named by Jones. Just 76 working days later the course was completed, due in large measure to the minimalist design. Even though some members began playing the course in December 1932, it was not formally opened until January 1933.

The business plan developed for Augusta National by Jones and Roberts envisioned 1,800 members, in that each member would pay $350 to join and an annual due of $60. Once the membership roles reached 1,000, an 18-hole course for women would be added. Also envisioned were tennis courts, outdoor squash courts, a bridle path, and private houses that would line the course. Roberts turned to Wall Street to find members and Jones tapped his many acquaintances. The country was in the midst of the Great Depression, however, and it was hardly the ideal time to sell memberships to a new golf club, even one associated with the great Bobby Jones. As a result, Augusta National had less than 100 members when it opened.

The lack of funds curtailed the ambitions of Jones and Roberts, and in retrospect the austerity it imposed kept the focus on the golf course and in time added to the mystique of Augusta National. It also forced the founders to consider hosting a professional tournament as a way to pay the bills. To ensure its success, Jones was persuaded to come out of retirement to participate. After failing to secure the U.S. Open for Augusta, the partners decided to host their own invitational. Jones rejected the idea of calling the tournament the Masters, which he thought too presumptuous, so it was called the Augusta National Invitation Tournament instead.

## FIRST TOURNAMENT: 1934

The first Augusta tournament was held in 1934. It was hardly an overnight success. Once the novelty of having Jones on the course faded, participation decreased steadily, from 72 players in the first tournament to 42 in 1938. The tournament was out of the way, played early in the season, and did not offer enough cash prizes to entice many professionals to make the expensive journey to inland Georgia. Ticket sales also dwindled. Because the club was desperate to sell tickets, it pampered its patrons by offering unobstructed views, pristine bathrooms, and excellent, low-priced food.

Poor cash flow had an immediate impact on the fortunes of Augusta National, which was delinquent in making its interest payments. The local Augusta bank that had financed the construction of the course and held the mortgage bonds grew concerned that it would not be repaid. Roberts allowed the bank to foreclose on the property in 1935, and on the courthouse steps he immediately bought it back at auction for a private company he formed, Augusta National Inc.

Even though the 1930s were a struggle, many aspects of Augusta National were established during this period. The members began wearing green jackets in 1937, and in 1939 Jones relented and the name of the annual tournament became the Masters. It was not until after World War II, however, that the Masters and Augusta National began to grow in stature. Because of the war the club was closed in 1943 and 1944, and the grounds were used for grazing cattle and turkeys. Members began playing the course again in 1945. A year later the Masters resumed, this time with increased prize money to entice greater participation from professionals.

## GROWTH IN POSTWAR YEARS: LATE FORTIES TO LATE SEVENTIES

Professional golf increased in popularity during the postwar years and as did Augusta National. The club was given a particular boost by General Dwight D. Eisenhower, who enjoyed a vacation with his wife at Augusta National in 1948 and became a member. He brought more prestige to the club four years later, when he was elected president of the United States. It was also during the postwar years, in 1949, that the winner of the Masters was awarded a green jacket.

Roberts shaped the modern golf tournament in the years following the war. The first field scoreboards were added to the course in 1947, and in 1949 the 11th hole became the first fairway to be roped to control spectators. In 1955 telephones were installed at each hole to report scores directly to the scoreboards. In 1960

## KEY DATES

**1931:** Land is purchased for the Augusta National golf course.
**1934:** The first Augusta National Invitation Tournament is held.
**1935:** Augusta National Inc. is formed to buy the course out of foreclosure.
**1948:** Dwight D. Eisenhower becomes a club member.
**1991:** Ron Townsend becomes Augusta National's first African-American member.

Roberts introduced the standards for posting the players' individual scores.

The 1970s brought a changing of the guard at Augusta National. Jones, who had been diagnosed with syringomyelia in 1948, had been wasting away for years, but remained president until his death in 1971. Roberts continued to run the Masters and control Augusta National with a tight grip until 1976, when on the eve of the Masters the 82-year-old announced his retirement. In 1977 Roberts suffered a stroke and in September of that year took his life with a self-inflicted gunshot wound.

## CONTROVERSY ABOUT MEMBERSHIP

While Augusta National and the Masters had become revered in golfing circles, it was not without some measure of controversy. The course was located in the heart of the old South in a city that was proud of its Confederate heritage. In 1969 Jim Murray of the *Los Angeles Times* denounced the Masters for never having any African-American players in column that featured the headline "As White as the Ku Klux Klan." Even though the Masters was considered an invitational tournament, most of its slots were determined by performance, and invitations were limited to international players, in keeping with Jones's desire to make the Masters a global event. Unwilling to bend the rules, Roberts, who claimed to hold no animosity toward golfers of color, waited for an African-American golfer to qualify. Finally, in 1974 the African-American golfer Lee Elder won the Monsanto Open on the fourth playoff hole and gained entrance to the Masters. He would qualify for five of the next six Masters.

Having carved out a special place in the sports world, Augusta National and the Masters were able to dictate their own terms. It was not until 1982 that the first and second rounds of the tournament were televised. Commercials remained limited to just four minutes per hour, making it essentially a break-even proposition for its longtime broadcast partner, CBS Sports, which continued to cover the event because of the associated prestige. Augusta National also carried enough weight that it was able to ban the sports announcers Gary McCord and Jack Whitaker, who overstepped the bounds of what its leadership considered acceptable commentary.

The race issue again came to the fore in 1990, when Hall Thompson, a member of Augusta National and the founder of Shoal Creek Golf Club in Birmingham, Alabama, which was about to host the Professional Golfers' Association Championship, told an interviewer that Shoal Creek explicitly banned African-Americans from its membership. A media frenzy followed and exclusive country clubs across the country scrambled to find suitable African-American members, who would factiously dub themselves "the class of 1990." Augusta National followed suit, and in 1991 Ron Townsend, the president of the Gannett Television Group, became the first African-American member.

Augusta National became embroiled in another controversy in September 2002, when Martha Burk, the head of the National Council of Women's Organization, began pressuring the club to admit a woman member. William Johnson, the chairman of Augusta National, refused to cave and even dropped the Coca-Cola Company, Citigroup Inc., and IBM Corporation as sponsors to keep them from being caught up in the flap. Even though the controversy did not extend beyond the 2003 Masters, Burk did not give up her crusade. Instead, she opted to pressure the corporations whose leaders were club members by forming Women on Wall Street, a corporate responsibility project that began showing results, including a $46 million settlement of a gender discrimination lawsuit against the investment firm Morgan Stanley.

Whether Augusta National would ever admit a woman member remained to be seen. The club and the tournament that defined it continued to cling tightly to tradition. Nevertheless, the Masters was the first golf tournament to be televised in high definition, and changes were made to the course to counter advances in golf technology and the long-shot ability of contemporary players. The green jackets and other traditions, however, would likely remain unchanged.

*Ed Dinger*

## PRINCIPAL COMPETITORS

Professional Golfers' Association of America; Pinehurst LLC; R&A Group Services Ltd.

## FURTHER READING

Amdur, Neil, "Clifford Roberts, a Founder and Longtime Chief of the Masters Golf Tournament Is Dead at 84," *New York Times*, September 30, 1977, p. 30.

Anderson, Dave, "Sports of the Times; Augusta's Rewarding 'Golf Nut,'" *New York Times*, April 14, 1991.

Murray, Jim, "As White as the Ku Klux Klan," *Los Angeles Times*, April 6, 1969.

Owen, David, *The Making of the Masters: Clifford Roberts, Augusta National, and Golf's Most Prestigious Tournament.* New York: Simon & Schuster, 1999.

Radosta, John S., "It's the Last Masters for the Master," *New York Times*, April 8, 1976, p. 49.

Shipnuck, Alan, *The Battle for Augusta National: Hootie, Martha, and the Masters of the Universe.* New York: Simon & Schuster, 2004.

Thomaselli, Rich, "Masters May Face Sponsor-less Future," *Advertising Age*, March 10, 2003, p. 39.

# Barnes & Noble College Booksellers, Inc.

120 Mountain View Boulevard
Basking Ridge, New Jersey 07920
U.S.A.
Telephone: (908) 991-2665
Fax: (908) 991-2846
Web site: http://www.bncollege.com/

*Wholly Owned Subsidiary of Barnes & Noble, Inc.*
*Founded:* 1965 as Student Book Exchange
*Employees:* 12,000
*Sales:* $1.8 billion (FY 2009)
*NAICS:* 451211 Book Stores

■ ■ ■

Barnes & Noble College Booksellers, Inc., is a wholly owned subsidiary of Barnes & Noble, Inc., and is a leading contract operator of college bookstores in the United States. In 2010 it operated 639 bookstores for colleges and universities, including many of the top U.S. institutions. Barnes & Noble College Booksellers replaces the traditional campus cooperatives at universities, medical schools, law schools, and community colleges, selling textbooks, trade books, school supplies, and emblematic items, including school logos and collegiate clothing. It serves about 4 million students and 250,000 faculty, with schools receiving a percentage of sales.

## BEGINNINGS AS STUDENT BOOK EXCHANGE: 1965

During the early 1960s, Leonard S. Riggio, a Brooklyn resident who had skipped two grades in school, was a night student at New York University and worked in the university's bookstore in Greenwich Village. Bored with his classes but an enthusiastic reader, he dropped out of school and in 1965 opened a competing store, the Student Book Exchange, which became one of New York's finest bookstores, with a wide selection of books, a knowledgeable staff, and excellent service. By 1970 Riggio had six other college bookstores, and in 1971 he bought Barnes & Noble, a bookstore located at 18th Street and Fifth Avenue in Manhattan for $1.2 million. The sale also included the rights to the Barnes & Noble trade name.

Barnes & Noble had been established in 1917 when G. Clifford Noble merged his business with a bookselling company founded by Charles Barnes in 1873. By the time Riggio purchased Barnes & Noble, however, its Manhattan bookstore was in decline. Riggio transformed it within a few years by increasing its inventory, offering 150,000 textbook and trade book titles. Soon it became known as the "world's largest bookstore."

In addition to offering a huge selection of books, Barnes & Noble, Inc., was a marketing innovator. It was the first bookseller to advertise on television in 1974 and was the first to discount bestsellers. During the 1970s Barnes & Noble College Booksellers expanded to meet student and faculty needs in all 50 states.

## COLLEGE BUSINESS NOT TAKEN PUBLIC: 1993

In 1986 Barnes & Noble bought the rival B. Dalton Bookseller and its more than 600 stores, with Leonard Riggio financing the purchase (estimated at $275 million to $300 million) by selling a stake in everything except Barnes & Noble College Booksellers to a group of minority investors.

Barnes & Noble, Inc., went public on the New York Stock Exchange in 1993, with Riggio having 29 percent of the equity and the provision that no other investor could own more than 20 percent of the company. Barnes & Noble College Booksellers, remained privately held and owned the rights to the Barnes & Noble brand, which it licensed in perpetuity to the public company. Barnes & Noble College Booksellers thus benefited from investments Barnes & Noble made in such areas as advertising and also received royalties on textbooks sold through its Web site. In 1995 the retailer Vendex International, N.V., Amsterdam sold its 32 percent stake in Barnes & Noble College Booksellers for shares in Barnes and Noble's trade publishing unit.

## ONE OF THE LARGEST U.S. PRIVATE FIRMS: 1999

At Brandeis University in Waltham, Massachusetts, a weeklong student boycott of the campus bookstore, operated by Barnes & Noble College Booksellers, ended on February 25, 1990. The boycott began after accusations were made against two managers of the store of discrimination against black students, who were purportedly suspected as shoplifters. At the time, Brandeis had 3,700 undergraduate and graduate students, only 90 of whom were African American. Barnes & Noble College Booksellers investigated the charges and praised the managers as "valued employees" but brought in a new management team. Barnes & Noble College

Booksellers also agreed to establish a new system to handle grievances, to make a concerted effort to hire more black students, and to implement a racial sensitivity and awareness-training program for all of its employees.

Controversy also arose in New York, in 1993, when Encore College Bookstores sued the state's College of Technology in Farmingdale, which had a campus bookstore operated by Barnes & Noble College Booksellers. Encore complained that it was denied access to professors' reading lists that were given to Barnes & Noble and was thus unable to stock the books needed by students. The State Supreme Court ruled against Encore.

In Texas in 1994, Robert Smith, a Texas A&M university official and one of the two lead negotiators in the $10 million contract awarded to Barnes & Noble College Booksellers by the state university system in 1990, was convicted of charges of solicitation of gifts as a public official. Smith had asked Barnes & Noble to cover the expenses of his wife's business trip to New York City, which it had done for Smith and Ross Margraves, chairman of the Board of Regents, during their 1990 negotiations. Similarly, in 1993 internal investigations at the University of Oklahoma found conflicts of interest about four trips sponsored by Barnes & Noble College Booksellers, which also signed a contract with the university in 1990. The university's president and vice president resigned.

By the end of the decade Barnes & Noble College Booksellers had grown into one of the largest private companies in the United States as ranked by *Forbes*, with estimated 1999 revenues of $830 million.

## THE END OF PRIVATE OWNERSHIP: 2009

In June 2003 Barnes & Noble College Booksellers moved from its Manhattan headquarters across the street from the Barnes & Noble flagship store on Fifth Avenue to Basking Ridge, New Jersey, and continued its expansion with additional university bookstores.

A federal report in 2005 found that textbook prices had increased at twice the inflation rate and that from 1986 to 2004 textbook prices had tripled. In response, Barnes & Noble College Booksellers began a pilot textbook rental program at three of its campus locations for the fall 2009 semester. Hardcover texts were rented at 35 percent of the list price, but paperbacks were not included because they became worn more quickly and easily. The program was limited by the reluctance of professors to commit to using the same textbooks for at least two years.

## KEY DATES

**1917:** Booksellers Charles Barnes and G. Clifford Noble merge their businesses to found Barnes & Noble in New York.

**1965:** Leonard Riggio opens the Student Book Exchange in New York City's Greenwich Village.

**1971:** Riggio buys the flagship Barnes & Noble bookstore and the Barnes & Noble trade name.

**1993:** Barnes & Noble, Inc., goes public; Barnes & Noble College Booksellers remains privately held.

**2009:** Barnes & Noble, Inc., completes acquisition of Barnes & Noble College Booksellers.

In August 2009 Riggio, the owner of Barnes & Noble College Booksellers and the chairman of Barnes & Noble, Inc., announced that Barnes & Noble would acquire Barnes & Noble College Booksellers as a wholly owned subsidiary. To avoid a conflict of interest in the transaction, Barnes & Noble set up an independent committee of directors to evaluate the purchase. At the time, the college business had a leading market position in the growing campus book business. About 35 percent of all the nation's college bookstores were run by Barnes & Noble College Booksellers, which had experienced a rise in same-store sales of 1 percent in FY 2009 (ended May 2, 2009) and had annual revenues of $1.8 billion. The sale was completed in September for $596 million, and Riggio remained as chairman. As part of the agreement, Barnes & Noble also acquired the Barnes & Noble trade name that it had been licensing from the College Booksellers.

At the time of the acquisition, Riggio commented: "With U.S. college enrollment projected to reach over 20 million students by 2015, and education-related consumption continuing to increase, a growing number of academic institutions are seeking to outsource their bookstores to an experienced operating partner who can deliver an attractive revenue stream, as well as consistent, high quality services for students and faculty. College's leading market position, superior quality, and Barnes & Noble branding make us the operator of choice for academic institutions who want a partner with a heritage of retail bookselling, respect for intellectual property, a strong customer service culture and a track record of client satisfaction."

In March 2010 Riggio's younger brother, Stephen Riggio, who had served as Barnes & Noble's chief executive officer since 2002, was replaced by William Lynch, the president of Barnes & Noble's Web division. Stephen Riggio stayed on as vice chairman of Barnes & Noble. At the same time, Mitchell Klipper was named chief executive officer of the company's retail group, which included the 639 college bookstores as well as 723 general retail centers. Leonard Riggio projected that the number of stores would "not change much" during the next couple of years as the country's largest bookstore chain embraced a digital future.

*Louise B. Ketz*

## PRINCIPAL COMPETITORS

A Book Company, LLC.; Follett Corporation; Nebraska Book Company, Inc.

## FURTHER READING

Carvajal, Doreen, "Trying to Read a Hazy Future: Another Metamorphosis for Barnes & Noble Chief," *New York Times*, April 18, 1999.

Dougherty, Philip H., "On Two Worlds of Publishing," *New York Times*, October 11, 1974.

Hadas, Edward, and Robert Cyran, "Pushing the Limits of Stimulus Plans," *New York Times*, August 10, 2009.

Rich, Motoko, "Barnes & Noble Promotes the Head of Its Web Division to Chief Executive," *New York Times*, March 18, 2010.

# Behr Process Corporation

---

3400 West Segerstrom Avenue
Santa Ana, California 92704
U.S.A.
Telephone: (714) 545-7101
Fax: (714) 241-1002
Web site: http://www.behr.com

*Wholly Owned Subsidiary of Masco Corporation*
*Founded:* 1947
*Employees:* 350
*Sales:* $1.63 billion (2008)
*NAICS:* 325510 Paint and Coating Manufacturing

■ ■ ■

Behr Process Corporation is a paint, varnish, and stain company whose products are exclusively sold by the home improvement big-box giant the Home Depot. As that company's "premium" paint supplier, Behr has sales figures that place it as the sixth largest paint and coatings manufacturer in North America. Founded in 1947 and maintained for 52 years as a family-owned company, Behr was acquired by Masco Corporation, a huge company best known for making Delta faucets and fixtures. However, Behr continued to operate fairly independently. Despite some high-profile lawsuits that threatened parent-company Masco's stock prices in 2002, Behr held its own in the 21st century, responding to the global economic crisis that began in 2008 with layoffs and plant closures. By 2010, as home sales began to pick up in the United States, signs pointed toward the company's recovery.

## A FAMILY COMPANY: 1947–99

Behr Process Corporation was founded in 1947 by Otho Behr Jr., who used his station wagon to distribute linseed oil to paint companies. Paint companies, however, were searching for a better alternative than linseed oil for effectively preserving redwood. Behr asked his father, a chemist, to help him develop a clear finish and stain for redwood. Soon the duo was producing stains and finishes in the family garage. By 1948 business was good enough to enable Behr to move his business into dedicated office space in Pasadena, California.

In the subsequent three decades, Behr remained a family-owned company that primarily sold its stains and finishes in California. However, a friendship between Behr partner Kevin Jaffe and the Atlanta founders of Home Depot resulted in a 1978 partnership in which Home Depot, which at the time had only two stores in the Atlanta area, would become a distributor of Behr products. It was a propitious partnership for Behr. The Home Depot, a one-stop shopping superstore for do-it-yourself homeowners, grew exponentially, and by 2010 was the world's largest home improvement chain and the second largest U.S. retailer after Wal-Mart. Behr, "at one time a relatively obscure regional stain manufacturer in California," wrote Joe Maty in *Paint & Coatings Industry*, "rode the home-center express to national prominence." As a result, the company enjoyed an annual sales growth of 25 percent in the last decade of the 20th century, an unheard of rate in the paint and coatings industry.

At the urging of Home Depot, Behr expanded into architectural paints in 1986. In that year the company first offered a full line of paints available exclusively at the big-box store. The company's director of marketing, Brian Sauer, told Maty that Behr's owners "saw that Home Depot was going to take off, and teamed up with them to make it happen. It's been an excellent partnership."

### PURCHASE BY MASCO: 1999–2002

Despite rumors that Behr itself was in acquisitions mode, in 1999 the Masco Corporation, a home improvement company that made Delta brand faucets as well as cabinets, locks, and other building materials, announced it would buy Behr Process Corporation as well as four other building products companies. Masco did not disclose what it paid for Behr, lumping the price of the company in with that of Mill's Pride, a cabinetmaker. The two companies together cost $3.1 billion. One of the prime motivators for acquiring Behr was its relationship with Home Depot. The five acquisitions allowed the new parent company to triple its business with the home improvement giant. Vice president of investor relations for Masco, Skip Cypert, told Monica Toriello in *National Home Center News*, "The fact that they're very strong with Home Depot means they have great growth ahead of them." For its part, Behr stockholders got stock options in a much larger company, and Behr continued to operate fairly independently of its new parent. Behr itself gained a subsidiary when Masco acquired Masterchem Industries, LLC, a paint primer and coatings manufacturing company, from Williams Holdings and made it a subsidiary of Behr.

Observers would later argue that the Behr acquisition was one in a line of questionable decisions made by the board of Masco. In fact, Behr had been sued in 1998, a year before the acquisition, by a group of homeowners in Washington State who had used its Super Liquid Raw-Hide and Natural Seal Plus wood sealants. Both products were advertised to block mildew on wood siding for years. Both products, however, actually

contained linseed oil, an ingredient that could work to promote mildew. Homeowners found their new wood siding treated with the product would begin to blacken with mildew within a year.

Behr attempted to argue that homeowners were applying the products incorrectly as well as claiming that the "guarantee" advertised on the label of Super Liquid Raw-Hide was actually "puffery," basically an advertisement designed to boost sales rather than imply a warrantee. A judge found, however, that the guarantee was not puffery and that the company had breached its warrantees. A jury awarded homeowners damages of between $14,000 and $87,000. Within months a judge ruled that Behr had "prey[ed] upon customers' ignorance" and awarded additional damages, for a total class-action suit with recovery expected to exceed $100 million.

In September 2002, when Masco lost its appeal in the case, shares of Behr's parent company declined 16 percent on the news that the company had filed with the SEC a statement that said that payouts in the class-action suit could be "material to its financial position and results of operations." Despite protestations and clarifications from Masco, the stock was slow to rebound. Within months the company settled the case for upwards of $2 million, but as part of the deal admitted no wrongdoing. Nevertheless, Behr continued to grow. Chris Cziborr reported in the *Orange County Business Journal* that Behr saw double-digit revenue growth in 2001 due in part to the home refinancing boom.

### CONTINUED GROWTH: 2003–10

New marketing tools helped Behr continue its phenomenal growth. In 2003 Behr introduced its ColorSmart interactive kiosks and online tools to help make color choices easier for consumers. In 2005 Behr redesigned its Web site to serve as a redecorating and color inspiration site, focusing on the needs of do-it-yourself homeowners. The ColorSmart tool was integrated into the new Web site to enable consumers to create projects with coordinated colors and save color samples and entire projects for future reference. Just two years later Behr introduced the newest interactive tool for consumers, an online application called Paint Your Place. The software, available in 2007 for a small yearly subscription and later distributed free of charge, allowed consumers to upload photographs of rooms and then test new paint colors by pointing and clicking.

Behr also continued research and development of new architectural coating products. In 2007 Behr began marketing a new premium paint called Behr Premium Plus. The new paint used nanotechnology, essentially

## KEY DATES

**1947:** Otho Behr Jr. begins selling linseed oil to paint companies and develops a clear varnish and a stain for use on redwood.

**1978:** Behr begins to sell products through The Home Depot.

**1986:** Behr expands into the production of architectural paints.

**1999:** Behr is acquired by Masco Corporation.

**2002:** Class action lawsuit over Behr products is settled.

narrowed its losses down to $7 million from $74 million in the first quarter of 2009. Paints and stains, however, were reported to have performed favorably. At the end of the quarter, sales began to pick up, reported CEO Tim Wadhams. In fact, encouraging new home sales in March 2010 probably meant that Behr could count on better economic fortunes ahead.

*Melissa J. Doak*

### PRINCIPAL SUBSIDIARIES

Masterchem Industries, LLC.

### PRINCIPAL COMPETITORS

Benjamin Moore & Co.; Kelly-Moore Paint Company, Inc.; The Sherwin-Williams Company.

### FURTHER READING

Covert, Erin, "Paint Your Place, Virtually," *Denton Record-Chronicle*, March 1, 2010.

Cziborr, Chris, "Paint Maker Behr Rides Fix-Up Wave," *Orange County Business Journal*, August 19, 2002, p. 4.

Fujii, Reed, "Santa Ana, Calif.–Based Paint Company to Settle Lawsuit for $107.5 Million," *The Record* (Stockton, CA), October 31, 2002.

"Judge Finds Behr 'Prey upon Customers' Ignorance'; Awards Treble Damages, Class Relief, and Judgment," *PR Newswire*, September 6, 2000.

"Jury Awards Damages over Wood-Protection Products That Caused Mildew Growth," *Associated Press Newswires*, May 25, 2000.

Lloyd, Mary Ellen, "Masco Lawsuit Impact Unclear: Some Say Shares Oversold," *Dow Jones News Service*, September 20, 2002.

"Masco 1Q Loss Narrows but Posts First Sales Growth in Years," *Dow Jones Business News*, April 26, 2010.

Maty, Joe, "Bold Brush Strokes," *Paint & Coatings Industry*, September 1, 2000.

Parker, Karen, "PCI 25 Reflects Industry Consolidation," *Paint & Coatings Industry*, July 1, 2009.

Toriello, Monica, "Masco Finds Five More to Its Liking," *National Home Center News*, September 20, 1999.

technology that allowed the company to change surface characteristics of its paints by manipulating materials at the molecular level. The new paint, the company promised, would provide one-coat coverage. A gallon of Behr Premium Plus cost $6 more than other Behr products.

The new interactive technologies that catered to consumers' desires to have assistance selecting paint colors and the promises of the premium paint paid off for Behr. In 2008 Behr Paints ranked highest in customer satisfaction with interior paint, according to a survey by J.D. Power and Associates. Nevertheless, the global economic recession hit Behr just as hard as it hit other paint and coatings companies in the United States. *Dow Jones Business News* reported that the housing crisis and the resulting global economic recession had seriously hurt the company: "Masco's top line depends on people opening up their checkbooks to buy new homes and renovate, the kind of spending that plummeted in the housing and economic downturns." As a result of this sales downturn, the company closed manufacturing facilities and cut jobs.

There were some signs in 2010 that Behr was on the road to economic recovery. Although analysts expected Masco to break even in the first quarter of 2010 (the company did not break out Behr's revenues from the parent company's), Masco only significantly

# Benjamin Moore & Co.

101 Paragon Drive
Montvale, New Jersey 07645
U.S.A.
Telephone: (201) 573-9600
Toll Free: (800) 344-0400
Fax: (201) 573-9046
Web site: http://www.benjaminmoore.com

*Wholly Owned Subsidiary of Berkshire Hathaway Inc.*
*Founded:* 1883
*Incorporated:* 1883 as Moore Brothers
*Employees:* 2,000
*Sales:* $1 billion (2008)
*NAICS:* 325510 Paint and Coating Manufacturing;
424950 Paint, Varnish, and Supplies Merchant
Wholesalers; 444120 Paint and Wallpaper Stores

■ ■ ■

Benjamin Moore & Co. is a leading manufacturer of high quality paints, stains, and protective coatings, with operations in both the United States and Canada. From its origins as a family-run paint business, the firm grew into an industry leader, ranking as the eighth largest U.S. paint company by 2009 in the annual *Paint & Coatings Industry* PCI 25. By 2010 Benjamin Moore products ranged from interior and exterior latex and oil-based paints to industrial maintenance coatings, safety-coated industrial enamels, porch and floor enamels, wood stains and finishes, and swimming pool paint, in a broad spectrum of colors. While other companies attempted to leverage their products into big-box home improvement stores in the 21st century, Benjamin Moore charted its own retail course, selling its paints through approximately 4,000 independent dealers in the United States and Canada, through Ace Hardware stores, and directly to consumers over the Internet.

## QUALITY FROM THE START: 1883

The company's origins date back to 1883, when Benjamin Moore and his brother, Robert Moore, started a family-run paint business, the Moore Brothers, in Brooklyn, New York. At the time, the paint and coatings industry was still in its infancy. Not until the mid-1880s did paint producers move decisively toward bulk production and distribution of their products. Chemical advances in such areas as film-forming compounds, emulsions, and inorganic pigment production helped the growing industry cover more and more ground (and surface area) with increasingly durable and adhesive products. Benjamin Moore rode the wave, growing rapidly beyond the regional market of New York and, within years, across the border into Canada and beyond.

The Moore brothers distinguished themselves from the competition by stringently adhering to their slogan: "quality, start to finish." Most other paint manufacturers laid claim to products of comparable quality, but the Moores were unique in their willingness to risk market share by charging a premium for their truly premium paints. This strategy would eventually pay off. Once the company had cornered the market niche that was willing and able to distinguish truly premium quality paints, by such criteria as greater durability, broader color spectrums and pigment quality, and easier application, they could depend on their reputation for

continued success. Indeed, the numbers demonstrated
that consumers were willing to pay top dollar to invest
in protective, and beautifying, coatings for their homes
and equipment.

From the outset, Benjamin Moore implemented a
distribution strategy that helped maintain its niche appeal to premium quality paint users and helped separate
it from the competition. Into the 1990s the company
sold its products only through independent Benjamin
Moore paint dealers. Generally, paint reaches the
consumer in one of three ways: Companies can make
private-label paints for retailers; they can sell their own
brands in hardware stores, home centers, and decorating
stores; or they can operate their own retail stores, selling
to consumers and painting contractors. While most
companies employ a combination of these methods,
Benjamin Moore for many years adhered to its strict
system of certifying specific dealers and selling its
products only through them.

The company continued to grow even when the nation encountered tough times, expanding through
World War I, the difficult Depression years, and into
the World War II era. In the mid-1940s the research
and development of latex-based paint products proved
beneficial to the paint industry in general. As legislation
in various states increasingly controlled solvent-thinned
paint products, water-based latex paints became more
attractive and more environmentally welcome.
Moreover, they were noted for ease of application and
cleanup, a beautiful finish, durability, and outstanding
protective qualities. Benjamin Moore capitalized on
consumer demand for the new product by introducing
its own latex line, which grew into several more specialized lines in the decades that followed.

## PAINT PRODUCTS FOR THE POST–WORLD WAR II ERA

Having focused efforts on numerous industrial coatings
for the war effort, Benjamin Moore was positioned to

market related products for civilian and industrial use in
the postwar era. In 1948 the company founded its
Technical Coatings Co. to formulate and manufacture a
complete line of primers and topcoats for general
industrial coatings as well as coatings used for both rigid
and flexible packaging, vacuum metalizing, wood finishing, and coil stock. Five decades later, that division
retained its high standing in the industry and continued
to grow, acquiring the general industrial coating business
of Cook Paint and Varnish Co. of Kansas City, Missouri, in late 1991.

Benjamin Moore's move into industrial coatings
was just one example of how the company accom-
modated new trends and industry regulations with its
marketing strategies and product lines. In 1968 it
removed lead from its paint formulations as required by
law after the harmful effects of lead poisoning were
made public. The passage of the Occupational Safety
and Health Act (OSHA) in 1971 created an entirely
new niche market of industrial operations seeking quality color-coded coatings to meet the new safety
standards. OSHA required that all industries color mark
physical hazards, safety equipment locations, and fire
and other protective equipment, according to the
American National Standards Institute (ANSI) code.
Benjamin Moore transformed those legal restrictions
into business opportunities, including OSHA/ANSI-
compatible colors in its IronClad Quick Dry Industrial
Enamel line of paints.

With the rise of computer technology in everyday
affairs during the 1980s, Benjamin Moore once again
adapted to the times, introducing computerized color
analysis systems to help its dealers match precise pigments to customers' needs. Previously, dealers had
depended on the company's proprietary Moor-O-Matic
color matching system, introduced in 1959, which used
charts, gradation sheets, and a good measure of eye
expertise to match up to 1,600 colors to particular
projects. The new computerized system, introduced in
the early 1980s, analyzed color specimens to provide a
formula indicating the base and the precise types and
amounts of colorants to match the sample. The system
could match virtually any color, with the exception of
certain intense or fluorescent colors beyond the paint
pigment spectrum. The computerized system was
developed over a seven-year period in collaboration with
Digital Equipment Corp. and consisted of a spectrophotometer (color analyzer) and a minicomputer loaded
with color-matching software fine-tuned to Moore's
paint products.

In 1985 Benjamin Moore also organized a financing
plan that would bring the $24,900 computerized system
within the budgets of interested dealers. After making

## KEY DATES

**1883:** Brothers Benjamin and Robert Moore launch a painting business in Brooklyn, New York.
**1959:** Moor-O-Matic Color System debuts.
**1968:** Benjamin Moore removes lead from its paint formulations.
**2000:** Berkshire Hathaway acquires Benjamin Moore.
**2005:** Benjamin Moore begins opening hundreds of retail stores.
**2006:** Benjamin Moore paints become available in Ace Hardware stores.
**2007:** ColorLock technology is introduced.
**2010:** Company begins selling paint directly to consumers over the Internet.

an initial 10 percent deposit on a system, Benjamin Moore dealers were offered a four-year payment plan by the company. Maurice Workman, Moore's president at the time, told the *Business Journal of New Jersey* that the computer sales were not income-producing for the paint company, but were offered as a means of increasing paint sales for its dealers. The bottom line, however, was beneficial to both Benjamin Moore and those dealers that saw improved sales from the technological sales assistant.

Financial assistance to its certified dealers was nothing new to Benjamin Moore. In the 1960s the company initiated its Temporary Co-Ownership (TCO) program, which provided minority entrepreneurs with the initial funding needed to open a neighborhood paint store, usually approximately $200,000. As the budding businesses turned profitable, the plan called for them to begin buying back their stock, until they fully owned the operation. After the 1992 Los Angeles riots and the media focus on neighborhood reinvestment projects, Benjamin Moore's longstanding program drew considerable attention and praise. Moreover, in mid-1992 the company announced that Triad Systems Corp. would provide automated business and inventory management systems for the outlets participating in its TCO program. The system would permit maximum efficiency and productivity at the store level and also would use a telecommunications package to transmit data (inventory, sales figures, etc.) to a centralized collection point. However, the main objective remained the bottom line: "This is not an altruistic move on our part; this is good business for Benjamin Moore," said Billy Sutton,

western division vice president for the company, in the *Los Angeles Times.*

## ENVIRONMENTAL RESPONSIBILITY, INTERNATIONAL GROWTH: 1980–94

Benjamin Moore had expanded its coverage through thousands of independent dealers in the United States and Canada from the 1950s onward. In the late 1980s and early 1990s, however, the company took more aggressive steps not only to expand its national market share, but to position itself for international growth potential. In 1985 the company opened a new plant in Pell City, Alabama, followed in 1991 by another in Johnstown, New York. In order to develop markets in British Columbia and, eventually, the northwestern United States, the company opened a facility in Aldergrove's Gloucester Industrial Estates (western Canada), replacing a plant it had opened in Burnaby in 1964. The plant, outfitted for production of both latex and alkyd trade sales paints, nearly doubled the company's production capacity on the West Coast. "The plant is designed as a completely closed loop system, for both water-bornes and solvent-bornes. Nothing will be released to either the sewers or the air," said Ron Hoare, senior vice president of the plant, in *Coatings.*

Such environmental conscientiousness, although not new to Benjamin Moore, saw more stringent implementation in response to new Volatile Organic Compounds (VOC) rules and regulations issued by the Environmental Protection Agency and other agencies since the 1980s. As such rules shifted according to region, Benjamin Moore and other paint producers tailored paint formulations to fit VOC standards for the various jurisdictions, making compliance more difficult, though no less prioritized, for the company. "Paint is really a very small part of the emissions problem," Walt Gozden, technical director of the Rohm & Haas Paint Quality Institute, told *Building Supply Home Centers* in July 1990. "But whether that is fair or not, paint manufacturers and retailers are going to have to comply with existing laws."

Benjamin Moore not only complied with environmental laws but continued to stand out as a particularly environmentally friendly paint manufacturer. When the Technical Coatings subsidiary set up a new facility at its Burlington, Canada, site in 1992, for example, VOC considerations were a top priority. In mid-1995 Benjamin Moore received a Pollution Prevention Award for its Milford, Massachusetts, facility's source reduction and recycling activities, which had been in operation since the 1970s.

Along with moves toward environmental efficiency, Benjamin Moore prepared for the 21st century by implementing state-of-the-art computerized management tools at all its facilities. In August 1992, the company began a transition from mainframe-based data processing to client-server computing by installing a nationwide network of 17 IBM AS/400s and 150 PCs. The company began using the software to automate its entire manufacturing operations, from order entry and inventory management to formula management and invoicing. That same year, Benjamin Moore invested approximately $3.5 million in a state-of-the art technical and administrative center in Flanders, New Jersey. The facility housed the company's central laboratories and data processing and engineering departments, as well as a model store for sales training and a "paint farm" for rigorous testing of paint products.

In April 1994 the company announced the formation of a joint venture with Southern Cross Paints, a paint manufacturer headquartered in Auckland, New Zealand, and its existing subsidiary, Benjamin Moore & Co. (NZ) Ltd. The new company, Benjamin Moore Pacific Limited, manufactured both decorative and industrial maintenance coatings. "This joint venture will enable us to meet the growing demands of our existing customer base as well as provide the newest technologies being developed in the coatings industry," stated David Arnold, sales and marketing director of Southern Cross Paints, in *American Paint & Coatings Journal*. For Benjamin Moore, the venture extended the company's growing global presence and added to the list of manufacturing locations that it already boasted in the early 1990s: Birmingham, Boston, Chicago, Cleveland, Dallas, Denver, Houston, Jacksonville, Johnstown, Los Angeles, Montreal, Newark, Richmond, Santa Clara, St. Louis, Toronto, and Vancouver, as well as thousands of dealers across North America.

## INTO THE 21ST CENTURY: ACQUISITION BY BERKSHIRE-HATHAWAY

In 1996 Benjamin Moore extended its commitment to environmental concerns when it joined the Coatings Care Program, a project spearheaded by the National Paints & Coatings Association. The goal of the program was to adopt the highest environmental, health, and safety standards in the industry. As a member of the program, the company was able to anticipate the stricter standards imposed by the revised VOC regulations, which went into effect in September 1999.

The company also was able to apply its environmental awareness to product development during the late 1990s. In 1999 it introduced its Pristine Eco-Spec line of acrylic latex interior paints. In addition to drying very quickly, the innovative new paint contained no solvents and, therefore, released no harmful VOCs, a particularly important quality for painters who worked indoors. At about the same time the company improved its color selection system with the launching of the Color Preview Studio, a revolutionary interactive store display that enabled customers to preview what colors would look like in a home environment. The Studio, which featured a three-dimensional "Room with a View" and more than 1,400 colors, debuted in Benjamin Moore retail locations in January 2000.

As it approached the year 2000, Benjamin Moore had positioned itself as one of the leading paint manufacturers in North America and one of the top 500 private companies. Net sales increased steadily in the last five years of the decade, rising from $564 million in 1995 to $779 million in 1999. By 1999 there were 73 company-owned stores nationwide, along with more than 3,700 authorized retailers in the United States and Canada. The company continued to make strategic acquisitions designed to enlarge its share of the retail paint outlet market, purchasing Janovics/Plaza Inc. in 1999 and Virginia Paint Company the following year. In 1999 it also implemented its Banner Store Program in Canada, to establish uniform standards for advertising and store displays among its sellers north of the border. By the end of the year more than 120 dealers had converted their storefronts to the new system, and another 100 were expected to comply in 2000.

The company began restructuring its operations in 2000, reducing the number of its manufacturing plants from 16 to eight and cutting about 10 percent of its workforce. On November 8, 2000, after more than a century as a major independent paint manufacturer and retailer, Benjamin Moore entered into a merger agreement with Berkshire Hathaway, the Omaha, Nebraska-based holding company led by Warren Buffett. The deal, worth approximately $1 billion, made the paint company a wholly owned subsidiary of Berkshire Hathaway. The buyout, however, was not expected to affect the management structure or operations of Benjamin Moore in any meaningful way, and company officials remained extremely optimistic about the company's future as the acquisition moved forward.

## CHANGES TO RETAILING STRATEGY: 2005

By 2005 Benjamin Moore was reconsidering its retailing strategy and announced plans to open hundreds of Benjamin Moore retail stores. Paint would be sold through these retail outlets as well as through the independent retailers it had always relied upon. Because Benjamin Moore paints were not sold in large retail home improvement stores like Home Depot and Lowe's, the company had been looking for ways to let customers know where to buy Benjamin Moore Paints. "Many people didn't know where to buy our products," director of retail development Alistair Linton told Renee Degross in the *Atlanta Journal-Constitution*. The company gave independent retailers the choice of becoming Benjamin Moore stores. Denis Abrams, president of the company, said, "We've had a long 123-year heritage of not supplying big-box generic operators. We're being very true to the premise of the company that paint is somewhat of a local business and the advice really comes from these independent operators who are tuned into local markets."

By January 2006 Benjamin Moore was again expanding its retail presence, buying the J.C. Lict chain of paint and decorating stores and allying with Ace Hardware Stores to sell Benjamin Moore paints within Ace stores. Although this was a departure from previous company policy, Vice President of Retailing Ed Klein gave the move a different spin in a comment to *Coatings World*, stating, "Benjamin Moore's business model, since its founding in 1883, has been to sell its products through independently-owned retail stores. Working with a strong retail cooperative like Ace continues that commitment while increasing brand awareness through additional distribution outlets." Some small paint store operators, however, saw the alliance as the "beginning of the end of the little paint retailer," as many of these stores would be in competition with the small, independent retailers that Benjamin Moore had used to distribute their paint for more than a hundred years.

## TECHNOLOGY AND MARKETING INNOVATIONS: 2007–10

In 2007 Benjamin Moore rolled out a new, low VOC line of paint, the Aura line, which cost 50 percent more than its standard paint. The new line embedded the color in the binding agent and therefore, was self-priming, requiring, at most, two coats to apply. The paint line was rolled out with sexy advertising featuring paint colors by zodiac sign and silhouettes of naked women. The company did not tout the environmental benefits of the new line, instead focusing on its ease of use, washability, and durability. The product won the "Best of What's New" award from *Popular Science* magazine that year for its ColorLock technology.

The company continued to build on this breakthrough, developing new products on that platform. In 2009 the company rolled out a zero-VOC interior paint called Natura, which was also available in thousands of hues and an array of sheens, unlike its competition, because it utilized the ColorLock technology.

The company incorporated new technologies in marketing as well. In August 2009 a free iPhone application became available that allowed users to take a picture of any color and instantly match it to one of Benjamin Moore's colors. By February 2010 the company announced it would sell directly to consumers over the Internet. Customer service representatives would be available to consumers via a toll-free number. "We've studied this e-commerce decision for a long time, and we believe now is the time to add it into our marketing mix," said Carl Minchew, director of product development, in *Health & Beauty Close-Up*. Minchew did not admit the decision might negatively affect retailers. "While we remain steadfastly committed to our retail partners," he said, "we hope they share our vision that this move will allow the brand to cast its net wider and capture new and more consumers, a benefit to us all."

Benjamin Moore made a variety of business decisions that allowed it to weather the recession that began in 2008 with relative ease. It had consolidated its manufacturing plants in the wake of its acquisition by Berkshire Hathaway, and by 2010 operated only 7 factories and 22 distribution centers. In an interview with Tim Wright in *Coatings World*, Dana Autenrieth, director of product marketing for Benjamin Moore, admitted that sales of interior decorative coatings were down in 2009, specifically because new housing starts were dramatically down. She predicted that 2010 sales would be up, however, and the company had not been forced to lay off any employees as of spring 2010. The company's willingness to experiment with new technologies and new marketing strategies left it well poised to take advantage of economic recovery.

*Kerstan Cohen*
*Updated, Stephen Meyer; Melissa Doak*

## PRINCIPAL COMPETITORS

Akzo Nobel N.V.; Behr Process Corporation; Kelly-Moore Paint Company, Inc.; The Sherwin-Williams Company; Valspar Corporation.

## FURTHER READING

Applegate, Jane, "Moore's Program Lays the Base Coat for Minority-Owned Paint Stores," *Los Angeles Times*, August 31, 1993, p. D3.

"Benjamin Moore, Ace Hardware Form Marketing Alliance," *Coatings World*, January 1, 2006.

"Benjamin Moore to Market Paint and Supplies Online," *Health & Beauty Close-Up*, February 8, 2010.

Berger, Amy, "Benjamin Moore Uses Computers to Analyze Colors," *Business Journal of New Jersey*, June 13, 1985, p. 20.

Casson, Clarence, "Environmental Issues Cloud Paint Strategies," *Building Supply Home Centers*, July 1990, p. 138.

Clemence, Sara, "Patrons Get a Brush with the Process," *Times Union* (Albany, NY), April 3, 2004, p. B11.

Degross, Renee, "Painting Outside the Big Box: Benjamin Moore Has Decided Its Venerable Brand Name Deserves a Place of its Own," *Atlanta Journal-Constitution*, May 4, 2005, p. C1.

"Moore Enters Joint Venture with New Zealand Producer," *American Paint & Coatings Journal*, May 9, 1994, p. 9.

"New B.C. Plant Might Sell Paint to Northwest United States; Benjamin Moore and Co.; British Columbia," *Coatings*, November 1991, p. 25.

Parker, Karen, "PCI 25 Reflects Industry Consolidation," *Paint & Coatings Industry*, July 1, 2009.

Stancavish, Don, "Omaha, Neb., Investor to Buy Montvale, N.J.–Based Paint Company," *Record* (N.J.), November 12, 2000.

Thurston, Charles, "iPhone Camera Meets Benjamin Moore Fan Deck," *Coatings World*, August 2009, pp. 24–25.

Wright, Tim, "The U.S. Interior Decorative Coatings Market," *Coatings World*, January 1, 2010.

# BILL BLASS

# Bill Blass Group Ltd.

236 Fifth Avenue, 5th Floor
New York, New York 10001
U.S.A.
Telephone: (212) 689-8957
Fax: (212) 689-1439
Web site: http://www.billblass.com/

*Wholly Owned Subsidiary of Peacock International Holdings, LLC*
*Incorporated:* 1968 as Bill Blass Inc.
*Employees:* 10
*NAICS:* 315222 Men and Boys' Cut and Sew Suit, Coat and Overcoat Manufacturing; 315233 Women's and Girls' Cut and Sew Dress Manufacturing; 315234 Women's and Girls' Cut and Sew Suit, Coat, Tailored Jacket and Skirt Manufacturing

■ ■ ■

Bill Blass Group Ltd. is the apparel company formed by the famed 20th-century American designer Bill Blass. Beginning in the 1970s Blass's fashions became a favorite of wealthy and prominent women, including Jacqueline Kennedy Onassis and Nancy Reagan. Extending from couture clothing to various other products through licensing agreements, the Bill Blass line included accessories, fragrances, and furniture. Blass sold his business in 1999 and died three years later. Following that time, the Blass house struggled, with a series of designers attempting to replicate the style of one of fashion's giants. Facing bankruptcy, the Blass couture house was shut down in late 2008, with hopes of reviving under new owners Peacock International Holdings.

## "OVERNIGHT" STARDOM: 1960–68

Born in 1922 in Fort Wayne, Indiana (which he told Leila E. B. Hadley in the *Saturday Evening Post* was "a miserable place to grow up in"), Blass knew at a very early age that he wanted to design clothing, and in his teens he was already selling sketches to firms in Manhattan's Seventh Avenue garment district. He left for New York City immediately after graduation from high school, soon finding a job as a $35-a-week sketch artist for a sportswear firm. After service in World War II, he became a designer in the Manhattan firm of Anna Miller and Co., Ltd. During the late 1950s Anna Miller merged her company with her brother's firm, Maurice Rentner Ltd.

Rentner, a manufacturer of high-priced clothing, was noted for catering to the "amply proportioned" woman. "Our 1959 collection was quite a shock to the buyers," Rentner's chairman recalled when later interviewed in the *New York Times* by Nora Ephron. "They came in looking for matronly stuff and we gave them Bill's young look.... They ate it up." Blass quickly rose in the firm to head designer, vice-president, and partner.

By 1963 Blass was a celebrated designer, having received the Coty American Fashion Critics' Award for the second time. His designs were known for quality fabric, simple lines, mix-and-match combinations of fabrics and patterns, impeccable tailoring, and brilliant

## COMPANY PERSPECTIVES

Bill Blass is recognized for bringing fine couture craftsmanship to American sportswear with precise tailoring and impeccable finishing. The intimate atelier of Bill Blass is reflected in each garment, from the comprehensive design process to the meticulous hand construction.

colors. His customers included Jacqueline Kennedy, Happy Rockefeller, and Marilyn Monroe. The beige chantilly-lace dress in which he clad model Jean Shrimpton for a Revlon lipstick ad proved a sensation. Put into production by instant demand, it achieved unprecedented sales in such stores as Bonwit Teller, Lord & Taylor, and Neiman-Marcus. Blass was also designing furs, swimsuits, rainwear, and children's wear for other companies, plus accessories such as shoes, hosiery, scarves, gloves, luggage, jewelry, and wrist-watches. He was even asked to design a tire. The designer established a Rentner licensing and franchising subsidiary, Bill Blass Inc., in 1968.

Blass claimed to be the first American designer of women's apparel to enter the menswear field. He told Barbaralee Diamonstein in *Fashion: The Inside Story* that he designed for the man over 35 who wanted to look "with it, but not ridiculous.... It was a terribly silly period. Grown men looked like their own sons, with long sideburns and bell-bottomed pants and body jewelry." Pincus Brothers-Maxwell began manufacturing, distributing, and marketing Bill Blass menswear, including suits, shirts, ties, shoes (and even a kilt) in 1967. A *Life* article called the line "a blend of Damon Runyon and the Duke of Windsor." "The man over 40 needs help," Blass explained in the magazine. "My [suit] jackets are more fitted and cut higher in the arm hole to make him look thinner and stay thinner." The designer was a recipient of the first Coty Award for Menswear in 1968.

### COMPANY ESTABLISHED IN 1970

Essentially traditional in taste, Blass, despite his commercial and critical success, also found designing women's apparel to be a challenge in this decade. "The single most difficult period for me was the 'sixties,'" he recalled in a 1981 *Vogue* article by Edith Law Gross. "For the first time, clothes came from the street.... Overnight, you had to make clothes that were cut off to here, that were amusing, bizarre, but above all young. I

survived by making crisp, attractive clothes that my customer also could relate to." In 1970 Blass won a third Coty American Fashion Critics' Award and, with it, lifetime membership in the Coty Hall of Fame. Also in 1970, he bought out his Rentner partners and renamed the company Bill Blass Ltd.

The 1960s were the first time that fashion designers became celebrities in their own right and hobnobbed with their wealthy customers. Before that time, Blass told Diamonstein, "The designers were anonymous, they weren't interviewed. They never talked to the press, and they rarely saw the buyers." A handsome and charming bachelor, the sophisticated Blass was perfectly placed to profit from the decade's relaxed social mores. He advanced his career by cultivating the right women, establishing precedent by inviting them to his shows and seating them in the front row. He was not, Cathy Horyn wrote in the *New York Times*, "at the intersection of American fashion and society. He was the intersection."

Blass was also making public appearances around the country, averaging more than 30,000 miles of travel each year, with models wearing his designs in tow. A fashion editor described him to Ephron as "a super-businessman [who] ... can sell the eyelashes off a hog." But he also knew when *not* to sell, having learned, he later told Gross, "one key thing: never sell anybody anything that isn't attractive on her."

### PRODUCT LICENSING, CELEBRITY CLIENTELE: 1970–90

The mainstay of Blass's clothing for women during the 1970s was the blazer. Trousers were prominent and were dressed up with fur-trimmed wrap coats and cardigan sweaters. The designer introduced his Blassport ready-to-wear sportswear division in 1972. Three years later he revived the cocktail dress and in 1978 added a signature perfume.

The total volume of Bill Blass sales by all licensees reached the $200-million level in 1980. By the early 1980s Blass's roster of licensees came to 30 in the United States alone. His name was now on perfumes and colognes, bed linen, towels, glassware, eyeglasses, Lincoln Continental automobiles, backgammon sets, and boxes of chocolates. Jeans were added in 1987, and the total worldwide sales volume of Blass-labeled goods reached $450 million in 1989. However, Blass was taking great care to make sure his name was not being used inappropriately, vetoing such propositions as Blass-designed stoves, refrigerators, orthodontic braces, and fabric-lined coffins.

## KEY DATES

**1960:** Bill Blass becomes chief designer of Maurice Rentner Ltd.

**1968:** Bill Blass Inc. becomes a Rentner subsidiary for the designer's licensed products, including a menswear line.

**1970:** Blass buys out his Rentner partners and renames the company Bill Blass Ltd.

**1980:** Annual sales of Blass-labeled goods reach $200 million.

**1993:** Bill Blass Ltd. is licensing 56 products with annual sales of $500 million.

**1999:** Blass sells the company and retires.

**2002:** Bill Blass dies at age 79.

**2007:** NexCen Brands acquires Bill Blass; designer Michael Vollbracht resigns.

**2008:** Bill Blass Couture shutters operations; Peacock International Holdings purchases the brand name and existing licenses.

The licensed revenues depended ultimately on the prestige of Bill Blass Ltd.'s own collections, whether these expensive productions made money or not. Blass's strength, he told Gross, was "making the sketch, and then I'm best at fitting. Because then I can spot absolutely what I want and what's wrong.... I'll tell you the secret of a great dress: it looks as though human hands hadn't touched it." Blass expanded his list of celebrity clients, which now included such politically prominent women as Nancy Reagan, Barbara Bush, Nancy Kissinger, and Pamela Harriman; the journalists Katharine Graham and Barbara Walters; and such performers as Candice Bergen, Anjelica Huston, Mary Tyler Moore, Jessye Norman, and Barbra Streisand.

In keeping with the decade, Blass's designs for the 1980s were more ornate and luxurious than those of the past. He employed such materials as panne velvet, satin, taffeta, cashmere, and sable, and he beaded sashes, skirts, blouses, and evening jackets. Blazers were replaced by jackets typically mixed, in suits, with different materials. Twin cashmere sweater sets were paired with long matching skirts of silk satin or lace bouffant. Beaded and embroidered evening dresses, at $5,000, were among his best sellers in the early to mid-1980s. Asked by Diamonstein why his clothes were so expensive, Blass replied, "I'm an avid believer that we have to have clothes made in this country. Therefore we

pay more money.... [The] cost of labor and fabrication is what makes the clothing expensive."

### SUCCESS AS A MATURE COMPANY: 1990–2000

Although now in his seventies, the indefatigable Blass was out on the road as always in 1993, when his couture "trunk show" traveled to 24 cities, with Blass himself accompanying it to Atlanta, Chicago, Detroit, Nashville, Philadelphia, San Francisco, and Washington. At Saks Fifth Avenue in New York City, he set a record for American designers by selling more than $500,000 worth of dresses. Bill Blass USA, a bridge line between couture and ready-to-wear, was launched in 1995 and licensed to Augustus Clothiers.

Pennsylvania House introduced a Bill Blass furniture collection of 50 pieces in 1997. The following year Blass, who had been licensing fragrances to Revlon for almost 30 years, bought out his contract and assigned it to Five Star Fragrances. The women's jeans license was awarded to The Resource Club Ltd., a private-label manufacturer. The Bill Blass USA line closed and was replaced by a better-than-bridge suit collection to be made and marketed by Zaralo.

Pared to 42, the Bill Blass licensees generated about $760 million in annual sales in 1998, and the designer collection was bringing in another $20 million to $25 million in retail. Blass hired George Ackerman, a former Donna Karan executive, to replace him as chief executive officer in March 1998. Shortly before year's end, however, Ackerman left the company for reasons that were not disclosed, and Blass, who had recently suffered a minor stroke, resumed his former duties. He announced in February 1999 that he was planning to sell his firm.

In October 1999 Blass concluded an agreement to sell his company to Haresh T. Tharani, chairman of The Resource Club, the firm's largest licensee, and Michael Groveman, the firm's chief financial officer, with the former becoming chairman and the latter chief executive officer. The purchase price was to be paid by issuing investment-grade bonds self-liquidating over 10 years, based on the Blass trademarks, brand equity, and licensing revenues. The designer committed himself to maintaining an active role in the company through a long-term contract "with financial interest." A new company, called Tharanco, was to be established to own and operate Bill Blass Ltd.

CAK Universal Credit Corp. financed the purchase by lending the new owners the money to buy the company. The loan was secured by the company's trademarks and licenses, which were placed into an entity that would receive all the cash from the licenses.

Robert D'Loren, cofounder of CAK, described the transaction as an alternative to going public, telling Lisa Lockwood in *WWD* that since the cyclical nature of the apparel business made Bill Blass Ltd. below investment-grade credit-worthiness, "What we do is structure a loan so credit becomes investment grade—triple B or better.... By creating investment grade asset-backed bonds, we have forged a vehicle that enables apparel industry leaders to leverage their assets at favorable terms, while allowing large financial institutions, which have strict investment requirements, to invest in these assets."

## CHANGES FOLLOW FOUNDER'S RETIREMENT: 2000–07

Blass had retired without naming a successor to head the company's design team. Groveman and Tharani led an extensive search to replace him as head designer, hoping to find someone who could help the brand evolve in new directions while retaining the essence of the Blass style. Eventually the company settled on another transplanted Midwesterner, Steven Slowik, who had worked in Paris for Salvatore Ferragamo before producing his own collection. Slowik's first collection, unveiled in September 2000, drew mixed reviews and was unpopular with the established Blass clientele. He was let go before the next season and his assistant, the Swedish designer Lars Nilsson, 34 years old, took the top job.

Nilsson won the favor of *Vogue* editor Anna Wintour and other fashion luminaries, including Blass himself, with his debut efforts in women's sportswear and evening wear. His designs revealed the inspiration of the master while incorporating more ornate embroideries and other Scandinavian touches. Sales appeared to be slowly recovering, although figures were down at certain key outlets such as the elite New York department store Bergdorf Goodman. Blass died of throat cancer on June 12, 2002, at age 79. His passing unleashed a torrent of tributes and returned attention to the company struggling to carry forward his vision and licenses.

Relations grew stormy between Nilsson and company executives, who reportedly wanted him to keep his spending under tighter control. On February 12, 2003, one day after Nilsson's fifth Blass collection premiered on the runway, he was fired. The company's move was poorly timed. It sparked an uproar in the fashion world and did lasting damage to Groveman's reputation as steward of the Blass holdings and legacy.

Stepping in next was designer Michael Vollbracht, a Seventh Avenue veteran who had worked with Blass for two years on a museum retrospective of the designer's iconic career and an accompanying book. As the firm's new artistic director, Vollbracht steered the company back toward its roots. The classic pinstriped pantsuits, refined evening gowns, and other traditional looks returned, as did some high-profile customers such as Oprah Winfrey, Paris Hilton, and first lady Laura Bush. The company appeared to be returning to its stride with a realigned selection of licenses and a timeless image, amplified by an advertising campaign with model Elettra Rossellini Wiedemann.

## CLOSING TIME: 2007–10

In January 2007 the brand management firm NexCen Brands Inc. acquired the Bill Blass line for $54.6 million. NexCen's CEO, Robert D'Loren, had headed CAK Universal, the credit firm that helped broker the firm's unusual sale seven years earlier. His company also owned The Athlete's Foot and several quick-service food franchises such as Great American Cookie. Groveman and Vollbracht were invited to remain involved in the haute couture end of the business. Vollbracht quit less than six months later, complaining that the new parent company, aiming for a younger look, had asked him to devote too much energy to grooming his underlings. Blass hired two creative directors to replace him, Peter Som to head women's fashion and Michael Bastian in the relaunched menswear department.

The next blow to the Blass house came from the corporate end. NexCen's stock fell 77 percent in one day after D'Loren announced in May 2008 that the company had neglected to disclose a pending $30 million loan repayment and that there was "substantial doubt" that the firm could remain afloat. Shortly afterward, NexCen bought out Groveman from Bill Blass Couture, to facilitate selling the company outright. Som left the company that October amid reports of unpaid vendors and cancelled runway shows.

On December 19, 2008, Bill Blass Couture ceased operations. More than 60 clothing makers and other employees were let go without severance. Days later, NexCen, under pressure to unload assets before year's end, sold the Bill Blass trademark and existing licenses to Peacock International Holdings for the bargain-basement price of $10 million. Peacock, owned by the Kim brothers of South Korea, is an apparel company specializing in neckties and men's shirts. In late 2009 the Bill Blass Group announced the hiring of a new design director, Jeffrey Monteiro, and its intention to return to producing ready-to-wear in 2010.

*Robert Halasz*
*Updated, Roger K. Smith*

## PRINCIPAL COMPETITORS

Christian Dior S.A.; Marc Jacobs International LLC; Oscar de la Renta, Ltd.; Polo/Ralph Lauren Corporation; Prada, S.p.A.

## FURTHER READING

Diamonstein, Barbaralee, *Fashion: The Inside Story*, New York: Rizzoli, 1985, pp. 46–52.

Ephron, Nora, "The Man in the Bill Blass Suit," *New York Times Magazine*, December 8, 1968, pp. 52, 182, 184–85, 187, 191–92, 195.

"The Fairchild 100," *WWD/Women's Wear Daily*, November 1999, pp. 60, 75–76.

Gross, Edith Law, "Bill Blass and Women: An American Affair," *Vogue*, March 1981, pp. 339, 360–61.

Horyn, Cathy, "Blass: An American Original, Seen Only in Silhouette," *New York Times*, August 24, 1999, p. B12.

Lockwood, Lisa, "Bill Blass Goes the Bond Route," *WWD/Women's Wear Daily*, October 28, 1999, p. 1ff.

Orlean, Susan, "King of the Road," *New Yorker*, December 20, 1993, pp. 86–92.

Reed, Julia, "Million Dollar Bill," *Vogue*, January 1990, pp. 200–07, 241.

Wilson, Eric, "The Long Fall of the House of Blass," *New York Times*, December 25, 2008, p. E1.

———, "Things Start to Stir at the Blass House," *New York Times*, December 17, 2009, p. E10.

The Blackstone Group

# The Blackstone Group
# L.P.

345 Park Avenue
New York, New York 10154
U.S.A.
Telephone: (212) 583-5000
Toll Free: (866) 800-8933
Fax: (212) 583-5712
Web site: http://www.blackstone.com

*Public Company*
*Founded:* 1985
*Employees:* 1,295
*Sales:* $1.77 billion (2009)
*Total Assets:* $9.41 billion (2009)
*Stock Exchanges:* New York
*Ticker Symbol:* BX
*NAICS:* 523110 Investment Banking and Securities
    Dealing; 523930 Investment Advice

■ ■ ■

A New York-based investment firm with offices in North America, Europe, and Asia, the Blackstone Group L.P. is one of the world's foremost managers of private capital and sources of financial advice. Its alternative management fund businesses include the management of private equity funds, real estate funds, funds of hedge funds, credit-oriented funds, collateralized loan obligation (CLO) vehicles, separately managed accounts, and publicly traded closed-end mutual funds. Its financial advisory services include mergers and acquisitions, restructuring and reorganization, and fund placement.

## STARTING OFF: 1985–1990

In 1985 Peter G. Peterson and Stephen A. Schwarzman, former colleagues at the investment bank Lehman Brothers, Kuhn, Loeb Inc., founded the Blackstone Group L.P. It was initially established with $400,000 in seed capital as a "boutique" investment banking firm providing advisory services in mergers and acquisitions. In 1987 Roger Altman, a top investment banker, left Shearson Lehman Brothers to join Blackstone. That year Blackstone engaged in its first high-profile undertaking, playing an advisory role in the merger of two investment banks, Shearson Lehman Brothers and E. F. Hutton, with the resulting firm capitalized at $3.7 billion. Blackstone received a fee of $3.5 million. In 1988 Blackstone was the adviser to CBS concerning its sale of CBS Records to Sony. Also in 1988, the firm hired on as a partner David Stockman, the former director of the Office of Management and Budget under President Ronald Reagan and a former managing director at Salomon Brothers.

From 1985 to 1987 Blackstone played only an advisory role. Starting in the latter year, Blackstone evolved into one of the most important private equity firms in the world, with an emphasis on the leveraged buyout strategy. This involved the acquisition of usually troubled companies using a major proportion of borrowed money, with the assets of the acquired company frequently employed as collateral for loans. Blackstone employed other investment strategies as well, such as venture capital, distressed investments, and mezzanine capital (a type of high-interest financing most often used in company expansions). For its acquisitions and investments, Blackstone utilized private equity funds and

## COMPANY PERSPECTIVES

We seek to deliver superior returns to investors in our funds through a disciplined, value-oriented investment approach. Since we were founded in 1985, we have cultivated strong relationships with clients in our financial advisory business, where we endeavor to provide objective and insightful solutions and advice that our clients can trust. We believe our scaled, diversified businesses, coupled with our long track record of investment performance, proven investment approach and strong client relationships, position us to continue to perform well in a variety of market conditions, expand our assets under management and add complementary businesses. Our businesses have yielded a significant positive impact on society through, for example, increases in employment, additional capital investment and research and development expense by our portfolio companies, increased tax revenue to federal and local governments and returns to our limited partners.

capital from pension funds, insurance companies, wealthy individuals, sovereign wealth funds, fund of funds, and other sources.

In 1987 Blackstone created its first private equity fund, Blackstone Capital Partners, with $800 million in capital. The biggest investors in the fund were the Prudential Insurance Company, Nikko Securities, and the General Motors pension fund. In 1998 Nikko put $100 million into Blackstone, enabling the latter to enlarge significantly its investment endeavors. After successfully fighting a hostile takeover attempt, freight railroad operator CNW chose in 1989 to be acquired by an investment group led by Blackstone Capital Partners. The savings and loan (S&L) crisis of the late 1980s and early 1990s saw the number of S&Ls, or thrifts, cut in half by 1995. In 1989 Blackstone and Salomon Brothers jointly gathered $600 million for the purchase of distressed thrifts. Blackstone entered the investment management business in 1987, when it partnered in a 50-50 arrangement with Larry Fink and Ralph Schlosstein, founders of the investment management firm Blackrock. In 1990 Blackstone established its Alternative Asset Management Fund (later renamed Credit and Marketable Alternatives), composed of management of funds of hedge funds, credit-oriented funds, CLOs, and publicly traded, closed-end mutual funds.

## EXPANSION AND NEW BUSINESSES: 1990–2000

During the 1990s Blackstone remained on a path of growth and moved into new businesses. The buyout surge of the 1980s ended with the recession of the early 1990s, so Blackstone added advisory services in corporate restructuring to its consultancy services in mergers and acquisitions. The creation of new capital funds reflected the firm's enlargement. Blackstone Capital Partners II (1994) began with $1.27 billion in capital, and Blackstone Capital Partners III (1997) started with investor commitments of $3.78 billion. Growing internationally, Blackstone in 1990 established partnerships with firms in Great Britain and France.

The Blackstone Group began a real estate business in 1990, when it joined with businessman Henry Silverman to acquire a 65 percent interest in the Ramada and Howard Johnson lodging franchises for $140 million. In 1991 the group bought Days Inns for $250 million along with other hotels and motels. Two years later Blackstone acquired Super 8 Motels for $125 million. During the 1990s Blackstone created three real estate funds: Blackstone Real Estate Partners I (1994), with $485 million in capital; Blackstone Real Estate Partners II (1996), with capitalization of $1.3 billion; and Blackstone Real Estate Partners III (1999), capitalized with $1.5 billion.

In 1991 the Blackstone Group and another investment firm, Wertheim Schroder & Company, acquired a 50 percent interest in Six Flags, a leading chain of amusement parks. Four years later Blackstone purchased Centerplate, a food vending services firm operating mostly in sports arenas, from Flagstar. In 1996 Blackstone bought an 80 percent interest in a rapidly expanding company, Ritvik Toys, a Montreal-based manufacturer and marketer of construction blocks for children. During that year Blackstone formed a partnership with the Loewen Group, the second largest North American manager of funeral homes and cemeteries, with the aim of acquiring similar properties. During 1999 the Blackstone Group opened yet another enterprise when it created a mezzanine financing business, mezzanine financing being a risky, high-interest form of lending generally offered in emergency situations such as when a company is in a cash crunch that makes conventional loans unobtainable.

During the late 1990s Blackstone invested in, among other firms, the Premcor Refining Group (1997), one of the largest oil refining companies in the United States, and American Axle & Manufacturing (1997), a producer of automotive parts. Blackstone also invested in advanced communications firms, including CommNet Cellular (1998), which operated, managed, and

## KEY DATES

**1985:** Investment bankers Peter G. Peterson and Stephen A. Schwarzman found the Blackstone Group L.P.

**1987:** Blackstone creates its first private equity fund, Blackstone Capital Partners.

**1994:** Blackstone establishes its first real estate fund.

**2006:** The company purchases Equity Office Properties, the largest office landlord in the United States, for $39 billion.

**2007:** Hilton Hotels is acquired for $26 billion in the largest acquisition ever of a hotel company; Blackstone becomes a publicly traded corporation.

financed cellular telephone systems; Centennial Communications (1999), which provided wireless and broadband telecommunications services in the United States, including Puerto Rico and the U.S. Virgin Islands; and Bresnan Communications, offering high speed Internet, digital cable services, and digital phone services.

## RECESSION FOLLOWED BY BUYOUT BOOM IN THE EARLY 21ST CENTURY

With its large capital reserves, Blackstone was one of only a few private equity investors able to make large deals during the recession of 2000 through 2002. In the latter year Blackstone, along with Thomas H. Lee Partners and Bain Capital, bought the publisher Houghton Mifflin for $1.3 billion. This transaction was among the first big club deals (in which several partners pool their assets) since the dotcom collapse in 2000.

With economic recovery coming in 2003, mergers resumed on a larger scale than ever, with the Blackstone Group fully involved. In 2003 Blackstone established another private equity fund, Blackstone Capital Partners IV. Capitalized at $6.4 billion, it was the largest private equity fund raised to that time. Later that year, the purchase of the auto parts business of TRW Automotive was the first investment made through that fund at a cost of $4.7 billion. Also in 2003, Blackstone invested significantly in the Financial Guaranty Insurance Company, a monoline bond insurer (one that guarantees the repayment of bonds).

The years 2005 through 2007 represented the peak of the buyout boom. In 2005 the Blackstone Group and six other private equity firms came together to purchase Sungard, one of the world's top software and technology services companies, in a leveraged buyout valued at $11.3 billion. This was the largest leveraged buyout since 1988 and the largest buyout of a technology firm to that time. It was also the largest club buyout up to that time. In 2006 Blackstone Capital Partners V, a new private equity fund, was created with $21.7 billion in committed capital. That year the company won a hard fought contest to purchase Equity Office Properties, the largest office landlord in the United States, for $39 billion. At that time it was the largest buyout in history.

## INTERNATIONAL EXPANSION AND IPO: 2007

At the same time, Blackstone made important real estate investments. Its most significant real estate acquisition was the Hilton Hotels Corporation buyout in 2007 for $26 billion, the biggest acquisition of a hotel company ever. The Hilton empire comprised 3,200 hotels with 545,000 rooms in 77 countries. Blackstone Real Estate Partners IV (2003), V (2006), and VI (2007) collectively brought together $17.6 billion for real estate acquisitions.

The first decade of the 21st century also saw the Blackstone Group enlarge its international presence. In Europe, it opened offices in London (2000), Hamburg, Germany (2003), and Paris (2004). In Asia, Blackstone established offices in Mumbai, India (2004), Tokyo (2007), and Hong Kong (2007). Because of the large and rapidly growing economies in India and China, Blackstone particularly sought investments in those nations. During 2007 Blackstone announced that it was acquiring a 50.1 percent stake in Gokaldas Exports, India's biggest garment exporting firm, for $116 million. Also in 2007, Blackstone stated that it would invest at least $600 million in the plastics and chemical maker China National Bluestar (Group) Corp. in exchange for a 20 percent stake in the Chinese firm.

In June 2007 the Blackstone Group became the first major private equity firm to go public. Through its IPO, the company raised $4.1 billion, the largest IPO in the United States since 2002. This move was a surprise, as Blackstone had been regarded since the 1980s as an example of how a private firm with a small number of brilliant managers could make bold, successful moves without worrying about the reaction of stockholders. Some believed that the only reason for Blackstone becoming a public corporation was the big financial rewards that the company's executives would make from the IPO.

## RECESSION AND CREDIT COLLAPSE: 2008–2010

The economic downturn starting late in 2007, followed by the collapse of key financial institutions in the fall of 2008, reduced the number of large transactions generated by the Blackstone Group. Yet because of Blackstone's vast resources, the credit crunch hampered its operations less than those of its competitors. Writing in *BusinessWeek*, Harry Maurer and Cristina Linblad captured this reality: "Call Blackstone the Last King of Private Equity. Amid a global deal slowdown,… [it] is powering $110 million into the $872 million effort to build a dam in Uganda."

Over the next two years, Blackstone managed to make a number of large purchases. In 2008 it bought AlliedBarton Security Services, a provider of security personnel, in a transaction valued at about $1 billion. During that year Blackstone joined with another private equity firm, Bain Capital, and NBC Universal, to buy the Weather Channel from Landmark Communications for an undisclosed sum estimated at just under $3.5 billion. In 2009 Blackstone bought the Busch Entertainment Corporation, with its 10 theme parks, from Anheuser Busch for $2.7 billion. At the end of 2009 Blackstone was managing $98.2 billion of assets.

To enhance its presence in China, Blackstone opened an office in Beijing in 2008. That year the firm's senior managing directors formed the Blackstone Charitable Foundation, which pledged to spend $50 million over the next five years to promote entrepreneurship and foster economic resurgence in the regions that suffered most from the international economic crisis. Its first grant established Blackstone LaunchPad, whose goal was to advance entrepreneurship through higher education. In 2009 the company acquired a 37.5 percent stake in Gateway Rail Freight, an Indian firm, for $62.5 million. Later in the year Blackstone and the municipal government of Shanghai agreed on establishing a joint venture private equity fund worth $732 million, the first Blackstone fund denominated wholly in Chinese currency, a sign of the growing worldwide respect for China's yuan.

*Michael Levine*

## PRINCIPAL SUBSIDIARIES

Blackstone Advisory Services L.L.C.; Blackstone Asia Opportunities Associates L.L.C.; Blackstone Capital Commitment Partners IV NQ L.P.; Blackstone/GSO Capital Solutions Associates LLC; Blackstone Real Estate Associates IV L.P..

## PRINCIPAL DIVISIONS

Credit and Marketable Alternatives; Financial Advisory; Private Equity; Real Estate.

## PRINCIPAL COMPETITORS

Bain Capital, LLC; The Carlyle Group, L.P.; Kohlberg Kravis Roberts & Co.

## FURTHER READING

Barboza, David, "For U.S. Private Equity, Yuan Is Ticket into China," *International Herald Tribune*, November 20, 2009.

Berke, Jonathan, "Full Plate for Blackstone Group," *Daily Deal*, February 6, 2002.

"The Blackstone Charitable Foundation Invests $50 Million to Support Entrepreneurship Globally," *Economics Week*, May 14, 2010, p. 23.

Callan, Eoin, et al., "Blackstone IPO Seven Times Subscribed amid Overseas Demand," *Financial Times*, June 21, 2007, p. 1.

Maurer, Harry, and Cristina Linblad, "News You Need to Know," *BusinessWeek*, December 31, 2007.

McNish, Jacquie, "Blackstone Rides to Success as White Knight," *Globe & Mail* (Toronto), February 11, 1993, p. B2.

Moriarity, George, "Lured by Internet, Blackstone Samples Venture Capital," *Investment Dealers' Digest*, October 11, 1999.

Pristin, Terry, "Blackstone Is Winner of Biggest Buyout: Private-equity Firm to Pay $39 Billion for U.S. Office Landlord," *International Herald Tribune*, February 8, 2007, p. 1.

Rudnitsky, Howard, "Triple Dipper: Blackstone Capital Partner Henry Silverman's Plans to Buy Days Inn of America," *Forbes*, November 25, 1991, p. 172.

# Blue Note Label Group

150 Fifth Avenue
New York, New York 10011
U.S.A.
Telephone: (212) 786-8600
Fax: (212) 786-8613
Web site: http://www.bluenote.com/

*Wholly Owned Subsidiary of Terra Firma Capital Partners Ltd.*
*Founded:* 1939
*Incorporated:* 1939
*Employees:* 25
*NAICS:* 512220 Integrated Record Production/Distribution

■ ■ ■

Blue Note Label Group is a legendary jazz label that operates as a subsidiary of the British-based EMI Group Ltd. Blue Note is renowned for its catalog of jazz greats that includes Miles Davis, Art Blakely, Thelonius Monk, John Coltrane, Herbie Hancock, and Dexter Keith Gordon, as well as its current list of music notables such as Norah Jones, Van Morrison, and Al Green. Blue Note albums are also celebrated for covers that established a look that continues to influence cover art in the 21st century.

## BLUE NOTE BEGINS

Alfred Lion, a Jewish émigré from Nazi Germany, attended the famous Spirituals to Swing concert held at Carnegie Hall on December 23, 1938. Lion had been captivated by jazz since hearing, at age 16, a live jazz concert in a skating rink near his Berlin home. After listening to the boogie-woogie mastery of Albert Ammons and Meade Lewis, Lion became determined to record them. Just two weeks later, with the help of Max Margulis, a left-wing writer and friend, Lion rented a studio. He recorded several solos by each of the musicians, followed by two duets. Blue Note, which was named for the expressive tone that characterized jazz and blues, had cut its first release.

The flyer that accompanied the 50 copies of the release grandly delineated Lion's credo: "Hot jazz ... is expression and communication, a musical and social manifestation, and Blue Note records are concerned with identifying its impulse, not its sensational and commercial adornments." In April and June 1939 Lion recorded a six-man group called the Port of Harlem Jazzmen. For the final session the sextet was joined by the soprano saxophonist Sidney Bechet. Bechet recorded an intense and moving version of "Summertime," and Blue Note had its first hit.

By the end of 1939 Blue Note had been incorporated. Lion's childhood friend, Francis Wolff, arrived in New York and joined him, helping to operate Blue Note from a tiny office on West 47th Street. While both men had to support themselves with outside jobs, Blue Note continued to function somewhat marginally, with single sessions followed by single releases.

However, the singular atmosphere created in the recording sessions was a new experience for the jazz artists. Lion and Wolff did not restrict the recordings to the three-minute cuts typical of other studios. They provided ample food and alcohol for the musicians. They held sessions at a time that was convenient for their artists, often at three or four in the morning, after the clubs the musicians worked at had closed. They also paid for rehearsal time before the actual recording. Blue Note was developing a reputation for its style. Regardless, financing and distribution were constant problems for Blue Note.

## THE EARLY YEARS

Lion was drafted into the U.S. Army shortly after the United States had entered World War II. While he was away, Wolff was hired by Milton Gabler, the owner of the Commodore Music Shop, a hang-out for jazz lovers. Gabler had his own record label and decided to let Blue Note use the production and distribution channels he had already developed. Access to Commodore's markets allowed Blue Note to survive the war and even accumulate some capital. By the time Lion returned from the war, in late 1943, Blue Note was ready to make recordings again.

Blue Note continued to record musicians who had established reputations, but it also fostered artists whose limited commercial appeal did not attract the major labels. During the late 1940s it gave a boost to the bebop style of jazz and its intricate melodies, new rhythmic phrasings, and freewheeling improvisations. Also, the saxophonist Ike Abrams Quebec functioned as a talent scout for Blue Note and helped bring soon-to-be musical luminaries such as Monk and Blakely to record at the studio. Blue Note's policy of listening to musicians helped keep it on the edge of musical innovation.

Besides being the Blue Note business manager, Wolff became the photographer for the label. His atmospheric shots, which were taken during studio sessions, provided intense and personal glimpses of the creative process. His portraits became the basis for the distinctive Blue Note covers.

As the decade came to an end, a new challenge faced the label. For almost 50 years recordings had been made on disc masters and released on 78 RPM shellac records. However, by the late 1940s most labels were beginning to use audio tapes, which allowed higher fidelity masters, and vinyl records, which provided greater durability and longer playing time. Blue Note struggled to afford the costs of this new technology, so it was one of the last labels to adopt the new formats. The label eventually released its first vinyl issue in 1951.

One of Blue Note's first extended play albums demonstrated the marketing creativity that helped make the label known for both its image and its music. Album covers by other labels were often utilitarian and unattractive. By contrast, Blue Note's early covers, many of which had been designed by Gil Melle and featured Wolff's haunting photography, were dramatic and distinctive. Then, too, Blue Note billed its albums with compelling titles, such as *Thelonius Monk: Genius of Modern Music*. Blue Note was on the verge of becoming known as the preeminent jazz label.

## THE BLUE NOTE ERA

Besides being instrumental in some of the early Blue Note cover designs, Melle played a role in introducing Lion and Wolff to the recording engineer Rudy Van Gelder in 1953. Working from a studio that he had built in his parent's home in Hackensack, New Jersey, Van Gelder was known for the unique sound and quality of his recordings. He also shared Lion's devotion to jazz and commitment to perfection. The label continued to record briefly at the WOR radio studio where it had cut most of its previous albums. However, having found a kindred spirit in Van Gelder, Lion soon switched all the Blue Note recording sessions to the New Jersey studio.

The pace of recording increased, while Lion maintained strict quality control. Furthermore, Blue Note continued to nurture the artistic creativity of its performers. According to Martin Gayford of the London *Daily Telegraph*, Bob Porter, a producer for Blue Note's competitor Prestige Records, once stated that "the difference between Blue Note and Prestige is 'two days of rehearsal.'" The label also expanded its roster of jazz notables, releasing albums by the Modern Jazz Quartet, James Louis Johnson, Horace Silver, and Miles Davis. Van Gelder's engineering provided the ideal sound quality that Lion wanted, including Blue Note's milestone live recording of an entire performance of the Art Blakely Quintet at Birdland Theatre, a quintessential New York jazz club.

Blue Note's reputation was also supported by its cover art. The label's covers received a further boost when in 1956 Wolff met and hired the commercial artist Reid Miles. Even though Miles did not particularly

## KEY DATES

**1939:** Blue Note cuts its first release.

**1953:** Rudy Van Gelder begins sound engineering for Blue Note.

**1956:** Reid Miles is hired to design Blue Note album covers.

**1967:** Alfred Lion retires from Blue Note.

**1984:** Bruce Lundvall revives Blue Note.

like jazz, the cover designs he created, which were based on discussions with Lion and used Wolff's photographs, became iconic classics.

From the mid-1950s to the early 1960s Blue Note continued to be the home of jazz innovators, and the label dominated the jazz industry with strong sales and occasional blockbusters. Its impressive roster continued to grow with notables such as Dexter Keith Gordon and John Coltrane, and younger players such as Herbie Hancock and Wayne Shorter. Furthermore, Blue Note maintained its support of the musical edge by recording new trends in music, such as the avant-garde albums of Ornette Coleman and Andrew Hill.

### BLUE NOTE'S DECLINE AND REBIRTH

However, the halcyon days of Blue Note's jazz-world prominence did not last through the 1960s. In 1965 Lion and Wolff sold Blue Note to Liberty Records, a primarily pop label. By 1967 Lion had retired and Miles had left to focus on other ventures. Four years later, in 1971, Wolff died. As rock and roll developed a greater audience, the dynamic energy and economic vitality of jazz was being eclipsed. In 1969 Liberty Records was acquired by United Artists and then in 1979 it was taken over by EMI. Meanwhile, the Blue Note label was eventually phased out.

In 1984 EMI hired Bruce Lundvall, a jazz fan and former executive of the Columbia, Elektra, and Capital record companies, to revive Blue Note. The label was relaunched in February 1985 with a recording of a Town Hall concert of old and new Blue Note artists. Uncertain of what do next, Lundvall decided to hire Michael Cuscuna as a consulting producer. Cuscuna had played a major role in keeping Blue Note's releases alive, for starting in 1975 he and the executive Charlie Lourie had issued a number of the label's former albums. In 1982 he founded Mosaic Records to provide collected reissues of several jazz performers.

Lundvall tried to emulate the old Blue Note style by signing less well known performers such as Cassandra Wilson and Joe Lovano and turning them into established artists. He also learned to listen to musicians' recommendations and record unknowns such as Jason Moran and Mark Shim. Meanwhile, Cuscuna managed the reissue of many classic Blue Note sessions and helped discover several unreleased recordings.

Lundvall tried to maintain a balance between selling records, nurturing talent, and supporting experimentation. According to Kim Campbell of the *Christian Science Monitor*, Lundvall survived criticism from what he referred to as the "jazz police" when he recorded music that was not considered pure jazz, such as the hip-hop album by Us3 that the label released in 1993, or signed the Irish singer Van Morrison in 2003. However, Lundvall, like Lion, trusted his instincts. When the unknown Nora Jones brought a demo to Lundvall's office, he signed her immediately. Jones's debut album sold over 1 million copies, and she eventually became a multiple Grammy winner. Blue Note also continued to maintain its catalog of classics.

When Blue Note celebrated its 70th anniversary in 2009, an all-star group of Blue Note artists made a 50-city tour that culminated at New York's Birdland Theatre. Festivals in Europe and the United States honored the label's passion and longevity. By 2010, however, Blue Note was facing serious organizational challenges. In 2007 Terra Firma Capital Partners Ltd., a private equity company, had bought EMI, Blue Note's parent company. By 2010 EMI was in financial jeopardy and Terra Firma had to raise over £100 million to save it from bankruptcy. That same year Lundvall, at the age of 74, was named chairman emeritus of Blue Note. While working part time and facing the changes wrought by the digitization of the music business, he was still looking for new talent to bring to Blue Note.

*Grace Murphy*

### PRINCIPAL COMPETITORS

Columbia Records Group; The Verve Music Group; Warner Bros. Records Inc.; Shanachie Entertainment Corp.

### FURTHER READING

"Alfred Lion, 78, the Founder of the Blue Note Jazz Label," *New York Times*, February 9, 1987, p. D11.

Blumenfeld, Larry, "Blue Note: Still Spry at 70," *Billboard*, March 28, 2009.

Campbell, Kim, "Keeping Blue Note in the Green," *Christian Science Monitor*, June 25, 2004, p. 13.

Cook, Richard, *Blue Note Records: The Biography*. Boston, MA: Justin, Charles & Co., 2003.

Davis, Clive, "Blue Notes in Black and White," *Times* (London), June 18, 1991.

Gayford, Martin, "Outrageous Graphics and Six-Handed Boogie-Woogie," *Daily Telegraph* (London), July 11, 2009, p. 2.

Kahn, Ashley, "Dr. Yes Will Hear You Now," *Wall Street Journal*, April 13, 2010.

Macnie, Jim, "Bruce Lundvall: The Billboard Interview," *Billboard*, January 16, 1999, p. B4.

Power, Helen, "Hands Looks to Investors as EMI Breaks Banking Covenants," *Times* (London), April 1, 2010, p. 68.

Watrous, Peter, "Jazz's Best-Known Label at 60," *New York Times*, January 10, 1999.

# Boston Basketball Partners L.L.C.

---

**151 Merrimac Street**
**Boston, Massachusetts 02114**
**U.S.A.**
**Telephone: (617) 854-8000**
**Fax: (617) 367-4286**
**Web site: http://www.nba.com/celtics**

*Private Company*
*Founded:* 1946
*Incorporated:* 1986 as Boston Celtics L.P.
*Employees:* 60
*Sales:* $144 million (2009)
*NAICS:* 711211 Sports Teams and Clubs

■ ■ ■

The owner of the Boston Celtics basketball franchise, Boston Basketball Partners L.L.C. oversees the financial and managerial operations of what is arguably the most successful team in the history of professional sports. Since its founding in 1946, the Celtics organization has won an unprecedented 17 National Basketball Association (NBA) championship titles. In a 13-year span between 1957 and 1969, the team won 11 championship titles, including eight in a row, a feat unparalleled among American professional team sports. Twenty-three former Celtics players have been inducted into the Naismith Memorial Basketball Hall of Fame, among them Bob Cousy, Bill Russell, Sam Jones, John Havlicek, Larry Bird, and Robert Parrish. Alongside the team's roster of great performers, the Celtics are typically associated with Arnold "Red" Auerbach, the Hall of Fame

coach who was the principal architect of the organization's early success. Founded by Walter Brown, the team has had a succession of owners over the course of its fabled history, including Boston Celtics L.P., which took the franchise public in 1986, and Boston Basketball Partners, which acquired the team in 2002.

## ORIGINS OF PROFESSIONAL BASKETBALL IN BOSTON: 1946–48

Boston Basketball Partners L.L.C. assumed ownership of the Celtics relatively late in the organization's history. Indeed, the Celtics recorded 16 league championships during the 56-year span between the team's founding and its acquisition by Boston Basketball Partners in 2002. Of all the owners, players, and coaches who helped build the Celtics dynasty, none was more pivotal than the team's founder, Walter Brown.

Owner of the Boston Bruins hockey team and the fabled Boston Garden, Brown cared little and perhaps knew even less about the game of basketball when he and a small group of arena operators gathered in New York City in 1946 to organize the Basketball Association of America. Like others in attendance, Brown was primarily concerned with keeping his arena filled with paying spectators, something that had been difficult to accomplish during the winter nights in Boston. Brown had made various attempts to keep the turnstiles spinning at Boston Garden when the Bruins had the night off, booking the Ice Follies, Ringling Brothers and Barnum & Baily Circus, a Notre Dame football game, midget auto races, rodeos, women's softball games, and book shows, but he was in search of a steady attraction.

## COMPANY PERSPECTIVES

◼

The words "Pride," "Mystique," "Tradition," "Teamwork," and the figure of a pint-sized, winking leprechaun leaning with one arm on his shillelagh and hoisting a basketball on his index finger, are a few of the ways that fans have come to know the Boston Celtics throughout the years.

A charter member of the Basketball Association of America (which evolved into the National Basketball Association) since 1946, the Boston Celtics have produced a legacy of success that no other professional sports franchise can match.

A glorious history of 17 world championship titles, unselfish, popular and loyal role players, an outdated building with its unique parquet floor, the plethora of classic, jubilant and memorable regular season and playoff games, and a fiery coach, general manager and president who, with his trademark cigar in his mouth, guided and led the charge, Arnold "Red" Auerbach, summarize this franchise.

Basketball seemed an odd choice considering that the game enjoyed little popular support, particularly in Boston, where the population was devoted to baseball and hockey. Basketball, in fact, had been eliminated from the Boston city school system in 1925, nearly two decades earlier. Nevertheless, Brown and his cohorts, all except one of whom owned hockey teams, organized the 11-member Basketball Association of America in the Commodore Hotel on June 6, 1946, and Brown left New York with a basketball franchise, as yet unnamed.

After considering several team names, including "Whirlwinds," "Unicorns," and "Olympics," Brown opted for "Celtics," hoping to grab the attention of Boston's large Irish population. John Davis "Honey" Russell was hired as the first Celtics coach, and the team soon began its inaugural season, losing its first game 59–53 to the Providence Steamrollers, the first of many losses during the franchise's fledgling years. The Celtics were 22–38 after their first season, and despite Brown's expectations of packing his arena with adoring fans, the team never filled half the seats in the Boston Garden, averaging only 3,608 people per game. The Celtics posted a losing record the following year but still made the playoffs. More important to the team's future was its financial condition, as the losses mounted for Brown

and the company he led, Boston Garden Arena Corporation.

## DIRE STRAITS FOR THE CELTICS: 1948–55

A coaching change was made before the 1948–49 basketball season, with Alvin "Doggie" Julian taking over for Honey Russell, but his impact was negligible and the Celtics again recorded a losing season, winning 25 games and losing 35. By this point the financial condition of the team was grave. During its third season the Celtics lost $100,000, bringing the total loss for its first three seasons to $350,000. Shareholders of the Boston Garden Arena Corporation wanted out and urged Brown to fold the franchise, but Brown persevered, convincing the disgruntled stockholders to give the Celtics franchise one more year to prove its financial viability. The following season was the worst in the franchise's short history, as the Celtics posted a dismal 22–46 record; the team's record was 89 victories and 147 losses during the first four years. As a result, attendance had declined and the franchise lost another $100,000, bringing its total loss for four years of operation to nearly $500,000. Boston Garden Arena Corporation stockholders were no longer receptive to Brown's pleas after the fourth season, and they sold their stakes in the franchise to Brown, leaving the disheartened founder saddled with debt and in charge of the failing Celtics.

To stave off a complete collapse of the franchise, Brown sold his home and other private investments, keeping the Celtics in business for another season. As later became apparent, Brown's decision to keep the team afloat, despite no obvious sign that its future would be any more successful than its past, was an immensely beneficial one. Two new faces arrived for the 1950–51 basketball season: coach Arnold Jacob "Red" Auerbach, who was hired as the Celtics third head man in five years, and guard Bob Cousy, who would convert his harshest critic—his new coach—into one of his staunchest supporters. Red Auerbach, age 32 when Walter Brown named him coach of the Celtics, would be chiefly responsible for creating the celebrated Celtics mystique that would intimidate opposing players and draw legions of Celtics fans into the Boston Garden for generations to come. With his ever-present victory cigar clamped in his mouth, Auerbach would guide the Celtics through the team's much-heralded glory years, orchestrating the action from courtside for the next 16 seasons, then wielding his managerial control for decades afterward. Under Auerbach's glare, the other new arrival—Cousy—would develop into one of the game's greatest players, transforming the Celtics

## KEY DATES

**1946:** Walter Brown, cofounder of the Basketball Association of America, establishes the Boston Celtics basketball franchise.

**1950:** Arnold "Red" Auerbach is named head coach of the Celtics.

**1956:** Rookie center Bill Russell joins the Celtics.

**1957:** The Celtics win their first National Basketball Association (NBA) championship.

**1964:** Walter Brown dies.

**1966:** Red Auerbach retires from coaching to become Celtics general manager; Bill Russell becomes the team's player-coach.

**1969:** The Celtics win their eleventh NBA championship in thirteen years.

**1978:** The Celtics acquire the draft rights to Larry Bird.

**1986:** The Celtics clinch the organization's 16th NBA championship.

**2008:** Led by Paul Pierce, Kevin Garnett, and Ray Allen, the Celtics notch their 17th NBA title.

organization from a perennial loser into the most successful franchise in the history of professional basketball.

Together, Cousy and Auerbach righted the floundering Celtics. In the team's first winning season, it posted a 39–30 record in 1950–51 and advanced to the playoffs. Perhaps more important, average attendance rose 2,000 per game during the season, enabling Brown to begin recouping his losses and beat back the financial pressures that threatened the franchise's existence.

### THE DYNASTY: 1956–76

The Celtics advanced to the playoffs each of the next five years, but a championship title—the hallmark of a sports organization's success—eluded the franchise. In retrospect, the Celtics were missing one key player, and that player, Bill Russell, arrived in camp in the autumn of 1956. The acquisition of the 6-foot, 10-inch Russell took the Celtics franchise over the top. During his rookie year (1956–57) attendance rose an average of 2,500 fans, and the Celtics won their first league championship. After losing the championship series the following season to the St. Louis Hawks (whom Boston had defeated to take their first championship), the Celtics captured an amazing eight titles in a row, ranking as the National Basketball Association's preeminent franchise between the 1958–59 and 1965–66 seasons.

Walter Brown died in 1964, near the end of the Celtics' string of championship titles. This marked the end of one era and the beginning of another. The connection between Walter Brown and the Celtics franchise had been resolute, but when that bond was severed, the team quickly passed through a series of owners. Lou Pieri, who had been co-owner with Walter Brown since 1950, and Marjorie Brown took charge of the Celtics organization for a year, followed by a succession of corporate owners. These were National Equities from 1965 to 1968; Ballantine Brewery from 1968 to 1969; Trans-National Communications from 1969 to 1971; Investors' Funding Corporation from 1971 to 1972; and Leisure Technology from 1972 to 1974.

Two years after Brown's death, another Celtics era ended when Red Auerbach relinquished his coaching duties and Bill Russell took over, becoming the first African American to either coach or manage a major professional sports team. Under Russell the Celtics won two more championship titles (1968 and 1969). The team went on to win two more league titles during the 1970s with Tom Heinsohn, a former Celtics player, coaching the team.

### A TRADE IS MADE, A FEUD BEGINS: 1978

Ownership of the franchise during the mid- and late 1970s had devolved to Los Angeles film producer Irv Levin, who, in 1978, traded the Celtics franchise to John Y. Brown and Harry Mangurian in exchange for the Buffalo Braves franchise. Aside from the peculiarity of trading one franchise for another, the deal between Levin and Brown/Mangurian was notable for another reason. The arrival of John Y. Brown to the Celtics organization ignited a bitter, intra-franchise feud and engendered the Celtics' most contentious year in its history.

Auerbach, who continued to embody the Celtics mystique and direct the franchise as its general manger, disliked John Y. Brown intensely, particularly because Brown had ignobly obtained the revered Celtics franchise through a swap. Even more irksome to Auerbach was Brown's disregard for his authority. As part of the franchise swap, several Celtics players were sent to the Braves franchise, the first time a player transaction had been made without Auerbach's knowledge since his arrival in 1950, nearly 30 years earlier. Angered, Auerbach began discussions with the New York Knicks and was offered a four-year contract as president of the rival organization for a salary that would make him the highest-paid National Basketball Association executive ever.

Auerbach relented, opting to remain in Boston after listening to advice from his wife and gaining assurances from Brown that he would not be excluded from future decisions affecting Celtics players. Less than a year later, though, Brown traded three first-round draft picks to the New York Knicks for Bob McAdoo without consulting Auerbach, bringing the running feud between the two to a climax. Enraged, Auerbach approached Brown and informed the Celtics owner that if he did not sell the team within two weeks he would leave. Two weeks later, Brown sold his interest in the team to Harry Mangurian. Brown then went on to successfully run for governor of Kentucky.

### THE LARRY BIRD ERA: 1979–90

Against the backdrop of this public dispute between Brown and Auerbach, the Celtics franchise had drafted a 6-foot, 9-inch forward from Indiana State University named Larry Joe Bird in 1978. Bird would establish himself during the 1980s as one of the greatest players in the history of the game. With the addition of Kevin McHale and Robert Parish (both of whom were acquired through a complicated trade involving Bob McAdoo), the Celtics franchise had formed the nucleus of a team that would win three national championships during the 1980s, extending the winning tradition into a fourth decade.

As the drive toward winning three championships during the decade gained momentum, ownership of the franchise once again changed hands. In 1983 Harry Mangurian sold the team to Don Gaston, Paul Dupee Jr., and Alan Cohen for $17 million. The new owners were intent on transforming the Celtics franchise into a profitable business, rather than treating it like a prestigious asset, as many of the owners who followed Walter Brown had done. Gaston, Dupee, and particularly Cohen wanted more from their acquisition and began looking for a way to substantially build on their investment.

Following a suggestion from David Stern, commissioner of the National Basketball Association, Gaston, Dupee, and Cohen formed a master limited partnership named Boston Celtics L.P. that enabled the three owners to avoid paying a substantial percentage of taxes on revenue the franchise generated and provided for the distribution of shares of Boston Celtics stock to the public, a first for a professional sports franchise. In 1986, 2.6 million Celtics shares, representing 40 percent of the team, were offered to the public at $18.50 per share, from which the three owners earned $44.74 million in proceeds. After the public offering Gaston owned 32.5 percent of the Celtics, Dupee owned 14.7 percent, and Cohen owned 11.8 percent, more than enough to

continue with their ownership unchallenged by all others.

### A LUCRATIVE PLAN TO REDIRECT BROADCAST REVENUES

In 1985 the Celtics franchise sold its television rights in a five-year deal to an independent UHF station, WLVI-TV, which immediately increased the station's estimated value from $50 million to $75 million, giving the three owners tangible evidence of the financial worth of their organization and the magnitude of revenue others were earning from their franchise. To redirect the broadcasting revenues into their pockets, Gaston, Dupee, and Cohen began planning to acquire their own broadcasting companies.

In 1987 the Celtics franchise purchased WFXT-TV for $10 million and formed Boston Celtics Communications Limited Partnership, a sister company, to oversee the broadcasting business. The Celtics then sold their own station the broadcasting rights to air Celtics games for $30,000 per game during the preseason, $150,000 per game during the regular season, and $200,000 per game during the playoffs. When WEEI-AM was acquired by Boston Celtics Communications L.P. in 1989, the three partners worked out a similar arrangement, giving the Celtics franchise radio broadcasting fees ranging between $1.4 million and $2.5 million per year.

### A SERIES OF DEPARTURES: 1991–95

By the beginning of the 1990s, as the Celtics' dominance on the basketball court began to wane, Gaston, Dupee, and Cohen oversaw a genuine sports empire, with revenue pouring in from the Celtics on the court and over the airwaves. When Mangurian sold the Celtics in 1983 the team was generating roughly $8 million in revenues per season. Ten years later the company was generating more than $80 million annually.

By the end of the 1993 fiscal year both Larry Bird and Kevin McHale had retired from the team, with Bird making his exit before the 1992–93 season and McHale leaving after the 1992–93 campaign. Their departures marked the end of yet another era in Celtics history, raising concern over the team's future and its ability to win additional championship titles. In 1993 Don Gaston transferred his ownership of the team to his son, Paul, who also assumed the role of chairman. A year later the company sold its radio station, and in 1995 it sold the television station WFXT to the Fox Network for accumulated proceeds of about $105 million. In 1995 Paul Gaston also purchased Alan Cohen's stake in the team for $16.3 million. The franchise played its last year at the Boston Garden during the 1994–95 basketball season, and it began its 1995–96 campaign at the new and larger FleetCenter, where both the Celtics and Boston Celtics L.P. hoped to establish a winning and lucrative tradition.

## HIGH PROFITS, LOW SCORES: 1995–99

For the year 1995–96, the Celtics posted net earnings of just over $54 million, the most profitable year in team history. The team's revenues for this period totaled $64.8 million, an increase of nearly 25 percent over the previous year. This robust financial performance was driven primarily by the sale of the team's television channel, as well as a rise of $13.2 million in season ticket revenues. Despite this financial success, the team floundered during its first year at the FleetCenter, completing the 1995–96 season with a 33–49 record. In December 1996 Boston Celtics L.P. purchased Paul Dupee Jr.'s ownership in the franchise for $22.9 million, increasing Paul Gaston's stake in the team to just over 44 percent.

Meanwhile the Celtics were sinking to new lows on the court. In 1996–97 the team finished with a dismal 15–67 record, the second-worst performance in the league. For the year, receipts on ticket sales fell to $31.8 million, a drop of 10 percent compared to 1995–96. At the season's conclusion, the organization hired Rick Pitino as its new head coach and president in a deal worth an estimated $50 million. As the coach who led the University of Kentucky to a National College Athletic Association (NCAA) basketball championship in 1996, Pitino brought renewed hope to the struggling franchise.

The Celtics also had high expectations for the draft lottery that year, with Wake Forest star Tim Duncan universally regarded to be the biggest prize of the incoming class of college players. Statistically, the Celtics had the best odds of landing the number-one pick. However, the team had to settle for the third pick in the draft and saw Tim Duncan go to the San Antonio Spurs. Despite this setback, Pitino's arrival had a positive impact on ticket sales. Attendance at the Fleet-Center rose 13.6 percent during the 1997–98 season, and gate revenues rose $3.8 million. The team finished 1997–98 with another losing record, failing to make the playoffs for the third straight year.

## NBA LOCKOUT AFFECTS SCHEDULE AND SALES

The 1998 off-season was a turbulent period for the NBA as a long-standing collective bargaining agreement between team owners and players expired on June 30, before the two sides could come to terms on a new labor deal. At the core of the dispute was the issue of player salaries; while league officials wanted to impose stricter limits on what NBA players could earn in a single year, players argued that the league's proposed scheme would further widen the financial gap between the league's elite and mid-level players. Unable to come to terms on a new agreement, NBA owners instituted a lockout in July 1998, and all league activities were suspended.

Although the two sides finally reached an accord in January 1999, the lockout had effectively reduced the playing schedule from 82 to 50 games. The Celtics posted a 19–31 record for the year, while the front office lost $10 million in revenue.

## MANAGEMENT CHANGES IN THE NEW CENTURY

The Celtics continued to struggle entering the new century. In early January 2001, with the team's record a meager 12–22, Rick Pitino resigned, walking out on the remaining six and a half years of his contract. He was replaced by his assistant, Jim O'Brien, who managed to guide the Celtics to a .500 record over the remainder of the season. O'Brien's squad finally came together in 2001–02, finishing the regular season at 49–33, the team's first winning season since 1992–93. The Celtics made it deep into the playoffs that year, fueled largely by the outstanding play of young forwards Antoine Walker and Paul Pierce, until finally losing to the New Jersey Nets in the Eastern Conference Finals.

In September 2002 a group of private investors led by Wycliffe Grousbeck, his father H. Irving Grousbeck, and Stephen Pagliuca launched a $360 million bid to acquire the Celtics. While the team had been valued at only $218 million earlier that year, NBA Commissioner David Stern considered the proposed offer to be a bargain. Writing in the *Boston Globe* on September 29, 2002, Shira Springer quoted the commissioner as telling the investment partners that they "should have paid $500 million" for the storied franchise. The deal was finalized on December 31, 2002, and the Celtics became the property of Boston Basketball Partners L.L.C. and once again became a private company.

In 2004 the Celtics named Doc Rivers as its new head coach. While the team earned its fourth straight postseason berth following the 2004–05 season, it failed to advance past the first round of the playoffs, losing to the Indiana Pacers in seven games. The Celtics stumbled over the next two seasons, falling to 24–58 in 2006–07 as star forward Paul Pierce played only 47 games due to injury. The team also suffered a deeply personal loss in October 2006 when Red Auerbach passed away at the age of 89. In tribute to the Celtics legend, the organization inscribed his name into the legendary parquet floor of the team's home court.

## TRADES, SETBACKS, AND SUCCESS: 2007–10

During the 2007 off-season, general manager Danny Ainge executed two blockbuster trades, acquiring star power forward Kevin Garnett from the Minnesota Timberwolves, and sharp-shooting guard Ray Allen from the Seattle Supersonics. Led by the "Big Three" of Garnett, Allen, and Paul Pierce, the revitalized Celtics stormed out of the gate to begin the 2007–08 campaign, starting the season 29–3 and finishing the year with a league-leading 66–16 record. After competing in an NBA-record 26 playoff games during the postseason, the Celtics secured the organization's seventeenth title banner in June 2008, defeating the Los Angeles Lakers in the NBA finals, 4–2.

The Celtics endured a number of setbacks during the 2008–09 season. The team lost Kevin Garnett to a knee injury midway through the season, and in April 2009 general manager Danny Ainge suffered a mild heart attack. Undermanned, the Celtics ultimately fell to the Orlando Magic in the second round of the playoffs. The franchise faced even greater uncertainty in 2009–10. It finished the regular season with a mediocre 27–27 record, prompting discussions that the team's core players had become too old to compete for a championship. The Celtics quickly quieted the skeptics during the postseason, however, eliminating the Miami Heat in five games and upsetting the heavily favored Cleveland Cavaliers in the second round of the playoffs. Much of the team's success was fueled by a rejuvenated Kevin Garnett as well as the inspired play of rising young point guard Rajon Rondo.

After eliminating the Orlando Magic in the 2010 Eastern Conference Finals, the Celtics squared off against the Los Angeles Lakers for the NBA championship. After splitting the first two games in Los Angeles, the Celtics went on to win two out of three games in Boston, returning to the West Coast with a 3–2 series lead. The Celtics suffered a fatal blow in game six, however, when starting center Kendrick Perkins went down with a season-ending knee injury. Although the Celtics led for much of game seven, Perkins's absence deprived them of a crucial interior presence on defense, and they ultimately lost the final game and the title. Still, the team's inspired postseason run exceeded the expectations of fans and commentators alike, making the 2009–10 season an overall success. With the impending free agencies of Ray Allen and Paul Pierce, however, it remained to be seen if the team could continue to compete at the highest level in the immediate future.

*Jeffrey L. Covell*
*Updated, Stephen Meyer*

## PRINCIPAL COMPETITORS

New Jersey Basketball, LLC; New York Knickerbockers; Philadelphia 76ers, L.P.; Toronto Raptors Basketball Club.

## FURTHER READING

Araton, Harvey, and Filip Bondy, *The Selling of the Green*, New York: HarperCollins, 1992.

Colston, Chris, "Health Blows Stagger Celtics; Ainge Suffers Heart Attack; Garnett May Miss Playoffs," *USA Today*, April 17, 2009, p. 1C.

Hackney, Holt, "Boston after Bird," *FW*, November 27, 1990, p. 68.

Hammonds, Keith H., "For Celtics Fans, It's Wait till Next Fiscal Year," *Business Week*, June 27, 1988, p. 89.

McLaughlin, Mark, "Win or Lose, Celtics' Performance Has Little Effect on Price of Stock," *New England Business*, June 20, 1988, p. 48.

Ryan, Bob, *The Boston Celtics: The History, Legends, and Images of America's Most Celebrated Team*, New York: Addison-Wesley, 1989.

Shaughnessy, Dan, *Ever Green*, New York: St. Martin's Press, 1990.

Springer, Shira, "Celtic Partners Stress Teamwork," *Boston Globe*, September 29, 2002, p. C1.

Turner, Broderick, "Celtics Are Caught at a Crossroads," *Los Angeles Times*, February 1, 2010, p. C4.

Webber, Alan M., "Red Auerbach on Management," *Harvard Business Review*, March/April 1987, p. 84.

# Brooks Brothers Inc.

———— ■ ————

**346 Madison Avenue**
**New York, New York 10017**
**U.S.A.**
**Telephone: (732) 225-4860**
**Toll Free: (800) 274-1815**
**Fax: (212) 885-6870**
**Web site: http://www.brooksbrothers.com**

*Wholly Owned Subsidiary of Retail Brand Alliance, Inc.*
*Founded:* 1818
*Incorporated:* 1903
*Employees:* 3,500
*Sales:* $809.30 million (2008)
*NAICS:* 448110 Men's Clothing Stores; 448120 Women's Clothing Stores; 448140 Family Clothing Stores; 448150 Clothing Accessories Stores

■ ■ ■

Brooks Brothers Inc., a subsidiary of Retail Brand Alliance, Inc., operates a chain of clothing stores in the United States and worldwide. A traditional source of suits and accessories for conservative businesspeople, Brooks Brothers also features designer men's and women's fashions. Its classic styles derive from English models, often dating back to the 19th century. Its contemporary styles are created by fashion designers such as Thom Browne.

## CLOTHING THE ELITE, 1818–1945

Dating from 1818, Brooks Brothers was one of the first stores in the United States to offer ready-made clothing.

Henry Sands Brooks bought a building and lot on the corner of Cherry and Catharine Streets in New York City for $15,250, and he opened his store there. After the founder died in 1833, his sons Henry and Daniel H. carried on the business, which they named H. and D.H. Brooks & Co. Henry subsequently died, and by 1850 when the name was changed to Brooks Brothers, control of the business had passed into the hands of Daniel and three younger sons of the founder. A new building replaced the original store in 1845.

Brooks Brothers opened a second store farther uptown, at the corner of Broadway and Grand Street, in 1857. Both stores offered custom and ready-made clothing and a variety of piece goods, including cashmeres, velvet, silk, and satin. During the Civil War the company's patrons, for both uniforms and civilian wear, included Union generals Ulysses S. Grant, Joseph Hooker, Philip Sheridan, and William Tecumseh Sherman. President Abraham Lincoln was a regular customer. He wore a frock coat bearing the Brooks Brothers label to his second inaugural, and it was said he was wearing this coat on the night of his assassination. Perhaps the identification of the firm with the Union cause accounted for the looting and sacking of the Cherry Street store during the draft-protest riot of 1863 that ravaged the city for three days.

The Cherry Street store was rebuilt but was closed in 1874. The Grand Street store moved to the south end of Union Square in 1870, but this was only a temporary location, for it moved back downtown to Broadway and Bond Street in 1874. Ten years later the store moved uptown, to Broadway and 22nd Street. Daniel Brooks, the last survivor of the founder's sons, retired in 1879.

## COMPANY PERSPECTIVES

As the country's oldest clothing retailer, Brooks Brothers is proud to uphold the same traditions and values for nearly two centuries. We believe these are the reasons why our customers consider us to be far more than a store. Brooks Brothers is an American icon.

Several former employees, as well as two of Daniel's nephews, then became partners in the firm. Two more nephews later became partners as well. The company was incorporated in 1903. A summer office in Newport, Rhode Island, was opened in 1909, and a Boston branch was opened in 1912. The flagship store made its last move uptown in 1915, when it opened in a new building constructed for it at Madison Avenue and 44th Street. Through it all, Brooks Brothers continued to clothe the nation's leaders, including Grant, Theodore Roosevelt, and Woodrow Wilson, all of whom took the presidential oath of office in the company's suits.

Brooks Brothers based its clothing on London styles and did most of its own manufacturing. Introduced about 1900, its standby "Number One Sack Suit" was loosely constructed, with straight-legged cuffed trousers and a three-button jacket that hung straight, without a tucked-in waist, and natural, unpadded shoulders. This suit style, imported from England, became popular among prep schoolers and eastern college undergraduates, although the company also made a two-button model.

In 1900 Brooks Brothers introduced to the United States shirts with button-down collar tabs, adapted from the shirt worn by English polo players to keep the collar wings from flapping during play. The polo coat, which was originally designed to throw on over the riding habit following a match and was white rather than camel, was introduced about 1910. The company also introduced from England the polo shirt, foulard tie, and deerstalker cap, the latter associated with Sherlock Holmes. The Shetland sweater was brought over in the 1890s. The company's pink shirt made its first appearance in 1900. India Madras for shirts and beachwear began to be displayed at this time. Brooks Brothers has also been credited for introducing the seersucker suit, a staple in tropical parts of the British Empire, to America.

Women began casting a hungry eye at Brooks Brothers furnishings about this time. The Shetland sweater was the first to fall into their hands, in 1912,

and the polo coat followed in the early 1920s. Hollywood actors and actresses were among the company's best customers. Fred Astaire bought 50 foulard ties at a time; Maurice Chevalier bought the company's hats; Rudolf Valentino was a steady customer; Katharine Hepburn bought seersucker slacks; and Marlene Dietrich purchased silk dressing gowns. Tank-style bathing suits for women, daring in the 1920s, were borrowed from Brooks's swimwear, and many a pink shirt found its way into a woman's wardrobe. By the late 1940s a corner of the first floor had been set aside for women shoppers.

As a privately held company, Brooks Brothers did not disclose its financial condition, but it was reported to have earned more than $1 million before taxes in 1923. After that date earnings dropped steadily for 10 years, and by 1935, according to one account, it had an operating deficit of more than $1 million. (According to another account the company lost money only during the 1938–40 period.) It was believed that the company needed to take in $3.6 million annually to break even at this point.

## NEW OWNERS AND NEW STYLES: 1946–88

Brooks Brothers was sold in 1946 to Julius Garfinckel & Co., Inc., a department store operator in Washington, D.C., that paid a little more than $3 million for 62 percent of the outstanding stock. (The minority shares were held by the department store John Wanamaker, which had bought them earlier from an old Brooks estate held in the custody of the Guaranty Trust Co.) With the sale, Winthrop H. Brooks, a great-grandson of the founder, stepped down as president, ending the family's guiding role in the business. Under Garfinckel's management, Brooks Brothers adopted more aggressive merchandising to boost sales and stabilized general operating expenses. The company's earnings rose steadily and reached $797,683 in fiscal 1955.

Brooks Brothers also made a few concessions to changing times, such as adding synthetic fibers to some of its wool suits. These included a polyester-worsted blend (Brooks-Knit) and an all-worsted stretch suit (Brooks-Ease). The company also introduced wash-and-wear shirts in the form of Dacron and oxford cotton (Brooksweave). It began offering suit jackets with the suggestion of a waist and slight shoulder padding.

The 1950s were a very good decade for Brooks Brothers. After the wide, two-button, double-breasted suits and heavily padded shoulders of the previous decade, men seeking progress up the corporate ladder, especially on Wall Street and among Madison Avenue

KEY DATES

**1818:** First Brooks store opens.
**1863:** Broadway store is looted in Civil War draft riots.
**1946:** Brooks Brothers is sold to Julius Garfinckel & Co.; Winthrop H. Brooks, a great-grandson of the founder, steps down as president, ending the family's guiding role in the business.
**1979:** First Tokyo store opens.
**1988:** British clothier Marks & Spencer PLC acquires Brooks Brothers for $750 million.
**2001:** Retail Brand Associates acquires Brooks Brothers from Marks & Spencer for $225 million; Claudio Del Vecchio becomes CEO.

advertising agencies, turned in the early 1950s to the look dubbed "Ivy League." This style, characterized by natural shoulders, narrow lapels, and narrow ties as the necessary accessory, was a natural fit for Brooks Brothers. The company, however, refused to take this look to the "jivey Ivy" extreme popular at the time, keeping its lapels three inches wide and its ties three and one-half inches wide.

Also trendy during this decade were the Bermuda-length shorts the company brought to America and shirts, jackets, and trousers of bleeding Madras. Women crowded the store to buy Bermuda shorts, pleated dress shirts, and sports shirts with rhinestone buttons. By the late 1950s, the Ivy League fashion in menswear was being challenged by the Continental look, a chestier two-button style. After John F. Kennedy, wearing a two-button suit, outpointed three-buttoned Richard Nixon and won the presidency, Brooks Brothers, in 1961, unveiled a new two-button suit. The suit retained the company's natural shoulders, notched lapels, and center vent, but it was trimmer and more tailored, with a longer roll to the lapels and slightly more waist suppression.

The 1960s most emphatically was not Brooks Brothers' era. Even those young men who were following a conventional career path took to sporting longer hair and long sideburns and fostering what was called the "peacock revolution" by favoring European-influenced two-button suits. These were characterized by higher armholes, a more defined waist, wider lapels, and more shoulder padding. Brooks Brothers gave ground grudgingly, slowly widening the lapels until they reached three and seven-eighths inches on the two-button model

and at least three and a half inches on the sack suit. The button-down shirt, a symbol of corporate uptightness, appeared to be dead.

"We knew we were losing our young people during the sixties," President Frank T. Reilly of Brooks Brothers told Stephen Birmingham in *Vogue* in 1978, "and we wondered what would happen to that generation of young men when they entered the business community. Well, we found out what would happen. They came back to Brooks Brothers for their working clothes, and they stayed back. In the end, our customers always come back." Even button-down shirts made a comeback. Custom tailoring, however, came to an end in 1976; this long-standing service was accounting for only about 0.5 percent of company revenue.

The Brooks Brothers chain grew from 10 stores in 1970, stretching from coast to coast and including a second Manhattan outlet in the financial district, to 13 in 1973. Gross annual revenues were in the neighborhood of $70 million, and the firm made a record profit in 1975. More than 40 percent of its suits were being made in its Long Island City plant in New York City's borough of Queens, and the rest were produced by other manufacturers to its specifications. The number of stores reached 24 in 1980. Three of these were in Tokyo, where the company first established a presence in 1979.

**MARKS & SPENCER SUBSIDIARY: 1988–97**

Garfinckel's sold Brooks Brothers to Allied Stores Corp. in 1980 for an estimated $228 million. In 1986 Brooks Brothers and other Allied holdings were passed to Campeau Corp., which sold the chain to the British clothier Marks & Spencer in 1988 for $750 million. At this point the Brooks chain had grown to 47 stores in the United States and 21 more in Japan. (The Japanese stores belonged to a 51 percent Brooks-owned joint venture that was separate from the Marks & Spencer subsidiary Brooks Brothers Inc.) Observers regarded the purchase price as wildly inflated. The firm was said to be poorly managed, carrying many slow-moving items while letting others that were selling briskly fall out of stock.

To reduce expenses, Marks & Spencer installed computer systems to monitor inventory and ensure timely distribution. It also closed Brooks Brothers' Paterson, New Jersey, shirt factory in 1989 and subcontracted most of the other clothing from the Long Island City plant to a Syracuse manufacturer. By mid-1993 all manufacturing was being done by outside contractors, except for three factories making shirts and ties.

The 1980s had not been kind to Brooks Brothers. The traders who thrived on Wall Street now preferred a "power look" that included broadly striped shirts and strong shoulders. By 1990, however, this had given way to softer, English-influenced clothing, but the new suits, unlike the sack, had double vents (instead of a single center vent) and high lapels. Marks & Spencer introduced its own English-cut suits to Brooks Brothers, featuring a darted front with either two or three buttons, slightly padded shoulders, and pleated trousers, which Brooks Brothers had not carried since the early 1960s. The parent company was well aware that the standard three-button Brooks suit was accounting for only 38 percent of the chain's sales, compared with 55 percent in the past.

There were other significant changes for Brooks Brothers. Management installed escalators in the flagship store as part of a $7 million remodeling effort and put its shirts and sweaters out on the counter instead of locking them up in wood-framed glass cases. The second floor, traditionally given over to the sack suit, now presented an expanded sportswear selection. Women's wear, which was accounting for 12 percent of sales, moved to the third floor. For the growing number of men who spent their spare hours working out in Manhattan's increasing number of health clubs, some suits, including double-breasted ones, were made much wider in the chest than at the waist. There was a wide selection of leather and suede jackets, and the company even offered sleeveless tank tops. Brooks Brothers also began opening factory outlet stores to market unsold merchandise, typically at 30 percent off. By the spring of 1994 there were 26 of these outlet stores, and they reportedly accounted for 25 percent of all U.S. sales.

To attract men not willing to pay $500 or more for a Brooks Brothers suit, the company developed what it called its Wardrobe Collection of "suit separates," consisting of jackets priced at $270 and trousers at $125. Separates also allowed a man whose waistline and shoulder proportions did not meet standard sizes to purchase clothing without making major alterations on the jacket or pants. New dyeing techniques allowed the company to match different bolts of fabric instead of having to use the same bolt to create a suit. Significantly, in 1993 Brooks Brothers introduced a wool-polyester suit that retailed for only $295, compared with its top-of-the-line Golden Fleece suit, selling for $895.

Brooks Brothers' sales in fiscal 1991 were $300.3 million, but operating profit fell to $10.9 million. The company, according to analysts, was trapped by its image, caught between longtime patrons who resented any change and a new generation with whom the firm had no credibility. In addition, a cost-cutting reduction in sales personnel inevitably meant less responsive service, and some customers maintained that the firm's practice of contracting out manufacturing had resulted in a decline in quality.

Nonetheless, the company's management stuck to its strategy of keeping its core clientele while making its goods more appealing and affordable to a new generation. Sales rose to $314.4 million in fiscal 1992 and $339 million in 1993, while operating profits rose from $18.3 million to $20.9 million. In fiscal 1994 sales came to $378.2 million and operating profit to $22.2 million. Fiscal 1995, however, saw a sharp downturn in operating profit to $9.2 million on sales of $403.1 million, leading to the resignation of company president William V. Roberti.

## CONTINUED RENOVATION IN THE LATE NINETIES

Under Joseph Gromek, the new chief executive, Brooks Brothers introduced its own eyewear frames and added such items as khaki pants and jeans to its clothing line, suitable for the so-called dress-down Fridays, which were adopted even on Wall Street. To deal with complaints that the firm was aloof and forbidding, it created a more open layout and better lighting for some stores and urged sales personnel to smile and greet visitors as they walked through the door. Old window displays were updated. Above all there was a great deal more use of color, including royal blue sports coats, purple gingham shirts, yellow handkerchiefs, and ties in lime green, fuchsia, turquoise, and orange. Shirt color choices included burgundy, turquoise, and sea-foam green. In women's wear, Brooks Brothers introduced suede jackets and velour tops in pastel colors, Lycra knit tops, and even bright orange winter coats.

Long reluctant to market itself in any blatant way, Brooks Brothers introduced a $1.5 million in-house advertising campaign in 1997. The Brooks Brothers credit card was reintroduced. The number of stores increased from 83 at the end of fiscal 1994 to nearly 100 at the end of fiscal 1996. Sales continued to rise, and operating profits rebounded, from $446.3 million and $16.7 million, respectively, in fiscal 1996 to $490.1 million and $24.8 million in fiscal 1997. (Sales and profit figures beginning in 1988 included the parent company's take from the Japanese Brooks Brothers joint venture.)

Buoyed by improved performance, Brooks Brothers moved to expand its markets and enhance its products and image. In 1998 it embarked on a program to increase its women's business by opening women-only stores. The goal was to hike the women's share of its sales from 12 percent to 20 percent. When it opened a new flagship store on Fifth Avenue in New York in 1999, it devoted half of the total floor space to women's apparel and accessories. In addition, the company announced plans to open 14 to 20 new U.S. stores serving men and women each year through 2001. It initiated online catalog sales and found unexpected success in sales of men's suits by 1999.

As it entered the new millennium, Brooks Brothers embarked on an effort to reinvent itself. It updated its tailored clothing and accessories lines, adding more casual wear and using new, high-technology fabrics and colors for dress shirts and ties. The goal was to move away from the staid Brooks Brothers image of dressing "the man in the gray flannel suit."

Millennial reinvention extended behind the scenes as well. In 1998 Brooks Brothers, as part of a five-year strategy to grow sales from $600 million to $1 billion, rearranged itself into four separate divisions: retail, outlet, direct mail, and international. To enhance its performance by upgrading the way employees handled everything from purchase orders to managing promotions, the company adopted an advanced software system of retail applications in 1999. The most dramatic move in this period, prompted by an $8.4 million operating loss in the first half of 1999, was the departure, voluntary or otherwise, of six key executives.

## NEW LEADERSHIP IN THE NEW MILLENNIUM

The wholesale executive turnover was an omen foreshadowing the end of the British Marks & Spencer stewardship of the iconic American brand. Some commentators argued that Brooks Brothers, while not floundering, had missed its potential because of Marks & Spencer's downgrading of the product lines and customer service in an effort to cut costs and attract bargain-hunting shoppers. Performance considerations aside, Marks & Spencer had decided to cut back on operations in Europe and the United States and to focus on its sales in its home base, the United Kingdom.

Consequently, in March 2001 Brooks Brothers went up for sale. There was great interest. It was courted by Texas Pacific Group, May Department Stores, and a dozen or so other retail and financial buyers. The terrorist attacks on New York and Washington, D.C., on September 11, 2001, interrupted negotiations, but they quickly resumed. On Thanksgiving Day, Retail Brand Alliance (RBA), Inc., based in Enfield, Connecticut, agreed to buy Brooks Brothers for $225 million in cash. This bargain price was considerably less than the $400

million selling price that Marks & Spencer had hoped for.

Formed earlier in 2001 by billionaire Italian investor Claudio Del Vecchio, RBA was a holding company controlling more than 1,000 women's jewelry and accessory stores. Brooks Brothers was to be its crown jewel. Del Vecchio's goal was to return Brooks Brothers to its traditional roots while incorporating contemporary high fashion styles and expanding the chain both domestically and internationally. As expected, CEO Joseph Gromek's long tenure was terminated. In a surprise move, Del Vecchio decided to personally take on the task of rebuilding the underperforming company and installed himself as CEO.

Del Vecchio immediately set about upgrading what he considered a tarnished brand. Within three months he had introduced handmade suits and top-of-the-line knitwear, and he upgraded back-office systems. Later in 2002 he took a powerfully symbolic action affirming not only Brooks Brothers' but New York's survival after the collapse of the World Trade Center towers in the 2001 terrorist attacks. The company's store in the Ground Zero zone survived nearly intact and had served as a relief center for rescue workers. Del Vecchio considered abandoning the location, which Brooks Brothers had occupied since 1935, but instead decided to keep and refurbish it. The store was reopened for business in September 2002. At the same time, a system-wide facelift of Brooks Brothers stores was initiated, and Del Vecchio reemphasized the suit business, the historical core of the company's merchandise, which had been almost abandoned under the previous ownership.

## A REALLY BIG PARTY

In 2003 Brooks Brothers reached an impressive milestone: 185 years in business. Del Vecchio decided to celebrate the odd number as though it were a bicentennial and use the occasion to emphasize the firm's newfound commitment to selectively drawing on its past to build both sales and brand luster. He unveiled a memento of the milestone, a coffee-table history of the company called *Generations of Style—It's All about the Clothing*. On September 9, 2003, an estimated crowd of 1,500 filled the Madison Avenue flagship store to celebrate the birthday. They were entertained by cohosts Del Vecchio and Katie Couric, as well as jazz great Wynton Marsalis. The occasion also served as the Brooks Brothers fall fashion roll-out, which featured clothing inspired by designs from the company archives.

For the rest of the first decade of the 2000s, Brooks Brothers, under Del Vecchio's leadership, followed a dual path of traditional-yet-trendy, high-end merchandise and continual expansion of its presence in the United States and worldwide. In 2007 it partnered with innovative, edgy designer Thom Browne to inaugurate the expensive and quickly very popular Black Fleece line. Counterbalancing Black Fleece, in 2009 Brook Brothers introduced a Makers & Merchants label spotlighting historical Brooks Brothers styles and emphasizing American craftsmanship. To reach the markets to which the new lines would appeal, Brooks Brothers unveiled a steady stream of new flagship and specialty stores, first in key West Coast cities, then in Tokyo, London, Florence, Paris, and other major cities around the globe. In the fall of 2009 it finalized a deal to open 40 stores in Mexico, giving it a foothold in the massive Latin American clothing market.

*Robert Halasz*
*Updated, Judson MacLaury*

## PRINCIPAL COMPETITORS

Barney's; Jos. A. Banks; Paul Stuart, Inc.

## FURTHER READING

Birmingham, Stephen, "Well-bred Clout," *Vogue*, April 1978, pp. 312, 318.

*Brooks Brothers Centenary, 1818–1918*. New York: Brooks Brothers, 1918.

Durant, John, and Mann, Lloyd, "Abe Lincoln Shopped Here," *Saturday Evening Post*, December 1, 1945, pp. 22–23, 121, 123, 125–126.

Elliott, Stuart, "Brooks Brothers Moves beyond the Gray Flannel Suit," *New York Times*, September 19, 1997, p. D5.

"Garfinckel's Buy," *Fortune*, August 1946, p. 136.

*Generations of Style—It's All about the Clothing*. New York: Brooks Brothers, 2003.

Maremont, Mark, "Marks & Spencer Pays a Premium for Pinstripes," *Business Week*, April 18, 1988, p. 67.

Millstein, Gilbert, "The Suits on the Brooks Brothers Men," *New York Times Magazine*, August 5, 1976, pp. 28–29, 33, 35, 38–39.

Palmieri, Jean E., "Brooks Bros. Planning 1st Women's-only Units," *Women's Wear Daily*, May 8, 1998, p.11.

Plimpton, George, "Fashion Is a Tradition at Brooks Brothers," *Gentlemen's Quarterly*, April 1959, pp. 74–75, 126–127.

# The Buckle, Inc.

2407 West 24th Street
Kearney, Nebraska 68845
U.S.A.
Toll Free: (800) 522-8090
Fax: (308) 236-4493
Web site: http://www.buckle.com/

*Public Company*
*Incorporated:* 1948 as Mills Clothing, Inc.
*Employees:* 7,000
*Sales:* $898.29 million (2010)
*Stock Exchanges:* NYSE
*Ticker Symbol:* BKE
*NAICS:* 448140 Family Clothing Stores

■ ■ ■

The Buckle, Inc., is a retailer of medium to better-priced casual apparel, footwear, and accessories for fashion-conscious young men and women. Operating over 400 retail stores in 41 states, the company markets a wide selection of mostly brand-name casual apparel including denims, tops, sportswear, outerwear, accessories, and footwear. The Buckle emphasizes personalized attention to its customers and provides customer services such as free hemming, free gift-wrapping, easy layaways, a private-label credit card, and a frequent shopper program. All of the company's central office functions, including purchasing, pricing, accounting, advertising, and distribution, are controlled from its headquarters and distribution center in Kearney, Nebraska.

## FOUNDING AND EXPANSION: 1948–89

The Buckle was founded in Kearney in 1948 as Mills Clothing, Inc. In 1967 Mills Clothing opened a second store in Kearney under the name Brass Buckle, and in 1976 the company opened another Brass Buckle outlet in Columbus, Nebraska. Meanwhile, the original Mills Clothing store was renamed Brass Buckle in 1970 and adopted the appropriate image as a jeans store offering a wide selection of denim apparel and coordinating shirts. All three outlets were furnished in a rustic motif, with built-in jeans bins and chrome display fixtures. In 1977 the Brass Buckle began focusing on the marketing of both men's and women's casual clothing. That same year the company opened its first mall location, and by the end of 1981 it had 17 outlets.

During the 1980s the company revamped its strategy for expansion in the retail market by targeting high-traffic shopping malls near large universities and colleges and in economically vital cities with more than 20,000 residents. Particularly because of its reliance on college-aged consumers, business was traditionally seasonal, with highest sales levels occurring during the periods November 15 to December 30 and July 15 to September 1. Combined, these two periods generated approximately 40 percent of the company's annual sales.

By 1987 The Buckle operated 45 stores in the north-central Midwest. The net sales for that year were $38 million. The following year the company opened 15 new outlets. For the year, its net sales had increased to over $86.7 million, resulting in a net income of $4.9 million.

As expansion efforts increased, so did The Buckle's financial leverage. Shadowing a rise in sales from its 1988 level of just under $50 million to $57.4 million by the end of fiscal 1989, the company's net income increased from $4.3 million to $4.8 million over the same period. Also, in 1989 The Buckle opened an additional six new outlets and began altering its product mix with the inclusion of more higher-end clothing items. This change, coupled with a slight rise in retail prices, caused the average annual sales per square foot in the company's retail outlets to increase from $221 to $238 over the course of the year.

### RENOVATION AND FURTHER EXPANSION: 1990–92

In 1990 The Buckle began a five-year renovation project to revamp its older stores with redesigned store layouts, enhanced lighting arrays, and new fixtures that presented a more modern attitude and appealed to savvy college-aged consumers. A special buying opportunity with one of The Buckle's suppliers helped stock the company's newly designed retail spaces with fresh merchandise, while also contributing to net income by providing the opportunity for a higher-than-usual initial price markup.

Continuing its plan of expansion, the company opened new stores and beefed up the sales in existing stores. Even though newer Buckle locations tended toward higher-end malls that commanded higher costs of occupancy, this increased overhead was largely absorbed by corresponding increases in sales and prices. In tandem with its expansion, the company worked to streamline record-keeping and scheduling and refined its centralized system to increase efficiency among its many outlets and decrease managerial overhead. By yearend 1990 the company was able to report a net income of $3.8 million on sales of $68.9 million. In 1991 The Buckle invested in a new computer system that further offset the increasing administrative and managerial func-

tions required of such a large-scale operation. By April of that year all of the company's retail outlets were operating under the name The Buckle, Inc.

The company learned early on that to maintain its leading edge in changing fashion trends it needed to have an adaptive, forward-thinking, and flexible managerial perspective. To this end, while contracting for a limited number of private-label apparel products with which to stock its stores, The Buckle concentrated on developing relationships with vendors of popular brands such as Levi's, Girbaud, Lawman, Esprit, Guess?, and others that held name recognition with the company's target market. In addition, it developed key relationships with both Pepe Clothing Co. and Lucky Brand Dungarees. By 1991 The Buckle was one of Pepe's largest customers. In turn, it received quality, fashion-focused apparel at wholesale prices lower than those offered by the more well-known manufacturers.

As The Buckle's outlets spread throughout the United States, it developed a centralized, semiautomated distribution system within its corporate headquarters in Kearney. Using an efficient bar-coding system, incoming merchandise was received, sorted, packaged for transit, and reshipped to individual outlets, usually within one business day of receipt. Beginning in 1992 the company started to warehouse a portion of its total inventory, thereby allowing individual stores to eliminate excessive inventories and replace items as needed. This warehouse and distribution system provided individual Buckle outlets with an ever-changing stock of products. It also provided customers with an uncluttered retail environment that had a constantly changing array of new fashions.

### GOING PUBLIC AND EXPANDING ITS MARKET: 1992–95

By the end of fiscal 1991 The Buckle had 5 million shares of stock privately held. In early 1992 the company decided to undertake its first public offering by presenting an additional 1.7 million shares on the NASDAQ. With 89 stores then in operation, the company used the funds generated from the sale of stock to fund further expansion and continue the final three years of its existing store remodeling program.

That same year the company welcomed the addition of 18 new Buckle outlets and an expanded market area that now included Tennessee, Ohio, Michigan, and Texas. The company also started its Buckle Kids line for younger customers, giving each store a more family friendly orientation. By the end of fiscal 1992 the company posted a net income of $7.9 million on sales of $112.9 million, which was a 30 percent jump over 1991 levels.

## KEY DATES

**1948:** Company is founded as Mills Clothing, Inc.
**1967:** Mills Clothing first uses the name Brass Buckle for a store.
**1991:** All company retail outlets operate under the name The Buckle.
**1992:** The Buckle, Inc., undertakes its first public offering, trading first on the NASDAQ and later on the New York Stock Exchange.
**2007:** The Buckle joins forces with Jones Soda to launch the promotion "Your jeans. Your Jones."

Through 1994 sales continued their steady climb, increasing from $129.6 million in 1993 to $145 million in 1994. Store openings also rose, with 27 new Buckle outlets in 1993 and an additional 16 outlets during 1994. In October 1994 The Buckle unveiled the Primo Card, a frequent-shopper program that rewarded loyal customers with percentage-off savings. Unlike other companies in the retail fashion industry, The Buckle reported a strong Christmas in 1994, with sales up 7 percent during the five-week holiday shopping season.

By the close of fiscal 1995 The Buckle reported a net income of $9.8 million. Its net sales had climbed to $172.3 million, an increase of almost 19 percent over the previous year. Advancements made during the fiscal year included the opening of 17 new outlets, the introduction of a private-label credit card, and The Buckle's inclusion as one of *Forbes* magazine's "World's Best Small Companies in America." At the end of fiscal 1996 The Buckle posted $206.4 million in net sales, an increase of nearly 20 percent over the previous year. In addition to opening 14 new stores and incorporating the state of Wyoming within its growing market area during the fiscal year, The Buckle had renovated the last of its existing stores. It now operated 181 stores in 22 states throughout the Midwest and was looking toward expansion on both coasts.

## INTO THE TWENTY-FIRST CENTURY

The Buckle had good reason to expect future success as it prepared to transition its business into the next century. Even though the company had increased its strength in several large metropolitan areas in the central United States, the market it knew and served much better than did its competitors was young people in the

smaller cities who were ready and willing to spend money on trendy clothes. One secret to The Buckle's success was to provide high-end and hard-to-find brands such as Lucky Brand Dungarees and Doc Marten that appealed to this fashion-conscious niche. Another key was its trained and experienced staff of sales employees. Furthermore, The Buckle had already proven its adaptability to the highs and lows of the retail sales cycle. Since 1982 it had only closed one store.

The Buckle's strategies and track record were soon tested by the economic downturn at the turn of the 21st century. By mid-2000 the bellwether statistic of sales by stores open more than one year had fallen against the previous year for eight consecutive months. The decline was partly attributable to the fact that young people were turning to lower-priced merchandise.

However, The Buckle eventually rallied to perform relatively well so that by mid-2004 its year-to-year growth per store was averaging 9 percent. The company's continued success was at least partly explained by an eclectic approach to merchandise that emphasized a wide range of name brands, fashions, and prices. Also, The Buckle's image was still built around denim. Jeans accounted for 30 percent of its annual sales. Increasingly, however, the store was stocking dozens of styles and brands of tops and bottoms for both young men and women. These came in a wide range of prices, as the store sought to avoid catering only to a one-priced niche. The trick to merchandise selection was that the stores only stocked a few copies in each style. This wide and shallow approach assured its customers that they were not likely to run into anyone wearing exactly the same item. In this way it successfully tapped into the universal desire of U.S. youth to be both hip and unique.

The Buckle's expansion strategy meshed well with its one-store-for-all-tastes approach. Most of its growth was in secondary, small-city markets such as Omaha, Nebraska, rather than in large metropolitan areas where more specialized retailers had the best success. Geographically, The Buckle continued expanding on both of the coasts and to the South and West. New England, however, remained unexploited. In all areas, location decisions were determined by a careful selection of prime sites in regional malls and shopping centers in population areas of at least 300,000 people.

## RIDING THE POPULAR CULTURE THROUGH A RECESSION

During the first decade of the 21st century The Buckle partnered with pop music groups and a wide range of unrelated product brands. In 2007 it joined forces with

Jones Soda and initiated the promotion "Your jeans. Your Jones," in which Buckle customers who tried on three pairs of jeans were rewarded with a can of Jones Soda. They could also visit The Buckle Web site to try to win 500 Buckle gift cards or the grand prize of a $1,000 Buckle shopping spree and a trip for two to Jones Soda's headquarters in Seattle, Washington, and help select a new soda label.

That same year The Buckle partnered with Atlantic Records and Viva La Rock, a marketing agency that worked with the entertainment industry and youth-oriented brands, to launch "Ticket to Style," a campaign promoting The Buckle's denims and introducing a new album by the group matchbox twenty. Buckle customers were invited to enter to win prizes in this matchup of the music and fashion industries. Playing off of its somewhat Goth-oriented image, in 2008 The Buckle collaborated with Affliction Clothing, an offbeat high-fashion brand, in a promotion built around Affliction's venture into mixed martial arts with an event called "Affliction Banned" that took place in Anaheim, California. The Buckle received more publicity when the employee Jordin Sparks took time off from her store to audition successfully for the television show *American Idol*. She wound up performing in a two-hour special broadcast of the show in 2007.

A sharp recession that began in late 2007 once again jolted the retail clothing industry in general and The Buckle in particular. Then in May 2008 a tornado struck Buckle facilities in Kearney. However, in spite of the economy and the weather, The Buckle proved its ability to be resilient. It was one of the few retailers to post sales growth when many others posted losses. In the depths of the recession, The Buckle reported that same-store sales were up 21 percent over the previous year. Through the end of 2009 the company had benefited from 13 straight quarters of positive same-store sales. The Buckle's long-term trend toward more female consumers held through this period, and by April 2010 women customers accounted for 61.5 percent of total sales. One factor that remained steady was the rock on which The Buckle's success had been built for many years: denim. With all the changes in fashions and popular culture in the 21st century, this icon of the youth culture in the United States showed no signs of losing its appeal.

*Pamela L. Shelton*
*Updated, Judson MacLaury*

## PRINCIPAL COMPETITORS

Abercrombie & Fitch Co.; American Eagle Outfitters, Inc.; The Gap, Inc.

## FURTHER READING

"Former Buckle Teammate Jordin Sparks Wins Hearts and Makes 'American Idol' History," Comtex News Network, May 24, 2007.

Kolb, Alex, "The Buckle, Inc.," Comtex News Network, March 10, 2009.

MacDonald, Laurie, "Buckled Up: Making It at the Mall," *Footwear News*, August 5, 1996.

Olson, Chris, "Slumping Nebraska-Based Retail Chain Hopes Its Problems Are Cyclical," *Knight Ridder/Tribune Business News*, June 8, 2000.

Rosenbloom, Stephanie, "Staying Alive in Retailing," *New York Times*, December 20, 2008, p. B1.

"The World's Best Small Companies in America," *Forbes*, November 6, 1995.

# Burger King Corporation

5505 Blue Lagoon Drive
Miami, Florida 33126
U.S.A.
Telephone: (305) 378-3000
Fax: (305) 378-7262
Web site: http://www.bk.com/

*Public Company*
*Incorporated:* 1954
*Employees:* 41,320
*Sales:* $2.54 billion (2009)
*Stock Exchanges:* New York
*Ticker Symbol:* BKC
*NAICS:* 722211 Limited-Service Restaurants

■ ■ ■

Burger King Corporation is the second-largest fast-food chain in the United States, trailing only McDonald's Corporation. The company franchises more than 10,000 restaurants, besides owning and operating over 1,000 of its own. Overall, there are more than 12,000 Burger King restaurants worldwide, with locations in all 50 states and in more than 70 countries. Although arguably most famous as the home of the Whopper, a popular hamburger first introduced in 1957, Burger King is recognized for the variety of its menu items, which include salads and other healthy dishes alongside sandwiches, French fries, and ice cream desserts. In 2006 Burger King became a public company and began trading on the New York Stock Exchange.

## RAPID GROWTH UNDER COMPANY FOUNDERS: 1954–67

The entrepreneurs James W. McLamore and David Edgerton founded Burger King Corporation in 1954 in Miami, Florida. Five years later they were ready to expand their five Florida Burger Kings into a nationwide chain. By the time they sold their company to Pillsbury in 1967, Burger King had become the third-largest fast-food chain in the country and was on its way to second place, after the industry leader McDonald's.

The story of Burger King's growth is the story of how franchising and advertising developed the fast-food industry. McLamore and Edgerton began in 1954 with a simple concept: to attract the burgeoning numbers of postwar baby-boom families with reasonably priced, broiled burgers that were served quickly. The idea was not unique: drive-ins offering inexpensive fast food were springing up all across the United States in the early 1950s. In fact, 1954 was the same year Ray Kroc made his deal with the McDonald brothers, whose original southern California drive-in started the McDonald's empire.

McLamore and Edgerton tried to give their Burger King restaurants a special edge. Burger King became the first chain to offer dining rooms (albeit uncomfortable plastic ones). In 1957 they expanded their menu with the Whopper, a burger with sauce, cheese, lettuce, pickles, and tomato, for big appetites. However, prices were kept low: a hamburger cost 18 cents and the Whopper 37 cents. (McDonald's burgers at the same time, however, cost only 15 cents.) In 1958 they took advantage of an increasingly popular medium, television.

## COMPANY PERSPECTIVES

For over 50 years, our restaurants have been serving high quality, great tasting and affordable food around the world. Our commitment to the food we serve is what defines us as a company and is at the center of our HAVE IT YOUR WAY brand promise.

The first Burger King television commercial appeared on Miami's VHF station that year.

By 1959 McLamore and Edgerton were ready to expand beyond Florida, and franchising seemed to be the best way to take their concept to a broader market. Franchising was booming in the late 1950s because it allowed companies to expand with minimal investment. Like many other franchisers, McLamore and Edgerton attracted their investors by selling exclusive rights to large territories throughout the country. The buyers of these territorial rights, many of them large businesses themselves, could do what they wanted to in their territory: buy land, build as many stores as they liked, sell part of the territory to other investors, or diversify. McLamore and Edgerton took their initial payments (which varied with the territory) and their cut (as little as 1 percent of sales) and left their franchisees pretty much on their own.

The system worked well, allowing Burger King to expand rapidly. By 1967, when the partners decided to sell the company they had founded, the chain included 274 stores and was worth $18 million to its buyer, the prepared-foods giant Pillsbury.

### DIFFICULTIES WITH
### FRANCHISEES UNDER PILLSBURY:
### 1967–77

The Burger King franchising system also worked well for the franchisees. Under the early Burger King system, some of the company's large investors expanded at a rate rivaling that of the parent company. Where this loosely knit franchising system failed, however, was in providing a consistent company image. Because McLamore and Edgerton did not check on their franchises and used only a small field staff for franchise support, the chain was noted for inconsistency in both food and service from franchise to franchise, which was a major flaw in a chain that aimed to attract customers by assuring them of what to expect in every Burger King they visited.

It was up to the new owner, Pillsbury, to crack down on franchise owners. However, some large franchisees thought they could run their Burger King outlets better than a packaged-goods company. For example, Billy and Jimmy Trotter bought their first Burger King outlet in 1963. By 1969 they controlled almost two dozen Burger King restaurants and went public under the name Self Service Restaurants Inc. In 1970, when the franchisees in control of the lucrative Chicago, Illinois, market decided to sell out, Billy Trotter flew to Chicago in a snowstorm to buy the territory for $8 million. By the time Pillsbury executives got to town the next day, they found they had been bested by their own franchisee.

The Trotters did not stop there. By 1971 they owned 351 stores with sales of $32 million. They bought out two steak house chains (taking the name of one of them, Chart House), established their own training and inspection programs, and decided on their own food suppliers. By 1972 they were ready to take over altogether. The Trotters made Pillsbury a $100 million offer for Burger King. When that initiative failed, they suggested that both Pillsbury and Chart House spin off their Burger King holdings into a separate company. When that also failed, they continued to acquire Burger King piecemeal, buying nine stores in Boston and 13 in Houston.

However, Pillsbury was not about to allow Chart House to gain other valuable territories. It sued the Boston franchisees who had sold to Chart House, citing Pillsbury's contractual right of first refusal to any sale. Eventually, Chart House compromised by agreeing to give up its Boston holdings in exchange for the right to keep its Houston properties.

### NEW LEADERSHIP: 1977

Pillsbury's suit was proof of a new management attitude that involved more central control over powerful franchisees. However, it was not until Pillsbury brought in a hard-hitting executive from McDonald's that Burger King began to exert real control over its franchisees. Donald Smith was third in line for the top spot at McDonald's when Pillsbury lured him away in 1977 with a promise of full autonomy in the top position at Burger King. Smith used it to "McDonaldize" the company, a process that was especially felt among the franchise holders.

Burger King had grown by selling wide territorial rights, whereas McDonald's had taken a different approach from the very beginning by leasing stores to franchisees and demanding a high degree of uniformity in return. When Smith came on board at Burger King in 1977, the company owned only 34 percent of the

## KEY DATES

**1954:** James W. McLamore and David Edgerton establish Burger King Corporation.
**1957:** The Whopper is launched.
**1967:** Burger King is sold to Pillsbury.
**1977:** Donald Smith is hired to restructure the firm's franchise system.
**1989:** Grand Metropolitan PLC acquires Pillsbury.
**2002:** A group of investors led by Texas Pacific Group acquire Burger King.
**2006:** Burger King launches an initial public offering.
**2010:** Burger King opens its first Whopper Bar.

land and buildings on which its products were sold. Land ownership is advantageous because land is an appreciating asset and a source of tax deductions, but more important it gives the parent company a landlord's power over recalcitrant franchisees.

Smith began by introducing a more demanding franchise contract. Awarded only to individuals, not partnerships or companies, it stipulated that franchisees may not own other restaurants and must live within an hour's drive of their franchise, effectively stopping franchisees from getting too big. He also created 10 regional offices to manage franchises.

Smith's new franchise regulations were soon put to the test. Barry W. Florescue, the chairman of Horn & Hardart and the creator of New York City's famous Automat restaurants, had recognized that nostalgia alone could not keep the original fast-food outlets alive and had decided to turn them into Burger Kings. Smith limited Florescue to building four new stores a year in New York and insisted that he could not expand elsewhere. When Florescue bought eight units in California anyway, Smith sued successfully. Florescue then signed with Arby's, and Smith again effectively asserted Burger King's control in court, based on the franchise contract. His strong response to the upstart franchisee kept Horn & Hardart from becoming too strong a force within Burger King.

## EXPANDING ABROAD AND REORGANIZING THE CORPORATE STRUCTURE

Increasing control over franchisees was not the only change Pillsbury instituted at Burger King during the 1970s. Like many other chains, Burger King began to expand abroad early in the decade. However, fast food and franchising were unfamiliar outside the United States, making international expansion a challenge. Burger King's international operations never became as profitable as anticipated, but within a decade the company was represented in 30 foreign countries.

At home the company focused on attracting new customers. In 1974 management required franchisees to use the "hospitality system" (multiple lines) to speed up service. In 1975 Burger King reintroduced drive-through windows. Even though original stands had offered this convenience, it had gradually been eliminated as Burger King restaurants added dining rooms. Drive-through windows proved to be a profitable element, accounting for 60 percent of fast-food sales throughout the industry by 1987.

Smith also revamped the corporate structure by replacing 8 of 10 managers with McDonald's people. To attack Burger King's inconsistency problem, Smith mandated a yearly two-day check of each franchise and frequent unscheduled visits. He also decided that the company should own its outlets whenever possible, and by 1979 he had raised the company's share of outlet ownership from 34 percent to 42 percent.

Smith also focused on the food served in his restaurants. He introduced the French fry technique that produced the more popular McDonald's-type fry. In 1978, primarily in response to the appeal that newcomer Wendy's had for adults, he introduced specialty sandwiches (such as fish, chicken, ham and cheese, and steak) to increase Burger King's dinner trade. Offering the broadest menu proved to be very successful, in that it boosted traffic by 15 percent.

A more radical expansion for the Burger King menu came next. After McDonald's proved that breakfast could be a profitable fast-food addition (offering a morning meal spread fixed costs over longer hours of operation) Smith began planning a breakfast menu in 1979. However, Burger King had a problem with breakfast: its flame broilers could not be adapted as easily to breakfast entrees as McDonald's grills could. Smith urged development of entrees that could be prepared on existing equipment instead of requiring special grills. He began testing breakfast foods in 1978, but it was not until the Croissan'wich in 1983 and French Toast sticks in 1985 that Burger King had winning entries in the increasingly competitive breakfast market.

## TROUBLED TIMES: EARLY TO MID-EIGHTIES

Smith left Burger King in June 1980 to try to introduce the same kind of fast-food management techniques at

Pizza Hut. By following in Smith's general direction, Burger King reached its number-two position within two years of his departure, but frequent changes at the top for the next several years meant inconsistent management for the company. Louis P. Neeb succeeded Smith, to be followed less than two years later by Jerry Ruenheck. Ruenheck resigned to become a Burger King franchise owner in Florida less than two years after that, and his successor, Jay Darling, resigned a little over a year later to take on a Burger King franchise himself. Charles Olcott, a conservative former chief financial officer, took over in 1987.

Regardless, Burger King did not stand still under its succession of heads. The company continued to expand abroad by opening a training center in London to serve its European franchisees and employees in 1985. Besides developing successful breakfast entries, Burger King added salad bars and a "light" menu to meet the demand for foods with a healthier, less fatty image. In 1985 the firm began a $100 million program to remodel most of its restaurants to include more natural materials, such as wood and plants, and less plastic. Burger King also completely computerized its cooking and cash register operations so even the least skilled teenager could do the job. Average sales per restaurant reached the $1 million mark in 1985.

However, even some of Burger King's post-Smith successes caused problems. The company introduced another successful new entree, Chicken Tenders, in 1986, only to find it that it could not obtain enough chicken to meet demand. Burger King was forced to pull its $30 million introductory ad campaign.

## MORE TROUBLED TIMES: MID- TO LATE EIGHTIES

Burger King was still bedeviled by the old complaint that its service and food were inconsistent. The company played out its identity crisis in public, changing ad styles with almost the same frequency that it changed managers. After Smith's departure in 1980, Burger King's old "Have it your way" campaign ("Hold the pickles, hold the lettuce. Special orders don't upset us.") was no longer appropriate. That ad campaign emphasized as a selling point what many saw as a drawback at Burger King: longer waiting times. However, under Smith's emphasis on speed and efficiency, special orders did upset store owners. As a result, the company turned to the harder sell "Aren't you hungry for Burger King now?" campaign. The hard-sell approach moved the chain into second place, and Burger King took an even more aggressive advertising line.

In 1982 Burger King directly attacked its competitors, alleging that Burger King's grilled burgers were better than McDonald's and Wendy's fried burgers. Both competitors sued over the ads, and Wendy's challenged Burger King to a taste test (a challenge that was pointedly ignored). In return for dropping the suits, Burger King agreed to phase out the offending ads gradually, but Burger King came out the winner in its $25 million "Battle of the Burgers": the average volume of its 3,500 stores rose from $750,000 to $840,000 in 1982, sales were up 19 percent, and pretax profits rose 9 percent.

Burger King's subsequent ad campaigns were not as successful. In 1985 the company added just over half an ounce of meat to its Whopper, making the 4.2 ounce sandwich slightly larger than the quarter-pound burgers of its competitors. The meatier Whopper and the $30 million ad campaign using celebrities to promote it failed to bring in new business. All three of the major campaigns that followed ("Herb the Nerd," "This is a Burger King town," and "Fast food for fast times") were costly flops. "We do it like you'd do it" followed in 1988, with little more success.

In 1988 the company faced another kind of threat. The parent company Pillsbury, which was the target of a hostile takeover attempt by the British company Grand Metropolitan PLC, devised a counterplan that included spinning off the troubled Burger King chain to shareholders, but at the cost of new debt that would lower the price of both Pillsbury and the new Burger King shares. Such a plan would have made it unlikely that Burger King could ever have overcome its ongoing problems of quality and consistent marketing.

Pillsbury's plan did not work, and Grand Met bought Pillsbury in January 1989 for $66 a share, or approximately $5.7 billion. Pillsbury became part of Grand Met's worldwide system of food and retailing businesses with well-known brand names. With Burger King, Grand Met got a company with some problems but whose 5,500 restaurants in all 50 states and 30 foreign countries gave it a strong presence.

## TURNAROUND UNDER GRAND MET

Grand Met's first move was to place Barry Gibbons, a successful manager of pubs and restaurants in the United Kingdom (UK), into the chief executive officer (CEO) slot. Soon thereafter, in September 1989, Grand Met acquired several restaurant properties from United Biscuits (Holdings) PLC, including the Wimpey hamburger chain, which included 381 UK outlets and 148 in other countries. By the summer of 1990, 200 Wimpeys had been converted to Burger Kings, bolstering the company's foreign operations, a traditional area of weakness. Over the next several years Burger King was much more aggressive with its international expansion, with restaurants opening for the first time in Hungary and Mexico (1991); Poland (1992); Saudi Arabia (1993); Israel, Oman, the Dominican Republic, El Salvador, Peru, and New Zealand (1994); and Paraguay (1995). By 1996 Burger King had outlets in 56 countries, a dramatic increase from the 30 of just seven years earlier.

Even though Gibbons was successful in accelerating the company's international growth, his overall tenure as CEO (which lasted until 1993) brought a mixture of successes and failures. In the new product area, the hamburger chain hit it big with the 1990 introduction of the BK Broiler, a broiled chicken sandwich aimed at fast-food eaters seeking a somewhat more healthful meal. Soon after appearing on the menu, more than 1 million were being sold each day. Also successful were promotions aimed at children. In 1990 the Burger King Kids Club program was launched nationwide, and more than 1 million kids signed up in the first two months. The program continued to grow thereafter. By 1996 membership stood at 5 million and the number of Kids Club meals sold each month had increased from 6.1 million in 1990 to nearly 12 million.

Also hugely successful was the long-term deal with the Walt Disney Company for motion picture tie-ins signed in 1992. Through 1996 (when Disney broke with Burger King to sign a deal with McDonald's), the partnership had involved Disney smashes such as *Beauty and the Beast*, *The Lion King*, and *Toy Story*. In 1996 Burger King signed a new Hollywood deal with Dream-Works Animation SKG Inc.

Gibbons, who was working under a mandate from Grand Met, also worked to improve Burger King's profitability. Soon after taking over as CEO, he cut more than 500 jobs, mainly field staff positions. He also began to divest company-owned stores in areas where the company did not have critical mass, particularly west of the Mississippi. Doing so helped increase profitability, although some observers charged that Gibbons was selling off valuable assets just to improve the company numbers. In any case, during Gibbons's last two years as CEO, profits were about $250 million each year, compared with at most $175 million a year under Pillsbury.

## NEW LEADERSHIP, CHANGE IN FOCUS: 1989–95

Where Gibbons failed, however, was in addressing Burger King's long-standing problem with image. The advertising program was still in disarray as the firm hired in 1989 D'Arcy Masius Benton & Bowles, which created still more short-lived campaigns: "Sometimes you've gotta break the rules" (1989–91), "Your way right away" (1991), and "BK Tee Vee" (1992–93). In the face of the improving profitability of the corporation, such marketing blunders led to abysmal chainwide sales increases, such as a 3.6 percent increase for the fiscal years 1991 and 1992 combined.

In mid-1993 James Adamson succeeded Gibbons as CEO, a position for which he had been groomed since joining Burger King as chief operating officer in 1991. Adamson, who actively sought out the advice of the company cofounder James W. McLamore, moved to build on Gibbons's successes as well as to rectify the failures. Adamson's most important initiatives addressed three key areas: quality, value, and image.

He improved the quality of products, such as in 1994, when the size of the BK Broiler, the BK Big Fish, and the hamburger were increased by more than 50 percent. He belatedly added a "value menu" after most other fast-food chains had already done so and he offered special promotions, such as the 990 Whopper. Related to both value and image was the long-awaited successful ad campaign "Get your burger's worth," created by Ammirati Puris Lintas, and emphasizing a back-to-basics approach and good value. The focus on the basics also led to a simplification of what had become an unwieldy menu. In all, 40 items were eliminated. The new focus was on burgers (with an emphasis on flame broiling), fries, and drinks. By early 1995 Adamson's program was paying off as same-store sales increased 6.6 percent for the fiscal year ending March 31, 1995. Morale among the franchisees had improved dramatically as well.

## MORE GROWTH AND RESTRUCTURING: 1995–98

Adamson resigned suddenly in early 1995 to head Flagstar Cos. of Spartanburg, South Carolina. In July Robert C. Lowes, who had been the CEO for Grand Met Foods Europe, was named the CEO of Burger King. Later that same year he became chairman of Burger King and gained a position on the Grand Met executive committee, a move that signaled Grand Met's commitment to Burger King and the strength of the company's resurgence. Lowes soon set some lofty goals for Burger King, including $10 billion in systemwide sales by 1997 (from $8.4 billion in 1995) and 10,000 outlets by 2000 (there were 8,455 in mid-1996). Management changes continued, however, and in 1997 Dennis Malamatinas, an executive from Grand Met's Asian beverage division, was named the CEO of Burger King. Later that year Grand Met merged with Guinness, creating Diageo

PLC. The new company's main focus was on its beverage and spirits business, leaving many analysts speculating that Diageo would eventually sell or spin off Burger King.

Despite the changes in ownership and management, Burger King remained dedicated to beating out its main competition, McDonald's. It introduced the new Big King burger to compete with McDonald's Big Mac and launched a $70 million French fry advertising campaign that included a free fryday give-away at its restaurants. By 1998 both domestic and international sales were increasing, along with market share.

Bolstered by its recent success, Burger King launched an aggressive restructuring campaign that included adopting a new logo; store remodeling with cobalt blue, red, and yellow décor; new packaging; drive-thru lane upgrades; and a new cooking system. The firm also began to turnaround its European operations, exiting the highly competitive French region and focusing on growth in the United Kingdom, Germany, and Spain. The company's Latin American, Mexican, and Caribbean operations also experienced modest growth.

## PROBLEMS LEAD TO A SALE: 2002

Burger King's success, however, proved to be short lived. In 1999 the company was forced to recall a promotional toy, the Pokémon ball, after it was discovered to be potentially dangerous for children. A class-action suit followed, claiming the company acted in a negligent fashion when it distributed the toy in its kids' meals. The firm's relationship with its franchisees was also deteriorating, marked by a highly publicized lawsuit with the franchisee La Van Hawkins. The Detroit-based entrepreneur claimed Burger King failed to help him develop and purchase restaurants as promised. The firm counter-sued, claiming that Hawkins owed the company $16 million. The civil rights activist Al Sharpton threatened to boycott Burger King as a result. To top it off, sales were falling, and the company experienced yet another change in management. Malamatinas left the firm in 2000, and Colin Storm was named interim CEO.

By this time, Burger King's parent company had announced plans to exit the fast-food industry. Many franchisees were experiencing financial difficulties (including bankruptcy) and had long since complained that Diageo had neglected Burger King in favor of its premium liquor business. These franchisees adopted the internal program "Project Champion," which was intended to force a sale of Burger King. They approached J.P. Morgan Chase & Co. to orchestrate the deal, and, eventually, Diageo agreed to sell Burger King.

In late 2002 Texas Pacific Group, Bain Capital, and Goldman Sachs Capital Partners purchased the fast-food chain for $1.5 billion.

According to Rod Smith of *Feedstuffs*, Burger King's franchisee association claimed that the new ownership marked "the first day of a new era" for Burger King. The new CEO John Dasburg also felt the acquisition had significant benefits. Dasburg remarked that it would "better position Burger King as a healthy, independent company for the first time in more than 30 years."

Even though company management appeared optimistic about its future, Burger King remained embroiled in intense competition. The firm continued to launch new advertising campaigns. For example, in 2002 it introduced the BK Veggie, the first fast-food veggie burger to be offered in the United States. That same year it revamped the BK Broiler, making a new product it called the Chicken Whopper. The firm also moved into its new world headquarters in Miami, dedicating the building to the founders Edgerton and McLamore. Management focused on capturing a larger portion of the fast-food market.

## REVITALIZING THE BURGER KING BRAND: 2003–05

In January 2003 Burger King hired Brad Blum, an executive with proven success in the restaurant industry, as its new CEO. Blum had previously served as head of the Olive Garden chain, where he oversaw a period of consistent sales growth between 1996 and 2002. As the eighth Burger King CEO in 11 years, Blum confronted a host of challenges, among them steadily declining revenues, an outdated marketing strategy, and a general decline of health and sanitation standards in many of the chain's restaurants.

In an effort to reverse this downward slide, Blum unveiled in May 2003 an aggressive new promotional campaign that was aimed at emphasizing the various health advantages of Burger King's flame-broiled cooking methods. As part of the strategy, the chain also promised to offer a wider range of healthy menu items, including reduced-fat sandwiches and grilled vegetable sides. At the same time, Blum was determined to expand the company's presence overseas, where Burger King lagged significantly behind McDonald's. Specifically, Blum hoped to exploit growth opportunities in emerging markets, such as eastern Europe and Asia.

A year into Blum's tenure, the results of the company's turnaround efforts were mixed. In February 2004 the company posted its first monthly sales increase in nearly two years, with revenues rising 4 percent, compared with the same period the previous year. In spite of this modest bump in sales, hundreds of individual Burger King franchisees continued to struggle during this period. In fact, several of the franchisees were on the verge of bankruptcy. Furthermore, many franchisees had become openly critical of the company's new sales campaign, in particular its emphasis on healthier food offerings. As Bruce Horovitz of *USA Today* noted in March 2004, the company's "schizophrenic marketing" strategy was ultimately alienating its customers, many of whom were baffled by the fast-food chain's efforts to become more health conscious.

In July 2004 Blum stepped down as Burger King CEO, after clashing with the board of directors over the company's long-term vision. He was replaced by Greg Brenneman, a former head of Continental Airlines. Adopting a new approach, Brenneman developed a marketing strategy that was based on larger quantities of food, which was intended to appeal directly to the chain's core demographic of young males. In March 2005 Burger King launched its Enormous Omelet Sandwich, a meat-laden breakfast that contained 730 calories and 47 grams of fat. At around this time the company revived its "Have it your way" slogan from the 1970s, in response to marketing research that showed that it was more recognizable to a broader base of consumers than the company's recent catchphrases.

## GOING PUBLIC, "THE KING," AND THE WHOPPER BAR: 2005–10

By mid-2005 Burger King had begun to show strong signs of recovery. For the fiscal year ending in June, the company's earnings topped $1.9 billion, compared with $1.8 billion the previous year. More significantly, the chain's profits had grown to $47 million, up from a mere $5 million in 2003. By early 2006 the company had enjoyed seven consecutive quarters of growth. In the midst of this turnaround, Burger King's owners began to make plans to launch an initial public offering (IPO) for the company, with the aim of raising up to $400 million. On the eve of the IPO, however, Brenneman suddenly resigned. Even though Brenneman's abrupt departure raised concerns among analysts and investors, the Burger King IPO took place in May 2006 under the new CEO John W. Chidsey. The stock offering generated $425 million on the first day of trading and was the largest IPO in history for a U.S. restaurant.

Following the IPO, the company continued to hone its image by utilizing edgy advertising spots and Internet marketing to promote the Burger King brand to younger consumers. At the core of the company's efforts was "The King," a roguish figure in a grinning mask

who became a ubiquitous pop culture presence, largely through television and online advertisements. At the same time the company continued to revamp its menu, introducing products such as the BK Stacker, a sandwich featuring up to four burger patties, and the Triple Whopper. Even though the new food items outraged nutrition experts (the quadruple BK Stacker had 1,000 calories and the Triple Whopper had 1,230 calories) they soon proved crucial to the company's fiscal health. By early 2008 Burger King had posted 16 straight quarters of growth, and shares in the company had increased 32 percent over the past year.

As the decade drew to a close, Burger King remained focused on developing new product and marketing innovations. In February 2010 the company launched the Whopper Bar, the first U.S.-based Burger King to sell beer, in Miami's South Beach. At the same time, the company unveiled a plan to open 200 to 300 similar restaurants in various international locations over a five-year span. Meanwhile, Burger King continued to push the envelope with its edgy advertising spots. Even though this audacious approach to branding occasionally sparked controversy, it was clear from brisk sales growth that Burger King had identified a winning marketing strategy going forward.

*Ginger G. Rodriguez*
*Updated, David E. Salamie;*
*Christina M. Stansell; Stephen Meyer*

## PRINCIPAL SUBSIDIARIES

B.K. Services, Ltd.; BK Acquisition, Inc.; BK Card Company, LLC; BK CDE, Inc.; Burger King Interamerica, LLC; Burger King Sweden, Inc.; Distron Transportation Systems, Inc.; Mid America Aviation, Inc.; Moxie's, Inc.; QZ, Inc.; The Melodie Corporation; TPC Number Four, Inc.; TPC Number Six, Inc.; TQW Company.

## PRINCIPAL COMPETITORS

McDonald's Corporation; Wendy's/Arby's Group, Inc.; YUM! Brands, Inc.

## FURTHER READING

Alva, Marilyn, "Can They Save the King?" *Restaurant Business*, May 1, 1994, p. 104.

Emerson, Robert L., *Fast Food: The Endless Shakeout.* New York: Lebhar-Friedman Books, 1979.

Gibson, Richard, "Burger King Overhaul Includes Refocus on Whopper," *Wall Street Journal*, December 15, 1993, p. B4.

Harrington, Jeff, "Burger King Executives Struggle to Turn around Company," *St. Petersburg (FL) Times*, October 16, 2000.

Hesse, Monica, "The Maddening Madness of Burger King's Mascot," *Washington Post*, April 3, 2010, p. C1.

Horovitz, Bruce, "Burger King Zaps Menu, Image," *USA Today*, March 22, 2004, p. 1B.

Kramer, Louise, "Burger King Gets Back to Basics in Latest Ad Blitz," *Nation's Restaurant News*, April 29, 1996, p. 14.

Martin, Andrew, "Gulp! Burger King Is on the Rebound," *New York Times*, February 10, 2008, p. 7.

Smith, Rod, "Burger King's Sale Readies System for Growth," *Feedstuffs*, January 6, 2003, p. 7.

Walker, Elaine, "Burger King Takes Aim at First Place in Fast-Food Battle," *Miami Herald*, May 10, 1999.

# BYD Company Limited

■

3001, Hengping Road
Longgang, Shenzhen City, Guangdong 518118
China
Telephone: (+86 755) 8421-8888
Fax: (+86 755) 8420-2222
Web site: http://www.byd.com

*Public Company*
*Founded:* 1995
*Employees:* 180,000 (est.)
*Sales:* CNY 39.5 billion ($5.80 billion) (2009)
*Stock Exchanges:* Hong Kong
*Ticker Symbol:* 1211
*NAICS:* 334210 Telephone Apparatus Manufacturing; 334413 Semiconductor and Related Device Manufacturing; 334419 Other Electronic Component Manufacturing; 335911 Storage Battery Manufacturing; 335912 Primary Battery Manufacturing; 336111 Automobile Manufacturing

■ ■ ■

BYD Company Limited is a Chinese research, development, and manufacturing organization that produces a variety of information technology (IT) and electronic components and, more recently, automobiles. Founded in 1995, by 2010 the company had 180,000 employees, nine production centers throughout China, and global branches that included offices in Europe, India, the Middle East, and the United States. Its subsidiary BYD Electronic Company Ltd. is a major manufacturer of rechargeable batteries (lithium, NiCad, and NiMH) for various applications, and it makes cell phone handsets and assemblies as well as chargers, LCD and LED products, keypads, opto-electonics, and other electronic parts. Its customers include Nokia, Motorola, and Samsung. BYD Automobile Company Ltd. began manufacturing gasoline-engine automobiles in 2003. This was followed by a plug-in hybrid model and then a totally electric car. BYD planned to be the world's largest automobile manufacturer by 2025.

## BEGINNINGS IN BATTERIES

In 1995, after being frustrated by the lack of funding at the government-affiliated research institute in Beijing where he had begun his engineering career, Wang Chuanfu and his cousin, Lu Xiangyang, founded BYD. The People's Republic of China was encouraging more private enterprise, and Wang borrowed $300,000 to open a battery manufacturing business in Shenzhen, a special economic zone close to Hong Kong. According to Wang, the company chairman, the letters BYD, the initials of the company's Chinese name, originally had no particular meaning in English, but the company now identifies the initials with the phrase "build your dreams." In a joking reference to BYD's meteoric growth, Wang has said that the letters actually mean "bring your dollars."

BYD quickly became a major source of mobile-phone batteries. Although the company's Japanese competitors used costly robotic arms to produce consistent quality in their battery cells, BYD used China's large labor pool on manual assembly lines to produce a high volume of inexpensive products.

Maintaining quality standards required eliminating 15 to 30 percent of the batteries made by these methods—much higher than the usual rate of discard—but the low cost of labor still produced batteries that could significantly undercut the price of other manufacturers. As of 2010 BYD batteries had never been recalled.

By 2000 BYD had become the first Chinese lithium-ion battery supplier for Motorola, a pioneer in the manufacture of cellular phones. In 2002 the company began supplying batteries to Nokia, which had become the world's largest manufacturer of mobile phones. BYD then expanded its product line, designing and manufacturing mobile-phone handsets and parts for Motorola, Nokia, Sony Ericsson, and Samsung. BYD had already established a global presence with branches in Europe, Japan, Korea, and the United States.

In July 2002 BYD went public, listing its stock on the Hong Kong Stock Exchange. That year the company was named the Best Managed Company by *Asiamoney* and 2002 Best Medium-sized Enterprise IPO Project by *Asset* magazine. BYD earned $80 million in 2002, and Wang, the orphaned son of poor farmers, now had a fortune valued at $306 million.

## ON TO AUTOMOBILES

Wang believed that BYD might soon reach its growth limit in the battery business. Although he did not know how to drive, Wang saw BYD's future in automobiles. In January 2003, for CNY 269 million, BYD acquired the majority stake in Shaanxi Qinchuan Auto Company Limited, a failing Chinese car manufacturer.

At the same time, BYD expanded its manufacturing and distribution capabilities, establishing a new plant in the Xi'an Hi-Tech Development Zone to serve western China, building a 560,000-square-meter industrial park in Shanghai, and then moving its automotive sales division to Shenzhen.

Relying on its battery-making expertise, BYD intended to establish itself as an electric and hybrid automaker. Its initial production automobile, however, was the gasoline-engine F3 sedan, released in 2005. BYD hired a team of Italian designers for its first foray into automobile manufacturing, and its efforts resulted in a vehicle that some contended was a copy of the Toyota Corolla. According to Malcolm Moore in the *Daily Telegraph* on September 28, 2009, Wang himself said that "60 percent of a new product is taken from publicly available information, 30 percent from existing products, 5 percent from the materials that are available, and only 5 percent from our original research."

Whatever the inspiration for BYD's automobile, by the fall of 2008 the F3 was China's top-selling sedan, outselling the Volkswagen Jetta and the Corolla itself. BYD was also exporting the F3, primarily to Russia and the Middle East. The company announced plans to introduce a new sport utility vehicle, a new multipurpose vehicle and the i-series of high-end autos. Despite the global economic slowdown, Chinese auto sales were growing exponentially. Although the country had only 42,000 cars in 1990, by March 2009 China had more than 1.1 million automobiles. The F3 maintained its position as the most popular sedan in China's developing market, with over 92,000 sales in the first quarter of 2010.

BYD used the same manufacturing model for its automobiles that is used for its batteries. A multitude of workers, including highly trained engineers investigating the relevant technologies, replaced the robotic machinery advantage of competitors. Unlike most of its rivals, BYD produced most of the car parts itself, from engines and auto bodies to seat belts and air-conditioning.

As it emphasized its entry into automobile manufacturing, BYD continued to develop its battery and electronic product lines, including solar-cell production. Although Sanyo and Sony sued BYD for patent infringement, BYD claimed the suits were motivated by competitive fears, and both suits were dismissed. In 2007 BYD spun off its electronic handset business, which then accounted for two-thirds of it sales. The separate listing on the Hong Kong Stock Exchange was planned to increase BYD's cash flow and reduce its debt.

## THE ELECTRIC FUTURE

BYD, though, was still focused on developing electric cars for a global market. The *Wall Street Journal* on January 12, 2009, cited Wang's strategy: "It's almost hopeless for a latecomer like us to compete with GM and other established automakers with a century of experience in gasoline engines. With electric vehicles, we're all at the same starting line." BYD, capitalizing on its cheap and abundant labor to keep costs down, launched the F3DM, a plug-in hybrid hatchback

## KEY DATES
■

**1995:** BYD is founded.
**2002:** BYD is listed on the Hong Kong Stock Exchange.
**2003:** BYD enters the automobile manufacturing business.
**2007:** BYD spins off its electronics division.
**2008:** BYD launches F3DM, a plug-in hybrid.

charged from household electricity, at the Geneva Auto Show in March 2008.

By late 2008 BYD was selling a small number of F3DMs to Chinese government agencies and banks. BYD had introduced its plug-in two years before General Motor's Chevrolet Volt and anticipated at least a one-year head start on the Toyota Prius plug-in. BYD followed the F3DM by introducing the F6DM, a plug-in hybrid sedan, and the E6, a purely electric model, at the January 2009 International Detroit Auto Show.

In developing its electric cars, BYD applied the ferrous technology used in its rechargeable lithium batteries. These batteries have a high reliability, lower cost, and greater durability than batteries using other materials, and they are more readily recyclable. CEO Wang, promoting BYD's "green" focus, famously demonstrated that the battery fluid was nontoxic by drinking some. BYD also billed these batteries as capable of a 50 percent charge in 10 minutes and a full charge overnight, as well as the ability to be recharged for 7 to 10 years of normal driving.

BYD continued to formulate major plans for its hybrid and electric car models. In May 2009 it announced a planned collaboration with Volkswagen for electric and hybrid cars. In September 2009 BYD entered into a joint development agreement with Wonder Auto Technology, a Chinese manufacturer of automobile electrical parts. In March 2010 it established a joint venture with Daimler Auto, the Mercedes-Benz manufacturer, to develop an electric car using Daimler vehicle architecture and BYD batteries. The next month the company took over a Japanese metal dies factory in order to improve BYD's auto-body production capabilities.

### OBSTACLES AND OPTIMISM

BYD's achievements, however, sometimes fell short of its announced goals. Although it billed its F3DM as

available for sale in 2009, by early 2010 the company had sold only a few cars to governmental agencies and then expanded to a small pilot program with taxis in Shenzhen. The E6, originally slated for the U.S. market in 2009, had its debut date pushed back to 2011. The expected Chinese government stimulus program for electric cars was also slow in materializing.

In addition, the company's unblemished recall record was damaged by a faulty Nokia cell-phone charger that posed a risk of electrocution. Although BYD promised to absorb all recall-related costs and no injuries had actually been reported, BYD's reliability was no longer completely without question. The recall was estimated to cost $14.6 million.

However, few doubted Wang's entrepreneurial skills and his ability to achieve his vision for BYD's future. In 2008 legendary U.S. investor Warren Buffet bought a 9.89 percent share of BYD. Originally Buffett had tried to purchase 25 percent of BYD, but Wang would not sell more than 10 percent. Buffett's confidence in BYD stimulated interest in Wang's company and propelled Wang to the top of *Forbes*'s list of China's wealthiest men. By late 2009 BYD shares were trading at 97 times their 2008 earnings, and by March 2010 Wang's worth was estimated at $4.4 billion.

Wang's lifestyle, however, remained extremely frugal, and like his employees, he lived in modest, company-owned housing. Company spending policies were also economical, including cost-saving measures like renting a suburban house for executives during the Detroit International Auto Show rather than paying for hotel rooms. Wang's policies reflect his stated disinterest in accumulating wealth and his belief in social responsibility. Soon after BYD went public, Wang distributed about 15 percent of his shares among the company's engineers and executives.

### GRAND PLANS

By 2010 BYD was ranked 8th on *Business Week*'s list of the 50 Most Innovative Companies 2010, and *Fast Company* ranked it 16th. BYD, secure in an expanding Chinese market, intensified its efforts to cultivate a global audience, particularly in the United States. In a ceremony in April 2010 Wang and California Governor Arnold Schwarzenegger announced the opening of BYD's North American headquarters in downtown Los Angeles. BYD planned its showrooms to demonstrate the range of its products, from electric cars to solar panels. The city of Los Angeles announced its intention to buy some of BYD's cars and buses.

The company had already begun investing in solar technology, calling it "new energy." In early 2010 BYD acknowledged its interest in a sizable solar-cell project. BYD and KB Homes, a large U.S. builder, announced a collaborative project to build homes that would include BYD solar panels and storage batteries. With a vision of becoming the foremost manufacturer of telecommunications and electronic products, as well as the world's leading automaker, BYD's plans for the future were well underway.

*Grace Murphy*

## PRINCIPAL SUBSIDIARIES

BYD Lithium Batteries Company Ltd.; BYD Automobile Company Ltd.; BYD Electronic (International) Company Ltd.; Golden Link Worldwide Ltd.

## PRINCIPAL COMPETITORS

Energizer Holdings, Inc.; Samsung SDI; Sanyo Electric Co., Ltd.; Toyota Motor Corporation; General Motors Company.

## FURTHER READING

Alberts, Hana R., "BYD Dives after Nokia Recall," *Forbes*, November 10, 2009.

Audi, Tamara, "Los Angeles Lures Chinese Auto Firm," *Wall Street Journal*, April 29, 2010.

Bunkley, Nick, "A Small Showing, but with Big Dreams," *New York Times*, January 12, 2009.

"BYD Swims against the Current and Sticks to Auto Industry," *SinoCast China IT Watch*, October 11, 2005.

Forney, Matthew, and Arthur Kroeber, "A Look Inside Buffett's Battery Bet," *Wall Street Journal*, December 10, 2009.

Gunther, Marc, "Warren Buffett Takes Charge," *Fortune*, April 13, 2009.

Moore, Malcolm, "Warren Buffett's Support Helps Make Wang Chuanfu China's Richest Man," *Daily Telegraph*, September 28, 2009.

Roy, Rex, "BYD Battery and Auto Manufacturer: A Shockingly Good Investment," *Automobile Magazine*, February 2010.

Shameen, Assif, "Corporate: Hong Kong's Battery and Electric-car Powerhouse BYD Soars Like a Rocket," *Edge Singapore*, September 14, 2009.

Ying, Tian, and Nipa Piboontanasawat, "Buffett-backed BYD's Profit Almost Quadruples as Car Sales Rise," *Bloomberg Businessweek*, March 14, 2010.

# Campbell Brothers Limited

---

Level 2, 299 Coronation Drive
Milton, Queensland 4064
Australia
Telephone: (+61 07) 3367-7900
Fax: (+61 07) 3367-8156
Web site: http://www.campbell.com.au/

*Public Company*
*Founded:* 1891 as Brisbane Soap Company
*Incorporated:* 1910 as Campbell Brothers Ltd.
*Employees:* 6,277
*Sales:* AUD 920.35 million ($817.73 million) (2009)
*Stock Exchanges:* Australian
*Ticker Symbol:* CPB
*NAICS:* 325611 Soap and Other Detergent Manufacturing; 424130 Industrial and Personal Service Paper Merchant Wholesalers; 424690 Other Chemical and Allied Products Merchant Wholesalers; 541380 Testing Laboratories; 541870 Sample Direct Distribution Services

■ ■ ■

Campbell Brothers Limited is an Australian firm that manufactures consumer products and chemicals and provides laboratory analysis and testing services. Headquartered near Brisbane, the company began in the 1860s as a soap and soda producer, extending its businesses to include testing services beginning in the 1970s for mining operations and then deepening its offerings in this area to include environmental testing, food safety, and other assaying needs. In 2010 the company's three divisions, ALS Laboratory Group, Campbell Chemicals, and Reward Distribution, had regional offices in nine national and international locations, with revenues that grew from more than AUD 271 million in 2000 to over AUD 960 million in 2009.

## FOUNDING AS SOAP COMPANY: 1860–1970

The progenitor of his family's soap and detergent business was Peter Morrison Campbell, a native of Scotland whose work in Scottish factories during the 1800s had been in this product line. When he resettled in Australia during the 1860s he became a wholesale trader of soap products. He did well enough to purchase land for his home and business in Bowen Hills, just outside of Brisbane in Queensland. By 1891 his alliance with two other companies, Kitchen & Sons and Apollo Ltd., resulted in the formation of Brisbane Soap Company. Campbell had majority controlling interest. The company's combined candle- and soap-making operations and distribution offices were located at his property in Bowen Hills. In 1910 the Brisbane Soap Company's operations were absorbed by the newly incorporated Campbell Brothers Ltd.

After Peter Campbell's retirement, his sons Malcolm Peter Morrison, Norman Carlisle, and Ronald Clifford became the "brothers" in Campbell Brothers Ltd., a private manufacturer of soap and soda in crystalline form. By making the latter product, the brothers were better able to control the quality of a primary ingredient of soap. In addition, in other chemical formations, soda could be used to produce household cleaners, water softeners, and other potential money-making products. Malcolm was the company's managing director (the Australian equivalent of CEO), Norman focused on the plant in Bowen Hills, and Ronald's job was to get another factory underway in Toowoomba, a four-hour train ride west of Brisbane.

During the 1920s the company was organized around its three main businesses: manufacturing soap for personal uses, formulating household cleaners, and producing chemicals for manufacturing. The brothers hired sales agents whose territory extended throughout eastern Australia's mining operations, farmland, sheep and cattle ranches, and growing cities. The brothers built a recovery plant, storage tanks for the soda, and stables to house the carts and horses that carried the increasingly large volume of products to docks in Brisbane and then elsewhere in Australia.

Thereafter, in addition to surviving the worldwide depression of the 1930s, and then replacing the carts with a fleet of trucks, one more significant event occurred during the company's first half-century. In 1952 Campbell Brothers became a public company, initially on the Brisbane Stock Exchange, as a means to obtain capital for expansion. According to Kyoko Sheridan in *The Firm in Australia*, from 1955 to 1967 Campbell Brothers Ltd.'s net capital assets more than tripled.

## LABORATORY SERVICES AND CONSUMER DETERGENTS: 1975–89

In response to market-driven opportunities and circumstances, Campbell Brothers entered the laboratory assaying field in 1975. Rather than the crucible-bound, dry process of testing samples of silver, gold, and alloys, the company focused on the wet process, using chemicals at laboratories to test minerals for mining

companies. The eastern and southern regions of Australia contained numerous mines tapping into coal, gold, manganese, and other resources. With Campbell Brothers' existing capital assets, knowledge base regarding chemicals, and regional connections developed partly through its sales agents, the company was able to diversify via its ALS Laboratory Group, based initially in Queensland. Among the new clients served by Campbell Brothers were owners of mines, equipment maintenance firms that had lubricants for possible reuse, investors interested in ore commodities, and others sharing a need for expert analysis.

Because of its ability to analyze the composition and quality of chemicals, ALS was seen as a complement to the other two, existing arms of its business, soaps and detergents. Campbell Brothers had continued to grow these product lines, with successful retail dishwashing and laundry detergent brands including Fluffy, Hurricane, and Moresoft. During the 1980s, however, suppliers of chemicals for the production of detergents were coming under scrutiny and increased regulation. Some of the largest companies (known as the "big soaps," including Procter & Gamble, Lever Brothers, and Colgate-Palmolive Company) had been targeted by government regulation and negative publicity for their use of phosphates and the effects on the environment. Although a much smaller company than the "big soaps," Campbell still had to address the issue and in fact, could do so in-house using the staff and equipment at ALS.

Environmental services and analytical laboratories became a booming field. As Ken Sternberg pointed out in *Chemical Week* in October 2009, "Besides technical expertise, a major advantage environmental services companies offer is state-of-the-art equipment chemical companies can't or won't buy." The financial outcome for Campbell's diversification: the 1988–89 edition of *Jobson's Year Book of Australian and New Zealand Public Companies* listed Campbell Brothers as having sales of AUD 34 million in 1987, up from AUD 19 million in 1982. After more than a decade, shrewdly targeted diversification had brought the company greater success.

## ACHIEVEMENT: 1990–2010

During the 1990s Campbell Brothers Ltd. experienced a period of financial and industrial well-being. In 1989 the company had acquired Bushland Products Pty. Ltd., a detergent maker in New South Wales. In 1990 the company purchased two laboratories in Western Australia, extending Campbell's expertise and operational ability in Australasia, Africa, and beyond. Revenues for the early 1990s were AUD 63.3 million, with three main subsidiaries: Bushland Products, ALS, and Reward Supply Company, which provided sample

## KEY DATES

**1891:** Peter Morrison Campbell helps to form Brisbane Soap Company.

**1910:** Campbell Brothers Limited is incorporated.

**1952:** The company has an initial public offering on the Brisbane Stock Exchange.

**1975:** The company's ALS Laboratory Group begins operations.

**2001:** The acquisition of Bondar Clegg makes Campbell Brothers the leader in laboratory analysis services to the mineral industry.

control, and management that ALS had performed at other sites for more than 30 years. In turn, the venture gave the company an opportunity to demonstrate its on-site capabilities at a place well-known for such mineral resources as copper, iron, and gold. This strategy of tackling field operations in a wide range of settings has enabled the company to accomplish enviable growth and awareness of its assets. Despite harsh conditions of climate and territory, despite challenging cycles tied to the world economy, minerals exploration and commodities, Campbell Brothers has established itself as a knowledge- and market-driven company committed to global earnings.

*Mary C. Lewis*

products, paper goods and plastic tableware to nursing homes, restaurants, and hotels. The company continued to expand, acquiring Chilean laboratory analyzer Geolab, the consumer products' division of Ajax Chemicals, and Woolseley Castle, another Australian detergent company. According to Richard Owen, writing in *The Australian*, Campbell's laboratory services business brought the company 29 percent of its sales in 1996. Roderick Campbell, the family's remaining link to the founder, remained a board member until his retirement in the late 1990s.

Then, in 2001, Campbell acquired the U.S. firm Bondar Clegg Group for an estimated AUD 8 million. With the addition of Bondar's laboratories in North and South America, Campbell Brothers became the world leader in minerals analytical laboratory services. By 2003 the company reported revenues of more than AUD 360 million. Nearly one-third of these revenues came from ALS. Similarly important news emerged in 2004 when Campbell agreed to sell Bushland Products and some popular detergent brands such as Fluffy and Moresoft to Colgate-Palmolive Company. In the *Courier-Mail*, Anthony Marx reported, "Campbell Brothers chairman Rodney White said the decision to sell followed a review of all company divisions and the move signalled an increased focus on service-based businesses." While Colgate-Palmolive's acquisition indicated the degree of brand distinction achieved by Campbell Brothers, the latter company seemed poised for a different business approach.

A significant area of that approach lay in laboratory services. In 2007 a joint venture was announced with the Russian company Norilsk Nickel Group. Campbell, taking on a 75 percent share, signed on to build a laboratory and related offices in the Transbaikal region of Siberia, providing the assaying equipment, quality

## PRINCIPAL SUBSIDIARIES

ALS Russia Holdings Pty. Ltd. (Australia); Australian Laboratory Services Pty. Ltd.; Carpi Ltd. (Papua, New Guinea); CBL Campbell Brothers NZ Ltd. (New Zealand); CBL Campbell Brothers USA Inc.; Panamex Pacific Inc. (American Samoa); Panamex Pacific Ltd. (New Zealand); Proclean Ltd.; Reward Supply Co. Pty. Ltd.

## PRINCIPAL DIVISIONS

ALS Laboratory Group; Campbell Chemicals; Reward Distribution.

## PRINCIPAL OPERATING UNITS

ALS Coal; ALS Environmental; ALS Minerals; ALS Tribology; Cleantec Commercial, Textile & Hygiene Systems; Cleantec Food Hygiene Systems (FHS); Deltrex Chemicals; Other Laboratory Services; Panamex Pacific.

## PRINCIPAL COMPETITORS

Coffey International Ltd.; Covance Inc.; Henkel Corporation; Lion Corporation; Nufarm Ltd.

## FURTHER READING

"Australia's Campbell Brothers to Acquire Ecowise for US $47 Mln," *AsiaPulse News*, November 13, 2009.

"Campbell Bros on Look Out for Acquisitions," *FEN (Factory Equipment News)*, May 28, 2003.

Layman, Patricia L., "For Detergent Producers, the Question Is, Which?" *Chemical Week*, July 23, 1980, pp. 44–46.

Marx, Anthony, "Campbell Sells Top Brands to Colgate," *Courier-Mail* (Brisbane), June 5, 2004, p. 77.

"Norilsk Nickel, ALS Laboratory Set Up JV for Geochemical Research," *Russia & CIS Business and Financial Newswire*, September 24, 2007.

Owen, Richard, "Campbell Cleans Up as Expansion Fuels Profit Surge," *The Australian* (Sydney), July 15, 1997, p. 25.

Sheridan, Kyoko, *The Firm in Australia*. Melbourne: Thomas Nelson and Sons Ltd., 1974, p. 164–65, 168, 176, 179–83.

Sternberg, Ken, "Cleaning Up: Lucrative Markets Abound in Environmental Services," *Chemical Week*, October 11, 1989, pp. 21–22.

Walsh, Liam, "Freeze Snows on Campbell Bros' Parade," *Courier-Mail*, February 24, 2010, p. 32.

Weber, Joseph, "The Cauldron Is Brimming with Profits," *BusinessWeek*, January 9, 1995, p. 69.

# Campbell Hausfeld

100 Production Drive
Harrison, Ohio 45030
U.S.A.
Telephone: (513) 367-4811
Fax: (513) 367-3176
Web site: http://www.campbellhausfeld.com/

*Private Company*
*Founded:* 1836
*Incorporated:* 1911
*Employees:* 350
*NAICS:* 332510 Hardware Manufacturing; 33391 Pump and Compressor Manufacturing; 333912 Air and Gas Compressor Manufacturing; 333991 Power Driven Handtool Manufacturing; 333992 Welding and Soldering Equipment Manufacturing

■ ■ ■

Campbell Hausfeld, one of the largest global manufacturers of professional and do-it-yourself power tools, is an Ohio-based company whose product line includes air compressors, pressure washers, pneumatic tools, paint systems, tire inflators, and welders. Founded in 1836 as a local maker of wagons and plows, the company now sells its products directly to the consumer as well as markets through national retailers such as Lowe's Companies, Inc., Wal-Mart Stores, Inc., The Home Depot Inc., and Tractor Supply Company. Campbell Hausfeld exports its goods to over 100 countries.

## THE FIRST 90 YEARS: 1836–1926

In 1836 Alexander Campbell, a blacksmith originally from Pennsylvania, began manufacturing wagons in Harrison, Ohio. By 1838 two of Alexander's brothers, James and William Campbell, had joined him in Harrison, and the following year the three formed a partnership to make carriages, plows, and other agricultural tools. During the next two decades the brothers struggled with the design for a corn drill, a tool that would make the planting of corn considerably easier. Even though the tool continued to have functional problems, the Campbells were awarded a patent in 1859. However, Alexander was still unhappy with the corn drill design, so he sold his interest in the company to his two brothers.

James and William corrected the problems with the corn drill by 1863, and they began manufacturing their first patented implement. James then took sole control of the company, and he changed the name first to the James Campbell Manufacturing Company and later to the Pioneer Corn Drill Works. During the later part of the 19th century Campbell's company introduced several innovations that adapted the drill for planting cotton and small seeds and for spreading fertilizer. By the end of the century the company had sold more than 75,000 corn drills.

Campbell sold the company to his three sons in 1900, and they changed the name to the Campbell Corn Drill Company. In 1911 the Campbell Bros. Manufacturing Company, Inc., was incorporated. During World War I the company diversified its operations through a partnership with Joseph Hausfeld and his

## COMPANY PERSPECTIVES

We want to make Campbell Hausfeld special to our end users and valued by our customers by creating innovative products that support our brand promise and creating end user loyalty by delivering a superior ownership experience.

Ohio Pattern Works and Foundry Company, which was founded in Cincinnati, Ohio, in 1892. The joint venture of manufacturing crucible furnaces did so well that by 1918 Hausfeld had relocated his business to Harrison. A new company, the Campbell Hausfeld, was formed when the two businesses merged in 1920.

The new company continued to diversify its product lines by adding various items such as sewer lids, Christmas tree stands, and decorative eagles to its original metal casting lines of planting drills and furnaces. In 1926, through the purchase of Paragon sprayers, it added agricultural tools for applying insecticides, weed killers, fertilizers, and paints to its manufactured goods.

### A NEW DIRECTION AND NEW MARKETS: 1940–86

Campbell Hausfeld entered a new market by purchasing the Pressure King Air Compressor fabrication machinery and patterns in 1940. This acquisition marked a shift in focus for the manufacturing company. Campbell Hausfeld was now in the business of making air compressors, which would become its signature product. In 1945 it augmented its focus by purchasing equipment to make spray air tools from its Chicago, Illinois, supplier.

The company continued to grow, first by acquiring the Melben Products Company in 1961 and then by moving to a new headquarters located on Campbell Road in 1965. Six years later, in 1971, Campbell Hausfeld was acquired by the Scott Fetzer Company of Cleveland, Ohio. Scott Fetzer, once primarily a vacuum cleaner manufacturer, had expanded dramatically during the 1960s and early 1970s by making over 30 acquisitions. Following the acquisition, Campbell Hausfeld became part of a much larger organization that focused on developing brand-name goods for consumer sales.

During the early 1970s Campbell Hausfeld increased its line of products by manufacturing chainsaws, initially under the Lombard brand name and later under the Campbell Hausfeld brand name. It expanded its product line further in 1974 by producing airless paint sprayers and two-stage air compressors. Beginning in 1981 the company introduced the first high-pressure washer for the do-it-yourself market.

Continuing its consumer-directed development, Campbell Hausfeld designed PowerPal, the first handheld air compressor. It also introduced PaintPal, an electrically powered paint roller that, according to the reviewer Vincent Blain of the Toronto *Globe and Mail,* "makes painting look as easy as mashing potatoes." This consumer focus used new marketing strategies that included commercials aired on sports channels to target the do-it-yourself audience.

The company was simultaneously expanding its global markets. In 1983 it entered into a joint venture with the Iwata Compressor Manufacturing Company, Ltd., of Tokyo, Japan, to sell Powerex air compressors. During this period the company increased its manufacturing capacities by opening new facilities in Leitchfield, Kentucky, and in Mt. Juliet, Tennessee.

In the acquisitional atmosphere of the 1980s Scott Fetzer, Campbell Hausfeld's parent company, boasted earnings that had risen 45 percent in 1984 and as a result it became the target of a number of investors interested in a takeover. After failed attempts by the financier Ivan Boesky (who was later prosecuted for insider trading) and Kelso & Company (a private equity firm noted for leveraged buyouts), Scott Fetzer was purchased in 1986 by Warren Buffet for $315 million. Buffet, the chairman and chief executive officer of Berkshire Hathaway Inc., had a reputation for buying undervalued companies with good management and consistent earnings that had made him an investor's idol. Scott Fetzer's largest division was Campbell Hausfeld and it was the nation's leading producer of air compressors. Its earnings more than doubled in 1986.

### FLEXIBILITY AND DURABILITY: 1980–2000

During the 1980s and 1990s Campbell Hausfeld continued expanding its product lines, production processes, and markets. It increased its presence in the air tool market, launched new versions of its high-pressure washers for consumer and commercial use, and created new lines of portable welders and generators. The company enhanced its production efficiency by cross-training its employees so that it had the ability to build several products on the same production line and be more responsive to consumer demands. At the same time, the company forged and solidified its retail relationships, including participating in a select group of

## KEY DATES

**1836:** The company is founded.
**1920:** The Campbell Bros. Manufacturing Company, Inc., and the Ohio Pattern Works and Foundry Company merge to form the Campbell Hausfeld.
**1971:** Campbell Hausfeld is acquired by the Scott Fetzer Company.
**1986:** The Scott Fetzer Company is acquired by Berkshire Hathaway Inc.
**2005:** Campbell Hausfeld launches its REVolution line of tool products.

Home Depot key retail suppliers asked to join that company's "Home Depot Olympic Family" and signing exclusive distribution agreements for its paint sprayer line with Tractor Supply Company.

In 1997 Campbell Hausfeld increased its branding emphasis with a new logo and the motto "Built to Last." Focusing further on the do-it-yourself market, in 1999 the company launched an e-commerce Web site that provided consumers with the opportunity to buy more than 7,500 Campbell Hausfeld service kits, parts, and accessories directly from the company. The site also included maintenance advice, troubleshooting tips, and a store and service center locator tool. An e-mail newsletter was developed in conjunction with the e-commerce program.

Three years later, in 2000, Campbell Hausfeld introduced a line of air compressors that were designed for the home workshop. As the company's primary product, Campbell Hausfeld wanted to increase consumer acceptance of this tool, so it chose a unique design process to accomplish this. Utilizing research with do-it-yourself consumers to establish both the performance features and a user-friendly design, Campbell Hausfeld had its engineers work closely with consumers through focus groups and performance testing. It then created a product whose development was a collaborative result of consumer input that preceded engineering design rather than following the traditional route that evaluated consumer response to an already conceptualized model.

Campbell Hausfeld continued to use innovative methods to discover what its customers wanted. Instead of relying on retailer feedback, the usual source of information for projecting consumer needs, Campbell Hausfeld focused on directly discovering consumer preferences to serve as the inspiration for product design. The company used market research strategies that included consumer panels, mail and Internet surveys, and phone interviews. It also developed a series of special consumer personas, such as, a woman do-it-yourselfer or an elderly craftsman. These personas were used to develop new products and add special features to existing items to appeal to new target groups.

## INGENUITY AND NEW PRODUCT DEVELOPMENT IN THE TWENTY-FIRST CENTURY

At the turn of the 21st century Campbell Hausfeld added new consumer products to its line. It launched the AT Power Series, a set of air tools designed to be light, durable, and easy to use. It created an air compressor that could operate vertically as well as horizontally, providing options for the limited space of a home workshop. It introduced a package of tire care and repair products that included gauges, repair kits, and inflators. It also produced HousePainter, a tool that eliminated application pressure guesswork by allowing the user to dial the task, from priming, to rolling, to spraying, to cleaning.

While increasing its emphasis on new target audiences, particularly women do-it-yourselfers, Campbell Hausfeld continued to provide new products for the commercial market. In 2002 the company created a new tougher series of professional pneumatic tools. It followed by introducing a powerful portable welder and a cost-cutting, gravity-fed paint spray gun. It also launched the Maxus line of contractor tools that included compressors, pressure washers, and welder/generators. With an industry-leading five-year warranty, these products were billed as high-performance, rugged machinery.

In one of the largest product launches in the company's long history, Campbell Hausfeld presented a new line of powerful, light, and uncomplicated tools in 2005. Almost half of the 30 new REVolution products were cordless because Campbell Hausfeld was appealing to markets that were new for a company that had built its reputation on commercial-grade machinery. Campbell Hausfeld worked with LPK Inc., an industrial design firm in Cincinnati, to create smaller, affordable, high-quality tools, including ultralight cordless drills and laser levels.

Beginning in 2008 the company faced a serious test of its reputation for reliability. Over 233,000 Campbell Hausfeld compressors (including its Husky brand) sold in the United States and 135,000 compressors sold in Canada were recalled. The compressors had protective covers that were not flame retardant and posed a fire risk. The following year the company recalled 16,000 compressors because an overheating shutoff mechanism failure also posed a fire hazard.

Meanwhile, the company continued enhancing the solid status that it had instilled in its products, many of which had been selected for Editor's Choice awards from *Popular Mechanics* magazine and garnered the Best Buy designation from *Consumer Reports*. In 2009 a Campbell Hausfeld professional-grade compressor was named as one of the "100 Best New Products" by *Professional Building* magazine. Campbell Hausfeld was quickly reclaiming the strong reputation that it had built for over 170 years.

*Grace Murphy*

## PRINCIPAL COMPETITORS

Air Components & Systems; Ashtead Group PLC; Briggs & Stratton Power Products Group, LLC; DeVilbiss Air Power Company; Dover Corporation; Midwest Air Technologies, Inc.; Tecumseh Products Corporation.

## FURTHER READING

Bianco, Anthony, "Warren the Buffet You Don't Know," *BusinessWeek*, July 5, 1999, p. 54.

Blain, Vincent, "Space Age Gadgetry for the Reluctant Painter," *Globe and Mail* (Toronto), April 27, 1985.

Boyer, Mike, "Light, Powerful and a Hit," *Cincinnati Enquirer*, December 6, 2005.

"Campbell Hausfeld Air Compressors Recalled," *UPI NewsTrack*, June 19, 2009.

"Campbell Hausfeld Introduces Home Workshop Series Air Compressors; Consumer-Focused Design Delivers Easy Operation and New Safety Features," *Business Wire*, October 12, 2000.

"Inmark Enterprises, Inc. Interactive Division Launches E-Commerce Web Site for Campbell Hausfeld," *Business Wire*, July 22, 1999.

"On Target; B-to-B Marketers Use Personas, Too," *Advertising Age*, June 5, 2006.

Johnson, M. Eric, "Giving 'Em What They Want," *Management Review*, November, 1998.

Stufft, Stacy, and Dan Pinger, "Campbell Hausfeld Turns 170," Cincinnati.com, October 23, 2006, http://rodeo.cincinnati.com/getlocal/gpstory.aspx?id=100127&sid=103254

"21st Century Tools Fit for a King," *Market Wire*, February 21, 2005.

# Capital Group Companies, Inc.

---

333 South Hope Street, 53rd Floor
Los Angeles, California 90071
U.S.A.
Telephone: (213) 486-9200
Fax: (213) 486-9217
Web site: http://www.capgroup.com/

*Private Company*
*Incorporated:* 1931 as Capital Research and Management
    Company
*Employees:* 8,000
*Sales:* $7.63 billion (2009)
*NAICS:* 523920 Portfolio Management

■ ■ ■

Based in Los Angeles, California, the Capital Group Companies, Inc., is a highly respected and privately held mutual fund firm that serves both individual and institutional clients. It consists of seven primary subsidiaries: American Funds, one of the United States' three largest mutual fund families; Capital Bank and Trust, which focuses on small company retirement plans; Capital Guardian, a manager of assets for North American pension funds and other institutional clients; Capital International, which manages assets of pension funds and other institutional clients outside of the United States; Capital International Asset Management, a unit devoted to selling mutual funds to individual Canadian investors; Capital International Funds, which offers investment funds to European individual investors; and Capital Research and Management, which

provides investment advice to the 30 American Funds. Capital is known for its no-stars culture, consensus-driven approach to building mutual funds, and taking a long view of the market. Rather than using a traditional fund manager system, the firm employs the multiple portfolio counselor system, which allocates parts of a fund to several managers. In this way the fund tends to be more diverse and the amount of overlap in holdings and trades are reduced. It is a formula that has proven successful since the Great Depression for the media-shy firm, which is mostly owned by its analysts.

## COMPANY FOUNDED: 1931

Capital was founded in 1931 as the Capital Research and Management Company by Jonathan Bell Lovelace. Lovelace was born into a prominent Alabama lumber family in 1895, and after serving in World War I he moved to Detroit, Michigan, to work as a statistician at the investment banking and stock brokerage firm E. E. MacCrone & Co. He eventually became a star investor who enjoyed excellent results because of his assiduous investment research skills.

By 1929, after watching a decade's worth of increasing stock market prices, Lovelace became convinced that the stock market had become disconnected to its underlying values and that a correction was inevitable. He was not, however, able to persuade his colleagues at MacCrone, and so in the late summer of 1929 he quietly cashed out by selling his 10 percent stake in the firm. He also sold most of his personal investments before the stock market crash of October 1929, which ushered in the Great Depression of the 1930s.

## COMPANY PERSPECTIVES

It's about the investor. Individuals, families, businesses and institutions look to our companies to guard and grow their hard-earned money. Whether in North America, Europe or Asia, investors and their advisers find their way to us and tend to stay. Why? Quality service and investment results.

Lovelace moved his family to Los Angeles, and after the carnage on Wall Street had run its course, he returned to the financial world with the launch of Capital Research, which included a number of his former Detroit associates. A year later he was recruited to reorganize a trust he had helped launch in 1926, the Investment Company of America (ICA). He negotiated an agreement and in late 1933 Lovelace began managing the ICA, which was the start of the American Funds family of mutual funds. What started out as a closed-end fund, with a limited number of shares, became by the end of the decade an open-end mutual fund that could issue and redeem shares at any time. With the passage of the Investment Company Act of 1940, which eliminated many of the questionable sales and trading practices of the past, mutual funds became an increasingly attractive investment option, and the American Funds products were well positioned to take advantage of that interest.

### GROWING WITH THE ECONOMY: EARLY FORTIES TO LATE FIFTIES

Capital opened a New York office in 1943. The firm expanded even further during the post–World War II economic boom. It formed American Funds Distributors Inc., which made the funds available for sale through third-party financial advisers on an exclusive basis, an approach that became a staple of the Capital business model. The firm continued to demonstrate a forward-looking approach in other ways as well. In 1953 it began investing beyond North America, one of the first U.S. firms to do so. In 1958, when the firm was managing $274 million, Capital took the radical step of dividing responsibility for its two funds among several stock pickers. Called the multiple portfolio counselor system, this system laid the groundwork for the no-stars, collegial approach to managing mutual funds.

The idea of splitting the funds came from the founder's son, Jon Lovelace. He had joined the firm in 1951, a year after graduating from Princeton University.

Even though he earned a degree in economics he had not planned on joining his father. His career ambitions were vague at best, ranging from forest ranger to painter, and he had worked in personnel at both Pacific Finance Co. and Lockheed before his father asked him to help out on a temporary basis at a time when the assets of Capital neared the $40 million mark. The younger Lovelace proved to have a mathematical mind and a memory that absorbed market information, making him ideally suited as an investment adviser. He also inherited his father's unassuming nature, making him more than willing to share responsibility as well as the credit for success. It was also during the 1950s that his father began distributing shares in the firm to senior executives to engender further camaraderie.

### COMPANY EXPANSION: 1960–80

Capital's multiple portfolio counselor system for portfolio management led to sustained growth during the 1960s. The firm opened its first international office in 1962, located in Geneva, Switzerland. In 1965 the Geneva office created the first non-U.S. market stock market indices. Called the Capital International Indices, it would later become known as the Morgan Stanley Capital International S.A. Indices. That same year Capital reached the $1 billion mark in managed assets. In 1968 the Capital Guardian Trust Company was formed to serve major U.S. institutional clients, and the American Funds Service Company was created to provide recordkeeping services for U.S. mutual fund shareholders.

After being prodded by his father to take charge of the firm, Jon Lovelace finally accepted the title of president in 1963. Even though he would never be a hands-on manager, he played a key role in determining the direction taken by the company. In 1967 he oversaw the creation of the holding company Capital Group, Inc. Besides employing multiple portfolio managers and expanding overseas, Jon Lovelace began assigning part of each fund to the research department to manage. He was also liberal in awarding equity and bonuses. As a result, the 50-percent stake in the firm he held in 1968 was whittled down to just 10 percent 30 years later. However, he greatly increased the value of his holdings because of the performance of his analysts, who had ample incentive to perform well and little interest in working for other fund companies. Moreover, Lovelace judged their performance based on four-year portfolio results rather than on much shorter assessment periods like the other fund companies, creating further comfort and loyalty while enhancing performance.

Jon Lovelace became chairman in 1975, although he was never particularly interested in the honor. He

## KEY DATES

**1931:** Jonathan Bell Lovelace founds the Capital Research and Management Company.

**1933:** Jonathan Bell Lovelace begins managing the Investment Company of America.

**1962:** Capital opens its first international office in Geneva, Switzerland.

**1974:** The Private Client Services division is formed.

**2008-09:** Capital opens offices in Beijing, China, and Mumbai, India.

stepped down from that role for a while before resuming the chairmanship and eventually giving up the title completely in 1993. He did not, however, quit the firm. Lovelace continued to work on four funds, for which he managed several billion dollars.

During the 1970s Capital pursued further international growth. In 1970 the Geneva office began managing a pair of global funds, Capital Italia Fund and Capital International Fund. In 1974 Capital began managing retirement plans based outside the United States, and four years later Capital Guardian Trust Company began managing international assets for its U.S. institutional clients. It was also during this period, in 1974, that Capital added wealthy individuals as clients by forming the Private Client Services division of Capital Guardian Trust Company. At the close of the decade, the firm established a London office.

### DOMESTIC AND INTERNATIONAL EXPANSION

Domestic and international growth highlighted the 1980s. Domestically, several U.S. offices were added in 1983, including Phoenix, Arizona; Irvine, California; Indianapolis, Indiana; San Antonio, Texas; and Hampton Roads, Virginia. Internationally, the firm's first Asian office was opened in Tokyo, Japan, in 1982. Named Capital International K.K., it was supplemented by an office in Hong Kong in 1983 and another office in Singapore in 1989. The firm also established an emerging markets growth fund in 1986 to provide institutions with an opportunity to invest in developing nations.

Assets managed by Capital topped the $200 billion mark by 1995. During the bull market of the late 1990s, however, Capital and its steady, conservative approach to investing fell out of favor with some investors

who turned instead to many of the new star fund managers. When the stock market crashed at the turn of the century, Capital regained its luster and its funds attracted an increasing amount of new business. Sales were further spurred by a federal probe into late-trading and market-timing practices by other fund companies.

By 2004 American Funds had more than $500 billion under management, and Capital Guardian Trust Company and Capital International managed another $300 billion between them. The popular Growth Fund of America, which had $95 billion under management, was only second in size to a passive Vanguard fund that tracked the Standard & Poor's 500 Index. In all, four of the 10 largest mutual funds in the United States were being managed by American Funds. By 2007 Growth Fund of America gained the top ranking, swelling to more than $160 billion, and seven of the country's largest funds were also part of the American Funds family.

### LOVELACE'S RETIREMENT

The new century brought the retirement of Jon Lovelace, but because of his unassuming demeanor, the firm was hardly dependent on him. Besides a surge in the amount of money under management, expansion took place on a number of other fronts for Capital. It added investment management services for individuals in Canada in 2000, and it offered the same to individuals in Europe in 2003 and to individuals in Japan in 2007. American Capital increased business in the retirement plan market, and in 2002 it became the top provider of more than 500 college savings plans. In 2007 the firm launched the American Fund Target Date Retirement Series of funds. Some reorganization also took place as Capital Research and Management Company split its equity investment business into Capital Research Global Investors and Capital World Investors. In addition, Capital opened new offices in Mumbai, India, in 2008, and in Beijing, China, in 2009.

Capital was not immune to a downturn in the economy as the first decade of the 21st century came to a close. It experienced a decline in assets and took steps to cut expenses. Approximately 10 percent of its workforce, or about 800 people, were laid off in 2009. The firm had always taken a long view on the market, and there was every reason to believe that from such a perspective Capital would enjoy continued success.

*Ed Dinger*

### PRINCIPAL SUBSIDIARIES

American Funds; Capital Bank and Trust; Capital Guardian; Capital International; Capital International

Asset Management; Capital International Funds; Capital Research and Management.

## PRINCIPAL COMPETITORS

American Century Companies Inc.; FMR LLC; Vanguard Group, Inc.

## FURTHER READING

Brewster, Deborah, "Why Capital Is Invisible, but Not Invincible," *Financial Times* (London), September 21, 2004, p. 14.

Ellis, Charles D., *Capital: The Story of Long-Term Investment Excellence.* Hoboken, NJ: John Wiley & Sons, 2004.

Grover, Mary Beth, and Jason Zweig, "Capital Research: Steak, No Sizzle," *Forbes*, August 28, 1995, p. 142.

———, "The Elusive Mr. Lovelace," *Forbes*, August 28, 1995, p. 150.

Phinisee, Tamarind, "Capital Guardian Trust to Trim Nearly 100 Positions in San Antonio," *San Antonio Business Journal*, June 9, 2009.

Sedoric, Tom, "Why We Should Remember Jon Lovelace," *New Hampshire Business Review*, November 6, 2009, p. 20.

Stein, Charles, "Investors Flock to 'Steady' Mutual-Funds Firm in Wake of Scandals, Bear Market," *Boston Globe*, September 17, 2004.

Strauss, Lawrence C., "Living Large, in a Fishbowl," *Barron's*, January 8, 2007, p. L5.

# Cardinal Health, Inc.

—— ■ ——

7000 Cardinal Place
Dublin, Ohio 43017
U.S.A.
Telephone: (614) 757-5000
Toll Free: (800) 326-6457
Fax: (614) 757-6000
Web site: http://www.cardinal.com

*Public Company*
*Founded:* 1971
*Incorporated:* 1971
*Employees:* 30,000 (est.)
*Sales:* $101 billion (2009)
*Stock Exchanges:* New York
*Ticker Symbol:* CAH
*NAICS:* 423210 Drug and Druggists' Sundries Merchant Wholesalers; 423450 Medical, Dental, and Hospital Equipment and Supplies Merchant Wholesalers; 551112 Offices of Other Holding Companies

■ ■ ■

Cardinal Health, Inc., is a leading provider of products and services supporting the health care industry. Cardinal Health companies develop, manufacture, package, and market products for patient care. They develop drug-delivery technologies and distribute pharmaceuticals, medical-surgical supplies, and laboratory supplies. Cardinal Health companies also offer consulting and other services that improve quality and efficiency in health care. Headquartered in Dublin, Ohio,

the company employs more than 30,000 people on five continents and produces annual revenues of more than $100 billion. It is one of the largest distributors of medical and surgical products worldwide.

Named for Ohio's crimson state bird, Cardinal Health, Inc., was founded in 1971 under the direction of Robert D. Walter. The company evolved from a rather inconsequential Ohio food distributor into a trend-setting leader of the pharmaceutical industry. A steady stream of acquisitions has helped to multiply Cardinal Health's sales from $429 million in 1986 to nearly $101 billion in 2009. In the mid-1990s Cardinal came within about $1 billion in annual sales of breaking into the top spot among wholesale drug distributors, having an estimated 18 percent of the $57 billion wholesale market compared with the 19 percent stakes held by leading competitors McKesson Corporation and AmerisourceBergen Corporation.

During the course of its growth spurt, Cardinal diversified from its core wholesale drug distribution business into specialty laboratory and pharmaceutical supplies, computer software, and retail drugstores. While it was not the country's largest drug distributor in terms of sales in the mid-1990s, Cardinal Health did rank highest in terms of market capitalization and profitability. According to Tibbett L. Speer in the August 5, 1996, issue of *Hospitals and Health Networks*, A.G. Edwards investment analyst Donald Spindel asserted, "Cardinal has been the most innovative and the fastest growing. To me, they're really the top company in the industry." By the end of the year 2000, three companies—Cardinal, AmerisourceBergena, and McKesson—controlled 90 percent of drug wholesaling.

# COMPANY PERSPECTIVES

By helping pharmacies, hospitals, laboratories, physician offices and ambulatory care centers improve their efficiency and collaborate across the healthcare system, we make it possible for our customers to focus on their patients. As the business behind healthcare, we improve the cost-effectiveness of the system, so that our customers can improve the quality of care.

There isn't a doctor, nurse or pharmacist in the world that chose a career in healthcare to track medication inventories, restock medical supply rooms or manage relationships with thousands of suppliers. They want to focus on treating and preventing disease.

We've made it our essential focus to address the business of healthcare, so our customers can focus on providing care to their patients.

## LEVERAGED BUYOUT IN 1971 PRESAGES TRANSFORMATION OF MID-OHIO DISTRIBUTOR

In 1971, just six months after his graduation from Harvard's MBA program, 26-year-old Robert Walter acquired Monarch Foods through a leveraged buyout. Walter hoped to build this small central Ohio grocery distribution company, which he renamed Cardinal Foods, into an industry leader through acquisitions. He soon discovered that he was too late, however, because the market had already begun to consolidate. To make matters worse, in the mid-1970s Cardinal was compelled to withdraw 10 tons of salmonella-infected, prepackaged roast beef from the market.

With consolidation within the wholesale segment of the grocery business out of the question, Walter attempted to shift his growth strategy, launching Mr. Moneysworth warehouse supermarkets. In the mid-1980s Cardinal had three Mr. Moneysworth outlets and planned to open stores in Ohio, West Virginia, and Kentucky.

Rather than abandon the distribution industry, Walter turned to a business segment that was more profitable, more fragmented, and ripe for consolidation: pharmaceuticals. The company made its first foray into pharmaceutical distribution in 1980 when it acquired a drug distributor in Zanesville, Ohio, 60 miles from Columbus, and became known as Cardinal Distri-

bution. Walter used the proceeds of a 1983 initial public offering on the New York Stock Exchange to launch an acquisition spree that would gain steam over the next decade. During the 1980s he targeted relatively small, privately held distributors in adjacent states and regions for his friendly acquisitions. Reasoning that these local managers knew their markets and would work hard to maintain growth, Walter focused on successful companies with exceptionally talented managers, whom he characterized in a 1993 interview with Reed Abelson in *Forbes* magazine as "the kings in our company." Walter operated Cardinal as a holding company, allowing affiliated companies to continue relatively autonomously. The new subsidiaries brought the parent company geographic growth and economies of scale. He told Abelson, "Knowing what I know now, I didn't know what I was doing. But it worked." Key acquisitions, which were focused in the eastern United States, included Ellicott Drug Co. in 1984, James W. Daly, Inc., in 1986, and John L. Thompson Sons & Co. in 1986.

## EXIT FROM GROCERY BUSINESS: LATE EIGHTIES

Walter gave up on the marginally profitable grocery business in 1988 when he sold the Cardinal Foods, Inc., Midland Grocery Co., and Mr. Moneysworth subsidiaries to Roundy's, Inc., a cooperative wholesaler, for $27 million. Instead of declining, Cardinal's annual revenues increased by one-third that year, and its net income more than doubled.

In contrast with his entry into the grocery distribution business, Walter's foray into drug distribution proved well timed, for retail drugstores and hospitals were increasing their purchases from distributors. Cardinal's acquisitions, while relatively small, were indicative of a budding trend toward consolidation in the distribution industry. Mergers and acquisitions shrank the number of participants in this market by more than half, from 135 in 1984 to 80 in 1989 and less than 60 by 1995. By the end of the decade, Cardinal had accumulated a 4 percent stake in the $22 billion wholesale drug business. Sales increased from $429 million in 1986 to $700 million in 1989, while net income grew from $6 million to $9 million during the same period.

Cardinal's profitable growth did not come exclusively from acquisitions. From 1986 to 1989, in fact, the company was able to increase productivity in nearly 80 percent of its operations. Computer automation was an important factor in this program. Cardinal employees developed IBM-compatible software to increase purchasing, inventory, and distribution efficiency. A company executive told Jagannath Dubashi

## KEY DATES

**1971:** Robert D. Walter acquires Monarch Foods in leveraged buyout.

**1980:** Walter acquires drug distributor in Zanesville, Ohio.

**1983:** Company goes public as Cardinal Distribution.

**1988:** Walter sells food group to Roundy's, Inc.

**1995:** Cardinal acquires Medicine Shoppe International.

**2000:** Cardinal acquires Bergen Brunswig Medical Corporation, establishes Cardinal.com and NewHealthexchange.com.

**2003:** Cardinal subsidiary Medicine Shoppe International acquires Medicap Pharmacy; Cardinal creates its Nuclear Pharmacy Services business.

**2006:** Walter announces retirement as CEO of Cardinal Health.

**2007:** Cardinal sells its Pharmaceutical Technologies and Services unit to the Blackstone Group.

**2009:** Cardinal spins off CareFusion as a separate public company.

in *Financial World* that the AccuNet system "can reduce the administrative costs of [a hospital's] pharmacy operations by as much as 80 percent." AccuNet not only helped Cardinal cut its own operating margins by 20 percent from 1988 to 1991, it also increased its level of customer service, offering its clients automated inventory management and up-to-date drug pricing information. Computer links with customers enabled Cardinal to fill and ship orders within 24 hours of receipt.

## LARGER ACQUISITIONS MARK THE NINETIES

Cardinal moved steadily up the ranks of the country's largest drug distributors with revenues exceeding $1 billion for the first time in 1991. It simultaneously increased its geographic reach in the early 1990s via significantly larger acquisitions. "Purchase or perish" was the theme in the market, which was dominated by seven major companies in 1993 that monopolized 78 percent of the industry's estimated $40 billion sales. The addition of four new subsidiaries moved Cardinal from its bulkhead in the northeastern United States into the mid-Atlantic and southeastern states. Acquisitions

included Ohio Valley-Clarksburg (1990, the mid-Atlantic), Chapman Drug Co. (1991, Tennessee), PRN Services (1993, Michigan), and Solomons Co. (1993, Georgia).

By the end of 1993 the company was ready to turn westward, but its rapid growth had caught the attention of well-established industry leaders McKesson Corp. and Bergen Brunswig Corp. When Walter made a move to acquire Alabama's Durr-Fillauer Medical, Bergen Brunswig quickly launched a bidding war with the upstart Ohio company. Under pressure from Bergen Brunswig, the price tag shot up from $250 million to $450 million in just four months. Although Walter lost the battle for Durr-Fillauer, he did not leave the contest empty-handed, as Cardinal drew five of the target company's top managers to its ranks. Moreover, some industry observers criticized Bergen Brunswig for overpaying and praised Walter's self-control throughout the ego-charged competition.

Walter more than made up for this minor setback with several major acquisitions from 1994 to 1996. The merger of Cardinal and Whitmire Distribution in 1994 added over $2.25 billion in annual sales and made Cardinal the third-largest drug distributor in the country. With its strong distribution network in the western and central United States, Whitmire was a long-sought piece of Cardinal's nationwide puzzle. The parent company's geographic scope, consisting of 32 distribution centers across the country, enabled it to compete for bigger business. In 1994 the company signed a $900 million contract to supply mass merchandiser Kmart's nearly 1,700 pharmacies. In 1995 it earned the right to supply pharmaceutical goods to the 175-store Wakefern grocers' cooperative.

The acquisition of Medical Strategies in 1994 added Healthtouch computerized kiosks to Cardinal's repertoire. These electronic point-of-purchase machines offered pharmacy customers access to up-to-date data on illnesses and treatment options. The kiosks generated income via advertising and promoted featured products with coupons. Cardinal claimed that its more than 1,000 Healthtouch machines "increase incremental sales of the featured products by 20 percent on average."

Cardinal entered the retail drug industry late in 1995, when the parent company traded $348 million worth of its stock for full ownership of St. Louis–based Medicine Shoppe International, a pharmacy franchiser with more than 1,000 stores. Less than six months later, Cardinal announced its $870 million stock swap for Pyxis, the nation's leading manufacturer of automatic drug-dispensing machines used in hospitals. Pyxis subsidiary Allied Pharmacy Management Inc. gave Cardinal entrée into the health care information network business. PCI Services, Inc., a pharmaceutical packager, was acquired in July 1996 for $145 million in cash and $56 million of borrowed money. Reflecting on his company's recent activities, Walter noted, "Cardinal has been progressively expanding its business beyond the purely logistical side of drug distribution to providing a full range of value-added information, marketing and educational services to our customers."

These acquisitions helped make Cardinal virtually impervious to the recession that gripped the country in the early years of the decade. While customers like hospitals and drugstores who themselves were under pressure from managed health care plans and other cost-conscious insurers whittled away at drug distributors' gross profit margins, reducing them from over 17.5 percent in 1960 to 6.5 percent in 1992, Cardinal's increasing share of the market and high level of efficiency helped it maintain consistent growth in sales and profit.

Cardinal also maintained healthy margins by focusing on the most profitable segments of its business. In the 1980s, for example, the company targeted independent drugstores that could not demand the volume discounts sought by larger chains. As these retailers began to disappear from the pharmaceutical landscape, Cardinal sought out new profit centers: Pyxis's groundbreaking dispensers, Medicine Shoppe's retail pharmacies, and Healthtouch information systems, for example. Nevertheless, Cardinal was not completely impervious to the cost-cutting pressures that plagued the industry; its gross margins declined from 7 percent in 1992 to about 5.8 percent in 1996.

Fueled by its record-setting acquisitions, Cardinal's sales and net income multiplied rapidly in the early 1990s. Revenues doubled from $874 million in 1990 to almost $2 billion by 1993, then nearly quadrupled to $7.8 billion by 1995. Net income made similar advances, growing from $13 million in 1990 to $34 million in 1993 and $85 million in 1995. Employment more than tripled during this period, and Cardinal's distribution centers nationwide increased from 6 to 32. In an early 1995 profile, Jennifer Reingold in *Financial World* characterized Cardinal as "by far the healthiest" of the drug distribution industry's five largest companies. Although it was not the sales leader at that time, Cardinal topped the industry in profits and market capitalization. Cardinal Health stockholders, including CEO Walter among the largest with about 8 percent of its stock, were well rewarded. In *Forbes* magazine's 1996 analysis of U.S. companies' 10-year total return, Cardinal ranked 25th.

Cardinal evolved beyond drug distribution into total health care by acquiring companies that served health care manufacturers and providers of patient care. In 1997 Cardinal acquired Owen Healthcare of Houston, Texas, a leading provider of pharmacy management and information services for hospitals. In 1998 the Federal Trade Commission blocked Cardinal's attempt to buy competitor Bergen Brunswig and McKesson's attempt to acquire AmeriSource Health. The decision was upheld by a federal judge. Cardinal did acquire R.P. Scherer, the world's largest maker of soft-gels and other drug-delivery solutions, located in Basking Ridge, New Jersey. The following year Cardinal bought Allegiance, the largest medical-surgical products distributor in the United States. Also acquired in 1999 was Automatic Liquid Packaging, a Woodstock, Illinois–based custom manufacturer of sterile liquid pharmaceuticals and other health care products.

## GROWTH IN THE NEW MILLENNIUM

Another record-breaking year followed for Cardinal in 2000. Operating revenues reached an all-time high of more than $25 billion. Net earnings grew 24 percent to $730 million. Contributing to the success were enhanced operations resulting in an improved market position and increased productivity, as well as the continuing implementation of a focused acquisition strategy. In August Cardinal completed the acquisition of Bergen Brunswig's medical supply distribution business, a distributor of medical, surgical, and laboratory supplies to doctors' offices, long-term care and nursing centers, hospitals, and other providers of care. Bergen Brunswig Medical Corporation was acquired for approximately $180 million. Other 2000 acquisitions included Rexam Cartons, Inc.; Enhanced Derm Technologies, Inc.; ENDOlap, Inc.; Ni-Med kit manufacturing; CurranCare, LLC; VegiCaps Division (from American Home Products Corporation); and a manufacturing facility in Humacao, Puerto Rico. Cardinal also established a two-pronged Internet strategy with the launch of cardinal.com, a comprehensive, Web-enabled site for health care product procurement, fulfillment, support, and information, and NewHealth Exchange.com, an independent, Internet-based business-to-business electronic health care exchange with McKesson, AmerisourceBergen, Fisher Scientific, and Owens & Minor.

In January 2001 Cardinal celebrated its 30th anniversary and began another banner year in financial records and value to customers. Stock prices rose 40.2 percent, and sales rose 28 percent to $38.7 billion. Chairman Walter credited the company's success to "strong internal growth combined with meaningful acquisitions and significant partnerships." For the year, nearly $30 billion was spent on 13 acquisitions, with each company meeting the company's standard of being "outstanding by itself, fitting closely into our strategy, and making Cardinal collectively stronger for the future." Bindley Western Industries, Inc., an Indianapolis, Indiana–based wholesale distributor of pharmaceuticals and provider of nuclear pharmacy services, was acquired in February. Other acquisitions included International Processing Corporation, Critical Care Concepts, American Threshold, FutureCare, SP Pharmaceuticals, Professional Health-Care Resources, and a manufacturing facility in Raleigh, North Carolina. To foster long-term partnerships with providers and manufacturers, Cardinal formed ArcLight Systems, LLC, a venture between Cardinal and several retail-chain pharmacies, to provide real-time pharmaceutical sales data to pharmaceutical manufacturers.

In August 2001 Cardinal had 48,900 employees in 22 countries on five continents. Forty-two percent of Cardinal employees lived outside the United States. The company's U.S. facilities were located in 41 states and Puerto Rico. Cardinal's operations were organized based on the products and services offered, comprising four reporting segments: Pharmaceutical Distribution and Provider Services, Medical-Surgical Products and Services, Pharmaceutical Technologies and Services, and Automation and Information Services. Through innovative products and services to tens of thousands of customers in the health care industry, Cardinal had more than adequately survived in its highly competitive industry. It was number 23 on *Business Week*'s list of 50 best companies and among the top 100 of *Internet Week*'s top commercial Web innovators. It was named one of the world's best companies by *Forbes* magazine in 2002.

## ACQUISITIONS CONTINUE INTO NEW CENTURY

Cardinal's record of friendly and profitable acquisitions continued as the new century progressed. In March 2002 the company acquired Magellan Laboratories, Inc., a privately held company offering a full range of contractual services related to drug research and development. The addition of Magellan to Cardinal's Pharmaceutical Technologies and Services segment allowed Cardinal to enhance its existing capabilities in early-stage drug development.

In May 2002 Cardinal acquired Boron, LePore & Associates, Inc., a full-service provider of strategic medical education to the health care industry, for a purchase price of approximately $200 million. Among other advantages, Cardinal expected the acquisition to allow access to marketing groups that advised companies on

the life cycle of products. Also in 2002 Cardinal took an important step in its corporate brand recognition and identity when it launched its worldwide brand and united all its employees under the name Cardinal Health.

In 2003 Cardinal finished acquiring Syncor International Corporation for a purchase price totaling approximately $900 million in stock. At nearly the same time, Cardinal also acquired Central Pharmacy Services of Atlanta and combined the two acquisitions to create its Nuclear Pharmacy Services business. The move promised to make Cardinal a leader in the sale of radioactive materials that aid in the diagnosis of cancer and other diseases. In October 2003 Cardinal purchased InterCare Group, plc, a leading European pharmaceutical services company, for $530 million. The purchase expanded Cardinal's international capabilities in pharmaceutical manufacturing and distribution, especially in sterile packaging such as pre-filled syringes. Finally in 2003, Cardinal's subsidiary Medicine Shoppe International acquired Medicap Pharmacy, a pharmacy franchiser with 181 locations spread throughout 34 states.

In 2004 Cardinal expanded its service to manufacturers when it acquired Beckloff Associates, a Kansas City, Kansas, firm specializing in consulting services that addressed the regulatory approval process for drugs, medical devices, and biologics in North America and Europe. In March 2004 Cardinal acquired the privately held Georgia-based firm of Snowden Pencer Tucker, a manufacturer of laparoscopic and other surgical instruments. In the summer of 2004 Cardinal paid $1.62 million to acquire Alaris Medical Systems, a company specializing in infusion products and services, such as computerized systems that control how much medication a patient can receive intravenously.

## ACCOUNTING AND MARKET INQUIRIES

In May 2004 the U.S. Securities and Exchange Commission formalized an inquiry into accounting practices at Cardinal. According to an article in the *New York Times* published on May 15, the inquiry focused on how Cardinal accounted for $22 million in settlement money that it had recovered from vitamin makers accused of overcharging it. Cardinal's chief financial officer, Richard Miller, resigned in July after federal investigators intensified their inquiry. In September that year Cardinal's audit committee announced that it would restate financial results of the company prior three fiscal years as well as the first three quarters of 2004. In early 2005 numerous Cardinal employees resigned, were reprimanded, or were fired after the accounting inquiry uncovered issues regarding classification of sales, cash recognition, timing of revenue recognition, and some balance-sheet adjustments.

In April 2005 Cardinal was one of several drug wholesalers throughout the country who received subpoenas from the office of the New York State Attorney General. The subpoenas marked the beginning of a broad inquiry into an active behind-the-scenes secondary market in which pharmaceuticals were purchased and resold by a series of companies several times before reaching consumers. Although not necessarily illegal, critics charged that the practice compromised the integrity of drug-supply chains and created openings through which counterfeit and dangerous drugs could potentially reach the market. Critics accused some companies of using the practice to stockpile certain drugs in anticipation of price increases or shortages. In May 2005 Cardinal announced that it was closing its secondary trading operations. In an article in the *New York Times* published on May 6, Cardinal characterized the closing as a response to poor financial results and asserted that it was not prompted by the recent investigations.

## ACQUISITIONS ADDRESS HOSPITAL NEEDS

In June 2006 Cardinal acquired family-owned F. Dohmen Wholesale, the fifth-largest pharmaceutical distributor in the United States. Later that summer Cardinal completed acquisition of Denver Biomedical, Inc., a Golden, Colorado, firm established in 1969 that designed and manufactured products for managing the chronic buildup of fluids in the chest and abdominal cavity. In 2006 Cardinal also acquired MedMined, Inc., a medical analytics firm that used data-mining technology and blood test results to predict which hospitalized patients were likely to develop infections.

In other developments in 2006, Cardinal's founder and chief executive officer, Robert D. Walter, resigned as CEO in April, and announced his intention to retire as chair of Cardinal's board of directors within two years. R. Kerry Clark, formerly a vice chairman at Procter & Gamble, replaced him.

## SETTLEMENTS, ACQUISITIONS, AND SALES

In December 2006 Cardinal announced it would pay $11 million to settle an investigation by the office of the New York State Attorney General into secondary market trading of pharmaceuticals. Cardinal's was the first settlement from a drug wholesaler in response to the

investigation. The company agreed to pay $7 million to the nonprofit firm Health Research, $3 million to the State of New York, and $1 million to cover costs of the investigation.

In January 2007 Cardinal announced plans to sell its Pharmaceutical Technologies and Services unit, its drug manufacturing arm, to the private equity firm the Blackstone Group, for $3.3 billion in cash. The move was part of an effort by new Cardinal management to streamline Cardinal's business operations by selling off underperforming units.

In 2007 Cardinal expanded its product offerings for acute respiratory care by acquiring Viasys Healthcare, Inc., for a purchase price of $1.42 billion. In addition to medical ventilators, Viasys manufactured products to diagnose and treat diseases of the lungs, as well as instruments to track brain, muscle, circulatory, nerve, and hearing function. About 40 percent of established Viasys customers were located outside the United States, allowing Cardinal to expand its international capabilities as well as its existing line of products.

## NEW SPIN-OFF AND SETTLEMENT OF OLD LAWSUIT

In June 2007 Cardinal announced its creation of a $600 million cash reserve intended to settle a class-action suit filed by investors contending that Cardinal violated federal securities laws when it issued what investors contended were false and misleading financial results. Cardinal denied the accusations. The lawsuit dated to an investigation formally begun in 2004 into Cardinal's financial reporting and guidance.

In August 2009 Cardinal spun off 80.1 percent of its subsidiary CareFusion Corporation, which specialized in clinical and medical products, into a separate publicly traded company. The CareFusion spin-off included several of Cardinal's most recognized brands: Pyxis for medication and supply management, Alaris for medication infusion, AVEA and Pulmonetic Systems for medical ventilation, and Snowden-Pencer for surgical instruments.

By 2010 Cardinal Health, Inc., made more than 50,000 deliveries every day to more than 40,000 customer sites. These deliveries accounted for distribution of one-third of all pharmaceutical, medical, laboratory, and surgical products in the United States from their manufacturers to health care providers and points of care. Every day Cardinal facilities manufactured four million individual surgical products used in 50 percent of surgeries and 90 percent of hospitals in the United States. These products included surgical instruments, drapes, masks, gowns, gloves, respiratory care products, and irrigation and fluid suction products. Cardinal consultants advised retail, hospital, and mail-order pharmacies on best practices. The company employed more than 1,000 pharmacists of its own, including 110 clinical specialists. Medicine Shoppe International remained Cardinal's leading franchiser of retail, apothecary-style pharmacies. By 2010 there were nearly 1,000 Medicine Shoppe and Medicap Pharmacy stores, including 300 outside the United States

*April Dougal Gasbarre*
*Updated, Carol D. Beavers; Joyce Helena Brusin*

## PRINCIPAL SUBSIDIARIES

Allegiance Healthcare; ALP (Allied Liquid Packaging); Beckloff Associates; Bergen Brunswig Medical Corporation; Cardinal Distribution; F. Dohmen Wholesale; Medicine Shoppe International, Inc.; R.P. Scherer.

## PRINCIPAL DIVISIONS

Pharmaceutical Distribution and Provider Services; Medical-Surgical Products and Services; Pharmaceutical Technologies and Services; Automation and Information Services.

## PRINCIPAL COMPETITORS

AmerisourceBergen Corporation; McKesson Corporation.

## FURTHER READING

"Cardinal Health Plans to Buy Drugstore Franchiser," *New York Times*, August 29, 1995, p. C3.

"Cardinal to Buy PCI in Stock Transaction Valued at $201 Million," *Wall Street Journal*, July 25, 1996, p. C20.

"Cardinal Will Settle Inquiry," *New York Times*, December 27, 2006.

Column, Lex, "US Medical Equipment," *Financial Times*, August 27, 2009.

Dubashi, Jagannath, "The Tie That Binds," *Financial World*, April 30, 1991, p. 66.

Freudenheim, Milt, "Cardinal Health to Buy Pyxis in Stock Swap," *New York Times*, February 8, 1996, p. Cl.

Holstein, William J. "Patient Safety through Technology: Interview with Kerry Clark, Chief Executive of Cardinal Health, Inc.," *New York Times*, February 17, 2007.

Reingold, Jennifer, "Cardinal Rule," *Financial World*, January 31, 1995, pp. 36–38.

Saul, Stephanie, "Large Drug Wholesaler to Close Its Secondary Trading Operation," *New York Times*, May 6, 2005.

———, "Subpoenas Seek Details on Resales of Drugs," *New York Times*, April 9, 2005.

Speer, Tibbett L., "Just Say Grow: Cardinal Health Looks beyond Drug Distribution and Sees a Healthy Future," *Hospitals and Health Networks*, August 5, 1996, pp. 34–35.

# Cephalon, Inc.

41 Moores Road
Frazer, Pennsylvania 19355
U.S.A.
Telephone: (610) 344-0200
Fax: (610) 738-6590
Web site: http://www.cephalon.com

*Public Company*
*Founded:* 1987
*Incorporated:* 1987
*Employees:* 3,026
*Sales:* $2.15 billion (2009)
*Stock Exchanges:* NASDAQ
*Ticker Symbol:* CEPH
*NAICS:* 541711 Research and Development in Biotechnology; 424210 Drugs and Druggist Sundries Merchant Wholesalers

■ ■ ■

Cephalon, Inc., is an international biopharmaceutical company that specializes in developing drug treatments for a range of disorders. Cephalon's activities encompass the discovery, research, and development of new treatments as well as the sales and marketing of finished products. Cephalon is perhaps best known as the maker of Provigil, a medication used in treating narcolepsy. The company also markets Fentora (a fast-acting painkiller for cancer patients), Treanda (a drug aimed at fighting leukemia and non-Hodgkin's lymphoma), and Vivitrol (an injectable therapy for treating alcoholism). Headquartered in Pennsylvania, Cephalon has estab-

lished a broad global presence over the years, acquiring subsidiaries throughout North America, Europe, and Australia.

## A SMALL RESEARCH HOUSE: 1987–91

Cephalon was founded in 1987 by two venture capital firms, Burr, Egan, Deleage & Co. and Hambrecht & Quist Life Science Partners. The firms recruited Frank Baldino Jr., a senior biologist who was conducting neuroscience research for DuPont, to head the company. In the early years, Baldino kept Cephalon focused on research. About 30 scientists worked in a 10,000-square-foot laboratory, specializing in the discovery of neurological growth factors that could be used to treat diseases such as multiple sclerosis, strokes, and amyotrophic lateral sclerosis (ALS, or Lou Gehrig's disease). The chemicals under development were intended to prevent the brain-cell death associated with the diseases.

As a small research house, Cephalon initially avoided involving itself in activities that would require maintaining a sales staff, managing clinical trials, and shepherding new drugs through the Food and Drug Administration (FDA) approval process. With no product to sell, Cephalon's only asset was its scientific expertise. That expertise proved sufficient to attract investors, and the company managed to fund its operations through research grants and contracts with larger pharmaceutical firms. The 1990 discovery of an enzyme, Clipsin, that plays a major role in Alzheimer's disease, for example, led to an agreement with Schering-Plough. Under the agreement, Schering-Plough provided Cephalon with $20 million to continue its Alzheimer's research in exchange for exclusive worldwide rights to any technologies developed.

By the end of 1990 Cephalon had accumulated a deficit of $7.26 million since it had begun operating in November 1987. However, the company continued on a path of confident expansion. In March 1991 the staff had grown to 49 employees who worked in an enlarged, 31,000-square-foot lab. That April Cephalon completed its initial public offering on the NASDAQ, raising $59.4 million at a price of $18 a share. However, the share price dipped to $14.75 several weeks later amid general concern that biotechnology stocks were overvalued. The company would have to produce tangible results to retain investor confidence.

## BANKING ON MYOTROPHIN IN THE MID-NINETIES

In late 1991 Cephalon received orphan drug approval for its product Myotrophin. Orphan drug status gives a company the right to market a product exclusively for seven years, and it is granted for drugs not considered profitable enough to justify development without such a guarantee. Thus Cephalon began an eight-year, ultimately unsuccessful occupation with Myotrophin. The drug, known as a neurotrophic factor, promoted the survival of neurons and was being developed as a treatment for ALS. Cephalon subsequently bought a plant in Maryland to manufacture Myotrophin for research purposes, and the company entered into an agreement with Chiron Corporation to manufacture the drug on a larger scale if it should be approved by the FDA.

Meanwhile, a successful $23 million equity offering in April 1993 showed that investors retained confidence in Cephalon. The company received $17 million in revenues that year from contracts with large pharmaceutical firms, and it grew to 222 employees by year's end. Besides Schering-Plough and Chiron, Cephalon worked with two other firms. In a collaboration

with SmithKline Beecham, Cephalon was researching the use of protease inhibitors, chemicals that impede the process of cell death, to aid in the treatment of Alzheimer's. It was also working with SmithKline Beecham on a line of drugs that had potential for stopping abnormal cell growth in cancer patients. With the Japanese firm Kyowa Hakko Kogyo Co. Ltd., Cephalon was developing chemicals to inhibit the action of kinases, a type of protein that causes cell death in Alzheimer's and Parkinson's patients. In addition, the first step toward the development of the narcolepsy treatment Provigil was taken in February 1993, when Cephalon bought all rights to develop, market, and sell Provigil's main ingredient, modafinil, from the French company Laboratoire L. Lafon. Such wide-ranging research efforts caused the accumulation of a $35.6 million deficit between 1987 and the end of 1993.

In 1994 failures at other clinics made Wall Street wary of biotechnology stocks, and Cephalon's share price fell from a high of $19.50 in the first quarter of 1994 to $5.75 in mid-1995. However, the company trusted in the potential of its own technologies. On June 12 Cephalon announced positive results of clinical tests of Myotrophin. The tests showed that Myotrophin appeared to slow the progression of ALS. Cephalon's shares rose 400 percent after this news. Although European tests, announced in the fall, showed less conclusive results, the company's stock continued to climb.

In 1995 Cephalon took a decisive step away from its research-only roots by establishing a sales force. Because Cephalon did not yet have a product to sell, the sales force sold other companies' drugs. In an arrangement with Bristol-Myers Squibb, Cephalon sold the company's drugs to neurologists, thus giving its own sales force the opportunity to establish the connections and experience that would pay off once Cephalon was marketing its own products.

The first major stumbling block for Myotrophin came at the beginning of 1996, when the FDA refused to allow Cephalon to expand tests of the drug. On January 19 shares fell 34 percent to $23.37 in reaction to the news. The FDA pointed to conflicting results between European and American tests as the basis for its decision. Critics of the tests also charged that the clinical trials of Myotrophin were poorly designed. The test groups were too small, they said, and records were kept in such a way that many patient deaths were not counted. Because the trials were testing disease progression, not mortality rates, patients who were taking Myotrophin were sometimes removed from the study before they died and hence were not included in the final statistics. The confusion over clinical trial results led a

## KEY DATES

**1987:** Biologist Frank Baldino Jr. founds Cephalon as a small pharmaceutical research house.

**1991:** Cephalon goes public with a $59.4 million IPO.

**1994:** News of positive test results for Myotrophin sends stock soaring.

**1995:** Cephalon establishes a sales force.

**1999:** Myotrophin is abandoned following difficulties gaining full FDA approval; Provigil and Actiq are launched.

**2001:** Rights to Gabitril are acquired.

**2004:** Cephalon completes acquisition of Cima Labs Inc.

**2006:** Cephalon receives FDA approval to market Fentora, a cancer pain lozenge.

**2007:** Cephalon agrees to pay $425 million for drug marketing violations.

**2010:** Cephalon acquires Swiss pharmaceutical firm Mepha Holding AG.

group of investors to file a suit against Cephalon charging that the company was misleading in its reporting of Myotrophin test results. The suit was eventually settled in August 1999 for $17 million, although Cephalon denied any wrongdoing.

In 1996 Cephalon sold the plant that it had been using to manufacture Myotrophin. However, Cephalon and its partner Chiron still hoped that the drug would gain final approval. In June 1996 the FDA made Myotrophin available to some ALS patients but strongly urged the company to conduct a third study of the drug. Cephalon was reluctant to do so, however, because it had already invested $180 million in a drug with a fairly small potential market. More bad news came in May 1997 when an FDA advisory panel rejected Myotrophin as an ALS treatment. Once again Cephalon stock plummeted 35 percent, to $13. Nevertheless, both Chiron and Cephalon planned to continue to pursue approval for Myotrophin, pointing out that the panel's recommendation did not amount to a final decision by the FDA.

In May 1998 the FDA ruled that Myotrophin was potentially approvable, contingent on additional clinical studies. However, Cephalon had already poured too many resources into Myotrophin to embark on another multiyear study. The company finally gave up on the drug in 1999, disappointing both the National ALS As-

sociation, which had hoped the drug could become an effective treatment, and ALS patients who had been given special access to Myotrophin. CEO Frank Baldino expressed regret that a potentially useful drug failed to gain FDA approval. He said additional tests would be justified for a drug designed to treat a disease that affected five or six million people, but only 25,000 to 30,000 people nationwide had ALS.

### DEVELOPING A SOLID PRODUCT LINE: 1998–2001

Fortunately, Cephalon's other drug development projects had been proceeding more successfully. The narcolepsy drug Provigil received preliminary approval from the FDA in December 1997 and final approval in December 1998. Company stock rose 12 percent as investors hoped the new product would make up for the Myotrophin fiasco. In February 1999 Provigil was launched in the United States. Sales of the drug exceeded expectations, reaching $25 million by the end of the year. Sales in 2000 were $72.1 million.

Cephalon hoped to expand the applications for Provigil beyond narcolepsy. In January 2000 test results were announced showing that the drug was effective in warding off fatigue in multiple sclerosis patients and shift workers. According to test results released in October 2001, Provigil also increased daytime wakefulness in patients suffering from obstructive sleep apnea, a disorder causing a person to wake frequently throughout the night because of obstructed breathing passages. Tests in 2000, however, failed to demonstrate that the drug was effective in treating attention deficit hyperactivity disorder (ADHD). Use of Provigil also expanded geographically through marketing collaborations with foreign companies, including an October 1998 agreement with Mercke GmbH to market Provigil in Austria and Switzerland and a November 2000 agreement with Choongwae Pharma Corporation in Korea.

Actiq, Cephalon's second major proprietary drug, received FDA approval in November 1998 and was launched in the United States in March 1999. At the time, the drug was manufactured and marketed by Abbott Laboratories. Cephalon acquired worldwide product rights to the drug in October 2000 through its merger with Anesta Corporation of Salt Lake City.

Actiq is prescribed to treat pain in cancer patients. Specifically, the drug targets sporadic flare-ups, known as breakthrough cancer pain, that overcome the medication already being used to treat chronic pain. Actiq provides fast-acting, short-term relief from breakthrough pain, which can last from 30 minutes to several hours.

Besides the acquisition of a new product, Cephalon's merger with Anesta gave the company access to a new drug-delivery technology, the Oral Transmucosal System (OTS). Using the OTS system, Actiq is absorbed through the mucous membranes of the cheek and passes directly into circulation without having to go through the liver. As a result, a flare-up of pain can be eased within 15 minutes. Sales of Actiq in 2000 were $15 million and growing as Cephalon worked to establish the product as the medication of choice for breakthrough cancer pain.

Like Provigil, Actiq developed a worldwide reach. In October 2000 the drug was approved for sale in the United Kingdom, and in June 2001 the drug was granted marketing authorization in 16 other European counties. Through marketing collaborations with companies such as Swedish Orphan AB, Elan Pharmaceuticals Ltd. in the United Kingdom, and Grupo Ferrer Internacional SA in Spain, Cephalon planned to launch Actiq commercially throughout Europe. Cephalon also granted rights to Orphan Australia to market and distribute Actiq in Australia and New Zealand.

Cephalon acquired a third major product in January 2001. All rights to Gabitril, a treatment for partial seizures related to epilepsy, were bought from Abbott Laboratories for $100 million. The drug had been approved by the FDA in September 1997 and was launched in the United States in 1998. Numerous epilepsy drugs already on the market competed with Gabitril, but the drug nevertheless garnered $23 million in sales in 2000. To widen the market for the drug, Cephalon began investigating the use of Gabitril as a mood stabilizer for various psychiatric disorders.

Besides its three main products in the United States, Cephalon marketed seven products through its European subsidiary. In the United Kingdom, those products included Anafranil (a treatment for depression and obsessive compulsive disorder), Lioresal and ITB Therapy (treatments for spasticity), Ritalin (an ADHD drug), and Tegretol (for epilepsy). The company also marketed two Parkinson's medications in Europe: Xilopar in Germany and Apokinon in France. A 30-person sales team in Europe supported Cephalon's activities there.

Research and development remained central to ensuring Cephalon's long-term profitability. In collaborations with such international partners as TAP Holdings, Kyowa Hakko Kogyo, H Lundbeck, and, as of December 2000, the R. W. Johnson Pharmaceutical Research Institute, the company was researching kinase inhibitors, compounds that either enhance cell survival or cause cell death. The compounds had potential for treating neurological and oncological diseases.

Cephalon's extensive library of proprietary compounds provided ample fodder for research. Products under development in 2001 included CEP-701, a compound that had been shown to cause the death of cancer cells by inhibiting the activity of a certain kinase, or protein. The compound was being developed to treat prostate and pancreatic cancer. Phase-one testing was also just beginning on a second compound, CEP-7055, which was found in preclinical studies to prevent the development of the blood supply required for tumors to grow. Cephalon hoped that the experience with Actiq would pave the way for success with these further cancer drugs. The company was also working on a compound, CEP-1347, that could inhibit the progression of Parkinson's and Alzheimer's diseases.

The deals leading to the acquisition of Actiq and Gabitril, as well as the resources invested in continued research, contributed to Cephalon's growing net loss. The company reported losses of $55.4 million for 1998, $70 million for 1999, and $101.1 million for 2000. Nevertheless, the establishment of three successful proprietary drugs finally gave Cephalon the prospect of stable sales revenue, while the products under development gave the company growth potential. CEO and founder Frank Baldino believed that the company was laying a solid foundation for profitability in the near future.

## DIVERSIFICATION AND RAPID GROWTH: 2001–10

In late 2001 Cephalon purchased French pharmaceutical company Laboratoire L. Lafon for $450 million. With the acquisition, Cephalon assumed 100 percent ownership of its narcolepsy drug, Provigil, while adding thirteen new drugs to its product line. Perhaps more important, the deal also gave Cephalon a foothold in Europe, where it hoped to begin marketing Provigil more aggressively. The move came at a time when the company's long-term vision was finally beginning to pay dividends. In 2001 Cephalon posted its first profit in the company's history, with sales of Provigil and Actiq alone rising to nearly $200 million for the year.

Over the next several years Cephalon continued to seek new business opportunities. In August 2003 the company launched a bid to acquire Minnesota-based drug firm Cima Labs Inc. At the heart of the merger was Cima's patented drug-delivery technology, an area where Cephalon hoped to carve out a sizable market niche. With the merger, Cephalon would also obtain the rights to Cima's cancer pain medication, OraVescent fentanyl, which was still undergoing clinical trials at the time of the acquisition talks. At around this time Cephalon also received FDA approval to begin marketing Provigil for a host of other disorders, including sleep apnea.

Cephalon's three leading drugs continued to post strong revenue growth. For the third quarter of 2003, sales of Provigil reached nearly $80 million, an increase of more than 50 percent over the third quarter of 2002. Sales of Actiq grew 87 percent over the same period, rising to $65.5 million, while Gabitril revenues topped $17.2 million for the quarter. For the year 2003 the company posted revenues of $714.8 million. As Cephalon continued its rapid rise, it found itself needing to expand. In March 2004 the company announced it would move its headquarters to a 200,000-square foot facility in Frazer, Pennsylvania, in addition to increasing its sales force to 500 employees. Explaining the move to the *Philadelphia Inquirer* on March 26, 2004, company executive Robert W. Grupp stated simply, "We are bursting at the seams here. We need office space immediately."

For the year 2004 Cephalon exceeded $1 billion in sales for the first time in the company's history. In spite of this achievement, the company faced numerous challenges heading into the second half of the decade. In August 2004 Cephalon finally received Federal Trade Commission (FTC) approval for its Cima Labs acquisition, in a deal worth roughly $515 million. As a condition of the approval, the company was compelled to license a generic version of its Actiq patent to rival drug company Barr Pharmaceuticals, Inc., in order to avoid antitrust violations. With Barr scheduled to begin marketing its generic Actiq by early 2007, Cephalon felt increased pressure to expand its portfolio of drugs.

In May 2005 the company announced that it would acquire cancer-drug specialist Salmedix Inc. for $160 million. A month later Cephalon entered into a pact with Massachusetts-based Alkermes Inc. to market and sell the alcoholism medication Vivitrol. The company received conditional FDA approval for the drug in early 2006 and began marketing the treatment by the middle of the year. Around this time the company reached agreements with four generic-drug manufacturers to retain its exclusive right to market Provigil for an additional five years. In September 2006 Cephalon received FDA approval for Fentora, a fast-acting cancer pain lozenge. Over time, the company hoped to receive broader FDA approval to market Fentora for other forms of chronic pain relief, including lower-back pain. In the short term, the company hoped that the new drug would compensate for the anticipated drop in Actiq sales. For the year 2006 Cephalon posted revenues of $1.76 billion, up from $1.21 billion in 2005.

In early 2007, however, Cephalon found itself at the center of a federal investigation, amid allegations that it had engaged in misleading marketing practices with several of its best-known drugs, including Provigil and Actiq. In November of that year the company reached a settlement with the U.S. Department of Justice and agreed to pay a fine of $425 million. In spite of this setback, Cephalon continued to introduce a range of new products during this period. It received approval in March 2008 to begin selling Treanda, a drug designed to treat a rare type of leukemia. The following November the company received additional authorization to market Treanda to patients suffering from non-Hodgkin's lymphoma. For the year, the company's sales reached $1.94 billion.

As the decade drew to a close, Cephalon remained firmly committed to its aggressive growth strategy. In August 2009 the company boosted its presence in Australia by acquiring biotechnology firm Arana Therapeutics Limited. In April 2010 Cephalon purchased Swiss pharmaceutical company Mepha Holding AG for $615.4 million. With the merger, the company hoped to increase its international presence significantly, using the new subsidiary as a springboard to untapped global markets. Cephalon also announced that it had surpassed $2 billion in sales for the year 2009. Clearly, Frank Baldino's business model had set the company on a trajectory for steady earnings growth well into the future.

*Sarah Ruth Lorenz*
*Updated, Stephen Meyer*

## PRINCIPAL SUBSIDIARIES

Anesta Corp.; Anesta AG (Switzerland); Arana Therapeutics, Inc.; Arana Therapeutics Pty. Ltd. (Australia); Arana Therapeutics (Vic) Pty. Ltd. (Australia); Cephalon (Bermuda) Limited; Cephalon Borinquen, Inc. (Puerto Rico); Cephalon B.V. (Netherlands); Cephalon Development Corporation; Cephalon France SAS; Cephalon Europe SAS (France); Cephalon GmbH (Germany); Cephalon Holdings Limited (United Kingdom); Cephalon International Holdings,Inc.; Cephalon Investments, Inc.; Cephalon Italia S.r.L (Italy); Cephalon Limited (United Kingdom); Cephalon Luxembourg S.a.r.l; Cephalon Pharma ApS (Denmark); Cephalon Pharma (Ireland) Limited; Cephalon Pharma SL (Spain); Cephalon Sp.z. o.o. (Poland); Cephalon Technologies Partners, Inc.; Cephalon Technology, Inc.; Cephalon Titrisation (France); Cephalon (UK) Limited; Cephalon Ventures Puerto Rico, Inc.; CIMA LABS INC.; East End Insurance Ltd. (Bermuda); Mepha Holding AG (Switzerland); PolaRx Biopharmaceuticals, Inc.; Promics Pty. Ltd. (Australia); Societe Civile Immobiliere Martigny (France); Zeneus Pharma S.a.r.l. (France).

## PRINCIPAL COMPETITORS

Amgen Inc.; Cortex Pharmaceuticals, Inc.; DRAXIS Specialty Pharmaceuticals Inc.; GlaxoSmithKline plc; Johnson & Johnson; Neurocrine Biosciences, Inc.; Sanofi-Aventis; Sepracor Inc.

## FURTHER READING

Armstrong, Michael W., "Cephalon Is Headed Public with $37.8 Million Offering," *Philadelphia Business Journal*, March 25, 1991, pp. 1–3.

Block, Donna, "Cephalon to Buy Mepha for $590M," *Daily Deal*, February 1, 2010.

George, John, "Cephalon Buys Rights to Anti-epileptic Drug," *Philadelphia Business Journal*, November 3, 2000, p. 4.

———, "Cephalon's Provigil May Have Wider Uses," *Philadelphia Business Journal,*, January 28, 2000, p. 9.

———, "Despite Loss, Cephalon Says It's on Right Road," *Philadelphia Business Journal*, March 2, 2001, p. 9.

Hower, Wendy, "New Issues Suffer as Wary Investors Cool to Biotech," *Boston Business Journal*, May 6, 1991, pp. 1–2.

Lloyd, Linda, "Cephalon Settles Charges for $425 million," *Philadelphia Inquirer*, September 30, 2008, p. C2.

Shaw, Donna, "Pennsylvania Biotech Company Cephalon's Research Continues to Boost Revenues," *Knight-Ridder/Tribune Business News*, May 17, 1994.

Tanouye, Elyse, "Cephalon Shares Sink on FDA Setback; Firm and Partner Chiron to Push Ahead," *Wall Street Journal*, May 12, 1997.

———, and Ralph T. King Jr., "Critics Question Drug Testing by Cephalon," *Wall Street Journal*, January 22, 1996.

# CIRCOR International, Inc.

---

25 Corporate Drive, Suite 130
Burlington, Massachusetts 01803-4238
U.S.A.
Telephone: (781) 270-1200
Fax: (781) 270-1299
Web site: http://www.circor.com

*Public Company*
*Founded:* 1999
*Incorporated:* 1999
*Employees:* 2,600
*Sales:* $642.6 million (2009)
*Stock Exchanges:* New York
*Ticker Symbol:* CIR
*NAICS:* 332912 Fluid Power Valve and Hose Fitting Manufacturing; 332919 Other Metal Valve and Pipe Fitting Manufacturing; 334513 Instruments and Related Products Manufacturing for Measuring, Displaying, and Controlling Industrial Process Variables

■ ■ ■

CIRCOR International, Inc., is a leading designer, manufacturer, and distributor of valves and related products and services for the safe and efficient operation of oil, gas, air, and steam systems worldwide. Marketed primarily to the energy, flow-technology, instrumentation, and aerospace industries, CIRCOR products are used in oil and natural gas distribution, in the aircraft and shipping industries, and for a wide range of industrial and commercial processes. The company, a

top-three provider of ball valves for the global oil and gas industry, also makes and supplies products for use in chemical processing, biotechnology, heating, and air conditioning. CIRCOR prides itself on a varied product portfolio and a streamlined, "lean" business model designed to minimize waste and maximize efficiency and growth. Headquartered in Burlington, Massachusetts, the company has 18 manufacturing sites in North America, Western Europe, North Africa, and China, with distribution in more than 100 countries. The company divides its business into two main groups: Energy Products and Instrumentation and Thermal Fluid Controls.

## THE PATH TO A NEW COMPANY

The story of CIRCOR, which was incorporated in 1999, actually begins more than 20 years earlier with the creation of a new industrial products division at the Watts Regulator Company of North Andover, Massachusetts. In 1978 Watts, an innovative plumbing and heating valve manufacturer, designed a ball valve that could control the flow of fluids, such as oil and gas, in industrial and chemical processes. The new valve had the potential to extend the company's reach into new markets. Internal product development could only drive growth so far, however. Determined to broaden its markets to include industrial and chemical processing in addition to water-based plumbing and heating, Watts in 1984 began acquiring companies whose products would both complement and grow its existing product lines. In 1988, with the acquisition of KF Industries, an Oklahoma-based valve supplier that would become

Watts's premier oil and gas subsidiary, Watts entered the oil and gas energy market.

Watts, now called Watts Industries, Inc., focused on growing and diversifying its industrial product offerings through acquisitions during the 1980s and 1990s. In 1984 it bought Spence Engineering, a manufacturer of steam regulators whose sales would more than double in its first decade as a Watts subsidiary. From 1989 to 1999 Watts acquired other companies specializing in steam regulation, gaining a firm foothold in the flow-technology industry. With the 1994 acquisition of Pibiviesse S.p.A., an Italian producer of valves with high pressure ratings for the petrochemical industry, Watts could provide products suitable for use in the exploration and production of international oil and gas pipelines. A year later Watts announced a joint venture with the Suzhou Valve Company, a leading Chinese valve manufacturer. The 1998 purchase of Hoke International, Inc., with its extensive line of valves and valve fittings for use in industry and instrumentation, would be Watts's largest acquisition to date.

Watts's move into the commercial and military aerospace industry came in 1990, with the acquisition of Circle Seal Controls, Inc., a manufacturer of valves and other fluid-control devices engineered to industry standards. Aerodyne Controls Corporation, acquired in 1997, supplied precision components to the aerospace and military industries. Its products included pneumatic control devices for regulating the flow of pressurized air. Atkomatic Valve Co., a 1998 acquisition, added heavy-duty solenoid valves able to withstand the impact of high-pressure, high-heat, and corrosive fluids. In 1999, spurred by the growth of its industrial products division and by a desire to focus on its core plumbing, heating, and water-quality products and services, Watts made a key decision. It would spin off its industrial oil and gas sector into a new, independent company, CIRCOR International, Inc.

## A NEW BEGINNING FOR AEROSPACE AND ENERGY

With the incorporation of CIRCOR in 1999, David A. Bloss Sr., formerly president and chief operating officer at Watts, was named chairman, president, and chief executive officer of the new company. Bloss would hold that position until his retirement in 2008, when Bill Higgins would take over the job. CIRCOR lost no time in announcing its renewed commitment to growth through a combination of specialized acquisition and internal product development. In addition, the new company worked to diversify its markets and expand them internationally. CIRCOR held its initial public stock offering on the New York Stock Exchange in March 2001.

During the early years, CIRCOR aggressively expanded its aerospace holdings. In 2005 the company acquired Loud Engineering & Manufacturing, Inc., a leading producer of landing gear and components for military aircraft, for $36 million. The same year the company bought the French aerospace valve manufacturer Industria S.A. These additions gave CIRCOR new access to military and aerospace markets in both the United States and Europe. In 2007, with the purchase of Survival Engineering, Inc., the company extended its product line to include specialized inflation and flotation systems for the aerospace and defense industries.

Over the next two years CIRCOR branched out even further, acquiring Motor Technology, Inc., a producer of aeronautical electrical components used in military and commercial aircraft, including Boeing aircraft, and Bodet Aero, a leading French manufacturer of electromechanical and fluid control systems. By 2008 CIRCOR aerospace technologies had been used on space shuttles and satellites. In 2010 CIRCOR partnered with Safran/Messier-Bugatti to produce precision control products for its Airbus A350 XWB. Sales of aerospace products brought in over $113 million in 2009, or 18 percent of total net earnings for the year.

Energy, however, became CIRCOR's biggest revenue producer, accounting for nearly 50 percent of the company's earnings over time and earning the company over $400 million in 2008, a jump of almost 30 percent from 2007. Early on, CIRCOR initiated a strategy to consolidate and integrate its growing industrial energy unit. In 2004 the company acquired Mallard Control Company, which included the Hydroseal brand, a producer of valves for the petrochemical industry. The next year CIRCOR merged the new acquisition into KF Industries and renamed the unit CIRCOR Energy Products. The year 2005 also saw CIRCOR gain full ownership of the Suzhou KF Valve Company. Sagebrush

## KEY DATES

**1999:** CIRCOR International, Inc., is established by Watts Industries, Inc.

**2000:** CIRCOR creates Instrumentation Products Group.

**2005:** CIRCOR purchases Loud Engineering & Manufacturing, Inc.

**2008:** CIRCOR names Bill Higgins chief executive officer.

**2009:** CIRCOR expands its energy markets to include Europe, Africa, and the Middle East.

Pipeline Equipment Company, a producer of pipeline flow control and analysis equipment for the North American market, was acquired in 2006. Three years later CIRCOR acquired the U.K.-based Pipeline Engineering & Supply Co. Ltd., a move that expanded CIRCOR's pipeline product line into Europe, Africa, and the Middle East. By 2010 CIRCOR energy products were manufactured on three continents and used for the exploration, distribution, construction, and maintenance of energy applications worldwide.

## THE GROWTH OF FLOW TECHNOLOGY AND INSTRUMENTATION

CIRCOR's early years were an active time for its instrumentation unit, which focused on the measurement and control of industrial processes like flow and temperature. Early in 2000 the company announced that it would consolidate the unit's product development and manufacturing operations, creating an Instrumentation Products Group to integrate Hoke International, Inc., Circle Seal Controls, Inc., GO Regulator, Inc. (acquired in 1999), Aerodyne Controls Corporation, and Atkomatic Valve Company. CIRCOR made several more acquisitions in the instrumentation sector, starting with Tomco Products, Inc., an industrial couplings manufacturer in 2003. The same year, the company spent $12 million to acquire DQS International B.V., a Dutch firm, and Texas Sampling, Inc. These acquisitions added equipment for sampling and monitoring fluids used in industrial processes to CIRCOR's portfolio.

The company also made good on its promise to expand into overseas markets with the 2001 acquisition of Regeltechnik Kornwestheim GmbH, a German manufacturer of industrial fluid control valves. Five

years later CIRCOR set its sights on a British company, Hale Hamilton Valves Limited, a provider of top-quality high-pressure valves and other flow-control devices to the defense and high-tech industries. Hale Hamilton products also opened opportunities for CIRCOR in the medical equipment market. By 2007 CIRCOR's flow-control products could be found everywhere from municipal heating systems to industrial shipping vessels. Record sales of the company's flow-technology products in 2008 brought in over $272 million, or 34 percent of the company's annual net earnings.

The 2009 economic climate was a challenging one for many U.S. companies, and CIRCOR was no exception. That year, the company reported a 19 percent decline in overall earnings from the previous year, primarily due to decreases in its flow-technology and energy sectors. However, the company expressed confidence in its industrial markets and in its overall business strategy. Chief Executive Officer Bill Higgins stated in the company's 2009 press release on fourth-quarter earnings that "the quality of earnings initiatives CIRCOR implemented in 2009 have enabled the company to enter 2010 a much leaner and stronger organization."

*Hanna Schonthal*

## PRINCIPAL SUBSIDIARIES

CIRCOR (Jersey) Ltd. (UK, 80%); CIRCOR Aerospace, Inc.; CIRCOR Energy Products, Inc.; CIRCOR Instrumentation Technologies, Inc.; CIRCOR German Holdings, LLC; CIRCOR Energy Products (Canada) ULC.

## PRINCIPAL DIVISIONS

Instrumentation and Thermal Fluid Controls; Energy Products.

## PRINCIPAL COMPETITORS

Cameron International Corporation; Flowserve Corporation; ITT Corporation; Parker Hannifin Corporation; SPK Process Equipment; Swagelok Company.

## FURTHER READING

"CIRCOR Aerospace Selected by Messier-Bugatti for A350 XWB Speed Transducers and Sensors," Financial EveryDay, January 31, 2010, http://www.financialeveryday.com/circor-aerospace-selected-by-messier-bugatti-for-a350-xwb-speed-transducers-and-sensors-2/.

"CIRCOR Leads Innovation in Alternative Fuels Industry," *Connections*, issue 6, Autumn 2002, http://www.circor.de/connections6/conn_iss6_p1.html.

"CIRCOR Reports Fourth Quarter and 2009 Results," Business Wire, February 24, 2010, http://www.businesswire.com/news /home/20100224006799/en.

Kofsky, Larry, "Valve Maker Circor Turns on the Spigot," CBS. Marketwatch.com, October 30, 1999, http://www. marketwatch.com/story/valve-maker-circor-turns-on-the-spigot.

Schutts, Larry, "CIRCOR International (CIR): Shares Define Bullish 'Flag' Pattern," BloggingStocks, July 14, 2008, http://www.bloggingstocks.com/2008/07/14/circor-inter national-cir-shares-define-bullish-flag-pattern/?utm_source =feedburner&utm_medium=feed&utm_campaign=Feed %3A+weblogsinc%2Fbloggingstocks+%28Blogging+Stocks %29.

# Cleveland Indians Baseball Company, Inc.

Progressive Field
2401 Ontario Street
Cleveland, Ohio 44115-4003
U.S.A.
Telephone: (216) 420-4487
Fax: (216) 420-4430
Web site: http://cleveland.indians.mlb.com

*Private Company*
*Founded:* 1901 as Cleveland Blues
*Employees:* 114
*Sales:* $170 million (2009)
*NAICS:* 711211 Sports Teams and Clubs

■ ■ ■

An original member of the American League, the Cleveland Indians Baseball Company, Inc., is one of major league baseball's most enduring and fabled franchises. In addition to winning World Series championships in 1920 and 1948, the Indians have also endured long periods of futility throughout their history, particularly during the 1970s and 1980s. During the 1990s the Indians emerged as a perennial contender for the American League pennant, and in 2001 the team set a major league record for consecutive sellouts at their home ballpark. In the early years of the new century, team executives were forced to slash payroll to restore the club to profitability, and by the end of the decade the Indians' payroll was among the lowest in the game.

## EARLY YEARS OF PROFESSIONAL BASEBALL IN CLEVELAND

Cleveland has had a big-league baseball team since 1869, when the Forest Citys first played a contest against the Cincinnati Red Stockings. In 1871 the Forest Citys joined the National Association, although the team disbanded a year later. The Cleveland team was resuscitated toward decade's end. It joined the National League in 1879 and became known as the Spiders in 1889. During the next decade Cleveland became home to what many consider the worst ball club in the history of the game. The 1899 Spiders had the misfortune of being owned by Frank DeHaas Robison, who purchased the St. Louis Browns and then, out of spite, transferred the best Spiders to his new team. Cleveland won only 20 games and lost 134. Attendance was so sparse that after July most Spider games were played on the road. The team disbanded at the end of the season.

The Western League, a minor circuit eager to challenge the Nationals, changed its name to American League in 1900 and looked to expand to larger cities for its first season in 1901. Cleveland was a perfect fit, and a franchise was sold to a group of local investors. A coal baron named Charley Somers became the official owner of the new team. Known briefly as the Blues, the Bluebirds, and then the Bronchos, the team next became known as the Naps, named after its star player Napoleon Lajoie. When Somers's finances soured, Lajoie was traded after the 1914 season, and a new name for the team was needed.

## COMPANY PERSPECTIVES

From its roots to the present, Cleveland baseball has been distinguished by great ballplayers and great moments. It is through the fortunes of the men that have played for the Indians, and the memories they have created, that the history of the Cleveland Indians is learned and appreciated.

## "INDIANS" NAME ADOPTED

According to popular legend, the Cleveland franchise became known as the Indians in honor of a Native American named Louis Sockalexis who had played briefly for the old Spiders in the 1890s. This explanation, however, is probably only a justification after the fact. The Cleveland newspapers fielded fan suggestions that included Commodores, Foresters, Harmonics, Rangers, Sixers, Some Runners, Speeders, and Tornadoes, but Indians was not among the published nicknames.

The talk of baseball that year was the miracle Boston Braves. When the sportswriters settled on Cleveland Indians as the team's new name in 1915, it was more likely an allusion to the Boston ball club's use of the nickname Braves than to Sockalexis, who played only 94 games in the city. Newspapers were reporting the team's new "temporary" name well before the first mention of a connection to Sockalexis. Then it was recalled that the team had been referred to briefly as the Indians when Sockalexis made his splash with the team. Unfortunately, Sockalexis was more troubled than talented, appearing only in 21 and 7 games, respectively, his last two seasons in baseball. After years of hard drinking, he died of a heart attack at the age of 41. Despite Sockalexis's personal troubles, the belief that the Indians were named in tribute to him is deeply held by the ball club and many of its fans. What is not in doubt is that the temporary nickname proved enduring.

In 1916 when Somers was in danger of losing the Indians to the bank, American League President Ban Johnson and a few of Somers's friends met at a Chicago bar to discuss the situation. For no apparent reason, Johnson decided that Sunny Jim Dunn should become the next owner, despite the fact that Dunn could come up with only $15,000. His partner in an Iowa construction business, Paddy McCarthy, thought he could add another $15,000. The bartender offered to kick in $10,000, and he, too, joined the growing consortium. Numerous other investors were solicited until Dunn had

$500,000 to purchase the Cleveland team and bail out Somers.

## TEAM SUCCESSES AND FAILURES: 1920–45

The Cleveland Indians would know both tragedy and triumph in 1920. On August 17 star shortstop Ray Chapman was hit in the left temple by a pitch, and he died 12 hours later without regaining consciousness. He is the only major league baseball player to die from an accident on the field. The team rebounded, however, and won the American League pennant, edging out the Chicago White Sox, who were forced to finish the 1920 season without eight of their best players following a gambling scandal that tainted the 1919 World Series. The Indians then defeated the Brooklyn Dodgers in the World Series to win the team's first national championship.

With the emergence of the New York Yankees in the 1920s, the Indians rarely challenged first place for the next generation. Alva Bradley, a businessman and the president of the Cleveland Chamber of Commerce, became the front man for a group of investors that bought the team in 1928. He is reported to have said, "I'm the perfect man to own the Indians—I know nothing about baseball!" He was certainly true to his word. He alienated fans by banning radio broadcasts in 1933. He changed managers so often that Cleveland became known as "the Graveyard of Managers." Only once under Bradley's ownership, in 1940, did the Indians seriously threaten to win the American League pennant. The team lost the championship to Detroit by one game.

Even the construction of a new ballpark did not help the franchise. After playing its entire history in League Park, which had been built for the Spiders in 1891, the Indians moved into cavernous Cleveland Stadium on July 31, 1932. With 76,000 seats, it was easily the largest baseball facility in the country. After drawing 80,000 for its opening game, the Indians saw attendance drop dramatically. Playing the entire 1933 season in the stadium, the Indians averaged fewer than 6,000 fans a game. The following year, to save money, the team returned to League Park for all but Sunday games and holidays.

Following the 1941 season the Indians were once again in need of a new manager. The youngest member of the team, 24-year-old shortstop Lou Boudreau, wrote to Bradley to express his interest in the job. With nothing to lose, Bradley invited the player to meet the board of directors. Boudreau, a University of Illinois physical education graduate with future plans for coaching, spoke to Bradley and his backers. Only one, George

```
┌─────────────────────────────────────────────┐
│                                               │
│               KEY DATES                       │
│                  ■                            │
│                                               │
│  1901:  The Cleveland Blues begin play in the │
│         American League.                      │
│  1915:  The ball club formally adopts the     │
│         Indians nickname.                     │
│  1920:  Team wins its first World Series.     │
│  1946:  Cleveland Indians franchise is sold   │
│         to Bill Veeck Jr.                     │
│  1948:  Ball club wins its second World       │
│         Series in franchise history.          │
│  1986:  Indians are sold to Richard Jacobs.   │
│  1994:  Indians play their first game at      │
│         newly opened Jacobs Field.            │
│  2000:  Team is sold to Lawrence J. Dolan.    │
│  2001:  Mark Shapiro succeeds John Hart as    │
│         team general manager.                 │
│  2008:  Indians trade ace pitcher CC Sabathia │
│         to the Milwaukee Brewers for          │
│         prospects.                            │
│                                               │
└─────────────────────────────────────────────┘
```

Martin, chairman of the board of Sherwin-Williams paints, voted for Boudreau. He liked the young man's confidence and good looks, and he argued that the move would spark debate and possibly ticket sales. The board voted again but this time with a unanimous result. Boudreau was hired as the new player-manager of the Cleveland Indians, much to the surprise of everyone in baseball, not the least of whom were his teammates.

The "Boy Manager" took over the team in 1942 and wasted no time in showing that he had a lot to learn. International events, however, worked in his favor. The United States was plunged into World War II, and baseball teams had to scramble to find able-bodied players. Boudreau was exempt from the draft because of arthritic ankles. He was one of the stars of the American League and popular with fans, so there was no thought to replace him as manager, despite less-than-stellar results. Only twice did the Indians post winning records under Boudreau from 1942 to 1946.

### THE VEECK ERA BEGINS: 1946

Another change in ownership after the war precipitated a golden era for the Cleveland Indians. On June 21, 1946, the club was sold for $1.6 million to Bill Veeck Jr. who was part of a 10-member syndicate. The son of a baseball executive, Veeck was a self-described hustler eager to run a baseball team in his own way, after years of working for the conservative ownership of the Chicago Cubs. He circulated with the fans to learn what

they wanted. He had the public address system fixed, he promised to put Indians' games on the radio even if he had to give away the rights, he had the women's rest rooms cleaned every two innings, and he allowed fans to keep baseballs that were hit into the stands, an act of generosity foreign to the previous ownership.

Veeck ran his team in a manner that was not only ahead of its time but was also peculiar to his personality. He might present an orchestra to entertain the fans before the game, or fireworks and circus acts after the game. He gave away nylon stockings or orchids on Ladies Day. He brought in flagpole sitters. He gave away livestock. He gave away used cars. He answered his own phone and took any call that came to his office. He stood at the turnstiles and shook countless hands. The fans loved him. In 1946 the Indians topped one million in attendance for the first time. The following season, now playing exclusively at Cleveland Stadium, they drew more than 1.5 million fans, second in the American League, despite finishing a distant fourth in the standings.

Veeck would do anything to improve his team or draw a crowd, even if it was controversial. Only 11 weeks after African-American baseball player Jackie Robinson broke baseball's color barrier with the National League Dodgers, Veeck signed 23-year-old Larry Dolby. Robinson, who was 28, had been prepared for Brooklyn by playing a year with the Dodgers' minor league team in Montreal and then going through spring training in 1947. In Cleveland, by contrast, Dolby was playing for the Indians only two days after signing. Although the move was lauded in most quarters, signing Dolby was hardly without controversy. Teammates were distant, a situation not helped when Dolby was unable to eat or room with the team on the road. Opposing players and fans were not above hurling racial epithets. Even umpires were hostile. The best that could be said for Dolby's first year with the Indians, in which he batted only 32 times, was that he endured it.

Veeck had no doubts about keeping Dolby, whom he felt certain would become a star player. Veeck did not, however, care for his young player-manager. When word leaked to the press that Veeck was trying to trade Boudreau to the St. Louis Browns, however, Veeck was smart enough to embrace the ensuing controversy. Even after the deal fell through, he milked it for every drop of publicity before announcing at a press conference, "Since the people are against trading Lou Boudreau, then I shout fervently that he will not be traded."

### A PINNACLE YEAR: 1948

In 1948 Boudreau was motivated to produce his best season. He was named the Most Valuable Player in the

American League as he led the Indians to their first World Series title in 28 years. It was a magical year for the team as it drew more than 2.6 million fans, a Cleveland record that would not be broken until 1995. Although the Indians remained one of the top teams in the American League for the next several seasons, 1948 was the pinnacle of achievement for the Cleveland Indians in the 20th century.

After the 1949 season Veeck was sued for divorce by his wife and was forced to sell the team to pay for the settlement. Over the next 35 years the Indians underwent numerous changes in ownership. The team enjoyed a stellar regular season in 1954, winning an American League-record 111 games, only to lose to the New York Giants in the World Series. The Indians fielded several competitive teams after that but were relegated for long stretches to the bottom half of the American League standings.

Attendance in the decaying Cleveland Stadium never approached the levels that Cleveland had reached under Veeck's leadership. Financially strapped, the Indians were poorly positioned to operate in the costly new era of free-agent players that began in the 1970s. Over the years, rumors circulated that the team would be relocated to Seattle, Atlanta, New Orleans, and other cities. During these years the Indians could boast of one achievement, at least. In 1974 it became the first major league team to hire an African-American manager, Frank Robinson.

## REGAINING A COMPETITIVE EDGE: THE EIGHTIES AND NINETIES

In 1986 the Indians were sold to real-estate developer Richard Jacobs for $35 million. Although improvement on the field was not realized immediately, the new management team invested heavily in player development and scouting as well as marketing. The Indians endured setbacks, such as losing a club record 105 games in 1991, but the most devastating moment since the death of Chapman occurred during spring training in 1993 when a boating accident took the lives of pitchers Tim Crews and Steve Olin, and severely injured Bob Ojeda. The final year in Cleveland Stadium was played with a pall cast over it, although the team played well in the second half of the season.

The Indians opened Jacobs Field, a state-of-the-art facility that ushered in a new era of excellence, in 1994. The team was in contention when a players' strike ended the 1994 season, and in 1995 the Indians continued their stellar play, finishing the year with baseball's best record. The team advanced to its first

World Series since 1954 but lost to the Atlanta Braves. As the Indians began to string together five consecutive division championships, and another World Series appearance, it set attendance records. The 1948 mark was finally broken in 1995 when 2.8 million fans attended Indians' games. The following year the team broke three million and began a consecutive regular-season sellout streak that stretched into the twenty-first century.

In 1998 the Indians became the first independent publicly traded Major League Baseball team when an initial public offering raised $60 million. The stock, however, did not perform well. It opened at $15 and soon dropped below $10. As successful as the Indians were, the club still reported a net loss in 1998 of $2.5 million. In May 1999, after Jacobs announced that he intended to sell the team, the stock rose to a level above $20.

In November 1999 the club announced that the team had been sold for $323 million to Ohio lawyer Lawrence J. Dolan. It was the largest amount ever paid for a baseball team, eclipsing the $311 million paid for the Los Angeles Dodgers the previous year. According to the *Wall Street Journal*, the price would have been higher if the Indians had played in a larger television market. Broadcast revenues for 1998 were only $19 million, compared to the Yankees' $50 million. The sale was approved in January 2000 by Major League Baseball. Shareholders of the Indians voted their approval of the deal the following month. On February 15, 2000, Dolan and family trusts assumed ownership of the team, delisted it from the NASDAQ, and took the company private once again.

## MANAGEMENT AND ROSTER CHANGES

Shortly after assuming control of the franchise, Dolan found himself confronting a number of daunting challenges. Prior to the 2000 season the club replaced longtime manager Mike Hargrove, who had led the Indians to five division titles and two World Series appearances in the 1990s, with team batting coach Charlie Manuel. Although Manuel's easygoing, self-deprecating style offered a stark contrast to Hargrove's businesslike focus, his ability to manage a major league team remained unproven.

Indeed, the 2000 season proved a major disappointment for the franchise, as the Indians missed the playoffs for the first time in six years. To make matters worse, the team lost its premiere slugger, outfielder Manny Ramirez, to free agency at the end of the season. Although the team offered the Ramirez a seven-year salary worth $119 million, that was ultimately trumped by an eight-year, $160 million offer from the Boston Red Sox. Around this time the team also traded away its star catcher, Sandy Alomar Jr., in order to avoid paying him an additional $2 million for a salary extension.

By 2001 the team's aging roster was also becoming a major cause for concern. Entering the season, the average age of the team's starting lineup was nearly 32 years old. At the same time, the club's payroll had swelled to $91.9 million, the fifth largest in the major leagues. Fan confidence in the hometown team appeared to be fading; in only the first week of the 2001 campaign, the team's consecutive home sellout streak came to an end at 455 games. Although the team still managed to earn a postseason berth at the end of the season, it failed to make it out of the first round of the playoffs. A short time later John Hart, regarded by many to be the principal architect of the team's run of success during the 1990s, stepped down as Indians general manager. He was replaced by Mark Shapiro, a Princeton University graduate in his mid-30s, who had been part of the Indians' front office for almost a decade.

Upon surveying the state of the Indians, Shapiro quickly determined that the club would need to embark in a different direction. At the core of Shapiro's new strategy was a focus on fiscal responsibility. From Shapiro's perspective, the team would need to come to terms with its financial limitations in order to construct a winning squad within its means. As a medium-market team, the Indians would never have the resources to pay for the game's elite players, a fact that had been painfully driven home by the loss of Ramirez in 2000. To remain competitive the Indians needed to bow out of the high-stakes free-agent market and place a greater emphasis on cultivating young, relatively inexpensive talent.

## CUTTING THE PAYROLL

By the spring of 2002 Shapiro had cut the team's payroll to just under $80 million, a reduction of more than 15 percent; by comparison, the payroll of the New York Yankees had grown to $135 million. In July of that year Shapiro made an even bolder roster move when he traded pitching ace Bartolo Colon to the Montreal Expos. Although the Indians received several promising prospects in the deal, the trade signified that the team had entered a rebuilding phase, alienating many fans. In the middle of its disappointing 2002 season, the team fired manager Manuel and replaced him with the team's third-base coach, Joel Skinner. At season's end Shapiro replaced Skinner with AAA manager Eric Wedge. In December of that year the Indians suffered another major public relations blow when Jim Thome, one of the team's most popular players from the 1990s, signed a free-agent contract with the Philadelphia Phillies.

Meanwhile, the team's new identity was beginning to take shape as a number of young stars began to earn spots on the major league roster. Among the more promising players to emerge during the early part of the decade were pitchers CC Sabathia and Cliff Lee, both of whom were under 25 years old at the beginning of the 2003 season. While the team's stockpile of young talent gave the front office reason for optimism, it nevertheless failed to impress the disenchanted fans of Cleveland. In 2003 attendance for home games dropped to roughly 1.7 million, compared to annual turnout of 3.6 million during the team's heyday in the late 1990s. On average, the Indians were attracting only 21,538 fans to each home game that year, despite dropping ticket prices. The Indians struggled in 2003, winning only 68 games. The franchise also suffered serious financial losses during the first half of the decade. Between 2000 and 2005, the team posted losses of roughly $65 million.

By the middle of the 2005 season, however, the young Indians finally began to emerge as legitimate contenders. In a three-month span between early June and early September the team notched a 50-32 record as a new generation of team leaders, among them center fielder Grady Sizemore and catcher Victor Martinez, began to emerge. This success came despite the fact that the team's payroll had dropped to $41.5 million, fifth lowest in the majors. Although the team fell just short of the playoffs, its ability to compete on a limited budget was beginning to attract favorable attention from a number of baseball insiders. Among the notable voices praising Cleveland's small-market business model was famed sportswriter and ESPN commentator Peter Gammons, who lauded Shapiro's work with the team in a 2005 interview with the *Cleveland Plain Dealer*. At the same time, attendance began to increase slightly, rising to nearly 2 million for both 2005 and 2006.

## RETURN TO THE POSTSEASON

In 2007 the Indians returned to the postseason for the first time since 2002, anchored by ace starting pitcher Sabathia. The team's defeat of the New York Yankees in the first round of the playoffs was particularly gratifying, especially considering that three Yankee starters (Alex Rodriguez, Jason Giambi, and Derek Jeter) earned more money that year than the entire Indians major league roster. Although the team ultimately fell to the Boston Red Sox in the American League Championship Series, the team's success had begun to bring fans back to the ballpark. Wedge was named American League manager of the year, and Sabathia earned his first Cy Young Award. Meanwhile, the *Sporting News* named general manager Shapiro the Executive of the Year.

In January 2008 the Jacobs Field sign was taken down from the ballpark as the team prepared to play its first season in the newly renamed Progressive Field. The Indians failed to build on their promising 2007 campaign, however, and by midseason it was forced to trade Sabathia. From a financial standpoint, the move was shrewd; the team had little chance of re-signing the star pitcher when he became a free agent at the end of the 2008 season, so it opted to trade him for young prospects while it could. Nonetheless, the trade irritated the team's fans, who saw it as evidence that the Indians were conceding defeat for the season. A year later, confronting a similar dilemma, Shapiro dealt pitcher Lee and catcher Martinez, and as the disappointing 2009 season came to an end he fired manager Wedge. By 2010 the Indians bore little resemblance to the club that had nearly reached the World Series only two years earlier. Whether or not the Indians were poised to rebound with another crop of young stars remained to be seen.

*Ed Dinger*
*Updated, Stephen Meyer*

## PRINCIPAL COMPETITORS

Chicago White Sox Ltd.; Detroit Tigers Baseball Club, Inc.; Kansas City Royals Baseball Corporation; Minnesota Twins Baseball Club.

## FURTHER READING

Arangure, Jorge, Jr., "Since Trade, Cleveland Finally Rocks," *Washington Post*, September 7, 2005, p. E3.

*Baseball: The Biographical Encyclopedia*, New York: Total Sports, 2000.

Mellinger, Sam, "Rapid Rebuilding; Indians GM Tore Up a Contender in 2001, but He's Built It Back Up with Young Guns and Low Payroll," *Kansas City (MO) Star*, May 21, 2006, p. C5.

Ocker, Sheldon, "Makeover Just Won't Do; Struggling Indians Can't Keep Shuffling Around Pitchers, Players," *Akron (OH) Beacon Journal*, May 24, 2009, p. C9.

Pluto, Terry, "Indians' Way of Business Gains Respect in Baseball," *Cleveland (OH) Plain Dealer*, November 15, 2007, p. D1.

———, *Our Tribe*, New York: Simon & Schuster, 1999.

Smith, Robert L., "Jacobs Field Sign Removed from Cleveland Indians' Ballpark; Now, Just a Memory," *Cleveland (OH) Plain Dealer*, January 19, 2008, p. A1.

Thomas, George M., "Build Winning Team, and Fans Will Come; Indians Struggling to Plump Attendance, Restore Fervor," *Akron (OH) Beacon Journal*, April 1, 2007, p. C8.

Thorn, John, and Pete Palmer, *Total Baseball*, New York: Warner Books, 1999.

Walker, Sam, "Attorney Set to Buy Cleveland Indians in $320 Million Deal," *Wall Street Journal*, November 5, 1999, p. B2.

# Cloverdale Paint Inc.

**6950 King George Boulevard**
**Surrey, British Columbia V3W 4Z1**
**Canada**
**Telephone: (604) 596-6261**
**Fax: (604) 597-2677**
**Web site: http://cloverdalepaint.com**

*Private Company*
*Founded:* 1933
*Employees:* 1,100
*Sales:* $237 million (2009 est.)
*NAICS:* 325510 Paint and Coating Manufacturing;
444120 Paint and Wallpaper Stores

■ ■ ■

Cloverdale Paint Inc. is a privately owned, regional paint company that operates five manufacturing plants and more than 100 retail outlets in western Canada and in the U.S. Pacific Northwest. Founded in 1933, the company began as a small, family-owned operation in a small town in British Columbia. The company grew throughout the 20th century, and by the 21st century sold its products to a variety of commercial, industrial, and do-it-yourself customers throughout western Canada and the northwestern United States, as well as in some foreign markets. Cloverdale and its subsidiaries employed about 1,100 people in 2010. In the first decade of the 21st century, Cloverdale embarked on a series of acquisitions, most notably of Rodda Paint Company, another family-owned company based in Portland, Oregon, as part of an aggressive growth strategy. This strategy allowed Cloverdale to move from 29th on the *Paint & Coatings Industry* annual list of the largest paint and coatings manufacturers in North America in 2001 to 14th in 2009.

## FOUNDING AND EARLY GROWTH: 1933

Cloverdale Paint was founded in 1933 by Rudy Henke on his farm near Cloverdale in British Columbia, Canada. His business steadily grew, attracting the attention of Hunter Vogel, who bought a 50 percent stake in the company in 1946. It was Vogel's vision that fueled the rapid growth of the company in the subsequent decades. Vogel's son, Walter "Wink" Vogel, joined the company in the 1950s, and the father and son team opened branches across western Canada, including in the Vancouver market. Their combined vision was responsible for phenomenal growth. In the late 1960s Cloverdale acquired Monarch Paint, expanding its retail presence, and built a factory in Surrey, British Columbia. In the seven-year span between 1968 and 1975, the company doubled in size.

Cloverdale's phenomenal growth was fueled in part by its acquisition of a color-matching machine, the first in the region, as well as research and development of industrial coatings in the 1970s, essentially opening up an entirely new market for the company. Cloverdale developed both baked and air dry enamels, specializing in maintenance coatings for machinery in the oil and gas industry as well as fabricators, equipment for the forestry industry, and marine applications.

At the same time, research and development teams continued to make technological advances in the company's architectural coatings. The subsequent decade saw continued expansion. Intelligent marketing decisions powered much of this growth. By the 1990s the company began to open retail stores over the border in Washington in the northwestern United States. The company also began marketing their architectural paints to large paint contractors and institutional buyers during this period, further fueling sales growth.

Environmental issues came to the forefront during the 1990s. A Canadian environmental law passed in 1994 required paint companies to collect unused waste paint, the largest proportion of household hazardous waste, and either recycle it or dispose of it properly. In British Columbia, 47 small paint companies, including Cloverdale, banded together into the BC Paint Care Association. Unlike larger retailers, which accepted waste paint at their retail locations, the Paint Care Association worked with municipalities in the province to set up waste paint collection sites within existing waste collection infrastructures. The collection sites were funded by charging customers a small "eco" fee when they bought a four-liter can of paint. More stringent air-quality regulations in both Canada and the United States also forced the company to turn its attention to developing or acquiring an environmentally-friendly paint with lower volatile organic compounds (VOCs) by the beginning of the 21st century.

## AN ACQUISITIONS STRATEGY IN THE EARLY 21ST CENTURY

In the first decade of the new century, Cloverdale looked to mergers and acquisitions as a key to the company's expansion. In 2001 Cloverdale acquired Northern Paint Canada, Inc., a manufacturer and paint wholesaler, from Reimer World Corporation. That acquisition helped

Cloverdale expand into the Canadian province of Manitoba. In 2002 Cloverdale Paint acquired Fargo Paint & Chemicals, another small Canadian paint company based in Calgary. This gave Cloverdale another manufacturing plant in Calgary. The company maintained Fargo's brands as part of its own product portfolio. Both companies became wholly owned subsidiaries of Cloverdale Paint.

The biggest merger occurred in 2004, when Cloverdale and Rodda Paint of Portland, Oregon, joined forces, with Rodda becoming a U.S. subsidiary of Cloverdale. The combined company, Charles W. Thurston reported in *Coatings World*, would produce 10 million gallons of paint per year, creating a "family-controlled powerhouse in northwestern North America." The companies hoped that the strategy would allow them to continue to compete with huge companies like Sherwin-Williams of Cleveland as well as large do-it-yourself big-box stores like Home Depot and Lowe's. The two companies maintained their names and brands. Cloverdale Paint was primarily sold in Canada, while Rodda Paint was marketed in Alaska, Washington, and Oregon. Wink Vogel remained the CEO of the combined companies, while Tom Braden, previously chairman of the board at Rodda, maintained minority ownership and sat on the combined company's board of directors.

Jonathan Brinckman, commenting on the merger in *The Oregonian*, noted that such mergers were part of increasing consolidation within the paint industry. Because paint is heavy and transportation costs are large, traditionally the industry was very decentralized. However, as profit margins narrowed, companies began to merge in order to maximize profits from some economies of scale. In 1975 approximately 1,500 paint companies were operating in the United States alone. By 2005 only about 350 remained in operation.

Rodda brought with it into the merger an award-winning, environmentally-friendly paint line called Horizon. Horizon was first introduced in 1995, and was the first low-VOC exterior paint and one of the first low-VOC interior paints to earn the Green Seal endorsement. Sales climbed each year in the decade after Horizon first came on the market, jumping especially after Rodda was named the Businesses for an Environmentally Sustainable Tomorrow (BEST) award-winning paint line by the Office of Sustainable Development of Portland in 2004. On receiving that designation, vice president of marketing for Rodda, Todd Braden, told *Coatings World*, "We believe that high quality, environmentally responsible paints are the future of the paint and coatings industry." In the first half of 2005, Rodda sold 55,000 gallons of the "green" paint

## KEY DATES

**1933:** Cloverdale Paint is founded by Rudy Henke.
**1946:** Partner Hunter Vogel buys a 50 percent share in the company.
**1994:** Cloverdale Paints joins with other small paint manufacturers in the BC Paint Care Association.
**2005:** Cloverdale Paints and Rodda Paint merge.
**2008:** Cloverdale acquires Guertin Coatings, Sealants and Polymers Ltd.

line, compared to just 23,000 gallons during the same period in 2004, a sales spike of nearly 140 percent.

After the merger with Rodda, Cloverdale continued its acquisitions strategy. In 2008 Cloverdale bought Guertin Coatings, Sealants and Polymers Ltd., a Winnipeg company that produced industrial coatings, resins, sealants and adhesives. As it had with Rodda, Cloverdale intended to maintain Guertin as a separate entity with its own products and brands. The acquisition gave Cloverdale a total of five manufacturing plants and more than 100 corporate branches in western Canada and the Pacific Northwest of the United States.

## POISED FOR FUTURE SUCCESS: 2010

In 2010 Cloverdale Paint appeared poised for continued success. Having grown its sales from $65 million in 2001 to an estimated $237 million in 2009, the company's acquisitions strategy seemed to be paying off, and its latest acquisition of Guertin Coatings suggested management would continue this strategy in the foreseeable future. In addition, Cloverdale's focus on low-VOC products, such as its Horizon paint line initially developed by Rodda, gave it somewhat of a niche market in the Pacific Northwest, and other low-VOC products were in the works. Lis Weller, marketing manager of Rodda Paint, told Tim Wright in *Coatings World* of new low-VOC wood lacquers that had recently come on the market in 2010.

While the global economic recession affected the company's bottom line, Cloverdale focused on diversifying into additional market sectors. Weller told Wright

that with increasing consolidation among competitors, especially large competitors like Home Depot and Lowe's, the company had focused during the recession on keeping cost to consumers, industrial clients, and contractors down by "trimming the fat" in the manufacturing process and reducing profit margins. A paint stewardship law in Oregon that required manufacturers to set up a system to collect post-consumer architectural paint by July 1, 2010, similar to the law passed in Canada in 1994, was an additional challenge. Nevertheless, while big-box retailers continued to expand their market share, Cloverdale managed to stay competitive in the early 21st century.

*Melissa J. Doak*

## PRINCIPAL SUBSIDIARIES

Rodda Paint Co.; Fargo Paint & Chemicals, Inc.; Guertin Coatings, Sealants & Polymers Ltd.

## PRINCIPAL COMPETITORS

The Sherwin-Williams Company; Benjamin Moore and Co.; Home Hardware Stores Limited.

## FURTHER READING

Brinckman, Jonathan, "Inside Oregon Business: Color Them Confident," *The Oregonian*, April 29, 2005, p. B1.

"Cloverdale Paint Purchases Guertin Coatings, Sealants and Polymers," *Paint & Coatings Industry*, May 2008, p. 30.

"Cloverdale Paints Inks Industrial Coatings Deal," *Chemical Week*, March 24, 2008, p. 41.

McCullough, Cody, "Portland 'Green' Paint Lines Continue to Boom," *Daily Journal of Commerce, Portland*, June 24, 2005.

"Paint Industry Begins Implementing BC Product Stewardship Regulations," *Business & the Environment*, March 1995.

Parker, Karen, "PCI Reflects Industry Consolidation," *Paint & Coatings Industry*, July 1, 2009.

"Rodda Wins 'BEST' Award for Horizon Paint Line," *Coatings World*, June 2004, pp. 10–11.

Thurston, Charles W., "Combined Forces: with Their Merger Completed, Rodda Paint and Cloverdale Look for Greater Regional Strength," *Coatings World*, September 2004, p. 37.

Wright, Tim, "The U.S. Interior Decorative Coatings Market: U.S. Paint Manufacturers Including Benjamin Moore, Kelly-Moore, Rodda Paint and Dunn-Edwards Discuss Key Issues in the Interior Decorative Coatings Market," *Coatings World*, January 2010, pp. 24–27.

# Coal India Limited

10 Netaji Subhas Road
Kolkata, West Bengal 700001
India
Telephone: (+91 33) 2248-8099
Fax: (+91 33) 2243-5316
Web site: http://www.coalindia.in

*Government-owned Company*
*Founded:* 1975
*Incorporated:* 1975
*Employees:* 409,332
*Sales:* INR 520.88 billion ($11.12 billion) (2009–10)
*NAICS:* 212111 Bituminous Coal and Lignite Surface
Mining; 212112 Bituminous Coal Underground
Mining; 212113 Anthracite Mining; 213113 Support Activities for Coal Mining

■ ■ ■

Coal India Limited (CIL) is the largest coal producer in the world, with proven fuel reserves exceeding 100 billion tons. The company is involved in diverse aspects of coal production, including extraction, exploration, and mine planning. CIL is wholly owned by the Government of India and accounts for more than 80 percent of the nation's total coal output. Coal India plays a central role in the Indian coal mining industry, and its performance and operations very much reflect the government's policies and priorities. By the 21st century, as the Indian economy enjoyed unprecedented growth, CIL found itself unable to keep up with rising demand. To address this challenge, the company began to explore new mining opportunities in foreign markets, notably in Africa and Australia.

## ORIGINS: FROM THE NINETEENTH CENTURY TO THE SEVENTIES

The Indian coal industry has its origins in the early 19th century, when mining activity became commercial in conjunction with the expansion of the railway network, particularly in the west of the country. The monopoly interests of the British East India Company were revoked in 1813. Initially the coalfields were operated by a large number of Indian private companies that possessed captive (company-owned) coalfields to support their iron and steel works. By 1900 there were 34 companies producing 7 million tons of coal from 286 mines. Production continued to grow in the first half of the 20th century, especially during World War I and World War II, and production reached 29 million tons by 1945. By then the number of companies had increased to 307 and the number of mines to 673. The trend continued for almost a decade after India's independence in 1947.

India's ambitious economic development plans led to a tremendous demand for energy, and in the absence of alternative sources, coal was targeted as the major source of power for industrialization. Under the government's second five-year economic development plan, covering the years 1957 to 1961, a target of 60 million tons was set for the end of the plan period. However, government economic planners were convinced that the private sector would be unable to meet this target. Therefore, the National Coal Development Corporation (NCDC) was formed, which took the old railway collieries as its nucleus and opened new mines as well. Production of coal increased from 38 million tons in 1956 to 56 million tons in 1961.

During the 1960s most of India's collieries continued to be operated by the private sector, with the exception of NCDC and the Singareni Collieries, both in the public sector. At the national level, three factors emerged to force the government to consider nationalizing the coal industry. First, there was a fear that contemporary mining methods were leading to great waste. Second, the government predicted that future demand for coal would be particularly heavy in view of its industrial development priorities. Finally, during India's third five-year plan period of 1962 to 1966, as well as the period from 1966 to 1969, despite the increase in production, there was a shortfall in private capital investment in the industry.

From 1971 to 1973 the government carried out a series of nationalizations of the privately owned coal companies in a major effort to increase production and overcome the country's shortage of coal. At the time of the nationalizations, total coal production in the country was 72 million tons, and the industry had been passing through cycles of shortages and surpluses that prevented effective planning for expansion and modernization. More than 900 mines were in operation, some of which were producing only a few thousand tons of coal a month, and methods of mining were obsolete.

## THE EARLY YEARS OF COAL INDIA LIMITED: 1972–80

Coking coal mines, with the exception of the Tata Iron and Steel Company, were nationalized in May 1972, and a new public-sector company, Bharat Coking Coal Limited (BCCL), was created to manage them. In May 1973 the non-coking coal mines were also nationalized and brought under the control of the Coal Mines Authority (CMA). The Department of Coal was set up in the Ministry of Energy to oversee the public-sector

companies. Further reorganization of the industry led to the formation of Coal India Ltd. (CIL), which also absorbed NCDC, in November 1975. The reorganization involved placing the majority of the public-sector coal companies under CIL. CIL originally had six subsidiaries, five of which were involved in production: BCCL at Dhanbad, Central Coalfields Limited at Ranchi, Western Coalfields Limited (WCL) at Nagpur, Eastern Coalfields Limited (ECL) at Sanctoria, and North Eastern Coalfields Limited (NECL) at Margherita. The sixth was the Central Planning & Design Institute at Ranchi. Together with the Neyveli Lignite Corporation (NLC), CIL was operated directly by the Indian government through the Department of Coal in the Ministry of Energy. All the subsidiaries of CIL had the status of independent companies, but the authority for framing broad policies and taking administrative decisions rested with CIL.

The structure of the Indian coal industry during the 1970s and 1980s was a reflection of the priorities placed by the government on coal as a source of fuel and energy in economic development. Most of the production was the responsibility of the five subsidiaries of CIL, but there were four other coal producers in the public sector: the Singareni Collieries Limited, the government of Jammu and Kashmir collieries, the Damodar Valley Corporation, and the Indian Iron & Steel Co. Ltd. These last four concerns were responsible for about 10 percent of the output. About 2 percent of the total output of coal was provided by the captive mines (company-owned mines that ensure coal supplies) of the Tata Iron and Steel Company, the only coal producer in the private sector.

Financially, the subsidiaries of CIL had an average authorized capital of INR 1.5 billion each during the late 1980s. Each employed between 100,000 and 180,000 people and had annual sales of between INR 1.1 and INR 1.7 billion. Their shares in the total production of coal varied from 25 percent for the Central and Western Coalfields to about 20 percent for Bharat Coking Coal and Eastern Coalfields. The financial performance of the subsidiaries also varied. BCCL reported cumulative losses of INR 4.5 billion over the five-year period of 1981 to 1986. Similarly, Eastern Coalfields reported cumulative losses of INR 3.6 billion over the same five-year period. In 1988 BCCL reported a loss of INR 900 million on sales of INR 5.3 billion. However, in the same year the Neyveli Lignite Corporation Limited announced a profit of INR 570 million on sales of INR 1.9 billion.

As a result of the nationalizations, some reorganization took place in the sector. The mines were regrouped and reduced to 350 individual mines. New technology

# KEY DATES

**1972:** Coking coal mines are nationalized; Bharat Coking Coal Ltd. (BCCL) is created to manage them.

**1973:** Non-coking coal mines are nationalized and brought under the control of the Coal Mines Authority (CMA).

**1975:** Coal India Ltd. (CIL) is formed as a holding company for five production subsidiaries.

**1980:** Coal mining production exceeds 100 million tons.

**1990:** CIL invests $250 million in longwall mining; the company approves five projects worth $712 million to increase production.

**1992:** The firm exports coal to Bangladesh for the first time.

**1997:** India begins to deregulate coal pricing and distribution.

**2001:** The Indian government starts a restructuring plan for CIL in hopes of returning its subsidiaries to profitability.

**2006:** CIL creates Coal Vidhesh Ltd. (CVL), a division dedicated to exploring investment opportunities in overseas coal markets.

**2009:** Indian government reveals plan to sell 10 percent stake in CIL through an initial public offering.

was introduced, and there was a shift from pick mining to blast mining, which resulted in considerable increases in production. The latter totaled 87 million tons in 1975, and 99 million tons in 1976. CIL's share of total production was about 88 percent. Nationalization was intended to provide the basis for modernizing the coal industry, but after the initial increase in production, output stagnated from 1976 to 1980. This was the result of shortages of power and explosives, labor unrest, absenteeism, excessive employment, and technical inefficiencies, as well as problems of flooding in the western coalfields and fires in the vast Jharia coalfield. During the 1980s Jharia possessed the largest known coking coal reserves in the country, and ongoing fires since around 1931 accounted for the loss of some 40 billion tons of coking coal by 1980. Consequently, CIL's financial performance was poor during this period, and it suffered losses from 1976 to 1981. These losses peaked at INR 2.4 billion in 1978–79 but came down to INR 882 million the following year, and came down even further to

INR 337 million the year after. Total losses for the five-year period were almost INR 6 billion.

## PRODUCTION CHALLENGES: 1980–83

Production picked up in 1980 when it finally exceeded 100 million tons, and it increased to 115 million tons by 1983. However, the problems suffered by CIL in particular and the coal industry in general had led to considerable shortages, especially for industrial users. This shortage was compounded by the poor quality of India's coking coal. This is coal from which the volatile elements have been removed, making it suitable as a fuel and for metallurgical purposes. It has difficult washing characteristics and requires the coal preparation plants to run extremely complex processes. The result was that the country had to import coal from abroad, a trend that persists. The bulk of the imported coal came from the United States, Australia, and Canada, and it was significantly more expensive than locally produced coal. This situation had two implications. First, it became feasible for CIL to adopt more expensive mining methods, because this was still less expensive than importing coal. Second, a need was perceived to improve the coal-handling facilities at India's major ports. This need was reflected in the country's sixth five-year plan, when it was projected that the ports would have to handle at least 4.4 million tons of imported coal by the mid-1980s.

During the sixth five-year plan, coal production grew at 6.2 percent per year, especially in the open-cast mines. Targeted production for the end of the plan period, in 1984 and 1985, was for 165 million tons per annum, although actual production fell short at 148 million tons. During the first two years of the plan, CIL made a profit for the first time in its history. This was largely because the Indian government increased the price of coal in both February 1981 and May 1982. The issue of pricing had always been a serious problem for the Indian coal industry and for CIL. Coal prices had been administered by the government since 1941, with the exception of a period of seven years, from 1967 to 1974. The pricing formula was based on an Indian industry-wide average with differentials for different grades, but in practice the price was usually set below the industry's average cost. This practice may explain in part CIL's poor overall financial performance.

Coal production in the year 1981–82 was 125 million tons, which was more than the targeted figure. Total production of coal and lignite was 146 million metric tons in 1983–84, and this increased steadily to 207 million tons in 1988–89. Despite the increase in production, problems related to operations, such as cost overruns, poor quality, and low productivity, meant that the targeted output was frequently revised downward. Part of the problem was the high cost of new equipment, which necessitated new investment and led to budget overruns. Furthermore, the number of mines, which had been reduced immediately following nationalization, had increased to 684 by 1982. This negated some of the initial cost-reduction benefits of reorganization.

## ADAPTING TO NEW MARKET CONDITIONS: 1984–93

Because coal was meeting over 70 percent of the energy requirements of the rapidly expanding Indian industry, CIL believed the output needed to increase by 25 million tons a year during the 1980s to keep up with demand. The structure of demand for coal had changed. The railways were no longer the primary source of demand for coal. Rather, the primary consumers were now steel plants, other industrial units, and thermal power stations. The reliance on coal-fired thermal power plants for power generation led to a steady increase in the demand for coal throughout this period. To satisfy this demand, CIL relied primarily on the expansion of open-pit mines. Mining coal from shallow seams was financially sound, but it resulted in a steady deterioration of coal quality over time. The seventh five-year plan, which began in 1985, included some important changes introduced by CIL in the structure of its production.

The plan had set a production target of 226 million tons for coal, and by 1988–89, output for coal alone, excluding lignite, had reached 195 million tons. As a result of the greater need for coal, new opportunities were created for international partnerships in the coal sector throughout the 1980s. CIL signed agreements with the Soviet Union, United Kingdom, Poland, and France for the construction and development of new mines and the introduction of new technology. The agreement with the Soviet Union called for investment in the Jayant open-cast project with a production capacity of 10 million tons a year, as well as a number of other projects. The output from both surface and underground mining was to be increased through additional investment. Open-cast mining (or surface mining) was expected to provide an increased share of total production, from about 30 percent in 1980 to 56 percent in 1990. One of the major factors in increasing underground production was the introduction of additional longwall faces. Longwall mining differs from the traditional board-and-pillar method of underground mining in that the seams are at a greater depth and the capital costs are higher because of the complexity and greater powered support in the mining.

During the 1990s a series of new developments occurred in an attempt to increase production of the Indian coal-mining industry. In February 1990 CIL decided to invest $250 million in longwall mining from 1990 to 1995. This development was projected to increase the powered-support longwall faces from 14 in 1990 to 28 in 1995, and 47 in the year 2000. Longwall coal production, allowing deeper seams to be worked, was also estimated to increase to 9 million metric tons by 1995. In April 1990 CIL also approved five additional projects, worth some $712 million, as part of its program to increase output to meet the needs of industry into the 21st century. During the 1990–91 fiscal year CIL lost INR 2.5 billion. However, by 1992, production began to increase, and the company was able to boast a small profit. During the year, CIL began exporting coal to Bangladesh for the first time in its history and secured contracts worth $5 million.

Despite increases in output of almost 9 percent per annum during the duration of the seventh five-year plan, serious coal shortages existed due to CIL's inability to meet specific needs, such as the provision of high-quality coking and non-coking coal. CIL's distribution system remained poor, and the Indian Railway system was already heavily overloaded. Consequently, there were cost overruns and a buildup of coal reserves at the pitheads. Furthermore, many of the targeted output figures were based on projects sanctioned but not completed by CIL, thus adding to infrastructural and distribution problems. This problem was compounded by poor coal quality, the system of pricing, and CIL's financial position. The Indian government knew that if coal was to be a major source of energy and fuel in the future, CIL had be able to generate sufficient resources internally to meet its investment requirements. In this context, the government continued to show concern about the financial performance of CIL well into the 1990s. About 100 of the 248 corporations owned by the Indian government were heavy loss makers, and CIL was no exception. As such, CIL was being seriously considered as a candidate for major restructuring during the early 1990s.

## RESTRUCTURING TO MEET RISING DEMAND: 1993–2000

In 1994 India amended its Coal Mines Nationalization Act to allow foreign companies to hold a 51 percent stake in Indian coal mines. The amendment also enabled foreign and private power companies to operate their own coal mines. Since 1973 the government had only allowed steel plants to run captive mines in the private sector. Indian officials hoped that the relaxed laws would encourage investment in Indian coal mining, an industry whose demand was growing at a rapid clip.

At the same time, the import duty on non-coking coal fell from 85 to 35 percent. The reduction enticed coal-consuming industries to seek imports of coal with a higher calorific value and lower ash content than Indian mined coal. With the threat of increased imports cutting into CIL's production, the company began to petition the government to allow it to fix its coal prices as well as its production targets.

By the late 1990s the Indian government was fearful that CIL and the entire mining industry would not be able to keep up with the rising demand for coal. India was known for its large amount of coal reserves, but in the past it had been unable to keep pace with the demand. In 1997 the country began reforming the industry to further encourage investment and exploration and to deregulate pricing and distribution in the industry. It also requested $1 billion from the World Bank to restructure CIL's operations. The loan was used to purchase new machinery and to build new coal-handling plants.

During that time, CIL was also feeling increased pressure from international competition. Major coal-producing countries, including Australia, South Africa, Indonesia, and Columbia, began eyeing the lucrative Indian market as a potential gold mine for their low-cost coal. As such, CIL management pleaded with its subsidiaries to cut costs and increase production. Profits, gross sales, and production fell in 1999.

In fact, by 2000 CIL had a poor image throughout the coal industry. Three major subsidiaries (Eastern Coalfields Ltd., Central Coalfields Ltd., and Bharat Coking Coal Ltd.) were in financial trouble, and the company was not meeting safety standards when compared with other international coal-mining companies. During 2001 the Indian government scrutinized CIL, its subsidiaries, and its management. Allegations ranged from misuse of company finances to illegal mining for profit. CIL's record of project completion also came under fire. Since nationalization, only 298 out of 401 government-sanctioned projects were completed, and more than 70 had been delayed.

As CIL neared the end of 2001, its future remained uncertain. The Ministry of Coal was considering merging the seven coal-producing subsidiaries of CIL into one unit in order to reduce tax-related costs. CIL pledged to focus on meeting demand, raising the productivity of its coal-mining operations, and restoring its subsidiaries to profitability.

## NEW PRESSURES IN AN AGE OF RAPID ECONOMIC GROWTH: 2001–10

By the early years of the new century, CIL accounted for approximately 85 percent of the nation's total coal output. During this period the company's production rate increased steadily, rising from 268 million metric tons of coal in 2001 to 307 metric tons in 2004. Unfortunately, this growth rate was unable to match an even swifter spike in demand over the same time frame. As a result, India was importing roughly 22 million metric tons of coal a year during these years, a figure that was projected to double by the end of the decade if the domestic coal industry was unable to boost production significantly. CIL's inability to keep up with demand made it the subject of intensified government scrutiny, and the nation's economic ministers exerted pressure on the company to identify new means of becoming more efficient.

In August 2004 the government requested that CIL's consulting subsidiary, Central Mine Planning and Development Institute Limited, produce a plan outlining how the company could mechanize a greater portion of its existing mining operations. While virtually all of the company's open-cast mines were mechanized by this point, only a small percentage of its underground mines had been fully modernized. In April 2004 the company operated 555 mines throughout India, 305 of which were underground. However, less than a third of CIL's underground mines were mechanized. According to government estimates, the company had the capacity to mechanize an additional 110 underground mines.

In addition to this emphasis on improved mining techniques, by mid-decade CIL began to seek other ways to expand its coal output capacity. In early 2005 the company launched a new online auctioning process for selling coal, a system that enabled the company to earn an additional $20 per metric ton of coal. By March of that year roughly 8 percent of the company's coal revenues were being generated by online sales. At the same time, CIL embarked on an ambitious overseas growth strategy aimed at expanding its total proven coal reserves. In the fall of 2005 CIL joined the Steel Authority of India Limited (SAIL) on an economic mission to Indonesia, with the goal of gaining government approval to establish mining operations in the island nation. In mid-2006 the company created a new division, Coal Vidhesh Ltd. (CVL), dedicated to pursuing growth opportunities abroad. Working in collaboration with two government-owned steel firms, SAIL and Vizag, CVL began to study overseas regions with high potential for coal exploration, notably in Bangladesh and Zimbabwe.

In spite of these positive steps, CIL continued to struggle during the second half of the decade. In December 2006 the Indian Supreme Court declared CIL's online auctioning process to be illegal, forcing the company to abandon one of its most profitable revenue streams. By October 2007 CIL was facing a new wave of financial pressures, including a government-mandated wage hike and an overall decline in domestic production. In the face of these challenges, CIL's global strategy became more critical, not only for its own growth but also for the sustained growth of the nation's economy. In March 2008 the company revealed its intention to purchase mines in a range of new markets, including Australia and South Africa, while also establishing research partnerships with firms in China, Australia, and the United Kingdom.

Meanwhile, major shifts in Indian economic policy created new avenues for CIL's future growth. In August 2009 the government announced a plan to divest roughly 10 percent of its ownership in CIL through an initial public offering. According to analysts, the move was aimed primarily at attracting foreign investment into India's coal industry. Scheduled for sometime in 2010, the IPO was projected to raise roughly INR 60 billion ($1.22 billion). In August 2009 the company earmarked $1.5 billion for investment in overseas assets. By the following April, CIL was in negotiations with Australian coal producer Peabody Energy to acquire four mines on the continent. Indeed, the increased attention to foreign expansion was becoming increasingly urgent. In a report issued in March 2010, CIL officials estimated that domestic coal demand would exceed the company's output by 235 million metric tons by 2011–12. Clearly, CIL would need to become fully committed to increasing its production capacity in order to meet the future needs of India's rapidly growing economy.

*Sarah Ahmad Khan*
*Updated, Christina M. Stansell; Stephen Meyer*

## PRINCIPAL SUBSIDIARIES

Bharat Coking Coal Limited; Central Coalfields Limited; Central Mine Planning & Design Institute Ltd.; Eastern Coalfields Limited; Mahanadi Coalfields Limited; Northern Coalfields Limited; South Eastern Coalfields Limited; Western Coalfields Limited.

## PRINCIPAL DIVISIONS

Coal Vidhesh Ltd.

## PRINCIPAL COMPETITORS

BHP Billiton Limited (Australia); RAG Aktiengesellschaft (Germany); Rio Tinto Limited (Australia).

## FURTHER READING

Chambers, Matt, "Coal India Looking for Coal Alliances," *Australian*, April 14, 2010, p. 32.

"Coal India Gets Funds to Expand," *Power Generation Technology and Markets*, September 26, 1997, p. 1.

Cooper, Mike, "Imports Alone Cannot Bridge India's Huge Coal Demand-Supply Gap: Coal India Director," *Platts International Coal Report*, March 15, 2010, p. 1.

"India: Minister Upset with CIL, Subsidiaries," *Business Line*, April 30, 2001.

"India: Whither Coal India?" *Business Line*, October 1, 2001.

"Major Changes in CIL on the Cards," *Statesman* (India), September 13, 2001.

Murty, B. S., and S. P. Panda, *Indian Coal Industry and the Coal Mines*. Delhi: Discovery Publishing House, 1988.

"New Projects to Spur Jump in Indian Coal Production," *Journal of Commerce*, March 16, 1992, p. 6B.

Nicholson, Mark, "India Opens Up Coal Mining to Avert Threatened Shortfall," *Financial Times* (London), February 13, 1997, p. 6.

Varma, S. C., "Coal: Its Extraction and Utilization in India," *World Coal*, July 1979.

# Consolidated Contractors Company

———■———

**P.O. Box 61092**
**62b Kifissias Avenue, Maroussi**
**Athens, 15110**
**Greece**
**Telephone: (30) 210 618 2000**
**Fax: (30) 210 619 9224**
**Web site: http://www.ccc.gr**

*Private Company*
*Incorporated:* 1952
*Employees:* 165,750 (2008)
*Sales:* $5.6 billion (2008) (est.)
*NAICS:* 213111 Drilling Oil and Gas Wells; 236210 Industrial Building Construction; 236220 Commercial and Institutional Building Construction; 237110 Water and Sewer Line and Related Structures Construction; 237310 Highway, Street, and Bridge Construction; 237990 Other Heavy and Civil Engineering Construction; 238120 Structural Steel and Precast Concrete Contractors; 541330 Engineering Services

■ ■ ■

Consolidated Contractors Company (CCC) is a leading transnational contractor, the largest Arab construction firm operating in the Middle East, and one of the 20 largest contractors in the world, operating predominantly in the petrochemicals industry. The company provides engineering, project-management, procurement, and complete construction services. Based in Athens, Greece, CCC employs approximately 165,000 people of more than 60 nationalities on four continents, although more than half of its employees work in the Middle East. The company is known for developing and building structures in some of the most volatile regions of the world. Less than 10 percent of the firm's activities involve investment dealings and utilities management.

## COMPANY ORIGINS: 1951–52

CCC's roots can be traced principally to two of its three cofounders, Hasib Sabbagh and Said Khoury, who joined together to create one of the first Arab construction companies. Sabbagh was born into a Catholic family in Tiberias in what was then Palestine, while Khoury was born a Greek Orthodox Christian in nearby Safad. Both men studied civil engineering at the American University in Beirut, which would later become a prime source of CCC employee talent. Both men also were involved in the establishment of contracting companies after graduation, Sabbagh in Haifa and Khoury in Safad.

Following the establishment of the state of Israel in 1948, however, Sabbagh and Khoury along with their families fled to Lebanon, where the two men teamed up in their first venture together, a contract to build an airport in Tripoli, Lebanon, in 1950. The following year, the partners secured a subcontract to construct an oil pipe storage yard in Syria for Iraq Petroleum Co., a predecessor of British Petroleum (BP), which was building a pipeline from Iraq to Lebanon across the Syrian Desert. This contract proved fortuitous for Sabbagh and Khoury, as it introduced them to the San Francisco–based Bechtel Corporation, the world's largest construction company.

In 1952 the young firm landed a deal as a subcontractor for Bechtel to construct an oil refinery and workers' camp in Aden, Yemen, for the Iraq-to-Lebanon pipeline. That same year, CCC was formally established, with headquarters in Beirut. Sabbagh, Khoury, and their friend Kamel Abdul-Rahman became sole owners and partners of CCC. After the company's successful work in Aden, "there was sort of an understanding that wherever Bechtel went in the Middle East, and sometimes before they went there, we would go too," Khoury later told Simon Clark in *Palestine Media Center* of the profitable relationship CCC developed with Bechtel. CCC subsequently followed Bechtel to projects throughout the Middle East, and along the way, Sabbagh and Khoury formed strategic business relationships with other key industry players that would later serve them well.

## MID-CENTURY: DEVELOPING A REPUTATION IN THE GULF REGION

As CCC followed Bechtel to construction sites, each new stop involved relocating immediate family, hiring office staff from the area, and gathering project teams, generally comprising Arabs hired in Beirut. In 1955 the firm for a time established itself in Kuwait, where Khoury settled his family two years later and helped the company's expansion in the Persian Gulf region. CCC's work during this period included laying pipelines and constructing bridges, roads, and airports.

During the 1960s CCC was involved in a range of major projects in the Gulf region, including a commercial harbor at a petrochemicals complex in Saudi Arabia, an oil-export pipeline in Yemen, and all of the liquefied natural gas trains, or the liquefaction and purification facilities, in Qatar. CCC developed business partnerships beyond its association with Bechtel throughout the Arab world and learned to accommodate itself to regional volatility. In some cases, however, an area grew too violent. Such was the case in 1966, when the firm left Aden, Yemen, after a civil war grew too dangerous to stay. Three years later, Sabbagh left Libya, where the company had constructed oil pipelines and plants for major companies such as the U.S.–based Occidental Petroleum Corp., after Muammar al-Qaddafi took control in a violent overthrow of King Idris. A decade before Saddam Hussein came to power in Iraq, CCC constructed the Abu Ghraib prison (now Baghdad Central Prison), which was completed in 1969.

In 1973 CCC established the National Petroleum Construction Company (NPCC) in Abu Dhabi to supply offshore services to oil and gas industries in the Gulf. NPCC became a public joint stock company, 70 percent owned by the conglomerate General Holding Corporation of the United Arab Emirates and 30 percent controlled by CCC. During the late 1970s, NPCC expanded through the building of its own pipe-coating operations and the development of its Offshore Services Division to deliver pipe-laying, installation, and hook-up services. As a result, NPCC grew quickly, becoming a major international engineering procurement construction contractor for onshore and offshore oil and gas projects.

## RELOCATION, REORGANIZATION, AND BUSINESS EXPANSION: 1975–90

In 1975 civil war broke out in Lebanon, and CCC briefly moved its headquarters from Beirut to London before relocating to Athens in 1976. Khoury remained in Kuwait, and Abdul-Rahman moved to France and sold his interest in CCC to the other two founders in 1976. CCC profited from its move to Athens, which placed it close to the economic development and subsequent construction boom in the Dubai area, where CCC became a major supplier of contracting services for the development of offshore oil and gas operations in the Persian Gulf. CCC also formed a joint venture, Consolidated Contractors Co., in Saudi Arabia with Prince Talal bin Abdul Aziz, father of the billionaire investor Prince Alwaleed bin Talal and the Saudi king's brother, and in 1976 became involved in a $950 million construction of a commercial harbor on the western coast of Saudi Arabia.

## KEY DATES

**1951:** The fledgling company lands a subcontract for the world's largest construction company, Bechtel, forming a key business partnership.

**1952:** Consolidated Contractors Company (CCC) is established in Beirut with Hasib Sabbagh, Said Khoury, and Kamel Abdul-Rahman as sole owners.

**1969:** CCC completes the construction of Abu Ghraib prison in Iraq.

**2008:** The company's annual revenues reach an estimated $5.6 billion.

**2010:** Cofounder Hasib Sabbagh dies.

In 1980 CCC made several reorganizational moves, beginning with the appointment of Fawzi Kawash, a friend of Sabbagh and Khoury, to the post of executive vice president. Next, the company endeavored to expand into markets in the United States, Europe, and Asia. During the same period, CCC entered into a partnership with Canadian OXY. The venture won a contract for oil exploration in South Yemen, with CCC holding a 40 percent interest. Khoury wanted to limit the company's risk, so CCC sold shares of its interest to Shell and American OXY, with CCC retaining a 10 percent stake. Ultimately, a substantial amount of oil was discovered.

During this period of restructuring and expansion, CCC made several acquisitions to help it diversify and develop its specialist services for the oil and gas industry. First, the company acquired what would be named CCC (Underwater Engineering) S.A.L. to provide specialist diving services to Middle East marine and offshore civil engineering firms. Next, CCC acquired in 1988 the U.S.–based Morganti Group Inc. as part of its efforts to move into North American markets. Morganti, a company with expertise in municipal construction, including hospitals, prisons, schools, government buildings, and water and sewage treatment facilities, had six wholly owned subsidiaries and annual revenues of $200 million in the United States.

### REBUILDING KUWAIT, BUILDING REVENUE GROWTH: 1990–95

In August 1990 Iraq invaded Kuwait, forcing CCC to close its business there and relocate its employees. In addition, it ceased all construction projects in neighboring Saudi Arabia at a significant loss to the company. The

Iraqi invasion of Kuwait had a direct impact on the Khoury family, who had lived in Kuwait since the 1950s. Said Khoury's two youngest sons, Wael and Samer, fled from the Iraqi army by driving 110 miles across the desert, leaving behind a country that had been their home for most of their lives.

While the conflict in Kuwait, and then Iraq, ensued, CCC continued its expansion and diversification efforts. In 1991 the firm acquired the British firm ACWA Services Ltd., a design, contracting, and engineering operation that provided services for water, air, and effluent treatment systems and reverse osmosis desalination plants. The following year, CCC created the Italian subsidiary Sicon Oil & Gas S.r.l. to serve as a procurement and engineering unit of CCC for upstream oil and gas developments. Sicon was created to follow the entire life of a project, from process design through start-up oversight and, along with ACWA, focused on engineering, procurement, and construction activities in the Middle East and Europe, specializing in oil and gas pipeline operations and water and effluent treatment systems.

Following the Kuwait invasion and the subsequent conclusion of war in Iraq, CCC took strides to recoup its losses through fresh projects in the Arab region. CCC constructed oil pipelines in Yemen that linked oil fields to Red Sea ports. It built electrical grids, roads, sewage systems, and national army housing in Egypt. It secured a bid to rebuild the international airport in Beirut, and it developed new roads through the desert in Mauritania in North Africa. Additionally, CCC became active in the reconstruction of Kuwait. By the mid-1990s, CCC had more than regained its footing as a major international contractor despite (or in some cases because of) the war in Kuwait and Iraq. In 1994 CCC garnered more than $1.3 billion in revenues and was ranked 26th among international contractors and 8th in Middle Eastern and U.S. markets by *Engineering News Record*. The gains CCC made during the early and mid-1990's largely came from the Gulf region and often involved consortiums with other firms like Bechtel, with which it partnered to rebuild the Beirut airport.

### GAZA PROJECTS: 1995–2000

The rebuilding of war-torn territory also provided CCC's founders an opportunity to return to the land of their birth. Following the historic handshake between Palestinian leader Yasser Arafat and Israeli Prime Minister Yitzhak Rabin in 1993, the CCC founders took steps to help their homeland, establishing and funding a $10 million program to train engineers in Gaza. Beginning in the late 1990s, the Khourys began making business investments there, helping to fund, for one, the first power plant in Gaza. Meanwhile, ACWA Services constructed a $2 million water purification facility in Gaza which sold drinking water at gas station dispensers, and CCC won a contract for construction work on Gaza City's seaport, a project stopped by violence but for which CCC would bid a second time.

In 1999 the construction of the first Palestinian power plant was formally approved, signified in a picture never to be repeated: Said Khoury was photographed with both Yasser Arafat and David Haug, the Middle East chairman of Enron Corp. The $150 million plant was to generate one-fifth of the power required by the 3.6 million people living in Gaza and the West Bank. However, by 2000 the Israeli-Palestinian conflict resumed, and in 2001 Enron collapsed in the second largest bankruptcy in U.S. history to date. Not ready to abandon the project, CCC bought Enron's stake in the power plant construction venture, and CCC along with the French firm Alstom, SA, remained and finished the job, despite ongoing violence. The plant was completed and online by 2002. Khoury became chairman of the Palestine Electric Company, and CCC took a substantial stake in the power company. Unfortunately, with poverty climbing in Gaza and the West Bank, the company had a difficult time receiving payments from its customers, and the plant became a substantial loss for the company.

## A SECOND GENERATION IN THE NEW CENTURY

By the early 2000s, CCC had annual revenues of about $2 billion and more than 60,000 employees working in 35 countries, from Kazakhstan to Kuwait. Major projects during this period included a $720 million shopping mall in Dubai, projected to be the largest in the world, and a $250 million section of an oil pipeline from Azerbaijan to the Turkey coast. CCC grew to a company of nearly 70,000 workers by 2004, with employees from nearly every country in Africa and the Middle East. It secured construction projects throughout the Middle East, including power plants, highways, bridges, harbors and docks, airports, water and sewage treatment facilities, and various facilities for the oil and gas industries, including refineries, petrochemical plants, and oil loading and off-loading terminals. Projects during this period included a 1,100-mile Azerbaijan/Turkey pipeline for a group led by BP Plc.

By the mid-2000s, a second generation of family members was making its mark on CCC, particularly Said Khoury's three sons, all of whom studied engineering at California State University at Chico. By 2004 Tawfic Khoury was in charge of legal and financial affairs in Athens, while Samer traveled and oversaw

Middle Eastern operations. Wael Khoury, based in London, was responsible for development of new markets. Sabbagh's two sons were also active in the company, with Suheil Sabbagh serving as director of group human resources and the younger Samir as manager of business development.

Meanwhile, founders Said Khoury and Hasib Sabbagh continued to honor a tradition they had established early in the company's history: hiring Palestinians, Jordanians, and Lebanese. At mid-decade, a full 80 percent of the management and engineering force were from these three nationalities. CCC also continued its use of business partnerships, working with such firms as Japanese engineering companies JGC Corp. and Chiyoda Corp., Europe's leading oil and gas services company the Paris-based Technip SA, and Bechtel, its first major partner in the 1950s.

## LANDMARK PROJECTS AND RECORD REVENUES: 2007–09

In 2007 CCC landed a portion of a $1.3 billion multi-partner contract with the Linde Group to construct a new ethylene cracker, expected to be the world's largest, for Borouge, a major provider of plastics. With the Gulf region experiencing rapid growth during the middle of the decade, and CCC benefitting, by 2007 the company boasted 160,000 employees and annual revenues of $4.2 billion. CCC was the second largest contractor in the Middle East and 13th largest worldwide, according to an annual *ENR: Engineering News-Record* review of international contractors.

CCC's growth in the first decade of the 21st century came largely as a result of oil, gas, and upstream petrochemical projects from which the firm garnered 80 percent of its revenues. The company came to be most active in Saudi Arabia, United Arab Emirates, and Qatar, where it employed more than half of its employees. In this same region, CCC landed two substantial contracts. In Qatar it was selected as part of a consortium led by VINCI to build the massive Qatar-Bahrain causeway, connecting Qatar and Bahrain, and in 2009 CCC secured its largest contract to date, worth $1.8 billion, as part of a six-group consortium to upgrade the Ras Laffan port in Qatar.

As of late 2009, according to *MEED: Middle East Business Intelligence*, CCC was the largest contractor in the Middle East, with an estimated $5.6 billion in annual revenues for 2008 and nearly 170,000 employees. It was also one of the largest private sector employers in the region, where its activities were dominated by contracts for oil, gas, and petrochemicals projects and real estate and infrastructure.

## A FOUNDER'S PASSING AND THE COMPANY'S FUTURE: 2010

In January 2010 CCC cofounder Hasib Sabbagh died at the age of 90. A year prior, *Arab Business* had listed Sabbagh as the 19th richest Arab, with a net worth of $4.3 billion, and one of the 50 most powerful Arabs in the world. Sabbagh had been a member of the Palestine National Council, an ally of President Jimmy Carter's pursuit for Middle East peace, an adviser to Yasser Arafat who encouraged the Palestinian Liberation Army president to engage in peace talks, and a philanthropist and proponent of education, particularly for Palestinian, Jordanian, and Lebanese causes.

Sabbagh had suffered a stroke several years before his death and had withdrawn from day-to-day activities with the company, serving as honorary chairman. He left behind a family-owned business run by his cofounder Said Khoury, chairman and president, and their sons, who with the cofounders comprised the remainder of the company board entering 2010. Suheil Sabbagh had said in 2005 that he anticipated the transition of the Sabbagh and Khoury sons from management to ownership status in the future. In addition, Said Khoury had said that CCC might sell shares if the number of family members with stakes grew substantially, although he provided no timeline for such an event.

As CCC management looked to the future in 2010, it was seeking to develop new business lines that could generate up to 10 percent of company annual revenues for at least five years. Among such opportunities were oil and gas industry operation and maintenance and utilities management. To secure revenue streams while it was engaged in contracting projects, CCC had partnered with two British firms: the Wood Group to service oil and gas operations, and the Erinaceous Group to manage utilities. The company was also pursuing oil and gas development in Nigeria, Yemen, and Gaza; developing real estate ventures in Jordan; and participating in the high-end resort Omagine in Oman. CCC planned to spread its resources so that revenue was more equally generated between the Gulf and three other international markets: Africa, where it had a dozen offices, Central Asia, where it was already active, and the Pakistan-India-Far East region. Given these strategic moves, near the turn of the decade, *MEED* gave the 60-year-old company a favorable review, suggesting it was well seasoned and well positioned to withstand any major problems and keep its position as the Middle East's leading contractor.

As it entered the new decade, CCC was likely to experience some shifts in executive management. Although Hasib Sabbagh had not been actively involved in the company for some time, his passing was expected to prompt changes within the company. At the time of his death Sabbagh owned 40 percent of the company. While CCC made no announcements in the early months following Sabbagh's passing as to what changes in ownership or management might be on the horizon, it did appear that the second generation of Sabbaghs and Khourys were prepared for ownership roles in the firm.

*Roger Rouland*

## PRINCIPAL SUBSIDIARIES

ACWA Services Ltd. (UK; 80%); CCC (Underwater Engineering) S.A.L. (United Arab Emirates); The Morganti Group Inc. (United States); National Petroleum Construction Company (United Arab Emirates; 30%); Sicon Oil & Gas S.r.l. (Italy).

## PRINCIPAL COMPETITORS

Balfour Beatty plc; Bechtel Corporation; Dutco Group of Companies; Fluor Corporation; VINCI.

## FURTHER READING

al-Alaya'a, Zaid, "Khoury Granted Unity Medal for Contributions to Yemeni Development," *Yemen Observer*, April 5, 2008, http://www.yobserver.com/front-page/10014019.html.

"Borouge and Linde / Consolidated Contractors Company (CCC) Formally Sign USD1.3 Billion Cracker Contract," *AMEinfo.com*, February 6, 2007, http://www.ameinfo.com/109854.html.

Clark, Simon, "Palestinian Builder CCC Dodges Mideast Conflicts, Reaps Profits," *Palestine Media Center*, July 25, 2005, http://www.palestine-pmc.com/details.asp?cat=4&id=2059.

Derhally, Massoud A., "Hasib Sabbagh, Palestinian Businessman Who Co-Founded CCC, Dies," *BusinessWeek Online*, January 13, 2010, http://www.businessweek.com/news/2010-01-13/hasib-sabbagh-palestinian-businessman-who-co-founded-ccc-dies.html.

Foreman, Colin, "Consolidated Contractors International Company," *MEED: Middle East Business Intelligence*, February 2, 2010, http://www.meed.com/consolidated-contractors-international-company/3000220.article.

"Hasib Sabbagh, Co-founder of Middle East Builder, Is Dead at 90," *Bloomberg News*, January 15, 2010.

"Hasib Sabbagh: Philanthropist with a Vision for Peace," *The National* (Abu Dhabi), January 15, 2010.

Hindley, Angus, "Arab Giant Achieves Global Reach," *MEED: Middle East Economic Digest*, July 29, 1994, p. 36.

"Honorary Doctorates at AUB: 2006 Honorary Degree Recipient—Said Khoury," *American University of Beirut*, 2006, http://www.aub.edu.lb/activities/doctorates/recipients/2006/khoury-profile.html.

King, Mary, and Deeb, Mary, eds., *Hasib Sabbagh*. Lanham, MD: Middle East Institute of University Press of America, 1996.

# Costain Group PLC

**Costain House, Vanwall Business Park**
**Maidenhead, Berkshire SL6 4UB**
**United Kingdom**
**Telephone: (+44 01628) 842-444**
**Fax: (+44 01628) 674-477**
**Web site: http://www.costain.com**

*Public Company*
*Founded:* 1865 as Richard Costain & Sons
*Employees:* 4,000 (est.)
*Sales:* £1.06 billion ($1.66 billion) (2009)
*Stock Exchanges:* London
*Ticker Symbol:* COST
*NAICS:* 237990 Other Heavy and Civil Engineering Construction; 237110 Water and Sewer Line and Related Structures Construction; 237310 Highway, Street, and Bridge Construction

■ ■ ■

The Costain Group PLC is a leading international engineering and construction company that has played a major role in some of the world's most notable projects, such as the Dubai Dry Dock, the Tsing Ma Bridge in Hong Kong, and the Channel Tunnel linking the United Kingdom with mainland Europe. Costain is organized into five broad divisions serving distinct markets and operates in Europe, the United States, Australia, Africa and the Middle East. The company's activities in the Middle East are significant, and its suc-cess in this region in the 1960s and 1970s played a large part in the group's rapid expansion. The Environment division, which boosted its orders 66 percent in 2009 by winning a number of major long-term contracts, serves the water, waste, and marine sectors. The Infrastructure division accounts for 13 percent of the group's overall activities, and serves the highway, rail and airport markets. The Energy and Process division undertakes projects for the hydrocarbons and chemicals, nuclear, and power sectors. It is one of the major contractors involved in the Sellafield decommissioning project. The Community division serves the health, education, and retail sectors, but Costain plans on reducing its opera-tions in these areas. The Land Development division, a joint venture with a subsidiary of Santander Bank, is a marina and land development project based in Alcai-desa, Spain.

## THE COSTAIN GROUP'S ORIGINS

Richard Costain was born in 1839 on the Isle of Man, where he became an accomplished joiner and craftsman. By 1865 Costain had saved enough money to move to Liverpool, England, where he established Richard Cos-tain & Sons. Recruiting masons and joiners from the Isle of Man, Costain's construction company built several terrace housing developments that transformed the English countryside. With each successful project, Costain would purchase a new tract of land and build more rows of houses for England's working class. Cos-tain died in 1902 and left the business to his son, William Percy Costain.

## COMPANY PERSPECTIVES

The Costain Group is embarking on a path of business excellence involving innovation, initiative, teamwork, and high levels of technical and managerial skills. We have a famous heritage, a well-defined culture with strong values and a strategy—"Being Number One"—designed to ensure a successful future. A key part of the strategy is to focus efforts and develop even stronger positions in our targeted markets. Costain has specialist project teams with detailed market knowledge and full understanding of individual customer needs.

William Costain is credited with building the Selsdon residential district in the 1920s, a development of more than 1,000 homes that sold for £425 each. In 1933 the company was floated as a public company with a share capital of £600,000. It traded as Richard Costain Ltd. In 1935 the company was awarded its first contract from GlaxoSmithKline plc (GSK) to build a £300,000 factory at Greenford. Fifty-five years later the Costain Group would build GSK's £50 million research center in Ware, England. Also in the 1930s the company built London's Dolphin Square, which was then Europe's largest apartment complex. Costain went on to build Europe's largest office block with the construction of Lambeth Bridge House, the headquarters of the Ministry of Works. In the same decade the company initiated its expansion into the Middle East beginning with the construction of eleven miles of Trans-Iranian Railway, seven tunnels, and two viaducts in 1935 for £1 million.

Costain was actively involved in World War II, arriving in France in March 1940 as No. 692 (Costain) Company, Royal Engineers. Along with the British Expeditionary Force, Costain built 26 aerodromes, part of the Mulberry Harbours, munitions factories, and 15,000 postwar prefabricated Airey houses. The company also produced more than 50 million precast concrete railway sleepers since beginning production in 1943. In 1948 Costain expanded its operations into central and southern Africa. In 1951 the company completed construction of the U.S. Embassy in Ankara, Turkey. In that same year, Costain built the Skylon and the Dome of Discovery for the Festival of Britain. Nearly 90 years after his grandfather founded the company, Richard Costain was knighted in 1954 in recognition of Costain's contributions.

## RAPID EXPANSION AFTER 1960

In a joint venture in the 1960s Costain built Port Rashid in Dubai, the largest deepwater port in the Middle East at that time. Costain's continued success in the Middle East during the 1960s and 1970s enabled the company to rapidly expand into other markets. During this period Costain also entered the coal-mining and property markets in the United States, the United Kingdom, India, and Australia. Between 1961 and 1973 Costain produced 34.5 million tons of washed coal from Scotland's Westfield mine. In 1967 Costain secured a construction contract with Tesco, one of the United Kingdom's largest supermarket and retail chains, and it has built more than 100 Tesco stores since that time.

In 1971 Costain was recognized for its international successes when it was awarded its first Queen's Award for Export Achievement. The first U.K. contractor to receive this accolade, Costain would go on to win nine more in the years to come. By the 1970s Costain had a presence in 25 countries worldwide, and its operations in these regions accounted for more than 50 percent of the company's sales. In 1972 Costain completed Hong Kong's first cross-harbor, steel immersed tube tunnel, spanning 1,850 meters. At the end of that decade Costain won a £300 million export contract for a chemical plant in Poland.

In 1983 Costain secured a two-year contract to build an army camp for the Sultanate of Oman's Armoured Regiment. The deal was worth £88 million, and it put Costain in a good position to challenge Britain's public sector and privately finance the building of the country's roads and railways. In 1988 Costain unveiled plans for three projects costing £7 billion, and the company proposed recouping costs by implementing tolls, rail fares, and freight charges. The projects included a second deck on London's M25 motorway, a 16-mile submerged tunnel under the Thames from Chiswick in West London to Tower Bridge, and a high-speed rail network that would link with the Channel tunnel.

## SHIFTING STRATEGIES IN THE NINETIES

The Costain Group's Amlohri coal-mining operation in northern India had quadrupled its production between 1990 and 1993, but the company's coal interests in the United States were not faring quite as well. After suffering heavy losses in the first half of 1994, the group decided to offload some of its more profitable U.S. coal businesses. In January 1995 Costain announced that it was selling its 80 percent share of the Dolet Hills Mining Venture in Louisiana to two subsidiaries held by

## KEY DATES

**1865:** Richard Costain founds a construction business in Liverpool, England.

**1933:** Costain is floated as a public company on the London Stock Exchange.

**1971:** Costain becomes the first contractor in the United Kingdom to win the Queen's Award for Export Achievement.

**2005:** Costain receives *Building* magazine's Major Contractor of the Year award.

**2009:** Costain is voted one of Britain's top 100 most admired companies.

Philipp Holzmann AG. Costain also sold Tradewater Railway to Western Kentucky Railway LLC for $8.8 million, and it sold its Columbus Southern Power coal-supply contract to Buckingham Coal for $7 million.

Costain was also in talks to sell all of its worldwide construction and contracting operations, but negotiations failed. In addition, after receiving offers that were too low, the group was unable to sell its losing mining interests, and in March 1995 Costain's share price tumbled by 30 percent. The group remained optimistic and adapted its strategy, deciding to implement cost-cutting measures and invest in its remaining U.S. coal assets. In April 1995 Costain signed a letter of intent to ship four million tons of coal over a two-year period to the Tennessee Valley Authority. Other contracts followed, including a 720,000-ton-per-year agreement with Big Rivers Electric and a 555,000-ton deal with Emerald International of Florence, Kentucky. In May 1995 Costain announced that its U.S. coal division had returned to profitability with a first-half profit of $1.1 million.

The Middle East remained a key business area for the group's contracting business, with the region accounting for approximately one-third of the contract division's international revenue. By 1995 Costain had offices in eight Arab states, and in April of that year it opened a new holding company, Costain Middle East, in Dubai. With a number of major contracts underway in Qatar, Abu Dhabi, and Oman, it came as no surprise when it was reported that Kuwait's Mohammed Abdulmohsin Kharafi & Sons (Kharafi) had acquired 13 percent of the group, a share that was eventually increased to 22 percent. Business in the region went from strength to strength as SIDC Metal Coating Co. awarded Costain the contract for construction of a $30 million continuous metal coating factory. In fact, the Middle East provided opportunities for all of Costain's business segments, and the company's wide geographic reach in the region ensured its sustainability into the new millennium.

## THE COSTAIN GROUP AFTER 2000

The British government had given Costain the green light for its civil engineering projects, including the ambitious Channel Tunnel Rail Link, and the group launched an aggressive advertising campaign to recruit 400 employees, 250 to be based in London. Costain was also planning to ramp up its activities in the Midlands and Scotland and to continue its international expansion. Stuart Doughty, the group's new chief executive officer (CEO), planned to increase annual sales by 15 percent over the next five years, and he expected to generate £85 million by 2003 through these initiatives. In March 2002 the group announced that its pre-tax profits had risen by 34 percent over the previous year. The company attributed this success to its new asset management strategy. The following month, in a joint venture with Balfour Beatty plc, Costain won the contract for the Stonehenge tunnel, a complex road scheme designed to link the national treasure with other ancient monuments dotting the English landscape.

By September 2002 U.K. projects accounted for 90 percent of the group's total work and had returned a £1 million profit, while its international business had operating profits of £1.9 million. Costain's two major international contracts at this time were the construction of the Kowloon Canton Railway Corp.'s depot and a joint venture with Alcaides Holding SA for the Alcaidesa development on the Costa del Sol, Spain. The following month Doughty unveiled the second stage of his strategy, which included streamlining the organizational structure and consolidating operations. The regional offices in Chandlers Ford and Peterborough were closed, and the staff relocated to the company's Maidenhead headquarters and to the new Midlands base in Birmingham. The group also estimated that it would need 400 additional employees to achieve its goals, and in November 2002 it launched an internship program for university students.

After it was announced in February 2003 that Costain was named the preferred bidder for construction of the Diamond Synchrotron Light Source in Oxfordshire, a contract valued at £60 million, the group's shares increased 5.6 percent. In a joint venture with Kharafi, Costain was also awarded an £18 million water contract in Botswana, the Palaype Village sanitation project. By September 2003 Costain had pre-tax profits of £6.1 million, while its sales were 17 percent higher than the previous year. In October 2003, as part of its business reconfiguration, Costain launched its highly successful iCosNet, an online business-collaboration portal.

In March 2004, with a 42 percent increase in profits, Costain deemed its recovery strategy a resounding success. In September the group secured two major water-supply upgrade contracts with Thames Water and Yorkshire Water. Costain's international projects in that year included a partnership with China Harbour, a leading Chinese construction firm, on various marine development and port-construction projects, including a major port redevelopment in Lagos, Nigeria. The year closed with Costain and Severn Trent Water winning a £1 billion contract from the Ministry of Defence to provide water services to 1,500 bases in the United Kingdom.

## SUCCESS IN HARD TIMES: 2005–10

In April 2005 Andrew Wyllie, a former director of the Taylor Woodrow construction company, took over the reins as CEO. Nearly 10 years after facing financial collapse, Costain was lavished with awards in 2005, including being named Major Contractor of the Year and a "2005 Superbrand." Its magazine, *Blueprint*, received the Award of Excellence from the National British Association of Communicators in Business. Costain had more than doubled its profits in 2005, and it estimated that it had enough projects in the pipeline to ensure work for the next five years.

However, business took a turn in July 2006 when Costain revealed that it was closing its international division, which had incurred losses of £2.9 million the previous year. Costain reported first-half losses of £20.7 million, and this figure rose to £61.7 million for the year after contract write-downs and closure costs. Wyllie planned to turn this around by focusing on core areas, such as oil and gas, and long-term projects with blue-chip customers.

In March 2007 Costain sold its West African subsidiary to Shoreline Energy International Ltd., deeming the region a noncore business area. By the close of 2007 the group had returned to profitability, and in January 2008 Costain announced that it would resume paying dividends. Going into 2009 the group had secured major deals, including a 10-year contract with Severn Trent, construction of the Port Talbot Peripheral

Distributor Road in Wales, a town revitalization project in Newbury, and a major waste-disposal project in Manchester.

By January 2010 Costain reported a 30 percent increase in its orders to £2.6 billion. The group continued to acquire new business, including two joint ventures for extensive motorway projects for the UK Highways Agency. In March, Costain opened a new office in northeastern England for its Energy and Process division, with long-term plans to focus on the hydrocarbons and chemicals, nuclear, and power sectors. Wyllie's strategy had returned the group to profitability during one of the world's most challenging economic environments, and Costain planned to continue on this path.

*Marie O'Sullivan*

## PRINCIPAL DIVISIONS

Environment; Infrastructure; Energy and Process; Community; Land Development.

## PRINCIPAL COMPETITORS

AMEC plc; Amey UK plc; Bechtel Corporation.

## FURTHER READING

"Costain Hopes to Rebuild after Major Losses," *Birmingham Post* (England), March 14, 2007, p. 23.

"Costain Pays First Dividend in 17 Years," *Investors Chronicle*, March 14, 2008.

"Costain Says No Further Write-downs Anticipated," Europe Intelligence Wire, March 13, 2007.

"Costain's Recovery 'in Line with Expectations,'" *Contract Journal*, January 16, 2008, p. 213.

"Costain Will Prove a Predictable Winner," *Independent* (London), June 26, 2009, p. 50.

Crosland, Jonas, "More Work for Costain," *Investors Chronicle*, February 17, 2010.

Geary, Joanna, "Loss Leaves Costain in a Precarious Position," *Birmingham Post* (England), August 31, 2006, p. 26.

Hawkes, Steve, "British Construction Group Upbeat on Iraq Deals after Lobbying Efforts," *Evening Standard* (London), March 26, 2003.

McAteer, Owen, "Business Echo: Costain to Open Office in the Region," *Northern Echo*, March 2, 2010.

"What's It Like Working at Costain," *Contract Journal*, April 18, 2007, p. 91.

# COTY

## Coty Inc.

**Two Park Avenue**
**New York, New York 10016**
**U.S.A.**
**Telephone: (212) 479-4300**
**Fax: (212) 479-4399**
**Web site: http://www.coty.com/**

*Wholly Owned Subsidiary of Joh. A. Benckiser GmbH*
*Founded:* 1904
*Incorporated:* 1922
*Employees:* 8,500
*Sales:* $3.50 billion (2009)
*NAICS:* 325620 Toilet Preparation Manufacturing

∎ ∎ ∎

Coty Inc. is a century-old fragrance company that manufactures and markets a wide range of perfumes, cosmetics, and other health and beauty products. Among the company's more famous brand-name fragrance and cosmetic lines are Calvin Klein, Vera Wang, adidas, Jovan, Stetson, and Joop. The company also markets a number of high-profile products endorsed by major celebrities, including Jennifer Lopez, Celine Dion, David and Victoria Beckham, Sarah Jessica Parker, and Kate Moss. Even though the company is based in New York, it registers the bulk of its sales in Europe. Coty Inc. is owned by the German holding company Joh. A. Benckiser GmbH.

## A PERFUME AND COSMETICS PIONEER: 1904–34

Born on the island of Corsica in 1875, François Spoturno was orphaned at an early age and reared by a grandmother. After leaving school, he drifted to Marseille and then to Paris, where he worked as a haberdashery salesman. Following a year's training in Grasse (the birthplace of the perfume industry), he took the name Coty from his mother's family name (Coti) and borrowed 10,000 francs from his grandmother to established Maison Coty, a makeshift laboratory that was housed in his small flat. He created his first perfume, La Rose Jacqueminot, in 1904 from concentrated flower oils that had been rejected by others because of their novelty. By 1908 he was successful enough to establish a factory on the outskirts of Paris. He eventually introduced face powder and packaged it with a powder puff in a round box.

Maison Coty owed its success to much more than its founder's training in and sensitivity to the materials from which commercial fragrances were derived. Coty catered to the rich and well-born, but he also sold small bottles that even the average Parisian could afford. He was the first to create a range of cosmetics in the same fragrance. Above all, Coty was a pioneer in every aspect of product design, including perfume bottles and cosmetics boxes. His close collaborator, Rene Lalique, created Art Nouveau crystal bottles that were works of art in their own right. Using red, black, and gold paper, Leon Bakst, the set designer for the acclaimed Ballets Russes, designed the powder box that as of 2010 was still being used for Coty's Airspun face powder. Coty was also quick to exploit foreign markets, opening a

## COMPANY PERSPECTIVES

■

Our mission is to deliver extraordinary fragrance and beauty products to consumers worldwide. As an organization, and as individuals, we value honesty, integrity, empowerment and openness. By consistently aiming for breakthrough excellence in creation, design and experience, we believe we will stay close to our consumers and communities.

Moscow store and establishing a London subsidiary in 1910. Two years later he founded a New York branch in a Fifth Avenue building that was adorned with stained glass windows designed by Lalique. Other agencies of what later became Coty S.A. were established in Buenos Aires, Argentina; Johannesburg, South Africa; Madrid, Spain; and Rio de Janeiro, Brazil.

When U.S. soldiers returned from World War I, they brought home Coty perfumes and face powder. These cosmetics became so popular that the United States was quickly considered to be important market. In 1922 Coty Inc. was formed, with laboratories and a large assembly plant established on Manhattan's West Side to avoid the heavy tariff on luxury goods. By 1929 the U.S. company was assembling and selling 23 perfumes, as well as powders, toilet soaps and waters, bath salts, brilliantines, hair and hand lotions, rouges, vanishing cream, shaving soap, and powder and rouge compacts. The firm was vigilant in forestalling price-cutting by retailers and achieved a 60 percent profit margin. Its net income rose from $1.1 million in 1923 to $4.1 million in 1928. In that year Coty S.A. had earnings of $1.6 million.

In 1925 Coty Inc. became a publicly traded company, and in 1929 it acquired a majority interest in the five European Coty companies. After Coty's death in 1934, his divorced wife, Yvonne Cotnareanu, received a controlling interest in Coty Inc. in lieu of the unpaid balance of an alimony settlement. Administration of the company remained in the hands of Benjamin E. Levy, who had become chairman of the board on its inception.

### THE DEPRESSION, THE WAR, AND THE POSTWAR YEARS: 1930–60

With the advent of the Great Depression, Coty saw its profits plummet. Sales in the United States fell from $50 million in 1929 to $3.5 million in 1933. Richard Rutter of the *New York Times* stated that management "compounded its mounting problems by slashing prices in a desperate effort to gain a mass market ... a near-fatal move in a field in which prestige and the luxury symbol were vital." Even so, Coty lost money on its U.S. operations only in 1935. With World War II imminent, the foreign companies were folded into the newly created Panama-based Coty International Corp. in 1939. The ownership remained the same, however, and the two corporations had interlocking directorships.

Levy retired in 1940 and was succeeded as chairman by Grover Whalen, a civic booster and promoter who was finishing his stint as president of the body that organized and ran the New York World's Fair of 1939–40. In his role as the company's public face, Whalen established the Coty American Fashion Critics' Award, an annual presentation that kept Coty's name before the public for 40 years. Administration was in the hands of Coty's president, Herman L. Brooks, from 1938 to 1946, when Cotnareanu, who spent the war years in the United States before returning to Paris, replaced him with Philip Cortney.

Cortney secured bank financing to keep Coty going and, in one of his first decisions, raised prices for the entire line. In spite of a long-range program to double the company's retail business, he cut off drugstores carrying Coty products if they would not agree to provide display space of at least 16 feet in length for exclusive stocking of these goods. Production lines were automated, packaging was restyled, and new lines of goods were added periodically, including, in 1955, a new toilet-goods line for men named Preferred Stock. Research laboratories were established in Morris Plains, New Jersey, and overseas.

In 1946, Coty's first postwar year, the company reported sales of $19.1 million and a net profit of $1.2 million. The company lost money in 1947, however, and even though it returned to profitability, sales stagnated. Fiscal year 1955 (the year ended June 30, 1955) was Coty's best postwar year, with a net income of $1.6 million on sales of $22.8 million. The firm lost money in fiscal years 1957 and 1958, with management blaming the results on the high cost of advertising, which rose from 7 percent to 16 percent of sales during this period. Moreover, firms such as Revlon, Inc., which reaped huge publicity from its sponsorship of the television game show *The $64,000 Question*, seemed to be getting better results for the money. In fiscal year 1962 Coty had a net income of only $386,985 on sales of $25.5 million. Coty International had a profit of $319,331 on sales of $7.4 million.

## KEY DATES

**1904:** François Coty creates his first perfume.
**1922:** Coty Inc. is founded in New York City.
**1939:** The five foreign Coty companies are reorganized as Coty International Corp.
**1963:** Coty and Coty International are sold to Chas. Pfizer & Co.
**1992:** Coty is sold to Joh. A. Benckiser GmbH.
**1996:** The addition of Benckiser's Lancaster Group makes Coty the global leader in production and sales of mass market fragrances.
**2001:** Bernd Beetz becomes the chief executive officer of Coty Inc.
**2002:** Coty Inc. launches Glow by JLo, a fragrance marketed specifically for the singer and actress Jennifer Lopez.
**2003:** Coty launches Celine Dion Parfums.
**2005:** Coty acquires Unilever Cosmetics International.

## CONTINUED SUCCESS AS A PFIZER SUBSIDIARY: 1963–91

In 1963 Coty and Coty International were sold to Chas. Pfizer & Co. for $26 million and became divisions in the pharmaceutical company's consumer products group. In 1965 Coty introduced Imprevu, its first new perfume in 25 years. This became the leading Coty fragrance by the end of 1968. Beginning in 1967 Coty Originals offered a comprehensive collection of newly designed makeup products at popular prices. Coty then added a high-priced, prestigious Dina Merrill line. In 1969 the division introduced the Bacchus line, a full collection of men's grooming aids, including aftershave lotion and cologne.

Coty and Coty International were united in 1973. Among the new products introduced in the early 1970s were the Styx, Sweet Earth, and Wild Musk fragrances and the Equatone beauty-treatment line. The production facility was moved from New York City to Sanford, North Carolina, at this time. Coty products were being marketed to franchised accounts, including distributors, independent drugstores, mass merchandisers, and department stores.

The battle for display space remained intense, but in 1984 Coty won a promotional award for its point-of-purchase Image Awareness campaign in 11,000 drug and mass merchandise stores. Departing from tradition, the campaign included posters, buttons, and aprons involving the whole store as well as a selection of traditional point-of-purchase materials, such as booklets, fragrance testers, and test cards within the cosmetics department. In 1985 Coty followed up with a similar Ingenious Solutions campaign. A specially designed consumer "colorkit" was provided for each of four fragrances: Nuance, Emeraude, Wild Musk, and Sophia. Each was graphically associated with an exotic locale.

Stetson, a highly successful men's scent, was introduced in 1981, and Lady Stetson was added in 1986. With more than $100 million a year in women's fragrance sales, Coty ranked second only to Revlon in this $3-billion-plus category in 1988. Besides the previously mentioned brands, Coty's brands also included L'Aimant and Sand & Sable. Its cosmetics and treatment products included Airspun face powder; Coty 24, Overnight Success, and Sheer to Stay lipsticks; Sweet Earth face-care-treatment products; and Thick 'N Healthy mascara. The men's fragrance line included Iron and Musk for Men. Coty ranked first in mass market men's fragrance sales in 1991, with a 22.6 percent share, and first in women's, with a 16.4 percent share.

## BENCKISER'S COTY: 1992–2000

Coty was purchased in 1992 by Benckiser Consumer Products, the U.S. arm of a family owned German household-products giant named Joh. A. Benckiser GmbH. That same year Coty introduced Gravity, a new upscale men's fragrance, and Truly Lace, a new bath-and-body fragrance collection. Vanilla Fields, a women's fragrance that proved hugely successful, was introduced soon after. In 1993 Benckiser merged into Coty its Quintessence Inc. unit, which it had acquired the previous year. Founded in Chicago by Bernard Mitchell in 1968 as Jo van Inc., this company had struck it big in 1972 with Jovan Musk Oil. The company was first sold to the Beecham Group in 1979 and then to its managers in 1988 in a leveraged buyout, when it became Quintessence.

Coty Inc. grew into a $1.5-billion-a-year company in 1996, when Benckiser made its Lancaster Group a Coty division. (The existing Coty, renamed Coty Beauty, became the other division.) Lancaster, which was founded in Monaco in 1946 and acquired from Smith-Kline Beecham PLC in 1990, consisted of the cosmetics brand of that name and an Isabella Rossellini line, as well as a number of designer and prestige fragrances, including Davidoff, Jil Sander, and Vivienne Westwood.

The consolidated Coty had become the global leader in mass market fragrance sales. In 1996 Lancaster introduced in Europe the leading Chinese cosmetics brand Yue-Sai Kan. In addition, it acquired Rimmel, a hip London-based cosmetics line. Coty Beauty's own line of color cosmetics was Margaret Astor.

The new introductions of 1997 were the Healing Garden, a line of four herbal-based aromatherapy fragrances that quickly developed into a collection of 34 stock keeping units, and Calgon Body Mists, Coty's first fragrance bath-and-body line. Like the company's traditional fragrance brands, these products were merchandised as minidepartments within a store. Calgon quickly moved into first place and Healing Garden into third place among mass market women's fragrances in the United States.

In 1998 Coty added a five-item Minitherapy for Feet line as an extension of the aromatherapy concept, and Isabella Rossellini launched a new cosmetics collection called Manifesto. During the year 45 percent of the company's sales were in mass fragrances, 31 percent in prestige-market beauty products, and 24 percent in mass cosmetics. Fifty-five percent of its sales volume came from western Europe and 30 percent came from North America. Lancaster represented 75 percent of the company's European sales. In North America, Calgon, Healing Garden, and Vanilla Fields ranked second, third, and fourth, respectively, among women's fragrances. Stetson, Aspen, and Preferred Stock ranked first, fourth, and fifth among men's fragrances.

In 1999 Coty introduced adidas Moves, a men's fragrance, to the United States and was planning to add its line of soaps as well. It also introduced Jovan Body Splash and a Dulce Vanilla fragrance, and it brought the Rimmel makeup line to the United States. The Lancaster Group's U.S. division introduced the Aromatopia line of 37 bath-and-body products in collaboration with May Department Stores Co., which took a one-year exclusive on the collection, to be sold in all 410 of its stores. For 2000 Coty was planning to introduce a new mass market perfume, Esprit, in 44 countries under a licensing agreement with the apparel marketer Esprit de Corp. Also planned for 2000 were line extensions of Aspen and adidas. In all, Coty was marketing 44 scents at the beginning of the new century.

## THE EMERGENCE OF A LIFESTYLE BRAND IN A NEW CENTURY

In April 2001 Bernd Beetz, a former executive with the French fragrance concern Parfums Christian Dior, became the new chief executive officer (CEO) of Coty. Shortly after taking over the leadership of the company, Beetz launched an ambitious and highly original growth plan, one founded on a steady expansion of the company's product line and the introduction of a range of innovative marketing tactics.

At the core of the company's new approach was something Beetz referred to as "lifestyle" branding, a marketing concept designed to create a connection between consumer self-image and certain Coty brand names. Beetz's short-term goal was to drive Coty's annual earnings growth to a figure somewhere near 10 percent by 2003, compared with the increase of roughly 4 percent the company experienced in 2000. In the long term he aimed to build Coty into a major global brand.

The first major step in Beetz's new strategy came in 2002, when Coty entered into an exclusive agreement with Jennifer Lopez to create a line of fragrances licensed under the performer's name. The company's first Jennifer Lopez fragrance, Glow by JLo, became available that same year. In July 2002 Coty announced a similar deal with the Canadian singer Celine Dion, with the aim of offering a diverse collection of scents and other beauty products. Celine Dion Parfums was launched the following March and was timed to appear in conjunction with the singer's new CD release and with her highly anticipated "A New Day" concert in Las Vegas, Nevada. To help promote brand awareness of the new line, Coty established a number of fragrance machines at Dion's Las Vegas venue.

## EXPANSION OF CELEBRITY BRANDING: 2004–10

By 2004 Celine Dion Parfums had become the world's number-one fragrance in the prestige brand category, and two of Coty's Jennifer Lopez scents, Glow and Still, were in the top five. In light of the near-instant success of its celebrity branding strategy, Coty launched two new products that year: Celine Parfum Notes and Miami Glow, a Jennifer Lopez fragrance aimed directly at young teenage girls. In February 2005 the company announced new licensing agreements with the actress Sarah Jessica Parker and the British soccer star David Beckham and his wife, Victoria. Three months later the company acquired Unilever Cosmetics International for approximately $800 million. With the purchase, Coty obtained the licenses to several major perfume brands, notably Calvin Klein and Cerruti.

After the acquisition of Unilever, Coty became the world's leading seller of fragrances, driven largely by its steadily expanding line of celebrity-endorsed scents. Reflecting on the resounding success of his marketing strategy to Cheah Ui-Hoon of the *Business Times Singapore*, Beetz recounted how "it was always clear to me that you can only get to a global leadership position if you played all three angles—designer, celebrity and lifestyle."

In 2006 Coty established a joint venture with the Singapore firm Luxasia to begin marketing Coty brands throughout Asia. That same year the company reorganized its prestige perfumes into a new division, Coty Prestige. During this period the company forged new licensing deals with a host of new celebrities, including Kate Moss and Gwen Stefani. By 2010 Coty had established a sales presence in more than 30 countries worldwide, with annual sales exceeding $3.5 billion. Clearly, Beetz's vision of transforming Coty into a global fragrance giant had come to fruition.

*Robert Halasz*
*Updated, Stephen Meyer*

## PRINCIPAL DIVISIONS

Coty Beauty; Coty Prestige.

## PRINCIPAL COMPETITORS

Avon Products, Inc.; Chanel S.A.; Christian Dior S.A.; The Estée Lauder Companies Inc.; LVMH Moët Hennessy Louis Vuitton S.A.; L'Oréal S.A.; The Procter & Gamble Company; Revlon, Inc.; Shiseido Co., Ltd.

## FURTHER READING

Barille, Elisabeth, *Coty: Perfumeur and Visionary.* Paris: Editions Assouline, 1996.

Born, Peter, and Janet Ozzard, "Coty Outlines Plans to Construct Network of Worldwide Brands," *WWD*, May 7, 1999, p. 1.

Day, Julia, "Benckiser Gears up for Brand Dominance," *Marketing Week*, August 5, 1999, p. 19.

Hellman, Geoffrey T., "Profiles: For City and for Coty—II," *New Yorker*, July 21, 1951, pp. 28–29.

Parks, Liz, "Coty Eyes Growth in New Fragrance Experiences," *Drug Store News*, December 8, 1997, p. 101.

Reece, Damian, "Unilever Sells Its Perfumes Business to Coty of the US," *Independent* (London), May 21, 2005, p. 44.

Rutter, Richard, "Personality: He Has Young Ideas in Old Line," *New York Times*, September 2, 1962, p. 79.

Sloan, Pat, "Coty's New Scent Gets Its Point Across," *Advertising Age*, July 11, 1988, p. 10.

Sloan, Pat, and Kate Fitzgerald, "Coty Targets Scent Invaders: Mass-Market Fragrances Take on Dept. Store Brands," *Advertising Age*, May 4, 1992, p. 4.

Ui-Hoon, Cheah, "Sweet Smell of Success; Coty Is Eyeing Asia, after Its Heady Conquest of the US Market with Its Fragrances," *Business Times Singapore*, February 25, 2006.

# Crayola LLC

1100 Church Lane
Easton, Pennsylvania 18044
U.S.A.
Telephone: (610) 253-6271
Toll Free: (800) 272-9652
Fax: (610) 250-5768
Web site: http://www.crayola.com/

*Wholly Owned Subsidiary of Hallmark Cards, Inc.*
*Incorporated:* 1902 as Binney & Smith Company.
*Employees:* 1,250
*Sales:* $675 million (2009 est.)
*NAICS:* 339943 Marking Device Manufacturing;
339932 Game, Toy, and Children's Vehicle
Manufacturing; 339942 Lead Pencil and Art Good
Manufacturing

■ ■ ■

For most of its history Crayola LLC was known by the
name Binney & Smith Company. The company was
incorporated in 1902, and in 1984 it became a wholly
owned subsidiary of Hallmark Cards, Inc. Crayola operates manufacturing facilities in Easton and Bethlehem,
Pennsylvania, as well as in Mexico City, Mexico. The
company also maintains sales and marketing facilities in
Canada, England, Australia, France, Mexico, Italy, and
Spain. The Crayola name for colored crayons is among
the most widely known brand names in the United
States and is found in more than 60 countries, from
Iceland to Belize. Annually, Crayola produces 120
shades of some 3 billion crayons that are labeled in 12

different languages. Crayola has branched into the
stationery segment with its markers, crayons, and chalks,
into the arts and crafts category with its paint sets and
activity kits, and into a licensed interior paint category
with its co-branded Benjamin Moore line of children's
paints. Over the course of its history the company has
controlled several other major brands, including Silly
Putty, Magic Marker, and Liquitex paints. Crayola sees
the visual arts as vital for teaching all subjects and is an
avid supporter of arts-in-education initiatives around the
country.

## THE EARLY YEARS: 1860–1900

Joseph W. Binney left England in 1860 for upstate New
York, where he founded, in 1864, Peekskill Chemical
Works for the grinding, packaging, and distribution of
ground charcoal and lamp black. In 1880 he set up
headquarters in New York City and was joined by his
son Edwin Binney and his nephew C. Harold Smith.
They were responsible for products in the black and red
color ranges, such as lamp black, charcoal, and a red
iron oxide paint that was often used to coat the sides of
barns. Joseph trained the young men in salesmanship for
the various pigments and colors he developed. When
Joseph retired in 1885, Edwin Binney and Harold
Smith formed the partnership of Binney & Smith
(B&S).

Meanwhile, a new and valuable black pigment had
been developed from natural gas deposits discovered
during the oil rush in Pennsylvania. This pigment was
more intensely black and stronger than any other pigment in use at the time. It soon became the main

ingredient in printing ink, stove and shoe polish, marking inks, and black crayons. B&S played an active role in the development and production of carbon black from the factories that sprang up in Pennsylvania, as well as in Indiana, Ohio, and West Virginia when other natural gas deposits were discovered in those states. B&S sold the greater part of the total production of carbon black, bought an interest in some of the operations, and stayed in touch with many new methods of production.

Binney and Smith proved to be complementary partners. Binney was focused on expanding the company's presence in the United States, developing new applications for carbon black and other pigments, and forming alliances that ensured the solid growth of the company. He also took care of the company's finances, which enabled Smith to exercise his talent as a master salesman. Smith traveled to several countries to introduce the new U.S. black and demonstrate its advantages over the local pigments in use during the 19th century for most of the paints, varnishes, and other protective finishes. The Chinese, for instance, collected the smoke and soot from the incomplete combustion of camphor leaves to make their stick inks and black lacquer finishes. By the end of the century practically all the printing inks, polishes, and paints that were used in China and in many other countries were made from the U.S. black.

In 1900 B&S bought an old water-powered stone mill on Bushkill Creek, near Easton, and used the mill to grind the scrap slate from the region's quarries. The ground slate was mixed with additional materials to create a superior slate pencil. Distribution of the slate pencils introduced B&S to the needs and potential of the educational market. The company listened and responded to schoolteachers' needs for better materials, especially for chalk that did not crumble and good, affordable colored crayons.

## CREATION OF AN-DU-SEPTIC CHALK AND CRAYOLA CRAYONS: 1902–03

In 1902 B&S was incorporated as Binney & Smith Company. That same year experiments at the Easton mill resulted in the production of An-Du-Septic, a white dustless chalk that was made by an extrusion process to "weight" dust particles. Meanwhile, an experiment consisting of mixing dry carbon black with various waxes led to replacing the company's Eclipse Marking Ink, a black liquid used on barrels and boxes, with trouble-free black crayons called Staonal ("Stay on all"), because they worked well on many types of surfaces, such as wood and paper.

Successful sales of Staonal triggered experiments for another product: the colored wax crayons schoolteachers needed to replace the poor-quality crayons that their students used. Artists had access to high-quality colored crayons, but they were imported and far too expensive for children's use. B&S chemists, aware that most of the pigments available at the time were highly toxic, developed synthetic, nontoxic pigments to replace organic colors. Furthermore, the company wanted to match the color uniformity and consistency of fine imported crayons while keeping costs low.

In 1903 B&S produced its first box of eight Crayola crayons (red, orange, yellow, green, blue, violet, brown, and black). Binney's wife, a former schoolteacher who recognized the significance of colored crayons in terms of childhood development, took particular interest in the new product. In fact, she coined the name "Crayola" from *craie* (the French word for chalk or stick of color) and *ola* (from *oleaginous*, a word referring to the oily characteristic of liquid petroleum before it was distilled into the paraffin used for crayons). Thus, B&S established itself in the avant-garde of suppliers for educational and artistic products.

## TWO BUSINESS DIVISIONS: 1900–55

During the next half century the company added many new products as the various carbon blacks were found to

## KEY DATES

**1864:** Joseph W. Binney begins producing charcoal and lamp black in his Peekskill Chemical Works in upstate New York.

**1885:** Binney & Smith is founded by Edwin Binney and C. Harold Smith, the son and nephew of Joseph W. Binney.

**1900:** Binney & Smith opens a mill in Easton, Pennsylvania, to produce slate pencils.

**1902:** Binney & Smith is incorporated.

**1903:** The first box of eight Crayola crayons marketed.

**1958:** The package of 64 Crayola crayons, with a built-in sharpener, is introduced.

**1984:** Hallmark Cards Inc. acquires Binney & Smith.

**1996:** Binney & Smith opens the Crayola Factory in Easton; the 100 billionth Crayola crayon manufactured.

**2007:** Binney & Smith changes company name to Crayola LLC.

work in an increasing number of manufactured materials. This part of the business (later known as the Pigment Division) continued to be handled by the New York office, whereas the business that led to the formation of the Crayon Division was overseen by the Easton office. The company's fortunes rose and fell with the conditions of the times (World War I, the postwar slump of the 1920s, the Great Depression, and World War II), and its extensive product list was the key to its survival. It is noteworthy that during the Great Depression, and for many years after that, B&S hired local farm families to hand-label crayons to supplement their winter incomes.

The highlight of this period was a 1911 request from the B.F. Goodrich Company of Akron, Ohio, for an annual supply of 1 million pounds of carbon. In the early years of the automobile, tires were white because of the zinc oxide that was in the rubber compound. Goodrich, however, experimented with Silvertown tires brought from England and discovered that the tread rubber wore considerably longer than that of the older white tire. The London manufacturer said it used a small amount of B&S carbon black to give its tires a distinguishing gray tint. Goodrich began experimenting with tires that contained varying amounts of No. 40 black mixed with rubber and found that increasing the

amount of carbon bound the rubber particles together to a greater degree than ever known and prolonged the life of the tire. To fulfill the order for Goodrich, B&S formed the Columbian Carbon Company.

The rapid development of many varieties of carbon black also spurred important advances in other industries. In the graphic arts, printing inks required the proper carbons for application to various new surfaces, such as highly finished papers, cellophane, and different plastic materials. Carbon black gave printing inks the special qualities needed for efficient operation at the rapid rate used to print modern newspapers. Furthermore, carbon black made it possible to develop the special lacquers required for automobiles. Carbon black was also used for shading or tinting cement to eliminate the glare of an untreated finish.

Even though the Pigment Division was experiencing rapid growth, the Crayon Division was quietly learning how to produce a superior crayon for both the retail trade and the education field. The first Crayola crayons were made in 16 colors. Crayola Rubens crayons for art students and Perma Pressed fine-art crayons that could be sharpened were eventually added to the product line. A new Crayola 48-crayon box that was introduced in 1949 featured new colors, such as bittersweet, burnt sienna, periwinkle, and prussian blue. Nine years later prussian blue was renamed midnight blue. By 1955 B&S had placed some 464 different items on the market.

## DEVELOPMENT AND EXPANSION: 1955–92

Sales in the Crayon Division increased steadily while the Pigment Division grew rapidly in size and products. Over the years the Pigment Division had relied increasingly on the Columbian Carbon Company for carbon black, bone black, iron oxides, new inks, and other products that accompanied developments in the oil and gas fields. As a result, Columbian became much larger than B&S. Wanting to own and direct its own sales activities, Columbian bought the B&S Pigment Division in 1955. Thereafter, B&S turned its attention to expanding its Crayola business through relevant acquisitions and new products.

In 1958 the Crayola 64-crayon box, which included 16 new colors and a built-in sharpener, made its debut on the *Captain Kangaroo Show*. With the 1964 purchase of Permanent Pigments Inc., the maker of Liquitex, B&S established its brand of fine art and decorative art supplies. As a world leader in acrylic paints, Liquitex provided artists with technically advanced, high-quality, versatile products in a broad range of colors, textures, and media. Thirteen years later, in 1977, B&S acquired the manufacturing rights for Silly Putty, which had started as a wartime experimental replacement for rubber and eventually became a popular toy. Craft and activity kits also became a vital part of the company's business.

In 1984 Hallmark Cards, Inc., the world's largest greeting card manufacturer and a privately owned corporation, acquired B&S as a wholly owned subsidiary. That same year marked the introduction of Crayola's Dream-Makers, an art education program for the nation's elementary schools. To the great delight of children, parents, and teachers, B&S placed washable markers on the market in 1987. This event was followed by the 1989 acquisition of the manufacturing rights for the Magic Marker brand of markers. The following year eight Crayola crayons (maize, raw umber, lemon yellow, blue gray, orange yellow, orange red, green blue, and violet blue) were retired into the Crayola Hall of Fame in Easton.

To show its leadership in the development of art products that emphasized international diversity, B&S launched Crayola My World multicultural crayons in 1992. The company hoped that by using crayons, markers, paints, and modeling compounds that reflected the variety of skin tones, children would build a positive sense of self as well as respect for cultural diversity. By 1992 Crayola crayons came in 80 colors.

## GROWTH AND ACCOMPLISHMENT: 1993–99

To celebrate the 90th anniversary of Crayola crayons, B&S offered in 1993, 16 new colors in the largest assortment of crayons to date: the Crayola 96 Big Box. However, instead of following its tradition of taking crayon color names from the U.S. Department of Commerce's National Bureau of Standards book *Color: Universal Language and Dictionary of Names*, the company decided to ask the public to name the new colors. Newspapers throughout the nation publicized the company's "Name the New Colors Contest." Between January and August 1993 the company received nearly 2 million suggestions.

That same year B&S acquired Revell-Monogram, a world leader in the manufacture of model kits, die-cast models, and modeling accessories. The company added a new dimension to its cultivation of children's creativity in 1996, when it opened the Crayola Factory, a hands-on children's learning complex, in downtown Easton. Featuring real crayon and marker manufacturing, rotating exhibits, and lots of places to play with color, the site began receiving tens of thousands of visitors each year.

In 1998 B&S decided to celebrate the classic Crayola 64-crayon box's 40th anniversary by reintroducing the original packaging, complete with a built-in sharpener and original package graphics. Between 1958 and 1998 over 185 million of these Crayola boxes had been sold, making it one of the most enduring and identifiable symbols of youth culture in the United States. In the same spirit, the Smithsonian Institution's National Museum of American History placed an actual 1958 Crayola 64-crayon box and an assortment of 20th-century Crayola advertising in the permanent collection of its Division of Cultural History. Another form of recognition occurred in February 1998, when the U.S. Postal Service included Crayola crayons in its "Celebrate the Century" program, which issued a commemorative stamp that depicted the original Crayola eight-crayon box introduced in 1903.

A significant moment in the company's development came with the launch of ColorWonder No-Mess Markers in 1999. The clear ink in these markers was invisible when drawn on any surface except the chemically coated paper that came with the markers. A full spate of products soon followed that applied the same proprietary technology, such as ColorWonder finger paint, spray paint, and glitter. Also in 1999 B&S made a rare name change of one of its colors. Indian red, which the company said was derived from a pigment imported from India, was renamed chestnut to allay complaints of cultural insensitivity toward Native Americans.

## NEW PRODUCTS IN A NEW CENTURY: 2002–10

In 2002 the company opened the retail outlet Crayola Works in Hanover, Maryland. More than a store, Crayola Works was an interactive studio designed for all ages, filled with activity stations and products not yet launched in the U.S. market. When sales lagged behind expectations, the store closed in early 2004. During this period B&S stepped up its licensing arrangements to capitalize on the unique appeal of its brand name. B&S partnered with Funrise to produce Discover and Draw kaleidoscopes and other optical toys. In a further stretch Crayola colors and logos were applied to a line of bedding linens, bath towels, and children's furniture.

For the 100th anniversary of Crayola crayons, B&S sent an "Art-rageous Adventure" tour bus around the country that culminated with a parade and festival in Easton in October 2003. The company held a naming contest for its four new crayon colors. To make way for the newcomers, four colors had to be retired. The company nominated five colors and held a contest to "save" the most popular of the five. Burnt sienna won the honor. The retired colors, along with the eight colors that had been retired in 1990, were offered in a special tin as part of a retail package that celebrated Crayola history.

Crayola headed into its second century with a burst of creativity. New products such as the ColorWonder series, a no-mess spin-art machine, and the battery-powered Crayola Cutter (which could safely cut a piece of paper from the center) were part of a concerted campaign to penetrate the craft market. With such tools and a host of toys and craft kits priced at $20 or less, the company positioned itself to grow in space by occupying new department store aisles and in time by generating sales during the holiday season as well as during the peak of its sales year at the end of summer.

To reduce confusion and accent its prize asset, B&S officially became Crayola LLC on New Year's Day 2007. In November 2009 PR.com reported that Crayola topped a mothers' poll of the "most loved brands of 2009." Clearly, Crayola occupied a secure, enviable market position.

*Gloria A. Lemieux*
*Updated, Roger K. Smith*

## PRINCIPAL COMPETITORS

Dixon Ticonderoga Company; Faber-Castell AG; Fisher-Price, Inc.; Hans Stockmar GmbH & Co. KG; MEGA Brands Inc.

## FURTHER READING

Cardona, Mercedes M., "Crayola Breaks Ad Effort to Target Parents' Nostalgia," *Advertising Age*, July 21, 1997, p. 35.

Cox, Jack, "After 100 Years, Crayola Colors Its Future Bright," *Houston Chronicle*, September 28, 2003, p. 12.

Goldstein, Seth, "Hallmark Inks Kid Vid Deal," *Billboard*, February 22, 1997, p. 8.

Horovitz, Bruce, "Crayola Draws on New Ideas," *USA Today*, December 6, 2006, p. B1.

Jana, Reena, "Crayola Brightens a Brand," *BusinessWeek Online*, January 26, 2007, http://www.businessweek.com/innovate/content/jan2007/id20070126_338855.htm.

Kitchel, A. F., *The Story of the Rainbow*. Easton, PA: Binney & Smith, 1961.

Mehegan, Sean, "Brand Builders: The Color of Money," *Brandweek*, September 15, 1997, p. 22.

"Smarty Pants Study Finds Moms Want Familiar, High-Quality Brands That Delight the Whole Family," PR.com, November 26, 2009, http://www.pr.com/press-release/195470.

# Dallas Cowboys Football Club, Ltd.

---

**1 Cowboys Parkway**
**Irving, Texas 75063-4924**
**U.S.A.**
**Telephone: (972) 556-9900**
**Fax: (972) 556-9304**
**Web site: http://www.dallascowboys.com**

*Private Company*
*Founded:* 1960
*Employees:* 220
*Sales:* $269 million (2009 est.)
*NAICS:* 711211 Sports Teams and Clubs

■ ■ ■

The Dallas Cowboys Football Club, Ltd., is the most profitable professional sports operation in the United States. Since entering the National Football League (NFL) as an expansion team in 1960, the franchise has appeared in more Super Bowls than any other team and is one of only two teams to have won five of them. Under the direction of owner Jerral (Jerry) W. Jones, the Cowboys have excelled off the field as well. Jones has run the team as a business, boosting revenue and profits through marketing deals and through the sales of stadium suites and tickets. Although Jones's individualistic and sometimes iconoclastic ways have led him into disputes with the NFL's power structure, they have benefited himself and his team handsomely. In 2009 the team moved into its new home facility, Cowboy Stadium in Arlington, Texas, the largest domed sports venue in the world.

## BUILDING THE FOUNDATIONS OF A FOOTBALL DYNASTY

The Dallas Cowboys Football Club entered the NFL as an expansion team in 1960. The driving force behind the team was one of its first co-owners, Clint Murchison Jr., who paid $600,000 for the franchise. Even before he, along with Bedford Wynne, was awarded the team, Murchison had settled on his coaching staff, hiring Tex Schramm, then a public relations employee with the Los Angeles Rams, to serve as the Cowboys' general manager, and tapping New York Giants defensive coordinator Tom Landry as head coach. Schramm and Landry would lead the team for the next 29 years.

The Cowboys' first years were difficult. With no permanent stadium or training facility, the young team finished the 1960 season winless. Although Dallas recorded its first victory in the 1961, it would not boast a winning season until 1966.

Despite its early on-field struggles, the team gained a great deal of exposure and a loyal fan base. With his marketing savvy, Schramm recognized the importance of image to the Cowboys' long-term success both on and off the field. When Dallas negotiated the terms of its entrance into the NFL, Schramm had lobbied hard for the Cowboys to be included in the league's eastern division, home to the New York Giants, who played in the single-largest television market in the country. As a result, Cowboys games reached millions of television viewers. Schramm made sure the team capitalized on the opportunity. "We captured people's imagination because we had good looking uniforms ... [and] a modest head coach that people respected. ... We were just the underdog people would be attracted to," Schramm told the *Dallas Morning News* in 1999.

The Cowboys also benefited from league-wide changes that began the same year Dallas joined the NFL. At the time, the NFL was under pressure from the American Football League (AFL), a rival association of teams founded in 1960. In fact, the AFL created the Dallas Texans in 1960, which competed directly against the Cowboys, although in 1963 the Texans moved to Kansas City, Missouri, and became the Chiefs.

## CONFLICT WITH THE NFL COMMISSIONER

Pete Rozelle, who had been named NFL commissioner in 1960, strove to rally the league against the upstart AFL. By the early 1960s the NFL had begun to lose some of its luster because of a growing competitive imbalance among its franchises. This situation arose largely because of the fragmented television coverage arrangements the NFL's individual teams had made. Until this point, each team had been free to negotiate its own broadcast deals and to keep whatever revenues were generated (with the exception of the NFL championship game, the rights fees for which were shared equally). As more popular teams in larger markets commanded better deals, they received more money, which they used to sign better players.

Rozelle was able to convince the club owners of the danger posed by this situation; if two or three teams gained total hegemony, fan interest (and therefore the league as a whole) would falter. National television contracts were soon negotiated, the proceeds of which were split evenly among all teams. In a similar vein, Rozelle launched NFL Properties in 1963 to promote the league as a whole. Under this arrangement, royalties from the sale of the merchandise of each NFL team were pooled, with all teams sharing equally in the profits. It was, according to the *Orange Country Register*, "at that point that the league really took off."

In 1966 Schramm joined with Lamar Hunt, the owner of the Chiefs, to negotiate a merger between the NFL and the AFL. The union was consummated in 1967, with the two leagues' 24 teams converging under the NFL's umbrella. All teams now shared a common

draft, all national television resources, and a championship game known as the Super Bowl.

While the NFL adjusted to these changes, the Cowboys began steadily to improve their record on the field. In 1966 Dallas won its first Eastern Conference title, although it lost the NFL Championship Game later that year to the Green Bay Packers. In 1967 the Cowboys again traveled to Green Bay, this time for the National Football Conference (NFC) title. (The winner would then play the American Football Conference champion in the first Super Bowl.) Although Dallas again lost, the game raised the team's profile further. Played in temperatures well below freezing, the game, known afterward as the Ice Bowl, was closely contested and became a symbol of pro football's gritty image. Dallas at last captured the NFC crown in 1970, although it lost to Baltimore in the Super Bowl.

## THE EMERGENCE OF AMERICA'S TEAM: 1971–80

Murchison attempted to boost the Cowboys' ticket sales, one revenue source that teams were allowed to keep for themselves, by constructing a new stadium. Located in Irving, Texas, a suburb of Dallas, Texas Stadium was completed in 1971 and could hold more than 58,000 fans. Even more noteworthy was Murchison's prescience in building 180 luxury suites in the stadium. Unlike standard seats, luxury suites offered spacious and comfortable accommodations with excellent views of the field. Air-conditioned and glassed-in, the suites provided a more upscale environment from which to watch the game. The suites carried a hefty price tag and were marketed to profitable corporations as an ideal spot to entertain clients or colleagues. The revenue generated by the sale of these suites not only helped the team's bottom line but also positioned it to attract a bevy of talented athletes who would lead the team on a glorious run through the 1970s.

In 1971 the Cowboys beat the Miami Dolphins 24-3 to claim their first Super Bowl title. After achieving its 10th consecutive winning season in 1975, Dallas again reached the Super Bowl, losing that game to the Pittsburgh Steelers. Nevertheless, Dallas rebounded in 1977 to claim its second Super Bowl, downing the Denver Broncos 27-10. The Cowboys returned to the Super Bowl again in 1978. They were edged out once again by the Steelers in what has been largely regarded as one of the more exciting title games in NFL history.

The Cowboys success during this period earned it legions of supporters nationwide. The Ice Bowl had given the team an image as a scrappy underdog, and its 1970s roster of charismatic stars (including quarterback

## KEY DATES

**1960:** Clint Murchison Jr. and Bedford Wynne are awarded the Dallas Cowboys expansion franchise and hire Tom Landry as head coach.

**1971:** Texas Stadium opens; Cowboys win first Super Bowl.

**1977:** Team captures second Super Bowl win.

**1984:** H. R. "Bum" Bright purchases Cowboys from Murchison.

**1989:** Jerry Jones acquires Cowboys and selects Jimmy Johnson as new head coach.

**1994:** Barry Switzer is named head coach.

**1995:** Cowboys win their fifth Super Bowl.

**1998:** Chan Gailey replaces Switzer as Cowboys' head coach.

**2009:** Franchise officially opens Cowboy Stadium in Arlington, Texas.

**2010:** Texas Stadium in Irving is demolished.

Roger Staubach, wide receiver Drew Pearson, and running back Tony Dorsett), captured the hearts and minds of fans around the country. A highlight film produced by the league in 1976 referred to the Cowboys as "America's Team." The name both fit and stuck.

## A FALL FROM GLORY: THE EIGHTIES

Although President Ronald Reagan declared that the 1980 elections marked a new morning in the United States, America's Team found the dawning decade to be a bleak one after the brilliance of the 1970s. Staubach retired in March 1980, and while the Cowboys would return to the NFC championship game in 1980, 1981, and 1982, they were unable to make it back to the Super Bowl. In 1984 Murchison sold the team for $60 million to an 11-member limited partnership headed by Dallas entrepreneur H. R. "Bum" Bright. Bright instituted few personnel changes; both Landry and Schramm remained in their positions. Nevertheless, the Cowboys' decline accelerated as the team missed the playoffs entirely for the first time in a decade.

In 1985 the team moved its headquarters and training facility to the newly constructed Cowboys Center in Valley Ranch but its on-field performance continued to flag. In 1986 the Cowboys had their first losing season in 20 years, and things turned ugly. Both Schramm and Bright publicly sniped at head coach Landry, who had by then become a Dallas institution. In 1988 the team recorded an embarrassing record of 3 wins and 13 losses. The team's profits spiraled downward with its record. Between 1983 and 1987 attendance at Texas Stadium fell 24 percent. To compound the problem, television revenues had decreased in the wake of declining ratings caused by fan disgruntlement with the labor disputes that plagued the league throughout the 1980s.

Despite these downturns, Arkansas oilman Jones bought the Cowboys and Texas Stadium in 1989 for $140 million, the highest price ever paid for an NFL franchise. Observers were amazed at the price. Their shock only grew when Jones implemented sweeping changes in the organization. Jones confidently pledged that the Cowboys would win the Super Bowl within five years and immediately set out to rebuild the team. In an act that brought him death threats, Jones fired Landry and replaced him with University of Miami coach Jimmy Johnson. Schramm resigned soon after, and Jones named himself general manager.

Jones was determined to return the Cowboys to profitability. To do this he cut expenses by laying off two-thirds of administrative personnel, among other measures, and he simultaneously strove to boost revenues. His first priority was to reverse the exodus of fans from Texas Stadium. After lowering regular ticket prices, Jones aggressively marketed vacant luxury suites. By the end of 1989 he had filled 27 of them, raising a total of $27 million. Jones used this money to attract excellent players, knowing that fans would return to watch a winning team. In 1989 he paid a record $10.4 million to secure the services of rookie quarterback Troy Aikman, and in 1990 he drafted Emmitt Smith as running back. Smith, Aikman, and wide receiver Michael Irvin would form the heart of the Cowboys' successful teams of the 1990s.

## THE BIRTH OF A NEW DYNASTY: 1991–95

Jones was universally despised during his first season as owner. To make matters worse, the Cowboys finished the 1989 season with a pitiful record of 1-15. The community "judged this man to be a fast-talking, hot-dogging, publicity-hounding Arkansas hillbilly with more dollars than sense," observed the *Houston Chronicle*.

Nevertheless, the Cowboys broke even in 1989 with revenues of $32 million. Good news in the accounting department was soon followed by good news on the field as the Cowboys returned to the playoffs in 1991, posting the team's best record since 1983. In 1992 Jones made good on his promise when the Cowboys won their third Super Bowl. Moreover, the next year the

Cowboys again claimed the Super Bowl title. By then Jones had nearly tripled the value of the franchise. With its net income in 1993 estimated to be $10.7 million, the Cowboys were ranked among the top-five profit producers of all U.S. sport franchises. Agent Lee Steinberg explained to *U.S. News & World Report*, "From the beginning, [Jones] has seen that everything—from his players to his stadium—has value beyond just that of a football team. Everything is part of a business that cross-fertilizes other ventures in that business."

Jones's financial success continued in the mid-1990s. By the close of the 1994 season he had increased the number of occupied luxury stadium suites from 100 to 300 and was planning to build more. Because NFL franchises could keep local television contracts, Jones renegotiated these deals, boosting them from $2.8 million to $6.2 million in 1994. Even more impressive was Jones's savvy in bringing in local advertising revenues. By aggressively selling stadium billboards and local corporate sponsorships, the Cowboys raised advertising sales from $400,000 to $8.5 million in 1994. In the process Jones forged an impressive profit-making cycle. The team's success generated revenue, which paid for talented players, who won more games, which improved the team's reputation, which generated more revenue. *Financial World* named the Cowboys the most valuable franchise in sports in 1994 and 1995.

Despite the Cowboys' success on the field, Jones replaced Johnson as head coach with Barry Switzer in 1994. The move was not entirely shocking, as both Jones and Johnson were exceptionally strong willed and had clashed repeatedly. Even with the coaching change, the Cowboys returned to the Super Bowl and won for a fifth time in 1995.

## SPONSORSHIP MONEY DISAGREEMENT

Jones continued to seek new ways to convert the team's on-field success into profit. He began to lobby the NFL to end the practice of pooling merchandise sales, because in 1994 and 1995 nearly one-third of all NFL paraphernalia purchased in the United States bore the Cowboy's logo. The league, however, refused. In response, Jones forged independent marketing alliances with sponsors in 1995. Nike Inc., PepsiCo, and American Express all made special agreements with the Cowboys that excluded the rest of the NFL. In fact, the NFL as a whole had sponsorship relationships with Reebok and Coca-Cola, both of which competed directly against Dallas's individual sponsors, and the revenues derived from the NFL's corporate sponsors were equally divided among all the teams, including the Cowboys.

Because Dallas's deals were struck formally between Texas Stadium and its various sponsors, the Cowboys were not technically breaking the NFL's resource-pooling policies. Nevertheless, the NFL was deeply threatened by Jones's actions. "The whole system is based on revenue sharing and access to players," league commissioner Paul Tagliabue told *USA Today*. In September 1995 the NFL filed a $300 million lawsuit against Jones; he responded with a countersuit for $750 million. In 1996 both parties agreed to drop their suits.

*Financial World* estimated that in 1998 the team netted $41.3 million on revenues of $413 million. Nonetheless, despite its high-profile status and considerable earnings, the team did not return to the Super Bowl after 1995. In part this was due to the aging of Dallas's core players. It was also a result of changes in the league's collective bargaining agreement that made it easier for teams to sign free agents away from their competitors. Although the Cowboys invested heavily in their marquee athletes, the league's salary cap prevented them from locking up many of the key players who had quietly but crucially contributed to the team's success. In 1998 Jones fired Switzer and installed Chan Gailey as head coach. This change, however, failed to right the listing ship, and Gailey was released after a disappointing 1999 season. Dave Campo was then chosen to lead the team into the new century.

Even with its on-field woes, Jones had placed the franchise in an enviable financial position. As one of the first owners to view the operation of an NFL team as a true business, he established a course that appeared likely to alter the face of the league for years to come.

## BUILDING A STADIUM FOR THE 21ST CENTURY

Entering the new century, the Cowboys franchise found itself at a crossroads. In the decade since Jones bought the team, the club's net worth had quintupled, rising from an original price tag of $140 million in 1989 to an estimated value of $713 million by 2000. In spite of the organization's robust financial health, however, numerous questions surrounded the team's future. The Cowboys finished the 1999 season with a mediocre 8-8 record as the team's long-heralded offense dropped to 11th in the league in points scored. Although the team managed to make the playoffs that year, it was overpowered in the wildcard round by the Minnesota Vikings. The following season, which was Aikman's last as quarterback, the team dropped to 5-11.

At the same time, the Cowboys suddenly found their traditional fiscal dominance being threatened by other teams. In September 2000 the organization dropped to second on *Forbes* magazine's annual rankings of NFL franchises, behind the Washington Redskins in overall value. It was the first time in seven years that Dallas failed to occupy the top spot. Washington's surge was driven primarily by revenues generated by its new stadium. Opened in 1997, the Redskins' home venue seated more than 80,000 fans at an average ticket price of roughly $80 a seat. In November 1999 the Redskins organization sold the stadium's naming rights to FedEx Corporation for $205 million, the largest deal of its kind at that time in sports history.

With several other franchises slated to open new, state-of-the-art stadiums in the early part of the decade, owner Jones determined that the Cowboys would need to revamp their own facilities in order to remain competitive. Although it was one of the league's most hallowed venues, Texas Stadium had become antiquated by the early 2000s, demanding more than $450,000 worth of annual repairs. More significantly, the Irving, Texas, landmark seated only 65,000 fans, far short of the capacity offered by more modern NFL stadiums.

In 2002 the team unveiled a preliminary proposal to the Irving City Council, recommending either a massive renovation of the existing Texas Stadium or the construction of a new venue entirely. A more ambitious plan emerged in March 2003, in which Jones envisioned a multiuse sports-and-recreational complex complete with a 100,000-seat stadium, a manmade lake, and a deluxe hotel. Initial estimates for the project ranged from $650 million to more than $1 billion. A handful of cities, notably Arlington, began lobbying heavily to become the new home of the Cowboys. Meanwhile, local comedians began referring to the proposed 200- to 300-acre venue as "Jerry's World."

## NEW STADIUM AGREEMENT REACHED

In January 2003 the club hired NFL legend Bill Parcells as its new head coach. That July the Cowboys franchise suffered a deep personal loss when the team's original general manager, Schramm, died at the age of 83. The team went on to have a successful campaign under Parcells's first year at the helm, returning to the postseason for the first time since 1999. The team, however, slipped again the following year, dropping to 6-10 and falling far short of the playoffs. Meanwhile, in November 2004 residents of the city of Arlington approved a ballot measure supporting the construction of the team's new stadium. The team and the city reached a formal agreement two months later. Under the terms of the deal, the Cowboys would invest $400 million toward the new venue, and Arlington's taxpayers would pay for the rest.

The team broke ground on the new stadium in April 2006. At around this time, the team began to regain its swagger on the field, led by young quarterback Tony Romo and new head coach Wade Phillips. The club's success on the field caused a sharp spike in Cowboys merchandise sales. By October 2007 Romo's jersey had become the number-one selling shirt in the league, while Cowboys merchandise in general outsold that of all other NFL teams. That season the Cowboys tied a franchise mark for best regular season performance, finishing at the top of the NFC East with a 13-3 record.

On December 20, 2008, the Cowboys played their last game in Texas Stadium. The new Cowboys Stadium was officially unveiled on May 27, 2009. The stadium's numerous architectural highlights included the world's largest retractable dome roof, an enormous video board offering fans a 360-degree view of the on-field action, and a 120-foot by 180-foot glass wall. The stadium grounds also featured a bronze statue of Landry, the Hall of Fame coach who led the team for nearly three decades. In June 2009 the venue hosted its first public event, a George Strait concert.

By the beginning of the 2009–10 season the Cowboys had once again regained their status as the top franchise in the NFL, with an estimated value of $1.65 billion. The team enjoyed another successful run that season, finishing first in their division and winning their first playoff game since the late 1990s. Although the team was defeated by the Vikings in the second round of the playoffs, the club had reason for optimism heading into the new decade. Meanwhile, on April 11, 2010, the team officially bid farewell to Texas Stadium. The demolition attracted thousands of onlookers, among them many former Cowboy greats. Having turned the page on an important chapter of its history, the Cowboys organization was now looking ahead to future glory at its new home in Arlington.

*Rebecca Stanfel*
*Updated, Stephen Meyer*

## PRINCIPAL COMPETITORS

New York Football Giants, Inc.; Philadelphia Eagles Limited Partnership; Pro-Football, Inc.

## FURTHER READING

Bell, Jarrett, "Cowboys' New Palace in Dallas; Stadium 'Transcends Football'," *USA Today*, September 18, 2009, p. 1C.

Campbell, Bill, "Underdog Image Helps Club Become America's Team," *Dallas Morning News*, September 12, 1999.

Cowlishaw, Tim, "Jones: Cowboys' Financial Footing on Firm Ground," *Dallas Morning News*, November 22, 1989, p. B1.

Formby, Brandon, "Clock Runs Out on a Dallas Legend," *Dallas Morning News*, April 12, 2010, p. A1.

Freeman, Denne H., "With Free Agency, Cowboys Won't Be in Lone-Star State," *Seattle Post-Intelligencer*, January 9, 1993, p. D4.

Kelly, Kevin, "Jerry Jones: The Man Who Fired Tom Landry," *Business Week*, April 24, 1989, p. 148.

Markiewicz, David A., "Texas Stadium Endures as a Financial Gold Mine," *Fort Worth Star-Telegram*, October 22, 1996, p. 1.

McGraw, Dan, "The Very Lonesome Cowboy Jerry Jones Refuses to Join the NFL's Corporate Huddle," *U.S. News & World Report*, September 26, 1994.

Robertson, Dale, "Jerry Jones Personifies a Real Dallas Maverick," *Houston Chronicle*, January 28, 1994, p. 4.

Swift, E. M., "Another Gusher for Jones," *Sports Illustrated*, December 12, 1994, p. 44.

# Davisco Foods International, Inc.

11000 West 78th Street, Suite 210
Eden Prairie, Minnesota 55344-8012
U.S.A.
Telephone: (952) 914-0400
Toll Free: (800) 757-7611
Fax: (952) 914-0887
Web site: http://www.daviscofoods.com/

*Private Company*
*Incorporated:* 1986
*Employees:* 385
*Sales:* $600 million (2009 est.)
*NAICS:* 311513 Cheese Manufacturing; 311514 Dry, Condensed, and Evaporated Dairy Product Manufacturing

■ ■ ■

Based in Eden Prairie, Minnesota, Davisco Foods International, Inc., is a family owned and operated manufacturer of commodity and specialty cheese and food ingredients. Davisco operates the Le Sueur Cheese Company in Minnesota. Other units include the Jerome Cheese Company in Idaho; the Lake Norden Cheese Company in South Dakota; the Whey Protein Institute, an advocate for the use of whey proteins; and Davis Family Farmers, which operates two major dairy production farms. Commodity products include whey protein 80 percent, lactose, and curd cheddar, mozzarella, and other cheeses. Each year Davisco produces 370 million pounds of cheese and is a major supplier to Kraft Foods, with which the company has maintained a

close relationship for more than 40 years. A pioneer in whey protein isolate research, Davisco offers several branded whey products, including BiPRO Whey Protein Isolate, BioZate Hydrolyzed Whey Protein, Alpa-lactalbumin Whey Protein Isolate, and Glycomacropep-tide Bioactive Whey Protein. All told, Davisco produces 65 percent of the world's supply of whey protein isolates. These ingredients are found in a wide variety of products, including shelf-stable baking mixes, infant formula, low-fat salad dressings, reduced-fat candies, and sports drinks. Davisco is headed by chief executive officer Mark Davis, the son of the company's founder, and whose own sons hold important positions in Davisco and other family business ventures.

## COMPANY FOUNDED IN 1943

Davisco was founded in 1943 by Stanley Davis when he bought the St. Peter Creamery in St. Peter, Minnesota. A St. Peter native, Davis had graduated from high school seven years earlier and moved to Norseland, Minnesota, to learn the buttermaking trade. He gained further expertise in 1941 when he enrolled in the dairy school at the University of Minnesota. Later in the year he found work in Texas but returned home when he learned that the St. Peter Creamery was for sale. Davis and his college instructor, Harvey Parsons, bought the business together. Parsons later sold his stake to a man named Eiler Grand, who eventually turned his attention to the egg business, and Davis became the sole owner of the creamery.

Initially the St. Peter Creamery simply accepted cream from farmers, who did their own separating, and churned it into butter. During World War II the U.S. government needed skim milk to ship overseas, and the creamery began buying milk, rather than just cream, and sold both butter and skim milk to the government at attractive prices. Although the war would soon end, the changes made to the way local creameries worked with farmers proved to be permanent.

Without the steady demand and prices offered by the government, however, the postwar years were challenging in the dairy industry, forcing companies to either expand and diversify or fall by the wayside. Davis made plans to produce ice cream and even purchased the necessary equipment, but he never initiated the product line and sold the machinery unused. In 1956 Davis invested in a spray dryer to turn skim milk into powdered milk, which he sold in addition to butter. It was a risky investment, given that groups of creameries usually purchased a dryer together, but it was a wise decision. As the decade progressed the small creameries that lacked dryers were either swallowed up by other operations or went out of business. The St. Peter Creamery, on the other hand, was able to take on larger milk routes and expand.

## MARK DAVIS JOINS COMPANY: 1959

The 1950s also marked the full-time involvement of the second generation of the Davis family when, in 1959, 18-year-old Mark Davis became a driver on a new bulk milk pickup route. He and his three brothers and sister were already well familiar with the creamery, having spent many Saturdays and Sundays helping out when necessary. The younger Davis also enrolled at Mankato State University and graduated with a degree in business administration and economics in 1963.

The Davis family reached a turning point in 1969 when Stan Davis decided to pool his milk supply with an old classmate, Allen Cords, who owned the Le Sueur Creamery and was a staunch believer that cheese was about to become a dominant dairy product. Hence, Stan and Mark Davis joined Cords to establish the Le Sueur Cheese Company, the three men each owning a third of the business. With Mark Davis serving as manager, the venture established a relationship with Kraft Foods, selling 500-pound blocks of cheese to the food products giant. Davis also began making use of the whey by-products that traditionally had been discarded. The plant expanded its cheese and whey production capabilities in 1970 and expanded further in 1978.

The Davis family added to its interests in 1970 when Stan and Mark Davis took on another partner, former employee Glen Anderson, to buy the Nicollet Creamery, which had been managed by Anderson and recently closed. It owned a dryer and became a second site for the contract processing of milk by-products, including soy milk. Anderson sold his share of the business to the Davis family in 1975. Spray drying became an increasingly important part of the business, so much so that in 1973 Stan Davis, a trained buttermaker, made the difficult decision to cease butter production at the St. Peter Creamery. Instead, the company acquired more dryers, built more storage space, and added to its revenues by drying on a per-pound contract rate.

The Davis family continued to expand its businesses during the 1980s. Stan Davis acquired the Land 'O Lakes plant in Lake Norden, South Dakota, in 1983, where he installed a spray dryer and added storage space. Rather than collect milk, the plant began to collect whey from area cheese plants and in effect became the world's first whey protein isolate plant. It was also in 1983 that Mark Davis made an important discovery. While attempting to sell whey protein to a pharmaceutical company, he was told that the product fell far short of what a British company was offering, a product called BIPRO. Davis tracked down the manufacturer in Wales and arranged to become the sole producer of BIPRO in the United States. The pure protein was especially well suited for food products and nutriceuticals (nutritional supplements).

## DAVISCO FORMED: 1986

After Cords retired in 1986, the Davis family decided to merge its three companies, St. Peter Creamery, Le Sueur Cheese Company, and Nicollet Food Products, to create Davisco Foods International, Inc. A year later the third generation of the Davis family joined the business when the first of Mark Davis's four sons went to work for Davisco. By 1993 all of the boys were employed there,

## KEY DATES

**1943:** Stan Davis and a partner acquire St. Peter Creamery.

**1959:** At age 18, Mark Davis joins his father's company.

**1969:** Company expands into cheese production by forming Le Sueur Cheese Company.

**1986:** Davisco Foods International, Inc., is formed.

**1993:** Company celebrates 50th anniversary.

**2009:** Davisco partners with the University of Minnesota to launch New Sweden Dairy.

starting in the barrel room at Le Sueur and working their way up. In the meantime, Davisco became a true international company, winning business in both Europe and Japan.

Davis enjoyed particular success in Japan, albeit not without some early difficulties. Upon learning that one of the products sold to a Japanese customer had turned hard because of moisture, Mark Davis and his production manager immediately traveled to Japan to troubleshoot the problem. The commitment to quality impressed the Japanese and solidified the relationship. Lasting alliances were forged with Mitsubishi Corp. and Meiji Milk Co., which used BIPRO as an ingredient in foods and pharmaceutical products.

Between 1987 and 1988, Davisco underwent a major business reorganization and expansion that set the stage for explosive growth in the 1990s. The Welsh developer of BIPRO was acquired in 1991, and the product became an increasingly important source of revenue. Davisco also expanded to Idaho in 1992, taking advantage of the state's milk production to build a cheese plant in Jerome, which opened a year later and was named New Plant of the Year by *Food Engineering Magazine*. A new milk evaporator was added two years later to increase production to 3.5 million pounds of milk each day.

### CREAMERY CLOSES: 1993

Davisco celebrated its 50th anniversary in 1993 and faced a difficult decision. The St. Peter Creamery either had to be expanded to remain competitive or be abandoned. In the end, the high electric rates in the area were the deciding factor, and Davisco moved the St. Peter Creamery equipment to the Le Sueur plant, where the operations were consolidated. The company soon moved its headquarters as well. With growing demand

and increased production, Davisco expanded its sales operation in the mid-1990s and soon outgrew its space. As a result, the company moved its headquarters to new offices in Eden Prairie, Minnesota. It also opened sales offices on the coasts of the United States and Mexico, and made further upgrades to its plants in the final years of the decade, including the investment of $26 million in Jerome and another $15 million to bring Le Sueur up to the same standards. Moreover, Davisco expanded its research operation to develop new whey products, and the Davis family began building a massive new cow operation.

The 21st century brought continued growth for Davisco. To accommodate demand in Europe, a regional headquarters was opened in Geneva, Switzerland, in 2001, making Davisco the first U.S. whey producer to take such a step. Davisco also differentiated itself in the global marketplace with further branding of its whey products, helping it to build a 65 percent worldwide market share for whey protein isolate. In recognition of its success, Davisco became the first recipient of the Exporter of the Year Award by *Dairy Field Reports* and the U.S. Dairy Export Council in 2006. In that same year, Mark Davis's efforts were also recognized, as he was inducted into the Minnesota Business Hall of Fame. In addition, the company's Alpha-lactalbumin product won a prestigious food industry award, named Most Innovative Food Ingredient by the Food Ingredients South America conference.

### LAKE NORDEN PLANT OPENS IN 2003

Production capacity was also increased in the new millennium. A $40 million mozzarella cheese plant was opened at Lake Norden in South Dakota in 2003 and seamlessly connected to the old facility. Two years later a 40-pound-block tower line was installed to produce cheddar, parmesan, and Monterey jack cheese when demand was low in the mozzarella market. A second phase was launched in 2007 with a $10 million capital investment to improve milk throughput. The powder warehouse was also expanded. Davisco's efforts were again recognized when the South Dakota plant was named the Plant of the Year by *Dairy Field Reports* in 2008.

Davisco was generating about $600 million in annual sales by this stage but continued to pursue growth on a number of fronts. It partnered with the University of Minnesota College of Veterinary Medicine in 2009 to launch New Sweden Dairy, LLC, to combine education and product research opportunities. A year later Davisco joined forces with other dairy processors to fund the construction of a facility in Brookings, South Dakota, to train students in dairy processing. Davisco also continued to broaden its product offerings. In 2009 it began working with the German company MEGGLE AG to produce pharmaceutical lactose in the United States. With stable family leadership, long-term partners at home and abroad, and products well entrenched in the marketplace, Davisco was positioned in 2010 to enjoy continued growth.

*Ed Dinger*

## PRINCIPAL SUBSIDIARIES

Jerome Cheese Company; Lake Norden Cheese Company; Le Sueur Cheese Company.

## PRINCIPAL COMPETITORS

Dairy Farmers of America, Inc.; Leprino Foods Company; Saputo Cheese USA Inc.

## FURTHER READING

Bardic, Allison, "Master Explorers," *Dairy Field Reports*, March 2001.

———, "Protein Powerhouse," *Dairy Field Reports*, January 2009.

Dudlicek, James, "Pride of the Plains," *Dairy Foods*, December 2008, p. 65.

Mans, Jack, "Whey to Export," *Dairy Foods*, April 1999, p. 68.

Matz, Roger, "Davisco Foods International," *Connect Business Magazine*, May 1998.

Vance, Daniel J., "How Now Brown Cow," *Connect Business Magazine*, September 2002.

# DCC plc

———■———

**DCC House**
**Brewery Road**
**Stillorgan**
**Blackrock, County Dublin**
**Ireland**
**Telephone: (+353 01) 279-9400**
**Fax: (+353 01) 283-1017**
**Web site: http://www.dcc.ie**

*Public Company*
*Founded:* 1976
*Employees:* 8,000
*Sales:* EUR 6.40 billion ($8.68 billion) (2009)
*Stock Exchanges:* Dublin London
*Ticker Symbol:* DCC
*NAICS:* 424410 General Line Grocery Merchant
Wholesalers; 423430 Computer and Computer
Peripheral Equipment and Software Merchant
Wholesalers; 423450 Medical, Dental, and Hospital
Equipment and Supplies Merchant Wholesalers;
424710 Petroleum Bulk Stations and Terminals;
424820 Wine and Distilled Alcoholic Beverage
Merchant Wholesalers; 562211 Hazardous Waste
Treatment and Disposal

■ ■ ■

DCC plc is a diversified group that operates across five
major divisions: DCC Energy, DCC SerCom, DCC
Healthcare, DCC Environmental, and DCC Food &
Beverage. DCC Energy is a liquefied petroleum gas
(LPG) and oil business serving the domestic, commercial, industrial, and agricultural sectors in Britain
and Ireland. DCC Energy markets and distributes such
well-known brands as BP, ESSO, Shell, and Texaco.
DCC SerCom markets and sells information technology
(IT) and entertainment products to retailers, computer
dealers, resellers, and software vendors throughout
Britain, Ireland, France, Iberia, and Benelux. SerCom
also provides procurement and supply-chain management services in Ireland, Poland, China, and the United
States, and partners with some of the world's leading IT
and electronics brands. Its own brands include Linx and
Exspect. DCC Healthcare is a broad-based provider of
health care, rehabilitation, mobility, and beauty products
and services in Britain, Ireland, mainland Europe,
Australia, and New Zealand. The division is also a leading supplier of physiotherapy products, which are
mainly marketed under its own Days Healthcare,
Physio-Med, and Metron brands. DCC Environmental
provides waste-management and recycling services
throughout Britain and Ireland. The division serves both
the industrial and commercial sectors, and its subsidiary,
Enva, is the leading hazardous-waste treatment business
in Ireland. DCC Food & Beverage serves the retail and
food-service sectors throughout Ireland and Britain, with
a product portfolio that includes health foods, wines,
snacks, frozen foods, confectionery, and kitchen
equipment. The bulk of DCC's profits are derived from
the procurement, sales, marketing, and distribution
businesses, while the remaining 15 percent is derived
from a variety of business support services. DCC's
strategy is to continue to grow through these two main
business streams and to extend the group's outreach
through focused global acquisitions.

## DCC'S BEGINNINGS

Development Capital Corporation (DCC) Limited was founded by DCC plc's former executive chairman, Jim Flavin, in 1976. By the late 1980s DCC had acquired shares in a broad range of businesses, prompting management to reassess the company's priorities and streamline its activities. By 1990 DCC was clearly defined as an industrial and commercial holding group, and the company set about acquiring majority or whole interests in selected business areas. Four years later, with a formidable presence as an industrial holding company, DCC was well poised to seek a listing on the Irish and London stock exchanges.

In 1996, after raising capital through a private placement via NatWest, DCC acquired 45 percent of Merits Health Products Company for $4.18 million, a manufacturer of wheelchairs, electric scooters, and other rehabilitation products. The purchase of Merits Health, based in Taiwan with a subsidiary in the United States, was a significant boost to DCC Healthcare's international business. In 1998 DCC Healthcare further expanded with the acquisition of BM Browne, a hospital supply company, and Eurocaps, a manufacturer of soft medical capsules. DCC's pre-tax profits for the fiscal year ending March 31, 1999, were EUR 46.4 million, with the group's energy and health care businesses returning the strongest results. In June of that year DCC acquired Thompson & Capper for $9.8 million, a vitamin and health supplement manufacturer based in Runcorn, England. In 2000 Thompson & Capper was merged with a sister company, Healthilife, to form Primacy Healthcare.

The beginning of 2001 saw a slowdown in the information technology business, but DCC was quick to dispel any speculation that the group's DCC SerCom division was affected, reporting a 22 percent increase in profits for the fiscal year ending on March 31. Contributing to this increase was a strong market demand for data-storage products, which were distributed by DCC's France-based company, Distrilogie. For that same year, the group also reported operating profits of 17 and 18 percent in its health care and energy divisions respectively. The trend continued into the first six months of the 2001 fiscal year. DCC

Energy became Scotland's leading oil distributor after acquiring BP's local operations. The purchase increased profits in this region by 44 percent to EUR 8.2 million, while DCC Healthcare's profits were up 8 percent to EUR 10.6 million

## BETTER BUSINESS PRACTICES IN THE NEW MILLENNIUM

According to an article in the November 2001 issue of the *Financial Times*, Flavin was looking forward to "very good growth for the full year." Two months later, DCC was rocked by scandal when Fyffes Plc filed a claim in the Dublin High Court against Flavin, who was a former Fyffes director, and three other defendants alleging insider trading. Fyffe's claimed that Flavin, DCC, and its subsidiaries, S&L Investments and Lotus Green, had price-sensitive information not available to the general public prior to a sale in February 2000 of a 9 percent stake in Fyffes.

Although Flavin vehemently denied any wrongdoing, the case would hang over Flavin like a black cloud throughout the first decade of the new millennium, and it placed DCC's corporate governance under scrutiny. Flavin was determined not to allow the threat of legal action to distract him, and he vowed to keep DCC on course. For the 2001 fiscal year DCC reported a 16 percent increase in profits, with more than 50 percent attributed to organic growth. The oil, gas, and food divisions all reported positive results, while the IT business showed only a 2 percent decrease in a market that was experiencing serious decline.

The acquisition of the U.K.-based storage component company AGP Distribution contributed to DCC SerCom's bottom line, and DCC was keeping a close eye on other acquisition opportunities in the U.K. and European IT markets. This was demonstrated with the July 2005 acquisition of Pilton Company Limited, a U.K.-based distributor of DVDs, computer games, and home entertainment products, and the August 2005 acquisition of Advanced Business Computing SA, a Belgian provider of IT infrastructure solutions.

In February 2004 DCC's reputation was restored when it won the Large Quoted Companies award from the Leinster Society of Chartered Accountants for excellence in financial reporting. In that same month, DCC raised $257 million in a U.S. private placement through the Royal Bank of Scotland (RBS) placement agent. In July 2004 DCC plc announced that it was expanding the DCC Food & Beverage division beginning with the acquisition of the U.K.-based wine sales and marketing company Bottle Green. This was followed in August with the acquisition of Allied Foods.

## KEY DATES

∎

**1976:** Jim Flavin founds Development Capital Corporation as a venture capital company.
**1994:** DCC plc is listed on the London and Irish stock exchanges.
**2007:** DCC plc sells its share in Manor Park Homebuilders Limited to Morevest Limited.
**2008:** DCC plc acquires U.K.-based Southern Counties Fuels Holdings Limited and Chevron's oil distribution business.
**2009:** DCC plc acquires Cooke Holdings Limited, Shell Oil's distribution business in Denmark, and Bayford Oil Limited.

The Fyffes claim reached Dublin's High Court in December 2004, and it affected DCC's time and resources for the next 12 months. In December 2005 the High Court ruled in favor of Flavin and DCC, stating that Flavin's actions in the sale were not unlawful. In a December 2005 issue of the *Irish Independent*, Flavin said that he held "a complete belief in the correctness of our actions in relation to the sales of these shares. At no stage were we looking over our shoulders."

DCC turned its attention to expanding the Environmental division in 2006, beginning with the acquisition in May of a 50 percent share in Scotland's William Tracey group of recycling and waste-management companies. This was followed in November 2006 with the acquisition of 90 percent of Realpower Limited, the holding company of Wastecycle Limited, a recycling and nonhazardous waste management business based in Nottingham, United Kingdom. For the first six months of the 2006 fiscal year, DCC posted a 20.2 percent increase in its pre-tax profits, and the company was expecting its full-year profits to match those of the previous year. The year closed with DCC once again winning the Large Quoted Companies award that it had won three years earlier.

For the 2006 fiscal year ending March 31, DCC reported revenues of EUR 4 billion ($5.3 billion), a 17.7 percent increase over the previous year. In May 2007 DCC returned to the U.S. private placement market through RBS, with a goal of raising $250 million. Acquisitions continued in 2007 beginning with the purchase in August of CPL Petroleum Limited, a leading U.K. oil distribution business. In November 2007 the Healthcare division was expanded with the acquisition of Britain's Squadron Medical Limited, a

supplier of medical and surgical products. DCC SerCom's European expansion continued with the December purchase of Banque Magnetique, a leading French distributor of consumer electronic products and computer peripherals. In that same month, DCC sold its 49 percent share in Manor Park Homebuilders Limited to Morvest Limited for an undisclosed sum.

## LEADERSHIP CHANGE

In February 2007 it was announced that Flavin would be replacing Alex Spain as DCC's executive chairman on July 1. The appointment was short-lived, however, as the Supreme Court reversed the High Court's decision on Fyffe's case in July 2007 and found Flavin and DCC guilty of insider trading. In April 2008 DCC was forced to pay EUR 41 million ($64.6 million) to settle the civil suit, and Flavin resigned the following month under increased pressure from the Irish Association of Investment Managers. "While I am resigning, I firmly hold the view that I have always acted honorably and in what I believe to be the best interests of the company and all its shareholders," Flavin said in a statement in May 2008. By the beginning of 2010, as reported by an article in the *Irish Independent* on January 20, Flavin had been cleared of all charges and was guilty of nothing more than an "error of judgment." Flavin, who had founded one of Ireland's largest listed public companies, was finally free to resume his career.

Michael Buckley, who was appointed to replace Flavin, continued to grow the group through acquisitions. The U.K.-based Southern Counties Fuels Holding Limited, Chevron's UK Oil Distributor business, and the Chevron Limited UK Equity Distributor business were added to the DCC Energy portfolio, while the acquisition of Findlater Grants from the C&C Group Plc, an Irish wine and liquor distributor, expanded the DCC Food & Beverage division. In 2009 the focus was once again on the DCC Energy division with the acquisitions of the British fuel-card business of Cooke Holdings Limited in January, Denmark's Shell Oil distribution business in August, Bayford Oil Limited in the U.K. in October, and Brogan Holding Ltd, a leading British fuel-card and fuel-distribution business, in December.

Riding the wave of one of Ireland's harshest and longest cold snaps in recorded history, which began in November 2009, DCC increased its full-year profit forecast in February 2010 as the demand for heating increased. In a trading statement issued on February 2, DCC had budgeted EUR 112.6 million for acquisitions, of which more than 80 percent was allocated to the DCC Energy division. It was also reported that DCC was close to raising $390 million, once again through a

U.S. private placement. With profit increases of between 5 and 10 percent forecast for the year ending March 31, 2010, DCC was well poised to extend its global presence.

*Marie O'Sullivan*

## PRINCIPAL SUBSIDIARIES

Allied Foods Limited; Aukbritt International Pty Limited (60%); Ausmedic Australia Pty Limited (60%); Banque Magnetique SAS Procurement (France); Bottle Green Limited Procurement (England); Broderick Bros. Ltd. (93.8%); Days Healthcare UK Limited Development (Wales); DCC Energy Limited Holding; DCC Energy Limited Procurement (Northern Ireland); DCC Environmental Limited Holding; DCC Food & Beverage Limited Holding; DCC Health & Beauty Solutions Outsourced (England); DCC Healthcare Limited Holding; DCC International Holdings B.V. (Netherlands); DCC Limited (England, Wales); Distrilogie SA (France); Emo Oil Limited Procurement; Enva Ireland Limited; EuroCaps Limited Development (England); Fannin Limited Procurement; Flogas Ireland Limited Procurement; Flogas UK Limited Procurement; Fuel Card Services Limited Sale (England); GB Oils Limited Procurement (England); Gem Distribution Limited Procurement (England); Kelkin Limited Procurement; KP (Ireland) Limited Manufacture (50%); Kylemore Foods Group (50%); Laleham Healthcare Limited (England); Metron Medical Australia Pty Limited (60%); Micro Peripherals Limited Procurement (England); Physio-Med Services Limited Procurement (England, 94%); Pilton Company Limited Procurement; Robert Roberts Limited Procurement; SerCom Distribution Limited Holding; SerCom Holdings Limited (98.5%); SerCom Solutions Limited Provision; Sharptext Limited Procurement; Squadron Medical Limited (England); The TPS Healthcare Group Limited (Scotland); Thompson & Capper Limited Development (England); Virtus Limited (51%); Wastecycle Limited (England, 90%); William Tracey Limited (England, 50%).

## PRINCIPAL DIVISIONS

DCC Energy; DCC SerCom; DCC Healthcare; DCC Environmental; DCC Food & Beverage.

## PRINCIPAL COMPETITORS

BP plc; Ingram Micro (UK) Ltd.; Maxol Group.

## FURTHER READING

Brown, John Murray, "DCC Lifted by Energy and Health," *Financial Times*, May 11, 1999, p. 24.

"Fyffes Presents Claim against Ex-director," *Financial Times*, January 29, 2002, p. 20.

"Combining Strengths to Take on the Province's Food Market," *News Letter* (Belfast, Northern Ireland), May 27, 2003, p. 14.

"DCC Acquires FindlaterGrants from C&C Group for about 9.6 Mln Euros Cash," *Europe Intelligence Wire*, September 15, 2008.

Gimbel, Florian, "DCC Displays Strong Underlying Growth," *Financial Times*, May 15, 2001, p. 30.

Iyer, Gayatri, "Irish DCC Returns to PP Market," *Private Placement Letter*, February 1, 2010, p. 2.

Kunert, Paul, "Micro P Parent Targets UK for Further Expansion Plans," *MicroScope*, July 15, 2003, p. 3.

Molloy, Thomas, Dearbhail McDonald, and Tim Healy, "Cleared Industrialist Flavin Returning to Commercial Life," *Irish Independent*, January 20, 2010.

Noonan, Laura, "DCC Taps US Market to Secure $390m in Funds," *Irish Independent*, February 15, 2010.

Penman, Andrew, and Michael Greenwood, "Sorted and the City: DCC Toasts Wine Deal," *Mirror* (London), July 8, 2004, p. 39.

# DIC Corporation

DIC Building, 7-20 Nihonbashi, 3-chome, Cuo-ku
Tokyo, 103-8233
Japan
Telephone: (+81 3) 3272-4511
Fax: (+81 3) 3278-8558
Web site: http://www.dic.co.jp

*Public Company*
*Founded:* 1908 as Kawamura Ink Manufactory
*Incorporated:* 1937 as Dainippon Printing Ink Manufacturing
*Employees:* 23,200
*Sales:* ¥757.85 billion ($8.31 billion) (2009)
*Stock Exchanges:* Tokyo
*Ticker Symbol:* 4631
*NAICS:* 325910 Printing Ink Manufacturing; 325998 All Other Miscellaneous Chemical Product Manufacturing; 325211 Plastics Material and Resin Manufacturing

■ ■ ■

Formerly known as Dainippon Ink and Chemicals, DIC Corporation is a global company based in Tokyo, Japan, that divides its business among four operations. The Printing Inks & Supplies Business Operation is mostly conducted through subsidiary Sun Chemical and offers a full range of printing inks as well as printing-related equipment, presensitized plates, and printing supplies. The Neo-Graphic Arts Materials Business Operation offers organic pigments, liquid crystal materials, toners, jet inks, coatings and bonding adhesives for optical disks, and specialty magnetic foils. DIC's Synthetic Resins Business Operation focuses on synthetic resins and additives and on chemicals used in the manufacture of automobiles, building materials, textiles, and electrical and electronic components. Finally, the Chemical Solution Materials Business Operation produces specialty compounds and colorants, pressure-sensitive adhesive materials, building materials, petrochemical-related products, plastic molded products, engineering plastics, hollow-fiber membranes, and coatings for interior materials, as well as food additives and dietary supplements. DIC is a public company listed on the Tokyo Stock Exchange.

## COMPANY FOUNDED IN 1908

DIC was founded in Tokyo in 1908 as Kawamura Ink Manufactory by Kijuro Kawamura. It was a time of significant change for Japan, which was beginning to embrace Western consumerism. A printing boom developed to keep pace with the popularity of picture postcards and to supply the bright and colorful packaging that began to be used in the food and cosmetics industries. To support woodblock, lithographic, and typographic printers, Kawamura set up shop to produce white, blue, yellow, and red milled inks. Because he had been born in 1880, the year of the dragon, Kawamura used the image of a dragon as the company's symbol and product trademark.

With demand brisk for his inks, Kawamura quickly branched out to serve other regions of Japan. In 1912 he changed the company name to Kawamura Kijuro Shoten. Three years later he expanded his product offerings. Because Germany was mired in World War I, he could no longer import pigments from Germany, so in 1915 the company began manufacturing its own inorganic pigments. In addition, it began producing offset printing inks. Offset printing was relatively new in Japan, and Kawamura's foresight to pursue the market paid off handsomely for the company, as offset printing and the higher image quality it offered gained rapid acceptance across Japan.

## ORGANIC PIGMENTS PRODUCED IN 1925

From the beginning Kawamura had harbored a desire to expand to China. That goal was realized in 1919 when an agency contract in Hankow, China, was finalized. After World War I Kawamura continued to deal with a shortage of pigment supplies. The company now looked to create its own organic pigments and succeeded by chemical means, converting coal tar intermediates such as beta-naphthol. In 1925, as a result, the company began producing its own supply of organic pigments. Not only did Karamura Kijuro Shoten become a full-range printing ink manufacturer, it laid the foundation for becoming a fine chemicals manufacturer.

The company launched operations in Indonesia in 1931, and at the end of the decade it opened an office in Beijing, China. In between, it expanded its product offerings. In 1936 it began producing varnishes, and in 1937 the company was reorganized and renamed Dainippon Printing Ink Manufacturing Co., Ltd. It was also a time of increasing political turmoil for Japan, which was soon involved in a war in China that helped lead to a greater conflict, World War II. Because of Japan's lack of petroleum supplies, aviation gasoline was strictly controlled. The mixture was a common solvent used in gravure ink, and to compensate, ink manufacturers were forced to develop water-based gravure ink. In 1940 Dainippon succeeded in developing a water-based gravure ink that would be widely used for the next decade until gasoline controls were lifted. Moreover, the research effort paid other dividends for Dainippon, which also found a substitute for natural resin in

gravure. This gave the company experience in synthetic resin production, which set the stage for later success in this field as well.

## POSTWAR EXPANSION

The war devastated Japan's economy, but it quickly recovered after the war, as did Dainippon. In 1950 the company, now under the leadership of the founder's son, Katsumi Kawamura, went public, and its shares began trading on the Tokyo Stock Exchange, setting the stage for renewed expansion. The company forged ties with American companies during this period. A joint venture with Reichhold Chemicals Inc. resulted in Japan Reichhold Chemicals Inc. in 1952. Two years later Dainippon established a technology cooperation agreement with Sun Chemical Corporation. Product expansion included the addition of plastic mold products, such as helmets, and the commercial production of plastic colorants and colored compounds. In 1958 Dainippon opened its first office since the end of the war, located in Hong Kong.

In 1959 the third generation of the Kawamura family became involved in the business, although it was not a blood relation. Shigekuni Kiriyama married the daughter of Katsumi Kawamura. Because the family lacked a male heir, Kiriyama was adopted, and he assumed his wife's surname so that he and his wife could inherit the business, a common practice for Japanese families lacking sons. Shigekuni Kawamura was Western educated and brought a different mindset to the running of a Japanese company. Born in 1928, he was just six months old when his family moved to Berkeley, California. His father worked for a Japanese shipping company, and Kawamura attended an American public school. He lived in California until turning eight in 1937 and thus spoke impeccable English. Moreover, he was a 1958 graduate of New York University's business school, having returned to the United States as a Fulbright scholar.

While his son-in-law learned the business, Katsumi Kawamura led Dainippon during the 1960s and most of the 1970s. In 1962 the company bought out its partner and renamed Japan Reichhold as Dainippon Ink and Chemicals, Incorporated. The decade also saw sales offices open in Singapore in 1965 and New York a year later. In 1969 Dainippon Ink & Chemicals (Europe) GmbH was established, and the following year brought Dainippon Ink & Chemical, Americas, Inc. (USA) and Dainippon Ink & Chemicals (HK) Ltd. On the production side, Dainippon pioneered new ways to manufacture epoxy resins and began producing polystyrene in the 1960s. Dainippon then developed UV-curable ink in 1970, and it entered the liquid

# KEY DATES

■

**1908:** Kawamura Ink Manufactory is founded in Tokyo, Japan.

**1937:** Company is reorganized as Dainippon Printing Ink Manufacturing Co., Ltd.

**1950:** Dainippon is taken public on the Tokyo Stock Exchange.

**1986:** Dainippon acquires Sun Chemical.

**2008:** Company name is changed from Dainippon Ink and Chemicals to DIC Corporation.

crystals market in 1973. The Linagreen Spirulina–based nutritional supplement was introduced in 1978.

## KOHL & MADDEN ACQUIRED IN 1976

Katsumi Kurwamura sought to take advantage of his son-in-law's American business-school education and become more aggressive than typical Japanese companies, urging him to learn more about mergers and acquisitions. The new approach was first put to use in 1976 when Dainippon acquired Kohl & Madden Printing Ink Corp., based in Hackensack, New Jersey, for $6 million. Kohl & Madden was a well-established company, founded in Chicago in 1906. Dainippon had hoped to use it as a platform on which to build a major printing ink company in the United States, but Shigekuni Kawamura, who succeeded his father-in-law as president in 1978, concluded that it would take too long to grow the business organically. Instead, in 1979 he paid $57 million for Polychrome Corp., an ink and printing-plate manufacturer based in Yonkers, New York. In the process he beat out another suitor, French chemical giant Rhone-Poulenc, and learned valuable lessons about the acquisitions process.

Dainippon opened sales offices in Sydney, Australia, in 1980, and in Seoul, South Korea, in 1985. It also began producing polyphenylene sulfide compounds in 1980 and developed fluorinated foam fire extinguishing agents in 1982, and late in the decade the company developed high-performance deoxygenating membrane. The most important step taken by Dainippon during the 1980s, however, was the hostile takeover of two former joint-venture partners. In 1986 Dainippon acquired the graphic arts materials division of Sun Chemical, paying $550 million. Karamura then turned his sights on Reichhold Chemicals, acquiring the company for $765 million in 1987. The addition of Sun Chemical made Dainippon the world's largest manufacturer of printing inks and graphic arts materials, while the addition of Reichhold made it the world's leading manufacturer of thermosetting resins. Kohl & Madden was also folded into Sun Chemical.

## A DECADE OF U.S. EXPANSION

Dainippon expanded both Kohl & Madden and Sun Chemical in 1994. The former merged with Graphic Fine Color of Annapolis Junction, Maryland, expanding the company's presence in the mid-Atlantic states. Sun Chemical, in the meantime, acquired United States Printing Ink Corp, a move that furthered a trend toward consolidation among suppliers to newspapers. Other acquisitions followed later in the decade. Kohl & Madden bought the printing inks business of United Printing Ink & Supply of Santa Fe, California, in 1998, followed a year later by the purchase of anther California company, American Printing Ink of Fremont. Also in 1999 Sun Chemical spent $90 million to acquire Heritage Ink of Edison, New Jersey, and a United Kingdom company, Gibbon Inks and Coatings. Dainippon bolstered its position in Australia with the acquisition of Colortron; it bought majority control in Tintas SA, a leading Colombian ink producer, and it added Coates, the printing inks division of TotalFina of France. On other fronts in the 1990s, Dainippon opened a sales office in Vietnam in 1996 and in 1998 launched a joint venture with Eastman Kodak Company called Kodak Polychrome Graphics. Company researchers also developed recyclable, pressure-sensitive industrial adhesive tapes and 100 percent vegetable oil–based printing ink.

The end of the 1990s brought the death of Shigekuni Kawamura, and Dainippon was forced to carry on without its dynamic president into the new century. Kohl & Madden acquired Fremont, California–based Thomas Printing Inks, Inc., a sheetfed ink manufacturer, in 2000. The early years of the decade brought an increased commitment to doing business in China. DIC Asia Pacific Pte Ltd was formed in Singapore in 2001 as a holding company for the graphic arts materials operations in the region, with the exception of the home market in Japan. In 2002 a plant opened in Nantong, China, for the production of printing inks and organic pigments, as did a plant for synthetic resins for use in coatings in Zhongshan, China. A plant was then opened in 2005 in Zhangiiagang, China, to produce synthetic resins and plastic colorants.

Dainippon adjusted its businesses mix mid-decade. It redeemed its capital interest in the Kodak joint venture in 2005 and also divested its interest in Reichhold through a management buyout. In that same year, Sun Chemical restructured its North American inks business. In 2008 Dainippon celebrated its centennial anniversary, and it marked the occasion by adopting a new name, DIC Corporation, as part of an effort to build a more global brand and foster greater cooperation among the DIC companies. Further changes followed in 2009 when DIC integrated its domestic printing inks business with Intec Inc. to create a joint venture, DIC Graphics Corporation. With the second century of its history now under way, there was every reason to expect DIC to continue to build its brand and enjoy strong growth across the globe in the years to come.

*Ed Dinger*

## PRINCIPAL SUBSIDIARIES

Sun Chemical.

## PRINCIPAL OPERATING UNITS

Printing Inks & Supplies Business Operation; Neo-Graphic Arts Materials Business Operation; Synthetic Resins Business Operation; Chemical Solution Materials Business Operation.

## PRINCIPAL COMPETITORS

Akzo Nobel N.V.; BASF Catalysts LLC; The Dow Chemical Company.

## FURTHER READING

Darlin, Damon, and Masayoshi Kanabayashi, "Dainippon Inks Takes Another Bold Step," *Wall Street Journal*, June 29, 2987, p. 1.

Hunter, David, "Dainippon See Payoff," *Chemical Week*, May 6, 1998, p. 17.

Nathans, Leah, and Brian Robins, "Then Came Kawamura," *Business Month*, October 1987, p. 40.

Power, Christopher, "Why Sun Chemical Is Playing Hard to Get," *Business Week*, June 2, 1986, p. 72.

Shibata, Yoko, "How Dainippon Ink Charted Takeover Trail," *Financial Times*, April 29, 1986, p. 36.

Tanzer, Andrew, "With Friends Like These," *Forbes*, June 30, 1986, p. 31.

# Dollar Thrifty Automotive Group, Inc.

---

7001 E 38th Street, Unit 7087
Tulsa, Oklahoma 74145
U.S.A.
Telephone: (918) 669-2503
Fax: (918) 664-8992
Web site: http://www.dtag.com/

*Public Company*
*Founded:* 1950 as Thrifty Rent-A-Car Systems; 1965 as Dollar Rent A Car Systems
*Incorporated:* 1989 as Pentastar Transportation Group, Inc.
*Employees:* 6,000
*Revenues:* $1.53 billion (2009)
*Stock Exchanges:* New York
*Ticker Symbol:* DTG
*NAICS:* 441120 Used Car Dealers; 532111 Passenger Car Rental

■ ■ ■

Dollar Thrifty Automotive Group, Inc. (DTAG), is an automobile rental agency that operates under the brand names of Dollar Rent A Car and Thrifty Car Rental. Both companies trace their origins to the mid-20th century. Thrifty was founded in 1950 as the Thrifty Rent-A-Car Systems, and Dollar Rent A Car Systems was formed in 1965. The two companies were merged in 1990, shortly after both were acquired by Chrysler Corporation. Chrysler later divested the two subsidiar-

ies, and in 1997 the combined car-rental agencies began trading publicly as the Dollar Thrifty Automotive Group. Based in Tulsa, Oklahoma, Dollar Thrifty markets car-rental services to a wide range of individual and corporate customers. Traditionally, both Dollar and Thrifty have represented a value-priced rental vehicle meant to appeal to a cost-conscious, value-sensitive market. With a total fleet of approximately 100,000 cars, the companies operate out of 600 locations throughout North America, while also maintaining offices in 80 countries worldwide. In 2010 the rival car-rental agency Hertz Global Holdings, Inc., launched a $1.2 billion bid to acquire DTAG.

## EVOLUTION OF THE U.S. CAR-RENTAL INDUSTRY: EARLY FIFTIES TO LATE EIGHTIES

Thrifty Rent-A-Car Systems was founded in Tulsa in 1950, and Dollar Rent A Car was founded in Los Angeles, California, in 1965. For decades, both companies operated as independent automobile rental agencies, each with its own area of specialization. Whereas Dollar operated primarily out of airport locations, Thrifty concentrated on offering its rental services at nonairport sites. Even though both companies conducted their businesses largely through franchising, they also owned a handful of rental offices in select North American cities.

In 1981 Thrifty Rent-A-Car Systems was acquired by a group of five private investors led by William E. Lobeck Jr. In 1987 Thrifty launched an initial public offering (IPO), and a year later Lobeck was elected the company's president and chief executive officer (CEO). By this time Thrifty had become the fifth-largest car-rental company in North America, with over 650 locations across the globe, and it had a fleet of more than 33,000 vehicles. In 1988 Thrifty posted net earnings of $9.1 million on revenues of $79.3 million. Dollar, by comparison, had 1,000 outlets worldwide and approximately 80,000 vehicles. In 1989 Dollar's total sales topped $600 million.

Meanwhile, major shifts in the U.S. automobile industry would soon exert a powerful impact on both Thrifty and Dollar. During the late 1980s Detroit's Big Three automakers (Ford Motor Company, General Motors Company, and Chrysler Corporation) began seeking ways to diversify as a means of propping up their meager income from flat car sales. As Dave Phillips of the *Detroit News* later recounted in April 1996, during this period the automakers began producing and selling almost everything. For instance, a Chrysler marine division made boats and outboard motors, General Motors manufactured earth-moving equipment, and Ford produced lawn and garden tractor equipment. The automakers' varied assets ranged from ownership of a data processing company and a credit card company to missile launchers and software developers.

Another area where the automakers identified enormous revenues potential was the car-rental industry. Toward the end of the 1980s major automakers began eyeing rental-car companies as possible acquisition targets, in the hopes of cashing in on the sector's brisk sales growth. At the same time, Chrysler, Ford, and General Motors hoped to take advantage of several key synergies that already existed between the two industries. For one, the car-rental sector accounted for roughly 10 percent of all automobile sales and was known to provide added exposure to certain car models. By becoming more involved in the car-rental business, the big automakers hoped to seize greater control over the future direction of the automobile market. Just as significantly, the bustling car-rental trade kept the manufacturers' assembly plants running during times of slow car sales. At the same time, auto-rental agencies remained a convenient place to unload cars that did not sell.

## AUTOMAKERS AND THE CAR-RENTAL INDUSTRY: 1987–94

As the decade came to a close, the major car companies began acquiring a sizable stake in the nation's leading car-rental companies. In 1987 Ford purchased a majority share in Hertz Corporation, the largest car-rental firm in the United States. The following year it acquired Budget Car Rental, the nation's third-leading rental agency, and General Motors purchased a minority stake in National Car Rental System, Inc. Not wanting to be shut out of this trend, Chrysler began identifying its own merger opportunities in the car-rental industry.

In 1989 Chrysler formed the Pentastar Transportation Group, Inc., with the aim of acquiring and operating rental-car subsidiaries. The company's first major acquisition was in May of that year, when it purchased Thrifty Rent-A-Car for $263 million. At the time of the merger, Thrifty was on the verge of acquiring Snappy Car Rental, Inc., a leader in the insurance replacement automobile rental sector, for $40 million. On completion of the deal, Thrifty and Snappy became the core brands of Chrysler's new Pentastar Transportation Group. The following year Chrysler acquired Dollar Rent A Car, giving the company a vital foothold in the airport auto-rental segment. Renamed Dollar Systems, Inc., the Dollar car-rental business immediately became the third brand operating as part of the Pentastar subsidiary. Between Thrifty, Dollar, and Snappy, Chrysler controlled more than 2,000 rental-car outlets worldwide.

In 1991 Chrysler acquired General Rent-A-Car, a relatively small rental agency with a presence at both airport and nonairport sites. With the acquisition of General, Chrysler increased its rental car fleet by 18,000. In fact, 80 percent of the new cars and trucks were actually Chrysler vehicles. Even though the addition of General boosted Chrysler's overall rental car business to 98,000 vehicles, the new company remained a separate subsidiary. Two years after completing the acquisition, Chrysler merged the operations of its General Rent-a-Car subsidiary into those of Dollar. In 1994 Chrysler sold Snappy Car Rental, Inc. That same year Dollar Rent A Car relocated its corporate headquarters from Los Angeles to Tulsa. Even though Thrifty and Dollar retained their unique brand names and areas of expertise, they now formed the backbone of Chrysler's Pentastar Transportation Group.

## DOWNSIDE TO THE CAR-RENTAL INDUSTRY

At the onset, Detroit's Big Three automakers benefited from this diversification, as their side businesses

## KEY DATES

**1950:** Thrifty Rent-A-Car Systems is founded in Tulsa, Oklahoma.

**1965:** Dollar Rent A Car Systems is founded in Los Angeles, California.

**1989:** Chrysler Corporation acquires Thrifty Rent-A-Car and reorganizes the brand under a new subsidiary, Pentastar Transportation Group, Inc.

**1990:** Chrysler acquires Dollar Rent A Car.

**1993:** Chrysler merges General Rent-A-Car operations into Dollar Rent A Car.

**1997:** Chrysler launches an initial public offering for Dollar Thrifty Automotive Group, Inc. (DTAG).

**1999:** DTAG forms Thrifty Car Sales, a chain of used-car dealers.

**2002:** DTAG merges the operations of Thrifty, Inc., and Dollar Rent A Car Systems into a single entity.

**2009:** DTAG renegotiates its vehicle supply contract with Chrysler.

**2010:** Hertz Global Holdings, Inc., launches a bid to acquire DTAG.

provided new automotive technologies and often improved their bottom lines. The car companies soon discovered, however, that these diverse subsidiaries also diverted management's time and attention away from their core vehicle production business. Data from publicly held U.S. car-rental companies also indicated that, during the first half of the decade, the industry was unable to keep pace with rising fleet costs. Furthermore, several of the domestic automotive manufacturers of the major U.S. vehicle-rental companies had been sold and were now publicly held. These changes in ownership led to higher car-rental rates, as a result of increased industry focus on profitability and shareholder returns rather than on transaction volume and market share.

Indeed, in only a few years the $16.4 billion rental-car business had changed a great deal. Describing this transformation in May 1998, Alex Taylor III of *Fortune* magazine wrote: "The big automakers, which owned the rental companies, realized that their subsidiaries made ideal captive customers for cars they couldn't sell, and they dumped vehicles on them. With so much excess inventory, the rental companies launched into a bloody round of competitive price cutting. Losses rocketed,

reaching an estimated $150 million in 1995." The automakers were also losers because the rental fleets on used-car lots stole new-car sales. Taylor noted that the Detroit Big Three, among others, sold their car-rental companies, which became independent public companies that could no longer depend on subsidies and "remodeled their businesses along the lines of airlines and hotels by using yield management."

In short, whereas between 1986 and 1996 car-rental companies had focused mainly on market share, they were now independent public companies that had to guarantee profits for their shareholders. Therefore, Pentastar Transportation Group faced a formidable challenge: not only that of increasing the revenues and improving the profitability of Dollar and Thrifty, whose loss of consolidated net income had gone from $40.5 million in 1993 to $146.3 million in 1996, but also that of keeping their individual identities.

### FORMATION OF DOLLAR THRIFTY AUTOMOTIVE GROUP, INC.: 1997

During the latter part of the 1990s shareholder pressure, booming stock prices, and a desperate need for capital to expand overseas prompted Detroit's Big Three auto manufacturers to divest a number of their noncore businesses, including their car-rental companies. General Motors sold its interest in National Car Rental in 1995 and divested itself of Avis in 1997. When Ford sold its interest in Budget Rent a Car in 1997 to a group of franchise holders and kept only a minor stake in the Hertz Corporation, Chrysler became the last of Detroit's Big Three to own car-rental companies.

As early as 1995, however, Chrysler had also begun to seek buyers for its car-rental subsidiaries. Finding itself unable to divest Thrifty and Dollar as separate entities, Chrysler reorganized in November 1997 the two car-rental companies into the Dollar Thrifty Automotive Group, Inc. (DTAG), making it a wholly owned subsidiary of the Pentastar Transportation Group, Inc. Pentastar was then merged into DTAG, which became the surviving subsidiary corporation. The new company continued to operate through its two nationally recognized subsidiaries, Thrifty and Dollar.

Indeed, the continued strength of the Thrifty and Dollar brands was key to the new company's future success. At yearend 1997 Thrifty's car-rental system comprised 636 U.S. and Canadian rental locations, of which 600 were franchised locations and 36 were company-owned stores. The Thrifty system also included 359 franchised locations in 63 other countries. In 1997 the company's total revenues reached $225.3

million, compared with $204.9 in 1996. Besides its U.S. suburban locations, Thrifty maintained a relationship with Montgomery Ward and operated rental facilities in many of the retailer's Auto Express Centers. In Canada Thrifty had a similar relationship with the Canadian Tire Corporation, Limited, a nationwide retail chain that sold automotive products, sporting goods, home and garden hardware, and plumbing supplies.

## BUILDING ON THE STRENGTH OF THE DOLLAR AND THRIFTY BRANDS

Even though Thrifty operated company-owned stores in a few U.S. and Canadian cities, its main focus was on franchising and franchise-support services. In fact, franchises were essential to its profitability and growth. For example, franchisees paid Thrifty an initial franchise fee based on factors such as population, number of airline passengers, total airport vehicle-rental revenues, and level of any other car-rental activity in the franchised territory. During the mid-1990s the company's average annual sales rate for franchisees was approximately 10 percent, with an average of 17 terminations and 25 new sales. In 1997 Thrifty's five largest U.S. franchisees generated administrative, fleet-leasing, reservation, and other fees that accounted for about 18 percent of Thrifty's total revenue. Thrifty also offered the franchisees a fleet-leasing program that provided them with a competitive and flexible source of fleet vehicles. In 1997 fleet-leasing fees accounted for about 58 percent of Thrifty's total revenue. Approximately 70 percent of Thrifty's revenue came from its franchises.

Thrifty's franchisees benefited from the company's continuously staffed worldwide reservation center headquartered in Tulsa. In 1997 the center processed more than 4.4 million telephone calls and 1.6 million reservations. The center was linked to all the major U.S. airline reservation systems and, through them, to worldwide travel agencies. Like Dollar, its companion subsidiary, Thrifty engaged SABRE to manage and monitor its data center network and daily information processing. The company also negotiated national account programs to allow its franchisees to take advantage of volume discounts for materials and services, such as tires, glass replacement, long-distance telephone service, and overnight mail. Furthermore, Thrifty helped new franchisees develop revenue opportunities, such as airport parking, used-car sales, and truck rentals.

Focusing mainly on the leisure market and on tour operators, Dollar had a fleet of some 61,336 vehicles in 1997, compared with a fleet of 52,571 cars in 1995.

About 76 percent of Dollar's 1997 rental revenues came from operations in Florida, California, Hawaii, and Nevada. The company also provided a high level of service to foreign-tour operators, especially those in the United Kingdom. Dollar realized significant income from rentals to tour customers because they reserved vehicles for longer periods and canceled reservations less frequently. The many tourist attractions of central Florida made this area the most important leisure destination for rentals. Dollar operated a company-owned store at Orlando International Airport and a facility at the Orlando Sanford International Airport, located 25 miles north of Orlando. Designed to serve mainly charter flights and to handle tour customers, this new facility oversaw the operation of 42 rental stations and parking for approximately 1,600 vehicles.

By this time, Dollar's line of services and products included fleet leasing, centralized reservations, insurance, supplies (such as ski racks, mobile telephones, and baby seats), and operational support. At yearend 1997 Dollar's vehicle rental system included 255 U.S. and Canadian locations consisting of 103 company-owned stores and 152 franchised stores. Dollar's total 1997 revenues were $617.5 million (of which 91 percent came from company-owned stores), compared with $499.2 million in 1996. Vehicle rentals by customers of foreign and domestic tour operators generated approximately 35 percent of these rental revenues. In 1997 Dollar was the exclusive U.S. car-rental company for three of its five largest tour-operator accounts.

## EMERGENCE OF A CONSOLIDATED CAR-RENTAL COMPANY

Shortly after incorporating DTAG, Chrysler announced that DTAG had filed with the U.S. Securities and Exchange Commission to sell up to 22.5 million shares of common stock. In December 1997 DTAG completed its IPO, generating roughly $460 million, of which Chrysler netted nearly $46 million. As it embarked on its new life as a public company, DTAG developed and implemented a six-point strategy aimed at increasing revenues, improving profitability, and expanding its worldwide presence.

First, to capitalize on the changing industry dynamics, DTAG identified the benefits that would accrue to smaller independent and regional rental operators that became franchisees of better-known brands such as Dollar or Thrifty. These benefits included better access to vehicle supply, more attractive financing, national marketing programs, and new technology. Second, DTAG expanded the market niches already established by the national brands of its two subsidiaries, Dollar and Thrifty. Third, DTAG took advantage of the operating efficiencies that resulted from its joint ownership of Dollar and Thrifty, such as volume discounts for advertising, insurance, and information systems as well as the consolidation of some administrative functions and the sharing of facilities. Additional benefits resulted from the coordinated disposal of used cars, the transfer of vehicles between fleets to adjust to variations in regional demands, the development of joint training programs, and the referral of overflow customers from one system to the other.

Fourth, joint investments in strategic information and reservation systems enabled Dollar to introduce, and Thrifty to improve, customer-frequency and loyalty programs. Fifth, international operations were expanded by having Dollar and Thrifty accept rental reservations for each other in their respective geographical areas. In addition, both Dollar and Thrifty licensed foreign vehicle-rental companies as master franchisees for specific countries or regions. Sixth, to develop opportunities for business expansion into related areas, DTAG applied its experience in fleet leasing and management, used-car disposal, and franchising. The company entered into joint ventures with new-car dealer groups and used its existing telecommunications capacity to provide telemarketing services. DTAG encouraged growth by linking incentive compensation to operating performance.

At yearend 1997 DTAG's consolidated revenues rose to $843.9 million, an increase of 20 percent over consolidated revenues of $705.6 million in 1996. For the first quarter of 1998 the company posted revenues of $191.3 million, compared with $177.1 million for the same period the previous year. The company's approach to serving both the airport and the local markets within each territory had enabled many of its franchisees and company-owned stores to have multiple locations. As a result, fleet utilization and profit margins could be improved by moving vehicles among locations for better administration of differences in demand among their markets. Even though DTAG traded as a single company, its principal operations remained divided into two distinct entities: Dollar Rent A Car Systems, Inc., and Thrifty, Inc. Without sacrificing the separate operating and brand identities of Dollar and Thrifty, DTAG planned to continue making investments in reservation, tour, and other information system improvements during 1998.

## DIVERSIFICATION AND EVOLUTION: 1998–2000

Toward the end of the 1990s, DTAG continued to seek new ways to expand its presence around the globe. In February 1998 Dollar entered into a strategic partnership with Europcar International, one of the major European car-rental groups. Under the terms of the deal, the two companies agreed to allow their respective locations in the United States and Europe to utilize both brand names, Dollar Rent A Car and Europcar, when renting vehicles to customers. In addition, Europcar agreed to reserve Dollar vehicles for its customers traveling to the United States, Canada, and Latin America. Previously, Dollar had operated under the name of EuroDollar in Europe, Africa, and the Middle East. The alliance with Europcar ended the EuroDollar relationship and enabled travelers wanting to reserve rental cars in these countries to contact Dollar for Europcar rentals.

At around this time DTAG began to explore ways to gain greater value from its outdated vehicles. Known as "risk vehicles" because the car-rental company was unable to sell them back to the manufacturers, these cars and trucks were traditionally sold at auction when they were no longer viable as rental vehicles, often at prices below market value. To establish a higher market value for its outgoing vehicles, the company created in early 1999 Thrifty Car Sales, with the aim of establishing up to 40 franchised used-car lots before the end of the year. According to estimates, the new business unit would enable DTAG to increase its earnings on car sales by $300 to $500 per vehicle. On average, Dollar and Thrifty had roughly 23,000 risk vehicles in their combined fleets each year.

DTAG also focused its attention on seizing a larger share of the domestic corporate travel market. One key to this ambition lay in building the company's presence in the nation's airports. Between 1998 and October 2000 Thrifty opened 25 new locations in airport terminals throughout the United States. Even though DTAG had traditionally operated at remote airport sites, thereby compelling airline passengers to wait for a shuttle to take them to the car-rental desk, the stronger presence within the terminals allowed the company to compete more directly with the larger rental agencies. During this time both Dollar and Thrifty also began emulating the swifter, more efficient pick-up and drop-off services provided by the bigger agencies. In 1998 Thrifty introduced its new express program, Blue Chip, which offered rapid transportation service for its customers. The following year Dollar launched an equivalent express service, Fastlane.

## ECONOMIC SETBACK AND RECOVERY: 2001–08

The terrorist attacks against the United States on September 11, 2001, had a disruptive and far-reaching impact on the car-rental industry. In the weeks following the attack, airport car rentals dropped significantly, forcing DTAG to delay its 2002 automobile deliveries by several weeks. For the third quarter of 2001 the company's net earnings dropped 83 percent, based on the decline in business during the final weeks of September alone. By December 2001 the company announced that it was cutting the salaries of its 40 top executives and implementing a freeze on pay raises. By early 2002, however, DTAG saw its earnings rebound, as the travel industry began to show signs of recovery. For the first quarter of 2002 the company's profits rose 31.7 percent, compared with the same period a year earlier.

Nonetheless, the general economic slowdown forced the company to consider ways to reduce costs. In late 2002 DTAG merged the operations of Thrifty, Inc., and Dollar Rent A Car Systems, Inc., into a single entity, with the aim of streamlining logistical and other support services for the two car-rental units. Even with this consolidation, Dollar and Thrifty continued to exist as distinct brand names. At around this time the company also unveiled a new expansion plan that was designed to increase its ownership over DTAG airport rental sites nationwide. In November 2004 DTAG purchased airport locations in Los Angeles and San Diego, California, and acquired several franchises in Boise, Idaho. In January 2005 the company acquired an additional three rental agencies in Florida. With these purchases DTAG increased its total number of airport acquisitions to 40 locations throughout North America since launching the new initiative. During this span the company also opened an additional eight new locations.

By early 2007 DTAG had increased its overall market value to $1.1 billion. However, with the onset of the global economic crisis that began later that year, the company's financial health began to take a turn for the worse. In February 2008 the company announced that its net earnings for fiscal 2007 would fall short of earlier forecasts, based largely on a decline in the travel sector. In the wake of this report, DTAG's stock value fell 37 percent, its largest single-day decline in its 10 years as a public company. As the recession stretched into 2008, the car-rental industry began to see a steep downturn in revenues. In November of that year DTAG announced that it would likely see an overall drop in revenues of between 4 percent and 5 percent for the year and post an operating loss.

## RECESSION AND COLLAPSE OF THE AUTOMOBILE INDUSTRY: 2008–10

In December 2008 DTAG failed to meet the $25 million minimum in market capitalization required of all companies trading on the New York Stock Exchange (NYSE). However, because a number of similarly sized companies also fell below this threshold, NYSE administrators agreed to lower the minimum market capitalization amount to $15 million on a temporary basis. Ultimately, DTAG suffered minimal financial damage relative to other major car-rental companies during the first quarter of 2009. The company posted losses of $8.9 million for the quarter, compared with $298 million for the same period in 2008. Still, the company found itself forced to seek additional ways to cut expenses, and during the first half of 2009 DTAG reduced its fleet of vehicles by 10 percent. At around this time the company's stock value plummeted to a low of $4.11 per share.

Meanwhile, the collapse of the nation's automobile industry introduced a host of new challenges for DTAG. After Chrysler declared bankruptcy in April 2009, DTAG found itself facing uncertainty over its future vehicle supply. The impact of Chrysler's collapse on DTAG was hard to overstate. Indeed, Chrysler had a long-standing pact with DTAG, whereby the car-rental firm was obliged to purchase 75 percent of all of its vehicles from the automaker. After Chrysler's bankruptcy, however, DTAG was suddenly in a position to renegotiate its existing contract. In October 2009 the two companies entered into a new agreement, one that allowed DTAG to acquire smaller percentages of vehicles from a larger number of suppliers. Under the terms of the new deal, DTAG was required to buy only 30 percent of its cars and trucks from Chrysler. At the same time, DTAG entered into similar agreements to purchase 34 percent of its vehicles from Ford and 20 percent from General Motors.

As DTAG continued to withstand the repercussions of the automobile industry collapse, it became the subject of acquisition talks. In April 2010 the car-rental giant Hertz Global Holdings, Inc., announced a bid to acquire DTAG, in a deal that was estimated to be worth $1.2 billion. As part of the agreement, Hertz would continue to market rental services under the Dollar and Thrifty brands. With the merger, Hertz would control 38 percent of the U.S. airport car-rental market, while increasing its worldwide holdings to 10,000 locations. Hertz's offer soon prompted a competing bid from Avis Budget Group, Inc., which asserted that Hertz's bid was dramatically undervaluing DTAG. Indeed, in the midst of this bidding war DTAG saw its stock value skyrocket to more than $50 per share in early May. Days after Avis launched its competing bid, a group of DTAG investors filed a lawsuit threatening to block the Hertz merger. Furthermore, in light of a growing trend toward consolidation in the car-rental industry, it was far from certain that U.S. regulators would approve any kind of major merger between DTAG and a larger company. In the face of all this uncertainty, DTAG's future had suddenly become very hard to predict.

*Gloria A. Lemieux*
*Updated, Stephen Meyer*

## PRINCIPAL SUBSIDIARIES

Dollar Rent A Car, Inc.; Dollar Thrifty Funding Corp.; DTG Operations, Inc.; Rental Car Finance Corp.; Thrifty, Inc.

## PRINCIPAL COMPETITORS

Avis Budget Group, Inc.; Enterprise Rent-A-Car Company; Hertz Global Holdings, Inc.

## FURTHER READING

De La Merced, Michael J., "Hertz May Have Rival in Bid for Dollar Thrifty," *New York Times*, May 4, 2010, p. B2.

"Dollar Opens 4 New Locations," *Journal Record*, June 16, 1998.

Hildebrand, Steven, "Dollar Thrifty Automotive Group, Inc.," *Wall Street Journal*, February 25, 1998, p. B5.

King, Sharon, "Hoping to Follow in Others' Tread Marks," *New York Times*, December 14, 1997, p. 8.

Peltz, James F., "Car Rental Agencies Driving up Profits with Higher Prices," *Los Angeles Times*, April 25, 1998.

Phillips, Dave, "Big 3 Shopping Spree Over," *Detroit News*, April 14, 1996.

Stoller, Gary, "Hertz to Acquire Dollar Thrifty," *USA Today*, April 27, 2010, p. 3B.

Taylor III, Alex, "Back in the Driver's Seat," *Fortune*, May 25, 1998.

Thompson, Chrissie, "Dollar Thrifty Slashes Its Chrysler Purchases," *Automotive News*, October 19, 2009, p. 6.

Yung, Katherine, "Big 3 Existing Car Rental Business," *Detroit News*, January 15, 1997.

WWW.EDWARDSVACUUM.COM

# Edwards Group Limited

Manor Royal
Crawley, West Sussex RH10 9LW
United Kingdom
Telephone: (+44 08459) 212-233
Fax: (+44 01293) 534-149
Web site: http://www.edwardsvacuum.com

*Private Company*
*Founded:* 1919 as Edwards Equipment and Services
*Incorporated:* 1954 as Edwards High Vacuum Limited
*Employees:* 3,000
*Sales:* £509.80 million ($798.80 million) (2008)
*NAICS:* 333911 Pump and Pumping Equipment Manufacturing; 333912 Air and Gas Compressor Manufacturing

■ ■ ■

Edwards Group Limited, a world leader in vacuum and abatement systems, is owned by the private equity groups CCMP Capital and Unitas Capital. The company supplies integrated solutions for the manufacture of microelectronic devices, and it designs, produces, and provides technical support for a wide range of high-technology vacuum equipment. Its staff of 3,000 is divided into two global teams serving the general vacuum industries and the semiconductor industries, and it supplies some of the world's leading semiconductor manufacturers. The company is credited with inventing the commercial oil-free "dry" vacuum pump and continues to excel in the development of innovative vacuum pumps and related technologies. Edwards operates in more than 20 countries worldwide, with Asia being an area of significant expansion in recent years. With major manufacturing centers in China, Japan, and Korea, and several remanufacturing and service centers in numerous other Asian countries, the region accounts for 60 percent of the company's business. In January 2010 CEO Nigel Hunton unveiled plans to relocate all of the company's manufacturing operations to countries within Asia and Europe, while retaining the United Kingdom as the company's base for research and development.

## THE ORIGINS OF EDWARDS GROUP LIMITED

In 1919 F. D. Edwards and his wife invested £20.00 to establish Edwards Equipment and Services, a vacuum equipment import business on Allendale Road in Camberwell, South London. By 1939 the company was manufacturing vacuum equipment, and by 1953 it had taken up residence in Crawley, Sussex, England. The following year Edwards High Vacuum Limited was formed, and the company began to grow through acquisitions. The Italian freeze-drying manufacturer Alto Vuoto SpA was acquired in 1955. In 1958 Edwards acquired J. H. Holmes and Son Ltd., a manufacturing subcontractor in Shoreham, Sussex, whose site would serve as the company's base for primary and dry pump manufacturing for more than 50 years. Additional factories in Eastbourne and Grand Island followed shortly thereafter.

The company went public during the 1960s, and in 1968 it was acquired by the British Oxygen Company

# COMPANY PERSPECTIVES

Edwards is a world leader in the manufacture and supply of vacuum and abatement solutions serving the most advanced industries, including solar, semiconductor, scientific, LED, pharmaceutical, and metallurgical.

With sales of $500 million and 3,000 employees in over 20 countries around the world, Edwards stays ahead by investing in talented people who provide innovative, high-quality products which set the industry standards in performance and technology. Now, with our newly founded independence, we are investing in product development and introductions that will meet the future challenges of our customers.

The welfare of our people and customers and the protection of the environment are our highest priorities. We adhere to a strict policy on Environment, Health and Safety Management where we are committed to excellence, and a Code of Conduct which guides our behavior as individuals and our ethics as an organization.

We thrive on challenges. It is part of our culture: challenging processes, changing technologies, product innovation. We are always striving to keep our leadership in vacuum and abatement, ensuring success for our customers and ourselves by going that extra mile to build a successful future together.

(BOC) Group Inc. In October 1971 Edwards expanded into Asia by entering into a 50/50 joint venture with Nissan Sanso to form Nissan Edwards Shinku KK. The joint venture was dissolved in 1993, with BOC Edwards assuming full management. In 1994 the company was renamed Nippon Edwards KK, and in 2003 it was renamed BOC Edwards Japan Ltd. Other Asian expansion efforts over the next two decades included a 1988 agreement with Japan's Seiko Seiki Ltd. for distribution of its magnetically suspended turbomolecular pumps, and a 1984 agreement with the Songwon Trading Company Ltd. in South Korea to act as the company's exclusive agent. This relationship was strengthened in 1992 when Songwon and Edwards entered into a joint venture to form Songwon Edwards Ltd. Also in 1984 Edwards patented its groundbreaking oil-free Drystar vacuum pump, launching the dry-claw pump into the semiconductor market.

European expansion included the 1977 acquisition of Kneise Apparatbau GmbH, a German freeze-drying manufacturer. It also included the 1992 acquisition of Plasma Products from Electrotech Ltd. and the 1995 acquisition of Calumatic BV, a pharmaceutical filling and handling systems manufacturer based in the Netherlands. Also in 1995 BOC Gases was awarded a contract by TwinStar Semiconductor Inc., a Texas Instruments and Hitachi joint venture, to be its sole supplier of industrial gases and related services at its first manufacturing facility in Richardson, Texas, and Edwards was selected to oversee all of TwinStar's vacuum pumping and point-of-use gas exhaust abatement systems. In 1997 the BOC Group continued its strategy of extending its product line with the acquisition of the slurry distribution equipment manufacturer Systems Chemistry Inc., a wholly owned subsidiary of SubMicron Systems Corporation.

## THE FORMATION OF BOC EDWARDS

In 1997 the BOC Group made the strategic decision to combine its electronic gases and semiconductor vacuum businesses to form BOC Edwards. By offering its wide range of products and services within one organization, the Group's profile with its semiconductor customer base was substantially enhanced. At the end of 1997 the BOC Group was operating in 40 countries and reported more than $800 million in sales to the semiconductor industry. The following year the newly formed company entered into an agreement with Semi-Gas Systems, another leading supplier to the semiconductor industry, to supply Semi-Gas Systems's gas-delivery equipment. The alliance garnered BOC Edwards further attention as a global leader in chemical-management systems and total process solutions for the semiconductor industry.

In May 1999 BOC Edwards won two major contracts within the European semiconductor industry, totaling over $1 million, to supply its iSIS 7000 slurry delivery system. In that same month, in a move designed to offer unrivaled service and technical support, BOC Edwards opened a sales and service center in Toufen, Taiwan, a prime location that placed the company among many of the world's largest foundries and close to several of its major customers. BOC Edwards continued to expand its product line with the purchase in Minnesota of FSI International's Chemical Management Division for £23 million ($38 million). Growth in the United States included opening a state-of-the-art electronic materials plant in Medford, Oregon. Opened in October 1999, the plant employed 50 high-technology professionals to serve semiconductor customers in the United States, Europe, and the Pacific Rim.

## KEY DATES

**1919:** F. D. Edwards establishes Edwards Equipment and Services.
**1954:** Edwards High Vacuum Limited (Edwards) is formed.
**1968:** BOC Group Inc. acquires Edwards.
**1997:** The Edwards vacuum business is merged with BOC's electronic gases business to form BOC Edwards.
**2007:** CCMP Capital and Unitas Capital acquire BOC Edwards, and the company is renamed Edwards Group Limited.

By 2000 the Internet and wireless communications were driving the burgeoning semiconductor market, and BOC Edwards pursued other expansion opportunities. The company expanded its FabMaX semiconductor on-site services business with the acquisition of Kachina Semiconductor Services in Phoenix, Arizona. In that same year BOC Edwards began a joint venture with Pelchem, the Chemical Division of NECSA (formerly AEC), South Africa, to establish a nitrogen trifluoride (NF3) gas-production facility. The highly prized gas had become a prime material for semiconductor production due to its lower perfluorocarbon (PFC) emissions, and BOC Edwards wanted to insure its availability.

In July 2000 Millipore Corp. and BOC Edwards collaborated on the development and marketing of an integrated bath regeneration system called CuBIS (Copper Bath Integrated Solution). In that same month, the company announced that it had begun a strategic alliance with Austin, Texas–based ISinc, Inc., a design and construction management provider to the semiconductor industry, to develop 3-D design tools and to share marketing activities.

## BOC EDWARDS'S STRATEGY AFTER 2001

In February 2001 BOC Edwards introduced two new models to its range of dry industrial vacuum pumps, the GV 260M and GV 410M. By June 2001, while the semiconductor industry was in recession, the company opened its 22,000-square-foot BOC Edwards Kachina facility in Hillsboro, Oregon, as part of its worldwide expansion. "There may be some pain in the beginning, but if we're serious about growth, we need to have capability in the Northwest," said Robert Adams, vice president of sales and marketing of BOC Edwards Kachina, to Aliza Earnshaw in the *Business Journal-Portland*.

Despite its successful expansion efforts, the downturn in the semiconductor industry still had an impact on BOC Edwards's bottom line. In August 2001 BOC Edwards reported a 14 percent drop in sales and a 25 percent decrease in operating profits. To offset these losses, the BOC Group announced that it would be eliminating 1,500 jobs, with 60 percent of these coming from BOC Edwards. The group was also forced to divest £120 million ($172 million) worth of its interests.

The range of the BOC Edwards product line was its strength, and the company seized opportunities in other markets, such as the fine chemicals and pharmaceutical sectors. Acquisitions in that year included Intellimetrics Ltd., a Glasgow, Scotland, manufacturer of on-tool monitoring and control equipment for vacuum and etch processes; the turbomolecular pump business from Seiko Instruments Inc.; and the vacuum and pressure interests of the Smiths Group, a £12.8 million ($19 million) deal that included Stokes Vacuum (United States), Hick Hargreaves (United Kingdom), Wilhelm Klein (Germany), and Hibon (France, Germany, Belgium, Czech Republic).

In 2002 acquisitions were once again part of the BOC Edwards expansion strategy. The company acquired Semco Corp. of Livermore, California, and Hydromatix, Inc., of Sante Fe, California, a manufacturer of liquid purification systems. These acquisitions were integrated into BOC Edwards's Chemical Management Division as the company announced that it was moving its chemical management business to a new, state-of-the-art facility in Chanhassen, Minnesota.

BOC Edwards also planned to ramp up its activities in Asia, the world leader of flat-panel display technology. In November 2001 BOC Edwards unveiled a new high-purity ammonia production system. The gas had applications in the semiconductor, LED, and flat-panel display markets, and this system would help to retain the company's competitive edge in the region. By 2003 the company had secured business at all of China's major semiconductor sites, with the majority of these near Shanghai and Beijing. BOC Edwards had also expanded its logistics and service operations in the region to provide full customer support.

China's special gas business was growing rapidly, and in January 2004 BOC Edwards signed an agreement with Nanjing Mucop Nanfen Special Gas Company to market its products in Northern China. The following month, the company signed a lucrative contract with LG Philips to supply fluorine gas at its manufacturing facility in Gumi, South Korea. In March

2004 BOC Edwards was contracted by a major Taiwanese semiconductor-chip manufacturer to provide all gas- and chemical-management site services. Expansion in the region continued as BOC Edwards announced in May 2004 that it would be constructing a high-purity silane transfill facility (which compresses bulk gas for shipment to customers) in Kunshan, Suzhou, China. In that same month, the company was awarded the contract to provide all vacuum and abatement solutions to a new foundry in North Asia, and it received a major vacuum systems order from Samsung Electronics in South Korea.

In October 2004 BOC Edwards acquired a 50 percent stake in Asia Union Electronic Chemical Corporation (AUECC) and was moving forward on a wet chemicals joint venture with Shangahi Huayi Company. In November the company announced that it was investing in seven gas facilities in Taiwan to position itself as the leading supplier of bulk gas to nine new manufacturers. The year closed with BOC Edwards announcing that it was moving its main Japanese operations to a new world-class facility in Yachiyo, Chiba, Japan. In 2005 BOC Edwards was again selected by LG Philips to supply most of the vacuum-pump systems at its new plant in Paju, Korea. The company's strategy was paying off, with BOC Edwards expecting business from the thin film transistor–liquid crystal display (TFT-LCD) industry to surpass 2004 levels.

## THE EVOLUTION OF EDWARDS GROUP LIMITED

In September 2006 the BOC Group was acquired by Linde AG, and plans were put in place to divest the BOC Edwards equipment business. The following month, the Ingersoll-Rand Company Limited acquired BOC Edwards's low-pressure air business. In March 2007 it was announced that Linde had signed a deal with the private equity firm CCMP Capital to sell BOC Edwards's vacuum and semiconductor business for $901.1 million. "This is the start of a new independent era for BOC Edwards in which we can focus on delivering world class products and services to our customers," CEO Nigel Hunton said in a company press release on March 12, 2007.

In April 2007 Linde sold BOC Edwards's Polish gases activities to Air Products and Chemicals, Inc. On May 31, 2007, the acquisition of BOC Edwards by CCMP Capital and Unitas Capital was completed, and the newly independent, privately owned company was rebranded Edwards Group Limited two months later. In August 2009 Edwards announced that it was selling its Kachina semiconductor facilities in Texas, Arizona, and Oregon, and its on-site service operations in Virginia,

Israel, and Ireland to Applied Materials of Santa Clara, California. In May 2008 Edwards signed an agreement with Air Liquide Electronics U.S. LP to divest most of its Chemical Management Division.

By the end of 2008 Edwards's core business was vacuum equipment and abatement solutions. Although the company was the largest vacuum supplier to the semiconductor industry, Edwards planned to turn its attention to new markets, such as solar panels and biofuels. In December 2009 Edwards completed the installation of an energy-efficient steel degassing system in New Delhi, India, the first of its kind in the country, using Edwards's dry-pumping technology.

In January 2010 Edwards announced that it was reducing its workforce in Sussex by 220 employees and relocating its manufacturing operations to Europe and Asia. In a press release that month, Hunton said that the company also planned to establish a new technology center in Sussex that would be supported by R&D efforts in Clevedon (United Kingdom) Yachiyo (Japan), and Shanghai (China). Although the bulk of the manufacturing business was going to be moved to Asia, where its semiconductor business was concentrated, expansion plans were in place for its U.K. sites in Clevedon, Eastbourne, Bolton, and Crawley. The restructuring put the company closer to its customers and reduced production lead times, while the United Kingdom was retained as the company's center for technological advances.

*Marie O'Sullivan*

## PRINCIPAL DIVISIONS

EXT Turbo Pumps; Industrial Dry Pumps; Large Oil Sealed Pumps; Measurement and Control; Semiconductor Pumps; Small Wet and Dry Pumps; Vacuum Fittings; Vacuum Valves.

## PRINCIPAL OPERATING UNITS

Asia-Pacific; Europe, Middle East and Africa; Americas.

## PRINCIPAL COMPETITORS

Alcatel Vacuum Technology (UK) Ltd.; Ebara Technologies, Inc.; Tuthill Corporation.

## FURTHER READING

"BOC Edwards Headed for Flat Panel Banner Year," *Business Wire*, July 11, 2005.

"BOC Edwards Makes Investments in Semiconductor Industry," *Chemical Market Reporter*, July 17, 2000, p. 5.

"BOC Edwards Opens New Sales and Service Center in Taiwan," PR Newswire, May 26, 1999, p. 8117.

"BOC Edwards to Be Rebranded as Edwards," Business Wire, July 17, 2007.

"CCMP Completes Acquisition of BOC Edwards from the Linde Group," Business Wire, May 31, 2007.

Collins, Don, "Vacuum Pumps for Pharmaceutical Processes," *Pharma*, May–June 2009, p. 42.

Earnshaw, Aliza, "BOC Moves Forward Despite Slowing Economy," *Business Journal-Portland*, June 8, 2001, p. 13.

"Exhaust Management Systems Use Vacuum and Abatement Technologies," *Product News Network*, March 19, 2010.

Sherwood, Bob, "Edwards Creates Vacuum in Sussex," *Financial Times*, January 18, 2010, p. 22.

———, "Edwards' Green Focus Pays Off," *Financial Times*, October 6, 2008, p. 26.

emerging·vision·inc.

# Emerging Vision, Inc.

—————— ■ ——————

100 Quentin Roosevelt Boulevard
Garden City, New York 11530
U.S.A.
Telephone: (516) 390-2100
Web site: http://emergingvision.com/

*Public Company*
*Incorporated:* 1992
*Employees:* 124
*Sales:* $50.68 million (2009)
*Stock Exchanges:* OTC
*Ticker Symbol:* ISEE
*NAICS:* 446130 Optical Goods Stores; 533110 Franchise Agreements, Leasing, Selling, or Licensing, without Providing Other Services

■ ■ ■

Emerging Vision, Inc., is a holding company with franchising, specialty retail, group purchasing, health care, financial service, and neutraceutical, or nutritional supplement, interests. It is one of the leading optical retailers in the United States, with nearly 200 retail locations doing business under the brand names Site for Sore Eyes and Sterling Optical. These retailers offer prescription and nonprescription eyeglasses, eyeglass frames, contact lenses, sunglasses, and a variety of other eye care products. Emerging Vision, Inc., also operates Sterling Vision Care, a specialty health management organization in California that offers the services of optometrists in offices adjacent to Sterling Optical retail stores. In other states, Emerging Vision's Insight Man-

aged Vision Care offers management plans for consumer vision needs. Emerging Vision's group purchasing subsidiaries, Combine Buying Group in the United States and The Optical Group in Canada, offer products at a discount to optical retailers.

## FOUNDERS PURCHASE OPTICAL COMPANY: 1992

Emerging Vision, Inc., began in 1992 when brothers Robert and Alan Cohen purchased the nearly 80-year-old firm Sterling Optical, which had begun as a single store in 1914 in New York's financial district. Thirty-five years later, a second Sterling Optical store opened in Washington, D.C. Over the following decades Sterling became the largest optical chain in the Northeast, and continued its growth across the Northeast, Mid-Atlantic, and Midwest by acquiring other retail optical chains.

In 1993 the Cohens made their new company's first acquisition when they purchased the California retail optical chain Site for Sore Eyes, which had begun as a single boutique in Berkeley in 1979. By in 1985, Site for Sore Eyes had grown to eight stores and had begun its own successful franchising campaign.

Among the many franchise locations Sterling Optical continued to open and actively support, one in its native New York proved especially noteworthy. In September 1998 Sterling Optical responded to a solicitation from the community development organization Local Initiatives Support Corporation, (LISC) to open a franchise in Harlem, New York, an area previously underserved by optical retailers. Jerry Darnell, chief operating officer of Sterling Optical's franchising division,

described the new store in an interview in the August
2000 issue of the trade magazine *Chain Store Age Executive with Shopping Center Age.* "There are inner-city
neighborhoods with ample disposable income that are
not being served. This is a huge opportunity for us
because there is a great need for our services." On opening day the new store booked more than 100 eye exams.

## A TURBULENT BEGINNING TO THE 21ST CENTURY

In April 2000 Sterling Vision changed its name to
Emerging Vision, Inc. Sterling Optical became a
subsidiary within the new parent company. The name
change marked Emerging Vision's new focus on building an Internet-based business-to-business optical supply
company that would sell services and eyewear to optical
distributors. The company engaged the services of an
investment banking firm, McDonald Investments, to
advise it on the most effective use of its resources as it
transitioned its business focus.

In June 2000 Emerging Vision engaged the services
of another investment banking firm, Legg Mason Wood
Walker, to oversee the sales of the company's Sterling
Optical retail stores, Insight Laser Centers, and ambulatory surgery center. The sales plan followed the
company's announced shift from specializing in retail
eyewear and vision services to becoming an online supplier of optical tools and services to manufacturers and
distributors.

In December 2000, however, Emerging Vision announced that it was cancelling the sale of its Sterling
Optical stores. Instead, it would split its new online
sales division and existing retail division into two
separate publicly held companies. It also announced
plans to retain its Insight Laser Centers. Company

executives told the *Long Island Business News* on
December 22 that the change in plan came after the
company reexamined its options. Sam Herskowitz, vice
president of marketing and advertising, commented that
"The whole thing is very positive. Sterling can now
focus on its core business, which is retail optical. Emerging Vision can focus on its business, which is the retail
portal."

A further modification of the corporate plan was
announced in March 2001, when Emerging Vision announced it would shut down its online sales operation,
Emergingvision.com, completely. Instead, the company
would concentrate on its more than 250 franchise locations and company-owned retail stores. The move followed a $40 million loss by Emerging Vision, Inc., in
the first nine months of 2000 and came at a challenging
time for many other online retailers. In an interview on
March 30 in the *Long Island Business News*, Herskowitz,
announced that Emerging Vision would explore ways to
grow its system of stores. "Adding stores where we
already have a presence and looking at new markets,
continuing to build the Sterling brand, which is a 90-
year old brand."

## ADJUSTMENTS AND A FAILED TAKEOVER BID: 2001–04

In June 2001, in response to a NASDAQ warning that
the company stood in danger of losing its listing on the
stock exchange, Emerging Vision sold its East Meadow,
New Jersey, ambulatory eye surgery center to Ambulatory Surgery, Inc., in exchange for assuming $880,000
in debt. Giving up the surgery center allowed Emerging
Vision to increase its net assets above the $4 million
minimum required for a listing on NASDAQ. The following month, however, Emerging Vision received word
from NASDAQ that its stock price had fallen below the
minimum $1 per share required for listing.

In July 2004 Emerging Vision survived a bid by its
largest shareholder to take control of the company's
board of directors. Real estate developer and
entrepreneur Benito Fernandez and his Horizon Investors Corporation of Albany, New York, owned 33.7
percent of Emerging Vision stock. An article in the July
23 *Long Island Business News* cited Emerging Vision's
delisting from the NASDAQ in 2001 and recent
revenue losses as major reasons for Horizon's challenge.
The subsequent failure of the takeover attempt, said
Emerging Vision CEO Christopher Payan, indicated "a
strong endorsement of management's operating strategy"
by other shareholders.

Shortly afterward, in September 2004, Emerging
Vision launched a $3 million marketing campaign

## KEY DATES

■

**1992:** Robert and Alan Cohen purchase Sterling Optical and establish the Sterling Vision Company.

**2000:** Sterling Vision Company changes its name to Emerging Vision, Inc.

**2001:** Emerging Vision abandons its online retail portal.

**2004:** The board of directors survives a proxy battle with the company's largest shareholder.

**2009:** CEO Christopher Payan, who had served in the position for eight years, is replaced by Glenn Spina.

intended to support the company's franchise subsidiaries, Sterling Vision and Site for Sore Eyes. Emerging Vision selected the EGC Group of Hicksville, New Jersey, to run the campaign, which included television, radio, movie theater, and print advertisements. "The goal of this campaign will be to have more bodies walking through the door," said Herskowitz in an interview in the *Long Island Business News* on September 10. Herskowitz also remarked on the challenges of a marketing campaign aimed at franchisees. "With a franchise, in many instances, it's like handling different accounts. Each franchise has its own concerns. They're in different markets, with different worries."

### SUCCESS AND ACQUISITIONS: 2005–08

In 2005 Payan announced that a five-point turnaround plan launched in 2003 had returned Emerging Vision to profitability for the first time in five years. The plan included rebuilding vendor relationships, refocusing on core services, and eliminating peripheral offerings, such as laser vision correction. Following the announcement, Emerging Vision engaged the services of the public relations firm Financial Dynamics to publicize the company's newly regained profitability.

In October 2006 Emerging Vision completed the purchase of its new subsidiary, Combine Optical Management Corporation, for $2.5 million in cash, $700,000 of which it paid at closing and $1.8 million to be paid over the next five years. Based in Florida and established in 1981, Combine Optical Management provided its approximately 1,000 retail members with vendor discounts on optical goods and business services. Emerging Vision announced that it would continue to

develop Combine's new nutritional supplement business, which distributed vitamins and other nutritional aids to individuals with a predisposition to develop certain eye diseases and disorders. Combine's existing management remained in place to operate the subsidiary. Prior to purchase by Emerging Vision, sales revenue for Combine Optical totaled approximately $15.2 million annually.

In 2007 Emerging Vision acquired The Optical Group, a group-purchasing operation based in Canada and established in 1988. The cash purchase price of CAN 3.8 million equaled about $3.6 million. Like Combine Optical Management, The Optical Group provided its approximately 525 retail members with group discounts on optical products and business services. Prior to purchase by Emerging Vision, sales revenue for The Optical Group totaled approximately CAN 41 million ($36 million) annually.

Emerging Optical continued to focus on the retail expansion of its business in 2007. A new print, mail, and electronic marketing campaign specifically targeted potential new franchisees already working in the optical industry. Midway through the year, six new franchise locations opened in three of Emerging Vision's strongest markets: California, Maryland, and New York. Payan commented in *Business Wire* that in addition to the brand equity and economic benefit of clustering stores in already proven markets, the recent expansion and "growth within these markets demonstrates the Company's dedication to the markets it serves and to its existing franchisees."

In 2008 the *Wall Street Journal* selected Sterling Optical as one of the 25 best-performing franchises in the United States. The *Journal* listed well-established franchises with overall financial health and what the newspaper called "a proven record of franchise success."

### NEW LEADERSHIP FACES DOWNTURN: 2009–10

In September 2009 the board of directors of Emerging Vision elected not to renew the contract of the company's CEO, Christopher Payan, who had served in the position for eight years. A company press release acknowledged his "instrumental role in the turnaround of Emerging Vision and the Company's expansion into new business sectors." In December the board announced the appointment of Glenn Spina as company CEO and president. Spina had previously served as president and CEO of a variety of national and international optical and medical retail companies. "We worked hard to select a leader with extensive retail optical management experience," said Emerging Vision board president Dr. Alan Cohen. "Mr. Spina's acute industry knowledge, experience and expertise are desirable assets to Emerging Vision's core retail and franchise businesses."

After years of restored financial health and losses in fiscal year 2008 that had totaled only $88,000, Emerging Vision indicated in reports filed with the Securities and Exchange Commission in April 2010 that it had experienced an increased net loss of $2.5 million during 2009. The losses came in the middle of a nationwide economic downturn that affected revenues throughout the economy's retail sector and posed a challenge to the company's new leadership.

*Joyce Helena Brusin*

## PRINCIPAL SUBSIDIARIES

Combine Buying Group; The Optical Group; Site for Sore Eyes; Sterling Optical; Sterling Vision Care.

## PRINCIPAL COMPETITORS

Eye Care Centers of America, Inc.; Luxottica Group S.p.A.

## FURTHER READING

"20/20: Excelling in the Business of Vision," *Chain Store Age*, January 2006.

Corry, Carl, "Sterling Continues Net Strategy with Name Change," *Long Island Business News*, April 28, 2000.

"Emerging Vision Completes Acquisition of Combine Optical Management Corporation," *Health & Medicine Week*, November 6, 2006.

Luhby, Tami, "Emerging Vision Refocuses on Retail," *Newsday*, March 29, 2001.

———, "Emerging Vision to Buy Canadian Optical Group," *Newsday*, August 25, 2007.

Powderly, Henry E., II, "Emerging Vision Completes Purchase of Combine Optical Management," *Long Island Business News*, October 6, 2006.

Solnik, Claude, "Emerging Vision Ends E-Commerce, Shuffles Execs," *Long Island Business News*, March 30, 2001.

———, "Emerging Vision's Board Staves off Challenge by Albany-based Horizon Investors," *Long Island Business News*, July 23, 2004.

———, "Sterling Optical's New View," *Long Island Business News*, December 22, 2000.

White, George, "Eyeing New Urban Markets," *Chain Store Age Executive with Shopping Center Age*, August 2000.

# eResearch Technology, Inc.

———————————————◼———————————————

30 South 17th Street
Philadelphia, Pennsylvania 19103
U.S.A.
Telephone: (215) 972-0420
Fax: (215) 972-0414
Web site: http://www.ert.com

*Public Company*
*Incorporated:* 1972 as Anthropometrics, Inc.
*Employees:* 353
*Sales:* $93.8 million (2009)
*Stock Exchanges:* NASDAQ
*Ticker Symbol:* ERES
*NAICS:* 541380 Testing Laboratories; 621511 Medical
    Laboratories

◼ ◼ ◼

Based in Philadelphia, Pennsylvania, eResearch Technology, Inc. (ERT), serves the pharmaceutical, biotechnology, and medical-device industries by offering software and support services in the regulatory approval process. ERT provides cardiac safety testing to measure the effect of drugs on key organs as a way to gauge a product's safety, and it offers cardiac safety counseling. ERT's electronic patient reported outcome (ePRO) service provides quick reporting of subject data in clinical drug trials. This information is also managed and delivered by the system. In addition, ERT offers a variety of project assurance services to make sure the company's solutions are having the desired impact, including study initiation, project management, site qualification, data manage-

ment, help-desk support, and software maintenance. Marketing and sales are handled by a global direct sales force. ERT customers include the world's 10 largest pharmaceutical companies, as well as 39 of the top 50. Novartis AG is ERT's largest customer. It accounted for 18 percent of ERT's net revenues in 2009 and is the only customer that accounts for more than 10 percent. ERT is a public company listed on the NASDAQ.

## ORIGINS: 1972

ERT traces its lineage to 1972, when a stock broker named John Aglialoro and his wife, June Carter, were looking for a business opportunity. They had a friend who was an exercise physiologist, and because at the time cardiovascular stress testing was primarily conducted in university settings, they decided there was an opening to provide cardiac testing and rehabilitation. They established a company called Anthropometrics, which became operational in 1973. About two years later Aglialoro and Carter formed a division called Cardiac Long Term Monitoring, which would evolve into ERT.

Cardiac Long Term Monitoring offered computer analysis of ambulatory electrocardiogram tapes, also called Holter tapes. It expanded its purview in 1975 when it helped in the development of an anti-arrhythmic agent by conducting a Holter study. In short order, Cardiac Long Term Monitoring established itself as a research company and became the country's largest provider of Holter monitoring services used by pharmaceutical companies seeking U.S. Food and Drug Administration (FDA) approval for new cardiovascular

Evaluation Services. In addition to testing pacemaker performance, it maintained a clinical division, which was eventually merged with the CDS clinical division.

CDS expanded to the United Kingdom in 1987, establishing an operation in Peterborough, Cambridgeshire, to better serve the needs of global clients by providing both Holter and ambulatory blood-pressure monitoring data collection, analysis, and reporting. The company continued to diversify its services at the start of the 1990s, employing computer analysis to detect changes on electrocardiograms and offering an new array of clinical laboratory tests.

Having expanded beyond its original purpose, Cardio Data Systems changed its name in 1990 to CDSResearch. To better reflect its work on global studies and an expanding customer base, which included pharmaceutical as well as biotechnology companies, the name became CDSResearch Worldwide in 1993. In addition, corporate headquarters moved that year to Philadelphia, Pennsylvania, where CDSResearch opened a Center City clinical research unit. The 45-bed facility was used to conduct pharmacokinetic, pharmacodynamic, and other Phase I regulatory approval studies. Also of note in 1993, Aglialoro and the other principal shareholders, displeased with the valuation of United Medical's stock, took the company private.

## COMPANY TAKEN PUBLIC: 1997

CDSResearch continued to expand during the balance of the 1990s. In 1995 it acquired a contract research unit of Premier Research Worldwide Inc. (PRWW), part of Premier Inc., a major hospital buying group. It also adopted the Premier Research Worldwide name. As such, the company was taken public in 1997 with Dr. Joel Morganroth as its chief executive officer. A well-respected cardiologist and clinical researcher, Morganroth had been a consultant for CDS since 1977 and had become the chief executive in 1993. Aglialoro and his wife, the majority shareholders in PRWW, were the only selling shareholders in the offering, which netted the company $34.2 million. The couple still retained a significant stake in PRWW, but by the end of the decade they liquidated their holdings. United Medical ultimately took the name UM Holdings, and it continued to invest in medical companies and other related ventures.

With its shares now listed on the NASDAQ, PRWW completed an acquisition, buying the assets and business of Bridgewater, New Jersey–based DLB Systems Ltd. from Safeguard Scientifics Inc. in October 1997, after previously investing $1 million in the company. DLB served pharmaceutical, biotechnology, and

drugs. The company changed the division's name to Cardio Data Services (CDS) and in 1979 played a key role in the National Institute of Health's Beta Blocker Heart Attack Trial, which led to the recommended use of the drug propranolol by analyzing 4,500 Holter recordings.

## RESEARCH AND DATA CORPORATION ACQUIRED

Aglialoro and Carter renamed Anthropometrics as United Medical Corporation and took the company public in 1981. In 1983 CDS acquired the Holter monitoring business of Fidelity Medical Services Inc. Another addition to the United Medical fold was Research Data Corporation, acquired in the early 1980s. It was little more than the purchase of a name, since the company brought no operations, but it would play a key role in the development of ERT. Research Data would later develop a program called Navigator that was used by the FDA to review data submitting for new drug approvals. At this stage, however, CDS and Research Data operated as separate divisions of United Medical. Another United Medical subsidiary was Pacemaker

## KEY DATES

**1972:** Anthropometrics, Inc., is founded.
**1981:** Anthropometrics is renamed United Medical Corporation and taken public.
**1993:** The Cardio Data Systems subsidiary is renamed CDSResearch Worldwide.
**2000:** eResearchTechnology, Inc., is formed.
**2009:** Rebranding effort focuses on the ERT name.

medical-device companies by offering clinical-trial and data-management software services that allowed clinical data from patients to be collected in real time via the Internet. In this way, researchers did not have to rely on monitors, who were sent out only sporadically to investigation sites, and risk working with outdated information. The addition of DLB's clinical research system broadened what PRWW had to offer clients and positioned it for greater worldwide growth. PRWW then worked to refine the software.

The DLB deal also brought with it the company's president, Joseph Esposito, who became PRWW's chief operating officer and president in 1998. Convincing researchers to abandon their old pencil-and-paper procedures in favor of the Internet took time, so only a handful of small studies in the late 1990s contracted to use the Web-based system. Nevertheless, PRWW was able to generate sales of $31.8 million in 1998, netting $700,000. A year later revenues increased to $42.8 million, and net income totaled $5.3 million. Esposito was exerting increasing influence on the company's affairs. He took the lead in selling PRWW's noncore holdings that had become little more than commodity businesses, such as a blood lab and a unit that provided basic Phase I clinical drug trial services, essentially dispensing experimental drugs to patients.

### CRO BUSINESS SOLD IN 1999

In 1999 Morganroth was elected chairman while continuing to serve as CEO, but Esposito continued to push PRWW in a new direction, repositioning the company as a business-to-business provider of integrated technology-based products and services. In keeping with this recasting, PRWW sold its domestic Clinical Research Organization (CRO) business unit to SCP Communications, Inc., for $18 million in late 1999 and it curtailed its international CRO operations. Clinical laboratory operations were also discontinued, and whatever contractual obligations remained were transferred to a third party.

These maneuvers set the stage for the establishment of a wholly owned subsidiary, eResearchTechnology, Inc. (ERT), in January of the following year. Serving as an e-technology marketing, development, and application services provider, it targeted the entire $30 billion research and development industry. The hope was that ERT was now well placed to participate in a market that the company anticipated would grow to $1 billion in annual sales. In 2001 Esposito took over as CEO, and Morganroth became chief scientist while continuing to serve as chairman.

The divestiture of the CRO business, which had accounted for $16.7 million in sales in 1999, led to a decline in revenues to $28 million in 2000 and a modest $120,000 net profit. Due to a downturn in the economy, sales dipped below $28 million in 2001, and ERT recorded a loss of $3.8 million. A year later the business returned to profitability, netting $6.15 million on sales of $41.5 million. Earnings more than doubled to $14.5 million in 2003 on sales of $68.8 million, and they doubled again in 2004 when ERT recorded earnings of $29.7 million on sales of $109.4 million. The company also received a patent in 2004 covering methods and systems used to process electrocardiograms.

### CHANGE OF LEADERSHIP IN 2006

Changes were in the offing, however, for cardiac safety regulations issued by the FDA and the International Conference on Harmonization. The resulting uncertainties prompted drug and device developers to delay contracting ERT's services. As a result, revenues dipped to $88.85 million in 2005 and remained flat the following year, while net income decreased from $15.4 million to $8.3 million. A contributing factor in the company's performance was the influx of new competition, which drove down prices and hurt margins. There was also a change at the helm in 2006, when in June of that year Esposito was replaced as president by Michael Mc-Kelvey, a former consultant who had spent 10 years at the U.S. Department of Commerce serving as forecast manager and senior economist in the Bureau of Economic Analysis.

Under McKelvey's leadership, ERT expanded its operations. In 2007 it acquired Covance Cardiac Safety Services, a unit of Covance Inc., the world's largest clinical research organization. As part of the deal, ERT became the exclusive provider of electrocardiogram services to all Covance business units for a 10-year term. Also in June 2007 ER acquired the ePRO assets from Healthcare Technology Systems, including an interactive voice-response system and 57 clinical assessments, a large number of which were proprietary. Additionally, ERT launched its EXPERT Technology Platform in

2007, a next generation of ERT's base technology.

Sales approached $100 million in 2007, and net income topped $15 million as the company stabilized and resumed growth. With the Covance assets fully integrated, 2008 was an excellent year, as ERT posted record revenues of $133.1 million and net income of $25 million. Unfortunately, economic conditions around the world began to worsen as the year came to a close. As a result, revenues fell to $93.8 million in 2009, and earnings were trimmed to $10.7 million.

To better position itself for the future, ERT initiated a rebranding strategy. Although its legal name remained eResearch Technology, Inc., the company focused on the ERT abbreviation and made other changes to sharpen its product positioning. Early in 2010 ERT's performance continued to decline. It also completed an acquisition, paying $81 million for the Research Services Division of CareFusion Corporation. This acquisition added a new line of business, respiratory diagnostics services, to supplement what ERT had to offer its global pharmaceutical customers. The company hoped this move would spur a resumption of growth in the near future.

*Ed Dinger*

## PRINCIPAL OPERATING UNITS

Cardiac Safety Solutions; ePRO Solutions; Clinical Research Consulting Group.

## PRINCIPAL COMPETITORS

Encorium Group, Inc.; Medifacts International, Inc.; Phase Forward Incorporated.

## FURTHER READING

DeHaan, Eloise, "United Medical Diversifies through More Acquisitions," *Philadelphia Business Journal*, April 21, 1986, p. 1.

"ERT, Philadelphia, Pa.," *CW Weekly*, February 23, 2009, p. 4.

George, John, "Premier Research Will Link 400 Cancer Sites," *Philadelphia Business Journal*, October 22, 1999, p. 6.

Helzner, Jerry, "Adventuresome Year: United Medical Grows beyond Its Original Mission," *Barron's National Business and Financial Weekly*, March 17, 1986, p. 54.

————, "Business with Heart: United Medical Scores Big Gains in Operating Net," *Barron's National Business and Financial Weekly*, March 5, 1984, p. 55.

Key, Peter, "eResearch Hopes for Big Future in Clinical Trials," *Philadelphia Business Journal*, November 16, 2001, p. B5.

# Essel Propack Limited

---

10th Floor, Times Tower, Kamala City
Senapati Bapat Marg, Lower Parel
Mumbai, Maharashtra 400 013
India
Telephone: (+91 22) 2481-9000
Fax: (+91 22) 2496-3137
Web site: http://www.esselpropack.com

*Public Company*
*Founded:* 1984
*Incorporated:* 1984
*Employees:* 2,700
*Sales:* INR 13.58 billion ($291.8 million; 2009 est.)
*Stock Exchanges:* Bombay (BSE) India (NSE)
*Ticker Symbol:* ESSEL PROPA
*NAICS:* 326130 Laminated Plastics Plate, Sheet, and
Shape Manufacturing; 326121 Unsupported Plastics
Profile Shape Manufacturing

■ ■ ■

Essel Propack Limited, based in Mumbai, India, is the world's leading manufacturer of laminated tubes. The company is affiliated with Essel Group, which embraces the sprawling corporate interests of chairman Subhash Chandra, one of India's boldest and most successful entrepreneurs. Essel Propack designs and manufactures custom tubing for household consumer goods giants such as Procter & Gamble, Johnson & Johnson, Colgate, and Unilever; much of the toothpaste purchased in North America, as well as in other markets worldwide, is packaged in the company's tubes. The company's

product line also includes plastic tubes and caps and closures for containers. It sold its medical supplies subsidiaries in late 2009. Essel Propack has regional headquarters in the People's Republic of China, the United States, and the United Kingdom, and it operates in 13 countries, including Colombia, Egypt, Germany, Indonesia, Mexico, Philippines, Poland, Russia, and Singapore.

## AN OFFSHOOT OF A FAMILY FIRM MAKES ITS MARK: 1984–99

Essel Propack traces its origin to an agricultural trading firm run by the Goel family. Subhash Chandra Goel (who later dropped his last name as a protest against India's entrenched caste system) began working for his family's firm in his teens, trading rice with commodity dealers and merchants in Bombay (now Mumbai), India. He helped establish a successor trading company, Rama Associates Ltd., in 1976. In the late 1970s the company moved in a new direction as it constructed massive plastic containers to help the Indian government store surplus crops. Chandra subsequently decided to extend the family's profitable plastics business, formally founding Essel Packaging in 1984.

The company decided to specialize in flexible laminated tubes, most widely used in squeezeable containers for household consumer products, especially toothpaste. This was one of the first of many new enterprises that would establish Subhash Chandra's reputation for entering and succeeding in industries that Indian companies had not previously entered. Chandra served as chairman of Essel Packaging as well as a swelling group of businesses in diverse industries, while his brother Ashok Kumar Goel became the company's vice chairman and managing director.

The company struggled for several years to establish itself. As a technologically advanced and capital-intensive business in an economy whose main competitive advantage seemed to be cheap labor, Essel Packaging was an anomaly. The company's growth was hampered by high interest rates on loans and by tight regulations imposed by left-of-center governments suspicious of capitalist enterprise. Markets in India for many packaged consumer items were poorly developed, so Essel Packaging aspired to boost growth by supplying leading international consumer goods producers as they sought to penetrate developing economies. Such companies were suspicious of potential manufacturing partners in less-developed economies, however, fearing that these firms could not uphold Western producers' high quality and safety standards.

The Goels risked losing their investment before Essel Packaging gained its first important customer, domestic producer Anchor, and started building a strong position in packaging in India. Essel Packaging next began moving into foreign markets. It started a joint venture in Egypt in 1993 to make it easier and cheaper to penetrate Egyptian markets by avoiding costly long-distance shipping of tubes. Meanwhile, Chandra appointed Cyrus Bagwadia as Essel Packaging's chief executive in 1995.

The company's next foreign venture—an important one—was its entry into the People's Republic of China in 1997. The company set up a manufacturing plant in Guangzhou province that year, and later one in Shanghai. The late 1990s seemed the ideal time for Essel Packaging to enter this vast market. Chinese people had traditionally used a variety of often homemade tools and substances to clean their teeth, but as the country

developed large-scale consumer retailing, packaged toothpaste was being widely promoted as a standard product. Company managers credited Chinese authorities for easing the company's progress in the country through reliable infrastructure, the generous assistance of outside investors, and swift local decision making. In China, Essel Propack was initially shut out of supplying international brands, so the company had to build up its business by persuading small domestic manufacturers to switch from aluminum to laminated tubes, in part by manufacturing thinner laminates that were less expensive and more eco-friendly.

Essel Packaging benefited from a trend among consumer goods manufacturers away from aluminum tubes and toward plastics and laminates. Aluminum tubes were inexpensive but difficult to clean, and they were prone to react toxically with their contents. With its background in plastics, the company was better equipped than many competitors to develop innovative packaging solutions. Essel Packaging's factories created laminates from several alternating layers of plastics and metals. Typically, production began by blowing molten polymers into thin films, which were rolled together with aluminum foil into laminates. Then the laminates were sliced, printed or stamped, and shaped into tubes. These laminates promised benefits such as greater flexibility and strength at lower package weight, along with the ability to print more vivid labels.

Essel Packaging gradually won the confidence of multinational firms such as Colgate-Palmolive, Unilever, Procter & Gamble, and Johnson & Johnson, obtaining contracts to package leading toothpaste brands such as Crest, Colgate, and Aquafresh in India and numerous other countries. Essel Packaging started laminated tube production in Germany in 1999 and in Nepal the following year. In addition, it set up a joint venture with the German firm Bericap in 1999 that made closures and caps for plastic containers at a plant in India.

## MERGER LEADS TO NAME CHANGE: 2000

Essel Packaging's next move to expand its industry profile came in 2000 through a merger with one of its chief rivals, Propack Holdings of Switzerland, forming a new company named Essel Propack Limited. Essel Packaging paid just $11 million, giving Propack executives a 22 percent share and two board seats in the merged company. The deal was conducted through a special-purpose vehicle registered in Mauritius to take advantage of the offshore territory's low tax rates. Propack was one of the few manufacturers of laminated tube production machinery, which Essel Packaging had

```
┌─────────────────────────────────────────────┐
│                                               │
│               KEY DATES                       │
│                    ■                          │
│  ┌─────────────────────────────────────────┐ │
│  1984:  Essel Packaging Ltd. is founded.      │
│  1993:  Essel Packaging participates in a     │
│         joint venture in Egypt.               │
│  1999:  Essel Packaging merges with Propack   │
│         Holdings A.G. to form Essel Propack   │
│         Limited.                              │
│  2002:  Essel Propack is chosen as the North  │
│         American laminated tube supplier to   │
│         Procter & Gamble.                      │
│  2004:  Essel Propack enters plastic tube     │
│         market by purchasing Arista Tubes.    │
│                                               │
└─────────────────────────────────────────────┘
```

been using practically since its founding. Essel Packaging also extended its international reach through acquiring Propack's operations in the People's Republic of China, Colombia, Indonesia, Venezuela, and the Philippines. The combination of the second-largest (Essel Packaging) and the fourth-largest (Propack) players created the unrivaled industry leader, with a daily production of around 10 million tubes and a 28 percent global share by 2002.

One of the strongest vindications of Essel Propack's reputation for quality was its selection in April 2002 by Procter & Gamble to supply its North American toothpaste tubing. Essel Propack located its American manufacturing in a vacant factory in Danville, Virginia, once again standing out for reversing customary trends. As many American companies outsourced production to foreign economies with lower labor costs, this Indian manufacturer was hiring employees in the United States, and even sending some of them to India to receive specialized training. The company regarded the Americas as its brightest long-term growth prospect as India's share of company income steadily dropped.

Ashok Kumar Goel resumed the role of chief executive when Cyrus Bagwadia retired in 2003. Subhash Chandra remained the chairman of Essel Propack and the other companies under the umbrella of the Essel Group. But Chandra now was devoting most of his attention to the group's prominent media and telecommunications companies, such as Zee Entertainment Enterprise Ltd. and Dish TV.

Essel Propack resumed its geographic expansion in 2004 by purchasing Arista Tubes, the United Kingdom's biggest manufacturer of plastic tubes. Essel Propack gained the use of Arista's co-extrusion process to produce seamless plastic tubes that were becoming increasingly adopted for cosmetics, pharmaceuticals, and

food packaging. The company was equipped to decorate plastic tubes by printing, metal foil stamping, and labeling. It established other plastic tube plants in Danville, Virginia, in 2006 and in Poland in 2007. The company did not ignore laminated tubes, purchasing a British manufacturer and beginning production in Russia in 2005.

Essel Propack chose medical devices as another field for diversification, which appeared to dovetail with its expertise in plastics manufacturing. In 2006 the company acquired the U.S.-based Tacpro Inc. and the Singaporean firm Avalon Medical Services Pte Ltd., both of which specialized in catheters and balloons used in minimally invasive surgery. The same year, Essel Propack acquired Packaging India Private Ltd., a specialty packaging firm headquartered in Pondicherry in southern India.

Essel Propack's expanded industry share and high-profile contracts were reflected in the company's financials. In 2003 the company reported total income of INR 5.82 billion ($124.8 million) with net profit after taxes of INR 705.6 million ($15.1 million). In 2006 income rose to INR 10.29 billion ($227 million) and after-tax net profit to INR 985.5 million ($21.8 million).

## PERSEVERING THROUGH ECONOMIC TURMOIL: 2007–10

Essel Propack suffered financially before and during the recession of 2008 and 2009. Already in 2007 prices for basic materials such as plastic polymers and crude oil were rapidly increasing, putting pressure on company earnings. Major clients were beginning to replenish their retailers more frequently, which forced Essel Propack to keep larger stocks of supplies, driving up expenses further. In 2008 currency devaluations in several of the countries where the company operated, as well as the devaluation of the Indian rupee against the U.S. dollar, imposed extra costs. Total income continued to grow each year, from INR 10.29 billion ($227.0 million) in 2006 to INR 12.09 billion ($292.3 million) in 2007 and INR 12.95 billion ($298.2 million) in 2008. Most of Essel Propack's packaging was for staple products that most consumers were not likely to stop purchasing even in hard economic times. Nonetheless, after-tax profit fell from INR 985.5 million ($21.8 million) in 2006 to INR 608.1 million ($14.7 million) in 2007, and then in 2008 the company registered a loss of INR 883.1 million ($20.3 million).

Essel Propack management showed its commitment to building its medical devices business by acquiring two more U.S.-based firms in the industry in 2008.

However, by August 2009 the cash-strapped company was seeking to dispose of the medical devices unit, intending to reinvest the proceeds in its core tube units. In January 2010 it was announced that the Irish-based company Creganna had purchased the unit, renamed Tactx Medical Inc.

Meanwhile, the company introduced three new laminated tube products in 2008 and 2009. Titanium had with thinner polymer layers, Egnite had a distinctive metallic sheen, and Etail had a significant share of recycled materials. By the second half of 2009 Essel Propack was beginning to recover, as the company maintained a worldwide industry share of over 30 percent in laminated tubes. Company revenues and earnings before taxes increased substantially in the second and third quarters of 2009, with strong hopes that this upward trend would continue, as the company reported preliminary income for the year of INR 13.58 billion ($291.8 million).

*Stephen V. Beitel*

## PRINCIPAL SUBSIDIARIES

Arista Tubes Inc. (USA, 100%); Arista Tubes Limited (UK, 100%); The Egyptian Indian Company for Modern Packaging S.A.E. (Egypt, 75%); Essel de Mexico, S.A. de C.V. (Mexico, 100%); Essel Packaging (Guangzhou) Limited (China, 100%); Essel Propack America, LLC (USA, 100%); Essel Propack LLC (Russia, 100%); Essel Propack MISR for Advanced Packaging S.A.E. (Egypt, 75%); Essel Propack Philippines, Inc. (Philippines, 100%); Essel Propack Polska Sp. Z.O.O. (Poland, 100%); Essel Propack UK Limited (UK, 100%); Lamitube Technologies (Cyprus) Limited (Cyprus, 100%); Lamitube Technologies Limited (Mauritius, 100%); MTL de Panama S.A (Panama, 100%); Packaging India Private Limited (India, 100%); Packtech Limited (Mauritius, 100%); Produxx Inc. (USA, 85%); Tubopack de Colombia S.A. (Colombia, 100%).

## PRINCIPAL COMPETITORS

Amcor Limited; Printpack, Inc.; Rexan plc; Reynolds Flexible Packaging.

## FURTHER READING

"Essel Propack Acquires Another US Medical Device Firm," *Medical Product Outsourcing*, October 2008, p. 106.

"Essel Propack: Brushing Away the Competition," *Plastics & Rubber Asia*, March 2002, p. 44.

Flynn, Meghan, "Made in America: The North American Division of This Global Manufacturer Has Big Plans for Diversification. Ted Sojourner Explains," *American Executive*, January 2010, p. 111.

Hardasmalati, Rumi Dutta, "Essel Propack to Exit Non-core Business," *Economic Times* (New Delhi, India), August 19, 2009.

"India: Essel Packaging to Buy Propack," *Business Line*, November 16, 2000.

"India: Mandarins and Babus: A Study in Contrast," *Business Line*, September 4, 2001.

Orr, Deborah, "Coming to America," *Forbes Global*, October 27, 2003, p. 42.

"Essel Propack: Company Profile," *Forbes Global*, October 27, 2003, p. 42.

Toloken, Steve, "Essel Slates $21 Million Tube Plant for Va.," *Plastics News*, July 8, 2002, p. 1.

"Essel Squeezes Out Profit with Local Focus; India Giant Makes Toothpaste Tubes in China," *Plastics News*, September 8, 2008, p. 18.

"Tube Stake: Essel Propack Emerges with Innovative Laminated Tubes," *Packaging Strategies*, August 15, 2009, p. 6.

Verespej, Mike, "Americas Are Key to Growth for Tube-making Giant Essel," *Plastics News*, December 4, 2006, p. 19.

# Etablissements Maurel & Prom S.A.

---

12, rue Volney
Paris, 75002
France
**Telephone: (+33 1) 53 83 16 00**
**Fax: (+33 1) 53 83 16 04**
**Web site: http://www.maureletprom.fr**

*Public Company*
*Founded:* 1813
*Incorporated:* 2005
*Employees:* 297
*Sales:* EUR 183.2 million ($263.9 million) (2009)
*Stock Exchanges:* Paris
*Ticker Symbol:* MAU
*NAICS:* 213111 Drilling Oil and Gas Wells; 213112 Support Activities for Oil and Gas Operations; 324110 Petroleum Refineries; 551112 Offices of Other Holding Companies

■ ■ ■

Etablissements Maurel & Prom S.A. is a leading French petroleum and natural gas exploration and production firm, with its headquarters in Paris. Founded in Bordeaux in 1813, the company operated for more than a century as a trading and shipping firm before sharply shifting its lines of business in the late 20th century. Maurel & Prom produces crude oil in Gabon and holds whole or partial stakes in exploration permits in Gabon, Congo, Tanzania, Mozambique, Nigeria, Colombia, Peru, Italy, and Syria, as well as a share in a mixed enterprise in Venezuela. Its subsidiary Caroil provides drilling services for other firms as well as for Maurel & Prom. The company enjoyed rapid growth in the first decade of the 21st century by exploiting largely undeveloped petroleum fields in Africa and Latin America.

## 1813: FOUNDING OF COMPANY

In the early 19th century two prominent interrelated merchant families in Bordeaux, France, the Maurels and the Proms, started trading between France and French outposts in West Africa. Etablissements Maurel et Prom was created in 1813, and members of the families moved to Africa to expand and supervise operations there. The company set up several trading posts on the African coast, its most important ones being at Saint-Louis and Gorée Island in modern-day Senegal. From Senegal and other areas of France's sprawling West African empire, the company's ships transported peanuts, rubber, cotton, and other raw materials, and they brought back machines, cloth, furnishings, and oil from Europe and the United States. Some company officials married into a socially elite group of mixed-race female merchants known as *signares*, giving Maurel & Prom better access to valuable trade goods.

Well into the 20th century, Maurel & Prom remained one of the handful of firms controlling most of the French colonial trade with Africa. In the 1970s, however, poor shipping industry conditions prompted the company to begin diversifying its operations. By the late 1980s the company had abandoned its African shipping lines and moved into agriculture, forestry, mining, and oil and gas exploration. In 1991 Maurel & Prom founded a joint poultry-farming venture, Promagra, with the French cooperative firm Transagra. Tensions soon developed between the partners, and the venture dissolved in acrimony within a few years. Maurel & Prom was sued for liability after Transagra's parent company, Agri Cher, failed, and Maurel & Prom in turn sued officials of Agri Cher to recover its own losses, without success.

## OWNERSHIP CHANGES LEAD TO A FOCUS ON PETROLEUM

In 1995 Electricité et Eaux de Madagascar (EEM), a diversified French holding company, purchased a 76 percent share in Maurel & Prom. EEM was guided by its chairman, Jean-François Henin, a French financier who had become notorious in the 1980s and early 1990s as the head of Altus Financial, an investment firm purchased in 1989 by Crédit Lyonnais, the government-controlled flagship of the French banking industry at the time. Henin had been forced to resign from Altus in 1993 after the unit racked up enormous losses that drove Crédit Lyonnais to the edge of collapse.

In the late 1990s Maurel & Prom was still involved in a wide range of businesses. The company owned two cable-laying ships and an oil-drilling vessel, the *Energy Searcher*. It owned majority shares in agricultural and forest plantations in the Republic of the Congo, as well as aquaculture businesses in France. Maurel & Prom was already exploring for oil and natural gas and operating wells in several countries scattered across Asia, Africa, and Latin America, most of them outside the traditional oil-producing regions. Newly introduced drilling methods such as horizontal wells helped producers such as Maurel & Prom to tap oil fields previously regarded as inaccessible.

The company gravitated toward some of the former French colonies in Africa where it had operated earlier as a trader and shipper. In early 1999 it entered Congo, joining with Canadian producer Heritage Oil Corp. as operator and co-owner of the Kouakouala and Kouilou licenses. Maurel & Prom worked jointly with Anzoil starting in 1994 to drill for oil and gas in Vietnam. The company courted controversy, including possible U.S. sanctions, by collaborating with the Canadian firms

Sherritt International and Pebercam in Cuba, which was touted as having tremendous potential for oil production.

Many of these countries presented significant risk for outside investors. For example, Congo was roiled by a series of civil wars between 1998 and 2004, along with corrupt and autocratic rule even in peacetime. In some places, test drills simply did not strike the hoped-for oil deposits, as happened in Senegal in 1999, prompting Maurel & Prom to pull out of that country temporarily.

By 1999 Henin had decided to focus his interests on oil and gas, believing that crude oil was undervalued. He was convinced that by continuing to obtain rights in little-regarded areas where Maurel & Prom could operate at low cost, the company could reap hefty profits. Henin resigned his posts at EEM and became an unpaid "partner in person" of the Maurel & Prom partnership, arranging its separation from its parent company and aiming to sell off its other businesses at suitable prices. In May 2000 EEM exchanged its shares with Maurel & Prom shares, reducing its ownership percentage to less than 5 percent.

## GROWTH INTO THE NEW CENTURY

The newly independent Maurel & Prom benefited right away from a surge in crude oil trading prices from under $10 per barrel in 1999 to a temporary peak of $37 per barrel in September 2000. Maurel & Prom's production and estimated reserves ramped up rapidly, seeming to vindicate the company's strategy. In Cuba, where the company operated six wells by 2001, production also increased rapidly. In 2001 Maurel & Prom assigned its rights in Cuban oil fields to Pebercam in exchange for a 20 percent share in its Canadian partner. The company also joined in ventures seeking oil in France and Russia and natural gas in Hungary. Finally, the company sold Energy Searcher, which had operated at a loss for a few years as major oil companies cut back on exploration expenses when oil prices bottomed out in the late 1990s.

The company's most striking success was at the M'Boundi field in Congo in 2001, soon reckoned to be West Africa's second-largest onshore oil field. This discovery was not only a major coup for Maurel & Prom but also a major contributor to Congo's status as the fifth-largest oil producer in sub-Saharan Africa. By the end of 2003 the company estimated its reserves in Congo at over 260 million barrels and in Cuba at over 50 million barrels. In both areas it was busily drilling numerous new wells, and successful strikes in many of these wells inspired plans for more drilling. The

## KEY DATES

**1813:** Etablissements Maurel et Prom is founded in Bordeaux, France, as a trading and shipping company.
**1995:** Electricité et Eaux de Madagascar acquires majority stake in Maurel & Prom.
**2000:** Maurel & Prom reemerges as an independent company focusing on petroleum.
**2005:** Maurel & Prom changes its legal status from partnership to public corporation.
**2009:** Maurel & Prom sells off its profitable subsidiary Hocol and reaffirms commitment to petroleum exploration.

M'Boundi field alone was yielding 8,000 barrels a day in 2003, and it would yield nearly 57,000 barrels a day by the end of 2005.

Maurel & Prom's successes in Congo and Cuba more than made up for its disappointments in other countries. The company's Vietnamese oil wells turned out to be dry, although it retained hope for significant natural gas production. It had to withdraw from its ventures in Russia and France. Activity on the company's tracts in Hungary was minimal. On the other hand, in 2003 alone the company started exploratory drilling in Peru, purchased shares in three onshore permit areas in the West African nation of Gabon, and began negotiating to obtain permits in Central African Republic and Guinea-Bissau.

Even with Maurel & Prom's rapid growth, leading financial firms were reluctant to arrange conventional loans for the company, which was still operating on a relatively small scale in high-risk regions. To help finance its oil drilling in Congo, Maurel & Prom turned to Natexis Banques Populaires to set up an innovative reserve-base lending facility valued at $50 million over three years starting in 2003. A key to this deal was that Natexis and its partner banks accepted anticipated proceeds from future oil production as collateral.

## CHANGE TO CORPORATE STATUS AMID CONTINUING EXPANSION

In 2005 Maurel & Prom changed its legal status from a partnership to a public corporation, prompted in part by Henin's desire to make the company a more attractive target for takeover by larger industry players. The

company's market value was soaring from around EUR 60 million ($53 million) to EUR 1.8 billion ($2.3 billion) between early 2001 and early 2005, and Henin was eager to cash in on the 26 percent share ownership he acquired in the reconfigured company. Maurel & Prom, however, broke off talks with several potential buyers because their bids were too low.

The company now boldly entered new markets to exploit promising opportunities and diversify away from Congo. Maurel & Prom obtained two permits valid for 11 years from the Tanzanian government in 2004 to explore for gas in its mostly untapped territory. The following year it purchased the Hocol group from the British firm Knightsbridge Exploration for $460 million. The group's assets included production facilities and exploration rights in Colombia and Venezuela. Despite guerrilla violence often directed against companies' equipment and personnel in Colombia and threats to nationalize foreign oil companies' operations in Venezuela, Maurel & Prom was attracted by the chance to pioneer in unexplored regions.

Also in 2005 the company concluded that profitable gas production in its tracts in Vietnam was unlikely and wound down operations there. By the end of that year Maurel & Prom had nearly completed its transformation into a focused petroleum firm, having divested itself of all unrelated units except for a share in a gold mining company in Mali. In 2006 Hocol's service contract in Venezuela was suspended, along with those of all other foreign companies, and Maurel & Prom negotiated to convert its operations there into a "mixed enterprise" majority that was owned by the Venezuelan state oil company PDVSA.

Maurel & Prom decided to cash in on its lucrative investment in Congo. In March 2007 the Italian producer Eni SpA agreed to purchase most of Maurel & Prom's assets and rights in the country for approximately $1.4 billion. Two major Indian oil companies, however, made a higher offer, enlisting Burren Energy (which now held minority shares in Maurel & Prom's Congo permits) to support its bid and wield its right to block the Eni bid. Nevertheless, after lengthy negotiations Burren elected to support the Eni bid instead.

Once the Eni deal was completed, Colombia became the dominant contributor to Maurel & Prom's bottom line. Over the next few years the company continued exploring in Congo, Gabon, and Tanzania. It also ventured into Sicily, where the company acquired a 25 percent share in an Italian producer in 2005, and Syria, where it obtained its first permit in 2006.

## CREDIT CRUNCH PROMPTS COMPANY'S REORGANIZATION

In 2008 and 2009 Maurel & Prom was financially buffeted by conflicting economic trends. The run-up of oil trading prices in 2008 temporarily boosted the company's profits before plunging again the following year. The international credit crunch of 2007–08 effectively reduced the company's credit lines to zero, prompting it to financially reorganize itself in 2009, making a new bond issue and developing a new reserve-base lending facility. The company announced the intended sale of Hocol to Colombia's state-owned Ecopetrol for $748 million in March 2009. Maurel & Prom kept some of its Colombian exploration permits, though. Its only significant production for the time being was in Gabon. The company saw hints of production breakthroughs in other countries, and early in 2010 Maurel & Prom bolstered its reserves by acquiring a 45 percent stake in Seplat, a Nigerian consortium that obtained valuable oil and gas exploration licenses in Nigeria from Royal Shell.

*Stephen V. Beitel*

## PRINCIPAL SUBSIDIARIES

Banque Congolaise de l'Habitat (10%); Caroil S.A.S.; Hocol—M&P Venezuela S.A.S.; Hocol Peru S.A.; Lagopetrol (26.35%); M&P Colombia BV; M&P Congo (99.9%); M&P Gabon Ltd.; M&P International S.A.; M&P Syrie S.A.S.; M&P Tanzania Ltd. (99.9%); New Gold Mali (26%); Panther Eureka Srl (30%); Pebercam Inc. (19.1%); Raba Xprom Energy (34.3%).

## PRINCIPAL COMPETITORS

Premier Oil plc; Soco International plc; Tullow Oil plc.

## FURTHER READING

Angrand, Jean-Luc, *Céleste; ou, Les temps des Signares*, Sarcelles, France: Éditions Anne Pépin, 2006.

Arnold, Martin, "M&P Rejected Indian Oil Offer as Too Low," *Financial Times* (London), February 24, 2005, p. 30.

"Maurel & Prom Hopes $460m Buy Will Tempt Bidders," *Financial Times* (London), June 13, 2005, p. 26.

"Coming of Age: For a Number of Sub-Saharan African Countries the Export of Crude Oil Provides Vital Revenue. And Like Some Other Recent Commodity Financings the Oil Sector Has Seen Both Record and Innovative Deals," *Trade Finance*, April 2004, p. 26.

"IOC Loses Out Race to Acquire Maurel and Prom's Stake in Congo," *PTI* (India), March 23, 2007.

"IOCs Sell Oil Fields to Nigerian-Led Consortium," *Africa News Service*, February 1, 2010.

Johnson, G. Wesley, "The Ascendancy of Blaise Diagne and the Beginnings of African Politics in Senegal," *Africa: Journal of the International African Institute*, July 1966, pp. 235–53.

"M&P Gets a Good Price for Hocol, More Deals Ahead," *Corporate Financing Week*, March 16, 2009, p. 11.

"M&P Moves into East Africa," *Oil Daily*, September 21, 2009.

Packard, Simon, "Maurel & Prom May Extend Rally as Investors Bet on Takeover," Bloomberg.net, December 3, 2004.

*Energie
vernünftig
nutzen*

# EVN AG

———— ■ ————

**EVN Platz**
**Maria Enzersdorf, Niederösterreich A2344**
**Austria**
**Telephone: (+43 2236) 200-0**
**Fax: (+43 2236) 200-2030**
**Web site: http://www.evn.at/**

*Public Company*
*Founded:* 1907 as Landes-Elektrizitätswerk
*Employees:* 8,937
*Sales:* €2.74 billion ($3.35 billion) (2009)
*Stock Exchanges:* Vienna, Frankfurt
*Ticker Symbol:* EVN
*NAICS:* 211111 Natural Gas Production; 221111 Electric Power Supply, Hydroelectric; 221122 Electric Power Distribution; 221210 Natural Gas Distribution; 221310 Water Supply and Irrigation Systems

■ ■ ■

Headquartered in Maria Enzersdorf, Austria, EVN (Energie-Versorgung Niederösterreich) AG is one of Europe's largest energy supply companies. EVN offers electricity, gas, heat, water, waste incineration, and related services to over 3 million customers in 18 countries. By taking advantage of the synergies among the its different business ventures in Austria and abroad, EVN is able to cover all stages of the value-added chain, from generation, to distribution, to sales of energy, in order to maintain profitability and sustainable growth. The company's business practices are based on and directed toward the security and reliability of energy supplies, a responsible use of natural resources, an ever-growing environmentally compatible infrastructure, and a superior product and service. Its major shareholders are the province of Niederösterreich (Lower Austria; 51 percent) and the German utility EnBW Energie Baden-Württemberg AG (35 percent).

## THE EARLY YEARS

In 1907 the Archduchy of Austria founded the electric company Landes-Elektrizitätswerk. The company was given the task of building the Wienerbruck hydroelectric power plant to cover the electricity needs of the local railway and the city of Sankt Pölten. Completed in 1911, Wienerbruck was the largest power station in the Austro-Hungarian Empire. The restructuring of Europe in the aftermath of World War I brought the end of the Austro-Hungarian Empire and the beginning of the Republic of Austria. Likewise, the former Archduchy of Austria was divided into two federal provinces, Lower Austria and Vienna. In 1922 these two provinces began a shared majority ownership of Landes-Elektrizitätswerk and renamed it Niederösterreichische Elektrizitätswirt-schafts-Aktiengesellschaft (Lower Austrian Electricity Business Stock Company; NEWAG). NEWAG was given a mandate to develop a regional network for electrical power and to distribute it throughout all of Lower Austria.

In 1938 Austria became part of the Deutsche Reich, and NEWAG was renamed Gauwerke Nieder-donau AG. During the regime of the National Socialists several independent and privately owned local utility companies were acquired by Gauwerke Niederdonau via a forced exchange of stock or cash. As a result, Gauwerke Niederdonau became a virtual electricity monopoly in Lower Austria. Between 1942 and 1944 Gauwerke Niederdonau built the first natural gas–fired power plant that featured a Velox boiler. At the time, this was a technical milestone, laying the foundation for expansion into the natural gas sector in the 1950s.

## NATIONALIZATION: 1940–70

In 1945 the Deutsche Reich collapsed. Austria regained independence from Germany, yet the country remained under Allied supervision. The Austrian economy lay in ruins, and in an effort to rebuild, the government instituted the nationalization laws of 1946 and 1947 to bring much of the economy, including the energy sector, under government control. In 1954, in cooperation with the province of Lower Austria, NEWAG (it had regained its former name after the war) founded Niederösterreichische Gasvertriebs (NIOGAS) GmbH, which would eventually control most of the enormous natural gas fields located in the province.

Beginning in the mid-1950s NEWAG set out to distribute electricity to the far remote alpine and rural areas in the province, a process that would be completed by 1963. Meanwhile, NEWAG slowly acquired most of the other utility companies in Lower Austria, except for Wiener Stadtwerke, which was owned by Vienna. At the same time, NEWAG built new hydroelectric plants to accommodate the growing demand of electricity throughout the province. In 1962 it acquired a 49 percent interest in Niederösterreichische Siedlungswasserbau (NÖSIWAG) GmbH, the newly founded water supply company in Lower Austria. Likewise, during the mid-1950s and 1960s NIOGAS acquired municipal gas works all over Lower Austria and converted the plants to natural gas, thus strengthening the monopoly of the energy market that NEWAG and NIOGAS maintained throughout the province.

## NEWAG AND NIOGAS MERGE

The close history and natural synergy of NEWAG and NIOGAS suggested a merger, and in 1972 the two companies formed a fully integrated affiliation. However, due to tax law complications the merger was not officially completed until 1987.

The 1970s and 1980s marked a period of growth and expansion. Natural gas consumption soared due to increased demands by municipalities, corporations, and private households, whereas demand for oil and coal decreased. In part this was because of environmental concerns over the use of fossil fuels and because of political concerns over a Western dependency on oil from the Middle East. Given that NEWAG and NIOGAS were ideally positioned to meet this growing demand, the two affiliated companies reported record sales and revenues. NEWAG operated several hydroelectric and gas-powered electric plants, and NIOGAS provided natural gas directly to its customers. In fact, NIOGAS was the first gas utility to provide natural gas to private households, thus offering customers even in remote areas a cleaner and more economical alternative to coal and oil.

During this period NEWAG participated with Lower Austria in the planning and building of Kernkraftwerk Zwentendorf, a nuclear power plant commissioned by the federal Austrian energy program. The plant was completed in 1978. However, because of a popular referendum against nuclear power, the plant never began operations. As of 2010, Austria was still an antinuclear country, and Kernkraftwerk Zwentendorf was a virtually unused building complex, evidencing an unprecedented and colossal financial mishap.

## KEY DATES

**■**

**1907:** The Archduchy of Austria establishes Landes-Elektrizitätswerk.

**1922:** Landes-Elektrizitätswerk is renamed Niederösterreichische Elektrizitätswirtschafts-Aktiengesellschaft (NEWAG).

**1954:** NEWAG and the province of Niederösterreich found NIOGAS.

**1987:** NIOGAS and NEWAG merge to form Energie-Versorgung Niederösterreich (EVN) AG.

**2004:** EVN begins expanding into southeastern Europe by acquiring a power generation plant in Bulgaria.

## LIBERALIZATION OF THE ENERGY MARKET

In 1987, following the completion of the legal merger between NEWAG and NIOGAS, the company was renamed Energie-Versorgung Niederösterreich (EVN) AG. The following year the Second Privatization Law was instituted to pave the way for private ownership in state-owned companies in the energy sector. In 1989 the Iron Curtain fell and suddenly the borders to the north and east of Lower Austria that had been closed for decades were now open. That same year EVN went public and began trading its shares via the Vienna Stock Exchange. The company offered 49 percent of its stock to private investors, while the province of Lower Austria continued to be the majority shareholder with the remaining 51 percent.

In 1995 Austria joined the European Union. Two years later the European Union issued directives for a deregulation of the energy market. The directives were intended to generate fair competition in an industry that had been ruled by regional monopolies such as EVN in Lower Austria. A deregulated energy market would allow national and international energy suppliers to move into any region within the Austrian market. As a result, competition was expected to be steep. To brace for such competition, EVN and Wien Energie GmbH formed EnergieAllianz in 1998. By 2002 the alliance included three other utilities: Energie AG Oberösterreich, Burgenländische Elektrizitätswirtschafts-Aktiengesellschaft, and Linz AG für Energie, Telekommunikation, Verkehr und Kommunale Dienste. In 2003 EVN established EconGas GmbH, a joint venture between EVN and several other provincial gas suppliers. EconGas

eventually became the largest natural gas supplier servicing wholesalers and corporate customers in Austria.

Initially, the liberalization of the energy market only affected corporate customers and municipalities. However, by 2001 the electricity market was completely liberalized, and the following year the gas market followed suit. From then on even private households could freely choose their energy supplier.

## EXPANSION AND DIVERSIFICATION IN THE NEW CENTURY

By the turn of the 21st century EVN's operations in Lower Austria covered all the important steps in the value-added chain for the generation and distribution of electricity and natural gas. With this in mind, EVN decided to expand its energy segment internationally. Paving the way was the growing liberalization and privatization of the energy market in southeastern Europe. EVN acquired plants in Bulgaria in 2004, in Macedonia in 2006, and in Albania in 2008. By 2008, 38.4 percent of EVN's total revenues were generated outside Austrian borders. Given southeastern Europe's enormous need to update and improve its energy infrastructure, the market in this region was expected to grow apace.

With successful acquisitions and alliances in the gas and electricity sector underway, EVN decided to invest in diversification. A new focus on environmental services led to an expansion into the water and waste incineration sectors. In 2001 EVN took over the remaining 51 percent of the water supplier NÖSIWAG and renamed it EVN Wasser. Two years later EVN acquired WTE Wassertechnik GmbH, a wastewater treatment facility, and Abfallverwertung Niederösterreich (AVN) GmbH, a waste incineration facility. EVN Wasser, WTE, and AVN made up EVN's Environmental Services segment, which operated throughout Austria and in 14 countries in central, eastern, and southeastern Europe.

In 2008–09 EVN reported revenues of €2.7 billion, which was an increase of 13.8 percent over 2007–08. EVN's Environmental Services segment generated 8.7 percent of the total revenues. Even though this meant that over 90 percent of the total revenues were still generated by EVN's Energy segment, the continued interest in sustainable use and reuse of energy and in the responsible disposal of waste were expected to have a positive impact on the Environmental Services segment. This could be evidenced in that the segment showed a 27.7 percent increase in revenues between 2007–08 and 2008–09, which indicated a potential for growth.

Despite the difficult global economic conditions between 2009 and 2010, EVN reported that total revenues increase by 4.5 percent in the first quarter of 2010. EVN's Energy segment profited from the comparatively cold European winter of 2009–10, which was reflected by an increase in the demand for electricity and gas. The Environmental Services segment also reported higher revenues, mostly because of contracts for wastewater treatment plants in Cyprus and Moscow.

*Helga Schier*

## PRINCIPAL SUBSIDIARIES

EVN Kraftwerks- and Beteiligingsgesellschaft mbH; evn naturkraft Erzeugungs- und Verteilungs GmbH; EVN Liegenschaftsverwaltung Gesellschaft mbH; EVN Netz GmbH; EVN Energievertrieb GmbH & Co. KG; EVN Wärme GmbH; EconGas GmbH; EVN Bulgaria EP AD; EVN Macedonia AD; EVN Wasser GmbH; EVN Umweltholding und Betriebs GmbH.

## PRINCIPAL DIVISIONS

EVN Energy segment; EVN Environmental Services segment; EVN Strategic Investment and Other Business segment.

## PRINCIPAL COMPETITORS

E.ON AG; EnBW Energie Baden-Württemberg AG; SUEZ Environment; Verbund; CEZ Group.

## FURTHER READING

"Commission Approves Austrian Electricity Merger Subject to Conditions and Obligations," Europa Press Releases RAPID, June 11, 2003, http://europa.eu/rapid/pressReleasesAction. do?reference=IP/03/825.

Dippelreiter, Michael, *Geschichte der österreichischen Bundesländer seit 1945*, vol. 6. Niederösterreich: Böhlau Verlag Wien, 2000.

Federal Competition Authority, "General Investigation of the Austrian Electricity Industry," Republic of Austria, December 2004, http://www.bwb.gv.at/NR/rdonlyres/4822 83D0-BC87-46E6-A985-559E03C23B83/19897/1stinterim reportengl.pdf.

Graham, Dave, "Austria's EVN to Build Three Albanian Power Plants," Reuters, January 25, 2005, http://www.reuters.com/ article/idUSL2557644520080125.

Schanda, Reinhard, and Günther Hanslik, "Liberalization of Austria's Electricity Market," October 22, 1998. http:// www.sattler.co.at/relaunch/gh_dt_electricity.htm.

"Spendenaffäre: Aufstieg und Fall des Viktor Müllner," Die Presse.com, February 5, 2010, http://diepresse.com/home/ politik/zeitgeschichte/537896/index.do?_vl_backlink=/home/ politik/zeitgeschichte/index.do.

# frog design

# frog design inc.

**660 3rd Street, 4th Floor**
**San Francisco, California 94107**
**U.S.A.**
**Telephone: (415) 442-4804**
**Fax: (415) 442-4803**
**Web site: http://www.frogdesign.com**

*Subsidiary of Aricent Inc.*
*Founded:* 1969 as Esslinger Design
*Employees:* 450 (est.)
*Sales:* $37 million (2005)
*NAICS:* 541420 Industrial Design Services; 541410
    Interior Design Services; 541430 Graphic Design
    Services; 541490 Other Specialized Design Services

■ ■ ■

Based in San Francisco, frog design inc. is a leading
product design services company that bills itself as a
"global innovation firm." The company also offers
corporate branding and strategic consulting services.
Over the years, frog has worked for major companies in
a wide variety of industries, including consumer
electronics, fashion, retail, media, telecommunications,
health care, education, and finance. Clients include
Apple, Disney, GE, Microsoft, SAP, Sony, and Yahoo!.
Taking a multidisciplinary approach, frog employs 450
designers, technologists, strategists, and analysts who
work at studios in San Francisco, Amsterdam, Austin,
Milan, Munich, New York, Seattle, and Shanghai. The
company is a subsidiary of Aricent Inc., a communications technology and services company, which is in turn

owned by the New York investment firm Kohlberg
Kravis Roberts.

## THE FOUNDING OF ESSLINGER

The forerunner of frog design, Esslinger Design, was
founded by Hartmut Heinrich Esslinger, a German born
in June 1944, when World War II was still 10 months
from completion in Europe. His father was a soldier
who survived the war and started a textile business and
clothing store, providing Esslinger with an opportunity
to read fashion magazines and attend fashion shows at a
young age. After studying electrical engineering at the
Technical University in Stuttgart, Esslinger told his
parents that he wanted to study design. They were
horrified. Nevertheless, he enrolled at one of the world's
premiere design schools, the College of Design in
Schwäbisch Gmünd, Germany, in 1968. A year later,
while still a student, he launched Esslinger Design.

Esslinger won a major student design award in
1969 that led him to be hired by Wega, a small
consumer electronics company. Setting up shop in the
garage of a rented house, Esslinger designed a television
set that used new plastic molding techniques and
incorporated foam-encased high-end stereo components
to provide excellent audio in an attractive-looking unit.
Called the System 3000, it was a hit at the Consumer
Electronics Show in Berlin in 1971 and established the
27-year-old Esslinger as a star designer.

It was a time of transition for industrial designers.
Prior to the early 1970s, design was little more than
beautification, but that changed with the oil embargo

COMPANY PERSPECTIVES

■

We help the world's leading companies create and bring to market meaningful products, services, and experiences.

that made petroleum products expensive and their availability uncertain. Designers had to display a better business sense by being judicious about their use of plastic and other materials. Not only did they have to keep cost control in mind, they also needed to be more environmentally conscious while still meeting the growing value demands of consumers.

## FIRST MAJOR CONTRACT IN 1972

Taking on his first partners, Andreas Haug and Georg Spreng, Esslinger had his choice of work from Wega and other clients. One of the company's first major contracts was with the dental company KaVo in 1972. Rather than just design a new light for an existing chair, Esslinger and his partners designed a entirely new dental system. Moreover, he convinced KaVo's owner to position the company as more than a dental-systems provider but as a provider of holistic treatment solutions. It was a vision that went well beyond designing a new light for an old chair, or even a new dental system, and played an important role in determining the future of both companies while forging a long-term relationship.

When Wega began looking for a buyer in 1973, Esslinger accepted a job offer from the Japanese electronics giant Sony, which a short time later acquired Wega as well. It was also during this time that Esslinger began advertising in Germany's most popular design magazine, *Form*. Still working out of a garage, Esslinger bought the back cover, where he placed an advertisement featuring a jumping Brazilian tree frog. Soon a green frog was adopted as the company's logo, an appropriate choice on a number of levels. Frogs were quite common in Esslinger's native Black Forest, and the word itself was an abbreviation for the Federal Republic of Germany.

Esslinger established a long-term relationship with Sony, designing more than 100 products, including the Sony Trinitron television. Rather than serving purely as an industrial designer for Sony, Esslinger also helped to craft what he called "globally acceptable and admired branding statements," such as "It's a Sony." Thus, Esslinger Design continued to expand beyond industrial

design to lay the foundation for becoming a "business designer."

## MOVE TO CALIFORNIA: THE EIGHTIES

A pivotal moment in the evolution of Esslinger Design came in 1981 when Apple's chief executive officer, Steve Jobs, persuaded Esslinger to open an office in California's Silicon Valley by offering a contract for $2 million per year. The move to California also brought the adoption of the frog design name. Esslinger and his team went to work on the design of computer cases. In 1984 Apple unveiled the Apple IIc personal computer with the frog-designed case, which was named "Design of the Year" by *Time* magazine and later inducted into the design collection of New York's Whitney Museum. This success was followed by the Mac SE, and in 1988 the frog-designed NeXT box was voted "Design of the Year" by *Business Week*.

The 1980s saw frog become involved in corporate branding. Esslinger and his wife, Patricia Roller, also attempted to launch a new venture in 1987 called frox inc., but it did not enjoy the kind of success to which he was accustomed. An electronics company, frox was ahead of its time in envisioning a digital system that integrated video and audio entertainment with computing power. In essence, it was a media center before the concept came into vogue. Esslinger devoted two years to the effort at the expense of frog before leaving the ventures to others, who eventually produced a prototype that was too expensive and unreliable for the market. The failure of frox, Esslinger contended, was attributable more to poor management than to the underlying technology.

In the 1990s frog expanded its purview, establishing a digital media design group in 1994. It would pioneer user-interface design for the World Wide Web as well as digital devices. Overall, frog enjoyed a number of successes during the decade. The firm began working with Disney to extend family visits to Disney resorts by redesigning the company's cruise ships to make them more appealing to all age groups. With that in mind, frog designed a classic ocean liner as it would be imagined by parents and their children that also included futuristic elements. The result of this "retro-futuristic" approach, as Esslinger described it, was *Disney Magic*, soon followed by a sister ship, *Disney Wonder*. The retro-futuristic approach was appropriated by a host of products, including automobiles and apparel.

## LATE-CENTURY SUCCESSES

The company enjoyed other successes as well in the 1990s. It worked with Lufthansa Airlines to create a

---

## KEY DATES

**1969:** Hartmut Esslinger founds Esslinger Design in Germany.
**1981:** Company moves to California and is renamed frog design inc.
**1984:** Apple IIc wins "Design of the Year" award.
**1994:** Digital media design unit is established.
**2004:** Esslinger sells the company.

---

new, more emotionally appealing image. Wholesale changes were made to plane interiors, check-in gates, and lounges to completely reengineer the flight experience for passengers. Late in the 1990s frog was hired by Germany's SAP to help make the company's enterprise resource-planning software more user friendly. Not only did the revised "humanized" software feature a more colorful interface that was easier to use, its speed and performance were improved.

Although frog enjoyed some triumphs during the 1990s, Esslinger considered it a dark time for design. "Everything was about money, greed and hype," he told Constance Loizos for an interview in *ID Magazine* in 2005. Moreover, frog had to contend with a host of U.S. and European competitors in new media design who were fat with cash from public stock offerings and were more concerned with winning jobs than with profits. Then came the bursting of the Internet bubble and a downturn in the economy. The company was forced to trim staff and close a pair of offices, but it was a well-established shop and was able to weather the difficult times.

In the new century frog continued to expand it service offerings. It established a Strategy Department in 2002 to provide clients with high-level business strategy and user insights. It also continued to score notable successes. In 2000, for example, frog redesigned the Dell.com website, which set the standard for e-commerce excellence. In 2003 it worked with Disney to develop a new line of consumer electronics for children, creating a new annual revenue stream of more than $500 million.

### ESSLINGER SELLS COMPANY: 2004

In 2004 Esslinger turned 60 and decided to sell a majority stake in frog, 60 percent, for about $30 million to Singapore contract manufacturer Flextronics Inter-

national. At the time, frog was generating annual revenues in the $35 million range and was highly profitable without need for a cash infusion. Some in the industry suggested that Esllinger and his wife were interested in selling because frog had lost its cutting edge in recent years. Esslinger maintained that merging with Flextronics allowed him to pursue a "bigger vision." He told Peter Burrows for a *Business Week Online* article dated August 13, 2004, "We were ahead of the curve when we started the company, and then a bunch of people copied what we did and began claiming that they were better than frog. That will never happen again. We're jumping ahead of the curve again." It wasn't just the financial backing Flextronics could supply that made it an attractive merger partner. Flextronics was one of the world's largest contract manufacturers, and teamed with frog it could create a vertically integrated product development outsourcer, one that could develop and manufacture hardware as well as user experiences.

Esslinger and Roller stepped down as dual chief executives but remained very much involved in frog, which under Flextronics expanded what it had to offer to clients in two important ways. First, it could generate market research and then develop prototype models to take the product development process a step further. Second, frog's relationship with Flextronics allowed it to bring the right manufacturing and parts suppliers into a project. Thus, frog became an ideal partner for a company that wanted to produce innovative yet affordable products. This approach helped frog to win such new clients as General Electric and Hewlett-Packard.

Flextronics had made other acquisitions, too, in recent years, and frog was tucked within its software development and solutions business. In 2006 Flextronics elected to sell 85 percent of the group for $900 million to Kohlberg Kravis Roberts & Co. and Sequoia Capital. The operation was then renamed Aricent. The change in ownership did not hinder frog's development as a design-consulting hybrid, however.

The strong growth of frog design prompted the firm to open a new design studio in Shanghai in 2007 to enter the Chinese marketplace and bolster its position in the Asia-Pacific region. A year later frog strengthened its presence in Europe with the opening of a studio in Amsterdam. The company remained a force in product design. In 2009 it designed the HP Touchsmart laptop with a touch screen for Hewlett-Packard. It also developed the Intel point-of-sale kiosk that brought together online and real-world shopping to create a new retail concept. While rivals claimed that frog's day had passed, the firm clearly demonstrated that it remained a viable concern.

*Ed Dinger*

## PRINCIPAL COMPETITORS

Agency.com Ltd.; Grey Global Group Inc.; Organic, Inc.

## FURTHER READING

Burrows, Peter, "frog design's New Lily Pad," *Business Week Online*, August 13, 2004.

———, "One Great Leap for frog design," *Business Week Online*, April 20, 2006.

Esslinger, Hartmut, *a fine line*, San Francisco: Jossey-Bass, 2009.

Loizos, Constance, "Q&A: Hartmut Esslinger," *ID Magazine*, January 1, 2005.

Rose, Jennie, "Form, Function, Emotion: Inside the Philosophy and Process of frog design," *New Architect*, May 2002, p. 14.

# Fruit of the Loom, Inc.

———■———

1 Fruit of the Loom Drive
Bowling Green, Kentucky 42103
U.S.A.
Telephone: ((270)) 781-6400
Fax: ((270)) 781-6588
Web site: http://www.fruit.com

*Wholly Owned Subsidiary of Berkshire Hathaway, Inc.*
*Founded:* 1851
*Incorporated:* 1955
*Employees:* 26,952
*Stock Exchanges:* New York
*Ticker Symbol:* BRK.A, BRK.B (Berkshire Hathaway)
*NAICS:* 315192 Underwear and Nightwear Knitting Mills

■ ■ ■

Fruit of the Loom, Inc., is a global manufacturer and marketer of family intimate apparel and activewear. The company's products include underwear for men, women, and children, as well as T-shirts, activewear, casual wear, and clothing for children. The company's namesake brand, Fruit of the Loom, is one of the oldest and best known in the world.

## BRAND INTRODUCTION IN THE MID–NINETEENTH CENTURY

The history of the company involves two separate entities: the B. B. & R. Knight Brothers textile company and the Union Underwear Company. The Knight

Brothers established a textile company in Pontiac, Rhode Island, in the mid–19th century. The company's high-quality broadcloth was recognized as one of the best fabrics for the homemade clothing and linens that were common at the time. In 1851, when trademarking was still in its infancy, the brothers gave their cloth the imaginative name "Fruit of the Loom."

Rufus Skeel, one of the merchants who sold the Knight Brothers' cloth commercially, operated a dry goods store in New York's Hudson Valley, and his daughter, an artist, painted pictures of local apple varieties. Over time, her paintings became associated with the Fruit of the Loom name. Soon, the apple accompanied the name on printed labels that identified the Knight brothers' increasingly popular cloth. The serendipitous combination of the two components helped make Fruit of the Loom the first branded textile product in the United States. When the federal patent and trademark office opened in 1871, the trademark (which had grown to include a cluster of fruits) received the United States' 418th patent.

As long as women made their own clothing and linens, Fruit of the Loom textiles remained in demand. The development of the manufactured apparel industry in the early 20th century, however, considerably diminished the fabric market. The market for piece goods declined as homemakers did less sewing and began to favor ready-made clothing and linens. Although the original product's market dwindled, the trademark still enjoyed popularity. Thus, in 1928 the Fruit of the Loom Company began to license the brand to manufacturers of finished garments.

## COMPANY PERSPECTIVES

■

For more than 150 years, Fruit of the Loom has fulfilled a promise to its consumers ... a promise of quality, value and trust. As a vertically integrated manufacturer, we control the quality of our garments every step of the way—we manufacture our own yarn, knit the cloth, cut the fabric, sew the garments, and package the product ourselves. When you buy Fruit of the Loom products, you can be assured of comfortable, up-to-date styles at value prices.

At about the same time that Fruit of the Loom lost its direct consumer market, a young immigrant named Jacob (Jack) Goldfarb decided to start his own clothing business. Goldfarb learned about the apparel industry through his work with the Ferguson Manufacturing Company. He noticed that Ferguson only made low-priced "sale items" available to those retailers who also purchased the company's higher-priced goods. Goldfarb reasoned that if he could provide retailers with strictly lower-priced, quality undergarments, he could establish a popular business.

He decided to concentrate on the unionsuit, the most popular style of men's underwear of the 19th century, and named his endeavor the Union Underwear Company. Like the term "unionsuit" itself, there is some controversy about the origin of the company name. Some historians assert that the term unionsuit referred to the "union" of a top and bottom, while others maintain that the name grew out of the fact that members of the Civil War–era Union Army wore the garment. Whether the name for the Union Underwear Company alluded to the United States or the construction of its clothing remains a mystery.

Oddly enough, Goldfarb started his manufacturing business without a factory. He purchased cloth from one supplier, had it delivered to a cutter, and then sent the parts to a sewing shop for finishing and shipping. Union Underwear's first garments were sewn by nuns in and around Indianapolis, Indiana, the site of the company's first finishing plant.

Goldfarb continued to work within this complex system even through the onset of the Great Depression. In 1930 he was approached by some promoters from Frankfort, Kentucky, who were looking for an industry that would provide employment and increase the city's tax base during the lengthy Depression. The municipal-

ity offered to build a plant for the business, which would bring all of Union's operations to a single location. Goldfarb agreed to the lucrative offer, and within five years his company employed 650 people at the new location.

Union Underwear and Fruit of the Loom's fortunes converged near the end of the decade. In his quest to become a national marketer, Goldfarb purchased a 25-year license for the Fruit of the Loom trademark in 1938. He was certain that the well-known brand would propel his products to national prominence.

Union Underwear built a second plant to produce broadcloth "boxer" shorts in Bowling Green, Kentucky, on the eve of World War II. When America joined the Allied effort in 1941, the company was enlisted to manufacture millions of pairs of G.I. shorts. Union Underwear received numerous commendations from the government for its contribution on the home front.

## POSTWAR BRAND EXTENSIONS AND INNOVATIONS

Goldfarb made several promotional innovations in the postwar era that set Union Underwear and the Fruit of the Loom label apart from other undergarment manufacturers. Before World War II, underwear was usually sold in single units, but in the late 1940s Goldfarb introduced a printed cellophane bag with three pair of shorts inside. The new packages were displayed to call attention to Union's branded undergarments. The move established a trend that has become an industry standard for most basic underwear. Furthermore, even though Goldfarb was only a licensee of the trademark, he became the only licensee to invest his own funds in consumer advertising.

The company expanded its product line from unionsuits and boxer shorts to include knit underwear in 1948, and it opened its third plant in Campbellsville, Kentucky, in 1952. The plant provided internal knitting and bleaching facilities for Union manufacturing for the first time, helping the company to gain more vertical control of production and facilitating the production of a wider variety of men's and boys' undergarments.

Goldfarb continued his promotional innovations when Union became the first underwear company to advertise on network television in 1955. The company purchased spots during Dave Garroway's *Today Show*. Union also utilized banners, posters, signs, price tickets, newspaper slicks, and a cooperative advertising program to support Fruit of the Loom sales. Consumer advertising campaigns were coordinated with such seasonal events as Father's Day, back-to-school time, and Christmas to maximize the company's advertising dollar.

## KEY DATES

■

**1851:** The B. B. & R. Knight Brothers textile company gives their cloth the imaginative name "Fruit of the Loom."

**1871:** Fruit of the Loom receives the United States' 418th patent and becomes the first branded textile product in the United States.

**1928:** Fruit of the Loom Company begins to license the brand to manufacturers of finished garments.

**1938:** Union Underwear purchases a 25-year license for the Fruit of the Loom trademark.

**1955:** Union Underwear becomes the first underwear company to advertise on network television.

**1968:** Union Underwear is purchased by Northwest Industries.

**1975:** Union Underwear makes advertising history with the first "Fruit of the Loom Guys" ads.

**1984:** William F. Farley acquires Union Underwear when he buys Northwest Industries.

**2001:** Berkshire Hathaway, owned by Warren Buffett, purchases Fruit of the Loom.

**2006:** Fruit of the Loom acquires competitor Russell Corp.

Around the same time, Union allied itself to the mass merchandisers that were beginning to spring up in the mid-1950s. The company's growth was soon tied to these new retailer's success: by the early 1990s, 45 percent of men's basic underwear was sold by discount stores.

## STRUCTURAL CHANGES IN THE FIFTIES AND SIXTIES

The mid-1950s saw the start of a string of acquisitions that would place Union Underwear in several different hands over the next three decades. In 1955 Union Underwear was taken over by the Philadelphia & Reading Corporation, a newly formed conglomerate. The new corporate structure provided Union with additional resources, enabling it to extend its manufacturing operations.

At that point Union Underwear had grown to become Fruit of the Loom's dominant licensee, and to most people the name had come to mean underwear more than fabric. The licensee, in fact, had grown larger

than Fruit of the Loom. In order to assure the availability of its well-known trademark, Philadelphia & Reading acquired the Fruit of the Loom Licensing Company in 1961.

In 1968 Union Underwear's parent was purchased by Northwest Industries. The consolidation furnished new capital, which further facilitated the company's growth. That same year Goldfarb stepped down as chair to be replaced by Everett Moore, who had joined the company in 1932 at the Frankfort plant.

## ADVERTISING IN THE SIXTIES AND SEVENTIES

Union Underwear strove to energize advertising for men's underwear in the late 1960s and early 1970s. In 1969 the company contracted sportscaster Howard Cosell to appear in five television commercials over three years. Next, British comedian Terry Thomas was named spokesperson, as advertisers hoped that an English representative would lend an air of quality and endurance to their commercials. The use of celebrity spokespersons brought more public attention to Fruit of the Loom underwear, but the company continued to seek more brand recognition and market share.

In 1975 Union made advertising history with the first "Fruit of the Loom Guys" campaign. The commercials featured three men in costume as a bunch of grapes, an autumn leaf, and an apple, all elements of the brand's trademark. The characters helped propel the Fruit of the Loom brand to 98 percent recognition and doubled Union's share of the market for men's and boy's underwear.

Moore retired that year and was succeeded by John Holland. In 1976 Union acquired the century-old BVD trademark. The company began to merchandise BVD as a completely separate line of underwear aimed at the more upscale department store market. Union also began to expand its product line in 1978 to include "Underoos"—decorated underwear for boys and girls—and began to supply blank T-shirts for the screen-print market during the 1970s. The expansion into plain T-shirts soon evolved into a huge business known as Screen Stars, which sold unbranded T-shirts, sweatshirts, and sweatpants to wholesalers who imprinted them for promotional uses.

## MID-EIGHTIES LEVERAGED BUYOUT AND REORGANIZATION

Union did not escape the trend toward leveraged buyouts in the 1980s. In 1984 William F. Farley acquired Union Underwear when he bought Northwest Industries for $1.4 billion. Farley privatized the parent company and renamed it Farley Industries. In the 1980s tradition of leveraged buyouts and junk bonds, Farley parlayed his acquisitions into larger and larger conquests until, by the end of the decade, he had fashioned a textile and apparel conglomerate with $4 billion in annual sales and 65,000 employees worldwide.

In 1985 the conglomerate was restructured, $260 million in shares were sold, and Union Underwear was renamed Fruit of the Loom, Inc., to relate the business more closely to its famous trademark. Farley, a former encyclopedia salesperson, worked to improve Fruit of the Loom's operational efficiency and squeeze more profits out of the company's number-one status as the holder of a 35 percent share of the undergarment market. Farley proceeded to sell the bulk of Northwest Industries' other businesses and cut costs at Fruit of the Loom. The proceeds of the asset sales were combined with revenues from bond issues to finance domestic modernization and expansion into Europe.

Over the course of the 1980s those manufacturing changes facilitated Fruit of the Loom's evolution from an underwear manufacturer into an apparel company. Farley and Chief Executive Holland decided to expand into men's fashion underwear, women's underwear, and socks over the course of the decade, and they put the Fruit of the Loom label on sportswear in 1987. Women's panties became one of the brand's most popular extensions. The company launched that division in 1984 and led the category with a 10 percent share within four years. Fruit of the Loom also made apparel history with its popular pocket T-shirt. Produced in a rainbow of colors, the wardrobe staple's flexibility made it a consumer favorite for decades.

In 1982 sales of men's and boy's white underwear accounted for 80 percent of the company's revenues, but by 1988 brand extensions made up more than 40 percent of revenues. The activewear market also grew much more rapidly than the underwear category. Activewear sales tripled in the 1980s, while the underwear market grew only about 6 percent annually.

## LOSSES IN THE LATE EIGHTIES

Capital improvements had enabled Fruit of the Loom to expand into newer, faster-growing markets, but they also left the company saddled with debt. Fruit's debt-to-equity ratio of 3.5-to-1 contributed to three out of four years of losses before the decade was over. Interest expenses also consumed 10 percent of annual sales revenues in 1989. At the same time, Fruit of the Loom was threatened on two fronts: low-priced imports began to eat into Fruit of the Loom's 38 percent market share

of basic men's undergarments, and the company's largest competitor, Sara Lee Corp.'s Hanes Knit Products, was raising the ante in the "underwars."

In an effort to promote its move from department stores to discount merchandisers, Hanes introduced "Inspector 12" into its advertising campaigns in 1982. The curmudgeonly quality-control character claimed that her brand fit better and shrank less than Fruit of the Loom's. Fruit of the Loom fired back with promotions that featured the tagline, "Sorry, Hanes, you lose!" The war escalated into a legal battle that ended with an out-of-court settlement wherein the two competitors agreed to pull the offensive ads.

The Fruit of the Loom Guys were phased out when the company launched its more modern campaign, "We fit America like we never did before," in 1988. The television spots featured family scenes, including a mother dropping her daughter off at the school bus, and also included the first views of a woman in a pair of panties on network television. The $25 million campaign, created by Grey Advertising, Inc., emphasized Fruit of the Loom's move into basic apparel for both sexes and all ages.

The brand extensions, expanded capacity, advertising blitz, and years of debt paid off in 1988 when Fruit of the Loom made its first profit since its acquisition by Farley. The mid-1980s capital investments had pumped up domestic operating margins to 20 or 25 percent, and European plants began earning profits in the early 1990s. Sales had actually grown 13 percent annually since 1976 to $1 billion in 1988, but debt had consumed all of the income.

In 1990 Fruit of the Loom unveiled the underwear industry's first network advertisements that featured a male model sporting the flagship white briefs. The commercials asked the musical question, "Whose underwear is under there?" The answer was provided by hunky celebrities Ed Marinaro, Patrick Duffy, and James DePavia. Lawyers for Grey Advertising spent two weeks battling one of the big three networks to air the commercials, which would have been banned just three years earlier. Over the next two years, Fruit of the Loom's celebrity "underwearers" included soap-opera star Don Diamont, action-adventure hero David Hasselhoff, and sitcom dad Alan Thicke.

## CONTINUED CHALLENGES IN THE NINETIES

In 1991 Fruit of the Loom introduced the campaign "It's your time" for its growing line of casual wear, which was extended to include garments for infants and toddlers. The company enlarged its array of brands that year through a licensing agreement with the upscale Munsingwear brand in the hope of expanding Fruit of the Loom's retail distribution.

The company's financial restabilization continued. Debt was reduced by more than $332 million with the help of sales totaling $1.4 billion, a stock offering of $100 million, a decline in capital expenditures, and the conversion of $60 million of debt into equity. Fruit of the Loom's European sales surged 43 percent in 1990 as these divisions hit stride.

Despite a lingering recession in the United States, the company once again found its capacity constrained. Farley and Holland predicted that Fruit of the Loom would invest $125 million in new equipment and increase the workforce by 3,000 at plants in the United States, Canada, and Europe in 1992. With strong ties to mass merchandisers, major product launches, and line extensions, Fruit of the Loom hoped to increase sales 15 percent each year, decrease debt load, and grow per-share earnings by one-third annually in the 1990s.

Fruit of the Loom's optimism, however, led to manufacturing overcapacity in 1993. Management responded by cutting back production. Unfortunately, customer spending was starting to rebound then from the recession of the early 1990s. In 1994 cotton prices unexpectedly rose and exacerbated the company's problems. Fruit of the Loom's stock price fell 50 percent between 1993 and 1995.

The company took several steps to correct its problems. In an effort to reduce its dependency on low-margin briefs and boxers, Fruit of the Loom focused on developing activewear and casual wear products, both by continuing to broaden the product lines of its traditional brands and by purchasing new brands. In 1993 the company acquired Salem Sportswear and arranged a licensing agreement to manufacture and market athletic wear under the Wilson logo. The following year it acquired sports logo clothing makers Artex Manufacturing Inc. and Pro Player. Also in 1994 it bought the bankrupt sportswear maker Gitano Group, Inc., for $100 million. By 1995 only 25 percent of the company's revenues derived from sales of men's and boys' underwear.

Fruit of the Loom also addressed operating inefficiencies in the early and mid-1990s. It invested in modernizing its manufacturing facilities, from spinning the yarn to assembling the finished clothing. In 1995 the company took more drastic measures to cut costs: It closed nine manufacturing facilities in the United States and laid off 6,000 employees. With the hope of cutting costs through lower-cost offshore labor, the company began moving its labor-intensive sewing operations to the Caribbean and Central America. One-time charges

related to the plant closings and relocations added to Fruit of the Loom's losses for 1995, which tallied in at $227 million.

The following year Fruit of the Loom helped fund its manufacturing relocations by selling the operating assets of its hosiery division to Renfro Corp. for $90 million. In 1997 the company laid off an additional 4,800 workers and closed another U.S. plant. By that time more than 60 percent of the company's production was taking place internationally.

Although the company returned to the black in 1996, with approximately $147 million in net earnings, in 1997 the company saw another loss. The net loss of $488 million was due in part to continuing costs of moving sewing operations offshore and in part to a charge of $102 million made to pay a legal judgment against Fruit of the Loom. The court judgment ended litigation dating from 1984 related to the Fruit of the Loom subsidiary Universal Manufacturing (which the company sold in 1986). However, sales were also down to $2.1 billion from $2.4 billion in 1996.

## CRISIS AT THE TURN OF THE MILLENNIUM

The company's performance fluctuated in the later 1990s. Reductions in labor expenses seemed to be reaping rewards in 1998. First-quarter profits were up 38 percent, and a price increase in men's underwear in April 1998 indicated potentially higher margins in a traditionally low-margin area for Fruit of the Loom. To further strengthen performance by reducing the tax burden, a new parent company, Fruit of the Loom, Ltd., was established in the Cayman Islands that same year. In 1999, however, production problems, lower sales, and depressed margins resulted in a loss of $9 million in the first quarter. A bright part of this picture was stronger sales in women's intimate apparel, partly due to a new marketing emphasis on the women's market, and in children's wear, because of promotions of Star Wars and Teletubbies licensed products.

Despite its best efforts, Fruit of the Loom remained burdened by inefficient mills and nearly $2 billion in liabilities, and the company was forced to file for bankruptcy protection in 1999. The company was further shaken up when William Farley, the colorful, longtime CEO, was forced out that year and replaced by William Bookshester, a member of the board of directors, as interim CEO, an appointment made permanent in 2000. The condition of the company was dire. Stock prices had declined from a peak of $48 per share in 1993 to less than $7 later in the decade. The company suffered a third-quarter loss of $166.4 million, seven times larger than expectations, and a decline of 8 percent in sales. To make matters worse, the company was hit with several class-action shareholder lawsuits alleging that former officers knowingly overstated the financial condition of the company to inflate the stock price. Some analysts now feared that the venerable brand was on the verge of ruin.

Looking for a way to stave off collapse, Fruit of the Loom considered selling its underwear and activewear businesses. Instead, the leadership decided that the best course was outright sale of the entire company. Competitors Warnaco, VF Corp., Hanes, and others quickly showed interest. By the spring of 2001 the company's financial position, while still weak, had improved enough to make it a more attractive acquisition.

In the meantime, Fruit of the Loom sued former CEO Farley, who while in that position had secured several bank loans, including one for $65 million, all guaranteed by the company. The suit contended that he had ceased repaying the loans and that the banks were asking Fruit of the Loom for repayment. Eventually, in a 2002 Delaware bankruptcy court settlement, Farley agreed to repay $23 million of the $65 million loan.

## WARREN BUFFETT RESCUES THE COMPANY

After U.S. commerce paused in the wake of the September 11, 2001, terrorist attacks in New York and Washington, D.C., it did not take long for the right buyer to show up. In November 2001 Berkshire Hathaway, Inc., the holding company and investment vehicle of billionaire investor Warren Buffett, agreed to pay $835 million in cash for Fruit of the Loom. In this deal, Buffett acquired a company whose stocks had become almost worthless due to slow sales, heavy debt, and mismanagement. The company was nonetheless a good fit with Buffett's investment style of buying firms with an established, well-defined product and market, which could be expected to generate steady if unspectacular profits if they were properly managed. Fruit of the Loom was established as an independent, wholly owned subsidiary of Berkshire Hathaway. Buffett retained as CEO John Holland, who had been called out of retirement the previous year. Buffett cited Holland's managerial talent as a major reason for buying the company.

Over the first three years under Berkshire Hathaway, Fruit of the Loom took a number of steps to expand its markets. Even before the acquisition was official, the company introduced a new television advertising campaign featuring the well-known Fruit Guys characters, who had been on a hiatus from advertising campaigns for several years. Thereafter the company resumed making them a regular feature in its advertising. In 2002 Fruit of the Loom initiated a private-label program that allowed promoters to put unique labels on the company's T-shirts. To reach the huge and rapidly growing U.S. Hispanic population, in 2003 Fruit of the Loom began targeting Spanish-speaking consumers with special television advertisements on the Telemundo, Telefutura, and Galavision networks. In 2004 Fruit of the Loom sought to ride the massive popularity of NASCAR, teaming up with successful race driver Robby Gordon to race a company-sponsored Chevrolet Monte Carlo in 24 NASCAR Busch Series races.

Unfortunately, by July 2004 the results of all these efforts under Berkshire Hathaway were not very impressive. Fruit of the Loom's marketing program was not as aggressive as some thought it should be, partly because Holland's background was in Fruit of the Loom's manufacturing side and not marketing. Advertising budgets had been cut, the Fruit Guys notwithstanding, and the company was emphasizing manufacturing efficiency and low production costs.

The first decade of the 2000s ended with two acquisitions that boded well for the future, expanding Fruit of the Loom's markets and product range and strengthening its revenue stream. In 2006, for $600 million, the company acquired competitor Russell Corp., maker of Jerzees, Moving Comfort, Spalding, Brooks, Mossy Oaks, and other established brands. The next year Fruit of the Loom bought VF Corp.'s intimate apparel business for $350 million cash. These moves were part of Buffett's strategy to enhance Fruit of the Loom's ability to market its intimate apparel to mass retailers like Wal-Mart and Target. The acquisitions also positioned the company to better compete with industry giant and principal competitor Hanesbrands, Inc.

*April S. Dougal*
*Updated, Susan Windisch Brown; Judson MacLaury*

## PRINCIPAL SUBSIDIARIES

Russell Corporation.

## PRINCIPAL COMPETITORS

Hanesbrands, Inc.; Jockey International, Inc.; Gildan Activewear, Inc.

## FURTHER READING

Barboza, David, "Berkshire Set to Acquire Apparel Giant; $835 Million to Be Paid for Fruit of the Loom," *New York Times,*

November 2, 2001, p. C1.

"Bill Farley Could Lose His Shirt and His Underwear," *BusinessWeek*, March 11, 1991, p. 86.

"Boyswear Brightens the Apparel Picture," *Discount Merchandiser*, December 1991, p. 52.

Fannin, Rebecca, "Underwear: Inspector 12 Takes on the Fruits," *Marketing & Media Decisions*, April 1988, pp. 55–56.

Greising, David. "Bill Farley Is on Pins and Needles," *BusinessWeek*, September 18, 1989, p. 58.

Levine, Joshua, "Marketing: Fantasy, Not Flesh," *Forbes*, January 22, 1990, pp. 118–20.

Oneal, Michael, "Fruit of the Loom Escalates the Underwars," *BusinessWeek*, February 22, 1988, p. 114.

"Profit Surges 38% on Moves to Reduce Labor Expenses," *Wall Street Journal*, April 16, 1998, p. A8.

Schifrin, Matthew, "Matchmaker Leon?" *Forbes*, March 28, 1994, p. 20.

Zipser, Andy, "Cherry-picking Fruit of the Loom," *Barron's*, May 20, 1991, pp. 30–31.

# Grace & Wild, Inc.

———■———

23689 Industrial Park Drive
Farmington Hills, Michigan 48335
U.S.A.
Telephone: (248) 471-6010
Fax: (248) 471-2312
Web site: http://www.gracewild.com/

*Private Company*
*Founded:* 1984 as Grace & Wild Studios, Inc.
*Employees:* 150
*Sales:* $100 million (2009 est.)
*NAICS:* 512110 Motion Picture and Video Production;
512191 Teleproduction and Other Postproduction
Services; 512240 Audio Recording Post-production
Services; 334613 Magnetic and Optical Recording
Media Manufacturing; 532490 Audio Visual Equip-
ment Rental or Leasing

■ ■ ■

Since its formative years, Grace & Wild, Inc., has
provided a noteworthy combination of technical
expertise, one-on-one service, and a passion for media.
By being part of the pioneering phase of video production and having an entrepreneurial flair, Harvey Grace
and Steven D. Wild started and developed a
multipurpose company. Headquartered in Farmington
Hills, Michigan, the company has undertaken numerous
projects, from producing commercials to recording
music to filming scenes for movies. The company also
has offices in Ferndale and Southfield, Michigan, and,
through its fiber connectivity and other resources, it can
provide remote production and postproduction services.
Grace & Wild's 2009 revenues are believed to have been
as high as $100 million, positioning the company
between two of its competitors: Ascent Media Corporation (with $600 million) and Wilson-Brown Produc-
tions, Inc. (with $200,000). Grace & Wild's clients
include world-famous corporations, award-winning
movie directors and advertising agencies, and nonprofit
groups and government agencies.

## MEDIA AND ENTREPRENEURSHIP: MID-SEVENTIES TO EIGHTIES

In 1984 Grace and Wild founded Grace & Wild
Studios, Inc. Both men had fairly extensive backgrounds
in broadcast media. Prior to the company's start, Grace
had been focusing on independent television and radio
station investment and management. Wild had
primarily been involved with the emerging field of
videotape. He was working at Magnetic Video Corporation in 1975 when the Farmington, Michigan, company
extended its operations to include not only audiotape
duplication but also videotape duplication. In 1977
Magnetic Video obtained the rights from Twentieth
Century–Fox Film Corporation to duplicate and
distribute 50 of its films as videocassettes. By that time
Magnetic Video had revenues of $3 million.

In 1978 Twentieth Century–Fox acquired Magnetic
Video for more than $7 million. Four years later
Twentieth Century–Fox and CBS agreed to a joint
venture whose outcome for Magnetic Video was CBS/
Fox Home Video. The new company where Wild was

COMPANY PERSPECTIVES

The production and post-production services offered by Grace & Wild present extraordinary possibilities to those in the business of communicating. In our vast universe you will find unique expertise in all forms of audio and visual content creation through delivery. We invite you to explore the work and the skills that define us.

director of studio operations was meant to take advantage of the public's increasing interest in watching movies at home. However, the idea needed refining for the mass market. For example, David Santry of *Business Week* noted in July 1978 that the viewing equipment had compatibility issues and that consumers had to pay $50 to $70 per videocassette. Still, the future of home video had begun.

After more than half a decade's involvement, Wild turned his attention to the entrepreneurial end of the video business. In 1984 Wild, Grace, and several other investors acquired CBS/Fox Home Video and renamed it Grace & Wild Studios, Inc. Following the acquisition, Grace and Wild established their headquarters in Studio Center, a vacated facility in Farmington Hills.

By 1986 the company had completed an extensive renovation of the facility. The renovations included upgraded areas for film editing and transfer from film to videotape and rooms that would improve clients' ability to meet, plan, and produce programming, ads, and motion pictures. The scale of the renovations made it evident that Grace and Wild were going beyond a mere prerecorded videocassette company.

### ACQUISITIONS AND DIVERSIFICATION: 1991–99

Grace & Wild undertook acquisitions as its next major business activity. Beginning in 1991 it acquired Film Works, a company that focused on special effects and animation. Two years later it bought ProVision, a video production facility in Ann Arbor, Michigan. By 1997 Grace & Wild had acquired a total of eight video, audio, graphics, and media equipment rental businesses.

A new name for the company, Grace & Wild Digital Studios, was announced in 1994. The addition of "Digital" to its name highlighted the company's awareness that technology was embarking on a digitally based journey. In fact, Grace & Wild was leading the

way: no other firm in the region had a full complement of digital editing equipment and no other company in the Midwest had the personnel to handle it.

This was evident when Grace & Wild acquired the processing company Film Craft Lab in 1995, renamed it Filmcraft Imaging, and established it as a new division. Another instance occurred when Postique and its arm Griot Editorial were acquired and established as new divisions. As Joseph Serwach of *Crain's Detroit Business* observed in September 1997: "While Postique offers some of the same video post-production services offered by Grace & Wild, Postique has its own niche and way of doing things, Wild said, adding that he wanted to see that diversity of ideas continue within the expanded company." These and other growth-oriented decisions made it apparent that Wild and his team were heading successfully toward the next century.

In October 1998 Wild articulated in the article "Think Big (with a Boutique Attitude)" the company's direction and management style. He noted that "companies that provide a wide range of services under one roof can offer conveniences that are sometimes lacking in smaller shops, which focus on one aspect of the process, such as graphics or editing." In addition, he noted that because Grace & Wild's division heads had been given decision-making responsibility and had actively engaged lines of communication, employees, company owners, and clients were experiencing a win-win situation.

### TECHNOLOGY AND LOYALTY

In 1999 Grace & Wild made CD and DVD duplication a part of its offerings. That same year the company established Division X, which specialized in 3D, animation, and computer-generated images. These developments helped Grace & Wild enter the 21st century with the "on" switch activated. Furthermore, advances in technology and equipment, increased affordability for consumers, and an upsurge of interest in home and portable media made it possible for the company to continue diversifying what it could to help its clients produce and market their products.

In 2001 high-speed and digital photography joined the company's roster. In 2002 a new name for the company, hdstudios, mirrored the recognition of high-definition technology's emergence. As they had done in 1994, Grace and Wild were pioneers by being the first firm in the region with a total range of high-definition equipment. Other improvements boosted their services, including a linkage in 2009 with Specs Howard, a school of broadcast arts whose branch tenancy at Studio Center brought clients local talent in need of intern-

## KEY DATES

**1984:** Harvey Grace and Steven D. Wild form Grace & Wild Studios, Inc.
**1994:** In its tenth year of operation, the company is renamed Grace & Wild Digital Studios.
**2002:** The company's new name becomes hdstudios and is the first in the region with fully operational high-definition services.
**2009:** The company enters its 25th year with the name Grace & Wild, Inc.

ships, apprenticeships, and freelance work; fiber optics that could empower connections on a near-global basis; and the capacity to create content for Web spots, mobile phones, and satellite radio.

While other media production companies were known to incur high costs and exert obstacles, Grace & Wild managed to build a reputation of efficiency. Regardless, the company encountered challenges when the economy faltered between 2008 and 2010. Wild and his management team made the onerous, but necessary decision in 2010 to downshift their staff to 150. Still, the company's ties with freelancers and the industry's esteem for Grace & Wild remained intact. So did its many clients. Among the advertisements that aired during this period were those featuring Price Pfister, the University of Michigan, Heinz ketchup, and USA.gov (U.S. Government Services Administration).

By 2007 a combination of improved tax incentives by the state of Michigan and initiates by the Michigan Film Office enticed several out-of-state companies to join companies such as Ford Motor Corporation and General Motors to begin employing Grace & Wild's expertise. From 2007 to 2009 Grace & Wild's projects with Hollywood alone went from three in 2007 to more than 10 in 2008 to several well-known films in 2009, with Clint Eastwood and Drew Barrymore being among the directors coming to Farmington Hills. As Corey Hall wrote in his 2009 profile for *Metromode*, "From Wild's perspective, the job is to keep the momentum rolling, and to make sure that Michigan and Hollywood

have a lasting relationship, not just a passing fling." Having celebrated its 25th anniversary in 2009 and returned to somewhat of a reunion with its original name, Grace & Wild, Inc., proved that business acumen, technological know-how, and a commitment to multidimensional media equal excellent prospects for sustainability.

*Mary C. Lewis*

### PRINCIPAL DIVISIONS

Grace & Wild Corporate; hdstudios; Postique; Griot Editorial; Division X; emerge; Filmcraft Imaging.

### PRINCIPAL COMPETITORS

Ascent Media Corporation; Audio & Video Labs, Inc.; Wilson-Brown Productions, Inc.

### FURTHER READING

Dupler, Steven, "Studio Center Welcoming New Tenants," *Billboard*, January 25, 1986, p. 35.

Hall, Corey, "Grace & Wild: A Studio Success before Hollywood Came Calling," *Metromode*, August 27, 2009, http://www.metromodemedia.com/features/GraceandWild0130.aspx.

Musburger, Robert B., and Gorham Kindem, *Introduction to Media Production: The Path to Digital Media Production.* Boston: Focal Press, 2005, pp. 71, 73–76.

"Prerecorded Videocassette Report: Fox Film, Fotomat, Allied Artists Take Closer Steps to Home Markets," *Merchandising*, January 1979, pp. 84, 86–87.

"Roberts to Head CBS/Fox Joint Venture," *Broadcasting*, April 19, 1982, pp. 30–31.

Santry, David G., "Inside Wall Street: Are Movie-Cassette Stocks Worth Buying?" *BusinessWeek*, July 17, 1978, p. 76.

Serwach, Joseph, "Grace & Wild Buys Postique for Growth and Diversity," *Crain's Detroit Business*, September 15, 1997, p. 6.

Shea, Bill, "'Perfect Time' for Film Biz, State Incentives Keep Studio Center Tenants Rolling," *Crain's Detroit Business*, March 14, 2010, p. 8.

Wild, Steven D., "Think Big (with a Boutique Attitude)," *Videography*, October 1998, p. 32.

Williams, Colin C., *Consumer Services and Economic Development.* New York: Routledge, 1997, pp. 172–77.

# Grupo Comex

———————— ■ ————————

Blvd. Manuel Avila Camacho #138 PH 1 and 2
Col. Lomas de Chapultepec,
Mexico D.F. CP 11000
Mexico
Telephone: (+55) 1669-1600
Fax: (+55) 1669-1660
Web site: http://www.thecomexgroup.com/

*Private Company*
*Founded:* 1956 as Comercial Mexicana de Pinturas
*Employees:* 5,000
*Sales:* US$1.47 billion (2009)
*NAICS:* 325510 Paint and Coating Manufacturing;
424950 Paint, Varnish, and Supplies Merchant
Wholesalers; 444120 Paint and Wallpaper Stores

■ ■ ■

Grupo Comex (Comex Group), based in Mexico, is the fourth-largest paint manufacturer in North America. The Comex Group manufactures not only paints but also industrial coatings, automotive finishes, adhesives, specialty coatings for wood and concrete, varnishes, sheet rock, and plaster. The company made its move into the United States in 2004, when it acquired Professional Paint Inc., a similar-sized group of paint manufacturers based in Denver, Colorado. The company operates under the Comex Paint name in Mexico and Central America and under the Professional Paint Inc. name in the United States and Canada. By 2010 Comex was the seventh-largest paint manufacturer by sales and

the fourth-largest paint manufacturer by gallons produced in North America.

## A SMALL, FAMILY-RUN BUSINESS

The Comex Group was founded in 1956 as a small family owned company in Mexico City named Comercial Mexicana de Pinturas. Operating with little equipment and hardly any space, the company began manufacturing small batches of paint out of the family garage using an old World War I grinding mill. Following a fire in 1959, Comex decided to separate its industrial and wood coatings manufacturing process from its architectural paint products by establishing two subsidiary companies. When it faced increasing opposition from retail outlets to carry Comex paint, the company branched into a new direction by opening up several independent retail stores to carry its brand. By the 1970s the company's manufacturing plant in Tepexpan was forced to expand to meet the growing demand for its products.

Over the subsequent two decades Comex grew exponentially in Mexico, becoming the country's top-selling paint brand and garnering half the market share. Company executives started searching for new ways to grow the company. In 1994 Comex decided to expand into neighboring Central American countries by seeking out independent business owners who were interested in becoming retail partners. The first Comex store was introduced in Guatemala in August 1994, in Belize in January 1997, in El Salvador in August 1997, and in Panama in June 1988. In 2000 the Comex Group brought these independent businesses under the

## COMPANY PERSPECTIVES

Having grown dramatically from a collection of small family-run businesses into a major industrial corporation, *Comex Group* manufactures paints and coatings that customers count on for quality across North and Central America.

Through our subsidiary companies we deliver the comprehensive cross-border solutions that customers require.

Superior performance, expert advice and the most convenient service distinguish *Comex Group* brands wherever they are sold.

We are passionate about partnering with customers to formulate architectural paints, industrial coatings, automotive finishes, waterproof coatings and wood-care products that achieve desired results and set the industry standard for excellence.

company's management, and in subsequent years it opened stores in Costa Rica, Honduras, and Nicaragua.

## EXPANSION IN THE UNITED STATES AND CANADA

By the 21st century Comex was searching for new ways to expand and strengthen its relationship with U.S. companies. In 2003 it signed an agreement with Ace Hardware Corporation of the United States. Ace agreed to retrofit Comex's Practico Home Centers in and around Mexico City with Ace retail formats, while Ace retailers already in Mexico would offer Comex products.

The company's most significant move came in 2004, when it purchased Professional Paint Inc. (PPI) of Lone Tree, Colorado, for $400 million. At the time, Comex held 52 percent of Mexico's architectural paint market. The company wanted to expand across the U.S. border because the per capita paint consumption in the United States was twice what it was in Mexico. Comex was one of several Mexican firms that had recently expanded into the United States, in part to market their products to the Hispanic population living in the country.

PPI had been founded in 2000, when it bought six North American paint companies from Williams PLC. Thereafter, PPI acquired several other paint and coatings companies in the United States and Canada, including the Jones-Blair Co. based in Dallas, Texas; Ideal Paints

based in Toronto, Canada; and Duckback Products, Inc., based in Chico, California. As a result of its acquisition of PPI, Comex acquired Frazee Paint, headquartered in San Diego, California; Kwal Paint, headquartered in Denver; Parker Paint, headquartered in Tacoma, Washington; Stellar Kwal Paint, headquartered in Dallas; General Paint, headquartered in Vancouver, Canada; Ideal Paint; and Duckback Products. The company also acquired a network of about 600 retail locations selling Kwal, Parker, Frazee, and General paint and Duckback wood and concrete stains across most of the United States and Canada. The acquisition translated into sales topping $1 billion, making the company the 15th-largest manufacturer of paints and coatings in the world.

## CONTINUING TO GROW THE MARKET

Comex's expansion drive was not satisfied with the PPI deal. In 2006 the company acquired another U.S. regional paint company, Color Wheel, which was headquartered in Orlando, Florida. That same year Comex invested in a plaster manufacturing plant in Mexico, becoming the third-largest manufacturer of plaster in that country.

Comex increased its marketing exposure in 2007, when it signed through its Frazee subsidiary a multimillion-dollar contract to sponsor the Chivas, a major league soccer team based outside of Los Angeles, California. The soccer team was a spin-off of Las Chivas, a popular soccer team in Mexico. Comex viewed company sponsorship of the team as a major marketing tool for reaching Hispanic-Americans living in the Southwest. The team's home stadium was renamed the Frazee Bell Gardens Sports Center and the Comex logo appeared on the players' soccer jerseys.

In 2008 Comex strengthened its foothold in Canada by acquiring the Para Paints and Crown Diamond brands from Akzo Nobel N.V. The following year it introduced the new paint line UltraTech Commercial Coatings, which was formulated to meet performance standards in high-use commercial areas such as hospitals, schools, and shopping malls. Besides being durable, UltraTech was safer for the environment because it emitted zero volatile organic compounds.

Like other paint and coatings manufacturers, Comex suffered from the global economic recession that began in late 2007, particularly because of the foreclosure crisis and the drop in new housing starts. Its sales dropped to $1.4 billion in 2008 from $1.5 billion the year before. To retain its market share, Comex began offering in 2009 spectrophotometer color matching and

## KEY DATES

**1956:** Comercial Mexicana de Pinturas is founded.
**1994:** The first Comex store outside of Mexico opens in Guatemala.
**2004:** Comex acquires Professional Paint Inc.
**2006:** Comex acquires Color Wheel.
**2009:** Comex introduces UltraTech Commercial Coatings.

decorating advice in its retail stores. It also provided paint color samples and decorating ideas based on the psychology of colors and the principles of feng shui on its Web site. This marketing scheme appeared to work, because by yearend 2009 it reported a slight increase in sales of nearly $1.5 billion.

*Melissa J. Doak*

### PRINCIPAL SUBSIDIARIES

Color Wheel Paint; General Paint; Frazee Paint; Parker Paint; Kwal Paint; Comex Mexico & Central America; Hardware Enterprises de Mexico.

### PRINCIPAL DIVISIONS

Professional Paint Inc.; Comex Paint.

### PRINCIPAL COMPETITORS

Behr Process Corporation; Benjamin Moore & Co.; Du-Pont Coatings & Color Technologies; Kelly-Moore Paint Company, Inc.; The Sherwin-Williams Company; The Valspar Corporation.

### FURTHER READING

"Ace Hardware Inks Deal with Retail Subsidiary of COMEX," *Coatings World*, October 2003, p. 12.

"Comex Launches UltraTech Commercial Coatings," *Coatings World*, March 1, 2009.

"Consorcio Comex Sets out to Tackle US Market, Invests US$400mn," *Corporate Mexico*, September 27, 2004.

D'Amico, Esther, "Paints and Coatings," *Chemical Week*, October 20, 2004.

Esposito, Christine Canning, "The Industry's Next Billion-Dollar Powerhouse? Comex and PPI Will Combine Forces in a Merger Deal That Creates a $1 Billion Paint Company," *Coatings World*, September 2004, p. 6.

Parker, Karen, "PCI 25 Reflects Industry Consolidation," *Paint & Coatings Industry*, July 1, 2009, http://www.pcimag.com/Articles/Feature_Article/BNP_GUID_9-5-2006_A_10000000000000618036.

Shanley, Will, "Mexico Firm Heads North for Growth," *Denver Post*, September 29, 2004, p. C1.

Thurston, Charles W., "Comex, Frazee Play Ball with Chivas USA," *Coatings World*, August 1, 2007, p. 18.

———, "Mexico's Comex Targets the Southeastern U.S. Market," *Coatings World*, July 1, 2006, p. 16.

"The 2007 PCI 50," *Paint & Coatings Industry*, July 1, 2007, http://www.pcimag.com/Archives/BNP_GUID_9-5-2006_A_10000000000000173476.

# Gucci Group NV

———————■———————

Rembrandt Tower, 1 Amstelplein
Amsterdam, 1096 HA
The Netherlands
Telephone: (+31 020) 462-1700
Fax: (+31 020) 465-3569
Web site: http://www.guccigroup.com

*Wholly Owned Subsidiary of PPR Group SA*
*Founded:* 1921 as Azienda Individuale Guccio Gucci
*Incorporated:* 1923 as Guccio Gucci
*Employees:* 11,371
*Sales:* EUR 3.39 billion ($4.26 billion) (2009)
*Stock Exchanges:* NASDAQ
*Ticker Symbol:* GUCG
*NAICS:* 316992 Women's Handbag and Purse
   Manufacturing; 316999 All Other Leather Goods
   and Allied Products Manufacturing; 448150 Cloth-
   ing Accessories Stores; 448120 Women's Clothing
   Stores; 448320 Luggage and Leather Goods Stores

■ ■ ■

Ever since Guccio Gucci opened his first shop in the early 1920s, Gucci Group NV has stood for excellent craftsmanship and an elite clientele. By focusing on luggage and accessories for men and women, and connecting these items with a compelling narrative stamped with a signature "GG," the company built its brand. A single store in Florence grew to shops in Rome, Milan, New York City, and several other locations, always bearing in mind that success at designs and sales needed the highest quality materials and attentive treatment of

clientele. Embargoes, wartime, and familial challenges were among the factors that impacted resources and management and led to the sale of the company, an initial public offering, and emergence as a subsidiary of a French-based conglomerate. By 2009 Gucci had evolved into a group of luxury retail brands with over 600 company-owned stores on five continents.

## GUCCI IN THE BEGINNING: 1923–37

Guccio Gucci, founder of the famous retail empire, was born in Florence, Italy, in 1881. As a youth Gucci left his hometown, which was a mercantile and arts center of Italy, and landed a menial job in the dining rooms at London's Savoy Hotel. During the pre–World War I era, the Savoy was becoming a notable gathering place for American and European upper classes. Observing the wealthy elite's lifestyles and habits while at his job, Gucci became aware that the key to attracting moneyed customers was the perception of quality and exclusiveness. Significantly, Gucci noticed the guests' top quality leather luggage.

Gucci returned to Florence, married a seamstress, Aida Calvelli, and began working in the retail field, in an antique store and then at a leather firm. Their household grew to five sons (one of them adopted) and one daughter. After serving in World War I, Gucci worked at a company in Florence that specialized in leather products bought by the gilded class. The firm's owner, a man named Franzi, became Gucci's mentor, and Gucci was chosen to open Franzi's new store in

Gucci Group NV is one of the world's leading multi-brand luxury companies with a portfolio of premier brands. Gucci, Bottega Veneta and Yves Saint Laurent are the flagship brands. They pave the way for younger, edgier, desirable brands with a strong potential (Balenciaga, Alexander McQueen and Stella McCartney) as well as two specialized brands (Boucheron and Sergio Rossi). With PPR (Pinault-Printemps-Redoute) as the parent company, an assertive entrepreneurial culture embraces the principle of decentralization and results in coherent, global, complementary expertise in luxury goods retail.

Rome. Not long afterward, in 1921, Gucci opened his own leather business in Florence.

Gucci's foray into his own business succeeded for three main reasons. One reason entailed his knowledge of fine leather and leather making, gained during his work for Franzi. The outcome of this in-depth knowledge was luxury luggage, including cases, trunks, and boxes for every conceivable purpose for men and women, on par with the best that Florence had to offer customers. At that time, the city was considered a required stop on European tours undertaken by rich and titled travelers of the 1920s. Once these special tourists and the local elite of Tuscany and Florence learned of Guccio Gucci's shop and his splendid luggage, his reputation soared as did his revenues. In her 2000 book *The House of Gucci*, Sara Gay Forden noted: "The business did so well that in 1923 Guccio opened another shop on Via del Parione and during the next few years expanded the shop on Via della Vigna Nuova."

Gucci's success also involved resourcefulness. During his firm's first year, he added a repair service, a source of additional revenue that increased a reputation for careful, first-class workmanship. While the Gucci store was becoming widely known, its owner had to draw upon resourcefulness again. Benito Mussolini's dictatorship of 1922 to 1943 caused 52 nations to impose harsh sanctions on Italy starting in 1935. Gucci turned a shortage of leather, an apparent misfortune, to his favor, designing and making handbags and luggage of both canvas and leather. In addition, belts and wallets, which required less leather, were becoming more fashionable, and Gucci capitalized on their popularity by including them as new product lines.

## BIRTH OF A LEGEND: 1938–53

Timing, including the timeline of his family's development, became another major factor of Gucci's success. His oldest son, Aldo, had been working for his father since 1925, running errands, cleaning the shop, and gaining sales and merchandise display skills. By 1938 Aldo was a young man who seemed ready to test his worth. Although he and his father sometimes disagreed, Guccio decided to permit Aldo to demonstrate what he could do. In 1938, the year of the company's 15th anniversary, he sent Aldo to open a Gucci shop in Rome, the company's debut outside Florence.

As it turned out, the timing of owning a shop in Rome was fortuitous. World War II got under way in 1939. Because the war involved many of Gucci's customers, who were British, German, French, American, as well as Italian, the conflict kept most of them away from his shops. Sales dropped precipitously, and plans for expanding into other Italian cities (proposed mostly by Aldo and somewhat doubted by Guccio) had to be indefinitely delayed. The shop in Rome, however, kept Gucci in business. The Allies declared the metropolis an "open city" and bombed elsewhere during the early part of the war.

By the end of World War II, Italy was in ruins, a situation that held little prospect for the sale of premium-priced leather goods. Guccio Gucci was able to arrange bank loans and revitalized his shops. Aldo Gucci, in charge of the shop in Rome during the postwar occupation by Allied soldiers, used salesmanship and other skills he'd acquired to ensure that British and American soldiers thronged the shop and purchased lots of special suitcases for their uniforms and gifts to send to women back home. Gucci's shops in Florence and Rome were doing well enough to provide the capital for a new store. In 1951 Guccio sent another son, Rodolfo, who had embarked previously on a film career to Milan, to head the shop.

Guccio and Aldo Gucci began to create a myth for the company's products. An exclusive signature, consisting of back-to-back linked stirrups in the founder's initials "GG," was printed on the luggage and handbags. A heraldic design on company stationery and on some items imparted an aristocratic, equestrian air. During the products' launching, a story arose that the Guccis had been saddle makers to the great Florentine families of the 1500s. This contrived history enhanced the Guccis' esteem and lent parity between them and their clientele at the stores in Florence, Rome, and Milan. Despite Aldo's interest in further expansion, Guccio was reluctant to do so. Still, just before Guccio died in 1953, Aldo opened a store in New York City: The Gucci mystique had gone international.

# KEY DATES

■

**1921:** The company is founded by Guccio Gucci in Florence, Italy.

**1953:** Internationalization begins with a new store in New York City; Guccio Gucci dies.

**1988:** Investcorp International acquires a 50 percent interest in Gucci.

**1993:** Investcorp buys Maurizio Gucci's remaining shares.

**1994:** Tom Ford is named creative director.

**1995:** Domenico De Sole is appointed CEO, and the company makes an initial public offering on the Amsterdam, New York, and London stock markets.

**1996:** Investcorp sells its remaining shares in the company.

**1999:** Gucci forms a strategic alliance with Pinault-Printemps-Redoute; Gucci acquires Yves Saint Laurent.

**2001:** Pinault-Printemps-Redoute acquires a majority interest in Gucci; Gucci acquires Bottega Veneta and forms partnerships with Alexander McQueen and Stella McCartney.

**2005:** PPR Group's ownership of Gucci Group reaches 99.5 percent.

## EXPANSION AND RENOWN:
### 1950–80

After Guccio Gucci's death, his sons Rodolfo, Vasco, and Aldo became equal shareholders. Rodolfo was the general manager, Vasco was supervisor of operations at the plant in Florence, and Aldo was the director of foreign operations. Demand was growing, and manufacturing and store expansion were needed to meet the demand. At this time Vasco expanded the factory in Florence and established a new production plant. Under Aldo's direction, new Gucci stores were opened during the early 1960s in London and Paris. Other openings followed in the 1970s, in Chicago, Philadelphia, San Francisco, Beverly Hills, Tokyo, and Hong Kong.

Gucci was heading to the forefront of high-end fashion retail, and magazine photographs of the rich and famous resplendent in Gucci items were evidence. Anyone who had the money sought the "GG" logo displayed on shoes, luggage, handbags, and scarf designs. Customers included Princess Elizabeth of England, Eleanor Roosevelt, Ingrid Bergman, Jacqueline Bouvier Kennedy, Sophia Loren, Frank Sinatra, Grace Kelly, and

others. Kelly, Princess Grace by then and seeking a floral scarf for a wedding gift in 1966, purchased one specially made for her by Rodolfo Gucci. The scarf became the springboard for a new product line and was a well-known example of the factors that reinforced the company's success.

The company's knowledge of products and of the elite, its resourcefulness, and its appreciation of timing kept the Guccis on a worldwide stage. While celebrities bought Gucci shoes, bamboo-handled handbags, and luggage, ordinary people became customers, too. This trend emerged via the Gucci moccasin for men and women. In *The House of Gucci* Forden reported, "By 1969, Gucci was selling some 84,000 pairs a year in its ten U.S. shops, 24,000 pairs a year in New York alone." Forden added: "Priced at thirty-two dollars, the Gucci loafer was one of the most affordable—and most visible—status symbols one could buy." There seemed no end to the Guccis' rise.

Vasco Gucci's death in 1974 signaled a turning point. After Aldo and Rodolfo purchased his widow's inherited stock, they fully owned the entire company. However, Aldo split a decisive 10 percent stake among his sons. The wares that the family owned were changing. In 1972 the Guccis diversified with a perfume company and a licensing agreement for watches. While expenses mounted for the perfume business, the other start-up did well, as Forden noted in *The House of Gucci*: "Overnight, sales of the Gucci watches soared from 5,000 units to 200,000. That watch even made it into *The Guinness Book of Records* for selling more than 1 million units in two years."

Staff problems arose in some of the U.S. stores, which were gaining a reputation for discourtesy and inattentiveness. Then in 1978, Gucci Shops Inc., the U.S. branch run by Aldo, reported revenues of over $48 million, but no profits. According to Forden in *The House of Gucci*, the costs of trying to make the perfume business successful, renovating a big new store in New York City, hosting galas, and the overall operation of 14 stores and 46 franchise shops had eliminated the profit margin. Another direction seemed necessary.

## REORGANIZATION: THE
## EIGHTIES

Having crafted and nurtured a reputation as a first-class manufacturer and retailer of luxury accessories, family feuds, power plays, and legal problems marred the Guccis' image during the 1980s. Aldo's son Paolo, who had concentrated on the production and design end, was bitter about his perceived lack of influence. Not long after a conflict-ridden board meeting in 1982, which focused on reorganizing and reincorporating the parent company as Guccio Gucci SpA, Paolo began unofficial investigations of his father's record-keeping procedures. He informed the Internal Revenue Service about discrepancies he found, which heightened the agency's scrutiny of Gucci Shops Inc. and its parent company.

Rodolfo, another of the founder's sons, died in 1983. His son Maurizio then began to take a keener interest in the company as he replaced Rodolfo as a major shareholder. Maurizio convinced Paolo to sign over his shares in the company and forced Aldo, who was clearly in legal trouble, to relinquish the position of president. By the mid-1980s Maurizio, president of the parent company, had more shares than anyone else and oversaw all the other Gucci entities including Gucci Ltd. (UK), Gucci Ltd. (Hong Kong), and Aldo's former territory, Gucci Shops Inc.

The company itself was still growing. Family squabbles and maneuvering, as well as customers' complaints about U.S. employees, had hurt the company's reputation. The firm's history and pervasive trademark, however, contributed to ongoing success, according to Gerald McKnight, author of the 1987 book *Gucci: A House Divided*. In the United States, McKnight pointed out, Gucci Shops Inc. reported a net profit in 1985 of over $5 million on revenues of $62 million. This included the buyout of six Gucci Boutiques in I. Magnin department stores, which had sold perfumes and small accessories since the 1970s. In Italy, McKnight reported further, Gucci shops' revenues for 1985 were over $200 million with a net profit of 8 percent. By the following year, 153 Gucci stores were selling over $500 million worth of merchandise.

During the decade's remaining years, legal difficulties continued. The U.S. Treasury proved that over $7 million worth of income taxes had been evaded while Aldo was head of Gucci's U.S. operation, with another approximately $11 million spirited by him out of the country. In 1986 Aldo was sentenced to a year and a day in prison and was fined $30,000. He had already paid back over $1 million to the U.S. Treasury. At the age of 81, he began serving his prison time in a penitentiary in Florida. It would be up to his nephew Maurizio, primarily, to move the luxury retail empire forward.

### NEW OWNERS: THE NINETIES

The conviction of Aldo began a period of vulnerability and change for Gucci operations. Maurizio had brought in Investcorp International from Bahrain in 1988. The Middle Eastern company's influx of $170 million in return for a 50 percent stake in Gucci, however, was

insufficient. Losses and past debts were involving Maurizio in lawsuits. In 1992 the parent company Guccio Gucci SpA sued the renamed Gucci America Inc. for nonpayments. An audit that year by Investcorp resulted in court action in Florence. Gucci was on the verge of liquidation, and change was essential.

As part of an agreement completed in 1993, the company's 70th year, Maurizio left Gucci and sold his remaining 50 percent interest to Investcorp. The family's control of the firm had ended. Then in 1995, an assassin killed Maurizio Gucci, and in 1998 his widow was convicted of the crime and imprisoned. Investcorp began rebuilding. Designer Tom Ford was named creative director in 1994 and attorney Domenico De Sole became CEO in 1995. De Sole had been an attorney for the Guccis during much of their struggle of the 1970s.

De Sole refocused the company's strategies. Gone was the previous decade's over-reliance on cheaper quality materials. Intent on promoting exclusivity, he closed some franchise and duty-free outlets. In a November 24, 1997, article in *Fortune*, Faye Rice wrote that De Sole told her, "Our [Gucci's] ad spending, which includes public relations and window display, increased from $6 million in 1993 to about $70 million this year [1997]." Headquarters moved from the extravagant site that Maurizio had built in Milan in 1991 back to Florence. De Sole also sought greater professionalism, increasing the budget for staff development. Rice noted: "Revenues have more than tripled since 1993 and this year [1997] are expected to hit $1 billion. Net profits more than doubled, to $168 million, over the past two years."

Investcorp capitalized on its investment with an initial public offering (IPO) in 1995 on the New York, Amsterdam, and London stock markets. Less than six months after the initial sale of a 30 percent stake, Investcorp's remaining 51 percent stake had more than doubled in value, and Investcorp sold its remaining shares. Gucci had moved its base to the Netherlands for its favorable tax laws, but under Dutch law, investors could buy a company's controlling interest without having to bid for all the stocks. Watching for indications of a hostile takeover became a shrewd decision for De Sole and others.

Sure enough, a Gucci rival, Prada, had secretly amassed a 9.5 percent stake. In 1999 Louis Vuitton Moët Hennessey (LVMH), a French luxury goods group, bought Prada's shares, gaining a 34.4 percent interest and, possibly, enough for controlling interest. Pinault-Printemps-Redoute, another French corporation and an LVMH competitor, increased Gucci's capital and purchased a 40 percent stake, effectively reducing the value of LVMH's stock to 20 percent. While LVMH challenged the legality, Pinault-Printemps-Redoute acquired Yves Saint Laurent (YSL) and sold YSL to Gucci in 1999. Gucci made two more acquisitions that year: YSL Beauté and Sergio Rossi, an Italian shoemaking firm.

## GUCCI GROUP'S MULTI-BRAND LUXURY RETAIL: 2000–10

Gucci Group began the 21st century as a dramatically different company. The name and "GG" signature were still prominent as were the red-and-green striped accessories, fine leather goods, and other products. The Gucci family's stake, however, was over, and the company had other prominent brands. Yves Saint Laurent, also run at the creative level by Tom Ford, had its own distinctive tradition and clientele, its own shops, and its own sources of additional income from, for instance, perfumes and beauty products. Sergio Rossi, maker of high-end footwear, had a fairly commanding presence among elite buyers, mainly in Europe. The newcomers to Gucci shared the luxury retail fashion niche.

With Pinault-Printemps-Redoute's financial backing, the brands in the group increased. In 2000 Gucci Group acquired Boucheron, a French-based jewelry firm specializing in platinum, diamonds, and other precious materials. In 2001 Pinault-Printemps-Redoute bought 100 percent of the shares of Gucci that LVMH owned, increasing its stake in Gucci to just over 53 percent. That year, the Gucci Group acquired the fashion house Balenciaga, as well as the Venice, Italy–based Bottega Veneta, another topnotch leather manufacturer and retailer. Partnerships signed in 2001 with Stella McCartney and Alexander McQueen of 50 percent and 51 percent respectively rounded out a comprehensive multi-brand luxury goods group.

The adjustments continued for Gucci Group. In 2003 François-Henri Pinault became CEO of Pinault-Printemps-Redoute, which renamed itself PPR Group SA, the same year that its controlling interest in Gucci Group exceeded 99 percent. Domenico de Sole and Tom Ford left Gucci in 2004. The creative imprint, which is crucial at a fashion-focused company, sprang from, among others, Frida Giannini, creative director at Gucci; Stefano Pilati, creative director at YSL since 2004; and Tomas Maier, heading design at Bottega Veneta since 2001. Along with innovative London-based designers Alexander McQueen and Stella McCartney, Gucci Group and its products were succeeding at a transition whose challenges deepened with the tragic death of McQueen in 2010. According to Eric Wilson in a February 19, 2010, article in the *New York Times*, the company planned to keep its commitment toward McQueen's brand.

For Gucci Group, the transition included a holdover: flagship stores as a primary retail choice. In the 2007 book *Fashion Marketing*, Christopher Moore and Anne Marie Doherty highlighted the assets for luxury retailers of company-owned shops. In 2009 Gucci Group had 609 such shops in more than 25 countries. The full inventory at these sites was one business advantage given by Moore and Doherty. Another advantage was the great media attention given to the stores, usually driven by the debut of new collections. For luxury goods companies, this kind of publicity was vital. Furthermore, at flagships, retailers had direct control over merchandise display methods and employees' performance, and they could standardize inventory and transaction equipment.

PPR's 2009 annual report indicated present and near term strategies for Gucci Group's divisions: Gucci, Bottega Veneta, YSL Couture, Boucheron, Balenciaga, Sergio Rossi, and the other brands. The report stated, "The [PPR] Group supports 'freedom within a framework,' which means substantial autonomy, within specific guidelines to the CEOs of the various divisions, who are responsible for design, merchandising and all aspects of the operating results of their respective brands." Europe was still the primary market in 2009. The Asia-Pacific region had become, except Japan, the second-largest market. The Gucci brand brought in over 66 percent of the group's revenue for 2009, Bottega Veneta brought in almost 12 percent, and YSL brought in 7 percent. With sturdy yet forward-thinking strategies in place, Gucci Group was establishing a mature pattern of growth.

*Thomas Derdak*
*Updated, Arianna Dogil; Mary C. Lewis*

## PRINCIPAL SUBSIDIARIES

Alexander McQueen Trading Ltd. (UK, 51%); Balenciaga America Inc. (US, 91%); Balenciaga Japan Co. Ltd.; Balenciaga SA (France, 91%); Balenciaga UK Ltd. (91%); Bottega Veneta Espana SL (Spain); Bottega Veneta France SAS; Bottega Veneta Germany GmbH; Bottega Veneta Hong Kong Ltd. (China); Bottega Veneta Inc. Ltd. (US); Bottega Veneta Japan Ltd.; Bottega Veneta Korea Ltd.; Bottega Veneta Macau Ltd. (China); Bottega Veneta Malaysia Sdn Bhd; Bottega Veneta Singapore Private Ltd.; Bottega Veneta Srl (Italy); Bottega Veneta UK Co. Ltd.; Boucheron.com (France); Boucheron International SA (Switzerland); Boucheron Parfum SAS (France); Boucheron SAM (Monaco); Boucheron SAS (France); Boucheron Suisse (Switzerland); Boucheron UK Ltd.; Les Boutiques Boucheron (France); Gucci America Inc.; Gucci

Australia Pty. Ltd.; Gucci Austria GmbH; Gucci Boutiques Inc. (Canada); Gucci Brazil Importacao Exportacao Ltda.; Gucci Caribbean Inc. (US); Gucci France SAS; Gucci Group (Hong Kong) Ltd.; Gucci Group Watches France, SAS; Gucci Group Watches Inc. (US); Guccio Gucci SpA (Italy); Gucci India Private Ltd. (99%); Gucci International NV (Netherlands); Gucci Group Japan Ltd.; Gucci Group Korea Ltd.; Gucci Ltd. (UK); Gucci Macau Ltd.; Gucci (Malaysia) Sdn Bhd; Gucci Mexico SA; Gucci Netherlands BV; Gucci New Zealand Ltd.; Gucci SAM (Monaco); Gucci Shops of Canada Inc.; Gucci Singapore Pte. Ltd.; Gucci Sweden AB; Gucci Thailand Co. Ltd.; Luxury Goods Logistics; Luxury Goods Spain SL; Luxury Timepieces Design SA (Switzerland); Luxury Timepieces España SL (Spain); Luxury Timepieces (Hong Kong) Ltd.; Luxury Timepieces International SA (Switzerland); Luxury Timepieces UK Ltd.; Sergio Rossi Espana SL (Spain); Sergio Rossi Retail Srl (Italy); Sergio Rossi SpA (Italy); Sergio Rossi UK Ltd.; Sergio Rossi USA Inc.; Stella McCartney America Inc. (50%); Stella McCartney France SAS (50%); Stella McCartney Italia Srl (Italy); Stella McCartney Ltd. (UK, 50%); Yves Saint Laurent America Inc.; Yves Saint Laurent Boutique France SAS; Yves Saint Laurent Germany GmbH; Yves Saint Laurent of Monaco SAM; Yves Saint Laurent Parfums SAS (France); Yves Saint Laurent SAS (France, 99.9%); Yves Saint Laurent Spain SA; Yves Saint Laurent UK Ltd.

## PRINCIPAL DIVISIONS

Bottega Veneta; Gucci; Other Brands; Yves Saint Laurent Couture.

## PRINCIPAL OPERATING UNITS

Autumn Paper Ltd. (UK, 51%); Balenciaga Fashion Shanghai Co. Ltd. (China); Birdswan Solutions Ltd. (UK, 51%); Bottega Veneta Asian Trade BV (Netherlands); Bottega Veneta (China) Trading Ltd.; Boucheron Joaillerie (USA) Inc.; Boucheron Taiwan Co. Ltd. (89.4%); Capri Group (Italy, 75%); Design Management Srl (Italy); Gucci (China) Trading Ltd.; Luxury Goods Italia SpA (Italy); Luxury Goods Outlet Srl (Italy); Sergio Rossi Manufacturing Srl (Italy); YSL Beauté Consulting SAS (France); Yves Saint Laurent Development Srl (Italy).

## PRINCIPAL COMPETITORS

Chanel SA; Compagnie Financière Richemont SA; LVMH Moët Hennessy Louis Vuitton SA.

## FURTHER READING

Collard, James, "The Master Craftsman: Understated and Expensive, Italian Luxury Brand Bottega Veneta Is Flourishing Despite Tough Times," *Times* (London), March 13, 2010, p. 30.

Forden, Sara Gay, *The House of Gucci: A Sensational Story of Murder, Madness, Glamour, and Greed.* New York: William Morrow & Company, 2000, p. 8–11, 14–18, 20, 22, 24, 28, 37–39, 63–69, 86–87, 106–07, 123–25.

———, "InvestCorp Buys All of Gucci," *Daily News Record*, September 28, 1993, p. 2.

Forden, Sara Gay, and Amy B. Barone, "Gucci's Envy Encore," *Women's Wear Daily*, January 16, 1998, p. 24.

Gumbel, Peter, "The New King of Luxury," *Fortune*, September 14, 2009, p. 74.

Hirschberg, Lynn, "How an Italian Designer with a Thing for Fabric Made YSL Sexy Again," *New York Times Magazine*, August 31, 2008, p. 20–25.

McKnight, Gerald, *Gucci: A House Divided.* New York: Donald I. Fine, 1987, p. 140–41, 154–55, 176–78, 231–32, 254–55.

Moore, Christopher M., and Anne Marie Doherty, "The International Flagship Stores of Luxury Fashion Retailers," *Fashion Marketing: Contemporary Issues*, edited by Tony Hines and Margaret Bruce. Boston: Butterworth-Heinemann, 2007, p. 277–79, 286–91.

Rice, Faye, "The Turnaround Champ of Haute Couture," *Fortune*, November 24, 1997, p. 305–07.

Wilson, Eric, "Alexander McQueen Line to Continue," *New York Times*, February 19, 2010, p. B2.

# Gulf States Toyota, Inc.

———— ■ ————

7701 Wilshire Place Drive
Houston, Texas 77040-5326
U.S.A.
Telephone: (713) 580-3300
Fax: (713) 580-3332
Web site: http://www.gstcareers.com

*Subsidiary of Friedkin Companies, Inc.*
*Founded:* 1969
*Incorporated:* 1969
*Employees:* 1,200
*Sales:* $5.1 billion (2008)
*NAICS:* 423110 Automobile and Other Motor Vehicle
   Merchant Wholesalers; 423120 Motor Vehicle Sup-
   plies and New Parts Merchant Wholesalers

■ ■ ■

A subsidiary of the Friedkin Companies, Inc., Gulf States Toyota, Inc. (GST), of Houston, Texas, is one of only two Toyota vehicle distributors in the United States not owned by Toyota Motor Sales. Each year the company's Vehicle Processing Center in Houston handles more than 250,000 Toyota, Lexus, and Scion brand cars, minivans, sport-utility vehicles (SUVs), and trucks, which are then sold through more than 150 dealers in Arkansas, Louisiana, Mississippi, Oklahoma, and Texas. All told, GST accounts for 13 percent of Toyota sales in the United States. In addition, GST supplies all of the 14 million Toyota parts sold in its five-state territory. Dan Friedkin, son of the company's

founder, Thomas H. Friedkin, serves as chairman of the company.

## FOUNDER A PILOT BY TRAINING

Thomas Friedkin was born in 1935, the son of an aviator. His father, Kenneth Friedkin, flew combat missions in England's Royal Air Force during World War II and trained fighter pilots. Following the war he opened a San Diego flight school, and in 1949, with a single leased DC-3 airplane, he founded Pacific Southwest Airlines. Trained to fly at an early age by his father, Thomas Friedkin became one of the airline's pilots. After his father died of a stroke in 1962, Friedkin took charge the airline and ran it until 1986, increasing annual revenues to $550 million before selling the business to USAir for $400 million. Although he received just $3.4 million of the purchase price, Friedkin was not short on funds, having already launched GST.

In addition to airplanes, Friedkin was obsessed with motor sports of all types, riding motorcycles, piloting speed boats, and driving race cars. One of his racing friends was Carroll Shelby, famous for having designed the Shelby Mustang for Ford Motor Company. In 1968 Shelby provided Friedkin with some inside information: Toyota was selling distribution licenses in the United States and had offered one to him. Shelby turned down the opportunity, convinced that the Japanese automaker had no chance of gaining a toehold in the U.S. market. Wasting no time, Friedkin flew to Japan and persuaded Toyota to grant him the Southwest territory. Thus, in 1969 Friedkin established GST.

### GST BEGINS IMPORTING TOYOTA CARS: 1969

GST opened a processing center on a 33-acre site at the Port of Houston in 1969, and in that same year the company accepted its first Toyota vehicle. GST grew alongside Toyota in the United States. The automaker had actually started importing cars into the country in 1957, although Toyota was not trademarked in the United States until 1967. The company focused on small cars, in particular the Corolla, introduced in 1966. Toyota vehicles, with a reputation of fuel efficiency, became increasingly popular in the 1970s because of the uncertainty of oil supplies and concerns about automobile engine emissions. GST enjoyed steady growth by selling Corollas and Coronas, which cost less than $2,000 and as little as $1,570. After three years GST was selling cars and trucks to 14 dealerships. By the end of the 1970s it was the top importer of cars and trucks in the United States, with nearly 66,000 vehicles sold.

Friedkin was not an especially hands-on owner, mostly allowing the managers he hired to run the business. Instead, he pursued a variety of other interests. Flying remained a chief pastime. He collected vintage planes and began a career as a stunt pilot in 1976 when the producers of a television program about World War II pilots, *Baa Baa Black Sheep*, asked if they could use his restored Corsair. He insisted on flying the plane, which led to his appearance in a number of films and membership in the Screen Actors Guild. Friedkin was also an avid outdoorsman and in 1972 started a game-hunting company in Botswana. Later he started an African safari company, Tanzania Game Tracker Safaris.

### PARTS FACILITY OPENS: 1986

GST continue to expand in the 1980s, mostly under the leadership of Jerry Pyle, who was hired by Friedkin in 1981 to serve as president and chief executive officer. Pyle had been previously employed by Ford and Chrysler, where he served in senior positions for 17 years. To better serve its roster of dealerships, GST opened a 302,000-square-foot Parts Distribution Center near Sealy, Texas, in 1986, offering an inventory of 45,000 different parts. Friedkin launched several companies affiliated with GST, including units to provide extended warranties, financing, insurance, and chemical sealants. He also established a used-car auction business and secured a Houston Lexus dealership in the 1980s when the luxury brand was introduced. GST reached the $1 billion mark in annual revenues in 1988, and Friedkin's personal worth at the time was estimated to be at least $150 million. As Toyota sales continued to grow, his net worth increased to about $225 million in 1990.

GST kept a low profile, preferring not to draw focus away from the dealerships it served. When it did spend money on advertising, the focus was on the dealerships. It was not until 1994, when GST celebrated its 25th anniversary, that a company executive granted a face-to-face interview with the media. Staff reporter Charles Boisseau interviewed Pyle for the *Houston Chronicle*. The CEO admitted, "We're very quiet," and he added, "It's desirable." *Forbes* magazine ranked GST number 80 on its list of the country's largest private companies, estimating its 1993 revenues at $1.53 billion. GST was now selling 100,000 vehicles a year through 140 dealerships. To support further growth, the company in early 1994 broke ground on a 107-acre, $18.5 million new vehicle processing facility in northern Houston. Rather than rely on the Port of Houston, the new site made use of rail and transport trucks to ship and receive vehicles.

GST was one of two independent distributors in Toyota's 12-region U.S. operation but its relationship with Toyota was solid. GST offered feedback unfettered by corporate politics, something that Toyota considered valuable. When it came time to design a new pickup truck, however, Toyota did not heed the advice of GST, which was well familiar with the truck market. Texas accounted for about 25 percent of all new pickup truck sales in the country. GST urged Toyota to offer high-powered engines and extended cabs. Toyota's full-size T-100 pickup trucks introduced in 1992 lacked both features, and sales proved disappointing, forcing GST to offer incentives to dealers to move the vehicles. Realizing its error, Toyota dispatched people to Houston to learn from GST how to appeal to the Texas market. Later versions of the T-100 offered extended cab options as well as V-6 and V-8 engines.

## KEY DATES

**1969:** Gulf States Toyota (GST) is founded.
**1986:** Parts Distribution Center opens near Sealy, Texas.
**1988:** GST reaches $1 billion in annual sales.
**2006:** San Antonio Tundra plant opens.
**2009:** GST moves to new corporate headquarters in Houston, Texas.

## AUTONATION BLOCKED: 1997

GST attempted to change with the times in the 1990s. With the emergence of the Internet, GST signed an agreement in 1996 with online host firm DealerNet to allow its 140 dealers to do business on the Internet. Like Toyota, it was less comfortable with the rise of the megastore approach to selling cars, in particular the rapid expansion of AutoNation USA, a dealership consolidator that was a banner of billionaire Wayne Huizenga's Republic Industries. In 1993 Toyota implemented new dealer policies, which included a nine-month waiting period between the acquisition of Toyota dealerships. Moreover, a single individual or company was limited to seven Toyota and three Lexus dealerships.

In February 1997 Republic acquired its first Toyota dealership, located in Miami, and later in that same month it agreed to purchase Houston's Joe Myers Automotive Group, which sold several brands of vehicles, including Toyota. Moreover, Republic had lined up the purchase of a Toyota dealership in Tempe, Arizona, and notified Toyota that within the next 18 months it hoped to have 59 Toyota dealerships in the fold. Because Toyota had only 1,200 dealerships, as opposed to the more than 5,000 held by Ford or General Motors, it was wary of being overly dependent on a single sales organization such as Republic. As a result, Toyota sought to slow down Republic and in conjunction with GST filed a petition with the Texas Motor Vehicle Board to block Republic's acquisition of the Joe Myers dealership. The deal was subsequently shelved.

By the dawn of the 21st century GST was selling 11 percent of all Toyota brand vehicles in the United States, or 155,406 cars in 2000, resulting in revenues estimated at $3.2 billion. Thomas Friedkin turned 65 at that time, and his son, 35-year-old Daniel Friedkin, began overseeing Friedkin Companies and later succeed his father as GST's chairman. More business was in the offing for GST as the decade progressed, due in large measure to Toyota opening a new $800 million plant in

San Antonio, Texas, to build its full-size pickup truck, the Tundra. The Texas location was strategic, as the choice was intended to spur sales in the all-important Texas market. The plant anticipated building 150,000 trucks, a third of which were expected to be sold through GST and the dealerships it served.

Toyota also looked to increase sales in the hinterlands by opening satellite stores in rural communities that were previously considered too small to support a full-fledged Toyota dealership. Because Toyota could sell its large pickups, as well as midsize pickups and SUVs, only in the United States because of their size, the company placed a good deal of pressure on dealers to increase sales volume in order to recoup its investment in new models.

## EXPANSION AND IMPROVING SALES

The Tundra plant opened in 2006. In order to keep pace, in that same year GST expanded its Vehicle Processing Center to 200 acres, supported by a $175 million private placement completed in 2005. In addition, GST's transport subsidiary upgraded its operations to bolster delivery of vehicles. In 2006 GST sold 226,960 Toyota vehicles, and sales continued to improve the following year. *Forbes* estimated 2007 revenues at $5.7 billion, earning GST the number 53 ranking on its list of the United States' largest private companies. Thomas Friedkin also make the magazine's list of the 400 richest Americans, ranked number 227 with a net worth $2 billion.

While the Tundra plant was coming on line, GST also developed a new corporate headquarters on a 16-acre site in west Houston. The 400,000-square-foot campus would include a 40,000-square-foot training center and also house the Gulf States Marketing and Gulf States Financial Services operations. Because of a downturn in the economy, the project had to be scaled back somewhat, but it still opened in the summer of 2009.

In light of the destruction caused by Hurricane Katrina in 2005, GST also made plans to build a second processing facility inland, located in Temple, Texas, at the Rail Park at Central Pointe. It would receive, accessorize, and distribute Toyota and Scion vehicles delivered by truck from the San Antonio Tundra plant and by rail from other North American Toyota plants. The project was scheduled to be operational in 2011. Not only would the Temple facility be better situated to deal with potential hurricanes, it would also support GST's future growth.

The Toyota brand was tarnished in 2009 and 2010 when millions of cars were recalled because of unintended acceleration problems as well as an issue with antilock brake software. GST was heavily involved in the recall effort, providing dealers in its five-state territory with the parts needed to correct the problems. It was a public relations nightmare that helped to drive down Toyota sales and adversely affect GST's balance sheet. Nevertheless, the company's long-term prospects appeared bright.

*Ed Dinger*

## PRINCIPAL SUBSIDIARIES

Gulf States Finance Company; Gulf States Financial Services, Inc.; Gulf States Marketing Inc.

## PRINCIPAL COMPETITORS

Ford Motor Company; Honda North America, Inc.; Nissan North America, Inc.

## FURTHER READING

Baird, Jane, "Toyota to Move Houston Car Processing Center from Port," *Houston Chronicle*, August 14, 1993.

Boisseau, Charles, "By Lying Low, Gulf States Toyota Finds Highroad to Success," *Houston Chronicle*, May 15, 1994, p. 22.

Chappell, Lindsay, "Gulf States' Owners Private, but Visible," *Automotive News*, March 31, 2008, p. 17.

Donovan, Doug, "Under the Radar," *Forbes*, October 8, 2001, p. 118.

"Gulf States Toyota to Build Processing Plant in Temple, Creating 500 Jobs," *San Antonio Business Journal*, November 16, 2007.

Hensel, Bill Jr., "Gulf States Toyota Is Expanding to Handle Tundra Truck Distribution," *Houston Chronicle*, August 31, 2006, p. 1.

Jackson, Kathy, "U.S. Distributors Gave Toyota a Toehold in a Mysterious New Market," *Automotive News*, October 29, 2007, p. T40.

Kaplan, David, "Toyota Recall: Houston Business Is Funnel for Parts," *Houston Chronicle*, February 5, 2010, p. 1.

Sarnoff, Nancy, "Gulf States Toyota Project Still Rolling," *Houston Chronicle*, January 25, 2009, p. 3.

Wendt, Ed, "New Toyota Car Processing Center Makes Houston Distribution Hub," *Houston Business Journal*, April 4, 1994, p. 10.

# Helmerich & Payne, Inc.

—————■—————

1437 South Boulder Avenue
Tulsa, Oklahoma 74119
U.S.A.
Telephone: (918) 742-5531
Fax: (918) 742-0237
Web site: http://www.hpinc.com

*Public Company*
*Founded:* 1920
*Incorporated:* 1926 (Oklahoma); 1940 (Delaware)
*Employees:* 5,000 (est.)
*Sales:* $1.89 billion (2009)
*Stock Exchanges:* New York
*Ticker Symbol:* HP
*NAICS:* 211111 Crude Petroleum and Natural Gas
  Extraction; 333132 Oil and Gas Field Machinery
  and Equipment Manufacturing

■ ■ ■

Founded in 1920, Helmerich & Payne, Inc. (H&P), is among the oldest contract drillers in the United States, a survivor in the volatile world of oil and gas exploration, contract drilling, and production. Part of H&P's success has come from its longtime commitment to diversified operations. The company owns more than 1.6 million square feet of commercial and industrial real estate, including the landmark Utica Square Shopping Center in Tulsa, Oklahoma. H&P's core business is as a contract driller for oil and natural gas. As of 2010 the company owned more than 200 land rigs in the United States, 32 internationally (with major operations in

Venezuela and Colombia), and nine offshore drilling platforms. Most of these rigs are Flexrigs, a technologically advanced drill rig that is the company's own invention. These rigs are in high demand, causing H&P's rig utilization rate to exceed that of its competitors by a significant margin. H&P is led by president and CEO Hans Helmerich, the grandson of company founder Walt Helmerich. In 2009 the company posted revenues of $1.89 billion.

## BARNSTORMING THE OIL BOOM: 1920

H&P was founded in 1920 by Walt Helmerich and William Payne. Helmerich was born in 1895 in Chicago. In 1914, bored with academic life at the University of Chicago, Helmerich left school to work in New Orleans and Beaumont, Texas, and eventually at the Western Electric Company in Chicago. When the United States entered World War I in 1917, Helmerich enlisted in the Army Signal Corps and became a pioneering member of the country's newly forming air force. He quickly rose to become a test pilot and flight instructor for the famous Curtis JN-4 "Flying Jenny" and a member one of the military's first acrobatic flying teams.

After the war, Helmerich took his piloting skills on the road, buying three planes and forming a barnstorming stunt flying team with two friends. Shortly before the troupe's first performance in 1919, both of Helmerich's partners were killed in a test flight. By then, Helmerich was married to Cadijah Colcord, the daughter of Oklahoma oil pioneer Charles F. Colcord. Offered a job

## COMPANY PERSPECTIVES

H&P owns and operates land rigs in the U.S. and in various international locations and offshore platform rigs mostly in the Gulf of Mexico. The Company endeavors to deliver well cost savings to its customers through ongoing improvements and leadership in drilling efficiency and safety. Its success is based on its ability to develop and apply new ideas, technologies and processes that create a differentiated, high-quality service offering. As a result, H&P has been able to deliver unprecedented drilling performance and value to its customers.

with brother-in-law Ray Colcord, Helmerich went to work overseeing the drilling of a well in Ossawatomie, Kansas, and then helped relocate Colcord's rig to South Bend, Texas.

The pair quickly struck oil with Colcord's rig, pumping 300 barrels a day. Helmerich purchased a share of the rig, and the profits, for $9,000. In 1920 Helmerich raised enough money, in part by selling the scrap metal from his airplanes, to buy his own drilling rig. Helmerich was joined by William Payne, who had worked as an oil scout for Charles Colcord. Payne's background was in bacteriology and chemistry, with an undergraduate degree from Oklahoma A&M, and graduate work in microbiology at Massachusetts A&M and Amherst. Payne gained practical experience working for a pharmaceutical company in Detroit and later as a bacteriologist for that city. During World War I, Payne joined the Army Sanitation Corps and helped isolate the influenza virus that caused an outbreak in 1918. After the war, Payne went to work for Colcord's North American Oil and Refining, then helped form Helmerich & Payne in 1920.

The partners originally plied the South Bend oil fields and carted their rig as far as New Mexico. In 1923 Helmerich sent his wife and newborn son, Walt Helmerich III, to live with her family in Tulsa, Oklahoma. By then H&P owned three rigs, and in 1926 the partners moved two of their rigs to Oklahoma in order to tap into the oil-rich Osage County field. Their first strike, a 2,350-foot wildcat producing 5,000 barrels per day in Braman, Oklahoma, led the partners to formally incorporate as Helmerich & Payne, Inc. Payne supervised the company's drilling activities, while Helmerich took charge of financing.

## STRUGGLING THROUGH THE DEPRESSION

The young company soon faced the Depression and an oil glut that saw the price of a barrel of oil fall from $1.43 per barrel to just $0.10 per barrel at the depth of the Depression. H&P began selling down its oil leases, while continuing to operate drilling rigs under contract. At the time, locating oil was as much based on luck as on science, with rates of about one producing well for every 50 drilled. Eventually, the company focused its operations on contract drilling. The company nevertheless continued its own exploration and drilling efforts, and in 1936 H&P made a major strike in the Hugoton natural gas fields in southeastern Kansas. Starting with four wells, H&P's Hugoton strike would provide a backbone for the company's growth. More than 60 years later, the Hugoton field still accounted for two-thirds of H&P's natural gas reserves. The company established another landmark in 1936, constructing a working rig on the lawn in front of Oklahoma's State Capital building. That well would continue producing until it was finally plugged in 1976.

William Payne left H&P in 1936, founding the Big Chief Drilling Company in Oklahoma City, and in 1965 Payne's success in the industry led him to be named Oklahoma's "Oil Man of the Year." Meanwhile, Helmerich struggled to obtain financing for H&P during the Depression. By 1939 H&P owed approximately $1 million in debt, and the company verged on bankruptcy. Helmerich refused to declare bankruptcy and managed to secure the loans to rescue the company. As part of the financing agreement, the company reorganized as a Delaware Corporation in 1940, and Helmerich was forced to relinquish partial control of H&P.

## POSTWAR GROWTH

Demand for oil and gas had plummeted during the Depression, while overproduction had kept prices low. With the outbreak of World War II, demand again surged. Yet contract drilling rates were low, especially for the highly competitive shallow drilling market, and H&P stepped up its own exploration efforts, turning now to deep drilling projects. Toward the end of the war, the company scored successes with three, deep wildcat wells in the Texas Panhandle, and several other 5,000-foot wells were also producing in the range of 300 to 500 barrels per day. In order to make the company more attractive to lenders, H&P reorganized in 1944 as the White Eagle Oil Company, which would be chiefly engaged in exploration and production. H&P was organized as the company's contract drilling subsidiary. The following year, the company made its

## KEY DATES

**1920:** Company is founded by Walt Helmerich and William Payne.

**1936:** Massive natural gas strike in Hugoton, Kansas, fuels period of company growth.

**1940:** Helmerich & Payne, Inc., incorporates in Delaware.

**1957:** Drilling lease in Venezuela is company's first international operation.

**1959:** Helmerich & Payne (HP) goes public.

**1964:** Company makes first major real estate acquisition, Tulsa's Union Square mall.

**1968:** Company constructs its first offshore drilling rig.

**1973:** OPEC crisis sets off a period of intense growth and profit.

**1998:** Helmerich and Payne introduces its first Flexrig, an advance over conventional drilling rigs.

**2008:** Company earns record profits of $461.7 million and surpasses $2 billion in operating revenues.

Secondary recovery output reached 80,000 barrels per year in 1954 and rose to 250,000 per year by 1958.

Meanwhile the company was expanding its operations, entering the international market with lease-partnerships in Venezuela in 1957. The company soon entered Bolivia, Cuba, and the Philippines. H&P also acquired Engineering Construction Company (ECCO), a pipeline construction firm. In 1959 the company reorganized again, dropping the White Eagle name and going public. H&P's revenues by then were $14.2 million. The following year, Walt Helmerich III replaced his father as the company's president.

### DIVERSIFICATION: 1960–69

With a fresh slump in the oil industry at the start of the 1960s, H&P began a new program of diversification to enable it to better weather the industry's traditionally cyclical nature. The company acquired Natural Gas Odorizing, Inc. (NGO), of Houston in 1960. NGO manufactured chemicals that added odor and taste to natural gas, which were necessary for detecting the presence of the volatile material. Over the years, NGO would become an industry leader, capturing as much as a 50 percent share of the gas odorant market. In 1962 H&P acquired Horton Company, a specialist in laying cable for the telephone industry. Horton's patented cable-laying plow was soon adapted for ECCO's pipeline work. The acquisition of Houston-based F. H. Maloney Company in 1964 brought H&P into manufacturing, with the production of molded rubber, machined metal, and other products for oil and pipeline companies. That same year saw H&P enter the commercial real estate market with the purchase of the Utica Square shopping center in Tulsa.

Throughout this period of diversification, H&P continued to expand its presence in the oil industry. Land-based drilling continued to decline during the 1960s, forcing the company to look in a new direction. Preparations for entering the burgeoning off-shore drilling market began in 1964, with the construction of the company's own off-shore rig. Launched in 1968, the rig was severely damaged during a storm the following year, and the company's drilling contract was canceled. In response, H&P traded the rig to offshore driller Atwood Oceanics, Inc., in exchange for a 28 percent interest in that company. Next, H&P, with sales passing $27 million by 1965, attempted a new acquisition, this time of a company larger than itself. By 1968 H&P had bought enough stock to make itself the largest single investor in Sunray DX, an oil and gas company. H&P and Sunray began merger discussions, but before these were completed, Sun Oil stepped in with an offer to purchase

first acquisition, Cardinal Oil Company, which had more than 240 producing wells and an average daily production of over 5,000 barrels. By 1949 the company was posting revenues of $6.7 million.

The company prospered in the postwar years. Automobile use was on the rise, sparking a huge demand for oil products. By 1952 the company was operating 17 deep-drilling rigs in six states. At the same time, the rise in demand brought on increased competition, and by the early 1950s the oil industry was entering a new slump. Drilling contracts fell, and H&P saw its profits threatened.

By the mid-1950s H&P was ripe for new management, and the company did not have to look far. In 1954 Helmerich's son, Walt Helmerich III, was named executive vice president. The younger Helmerich, a graduate of Harvard Business School, and one of the company's first college graduates, quickly assembled a new management team and set to work improving the company's operating efficiency. The company also began hiring its first drilling engineers, who introduced new technology to the company's exploration and drilling operations, particularly in secondary recovery techniques that would extend each well's production output.

Sunray. H&P attempted to block the acquisition but failed. Nevertheless, H&P retained a significant share of Sun/Sunray stock and realized a handsome profit through the merger. The company retained that investment, which helped increase revenues to $38 million by the end of the decade, while continuing to expand its stock portfolio with investments in other public companies.

## DEREGULATION, INCREASED EXPLORATION FUEL GROWTH: 1970–79

With drilling contracts continuing to suffer during the early 1970s, H&P accelerated its exploration activity, but the company had not kept pace with advances in technology made by the larger oil companies and needed to aggressively recruit geologists and other engineers. This effort soon paid off with the opening of three wells in Buffalo Wallow Field in Texas, which combined for a potential output of 75 billion cubic feet of natural gas. By the late 1970s, the company's gas output topped its oil production for the first time. The company, along with the entire oil industry, was given a fresh boost by the oil crisis of 1973.

With oil prices rising, and the search intensifying for alternative sources of oil reserves, H&P's international operation grew. By the end of the decade, H&P was operating 12 of its own rigs in Venezuela alone, while drilling under contract for another nine rigs. The company's rigs were also drilling wells in Belize, Bolivia, Colombia, Ecuador, Guatemala, and Peru. H&P's revenues climbed to $77.5 million in 1976 and neared $150 million by 1979. As the decade closed, the total number of H&P-owned rigs topped 50, with utilization rates of 99 percent. Deregulation of the oil industry stimulated a boom in the search for oil. Meanwhile, oil prices were skyrocketing, reaching as high as $50 per barrel. As more and more sources of oil were developed, OPEC, watching its share of the oil market dwindle from 70 to 30 percent, reacted in panic. Quickly, the market was flooded with oil.

## NEW GENERATION, NEW TECHNOLOGY: 1980–99

By the end of the 1980s, nearly 80 percent of the oil industry had gone bankrupt. For H&P, which saw its 1982 revenues climb to $338 million and net profits soar to $75.6 million, the tide began to turn by 1983. Revenues began to drop, to $208 million in 1984, down to $160.5 million by 1988. The company struggled to retain profits: net income slid to $48 million in 1983 and to $7 million in 1986. However, in 1989, with revenues of $171 million, H&P was the only drilling company in the world to post a profit ($22.7 million).

The company could credit its survival to a conservative fiscal policy set in place during the late 1970s. Where other drilling companies attempted to cash in on the oil boom with rapid expansion, Helmerich focused instead on increasing its production of natural gas. Meanwhile, the company's stock portfolio, its real estate investments, and its NGO and other subsidiaries, helped cushion the company's bottom line and allowed it to continue investing in upgrading and building state-of-the-art drilling rigs, and to step up its presence in off-shore drilling. By 1991 the company had spent some $112 million in upgrading and expanding its equipment, while managing to pay for its new rigs by securing long-term contracts with the major oil companies. By then, the third generation of Helmerichs took over the company's leadership with the appointment of Hans Helmerich as president and CEO. Walt Helmerich III remained as company chairman.

With so much of its competition out of business, H&P could now compete for some of the industry's largest drilling contracts, including a contract with BP Exploration for the vast Cusiana Field discovered in Colombia at the start of the decade. H&P became a leader in international drilling, particularly in South America. During the first half of the 1990s the company continued to expand, raising its total number of operating rigs to more than 75 by 1996. The company's revenues also made a strong return, reaching $239 million in 1992, climbing to $329 million in 1994, and jumping to $393 million by 1996. The sale of its NGO subsidiary helped boost the company's profits to nearly $73 million in that year.

During the late 1990s H&P made a fateful investment in technological innovation by creating a new type of drilling rig. Known as the Flexrig, the automated, electronically-controlled device was intended to improve safety, reliability, and flexibility while reducing the physical strain on rig operators. The first Flexrigs, which entered the field in 1998, were capable of drilling at a range of depths, particularly the relatively shallow depths that are increasingly used in oil and gas extraction. Their ease of disassembly could allow crews to move the rigs relatively quickly, saving time as well as labor and equipment costs. The advanced rigs were slow to catch the attention of the market at first, but with the nation's fleet of conventional rigs growing older, Hans Helmerich and his colleagues were confident that the investment would pay off. The following decade would confirm that this confidence was justified.

## AHEAD OF THE PACK: 2000

The company became involved in a major international incident in October 2000 when two of its employees were among 10 oil workers kidnapped by Colombian rebels in Ecuador. A longtime employee, Ron Sander, was found dead several months later, apparently shot in the back to illustrate the kidnappers' frustration that ransom money had not been delivered. The other hostages survived and were freed after five months in captivity.

In early 2001 H&P released its exploration and production subsidiary to its shareholders, while simultaneously announcing that the new entity would merge with another energy firm, Key Production Company. The "spin-merge" produced a new independent company called Cimarex Energy, leaving H&P to focus on its most lucrative business, contract drilling.

The company emerged from this transition well prepared to capitalize on the technological advantage created by the Flexrig. No rig on the market could match its record for safety, precision, or efficiency. An Oklahoma industry analyst called it "the Rolls-Royce of the drilling industry." According to company estimates, the technology reduced the length of the average job from 20 days per well to 12.8. Thus, even though daily rates for Flexrigs were roughly 30 percent higher than conventional rigs, the customer could count on substantial cost savings over the life of a job. While other drilling companies were idling their rigs during periods of falling oil and gas prices, H&P's fleet remained in demand, with the industry's highest utilization rates. By the time competing firms had committed to modernizing their own rigs, the Flexrig was already in its third or fourth generation, ensuring H&P's technological edge.

The company formulated a pragmatic strategy for increasing its Flexrig fleet: it committed to building new models only once it had lined up three-year leasing contracts for them. Under this arrangement, the customer essentially underwrote the manufacturing cost. By the end of the third year, H&P had recouped its capital investment, and most rigs continued in operation after the initial lease term. By 2007 the company was producing four new Flexrigs per month. Between 2005 and 2010 the company more than doubled its rig fleet from 128 to 262 available units. Financial performance grew nearly as fast: the company set earnings records in three consecutive years from 2006 to 2008, topping $461 million in profits for fiscal 2008 on revenues in excess of $2 billion. That year, H&P acquired TerraVici Drilling Solutions for roughly $22 million.

## SUSTAINING GROWTH THROUGH MARKET, POLITICAL WOES: 2009–10

In 2009, with oil and natural gas prices steeply declining, H&P became entangled in a conflict with the Venezuelan national oil company, Petróleos de Venezuela, over unpaid fees that at one point topped $100 million. Venezuelan leader Hugo Chávez, under pressure to maintain social programs his government had funded with oil revenues, declared his government would pay only a fraction of what it owed oil contractors. Chávez threatened to take over the operations of any foreign organization that suspended work in protest over the arrears. H&P, with half a century's experience working in Venezuela, handled the situation with some finesse: it let eight of its 11 rigs in the country stand idle once their contracts expired. None of the rigs were taken over, and by the end of the fiscal year the company had collected roughly a third of Venezuela's outstanding balance.

Along with the Venezuelan situation, the drop in commodity prices affected H&P's bottom line and rig utilization rate in 2009. Nevertheless, the company retained a steady leadership position in a notoriously fluctuating industry. In a clear sign that the market was acknowledging this track record of leadership, Standard & Poor's named H&P to the S&P 500 in early 2010.

*M. L. Cohen*
*Updated, Roger K. Smith*

## PRINCIPAL SUBSIDIARIES

Helmerich & Payne Properties, Inc.

## PRINCIPAL COMPETITORS

Nabors Industries, Inc.; Patterson-UTI Energy, Inc.; Transocean Ltd.

## FURTHER READING

Davis, Kirby Lee, "Tulsa-based Helmerich and Payne Faces Hard Line in Venezuela," *Journal Record* (Oklahoma City, OK), March 10, 2009.

———, "Tulsa-based Helmerich and Payne Profits Drop, but Top Expectations," *Journal Record* (Oklahoma City, OK), November 20, 2009.

Harlin, Kevin, "Helmerich & Payne's Rigs Give Gas Driller a Leg Up," *Investor's Business Daily*, July 26, 2007, p. B3.

Jones, James A., "Helmerich & Payne Hikes Oil Drilling as Gas Prices Rise," *Investor's Business Daily*, April 29, 1996, p. A35.

Krauss, Alan, "Helmerich & Payne Scores Even during Oil Industry Slump," *Investor's Daily*, January 11, 1990, p. 30.

Percefull, Gary, "Helmerich & Payne Knows It's a Jungle out There," *Tulsa World*, October 1, 1989, p. G1.

Ray, Russell, "Tulsa, Okla.–based Firm's High-Tech Rig Fits Today's Drilling Needs," *Tulsa World*, May 11, 2002.

Roberts, James, and Chris Hernandez, *Helmerich & Payne, Inc.: The First 75 Years*. Tulsa: Helmerich & Payne, Inc., 1995.

Rutherford, Dan, "Stock of Tulsa's Helmerich & Payne Skyrocketing," *Tulsa World*, October 18, 1996, p. E1.

Schein, Chris, "Decade of Work Pays off for Driller," *Tulsa World*, January 26, 1992, p. G1.

# Hospital for Special Surgery

—∎—

535 East 70th Street
New York, New York 10021
U.S.A.
Telephone: (212) 606-1000
Fax: (212) 606-1930
Web site: http://www.hss.edu

*Nonprofit Company*
*Founded:* 1863 as Hospital for the Relief of the
Ruptured and Crippled
*Incorporated:* 1863 as New York Society for the Relief of
the Ruptured and Crippled
*Employees:* 1,238
*Operating Budget:* $534 million (2009)
*NAICS:* 622310 Specialty (Except Psychiatric and
Substance Abuse) Hospitals

■ ■ ■

Based in New York City, Hospital for Special Surgery
(HSS) is the oldest orthopedic hospital in the United
States and is regarded as one of the world's best institutions in the field of musculoskeletal medicine. In addition to serving the general public, HSS, which performs
22,000 procedures each year, serves as the physician and
athletic trainer for several New York–area professional
sports teams, including the New York Giants, New York
Mets, New York Knicks, and New Jersey Nets, as well as
several area colleges, USA Swimming, and the U.S.
National Rowing Team. Academically, HSS is affiliated
with the New York–Presbyterian Healthcare System and
Weill Cornell Medical Colleges. Additionally, HSS is

well known for its research efforts in arthritis and tissue
degeneration, autoimmunity and inflammation, biomechanics, musculoskeletal integrity, and tissue engineering, regeneration, and repair. It pioneered the first total
knee replacement, perfected minimally invasive hip and
knee procedures, developed a technique to avoid spinal
fusion in minimally invasive spine surgery, and made
advances in the evaluation of magnetic resonance imaging (MRI). Aside from orthopedic services, HSS
maintains specialized centers in such areas as cartilage
repair, hip pain, osteoporosis prevention, spinal care,
and rheumatic disease.

## CIVIL WAR–ERA ROOTS

HSS was founded in 1863 by Dr. James Knight as the
Hospital for the Relief of the Ruptured and Crippled.
Born in 1809 in Maryland, Knight graduated from
Washington Medical College in Baltimore, where he
practiced as a family physician until 1840 when he
began to devote his attention to orthopedic surgery. He
moved to New York to work in the orthopedic clinics of
the medical department of the University of the City of
New York and serve as the medical director for the Association for Improving the Condition of the Poor. Unlike many of his colleagues, Knight did not consider the
crippled as hopeless cases. He was further spurred to action by the increasing appearance of crippled people on
New York streets due to the upheaval caused by the
Civil War.

With support from Robert M. Hartley, Knight
incorporated the New York Society for the Relief of the
Ruptured and Crippled in April 1863. Less than a

month later he began seeing patients at his private residence located at Second Avenue and 6th Street. The makeshift hospital included 28 beds, and his conservatory became a workroom where Knight produced his own prosthetics. In the first year, the hospital treated well over 800 patients. The hospital served the needs of children, and, even after adults began receiving treatment following the Civil War, incurable children were the institutional focus.

## PERMANENT HOSPITAL OPENS: 1870

Knight did not maintain any operating-room facilities, even after the hospital moved to a permanent facility at 42nd Street and Lexington Avenue in 1870. Planned by Dr. Knight, it was a 200-bed children's hospital, but it included no operating room because he was adamant about pursuing what was called "expectant treatment." He relied entirely on diet, exercise, electrical stimulation, sunshine, and fresh air. He avoided surgery at all costs, understandable given the unsanitary conditions of operating rooms at the time and the lack of knowledge concerning infections.

As the hospital expanded, many of Dr. Knight's younger colleagues did not share his mistrust of surgery, and a rift developed between Dr. Knight and his followers and the progressive wing of the staff led by his assistant, Dr. Virgil Pendleton Gibney, the first professor of orthopedic surgery at Columbia Medical College. Born in Kentucky and a graduate of Bellevue Medical College in 1871, Gibney advocated the use of casts and traction as well as surgery, if necessary. Drs. Knight and Gibney worked together for 13 years, not always harmoniously, before Gibney left abruptly. He soon returned, however: In October 1887 Dr. Knight died and was replaced by Gibney as the hospital surgeon-in-chief.

Gibney quickly made his mark on the hospital even as he maintained a private outside practice. He added a hernia department and in 1889 opened the institution's first operating room. Moreover, he recruited some of the city's best surgeons and established the first orthopedic residency program in the United States. As the 20th century dawned, Gibney oversaw the opening of the hospital's first adult ward, which only served women patients. Other turn-of-the-century additions included a custom brace shop, a pathology laboratory, and an anesthetist.

## HOSPITAL MOVED TO ACCOMMODATE GRAND CENTRAL: 1912

In 1912 the Hospital would be forced to relocate to a site further east on 42nd Street between Second Avenue and First Avenue, giving way to the New York Central Railroad, which needed the property to complete the construction of the massive Grand Central Terminal. In that same year, the Alumni Association of the Hospital for the Ruptured and Crippled was founded. The new six-story building included a New York City Public School to educate children who were long-term patients, and it would remain in service until the mid-1960s. A few years later, during World War I, the Hospital would also open its doors to wounded and injured military personnel, providing them with its expertise in orthopedics and hernia care.

With his health beginning to fail, Gibney retired in 1924 and passed away three years later at the age of 80. Before his retirement the Hospital opened its first arthritis clinic, modernized its radiology department, and established the Department of Physio-Therapy, which laid the foundation for today's physical therapy. In that same year, Dr. R. Garfield Snyder was appointed as the first physician-in-chief and the first chief of arthritis. A longtime friend and colleague, 63-year-old Dr. William B. Coley, succeeded Gibney as surgeon-in-chief at the start of 1925. The first general surgeon to hold the post, he served eight years. Dr. Eugene H. Pool took charge in 1933 for a two-year stint, during which time the women's auxiliary was formed to better organize the volunteer efforts on which the Hospital depended. Like Coley, however, Pool was a general surgeon, and the Hospital's reputation as the country's prominent orthopedic center was beginning to decline. Pool was therefore given the job of recruiting the best possible orthopedic surgeon to serve as his replacement and become the new surgeon-in-chief.

Dr. Philip D. Wilson, a prominent orthopedic surgeon from Boston, was named director of surgery in 1934 and succeeded Pool as surgeon-in-chief in 1935. Wilson brought sweeping changes to the Hospital. He

## KEY DATES

**1863:** Dr. James Knight founds the Hospital for the Relief of the Ruptured and Crippled.
**1887:** Dr. Knight dies.
**1912:** Hospital is moved to make way for the Grand Central Terminal.
**1940:** Name is changed to Hospital for Special Surgery.
**1955:** Hospital is moved to present-day location on East 70th Street.
**1980:** Major expansion is completed, doubling the number of operating rooms and adding capabilities to perform total joint procedures.
**1995:** New East Wing inpatient hospital is constructed over the FDR Drive, creating space for four new operation rooms.
**2007:** *U.S. News & World Report* names HSS the United States' top orthopedics hospital, as well as in the following year.

transformed the hernia department into the general surgery department and focused on musculoskeletal conditions. He organized the surgical staff into general surgery and orthopedics, and he improved the care of patients. Moreover, he increased the emphasis on professional education and established fellowships to encourage research in orthopedics. During Wilson's tenure the Hospital changed its name. In 1940 it dropped the words Ruptured and Crippled and called itself the Hospital for Special Surgery.

## POST-WAR POLIO TREATMENT CENTER

Despite the loss of staff to the military during World War II, the Hospital continued to serve its primary purpose. It was during the war, in the summer of 1943, that the number of polio cases increased dramatically, and the Hospital became a major treatment center and would remain so during the post-War years. A rheumatic disease service was also established during the war.

Wilson continued to expand the Hospital after the war came to an end in 1945. One of the country's first bone banks was added in 1948. In that same year, Wilson began negotiations to align the Hospital with a university center that had a medical school and hospital as a way to ensure the Hospital maintained its place as a leading orthopedic institution. In 1949 the Hospital

reached such an agreement with New York Hospital and Cornell University Medical College. The Hospital maintained its independence while providing orthopedic and rheumatological services. As part of the agreement, a new building that would contain 170 beds for orthopedic and arthritis patients was to be built on New York Hospital–owned property on the East River between 70th and 71st Streets that was deeded to HSS. In 1955 HSS moved to its new $6 million home, and the affiliation with the New York Hospital–Cornell Medical Center began in earnest. A short time later Wilson retired as surgeon-in-chief and became the new director of research.

Wilson's successor, Dr. T. Campbell Thompson, continued to expand HSS. The new building allowed for the addition of a fracture service and a school of practical nursing. HSS also furthered its efforts in basic research with the opening of the Alfred H. Caspary Research Building in 1960. The relationship between HSS and New York Hospital–Cornell Medical Center became contentious in 1962, threatening the partnership. A year later Thompson resigned during a hiring controversy and was replaced by D. Robert Lee Patterson Jr., who served as surgeon-in-chief until 1972.

## KNEE REPLACEMENT UNVEILED: 1970

Patterson proved to be a forward-thinking leader who recognized how technology and bioengineering were going to influence orthopedics. HSS was soon in the vanguard in the development of knee replacement, its researchers producing a prototype in 1970 that lead to the HSS Total Condylar Knee Replacement, first implanted in 1971. Elbow and wrist implants followed, and HSS began employing computers with biomechanics to design a range of new prosthetic implants.

HSS advanced on other fronts in the 1970s. Patterson was succeeded by Dr. Philip D. Wilson Jr., son of the former surgeon-in-chief. Postgraduate fellowships were added, Cornell Medical College students began rotating through HSS clinical services, and the residency program became prestigious. The research department was also expanded, and significant advances were made in the study of immunology. Additionally, the decade brought the first Sports Medicine Clinic, established by Dr. John Marshall, who performed pioneering work for both professional and recreational athletes.

HSS completed a major expansion in 1980, doubling the number of operating rooms and adding capabilities to perform total joint procedures. The Belaire building was also opened during the 1980s, adding a new rehabilitation center and physician offices.

Further expansion to the Hospital in the final years of the century allowed for the addition of the Sports Medicine, Research and Performance Center, the Osteoporosis Center, the Pediatric Rheumatic Disease Unit, the Orthopedic Trauma Service, the Women's Sports Medicine Center, the Barbara Volcker Center for Women and Rheumatic Disease, and the Department of Physiatry. Ambulatory hand surgery operating rooms were added as were other operating rooms. A new East Wing inpatient hospital was constructed over the FDR Drive in 1995 that also created space for four new operation rooms. The end of the century saw the launch of a $115 million campaign to expand the research facilities and to hire and retain talented scientists.

HSS continued to grow in the new century and build upon its stellar reputation. Three floors were added to the West building, and plans were made to expand over the FDR Drive from the Caspary Research Building. *U.S. News & World Report* named HSS the United States' top orthopedics hospital in 2007 and 2008. With the addition of new facilities, there was every reason to expect HSS to maintain its place among the leading medical facilities in the world.

*Ed Dinger*

### PRINCIPAL OPERATING UNITS

Anesthesiology ; Endocrinology; Neurology; Nursing; Orthopedic Surgery; Pain Management; Pathology; Pediatrics.

### PRINCIPAL COMPETITORS

Beth Israel Medical Center; NYU Hospital for Joint Diseases.

### FURTHER READING

"Aiding the Crippled," *New York Times*, September 29, 1955.

"Dr. James Knight's Death," *New York Times*, October 25, 1887.

"Dr. Virgil P. Gibney, Noted Surgeon, Dead," *New York Times*, June 17, 1927.

"Evolution of a Hospital," *New York Times*, March 8, 1951.

Levine, David B., "Hospital for Special Surgery: Origin and Early History First Site 1863–1870," *HSS Journal*, September 2005.

———, "The Hospital for the Ruptured and Crippled: Knight to Gibney, 1870–1887," *HSS Journal*, February 2006.

———, "History of HSS: Gibney as Surgeon-in-Chief: The Early Years, 1887–1900," *HSS Journal*, September 2006.

———, "History of HSS: The Hospital for the Ruptured and Crippled Entering the Twentieth Century c. 1900 to 1912," *HSS Journal*, February 2007.

———, "The Hospital for the Ruptured and Crippled Moves East on 42nd Street, 1912 to 1925," *HSS Journal*, September 2007.

———, "The Hospital for the Ruptured and Crippled: William Bradley Coley, Third Surgeon-in-Chief 1925–1933," *HSS Journal*, February 2008.

———, "The Hospital for the Ruptured and Crippled Eugene H. Pool, Fourth Surgeon-in-Chief 1933–1935 Followed by Philip D. Wilson, Fifth Surgeon-in-Chief 1935," *HSS Journal*, September 2008.

———, "The Hospital for the Ruptured and Crippled Renamed The Hospital for Special Surgery 1940; The War Years 1941–1945," *HSS Journal*, December 2008.

———, "The Hospital for Special Surgery Affiliates with Cornell University Medical College and New York Hospital, 1951; Philip D. Wilson Retires as Surgeon-in-Chief, 1955," *HSS Journal*, September 2009.

———, "The Hospital for Special Surgery 1955 to 1972: T. Campbell Thompson Serves as Sixth Surgeon-in-Chief 1955–1963 Followed by Robert Lee Patterson, Jr. the Seventh Surgeon-in-Chief 1963–1972," *HSS Journal*, February 2010.

"No Patient Was Injured," *New York Times*, August 2, 1887.

# Ingersoll-Rand PLC

——— ■ ———

**170/175 Lakeview Drive**
**Airside Business Park**
**Swords, County Dublin**
**Ireland**
**Telephone: (+353 1) 870 7400**
**Fax: (+353 1) 870 7401**
**Web site: http://www.ingersollrand.com/**

*Public Company*
*Founded:* 1871 as Ingersoll Rock Drill Company
*Incorporated:* 1905 as Ingersoll-Rand Company
*Employees:* 57,000
*Sales:* US$13.19 billion (2009)
*Stock Exchanges:* New York
*Ticker Symbol:* IR
*NAICS:* 333415 Air-Conditioning and Warm Air Heating Equipment and Commercial and Industrial Refrigeration Equipment Manufacturing; 333412 Industrial and Commercial Fan and Blower Manufacturing; 333912 Air and Gas Compressor Manufacturing; 333131 Mining Machinery and Equipment Manufacturing; 561621 Security Systems Services (Except Locksmiths)

■ ■ ■

Ingersoll-Rand PLC has been a groundbreaking company since the late 1800s. The company evolved from a machine shop in New York City in 1871, to four factories in three states during the 1920s, to 94 plants on six continents in 2010. Inventions, acquisitions, and joint ventures resulted in the company's six main brands: Ingersoll-Rand rock drills, tools, compressed air systems, and microturbines; Schlage locks, security systems, and heating, ventilation, and air conditioning (HVAC) systems; Club Car's low-speed vehicles for golf courses, campuses, warehouses, and military installations; Thermo King's refrigeration and heating units for trucks, ocean, and railway containers; Hussmann's refrigeration units for stores' perishables; and Trane's HVAC systems for homes and businesses. These brands, which are enfolded within the Climate Solutions, Industrial Technologies, Residential Solutions, and Security Technologies business segments, indicate Ingersoll-Rand's iconic presence, steering, and sustaining prosperity.

## INNOVATORS: 1871–88

Ingersoll-Rand grew out of four inventors' efforts: Simon Ingersoll, Henry C. Sergeant, William L. Saunders, and Addison C. Rand. While laboring as a farmer to support his family, Ingersoll was given a commission to design a drill that would work on rock. In a machine shop in New York City owned by the entrepreneur José F. de Navarro, Ingersoll completed a drill and received a patent in 1871, but the tool needed improvements on its functionality.

Henry C. Sergeant, a partner in de Navarro's shop, made an important change in the drill design by separating the front head from the cylinder. Sergeant then persuaded de Navarro to invest. The businessman bought Ingersoll's patent and organized the Ingersoll Rock Drill Company in 1871, with Sergeant as its first president. According to George Koether, the author of

# COMPANY PERSPECTIVES

∎

In recent years, Ingersoll Rand has transformed itself into a multi-brand commercial products manufacturer serving customers in diverse global markets, and away from the capital-intense, heavy-machinery profile of its past.

Today, we are a global diversified industrial firm providing products, services and solutions to enhance the quality and comfort in homes and buildings, transport and protect food and perishables, secure homes and commercial properties, and enhance industrial productivity and efficiency.

Our customers count on the reliability of our family of industrial and commercial brands, such as Club Car golf cars, Hussmann stationary refrigeration equipment, Ingersoll Rand industrial equipment, Schlage locks, Thermo King transport temperature-control equipment and Trane air conditioning systems and services. Through these brands we enable companies and their customers to create progress.

*The Building of Men, Machines, and a Company*, Ingersoll returned to his farm in Connecticut, where he worked on inventions and sold the patents. When he died in 1894, he was nearly destitute. Sergeant, however, was a successful inventor-businessman. By 1868 the 34-year-old had started a machine shop in New York City, where he developed other inventors' ideas.

For several years Sergeant focused on improving Ingersoll's drill by using compressed air instead of steam to operate it. With de Navarro funding other investment and development opportunities, Sergeant's skillfulness with drill improvements, steam pumps, and other machinery remained a key feature of the company's stability. In 1885 Sergeant developed a completely different rock drill and formed the Sergeant Drill Company to manufacture it. Three years later, in 1888, he merged the two companies, becoming president of the Ingersoll-Sergeant Drill Company. After several years he became a board director and devoted himself to inventing.

During this period another inventor, Addison C. Rand, became an important part of drilling firms in New York. Rand's brother, Alfred T. Rand, was instrumental in founding the Laflin & Rand Powder Company, a mining company. According to Koether, Alfred Rand foresaw the value that machinery would have for the progress of mining, and Addison Rand foresaw the significant impact of air compressors on his brother's business. Addison Rand formed the Rand Drill Company, which produced and marketed the Little Giant tappet drill, the Rand Slugger drill, and air compressing machinery for his brother's company and other mining firms.

## THE FORMATION AND EARLY ACTIVITIES: 1905–13

In 1905 Michael P. Grace brought Ingersoll-Sergeant Drill Company and Rand Drill Company together through stock purchases and a merger. The two companies specialized in slightly different segments of the drill market (Ingersoll-Sergeant specialized in construction work, and Rand focused on underground mining), and their interests were complementary. With the Grace family owning the largest single block of stock, the new company was incorporated as Ingersoll-Rand Company in 1905.

William L. Saunders became Ingersoll-Rand's first president and brought many accomplishments with him. An engineer, he had developed a compressed air drilling apparatus for subaqueous use while in his 20s. The widely used invention improved the construction of aqueducts, piers, and oil platforms. His achievements also included an inspection dive at an underwater site so he could tailor an appropriate design for a subaqueous drill. He was active in engineering societies and established an award given by the American Institute of Mining and Metallurgical Engineers. He also established *Compressed Air*, the company's industrial trade journal, in 1896 and served as its editor.

As president of Ingersoll-Rand, Saunders expanded the company's line of rock drills and air compressors. He promoted the development of several types of these machines and led Ingersoll-Rand into related product areas. For example, in 1907 Ingersoll-Rand added pneumatic tools to its product lines by acquiring Imperial Pneumatic Tool Company of Athens, Pennsylvania. In 1909 the company bought A.S. Cameron Steam Pump Works, thereby entering the industrial pump business. Four years later centrifugal pumps joined Ingersoll-Rand's product list. Under Saunders Ingersoll-Rand also acquired J. George Leyner Engineering Works Company. This firm had developed a small, hammer-type drill that could be operated by one person. Ingersoll-Rand began producing the so-called jackhammer in 1913, and it quickly became a popular brand.

# KEY DATES

**1871:** Ingersoll Rock Drill Company is established.
**1905:** Ingersoll-Sergeant Drill Company and Rand Drill Company merge to form Ingersoll-Rand Company.
**1974:** Ingersoll-Rand purchases the Schlage Lock Company.
**1995:** Ingersoll-Rand purchases the Clark Equipment Company.
**1997:** Newman Tonks Group PLC and Thermo King are added to Ingersoll-Rand's holdings.
**2000:** Hussmann International Inc. is acquired.
**2006:** The company celebrates a century of trading on the New York Stock Exchange.
**2007:** Ingersoll-Rand sells its Bobcat and compact equipment operating units.
**2008:** Ingersoll-Rand acquires Trane Inc.
**2009:** Ingersoll-Rand reincorporates in Ireland.

## THE DOUBLEDAY ERA: 1913–57

In 1913 George Doubleday became the president of Ingersoll-Rand. During his 23-year stint, Doubleday strove to make Ingersoll-Rand the leader in drills, air compressors, jackhammers, pneumatic tools, and industrial pump products. Ingersoll-Rand's plants in Phillipsburg, New Jersey; Easton and Athens, Pennsylvania; and Painted Post, New York, handled increasing business. In these locations Ingersoll-Rand, the Central Railroad of New Jersey, and others were major employers. As such, the towns' residents, their income levels, their training, and the overall quality of their lives were critically intertwined with the companies. To acquire their goals, firms such as Ingersoll-Rand needed a skilled workforce that took pride in personal efforts.

Doubleday instituted advances in products and their marketing, such as a diesel electric engine. In the book *Iron Rails in the Garden State: Tales of New Jersey Railroading*, Anthony J. Bianculli stated: "The Jersey Central manifested its innovative spirit again in 1925 when it placed into operation the world's first diesel-electric locomotive. Number 1000, a switching engine, was built by Ingersoll-Rand at Phillipsburg, with major components from the American Locomotive and the General Electric Companies." Two years later crews creating Mount Rushmore used Ingersoll-Rand's jackhammers and air compressors. In 1933 Ingersoll-

Rand introduced a new portable-compressor line, which was later improved during the 1950s with a rotary portable unit. Meanwhile, progress with some of Ingersoll-Rand's drills placed the company in the "big drill" field: the Quarrymaster for quarrying, open-pit mining, and excavation in 1947; the self-propelled jumbo Drillmaster in 1953; and the Downhole drill in 1955.

Other accomplishments occurred while Doubleday was in charge. General Electric's centrifugal-compressor business was acquired in 1933, which gave Ingersoll-Rand the top rung in that sector of the business. In 1948 the company designed the first natural gas transmission centrifugal compressors. In 1954, when the U.S. Navy launched the world's first nuclear-powered submarines, the vessels were using Ingersoll-Rand's compressors and pumps. When Doubleday retired in 1955 after 19 years as board chairman, Ingersoll-Rand's cash flow exceeded $100 million, it had no debt, its operating profit margin was 37 percent, and its net profit margin was 19 percent.

Doubleday had reached those numbers, however, by abandoning his original marketing orientation. The company had more than $197 million in assets in 1957 but expansion that year was below the $5 million mark. When Doubleday was chairman, the company's cash flow in the late 1940s was around $42 million but he had not used the available funds for upgrades on factories, research and development, or increasing foreign parts inventory.

## DIVERSIFICATION: 1959–74

Robert H. Johnson, the next head of the company, was named chairman and chief executive officer (CEO) in 1959. A 35-year veteran of Ingersoll-Rand with a sales background, Johnson's first move was a competitive price-cutting of company products. He spent $25 million boosting inventories abroad, and by the mid-1960s foreign sales doubled. He also increased the budget for research. Expenditures on plants and equipment rose from an approximate average of $2 million per year to $15 million by 1965. Excess cash (more than 65 percent of total assets in 1966) went toward carefully planned acquisitions and investments. Lawrence Manufacturing Company, which produced mechanical moles for urban underground utility tunneling, was an example of an investment.

Johnson's successor as CEO in 1967, 52-year-old William L. Wearly, came to Ingersoll-Rand as a consultant in 1962 and was Ingersoll-Rand's first nonveteran leader. A new generation of managers came as well: President D. Wayne Hallstein was 49, and the four newest vice presidents were under 44. Wearly and his team benefited from Johnson's previous investments in upgrades and parts inventories, which increased manufacturing capacity and bolstered Ingersoll-Rand's sales. Capacity overseas also rose through acquisitions Wearly's team made in England, Italy, Canada, South Africa, and Australia.

Wearly then took Ingersoll-Rand into new, diversified areas that offset the cyclical nature of the capital goods market. Especially important was Ingersoll-Rand's acquisition of Torrington Company in 1968, which brought needle and roller bearings, knitting needles, metal-forming machines, universal joints, and roller clutches to the company catalog. Also notable was the 1974 acquisition of the Schlage Lock Company, a maker of locks, door hardware, and home and business security devices. These acquisitions, especially of Schlage, signaled a fresh direction for Ingersoll-Rand.

## INITIATIVE AND NEW VENTURES: 1970–90

During the early 1970s factors such the exploration and development of new energy sources, capital from oil and gas in the Middle East, growing East-West trade, and Third World industrialization increased demand for almost all Ingersoll-Rand products. By mid-decade the boom became a bust. Capital spending slowed after the energy crisis of 1973. Coal and railroad strikes hurt Ingersoll-Rand, which was still a major supplier of coal mining machinery. These and other elements left Ingersoll-Rand with too much capacity and inventory.

In 1980 Thomas Holmes, a 30-year employee, became the CEO and Clyde Folley became the chief financial officer. The new executive team faced a global economic recession in the early 1980s, which decreased Ingersoll-Rand's earnings and sales, especially on oil drilling and construction equipment. Overall, in 1983 Ingersoll-Rand lost $112 million. In response, the company closed 30 production plants, cut staff by one-third, and spent its tight cash supply only in product areas where returns were highest (bearings, locks, and tools) rather than on engineered and coal mining equipment and air compressors. Furthermore, management compensation was tied to return on assets instead of on sales and inventory controls were centralized. The executive team then initiated joint ventures with competitors.

Dresser-Rand, a 50-50 partnership, was formed in 1986 with Dresser Industries, a major mining and oil equipment company. As Robert Wrubel of the *Financial World* noted in July 1987, "Wisely, Folley made the joint venture a partnership rather than a corporation, so Ingersoll retains the tax basis of the assets devoted to the partnership and uses any losses to reduce its own taxable income." Dresser-Rand was profitable within its second year of operation. In 1987 Ingersoll-Rand formed other joint ventures, in mining with B.R. Simmons and in pneumatic equipment with China's Xuanhua Pneumatic Machinery Ltd. Joint ventures trimmed Ingersoll-Rand's staff and losses as the company competed effectively with Japanese and West German rivals. Also, pooling talent helped the company's technological status.

Ingersoll-Rand had once again weathered recession by the time Holmes stepped down in 1988. Prosperity allowed Theodore Black, the next CEO, to focus on Ingersoll-Rand's strengths. Product development was emphasized, and in 1988 improved air compressors, new papermaking technology, and a new type of camshaft were introduced. Between 1988 and 1990 Ingersoll-Rand made appropriate acquisitions, including a Swedish maker of water jet cutting systems, a Canadian manufacturer of paving equipment, a German maker of hydraulic drills, and ARO Corporation, a maker of centrifugal pumps, valves, and other fluid products. Ingersoll-Rand remained committed to computerized production and design techniques, whose outcomes featured significantly less labor and more, higher-quality goods.

## GEOGRAPHIC DIVERSITY AND RESEARCH AND DEVELOPMENT: 1991–94

Another recession during the early 1990s barely registered on Ingersoll-Rand's balance sheet. Its profits fell 19 percent in 1991 to $150.6 million, whereas its competitors posted substantial losses: $404 million for Caterpillar Inc. and $36 million for Timken Company. According to Paul Klebnikov of *Forbes*, Ingersoll-Rand's success was partly attributed to its geographical diversity. In the early 1980s, 30 percent of the company's sales were for products manufactured outside the United States. However, through various acquisitions during the 1980s, these overseas sales increased to 70 percent by 1992. The Dresser-Rand partnership was also paying off. Its sales exceeded $1.2 billion by 1991 and $40 million of Ingersoll-Rand's 1991 profits came from Dresser-Rand.

Dresser Industries and Ingersoll-Rand recognized another area of cooperation in 1991: combining their industrial pump manufacturing divisions into one entity. The new entity's potential sales were $800 million annually, with likely domination of this industry in the United States. The U.S. Department of Justice initially opposed the joint venture under the Sherman Antitrust Act. However, Dresser and Ingersoll-Rand contended that foreign competition in Japan, Germany, and elsewhere was an influential, mitigating factor. After successful negotiations the merger was approved in 1992 with a divestiture provision for Ingersoll-Rand and Dresser of about $10 million in pump operations to lessen the impact on domestic competition. Ingersoll-Rand owned 51 percent of the newly named Ingersoll-Dresser Pump Company.

In 1993 James E. Perrella, a 16-year veteran of the firm, became chairman and CEO. As Wearly and Black had done, Perrella carried out some strategic acquisitions in 1993 and 1994, which increased Ingersoll-Rand's presence in the European market and brought additional complementary businesses into the company fold. These moves included purchases in 1994 of the French-based Montabert S.A., a manufacturer of hydraulic rock-breaking and drilling equipment, for $18.4 million and the Ecoair air compressor operation from MAN Gutehoffnungshütte AG for $10.6 million. That same year Ingersoll-Rand also invested $17.6 million in a joint venture with MAN to manufacture airends, an important component in certain industrial air compressors. By yearend 1994 Ingersoll-Rand's sales reached $4 billion.

## KEY ACQUISITIONS AND SOLID STRATEGIES: 1995–2003

One of Ingersoll-Rand's biggest acquisitions during this period came in 1995, when it purchased Clark Equipment Company, an Indiana-based manufacturer of small and medium-sized machines for agriculture and construction. The $1.5 billion purchase seemed particularly complementary given Clark's focus on construction and Ingersoll-Rand's construction-related tools and equipment that accounted for about 18 percent of company sales before the takeover. Through the acquisition, Ingersoll-Rand gained Clark operations such as Blaw-Knox (the world's leading manufacturer of asphalt road paving equipment), Melroe (the world leader in loaders such as the Bobcat brand), and Club Car (the second-largest golf car manufacturer in the world). Ingersoll-Rand's sales in 1995 were $5.7 billion, a record increase of 27 percent over 1994.

Several more acquisitions followed. In 1997 Ingersoll-Rand bought Newman Tonks Group PLC, an architectural hardware producer based in the United Kingdom, and Thermo King, the largest transport temperature control manufacturer in the United States. Two years later, in 1999, Ingersoll-Rand bought the electronic security system makers Harrow Industries and Recognition Systems. The company's sales neared the $7.7 billion mark, a clear sign of success. Perrella retired that year and Herbert L. Henkel took the helm.

Like Perrella, Henkel made growth a priority. As a result, Ingersoll-Rand increased its product arsenal and divested significantly. In 2000 the company sold its Ingersoll-Dresser pump division and Corona Clipper, a hand tool manufacturer. In 2003 the firm sold its engineered solutions arm to Timken Company for $840 million. Product additions achieved through acquisitions included Hussmann International Inc., a leading refrigeration manufacturer, in 2000 in a $1.7 billion deal. The following year the company acquired the lock maker Kryptonite Corp., the Netherlands-based Grenco Transportkoeling B.V., National Refrigeration Services Inc., Taylor Industries Inc., and several infrastructure-related firms.

Ingersoll-Rand then made several internal changes. A cost-cutting program led to the closure of 20 plants. The firm sold Torrington Company, which it had acquired in 1968. The company also changed its incorporation site from New Jersey to Bermuda, gaining some tax advantages. At the same time, a slowdown in global economies, similar in nature to occurrences during the mid-1970s and early 1990s, affected earnings somewhat. Nevertheless, Ingersoll-Rand's internal changes, diverse product lines, and solid business strategies seemed effective choices for progress.

## A NEW CENTURY: 2004–10

In 2004 Ingersoll-Rand sold its Dresser-Rand partnership and its Drilling Solutions unit. The following year it established a joint venture with the door lock maker and distributor Fu Hsing Industrial Company of Taiwan, bought a majority interest in the security technologies and services firm Shenzhen Bocom System Engineering Company Ltd. of China, and acquired the security-focused manufacturer Dolphin Electromagnetic Technologies of India. Other acquisitions during this period included Integrated Access Systems, Electronic Technologies Corp., FX Technologies, and Security One Systems. By yearend 2005 Ingersoll-Rand had 66 such entities in North America and Europe.

In 2006 Ingersoll-Rand celebrated being on the New York Stock Exchange (NYSE) for 100 years. A century had passed since the Grace family merged the Ingersoll-Sergeant Drill Company with the Rand Drill Company and Ingersoll-Rand held its first stock offerings at the NYSE. However, rather than looking back on its accomplishments, Ingersoll-Rand was focused on moving forward. Its 100th year of trading included the acquisitions of ZEKS, a manufacturer of dehumidifers, air filters, and other features of compressed air technology. It also purchased the Ireland-based Geith International, a maker of utility vehicle attachments.

In 2007 Volvo AB bought a road-working unit from Ingersoll-Rand for $1.3 billion. That same year Ingersoll-Rand sold its utility equipment, attachments, and Bobcat units to Doosan Infracore of Korea for $4.9 billion. At yearend 2007 the company reported net revenues of $8.7 billion. In 2008 the purchase of Trane Inc. for $10 billion complemented Ingersoll-Rand's HVAC businesses and reflected a redirection. For the year the company reported net revenues of $13.2 billion, an increase of 51 percent. The following year the company reincorporated in Ireland. Corresponding with this move, the company began refining its manufacturing focus to climate control products, security systems, microturbine technology and related components, and equipment for transporting and protecting perishables. Reporting net revenues of $13.1 billion in 2009, a decrease of only 0.2 percent from the year before, Ingersoll-Rand clearly had a firm global stance and was well positioned to continue its expansion during the next decade.

*Ginger G. Rodriguez*
*Updated, David E. Salamie; Christina M. Stansell;*
*Mary C. Lewis*

## PRINCIPAL SUBSIDIARIES

Airtec Limited; American Standard Inc.; CISA PLC; Clean Air Inc.; Club Car Inc.; Compagnie Ingersoll-Rand S.A.; Electronic Technologies Corporation USA; Fu Hsing Industrial (Shanghai) Company Ltd. (51%); Fu Jia Hardware Products (Shanghai) Company Ltd. (51%); Harrow Industries LLC; Hussmann Corporation; Hussmann (Europe) Limited; Hussmann International Inc.; Ingersoll-Rand AB; Ingersoll-Rand Air Solutions Hibon Sarl; Ingersoll-Rand (Australia) Pty. Ltd.; Ingersoll-Rand Company; Ingersoll-Rand Company; Ingersoll-Rand Company South Africa Pty. Ltd.; Ingersoll-Rand Company; Ingersoll-Rand Company Inc.; Ingersoll-Rand de Puerto Rico Inc.; Ingersoll-Rand Deutsche Holding GmbH; Ingersoll-Rand do Brasil Ltda.; Ingersoll-Rand Energy Technologies LLC; Ingersoll-Rand Equipment Manufacturing Czech Republic Limited; Ingersoll-Rand Global Holding Company Ltd.; Ingersoll-Rand Holdings Ltd.; Ingersoll-Rand (India) Limited (74%); Ingersoll-Rand International Limited; Ingersoll-Rand Irish Holdings; Ingersoll-Rand Italia S.r.l.; Ingersoll-Rand Philippines Inc.; Ingersoll-Rand S.E. Asia (Private) Limited; Ingersoll-Rand Security & Safety GmbH; Ingersoll-Rand Security & Technologies; Ingersoll-Rand Security Technologies; Ingersoll-Rand Technical and Services Limited; Ingersoll-Rand UK Ltd.; Integrated Access Systems Inc.; Ives Trane NY Inc.; Krack Corporation;

Newman Tonks Management Services Ltd.; Refrigeration Services & Design Inc.; Schlage Lock Company; Security One Systems Inc.; Shenzhen Bocom System Engineering Company (China, 80%); Thermo King de Puerto Rico Inc.; Thermo King do Brasil, Ltda.; Thermo King European Manufacturing Limited; Thermo King Ireland Limited; Thermo King Services Limited; Thermo King Total Kare Limited; Thermo King Transportkoeling B.V.; Trane Air Inc.; Trane America LLC; Trane (Ireland) Limited; Trane (UK) Ltd.; Von Duprin LLC; ZEKS Compressed Air Solutions LLC.

## PRINCIPAL DIVISIONS

Hussmann Canada Inc.; Ingersoll-Rand Canada Inc.; Ingersoll-Rand Energy Systems; Ingersoll-Rand Equipment & Services; Ingersoll-Rand Von Duprin-Exit Device; LCR-Door Closer; Locknetics Security Engineering; Reftrans S.A.; Thermo King Container-Denmark A/S; Thermo King Corporation.

## PRINCIPAL OPERATING UNITS

Ingersoll-Rand Climate Solutions; Ingersoll-Rand Industrial Technologies; Ingersoll-Rand Residential Solutions; Ingersoll-Rand Security Technologies.

## PRINCIPAL COMPETITORS

ASSA ABLOY AB; Carrier Corporation; Johnson Controls Inc.

## FURTHER READING

Bianculli, Anthony J., *Iron Rails in the Garden State: Tales of New Jersey Railroading.* Bloomington: Indiana University Press, 2008.

Blankenship, Steve, "Microturbine Exec Optimistic about Growing Market Acceptance," *Power Engineering*, November 2005, p. 148.

Campanella, Frank W., "Solid Gains in Backlog Bolster Ingersoll-Rand," *Barron's*, February 26, 1973, p. 31.

"Jingle, Jingle," *Forbes*, April 15, 1958, p. 30.

Klebnikov, Paul, "A Traumatic Experience: Ingersoll-Rand Prospers Today Because It Stumbled So Badly a Few Years Ago," *Forbes*, January 18, 1993, p. 83.

Koether, George, *The Building of Men, Machines, and a Company.* Woodcliff Lake, NJ: Ingersoll, 1971.

Lipin, Steven, "Clark Accepts Ingersoll Bid of $1.5 Billion for Takeover," *Wall Street Journal*, April 10, 1995, pp. A3, A5.

Sorkin, Andrew Ross, and Michael J. de la Merced, "Ingersoll-Rand to Acquire Air-Conditioning Company," *New York Times*, December 18, 2007, p. C3.

Woods, Chelsie, "IR Does It One More Time," *Security Systems News*, July 2005, p. 1, 17.

Wrubel, Robert, "Overcoming the 'Mango' Factor," *Financial World*, July 28, 1987, p. 18.

# International Brotherhood
# of Teamsters

—■—

**25 Louisiana Avenue NW**
**Washington, D.C. 20001**
**U.S.A.**
**Telephone: (202) 624-6800**
**Fax: (202) 624-6918**
**Web site: http://www.teamster.org/**

*Labor Union*
*Founded:* 1903
*Members:* 1.4 million
*NAICS:* 813930 Labor Unions and Similar Labor
Organizations

■ ■ ■

The International Brotherhood of Teamsters (IBT) is the fourth-largest labor organization in the United States. In 2010 it had 1.4 million members in nearly 1,900 locals and affiliates in the United States, Canada, and Puerto Rico. IBT members include truck drivers, locomotive engineers, hospital workers, printers, farmworkers, airline pilots and flight attendants, police officers, custodians, and school principals. The IBT organizes new members and negotiates collective bargaining agreements with employers from almost every major industry in the United States.

## EARLY ROOTS: 1898–1902

At the turn of the 19th century, people depended on horse-drawn wagons to move produce and goods locally. Teamsters, who drove the teams of horses, generally worked 12 to 18 hours a day, every day of the week for an average wage of $2 per day. Not only was their pay low but also they were held responsible when the merchandise was damaged or lost or when the shipper did not pay.

Individual teamsters began forming local groups to improve their working conditions. In 1899 the Team Drivers International Union (TDIU), composed of several local unions in the Midwest, received a charter from the American Federation of Labor, which was a loose confederation of national unions. The Team Drivers membership numbered 1,700. Under the charter, anyone who drove a team for someone else or who owned up to five teams of horses and had others working for them could be a member.

Soon, the teams owners took control of the union. The two groups (the employees and the owners) often had different concerns, as might be expected. The drivers who owned no teams felt their issues were not being addressed. Many of these members belonged to local unions in Chicago, Illinois, and in 1902 the Chicago locals pulled out of the Team Drivers and founded their own organization, the Teamsters National Union (TNU).

Membership in this union was limited to nonowner teamsters, teamster helpers, and owners of no more than one team of horses. The TNU pushed for higher wages and shorter hours, issues that attracted nonowners, and in a few months its membership was larger than the TDIU. Another difference was that for the TNU, a teamster was a skilled craftsman, and the unskilled immigrants and farmworkers coming to the cities were not

## COMPANY PERSPECTIVES

For more than a century, the Teamsters Union has helped millions of workers achieve the American Dream. Our success is a testament to those who came before us, who stood together to form a union and a labor movement. These workers fought for the rights and privileges that today most Americans take for granted. Without the solidarity of unions, there would be no weekends, no pensions and no health insurance.

welcome in the union. Finally, according to Arthur A. Sloane in *Hoffa*, the Chicago-based TNU colluded with employers and was considered a criminal association.

## FROM HORSES TO TRUCKS: 1903–30

Samuel P. Gompers, the head of the American Federation of Labor, urged the two unions to get back together, and in 1903, at Niagara Falls, New York, they merged to create the International Brotherhood of Teamsters (IBT). The issue of owners versus nonowners was settled with the merger: no one owning more than one team of horses could belong to the IBT. The former TDIU head Cornelius Shea of Boston, Massachusetts, was elected president.

Four years later, with the loss of a bloody strike against the Montgomery Ward Company and charges of racketeering, Shea lost his reelection bid. The new president, Daniel J. Tobin, was also from Boston and would lead the union for the next four and one-half decades.

Tobin's early years focused on organizing the skilled drivers, particularly beer wagon drivers and those delivering bakery and confectionery goods. The union was successful in improving working conditions for its members (reducing hours of work, winning the right to overtime pay, and standardizing contracts), but big changes were also occurring within the industry. Motor trucks were replacing horses, and in 1912 the first transcontinental freight delivery by truck occurred. That same year IBT membership reached 40,000, and Tobin urged the organization of both truck and wagon drivers.

IBT membership hit 60,000 in 1915, and in 1920 the union expanded by affiliating with the Canadian Trades and Labor Congress, Canada's national confederation of unions. That same year Tobin convinced the members to double the per capita dues

paid to the national union by all the locals. The increase, from 15 cents to 30 cents, strengthened the organizing efforts and raised benefits paid to workers striking to win a contract. By 1930 membership had reached 105,000, even though the IBT continued to ignore the drivers making long-distance hauls between cities.

## ORGANIZING OVER-THE-ROAD TRUCKERS: 1933–37

The Great Depression left thousands of drivers out of work, and in 1933 Teamster membership had dropped to 75,000. However, the militant leaders of the Teamsters local in Minneapolis, Minnesota, were about to change the power of the union. These men, who favored Leon Trotsky over Franklin D. Roosevelt, were Ray Dunne, his brothers Miles and Grant, and Farrell Dobbs. In organizing the city drivers, they ignored the national union's focus on skilled workers and worked to get any group of drivers into the union. They organized the city coal yard workers, following a bitter strike, and then turned to over-the-road drivers.

Dobbs, in particular, saw the importance of long-distance trucking as it replaced railroads as the means for handling freight. Their strategy was simple: Teamster members at the Minneapolis truck terminals would not unload any trucks unless they were driven by Teamster members. Out-of-town owners had to allow their drivers to join the Teamsters and then negotiate with the union. The new drivers would then go on to organize the next terminal. The leapfrog organizing of truck terminals was not limited to the Midwest. David Beck, in Seattle, Washington, used it to organize almost all the long-haul drivers from Washington to southern California.

Dobbs and the Dunnes were not organizing truck drivers only. They recruited loading dock and other types of workers by permitting Teamster drivers to deliver to and pick up only from warehouses where the Teamsters represented the workers. Once they had those workers in the union, the local negotiated contracts that allowed them to accommodate union-made goods only, thus bringing in many factory workers. By 1937 the IBT membership had jumped to 277,000.

## NEW TEAMSTER STRUCTURES: 1936–38

Structurally, Teamster locals were strong, autonomous, and independent. Traditionally, they organized, provided services to, and negotiated bargaining agreements for people who worked in a specific trade in a specific city, such as the bakery truck drivers in Des Moines, Iowa, or

## KEY DATES

◾

**1899:** The Team Drivers International Union is chartered by the American Federation of Labor.

**1903:** The Team Drivers International Union and the Teamsters National Union merge to create the International Brotherhood of Teamsters (IBT).

**1957:** Jimmy Hoffa is elected president; AFL-CIO expels the IBT on corruption charges.

**1975:** Hoffa disappears.

**1989:** The IBT accepts a consent decree from the U.S. Department of Justice to conduct direct election of officers.

**1991:** Ron Carey is elected president in the IBT's first national election.

**1998:** James P. Hoffa is elected president.

**2005:** The IBT breaks away from the AFL-CIO and cofounds the Change to Win Coalition of labor unions.

the laundry truck drivers in Portland, Oregon. The union would bargain with the employer or employers in that city who hired their members. Joint councils were established where there were three or more locals, to coordinate Teamster activities in the area, especially organizing, and to decide certain jurisdictional matters.

The over-the-road drivers who joined the Teamsters as a result of the work of Dobbs and Beck did not live and work in one place. Both leaders realized how important it was to develop a means to negotiate area-wide contracts to ensure consistency in wages and benefits. If that did not occur, the owners could easily move a terminal to an area where the negotiated wages were low.

Beck negotiated the first area-wide trucking agreement in 1936, covering over-the-road drivers in Washington, Oregon, Idaho, and Montana. In 1938 Beck also introduced a new structure to the union: a multistate conference divided into trade divisions to provide specialized organizing help to joint councils and local unions. This new administrative entity would help expand Teamster membership and provide regional power bases outside the control of the IBT president.

In the Midwest, Dobbs formed the North Central District Drivers Council in 1937. The council comprised 70 locals representing most of the several hundred trucking workers in the 12 midwestern states.

One of the men working with Dobbs was a young Teamster organizer from Detroit, Michigan, Jimmy Hoffa.

To negotiate a master regional agreement, Dobbs concentrated on Chicago, because almost all truck routes in the Midwest went through there, and then he took the terms of that contract to the rest of the region. Because most trucking employers would have to abide by the terms of the Chicago agreement, they wanted to participate, so they set up the Central States Employers Negotiating Committee. The regional agreement was signed in 1938, granting road drivers 2.75 cents per mile and 75 cents per hour for lost time. It also established a grievance committee and made membership in the Teamsters a condition of employment for all drivers.

The labor scene changed significantly during the 1930s. New federal laws established minimum wages and maximum hours of work for each industry, provided protection against management interference or intimidation aimed at union activity, and established legal sanction for collective bargaining, the framework for the minimum wage, a 40-hour week, and overtime. Workers in the same industry, no matter what their actual jobs were, joined industrial unions. This approach was to counter the skilled trades organizing of the Teamsters, building trades, and other craft unions. In 1934 John L. Lewis, the head of the United Mine Workers, along with auto workers, garment workers, steel workers, and others, founded the Congress of Industrial Organizations (CIO).

In 1935 Congress passed the Motor Carrier Act, making regulation of the trucking industry a responsibility of the federal government. At the time, there were approximately 3.7 million registered trucks on the road, and the industry had revenues of about $500 million. In 1938 the Interstate Commerce Commission adopted the Motor Carrier Safety provisions, which established maximum hours of driving and minimum hours of rest between driving shifts.

### GROWING THE MEMBERSHIP AND CHANGING THE LEADERSHIP: 1940–60

By the beginning of the 1940s IBT membership had reached 456,000. The trucking industry was considered essential to the war effort, and after World War II the industry grew tremendously. By 1947 gross operating revenues of the motor carriers had risen to $2.2 billion. The union's membership grew to 890,000, and the Teamsters expanded their organizing efforts. While continuing to organize truck drivers, especially in the nonunion South, the Teamsters also moved into the auto, food processing, dairy, and vending industries. By the late 1940s IBT membership had doubled to 1 million members.

In 1952 Tobin retired after 45 years as president and was succeeded by David Beck. The following year Beck moved IBT's headquarters from Indianapolis to Washington, D.C., erecting a huge marble building across the street from the U.S. Capitol. From there, the union, along with the automobile, concrete, and rubber industries supported plans for a national highway construction program. The result was the beginning of the modern interstate highway system, a 16-year, $41 billion project that would cement trucking's supremacy over the railroad for hauling freight.

In 1955 the American Federation of Labor and the Congress of Industrial Organizations merged to form the AFL-CIO. Meanwhile, various committees in Congress were holding hearings on labor racketeering, particularly within the Teamsters. Even though the early investigations ended with no findings, in 1957 the U.S. Senate created a bipartisan, special Select Committee on Improper Activities in the Labor or Management Field. The committee was chaired by Senator John Little Mc-Clellan, a Democrat from Arkansas. Its chief council was Robert F. Kennedy, and its first target was David Beck for misuse of Teamster funds. Beck eventually went to jail for falsifying income tax returns.

Jimmy Hoffa succeeded Beck as president in 1957, despite pending federal trials for perjury and wiretapping, 34 new charges from the McClellan committee, and a suit in federal court for improper selection of convention delegates. Three months latter the AFL-CIO expelled the Teamsters, its largest affiliate with 1.5 million members, for corrupt leadership. It did not charter a rival union, however.

## CHANGES IN THE TRUCKING INDUSTRY AND ORGANIZING PUBLIC EMPLOYEES: 1960–70

The 1960s saw the continuing centralization and standardization of bargaining for truckers and increased organizing of public employees. By 1961 the trucking industry directly employed over 7 million people and its carriers available for public hire had gross revenues of $7.4 billion. However, the railroads were fighting to take back more of the freight hauling, and air freight competition was accelerating.

In 1964 Hoffa negotiated the first national bargaining agreement for the trucking industry, covering 400,000 intracity and over-the-road drivers employed by some 16,000 trucking companies. According to Sloane, Hoffa was both a realist and a negotiator, and he fol-lowed "an ability-to-pay" approach, protecting the industry as well as his members. As technology and innovations such as sleeper cabs and piggybacking changed the industry, his objective was to minimize displacement and ensure that the workers shared in whatever productivity gains resulted.

That same year Hoffa was found guilty of jury tampering, conspiracy, and mail and wire fraud. After appeals, he went to federal prison in 1967, and the general vice president Frank Fitzsimmons assumed control in his absence. Meanwhile, public employees, especially those working for state and local governments, were becoming more militant. Sanitation workers, teachers, nurses, and other hospital workers joined unions and made the concept of public employee collective bargaining more acceptable. By the end of the 1960s the Teamsters had several hundred thousand members in the public sector.

## GROWING DISSENT AND GOVERNMENT OVERSIGHT: 1970–89

Fitzsimmons was elected general president of IBT in 1971, and by 1975, the year Hoffa disappeared, the union numbered 2.2 million members. The new members included local police, airline pilots, office workers, dental mechanics, and farmworkers.

However, some members, especially the truckers, were not happy with the union leadership and its priorities, and various dissident groups such as the Professional Drivers Council, the Teamsters United Rank and File, and the Teamsters for a Decent Contract appeared to challenge the leadership. Grassroots organizations began building bases within local unions and electing reformers to leadership positions with the hope of eventually influencing national issues. In 1976 the various groups came together to establish the Teamsters for a Democratic Union (TDU).

The 1980s were a turbulent time for the Teamsters. Four men served as general president during the decade, the union rejoined the AFL-CIO, and membership dropped as a result of deregulation of the trucking industry.

By 1989 membership was down to 1.5 million. In March of that year the Teamsters signed a consent decree with the U.S. Department of Justice. The agreement settled a suit charging that the union had allowed organized crime to infiltrate and dominate the organization. It called for a court-appointed panel to oversee the union's internal affairs for the next three years. It also required that top officers be elected by direct, secret vote of the membership, a longtime TDU demand.

## NEW LEADERSHIP:1990–2000

Charges against Teamster officials resulting from the government investigations gave a boost to the dissidents and led to victories at the local level, such as that of Ron Carey, the president of a New York local and a former UPS driver. With promises to clean up the union and backing from the TDU, Carey and his slate won the first direct election in 1991 and was reelected in 1996, defeating James P. Hoffa, the son of Jimmy Hoffa.

In 1997 the government invalidated Carey's win because of election finance illegalities. Hoffa won the new election in 1998. After taking office, he surprised many observers by building coalitions with environmentalists and other progressive groups on trade and human rights issues. He established the Respect, Integrity, Strength, and Ethics (RISE) program to fight internal corruption, a move that was intended to encourage the end of government oversight. Hoffa won reelection to a full term in 2000 and remained as president of the union throughout the first decade of the 21st century.

## UNION WORK IN THE TWENTY-FIRST CENTURY

The IBT was constantly focused on the activities of organizing and collective bargaining. The deregulation of the trucking industry, begun in the 1970s, continued to offer challenges to the Teamsters. The growing numbers of independent truckers, which neither trucking companies nor shipping lines would claim as employees, constituted a poverty-class of workers. By 2000 the union was having some success of bringing these workers into the fold.

In 2003 the Brotherhood of Locomotive Engineers voted to merge with the Teamsters. This was followed in 2004 by the Brotherhood of Maintenance of Way Employees. These two mergers added 70,000 members to the IBT. That same year the Graphic Communications International Union also voted to join the Teamsters, adding another 60,000 members.

In 2007 the Teamsters won a new master contract with UPS that added coverage of the 15,000 employees of the new UPS unit created when it acquired overnight shipping. In 2009 the Teamsters and UPS entered into an unusual alliance supporting mutually beneficial legislation that would make it easier for the Teamsters and other unions to organize the UPS rival FedEx. In a bizarre case of a union supporting an employer in an unfair labor practice, the Teamsters allowed the company to require members working for UPS to write letters to Congress in support of the bill.

The first decade of the 21st century was a turbulent period for the U.S. labor movement. After years of trying to battle the decline in organized labor, union leaders knew that the movement was in deep trouble. The election of the reform candidate John Sweeney as president of the AFL-CIO in the 1990s failed to solve most of the problems. As a result, in 2005 the IBT and four other major unions (the Laborers' International Union of North America, the Service Employees International Union, the United Farm Workers of America, and the United Food and Commercial Workers International Union) each voted to withdraw from the AFL-CIO. These five unions then created the Change to Win Coalition with the goal of rebuilding and expanding the labor movement. The Teamsters and the other member unions contributed funds to apply innovative organizing techniques to reverse the trend of deunionization and to bring into the fold the harder-to-organize sectors of the workforce. However, by 2010 the Change to Win Coalition, which was battered by the global economic recession that began in late 2007, was faltering in its effort to revitalize the labor movement.

## GOVERNMENT AND THE TEAMSTERS

Even though the Teamsters finally endorsed Al Gore, the Democratic nominee for U.S. president, in 2000, the winner in that extremely close election, George W. Bush, and his fellow Republicans had not forgotten that the Teamsters were traditionally loyal to their party. As a result, they aggressively courted the Teamsters and a few other unions in the hopes of politically splitting the union movement and giving President Bush a recount-proof majority for reelection in 2004. In a potent symbolic gesture, Hoffa was invited to sit in First Lady Laura Bush's box for the 2002 State of the Union address. In a more concrete benefit, Bush added to his massive tax cut bill of 2003 a pension provision that the Teamsters and other unions had long sought. Such blandishments persuaded the Teamsters to increase their political contributions to the Republicans that year.

However, despite their grand strategy, Republicans committed several tactical mistakes. In 2001 President Bush began allowing Mexican trucks to make long-haul deliveries under the North American Free Trade Agreement, a move opposed by the Teamsters, who were concerned about job loss and safety issues. The U.S. secretary of labor Elaine Chao frustrated the Teamsters at the 2003 winter labor meeting when she opposed a long-sought increase in the minimum wage and flaunted a list of antilabor steps that the Bush administration had taken. In another instance, the Republican House minority leader Tom DeLay allowed his staff to send out a union-bashing fund-raising letter that denounced efforts to organize federal workers as "sickening." DeLay had been seeking the IBT's support for a law allowing exploration for oil and gas in environmentally sensitive areas of Alaska. When Hoffa expressed dismay about the letter, DeLay quickly scuttled the letter. Nevertheless, the bill still failed.

Even though the IBT tended toward the conservative side on the environment, it took more traditionally liberal positions in some important social issues. In 2006 Hoffa was joined by workers, students, and civil rights and community leaders in a campaign publicizing the need for a living wage, affordable health care, a secure retirement, and greater democracy in the workplace. As the first decade of the 21st century came toward a close, health care reform became a major legislative goal of President Barack Obama's administration. The Teamsters and its fellow Change to Win Coalition unions lobbied hard and helped to mobilize grassroots support. Organized labor rejoiced with the signing of the Patient Protection and Affordable Care Act by President Obama in March 2010.

*Ellen D. Wernick*
*Updated, Judson MacLaury*

## PRINCIPAL DIVISIONS

21 industrial divisions representing a wide range of occupations.

## FURTHER READING

Brooks, Thomas R., *Toil and Trouble: A History of American Labor*, 2nd ed. New York: Delacorte Press, 1971.

Butterfield, Bruce, "Teamsters Avert Trial by Accepting Reforms," *Boston Globe*, March 14, 1989, p. 1.

Cooper, Mark, "Where's Hoffa Driving the Teamsters?" *Nation*, July 24, 2000, p. 11.

Edsall, Thomas B., "Two Top Unions Split from AFL-CIO," *Washington Post*, July 26, 2005. p. A1.

Eggen, Dan, "UPS Employees Say They Were Forced to Lobby against FedEx," *Washington Post*, August 7, 2009, p A3.

Fink, Gary M., ed., *Labor Unions*. Westport, CT: Greenwood Press, 1977.

Larkin, Jim, "Teamsters: The Next Chapter," *Nation*, January 4, 1999, p. 17.

Nicholson, Tom, et al., "Taking on the Teamsters," *Newsweek*, January 8, 1979, p. 54.

Sloane, Arthur A., *Hoffa*. Cambridge, MA: Massachusetts Institute of Technology Press, 1991.

Whoriskey, Peter, "Teamsters Union Approves Wage Cuts for Truckers," *Washington Post*, January 9, 2009, p. D1.

# K-Tron International Inc.

———————— ■ ————————

Routes 55 and 553
Pitman, New Jersey 08071
U.S.A.
Telephone: (856) 589-0500
Fax: (856) 589-8113
Web site: http://www.ktroninternational.com/

*Wholly Owned Subsidiary of Hillenbrand Inc.*
*Incorporated:* 1964 as Kane Electronics
*Employees:* 639
*Sales:* $190.77 million (2009)
*NAICS:* 334513 Instruments and Related Products Manufacturing for Measuring, Displaying, and Controlling Industrial Process Variables.

■ ■ ■

Based in Pitman, New Jersey, K-Tron International Inc. is a global material handling equipment manufacturer and systems provider that serves the process, electric utility, pulp and paper, mining, and other industries. The company divides its business between two groups: the K-Tron Process Group and the K-Tron Size Reduction Group. The K-Tron Process Group offers the K-Tron Feeders brand of weight and volume manufacturing process feeders; the K-Tron Premier brand of pneumatic conveying and bulk handling equipment; and the Wuxi K-Tron Colormax brand of feeders, pelletizers, and other equipment used in plastics compounding and injection molding processes. The subsidiary K-Tron Electronics designs and manufactures the electronic assemblies for the K-Tron Process Group

brands and for third-party equipment manufacturers. The K-Tron Size Reduction Group includes three subsidiaries: Pennsylvania Crusher Corporation, a maker of coal-crushing equipment for coal-fired power generation plants; Gundlach Equipment Corporation, which produces coal reduction equipment for use at both the mine site and the preparation plant and reduction equipment for salt processing plants, fertilizer plants, and other applications; and Jeffrey Rader Corporation, a maker of wood hogs, chip sizers, and other size reduction equipment used in the forest products and pulp and paper industries. K-Tron, which maintains plants in the United States, Switzerland, and the People's Republic of China, is a wholly owned subsidiary of Hillenbrand Inc., a provider of coffins and other solutions to the funeral industry.

## POST–WORLD WAR II ORIGINS

In 1949 the manufacturing engineer John R. Monsell formed John R. Monsell Company in a Pitman, New Jersey, garage to manufacture pneumatic scales. These scales were used in metropolitan lift stations that pumped wastewater to a high elevation to allow gravity to deliver it to treatment plants. To make the tanks he needed to house machinery underground, he turned in the early 1960s to another New Jersey business, Kane Steel, a steel fabricator and supply company. The company provided him with sections that he then welded together in his shop.

Kane Steel was founded in 1955 by Edward Kane, an entrepreneur and self-taught mechanical engineer. Because Kane had more cash at his disposal than Monsell, the two men began to bid together on Monsell's projects. When Monsell ran into financial difficulties and was forced to declare bankruptcy, Kane bought the assets of the John R. Monsell Company from the bankruptcy court in 1964 and formed the new enterprise Kane Electronics with Monsell in charge. A few years later the K-Tron name was adopted, with the "K" standing for Kane and "Tron" an abbreviation for electronics.

Not only did Kane serve as K-Tron's chairman but also he became the chief mechanical engineer. About a year after the founding of the reconfigured company, Monsell died from complications caused by an untreated boil on his neck. To replace him, Kane brought in the engineer Don Stein, whose tenure with the company extended beyond 1985, when Kane resigned as chairman.

## A TURNING POINT WITH THE DIGITAL SENSOR

A significant turning point in K-Tron's history occurred in the early 1970s, when the company developed a digital sensor for pneumatic control machinery. Displayed at the Philadelphia Chemical Engineering show and at a plastics manufacturing show, the sensor caught the attention of some major companies. Proctor & Gamble, for example, was extremely interested in finding a digital sensor for use in combining the ingredients for Duncan Hines cake mixes. Analog sensors, which were sensitive to shifting temperatures, were not reliable for use on continuous line operations in which scales could not be reset to zero with each operation. Because K-Tron's digital sensor was not affected by temperature, it proved to be more suitable for continuous line functions.

Also taking notice of K-Tron's new sensor was General Electric, which took it to Belgium to be installed at a General Electric plant. K-Tron then opened a sales office in Belgium and displayed the sensor at a trade show in Milan, Italy. Shortly thereafter, K-Tron lined up agents to represent it throughout Europe. Wanting to expand its presence in Europe, K-Tron acquired Soder AG in 1975. Founded in 1900 in Niederlenz, Switzerland, Soder originally manufac-

tured mills for the food industry and eventually became involved in the manufacture of weigh feeders. It also possessed high-quality mechanical design capabilities, so much so that Kane retired as chief mechanical engineer and all mechanical design was transferred to the Swiss branch. A year after the acquisition, K-Tron introduced loss-in-weigh feeders that employed digital weighing.

## PUBLIC OFFERING OF K-TRON: 1980

To supply the growing capital needs of what was fast becoming a global company, Kane took K-Tron public in 1980. In a stock offering underwritten by Lehman Brothers, the company grossed $10 million, although Kane and some Swiss investors retained majority control. Most of this money was then invested in an effort to become involved in the platform scale business.

K-Tron attempted to apply its technology to platform scales for weighing packages and calculating postage as well as to a unit that could weigh and count currency and coins, but the company misread the market. The scales may have been more accurate than analog products, but as a result they were overly expensive for the tasks they performed. In the end, consumers and companies opted not to spend the extra money and remained content with less accurate but cheaper products. It was a costly failure and played a role in Kane stepping down as K-Tron's chairman in 1985. Kane was also experiencing health problems that proved to be the deciding factor in his resignation. He retained his stake in the company for three more years before selling out.

Succeeding Kane as chairman was Leo C. Beebe, who also took over as chief executive officer (CEO). A former Ford Motor Company executive of 28 years and the dean of the School of Business Administration at Glassboro State College, later renamed Rowan University, Beebe had been a K-Tron board member since the early 1980s. Once in charge, he quickly sold off the platform scale business to return K-Tron's focus to its core industrial feeder business. A year later the company returned to profitability and sales reached $70 million in 1990, a 180 percent increase from 1985, due primarily to oversea sales, which accounted for 65 percent of revenues.

Under Beebe's leadership, K-Tron remained profitable. In 1992 the 74-year-old Beebe stepped down as CEO, but he retained the chairmanship. The new CEO was Marcel O. Rohr, a Swiss citizen, who had been employed at Soder since 1978. He relocated to Pitman in 1986 but returned to Switzerland in 1989 to

## KEY DATES

**1949:** John R. Monsell Company is formed.
**1955:** Edward Kane founds Kane Steel.
**1964:** Edward Kane buys Monsell's assets from bankruptcy court to form Kane Electronics, which is eventually renamed K-Tron International Inc.
**1980:** K-Tron goes public.
**2010:** K-Tron is acquired by Hillenbrand Inc.

head K-Tron's European operations. His path to the company's top post was part of a long-term succession plan put in place by Beebe and the board.

## ACQUISITION OF COLORTRONIC: 1992

Unfortunately for Rohr, he made a grievous mistake with the 1992 acquisition of the German company Colortronic GmbH, a maker of feeder machines and other equipment used in a different part of the market. To pay the $13 million price tag for Colortronic, K-Tron went into debt. When the German economy slumped, as did the economies in the countries where K-Tron did business, the company quickly found itself in dire straits. Losses topped $16 million between 1994 and 1995, and the total debt increased to an unmanageable level of $69 million. At one point Colortronic was losing $100,000 a week.

With K-Tron on the verge of bankruptcy and the German banks threatening foreclosure, Beebe came out of retirement in 1995 and took the helm for a second time. Given a 9:00 a.m. deadline to dispose of Colortronic, Beebe was able to complete a sale 4:30 that morning. Colortronic not only fetched $9 million in cash but also its sale reduced K-Tron's debt load by $14 million. Once again, Beebe turned K-Tron around. By 1997 the company was ready to resume expansion. In that year, it acquired Hurricane Pneumatic Conveying Inc.

Now 80 years of age, Beebe retired again at the start of 1998. Edward B. Cloues II replaced Beebe as chairman and CEO. The 50-year-old Cloues was a former corporate attorney familiar with mergers and acquisitions but whose immediate focus was on cutting costs and pursuing organic growth. As the 1990s came to a close, he consolidated a few of the company's operations and downsized some of its workforce. He also

introduced the Smart Force Transducer System and the SmartConnex Control System.

## NEW CENTURY, NEW GROWTH

At the start of the 21st century, Cloues was ready to pursue external growth. Colormax Ltd., a maker of pneumatic conveying equipment and material handling systems, was acquired in 2000. A year later K-Tron's product offerings were supplemented by the acquisition of Pneumatic Conveying Systems Ltd. To provide some diversity for the company, Cloues acquired in 2003 Pennsylvania Crusher Corporation, a maker of equipment for the coal industry, and Jeffrey Specialty Equipment Corporation, a maker of equipment for the coal, pulp and paper, and other types of industries.

Expansion continued in 2006 with a pair of acquisitions: J.M.J. Industries, which became Gundlach Equipment Corporation, and Premier Pneumatics Inc. That same year K-Tron brought together several units to create the K-Tron Process Group. Two more acquisitions were completed in 2007. The five-year-old Wuxi Chenghao Machinery, already one of China's lead feeder and ancillary equipment makers serving the plastics compounding and injection industries, was acquired. Later in the year K-Tron paid $16 million for Rader Companies Inc., a maker of pneumatic conveying systems, screen equipment, and storage and reclaim systems used in the pulp and paper industries. In 2009 Jeffrey and Rader were brought together to create Jeffrey Rader Corporation.

The success of K-Tron was recognized by *Forbes* magazine, which listed it number 19 among its 200 Best Small Companies in 2007. K-Tron netted $21.3 million on sales of $201.7 million in 2007. A year later the company generated $243 million in sales and $25.8 million in earnings. Sales dipped to $190.8 million in 2009, due to lower sales in the process business line and the effects of a stronger U.S. dollar. Nevertheless, earnings held up. K-Tron reported a net income of $21.6 million for the year.

K-Tron's performance also attracted the attentions of a suitor. In January 2010 the Indiana-based Hillenbrand Inc. acquired K-Tron for $435 million. Involved in the funeral industry, Hillenbrand manufactured caskets and related items, and while K-Tron's business appeared dissimilar, the two companies were both manufacturing concerns and Hillenbrand believed that K-Tron's product line would provide much needed diversity. Even though it now had a corporate parent, K-Tron continued to operate as an independent business and was determined to remain a major global player in the industrial equipment field.

*Ed Dinger*

## PRINCIPAL OPERATING UNITS

K-Tron Process Group; K-Tron Size Reduction Group.

## PRINCIPAL COMPETITORS

Badger Meter Inc.; Heat and Control Inc.; Key Technology Inc.

## FURTHER READING

Fernandez, Bob, "Coffin Maker Buys Pitman's K-Tron for $435 Million," *Philadelphia Inquirer*, January 11, 2010.

Galante, Joseph, "A Measure of Success," *Philadelphia Inquirer*, June 29, 2007.

Greenburg, Zack O'Malley, "Counted, Weighed, Divided," *Forbes Global*, October 29, 2007, p. 60.

Myra, A., "K-Tron Fashions a Convincing Comeback," *Business News New Jersey*, May 18, 1998.

Raver, Diane, "Hillenbrand Inc. Diversifies," *Batesville (IN) Herald-Tribune*, January 12, 2010.

Rolfes, Paul, "K-Tron International: A Quiet Giant," SmallCapInvestor.com, July 17, 2008, http://www.smallcapinvestor.com/guides/mutualfunds/2008-07-17-ktron_international_a_quiet_giant.

Rouse, Ewart, "After Years of Stumbling, K-Tron Is Back on Its Feet," *Philadelphia Inquirer*, July 22, 1998, p. C1.

Skomial, Marcin, "Leo C. Beebe, 83, Led Industrial Equipment Maker," *New York Times*, July 7, 2001, p. A11.

Webber, Maura, "Beebe Returns as K-Tron Chief, Puts Company Back on Course," *Philadelphia Business Journal*, April 26, 1996, p. 1S.

# Kable Media Services, Inc.

14 Wall Street, Suite 4C
New York, New York 10005
U.S.A.
Telephone: (212) 705-4600
Fax: (212) 705-4667
Web site: www.kable.com

*Wholly Owned Subsidiary of AMREP Corporation*
*Founded:* 1932 as Kable News Company
*Employees:* 1,860
*Sales:* $136.2 million (2009)
*NAICS:* 424920 Book Periodical and Newspaper
  Merchant Wholesalers

■ ■ ■

One of the largest periodical and magazine circulators, Kable Media Services, Inc., meets all the circulation needs of its publishers, including newsstand distribution, subscription fulfillment, lettershop (printing and direct mailing) services, and graphic arts, as well as temporary staffing needs for clients of various industries. Its operations and data center are located in Mt. Morris, Illinois, and its executive offices are on Wall Street in New York City. It also has locations in Cerritos, California; Fairfield, Ohio; Louisville, Colorado; Palm Coast, Florida; and Horsham, United Kingdom. Kable is a wholly owned subsidiary of AMREP Corporation, a landholder and real estate developer in New Mexico. AMREP Corporation was formed in 1961 and has been listed on the New York Stock Exchange since 1972.

## NINETEENTH-CENTURY BEGINNINGS

In the late 1800s the Kable family of the rural community of Mt. Morris, Illinois, established the Kable Printing Company, which quickly gained a reputation for efficient printing of mass-market magazines. Around 1930 the newspaper and magazine publishing magnate William Randolph Hearst entered the field of independent distribution of single-copy magazine sales to consumers. Two years later Harry Kable, president of Kable Industries, as the company had renamed itself, decided to enter the field of magazine distribution for some publications it was printing. On April 30, 1932, Harry Kable started the Kable News Company with one client: Hugo Gernsback and his publication *Radio-Craft*, which was later renamed *Radio-Electronics*. Kable's billing for its first month was $12,364.93. The Kable News Company quickly added more publishers and magazines, and its first year's billing was $750,000. Five years later it billed $6 million.

During the 1940s Kable News Company expanded its business to include the distribution and sale of golf balls, cigarette filters, razor blades, and bridge score cards. In September 1944 it started a new division, Kable-Colcord Inc., which provided advertising and promotion services for its magazine publishers.

Comic books that reprinted comic strips had begun circulation in 1934, and Kable News Company was one of the distributors. Original comic books had been around since the beginning of the century, and in 1941 Archie Comics, drawn by Bill Montana, appeared, with Kable as its national distributor. Kable also was a

## COMPANY PERSPECTIVES

Kable Media Services, Inc., is a strong and enduring company. We have succeeded because of our devotion to basic values, the ethics and integrity of our people, the quality of our work, and the principles of our charter.

We believe that business enterprises exist to strengthen and enhance the quality of our lives and our communities, and that the network of relationships and interests which nurture and sustain thriving companies must be carefully and effectively balanced over the long term, so that the many people and groups who have a stake in the success of the enterprise are amply and equitably rewarded for their contributions.

Our Mission is to be a world class supplier of circulation and direct marketing services to the publishing, media and direct marketing industry.

distributor of comic books in the superhero, crime, and horror genres. More than a decade later, a government panel was formed to investigate juvenile delinquency and its causes, and comic books of the day were thought to be a contributing factor. On June 4, 1954, George B. Davis, president of Kable News Company, appeared before the U.S. Senate Judiciary Subcommittee on Juvenile Delinquency. When Davis asked the subcommittee what specific crimes had ever been attributed to such reading matter, he was told that the teenage killers in two Canadian homicides had been affected by crime comics. Davis testified that there was an undesirable trend in comic books that was indeed pushing the limits, but he did not feel that measures against comic books were warranted, because such measures would destroy the imaginations of children.

### EXPANSION AND ACQUISITION: THE SIXTIES AND SEVENTIES

The Kable News Company celebrated its 25th anniversary in 1957, having survived the so-called comic book disaster. Prompted by concerns after the 1954 Senate hearings, publishers established the Comics Code Authority (CCA). Distributors, including Kable, often refused to carry comics without the seal of the CCA, which in the early 1960s was headed by John L. Goldwater, the publisher of Archie Comics. Following the "disaster," expansion at Kable News slowed but did not

stop. In 1964 the Kable News Company took a 15-year lease on an entire floor of a new office building in midtown Manhattan and moved from Fifth Avenue to Third Avenue.

In 1969 the AMREP Corporation acquired the Kable News Company and created Kable Media Services, Inc., which began performing subscription fulfillment services to accommodate some of its publishers. Its average retailers had changed from the newsstands to large chain stores, such as supermarkets, drug stores, and discount and convenience stores, which sell a variety of merchandise, with publications accounting for only a small percentage of sales. The newsstand industry was changing, from 800 wholesaler agencies in 1932 to what would eventually be fewer than 100 owners in 2010, with just 3 owners representing 90 percent of North American newsstand sales.

The industry had begun newsstand and other distribution services for publishers of mass-market paperback editions of popular books. In 1972 Kable became the distributor of the 750,000-copy printing of Grove Press's paperback book *Clifford Irving: What Really Happened*, which was Irving's account of the publishing scandal in which Irving was convicted of defrauding the publisher McGraw-Hill with an "autobiography" of the industrialist Howard Hughes that Irving falsely claimed was based on extensive interviews with the reclusive Hughes.

Kable continued to take on new magazine titles. In 1979 it began distribution of *Talk* magazine, which for the previous ten years was *Girl Talk*, a free magazine distributed in beauty salons. The revamped, redesigned magazine was priced at $1.25 for newsstand distribution of 250,000 copies in addition to the 125,000 for beauty salons.

### END OF ONE CENTURY, START OF ANOTHER: 1983–2010

In the early 1980s more and more hardcover book publishers decided to sell their own paperback reprint editions instead of selling reprint rights to mass-market publishers. The hardcover publishers sold the paperbacks to bookstores and hired magazine wholesalers (independent distributors or IDs) to get them into mass-market outlets. Sol Stein, president of the independent publisher Stein & Day, launched a line of mass-market reprints in January 1984, which Kable distributed to IDs while the Stein & Day sales force supplied bookstores. In 1985 a suit was filed against Kable by Stein & Day, who claimed Kable had failed to pay money it owed the publisher. A senior vice president of Kable admitted that some money was owed to Stein

## KEY DATES

**1932:** Harry Kable founds Kable News Company.

**1941:** Kable is the national distributor of Archie Comics, drawn by Bill Montana.

**1954:** George B. Davis, president of Kable News Company, appears before the U.S. Senate Judiciary Subcommittee on Juvenile Delinquency.

**1957:** Kable News Company celebrates its 25th anniversary.

**1969:** The AMREP Corporation acquires the Kable News Company, creating Kable Media Services, Inc.

**1985:** Publisher Stein & Day files a suit against Kable.

**2007:** AMREP acquires Palm Coast Data, a leader in subscription and membership fulfillment services.

& Day but it was far from the amount claimed by Sol Stein. Kable filed a counterclaim against Stein & Day for breach of contract and against Sol Stein for defamation. Two years later Stein & Day filed for bankruptcy.

Kable went on to pursue new business, including a partnership with Ronald Busch (former president of Pocket Books and Ballantine Books) and his newly formed small publishing house, Tudor Communications. In 1988 Kable Media Services acquired Publishers Aide, a West Coast fulfillment company, and merged its operations with its own fulfillment division (the part of the company that receives, processes, and ships orders). In 1994 it acquired a competing national distributor, Capital Distributing, and in 1995 it expanded again by acquiring Fulfillment Corporation of America in order to add staff and management services to its growing Fulfillment Services Division.

In the mid-1990s a trend in magazine sales was emerging, in which older, family-owned wholesale distributors were disappearing. James Sterngold in the *New York Times* reported that from mid-1995 to mid-1996, about 85 distributors had merged with huge wholesalers or had disappeared, leaving about 100 distributors. The Council for Periodical Distributors Associations predicted that by the end of 1996, 10 to 20 of the remaining wholesalers would control about 90 percent of the business of supplying magazines to supermarkets and other retail chains, with chain stores

now being the single largest source of retail magazine sales. Sterngold pointed out that total magazine sales revenue in 1995 was $4.1 billion, with 41.2 percent coming from supermarkets and big chain stores. Daniel Friedman, chairman of Kable News Company, was quoted by Sterngold as saying: "At one time the publisher was king in this industry... . Then the distributor was king. Now the retailer is king."

In January 2007 AMREP Corporation acquired Palm Coast Data, a leader for 50 years in subscription and membership fulfillment services. Palm Coast Data was joined with Kable Fulfillment Services, a move that, according to the company's Web site, "streamlined operations, improved service to clients, created cost efficiencies, and eliminated operating redundancies in the magazine subscription, membership, and direct mail fulfillment services departments."

By decade's end, Kable's newsstand clients were generating more than $700 million in annual retail sales. Kable attributed its success to its numerous unique but interrelated divisions making up the Kable Media Services collection of circulating and marketing services for publishing and direct response industries. Kable Distribution Services distributed more than 600 magazines, annuals, and digests, including Archie Comics, *Psychology Today*, *Ms.*, and *Bloomberg Markets*, for over 200 publishers. Kable Specialty Services contained a direct-to-retail department working with all major book chains and nontraditional retail outlets, such as Sam's Club and Home Depot. Kable International Sales and Distribution Division was part of the company's distribution services, working in more than 120 countries. Kable Fulfillment Services provided magazine subscription and related services for publishers and direct marketers. Kable Staffing Resources provided temporary, direct hire, and staffing/management services for the light industry sector and also managed Kable Comprehensive Healthcare Staffing. Other divisions in the Kable family included Kable Specialty Packaging Services and Kable Product Services.

On its Web site, Kable Media Services, Inc., refers to itself as "an aggressive company dedicated to innovation and growth." Parent company AMREP Corporation reported in a press release that Kable Media's revenues increased from $32.3 million for the first quarter of 2008 to $34 million for the same period in 2009. More than a year later, however, AMREP reported decreased revenues for Kable, from $35.1 million for third quarter 2009 to $28.4 million for the same period in 2010. With the global economic downturn at the end of the first decade of the new century, magazine publishers suffered from lower advertising revenues and decreased newsstand sales, events directly affecting Kable's operations. With its motto "EXCELLENCE is no accident!" and its long history of success, Kable Media seemed capable of weathering the challenges the publishing industry faced in the years to come.

*Louise B. Ketz*

## PRINCIPAL SUBSIDIARIES

Palm Coast Data.

## PRINCIPAL OPERATING UNITES

Kable Distribution Services; Kable Specialty Services; Kable Specialty Packaging Services; Kable International; Kable Fulfillment; Kable Product Services; Kable Staffing Resources; List Services; Graphic Arts; Membership; Internet Services.

## PRINCIPAL COMPETITORS

Hudson Group; Levy Home Entertainment LLC; Source Interlink Companies, Inc.

## FURTHER READING

"AMREP Reports First Quarter Fiscal 2009 Results" (press release), Princeton, NJ: AMREP Corporation, September 9, 2008, http://www.amrepcorp.com/pr_2008_0909.asp.

Applebaum, Judith, "Paperback Talk," *New York Times*, November 6, 1983.

Dougherty, Philip H., "Advertising: New Magazine Tack," *New York Times*, September 4, 1974, p. 64.

Nyberg, Ami Kiste, *Seal of Approval: The History of the Comics Code*. Jackson, MS: University Press of Mississippi, 1998.

Sterngold, James, "Changing Face of Supermarket Magazine Sales," *New York Times*, May 6, 1996.

"10-Q: AMREP Corp.," Edgar Online-Glimpse, March 10, 2010.

# King & Spalding LLP

1180 Peachtree Street NE
Atlanta, Georgia 30309
U.S.A.
Telephone: (404) 572-4600
Fax: (404) 572-5100
Web site: http://www.kslaw.com/

*Private Company*
*Founded:* 1885
*Employees:* 800
*Revenues:* $677.3 million (2009)
*NAICS:* 541110 Offices of Lawyers

∎ ∎ ∎

Since its inception in 1885, King & Spalding has been a top-ranked law firm in Atlanta, Georgia. The firm has evolved from a general practice of law with specializations in railroad consolidation, intellectual property, and banking, to a practice in the 21st century with nearly 800 lawyers concentrating on more than 75 areas. The firm consists of seven divisions: Corporate/Transactional, Finance and Restructuring, Government and Regulatory, Industry-Related Practices, Intellectual Property, International, and Litigation and Alternative Dispute Resolution. Besides its Atlanta headquarters, King & Spalding has seven other offices in the United States (Austin and Houston, Texas; Charlotte, North Carolina; New York City; San Francisco and Redwood Shores [Silicon Valley], California; and Washington, D.C.) and

six offices overseas (Abu Dhabi and Dubai, United Arab Emirates; Frankfort, Germany; London, England; Paris, France, and an affiliated office in Riyadh, Saudi Arabia). As of 2009, King & Spalding represented half of the Fortune 100 companies and, according to *American Lawyer*, was ranked within the top 50 law firms for gross revenue between 2007 and 2009.

## THE PARTNERSHIP'S START: SPALDING AND KING

In 1885 Alexander C. King and Jack J. Spalding founded the law firm that would bear their names. Both men chose Atlanta to live and work in, both were strongly interested in Atlanta's progress and the legal profession, and both (as a result partly of the Civil War and its immediate aftermath) had studied law mainly on their own. Otherwise, Spalding and King were distinct contrasts. King was known for his keen knowledge of law and unassuming personality. Spalding was known for his numbers-crunching skill and business-like approach. In *The First Hundred Years: A Centennial History of King & Spalding*, Della Wager Wells concluded, "Spalding, the diplomat and financial negotiator, picked up where his partner's scholarly techniques left off, and together they created a well-rounded partnership which was destined to endure and thrive." The pair named their firm King & Spalding because King had been admitted to the Georgia bar two years before Spalding.

Spalding and King's first location at 6¹/₂ Whitehall Street had no heat or restroom. Walter W. Driver Jr., a partner and former chairman of the firm, noted in *King & Spalding LLP, Growing with Our Clients since 1885,*

## COMPANY PERSPECTIVES

At King & Spalding LLP, long-standing client relationships are one of the surest barometers of a law firm's success in meeting its clients' needs for legal services. King & Spalding lawyers pride themselves on developing continuing client relationships that are productive, professional and collegial. King & Spalding continues to build on the firm's fundamental roots and values. Our mission statement reflects our commitment to three core objectives: legal work of the highest quality, attentive and responsive client service and community stewardship.

"Their [King & Spalding's] financial arrangement was simple: They placed legal fees in a drawer and split their collections before going home at night. Compensation of partners, as we all know, has become slightly more complicated since then." Patrick Calhoun joined the firm in 1887, and his impact was considerable. During his tenure, the firm's style (its name) gave Calhoun first placement.

For Calhoun, King & Spalding, railroads were the chief enterprise. Before and after the Civil War, rail transport was a leading factor in Atlanta's growth. Beginning in the late 1880s, King and Calhoun worked as general counsel or assistant general counsel for a number of railroad lines, focusing on consolidations, settlements of disputes, and other litigation. The bank panic of 1893 caused many railroads to require receivership, so the law firm sometimes owned a few of the lines. The firm specialized in these matters and would continue in this arena for the next 40 years.

During the 1890s and the first decade of the 20th century the firm experienced several changes. In 1894 Calhoun left the firm. In 1903 John D. Little joined the firm, which became King, Spalding & Little. He left five years later. In 1909 E. Marvin Underwood joined the firm, and its name became King, Spalding & Underwood. Because the firm was gaining more prominence in Atlanta, the three partners decided to relocate their offices to a prime site for lawyers: the Gate City National Bank Building. In 1911 the firm was paid a legal fee of $1 million for its work with railroad lines, the largest fee to date. Even though the payment was mostly in shares of stock, it was an eye-opening indication of the firm's influence in the city.

## MORE CLIENTS, MORE CHANGES: 1912–38

Hughes Spalding Sr. became a junior member of his father's firm in 1912. By 1929 the "Spalding" in the firm's name referred to Hughes, who would continue in an increasing leadership role there for half a century. During the initial phase of his work, the firm obtained a significant client: the Coca-Cola Company, which would become synonymous with industry in Atlanta. Even though the Spaldings and their firm were better known among their peers, Coca-Cola was gaining in popularity and prosperity and came to the firm's attention because of litigation against the beverage maker. King & Spalding won not only the suit but also the respect of Coca-Cola, which decided to hire the firm during the early 1920s. As Driver pointed out in his history of the law firm, Coca-Cola wanted Spalding and his partners' representation, not their opposing counsel.

The 1920s was a decade of great progress and prosperity for both Atlanta and the nation. During this period Jack Spalding and his partners established an important relationship with the Georgia Railway and Electric Company. Still committed to the idea of railways, Jack Spalding added electric power to his interest in development for Atlanta and was offered the job of president of the recently founded Atlanta Water & Electric Company. He declined the offer and instead pursued a strategy of consolidation of this company with the Georgia Railway and Electric Company and other, smaller hydroelectric firms. In 1925 Spalding and his associates successfully finalized the agreement for the consolidated Georgia Power Company. This agreement culminated the efforts from the previous decade, for which Spalding and his team were paid $1 million in shares of stock.

This was also a time of shifting personnel at the law firm. In 1914 Underwood became the U.S. assistant attorney general. King also left the firm to serve as the U.S. solicitor general in 1920 and then as a U.S. circuit judge, a position he held until 1925. Jack Spalding reorganized and renamed the firm, taking on Daniel MacDougald and John A. Sibley as partners under the style Spalding, MacDougald & Sibley. After leaving the federal bench, King rejoined the firm briefly, but he died in 1926. Jack Spalding retired from the firm in 1929. He remained active in civic and political affairs, serving as a county commissioner and as a delegate to several gatherings of the Democratic National Convention. He died in 1938, three years after the firm celebrated its 50th anniversary. That same year Hughes Spalding Sr. became a partner.

## KEY DATES
∎

**1885:** Jack J. Spalding and Alexander C. King become partners in a law firm in Atlanta.

**1887:** Patrick Calhoun joins King & Spalding, becomes the first new partner in the firm.

**1911:** King, Spalding & Underwood receives its first $1 million legal fee.

**1926:** Alexander C. King dies.

**1938:** Jack J. Spalding dies; Hughes Spalding Sr. becomes managing partner.

**1977:** Griffin C. Bell leaves King & Spalding to become the U.S. attorney general.

**1979:** The firm opens a branch in Washington, D.C., its first office outside Atlanta.

**2003:** The firm opens its first overseas office, in London.

### THE SPALDING-SIBLEY-MEADOW ERA

King & Spalding's representation of Coca-Cola formed a significant portion of the law firm's growing practice and reputation. Its work on behalf of the beverage maker mirrored nearly all of what evolved into the firm's seven divisions, including its Corporate/Transactional, Government and Regulatory, Intellectual Property, International, and Litigation and Alternative Dispute Resolution divisions. In his company history, Driver specified one such example. During the pre–World War II years a tax law in Georgia compelled Coca-Cola to move its headquarters to Delaware. After extensive public relations by Hughes Spalding and John Sibley's many visits to legislators, the law was changed and Coca-Cola returned to Atlanta. When John Sibley's son James Sibley joined the law firm, he became the relationship partner for Coca-Cola in 1942.

While the law firm continued to communicate with public officials and work closely with corporate clients on a range of matters, it also began to provide banking and finance offerings. Besides becoming Coca-Cola's relationship partner in the early 1940s, James Sibley garnered the same position with Sun Trust, a bank in Atlanta. Several years before, three banks had merged and when the banking laws were revised in 1933, Hughes Spalding oversaw their demerger, which resulted in Sun Trust's establishment. Within a decade, Spalding joined the bank's board, moved the law firm's offices to the bank's building, and Sibley was named the relationship partner for the bank. From this foundation grew an extensive amount of finance and finance-related work with Sun Trust and many other clients.

Another attorney with a lasting impression on the firm was William K. Meadow. Beginning as an associate in 1935, Meadow became a partner in 1945. His 52-year-career at the firm was second only to the record established by Hughes Spalding, who served for 57 years. Much of Meadow's practice concentrated on defending insurance companies and handling general litigation. Meadow's death in 1987 at the age of 95 ended the link between the earlier generations at King & Spalding and the lawyers who would work there in years to come. A veteran of World War I, his career seemed to belong to a fairly uncomplicated past. As Tom Bennett reported in Meadow's obituary in the *Atlanta Journal and Constitution*, Meadow had no formal partnership agreement with Hughes Spalding, trusting instead that he only needed to speak to Spalding to know its details.

### SERVICE, DIVERSITY, AND COST-CONSCIOUSNESS: 1970–90

Since the firm's early days, Jack Spalding and Alexander King viewed public service as an essential aspect of their firm. In addition, this element was tied to the associations they made with prospective and actual clients, heads of industries, and leaders in charitable and social affairs. From the boards that they and their descendants served on to the committees they volunteered for and the groups they donated money to, the partners of King & Spalding established a network that thrived as the firm progressed. This network carried direct, positive consequences for the firm, serving to grow its profitability and enduring future. The network had political outcomes, too, which became nationally visible during the 1970s.

When Jimmy Carter became the nation's president in 1976, he named Griffin B. Bell to head the U.S. Department of Justice. Bell received approval in 1977 and went on to continue a distinguished career that he began with King & Spalding in 1953. He would work for the firm on three occasions, leaving to become a federal judge in 1961, leaving again to work for President Carter in 1977, and returning to King & Spalding for the last time in 1979. Bell's specialties included product liability litigation and special governmental investigations.

Charles H. Kirbo, one of Bell's colleagues at King & Spalding, unofficially joined the Carter administration. Even though he was devoted to helping Carter, having been his attorney and friend for several years, Kirbo was not interested in an official position. With a similar personality as his predecessor Alexander King,

Kirbo preferred an advisory background role on a range of legal matters. Known for his courtroom skill and his diplomatic approach to negotiations, Kirbo became a partner at King & Spalding in 1960 and remained there until his death in 1996.

During the 1970s and 1980s the principal civil rights challenge at King & Spalding came in the area of gender. In 1979 the associate Elizabeth A. Hishon filed a sex discrimination suit against the firm after she was denied a partnership. In 1984 the U.S. Supreme Court ruled in her favor: private law firms were still subject to federal civil rights laws. *Hishon v. King & Spalding* (467 U.S. 69) assumed tremendous importance legally and in terms of hiring practices. Over time, this was reflected at King & Spalding as indicated in the 2007 *Diversity Report*, which was compiled by African-American and Asian-American lawyers who worked at the firm. Other changes were also occurring. Competition for jobs and cost-conscious measures resulted in a New York–style pace. In October 1985 (the firm's centennial year) Tracy Thompson noted in the *Atlanta Journal and Constitution*, "Along with a package explaining insurance benefits and the like, first-year associates are handed a key to get into the office on weekends and at night. They are expected to use it."

## DIVERSIFICATION: 1990–2000

During the 1990s King & Spalding's clientele consisted primarily of large corporations, nonprofit organizations such as hospitals, and government entities. Among its most well-known clients of this period was the Atlanta Committee for the Olympic Games, which staged the 1996 Summer Olympics in Atlanta. The firm also operated as bond counsel for Georgia counties raising money through the sale of certificates of participation, and as such was able to achieve considerable financial gains.

After relocating to occupy 12 floors of a new downtown site designed by the celebrated architect Philip Johnson, King & Spalding continued to expand outside of Atlanta. In 1979, partly in response to the needs of its client Coca-Cola, the law firm opened an office in Washington, D.C. By 1998 the Washington branch had 65 full-time lawyers specializing in areas that ranged from tax to litigation to environmental law. A New York office opened in 1990 to handle issues that included financial services and securities litigation, and a Houston office opened in 1995 to focus mainly on matters of energy for clients that included Texaco.

By June 1997 Christopher Seward of the *Atlanta Journal and Constitution* stated that "King & Spalding did $165 million in billings last year [1996] at offices in Atlanta, Washington, New York and Houston, with profits of $588,235.... Its closest rival is Alston & Bird,

which had $106 million in billings." With over 350 lawyers and $60 million more in billings than its nearest competitor, King & Spalding was ending the 1990s with a bright future ahead for itself and its clients.

## INTERNATIONAL AND ELECTRONIC FRONTIERS

Maintaining a dynamic law firm at the turn of the 21st century required a great deal from King & Spalding. Just as Spalding, King, Calhoun, Bell, and others in the firm had done over the course of 115 years, a disciplined approach, a devotion to the law, and a willingness to adjust to changing times enabled the firm to head confidently into the new century. This approach enabled King & Spalding to weather the global economic crisis that began in late 2007 better than most other law firms. Despite the challenges inherent in the worldwide recession, and the subsequent need to streamline budgets and lower expectations for profits, the firm did noticeably well.

In March 2010 Meredith Hobbs of the *Fulton County Daily Report* indicated that between 2009 and 2010 King & Spalding's revenues increased 4 percent and per partner profits grew 17 percent. Hobbs stated, "According to [Robert] Hays [the firm's chairman], the recession actually allowed his firm to get more work and improve its client base last year because cost-conscious legal departments were looking for firms capable of doing high-quality work at a better price." King & Spalding's partners tended to charge somewhat lower rates than at other firms. In addition, Hays noted that the firm billed more hours because demand for its work had risen.

Part of this demand occurred because the firm expanded its sites. After opening a location in Dubai in 2007, King & Spalding established offices in 2008 in four U.S. cities (Austin, Charlotte, San Francisco, and Silicon Valley) and in three overseas locations (Abu Dhabi, Frankfort, and Riyadh). The overseas offices were complements of branches already in place in London, which opened in 2003, and in Paris, which opened in 2006. In September 2008 David Bario observed in *American Lawyer* that when Hays became chairman in 2006, the firm seemed to renew itself. A strategic plan emerged, one that involved markets that were previously not targeted, such as biotechnology, energy, and health care.

Also new was a dramatically different way of doing business with new clients. As Bario remarked, "If a single new office illustrates how King & Spalding is managing its expansion differently than in the past, it's probably Dubai." In that office and others, the firm adopted ways of structuring transactions and investments that respected Islamic laws. Growth in this part of the firm's practice boosted its work in multiple ways, from energy transactions to international arbitration to real estate capital agreements to investment funds. As of 2010, the firm embraced Internet-based legal issues, with practices that focused on e-commerce, e-discovery, and related matters.

*Judson Knight*
*Updated, Mary C. Lewis*

## PRINCIPAL DIVISIONS

Corporate/Transactional; Finance and Restructuring; Government and Regulatory; Industry-Related Practices; Intellectual Property; International; Litigation and Alternative Dispute Resolution.

## PRINCIPAL COMPETITORS

Alston & Bird LLP; Kilpatrick Stockton LLP; Sutherland Asbill & Brennan LLP.

## FURTHER READING

"The AM Law 100—Thirteen Firms Gross over $1 Billion," Law.com, 2010, http://www.law.com/jsp/tal/PubArticleTAL. jsp?id=1202430111960.

Bario, David, "Midnight Train from Georgia: Long Tied to Its Atlanta Roots, King & Spalding Has Opened Eight Offices in 18 Months," *American Lawyer*, September 2008, pp. 88–93.

Bennett, Tom, "William K. Meadow, 95, Oldest Attorney at King & Spalding," *Atlanta Journal and Constitution*, November 29, 1987, p. E6.

Driver, Walter W., Jr., *King & Spalding LLP, Growing with Our Clients since 1885*. Exton, PA: Newcomen Society, 2004.

"Global 100—Most Revenue 2009," Law.com, 2010, http://www.law.com/jsp/tal/PubArticleTAL.jsp?id=1202433980888.

Hobbs, Meredith, "K&S Attributes Revenue, Profit Jump to More Demand," *Fulton County Daily Report*, March 16, 2010.

Seward, Christopher, "Top Billing: King & Spalding Reigns in State's Legal World," *Atlanta Journal and Constitution*, June 5, 1997, p. E1.

Thompson, Tracy, "Competition Is Changing Tradition at City's Most Prestigious Law Firms," *Atlanta Journal and Constitution*, October 25, 1985, p. A1.

Warner, Jack, "Obituaries: Charles H. Kirbo, Lawyer, Carter Ally," *Atlanta Journal and Constitution*, September 3, 1996, p. B6.

Wells, Della Wager, *The First Hundred Years: A Centennial History of King & Spalding*. Atlanta, GA: King & Spalding, 1985.

# Knowledge Learning Corporation

650 Northeast Holladay Street, Suite 1400
Portland, Oregon 97232
U.S.A.
Telephone: (503) 872-1631
Toll Free: (888) 525-2780
Fax: (503) 872-1385
Web site: http://www.knowledgelearning.com

*Division of Knowledge Universe*
*Founded:* 1983 as Children's Discovery Centers of
America
*Employees:* 36,000 (est.)
*Sales:* $1.6 billion (2009 est.)
*NAICS:* 611110 Elementary and Secondary Schools;
624410 Child Day Care Services; 721214
Recreational and Vacation Camps (except
Campgrounds)

■ ■ ■

Knowledge Learning Corporation is the largest for-profit child-care and early-education provider in the United States. Based in Portland, Oregon, Knowledge Learning operates more than 1,800 child-care, preschool, kindergarten, and primary school facilities across the country. The company's educational and care programs include Knowledge Beginnings, Children's Creative Learning Centers, and KinderCare Learning Centers. In addition, the company provides before- and after-school care and organizes and supervises camps during the summer months. A number of Knowledge Learning's child-care centers are funded by corporate clients for the benefit of their employees. The company is a division of Knowledge Universe, an educational company founded by Michael Milken of Drexel Burnham Lambert fame, his brother Lowell, and Oracle CEO Larry Ellison.

## COMPANY ORIGINS AND EARLY GROWTH: 1983–88

Knowledge Learning, originally known as Children's Discovery Centers of America (CDC), was established in the small town of Monroe, Connecticut, in 1983 by an entrepreneur named Tommy Thompson who had already been involved in a number of successful startups. He was attracted to the industry because of the rising need for day care. With backing from New York venture capitalists, he acquired a small Connecticut chain of day-care centers, operating as Children's Discovery Centers, and used that name to create Children's Discovery Centers of America, Inc. Thompson became the chairman and CEO of CDC, with James DeSanctis serving as his chief financial officer. Within a year they were running 12 facilities, and in 1985 they took the company public. Around the same time as the IPO, CDC made a major acquisition, the purchase of Mary Moppets Day Care Schools, an Arizona chain that combined company-owned with franchised units. The timing of both the IPO and the entry into the Arizona market, however, proved disastrous. A change in Arizona regulations mandated a higher ratio of personnel per child in day-care facilities, resulting in much higher labor costs and adversely impacting the entire industry in the state.

With the Mary Moppets subsidiary draining the resources of CDC, Thompson resigned and DeSanctis

## COMPANY PERSPECTIVES

At Knowledge Learning Corporation, we are committed to enhancing the educational opportunities for children, families, and the dedicated professionals who serve them.

To fulfill this mission we provide programs and environments that enrich children's development, promote respect for children, and celebrate the joy of childhood. We support families in balancing their personal and professional lives while achieving fulfillment in their parenting roles. We elevate the education profession through development and implementation of curriculum and training resources that promote excellence and honor the art of teaching. We utilize sound and ethical business practices that uphold the highest standards of fiscal accountability. And we expand our business to strengthen our ability to benefit families and clients, create new opportunities for our employees, and enhance shareholder value.

took over as chairman and CEO. Under his leadership, the company continued to struggle, posting a significant loss in 1986. DeSanctis and CDC's backers agreed that a change was needed, and a search was conducted to find a new chief executive with experience in turning around troubled companies. The man chosen was Richard A. Niglio, who was installed as chairman, CEO, and president in March 1987. He had considerable experience in turning around multi-unit operations, albeit in the restaurant field. He served as president and CEO of Mr. Donut of America from 1971 until 1982, then he became chairman and CEO of the San Francisco–based Victoria Station restaurant chain after it entered bankruptcy in 1982. In May 1988 Niglio moved CDC's headquarters to San Rafael, California, where he had previously relocated while heading Victoria Station.

Although Niglio planned to maintain CDC's presence in New England, he saw California as an even more promising market. In reality, the child-care industry across the country held great potential. America's birthrate was increasing steadily, an echo effect of the post–World War II baby boom, and with more mothers now entering the workforce, the need for child-care facilities was growing rapidly. According to statistics compiled by the National Association for the

Education of Young Children, child-care center enrollment increased 400 percent from 1976 to 1990. Moreover, the industry was highly fragmented. Operating just 53 facilities, CDC was the fifth-largest child-care company. The five largest companies combined controlled less than 10 percent of the estimated 40,000 to 50,000 centers operating in the United States. The top two companies, KinderCare (with over 1,000 centers) and La Petite Academy, achieved growth by opening new centers. Niglio opted instead to acquire established child-care centers. Furthermore, he focused on providing affordable, quality child care. "Safety, supervision and cleanliness are the minimums," he told the *San Francisco Business Time* in 1988. "Above and beyond those, it gets down to curriculum and program and that can make a substantial difference with children. We've spent a great deal of our resources developing what we think is the greatest curriculum that exists."

### A SERIES OF STRATEGIC ACQUISITIONS: 1989–93

To support his expansion plans, Niglio raised $4.5 million in a private placement of stock. CDC became profitable in 1988 and 1989, but in 1990, with the economy faltering, it fell into financial difficulties, mostly related to the Mary Moppets operation, which was finally sold off. As a result of a one-time charge against earnings, CDC lost $1.8 million on revenues of $16.5 million in 1990. Nevertheless, the fundamentals of the business remained sound, and by the end of 1990 Niglio was able to complete the company's largest deal, a tax-free stock swap for Magic Years Child Care and Learning Centers Inc. The move also expanded CDC's scope. While most of its 59 facilities were community-based, Magic Years' 32 centers were located at work sites, primarily hospitals and other health-care facilities. Eighteen of the units were employer-sponsored centers. CDC now operated in 13 states with a total license capacity of its units standing at 8,000. Niglio was eager to maintain the company's momentum, especially in light of the problems suffered by its chief rivals. Kinder-Care, for instance, was lapsing into bankruptcy after making poor investments in high-yield bonds with Drexel Burnham Lambert, an ironic situation given Milken's eventual purchase of CDC. La Petite Academy would suffer its own problems and ultimately be taken private. As a result of these developments, CDC found itself the only company in the field capable of making sizeable acquisitions.

After completing the Magic Years merger, CDC made another stock offering of $4 million to be used in making further purchases. Niglio targeted operations with six to ten centers that were on the verge of needing

## KEY DATES

**1983:** Children's Discovery Centers of America (CDC) is founded.

**1985:** CDC goes public and acquires Mary Moppets Day Care School.

**1987:** Richard Niglio becomes chairman and CEO.

**1990:** CDC acquires Magic Years Child Care and Learning Centers, Inc.

**1996:** Knowledge Universe is founded.

**1998:** Knowledge Universe acquires CDC and renames it Knowledge Learning Corporation.

**2003:** Knowledge Learning acquires Aramark Educational Resources for $265 million.

**2005:** Knowledge Learning merges with KinderCare Learning Centers, Inc., becoming the largest for-profit child-care and education provider in the United States.

**2007:** Knowledge Learning acquires Children's Creative Learning Centers, Inc.

a more sophisticated infrastructure. While they would keep their local names and retain management, the acquisitions would adopt CDC's curriculum and employ its computer-management systems. In 1992 the company added 41 facilities, ending the year with a total of 131 in operation and generating revenues of $25.7 million. The company was also on the verge of returning to profitability after posting losses in three consecutive years, due in large measure to CDC's rapid expansion.

CDC continued to add child-care centers in 1993, adding 26 new facilities while closing three. Niglio floated another stock offering, this time selling 1.3 million shares at $10 a share. Just a year earlier CDC's stock traded in the $3 range. The rise in value to $10 was in many ways a reflection of investor recognition that the child-care business was likely to continue to expand for a number of years. CDC picked up the acquisition pace in 1994, adding 42 facilities while closing three. With 193 facilities in operation by the end of 1994, the company grew revenues to $55.3 million, a significant increase over the 1993 total of $38.6 million. Moreover, net profits more than doubled, growing from $1.1 million in 1993 to $2.8 million in 1994. In addition to day care, CDC was also becoming involved in managing before- and after-school programs for older children, ages 6 to 12, as well as operating a few private elementary schools.

## ENTERING NEW TERRITORY WITH PRODIGY: 1995–96

In January 1995 CDC completed the cash and stock purchase of Prodigy Consulting Inc. and its affiliated partnerships. a major acquisition that began to diversify its interests. In addition Prodigy added some $6 million in annual revenues to CDC's balance sheet. Founded in 1988, Prodigy operated seven child-development centers in suburban Atlanta. It also managed ten employer-sponsored facilities spread across seven states, a segment of the child-care market in which CDC was eager to make inroads. Prodigy concentrated its efforts on such blue-chip clients as Amoco, Chrysler, General Motors, IBM, UAW, and Xerox. In the first two months of 1995, CDC won five additional contracts to operate employer-sponsored child-care facilities, including an agreement with the Federal Aviation Administration in Seattle. Moreover, CDC acquired eight community-based child-care facilities during the first quarter of 1995. By the end of the year the company added 52 units and closed six, for a net increase of 46 and bringing the total operation to 239 facilities. As a result revenues also continued a steady climb, reaching $77.6 million for the year, along with a $2.6 million profit.

Even before the completion of 1995, however, business conditions began to change. The field became more competitive, leading to much higher prices for available acquisitions. Moreover, CDC was having trouble digesting all of its 1995 purchases. Due to these factors, the company slowed its rate of growth in 1996, adding only nine facilities for the year. Although revenues improved to $87.8 million in 1996, profits fell significantly, dipping below $1 million. One area in which CDC remained aggressive was in elementary school programs, adding five operations in 1996, as well as 26 new kindergarten programs. The company was also eager to create internal growth by adding grades to some operations, a simple way to boost total enrollment and revenues.

## A MERGER AND A NEW BRAND IDENTITY: 1997–99

Although profits rebounded in 1997, improving to $2.5 million, CDC's revenues only grew at a modest rate, reaching $93 million. After a period of retrenchment, CDC was poised to return to a growth mode in 1998. The company was particularly anxious to continue its entry into elementary education, with the goal of offering all elementary grades, and possibly higher. With the poor state of the country's education system becoming a salient topic of public discussion, CDC was clearly beginning to position itself as an education company rather than a day-care chain. To realize these aspirations, however, required funding, and CDC was not alone in recognizing the potential of the for-profit private-education business. One of the new players in the field was Knowledge Universe, and rather than compete against it, CDC decided to join forces when the corporation came calling. In May 1998 a subsidiary of Knowledge Universe took CDC private; the company subsequently became a division of Knowledge Universe. As part of a transition to a new management team, Miglio agreed to step down and accept a two-year consulting contract.

The driving force behind the creation of Knowledge Universe was Michael Milken, the controversial king of junk bonds who served 22 months in federal prison and paid a $1 billion fine for six counts of felony securities fraud. After his release from prison in 1993, much of his attention was spent on the Milken Family Foundation, which was involved in education through the awards granted to top teachers and minority students. He also came to see for-profit education as a business opportunity, revealing to *Fortune* magazine in 1996 his vision for a "cradle to cane" enterprise, encompassing not only schooling for children but also technical training and continuing education for adults. Even capturing a small percentage of this vast market could mean tens of billions of dollars. To make his vision a reality he contacted Lawrence Ellison, founder and CEO of Oracle. A subsidiary of Oracle was one of the world's largest computer-training companies, making Ellison a likely partner. Milken also enlisted his brother Lowell, and together the three men formed Knowledge Universe with $500 million in financing. The company essentially served as a vehicle for investing in the education industry.

The initial focus of Knowledge Universe was in an area with which Ellison already felt comfortable: IT training. The first acquisition took place in September 1996, with a U.K.–based IT training company called CRT, followed by similar purchases over the next two years. It was because of Lowell Milken's interest in early childhood education that the company began to look for a suitable investment in the child-care business. They settled on CDC, then paid $80 million to take the company private. It took on the name of the acquiring subsidiary before becoming Knowledge Learning. With the deep pockets of its corporate parent to back it, and free of shareholder pressure to produce short-term results, the company was again positioned to grow rapidly through acquisitions. Instead of targeting single units or small chains, however, Knowledge Learning was now able to consider buying operations that were larger than itself. Aside from this shift in strategy, the company also began to focus more on children's educa-

tion, an area that had originally been an offshoot of its child-care operations.

## A BROADER FOCUS: PUBLIC EDUCATION

Staking out market share and building a megabrand were of greater concern than becoming highly profitable in the immediate future. The Knowledge Universe holding company was spreading in all directions, quickly becoming a billion-dollar company in annual revenues. Moreover, no other company was attempting to vertically integrate the education market, leaving it virtually unopposed. While Knowledge Universe was very much interested in acquiring more child-care facilities and developing private schools, extending its reach from preschool through high school, the real opportunity lay with the public schools, which represented about half of America's $665 billion education market. The increasing popularity of charter schools provided a wedge into the public K–12 market. These schools were publicly funded but privately operated.

In much the same way that for-profit hospital chains had become a major factor in health care, Knowledge Universe foresaw a day when for-profit schools might do the same thing in education. Indeed, the company was committed to Milken's "cradle to cane" vision, and Knowledge Learning was positioned to play a key role. Through its day-care and preschool operations, the division would be able to establish the Knowledge Universe brand with both children and parents, who thereafter would be more inclined to turn to affiliated elementary schools, secondary schools, and so on down the line. Such full market coverage of education was an enticing prospect, so much so that it appeared inevitable that major mass-media companies like Disney or AOL–Time Warner would begin to provide some stiff competition.

## GAINING AN EDGE ON THE COMPETITION: 2000–04

Entering the new century, Knowledge Learning emerged as one of the largest child-care providers in the nation. As the decade progressed, the company began to identify key acquisition opportunities that would enable it to expand its reach even further. In March 2003 Knowledge Learning agreed to purchase Aramark Educational Resources, the child-care unit of Philadelphia-based Aramark Corporation, for $265 million. Although Aramark's child-care division had seen its sales figures slip in recent years, it remained a profitable enterprise, posting net earnings in 2002 of more than $29 million on revenues of $456 million.

The acquisition of Aramark Educational Resources also gave Knowledge Learning access to roughly 95,000 new customers in 28 states, while increasing its total of child-care centers and educational facilities to more than 1,200 sites nationwide. Upon completion of the merger, Knowledge Learning named Thomas Heymann, former head of the Disney Store, to serve as the combined company's new CEO.

Knowledge Learning embarked on an even more ambitious business venture in November 2004 when it reached an agreement to acquire KinderCare Learning Centers, Inc., a major early childhood education company with a broad geographical reach, in a deal worth roughly $1.1 billion in cash and debt. In many respects, the acquisition matched up well with Knowledge Learning's long-term growth strategy. The largest single child-care provider in the United States, KinderCare operated more than 1,200 facilities and preschools across the country and served approximately 118,000 children.

In spite of the acquisition's enormous potential, however, the deal involved a number of risks. Many industry analysts felt that Knowledge Learning was paying too much for the rival company, pointing out that the overall price tag came to roughly $25 a share, nearly double KinderCare's stock value at the time of the agreement. On the other hand, Knowledge Universe chairman Milken saw enormous growth potential in the private early-education industry, as the population of toddler-age children in the United States was expected to increase by 1.2 million between 2004 and 2010. At the same time, the deal came at a time when American parents were spending more money on supplemental educational programs and products. Indeed, by mid-decade, education had become the second-largest economic sector in the country, comprising almost 9 percent of U.S. gross domestic product.

## LARGEST U.S. PRIVATE EDUCATION COMPANY, AND GROWING: 2005–10

The KinderCare acquisition was finalized in January 2005. With the purchase, Knowledge Learning Corporation became the largest for-profit private education company in the United States, with more than 2,000 facilities nationwide and annual revenues of $1.4 billion. The deal prompted Knowledge Learning to overhaul its corporate structure. Less than two weeks after completing the merger, the company announced that it would be relocating its headquarters to Portland, Oregon, where KinderCare had been based since 1997. As part of the move, Knowledge Learning consolidated all of its corporate offices into the new location, shutting down

administrative facilities in San Rafael, California; Golden, Colorado; and Minneapolis, Minnesota. In June 2005 Knowledge Learning leased a new 80,000-square-foot office facility at Portland's Liberty Centre, in addition to occupying a smaller space in the nearby Oregon Square Building.

As the decade drew to a close Knowledge Learning continued to seek new growth opportunities. In 2007 the company acquired Children's Creative Learning Centers, Inc., a firm specializing in providing day-care services for corporations, universities, and other major institutions. In September 2008 Knowledge Learning launched a $186 million bid for Nobel Learning Communities, Inc., a Pennsylvania-based private-school operator. In March 2009, after months of negotiations, Knowledge Learning lowered its offer to $136 million, based largely on Nobel's slumping stock price. Although Nobel ultimately rejected the offer, Knowledge Learning had clearly positioned itself to be a dominant player in the private-education sector for years to come.

*Ed Dinger*
*Updated, Stephen Meyer*

## PRINCIPAL DIVISIONS

Champions; Children's Creative Learning Centers, Inc.; KinderCare Learning Centers, Inc.; Knowledge Beginnings, Inc.

## PRINCIPAL COMPETITORS

Bright Horizons Family Solutions LLC; Child Development Schools, Inc.; Imagine Schools, Inc.; Learning Care Group Inc.; Mosaica Education, Inc.; National Heritage Academies, Inc.; Nobel Learning Communities, Inc.

## FURTHER READING

Atlas, Riva D., "Milken Sees the Classroom as Profit Center," *New York Times*, December 18, 2004, p. C1.

Baker, Russ, "The Education of Mike Milken: From Junk-bond King to Master of the Knowledge Universe," *Nation*, May 3, 1999, p. 11.

Carlsen, Clifford, "Growing Child-care Chain Poised for Expansion Spurt," *San Francisco Business Times*, October 29, 1993, p. 3.

Diakantonis, Demitri, "Nobel, KLC Lose Gloves," *Daily Deal*, March 20, 2009.

Fernandez, Bob, "Aramark Sells Child-care Unit," *Philadelphia Inquirer*, March 5, 2003, p. D3.

Galagan, Patricia, "Bullet Train," *Training & Development*, July 1999, p. 22.

Hunsberger, Ken, "Knowledge Learning Will Settle in Portland," *Oregonian*, January 12, 2005, p. C1.

Martin, Judith, "Lifelong Learning Spells Earnings," *Fortune*, July 6, 1998, p. 197.

Morris, Kathleen, "Professor Milken's Lesson Plan," *Business Week*, August 4, 1997, p. 32.

Whiteman, Lou, "Nobel Disappointed with New Bid," *Daily Deal*, March 12, 2009.

# Koenigsegg Automotive AB

262 91
Ängelholm,
Sweden
Telephone: (+46 431) 45 44 60
Fax: (+46 431) 45 44 61
Web site: http://www.koenigsegg.com/

*Private Company*
*Founded:* 1994
*Employees:* 45
*NAICS:* 336111 Automobile Manufacturing; 336211 Motor Vehicle Body Manufacturing; 336322 Other Motor Vehicle Electrical and Electronic Equipment Manufacturing

■ ■ ■

Koenigsegg Automotive AB is a leading designer and producer of supercars. Founded in 1994, it is also one of the youngest. Headquartered near Ängelholm, Sweden, the company is located on property that formerly housed a Swedish Air Force jet fighter squadron. The market for hand-made supercars such as Koenigsegg's, which assembles each car for a specific buyer, is small and exclusive. As a result, Koenigsegg has pursued this niche market exclusively, with one exception, when it headed a consortium in 2009 that tried unsuccessfully to purchase Saab Automobile from General Motors Company.

## ESTABLISHING A NEW SUPERCAR

Koenigsegg was founded in 1994 by Christian von Koenigsegg, who had attempted to sell new technologies in several other fields before deciding, at the age of 22, to create the ultimate car. The initial plan was to build a two-seater car with a hard top and midengine layout (the engine placed between the rear and front axles) that used technology adapted from Formula One race cars. The company assembled a team of designers and engineers and by 1996 it began testing its first prototype.

The prototype, the Koenigsegg CC, was tested and then unveiled at the Cannes Film Festival in 1997. By this time, another feature of the company's cars was a lightweight construction using carbon fiber (a composite material) and hand-made metal. Three years later, after more development and testing, the company premiered its first production prototype at the Paris Motor Show. After receiving good reviews and performing well in tests conducted by the *Car and Driver* magazine, the company sold its first car, a Koenigsegg CC 8S, in 2002. The company built five cars that first year of production and began displaying them at auto shows outside Europe for the first time.

In 2004 Koenigsegg introduced the CCR, which had greater horsepower. The following year the CCR took the top speed mark for road cars from the McLaren F1, which had held the record for the past seven years. The third-generation Koenigsegg, the CCX, followed in 2006, and a year later the company introduced the CCXR, the world's first green supercar.

## COMPANY PERSPECTIVES

■

Koenigsegg manufactures exclusive super sports cars for a select elite of enthusiasts. Space age materials and uncompromising quality both in finish and function make these cars among the very best. They reach higher top speeds and are more powerful than any other series-produced car today.

Because it used E85 Biofuel, a high-octane ethanol, the car's horsepower was actually boosted by the biofuel.

By 2008 the company's annual production was up to 35 cars, and the CCX became the first Koenigsegg to be "street-legal" in the United States, meaning that it was capable of passing all official tests and inspections for use on U.S. public roads. The company had 45 employees and sold a total of 18 cars that year. In March 2009 it unveiled its prototype for the Quant, its first four-seat, four-door car, at the Geneva Motor Show. The Quant also carried the green theme forward: it would be the company's first electric car as well as its first solar vehicle, in that the battery power would be supplemented by an invisible paint coating that drew energy from sunlight.

In 2009 Koenigsegg's ownership profile included a 49-percent stake that was held by Eker Group AS of Norway and a 22-percent share owned by the investor Mark Bishop of San Diego, California. That same year the company's public profile grew in an unexpected direction when it emerged as one of three bidders for Saab Automobile, the renowned but money-losing Swedish automaker that General Motors was planning to divest. In June of that year General Motors announced that it had agreed to sell Saab for an undisclosed sum to a consortium led by Koenigsegg.

### THE SAAB DEAL

Following the purchase, Saab would settle the $1.3 billion in debt it owed to more than 600 creditors, including auto suppliers, the Swedish government, and General Motors for 25 cents on the dollar. The new owner would get a $600 million loan from the European Investment Bank and assets from General Motors that included platforms, powertrain (engine and transmission) technology, and some $500 million in cash and other assets. All this would give Koenigsegg a head start in achieving a necessary 140,000 car sales a year and completing development and production on two new Saab models.

"Closing this deal represents the best chance for Saab to emerge a stronger company," Carl-Peter Forster, the president of General Motors Europe, said in a press statement that was published in *Ward's Auto World*. "Koenigsegg Group's unique combination of innovation, entrepreneurial spirit and financial strength, combined with Koenigsegg's proven ability to create world-class Swedish performance cars in a highly efficient manner, made it the right choice for Saab as well as for General Motors."

However, beginning in August 2009 there was concern that the deal would not be completed. Bishop was reported to have sold his stake in Koenigsegg. Without Bishop, Koenigsegg had only 70 percent of the needed financing to complete the Saab deal. Unable to close the shortfall on its own, the company asked the Swedish government for assistance. In September the Swedish government, which was reluctant to bail out failing companies, responded by declining to help the carmaker.

Regardless, Koenigsegg was still able to close the gap when it signed a deal with Beijing Automotive Industry Holding Company (BAIC), one of China's leading commercial vehicle manufacturers. John Reed of the *Financial Times* noted that BAIC would invest approximately $400 million in Koenigsegg, part of which would give it a noncontrolling minority stake in the European carmaker, and in return the two would "explore growth opportunities" for Saab in China. "This is an important step on the road to a new Saab Automobile," von Koenigsegg told Reed. "We have a solid business plan, an important partnership and we are now in a position to go ahead without any governmental financing."

Then in November the Saab deal collapsed unexpectedly when Koenigsegg pulled out of talks with General Motors. According to John Reed and Andrew Ward of the *Financial Times*, the company said: "Unfortunately, delays in closing this acquisition have resulted in risks and uncertainties that prevent us from successfully implementing the new Saab Automobile business plan." Despite this setback, General Motors announced in December that the Netherlands sports carmaker Spyker Cars would be buying Saab for $400 million.

### LOOKING AHEAD

Meanwhile, Koenigsegg continued to expand its line of supercars. In September 2009 it introduced the Trevita, which featured a carbon-fiber body that was coated with a diamond finish. The company planned on producing only three of the cars. In March 2010, marking its 15th

```
┌─────────────────────────────────────────┐
│                                         │
│            KEY DATES                    │
│               ▪                         │
├─────────────────────────────────────────┤
│  1994:  Koenigsegg Automobile AB is     │
│         launched.                       │
│  2002:  Koenigsegg's first automobile   │
│         is sold.                        │
│  2007:  Koenigsegg introduces the CCXR, │
│         the world's first green         │
│         supercar.                       │
│  2008:  Koenigsegg meets U.S.           │
│         specifications and delivers its │
│         first car to the United States. │
│  2009:  Koenigsegg ends a six-month     │
│         effort to assemble financing to │
│         purchase Saab Automobile from   │
│         General Motors Company.         │
│                                         │
└─────────────────────────────────────────┘
```

year, Koenigsegg unveiled a new model, the Agera, at the Geneva Motor Show. The company anticipated producing 16 to 20 cars of the new model per year.

The company was also moving ahead with its plans to go into production of the Quant, its prototype solar-electric car. This model promised to keep Koenigsegg abreast of sports carmakers such as Ferrari and Porsche, which were unveiling their own hybrid vehicles. Furthermore, Koenigsegg was working to meet new European Union emissions standards that were scheduled to go into effect in 2012.

*Eric Laursen*

## PRINCIPAL COMPETITORS

Aston Martin; Automobili Lamborghini S.p.A.; Bugatti Automobiles S.A.S.; Dr. Ing. h.c.F. Porsche AG; Maserati S.p.A.; McLaren Automotive; Mercedes-Benz USA, LLC; Pagani Automobili S.p.A.; Saleen Performance Vehicles.

## FURTHER READING

Edmondson, Ian, and Sharon Terlep, "New Swedish Owner Could Give Saab a Fresh Lease on Life," *Wall Street Journal*, June 17, 2009, p. A1.

"Koenigsegg Agera," *Motoring Monthly*, April 15, 2010.

Reed, John, "BAIC to Help Koenigsegg Expand Saab in China," *Financial Times* (London), September 9, 2009.

Reed, John, and Andrew Ward, "Koenigsegg Pulls out of Talks to Buy Saab," *Financial Times* (London), November 24, 2009.

Ulrich, Lawrence, "Tiny Carmaker Lands Saab," *New York Times*, June 21, 2009, p. 8L.

———, "Who Wants to Drive a Millionaire?" *New York Times*, July 6, 2008, p. 1L.

Vaughn, Mark, "Better Than Abba: CCX Is the Latest and Best from Swedish Supercarmaker Koenigsegg," *AutoWeek*, October 30, 2006, p. 20.

Ward, Andrew, "Funding Gap Casts Saab Deal Shadow," *Financial Times* (London), August 19, 2009, p. 12.

# Kohlberg Kravis Roberts & Co. L.P.

—————■—————

9 West 57th Street, Suite 4200
New York, New York 10019
U.S.A.
Telephone: ((212)) 750-8300
Fax: ((212)) 750-0003
Web site: http://www.kkr.com

*Public Company*
*Founded:* 1976
*Employees:* 1,433 (est.)
*Total Assets:* $52.2 billion (2009)
*Stock Exchanges:* Amsterdam
*Ticker Symbol:* KKR
*NAICS:* 523120 Securities Brokerage

■ ■ ■

Kohlberg Kravis Roberts & Co. L.P. (KKR) is one of the largest private-equity firms in the United States. In 2009 the company oversaw the management of more than $50 billion in investment funds, while its portfolio of companies in the United States and Europe boasted aggregate revenues of more than $100 billion and included such industry giants as hospital operator HCA Inc., Texas utility TXU, and the Toys R Us retail chain. A pioneer of the leveraged buyouts (LBOs) that privatized many American corporations in the 1980s, KKR has a number of deal-making firsts to its credit. In 1979 the firm staged the first large public-to-private transaction. KKR's most famous LBO was its 1989 acquisition of RJR Nabisco Inc. for an unprecedented $30.6 billion. The magnitude of the buyout stunned industry observers at the time and formed the basis of the 1990 book *Barbarians at the Gate* by Bryan Burrough and John Helyar. In the 21st century KKR moved toward becoming a public company, selling shares on the Amsterdam stock exchange through its overseas business unit KKR & Co. (Guernsey) L.P.

## A DECADE OF MEGABUCK DEALS: 1976–86

Jerome Kohlberg Jr. was in charge of the corporate finance department at the Wall Street firm of Bear, Stearns & Co. when he devised or first utilized, in 1965, the technique later to be called the leveraged buyout. Kohlberg believed a company would be better managed if it were owned by a small group of highly motivated investors (often including the top company executives) rather than thousands of shareholders who rarely had the knowledge or time to make sure the business was being run effectively. It would remain a key principle of KKR's operations throughout the firm's history. To raise the money, the investors would borrow heavily, as much as 10 times the cash they actually contributed, usually pledging as collateral the assets of the company they intended to acquire. They would reap their profit by later selling the company to new owners or issuing stock to the public.

George Roberts and his cousin Henry Kravis became protégés of Kohlberg at Bear, Stearns, although Roberts relocated to the company's San Francisco office. They conducted 14 buyouts between 1969 and 1975 with generally mediocre results in a time of recession and falling stock prices. One of the companies they bought for $27 million, Cobblers Industries, went

## COMPANY PERSPECTIVES

■

When our founders started KKR in 1976, leveraged buyouts were a novel form of corporate finance. With no financial services firm to model ourselves after, and little interest in copying an existing formula, we set out to build a firm based on principles and values that would provide a proper institutional foundation for years to come. Today, we believe we have succeeded.

The KKR name is associated with the successful execution of many of the world's largest and most complex private equity transactions worldwide. We have a focus on operational value creation, a global network of strong business relationships, a reputation for integrity and fair dealing, and a distinguished track record of generating attractive investment returns.

We attribute our success, in large part, to our culture and values. We have created a single, integrated culture that rewards investment discipline, creativity, determination, and patience, and encourages the sharing of information, resources, expertise, and best practices across our offices.

bankrupt. However, investors in Vapor Corporation, purchased in 1972 for about $37 million, recovered their stake twelvefold when the company was sold in 1978. Industrial Components Groups, a division of Rockwell International purchased in 1975, yielded 22 times the original investment in five years.

Restive at Bear, Stearns, Kohlberg persuaded Kravis and Roberts to join him in the partnership that opened its doors in 1976. KKR created an equity fund that KKR, as general partner, used to purchase companies. Adding to the pool were major lenders entitled to fixed returns and, where law permitted, sweeteners like warrants or common stock free or at bargain prices. A favorite inducement for banks was preferred stock, which offered an 85 percent tax exemption on dividends. Because of the huge debt incurred in LBOs, a prospective target had to be able to generate the high cash flow needed to make interest payments. This excluded high-technology companies with heavy research-and-development expenditures. The most attractive prospects were businesses like supermarket operators, provided they had little prior debt and a market niche that protected them from severe competitive pressures.

In 1977 KKR bought three companies, but investors were hard to find and the firm made no deals the next year. In 1979, however, KKR bought Houdaille Industries for about $355 million, by far the largest LBO transaction to that time and KKR's first buyout of a major publicly held company. Prior to then no LBO had been completed for much more than $100 million. For investing $12 million of its own money, KKR received 37 percent of the voting common stock. Investors, including big banks, now began to come on board. By the fall of 1980 the firm had paid nearly $800 million to acquire seven companies with combined annual sales totaling about $1.3 billion.

Another breakthrough for KKR came in 1981, when Roberts tapped a conservative investor (Oregon's public employees' pension fund) to contribute $178 million for the leveraged buyout of Fred Meyer Inc., one of the seven companies KKR acquired that year. Soon other state pension funds, looking for a better yield than what they were earning from bonds, were willing to sign on. By 1986, 11 state pension funds were partners in KKR equity pools. When KKR initiated a $5.6 billion fund, which was its largest ever, in 1987, the 11 pension funds provided 53 percent of the money.

In addition to pension funds and other limited partners willing to provide equity (about 10 percent of an LBO) and banks willing to make loans (60 percent), KKR needed subordinated lenders (30 percent), who earned a higher fixed rate by taking more risk because they were the last to get paid. Historically, insurance companies tended to be the main source of subordinated debt. By the mid-1980s, however, firms such as Drexel Burnham Lambert Inc. had assembled big money by attracting private investors to high-yield junk-bond funds that would assume the necessary risk.

For its own part, KKR collected the standard investment banking fee of around 1 percent for making a deal, which it usually invested in the stock of the acquired company. It also collected annual consulting fees from the acquired company. KKR partners sat on the boards of these companies and collected directors' fees. KKR also received a 1.5 percent annual management fee on the money in an equity fund not yet invested. But the real payoff for the firm, as general partner, was its 20 percent share of the capital gains from the eventual resale of the acquired company. KKR even took a fee (1 percent) when it sold a company at a loss. Everybody in the firm, from the partners to the secretaries, had a stake in the rewards.

By 1983 KKR was claiming an average annual return of 63 percent to its equity partners. That year KKR's fourth equity fund accumulated $1 billion from investors, enabling its roster of companies to reach 18,

## KEY DATES

∎

**1977:** Kohlberg Kravis Roberts & Co. L.P. (KKR) completes its first leveraged buyout (LBO).

**1979:** The firm's first major deal is made, for Houdaille Industries.

**1982:** The first equity capital fund is raised.

**1986:** The firm acts as "white knight" to Safeway grocery store chain.

**1989:** KKR executes the largest LBO in history ($31.4 billion) of RJR Nabisco, Inc.

**1996:** KKR makes its first European acquisition.

**2000:** The acquisition of Shoppers Drug Mart is the largest in Canadian history.

**2002:** Legrand SA is acquired.

**2006:** KKR creates KKR Private Equity Investors, a publicly traded investment fund.

**2007:** KKR orchestrates acquisition of Texas utility TXU for $45 billion, the largest LBO in history.

**2009:** KKR merges operations with KKR Private Equity Investors to begin public trading on Amsterdam exchange; KKR Private Equity Investors is renamed KKR & Co. (Guernsey) L.P.

acquired for a total of $3.5 billion. KKR was using this money for ever-bigger deals. In 1985 the firm acquired Storer Communications for a record $2.5 billion. When Storer was sold in 1988, KKR's partners achieved an annual return of around 50 percent. Also in 1985 KKR conducted its first hostile takeover. Previously it had made an acquisition only when management (which got a stake in the deal) agreed.

KKR launched a new $2 billion fund in 1986. The acquisition of Safeway Stores Inc. that year was the best transaction KKR ever made, according to a *Fortune* article that appeared 10 years later. The firm paid $4.3 billion but put down only $130 million itself and reaped more than $5 billion in realized and paper profits. KKR's remaining one-third stake in the company was valued at more than $3.5 billion in early 1997 and more than $7.4 billion by 2001. Even bigger was KKR's 1986 takeover of Beatrice Cos. for about $6.2 billion. The firm put up $402 million in equity capital, while Drexel provided $2.5 billion in junk bond financing. According to KKR, when the final returns from this deal were realized in 1992, limited partners enjoyed an annual return of 43 percent.

## THE GOING GETS TOUGHER: 1987–89

By this time, however, Kohlberg was on his way out. After spending 1984 recovering from a serious illness, he returned to find that he was not needed or wanted by his younger partners. Kohlberg was disturbed by KKR's increasingly aggressive search for deals that disturbingly echoed the tactics of corporate raiders. He vetoed so many prospective deals that he became known at KKR as "Doctor No." Kohlberg resigned in 1987 to form his own company but remained a limited partner in KKR. In 1990 Kohlberg sued his partners, alleging that they had illegally reduced his ownership stake in several buyout deals. The suit was settled under undisclosed terms.

Of the remaining founders, Kravis was the one who cast the higher profile. While Roberts, in California, avoided the limelight, "King Henry," as the media dubbed Kravis, married his second wife, fashion designer Carolyne Roehm. The couple was prominent on the social scene, contributing heavily to charities and maintaining a Manhattan duplex apartment plus homes in Colorado, Connecticut, and Long Island.

There seemed to be no limit to KKR's dominance at this time. Having raised $5.6 billion for its 1987 fund, the firm bought eight companies in the next two years for $43.9 billion, among them the more than $1 billion purchases of Owens-Illinois, Duracell, and Stop & Shop. If ranked as a single industrial company, the businesses KKR controlled would have placed it among the top 10 U.S. corporations. When stock prices plunged in October 1987, KKR secretly bought chunks of several top-level U.S. corporations but was unable to sell their chiefs on the LBO idea.

KKR's biggest LBO, which was indeed the biggest of all time, was its acquisition of RJR Nabisco, Inc., for $30.6 billion. The bidding started with a $17.5 billion offer from Shearson Lehman Hutton. Other interested parties included Merrill Lynch and Forstmann Little, neither of which charged a fee when it sold companies, an annual fee to manage them, or directors' fees for having their executives sit on the boards of the companies they controlled.

KKR topped Shearson, only to have the ante raised in turn by Forstmann Little. In what unsympathetic outsiders described as high-stakes macho posturing and a fitting end to a decade of greed, Kravis won the battle but clearly overpaid for his prize. KKR had to take 58 percent of the company itself. In 1990 it needed to pump in $1.7 billion more for a $6.9 billion recapitalization of RJR, which, after going public in 1991, lost more than $3 billion of its market value in the next two years. In 1995 KKR traded its remaining stake in RJR for ownership of Borden Inc.

KKR made other mistakes in 1987 and 1988. Jim Walter Corporation (later Walter Industries), purchased for about $2.4 billion, later went bankrupt. Seaman Furniture Co., acquired for about $360 million, had to be restructured in 1989 to avoid bankruptcy and was in bankruptcy during 1992 and 1993. Hillsborough Holdings Corporation, purchased for $3.3 billion, went bankrupt in 1989. American Forest Products, acquired from Bendix for $425 million, was sold at a loss.

## ADAPTING AND THRIVING IN THE NINETIES

After the completion of the RJR Nabisco deal in February 1989, KKR did not make another LBO acquisition for three years, not because of any loss of nerve but due to the collapse of the junk bond market, a growing reluctance of banks to lend for this purpose, and fewer corporate raiders to put companies into play. To some degree, KKR was a victim of its own success, because companies increasingly had put their houses in order before they became vulnerable to a takeover. "Paying off debt, getting rid of divisions that are not up to snuff— companies can do that for themselves now," a University of Chicago professor told a *New York Times* reporter in 1995.

Without lucrative LBOs to put into effect, KKR became less attractive to partners like the state pension funds, which then began complaining about its fees. In 1989 KKR had reported an annualized rate of return of 19.5 percent, well below its average. Investors wanted higher yields to compensate for high risk and the need to keep their money tied up until there was a payoff in the form of a company sale. Bad publicity concerning fired Safeway workers riled some limited partners, especially public pension funds whose constituents included unionized workers.

One alternative KKR tried was "leveraged buildups." The firm bought a piece of Macmillan Inc. in 1989 and turned it into K-III Holdings Inc., a publishing and information resources conglomerate that had made 52 acquisitions by 1997, when it was renamed Primedia Inc. This venture was unusual in that KKR took and continued to hold most of the equity itself. A similar transaction was KKR's 1991 injection of $283 million into Fleet/Norstar Financial Group for the purchase of the assets of the failed Bank of New England. KKR also took "toehold" minority positions in companies such as ConAgra Inc., Texaco Inc., and First Interstate Bancorp, remaining a passive investor.

KKR consoled itself and stilled its critics by taking six prior LBO acquisitions public in 1991 for a combined estimated $6 billion, which meant a sixfold return to the investors in five years, not counting the firm's own fees. In 1992 KKR purchased American Re-Insurance Co. for $1.2 billion, an LBO acquisition at $10 per share. Keeping a one-fourth stake, KKR took the company public only four months later at $31 per share. Also in 1992 the firm raised $1.8 billion for a new fund.

Even so, as the 1990s continued, disillusionment over KKR's performance became more vocal. A *Fortune* article claimed in 1994 that since the early 1980s the firm had barely outpaced the Standard & Poor 500 stock index, at least for its two largest investors, the Oregon and Washington state pension funds. In its 1996 annual report Oregon's state treasury said it was disappointed with the returns on more than half of its $2.1 billion investment in KKR funds, of which $1.2 billion was in the 1987 fund. Burdened by poor-performing investments in RJR Nabisco and K-III, this fund had an average annual yield of only 12.6 percent through 1996.

As the stock market roared ahead in the mid-1990s, KKR improved its record by cashing in some more of its acquisitions. The sale of Duracell, which had gone public in 1991 as Duracell International Inc., to Gillette Co. in 1996 for stock valued at $7.9 billion brought KKR $3.7 billion for an original investment of $350 million. Between the beginning of 1995 and September 1996 it sold, for $7 billion, stock originally acquired for $1.3 billion. This included American Re for $3.3 billion and Stop & Shop for $1.8 billion. In 1996 alone the firm sold five companies for $5.3 billion.

These gains were counterbalanced by some losers. Flagstar Corporation, in which the firm had invested $300 million in 1992, filed for bankruptcy in 1997. KKR put up $250 million for the $1.15 billion LBO in 1995 of the Bruno's Inc. grocery chain but wrote off the entire sum in early 1998, when the company's debt had reached about $1 billion. Spalding & Evenflo Cos., in which KKR had invested $420 million, was barely covering its interest payments in early 1998. Primedia (the former K-III) was still losing money after almost a decade because of the heavy cost of making payments on its acquisition debts.

KKR raised a record $6 billion for its 1996 fund. To raise this sum, the firm agreed for the first time to deduct losses from its profits and to reduce its transaction fees. Among the subscribers was the Oregon pension fund, which, despite its misgivings, committed to $800 million after a sales call by Roberts. For KKR the year was the firm's most lucrative ever, with Kravis and Roberts each believed to have collected $300 million. Kravis's personal fortune was estimated at more than $1 billion.

## EXPANDING INTO OVERSEAS MARKETS: 2000–04

KKR made dramatic forays into Canada in the early years of the 21st century, completing the two largest LBOs in the country's history in 2000 and 2002. Shoppers Drug Mart was acquired in 2000 for about $1.7 billion. Two years later KKR took the directories unit of Bell Canada Enterprises private for CAD 3 billion ($1.9 billion). *Buyouts* magazine described the deal in 2003 as an "asset that offered stable, predictable cash flow and low capital requirements," all key selling points for KKR. It was, at the time, Canada's largest-ever LBO.

The firm also entered the European LBO market at the turn of the century, completing some of the largest deals the continent had seen. KKR initiated this effort in 1996, amassing a EUR 3 billion fund by 1999. Early acquisitions included a British newspaper publisher called *Newsquest*, the insurance company Willis Corroon, and the engineering firm TI Group. KKR made its biggest European LBOs to date in 2002. It took Legrand SA, a French manufacturer of electrical equipment, private for EUR 3.6 billion, and it bought seven Siemens subsidiaries for EUR 1.7 billion. The Siemens companies were amalgamated under a holding company, Demag Holding s.a.r.l., and included Demag Cranes & Components, Gottwald Port Technology, Mannesmann Plastics & Machinery, Stabilus, Networks Systems, and Ceramics and Metering, with a combined annual sales volume of EUR 3.5 billion.

During this same period KKR managed, for the most part, to avoid the telecom and dot-com debacle. In 2001, however, it had to write off its barely two-year-old, $210 million investment in Birch Telecom Inc. KKR made relatively small investments in Desktop.com, Starmedia, Mypoints.com, PlanetRX, and LivePerson as well. Its forays into the online world included a relatively modest partnership with Accel Partners to create Accel-KKR Internet Co., a venture capital firm charged with merging companies' online and offline capabilities.

KKR looked forward to completing a $610 million purchase of International Transmission Co., an electricity transmission company, in the first quarter of 2003. It was the largest deal of its type at the time, and KKR indicated that it would continue to look for deals in the electricity transmission industry.

Although the firm continued to enjoy success in the early years of the 21st century, the question of succession at KKR loomed large. Founding partners and cousins Henry Kravis and George Roberts were both due to turn 60 years old by January 2004, and even though both expected to continue with the company thereafter, they concomitantly worked to prepare the

firm to outlast them. These preparations included shifting equity stakes in the firm to other partners, or "members," as KKR called them. The principal owners also cultivated a cadre of legal, accounting, and investment-banking professionals to carry on their legacy. An effort, however, to encourage longtime institutional investors Washington State Investment Board and Oregon Investment Council to purchase ownership stakes in KKR failed. In fact, the firm's Millennium Fund drive actually accumulated less money than its previous pool. Jacqueline Gold posited in *Crain's New York Business*, "Without the charismatic and reassuring presence of its name partners, putting together a multibillion-dollar pot will be that much harder" in the future.

## MOVING TOWARD AN IPO: 2005–10

By mid-decade KKR found itself facing a range of new challenges in a rapidly changing economic landscape. At the time, the company remained one of the leading private-equity firms in the United States, earning roughly $40 billion annually. In addition, KKR completed several major deals in 2004 and 2005, including acquisitions of mattress maker Sealy Corporation and the Toys R Us retail chain. Still, with many of its rivals diversifying into new fields such as hedge fund management, while simultaneously forming strongholds in emerging markets like Southeast Asia and India, KKR was compelled to alter its corporate philosophy in order to remain competitive. In September 2005 KKR established its first offices in Asia, opening branches in Tokyo and Hong Kong, and explored new opportunities in India. At the same time, the company developed a new strategy focused on expanding its portfolio of technology holdings, acquiring the semiconductor division of Agilent Technologies, along with software and IT firm SunGard Data Systems, for a combined $14 billion in 2005. In April 2006 KKR paid roughly $900 million for an 85 percent stake in Flextronics Software Systems, a leading Indian software maker. At the time, the deal represented the largest LBO in Indian history, and it was regarded by many analysts to be an important milestone in the development of the nation's private-equity market.

During this period KKR also began to explore new ways to raise capital. In May 2006 the company's publicly traded investment fund, KKR Private Equity Investors, launched an initial public offering on the Amsterdam stock exchange with the aim of raising $5 billion. By listing in Europe, KKR was taking advantage of the continent's more lenient regulatory policies, which allowed private-equity firms the power to operate simultaneously as public funds. The creation of a publicly traded division promised to open the KKR portfolio to a wider range of investors. Whereas traditional KKR funds required a minimum investment of $25 million, KKR Private Equity Investors provided potential shareholders with a more flexible means of purchasing stock in the company.

As KKR reshaped its core business philosophy, it also remained committed to expanding its holdings. During the first half of 2006 the company embarked on an acquisition spree, spending more than $215 billion on 30 companies. In July of that year KKR broke its own record for a leveraged buyout, joining three other investment firms to acquire hospital group HCA Inc. for $33 billion. Even with these successful deals, the company suffered some key setbacks during this time. In October 2006 KKR's attempt to purchase Australian retail giant Coles Myer was rejected by the company's board. At around that time, the company launched a bid to acquire the French media firm Vivendi in a buyout worth an estimated EUR 40 billion ($51 billion), but the proposed bid ultimately fell apart. Undeterred, KKR continued its aggressive pursuit of new opportunities heading into 2007. In February of that year KKR joined private-equity firm TPG to acquire Texas utilities giant TXU for $45 billion, once again smashing its own record for an LBO. A month later the company acquired retail chain Dollar General for $6.9 billion, the highest price paid for a U.S. retailer in history. In April KKR acquired credit card behemoth First Data for $25.6 billion. By mid-2007 KKR had stakes in 36 major companies, with combined revenues of more than $100 billion a year. The company was managing roughly $53 billion in investment assets.

In July 2007 KKR signaled its intention to become a public company, filing preliminary papers with the Securities and Exchange Commission (SEC). A month later, however, as the nation's private-equity markets were rapidly deteriorating, the company announced that it would delay its initial public offering. By March 2008 KKR's IPO was in doubt as prospects for the financial sector became increasingly bleak. After several false starts, in November of that year KKR once again postponed its IPO in the hope that financial markets would improve in the near future. For the year, KKR suffered losses of $1.2 billion. By mid-2009 several of the key acquisitions from KKR's 2007 buying spree, including the five largest companies, had lost value. One notable exception was Dollar General, which had increased in value by nearly 31 percent over a two-year span.

In October 2009 KKR aborted its plan to list publicly on the New York Stock Exchange (NYSE), opt-

ing instead to merge with its European unit, KKR Private Equity Investors. As part of the deal, KKR relinquished a 30 percent stake in the company for roughly $3 billion in assets controlled by KKR Private Equity Investors. In this way KKR was able to list itself on the Amsterdam exchange while retaining the right to switch its listing to the NYSE within six months. As part of the deal, KKR Private Equity Investors was renamed KKR & Co. (Guernsey) L.P. By February 2010, with the global financial markets slowly recovering, shares in KKR Guernsey had quintupled, and KKR was once again prepared to list its shares on the NYSE. The company's cautious maneuverings in the midst of uncertain economic conditions seemed to have paid off, at least in the short term.

*Robert Halasz*
*Updated, April D. Gasbarre; Stephen Meyer*

## PRINCIPAL SUBSIDIARIES

KKR Asset Management; KKR Financial LLC; KKR MENA Limited (United Arab Emirates); Kohlberg Kravis Roberts & Co. (Fixed Income) LLC.

## PRINCIPAL COMPETITORS

Bain Capital, LLC; The Blackstone Group L.P.; The Carlyle Group, L.P.; Clayton, Dubilier & Rice, Inc.; Forstmann Little & Co.; HM Capital Partners LLC; Thomas H. Lee Partners L.P.; TPG Capital, L.P.; Warburg Pincus LLC.

## FURTHER READING

Anders, George, *Merchants of Debt: KKR and the Mortgaging of American Business.* Frederick, MD: Beard Group, 2002.

Arenson, Karen W., "Kohlberg's Leveraged Success," *New York Times*, September 29, 1980, pp. D1, D5.

Arnold, Martin, "KKR Unveils $2.2bn Listing Plan as Market Recovery Ends Delay," *Financial Times*, March 13, 2010, p. 1.

Bianco, Anthony, "KKR Hears a New Word from Some Backers: 'No,'" *BusinessWeek*, April 15, 1991, pp. 80–82.

Burrough, Bryan, and John Helyar, *Barbarians at the Gate.* New York: Harper & Row, 1990.

Carey, David, "Mediocrity at the Gates," *Daily Deal*, May 31, 2001.

Hylton, Richard D., "How KKR Got Beaten at Its Own Game," *Fortune*, May 2, 1994, pp. 104–06.

Lipin, Steven, "KKR Is Back, and It Boasts Big War Chest," *Wall Street Journal*, September 16, 1996, pp. C1, C15.

Rustin, Richard E., "Kohlberg Kravis Hones Its Takeover Technique," *Wall Street Journal*, September 25, 1980, pp. 35, 38.

Teitelbaum, Richard, "KKR Dominates 'Golden Age' of Equity," *International Herald Tribune*, July 2, 2007, p. 14.

Truell, Peter, "At KKR the Glory Days Are Past," *New York Times*, August 10, 1995, pp. D1, D4.

# Lucasfilm Ltd.

P.O. Box 29901
San Francisco, California 94129
U.S.A.
Telephone: (415) 623-1800
Web site: http://www.lucasfilm.com

*Private Company*
*Incorporated:* 1971
*Employees:* 1,800 (est.)
*Sales:* $1.20 billion (2009 est.)
*NAICS:* 339932 Game, Toy, and Children's Vehicle Manufacturing; 512110 Motion Picture and Video Production; 512120 Motion Picture and Video Distribution; 512191 Teleproduction and Other Postproduction Services

∎ ∎ ∎

Lucasfilm Ltd. is an independent film and television production and distribution company developed by George Lucas, the creator of the popular and profitable Star Wars and Indiana Jones film series. Responsible for some of the biggest blockbusters in cinema history, the company ranks among the largest motion picture companies in the United States. Divisions of Lucasfilm include Industrial Light & Magic (ILM), the world's foremost visual effects production facility; Skywalker Sound, a premier sound-engineering facility; animation studios in the United States and Singapore; LucasArts, an interactive multimedia producer of Star Wars games and other computer software for entertainment and education; and Lucas Licensing, which oversees the

licensing responsibilities for Lucasfilm's lucrative intellectual properties. In 2005 Lucas moved several of these operations into new facilities in San Francisco's Presidio district, near the Golden Gate Bridge.

## GEORGE LUCAS BREAKS INTO THE MOVIE BUSINESS: 1971

Company founder George Lucas was born in 1945 in Modesto, California, and was educated at the University of Southern California's (USC) film school. Having won a scholarship to observe Francis Ford Coppola direct the film *Finian's Rainbow*, Lucas would later recall in a *New York Times* interview, "Francis forced me to become a writer and to think about things other than abstract and documentary films." In 1971 Lucas wrote and directed his first feature film, *THX 1138*, the story of a future world in which people live in underground cities run by computers. Inspired by a short film he wrote while a student at USC, *THX 1138* was produced by Coppola's American Zoetrope studios. At the same time, Lucas created his own film company, Lucasfilm Ltd., with offices in Hollywood, across the street from Universal Studios.

In 1973 Lucas experienced his first commercial success as director and co-writer of the film *American Graffiti*, a humorous look at one evening in the lives of some recent high-school graduates in the early 1960s. In addition to receiving a Golden Globe award and prizes from the New York Film Critics and the National Society of Film Critics, *American Graffiti* received five Academy Award nominations. Moreover, Lucas became known as one of the most popular directors in Hollywood, and his company began to expand. During this time, for example, Lucas founded Sprocket Systems, which later became Skywalker Sound, a full-service audio post-production facility. He also created Industrial Light & Magic to develop the use of computer graphics in film, focusing particularly on the striking visual effects that would be used in the upcoming film *Star Wars*.

### *STAR WARS* IS BORN: 1977

Lucas wrote and directed the first *Star Wars* film in 1977. Made by Lucas and Lucasfilm for 20th Century-Fox, the film reportedly incurred production costs of about $6.5 million. A fantasy/science fiction tale featuring a young hero, a princess, a pilot, a villain, and a host of robots and creatures, *Star Wars* became a number one box-office attraction as well as an important part of U.S. culture and film history. The film's characters also became the basis for a very profitable line of children's toy figures and other merchandise. In fact, profits from *Star Wars* allowed Lucas to fully finance subsequent films in the series and to retain a higher portion of the profits. Over the next six years, Lucas wrote and executive produced the Star Wars sequels *The Empire Strikes Back* (1980) and *The Return of the Jedi* (1983). For more than a decade, all three films remained among the top 15 box-office attractions of all time and would continue to generate record toy sales.

In the early 1980s a wholly owned subsidiary, LucasArts Entertainment Company, was added to Lucasfilm's holdings, providing, according to company literature, "an interactive element in George Lucas's vision of a state-of-the-art, multi-faceted entertainment company." LucasArts developed, in part, under the leadership of R. Douglas Norby, who joined Lucasfilm in 1985 after serving as chief financial officer at Syntex Corporation. As president and chief executive officer of LucasArts until 1992, Norby helped the subsidiary become a leading developer of entertaining and interactive multimedia computer software for schools, homes, and arcades. Such products combined Lucas's storytell-

ing and character development strengths with the newest, most advanced technologies available. Early game efforts included: *Battlehawks 1942, Their Finest Hour: The Battle of Britain, Loom, Maniac Mansion, Secret Weapons of the Luftwaffe*, and *The Secret of Monkey Island*. The company also produced software products based on the Star Wars and the Indiana Jones series. *X-Wing* would become the best-selling CD-ROM entertainment title of 1993, and in 1994 *Rebel Assault* became one of the best-selling CD-ROM software products of all time. The company also produced educational products in partnership with such organizations as Apple Multimedia Lab, the National Geographic Society, and the Smithsonian Institution.

LucasArts was also charged with overseeing the licensing and design of toys and other products based on Lucasfilm ideas and characters. Comic books and novels extending the Star Wars and Indiana Jones universes were successful ventures for LucasArts. In 1991 the *New York Times* indicated that LucasArts-licensed Star Wars toys had grossed more than $2.6 billion dollars around the world.

### LUCAS BREAKS FROM HOLLYWOOD TRADITION: 1981

As Lucasfilm continued to profit, George Lucas gradually began to separate himself from traditional Hollywood. In 1981 he relinquished membership in the Academy of Motion Picture Arts and Sciences, the Writers Guild, and the Directors Guild and began moving his offices to Skywalker Ranch, a 3,000-acre secluded production facility located in San Rafael, 25 miles from San Francisco. Named for the *Star Wars* character Luke Skywalker, the ranch became the business and production hub of the Lucas financial empire. Discussing his intentions for the new ranch complex in an interview in the *New York Times*, Lucas said, "As opposed to Hollywood, where the film makers support the corporate entity, Lucasfilm will support the overhead of the ranch. We'll make money out of the money by buying real estate, cable, satellite, solar energy—without buying anything we're ashamed of, like pesticides—and then the corporation will give us the money to make films."

Despite their detachment from Hollywood, Lucas and Lucasfilm continued to create widely successful films, producing another huge global hit in the Indiana Jones movies, which were directed by Lucas's friend and colleague Steven Spielberg. The three movies, *Raiders of the Lost Ark* (1981), *Indiana Jones and the Temple of Doom* (1984), and *Indiana Jones and the Last Crusade* (1989), featured the adventures of Indiana Jones, an heroic archaeologist whose work brings him into contact with villains, dangerous situations, and romance.

## KEY DATES

**1971:** Lucasfilm Ltd. incorporates; George Lucas writes and directs his first feature film, *THX 1138*.

**1973:** Lucas experiences commercial success with the film *American Graffiti*.

**1975:** Industrial Light & Magic is established to produce visual effects for the upcoming *Star Wars* film.

**1977:** *Star Wars* is released and wins six Academy Awards.

**1981:** *Raiders of the Lost Ark* is released.

**1983:** *Return of the Jedi* is released to complete the Star Wars trilogy; the Computer Division reorganizes to form Pixar and Games.

**1986:** Lucasfilm sells Pixar to Steven Jobs of Apple Inc.

**1989:** LucasArts Entertainment Company is established, which includes the Games Division.

**1999:** *Star Wars Episode One: The Phantom Menace* is released.

**2005:** Lucasfilm moves into new facilities, the Letterman Digital Arts Center in San Francisco; Star Wars becomes the leading toy line in the United States.

Not all Lucasfilm productions achieved commercial success. Such motion pictures as *More American Graffiti* (1979), *Howard the Duck* (1986), *Labyrinth* (1986), and *Radioland Murders* (1994) met with disappointing ticket sales and critical reviews. Nevertheless, George Lucas remained a leader in his field. In 1992 he received the Academy of Motion Picture Arts and Sciences' prestigious Irving G. Thalberg award for pioneering work in film technology. Moreover, any losses the company incurred through its few commercial disappointments were offset by Lucasfilm's involvement in all aspects of movie production. ILM in particular began to thrive and gradually became the company's most profitable division.

## SPECIAL EFFECTS DIVISION ADVANCES INDUSTRY TECHNOLOGY: 1985

Described by Lucasfilm as "the largest and most advanced digital effects system in the entertainment industry," ILM not only mastered the traditional arts of blue screen photography, matte painting, and model construction, but also pioneered the development of motion control cameras, optical compositing, and other advances in special effects technology. Its use of computer graphics and digital imaging in feature films also involved developing such breakthrough techniques as "morphing," which allowed the seamless transformation of one object into another. ILM's film credits in the 1980s and 1990s included most of the Star Trek movies, *ET: The Extraterrestrial* (1982), *Cocoon* (1985), *Back to the Future* (1985), *Who Framed Roger Rabbit?* (1988), *Ghost* (1990), *Terminator 2: Judgment Day* (1991), *Jurassic Park* (1993), *Schindler's List* (1993), *Forrest Gump* (1994), and many others. In fact, by the end of 1994, ILM had handled special effects for more than 100 feature films, several of which won Academy Awards for best visual effects and technical achievement.

ILM also began working with Walt Disney Productions in 1985, developing over the years such theme park attractions as Captain EO (1986) for Disneyland, Body Wars (1989) for Disney World's EPCOT Center, and Space Race (1991), a simulator ride for Showscan.

Skywalker Sound was also thriving during this time, with sound post-production studios in Santa Monica, West Los Angeles, and at the Skywalker Ranch complex. At these facilities, which comprised sound and foley stages, mixing and editing studios, and screening rooms, all renowned for their technical sophistication and versatility, the sound was recorded for such popular films as *Jurassic Park, Mrs. Doubtfire* (1993), and *Quiz Show* (1994). Skywalker also worked on many television commercials.

## THE EMPIRE CONTINUES TO EXPAND: 1993

In February 1993 Lucasfilm announced a reorganization, opting to spin off ILM and Skywalker Sound into units of a new company called Lucas Digital Ltd. Film producer Lindsley Parsons, Jr., a former manager of production at MGM/UA Entertainment, CBS Theatrical Films, and Paramount Pictures, was named president and CEO of Lucas Digital, while George Lucas served as the company's chairperson. Two months later, Lucas Digital's ILM subunit teamed up with Silicon Graphics Inc., of Mountain View, California, to create the Joint Environment for Digital Imaging (the acronym JEDI referring to the heroic knights of the Star Wars trilogy). The joint effort was created to serve as a film production unit as well as a test lab for new technology in visual effects.

During this time, Lucasfilm also made a name for itself in the field of television production, notably through the 1993 television series *The Young Indiana Jones Chronicles*. Written and executive produced by George Lucas, the series won the Banff Award for Best Continuing Series, a Golden Globe nomination for best dramatic series, an Angel Award for Quality Programming, and 10 Emmy Awards.

Another of Lucasfilm's activities involved its THX Group, which, according to Lucasfilm literature, was "dedicated to ensuring excellence in film presentation." The commercial portion of the certification program, developed in 1982, involved certifying the quality of the listening environment in commercial theaters. THX-certified theaters were required to meet Lucasfilm standards for such factors as speaker layout, acoustics, noise levels, and equalization of the signal. The THX system also had applications in the home theater, a concept that was gaining popularity in the mid-1990s. Lucasfilm's home THX system certified equipment to ensure that it maintained the quality of film sound as it was transferred to the home. THX became an independent company in 2001.

In the mid-1990s George Lucas remained very involved in the arts and education, serving as chairperson of the George Lucas Educational Foundation as well as on the board of directors of the National Geographic Society Education Foundation, the Artists Rights Foundation, the Joseph Campbell Foundation, and the Film Foundation. He was also a member of the USC School of Cinema-Television Board of Councilors. Moreover, Lucasfilm remained poised for growth, announcing plans in 1994 to produce three more installments of the Star Wars series and one more installment of the Indiana Jones series. Plans were to film the three Star Wars films simultaneously and to release them biannually, beginning in 1998 or 1999. Steven Spielberg agreed at that time to direct the fourth Indiana Jones movie.

## NEW TECHNOLOGIES AND NEW STAR WARS MOVIES: 1999

George Lucas's announcement that he would re-release the original Star Wars series, remastered and enhanced, and that he would direct three additional Star Wars films that would reveal the history behind the original trilogy, sparked a host of commercial deals. Companies clamored to tie into the Star Wars legacy. In 1996 Lucasfilm and PepsiCo aligned forces in a global marketing deal worth approximately $2 billion. Random House and Scholastic joined as well, signing agreements with Lucasfilm to develop books based on the forthcoming prequels. Under the agreement, Scholastic would publish three sets of Star Wars books for each new format, and a novelization of each new film. Fox also

secured a deal. It agreed to distribute all three of the upcoming movies and received, for an undisclosed sum, the network broadcast rights to the first of the three films. Unity, a communications agency, was hired to mastermind the global marketing launch of *Star Wars Episode One*, in 1999. The much sought after multi-year, multi-million dollar toy rights went to Galoob and Hasbro, prompting Hasbro to purchase Galoob. Nintendo snagged another hot deal: the rights to Star Wars video games.

The 1997 re-release of *Star Wars*, the first movie in the original trilogy, grossed more than $250 million domestically, a good start to the upcoming string of re-releases and prequels. George Lucas stunned the movie industry in 1999 when he announced that Lucasfilm would bankroll the first digital projectors to be used in theaters. The projectors' debut would be timed to show the first of the three Star Wars prequels. The first movie in the prequel series, *Star Wars Episode One: The Phantom Menace*, was released on May 19, 1999.

Later in 1999, Lucasfilm was selected by the trustees of the new Presidio National Park, intended to become a part of Golden Gate National Recreation Area in San Francisco, California, to develop a motion picture complex at the site. Additional strides in technology were taken, over the years, by ILM, the largest f/x studio in the film business. The company supplied complex computer graphics for several notable films, including *The Mummy* (1999), *A.I. Artificial Intelligence* (2001), *Pearl Harbor* (2001), and *Harry Potter and the Chamber of Secrets* (2002).

## LUCASFILM BY THE BAY: 2005

Although the releases of *Star Wars Episode One: The Phantom Menace* and *Star Wars Episode Two: Attack of the Clones* (2002) were financially successful, there were lessons to be learned. Toys and games sold as forecast, but apparel and some other products did not sell as anticipated. After a disappointing run of apparel sales after *Episode One* release, retailers vowed to be more cautious. Also, just days after releasing *Episode One* in the United States, Lucasfilm found that hawkers in many foreign countries managed to procure bootleg copies of the film to sell on the streets. In order to avoid the same problem, Lucasfilm decided to release the second movie worldwide on the same day: May 16, 2002. Lucasfilm created its own "underground" Web site, complete with fake news stories and features in order to keep ahead of the game and scoop the unauthorized Internet sites.

*Episode Two* was one of the highest-grossing films of 2002, although it was beaten by *Spiderman* and *The*

*Lord of the Rings: The Two Towers.* The last release in the six-film cycle, *Star Wars Episode Three: Revenge of the Sith* (2005), took the number-one spot for domestic gross box office receipts in 2005. As of 2010, the six movies had earned a combined worldwide total of over $4.3 billion in ticket sales.

The films themselves, of course, constitute only one stream of Star Wars revenue for Lucasfilm. Over time, merchandising based on the films' characters and fictional universe has proven substantially more lucrative. The year of *Episode Three*'s release, 2005, was the most successful year in the history of LucasArts, the company's games division. Star Wars toys and games stood atop the licensed toy market by a wide margin. Action figures, light sabers, video games, role-playing games, Lego sets, and novelties such as the Darth Vader Voice Changer have helped the company take in far in excess of $10 billion in retail sales over the three-decade-plus life cycle of the Star Wars brand.

In June 2005 Lucasfilm unveiled its new Letterman Digital Arts Center in San Francisco's Presidio. The 23-acre production campus featured the world's largest computer network devoted to entertainment, including an industrial-size "render farm" to convert data into sophisticated computer-generated imagery (CGI). Industrial Light and Magic, LucasArts, and Lucasfilm Animation soon took up residence in the new facility. The proximity was intended to stimulate increased collaboration between the filmmaking and video-gaming segments of the business. ILM and LucasArts also shared a common software platform, a proprietary application named Zeno, in order to facilitate further coordination. Later in 2005, Lucasfilm opened a second animation studio, this one in Singapore. The offshore image factory was set to work creating *Clone Wars*, an animated television series based on the Star Wars saga. Lucas hinted in 2006 that the company would be reducing its emphasis on theatrical blockbusters because of the expense and investment risk.

Nevertheless, the company spent much of 2007 preparing for the release of *Indiana Jones and the Kingdom of the Crystal Skull* the following spring. Attending the release was a host of corporate tie-ins, from Hasbro and Lego to Burger King and M&M's. Howard Roffman, head of Lucas Licensing, told *Daily Variety*, "It's been 19 years since the last film, and we are sensing a huge pent-up demand for everything Indy." The fourth Indiana Jones vehicle, once again directed by Steven Spielberg and starring the 65-year-old Harrison Ford, earned more than $700 million worldwide. The film's distributor, Paramount Pictures, invested more than $150 million in marketing.

## DEVELOPING FURTHER FILM AND TELEVISION PROJECTS: 2008–10

That galaxy far, far away returned to the big screen in a new way in August 2008 with *Star Wars: The Clone Wars*. After viewing footage for the animated TV series preparing to premiere on Cartoon Network, Lucas and Warner Brothers executives decided to introduce the project in theaters. The CGI film was produced for under $10 million, a relatively low budget by the standards of the live-action Star Wars sextet. It opened to poor reviews and grossed only $69 million. However, the half-hour TV series, shot in 3-D, won high ratings and powered another merchandising bonanza.

In 2009, for the first time in 15 years, Lucasfilm began shooting a theatrical film that was neither a Star Wars nor an Indiana Jones project. It was *Red Tails*, a fiction film directed by Anthony Hemingway and based on the story of the Tuskegee Airmen, an African-American aviation squad that flew during World War II. The movie was set for release in 2010. In addition, the company was developing a live-action television series based on the Star Wars series, with its debut tentatively scheduled for 2011.

*Terry W. Hughes*
*Updated, Tammy Weisberger; Roger K. Smith*

## PRINCIPAL DIVISIONS

Industrial Light and Magic (ILM); Lucasfilm Ltd.; Lucasfilm Animation; Lucasfilm Animation Singapore; LucasArts; Lucas Licensing; Lucas Online; Skywalker Sound.

## PRINCIPAL COMPETITORS

Digital Domain Productions, Inc.; DreamWorks Animation SKG; The Walt Disney Company; The Weinstein Company.

## FURTHER READING

Carlton, Jim, "George Lucas Chosen to Develop Presidio Park in San Francisco," *Wall Street Journal*, June 16, 1999, p. 4.

Eller, Claudia, "Risky Quest for Treasure," *Los Angeles Times*, April 21, 2008.

Graser, Mark, "Lucas Empire Continues Growth at Light Speed," *Daily Variety*, April 11, 2002, p. A1.

Grover, Ronald, "The Emperor Strikes Back; How Lucas Is Maximizing the Take on Attack of the Clones," *Business-Week*, May 6, 2002, p. 38.

Harmetz, Aljean, "But Can Hollywood Live without George Lucas?" *New York Times*, July 13, 1981, Sec. 3, p. 11.

Jensen, Jeff, "PepsiCo Beams into 'Star Wars': $2 Billion Deal Offers Model for Future Alliances Tied to Lucasfilm Franchise," *Advertising Age*, May 20, 1996, p. 62.

"The New Force at Lucasfilm," *BusinessWeek Online*, March 27, 2006.

Peterson, Karyn M., "Power of The Force," *Playthings*, August 1, 2008, p. 10.

Pollock, Dale, *Skywalking: The Life and Films of George Lucas: Updated Edition*. New York: Da Capo Press, 1999.

Snyder, Beth, "Toy Fair Girds for 'Phantom Menace' Burst— Marketing to Kids: Demand for Star Wars Toys about to Explode," *Advertising Age*, February 8, 1999, p. 46.

# M. A. Mortenson Company

**700 Meadow Lane North**
**Minneapolis, Minnesota 55422**
**U.S.A.**
**Telephone: (763) 522-2100**
**Fax: (763) 287-5430**
**Web site: http://www.mortenson.com**

*Private Company*
*Founded:* 1954
*Employees:* 2,200
*Sales:* $2.68 billion (2008)
*NAICS:* 236220 Commercial and Institutional Building Construction; 236210 Industrial Building Construction

■ ■ ■

Family owned and operated, M. A. Mortenson Company is one of the leading general contractors in the United States. It is involved in a wide range of projects, including office buildings, university facilities, medical centers, airport terminals, wastewater-treatment facilities, hotels, manufacturing and industrial facilities, and sports and event centers. Based in Minneapolis, Minnesota, the company maintains regional offices in eight U.S. cities as well as Shanghai, China. Mortenson divides its business among five industry groups: the Federal Contracting Group, Full Service Facility Solutions, Mortenson Development, Inc., the Renewable Energy Group, and the Sports Group. In addition to construction services, Mortenson possesses design-build capabilities and offers real-estate development, precon-

struction, diverse workforce planning services, program management, and full-service facility solutions. Chairman Mauritz A. Mortenson Jr. is the son of the company's founder.

## COMPANY IS FOUNDED, 1905

Mauritz A. Mortenson Sr. was born in 1905, the son of a Swedish immigrant who settled in Minneapolis, Minnesota, and left farming to become involved in construction. Known as Mort, Mauritz Mortenson eventually became a superintendent with the James Leck Company. He earned a certificate in building construction in 1925 and completed some course work in structural engineering at the University of Minnesota. With a pair of associates he launched Northland Construction Company in 1931, but times were tough, and just a year later he was fortunate to return to work at James Leck. He did not attempt to start another construction firm until he was 48 years old, launching M. A. Mortenson Company on April 1, 1954, hopeful that the fast growing Minneapolis–St. Paul market could provide enough work for his fledgling business.

Mortenson Company was a shoestring affair. Working from his dining-room table, Mort Mortenson put together his bids while his wife served as secretary. The first job he landed was a $370 remodeling project for the Paul Bunyan Bait Company. He soon won his first competitive bid: $127,344 to build a Sunday school addition to Gustavus Adolphus Lutheran Church. By the end of his first year in business, Mortenson had secured eight projects worth about $410,000. Thus, in 1955 he was able to free up his dining room and move into a cramped downtown office, although his wife continued to keep the books at home. The following year the company was established enough that Mortenson could move into a two-room office suite and hire a secretary. Moreover, he hired a couple working out of their home to relieve his wife of the bookkeeping responsibilities.

## FIRST HOSPITAL PROJECTS: 1956

It was also in 1956 that Mortenson Company completed its first project at the University of Minnesota, a chemical storehouse. This gave the company a start in the educational facility field and established a relationship with the University of Minnesota that would extend into the next century. In addition, in 1956 Mortenson Company won its first hospital projects, an administrative wing at Swedish Hospital and a polio rehabilitation center at Sister Kenny Institute, opening up the medical center sector for the young company. The year also saw Mortenson secure its first projects outside of the Twin Cities: a Diamond Match warehouse in Cloquet, Minnesota, and the Leach Elementary School in the same community.

Mort Mortenson Jr. joined his father's company in June 1960 after earning a civil engineering degree from the University of Colorado and serving a two-year stint in the United States Navy. Although the company only employed 11, it was growing rapidly, and the offices were moved to a property on the outskirts of downtown Minneapolis that offered space to house equipment and warehouse building materials. The extra capabilities allowed the company, starting in 1960, to construct three buildings for leasing that would provide a steady source of income over the years. They included the Builders

Exchange, an office and warehouse building used by Marlin-Rockwell Company, and a Westinghouse warehouse and distribution center. The year 1960 also brought the Mortsenson Company its first million-dollar contract, a high school addition worth $1.6 million. Because of the growing population, the result of the post–World War II baby boom, a large number of public schools were built, and Mortenson Company landed a considerable number of these projects as well as college and university projects that were spurred by the passage of the Higher Education Facilities Act in 1963.

Another new area of involvement for the company in the 1960s was heavy construction projects. In 1966 the firm won three construction contracts related to a power-generating plant in Bayport, Minnesota. Other area power projects soon followed, and eventually Mortenson Company secured work on power plants and wastewater-treatment plants throughout the United States. Moreover, the jobs paved the way for the company to take on other heavy construction assignments, such as hydropower, water-treatment, and dam projects. Later in the 1960s Mortenson added its first transportation project, a hangar and cargo building for United Airlines.

## NEW PRESIDENT: 1969

In 1969 Mort Mortenson Jr. was named president of the company, and a year later Mort Mortenson Sr. retired. In June 1970 the company made the coveted *Engineering News-Record's* Top 400 ranking for the first time, listed at number 399. Under the leadership of Mort Mortenson Jr., the company enjoyed further growth. It continued to win a large percentage of major area projects, and it looked beyond the borders of Minnesota for new work. In 1975 the company won its first out-of-state contract, the construction of the Hansen Ford Dealership in Grand Forks, North Dakota.

As the company sought to increase its market reach and the scope of the projects it undertook, Mort Mortenson Jr. assembled his first management team in 1975 while organizing the business into three divisions: Commercial/Industrial, Diversified Services, and Heavy Construction. In 1978 an Estimating Group was added as well. At the start of the 1970s Mortenson Company generated less than $16 million in annual revenues, and by the end of the decade revenues topped $100 million, totaling $106.4 million.

To keep pace with its steady growth, Mortenson Company moved its headquarters to a new and larger property in 1980. Mort Mortenson Sr. came out of retirement to oversee the construction of an office complex that would include the company's new

## KEY DATES

**1954:** Company is founded by Mauritz A. Mortenson Sr.
**1960:** M. A. Mortenson Company wins its first $1 million contract.
**1969:** Mauritz A. Mortenson Jr. is named president.
**1981:** First branch office opens in Denver.
**2001:** Chicago office opens.

headquarters as well as homes for other corporate tenants. It was the start of real-estate development projects for Mortenson Company. In 1981 the firm opened its first branch office, located in Denver. There was no market research that went into the decision, merely a gut feeling that it would be a good location, even despite a downturn in Colorado's economy at the time. While the new branch was introducing itself to the market, it was fortunate to have a project to pursue, the Wyoming State Office Building in Cheyenne, Wyoming, that Mortenson Company had recently won. Also of importance in 1981, the company received its first contract outside the continental United States: the $77.3 million Tripler Army Medical Center in Honolulu, Hawaii. It was the largest hospital the company had yet attempted, and because of its size and the distance away from home, it was a seminal achievement in the history of Mortenson Company.

### TOP 100 RANKING: 1982

The firm cracked the *Engineering News-Record* top 100 list in 1982, slotted at number 96. Expansion continued the following year with the opening of an office in Seattle, the outgrowth of winning a contract to construct a Veteran's Administration Medical Center in the city. To help land more government contracts, the company established a Federal Contracting Group in 1988. In the meantime, an office was established in Tampa, Florida, in 1984, after the firm won a pair of area projects. Problems with the performance of subcontractors and retaining skilled construction trade workers proved the undoing of the Tampa branch, which closed in 1987. During this period the firm also attempted to establish an office in Grand Rapids, Minnesota, in 1986 to serve the pulp and paper industry, but it, too, lacked staying power.

The 1990s began with a recession, but because of a deep backlog of projects, Mortenson Company increased revenues from $496.5 million in 1989 to $665.9 mil-

lion in 1990. A branch office was opened that year in Milwaukee, Wisconsin, and the third generation of the Mortenson family became involved in the company on a full-time basis when David Mortenson joined his father and eventually became a vice president in the Seattle office. His brother Mark, a lawyer by training, joined the company in 1997 to head financial planning.

Mortenson Company expanded on a number of fronts in the 1990s. It completed its first major sports project, the Target Center arena for the Minnesota Timberwolves of the National Basketball Association. A new group, nicknamed "Mort's Sports," was formed to pursue other sports projects. Soon Mortenson Company was working on Joe Robbie Stadium in Miami to make the football stadium suitable for baseball, building a new domed stadium in St. Louis, renovating the Seattle Kingdome, constructing Coors Field in Denver, and completing facilities in the Disney Wide World of Sports Complex in Orlando, Florida. The firm worked with Disney in a different context as well during this period. In 1999 it teamed up with Disney and Stanford University to make use of 3D modeling in the construction of the Walt Disney Concert Hall.

### CENTER FOR CONSTRUCTION INNOVATION OPENS: 1994

Several new branch offices were opened in the 1990s. Three major projects led to the addition of a Honolulu office in 1993. In that same year, offices opened in San Francisco and Los Angeles, which oversaw the Walt Disney Concert Hall project. Meanwhile, Mortenson Company's heavy construction business, a specialty for the previous three decades, was no longer a strong suit, and in the 1990s the personnel in this group was dispersed among the other industry groups and branch offices. In another development of note in the 1990s, the company formed its own think tank of sorts in 1994, the Center for Construction Innovation, which examined best practices in design and construction to incorporate into Mortenson Company.

Mortenson Company ended the century by posting its first $1 billion year in revenues in 1999, and the firm continued to expand as the 2000s dawned. A branch office was opened in Chicago in 2001. It was followed three years later by a new branch in Phoenix, Arizona. Mortenson Company also looked overseas, opening offices in Australia and in Shanghai, China. Seeking new growth opportunities, the company established a Renewable Energy Group and quickly became the largest designer-builder of wind-energy facilities in North America. In 2008 Mortenson Company ranked number 27 on the *Engineering News-Record*'s list, the first time it cracked the top 30. Diversified and well respected,

Mortenson Company was well positioned to enjoy continued success in the new century.

*Ed Dinger*

## PRINCIPAL OPERATING UNITS

Federal Contracting Group; Full Service Facility Solutions; Mortenson Development, Inc.; Renewable Energy Group; Sports Group.

## PRINCIPAL COMPETITORS

Hunt Construction Group, Inc.; Turner Construction Company; Walsh Group.

## FURTHER READING

Anderson, Mark, "Minnesota-based M. A. Mortenson Co. Positioned for Hotel Recovery," *Finance and Commerce Daily Newspaper*, November 9, 2006.

Johanson, Mark, "M. A. Mortenson Quietly Builds Construction Empire," *Minneapolis–St. Paul City Business*, August 14, 1992, p. 22.

Johnson, Adam, "Minnesota Twins Announce Firms to Design, Build New Ballpark," *Finance and Commerce Daily Newspaper*, November 21, 2006.

Pine, Carol, *Building a Legacy: M. A. Mortenson Company: 50 Years, 1954–2004*, Minneapolis, MN: M. A. Mortenson Company, 2004.

# Mayo Foundation for Medical Education and Research

————————■————————

200 First Street S.W.
Rochester, Minnesota 55905
U.S.A.
Telephone: (507) 284-2511
Fax: (507) 284-0161
Web site: http://www.mayo.edu

*Nonprofit Company*
*Founded:* 1919
*Incorporated:* 1919 as Mayo Properties Association
*Employees:* 57,000
*Sales:* $7.2 billion (2008)
*NAICS:* 622110 General Medical and Surgical Hospitals; 541710 Research and Development in the Physical, Engineering, and Life Sciences; 611310 Colleges, Universities, and Professional Schools; 621491 HMO Medical Centers

■ ■ ■

The Mayo Foundation for Medical Education and Research oversees activities at health care institutions around the country that bear the Mayo name. These include the world-renowned Mayo Clinic in Rochester, Minnesota; Mayo clinics in Scottsdale, Arizona, and Jacksonville, Florida; four clinic-affiliated hospitals; the Mayo Health System, an affiliated network of hospitals and medical practices in the American Upper Midwest; five medical schools; and a retirement community. A board of 30 trustees, including physicians, administrators, and community members, governs the Mayo Foundation.

## 1919 THROUGH EARLY EIGHTIES: FIRST YEARS AS A FOUNDATION

In 1914 brothers Charles H. Mayo and William J. Mayo oversaw the construction of the first building to bear the Mayo Clinic name and the first in the world designed specifically for a group medical practice. Now 75 people strong, the Mayo partners were seeing an average of 30,000 patients annually. The following year the independently wealthy Mayo brothers, in an effort to preserve the education and research tradition they had founded, established a nonprofit endowment through the University of Minnesota, which they named the Mayo Foundation for Medical Education and Research. This foundation was funded by nearly $2 million from the brothers' personal savings. Eventually renamed the Mayo Graduate School of Medicine, this organization was the world's first formal graduate training program for physicians.

In 1919, "in an act without precedent in American medicine," according to *Mayo Clinic*, "the two brothers transferred all of the assets of the Mayo Clinic into an endowment to advance medical science (originally named the Mayo Properties Association, this endowment became the Mayo Foundation in 1964). Thus began Mayo's tradition of giving, an essential part of our position in world medicine." Because the foundation was nonprofit, Mayo physicians from this point forward would be paid a salary and would not share directly in the proceeds of their practice. Funds left over after operating expenses were met were contributed to education, research, and patient care.

From 1919 until 1939, Dr. Will Mayo served as president of the foundation. Among the highlights of this era were the construction in 1922 of a state-of-the-art surgical pavilion, which doubled the capacity of its affiliate Saint Marys Hospital; the beginning of air transportation to Rochester in 1928; and the public donation of Mayo Foundation House, the former residence of Dr. Will Mayo and his wife, so that it might be used as "a meeting place for the exchange of ideas for the good of mankind."

With the deaths of Charles Mayo in May and Will Mayo in July 1939, an enormous loss was felt around the country. Harold Severson in *Rochester: Mecca for Millions* reported that "messages of condolences poured in from people in all walks of life—from President and Mrs. Franklin D. Roosevelt to a little old woman in Texas who sent a potted plant and a note to Mrs. Charlie Mayo expressing her deep sorrow on the death of the man who had been so kind to her years ago."

Harry Harwick, chief administrative officer since 1908, assumed the chairmanship of the foundation upon Will Mayo's death. He presided over a thrilling era of Mayo's development, which included the creation of the first post-anesthesia room (a forerunner of modern intensive care units) in 1942 and the awarding of the Nobel Prize in 1950 to two Mayo researchers for their synthesis of cortisone. Later, the foundation opened two more medical schools: the Mayo Medical School in 1972 and the Mayo School of Health-Related Sciences, which specialized in training students in allied health programs, in 1973. Numerous other medical advances continued to keep the Mayo name in the spotlight of world medicine into the early 21st century.

## MID-1980S AND BEYOND:
## MERGING AND EXPANDING IN A
## MORE COMPETITIVE ERA

Until the mid-1980s, the structure of the Mayo Foundation, including its longstanding alliance with Saint Marys Hospital, remained essentially unchanged. With improvements in health care, concurrent declines in patients' average hospital stays, rising medical costs, and tighter governmental controls, however, there was a much more pressing need for conserving resources and maintaining revenue levels. Therefore, the Mayo Foundation, Saint Marys, and a third entity, Rochester Methodist Hospital, entered into negotiations about integrating. On May 28, 1986, their organizational merger was complete, and the newly expanded Mayo Medical Center was now the largest nonprofit medical concern in the country. At the time of the merger, combined revenues exceeded half a billion dollars, with pooled assets listed at around $1 billion. One proviso of the agreement was that Saint Marys would retain its separate legal identity as a Catholic hospital and continue to receive support from the Sisters of St. Francis.

Also in 1986, the Mayo Foundation began expanding outside of Minnesota. The Mayo Clinic Jacksonville opened in Florida that year, and Mayo Clinic Scottsdale opened in Arizona the following year. The foundation acquired St. Luke's Hospital in Jacksonville in 1987, thereby gaining the clinic-hospital pairing that worked so well in Rochester. Also in 1987 the original Mayo Clinic in Rochester went smoke free, becoming one of the first medical facilities in the country to do so.

In addition to its expansion, Mayo also found new sources of income by providing specialized lab services to outside doctors and hospitals (through a unit called Mayo Medical Laboratories) and by launching such commercial enterprises as the *Mayo Clinic Family Health Book* and the *Mayo Clinic Health Letter*, both of which were first published in 1983. In 1986 the foundation created another new unit, called Mayo Medical Ventures, which in addition to assuming responsibility for the publishing ventures, managed technology transfer agreements, patent applications, and licensing deals, and created pharmacies and a medical supply outlet in Rochester. In addition, Mayo began actively soliciting charitable contributions, whereas previously it operated as a self-funding organization. By 1992 outside philanthropy to Mayo totaled more than $58 million, approximately the same amount the foundation spent on education and research.

The mid-1980s also saw the Mayo Foundation begin to participate in the burgeoning managed health care sector, which was bringing profound changes to the industry. In 1986 the foundation created a subsidiary called Mayo Management Services, Inc. (MMSI), to operate a Minnesota-based health maintenance organization (HMO) called Mayo Health Plan. Two years later MMSI entered the plan administrative services sector when it began providing claims administration for St. Luke's Hospital in Jacksonville. In somewhat of a return to its general practice roots, the Mayo Foundation in 1992 began building a regional network of community-

## KEY DATES

■

**1914:** Construction begins of the first building bearing the Mayo Clinic name and the first in the world designed specifically for a group medical practice.

**1915:** The Mayo brothers establish the Mayo Foundation for Medical Education and Research (later called the Mayo Graduate School of Medicine), the world's first graduate training program for physicians.

**1919:** The Mayo brothers transfer the assets of the Mayo Clinic to a nonprofit foundation, initially called the Mayo Properties Association.

**1964:** The Mayo Properties Association is renamed the Mayo Foundation.

**1986:** The Mayo Clinic, Saint Marys Hospital, and Rochester Methodist Hospital are integrated to form Mayo Medical Center, the largest nonprofit medical concern in the country; Mayo Clinic Jacksonville opens.

**1987:** Mayo Clinic Scottsdale is established.

**1992:** Foundation begins building a regional network of community-based clinics and medical centers, the Mayo Health System.

**2001:** The 20-story tall Gonda Building opens on the Rochester campus and creates one of the largest interconnected medical facilities in the world; Mayo researchers create rapid test to detect anthrax.

based clinics and medical centers, called the Mayo Health System, with the acquisition of Decorah Medical Associates in northeastern Iowa.

By the late 1990s this system included 500 physicians, 7,600 allied health staff, and 13 hospitals with nearly 900 beds and was providing health care services to 54 communities in Minnesota, Iowa, and Wisconsin. The Minnesota portion of the Mayo Health System served as the core of the Mayo Health Plan HMO. Strategically, the Mayo Health System served in part as a conduit to the Mayo Clinic, because the primary care physicians in Mayo's new network were the doctors referring patients to its specialized facilities. The network's regional makeup also made sense, because half of the patients who went to the Mayo Clinic lived within 120 miles of Rochester. In 1995 MMSI entered

the commercial market, offering and administering a variety of customized, self-insured health plans. With the Mayo Health System as its core network, supplemented by providers outside the system, MMSI began managing health plans for such regional employers as Hormel Foods Corporation and the Ashley Companies.

### NEW SOURCES OF REVENUE

The pressure on the Mayo Foundation to find alternative revenue sources was highlighted in 1993 when the foundation had an operating loss of $6.2 million, its first year in the red since the Great Depression. Contributing to the loss were higher patient care costs and lower Medicare reimbursement levels. In early 1994 the Mayo Clinic announced that it would cut 450 jobs in an effort to save $18.5 million. Through the remainder of the 1990s, the Mayo Foundation's earnings suffered from the growing number of patients who were covered either by Medicare or a managed care plan. Earnings fell 50 percent in 1998 from the previous year, to $86 million, in large part as a result of an estimated $85 million loss on Medicare patients. In the meantime, during 1998, the Scottsdale operations were augmented with the opening in nearby Phoenix of Mayo Clinic Hospital, a five-story facility with 178 beds and complete emergency room/urgent care services. The Scottsdale system included both a clinic and a hospital, as well as a regional network of seven primary care centers similar to the Mayo Health System.

As the 21st century neared, the Mayo Foundation continued to seek out alternative ways of generating revenue and of simply making the Mayo Clinic name more widely known. In 1998 the foundation partnered with Winn-Dixie Stores, Inc., to begin installing Mayo Clinic kiosks featuring free health information in more than 600 grocery stores and pharmacies owned by the Jacksonville-based chain. The two organizations had a longstanding relationship, highlighted by Winn-Dixie having donated the land on which the Mayo Clinic in Jacksonville was built. Also in 1998, in a partnership with a leading housewares retailer, the *Mayo Clinic/ Williams-Sonoma Cookbook* was published.

By this time the Mayo Foundation also had established a Web site, the Mayo Clinic Health Oasis, to provide specialized medical information to consumers. The site generated strong traffic but little revenue because advertising and sponsorship opportunities were not being aggressively pursued. In late 1999, however, the foundation entered into a joint venture with a San Francisco–based private equity company, the Shansby Group, to develop an interactive Web site that was intended to compete more aggressively in the burgeoning online health care sector. The aim was not to practice medicine on the Internet. Dr. Patricia Simmons, chair of the foundation's Internet steering committee, told the *Minneapolis Star Tribune*, "I'd look at this as an activity that will fill the gap between having an encyclopedia of health information and having a real thorough medical visit with a physician. We will tailor the information to help people manage their own health." The joint venture, of which Mayo retained majority control, was the foundation's first major for-profit venture. Having stayed on the cutting edge of the medical field for more than 100 years, it appeared that the Mayo Foundation would not let the electronic revolution pass it by.

## NEW GONDA BUILDING: CENTERPIECE OF BUILDING AND RESEARCH BOOM

In October 2001 the 20-story Gonda Building opened on the downtown Rochester campus. Joined on one side to the Mayo Clinic building and on the other to the Rochester Methodist Hospital, the Gonda Building made the Mayo Clinic one of the largest interconnected medical facilities of its kind in the world. More than 3.5 million square feet of space allowed teams of medical specialists to work together in close proximity and increase both patient convenience and quality of care.

In late 2001 researchers at the Mayo Clinic gained national attention with the development of a rapid test to detect the presence of anthrax in human and environmental samples. A process that previously had taken several days was reduced to less than one hour. Development of the rapid test increased the ability of public health and law enforcement officials across the country to respond effectively to bioterrorism threats, such as the anthrax attacks that occurred in the eastern United States that same year.

In 2002 the National Cancer Institute (NCI) expanded on its previous designation in the Mayo Clinic's Rochester campus as a comprehensive cancer treatment center. The NCI was also included in the Mayo campuses in Scottsdale and Jacksonville, making the Mayo Clinic the first multicenter clinic in the United States to be named a comprehensive cancer treatment center. Also in 2002 the Rochester campus became home to the new Mayo Proteomics Research Center. One of only a dozen such centers around the world, it would focus on researching the role proteins played in cell behavior.

The Mayo Clinic College of Medicine, which brought together educational and research programs at the clinic in Rochester with those in Jacksonville and Scottsdale, was introduced in 2003. The new College of Medicine featured five professional schools across all three campuses to educate scientists, medical students, medical residents, fellows, nurses, and allied-health professionals.

In 2003 the completion of the C. V. and Elsie R. Griffin Cancer Research Building on the Jacksonville campus opened 103,000 square feet of office and laboratory space to 400 cancer researchers working in 20 laboratories. The building was the first on any Mayo campus to be wholly dedicated to cancer research.

## INCREASED OUTREACH INCLUDES HOLLYWOOD

The introduction of *Medical Edge Radio from Mayo Clinic* on stations across the United States in 2004 increased the clinic's public outreach significantly. Although they were relatively short, the 60-second installments featured recent medical research and individual patient stories. In February 2005 Mayo launched another public outreach tool with the first issue of its online research magazine, *Discovery's Edge*. Alongside patient and researcher profiles, the magazine tracked research trends and described new developments in medical technology.

In April 2005 MMSI announced plans for the Mayo Clinic Nicotine Dependence Center to provide phone counseling services to members of the entertainment industry who were struggling with nicotine addiction. Sponsored in part by the Entertainment Industry Foundation, and known as "Hollywood Quits," the program was intended to help the estimated one out of three people working in the entertainment industry who were habitual tobacco users. In a press release on April 6, 2005, Entertainment Industry Foundation officers explained they had chosen to partner with the Mayo Clinic because of the "combination of academic and operational expertise" it offered and its 17 years of leadership in the treatment of nicotine addiction.

## RESEARCH ON CANCER AND GENETICS MOVES AHEAD

The completion of the Mayo Clinic Collaborative Research Building on the Scottsdale campus in 2005 combined the Mayo Clinic's academic, clinical, research, and technological resources with the capabilities of the neighboring biotechnology firm Translational Genomics Research Institute. The new building offered 110,000 square feet to house collaborative efforts on advanced cancer and genetics research.

In 2006 the U.S. Department of Health and Human Services, on behalf of the Indian Health Service (IHS), forged an agreement with Mayo Clinic to work on ways to reduce cancer and other diseases in Native American and Alaska Native communities around the United States. The agreement was the most comprehensive one ever between the IHS and any other health organization.

## HEALTH CARE COSTS AND PATIENT SERVICES

In September 2007 the Mayo Clinic released a proposal to address the growing need for affordable and accessible health care in the United States. Developed by 400 health care experts over 18 months, the Mayo proposal rejected the idea of a government-run single-payer system and instead suggested that private health insurance companies be required to offer standard plans with a variety of options for consumers. The proposal was modeled on the Federal Employees Health Benefits Plan available to federal workers. No applicants would be turned away, and employers would contribute toward the cost of employee premiums. Low-income applicants would receive government assistance with payments according to a sliding scale. Media coverage of the Mayo proposal included an article in the September 15, 2007, edition of the *New York Times*.

Mayo continued keeping its sights on affordable health care. In April 2008 the *Dartmouth Atlas of Health Care*, published by the Dartmouth Institute for Health Policy and Clinical Practice, examined Medicare spending patterns at five top teaching hospitals in the United States. Costs at the Mayo Clinic ranked lowest among the five, at $53,000 per patient. Costs at the Cleveland Clinic emerged as second lowest, at $55,000 per patient. In contrast, per-patient costs at the most expensive teaching hospital, the University of California at Los Angeles, averaged $93,000 per Medicare patient. An editorial in the April 10, 2008, edition of the *New York Times*, written by staff members of the Mayo and Cleveland clinics, cited several reasons for the clinics' ability to provide high-quality, low-cost care. Among these, noted the writers, doctors at the Mayo Clinic received an annual salary as opposed to a fee for each patient service provided. Patients at both of the lower-cost teaching hospitals also spent less time in intensive-care units and less total time in the hospital.

In addition to innovation, expansion continued. By 2007 the Mayo Health System, begun in 1992 and consisting of community-based clinics and medical centers, served 62 communities in Iowa, Minnesota, and Wisconsin. By 2009 the Mayo Clinic had opened two walk-in Express Care Clinics at retail establishments in Rochester, one at a supermarket and another at a shopping mall. The move came in response to patient and employee requests for more convenient medical care for relatively minor medical problems. The clinic openings reflected a nationwide trend in which other prominent health care providers, such as the Cleveland Clinic, also responded to consumer demand and rising medical costs by opening walk-in clinics in convenient locations outside a main hospital campus.

*Jay P. Pederson*
*Updated, David E. Salamie; Joyce Helena Brusin*

## PRINCIPAL SUBSIDIARIES

Mayo Clinic College of Medicine; Mayo School of Graduate Medical Education; Mayo Graduate School; Mayo School of Continuing Medical Education; Mayo School of Health Sciences; Mayo Management Services, Inc.; Mayo Medical Laboratories; Mayo Medical Ventures.

## PRINCIPAL OPERATING UNITS

Mayo Clinic Rochester; Mayo Clinic Jacksonville; Mayo Clinic Scottsdale; Saint Marys Hospital, Rochester; Rochester Methodist Hospital; St. Luke's Hospital, Jacksonville; Mayo Clinic Hospital, Phoenix; Charter House, Rochester; Mayo Health System.

## PRINCIPAL COMPETITORS

Cleveland Clinic; Columbia/HCA Healthcare Corporation; Henry Ford Health System; The John Hopkins Health System; Marshfield Clinic; Memorial Sloan-Kettering Cancer Center; Massachusetts General Hospital, Boston; Mercy Health Services; Ronald Reagan UCLA Medical Center; University of California San Francisco Medical Center; Stanford Hospital and Clinics.

## FURTHER READING

Berry, Leonard, and Kent Seltmann, *Management Lessons from Mayo Clinic: Inside One of the World's Most Admired Service Organizations.* New York: McGraw-Hill, 2008.

Clapesattle, Helen, *The Doctors Mayo* (2nd ed.). Minneapolis: University of Minnesota Press, 1963.

Freudenheim, Milt, "Hospitals Begin to Move into Supermarkets," *New York Times*, May 11, 2009.

———, "Mayo Clinic Recommends Universal Health Insurance Plan," *New York Times*, September 15, 2007.

Gelbach, Deborah L., "Mayo Clinic," *From This Land: A History of Minnesota's Empires, Enterprises, and Entrepreneurs.* Northridge, CA: Windsor Publications, 1988.

Hodgson, Harriet W., *Rochester: City of the Prairie*. Northridge, CA: Windsor Publications, 1989.

Johnson, Victor, *Mayo Clinic: Its Growth and Progress*. Bloomington, MN: Voyageur Press, 1984.

*Mayo Clinic*. Rochester, MN: Mayo Foundation, 1990.

"Quality Care at Bargain Prices" (editorial), *New York Times*, April 10, 2008.

Severson, Harold, *Rochester: Mecca for Millions*. Rochester, MN: Marquette Bank & Trust Company, 1979.

Shepherd, John T., and Walter F. Mondale, *Inside the Mayo Clinic: A Memoir*. Afton, MN: Afton Historical Society Press, 2004.

The **McGraw·Hill** Companies

# The McGraw-Hill
# Companies, Inc.

**1221 Avenue of the Americas**
**New York, New York 10020-1095**
**U.S.A.**
**Telephone: (212) 904-2000**
**Fax: (212) 512-4502**
**Web site: http://www.mcgraw-hill.com**

*Public Company*
*Founded:* 1909
*Incorporated:* 1925 as McGraw-Hill Publishing
    Company, Inc.
*Employees:* 21,077
*Sales:* $6 billion (2009)
*Stock Exchanges:* New York
*Ticker Symbol:* MHP
*NAICS:* 511120 Periodical Publishers; 511130 Book
    Publishers; 511210 Software Publishers; 514191
    Online Information Services; 513120 Television
    Broadcasting

■ ■ ■

Perhaps best known for its textbooks, The McGraw-Hill
Companies, Inc., was formed initially from the merger
of McGraw Publishing Co. and Hill Publishing
Company. The business has always aimed to provide
technicians, scientists, and business people complete, accurate, and up-to-date information of both specialized
and general interest. The company carried on that tradition in the late 20th and early 21st centuries with mergers and acquisitions that increased market share, reached
new markets, and expanded its global reach. Guided by

Harold "Terry" McGraw III, great-grandson of founder
James H. McGraw, the company employs the latest
media technologies to keep its customers in education,
business, industrial, professional, and government
markets abreast of their disciplines.

## BEGINNINGS: LATE NINETEENTH
## CENTURY

Born in 1858, John A. Hill, a typesetter, silver prospector, newspaper publisher, and railroad engineer, came to
the attention of the publisher of *American Machinist*
with his contribution of letters and articles on practical
aspects of railroading. When the publisher began
*Locomotive Engineering* in 1888, Hill was his choice for
editor. By 1889, Hill had become part owner of both
magazines, and in 1897, divesting his interest in
*Locomotive Engineering*, he took over full ownership of
*American Machinist* and established the American
Machinist Press in 1898. In 1902 he incorporated Hill
Publishing Company, going on to acquire *Power,
Engineering and Mining Journal* and *Engineering News*.
By 1909 Hill was a leading trade publisher of not just
magazines but of books such as Colvin and Stanley's
*American Machinist's Handbook* (1908) and Herbert
Hoover's *Principles of Mining* (1909).

Hill's chief competitor was onetime teacher and
subscription salesman James H. McGraw. McGraw was
an advertising salesman for the American Railway
Publishing Company in 1884, where he rose to the
position of vice president by 1886. On resigning from
American Railway, McGraw began to acquire magazines
that reported on technological progress. Titles included

> ## COMPANY PERSPECTIVES
> Our mission is to provide essential information and insight that help individuals, markets and societies perform to their potential.
>
> We achieve growth by ... Purpose: Being essential to markets—influencing, transforming and expanding them. Strategic Intent: Focusing on content, services and being a solutions provider. Balanced Portfolio: Providing leadership in the diverse markets we serve. Financial Performance: Generating consistent revenue and profit growth. Shareholder Return: Providing a superior return to our shareholders in the form of increasing dividends and share appreciation.

the *American Journal of Railway Appliances*; *Electrical Industries* (later retitled *American Electrician*); *Electrical World*; *Electrical Engineer*; *Electrochemical Industry*; and *Engineering Record*. In 1899 McGraw incorporated McGraw Publishing Company. Its first engineering handbook, the *Standard Handbook for Electrical Engineers*, was published in 1907.

In the years following the Civil War, the United States evolved from an agrarian to an industrial society. Both McGraw and Hill found a growing market of technicians concerned with the practical applications of science to transportation, lighting, and engineering, among other facets of daily life. In 1909 Edward Caldwell and Martin M. Foss, the respective heads of the book departments of the two firms, agreed that a merger would serve both companies well. After the two men persuaded their bosses, a coin toss decided whose name would come first in naming the new company, the loser becoming president. The McGraw-Hill Book Company, with John A. Hill as president, was thus born, locating itself in McGraw Publishing's building in New York City.

The two companies, however, were still distinct entities: the magazines that formed the chief interests of both and supplied articles for many of the books remained separate concerns. In 1914, as World War I broke out in Europe, Hill moved his company into an air-conditioned building in New York City, one specially constructed to house his publications and their printing facilities. By 1910 the McGraw-Hill Book Company had established itself with its first publication, *The Art of Engineering*, and its first series, "Electrical Engineering Texts." This series marked the beginning of a company trend toward publishing series of books by multiple

authors covering an entire range of knowledge in a specific field.

## A NEW ERA: 1916–28

A more complete merger of the McGraw and Hill interests came in 1916 when John A. Hill died at the age of 57. Arthur Baldwin, Hill's attorney, led Hill Publishing for a brief time following Hill's death. McGraw became president of the book company. The two established the McGraw-Hill Publishing Company in 1917, with its offices located in the Hill Building, publishing *Electrical World*, *Electric Railway Journal*, *Electrical Merchandising*, *Engineering Record*, *Metallurgical and Chemical Engineering*, *The Contractor*, *American Machinist*, *Power*, *Engineering and Mining Journal*, *Coal Age*, and *Engineering News*. This concentration of interests, along with the enlargement of the book company, now a subsidiary of McGraw-Hill Publishing, made McGraw-Hill the largest technical publisher in the world at that time.

The United States entered World War I in 1917, and this was a particularly good time for technical publishers. The first McGraw-Hill title to benefit from increased wartime demand was the *American Machinists' Handbook*, originally published before the war. There was also increased demand for engineering books in radio communication, aviation, construction and maintenance, chemical warfare, trench construction, automotive transportation, aerial photography, and antisubmarine tactics. McGraw-Hill responded quickly to this market. An example was its record response to the U.S. Army Educational Commission's order for 150,000 technical books, which were printed, bound, specially packed, and shipped to France in a matter of days.

After World War I, McGraw-Hill expanded rapidly. With Foss in charge of editorial and sales activities and Caldwell heading up finances and production, the book company had grown by establishing close contacts with the faculties of various universities and engineering schools, not only to make sales but also to find new authors. With the addition of a series designed for educational use, McGraw-Hill formed a college department in 1927, thus establishing a lasting emphasis on textbooks. Foss was equally innovative in finding new ways to market the technical books that seldom found space in general bookstores. By both advertising at cost in the parent firm's magazines and sending letters and circulars to subscribers, Foss offered interested parties a chance to examine a book for ten days without payment, an approach that quickly resulted in increased book sales.

## KEY DATES

**1909:** The McGraw-Hill Book Company forms in New York with the merger of the Hill Publishing Company and the McGraw Publishing Company.

**1927:** Company forms a college department, establishing a lasting business in textbooks.

**1928:** Company acquires A. W. Shaw Company of Chicago and turns Shaw's monthly *Magazine of Business* into a weekly, *Business Week* (later named *BusinessWeek*.

**1929:** Company's stock begins trading publicly.

**1946:** International division is established.

**1966:** Standard & Poor's Corporation is purchased.

**1983:** Joseph L. Dionne becomes president and CEO and refocuses the company from a "simple publishing company" into an "information turbine," reorganizing it into market-focus groups.

**1998:** Harold "Terry" McGraw III succeeds Dionne as CEO and consolidates the company, trims senior management tier, and initiates global expansion of Standard & Poor's.

**2007:** Controversy over ratings of structured finance vehicles sparks reorganization and tighter corporate control of Standard & Poor's.

**2008:** *BusinessWeek* is sold to Bloomberg L.P.

The publisher also grew through acquisition during the 1920s, purchasing the Newton Falls Paper Co. in 1920. McGraw-Hill opened offices in Great Britain and California as well. With the purchase of the A. W. Shaw Company of Chicago in 1928, McGraw-Hill extended its reach into the field of business books and magazines. The editorial staff turned one of Shaw's monthlies, the *Magazine of Business*, into a weekly, covering and interpreting news of specific interest to business people. Now named *Business Week* (and later known as *Business-Week*), it would become the best known of all McGraw-Hill publications.

During the 1920s James McGraw began to shift some of his authority in the company to other people. The first shift came when he named himself, his son James McGraw, Jr., and Malcolm Muir to a governing board of trustees. Then, in 1925, McGraw turned over the presidency of the book company to Edward Caldwell, who was succeeded by Martin M. Foss the next year. In 1928 Malcolm Muir became president of the

publishing company, and James McGraw remained chairman of the board.

## NEW VENTURES: 1929–45

McGraw-Hill stock was first traded publicly in 1929. Just after the stock market crash that same year, *The Business Week* (as it was then known) predicted, in its November 2, 1929, issue, that "business will gradually and steadily recover as businessmen regain their perspective and go back to work." Following this optimistic line of thought, McGraw-Hill established four new magazines in 1930, opened a West Coast office and book depository in San Francisco, and, under the imprint of Whittlesey House (named after James McGraw's father-in-law), entered the trade book field for the first time. The first title under the new imprint, selected to distinguish this division from trade publications, was Ernest Minor Patterson's *The World's Economic Dilemma*.

McGraw-Hill commissioned a new office building designed by Raymond Hood and located on West 42nd Street in New York City. Nicknamed "Big Green" because of the blue-green cast of its Art Deco exterior, the new McGraw-Hill building aroused controversy because of the horizontal banding of its windows, now a standard feature of many modern office buildings. When first occupied in 1931, Big Green included a complete production plant taking up four floors. The increasing severity of the economic depression during the early 1930s, however, forced McGraw-Hill not only to make deep cuts in personnel and salaries but to sell its press machinery and equipment in 1933. In 1932 the parent company's deficit ran to $239,137.

That same year, Whittlesey House had its first bestseller, *Life Begins at Forty*, by Walter B. Pitkin. The company's other publications made themselves useful sources of information for business people by providing hard facts and analysis of the economic situation. The vocational-education department of the book company helped those seeking new skills. Established in 1930, it concentrated on mechanical arts, agriculture, and home economics. The 1930s also saw major shifts at the executive level of McGraw-Hill. In 1935 James H. McGraw handed the chairmanship over to James McGraw, Jr. During the next two years Malcolm Muir failed to get along with the McGraw family. In 1937 he left to run *Newsweek* magazine, and James H. McGraw, Jr., became both president and chairman of the board. By 1937 the company had an annual profit of more than $1 million.

With the coming of World War II in the 1940s, McGraw-Hill was in an advantageous position. Because its technical publications were especially important to the war effort, its paper requirements received special priority. The company's magazines began to cover a range of relevant wartime topics from accelerated training in the use of metalworking power tools to dehydrated foods. The company also added titles in the fields of aviation, health, and atomic energy. In addition, the company began to publish special wartime titles, such as *En Guardia*, a Spanish-language paper promoting Latin American relations, and *Overseas Digest*, excerpting articles from other McGraw-Hill titles for distribution to military personnel posted abroad.

It was in the area of special training manuals, however, that McGraw-Hill was to make a special effort. As untrained men and women poured into industry and the armed services, accelerated technical training became increasingly important to the war effort. By 1943 the book company had published 231 titles for the Engineering and Science Management War Training Program. Of the 304 books published by 1944 to further the war effort, many dealt with radio and electronics, a newly important part of warfare. One title, *Mathematics for Electricians and Radiomen* by Nelson M. Cooke, first published in 1942, continued to be successful after the war and by 1964, under the new title of *Basic Mathematics for Electronics*, had total sales in excess of 485,000 copies.

Although McGraw-Hill had been present in the United Kingdom and Germany as well as other countries since before World War I, the company made use of the opportunities World War II offered to increase its foreign activities. In 1943 the book company opened a book-export department, which by 1944 had a foreign-language translation office. The same year, McGraw-Hill acquired the Embassy Book Company Ltd. of Toronto, which was renamed the McGraw-Hill Company of Canada, Ltd., and later designated McGraw Ryerson. In 1945, to provide its magazines with international coverage, the company started the World News Service.

## AFTER WORLD WAR II: 1946–59

After the war the book company prospered under the presidency of Curtis G. Benjamin, who succeeded James S. Thompson, president for only two years. Benjamin developed a text-film department, a venture inspired by the use of educational films during World War II to supplement textbook materials. As teachers discovered the value of motion pictures and filmstrips in the classroom, the market expanded, and by 1965 McGraw-Hill was the leader in the field. Another wartime dividend for the company was the 13-volume "U.S. Navy Flight Preparation Training" series printed for the

Bureau of Aeronautics during the war.

With the growth of commercial aviation in the postwar period, McGraw-Hill found a large market for civilian editions of the series. Building on the close contacts with governmental agencies in research and development made during World War II, the company contracted to publish the "Radiation Laboratory" series, 27 volumes concentrating on the results of wartime research into radar. According to Charles A. Madison's 1966 *Book Publishing in America*, this series, published in 1949 and costing more than $1.2 million to produce, "set a precedent for the commercial publication of government-financed projects." Although McGraw-Hill lost money on another project, the "National Nuclear" series, the company made an arrangement with the U.S. Atomic Energy Commission to produce an eight-volume compilation of scientific reference materials that was presented at the first International Conference on the Peaceful Uses of Atomic Energy at Geneva in August 1955.

Another project started in the late 1940s was the publication of James Boswell's manuscripts. Consisting of the voluminous collection of original manuscripts of the 18th-century Scottish author collected by Colonel Ralph H. Isham, the project was guided through negotiations with its purchaser, Yale University, by Edward Aswell, Whittlesey House's editor-in-chief since 1947. Publication of a projected 40 volumes began in 1950. It was not to be under the Whittlesey imprint, however, as Yale preferred to have the McGraw-Hill name on the books. This began the relegation of Whittlesey House to juvenile titles. Another milestone, this one commercial, proved to be the publication in 1950 of Betty Crocker's *Picture Cook Book*, which achieved sales of more than 235,000 copies in its first two years.

By the time its cofounder, James H. McGraw, died in 1948 at age 87, McGraw-Hill Publishing was well on its way to developing a departmentalized organizational structure. An independent technical-education department had been established in 1941, then a text-film department in 1945. The acquisition of the Gregg Publishing Company, publisher of vocational textbooks, in 1949 transformed the company's business-education department into the Gregg division. In response to the need for training literature during the Korean War, beginning in 1950, the book company established a technical-writing division to produce specialized materials for both government and industry. The next year, following a reorganization of the handbook, technical, and professional publishing department, the industrial- and business-book department was born, and the medical publishing department was formed in 1945. It was not until 1954, when it acquired Blakiston Company from Doubleday, which specialized in medical titles, that McGraw-Hill began to have a major share of the medical market under the newly named Blakiston division.

What proved by far to be the most important division for company progress in the postwar period was the international division, established in 1946. In less than 15 years, book exports trebled, with a profitable business in text-films, filmstrips, and the sale of foreign-language rights. A major force in the international growth of the company was Curtis Benjamin, who proceeded along lines mapped out by James Thompson. Benjamin succeeded, along with B. G. Dandison, head of the international division, in making the company successful in foreign countries: In 1962 McGraw-Hill was presented by President John F. Kennedy with a presidential E-for-Export award, making McGraw-Hill the first commercial publishing firm to be so honored.

James McGraw, Jr., who had headed up the company since 1935, retired in 1950 and was replaced by another son of the first McGraw, Curtis. Curtis led the company for three short years before his sudden death in 1953. He was succeeded by his brother, Donald C. McGraw.

Just before the death of Curtis, the company purchased the National Petroleum Publishing Company, the W. C. Piatt Company, and Piatt's Price Service, Inc., all from Warren C. Piatt. The book company then began three major encyclopedia projects in the late 1950s, each continuing on into the 1960s: *The McGraw-Hill Encyclopedia of Science and Technology*, *The Encyclopedia of World Art*, and *The New Catholic Encyclopedia*. When in 1959 the publishing company commemorated its 50th year, revenues exceeded $100 million.

## GROWTH AND DIVERSIFICATION: 1960–79

While Curtis Benjamin remained chairman of the board and CEO of the book company, Edward Booher, who had joined the company in 1936, became president in 1960. They doubled overall sales within five years, contributing 39 percent of the total income of the parent company in 1965. The F. W. Dodge Corporation, information provider to the construction industry, was purchased in 1961. The following year, the general book division was formed by merging the industrial-and-business-book department with the trade department. The purchase of Webster Publishing Company in 1963 marked the company's entry into the elementary school and high school textbook markets.

In 1964 the book company and the F. W. Dodge Corporation merged with McGraw-Hill Publishing Company to form McGraw-Hill, Inc. The reorganization created a single corporation, the parent company, with three operating divisions: book publishing, the Dodge complex, and magazines and news services. The company established an Australian publishing unit the same year. With the acquisition of the California Test Bureau in 1965, McGraw-Hill strengthened its K-12 educational services just in time to benefit from the postwar baby boom. The company moved into two new fields in 1966: One was legal publishing with the purchase of Shepard's Citations, Inc., and the other was financial information services through the acquisition of Standard & Poor's Corporation. Other acquisitions were Schaum Publishing Company, Capitol Radio Engineering Institute, and *Postgraduate Medicine* magazine, all in 1967. The company also expanded into Mexico in 1967 and into Japan in 1969.

A key figure in this expansion was Shelton Fisher. Beginning as promotion manager for *Business Week* in 1940, by 1968 Fisher had succeeded Donald McGraw as president and CEO of McGraw-Hill. His goal was to change the perception of McGraw-Hill as an old-fashioned publisher of trade magazines into that of a dynamic media giant. Fisher further extended the company's reach into Canada, Brazil, and India, bought four television stations from Time Inc., and moved the company out of Big Green and into a new, 50-story international headquarters in 1972. While increasing the company's prestige, the large capital outlay came at a time when a recession caused a loss in revenues for the McGraw-Hill magazines. After a period of uncertainty during which the McGraw family worked out a succession, Harold McGraw, Jr., became president of the parent company and Fisher assumed the chairmanship. This changed within a year when Fisher retired and Harold McGraw, Jr., became chairman in addition to his other positions.

The picture of McGraw-Hill, Inc., at the end of the 1970s, according to John Tebbel's *History of Book Publishing in America*, was of "an extremely healthy, well-managed conglomerate, composed of several operating divisions." Along with the book and publications companies, there was the information system company, composed of the F. W. Dodge division, Sweet's division, and Datapro Research Corporation. Two other divisions were Standard & Poor's Corporation and the McGraw-Hill Broadcasting Company. Total operating revenues amounted to more than $761 million, crossing the $1 billion threshold in 1980.

Its very success made McGraw-Hill the target of a takeover attempt by the American Express Company in 1979. The chairman of American Express, James D. Robinson III, and its president, Roger H. Morley, were shocked by the ferocity with which Harold McGraw fought the attempted stock buyout. Concerted action by the McGraw family, along with various legal actions, defeated the bid for ownership. Although American Express had failed, McGraw-Hill remained a prime target for a takeover. Harold McGraw was planning to retire in four years and, while another generation of McGraws waited in the wings, none were as yet ready to run the corporation. By appointing Joseph L. Dionne, who had been in charge of planning, to the newly created position of vice president of operations, McGraw sought to improve management organization and put someone in charge who could generate the fast growth needed to discourage further takeover attempts.

## DAWN OF THE ELECTRONIC AGE: 1980–90

Dionne became president and CEO in 1983, while McGraw remained chairman. A former history teacher, Dionne proved a visionary intent on transforming McGraw-Hill from "a simple publishing company" into an "information turbine" for the digital age. Under this model, McGraw-Hill's content would flow seamlessly throughout the company's vast information-gathering and disseminating "machine." As Suzanne Oliver described it in a 1990 *Forbes* article, "Housing statistics, say, could go into the turbine and come out as a feature story in a magazine and then as a new bond rating on a home builder. Like a packing house of old, McGraw-Hill would turn the same basic raw material into dozens of different products." Under Dionne's guidance, the company was reorganized into "market focus groups" as opposed to groupings by media. In 1985 Dionne created 20 market-focused business units.

Although still committed to print publishing, Dionne planned to reduce the 80 percent of the business that was print-oriented in 1983 to 65 percent or 70 percent over several years. The company had made a halting step toward this goal with the acquisition of Data Resources, Inc. (DRI), in 1979. Dionne was convinced that DRI held not only a vast share of the world's business and economic data but also the expertise required to translate McGraw-Hill's hard copy into malleable electronic information. Although the DRI acquisition would prove to be a misstep (the company actually made most of its money from renting computer space), Dionne pressed on with his plan. During this same period, McGraw-Hill entered the computer publishing field by acquiring *BYTE, Unixworld*, and *LAN Times* magazines, as well as Osborne Books, all of which provided support information to computer users. As the company moved into the electronic information marketplace, much of the data

supplied by the news service, magazines, Standard & Poor's, Dodge, Piatt, and Shepard's was made available in computerized form and in various configurations.

Despite his reservations, Harold McGraw approved of the direction in which Dionne was taking the company. In 1988 Harold McGraw became chairman emeritus and Dionne added the title of chairman to those of president and CEO. In its attempt to weather the communications revolution, McGraw-Hill had undergone three major reorganizations in four years, resulting in an organization centered around 14 market-focus groups. These reorganizations, the automation of F. W. Dodge, and the shutdown of the general-book division, ending the company's involvement in the trade book market, resulted in a layoff of more then 1,000 workers.

The company expanded globally and had success with the Standard & Poor's Marketscope and with other online, real-time services. Early in 1990, however, two online services, McGraw-Hill News and Standard & Poor's News, were discontinued. Some acquisitions resulted in costly write-offs, notably Nu-merax Inc., an electronic data and services operation. McGraw-Hill continued, however, to invest in strong growth markets and divest itself of publications and units connecting it with its past. *American Machinist & Automated Manufacturing, Coal Age*, and *Engineering & Mining Journal* were sold in 1987. Although it took years of acquisitions and divestments, more than a few stumbles, and intensive development from within, Dionne's model proved not only successful but prescient.

In 1988 McGraw-Hill celebrated its centennial, acquired Random House's college division for over $200 million, and created the Harold W. McGraw Jr. Prize in Education to honor the chairman emeritus's efforts on behalf of education and literacy. Operating revenues for the year were just shy of $1.7 billion. The next year, 1989, McGraw-Hill entered into a 50/50 joint venture with Macmillan, combining the elementary, secondary, and vocational education businesses of both companies. In 1990 a new electronic textbook publishing system known as Primis was implemented, allowing teachers to custom design textbooks with the results printed, bound, and shipped within 48 hours. Primis quickly became America's leading custom publisher.

## KEEPING THE WORLD UP TO SPEED: THE NINETIES

The early 1990s found McGraw-Hill growing steadily in its quest to provide information in a wide range of formats for persons of all ages. In 1993 the company bought out Macmillan's half of the Macmillan/

McGraw-Hill School Publishing Company for $160.8 million, and by the following year McGraw-Hill's three business segments (Educational and Professional Publishing, Financial Services, and Information and Media Services) helped the company rake in almost $2.8 billion in revenue, a sizeable leap from the previous year's $2.2 billion. The Educational/Professional unit accounted for the most revenue (42 percent), while Financial Services dominated income with over 48 percent, despite the worst bond market since 1927 and rising interest rates.

For McGraw-Hill, Inc., 1995 proved a pivotal year in which the company ceased to exist, at least in its previous form. To reflect its ongoing diversity, the company changed its name from McGraw-Hill, Inc., to The McGraw-Hill Companies, Inc., followed by a broadcast media campaign showcasing how the company was "keeping the world up to speed." Other milestones for 1995 were an all-time high stock price and a two-for-one stock split, as well as additional ratings services and new alliances for Standard & Poor's. Along with a myriad of new CD-ROM products, including Harrison's *Principals of Internal Medicine* (the world's best-selling medical textbook), there was a joint venture between the company's secondary school publisher Glencoe/McGraw-Hill, National Geographic, and Capital Cities/ABC. In addition, the company acquired UCB Canada and Hospital Practice and opened new offices in Asia, Europe, and the Middle East.

McGraw-Hill's most famous periodical, *Business-Week*, experienced a phenomenal year in 1995 with exceptional circulation (over one million with a readership of nearly seven million) and pumped up advertising volume and revenue. Additionally, *BusinessWeek Online* gained in popularity and *BusinessWeek Enterprise*, a magazine for small-business executives, published international editions in Asia, Europe, Latin America, and the Middle East. With so many new opportunities swirling about, McGraw-Hill, inevitably, let others go: Shepard's publishing operations and SRA Technology were sold, while Open Computing ceased publication. Despite a disastrous showing in Mexico after the peso's collapse, McGraw-Hill still managed to increase overall earnings by nearly 12 percent to $227.1 million while revenue topped $2.9 billion, a 6.3 percent increase over 1994's stellar performance.

In 1996 McGraw-Hill continued to expand its operations globally, with several high profile acquisitions, including Open Court Publishing Company for its K-8 elementary education division, *Healthcare Informatics* and *InfoCare* magazines from Wiesner Publishing for its Healthcare Information unit, and the Times Mir-

ror Higher Education Group, which prompted the formation of the Higher Education and Consumer Group to house it and McGraw-Hill's well established college division. The Times-Mirror acquisition made McGraw-Hill America's top college publisher, with leading positions in 12 disciplines and a particular strength in business. The college division's emphasis on business and finance meshed well with the corporation's financial services operations. Around that same time, the Financial Information Services unit was renamed to reflect its most important asset, Standard & Poor's, to Standard & Poor's Financial Information Services.

## A MCGRAW AT THE HELM: LATE NINETIES

When CEO Joe Dionne retired in 1998, he could look back on a 15-year record of innovation and growth. He was succeeded in April 1998 by Harold "Terry" McGraw, a great-grandson of the founder who had logged 13 years at McGraw-Hill before ascending to president in 1993. Although McGraw's climb to the top spot was viewed by some with skepticism, he quickly proved to be a "big picture" leader for a new era. He focused on enlivening the company's identity through a $4.5 million promotion targeting industry analysts and investors. In-house, he concentrated on cutting costs and investing in growth businesses. He consolidated McGraw-Hill's divisions from 15 down to 3 and sacked two-thirds of the company's senior managers. A 1998 article in *Crain's New York Business* called Terry McGraw's global expansion of Standard & Poor's "his most meaningful accomplishment." His efforts paid off in higher returns: While revenues increased only slightly from 1997 to 1998, earnings increased by 15.6 percent.

In 2000 McGraw-Hill moved to challenge Pearson Education for the top spot in educational publishing with the acquisition of Tribune Education. The nation's top publisher of K-12 supplements, Tribune was one of McGraw-Hill's largest purchases in years, at $635 million. The horserace for leadership of the textbook industry continued, however, when rival Thomson Corp. acquired Harcourt's higher-education and professional/corporate divisions from Reed-Elsevier in 2001.

With sales of $4.6 billion in 2001, McGraw-Hill stood as America's top K-12 education publisher and led the world in financial analyses and risk assessments though its Standard & Poor's financial services. With a 20 percent decline in net income from 2000 to 2001, however, the company announced a year-end restructuring that cut 5 percent of the global workforce, or 925 employees. McGraw-Hill continued to cut costs and refocus over the next two years, when it sold its MMS

International unit, which provided real-time fixed-income and foreign-exchange commentary and analysis, and then sold its 45 percent stake in its Manhattan headquarters building.

In early 2004 it sold its retail educational book division, and then it reorganized its entire professional book group from three divisions into two. McGraw-Hill also sold another peripheral operation, the municipal bond broker J. J. Kenny Drake. The company, however, was also adding to its data and research offerings, acquiring Capital IQ, a financial data provider, for Standard & Poor's. It also purchased J. D. Power and Associates, supplier of well-known automobile and truck surveys, in 2005 and bought Automotive Research Asia, an auto industry consultancy, for J. D. Power the following year.

## BELT-TIGHTENING AND THE RATINGS BOOM: 2000–05

Fallout from the economic and other crises of the early years of the new millennium was affecting McGraw-Hill. In 2002 the Commodity Futures Trading Commission, which was conducting an investigation of energy-trading practices, subpoenaed documents, employee information, customer lists, and other materials from Platt's, the company's energy research and information unit. McGraw-Hill refused to turn over some of the information sought, arguing the request violated the First Amendment. A federal judge ruled in 2005 that the company had to turn over the data. Controversy also touched another McGraw-Hill data-and-research provider, Standard & Poor's. In 2004 a former Standard & Poor's analyst pleaded guilty in an insider-trading case that involved improper use of information he had gathered on the job.

Data and research, especially for the financial sector, were becoming an ever more important component of McGraw-Hill's profits. In January 2004 the company reported a 19 percent boost in fourth-quarter net income, to $159.9 million. Revenue for financial services, including Standard & Poor's, led the way with a 21 percent jump. Education and testing services still dominated the revenue mix, with revenue from this area having quadrupled since 1990 to account for 49 percent of the company total. Revenue from sales of research on stocks and bonds had tripled to compose 34 percent of total sales, while only 17 percent came from McGraw-Hill's advertising-based information and media unit.

The formula was proving successful: The company had delivered a 10.4 percent total annual return to shareholders over the past five years, compared with 1 percent per year for the benchmark Standard & Poor's (S&P) 500 index. Within the McGraw-Hill fold,

Standard & Poor's itself was expanding geographically as well as into new corners of the financial information business. It formed a joint venture with Citic Securities Co. in 2006 to develop and promote benchmark indexes for the Chinese securities market.

Meanwhile, Standard & Poor's, along with competitors Moody's and Fitch, was expanding its ratings service from corporate and government bonds to encompass "structured finance" deals: securities created from all or parts of mortgages, credit card debt, and other streams of income, such as mortgage-backed securities and collateralized debt obligations. By 2005 most of Standard & Poor's revenue came from supplying ratings on this fast-growing category of investments. "Structured finance showed strength across all asset classes and in all of our international regions," Terry McGraw told Richard Beales and Gillian Tett in the *Financial Times*.

Standard & Poor's now accounted for some 70 percent of McGraw-Hill's total corporate profits. Noting that the company's stock price was not rising as fast as that of rival Moody's, a stand-alone concern that had no other businesses but its rating service, some observers like Andrew Bary in *Barron's* suggested that McGraw-Hill's shareholders would benefit if Standard & Poor's was spun off. Terry McGraw opposed the idea, arguing that diversification had advantages and citing the stock's strong performance.

## STANDARD & POOR'S AND THE MORTGAGE COLLAPSE: 2006–08

In March 2006 Standard & Poor's launched 10 indexes to track housing prices in different regions of the United States, along with a nationwide composite index, all of which it expected to serve as the basis for futures and options contracts. Unfortunately, the housing bubble of inflated home values, and much of the business derived from it, was starting to deflate. In June Standard & Poor's revised its criteria for evaluating pools of mortgages that allowed home buyers to use other loans to finance their down payments.

By the following year Standard & Poor's and its rivals were becoming embarrassed by revelations that they had assigned investment-grade ratings to securitized products made up of shaky subprime mortgages. McGraw-Hill's stock price dropped 6 percent in February and March 2007 on these concerns. Some observers were calling into question the rating agencies' revenue model, by which they were paid to issue judgments by the same institutions that packaged and underwrote the securities and often worked with those institutions to make sure the final product received a respectable rating.

In July Standard & Poor's downgraded hundreds of debt issues backed by risky home loans. The U.S. Securities and Exchange Commission (SEC) and the state attorneys general of New York and Ohio announced in September that they were investigating the mortgage market and the rating agencies. Standard & Poor's was subpoenaed to turn over documents by New York State Attorney General Andrew Cuomo. Standard & Poor's, Moody's, and Fitch all agreed to cooperate in the probe. The Senate Banking Committee and the House Financial Services Committee were also planning hearings into the ratings firms' role in the subprime mortgage business.

To partially end the New York inquiry a year later, the agencies agreed to change their compensation structure. Instead of being paid by the banks only if they were selected to rate bonds backed by individual home loans, they would be paid for all work they performed, including initial reviews and discussions. McGraw-Hill itself was taking measures to tighten control of Standard & Poor's, having seen its stock drop from a peak of $72.50 in June 2007 to $41.67 in August 2008. That month, four key executives of the unit departed as part of a broad management shakeup.

Even as the company worked to contain and correct problems at Standard & Poor's, it was again cutting costs to address a difficult economic environment and eroding profits. McGraw-Hill Education group underwent 2 major restructurings in 18 months. The first, in 2006, resulted in 405 jobs eliminated. The group saw gains in sales and earnings the following year. Nevertheless, in January 2008 McGraw-Hill announced that the education group would be cutting another 611 jobs, about 3 percent of its global workforce, and taking a $43.7 million charge. Net income for the entire company declined 30 percent during the first six months of 2008, and for the rest of the year McGraw-Hill continued to tighten its belt, cutting a total of 1,045 jobs.

### NEW BUSINESS PROSPECTS: 2008–09

Some positive signals were peeping through. While states' spending on schools, reduced due to the recession and collapse in property tax revenues, was dampening K-12 sales, the company in January 2009 forecast an offsetting boost from the higher education market, building on 3 to 4 percent growth chalked up the previous year. McGraw-Hill was looking for ways to take advantage. One avenue was the fast-growing textbook rental market. The company entered into a deal with Chegg, an online textbook-rental business, to supply 25 of its books to Chegg in return for a portion of the rental income.

Another route was Connect, a new service the company launched in 2009 that delivers college coursework to students over the Web, including notes and video lectures, and enables them to answer practice exam questions. The product aimed to help McGraw-Hill keep pace with the transition in college study from textbooks to greater use of interactive, multimedia tools. Connect "is where we see this all going," Ed Stanford, president of McGraw-Hill Higher Education, told Kelly Nolan in the *Wall Street Journal*.

The company was continuing to penetrate Web-based businesses in other ways, while also managing its exposure to these businesses. In 2005 McGraw-Hill joined with a group of large publishers in a copyright lawsuit against Google aimed at the company's Google Print Library project, set up to scan millions of books and make their content searchable online. A year later McGraw-Hill teamed with Hearst Corp. to invest in Gather Inc., a start-up social-networking site aimed at adults.

*Business Week* was looking to integrate its traditional, print magazine with the Web but was hampered by declining ad revenues in the print edition. In 2005 it closed its European and Asian editions and announced layoffs. For all of 2008, the entire *Business Week* operation lost $43 million. Ad pages declined by a third in the first quarter of 2009. In July McGraw-Hill hired an adviser to explore selling *Business Week*. A purchaser emerged in October: Bloomberg L.P., which McGraw-Hill had been rumored three years earlier to be considering buying. The final deal called for Bloomberg to take over the 80-year-old magazine in exchange for $5 million and the assumption of some $31.9 million in liabilities.

McGraw-Hill remained dependent on Standard & Poor's for as much as three-quarters of its earnings. The rating agencies as a group were still the focus of lawsuits and congressional and regulatory action. Consequently, much of McGraw-Hill's attention was still focused on Standard & Poor's. The company announced a series of organization and procedural changes in early 2008 aimed at bolstering confidence in the agency's practices. These included rotation of lead analysts every five years so that relationships with companies, governments, and packagers of structured finance vehicles did not become entrenched. The company also hired a chief credit officer to better monitor the quality of Standard & Poor's ratings.

## RECOVERY: 2009–10 AND BEYOND

In the first few months of 2010, McGraw-Hill had reason to both mourn and celebrate. In March the company observed the passing of former chairman and CEO Harold W. McGraw Jr., at age 92. He did live to see McGraw-Hill experience a financial recovery as its own cost-cutting measures paid off. For fourth-quarter 2009 the company reported its first increase in quarterly diluted earnings in two years, a 43.2 percent boost from the same period in 2008. "Continued recovery in the corporate new issue market here and overseas at Standard & Poor's Credit Market Services and an upswing in higher education, professional and international markets enabled us to finish 2009 positively and set the stage for more growth in 2010," Terry McGraw said in a press statement. "Increased revenue and tight cost controls contributed to substantial improvement in our operating margin."

In January McGraw-Hill announced it was working on applications for the iPad, Apple Inc.'s new tablet computer. As quoted by Jeffrey A. Trachtenberg in the *Wall Street Journal*, Terry McGraw predicted, "In the near future you'll undoubtedly see a McGraw-Hill e-book for the college market running on the Apple tablet." With its long history of innovation and diversification, McGraw-Hill seemed ready to face the future challenges posed by the publishing industry.

*Wilson B. Lindauer*
*Updated, Taryn Benbow-Pfalzgraf;*
*April Gasbarre; Eric Laursen*

## PRINCIPAL SUBSIDIARIES

Capital IQ, Inc.; ClariFI, Inc.; CTB/McGraw-Hill LLC; Editora McGraw-Hill de Portugal, Ltda.; Editorial Interamericana, S.A. (Colombia); Funds Research SRL (Argentina); Funds Research USA, LLC; Grow.net, Inc.; International Advertising/McGraw-Hill, Inc.; J. D. Power and Associates; Lands End Publishing; McGraw-Hill Australia Pty Limited; McGraw-Hill Broadcasting Company, Inc.; McGraw-Hill Cayman Finance Ltd.; McGraw-Hill Holdings Europe Limited; McGraw-Hill Information Systems Company of Canada Limited; McGraw-Hill/Interamericana de Chile Limitada; McGraw-Hill/Interamericana de Venezuela S.A.; McGraw-Hill Interamericana Editores, S.A. de C.V. (Mexico); McGraw-Hill Interamericana, Inc.; McGraw-Hill/Interamericana, S.A. (Panama); McGraw-Hill International Enterprises, Inc.; McGraw-Hill News Bureaus, Inc.; McGraw-Hill New York, Inc.; McGraw-Hill Publications Overseas Corporation; McGraw-Hill Real Estate, Inc.; McGraw-Hill Ryerson Limited;

McGraw-Hill Ventures, Inc.; Money Market Directories, Inc.; S & P India LLC; Standard & Poor's (Dubai) Limited; Standard & Poor's Europe, Inc.; Standard & Poor's Financial Services LLC; Standard & Poor's Hong Kong LLC; Standard & Poor's International, LLC; Standard & Poor's International Services, Inc.; Standard & Poor's Investment Advisory Services (HK) Limited; Standard & Poor's Investment Advisory Services LLC; Standard & Poor's, LLC; Standard & Poor's Securities Evaluations, Inc.; Standard & Poor's Maalot Ltd. (Israel); Standard & Poor's, S.A. de C.V. (Mexico); Standard & Poor's South Asia Services (Private) Limited (India); Sunshine International, Inc.; Tata McGraw Hill Education Private Limited (India); WaterRock Insurance, LLC.

## PRINCIPAL OPERATING UNITS

Education: CTB/McGraw-Hill; Glencoe/McGraw-Hill; The Grow Network/McGraw-Hill; Macmillan/McGraw-Hill; McGraw-Hill Contemporary; McGraw-Hill Custom Publishing; McGraw-Hill Digital Learning; McGraw-Hill Education (Asia); McGraw-Hill Education (Australia); McGraw-Hill Education (Europe); McGraw-Hill Education (Spain); McGraw-Hill Higher Education; McGraw-Hill Interamericana (Latin America); McGraw-Hill Professional; McGraw-Hill Professional Development; McGraw-Hill/Ryerson (Canada); Open University Press (UK); SRA/McGraw-Hill; Wright Group/McGraw-Hill; Tata/McGraw-Hill (India). Financial services: Standard & Poor's. Information and media: Aviation Week Group; Broadcasting Group; J.D. Power and Associates; McGraw-Hill Construction; Platts.

## PRINCIPAL COMPETITORS

Pearson PLC; Thomson Reuters Corp.; Moody's Corp.; Morningstar, Inc.; Bloomberg L.P.; Reed Elsevier Group PLC; Wolters Kluwer N.V.

## FURTHER READING

Burlingame, Roger, *Endless Frontiers: The Story of McGraw-Hill.* New York: McGraw-Hill, 1959.

Clifford, Stephanie, and David Carr, "Bloomberg Buys BusinessWeek from McGraw-Hill, Moving into Consumer Media," *New York Times*, October 14, 2009.

Colter, Allison Bisbey, "S&P's Rating of Mortgage Pools Is Revised amid Exotic Lending," *Wall Street Journal*, June 15, 2006.

Fabrikant, Geraldine, "At McGraw-Hill, an Heir Takes Over and the Company Flourishes, *New York Times*, June 27, 2005.

Lehmann-Haupt, Christopher, "Harold W. McGraw Jr., 92, Chairman of McGraw-Hill," *New York Times*, March 25, 2010.

Lucchetti, Aaron, and Serena Ng, "Credit and Blame: How Rating Firms' Calls Fueled Subprime Mess," *Wall Street Journal*, August 15, 2007.

McGraw, Harold III, "The Global Information Revolution," *Vital Speeches*, August 15, 2000, p. 655.

Milliot, Jim, "New Media Helps Spur Sales at McGraw-Hill Cos.," *Publishers Weekly*, April 15, 1996, p. 20.

Oliver, Suzanne, "Management by Concept," *Forbes*, November 26, 1990, p. 37.

Picker, Ida, "Joseph Dionne of McGraw-Hill Cos.: A Place in Cyberspace," *Institutional Investor*, December 1996, p. 27.

Tebbel, John, *A History of Book Publishing in the United States*, 4 vols. New York: R. R. Bowker Company, 1972–81.

# Meridian Bioscience, Inc.

3471 River Hills Drive
Cincinnati, Ohio 45224
U.S.A.
Telephone: (513) 271-3700
Toll Free: (800) 543-1980
Fax: (513) 271-3762
Web site: http://www.meridianbioscience.com/

*Public Company*
*Founded:* 1976
*Incorporated:* 1986
*Employees:* 423
*Sales:* $148.27 million (2009)
*Stock Exchanges:* NASDAQ
*Ticker Symbol:* VIVO
*NAICS:* 325413 In-Vitro Diagnostic Substance Manufacturing; 325414 Biological Product (except Diagnostic) Manufacturing

■ ■ ■

Meridian Bioscience, Inc., produces diagnostic test kits for respiratory, gastrointestinal, viral, and parasitic infectious diseases, including pneumonia, influenza, ulcers, mononucleosis, strep throat, and chicken pox. Its kits test samples of blood, urine, stool, and other body fluids or tissues for the presence of antibodies and antigens of specific infectious diseases. It also provides transport media that store and preserve sample specimens from patient collection to laboratory testing. In the area of research, Meridian produces and distributes bulk antigens, antibodies, and reagents used by researchers. It

also manufactures proteins and other biologicals for pharmaceutical and biotechnology companies. Meridian's products are used in reference laboratories, hospitals, physicians' offices, and veterinary testing centers in the United States, Canada, and more than 60 countries throughout the world.

## MERIDIAN DIAGNOSTICS: 1976–2000

In 1966 William J. Motto took a job selling diagnostic products, and over a period of 10 years he visited about 4,000 U.S. hospitals, learning what their needs were. In 1976 he founded Diagnostic Products with a $500 investment. His first product was a rapid fungal test. In his previous job he had seen the difficulties hospitals had in collecting stool samples, and he developed what he believed was a practical solution. Motto designed a plastic container with a preservative, called Parapak, and he sold out his first 2,000 units to a hospital in Kentucky. Diagnostic Products next developed a strep throat test, introducing its *C. difficile* detection kits in the early 1980s.

In 1986 Diagnostic Products went public and changed its name to Meridian Diagnostics. By April 1991 the company had grown enough to enter into an agreement with Disease Detection International, Inc., of Irvine, California, to manufacture, market, and sell test kits for pregnancy, strep throat, and herpes. Meridian was given exclusive worldwide rights to manufacture and sell tests using Disease Detection's technology in exchange for $210,000, including a $100,000 advance against royalties. Disease Detection would receive 6 percent royalty on all such products sold by Meridian.

## COMPANY PERSPECTIVES

Our mission is to efficiently apply our human, scientific and financial resources to provide innovative high value products and technologies that improve the diagnosis and treatment of infectious diseases and metabolic disorders.

Meridian introduced important products to market during the late 1990s, including a test in 1997 that revealed Shiga toxin. Shiga toxin causes hemolytic uremic syndrome (HUS), a condition that follows a gastrointestinal infection such as *E. coli* and may cause kidney failure. The following year Meridian was granted the first U.S. patent for the *Helicobacter pylori* Stool Antigen test, the first totally noninvasive test for diagnosing *H. pylori* infection, the primary causative agent of stomach ulcers.

At about the same time, the company was growing through acquisitions. In September 1998 Fresenius AG of Germany, the world's largest producer of diagnostic products, sold its 5.2 million shares of Gull Laboratories of Salt Lake City to Meridian Diagnostics. A subsidiary of Gull, Biodesign International, provided Meridian an entrance into the life science market.

### EXPANDING INTO LIFE SCIENCE: 2001

On January 24, 2001, Meridian shareholders formally approved a name change from Meridian Diagnostics to Meridian Bioscience, Inc. The company expanded its Life Science Division in 2000 with the acquisition of Viral Antigens, Inc., which later received a patent for anti-rubella IgM antibodies. In addition, Meridian entered into an exclusive supply agreement with Ora Sure Technologic to bring its Uplink technology to market. Meridian Life Science, Inc., was formed as a wholly owned subsidiary of Meridian Bioscience in 2001 to produce proteins and other biologicals for pharmaceutical and biotechnology companies engaged in research for new drugs and vaccines. Meridian Life Science, located in Memphis, Tennessee, and Portland, Maine, supplies monoclonal and polyclonal antibodies, purified antigens, assay development reagents, and custom antibody services to pharmaceutical, diagnostic, and biotechnology companies and to academic researchers.

Early in 2001 the Food and Drug Administration (FDA) cited Meridian Bioscience for failing to validate a

lyophilization (freeze-drying) process gained with the acquisition of Gull Laboratories in 1998. After an FDA reinspection of manufacturing and quality procedures at Meridian's headquarters plant, Meridian voluntarily removed 30 of its diagnostic tests from the marketplace. Meridian then signed an agreement with Zeus Scientific to manufacture test kits sold under the Meridian brand name for the detection of measles, mumps, chicken pox, Lyme disease, herpes, Epstein-Barr virus (EBV), mycoplasma, and Legionella.

The company's overseas business received a boost in July 2002, when the Japanese distributor TFB, Inc., began distributing Meridian's ImmunoCard STAT Adenovirus test. This 10-minute test is used to detect the virus that causes conjunctivitis, pharyngitis, and gastrointestinal disease. That same month, Meridian Bioscience issued a letter of intent to acquire Biotrin Holdings PLC, headquartered in Dublin, Ireland. Biotrin works with biomarkers in the field of predictive toxicology. It also has a patented diagnostic test for parvovirus, a pathogen that can cause serious complications during pregnancy and for transplant patients.

Between September 2004 and February 2005 Meridian Bioscience distributed quality assurance kits that inadvertently contained a dangerous strain of Asian flu that had killed more than two million people worldwide in 1957. Quality assurance kits are used to verify that laboratories can identify what they say they can identify. The College of American Pathologists had contracted with Meridian to send samples of a type A influenza virus in a test kit to 3,700 laboratories in the United States, Canada, and 16 other countries. The flu strain that Meridian included was A(H2N2), which had not been seen since 1968, when vaccines no longer included the strain, leaving anyone born since that time without immunity. Meridian believed A(H2N2) was a low-level biosafety microbe. However, the National Institutes of Health and the Centers for Disease Control were at the time considering raising the biosafety level of the microbe, as Canada and other countries had done. The strain was identified by a Canadian lab, and, once the potential threat was recognized, most of the distributed kits and Meridian's stockpile of A(H2N2) were destroyed without any reported cases of the illness.

### NEW PARTNERSHIPS: 2005–09

In 2005 Meridian acquired OEM Concepts, Inc., and in 2006 Meridian Life Science completed its manufacturing of a recombinant protein for the NIH for use in clinical trials of a vaccine for parvovirus. In January 2007 the company completed manufacturing of a clinical infectious inoculum of respiratory syncytide virus (RSV). RSV is the most important cause of

## KEY DATES

**1976:** William J. Motto founds Diagnostic Products, later renamed Meridian Diagnostics.

**1998:** Meridian is granted the first U.S. patent for a test for *H. pylori*, which causes stomach ulcers.

**2001:** Meridian Diagnostics changes its name to Meridian Bioscience, Inc.

**2005:** Meridian inadvertently includes the deadly 1957 Asian flu virus in quality assurance kits distributed to 3,700 laboratories worldwide.

**2010:** Meridian announces it will begin molecular testing.

pneumonia and bronchiolitis in infants and small children. The RSV clinical material produced was used to conduct human challenge studies to determine the optimal infectious levels. Alnylam Pharmaceuticals used the RSV clinical material to evaluate its treatment of RSV infection, and Richard L. Eberle, president of Meridian Life Science, commented: "The combination of Alnylam's clinical expertise with our scientific and technical capabilities led to the development and production of important clinical viral materials."

Meridian continued to expand its international operations through licensing and distribution agreements as well as subsidiaries. On October 25, 2006, Meridian signed an agreement with Eiken Chemical Company Ltd. in Tokyo to license Eiken's gene amplification technology, the Loop-mediated Isothermal Amplification (LAMP) Method, allowing Meridian to enter the nucleic-acid testing market. In September 2008 Meridian Bioscience began an exclusive Canadian distribution agreement with Somagen Diagnostics of Alberta.

In 2008, through its subsidiaries in Belgium, France, the Netherlands, and Italy, Meridian began distributing rapid tests for the Epstein-Barr virus infections TRU EBV-M and TRU EBV-G, the first rapid tests that used recombinant antigen technology to detect IgM and IgG antibodies specific to EBV, the primary cause of infectious mononucleosis.

In September 2009 Meridian Bioscience Europe signed an agreement with Bühlmann Laboratories AG of Switzerland for distribution in Italy of an innovative test for inflammatory intestinal conditions, known as Quantum Blue Calprotectin. Calprotectin is a gastrointestinal inflammatory marker, and the test is instrumental in differentiating inflammatory bowel disease (IBD) and irritable bowel syndrome (IBS). The test also allows for the avoidance of colon endoscopies for ulcerative colitis or Crohn's disease.

### MOLECULAR TESTING BEGINS: 2010

In January 2010 Meridian Bioscience announced first quarter earnings of $8.9 million because of high sales of influenza test kits. Meridian had only just received clearance from the FDA to market its two new upper respiratory tests: TRU FLU and TRU RSV. Based on rapid test technology, TRU FLU detects both influenza A and influenza B, and TRU RSV detects respiratory syncytial virus. The CDC predicted that in 2010, 60 million people in the United States would contract influenza and 36,000 would die. While test kits for upper respiratory infections dominated sales in the United States, tests for food-borne infections also grew. Income for Meridian Life Science, which manufactured reagents and biologicals, also grew from $5.1 million in 2009 to $5.5 million.

Also in January, Meridian CEO John Kraeutler announced that the company would begin molecular testing. Molecular tests were so sensitive that they could detect a single bacterium or virion in a tiny sample. Meridian started clinical trials of its molecular test for *C. difficile*, and molecular tests marketed under the brand name Illumigene provided multi-analyte testing. Most of the molecular assays on the market were based on polymerase chain reaction (PCR) technology, in which the sample's temperature had to be raised and lowered several times to amplify it to be tested, which required large pieces of capital equipment. Meridian's product remains at a constant temperature and is simple enough to be run one at a time.

However, on March 17, 2010, Meridian Bioscience shares fell 15.2 percent after it lowered its 2010 sales forecast following the end of the swine flu (H1N1) pandemic in early December 2009. Kraeutler stated: "Due to the abrupt end to the H1N1 pandemic, lab and distributor inventories of these types of rapid flu tests are higher than normal. This may impact purchases ahead of the next season."

In 2009 *Forbes Small Business* magazine ranked Meridian Bioscience at number 34 on its list of the 100 Fastest-growing Small Public Companies and number 55 on its list of the 200 Best Small Companies. With a range of products that provide accuracy, simplicity, and speed in the early diagnosis and treatment of common medical conditions, Meridian occupied a strong market position, offering solutions that improve patient care while reducing the costs of health care.

*Louise B. Ketz*

## PRINCIPAL SUBSIDIARIES

Meridian Life Science, Inc.; Meridian Bioscience Europe.

## PRINCIPAL COMPETITORS

3M; Abbott Laboratories; Becton, Dickinson and Company; Conceptus, Inc.; Cyberonics, Inc.; Inverness Medical Innovations; Quidel Corporation; Siemens Healthcare Diagnostics Inc.; Thermo Fisher Scientific, Inc.

## FURTHER READING

Altman, Lawrence K., and Mark Santora, "Risk from Deadly Flu Strain Is Called Low," *New York Times*, April 14, 2005.

"Companies: Meridian Bioscience, Inc.," *New York Times*, 14 March 2009.

"FSB 100: America's Fastest-Growing Small Public Companies," *Fortune Small Business*, July/August 2009.

"Medical Concerns' Pact on Test Kits," *New York Times*, May 1, 1991.

"Meridian Bioscience Europe to Distribute Bühlmann Calprotectin Test in Italy," *Medical News*, October 1, 2009.

Smith-Morrow, Julie A., "William J. Motto and the Origins of Meridian Bioscience, Inc.," *American Biotechnology Laboratory*, September 2004.

Vanac, Mary, "Meridian Bioscience FDA Clearance to Add Swine Flu Claims to Rapid Flu Testing Device," *MedCity News*, September 17, 2009.

———, "Meridian Bioscience Sees Molecular Tests as Makeover of 'Just a Little Kit Company' Image," *MedCity News*, January 29, 2010.

# Mermaid Marine Australia Limited

———— ■ ————

**Eagle Jetty**
**20 Mews Road**
**Freemantle, Western Australia 6160**
**Australia**
**Telephone: (61 (8)) 9431-7431**
**Fax: (61 (8)) 9431-7432**
**Web site: http://www.mma.com.au**

*Public Company*
*Founded:* 1982
*Incorporated:* 1984
*Employees:* 179
*Sales:* AUD 163.88 million ($136.77) (2009)
*Stock Exchanges:* Australian
*Ticker Symbol:* MRM
*NAICS:* 488320 Marine Cargo Handling; 488330 Docking and Undocking Marine Vessel Services; 488390 Other Support Activities for Water Transportation; 541614 Process, Physical Distribution, and Logistics Consulting Services.

■ ■ ■

Mermaid Marine Australia Limited is Australia's largest provider of marine services to the oil and gas industry and one of Australia's 10 largest transportation and shipping firms as ranked by market capitalization. Based in Western Australia, the company operates a varied fleet of more than two dozen vessels and provides marine services for a blue-chip customer base predominantly operating in the North West Shelf and Browse Basin regions. The company conducts its business through two divisions: vessels and supply bases. The vessels segment provides crewed vessel charters, tugs, and barges for offshore construction services and management and logistics services which cover all phases of the offshore oil and gas industry development cycle. The supply base segment involves operations of the firm's two full-service supply bases, at Dampier and Broome in Western Australia, which provide docking and slipway services, ship maintenance and repair services, and other marine support facilities and services.

## COMPANY ORIGINS: 1982

Mermaid Marine Australia was launched with a single vessel in 1982 by Captain James Carver, a seasoned Shipmaster with an exhaustive knowledge of the marine industry. Before establishing Mermaid, Carver served as the first Shipmaster for Woodside Petroleum, an independent Australian oil and gas exploration and production firm that evolved into the country's largest. Not only did Carver establish his own career with Woodside, but after Mermaid Marine was founded, Carver's company also developed a productive long-term relationship with the oil and gas firm.

Woodside had begun its operations during the 1950s, exploring for oil in Southern Australia before moving to what would become known as the North West Shelf. During the early 1970s, Woodside made significant gas discoveries near Broome and Dampier, two Western Australia locations where Mermaid would later establish supply bases. Capitalizing on its discoveries, Woodside in 1980 signed a long-term contract with the State Energy Commission of Western Australia to provide gas to homes and industries. Two years later, to service the needs of exploration companies like Woodside, Carver launched his own company, drawing upon his experience in oil and liquid natural gas (LNG) activities in Western Australia. This experience included involvement in varied construction, exploration, and production programs for a majority of the oil and gas projects on the North West Shelf.

As oil and gas exploration expanded during the 1980s and 1990s along the Shelf, Mermaid grew as well. In 1989 Woodside began shipping LNG to Japan, solidifying the North West Shelf's position as Australia's largest resource development for the next two decades. Between 1992 and 1994, Carver completed his development of the Slimdrill, an award-winning oil-drilling rig that became the basis for a Mermaid subsidiary. The captain also guided the expansion of his company's fleet, which by 1998 had grown to 15 vessels and included tugboats, workboats, and barges involved in berthing assistance and support for exploration, supply, and survey activities. The majority of the Mermaid's vessels were engaged in the waters off Australia's northwest coast while smaller numbers were involved in long-term contracts further away: in the Pacific Ocean near New Zealand, in the Tasman Sea, and in Bass Strait. During the late 1990s Carver also lined up land for the company's development of supply bases for exploration and production fleets. With Mermaid prepared to significantly expand its business operations to include onshore activities, Carver decided the time was right for the company to go public.

### GOING PUBLIC: 1999

In a 1998 lead-up to an initial public offering, Alan Gordon Birchmore, who earlier in the decade ran a major Australian gold-mining firm, was tapped as Mermaid's chairman of the board. Carver became chief executive officer of the company he founded. In 1999 Mermaid signed a 21-year land-lease, with an option for another 21 years, for seafront property on Kings Bay to develop a supply base at Dampier. The firm signed a

similar lease for property on Roebuck Bay to set up a smaller base near a government wharf at Broome. After raising AUD 6.5 million from the private placement of 13 million shares of stock, or 30 percent of the company's share capital, Mermaid Marine went public in June 1999 and was listed on the Australian Stock Exchange.

Mermaid's strategy, as identified by Birchmore in the company's first annual report to shareholders, was to leverage its prime real estate in order to further develop and expand its marine services. In 2000 Mermaid began construction at Dampier, an ideal supply base location near onshore facilities and offshore operations of major players in the oil and gas industry. That same year, Mermaid established a smaller multi-use supply base at Broome. With these two locations, which sufficiently covered about 75 percent of the northwestern Australia oil and gas area, Mermaid was literally well positioned to accommodate and service future oil and gas developers in Western Australia. Because seafront property in northwestern Australia was extremely limited (and there was not another base within 1,000 miles of Dampier that offered repair services) Mermaid's base locations provided a strong competitive advantage.

### TRANSITIONING TO AN "INTEGRATED OIL AND GAS COMPANY"

As the new century opened, oil prices were falling, prompting a slowdown in offshore activity. As a result, Mermaid's annual revenues slid more than 40 percent in the company's fiscal year ending in June 2000, and the company posted a net loss of AUD 200,000. That same year, Carver ceded his post as chief executive officer to Mark Bradley, a former managing director of Clough Offshore, and Carver became executive director. To garner an additional revenue stream, the company joined with OIS MOC in 2000 to establish a 50-50 joint venture, Mermaid Labour & Management, a marine services work-for-hire subsidiary.

The year 2001 was a transitional year for Mermaid. As Birchmore summarized in that year's annual report, the company, from its founding to the turn of the century, consistently expanded its fleet "but offered no greater leverage than an ability to successfully and profitably operate a vessel fleet." However, upon entering the supply base business, Mermaid effectively began transitioning to an "integrated oil and gas services company" involving a portfolio of mutually complementary businesses, "each holding a competitive edge in their various sectors." By 2001 Mermaid's fleet of 17 was the largest in the North West Shelf area but,

## KEY DATES

**1982:** The company is founded by Shipmaster James Carver.
**1999:** Mermaid Marine Australia Limited goes public.
**2000:** Broome Supply Base is established.
**2002:** Dampier Supply Base opens.
**2007:** Mermaid begins international operations.

unlike in the past, the fleet was not the sole means of income for the company. In 2001 Mermaid added a new business line, forming a joint-venture shallow-water pipelay operation with Clough Engineering. Mermaid acquired a half-interest in Clough's pipe-laying ship in exchange for giving Clough a 20-percent interest in Mermaid, a deal that made Clough the largest Mermaid stakeholder for a short period.

In early 2001 Mermaid landed its first customer for the newly opened Broome Supply Base, the Japanese exploration firm INPEX Corporation. Within seven months of its opening, the Broome base became profitable, housing and supporting four major oil and gas firms. In August 2001 Mermaid opened its new AUD 6 million Dampier slipway, which was part of its AUD 22 million port-development plan. The Dampier Supply Base was officially opened the following year and also included a land-backed wharf, pipe-spooling yard, maintenance and repair service facilities, and berthing locale for tug and work boats. Dampier was designed as an alternative docking location (for routine and emergency docking) to reduce traveling time for both Mermaid vessels and those from exploration companies. Mermaid hoped to not only draw ships from the immediate region to Dampier but also larger vessels operating in the Timor Sea that would opt for Dampier rather than traveling further to Singapore.

## AN INFLUX IN CAPITAL LEADS TO UPGRADED FLEET AND SUPPLY BASES: 2002

In its 2002 fiscal year, Mermaid recorded earnings of AUD 85,000, one-quarter of the previous year's net. Falling oil prices translated to a poor market for vessels, and the company also failed to earn its traditional share of offshore construction support work. In order to accelerate its growth plan, Mermaid turned to the capital and operational resources of major investors Clough Engineering and PSA Marine Ltd. of Singapore, the lat-

ter of which acquired a 20 percent stake in Mermaid in 2002. The two major investments were expected to provide Mermaid with the financial resources to assume larger projects. That same year, Jeffrey Weber, a former BHP Transport executive, was brought on board as chief operations officer to oversee supply bases, vessel activities, slipway operations, and the labor-hire business.

In 2003 Mermaid began an ongoing program of retiring older vessels and adding newer, more powerful ones. In May 2004 Mermaid entered a three-year agreement with BHP Billiton to provide marine services for BHP's oil and gas Griffin's facility off the coast of Western Australia. With such new projects developing throughout its service area, Mermaid officials believed the company was in the right place at the right time. During its fiscal 2004 year, the Mermaid-Clough venture landed six of seven available pipe-laying contracts as the company earned AUD 4.3 million on climbing revenues of AUD 42.3 million. In late 2004, Mermaid formed a joint venture with Toll Energy Logistics, a provider of integrated logistics services, to seek common offshore business activities.

For the year ending June 2005, Mermaid's revenues rose to AUD 48.26 million, although income slipped to AUD 2.52 million. In October 2005 Mermaid sold its 200-person labor-hire business to (and acquired a five-vessel fleet of offshore vessels from) Integrated Group. This transaction gave Mermaid a total of 24 vessels, representing the largest oil and gas support fleet in Australia. Integrated received AUD 19.4 million as part of the deal, and its personnel service agreed to provide exclusive manning services to Mermaid's fleet for seven years.

## SUPPLY BASE EXPANSION PROJECTS AND MANAGEMENT CHANGES: 2006

As the number of exploration firms engaged in northwest Australia increased in the middle of the decade, so did the number of service firms. Mermaid's competitors were growing in number, but they were generally smaller companies offering only a portion of Mermaid's portfolio of services. To keep up with the region's growth in exploration, Mermaid began expanding both Dampier and Broome. At Dampier, the company doubled the size of the wharf and constructed a roll-on roll-off cargo ramp and additional storage facilities. To develop and oversee an expanded Broome Supply Base, Mermaid and Toll Energy formed a new joint venture, Toll Mermaid Logistics Broome in 2006

Tony Howarth succeed Birchmore as chairman in 2006. Birchmore retired and became a non-executive director. That same year, Carver returned to an executive director's seat after five years away from day-to-day operations. Mermaid logged AUD 9.2 million in earnings in 2006, nearly tripling the previous year's net, on revenues of AUD 71.1 million. Part of the rise in revenues was due to an expanded fleet size. Since taking control of the five Integrated ships, Mermaid had begun earning nearly AUD 1 million per month. Mermaid's success did not go unnoticed. While Clough and PSA Marine no longer owned large stakes in the company, Mermaid had attracted several investment banks as its largest shareholders.

## 2007: A FAILED MERGER AND FINANCIAL SUCCESS

In late 2006 Mermaid Marine began serious merger discussions with P&O Maritime Services Pty Limited, a division of the Dubai Government's DP World group, to create what would become Australia's largest marine services firm, with annual revenues of more than AUD 200 million and a fleet of 140 vessels. By December 2006 the two companies had reached a preliminary agreement: Mermaid would issue 221 million shares to DP World, and Mermaid shareholders in exchange would receive stock in three P&O companies controlled by DP World. Initially, Mermaid directors favored the deal, which would have made DP World owner of 60 percent of Mermaid shares, because it would infuse capital into Mermaid and provide ample opportunities for geographical expansion.

In early 2007 Birchmore left the company board for personal reasons and sold about half his shares for AUD 6.3 million. Company founder James Carver sold half of his 7 percent stake in Mermaid for AUD 5.3 million, and non-executive director Mark Bradley likewise sold half of his shares for AUD 3 million. Both Carver and Bradley had planned to resign and divest shares when the merger with DP World took effect.

The merger appeared all but concluded until Mermaid's stellar half-year earnings were released. In February 2007 the company reported it had earned AUD 6.34 million (compared to AUD 1.47 million a year prior) on revenues that nearly doubled the previous half-year's sales. New vessels in the company fleet helped propel increased profitability, although all lines of business generated increased revenues. Before the end of February 2007, Mermaid called off the merger, citing recent financial results that far exceeded expectations and claiming the previously agreed-upon deal was not in the best interest of stockholders because it undervalued Mermaid, whose stock had risen to an all-time high. Merger talks were briefly restarted, but by early March 2007, negotiations were permanently terminated.

## THE LAUNCH OF INTERNATIONAL OPERATIONS; RECORD REVENUES: 2007–08

Left to its own means, Mermaid established a Singapore office in 2007 as a gateway to its own international business. Mermaid's objectives included establishing a foothold in Southeast Asia and adding to its fleet. In terms of the former, the Asian market offered a business cycle that complemented the cycle in Mermaid's home territory: exploration and production activity increased in Southeast Asia in autumn and winter, as opposed to the spring and summer when activity was more prolific in Western Australia. Hence, the company planned to make greater year-round use of its fleet with an established business in Singapore's gas market. The company also acquired its first drilling vessel that year and expected similar acquisitions to follow and be put to use in Southeast Asia.

As expected, 2007 was a banner year for Mermaid. The company earned AUD 12.5 million on record revenues of AUD 103.1 million. For the first time ever, the company paid a dividend to shareholders. The strong financial results were fueled by increased exploration activity in both the North West Shelf and Browse Basin by blue chip exploration companies that moved into deeper waters.

After establishing an international office, Mermaid in 2008 launched its first international vessel, which began supporting a shallow-water seismic operation for Geokinetics in Egyptian waters. That same year, Mermaid vessels also began operating in Angola. In 2008 Mermaid's earnings rose again, to AUD 17.9 million, on revenues of nearly AUD 150 million. The company responded by doubling its dividend.

## THE GORGON PROJECT AND BEYOND: 2010

After spending years acquiring governmental permissions, during the late 2000s, Chevron and its partners received environmental approvals to begin work on the mammoth Gorgon gas project fields that were estimated to have a lifespan of up to 60 years and replace the North West Shelf as Australia's major resource development. To cash in on the development, in 2008, Mermaid signed an AUD 100,000 million contract to sublet 50,000 square meters of its Dampier Supply Base, which would serve as a supply base for Chevron's initial Gorgon project in Western Australia. Mermaid agreed to make infrastructure improvements to support Chevron, which owned nearly half of the Gorgon's developmental rights. To fund the infrastructure improvements, Mermaid conducted a share float through a book-build, which garnered the company AUD 36.3 million.

Between 2003 and 2008, Mermaid expanded its fleet from 17 to 26 vessels, spending more than AUD 100 million on fleet renewal, upgrades, and new-builds. During the same period, income rose from a negative AUD 10.7 million to AUD 17.9 million, and revenues climbed from AUD 42.6 million to AUD 149 million. Meanwhile, the company's stock price steadily rose, hitting a high in December 2007 at AUD 2.20 before slumping with the equities market.

By the turn of the decade, Broome Supply Base had grown into a key component of the company's growth strategy. To complement existing Broome operations, Mermaid and Toll Energy began jointly developing a new greenfield supply base in the Broome Port Authority precinct to serve exploration activities that continued in the Browse Basin.

In January 2010, the recently formed subsidiary Mermaid Offshore Services (MOS) and KD Marine formed an alliance to jointly provide air diving, integrated saturation, daughter craft, and remotely operated underwater vehicle (ROV) services from Mermaid's new dive support vessel in European markets. KD Marine agreed to provide the daughter craft and launching system for the ROV. The services were especially geared toward projects at restricted work sites, with the ROV able to support inspection and diving operations. The joint venture was expected to further boost activities of MOS, based in Thailand, which had recently expanded its sub- and sea-engineering services to locations in Brazil, China, India, the Middle East, Sakhalin Island in Russia, and the United Kingdom Continental Shelf.

As it entered a new decade, Mermaid appeared well positioned to continue both its international expansion and its industry dominance in northwest Australia. Managing director Jeffrey Weber said in 2010 that the company clearly had enough work for the next five years to maintain its earnings growth, and investors at that time seemed to approve Weber's claim, with Mermaid stock having risen nearly 170 percent in value between 2009 and 2010. Moreover, with North West Shelf activity showing no signs of slowing, and with the Gorgon project just ramping up for perhaps decades of development, Mermaid appeared physically well placed to take advantage well beyond five years. In addition, the company's initial foray into international waters also opened prospects for much wider geographic expansion. When Mermaid turned down the merger offer with DP World in 2007, the company was just beginning to stand on its own as a burgeoning financial success. In rejecting the Dubai energy giant's offer, Mermaid reinforced its independence and then illustrated it was fully able to generate consistent profits and expand into international waters on its own.

*Roger Rouland*

## PRINCIPAL SUBSIDIARIES

Dampier Stevedoring Pty Ltd.; Mermaid Labour and Management Pty Ltd.; Mermaid Manning and Management Pty Ltd.; Mermaid Marine Asia Singapore Pte Ltd.; Mermaid Marine Charters Pty Ltd.; Mermaid Marine Group Pty Ltd.; Mermaid Marine Offshore Pty Ltd.; Mermaid Marine Pty Ltd.; Mermaid Marine Vessel Operations Pty Ltd.; Mermaid Supply Base Pty Ltd.

## PRINCIPAL DIVISIONS

Supply Base; Vessels.

## PRINCIPAL COMPETITORS

Farstad Shipping ASA; John Swire & Sons (H.K.) Ltd.; Mitsui O.S.K. Lines, Ltd.; Nippon Yusen Kaisha (NYK Line); Richfield International Limited; Svitzer Australasia Services Pty Ltd.; Tidewater Inc.; Wan Hai Lines Co., Ltd.; Wilh. Wilhelmsen ASA.

## FURTHER READING

"Australia's Mermaid Marine Quadruples 2007 Revenue," *AsiaPulse News*, November 22, 2007.

"CEO Hot Seat: Jeff Weber," *AFR Smart Investor* (Melbourne, Australia), March 1, 2010.

Chinnery, Kevin, "Newly Boosted Mermaid to Focus on Offshore and Resource Ports," *Australasian Business Intelligence*, December 12, 2002.

Klinger, Peter, "Birchmore Joins Big Mermaid Sell-down," *Australasian Business Intelligence*, March 12, 2007.

"Mermaid Marine Australia to Service BHP Oil, Gas Facility," *Asia Africa Intelligence Wire*, May 10, 2004.

"Mermaid Marine Chairman Retires; Sees Company Well Placed for Growth," *Ozequities News Bites*, August 1, 2006.

"Mermaid Marine Not to Proceed with DPW Australia Merger," *RWE Business News Information Service*, February 22, 2007.

"Mermaid Marine to Sub-let Dampier, Major Upgrade," *RWE Business News Information Service*, April 30, 2008.

Sprague, Julie-Anne, "Oil Price Rise Delivers Swelling Demand," *Australasian Business Intelligence*, July 6, 2008.

Weir, Michael, "Mermaid, P&O Back in Merger Talks Again," *Australasian Business Intelligence*, February 26, 2007.

# The Metropolitan Museum
# of Art

1000 Fifth Avenue
New York, New York 10028-0198
U.S.A.
Telephone: (212) 535-7710
Fax: (212) 472-2764
Web site: http://www.metmuseum.org

*Nonprofit Organization*
*Incorporated:* 1870
*Employees:* 2,500
*Sales:* $290.8 million (2009)
*NAICS:* 712110 Museums

■ ■ ■

The Metropolitan Museum of Art ("The Met") is the nonprofit organization that is responsible for the operation of one of the world's largest and most comprehensive art museums. Located in Central Park, the Met's 2-million-square-foot main building is owned by the city of New York, while the collections are held for the benefit of the public by the corporation's trustees. In addition, the city pays for the museum's heat, light, and power, as well as funding a portion of the costs of maintenance and security. The corporation is responsible for its share of maintenance and security, plus the costs of acquisitions, conservation, special exhibitions, scholarly publications, and educational programs. The Met also receives an annual grant for basic operating expenses from the New York State Council on the Arts. Moreover, it receives funding through gifts and grants, endowment support, paid

admissions, the selling of memberships, as well as ancillary income derived from merchandising, parking garage fees, auditorium admissions, and the museum's restaurants. The Met is New York's most popular cultural attraction, visited by approximately 5 million people each year. Aside from its Central Park location, the Met owns and operates a branch museum, The Cloisters, located in northern Manhattan, one of the sites of the museum's Department of Medieval Art. Supplementing the Met's gift shop income are 7 satellite retail operations around the metropolitan area and 14 licensed shops around the world. Aside from the usual souvenirs of tee-shirts and post cards, Met merchandise includes expensive reproductions of the artwork found in the museum.

## NINETEENTH CENTURY ORIGINS

Since its founding on the southern tip of Manhattan, New York City has been very much devoted to the making of money. It also grew to harbor aspirations for culture, or at least the accolades that were accorded a cultural center. A strong theatrical tradition was born during the Colonial period, and by the 1840s four different theaters were presenting opera. The Academy of Music, which opened in 1854, would become the hub of fashionable society. When it came to the appreciation of the fine arts, however, New Yorkers showed little interest. At the opera, at least, the wealthy had a venue where it could appreciate itself. The New York Historical Society, founded in 1804, which collected and displayed a limited amount of art, was as close to an art museum as the city had to offer. The only serious collector of American art in New York at the time was a wholesale grocery merchant named Luman Reed, who exhibited the pictures he purchased on the third floor of his home one day a week.

After Reed's death in 1841, his collection formed the basis of the New York Gallery of Fine Arts. This early attempt to create an art museum failed to maintain sufficient funding, however, and closed in 1854. The nonprofit American Art Union, established on lower Broadway in 1838, provided a place for artists to display their work and charged the public a nominal admission fee. Following legal problems, it closed its doors in 1852, but during its short history the Art Union was instrumental in establishing New York as the country's most important marketplace for American art. In 1859 the Cooper Union was established in New York for the advancement of science and art. It offered a public reading room where collections of arts and artifacts were displayed, destined one day to become part of the Smithsonian Institution.

During this period, New York boasted a number of museums, as did most large cities, but they were devoted to natural science rather than the display of the fine arts. The popular dime museums of the 19th century, epitomized by P. T. Barnum's American Museum, also specialized in the exhibition of "curiosities." The idea of establishing a New York museum dedicated to the fine arts finally came to fruition in the years following the Civil War, prompted in large part by the success of the 1864 Metropolitan Art Fair, a charity auction that benefited the U.S. Sanitary Commission, ancestor of the American Red Cross.

The seeds for a major New York art museum were actually planted in Paris in 1866 during a Fourth of July luncheon at which John Jay, a prominent lawyer and the grandson of the first chief justice of the U.S. Supreme Court, commented in a post-meal speech that it was "time for the American people to lay the foundations of a National Institution and Gallery of Art." Among the Americans gathered that day were a number of New Yorkers who responded to Jay's call and that very night agreed to create such an institution in their native city.

Several of these New Yorkers were members of the Union League Club, which had been created to support Abraham Lincoln but was also involved in nonpolitical matters. The club referred the idea of a museum to its art committee, which deliberated for three years before recommending the establishment of a metropolitan art museum, provided that it was "free alike from bungling government officials and from the control of a single individual." A plan for the museum was then developed, and legal documents were drawn up. On January 31, 1870, the Board of Trustees for the new museum was selected, their numbers including merchants, lawyers, city officials, as well as a few practicing artists. On April 13, 1870, the New York Legislature agreed to incorporate the Met, mandating that it serve an educational mission to the public.

The Met's first president, railroad tycoon John Taylor Johnston, initiated a $250,000 fundraising campaign, but in the first year succeeded in raising only $110,000, the largest donation of $10,000 coming out of his own pocket. After a second year of effort, the Met was still $24,000 short of its goal, while at the same time Philadelphia and Boston were making great strides in funding their own museums. At this point the Met had no art and no place to display it. A permanent home for the Met would be provided by the city in the new Central Park, which many of the trustees considered too remote, preferring instead the present-day site of Bryant Park. City funding also paid for the construction of a building, which was begun in 1874. In the meantime, the Met secured its first collection of art, due to William T. Blodgett, a member of the executive committee, who on his own initiative bought three private collections of Dutch and Flemish paintings at the cost of $116,000. To display these works as well as other gifts and loans, in 1871 the museum leased a temporary home at 681 Fifth Avenue, a townhouse that had previously been the site of Dodworth's Dancing Academy.

Even before the Met opened its first exhibition, it began merchandising, selling $25 sets of Old Masters engravings. After two years the Met relocated downtown to West 14th Street, an area that was still a fashionable residential neighborhood. A move to the former Douglas Mansion was made necessary in large part by the purchase of the Cesnola Collection of antiquities in 1874, excavated by the American Counsul to Cyprus, and amateur archaeologist, General Luigi Palma di Cesnola. He sold a second collection to the Met in 1876, and three years later he was hired to become the

## KEY DATES

**1870:** The museum is incorporated.
**1872:** The first exhibition is presented in temporary quarters.
**1880:** The Central Park facility opens.
**1904:** J. P. Morgan becomes president of corporation.
**1938:** The Cloisters, a branch of the museum, opens.
**1950:** Annual attendance at the main museum reaches 2 million.
**1970:** A master plan for a major rebuilding project is announced.
**1975:** The Lehman Wing becomes the first part of the master plan to be completed.
**1994:** The major part of the master plan is completed, doubling the museum in size.
**2008:** Philippe de Montebello retires after 31 years as director and is replaced by Thomas P. Campbell.

museum's first paid director. His tenure would last 25 years.

### A NEW HOME IN 1880

The Met's permanent building in Central Park opened in 1880 and was quickly found wanting. Over the next 100 years three master plans would be developed and abandoned for lack of funding, forcing the museum to make do with piecemeal improvements. In 1888 the exhibition space was doubled by enlarging the southern end of the building. In 1894 a North Wing opened. In 1905 a Fifth Avenue facade would be added. In 1926 the present Fifth Avenue facade and entrance structure would be completed.

Although the Met now had a permanent home and city support for its upkeep, it still lacked the necessary funds to add to its collections and maintain them, as well as fulfill its educational mission. While many wealthy patrons donated artwork to the museum, much of it was of inferior quality and more of a nuisance than a help. The Met made no secret that in most cases it preferred patrons' money over their art. When the museum received one of its most important bequests, however, it came from an entirely unexpected source. In 1901 New Jersey locomotive manufacturer Jacob S. Rogers, who had only been a supporter of the museum as a $10 per year member, died and left the bulk of his

estate to the Met, totaling nearly $5 million. The result was an annual income of close to $200,000 that instantly transformed the institution into the richest museum in the world.

Cesnola died in 1904. The next day a new era began for the Met when famed banker J. Pierpont Morgan was named president of the corporation. With Sir Caspar Purdon Clarke serving as the museum's director, succeeded by his assistant Edward Robinson in 1910, the Met began to grow into a world-class organization supported by a strong professional staff. The publication of the Metropolitan Museum, *Bulletin*, began in 1905, and the Egyptian and Classical departments were organized, as well as the Department of Decorative Arts. Over time other departments were spun off: Arms and Armor in 1912; Far Eastern Art in 1915; the American Wing in 1924; Near Eastern Art in 1932; and Medieval Art in 1933.

Morgan was instrumental in naming other prominent millionaires to vacant board positions, an act that proved crucial as annual operating costs almost doubled to $362,000 during the eight years he served as president before his death in 1913. To make up the Met's budget deficit, Morgan simply bullied the board into making contributions. Despite his devotion to the museum, however, he left it no money in his will. A large portion of his wealth, which amounted to far less than anyone suspected, was tied up in his art collections. Much of Morgan's art was sold off to satisfy inheritance tax and other liabilities, and in the end just 40 percent came to the museum, albeit one of the most valuable bequests ever made to the Met.

The Met accumulated art at such a pace during the Morgan era that by 1915 the amount of city appropriations to maintain the collections had failed to keep pace, forcing the museum to turn to the public to raise additional funds. Nevertheless, the Met was able to acquire a considerable number of treasures that came available during the turbulence of World War I.

Despite increased funding from the city, the museum's money woes continued into the 1920s. By the end of the decade it boasted the highest attendance in its history, as well as its largest deficit. With the advent of the Great Depression, followed by the start of World War II, the Met struggled through the 1930s. Attendance fell off steadily as did memberships. City funding was cut from $501,495 in 1930 to $369,592 in 1939, although by the end of the decade it cost more to operate the museum, which now included The Cloisters, the northern Manhattan medieval museum created by John D. Rockefeller Jr. Moreover, 17 years had passed since the last improvement had been made to the main Central Park facilities. The buildings were improperly heated and ventilated, and the galleries were poorly lit and maintained. The museum, whose trustees in 1939 averaged 60 years of age, was becoming regarded as stodgy, and other institutions began to challenge the Met's preeminence. The Museum of Modern Art, for instance, was organized in large part because of the Met's disinterest in contemporary works.

To rejuvenate the Met and lead it into a new era, the trustees named Francis Henry Taylor to become the museum's new director in the fall of 1939. Taylor, who had introduced exciting new ideas while serving as the director of the Worcester Museum, was devoted to the goal of getting as many people as possible to attend the Met. He abolished the turnstiles and instituted free admission for every day of the week, thus ending 70 years of Monday and Friday paydays. Much of Taylor's plans for construction and rehabilitation, however, were interrupted by the United States' entry into World War II. A large portion of the museum's most treasured items, in fact, were stored in a Pennsylvania mansion during the first three years of the war, a precaution against German air raids. Following the war, Taylor began to organize a series of exhibitions that attracted people who had never before visited an art museum. The American people in the postwar years began to visit all museums in record numbers, resulting in greater news coverage for exhibits, which fueled even greater interest. By 1950 attendance at the Met's main museum reached 2 million, double the 1940 total.

## POSTWAR FUNDRAISING CHALLENGES

One of Taylor's innovations was the opening of a restaurant in the Met, an idea that at the time occasioned scorn. Fundraising, however, proved not to be Taylor's strong suit. A 75th anniversary drive only netted a disappointing $1 million, one-fifth of its stated goal. The city agreed to help fund the costs of construction and rehabilitation of the museum buildings, but at only half of the total cost and none of the costs of installation. Moreover, it would budget no more than $1 million in a single year. Much needed renovations to the Met, as a result, had to be staggered. Finally, in January 1954, remodeling was completed, and the Met featured 6 new period rooms and 95 renovated galleries. Despite this success, Taylor resigned as director of the Met by the end of the year, choosing to return to the Worcester Museum.

The Met was able to continue its acquisition of art through endowment funds earmarked for that purpose, and it was also able to take advantage of the liberal tax laws of the day that encouraged patrons to donate works to the museum in exchange for generous tax breaks.

Raising money to air condition the galleries and fund much-needed construction, however, was difficult for director James Rorimer. The size of the Met collections had grown so large by now that only a small portion of them could be displayed.

Rorimer was replaced by Thomas Hoving, who was pivotal in transforming the Met into a business. He too created a master building plan for the Met, centered around its centennial celebration in 1970, but unlike his predecessors he was able to scrape together enough public and private money to achieve the goal, as well as to overcome strong opposition to the Met encroaching on Central Park land. He was so determined that he even threatened to take the Met's collections across the Hudson River to a new home in New Jersey. Hoving is credited with building the Met into one of New York City's top tourist attractions. With blockbuster exhibitions, lavishly promoted, he infused the values of showmanship into the presentation of art treasures.

It was Hoving's search for income streams that resulted in the Met's parking garage, which became an important moneymaker for the museum. While construction of the master plan began, he modernized the Met's merchandising, in particular growing a mail-order business, marketing linens and other soft goods, as well as selling reproductions of choice clothing. The Museum Store began its evolution from a simple gift shop to a worldwide retail enterprise.

## THE MONTEBELLO ERA

The first major part of the master construction plan to be completed was the Lehman Wing, which opened in 1975. Two years later Hoving resigned and would not see other phases completed, including the Sackler Wing in 1978, the American Wing in 1980, the Michael C Rockefeller Wing in 1982, the Lila Acheson Wallace Wing in 1987, the Tisch Galleries in 1988, and the Henry R. Kravis Wing and Carroll and Milton Pétrie European Sculpture Court in 1990.

These projects took place under the direction of Philippe de Montebello, the French-born art historian who became the embodiment of the Met's classically elitist ethos. By the end of Montebello's 31-year tenure at the helm, he had served longer than any director of a major museum anywhere in the world. His baritone voice could be heard in five languages, appreciating highlights of the permanent collection with great authority on the museum's audio guides. Montebello believed firmly in the museum's mission of cultural enlightenment and resisted the trend towards commercialization that prevailed in the art world during the 1980s and 1990s.

Nevertheless, the museum, as both a cultural institution and a business, grew robustly during his leadership. This growth spread to every aspect of the Met's operations: the collections, exhibitions, and public programs; the libraries, research, and educational services; conservation work; publications; the retail business, which spread through satellite shops around the New York metropolitan area as well as foreign cities such as Bangkok, Tokyo, Vienna, and Mexico City; and, of course, the endowment.

By 1994 the 1970 master plan had been completed, doubling the museum's available exhibition space. The Met had become a massive facility with resources that rivaled or surpassed anything available elsewhere in the world. It also required a constant flow of money, which was supplied by its well-run business operations. Fundraising reached a new magnitude in the mid-1990s, when a booming economy resulted in unprecedented levels of donations to all of the arts. In 1995 the Met launched a $300 million capital campaign. The response was so strong that two years later the museum more than doubled its goal. By the end of the decade the Met had an annual budget in excess of $200 million, which it was more than capable of meeting through its different lines of funding, endowments, and income.

The terrorist attack that struck New York on September 11, 2001, had an adverse impact on museum attendance and the overall health of the business. Like other city institutions, it suffered from a lasting decline in foreign tourism. The recession that followed the attacks led to reduced contributions from the city. Moreover, the Met would now incur increased security costs. The museum cut back some staff and services in 2003. It also initiated some new endeavors to raise revenue, such as allowing patrons to visit on Mondays, when the museum was traditionally closed, for a $50 entrance fee. In 2006 it raised its suggested donation price from $15 to $20, making the Met one of the world's most expensive museums. (As a public institution, however, it cannot turn patrons away for lack of funds.)

Fortunately for the museum, Montebello was not only a world-class cultural leader, he was also a wildly successful fundraiser. The Met's ongoing capital campaign took in more than $1 billion in 2007. These resources allowed the museum to continue expanding and redesigning its space. In 2007 the Met opened new Greek and Roman galleries, renovated its permanent exhibitions of Oceanic and Native American art, expanded its 19th- and 20th-century European painting and sculpture galleries, and spruced up its Fifth Avenue facade. With the completion of these major projects, Montebello announced that he would retire at the end of 2008. The search for his successor, which was very intensely watched in the art world, ended with the surprise selection of Thomas P. Campbell, a tapestry curator with the Met's European Sculpture and Decorative Arts department. Approving the choice, Montebello said it indicated that the Met would continue to prize intellectual and cultural rigor above the values of marketing.

As Campbell took over, the Met remained a very strong and healthy institution, but the adverse economic situation at the end of the decade would demand some cutbacks and careful choices. The museum would house fewer pricey traveling exhibitions. Instead it would find new ways to display and call attention to works from its massive permanent collection, less than 1 percent of which is visible to the public at any given time. In 2009 the global financial crisis had reduced the value of the endowment by nearly 30 percent, forcing an overall reduction of more than 100 jobs. Several of the Museum Shops closed, and the museum imposed a hiring freeze. Development, however, went on. The renovated American Wing was unveiled in May 2009, with First Lady Michelle Obama in attendance at the ribbon cutting. Although the museum faced its most difficult period in many years, there was little doubt that it would remain capable of fulfilling the mission set forth by its founders so many years ago.

*Ed Dinger*
*Updated, Roger K. Smith*

## PRINCIPAL COMPETITORS

Museum of Modern Art.

## FURTHER READING

Cox, Meg, "At the Metropolitan Museum, Artwork Is to Be Seen, Bought—and Manufactured," *Wall Street Journal*, July 10, 1985, p. 1.

Danziger, Danny, *Museum: Behind the Scenes at the Metropolitan Museum of Art.* New York: Viking Press, 2007.

Hibbard, Howard, *The Metropolitan Museum of Art.* New York: Harper & Row, 1980.

Hoving, Thomas, *Making the Mummies Dance: Inside the Metropolitan Museum of Art.* New York: Simon & Schuster, 1993.

Kennedy, Randy, "74 Are Laid Off at Met Museum; More May Follow," *New York Times*, March 12, 2009.

Lerman, Leo, *The Museum: One Hundred Years and the Metropolitan Museum of Art.* New York: Viking Press, 1969.

McGrath, Charles, "Twilight of the Sun King," *New York Times*, July 29, 2007.

Rosenbaum, Lee, "Museum Confronts an Altered Landscape," *Wall Street Journal*, October 11, 2001, p. A19.

Souccar, Miriam Kreinin, "Darkening Picture," *Crain's New York Business*, November 4, 2001, p. 3.

Tomkins, Calvin, *Merchants and Masterpieces: The Story of the Metropolitan Museum of Art*. New York: H. Holt, 1989.

# Metropolitan Opera Association, Inc.

---

Lincoln Center, No. 423
New York, New York 10023
U.S.A.
Telephone: (212) 799-3100
Fax: (212) 870-4508
Web site: http://www.metoperafamily.org

---

*Nonprofit Organization*
*Founded:* 1880
*Employees:* 3,000
*Sales:* $209.37 million (2008 est.)
*NAICS:* 711110 Theater Companies and Dinner
    Theaters

■ ■ ■

Since 1932 the Metropolitan Opera Association, Inc., has run New York City's internationally acclaimed Metropolitan Opera (the Met). With an annual operating budget of approximately $300 million, the Metropolitan Opera stages more than 200 performances during a 30-to-32-week season. In addition to the more than 800,000 people who attend performances at the Met's home in the Lincoln Center for the Performing Arts, millions more across the world partake through weekly radio broadcasts and occasional televised productions, as well as through touring shows and recordings. A separate, independent organization, the Metropolitan Opera Guild, helps raise a significant portion of the approximately $70 million in contributions made to the Metropolitan Opera each year. The guild also handles the Met's merchandising. Because ticket sales cover only

40 percent of the Met's operating budget, and government grants account for less than 2 percent, fund-raising and ancillary income are of paramount importance. After enduring many periods of financial struggle during its more than 125 years of existence, the Metropolitan Opera has attained sound financial stability.

## CREATION OF THE
## METROPOLITAN OPERA: 1880

In the 1840s in New York, as many as four theaters presented opera, creating what was deemed New York's first golden age of opera. With its opening in 1854, the Academy of Music, located near fashionable Union Square, became the leading opera house, the place where high society gathered to admire itself. As post-Civil War industry produced a generation of *nouveau riche*, however, the Academy's 18 boxes were unable to accommodate the newcomers who, in any case, were less than enthusiastically received by the old-line Knickerbocker aristocracy. The Academy's begrudging offer to build 26 additional boxes was considered inadequate, and in April 1880 the Metropolitan Opera was incorporated by several wealthy benefactors. In all, 70 shareholders were enlisted to provide the $1.7 million required to buy the land and build an opera house at 39th and Broadway.

The mansions of the wealthy and the entertainment district, which had been marching uptown for many years, would soon leave the Academy in the backwaters of Manhattan. By 1886 it abandoned the field to the Met, as New York's reconstituted high society and new opera house reigned virtually unopposed for the next 20 years.

From the outset, the Metropolitan Opera House, which opened in 1883, was considered inadequate, despite its fine acoustics. The configuration of the building's property lines resulted in cramped dressing rooms and limited rehearsal and storage space. In fact, scenery stored under the stage contributed greatly to a fire that in 1892 destroyed the interior of the theater. The expense of rebuilding also led to a new organization, the Metropolitan Opera and Real Estate Company, which would in effect act as landlord to the independent producers who actually ran the opera season, presumably at a profit. The shareholders of the Metropolitan Opera and Real Estate Company, who paid for taxes, maintenance, and repairs of the theater through a yearly assessment, received use of a box for every performance of the opera season in lieu of rent. It was this subsidy that permitted the producers to return a profit, or at least keep losses to a minimum. The Metropolitan Opera Company became the official producing entity in 1908.

## COMPETITION FROM HAMMERSTEIN

For three seasons in the early 1900s, the Metropolitan Opera faced stiff competition from a maverick impresario named Oscar Hammerstein (the grandfather of the lyricist Oscar Hammerstein II) and his Manhattan Opera House. Although Hammerstein did not curry favor with high society, his opera house, which featured exciting new French opera and fresh talent, began to draw fashionable patrons. In what was nothing less than an opera war, both Hammerstein and the Metropolitan Opera spread their operations to other cities. In the end, Hammerstein was choked by debt and on the verge of ruin; nevertheless, the Metropolitan Opera generously paid him $1.2 million to quit the business. Although grand designs of controlling opera in other major cities,

including Chicago and Philadelphia, were never realized, the Metropolitan Opera firmly established itself as the United States' major producer of opera and a true international venue.

For 20 years, until the stock market crash of 1929, the Metropolitan Opera would enjoy a period of artistic achievement and financial stability. Until 1920 the major attraction was tenor Enrico Caruso. Gustav Mahler and Arturo Toscanini became principal conductors at the Met, which presented the American premieres, and in some cases the world premieres, of many notable operas.

Along with the U.S. economy, the Metropolitan Opera thrived in the 1920s, so much so that it could decline an offer of funding from the Juilliard Musical Foundation, created by textile mogul and longtime Met boxholder Augustus D. Juilliard. (The Met's lack of interest in meeting the foundation's requirements would free up the funding that allowed Juilliard to establish the Juilliard School of Music.) Rising production costs during this period were offset by increased ticket prices and new sources of secondary income: The Victor Talking Machine Company paid an annual fee to sign Met singers for recordings, and the National Broadcasting Company (NBC) paid for the exclusive right to bring Met singers to the radio. In addition, the Metropolitan Opera rented out its house, sold the rights to its concessions and programs (plus a share of advertising revenues), and earned $15,000 a year from a piano endorsement. Times were so flush that building a new opera house seemed almost a certainty. The collapse of Wall Street in 1929, however, would delay that dream for many years.

The high-water mark during this affluent period for the Metropolitan Opera was the 1927–28 season, when the company realized a profit of $141,000, with subscription revenues that totaled $55,000 per week. During the 1929–30 season, however, the Met lost money for the first time in 20 years, despite record receipts. With the economy in shambles, the Metropolitan Opera saw subscriptions drop and tours canceled. Otto Kahn, longtime president and chairman of the Metropolitan Opera Company, was replaced by his attorney Paul D. Cravath, who also represented Westinghouse and RCA. Cravath quickly signed a generous radio contract for the Met, which received $5,000 for each of 24 live broadcasts of operas.

The first radio broadcast of a Met opera, *Hansel und Gretel*, occurred on Christmas Day 1931, and was carried by the largest network of stations ever assembled at the time. The entire Red and Blue Networks of NBC were augmented by shortwave transmission over the British Broadcasting Corporation as well as Canadian

## KEY DATES

**1883:** Metropolitan Opera House opens.

**1892:** Fire destroys interior of house and leads to reorganized Metropolitan Opera and Real Estate Company.

**1908:** Metropolitan Opera Company becomes official producing entity.

**1931:** First radio broadcast of a Metropolitan Opera production is aired on Christmas Day by the largest network of stations yet assembled.

**1932:** Company is reincorporated as nonprofit Metropolitan Opera Association.

**1940:** Association buys the Metropolitan Opera House from the Metropolitan Opera and Real Estate Company.

**1948:** First telecast from the stage of the Metropolitan Opera is aired.

**1966:** Metropolitan Opera moves to new home in Lincoln Center.

**1990:** Metropolitan Opera extends radio broadcasts to 22 foreign countries.

**2006:** "Metropolitan Opera: Live in HD" begins simulcasts at movie theaters around the world.

and Australian networks. By the 1933–34 season, the Saturday afternoon broadcasts had found a sponsor, Lucky Strike Cigarettes. A year later Listerine backed the show. Aside from the much needed revenue that radio brought the Metropolitan Opera, it also lent the company national stature. No one was sure about the number of listeners until the Met appealed for contributions over the radio. The enthusiastic and widespread support of the broadcasts could now be measured in the tangible form of money.

### ESTABLISHMENT OF METROPOLITAN OPERA ASSOCIATION: 1932

As the losses mounted in the 1930s, the Metropolitan Opera had no choice but to change its approach to business. The concept that opera could be made profitable was abandoned. To produce a season was now a matter of funding, not investment. In 1932 Cravath reorganized the producing entity by reincorporating it as the Metropolitan Opera Association, a nonprofit corporation that would be free of federal entertainment taxes. Because it was now deemed an educational

enterprise, the Met was also able to apply for funding from the Juilliard Musical Foundation. The 50th season of the Metropolitan Opera was saved only by a fundraising campaign that scraped together $300,000 from various sources, including $100,000 from the radio audience and $50,000 from the Juilliard Musical Foundation.

In 1935 actress and philanthropist Eleanor Belmont, wife of banker August Belmont, founded the Metropolitan Opera Guild to raise money for the Metropolitan Opera, as well as to develop an audience for opera through education. By 1937 regular matinee performances for students were held, and soon the guild would bring opera to the schools. By the end of the 20th century the guild would contribute more than $75 million to the Metropolitan Opera. With an annual budget of approximately $17 million, the guild would boast 100,000 members, becoming the largest organization of its kind.

Although it was far from healthy, the Metropolitan Opera saw its income steadily increase in the late 1930s, enough to ward off the very real danger of collapse as it waited for the U.S. economy to recover. Then in the summer of 1939 the association was informed that a number of boxholders who constituted the Metropolitan Opera and Real Estate Company refused to pay the annual assessment levied on their shares. Therefore, the lease on the opera house would not be renewed when it expired in 1940 and the property would be put up for sale. Cravath's successor, Cornelius Bliss, is credited with saving the Metropolitan Opera by negotiating a selling price of $1.97 million for a property that was assessed for tax purposes at $5.4 million, and spearheading an effort to persuade shareholders to accept the deal. He also initiated a million-dollar fund-raising campaign to provide the financing. Thus, on May 31, 1940, the Metropolitan Opera Association assumed title to the opera house itself.

### TEXACO BECOMES SPONSOR: 1940

Also in 1940 the Metropolitan Opera radio broadcasts finally landed a long-term sponsor in the Texas Company (Texaco; later ChevronTexaco), which had recently suffered bad press over its dealings, however legal, with Axis countries in the period before the United States entered World War II. Because a prominent display of philanthropy was deemed an appropriate public relations response, the oil company decided to back the Met. The goodwill that would accrue to Texaco over the next 60-plus years for sponsoring the weekly opera broadcasts cannot be estimated. Furthermore in 1940, the Metropolitan Opera would first turn to television, another medium in which Texaco would eventually serve as sponsor. An initial concert of selected material was telecast from the NBC studios. The first telecast from the stage of the Metropolitan Opera would be November 29, 1948, when the American Broadcasting Company presented the season's opening night production of *Otello*.

World War II hurt attendance and, until New York State tax laws were modified, the Metropolitan Opera was burdened with heavy real estate taxes. Another public appeal for money was made in 1943–44, but with the end of the war and the resumption of touring and increased ticket sales, the Metropolitan Opera was able to post a modest $6,000 profit. Although the 1946–47 season produced $3 million in income for the first time since the 1920s, the Metropolitan Opera still lost more than $200,000. Even though scenery and costumes were becoming threadbare as operas that had been mounted 20 and 30 years earlier were recycled, rising production costs had clearly outstripped the amount of revenue that could be generated through ticket sales and ancillary income. Periodic fund-raising appeals to the radio audience in order to avert pending disaster became a way of life at the Met.

## A NEW OPERA HOUSE

The tonic that would restore the Metropolitan Opera to financial health, in the opinion of many, was a new opera house, offering not only increased seating capacity but storage facilities and updated technology. The idea had been advanced a number of times over the decades but finally took shape in the 1950s. Federal urban renewal legislation gave the government broad powers of eminent domain to seize property. Robert Moses, New York's legendary and autocratic builder of parks and roadways, was in charge of the Title I program in the city. He identified a slum in the vicinity of Columbus Circle and offered to make the space available to the Met.

In the meantime it appeared that Carnegie Hall might be torn down and that the New York Philharmonic might be in need of a new home. The Met and the philharmonic joined forces and turned to the Rockefeller family, whose foundation had already decided to fund the performing arts. What resulted eventually was Lincoln Center, Inc., and the building of a complex that not only included a 3,750-seat Metropolitan Opera and Philharmonic Hall (later renamed Avery Fisher Hall), but also a multipurpose theater (the New York State Theater), a library, and an educational facility that would eventually house the Juilliard School of Music.

Plans for a new opera house had always assumed that the project would be funded by selling the old facility. Because of Lincoln Center, the Metropolitan Opera Association would be able to raze the old building and lease its valuable midtown property. It was not surprising that efforts to "Save the Met" were not welcomed by the association's management as it prepared to move into its new theater. In the end, the old opera house began to crumble on its own accord, and the Metropolitan Opera Association was able to sign a long-term lease for the property that would create an endowment fund the organization had never previously been able to accumulate. Rather than a contingency fund to meet deficits, the endowment was intended to expand the opera company's repertory and allow the production of new operas as well as the revival of older works that had limited box-office appeal.

Although Philharmonic Hall was completed in 1962, the new Metropolitan Opera venue did not open until 1966. The finances of the Metropolitan Opera Association, however, were still shaky. Banker George S. Moore became president of the organization in 1967 and began to put the Metropolitan Opera on a sound financial footing. Production budgets were adhered to and ticket prices raised. Moore cut costs, going so far as to postpone the opening of the opera season and canceling a production of *Don Giovanni*. When longtime general manager Rudolf Bing left in 1972, the Metropolitan Opera entered another crisis state. It lost star performers and attendance fell, as did contributions. To many observers in the late 1970s it seemed that only a massive government subsidy, as much as 30 percent of the Met's fund-raising budget, would be able to keep the Met, and American opera, alive.

## A NEW MEDIUM: TELEVISION

It was in 1977 that the Metropolitan Opera began regular telecasts on the Public Broadcasting Service (PBS), with Texaco serving as the sole corporate sponsor. The initial show, a production of *La Bohème*, was seen by some four million viewers. Not only were more people now exposed to opera through television, the Metropolitan Opera was exposed to more people. Aggressive marketing and fund-raising, as well as tighter management, paid off in the early 1980s as the Metropolitan Opera achieved its best fiscal health since the 1920s. It was now in a position to begin work on a new $100 million endowment fund.

Unlike other prosperous times in its history, the Metropolitan Opera did not slip backward; rather, it continued to thrive on its success. By 1989 merchandising sales alone exceeded $6 million, allowing the Metropolitan Opera Guild to contribute a record $4.1

million. In 1990 the Texaco-Metropolitan Opera International Radio Network began to deliver live broadcasts to 22 countries in Europe, thus solidifying the Met's international presence. Also in 1990 the Metropolitan Opera Association was solvent enough to complete 82 capital projects at a cost of $15 million.

## VOLPE LEADS MET INTO THE NEW MILLENNIUM

Joseph Volpe, who began work at the Met in 1964 as an apprentice carpenter, was named general manager in 1990. Under his watch the Met strengthened its position, financially and artistically, at a time when other major opera companies around the world were struggling. Thus, Volpe became the most powerful man in opera and his job the most coveted. When Lincoln Center began to make plans for a $1.5 billion renovation, making it one of the largest American arts projects ever, Volpe and the Metropolitan Opera Association temporarily withdrew from the project in January 2001 in protest over a proposed new $200 million home for the New York City Opera. Volpe feared that the New York City Opera was not financially solid enough to pay the cost and that the Met, as the largest stakeholder in Lincoln Center, might wind up footing some of the bill for the new facility. Another contentious point was that, despite contributing 30 percent of Lincoln Center's shared operating costs (and receiving 30 percent of common revenues), the Metropolitan Opera had no more say in the renovations than the smallest of the center's 12 constituent groups.

Volpe's surprise notice of withdrawal from the Lincoln Center renovation came just a week after the city had committed $240 million to the project. The Met immediately prepared to undertake its own renovation plans, which were to include expanding the lobby. Fortunately for both parties, under new ground rules that gave it a greater voice in Lincoln Center, the Met quickly rejoined the project. Although relations between the two cultural giants remained somewhat contentious, the project moved forward and was substantially complete by 2010.

With the initiation of the renovation project behind him, in 2004 Volpe decided it was time to wrap up his 40-plus year career at the Met, and he announced that he would resign effective in 2006. A few unfortunate events in this period no doubt reinforced his decision. Representatives of wealthy Texas oil heiress and major Met benefactor Sybil B. Harrington, who died in 1998, charged that the opera company had violated the terms of a bequest she had made in support of "traditional" productions of standard operatic fare. They charged that the Met's 2001 production of *Tristan und Isolde*, using

$5 million which Harrington's estate had provided, was nontraditional in spirit, and they initiated a lawsuit to recover the money.

## END OF CHEVRONTEXACO SPONSORSHIP AND VOLPE'S ERA

In 2004, citing economic hardship, ChevronTexaco withdrew its support of the Saturday afternoon live Met radio broadcasts, ending the longest continuous commercial sponsorship in broadcast history. The Annenberg Foundation jumped into the breach with a $3.5 million gift, but that funded only one more season of broadcasts. Then in 2005 Beverly Sills, the longtime opera diva who had become chair of the Met in 2002, resigned her post.

As Volpe prepared to wind up his 14-year tenure as general manager, it was clear that his legacy was much more than service as a strong-willed administrator and helmsman of the flagship American opera company. He had more artistic acumen and impact than he was generally credited with. Although he often insisted on lavish, crowd-pleasing productions of opera warhorses, he also brought in innovative European directors such as Jürgen Flimm and Herbert Wernicke to lead ground-breaking productions.

During Volpe's tenure the Met gave a moving and productive benefit performance for the victims of the September 11, 2001, World Trade Center attacks. Under his leadership the Met presented probably the most monumental production in its history, a 2002 staging of *War and Peace* that starred Dmitri Hvorostovsky and Anna Netrebko plus 50 other soloists. In the final scene there were 346 people onstage (as well as one horse). The action was so intense that on opening night an overexuberant supernumerary actually leapt off the stage, breaking a violinist's bow in the orchestra pit. Sadly, the artistic successes of the first decade of the 21st century did not stem losses at the box office (which were affecting all of the performing arts), and resulted in a third straight year of midseason cuts in the Met budget in 2005. As Volpe prepared to retire, the Met's losses had become widely noted in the music world.

Volpe could not claim all the credit for the Met's artistic successes during his tenure. Working within an often tense relationship with Volpe, music director James Levine was able to realize some of his own sometimes edgy musical goals, presenting productions of Arnold Schoenberg's stark *Moses und Aron* and Igor Stravinsky's *The Rake's Progress*; awarding commissions to such composers as John Harbison, Tan Dun, and Tobias Picker; and expanding the schedule of Carnegie Hall concerts for the upgraded Met Orchestra. In 1995

Levine outfoxed Volpe and won installation of an electronic titling system. In 2004 Levine was accorded the signal honor of appointment as music director of the Boston Symphony Orchestra, while continuing to hold down the analogous post at the Met through and beyond Volpe's tenure.

## PETER GELB TAKES OVER

In 2004 the Met named Peter Gelb, director of Sony Classical USA since 1993, to take over as general manager in 2006. The son of Arthur Gelb, managing editor of the *New York Times*, Peter Gelb had been an assistant to impresario Sol Hurok, pianist Vladimir Horowitz's manager, and, beginning in 1988, the executive producer of *The Metropolitan Opera Presents*, the Met's PBS television series. Gelb joined the Met in 2005 and began working with Maestro Levine and the Met leadership to begin the transition to his tenure.

Building on Volpe's more innovative efforts but going far beyond them, Gelb began the task of revitalizing the Met, reconnecting it to the world, and attracting a younger audience not necessarily enamored of opera. A primary means to this end was the continuation of Volpe's policy of introducing new directors, but now with an emphasis on the realms of stage and film to emphasize theatricality in Met productions. Gelb's introduction of theater composers Michael John LaChiusa and Adam Guettel; jazz musician Wynton Marsalis; and major conductors who had never before appeared at the Met, such as Riccardo Muti, Daniel Barenboim, and Esa-Pekka Salonen, caused traditionalists to fear that a revolution was afoot at the Met.

Hardly comforting to them was Gelb's repositioning of the company as a media giant that included a Peabody Award-winning program of high-definition (HD) video transmissions of numerous productions to movie theaters around the world. Begun in December 2006, "Metropolitan Opera: Live in HD" attracted 1.7 million viewers in the 2008–09 season. Further enhancing its reach was the launching of a Met satellite radio station and the long-term resurrection of live Saturday radio broadcasts under the sponsorship of Toll Brothers, a luxury-home builder making an initial foray into arts philanthropy.

All the flashy new media, personnel, and productions cost money. The Met's operating budget grew more than 21 percent in Gelb's first two years, and it was rapidly drawing down on its endowment. With the recession of 2008–09, donations and ticket sales dropped sharply. The production and musical unions were expected to absorb part of the losses with pay cuts to be negotiated in 2010. On a brighter note, that same year philanthropist Ann Ziff donated $30 million, the largest single gift from an individual in Met history. Such generosity showed confidence in the Met's future and in Gelb's approach. Music critic Alex Ross wrote in the March 29, 2010, *New Yorker* that "Gelb has transformed the Met's public reputation, remaking a conservative bastion into an arena of chic spectacle." Whether chic would translate into box-office success and solid artistic achievement remained to be seen.

*Ed Dinger*
*Updated, Judson MacLaury*

## PRINCIPAL SUBSIDIARIES

Impresario, LLC.

## PRINCIPAL COMPETITORS

New York City Opera.

## FURTHER READING

Blumenthal, Ralph, "Midlife Hits Lincoln Center with Call for Rich Face Lift," *New York Times*, June 1, 1999, p. 1.

Briggs, John, *Requiem for a Yellow Brick Brewery: A History of the Metropolitan Opera*, Boston: Little, Brown, 1969, 359 p.

Eaton, Quaintance, *The Miracle of the Met: An Informal History of the Metropolitan Opera, 1883–1967*, New York: Meredith Press, 1968, 490 p.

Ellison, Nancy, with Joseph Volpe, *In Grand Style: The Glory of the Metropolitan Opera*, New York: Rizzoli, 2006, 239 p.

Fiedler, Johanna, *Molto agitato: The Mayhem behind the Music at the Metropolitan Opera*, New York: Nan A. Talese/ Doubleday, 2001, 393 p.

Kolodin, Irving, *The Metropolitan Opera, 1883–1966: A Candid History*, New York: A.A. Knopf, 1966, 762 p.

Mayer, Martin, *The Met: One Hundred Years of Grand Opera*, New York: Simon and Schuster, Metropolitan Opera Guild, 1983, 368 p.

"Mighty Joe Opera," *Forbes*, June 15, 1998, p. 302.

Pogrebin, Robin, "Making Waves Is Nothing New for Met's Maverick," *New York Times*, January 25, 2001, p. B6.

Ross, Alex, "A Bumpy Season at the Met," *New Yorker*, March 29, 2010.

# Michigan Turkey Producers Co-op, Inc.

---

**2140 Chicago Drive S.W.**
**Grand Rapids, Michigan 49519-1215**
**U.S.A.**
**Telephone: (616) 245-2221**
**Fax: (616) 247-1548**
**Web site: http://www.miturkey.com**

*Private Company*
*Founded:* 1998
*Incorporated:* 1998
*Employees:* 385
*Sales:* $120 million (2009 est.)
*NAICS:* 311615 Poultry Processing

■ ■ ■

Michigan Turkey Producers Co-op, Inc. (MTP), is a Grand Rapids, Michigan–based turkey slaughtering and processing operation making use of turkeys raised by member farmers in Western Michigan. MTP sells ready-to-cook and cooked turkey products under the Golden Legacy label, emphasizing breast meat but also offering ground turkey as well as turkey steaks, fillets, burgers, and sausage. Additionally, the company produces an "all natural" organic line of turkey products and maintains a private label program.

MTP products are sold across the United States, as well as in Canada, Mexico, South Africa, China, Taiwan, Western Samoa, the Dominican Republic, and Russia. A subsidiary, Michigan Turkey Producers, LLC, operates the co-op's processing plant in Wyoming, Michigan, as well as a nearby cooked turkey plant. MTP

farmers produce 4.6 million birds, or 96 percent of the turkeys raised in Michigan. The co-op's processing facility differentiates itself from the competition by completely relying on the process of deboning by hand, resulting in higher quality cooked products. MTP also uses a proprietary bird-stunning system that employs carbon dioxide instead of traditional electronic stunning, a method that not only reduces bruising and blood spots but also the number of employees needed to handle the birds for slaughtering.

## TURKEY GAINS IN POPULARITY AS CENTURY CLOSES

The turkey industry began to take shape in western Michigan in the early years of the 20th century when farmers took advantage of the rich farmland and temperate climate to begin raising turkeys. A longtime staple at the holiday season, turkey became increasingly popular during the rest of the year in the latter decades of the century as consumers became more health conscious. Per capita consumption in the United States was 8.3 pounds in 1975. That number would grow to 17.6 pounds three decades later. To help supply the demand, Bil Mar Foods Inc., a Zeeland, Michigan–based division of Sara Lee Corporation, recruited area growers in the mid-1990s to provide it with turkeys for a new product line, enticing them with offers of low-cost bird housing and feed.

There was soon a glut of turkey on the market, however, and in July 1997 Bil Mar informed the growers that it would move its turkey slaughtering and boning operation to Iowa. Moreover, the company's processing plant in Borculo, Michigan, would truck in out-of-state turkeys. As a result, Bil Mar would not renew contracts with five independent turkey farms in western Michigan after they expired in January 1998 and would also cancel contracts with 10 other growers 6 years early. The farmers' offer to cut production fell on deaf ears, and Sara Lee paid them a settlement for canceling the production contract.

It was a bitter pill to swallow for the farmers, who had invested hundreds of thousands of dollars, and in some cases millions, to fulfill their contracts with Sara Lee. With everything they owned tied up in turkey production, three of the growers, Harley Seitsema, Harold Walcott, and Harry Smith, decided to start a cooperative to process and market their turkey products. They recruited a dozen other farmers, and in October 1998 the 15 initial members, operating 40 farms, signed articles of incorporation to form Michigan Turkey Producers Cooperative, Inc. They then hired a research company, Sparks Commodities Inc., to conduct a feasibility and market study in anticipation of opening a processing plant. The United States Department of Agriculture Rural Development unit supplied $95,000 to fund the studies, and Michigan State University poultry economist Allan Rahn played a key role as well. In the end, the studies indicated there was a market for the meat, and the co-op would not be putting more meat on the market than what was already there.

## FINANCING SECURED THROUGH LLC

MTP took the next step of establishing a processing plant. Members pooled their Sara Lee settlement money, but they lacked the necessary funds to open a processing plant. Bank financing for the $20 million project was arranged, provided the co-op could raise 30 percent of the necessary funds. MTP sold shares of stock to members based on the price of $1.50 per shackle (the hooks that carries a turkey through the processing plant). Each share was worth 1,000 shackles. Two months later, however, the agricultural economy began to struggle, and the bank demanded the co-op have 50 percent equity in hand. In response, the co-op raised the per-shackle commitment to $2, but because it was still short on funds it formed Michigan Turkey Producers, LLC, and brought in outside investors. MTP became one of the members of the LLC.

In November 1997 MTP acquired a 170,000-square-foot former Simplot french fry potato processing plant in Wyoming, Michigan, for $4.5 million. About $12 million was then spent on renovating the facility and acquiring the old production equipment from Bil Mar. The co-op acted quickly to purchase the Bil Mar assets as a package before they could be sold piecemeal at auction. The Wyoming City Council also helped the fledgling operation by providing a 12-year, $11 million tax abatement for the plant. The Wyoming facility was ideally suited for the co-op because it already had the necessary ammonia compressors in place and offered more than adequate refrigeration and freezer capacity.

There was a ready supply of labor in the Wyoming area. Without running an ad, the new plant received 1,400 applications for 225 jobs. The facility's design also helped to retain the workers. The kill room in a typical processing plant that relied on electrical stunning to kill the birds led to a chaotic environment, where panicked birds flailed and thrashed, resulting in worker injuries as well as damaged meat. Employee turnover was incredibly high, with most workers quitting before lunch on their first day on the job. The Wyoming plant eliminated much of the stress by using an innovative carbon dioxide stunning method, meaning an employee never had to handle the birds in a live state. Annual worker turnover would run below 10 percent, while many other plants experienced a 100 percent turnover in line workers.

The co-op hired a former Bil Mar executive, Dan Lennon, to serve as plant manager and president. While the plant was being renovated and the Golden Legacy and Silver Legacy labels were designed, an arrangement was made to sell the co-op's turkeys to processing companies in Iowa and southern Indiana for 1999 to keep members in business. Although freights charges made it a break-even proposition, it was still an important stopgap measure.

## PROCESSING PLANT OPENS: 2000

The Wyoming facility became operational in March 2000, processing and deboning toms to produce MTP's first product, ground turkey, which was easy to produce. The co-op had expected that it would take a year before it could crack the retail market but was pleasantly surprised when the Meijer supermarket chain, after

## KEY DATES

**1997:** Sara Lee Corporation cancels contracts with Michigan turkey growers.
**1998:** Michigan Turkey Producers Co-op, Inc., is formed.
**2000:** Processing plant opens.
**2003:** First cooked turkey contract is won.
**2006:** Cook plant opens.
**2009:** Meijer agrees to carry the company's Golden Legacy brand turkey products in all of its midwestern stores.

participating in a taste test, expressed a willingness to carry the Legacy brand on its shelves. Moreover, Brooklyn, New York–based Boar's Head Provisions contracted with the co-op to supply its plant in Holland Township, and Gerber Products Co. agreed to buy 3 million pounds of turkey for use in its baby foods. As a result of these deals, MTP generated sales of about $75 million in 2000.

In addition to ground turkey, MTP began offering cut-up portions, including breast, drum, thigh, neck, and wing meat. The co-op did well as a producer of uncooked turkey products, but Lennon harbored a vision of becoming a value-added supplier, which meant becoming involved in cooked products. That need to expand beyond a mere commodity business became even more apparent in 2003 when the market for uncooked turkey waned. Because of the high quality of its turkeys, MTP weathered the poor economic conditions. The co-op, however, realized that it needed to move into the cooked products arena to fuel growth.

Despite lacking the necessary facilities, MTP established itself in the value-added products market in 2003 when the state of Michigan issued a bid for cooked meat to supply its institutional operations. By taking on several industry partners in a co-packing relationship to arrange the cooking and packaging of its meat, MTP won the contract. Originally its partners had used their own meat but later began relying on turkeys produced by MTP member growers. It was obvious, however, that the co-op needed its own cooking capabilities to realize its full potential.

### COOK PLANT OPENS: 2006

MTP began actively scouting for a plant site for cooking its turkeys and soon found several possibilities. In the end MTP settled on a former distribution facility that already had coolers and freezers in place. Better yet, it was located just 2.5 miles from the Wyoming processing plant on 13 acres of land in an industrial park. The facility was purchased in March 2005 and essentially gutted as the processing areas were laid out. Following a nine-month renovation, the new cook plant became operational in late January 2006 after it passed inspection. Its eight production lines began turning out four product lines that catered to the needs of distributors and retailers: whole-muscle breasts, whole-muscle pan roasts, slicing logs, and foodservice rolls. The products were then shipped to national foodservice distributors, which accounted for about 70 percent of sales, as well as retailers, especially club retailers, who began carrying MTP products under private labels.

The new plant was designed with state-of-the-art food safety in mind. Employees working on raw and cooked products were segregated: The plant included separate parking lots, entrances, and break rooms, and employees wore different color uniforms. Nothing was suspended from the ceilings of the processing rooms, eliminating possible debris collection points and airborne contamination. Ovens, on the other hand, were suspended, providing workers with easy access for cleaning and other maintenance. To further ensure food safety, the new plant also employed a post-pasteurization process that called for packaged products to travel on a conveyor to undergo a hot water dip, immediately followed by immersion in chilled water. Not all of the available space in the new cook plant was in use, but it was process ready, providing MTP with future flexibility. In addition, the facility included eight acres of undeveloped property that could accommodate future expansion.

By 2006 MTP was processing 171 million pounds of turkey per year, a number that held steady for the next two years. In 2008 MTP held the number 14 position on the WATT Poultry USA top turkey company rankings. It was a far cry from the 1.35 billion pounds processed by category leader Butterball, LLC, but not far from Sara Lee's 220 million pounds and a Top 10 ranking.

### RETAIL BUSINESS EXPANDS: 2009

After just a decade in business, MTP was well established in the marketplace, selling its products across the United States as well as overseas. The co-op continued to grow, adding organic products, and in 2009 it expanded its relationship with Meijer, which agreed to carry MTP's Golden Legacy all-natural oven-browned turkey products and honey-smoked turkey breast products in the deli cases of all of its 98 stores in five midwestern states. It was the first time MTP had such a retail account for one of its fully cooked items. It was a development that could very well lead to the addition of new products and further opportunities in the years to come.

*Ed Dinger*

## PRINCIPAL SUBSIDIARIES

Michigan Turkey Producers LLC.

## PRINCIPAL COMPETITORS

Butterball, LLC; Cargill Value-Added Meats; Perdue Farms, Inc.; Sara Lee Corporation.

## FURTHER READING

Burdick, John, "Bil Mar Turns Down Offer to Help Turkey Farmers," *Holland Sentinel*, July 25, 1997.

Jackson, Paul W., "Michigan Turkey Producers Go Mainstream," *Michigan Farm News*, March 30, 2009.

Karapetian, Alicia, "Home Grown," *Poultry*, February-March 2007, p. 28.

Kopenkoskey, Paul R., "After Losing Bil-Mar Business, Turkey Farmers Launch Their Own Venture," *Holland Sentinel*, June 20, 1999.

"Michigan Turkey: Establishing a Legacy," *Urner Barry's Reporter*, Winter 2007, p. 1.

"The Mother of Invention," *Food Engineering*, September 2001, p. 46.

O'Keefe, Terrence, "MTP Cooks Its Way to Value," *Watt Poultry USA*, September 2006, p. 16.

Sanchez, Mark, "Turkey Farmers Preparing Study of Own Plant," *Holland Sentinel*, October 14, 1998.

Vincent, Jennifer, "Michigan Turkey Producers Co-Op Opens," *Michigan Farm News*, March 15, 2000.

Wieland, Barbara, "Product Debut Gives Turkey Farmers Chance to Survive," *Grand Rapids Press*, November 20, 2000, p. A1.

# Millicom International Cellular S.A.

15 rue Leon Laval
Leudelange, L-3372
Luxembourg
Telephone: (+352 27) 759-101
Fax: (+352 27) 759-359
Web site: www.millicom.com

*Public Company*
*Founded:* 1990
*Incorporated:* 1992
*Employees:* 6,600
*Sales:* $3.37 billion (2009)
*Stock Exchanges:* NASDAQ Stockholm
*Ticker Symbol:* MIC
*NAICS:* 517110 Wired Telecommunications Carriers;
    517212 Wireless Telecommunications Carriers
    (except Satellite)

■ ■ ■

Millicom International Cellular S.A., based in Leudelange, Luxembourg, provides mobile telecommunications service in Central and South America and Africa. The company targets developing markets by offering a prepaid mobile-phone service that is convenient and affordable for many low-income consumers and postpaid service plans for more affluent customers. Through its Amnet unit, the company also offers cable television, broadband Internet, and landline telephone service in Central America. In early 2010 the company had operations in Bolivia, Chad, Colombia, Costa Rica, Democratic Republic of Congo, El Salvador, Ghana, Guatemala, Honduras, Mauritius, Nicaragua, Paraguay, Rwanda, Senegal, and Tanzania.

## A MULTINATIONAL MARRIAGE OF PIONEERING MOBILE PROVIDERS: 1979–93

Millicom International Cellular traces its roots to two pioneering mobile-phone companies, both connected to the Swedish corporation Industriförvaltnings AB Kinnevik. In 1979 Kinnevik purchased a mobile-phone company that it renamed Comviq GSM, which offered its first services in Sweden in 1981. That same year, Kinnevik chairman Jan Stenbeck founded Millicom Inc., based in the United States. Three years later the U.S. Federal Communications Commission granted it one of the first three licenses to develop cellular telephone networks. Millicom also offered pagers, becoming one of the first companies to introduce "textual beepers" in 1984. During the 1980s Comviq acquired cellular licenses in several developing countries from Sri Lanka to Costa Rica. Millicom partnered with the British firm Racal Electronics plc in a joint venture that later grew into the industry giant Vodafone Group plc. Between 1983 and 1989 Millicom's annual revenues soared from less than $1 million to $120 million.

In the late 1980s and early 1990s mobile phones, initially regarded as expensive toys for high-flying businesspersons, became much more affordable and attractive to mass consumers. Millicom Incorporated was one of the first cellular providers to promote setting up PCN networks. These networks could handle much larger calling volumes than old-fashioned cellular networks and

# COMPANY PERSPECTIVES

Millicom is today one of the fastest-growing cellular operators in emerging markets, and we believe we can continue to grow more rapidly than our competitors. Our ability to take or hold market share is made possible by our inherent culture of cost control and innovation and by our successful marketing-oriented strategy that is specifically tailored to emerging markets and has become embodied in our Tigo brand. Tigo today is known to represent affordability, accessibility, and availability, the three pillars of our "Triple A" business strategy, which are real product differentiators in the market place

could support more sophisticated services and more flexible calling plans, which could attract a larger customer base. In 1990 Kinnevik and Millicom Incorporated agreed to combine their international cellular operations, creating Millicom International Cellular S.A. (MIC), based in Luxembourg. Kinnevik transferred its international licenses to the new company.

In 1993 MIC arranged to merge Millicom Incorporated's cellular operations into a U.S.-based subsidiary that could issue stock on the NASDAQ beginning on December 31 of that year. Millicom Incorporated's other operations were spun off into American Satellite Network Inc. Kinnevik retained a 38 percent share in Millicom International and seats on its board of directors. Millicom International (Millicom) had sold its 20 percent ownership in Comviq, keeping the option to repurchase these shares. In 1996 Millicom swapped this option for a stake in NetCom Systems AB (later renamed Tele2 AB), another Kinnevik-connected firm, supplying telephone and Internet access in northern Europe.

## WORLDWIDE EXPANSION: 1993–2000

Millicom began to focus on seeking opportunity in developing economies. By 1997 the company was operating in Estonia, Lithuania, Russia, India, Pakistan, the Philippines, Sri Lanka, Vietnam, Laos, Cambodia, and several African and Latin American countries. In the 1990s many of these countries were emerging (or still suffering) from long periods of warfare and repressive regimes and were loosening restrictions on foreign economic investment. Millicom accepted the risks of

continuing violence, political instability, and regulatory problems for the possibility of tremendous growth and high profits in markets where few people were using mobile phones. Many consumers and officials in developing countries saw the spread of mobile wireless technology as a way to avoid having to establish and maintain limited and expensive landline telephone service.

The company typically participated in a joint venture to establish a foothold in a market, and then it often sought to buy out its partners' interests if the venture was succeeding. Partnering with domestic firms helped Millicom defend itself against political and business opponents. Typically the company entered a new market with mobile-phone service. It later added Internet service and more sophisticated data transmission services when conditions seemed right.

Starting in 1997 many of Millicom's subsidiaries promoted prepaid service that lower-income consumers could purchase in small quantities without tying themselves to expensive contracts. By the end of the year 2000, prepaid service accounted for over 70 percent of the company's mobile-phone customers, boosting the total number of subscribers to over three million from around 500,000 just four years before. Revenues accordingly rose from $131.4 million in 1995 to $570.8 million in 2000. However, the company often ran deficits, which it attributed to servicing its high-yield bond issues and the high costs of setting up new networks. From time to time Millicom sold off some of its holdings to raise capital. For example, in 1994 it sold its 50 percent share in Telefonica Celular de Chile, and four years later it sold its minority shares in Estonian and Lithuanian operators.

Millicom retained some cellular licenses and telecommunications interests in Western Europe. In 1998 the company merged these holdings with several Kinnevik units, receiving a 35 percent share in the newly formed Société Européene de Communication SA. Millicom's subsidiary Multinational Automated Clearing House (MACH) helped hundreds of GSM providers to reconcile the calling records of mobile-phone users roaming between networks and to perform numerous other business services. In 1999 Tele2 (UK) Ltd., another Millicom subsidiary, launched high-speed wireless Internet services that served as a model for introducing such services in other markets.

## A PERIOD OF ADJUSTMENT AND RESTRUCTURING: 2000–05

After the year 2000, Millicom continued to seek greater penetration of its established markets, gradual rolling

## KEY DATES

**1979:** Millicom Incorporated is founded in the United States.

**1990:** Millicom International Cellular S.A. is established in Luxembourg.

**1993:** Millicom International merges with Millicom Incorporated's cellular operations.

**2006:** Proposed sale of Millicom to China Mobile Communications falls through.

**2008:** Millicom acquires Amnet Telecommunications Holding Limited, a broadband and cable television provider in Central America.

out of more advanced services, and entry into selected new markets. Company management was convinced that long-term success would stem not from introducing the most sophisticated technology first, such as 3G networks, but from supplying the most customers with basic voice service. Millicom's financial growth was modest from 2000 to 2003. During that time revenues rose from $570.8 million to $647.1 million, and EBITDA (earnings before interest, taxes, depreciation, and amortization) rose from $229.1 million to $320.8 million. Financial growth fell somewhat behind growth in customers and calling time, in part because the company was burdened with high amounts of debt.

To raise capital, Millicom sold several valuable assets from 2001 through early 2003, including MACH, its Russian subsidiary FORA Telecom B.V., and subsidiaries in Colombia and the Philippines. In 2003 Millicom exchanged some of its existing bond issues and made a new bond issue, considerably reducing the company's debt load. These measures enabled the company to spend money on introducing GSM networks and promoting the new brand name Tigo in Central and South America. This stimulated a renewed surge of growth in 2004 as revenues and EBITDA both rose by 42 percent, to $921.5 million and $455.9 million, respectively.

Throughout the decade Millicom adjusted its geographical mix of markets. Most notably, the company invested more heavily in Africa, which it increasingly regarded as a strong driver for long-term growth. In many poor African and Asian countries, market penetration was still 10 percent or less. The company bet that many inhabitants would come to see mobile phones as a vital tool and consumer necessity even as they struggled to find sufficient work and food.

In 2000 the company was already operating in the Democratic Republic of Congo, Ghana, Senegal, Sierra Leone, and Tanzania. Millicom pulled out of the Democratic Republic of Congo in 2002 only to return three years later, and the company entered Mauritius in 2004 and Chad in 2005. Between 2000 and 2004 Africa's share of company revenues jumped from 6 percent to 16.3 percent. For the time being, Millicom renewed its commitment to its Asian markets, renewing its cellular licenses in Pakistan in 2004 and raising $400 million to finance operations there and in Vietnam. In 2004 Asia accounted for 37.5 percent of the company's revenue, up from 27 percent in 2000.

### STAYING INDEPENDENT AND RENEWING GROWTH: 2005–10

In January 2006 Millicom management decided to formally consider acquisition offers the company had received. The most serious offer came from China Mobile Communications, the dominant Chinese wireless telecommunications provider. After prolonged negotiations in May and June 2006, China Mobile backed away at the 11th hour from its tentative agreement to acquire Millicom, apparently fearing it was being asked to pay too much. Although Millicom share prices fell sharply after this announcement, the company believed its continuing growth justified its high asking price and its decision to suspend acquisition talks when China Mobile balked.

Indeed, from 2005 through 2008, Millicom enjoyed a remarkable spurt of growth. The number of subscribers leaped from around 7.5 million to over 32 million, and revenues climbed from $912.4 million to $3.41 billion and EBITDA from $445.9 million to $1.47 billion. This growth was all the more impressive because the company left some of its oldest and largest markets, particularly in Asia. In Vietnam, after the company's contract with its government-run partner expired in 2005, it was unable to reach an agreement to continue its operations there. In late 2006 Millicom sold its Pakistani operations to China Mobile Communications, which had just walked away from a deal to acquire Millicom itself. Millicom management had come to regard profit margins in the country as too low, despite tremendous investments over two decades.

Millicom therefore refocused on its operations in the Americas and Africa. The Tigo brand was spread across Africa starting in 2005. Millicom did not offer headsets in many of its African markets, allowing customers to use their existing phones or acquire them elsewhere. The company's prepaid service could be purchased at innumerable formal and informal points of sale, including "mom-and-pop shops or somebody standing under an umbrella," as chief executive Marc Buels told Reinhardt Krause in *Investor's Business Daily* in September 2008. To appeal to lower-income consumers, the company began billing users by the second instead of by the minute. Millicom also offered a one-dollar-a-day unlimited calling service in Africa, which attracted a growing percentage of customers. In the somewhat more affluent Latin American markets, in 2008 the company introduced broadband 3G service and value-added features such as video calls, music downloads, and cash payments and transfers. In 2008 Millicom acquired Amnet, a provider of cable television, high-speed Internet, landline telephone, and corporate data services in Central America, including the new markets of Nicaragua and Costa Rica.

After years of expressing its commitment to Sri Lanka, Cambodia, and Laos, by 2009 the company had arranged to dispose of its subsidiaries in those countries as well, completing its withdrawal from Asia. In Africa, even as it sold off its subsidiary in Sierra Leone, the company obtained the third national cellular license in Rwanda, where it began offering mobile-phone service in December 2009. This market, like many other African markets, attracted Millicom because it was densely populated and rapidly growing economically but had low rates of mobile-phone usage.

For 2009 Millicom reported revenue of $3.37 billion. In 2010 the company still boasted over 30 million subscribers and was ranked either first or second in all of its markets except Rwanda and Colombia. Although these figures remained well below those of the leading international mobile service providers such as Telefónica and Vodafone, Millicom's ability to develop and exploit soaring demand for wireless communications in underdeveloped markets was helping the company continue to grow and remain profitable despite the international economic recession of this period.

*Stephen V. Beitel*

## PRINCIPAL SUBSIDIARIES

Amnet Telecommunications Holding Limited (Bermuda); Cam GSM Company Limited (Cambodia, 58.4%); Colombia Móvil S.A. E.S.P. (Colombia, 50%); Comunicaciones Celulares SA (Guatemala, 55%); Emtel Limited (Mauritius, 50%); MIC Latin America B.V. (Netherlands); MIC Tanzania Limited (Tanzania); Millicom (S.L.) Limited (Sierra Leone); Millicom Africa B.V. (Netherlands); Millicom Ghana Company Limited (Ghana); Millicom Holding B.V. (Netherlands); Millicom International Operations B.V. (Netherlands); Millicom International Operations S.A.; Millicom Lao Co. Limited (Lao People's Democratic Republic, 74.1%); Millicom Rwanda Limited (Rwanda, 87.5%); Millicom Tchad S.A. (Chad, 87.5%); Navega S.A. (Guatemala, 45%); Oasis S.P.R.L (Congo); Sentel GSM S.A. (Senegal); Telefonica Celular de Bolivia SA (Bolivia); Telefonica Celular del Paraguay SA (Paraguay); Telefonica Celular S.A. (Honduras, 66.7%); Telemovil El Salvador SA (El Salvador); Tigo (Pvt) Limited (Sri Lanka, 99.9%).

## PRINCIPAL COMPETITORS

América Móvil, S.A.B. de C.V.; Mobile Telecommunications Company KSC (Zain Group); Telefónica, S.A.; Vodafone Group Plc.

## FURTHER READING

Clark, Robert, "Hands-on Operator," *Wireless Asia*, May 2001, p. 30.

House, Richard, "Jay Metcalfe of Millicom International Cellular: On the Telecom Frontier," *Institutional Investor*, February 1996, p. 23.

Krause, Reinhardt, "Luxembourg's Millicom Bets on Its Tigo Brand in Latin America, Africa, Asia: The Wireless Provider Aims to Offer Markets a Low-Cost, Easy-to-Get Mobile Service," *Investor's Business Daily*, May 22, 2007, p. A6.

———, "Luxembourg's Millicom International: In Rich, and Poor, African Markets It Sees Cell Phone User Penetration Rates Soaring Despite Many Challenges," *Investor's Business Daily*, September 4, 2008, p. A5.

McVicker, Dee, "A World Unwired: Juggling Business Plans to Attract Customers Worldwide Is No Easy Trick; Returns Can Drop Out Completely," *Tele.com*, October 16, 2000, p. 55.

"Millicom Plans to Sell Comviq Stake to Finance Emerging Networks," *Mobile Communications*, July 13, 1995.

Phillips, Jim, "Pioneer Seeking License for Personal, Portable System," *Houston Business Journal*, February 19, 1990, p. 17.

"Rwanda's Third Network, Tigo, Goes Live," *African Business*, November 2009, p. 47.

Timmons, Heather, and Donald Greenlees, "Art of the Deal Meets The China Syndrome," *New York Times*, July 14, 2006, p. C6.

Trachtenberg, Jeffrey A., "Getting the Message," *Forbes*, April 23, 1984, p. 144.

# National Football League

280 Park Avenue, 15th Floor
New York, New York 10017
U.S.A.
Telephone: (212) 450-2000
Toll Free: (888) 635-2273
Fax: (212) 681-7599
Web site: http://www.nfl.com

*Nonprofit Company*
*Founded:* 1920 as American Professional Football
  Conference
*Employees:* 400
*Sales:* $8 billion (2009 est.)
*NAICS:* 711211 Sports Teams and Clubs

■ ■ ■

The governing body for the most popular spectator sport in the United States, the National Football League (NFL) serves as a trade association for 32 franchised football teams based in the United States. NFL team owners operate their clubs much like stand-alone businesses, but they share large portions of their revenue with the other franchises. Over the years the NFL has negotiated television and radio broadcast rights for the teams and maintained the right to market team names and logos through exclusive licensing agreements. In the 21st century the NFL has taken advantage of new media outlets to expand its market share. For example, it has employed cell phones and the Internet to increase its availability to a wider fan base, and it has launched its own television network to expand its program offerings.

By 2009 the league had swelled into an $8 billion-a-year business.

## ORIGINS OF ORGANIZED AMERICAN FOOTBALL: 1870–1920

U.S. football evolved as a hybrid of soccer and rugby during the early 1870s, gaining distinction from its two influences in 1876 when the first rules for the sport were written. By the 1890s the new version of football was a popular activity at local athletic clubs, particularly in Pennsylvania where intense rivalry between two clubs led to the first payment to a player. In 1892 William "Pudge" Heffelfinger was paid $500 by the Allegheny Athletic Association to play one game against rival Pittsburgh Athletic Club, marking the advent of professionalism in U.S. football. Five years later the Latrobe Athletic Association football team hired all professional players, becoming the first team to field professionals for a full season. Other purely professional football clubs were organized in the ensuing years as the epicenter of football activity moved from Pennsylvania to Ohio. Ohio was home to at least seven professional teams during the first decade of the 20th century, but the growth of football in Ohio and elsewhere bred a host of problems, each attributable to the professionalism that spurred the sport's growth.

As the number of professional teams proliferated and competition became more heated, the salaries paid to players escalated rapidly. The lure of these rising salaries prompted players to switch continually from one team to another, going wherever the highest bid beckoned. In the search for talent, football clubs began

The National Football League is America's most popular sports league, comprised of 32 franchises that compete each year to win the Super Bowl, the world's biggest annual sporting event. Founded in 1920, the NFL developed the model for the successful modern sports league, including extensive revenue sharing, competitive excellence, strong franchises across the board, and national distribution. The NFL is the industry leader on a wide range of fronts. *Business Week* magazine calls the NFL 'one of America's best-run businesses.'

scouting college players, hiring some while the players were still enrolled in school. The outbreak of these problems created confusion within the sport, compounded by the widely varying schedules each team maintained. By the end of the 1910s there was need for the order and discipline that the establishment of a uniform set of rules and conduct could bring to the sport. The strongest cries for organization and structure emanated from the stronghold of professional football in Ohio, where the foundation for the NFL was laid.

Several attempts to organize a professional football league had been made early in the century, but each had failed until an attempt to form a league took root in 1920. In August the first organizational meeting for what later became the NFL was held in Canton, Ohio, at the Jordan and Hupmobile automobile showroom. In attendance were representatives of the Akron Pros, the Canton Bulldogs (arguably the best professional team in the country), the Cleveland Indians, and the Dayton Triangles. Their meeting marked the establishment of the American Professional Football Conference, which was renamed the American Professional Football Association (APFA) at a second meeting one month later. At this meeting, also held in Canton, the participants of the first meeting were joined by representatives of teams from three other states, including Indiana's Muncie Flyers, the Rochester Jeffersons from New York, and the Racine Cardinals from Illinois.

### THE NFL TAKES SHAPE: 1920–60

By the end of the APFA's first year there were 14 teams within the league. The scheduling of games, both the overall number of games and the number of games contested between APFA teams, was left for each team to decide on its own. The league did not begin to exert

control over its constituents until its second year of operation when a new president, Joe Carr of the Columbus Panhandles, was elected at the APFA meeting in April 1921. Carr, who presided over the league for the next 18 years, became the NFL's first architect, establishing the framework that gave the league control over affiliated teams. He made his mark early in his tenure by drafting a league constitution during his first year in office. Carr developed bylaws, assigned teams territorial rights, restricted player movements, and developed membership criteria for team franchises. Carr's inaugural year also included the debut of league standings, which enabled the designation of a league champion, previously an issue of considerable debate. In 1922, by which time membership within the league had increased to 22 teams, the APFA was renamed the National Football League.

Carr continued to give shape and structure to the NFL during the 1920s, making alterations that would endure for decades. He instituted the first roster limit (16) in 1925, and in 1927 he resolved a fundamental weakness of the league by eliminating the financially weaker teams and consolidating the more talented players into a reduced number of financially stronger teams. Carr's most critical changes occurred during the 1930s, as the country endured the effects of the Great Depression.

The pernicious economic environment whittled the number of league teams to eight in 1932, the lowest during the 20th century, but amid the despair the NFL achieved important strides. In 1932 the first tie for first place occurred, prompting the need for the first NFL play-off game. The following year Carr labored to give the NFL its own identity. Since its inception the NFL generally had followed the rules of college football, but in 1933 Carr began developing separate rules that addressed the needs and style of the professional game. Some of these changes were born from the first championship game in 1932, which had to be held indoors because of freezing temperatures and heavy snow. The alterations included hash marks and goal posts fixed on the goal line rather than the end line, both of which were innovations required because of the limited space available for the 1932 championship game. Furthermore, the forward pass was legalized from any point behind the line of scrimmage. Organizationally, the league was divided into two divisions in 1933, the Western and Eastern divisions, with the winners of each scheduled to meet in an annual championship game. The NFL also took charge of an annual draft of college players, instituted for the first time in 1936, the same year all member teams played the same number of games in one year for the first time. The decade ended with Carr's death and the first television broadcast of an

## KEY DATES

**1920:** Several professional football teams join to form the American Professional Football Conference; one month later, the organization is renamed the American Professional Football Association (APFA).

**1921:** Joe Carr is elected first league president.

**1922:** APFA is renamed the National Football League (NFL).

**1939:** First televised NFL game takes place between the Brooklyn Dodgers and the Philadelphia Eagles.

**1960:** Pete Rozelle becomes NFL commissioner.

**1963:** NFL Properties, Inc., is created to oversee league's licensing and merchandise operations.

**1967:** NFL and rival American Football League (AFL) play first World Championship Game, or Super Bowl.

**1970:** NFL and AFL officially merge.

**1998:** ABC, FOX, CBS, and ESPN pay a combined $17.6 billion for rights to broadcast NFL games.

**2002:** The NFL adopts the "Rooney rule" to help promote diversity within the league's coaching and management ranks.

**2010:** Super Bowl XLIV between the New Orleans Saints and Indianapolis Colts sets an American television broadcasting record, attracting 106.5 million viewers.

NFL game. In 1939 NBC aired a game between the Brooklyn Dodgers and the Philadelphia Eagles at a time when there were 1,000 television sets in New York.

By the end of the 1930s the NFL played a vital role in the sport of football, lending cohesion and legitimacy to what was becoming a national pastime. From the legacy of Carr's achievements, the NFL gained the structure to support its increasing influence over the game during the postwar period, when football developed into a multibillion-dollar business. One of the chief factors igniting such growth was the increasing fees paid by broadcasters to air NFL games. The value of radio and television deals increased in part because of the expansion of the NFL. After its early popularity in Ohio, football moved eastward into the large cities following Carr's consolidation of the league in 1927. In 1946 the NFL became national in scope for the first time when the Cleveland Rams moved to Los Angeles.

In 1950 the Los Angeles Rams became the first team to have all of its home and away games televised, an arrangement other teams secured as the 1950s progressed. Following the promulgation of a congressional bill legalizing single-network television contracts by professional sports leagues in 1961, the NFL reached a single-network agreement with CBS in 1962 for broadcasting all regular-season games. The NFL-CBS contract, valued at $4.6 million annually, marked the beginning of an ever-increasing bidding war waged by the networks to secure the rights for NFL games. Two years later CBS paid $14.1 million for broadcasting rights.

## DOMINATING THE AMERICAN SPORTS SCENE: 1960–2000

The exponentially increasing television deals were indicative of the growing popularity of football. By the mid-1960s football was the country's favorite sport, eclipsing baseball (41 percent to 38 percent, according to a survey) for the first time. To take advantage of the widespread interest in the sport, the NFL developed ancillary businesses for the modern, lucrative era of football. In 1963 the league formed NFL Properties, Inc., to serve as the licensing arm of the NFL. The following year the league purchased Ed Sabol's Blair Motion Pictures, renaming it NFL Films. Football's growth in popularity and its attendant revenue-generating potential also spawned the organization of competing leagues, nothing new to the NFL. Since its inception, the league had butted against rival leagues, including four leagues (each named the American Football League) between 1920 and 1940.

By the 1960s, however, a new version of the American Football League (AFL) had taken root and proved to be a meddlesome entity with which the NFL was forced to contend. Rivalry between the two leagues was litigious and resulted in an antitrust suit filed by the AFL against the NFL during the early 1960s. The legal battle dragged on for nearly four years. The courts ultimately ruled against the AFL, but the ruling did not signal the end of the AFL. The rival league continued to flourish, securing a $36 million, five-year deal with NBC for television rights beginning in 1965. The resilience of the AFL led to a series of secret meetings between two team owners from the two leagues in 1966. Their discussions centered on a potential merger between the AFL and NFL, which was announced in mid-1966. Under the terms of the agreement, the merger created an expanded league comprising 24 teams, although the two leagues maintained separate schedules until they officially merged in 1970 to form one league with two conferences. In the interim, the two leagues played a World Championship Game beginning in January 1967, the first of what later became known as the Super Bowl.

Overseeing the merger between the AFL and the NFL was Pete Rozelle, who held the title of NFL commissioner. Rozelle was selected as commissioner in 1960 and held the same title after the merger. Rozelle's tenure, which stretched until 1989, was as influential on the development of the NFL as Carr's effect on the league. When Rozelle took control, he inherited a fragmented league in which the team owners maintained substantial control. The league governed the game, but the team owners operated their franchises essentially like stand-alone businesses. Operating as such, the teams negotiated individually with broadcasters for the rights to air games, a state of affairs Rozelle disliked. He perceived a sporting event's greatest strength as representing a piece of programming, and to give the sport its greatest bargaining power when negotiating with broadcasters, he realized that the franchises needed to cease operating as fiefdoms and combine their strength under the NFL. To accomplish this, Rozelle convinced the owners to share their broadcasting revenue evenly among all franchises and to give the NFL control over negotiating broadcasting rights. Rozelle accomplished this diplomatic feat during the early 1960s, fueling the dramatic rise in broadcasting rights during the early part of the decade. Broadcasters, in the wake of Rozelle's shrewd maneuver, found themselves with "about as much clout as the Dalai Lama has dealing with the Chinese army," in the words of ABC sports broadcaster Roone Arledge, quoted by Michael Lewis in *Time* magazine on December 7, 1998.

Rozelle transformed football into big business, taking a league that along with its franchises generated less than $20 million annually in 1960 and developing it into a multibillion-dollar-a-year business by the end of his stewardship as commissioner. He did so by acting as a skilled promoter of the game, which again was a product of his emphasis on football as a piece of programming. With the millions of dollars the networks were paying for the rights to the NFL, they were obliged to promote the game to ensure the success of their investment. Together with Roone Arledge, the head of ABC Sports, Rozelle created Monday Night Football, which debuted on ABC in 1970 and become one of the longest-running shows in the history of television. Rozelle also expanded, moving into new markets (a new term in the sports world) with the establishment of a franchise in New Orleans in 1967 and in Tampa Bay and Seattle in 1976. The NFL expanded internationally as well. It played its first game outside North America in 1976 at a preseason match in Korakuen Stadium in Tokyo.

Despite the list of achievements during Rozelle's 29-year career as commissioner, the NFL also suffered its low points. Two players' strikes in 1982 and 1987 marred the league's otherwise stellar progress. A litigious relationship with a rival league, the United States Football League (USFL), also diverted the league's attention, resulting in a $1.7 billion antitrust lawsuit filed against the league. The jury, however, rejected all of the USFL's television-related claims in 1986. The 1980s also bore witness to a contentious battle between the NFL and the owner of the Oakland Raiders, Al Davis, formerly head of the AFL. Davis, who wanted to move his team to Los Angeles, prevailed despite repeated attempts by the NFL to stop the team's relocation. In addition, television ratings for the NFL dipped during the mid-1980s amid escalating expenses arising from increasing player salaries. Integral to the league's ability to withstand the turbulence was the willingness of broadcasters to pay increasing amounts for the right to air NFL games. Because of this, the league demonstrated encouraging vibrancy by the end of the 1980s. When Rozelle retired in 1989, a new four-year contract was signed with the three major networks, ABC, CBS, and NBC, and two cable networks, ESPN and TNT, valued at $3.6 billion, the largest in television history.

Rozelle's successor, Paul Tagliabue, took charge of the league in 1989, becoming the seventh chief executive to lead the NFL. Under Tagliabue's control the NFL expanded during the 1990s, both domestically and abroad. In 1991 the NFL decided to expand to 30 franchises, leading to the debut of the Jacksonville Jaguars and the Carolina Panthers in 1994. The league also launched the World League of American Football in 1991, after years of staging preseason games at international venues. When the new league began playing Europe, the NFL became the first sports league to operate on a weekly basis on two continents. Initially the World League faltered, taking a two-year hiatus before resuming operation as the NFL Europe League in 1998.

Although the NFL continued to contend with rising player salaries, which was a perennial problem predating the league's existence, broadcasters consistently demonstrated a willingness to keep pace with the league's rising expenses by paying vast sums for broadcasting rights. In 1998, as the NFL prepared for the century ahead, the market value of its programming showed no signs of weakening in the least. In a record-setting, eight-year deal with ABC, FOX, CBS, and ESPN, the networks paid a staggering $17.6 billion for the broadcast rights to NFL games. Clearly, the strength of NFL programming was sufficient to ensure the league's continued success into the next millennium.

## EXPANDING THE NFL BRAND IN THE DIGITAL AGE: 2000–10

NFL executives confronted a range of new challenges as the league entered the 21st century. One issue that became central during this period was that of minority hiring, particularly in the areas of coaching and management. The NFL had made significant strides toward greater diversity over the previous two decades. In 1980 there were no African-American head coaches and only fourteen assistant coaches in the league, but by the end of the 1990s there were two African-American head coaches and roughly 125 coordinators and assistants. Still, the disproportionate number of head-coaching positions continued to be awarded to white candidates even though nearly 70 percent of NFL players were African American.

This disparity eventually sparked a groundswell of activism. In September 2002 attorneys Johnnie Cochrane and Cyrus Mehri produced a landmark report entitled "Black Coaches in the National Football League: Superior Performance, Inferior Opportunities." The document illustrated that African-American candidates faced a range of deeply entrenched discriminatory practices when applying for head coaching positions. Urged by the report's findings, Commissioner Paul Tagliabue promptly implemented a series of initiatives aimed at promoting awareness of the issue among league owners. In October 2002 Tagliabue created a new diversity committee aimed at exploring new ways to increase the numbers of minorities in coaching in management position. That December, the league introduced a new rule requiring teams to interview at least one minority candidate when seeking to fill head coaching vacancies. The requirement became known as the Rooney rule, after diversity committee chair and Pittsburgh Steelers owner Dan Rooney. In March 2003 a group of minority coaches and officials joined together to form the Fritz Pollard Alliance, an organization dedicated to promoting greater diversity among NFL front offices.

During this period, the NFL was also fighting to improve its image on other fronts. In February 2004 the league suffered one of the most embarrassing moments in its history when singer Janet Jackson inadvertently exposed one of her breasts during the Super Bowl XXX-VIII halftime program. Described as a "wardrobe malfunction" by Jackson's representatives, the incident sparked an investigation by the Federal Communications Commission (FCC) and promoted the league to overhaul its Super Bowl entertainment policies. The NFL found itself contending with increasing incidents of player misconduct toward the end of the decade, both on and off the field. The most disturbing example occurred in 2007, when Atlanta Falcons quarterback Michael Vick was arrested on charges of orchestrating an illegal dogfighting ring. Recently elected NFL commissioner Roger Goodell, who had succeeded Paul Tagliabue in September 2006, took immediate action, publicly condemning Vick's actions and suspending the troubled quarterback indefinitely. Goodell's response to the Vick incident earned widespread praise among team executives, including Falcons' owner Arthur Blank, who hailed the commissioner for "coming out strongly and definitively against player conduct," according to Mark Maske in a *Washington Post* article on September 2, 2007.

In spite of these public relations issues, the NFL continued to dominate U.S. sports entertainment at decade's end, with annual revenues topping $8 billion in 2009. The advent of digital media had helped the league expand its reach considerably, as streaming video and cell phone alerts became increasingly vital to the viewing experience of the average fan. In addition, the league's popular TV channel, the NFL Network, was rapidly becoming an important revenue stream. First launched in 2004, the NFL's television outlet allowed the league to expand its coverage of football-related events and gave it greater leverage when negotiating broadcasting rights with other networks.

As the league continued its brisk growth, however, new challenges emerged. In January 2010 the NFL became embroiled in an antitrust suit when the apparel firm American Needle sued the league over its rigid licensing policies. After a series of lower-court decisions, the company appealed the case to the Supreme Court, which was expected to reach a decision by June of that year. At the same time, league owners were involved in intense negotiations with player representatives over a new collective bargaining agreement, and the possibility of a lockout prior to the 2011 regular season loomed on the horizon. Even the resounding success of Super Bowl XLIV, which set a new U.S. broadcast record with 106.5 million viewers when it aired on February 7, 2010, could not fully erase the uncertainty that confronted the league in the coming months.

*Jeffrey L. Covell*
*Updated, Stephen Meyer*

### PRINCIPAL SUBSIDIARIES

NFL Enterprises LLC; NFL International LLC; NFL Properties LLC; NFL Ventures, L.P.; NFL Ventures, Inc.

## PRINCIPAL COMPETITORS

Major League Baseball; National Association for Stock Car Auto Racing, Inc.; National Basketball Association, Inc.; National Hockey League.

## FURTHER READING

Belson, Ken, and Alan Schwarz, "Antitrust Case Has Implications Far Beyond N.F.L.," *New York Times*, January 7, 2010, p. B13.

"League's 1991 Sales Show No Recession," *Sporting Goods Business*, December 1991, p. 14.

Levingston, Steven, "NFL Plays Smash-Mouth Ball When It Comes to Branding: League Seeks to Extend Dominance through Cable, Internet," *Washington Post*, February 5, 2006, p. A7.

Lewis, Michael, "High Commissioner—Pete Rozelle," *Time*, December 7, 1998, p. 188.

"NFL Sacks Itself," *Fortune*, January 21, 1985, p. 10.

Maske, Mark, "Commissioner Goodell Has Great Expectations for NFL," *Washington Post*, September 2, 2007, p. D11.

Maske, Mark, and Leonard Shapiro, "Minority Hiring Is Lauded; NFL Makes 'Substantial Progress' in Coaching Ranks," *Washington Post*, January 22, 2004, p. D1.

Mihoces, Gary, "Half Provides Kind of Exposure NFL Doesn't Want," *USA Today*, February 2, 2004, p. 1C.

Rhoden, William C., "Working with the N.F.L. on Diversity," *New York Times*, December 24, 2009, p. 10.

Shapiro, Leonard, "Minority Hiring Discussed at NFL; League Will Add Issue to Meetings Next Week," *Washington Post*, October 23, 2002, p. D3.

# Netflix, Inc.

---

**100 Winchester Circle**
**Los Gatos, California 95032**
**U.S.A.**
**Telephone: (408) 540-3700**
**Toll Free: (866) 716-0414**
**Fax: (408) 540-3737**
**Web site: http://www.netflix.com**

*Public Company*
*Incorporated:* 1997 as NetFlix.com, Inc.
*Employees:* 4,080
*Sales:* $1.67 billion (2009)
*Stock Exchanges:* NASDAQ
*Ticker Symbol:* NFLX
*NAICS:* 532230 Video Tape and Disc Rental

■ ■ ■

Netflix, Inc., is the world's leading digital video disc (DVD) rent-by-mail company. The company serves more than 12 million subscribers and operates 50 processing facilities throughout the United States. Netflix offers many subscription plans, allowing customers to rent anywhere from one to eight DVDs at any given time and ranging in price from $4.99 to $47.99 per month. A portion of the extensive Netflix video library is also available for viewing on the Internet, through the company's "Watch Now" feature. In addition, Netflix allows subscribers to watch content directly on their televisions through a variety of platforms, including the Roku video player and the TiVo digital video recorder;

gaming consoles such as Sony Playstation 3, Wii, and Xbox; and various Blu-ray DVD players.

## A NEW MODEL FOR DVD RENTALS: 1997

NetFlix.com, Inc., was founded in Scotts Valley, California, in 1997 by Marc Randolph and Reed Hastings to rent and sell DVDs over the Internet. Randolph had previously helped found a computer mail-order company called Micro Warehouse and then served as vice president of marketing for Borland International, while the one-time math teacher Hastings had founded Pure Software, which he had recently sold for $700 million. Hastings, who supplied the firm's start-up cash of $2.5 million, had reportedly hit on the idea for rental-by-mail when he was forced to pay $40 in fines after returning an overdue videotape of the movie *Apollo 13*.

The DVD format, which can store a high-quality copy of an entire feature film on a single five-inch disc, had been introduced in the spring of 1997 and less than 1,000 titles were then available. Even though the hardware needed to play DVDs was fairly expensive and owned by relatively few Americans, Randolph and Hastings thought the disc had the clear potential to replace the bulkier, lower-resolution videotape as the consumer format of choice.

Key to the firm's initial strategy was the fact that few video stores carried DVDs, making renting them in person a hit-or-miss affair. The company was also able to take advantage of the small size and light weight of the discs, which could be shipped to users inexpensively.

The firm experimented with more than 200 mailing packages before finding one that could safely ship a disc (in a plain case without cover art and inserts) for the cost of a single first-class stamp. A stamped return mailer was also enclosed. NetFlix promised to virtually guarantee that titles would be in stock, with reasonably quick delivery offered through the U.S. Postal Service. The company pledged to buy more than 1,000 copies of new releases, which could be reserved in advance for shipment on the day they were made available in stores.

### READY FOR BUSINESS: 1998

NetFlix opened for business in April 1998 with 30 employees and 925 titles for rent, which accounted for nearly the entire catalogue of DVDs in print. The firm offered some soft-core Playboy titles but shied away from hard-core pornography to avoid the potential for legal problems in certain states. NetFlix initially offered a seven-day DVD rental for $4, plus $2 shipping, with the cost going down when additional discs were rented. Discs could be kept longer for an additional fee. New DVDs were also offered for sale at a discount of up to 30 percent. Consumers could decide to purchase a rented disc once they got it home by having the balance of the retail price charged to their credit card. The firm's Web site offered a number of informational features including movie reviews, and once a customer had rented several titles a profile would be generated that automatically suggested additional films of interest based on the characteristics of ones already chosen.

To promote its debut, NetFlix sponsored a sweepstakes to win an "L.A. Weekend" all-expense-paid trip to Los Angeles, California, as a cross-promotion with Warner Brothers for the newly available DVD of the film *L.A. Confidential.* The initial response to Net-Flix's service was strong, and its Internet site was briefly forced to shut down 48 hours after it went online. Net-Flix was one of the first companies to rent DVDs by mail, with only a handful of other competitors in operation, including Magic Disc, DVD Express, and Reel. com.

A month after the company opened its virtual doors, it announced a promotional venture with Toshiba America to offer three free DVD rentals to purchasers of new Toshiba DVD players, and similar offers were soon made to buyers of Pioneer DVD players and select Hewlett-Packard and Apple computer models that included DVD drives. Later in the year Sony was also signed up, with additional companies following.

### HONING THE NETFLIX BUSINESS MODEL: 1998–99

The company received a tremendous promotional boost in September 1998, when it made available 10,000 copies of a DVD of President Bill Clinton's Grand Jury testimony in the Monica Lewinsky affair. They were sold for just two cents each, plus $2 shipping and handling. The offer was widely covered in the news media, although the success was marred slightly by a mix-up at the manufacturing plant, which shipped pornographic DVDs in place of a few copies of the disc.

In December NetFlix announced that it would stop selling DVDs. It began directing customers interested in purchases to Amazon.com, Inc., which had recently begun offering DVDs as well. In exchange for bowing out of this business area, NetFlix would be promoted on Amazon's highly trafficked site. The firm cited the relatively modest sales figures, the sizable competition, and the huge effort that would be required to remain competitive. By this time NetFlix's library had grown to 2,300 titles, and home DVD player sales were taking off, although prices remained high and only 1 percent of U.S. households owned the device.

In January 1999 NetFlix began partnering with the online movie information provider All-Movie Guide, which would direct people looking up a title NetFlix carried to the firm's Web site. In March the film critic Leonard Maltin signed on to write an exclusive monthly film column for the site, with five "must-rent" DVD titles listed each time. The company was now buying 10,000 or more copies of some popular titles and had a total inventory of more than 250,000 discs. Its staff had grown to 110.

In July Hastings, the chief executive officer (CEO) of NetFlix, announced that the company had secured $30 million in new financing from Group Arnault, a French luxury goods investment firm that was starting to back e-commerce ventures. The money would be used to fund new brand-building and marketing endeavors. A number of new competitors were beginning to emerge, and the Group Arnault backing was seen as crucial to establishing NetFlix's dominance of the DVD rental category. Shortly afterward, the firm an-

## KEY DATES

∎

**1997:** NetFlix.com, Inc., is formed in California by Marc Randolph and Reed Hastings.

**1998:** The company begins offering DVD rentals and sales.

**1999:** Group Arnault invests $30 million in the firm and a subscription plan debuts.

**2000:** Revenue sharing deals are signed with Warner Home Video and Columbia Tri-Star; CineMatch is introduced.

**2001:** A partnership with Best Buy Co., Inc., gives NetFlix exposure in the chain's 1,800 stores.

**2002:** The company goes public and changes its name to Netflix, Inc.

**2003:** Subscribers top 1 million, and Netflix has its first profitable quarter.

**2007:** Netflix begins streaming instant video via the Internet.

**2008:** Netflix begins marketing the Roku viewing box, enabling subscribers to watch online content on their televisions.

nounced a new cross-promotional initiative with Musicland Stores Corp. and plans to offer free rental coupons in the box of most new DVD players sold.

### INTRODUCING THE SUBSCRIPTION PLAN: 1999–2000

In September 1999 NetFlix introduced the Marquee Program, which allowed members who paid $15.95 per month to preselect four DVDs, with no late fees or due dates. Customers could also rent new discs each time they returned one and could put themselves in a queue for checked out titles in which they were interested. CEO Hastings commented that the new service was possible because the company had achieved the economies of scale, with 10,000 orders processed each day by its own proprietary software system. Despite NetFlix's growing popularity, for fiscal year 1999 it reported losses of $29.8 million on revenues of only $5 million. Like many Internet start-ups, NetFlix was still spending heavily to entice customers to its Web site, betting that it would become profitable after the brand was better established.

In February 2000 NetFlix introduced the new service CineMatch, which compared rental patterns among its customers and looked for similarities in taste.

Using this information, the company recommend titles to people whose profiles were similar. It could also be programmed to combine the attributes of two users, such as a married couple, and recommend titles that both might like. The information gleaned from the CineMatch system, which required customers to rate 20 films using a five-star scale, was also shared with movie studios to help them plan marketing campaigns. Early the next year NetFlix changed the Marquee Program to offer unlimited rentals for $19.95 per month, with a maximum of four titles out at a given time, although this was later dropped to three. Shipping and handling were included in the price. At the same time, the firm phased out single-title rentals, as 97 percent of its business was now derived from the Marquee Program. The company was currently distributing more than 100,000 DVDs per week.

In May 2000 NetFlix announced plans for an initial public offering of $86.3 million worth of common stock but withdrew it in July. Investors had become increasingly skeptical of the e-commerce business model, and NetFlix's lack of profits was a red flag to many. Despite this setback, the company continued to expand. By year's end it had over 7,000 titles available to a customer base of 250,000.

### FORGING STRATEGIC REVENUE SHARING AGREEMENTS: 2000–01

In December 2000 a major goal was achieved when revenue sharing agreements were reached with Warner Home Video and Columbia Tri-Star. In exchange for a percentage of rental receipts, the movie studios gave NetFlix better prices on large quantities of DVDs, which the firm needed to have on hand to fulfill requests for new releases. A number of other studios, including DreamWorks SKG and Artisan Entertainment Inc., were soon signed up as well. The company also unveiled its first television ads at this time, running them in a limited number of markets that had high per capita numbers of DVD players.

In January 2001 NetFlix signed a deal that gave it exclusive distribution of the DVD version of the recent art house hit *Croupier*, which it would have for three months before the title was available elsewhere. Other such deals were reportedly in the works. An important aspect of NetFlix's business was the availability of titles that were not found in mainstream video stores such as Blockbuster Inc. The company also had great success tapping into the underserved markets for independent and foreign films. One particular area of success was in renting so-called Bollywood films from India. The firm offered about 1,000 titles in this category, and these circulated frequently. NetFlix also found that subscribers were renting many lesser-known films after they had been suggested by the company's recommendation system. Because they were not paying for each movie individually, NetFlix customers could take a chance on an interesting-sounding title with which they were not familiar.

During the spring of 2001 the company began offering a free six-week trial membership via the Internet Movie Database, a popular movie information Web site, and selling off overstocked titles through the e-tailers Wherehouse.com and Half.com. In September NetFlix partnered with Best Buy Co., Inc., to create a co-branded DVD rental service in the company's 1,800 stores and on its Web site. Best Buy also owned several other retail chains, including Sam Goody, Media Play, and Suncoast. By late 2001 NetFlix secured additional venture capital funds, and the company began predicting profitability by the fourth quarter of the fiscal year.

Following the September 11, 2001, terrorist attacks against the United States, the company's monthly subscription rate doubled, due as much to fearful Americans seeking refuge at home as to the dropping price of DVD players, which now could be purchased for less than $100. Despite its rapidly growing customer base, the company lost $21.1 million for the year on revenues of $74.3 million.

## GOING PUBLIC

In February 2002 NetFlix announced that it had attained the long-anticipated subscription figure of 500,000. This included some who chose the recently added NetFlix Lite, which cost $13.95 per month and limited users to two rentals at a time. In March the company revived its plans for an initial public offering (IPO), and when it sold 5.5 million shares in late May it raised $82.5 million, more than some had expected. The money was targeted to pay down $14.1 million in debt and cover promotional expenses. In conjunction with the IPO, the firm also quietly amended its name to Netflix, Inc.

Earlier in the year the company had opened new regional distribution facilities near Los Angeles and Boston, Massachusetts, to speed delivery to those areas. These facilities had quickly proven their worth, and by June other facilities were open in Atlanta, Georgia; Denver, Colorado; Detroit, Michigan; Houston, Texas; Minneapolis, Minnesota; New York City, New York; Seattle, Washington; and Washington, D.C. Netflix spent approximately $60,000 on each site for computers, bar-code scanners, and printers, and the facilities were set up to handle 50,000 orders per day. The loca-

tions were situated so that the company could achieve overnight first-class mail delivery to as many customers as possible. Netflix's per capita subscription rate was much higher in San Francisco, California, by almost 5 percent, and this was largely attributed to the overnight response to customer orders. In contrast, subscribers on the East Coast had to wait approximately four days for an order to reach them, reducing the number of DVDs they could receive each month. Each distribution site did not maintain a full inventory, so when an order for an out-of-stock disc was received, the company's computers found the closest location of a copy and automatically generated a shipping order to forward it.

During the summer of 2002 the company also experimented briefly with a brick-and-mortar DVD rental store in Las Vegas, Nevada. Called Netflix Express, the 600-square-foot operation was located in a supermarket and was open for less than a month. Netflix now had 670,000 subscribers and offered 11,500 different titles. It had also signed revenue-sharing agreements with more than 50 film distributors, who received approximately 20 percent of the company's subscription fees.

## COMPETING WITH COMPETITORS

As Netflix garnered more media attention and its subscriber numbers soared, the competition began to heat up. During the summer of 2003 Blockbuster began offering an unlimited, no-late-fee subscription service for DVD rentals in some stores. It also bought an online DVD rental company and renamed it FilmCaddy.com. Netflix was also being targeted by Wal-Mart Stores, Inc., which had started its own unlimited online DVD rental service. Priced at $18.86 per month, the service undercut Netflix by just over a dollar. Wal-Mart claimed it had 12,000 titles available, comparable to what Netflix offered. Another major player, Columbia House, was reportedly eyeing a similar plan as well. With these threats, and with Netflix's subscriber cancellation rate inching upward, the company's stock price dropped by more than half.

Responding to these challenges, Netflix announced that it would open a dozen more distribution facilities by the end of 2003 to serve major metropolitan areas such as Chicago, Illinois; Dallas, Texas; and Portland, Oregon. The firm was targeting 5 million subscribers by 2009 and had plans to begin distribution in Canada. Annual figures for 2002 showed double the previous year's revenues, $152.8 million, and losses of just $1.6 million, which was a dramatic improvement over 2001.

The subscriber cancellation rate was also dropping, to 6.3 percent for the final quarter of the year.

## ONE MILLION SUBSCRIBERS: 2003

Netflix hit the 1 million subscriber mark in February 2003, by which time it had also opened five additional shipping facilities. Its stock price was on the rebound and in the spring it was $22 a share, almost 50 percent more than it had commanded at the IPO. June saw the firm report its first profitable quarter to date, and it also became one of the first Silicon Valley companies to count stock options as expenses, a move that came in the wake of the public outcry over a number of corporate accounting scandals. The company gave stock options to all of its salaried employees, and this was expected to add $2 million in costs in the latter half of the fiscal year. Also in June Netflix was awarded U.S. patents for its software systems that tracked DVD rentals and compiled customer requests. By midsummer the company had more than 1.1 million subscribers and a library of 15,000 titles from which to choose.

By the end of 2003 Netflix had expanded its subscriber base to 1.5 million customers. Furthermore, its fourth-quarter revenues increased to $81.2 million, which was a substantial increase over the same period in 2002, when the company's sales were $45.2 million. More significantly, the company posted a profit of $2.3 million for the quarter, after suffering a fourth-quarter loss of $2.2 million a year earlier. These brisk earnings were not lost on investors. By December 2003 Netflix saw its stock value skyrocket to roughly $50 a share, an increase of 400 percent over the course of the year.

## EMERGING TECHNOLOGIES, NEW COMPETITION: 2004–10

Regardless, Netflix faced many challenges heading into the second half of the decade. In early 2004, as it contended with rising marketing costs, the company was forced to increase its monthly subscriber fee from $19.95 to $21.99 per month. This price hike came at an inopportune time, as Blockbuster was able to offer its DVD-by-mail service for only $19.99 per month. Furthermore, by October 2004 rumors had begun to circulate that Amazon was on the verge of entering the online DVD rental business. Amazon had already established an online rental service in the United Kingdom, and an eventual entry into the U.S. market seemed inevitable to many observers. To confront this potential threat, Netflix announced that it would reduce its subscriber fee to $17.99 per month. Blockbuster promptly followed suit, lowering its monthly rate to $17.49. As increased competition exerted greater pressure on Netflix, many analysts downgraded its stock value, with some suggesting the company was ripe for a takeover.

Arguably more daunting for Netflix during this period was the rapid emergence of streaming-video technology. By mid-decade an increasing number of regional cable television providers were beginning to offer video-on-demand to their subscribers. Even though the volume of programming available in this format still remained relatively small, the ease and convenience of the streaming technology was hard for Netflix to ignore. As the popularity of streaming video increased, the company began to consider ways that it could exploit on-demand technology to reach a wider customer base. In September 2004 Netflix formed a strategic partnership with TiVo Inc., the company that had revolutionized the digital video recorder (DVR) for cable television, to develop a means of streaming secure video content to personal computers via the Internet.

As the decade drew to a close, streaming video became an increasingly important component of the company's long-term growth strategy. In January 2007 Netflix finally launched its "Watch Now" online service, making select videos available to subscribers instantly over the Internet. The new feature remained relatively modest in scale compared with the company's established DVD-by-mail service. Even though the Netflix library had grown to 85,000 titles, only 5,000 were available for online viewing. By October the company was processing roughly 1.6 million DVDs per day. By contrast, only 40,000 titles per day were being viewed over the Internet.

Even so, the "Watch Now" option grew steadily in popularity, and Netflix began to explore new platforms for broadcasting online content. In January 2008 Netflix joined the South Korean firm LG Electronics Inc. to develop a device capable of streaming videos from its instant library directly onto a television. In May Netflix and the California-based technology firm Roku, Inc., began marketing a similar video player. Priced at $99, the Roku box was widely hailed for its simplicity, affordability, and quality. Two months later Netflix partnered with Microsoft Corporation to develop streaming video capability for the Xbox game console. The company reached a similar agreement with Sony Corporation in late 2009, when it began offering programming through the Sony PlayStation 3. Beginning in April 2010 Netflix also made content available via the Nintendo Wii console. By this point the company had over 12 million subscribers. With more than 42 percent of them regularly viewing Internet-based content, it seemed clear that streaming video had the potential to become the core of the company's business plan heading into the next decade.

*Frank Uhle*
*Updated, Stephen Meyer*

## PRINCIPAL COMPETITORS

Amazon.com, Inc.; Blockbuster Inc.; Hastings Entertainment, Inc.; Movie Gallery, Inc.; Redbox Automated Retail, LLC.

## FURTHER READING

Barker, Robert, "Can Netflix Keep Spinning Gold?" *Business-Week*, April 21, 2003, p. 112.

Burr, Ty, "DVD-by-Mail Company Bites at Blockbuster," *Boston Globe*, May 4, 2003, p. N1.

Espe, Eric, "Retailer's Plan: 'DVD' and Conquer," *Business Journal*, July 20, 1998, p. 3.

Liedtke, Michael, "Netflix Gets Thumbs up in Stock Market Debut," Associated Press, May 23, 2002.

Rivlin, Gary, "How Long Will Netflix Stay in the Picture?" *International Herald Tribune*, February 23, 2005, p. 21.

Seitz, Patrick, "Netflix Is Moving to Get Big Fast," *Investor's Business Daily*, July 2, 2002, p. 8.

Snider, Mike, "Streaming Movies Grows Dramatically," *USA Today*, January 29, 2009, p. 9B.

Taylor, Chris, "The Movie Is in the Mail: Netflix Is Riding a Boom in Online DVD Rentals, but Will Blockbuster Muscle in on the Business?" *Time*, March 18, 2002, p. 67.

Thompson, Nicholas, "Netflix's Patent May Reshape DVD-Rental Market," *New York Times*, June 26, 2003, p. 4.

Walker, Nancy, "Now Showing, in Your Mailbox," *Washington Post*, August 11, 2002, p. H1.

# New York City Off-Track Betting Corporation

1501 Broadway
New York, New York 10036
U.S.A.
Telephone: (212) 704-5110
Toll Free: (800) 682-8118
Web site: http://www.nycotb.com/

*Government-Owned Company*
*Incorporated:* 1971
*Employees:* 1,300
*NAICS:* 713290 Other Gambling Industries

■ ■ ■

The New York City Off-Track Betting Corporation (OTB) is a quasi-government operation that is run for the benefit of the city and New York state. Each year approximately $1 billion is wagered on horse races at more than 60 off-track betting parlors, three teletheaters, and several restaurant locations, as well as via bet-by-phone and Internet accounts. Besides races run at area tracks, both thoroughbred and harness, OTB also provides wagering on out-of-town locations. Weighed down by its obligations to fund the state and city governments as well as the racing industry, OTB filed for bankruptcy protection in 2009.

## CALLS FOR OFF-TRACK BETTING

Early in the 20th century horse racing was briefly banned in New York state, but this prohibition did little to suppress gambling. Even though some began advocating for the legalization of off-track betting, arguing that people would always feel compelled to wager, before the

1950s it remained a challenging position to hold for politicians.

In 1944, for instance, the New York City mayor Fiorello LaGuardia denounced the idea in one of his weekly radio addresses, maintaining that off-track betting would pave the way for legalized roulette, faro, dice, and other gambling. Moreover, he stated that the city could balance its budget without proceeds from gambling. The truth was that the state of New York was already very much dependent on its share of gambling at the local tracks, taking 5 percent of the handle (the amount bet on a race). Racetracks themselves accounted for another 5 percent of the takeout. LaGuardia's successor, Mayor William O'Dwyer, was able to get an extra 5 percent share for the New York City in 1946, which raised the total takeout to 15 percent. Over the next several years, however, the city was unable to fend off politicians at the state level who managed to wrest away the 5 percent, thereby doubling the state's share to 10 percent.

Starting in the 1950s New York City mayors began to actively lobby for an off-track betting operation that could benefit the city coffers, which were beginning to increasingly feel a financial strain. They argued that not only would the city not have to ask for more state funding but also that off-track betting would drive out illegal bookmakers and decrease the burden on the police.

## POLITICS OF OFF-TRACK BETTING

The battle lines for off-track betting were essentially drawn between city Democrats and upstate Republicans.

Also involved were a pair of unlikely allies: church groups opposed to gambling and the racetracks opposed to giving up a share of the takeout. The tracks simply did not believe that off-track betting would increase the betting market, as advocates argued.

In 1963 Mayor Robert Wagner placed an off-track betting referendum question on the ballot for city voters. Even though it had no legal effect, its support by a three-to-one-margin exerted pressure on upstate politicians, especially after Senator Jacob Javits, a leading Republican and the state's senior senator in the U.S. Congress, called for the legislature to accede to the voters' wishes. Nevertheless, over the next several years off-track betting bills died in committee or were defeated by the legislature. All the while, city officials prepared to create a corporation to run the off-track betting operations and as early as 1964 they envisioned a computerized wagering system. They also dreamed of realizing $200 million a year from the enterprise.

The breakthrough came at the end of the 1970 legislative session, when the city projected a $630 million budget shortfall. City-backed legislation was passed permitting the creation of the New York City Off-Track Betting Corporation (OTB), a public-benefit corporation that would be run by a board of directors appointed by the mayor. The off-track betting takeout would be 17 percent, with 0.5 percent of the handle going to the state, 1.5 percent to the tracks and horsemen, and the remaining 15 percent retained by the corporation to cover costs and generate a profit, which would then be split between the city and the state. In an attempt to lessen the impact on the tracks, off-track betting facilities were mandated to be uncomfortable: no food, no drink, no chairs, and no bathrooms.

The racing industry, which took no solace in the knowledge that off-track betting patrons would be made to suffer, was outraged by this development and turned to the courts to have off-track betting declared unconstitutional, an effort that ultimately failed. A long-term conflict between off-track betting and the industry ensued, resulting, at the best of times, in an uneasy coexistence. Labor unions representing track employees were also hostile to the new venture because they were afraid that a long-term slide in track attendance would only be aggravated by off-track betting and cost them jobs.

## EARLY YEARS OF OTB: 1971–73

To establish off-track betting, Mayor John Lindsay chose Howard Samuels, a former state senator. Samuels had considerable business experience, having cofounded Kordite Company, best known for the creation of Baggies. Samuels made several million dollars when the company was sold to Mobil Oil. OTB began operations on April 8, 1971, less than a year after the passage of off-track betting legislation, becoming the first legalized off-track betting operation in the United States.

Its start was modest, with only two betting facilities available to take wagers on that night's harness races at Roosevelt Raceway: several windows at Grand Central Terminal and an OTB shop in Forest Hills, Queens. Mayor Lindsay held the honor of placing the first off-track bet, $2 on a pacer by the name of Moneywise at four-to-one odds. Other patrons, lacking the privileges of rank, waited in line as long as two hours to place their bets. Because OTB's computer system was not yet deemed reliable, employees used three-part betting slips that took time to fill out and were then manually checked. Moreover, it was evident that the slips could easily be altered to create winning tickets.

After the first day's handle of $66,091, OTB began to ramp up its operations. By the end of its first year in operation, OTB boasted more than 50 parlors located in all five boroughs, with a daily handle of $1.2 million. It remained a controversial venture, however, with its computer system proving to be slow and unreliable and attendance at local tracks falling, thereby cutting into the takeout of both the state and tracks. Critics also contended that OTB was trying to dress the books. In March 1972 Steve Cady of the *New York Times* stated that "by scrimping on services (no security guards or cleaners in the shops), hiring part-timers for four-hour shifts and deferring payments on such obligations as a $5 million fee for computer installation, OTB has sought to make itself appear more profitable at an earlier date than it really is."

OTB also faced a challenge from the New York Racing Authority (NYRA), a nonprofit corporation that represented the interests of the three state thoroughbred tracks: Aqueduct, Belmont, and Saratoga. Samuels attempted to negotiate with the NYRA and the harness

## KEY DATES

**1963:** New York City voters support an off-track betting referendum.
**1970:** New York State Legislature passes legislation leading to the creation of off-track betting.
**1971:** The New York City Off-Track Betting Corporation (OTB) begins operations.
**1986:** The first OTB teletheater opens.
**1995:** Home simulcasting of races is initiated.
**2001:** Agreement to sell OTB is reached but not executed.
**2008:** The state of New York takes over the public corporation.
**2009:** New York City OTB files for bankruptcy protection.

tracks a more equitable split in the OTB takeout, and it appeared that the two sides were on the verge of an agreement. However, relations quickly deteriorated when a racing industry-supported bill was presented in the New York legislature that called for the creation of a board, dominated by racing officials, that would consolidate all the state's track and off-track betting commissions. Samuels vowed to fight the obvious attempt to take over OTB, suggesting that the tracks would be better served by cooperating with OTB to stimulate bettor interest, especially by permitting televised races.

### DISAPPOINTMENT, CRITICISM, AND COMPETITION: 1974–91

During his tenure as the head of OTB, Samuels was able to fend off attempts to gain control of the organization. However, he was unsuccessful in expanding the scope of the corporation to include the taking of bets on other sporting events, such as football, baseball, basketball, and hockey. His successor at OTB, Paul Scevane, who took over in March 1974, floated the idea of a betting card format, in which bettors attempted to pick the highest number of winners on a slate of games, but this concept failed to gain backing, and OTB's quest to become an all-purpose bookie gradually faded.

The corporation was having enough trouble fulfilling its stated mission of generating large revenues for the city's coffers. The dream of gaining $200 million a year from OTB was dismissed from the outset of operations. In fact, annual profits peaked in 1974, when $43 million was turned over to the city. Despite the

disappointment of declining profits, the city continued to collect its 5 percent share of the takeout. Even that amount would begin to fall off as OTB's annual handle peaked in 1988, totaling $1 billion. Thereafter, it began a steady slide.

OTB received mounting criticism over the years: its parlors were shabby, technology antiquated, management inept, and workforce inefficient. Like so many city institutions, it had become a source for political patronage by providing high-paying, high-sounding, do-little jobs to supporters. During the early 1980s the comptroller's office began urging OTB to cut costs, including the consolidation of branch offices, but little progress was made. OTB attempted to improve its finances by upgrading its product to spur revenues. For example, live calls from the racetracks were piped into OTB parlors. Then in 1986 OTB opened its first teletheater, the Inside Track, in Manhattan.

These changes did little to offset the increased competition over gaming dollars from the state lottery and from casinos in Atlantic City, New Jersey, and on Native American lands. Illegal bookmaking operations, which featured satellite-televised races, comfortable accommodations, and credit, were also flourishing in the city. Moreover, the demographics of the typical OTB bettor were troubling. A survey conducted in 1991 indicated that almost 70 percent of patrons were over 45 years old.

### RESTRUCTURING AND NEGOTIATING: 1994–98

By cutting the number of OTB shops from 157 to 90, it came as no surprise that OTB's annual handle slipped from $959.2 million in 1990 to $742 million in 1994, and despite cost-savings measures, the corporation actually lost over $7.4 million that year. During Rudolph Guiliani's run for mayor in 1993, the state of OTB became a salient campaign issue when he questioned how a bookie operation could possibly lose money.

Even though mayoral candidate Guiliani vowed to sell OTB to private interests, after his election he allowed the corporation a chance to redeem itself. Under the leadership of Robert Palumbo, who was soon succeeded by the former New York Giants football coach Allie Sherman, OTB began to show improvement. A first step was to simply clean the OTB parlors, which were notoriously dingy and marred by graffiti. Sherman also lowered OTB's overhead by closing 12 poorly performing parlors, cutting back on the number of parlors opened on Sunday to reduce double overtime for labor, and eliminating staff through buy-out packages.

More important to revitalizing the fortunes of OTB was a new law that allowed OTB to simulcast out-of-state races in its parlors and the March 1995 introduction of experimental in-home simulcasting of races on the city's public access cable channel, which spurred growth in new telephone accounts for both OTB and the NYRA. As a result of these developments, OTB posted a $4.6 million profit for 1995 while improving the handle to $821 million.

OTB outlets featuring simulcasts were added to several restaurant locations in 1997. Even though it appeared that the simulcasts mutually benefited OTB and the NYRA, especially in light of the rise of Internet wagering on horse races, the two sides soon fell out over the arrangement. NYRA officials blamed in-home signals for a significant drop in track attendance, which OTB officials pointed out was a nationwide trend unconnected to the telecasts. After an agreement covering the pricing of track signals expired in July 1997, OTB and the NYRA engaged in protracted and sometimes heated negotiations. In July 1998 the NYRA stopped home telecasts, and in October it stopped the feed to OTB parlors and teletheaters as well as affiliated bars and restaurants. The impasse was not settled until November 1998, when the parties finally agreed on a four-year contract.

## IMPROVED PROFITS AND THREATS OF BEING SOLD: 2000–02

In 2000 OTB's annual handle topped the $1 billion mark, and the corporation contributed $39.2 million to New York City. As he entered the final year of his administration, Mayor Guiliani sought to fulfill a long-term pledge to sell the enterprise to commercial interests, while retaining a minority interest for the city. With a minimum offer of $250 million, two bidders ultimately emerged: Magna Entertainment Corp. of Ontario, Canada, and Churchill Downs Inc. of Louisville, Kentucky, in partnership with the NYRA.

The sale faced several obstacles, including a lawsuit from labor unions representing 1,700 OTB employees, which maintained that the city had not properly evaluated the impact of the sale on city employees as required by law. Any deal would also require approval from the state legislature, which was far from certain. In addition, both suitors for OTB were under somewhat of an ethical cloud. The NYRA was under investigation by the state attorney general's office and by federal authorities for possible tax evasion and money laundering at its three thoroughbred tracks. One of Magna's partners, Robert W. Green, a British bookmaker and track owner, was tainted by his close association with a New Jersey businessman who had just been convicted of money laundering and bank fraud.

A deal to sell OTB to Magna twice fell apart before Mayor Guiliani was able to announce in August 2001 that a $262 million deal had been struck. Critics claimed that the sale was shortsighted, and opponents, which included the NYRA and the OTB union, vowed to stop the transaction in the state legislature. The matter was momentarily forgotten following the September 11, 2001, terrorist attacks that destroyed Manhattan's World Trade Center. When Michael Bloomberg was elected mayor in 2002, he raised the novel idea of selling OTB's future revenues for a single, up-front payment. Bloomberg appointed a new OTB director, Raymond Casey, and declared he would hold off selling OTB for at least a year, hoping the outfit could return to profitability.

## FLIRTING WITH INSOLVENCY: 2003–08

With stagnant demographics and a mandate to fill government coffers, OTB had little latitude to steer toward growth. It remained a football in the perennial squabbles between the state and city governments. In 2003 the New York legislature passed a law that allowed OTB to telecast out-of-state races, potentially bringing in additional revenue, but the legislation also increased the fees the state government took from those wagering operations. Furthermore, OTB's financial contribution to the city plummeted 90 percent in three years, from $12.5 million in 2001 to $1.3 million in 2004, prompting renewed talk from the Bloomberg administration about selling off the ailing quasi-government entity.

By 2007 OTB was running an annual deficit of $40 million or more. Bloomberg warned that instead of fulfilling its mission to provide cash to the city, OTB could soon require city subsidies to keep its doors open. In early 2008 he asked the OTB board to draft a contingency plan for shuttering all the city's betting parlors if no funding solution could be reached. The board voted in February 2008 to close the parlors on June 15, at a cost of over 1,000 jobs.

As the date approached, Bloomberg and the New York governor David Paterson entered into frantic negotiations in search of a mechanism for saving the corporation. On June 15 a deal was sealed authorizing New York state to take over OTB. The agreement allowed the parlors to stay open, while the city retained a portion of the revenue stream from winning bets as well as a fee for televising races on a city-owned television station.

## STRUGGLING TO SURVIVE: 2009–10

Even after this reshuffling of ownership, OTB continued to struggle. New York's horse racing industry had simply withered in the decades since OTB's creation. In 2009 Paterson appointed a new chairman, Meyer Frucher. Before the year was out, however, the corporation had filed for bankruptcy protection under Chapter 9 of the federal bankruptcy code, which applied to public-sector organizations.

Frucher, who was given the task to create a plan to return OTB to solvency, believed the keys were revamping the overall business model and reducing the statutory allocation of profits to the state and city governments and the racing industry. The plan he formulated would close down roughly two-thirds of the city's 68 brick-and-mortar betting parlors and replace them with Internet kiosks at licensed sports bars and other venues that might be able to attract the business of women and younger people. However, the agency's mounting debts made it highly questionable that such a plan could be executed. As a result, another shutdown date loomed in April 2010.

Frucher, Paterson, union leaders, and state legislators again negotiated to avert a collapse of OTB, an outcome that onlookers said could threaten the survival of the state's racetracks. The OTB board twice shied away from shutting down, and on April 17 it announced an emergency rescue plan that it said would keep the organization running another year or more. OTB would defer some of its pending payments to the industry and move forward with its plan to cut costs and selectively close parlors. In spite of this plan, OTB's future looked uncertain.

*Ed Dinger*
*Updated, Roger K. Smith*

## PRINCIPAL SUBSIDIARIES

NYC OTB Racing Network.

## PRINCIPAL COMPETITORS

New York Racing Authority; Penn National Gaming, Inc.; Churchill Downs Incorporated; Youbet.com.

## FURTHER READING

Cady, Steve, "OTB: 11 Months Later," *New York Times*, March 15, 1972, p. 59.

Lentz, Philip, "A New Parlay for OTB," *Crain's New York Business*, May 1, 1995, p. 3.

Lipton, Eric, "Conglomerates in Horse Racing Compete to Buy OTB Parlors," *New York Times*, June 4, 2001, p. B1.

McDonald, John, "How the Horseplayers Got Involved with the Urban Crisis," *Fortune*, April 1972, p. 94.

Moore, Martha T., "Off-Track Betting Heads off the Rails," *USA Today*, April 9, 2010, p. A3.

Santos, Fernanda, "Late Deal Pulls OTB from Brink of Shutdown," *New York Times*, June 16, 2008, p, B1.

Sulzberger, A. G., "Bleeding Cash and Deep in Debt, OTB Files for Bankruptcy Protection," *New York Times*, December 3, 2009, p. A30.

Tierney, John, "For New York City's OTB, a Sure Bet Ends up a Loser," *New York Times*, November 14, 1994, p. A1.

Unger, Howard Z., "Track Marks: The Death of New York Horse Racing," *Village Voice*, January 20, 1998, p. 150.

Viuker, Steven J., "High Stakes," *Barron's*, June 10, 1996, p. 20.

# NHK

———————————■———————————

2-2-1 Jinnan
Shibuya-ku, Tokyo 150-8001
Japan
Telephone: (+81 3) 3465-1111
Fax: (+81 3) 3469-8110
Web site: http://www.nhk.or.jp/

*State Administered Company*
*Founded:* 1925 as Tokyo Broadcasting Station
*Incorporated:* 1926
*Employees:* 15,400
*Sales:* ¥669.9 billion ($7.2 billion) (2009)
*Total Assets:* ¥823.5 billion ($8.8 billion) (2009)
*NAICS:* 515112 Radio Stations; 515120 Television
    Broadcasting

■ ■ ■

Nippon Noso Kyokai (Japan Broadcasting Corporation), better known as NHK, is Japan's national public broadcasting network. Founded in 1925 and nationalized under the 1950 Broadcast Law, the company is administered by a board of governors appointed by the prime minister and is supported by public fees, which are collected from viewers through a funding arrangement called "receiving fees." The company operates more than 50 television stations and three public radio networks throughout Japan. NHK also offers international programming through NHK World TV and NHK World Radio Japan. Since the 1990s, NHK has moved away from its traditional analog transmission format to develop a more comprehensive digital broadcasting system, while also offering television and radio programming over the Internet.

## THE BIRTH OF BROADCAST MEDIA IN JAPAN: 1925–45

NHK traces its origin to the Tokyo Broadcasting Station, which aired Japan's first radio transmission on March 22, 1925. Tokyo Broadcasting was established with a license from the Ministry of Posts and Telecommunications. The radio station was then incorporated under government charter in August 1926 as Nippon Hoso Kyokai, the Japan Broadcasting Corporation. As Japan's national broadcaster, NHK was in a unique position to reach the Japanese people, spread over four large, mountainous islands, roughly all at the same time. Through NHK the country as a whole was able to hear live broadcasts of such important events as the enthronement of Emperor Hirohito in November 1928.

In June 1930 the company formed a research laboratory to explore technological advances that would further the broadcasting industry. That same year the first international radio transmission was received successfully from London, England, setting the stage for regularly scheduled overseas broadcasting. Under the name Radio Tokyo, the company began broadcasting daily English- and Japanese-language programs to the Pacific Coast of North America on June 1, 1935.

After establishing a second radio network in April 1931, NHK became more involved in current events, providing newspaper-format news programming and

## KEY DATES

**1925:** Tokyo Broadcasting Station begins airing radio programs in Japan.

**1926:** Nippon Hoso Kyokai (NHK), also known as the Japan Broadcasting Corporation, is incorporated under a government charter.

**1935:** NHK begins airing English- and Japanese-language broadcasts to North America under the name Radio Tokyo.

**1945:** Emperor Hirohito uses NHK broadcast to announce Japan's surrender to the Allied Forces.

**1950:** Passage of the Broadcast Law ensures NHK's neutrality as a news provider.

**1953:** NHK introduces the first television broadcasts.

**1978:** NHK begins testing new satellite-broadcasting technology, known as DBS.

**1984:** NHK launches the first DBS broadcasts.

**2005:** An embezzlement scandal leads to the resignation of NHK president Katsuji Ebisawa.

**2010:** NHK operates at a fiscal deficit for the first time in a decade and a half.

coverage of the 1932 Olympic Games in Los Angeles. Three years later NHK began broadcasting school lessons as part of a national effort to standardize the country's educational curriculum and extend learning to remote areas.

With the rise of militarism in Japan, NHK and other media eventually fell under the control of the government. Through the late 1930s, NHK gradually lost its impartial tone and soon was dominated by imperialist rhetoric. It was through the network that Japanese public opinion was effectively galvanized against European imperialists who, it was charged, had colonized Asia.

At this time experimental television broadcasting was being carried out at NHK's laboratories. Before any regular application could be established, however, the Japanese became distracted by the country's war in China and, later, the war in the Pacific. Virtually all technological development was diverted to military projects, including the establishment of military communications throughout Japan's theater of war operations.

NHK, in the meantime, had become largely an instrument of government propaganda, although efforts were also made to provide the people with helpful information. For example, toward the end of the war, when Japan was suffering from shortages, NHK broadcast directions on how to produce food and tea from common plants so people could avoid starvation.

When Emperor Hirohito addressed the nation in August 1945, he did so over NHK. It was the first time anyone but a small circle of advisors had ever heard his voice. He announced the surrender of Japan to Allied forces ending World War II in the Pacific.

## EXPANDED PROGRAMMING IN THE POSTWAR ERA: 1945–75

No longer under the control of the government, NHK broadcast important news to the Japanese people about the occupation, the formation of a new government, and the establishment of new laws. One of those new laws, enacted in June 1950, was the Broadcast Law, which established NHK as a special corporation under the direction of a board of governors. This law laid out special provisions designed to guarantee the impartiality and journalistic integrity of NHK so it could never again be used as a propaganda device.

Resuming work on technological development, NHK conducted a successful trial of color television broadcasting in March 1952. The first rudimentary stereo radio broadcasts were also tried that year, using two different AM frequencies. Experiments with FM broadcasts commenced five years later in Tokyo, and regular FM programming began in 1969.

The shortwave station, Radio Tokyo (having suspended transmission at the end of World War II), resumed operation on February 1, 1952, under the name Radio Japan. Its new mission in the postwar era was to promote better understanding of Japanese culture and to provide Japanese people living abroad with news and entertainment from their homeland. The station broadcast in several languages, including English, Russian, Chinese, Arabic, and Indonesian.

NHK entered a new era in February 1953 when the broadcaster began providing television services, initially aired four hours per day. Although there were few commercial reasons to start a television station (Tokyo could only claim about 900 television sets), NHK forged ahead. The company provided a catalyst for other television broadcasters to enter this new medium, spurring growth in the industry. Only months after hitting the airwaves, NHK provided a live telecast of the coronation of Queen Elizabeth II in England. The next year the company began recorded programming with kinescopes, enabling it to repeat broadcasts and produce fully rehearsed programs.

The television service became immensely popular, particularly after the entry of Fuji Television, Nippon Television, and Tokyo Broadcasting. The rapid commercialization of the new medium enabled these television services to quickly incorporate new technologies, including color broadcasting, which NHK introduced in August 1960. Nationwide color broadcast capability was completed in 1966, and by 1971 all General TV programs were being broadcast in color.

NHK began educational television programming with the opening of a second network, Educational TV, in January 1959, and another network, Nippon Educational Television (NET), began broadcasting to a similar audience only a few weeks later. NET and NHK continued to operate educational programs in tandem for several years until 1973, when NET formally became the commercial network TV Asahi.

NHK was an early pioneer of satellite transmission technology. Virtually as soon as the first public circuits were opened, NHK began news feeds from the United States, Europe, and Africa. The first use of live satellite coverage came on November 22, 1963, when reports on the assassination of U.S. President John F. Kennedy were carried live on NHK.

With the proliferation of television broadcasting in Japan, particularly within the heavily populated urban areas, the airwaves were soon depleted of available frequencies. Therefore, NHK began experimental transmissions in the new UHF frequencies. The first of these put to practical use were on special NHK stations in Tokyo and Osaka during 1971.

NHK's charter in the Broadcast Law mandated the company's responsibility for airing programs of a more culturally complex nature than commercial television could afford to support. Aside from educational programming, NHK carried symphonies, opera performances, interviews, and documentaries. This programming, however, needed an appropriate venue, and NHK obliged in 1973, with the construction of a massive broadcasting complex and a theater, NHK Hall.

While culturally enriching, these programs did not draw tremendous audiences, but the shows did serve to make these subjects more popular than they might have been. To provide some variety in their programming format, NHK began airing baseball games, which are extremely popular in Japan, as well as boxing, soccer, and the Olympic Games.

## TECHNOLOGICAL INNOVATIONS: 1975–90

NHK was one of the first networks to try direct broadcasting, or beaming a signal directly to viewers' televisions from a satellite. The digital broadcasting satellite (DBS), as it was called, provided several advantages over the terrestrial network, the most important of which was high-quality reception throughout Japan. Because 70 percent of Japan is mountainous, it had thus far been difficult for many viewers living in valleys and less populated areas to receive decent radio and television transmissions. Even NHK, with the most complete network in Japan, covering approximately 95 percent of the country, would benefit from DBS, which would enable huge areas to receive high-quality signals at a much lower cost than a network of ground-based relay stations.

NHK's first DBS tests took place in July 1978. Based on these tests, NHK developed the MUSE system, designed for the transmission of high-definition television (HDTV) signals. Hi-Vision, as HDTV is called in Japan, was demonstrated at the Tsukuba Science Expo in 1985. Using its research facility, NHK became a participant in a Japanese consortium, the Hi-Vision Promotion Association (HPA), working to broadcast HDTV.

Two DBS satellites were launched in January 1984 and February 1986 aboard Japanese N-2 and H-l rockets. This allowed NHK, among other users, to begin experimental DBS broadcasts in May 1984. A regular 24-hour service began three years later and had about 150,000 viewers. When the second DBS channel went on line on June 3, 1989, it served more than 1.5 million viewers. The service was available to anyone with a television and a parabolic antenna. Two more satellites were launched in 1990 and 1991. These satellites beamed two NHK channels (by 1992 the number of viewers had grown to six million) and a third operated by the commercial consortium, Japan Satellite Broadcasting Corp.

In October 1983 NHK began teletext broadcasting, which delivers subtitles to hearing impaired viewers, in Tokyo and Osaka. An improved service was introduced two years later, and by 1986 the entire network was equipped for teletext service. In addition, in 1985 the company started an Emergency Warning Broadcasting System. Intended for use in the event of natural or other disasters, the system was employed several times to warn viewers of severe weather, tsunamis, and, on one occasion, a volcanic eruption.

By the early 1990s the broadcaster operated two DBS stations, Satellite Television Channel One and Channel Two, in addition to its two terrestrial television stations, General TV and Educational TV. Some of the more popular programs on NHK television at the time were *Asia Now*, *NHK Morning Magazine*, and American National Football League games. NHK also managed news-oriented Radio 1 and the educational Radio 2 on medium wave (AM), an FM music network, and the shortwave-frequency Radio Japan. At the same time, NHK operated shortwave relay stations in Canada, Singapore, French Guiana, Sri Lanka, Gabon, and Britain.

Since its establishment under the Broadcast Law of 1950, NHK had been administered by a board of governors chosen by the prime minister and approved by both houses of Parliament. The 12-member board was responsible for appointing the president and a group of auditors, who surveyed the president's business practices. In addition, NHK's strategic and operating policies, including the annual budget and programming plans, were determined by the board. The budget and operational plans were then submitted to the Minister of Posts and Telecommunications, who reviewed the material, which was passed on to the Cabinet and, finally, to Parliament for approval.

Accepting governmental financial support only for overseas shortwave services, NHK's operating budget was financed through receiving-fee contracts with television owners, originally collected door-to-door or through bank transfer. In the 1970s, however, automatic bank transfers were introduced, and in the early 1990s this was the method of payment used by more than 60 percent of the contracted households. At the time, NHK was charging ¥1,320 each month for regular channels and an additional ¥930 for DBS reception.

Through this unusual funding mechanism, NHK was able to operate Japan's largest broadcast network, completely without commercial support. In addition, the company remained at the forefront of technological advancements in the industry. NHK had become more than a broadcaster. It was in many ways a broadcast laboratory.

## ADAPTING TO THE DIGITAL AGE: 1990–2010

With the rapid improvement of digital technology during the 1990s, NHK found its analog-based high-definition television (HDTV) on the verge of becoming obsolete. As the industry's shift to all-digital media platforms began to seem inevitable, NHK's status as the lead innovator in Japanese broadcasting was suddenly in question. To confront this challenge, the company devoted greater resources to the development of new digital formats. The decision to abandon its analog system was a difficult one from an economic standpoint.

By mid-decade the company had amassed roughly 550,000 subscribers for its analog-based satellite TV service, HI-vision. Still, NHK realized that the future of broadcasting would rely on ultra-definition TV, or UDTV, a purely digital form of transmission.

As part of its effort to speed the development of the new technologies, NHK entered into several key strategic pacts at mid-decade. In April 1996 the company formed a strategic partnership with the British Broadcasting Corporation (BBC). As part of the deal, the companies agreed to share certain programming and exchange information on emerging digital formats. In September of that year NHK entered into a similar accord with the Cuban Institute of Radio and Television (ICRT). In November 1997 the company began experimenting with broadcasting select television and radio programming over the Internet. The following April NHK launched its debut digital television channel, NHK World TV, with the aim of broadcasting Japanese programming overseas. By October 1998 the new channel was available in approximately 175 countries across the world.

At decade's end NHK's overall financial picture remained strong. The company had enjoyed annual surpluses throughout the decade, and in 1998 alone the company had a surplus income of ¥16.7 billion ($123.8 million), more than double its anticipated surplus of ¥7.7 billion ($59.1 million). Nevertheless, as it entered the 21st century, NHK found itself at a crossroads. As broadcasting technology continued to evolve, NHK would need to expand its research and development budget considerably to remain competitive. At the core of the company's strategy for the future was the development of a terrestrial, as opposed to satellite, digital network. At an estimated cost of ¥400 billion ($3.4 billion), the digital terrestrial broadcasting system would clearly come at an enormous cost to the company's bottom line. At the same time, NHK remained committed to its focus on quality programming, a position it considered essential in the midst of a rapid proliferation of media, both in traditional television and radio formats and on the Internet.

In 2003 NHK celebrated the 50th anniversary of its debut television broadcast. To commemorate the occasion, the broadcaster announced the opening of a new digital broadcasting museum and archives outside of Tokyo, which would house roughly 600,000 of NHK's television programs, as well as 40,000 of its radio programs. As the company commemorated its historic role in the development of modern Japanese broadcasting, however, it suddenly found itself mired in scandal. In 2004 it was revealed that several NHK employees had embezzled funds from the company's operating budget. The controversy inflicted significant damage on the broadcaster's public image, and by December of that year roughly 110,000 NHK subscribers had stopped paying their fees in protest. A month later NHK president Katsuji Ebisawa abruptly resigned. His successor, Genichi Hashimoto, found himself confronting a public relations disaster that was rapidly spiraling out of control. In February 2005 the number of NHK subscribers refusing to pay their annual license fees exceeded 500,000, and by July of that year the figure had grown to 1.17 million.

To offset these lost revenues, NHK was forced to implement a series of cost-cutting measures. In late 2005 the company announced a 10 percent reduction in its workforce over a three-year period. The company also began to explore a variety of new legal avenues designed to help it collect delinquent subscriber fees. At the same time, NHK formed a new advisory panel to reform the company's corporate culture. In the midst of these efforts, the broadcaster was rocked by new revelations of fraud in April 2006, when a sports producer was charged with embezzlement. Although the sums involved were relatively small, the case represented the 242nd instance of corruption at NHK since the beginning of the decade. In March 2007 a new scandal shook the broadcaster when three NHK employees were caught in an insider trading scam. In the wake of the revelations, Genichi Hashimoto stepped down as company president. He was replaced by Shigeo Fukuchi, who had formerly worked as an advisor to Asahi Breweries Ltd. In the eyes of some observers, the choice of someone outside of a broadcasting industry tainted by corruption represented a shrewd public relations maneuver as the company set out once again to regain the public's trust.

Meanwhile, NHK continued to seek ways to expand its programming to take advantage of new technologies. In December 2008 the company began offering on-demand videos on the Internet, using a new fee-based payment system. The following February the company introduced 24-hour broadcasting on NHK World TV. In the midst of these developments, NHK continued to face financial uncertainty. A continued shortfall in annual fees, combined with the high costs of converting to an all-digital format by 2011, left the company operating at a deficit of ¥5.5 billion ($61 million) in 2010. As it struggled both to remake its public image and to adapt to a changing technological landscape, NHK clearly had many challenges ahead as it forged into a new decade.

*John Simley*
*Updated, Stephen Meyer*

## PRINCIPAL SUBSIDIARIES

Japan Broadcast Publishing Co. Ltd.; Japan International Broadcasting; NHK Art, Inc.; NHK Business Create Inc.; NHK Business Services Inc.; NHK Culture Center, Inc.; NHK Enterprises, Inc.; NHK Educational Corporation; NHK Global Media Services, Inc.; NHK Integrated Technology Inc.; NHK Media Technology, Inc.; NHK Plannet, Inc.; NHK Promotions, Inc.

## PRINCIPAL COMPETITORS

Fuji Television Network, Inc.; Nippon Television Network Corporation; Tokyo Broadcasting System Holdings, Inc.

## FURTHER READING

Alford, Peter, "Signs of Bad Old Ways at NHK," *Australian*, April 19, 2006, p. 22.

"The Changing Face of Television," *Look Japan*, March 1993.

"NHK Boss Picked for Reform: Public Broadcaster's Next President Comes from Outside," *Daily Yomiuri*, December 27, 2007, p. 3.

"NHK Considers Digital Service via BS-4 Satellite," *BBC Summary of World Broadcasts*, February 21, 1997.

"NHK Inaugurates World TV Satellite Service," *BBC Summary of World Broadcasts*, April 10, 1998.

"NHK's Credibility Shaken by Scandals," *Daily Yomiuri*, August 7, 2004, p. 4.

Osaki, Tad, "NHK Marks Fiftieth Anniversary," *Daily Variety*, February 3, 2003, p. 14.

Schilling, Mark, "Lost Fees Put NHK in Red," *Daily Variety*, January 15, 2010, p. 46.

Segawa, Natsuko, "NHK Hunts for Profits, New Markets," *Nikkei Weekly*, February 21, 2000, p. 3.

Suzuki, Yoshikazu, "Scandal a Setback for NHK's Efforts to Rebuild Confidence," *Daily Yomiuri*, January 26, 2008, p. 4.

Weng Kin, Kwan, "New Channel to Lift Japan's Profile Abroad," *Straits Times* (Singapore), February 13, 2009.

# Nippon Paint Company Ltd.

---

**2-1-2, Oyodo-Kita, Kita-Ku**
**Osaka, 531-8511**
**Japan**
**Telephone: (+81 6) 6458-1111**
**Fax: (+81 6) 6455-9261**
**Web site: http://www.nipponpaint.com**

*Public Company*
*Founded:* 1881 as Komyosha
*Incorporated:* 1898
*Employees:* 6,078
*Sales:* $1.4 billion (2009)
*Stock Exchanges:* Tokyo
*Ticker Symbol:* 4612
*NAICS:* 325188 All Other Basic Inorganic Chemical Manufacturing; 325510 Paint and Coating Manufacturing; 444120 Paint and Wallpaper Stores

■ ■ ■

Nippon Paint Company Ltd. is Japan's oldest and second largest paint company. Nippon Paint is focused on producing paints and coatings for automobiles, industrial products, and ships, as well as architectural paints for contractors and do-it-yourselfers. The company also manufactures and sells paints for steel and other metal structures, electrical equipment, and roadways as well as coil coatings. While the company remains focused on paints and coatings, in recent decades it has diversified, branching into the manufacture and sale of other chemicals, including pharmaceuticals, printing materials, and electronic

components. The company runs about 30 manufacturing operations throughout the world, principally in Asia, with the goal of being a truly multinational corporation. Its eight locations in China can take advantage of the influx of automakers into that country in recent years.

## FIRST CENTURY: 1881–1980

Japanese brothers Huruta and Jujiro Moteki began their industrial careers in the 1870s by producing zinc oxide, an inorganic compound used to treat burns and as a cosmetic. Buoyed by their success, they then joined with Heikichi Nakagawa, the chief engineer of the Imperial Navy Dockyard's painting team, to experiment with Western-style oil-based paint. In 1881 the trio formed their own company, Komyosha, to manufacture these paints. In 1897 the company obtained its first patent for their method of producing zinc oxide. In 1898 the company was incorporated and renamed Nippon Paint Manufacturing Co., Ltd., the first Western-style paint company in Japan.

Nippon Paint focused on expansion from its start. The company's first new factory was built in 1896 in Tokyo, just 15 years after the company's founding. A branch plant was opened nine years later in Osaka. In 1914 its primacy in the Japanese paint market assured, Nippon Paint began expanding to other locations in Asia and the South Pacific. Subsidiaries in Manchuria (1939), Taiwan (1940), and China (1942) were established by mid-century. The company's first manufacturing plant outside of Japan was established in Singapore in 1962. Nippon Paint opened an office in New York in 1968. In subsequent decades Nippon researchers discovered how to isolate a coagulation chemical from a plant. In 1989 Nippon introduced a new type of copy machine toner, and in 1990 the company developed both a new way to produce LCD display colors and biotechnology-based dyeing methods. In 1991 the company introduced Ferri Sphere magnetic particles that could be used to diagnose certain medical conditions, including cancer. Research and development also succeeded in creating new paints, including an automotive paint with a deep texture that resulted in a metallic finish.

## CHALLENGES: 1991–99

The economic boom of the 1980s, however, did not translate into continued profitability during the 1990s. Despite tensions in the Middle East and the Gulf War, Nippon Paint had continued its expansion into Asia, taxing the company's resources. In addition, an economic slowdown in Japan cut down on orders from Japanese car makers for the company's automotive coatings. In 1994 the company reported its pretax profits had declined 40 percent over the previous year. At this time, Japan's Fair Trade Commission discovered that 10 leading Japanese paint companies, including Nippon, had fixed the price of materials used in ship paints, one market segment that was growing because of government demand for ships during the Gulf War. As a result, prices for ship paints had risen as much as 10 percent. The Commission ordered the price-fixing cartel broken up and warned several companies, including Nippon, that they were suspected of fixing prices for auto-body and industrial paints as well.

The price-fixing scandal did not help Nippon Paint's bottom line. To recover from the slump, the company focused on two key areas: expansion into Asia, particularly China, and increasing its coil coatings production worldwide. Coil coatings are a type of paint applied to metal strips before the metal is formed. These coatings must be exceedingly durable, because the painted strip is then cut and formed into a product without damaging the finish. While Nippon Paint did continue its expansion into China and did gain a greater market share of coil coating, the company's profits continued to drop throughout the 1990s. In 1999, however, due to robust sales of Nippon's new, more environmentally friendly products as well as cost-cutting efforts, profits once again rose.

In fact, much of the research and development efforts of the company focused on creating more environmentally-safe coatings and coatings systems, which the company viewed as a fairly unexplored market. In 1991 the company developed a new metal-coating system that used water-based rather than

expanded into Australia, Korea, Pakistan, the Philippines, and Australia.

Part of Nippon Paint's strategy throughout the mid- to late-20th century was to enter into partnerships with companies around the world. Companies in other parts of the world might produce or distribute Nippon Paint locally, or the companies might collaborate on development of new products. In the mid-20th century, Nippon entered "technical tie-ups" with American Chemical Products, Inc., Copon Associates, and PPG Industries, all of the United States as well as a technical "assistance" contract with the Sherwin-Williams Company.

## RESEARCH AND DEVELOPMENT FUEL GROWTH: 1981–90

By the 1980s Nippon Paint was the second-largest Japanese paint company after Kansai Paint. In 1984 the company launched an advertising campaign and branding effort designed around the slogan, "Nippon Paint, a company that can be trusted." Business boomed. The *Jiji Press* reported that the company's profits rose every year from 1978 to 1985. Several new plants, office buildings, and research and development laboratories were built during the 1980s. The company was able to achieve such positive results through a combination of increasing sales to the automobile and metal-processing industries and streamlining and cost-cutting efforts companywide.

Nippon Paint also branched out of paints and coatings into other products in an effort to diversify into non-coatings lines. For example, in 1987 company

```
┌─────────────────────────────────────────┐
│                                         │
│            KEY DATES                    │
│               ■                         │
│  ─────────────────────────────────      │
│                                         │
│  1881: Komyosha is founded in Japan as a │
│        manufacturer of Western-style oil-based paint. │
│  1927: Company name is changed to Nippon Paint. │
│  1942: North China Nippon Paint Co., Ltd., is │
│        established.                     │
│  1962: Manufacturing plant in Singapore opens. │
│  1997: Companies in Singapore and Taiwan achieve │
│        ISO 14001 certification.         │
│  2004: Nippon is largest paint producer in China. │
│                                         │
└─────────────────────────────────────────┘
```

solvent-based paints and which completely recycled all water used in the system. In mid-decade, both the Singapore and Taiwan subsidiaries achieved ISO 14001 environmental certification, showing that the company minimized harmful environmental effects caused by its activities. In 1998 the company touted its newly introduced Cationic Electrolyzed Activate Deposition Paint as "super environmentally friendly." By 2002 an environmentally friendly steel coatings system that used lead-free and recyclable materials was introduced. In 2006 a completely water-based coating system for automotive repairs was introduced. In that year, company representatives stated that Nippon aimed to ensure that 100 percent of its products be "environmentally friendly" by 2010.

### EXPANSION: 2000–10

In the first decade of the 21st century, Nippon continued to pursue worldwide expansion as its primary growth strategy, particularly throughout Asia. By 2004 Nippon was the largest producer of paint in China. The following year, the company developed a long-range plan that outlined the path to becoming Asia's largest coatings supplier by 2010. Nippon also expanded further into North America. In 2006 the company bought the automotive coatings business of the U.S. company Rohm & Haas as well as the plastic paints producer Bee Chemical.

In 2009, in the midst of the global economic recession, Nippon Paint struggled to remain profitable. New company president Kenji Sakai told *Japan Chemical Web* in June 2009 that a key to Nippon's success during the recession and beyond was not in scaling back company expansion, but rather in reducing overhead and operating costs. "I liken the situation to a person with metabolic syndrome," he said. "If we become leaner, we will be more profitable." The company put together a plan of emergency measures, called "Survival Challenge," to reduce company costs, but at the same, the company took steps to further expand into China, opening plants to produce paint materials in order to avoid the costs of importing these materials to its three paint production centers in the country. It remained to be seen whether Nippon's growth strategies were feasible and if, and when, the company could return to profitability.

*Melissa J. Doak*

### PRINCIPAL SUBSIDIARIES

Guangzhou Nippon Paint Co., Ltd. (China); Langfang Nippon Paint Co., Ltd. (China); Nippon Paint Co., Ltd. (China); Nippon Paint Co., Pte., Ltd. (Singapore); Nippon Paint, Inc. (United States); Nippon Paint Limited (United Kingdom); Nippon Paint Sdn. Bhd. (Malaysia).

### PRINCIPAL COMPETITORS

Akzo Nobel, N.V.; BASF Coatings GmbH; E. I. du Pont de Nemours and Company; Kansai Paint Co., Ltd.

### FURTHER READING

"Aspirations of New Presidents: Kenji Sakai, President of Nippon Paint," *Japan Chemical Web*, June 30, 2009.

"Business Brief—Nippon Paint Co.: Pretax Profit in Fiscal Year Fell Slightly to $88.9 Million," *Wall Street Journal*, May 22, 1992.

"Interview with Kenji Sakai, Representative Director and President, Nippon Paint," *Japan Chemical Web*, January 25, 2010.

"Japan's FTC Orders Breakup of Paint Price Cartel," *Dow Jones News Service*, January 21, 1994.

Morse, Andrew, "Japan's Car-Parts Makers Go Global—Spurt of Acquisitions Aims to Widen Suppliers' Reach," *Wall Street Journal*, December 7, 2006, p. C4.

"New Metal Coating System from Nippon Paint Completely Recycles Washing Water," *Japan Chemical Week*, August 2, 1991.

"Nippon Paint Aims for No. 1 in Asia, Emphasizes China, India," *Japan Chemical Week*, December 29, 2005.

"Nippon Paint Boosting Paint-Material Production in China," *Japan Chemical Web*, August 6, 2009.

"Nippon Paint's Profits Continue to Rise," *Jiji Press English News Service*, December 6, 1985.

"Spotlight on Paints & Coatings, Part 4," *Japan Chemical Week*, October 16, 1996.

# OMRON Corporation

—■—

**Shiokoji Horikawa, Shimogyo-ku**
**Kyoto, 600-8530**
**Japan**
**Telephone:** (+81-75) 344-7000
**Fax:** (+81-75) 344-7001
**Web site:** http://www.omron.com

*Public Company*
*Founded:* 1933 as Tateisi Electric Manufacturing
     Company
*Incorporated:* 1948 as Tateisi Electronics Company
*Employees:* 32,583
*Sales:* ¥524.69 billion ($5.62 billion) (2009)
*Stock Exchanges:* Osaka
*Ticker Symbol:* 6645
*NAICS:* 334220 Radio and Television Broadcasting and
     Wireless Communications Equipment Manufactur-
     ing; 334413 Semiconductor and Related Device
     Manufacturing; 335314 Relay and Industrial
     Control Manufacturing; 339112 Surgical and
     Medical Instrument Manufacturing; 541512
     Computer Systems Design Services

■ ■ ■

OMRON Corporation is a world leader in the development, production, and distribution of electronics. Divided into five business sectors, the company manufactures electronic devices and tools for the automotive, banking, medical, and government sectors. OMRON is best known for its factory automation systems, building control components such as printed circuit board relays, security system sensors, and seismic sensors for a range of industries. The company's components are also used in digital blood pressure monitors and thermometers; automatic teller machines, point-of-sale systems, electronic cash registers, vending machines, and automated airport check-in systems; and a range of home appliances, communication devices, and other consumer products. Headquartered in Japan, OMRON has manufacturing facilities and sales offices throughout North America, Europe, and Asia.

## ORIGINS AND EARLY GROWTH: 1932–37

Born in 1900, Kazuma Tateisi graduated from the electrical engineering department of what eventually became Kumamoto University. Tateisi worked briefly as an electrical engineer for the Japanese government on a Hyogo hydroelectric plant, and then began working for the Inoue Electric Manufacturing Company in 1922.

The New York stock market crash of 1929 triggered a depression in Japan the following year. When Tateisi was laid off, he rented a factory and began manufacturing household appliances. Sales of his knife grinder and pant press, items Tateisi developed himself, were low. However, in 1932 Tateisi used the knowledge of induction relays he had acquired at Inoue to invent and develop a timing device that limited x-ray exposure to less than one second. He began production of the timer through a joint venture with Dai Nippon X-ray Inc.

Early in 1933 Tateisi moved to Osaka to be nearer to Dai Nippon. That May he founded the Tateisi Electric Manufacturing Company. The lack of capital

## COMPANY PERSPECTIVES
■

Ever since its establishment, OMRON has sought to promote innovation and benefit society. Anticipating the needs of future generations is the wellspring of our daily inspiration and a way of doing business that is deeply rooted in OMRON's corporate DNA. For as long as OMRON exists as a company, this will remain our mission.

No matter what challenges the future brings, we will continually develop new solutions to help build a safe and sustainable society where people enjoy peace of mind. Years of experience have taught us that true innovation is impossible if we fear failure or settle for conventional thinking. Working for the benefit of society—with an unwavering dedication to this core value, OMRON will apply its unique competencies in sensing and control technology to the realms of safety, security, environmental protection and healthcare in pursuit of a brighter future for all.

and contractual limitations with Dai Nippon hampered the young company, but in early 1934 Tateisi began marketing an induction-type protection relay, which was an essential component of the timer. The component found a large market and successfully raised revenue.

Later that year a typhoon struck Japan's western coast, causing extensive damage to factories that were located there. Hitachi, the chief manufacturer of induction-type protection relays, could not meet the immediate demand, and orders for the repair or substitution of relays overwhelmed Tateisi's small factory. The company quickly transferred the manufacturing of its timers to Dai Nippon and concentrated on the relay.

Demand for the relay devices continued after the recovery from the typhoon as industrial development in Japan increased overall, allowing Tateisi to expand his output and facilities. In 1937 Tateisi built a larger factory with offices and a warehouse. He also established a branch office in Tokyo and purchased another factory, where parts from the Osaka plant were assembled.

### GROWTH DURING AND AFTER
### THE WAR: 1940–50

Research conducted during World War II led to the development of a product line that would become an area of extensive postwar growth for the company. At the request of Tokyo University, Tateisi began in 1941 researching microswitches, also known as precision switches. Three years later, in 1944, the company supplied 300 microswitches to the university. Tateisi also produced flap switches for aircraft and acted as a subcontractor to Mitsubishi Heavy Industries. In 1944 he converted a movie studio into the Kyoto branch factory. A year later the Tokyo branch office and the main factory were destroyed during an air raid, forcing all production to the Kyoto branch, which remained the company's headquarters until 1968.

The company's initial peacetime production centered on small household consumer appliances under the name Omlon (which later became OMRON), an independent subsidiary. In 1947 the government, which was seeking to prevent the frequent electrical overloads common at the time, asked appliance manufacturers to develop a current limiter. Production for the government required incorporation, which Tateisi completed in 1948 by establishing the Tateisi Electronics Company. In 1949 the Allied powers enacted the Dodge Line, requiring the Japanese government to take anti-inflationary action. These measures revoked the funds that had provided the market for Tateisi's limiter.

This action struck a serious blow to Tateisi's 33 employees, who had devoted all production capability to the limiter. Debt forced reductions in operations and reorganization in the company's subsidiaries. Likewise, sales dropped 57 percent that year. Efforts to rebuild amid economic instability continued until the intervention of the United Nations during the Korean War stimulated the economy and increased demand for relay devices. This renewed demand allowed Tateisi to reopen the Tokyo branch office and build a new office in Osaka.

### BREAKING INTO THE
### AUTOMATION FIELD: 1950–60

The Korean War created demand that boosted the Japanese industrial economy. Tateisi's company benefited from the war as well. In fact, the demand for his products was such that by 1953 he employed 65 people. While focusing on his main product line, he also remained vigilant for new developments within and outside his specific industry. One development that grabbed his attention was cybernetics (automatic control systems). After researching the possibilities of automation, and even conducting a tour of several U.S. companies, he became convinced that an automation revolution was close at hand in Japan. Determined to be a leader in his industry, he began reorganizing the company.

## KEY DATES

**1933:** Kazuma Tateisi founds the Tateisi Electric Manufacturing Company.

**1934:** Tateisi markets its first induction-type protection relay.

**1948:** The company incorporates as Tateisi Electronics Company.

**1958:** Tateisi Electronics begins using the OMRON trademark on all its products.

**1962:** Tateisi Electronics goes public.

**1968:** Tateisi Electronics changes its name to OMRON Tateisi Electronics Co.

**1979:** Takao Tateisi succeeds Kazuma Tateisi as company president.

**1990:** OMRON Tateisi Electronics Co. changes its name to OMRON Corporation.

**2003:** Hisao Sakuta becomes the new president of OMRON.

**2005:** OMRON launches the OKAO Vision Face Recognition Sensor.

The development of new products had assumed a rapid pace, and a centralized company could not efficiently administer market-oriented production. Tateisi introduced the Producer system (P-system), which delegated individual products to independent companies. Under the P-system, the managers of individual factories and subsidiaries were responsible for production and labor relations, while the head office retained all other decision making. This decentralization allowed a varied product line and profitability on items with slim margins. The company continued to pursue this approach to production, creating separate sales and research subsidiaries in 1955.

In 1958 OMRON became a registered trademark and was used on all of the company's products. That same year the company developed its first control system, which combined several of its components. In 1959 a P-system company began production of the control systems. With these and other innovations, Tateisi's company saw its sales increase 10-fold between 1955 and 1959, to ¥1.3 billion.

With the help of government financing, Tateisi completed his Central Research Institute in 1959, which helped speed the development of new items, especially the contactless switch in 1960. The tremendous success of this switch solidified the company's future commit-

ment to research and development and gave it prominence in the area of high-tech research.

### DIVERSIFICATION AND DEVELOPMENT: 1961–70

In 1961 Tateisi introduced a stress meter, the first of many low-cost cybernetic devices for medicine and biology. Complex vending machines, introduced in 1963, were also a long-term success for the company. Capable of dispensing several different items and accepting a variety of currencies, the machines' currency calculation and detection equipment soon found applications in areas beyond food vending. The device proved to be a major breakthrough for the company, as it offered electronic processing of financial transactions, an enormous area of growth in the decades to come.

When the company went public in 1962, it had to consolidate the management and financing of the P-system companies to be traded on commodities markets, a process that was completed in 1965. Even though this sacrificed many of company's cost advantages, Tateisi took advantage of its public status. Thanks in part to a period of national economic growth, the company had the means to invest more heavily in its structural facilities. As a result, it established eight new factories, four offices, and seven retail branches.

During the mid-1960s international sales grew through long-term export contracts. Tateisi opened a representative office in New York, and his company eventually earned the respect of U.S. buyers as a quality producer of vending machines and other electronically monitored control devices just as market demand for such items intensified.

Between 1959 and 1967 annual sales increased almost 10-fold, to ¥10 billion. In 1968 the company built new headquarters in Kyoto and changed its name to OMRON Tateisi Electronics Co. in celebration of its 35th anniversary. That same year OMRON introduced a contactless pinboard sequence programmer, which allowed systems flexibility and increased the number of individual tasks to which they could be applied. In 1969, after examining its sales history and development of future products, the company decided to set a five-year sales goal of ¥100 billion and to extend its international presence even further.

One country in particular that OMRON wanted to strengthen its position was in the United States. In 1970 it established the first Japanese research and development center in California. The center was greeted with some hostility from Americans, who saw it as another example of the growing economic threat that Japan's booming economy represented. Despite its reception, the center eventually helped develop large-scale integrated circuits and liquid crystals, further advancing OMRON in the area of electronics research.

## A PERIOD OF RESTRUCTURING: 1973–88

The oil crisis of 1973 sparked a period of slow growth nationwide. The mid-1970s were the most stagnant years since the Dodge Line of 1949. Meanwhile, OMRON was caught expanding its production and was forced to lay off workers and to cut production in the P-system companies. In an attempt to build immunity to such fluctuations, OMRON decided that its management needed to be downsized and the company restructured. Even though many Japanese companies increased their export drive to overcome this economic shock, OMRON delayed such efforts until its reorganization of 1976 was completed.

The reorganization was expensive but successful. Sales decreased and the company reported negative net profits between 1975 and 1976, but after three years it was back on course. In 1978 OMRON's sales reached ¥101.1 billion. The following year Takao Tateisi succeeded Kazuma Tateisi as president, and a new sales goal of ¥500 billion was set for 1990.

By 1980 the goal still looked reasonable. Over the last two years demand for control systems increased 20 percent each year and overall sales grew steadily. However, growth slowed substantially in 1981 and actually reversed in 1982. Sales slowly increased but it was six years before the company was fully recovered. Even though OMRON was still sensitive to the global economic climate, it had satisfactory returns in many areas. Exports had slowed because of yen appreciation, but overall sales of ATMs, switches, relays, office automation equipment, and medical devices increased rapidly, while control systems continued to increase more moderately.

The brisk pace of 1984–85 hinted at recovery, and the corporation set record net profit levels. Regardless, sales of control systems, OMRON's largest sector, did not increase and electronic funds transfer systems (EFTS), the second-largest sector, actually decreased. Further frustration came from the appreciating yen, which limited export potential.

In 1987 Takao Tateisi stepped down as OMRON president and was replaced by another scion of the founding family, Yoshio Tateisi. By that time, international sales accounted for only 17 percent of the company's sales, down from 25 percent at the beginning of the decade. However, OMRON's limited vulner-

ability to fluctuations in the exchange rate did offer opportunities, and the company mobilized to capitalize on them. The strong yen led many companies in Japan to reinvest in their manufacturing facilities and information systems, which improved OMRON's domestic sales. OMRON also invested in itself, nearly doubling its long-term debt during the decade to ¥34.8 billion and lowering its earnings for 1985 and 1986. The exchange rate also allowed the company to increase overseas production and buy more components from Taiwan and South Korea. In 1988 these investments finally improved earnings, which nearly doubled in one year, and sales jumped to ¥315 billion.

## THE TRANSITION TO SYSTEMS DEVELOPMENT: 1989–99

OMRON had also used the slow growth period to restructure. Its most important move was its transition from a component manufacturer to a producer of integrated control systems. As it entered the late 1980s, OMRON relied on research and development and its expertise in combining cybernetic technology, advanced controls, computers, and telecommunications technology to position all of its sectors for the next growth period. Such flexibility in applications was crucial as customers' needs grew more complex. The retail industry, for instance, increased its demand for faster seller recognition, order placement, and stock control. Other industries interested in EFTS technology included insurance and securities companies that needed to gain rapid access to markets.

OMRON's most significant move toward systems development came in 1988, when the company integrated the control components (65 percent of sales) and the EFTS divisions (19 percent), believing that technical integration of the company's two largest divisions would be vital to future growth. These divisions were regrouped as industrial-related strategic business units (SBUs) and social-related SBUs. The latter was certain to employ the company's office automation and information systems divisions, which made up 10 percent of sales in 1988. In recognition of these changes, the company changed its name to OMRON Corporation in 1990.

Following the collapse of the Japanese financial bubble during the 1980s, OMRON and other high-tech Japanese companies faced a much more difficult operating environment during the 1990s. The bleakest period for OMRON was between 1992 and 1994, when net income dropped from ¥21.5 billion in 1991 to ¥6.2 billion in 1992, ¥4.6 billion in 1993, and ¥4.7 billion in 1994. The company recovered by 1995, when it reported a net income of ¥12.2 billion. Cost-cutting measures taken by OMRON to improve its results included sharply reducing capital spending, streamlining operations (including the reduction of products offered by more than 30 percent), and cutting the workforce by 1,500 through attrition over a three-year period starting in 1994. The company also stepped up its efforts to develop higher value-added products.

With domestic demand stagnant, OMRON looked for opportunities for growth through export. The rapidly emerging nations of Southeast Asia were particularly targeted because of potential sales and because manufacturing could be carried out in those nations more inexpensively than in Japan. Likewise, China became a key for overseas growth and OMRON established a regional headquarters there in 1995. In 1996 OMRON expanded its facilities in Indonesia and opened three new factories in Shanghai. In early 1997 the company announced plans to double its presence in Asia, outside Japan, by 2001. OMRON had already become a much more export-oriented firm, increasing its sales outside of Japan from 16.5 percent in 1990 to 25.6 percent in 1997. The company aimed to further increase export sales to 30 percent by 2001. Another goal was to raise the overseas procurement rate from 10 percent to 30 percent during the same period.

The beginning of the Asian financial crisis in mid-1997 and the subsequent recession of the Japanese economy wreaked havoc on OMRON's plans. During the fiscal year ending in March 1999, OMRON saw its export of control components fall because of weak global demand and a strong yen. Revenues also fell for the year, as did net income, which declined from ¥18.3 billion in fiscal year 1998 to ¥2 billion in fiscal year 1999. In March 1999 OMRON announced another restructuring plan, this one to lower the company's workforce from 18,800 to 16,800 by March 2002 and to reduce the number of directors from 30 to less than 10.

## EXPLORING NEW MARKETS IN THE TWENTY-FIRST CENTURY

OMRON continued to struggle during the early years of the new century, as its streamlining efforts failed to produce adequate reductions in the company's expenses. The company hit its low point for the fiscal year ending in March 2002, when it suffered its first annual loss in more than a quarter century. For fiscal year 2001 OMRON posted a net loss of ¥15.7 billion ($118.3 million), on sales of ¥533.9 billion ($4 billion). To reverse this trend, the company unveiled in March 2002 a broader, more aggressive restructuring plan, one that was designed to reduce operational efficiencies throughout the entire company. In a reorganization effort that lasted

18 months and cost roughly ¥30 billion ($226 million), OMRON shut down three manufacturing facilities in Japan and eliminated 11 subsidiaries, either through divestment or consolidation. In May 2002, with the aim of trimming its workforce, the company also introduced the first early retirement program in its history. By early 2003 OMRON began to show signs of recovery. Even though overall revenues dropped to ¥522.5 billion ($4.3 billion) for the fiscal year ending in March 2003, the company was able to post a modest profit of ¥511 million ($4.2 million) for the year.

Three months into the new fiscal year Hisao Sakuta succeeded Yoshio Tateisi as president of OMRON. The changeover was noteworthy, in that Sakuta was the first person outside of the Tateisi family to assume leadership of the company. OMRON continued to show significant gains during Sakuta's first year at the helm. Revenues rose to ¥575.2 billion ($5.1 billion) for the fiscal year ending in March 2004, and net earnings swelled to ¥26.8 billion ($237.8 million). Much of this improvement was driven by a general upswing in the Japanese economy, as increased demand for OMRON's products lifted sales throughout the company's principal operating divisions. At the same time, the improvement to OMRON's bottom line was aided by substantial reductions in costs, particularly in the area of personnel, where the company was able to cut payroll expenses by ¥15.5 billion ($137.49 million) between March 2002 and March 2004.

Another significant factor propelling the company's growth was its increased presence abroad. One notable area of foreign expansion during this period was in China, where the company hoped to capitalize on the rapidly emerging labor and consumer markets. In April 2004 OMRON announced a plan to invest ¥30 billion ($276 million) in China over a three-year period. The money would primarily be dedicated to improving the company's existing manufacturing facilities, developing an extensive sales network in the nation, and developing strategic partnerships with established mainland firms. Ultimately, the company hoped to increase sales from its Chinese operations from $330 million in 2003 to $1.3 billion by 2007. Indeed, according to the company's plan, China would eventually become the company's most productive region in the world, accounting for 20 percent of its total revenues. During this period OMRON continued to launch a range of new products. In March 2005 the company introduced the OKAO Vision Face Recognition Sensor, a face-recognition security tool for use with cell phones and other mobile devices.

OMRON enjoyed record profits throughout the middle of the decade, along with steadily improving sales figures. For fiscal year 2006 the company posted net earnings of ¥38.3 billion ($325.8 million), on revenues of ¥723.9 billion ($6.2 billion). For fiscal year 2007 the company's profits rose to ¥42.4 billion ($372 million), and its sales ballooned to ¥762.9 billion ($6.7 billion). In the wake of the global economic downturn that began in late 2007, however, the company's financial fortunes took a serious hit, culminating in a loss of ¥29.2 billion ($292.2 million) in fiscal year 2008. Even though sales continued to sag during fiscal year 2009, in which it reported another loss of ¥19.5 billion ($198.1 million), by fiscal year 2010 the company managed to post a modest profit of ¥22.8 billion ($243.9 million). As the global economy began to show signs of recovery, OMRON's long-term future once again seemed secure.

*David E. Salamie*
*Updated, Stephen Meyer*

## PRINCIPAL SUBSIDIARIES

OMRON Corporation has more than 150 subsidiaries throughout the globe. The majority are located in Japan, Asia, and the Pacific region, with the remaining subsidiaries in Europe and North America.

## PRINCIPAL DIVISIONS

Automotive Electronic Components; Electronic and Mechanical Components; Healthcare; Industrial Automation; Social Systems, Solutions, and Service.

## PRINCIPAL COMPETITORS

CTS Corporation; Custom Sensors & Technologies, Inc.; DENSO Corporation; Honeywell International Inc.; Kyocera Corporation; Murata Manufacturing Co., Ltd.; Robert Bosch GmbH; Rockwell Automation, Inc.; TDK Corporation.

## FURTHER READING

Baker, Gerard, "Restructuring Helps Omron to Rise 42%," *Financial Times* (London), November 9, 1994, p. 33.

Dawkins, William, "Omron Shrugs off Domestic Doldrums," *Financial Times* (London), November 7, 1995, p. 27.

*Fifty Years of OMRON: A Pictorial History.* Kyoto, Japan: OMRON Tateisi Electronics Co., 1985.

Hashimoto, Ryusuke, "Recovering Omron Turns to China to Spark Growth," *Nikkei Weekly* (Tokyo), January 19, 2004.

Johnstone, Bob, "Mechatronic Marvels," *Far Eastern Economic Review*, July 29, 1993, p. 30.

Maruyama, Hiroya, "Omron Eyes All-Time High Net Profit," *Nikkei Weekly* (Tokyo), March 22, 2004.

Ohara, Kentaro, "Consolidation Pays Omron Dividends," *Nikkei Weekly* (Tokyo), June 19, 2006.

"Omron Vows Reforms under New Leadership," *Daily Yomiuri* (Tokyo), July 4, 2003, p. 16.

Robinson, Gwen, "Omron Set to Expand in Asia," *Financial Times* (London), January 22, 1997, p. 32.

Wagstyl, Stefan, "Omron Fights to Retain Competitive Edge," *Financial Times* (London), February 25, 1992, p. 27.

# Organización Soriana
# S.A.B. de C.V.

■

**Alejandro de Rodas 3102-A**
**Monterrey, Nuevo Leon 64610**
**Mexico**
**Telephone: (+52 81) 8329-9000**
**Fax: (+52 81) 8329-9127**
**Web site: http://www1.soriana.com**

*Public Company*
*Founded:* 1968
*Incorporated:* 1971
*Employees:* 76,800
*Sales:* $6.39 billion (2008)
*Total Assets:* $4.43 billion (2008)
*Stock Exchanges:* Bolsa Mexicana de Valores
*Ticker Symbol:* Soriana
*NAICS:* 445110 Supermarkets and Other Grocery
(Except Convenience) Stores; 452910 Warehouse
Clubs and Supercenters; 441310 Automotive Parts
and Accessories Stores; 445120 Convenience Stores;
448140 Family Clothing Stores; 522120 Savings
Institutions

■ ■ ■

Organización Soriana S.A.B. de C.V. is the second-largest Mexican retailer. The grocery chain has over 470 stores located in more than 135 cities. It began primarily in northern Mexico but has expanded into central and southern Mexico, and it has a few stores in the United States. Its hypermarkets sell food and many other consumer products and provide a range of services that include banking, auto centers, doctors' offices, and photo shops. In addition to its hypermarkets, Soriana operates stores in a variety of other formats, including Supermercados Soriana, targeting high-income customers; Mercados Soriana, located generally in rural areas; City Club, a members-only outlet store; and Soriana Express, a small-town convenience store.

## SORIANA'S ROOTS

In 1905 in Torreon, Coahuila, a northern Mexican town at the crossroads of two railroads, Spencer Borque founded a fabric store called Soriana, named after the Spanish province of his family's origins. The business expanded through the next decades, gradually selling clothing and household goods as well as textiles. In the 1930s, when Pedro Martin and his sons, Francisco Martin Borque and Armando Martin Borque, came from Spain to join the family business, Soriana began offering wholesale goods to a wider region, providing products to stores in many of the towns of northern Mexico.

Later, in the 1950s, Soriana left the wholesale business and focused once again on retail operations, this time with the newly popular discount store. Using the then-innovative concept of self-service stores, enabling prices to be significantly less than those of department stores, Soriana expanded from its initial single retail location in Torreon to a chain of discount stores.

The brothers, Francisco Martin Borque and Armando Martin Borque, then founded the first Soriana hypermarket in 1968. Located in Torreon, this store carried both groceries and a variety of other merchandise and was significantly larger than supermarkets that sold only food. Its opening is considered the current company's formal founding.

### TRANSFORMATIONS: 1970–94

Upon the success of its first hypermarket, Soriana extended its operations and its organization. The company opened stores in Durango, Chihuahua, and Monterrey. Soriana, although still family owned, was no longer a small family business, and it was incorporated in 1971. The company created a system of distribution centers to ensure its stores' supplies and adopted computerized information systems for tracking its products and its accounts. Soriana also diversified its holdings, investing in restaurants, clothing manufacturing, shipping, and agriculture.

By 1984, however, a serious family rift occurred, and the two brothers split the company. Francisco and his family took assets that included eight markets near Monterrey, a restaurant chain, and a ranch. Armando and his family took the properties around Torreon and used the name Hipermart. In 1987 both organizations went public and were listed on the Mexican stock exchange (Bolsa Mexicana de Valores).

Francisco initiated significant changes with his company, bringing in professional management and employing only one of his sons, Ricardo, his youngest, in the retail chain. Francisco also traveled, always looking for new business ideas, and he soon increased his stores to 16. Despite these efforts, however, both his organization and his brother's had struggles. The North American Free Trade Agreement (NAFTA) was implemented in 1994, and around this time Mexico was inundated with giant corporate retailers such as the United States' Wal-Mart, France's Carrefour, and the Netherlands' Ahold. To compete with these immense organizations, Ricardo Martin and his cousin Alberto negotiated to bring the two Soriana companies back together. In 1994 the aging patriarchs, Francisco and Armando, authorized the reunion of the two Sorianas. A unified Organización Soriana was now poised to challenge its rivals.

Soriana began 1994 with 26 stores and ended it with 48. At the year's end, however, the value of the peso fell dramatically. Nonetheless, despite Mexico's economic crisis, Soriana was able to grow. Unlike many of its competitors, Soriana had avoided international investors, and it had no dollar-dependent debts that would have to be serviced with devalued pesos. Additionally, much of Soriana's business was located in the north of Mexico, near the U.S. border. U.S. buyers thronged to Mexico for goods that had become even less expensive than before. The devalued peso and NAFTA also resulted in foreign companies locating more manufacturing plants in the northern Mexican provinces, increasing payrolls and adding customers in Soriana's prime service areas.

### EXPANSION AND ORGANIZATION

Soriana determined to expand its locations to provide a nationwide presence, and it planned to operate 100 stores by 2000. In addition to its sizable goals, the company maintained its focus on high performance. It installed computer-based registers in its hypermarkets with systems that supported corporate inventory control and accounting systems and thereby informed the local managers' stocking and staffing decisions. It developed its distribution networks, expanding and modernizing the Mexico City and Guadalajara distribution centers and constructing a new supply hub near Monterrey.

The company also established an electronic point-of-sale program that provided information on customer buying habits and preferences. In 1998 it introduced its own store-label goods. It then launched a Soriana credit card, a bank debit-card program, and money-transfer services. By 2000, with the opening of its 100th store in Tepic, Nayarit, Soriana had achieved its millennial goal.

Soriana was, however, careful in implementing its $400 million expansion program. It refrained from any foreign partnerships, distinct from its competitors, which included Cifra (allied with Wal-Mart) and Grupo Gigante, S.A. de C.V. (involved in joint ventures with Carrefour). Soriana was also conservative in its financing and avoided funding its growth through debt. This was possible because the company carefully controlled costs and demonstrated a remarkable return on equity that went from 5.9 percent in 1994 to 17.9 percent by 1998.

Soriana also saw opportunities where other retailers saw obstacles. Although sales for most chain retailers had shown steady increases during the late 1990s, many Mexicans, responding to the country's financial crisis, continued shopping in the lower-cost street markets. Because taxes and other expenses could be avoided by the sidewalk peddlers, many established retailers saw this "gray market" as a threat. Demonstrating the company's

---

## KEY DATES

**1905:** First Soriana store is established in Torreon.
**1968:** First Soriana hypermarket is opened.
**1984:** Soriana splits into two organizations.
**1994:** Soriana is reestablished as a single organization.
**2007:** Soriana acquires Grupo Gigante.
**2010:** Soriana Express is opened.

---

singular perspective, Soriana's CEO, cited by reporter Jeff Wright in the April 1, 1997, issue of *Business Mexico*, said that sidewalk sales did not represent a threat to Soriana but an area for growth and a new market share to be won.

Having operated only hypermarkets until 2001, Soriana decided to diversify store formats and extend its appeal to different consumer groups. It began by opening City Club, which had substantial member discounts. It then added Mercados Soriana, which was smaller in size and located in smaller towns. In 2005 Soriana included Supermercados Soriana, which was positioned in high-income neighborhoods.

## SORIANA VERSUS THE GIANT

While Soriana was expanding its reach and increasing its profits, it was facing stiff competition, particularly from the U.S.-based Wal-Mart. Wal-Mart first began operating in Mexico in 1981, and the store increased its presence in the Mexican retail marketplace in the early 1990s through a joint venture with Cifra, a leading Mexican retailer. It bought a majority interest in Cifra in 1997 and renamed the company Wal-Mart de Mexico, often called Walmex.

By 2002 Walmex already had 579 stores in Mexico, over half of Mexican supermarket sales, and the purchasing clout to undercut the prices of all its competitors. Soriana, however, was not willing to concede the battle for Mexico's retail market. According to Geri Smith in *Business Week* on September 23, 2002, Soriana CEO Ricardo Martin said that he believed that Walmex was "formidable, but we aren't afraid of the challenge."

Hoping to halt Walmex's increasing share of the Mexican retail market and buoyed by rising criticism of its aggressive tactics, Soriana moved to form a consortium with Grupo Gigante and Controladora Comercial Mexicana, two other large Mexican retailers. The combined sales of the three companies equaled

about 95 percent of Walmex's total sales, and their alliance would allow them to have the purchasing volume to obtain competitive pricing of supplies.

Although Sinergia, as the retail alliance was called, was supported by the association of Mexican retailers, it was initially blocked by the Comisión Federal de Competencia (CFC; Federal Competition Commission), Mexico's antitrust agency. In July 2004, however, the CFC allowed the three companies to merge some operations and form a joint purchasing organization.

The alliance was not Soriana's only salvo in its battle with Walmex. Soriana also adapted its selling strategies to appeal specifically to Mexican shoppers. Soriana countered the stark warehouse atmosphere typical of the Walmex stores with wide aisles, a mix of natural and artificial light, covered parking, raffles for luxury cars, loyalty cards with redeemable points, delivery services, on-site bakers and butchers, and a dizzying variety of discount price promotions.

## FORGING AHEAD

When Walmex, in 2007, followed the lead of several other Mexican chain stores and obtained a license to offer banking services, Soriana quickly launched its own financial services. In partnership with Banamex (part of Citigroup), it offered credit cards and small loans to low-income customers. Soriana also continued to enhance its other store conveniences, including providing electronic top-up for cellular phones.

Simultaneously, Soriana worked to be an innovator in other areas. It was the first large Mexican retailer to use biodegradable plastic bags in all its stores. It also planned the development of a $300 million wind-driven power plant, capable of generating all of Soriana's energy needs in a cost-cutting and environmentally friendly investment.

The next stage for Soriana was a move to operate in Mexico City, which was new territory for the organization. In 2007, continuing its expansion, Soriana acquired its Sinergia partner, Grupo Gigante, for $1.35 billion. That company's 206 stores included several in the United States and 47 in Mexico City. Soriana then planned, between January 2007 and June 2008, to invest $700 million, open 60 more stores, and achieve a total of 400 operating units.

Most of the new financing for Soriana's acquisitions and expansions was funded by commercial paper (an unsecured short-term debt instrument issued by banks and corporations), and this created some concern for the company shareholders and some stock analysts. Soriana also experienced a drop in sales because of the global recession. Despite this, Soriana increased its profits in

2009 through increased efficiencies in its operations, including minimizing administration costs, improving distribution methods, and curtailing labor costs. As 2010 began Soriana opened the new decade with more than 470 stores and another new format: Soriana Express, a basic convenience store for small towns. By January 2010 Soriana had reduced its debt by $308 million from a year earlier and its stock was on the rise again.

*Grace Murphy*

## PRINCIPAL OPERATING UNITS

Soriana; Soriana Super; Soriana Mercado; Soriana Express; City Club; Super City.

## PRINCIPAL COMPETITORS

Wal-Mart de Mexico, S.A. de C.V.; Controladora Comercial Mexicana, S.A. de C.V.; H-E-B; Grupo Electra.

## FURTHER READING

Barrera Diaz, Cyntia, and Gabriela Lopez, "Walmart's Mexican Unit Aided by Rivals' Problems," *International Herald Tribune*, October 29, 2008.

Malkin, Elisabeth, "Mexican Retailers Unite against Walmart," *New York Times*, July 9, 2004.

"Mass Grocery Retail: Mexico Food & Drink Report Q1 2010," *Business Monitor International*, January 2010.

"Mexico Retailer Soriana to Invest $300US Million in Wind Project," Associated Press, January 22, 2007.

"Mexico: Soriana Profits Up on Margin Improvements," *Just-Food Global News*, July 27, 2009.

"Mexico Soriana Sees Same-Store Sales Up in 2010," Reuters, February 8, 2010.

Morais, Richard C., "One Hot Tamale (Soriana, Emerging Super Market)," *Forbes Global*, December 20, 2004, p. 62.

Smith, Geri, "War of the Superstores," *Business Week*, September 23, 2002.

Wall, Allan, "Mexico's Soriana Stores—A True Success Story," Mexidata.info, August 6, 2007, http://mexidata.info/id1470.html.

Wright, Jeff, "Mexican Retailers Reaping Rewards of Long-Lost Consumer Buying Power," *Business Mexico*, April 1, 1997.

CYMBALS SOUNDS GONGS

# Paiste AG

———————■———————

Kantonsstrasse 2
Nottwil, CH-6207
Switzerland
Telephone: (+41 41) 939-3333
Toll Free: (800) 472-4783
Fax: (+41 41) 939-3366
Web site: http://www.paiste.com

*Private Company*
*Founded:* 1901
*Employees:* 90 (est.)
*Sales:* $13 million (2009 est.)
*NAICS:* 339992 Musical Instrument Manufacturing;
423990 Other Miscellaneous Durable Goods
Merchant Wholesalers

■ ■ ■

Paiste AG is one the world's premier producers of cymbals and gongs. Headquartered in Switzerland, the family-owned company maintains a second factory in Germany (Paiste GmbH & Co. KG) and an office in the United States (Paiste America, Inc.). Its line of cymbals includes approximately 400 different models designed for a customer base that ranges from marching-band members to rock drummers. Consistency of product, which allows a musician to replace a cymbal with confidence that it will sound like its predecessor, has long been a hallmark of the company. Paiste is also well known for innovation, such as the development of the first flat ride cymbal in 1967 and the introduction of unlathed cymbals (the RUDE

series) in 1980. The 21st century found the business returning to its primary focus of manufacturing, as it terminated its internal distribution efforts in favor of relationships with external distributors. Under the leadership of the fourth generation of the Paiste family, and more than 100 years after its founding in 1901, the company appeared to be well positioned to thrive for many years to come.

## TURBULENT BEGINNINGS

Michail Toomas Paiste founded Paiste as a music store and publishing business in St. Petersburg, Russia, in 1901. The onset of the Russian Revolution led him to return to his native Estonia in 1917, temporarily leaving his children in boarding schools near the newly named Leningrad. His son, Michail M., was relocated to a refugee camp by the Red Cross, and he was soon wandering the world from China to New York until finally being reunited with his parents in Estonia in 1927. Just 17 at the time, his unorthodox upbringing had exposed him to the music of many cultures and made him particularly suited to joining the family business. He did so that year and quickly became the individual who defined Paiste.

The senior Paiste had begun designing and making cymbals in Estonia as a sideline, but his son saw greater potential in the enterprise. Modern music was rapidly changing, and the contemporary drum set was emerging. Michail M. decided to meet the new market demands by developing his own Turkish-style cymbals and making them the primary focus of the business. (It was also during that time that the gong section of the company was started.) His instincts and workmanship proved a winning combination as Paiste gained widespread recognition and began to export its products throughout Europe and the United States. Once again, however, war intruded on the family's fortunes.

The Paistes were uprooted a second time as World War II broke out in 1939, causing them to relocate to Poland. They were able to reestablish the business but were challenged by a shortage of raw materials and the wartime break in international relations. The former difficulty turned out to hold an unexpected long-term benefit, however, in that it necessitated the particular attention to craftsmanship that would become a company trademark. Fourth-generation CEO Erik Paiste explained to *Music Trades* in November 2009, "There were times when my grandfather was trying to make cymbals during the war and was not in the position to get quality raw materials, so superior workmanship was especially necessary. He had to rise above the tools and materials he had to work with. This is why we have this vast body of know-how in creating perfect cymbals."

Yet another upheaval for the family came in 1945 as the Soviet Union occupied Poland and forced them to flee to Germany as refugees. The business had to be rebuilt from the ground up for the third time since its inception. Perseverance and reputation combined to bring success, and Paiste was flourishing again in the 1950s. The tumult of the early years was not forgotten, though, leading Michail M.'s sons, Robert and Toomas, to set up the company's headquarters in politically neutral Switzerland in 1957. The German plant was retained, and Paiste was poised on the brink of a new, vastly more secure era.

## PROGRESS AND INNOVATION

Finally in a position to apply its first-rate craftsmanship to commensurate raw materials, Paiste introduced its first professional cymbal series, the Formula 602, in 1959. The company came up against an unexpected hurdle when it was discovered that music stores were often already stocking another brand and had no particular incentive to change. Robert and Toomas took

a creative approach to the problem by contacting drummers directly and giving product demonstrations. The duly impressed musicians then began to request Paiste cymbals from the shops, and the shops responded to the customers. It was clearly a clever business move, but it was also an apt illustration of the company's relationship with musicians. This affiliation would grow as drummers played an increasing role in the testing and development of new products.

As Paiste's reputation intensified, so did its commitment to innovation. Its many contributions to cymbal design and manufacture included pioneering the use of an 8 percent bronze alloy for production (1963) and developing the flat ride cymbal (1967), as well as flattened bells (1975), unlathed cymbals designed for such comparatively abrasive music styles as punk and heavy metal (1980), non-chip colored cymbals (1983), an inverted bell Chinese cymbal (1983), and a patented alloy that was reportedly the first bronze alloy specifically created for cymbals (1989). Additionally, the company was diligent about selection, continually introducing new lines to appeal to drummers across the entire spectrum of musical genres. Orchestra members, marching band players, and jazz, country, rock, and classical percussionists could all find a variety of sounds to suits their needs. Indeed, some 400 different models of cymbals became available at any given time. Gongs, too, were an integral part of the business. Manufactured only at the plant in Germany, Paiste offered gongs for symphonies, meditation, or chakra stimulation, including the world's largest, the 80-inch symphonic gong.

Paiste established a presence in the United States with the 1981 opening of an office in Brea, California. The company also was actively and internally involved in distribution. The latter focus changed after the untimely death of Toomas in 2002, leaving his son, Erik, in charge of the family business. Erik determined that the company would be best served by farming out the distribution side and returning to its roots in development and manufacturing. Thus, deals were struck with such outside distributors as Yamaha, Davitt & Hanser, and St. Louis Music (SLM), leaving Paiste free to do what it did best: make cymbals and gongs.

## THE CONSISTENCY QUOTIENT

One of the key features of Paiste cymbals was consistency. That is, each new cymbal within any product line was specifically crafted to replicate the overall sound and character of its prototype. This uniformity meant, for instance, that a professional drummer who broke a favorite hi-hat could order a replacement secure in the knowledge that it would produce the same results. It also enabled fans to

## KEY DATES

**1901:** Paiste is founded in St. Petersburg, Russia.
**1917:** Business moves to Estonia and begins to focus on cymbal design and manufacture.
**1945:** Company is reestablished in Germany.
**1957:** Paiste establishes corporate headquarters in Switzerland.
**1981:** A U.S. operation is opened in Brea, California.
**1984** Patent granted co. for first bronze alloy created specifically for cymbals.
**2001:** Erik Paiste, grandson of founder, assumes leadership of company.

reproduce the sound, if not necessarily the expertise, of favorite drummers simply by purchasing the drummer's particular cymbal combination. Such reliability was not applauded by all, as some critics preferred cymbals with distinct character. But it was a quality upon which Paiste prided itself, and it earned the company a loyal following.

Consistency was attained through a painstaking, handcrafted process at Paiste's headquarters in Switzerland. (Its German operation manufactured the lower-end Paiste Sound Technology line by machine.) The sound development team, composed of drummers and product specialists, started by creating prototypes of new cymbals as they became needed. A prototype, or sound master, for every step in the production process from heating and pressing to hammering to lathing to finishing was then made so that each artisan along the way had a point of reference to consult. Finally, every finished cymbal was played in a testing room to be certain that it conformed precisely to the character of the sound master. Any that failed to make the grade were destroyed and sold as scrap metal. It was an unforgiving protocol that yielded positive results.

Such meticulous measures could only be achieved via a top-notch workforce. Toward that end, the Swiss facility employed approximately 40 to 50 people, most of whom remained for decades. Dedication and skill were required, as it took up to five years to acquire the expertise to craft all the cymbals in a product line. Equally vital was the company's clear recognition of, and respect for, the contributions of its employees. Production director Michael Lehmann told Robert Brookes of SwissInfo in 2007, "The most important asset of our company is the knowledge of our employees

and you could never transfer that somewhere else." Thus, the atmosphere of mutual admiration and commitment between management and worker was integral to Paiste's success.

## ONGOING EVOLUTION

While consistency was crucial to the Paiste brand, change was also paramount. Innovations in the percussion field and getting out of the distribution business were not the only ways the company continued to keep up with the times.

One notable trend that Paiste embraced was that of regarding cymbals as musical instruments. For years, many retailers had regarded them as a kind of accessory. They were often minimally displayed behind the counter, rather than shown on the floor of a store where they could be played by prospective customers, as were, for example, guitars. As that attitude started to change in the 1980s, partially because of Paiste's efforts, Erik was full of enthusiasm. "To be in the cymbal business, you have to treat cymbals as a serious musical instrument, not merely something you hit," he told *Music Trades* in 1989. He added, "When drummers can experience the wide variety of cymbal sounds available, they get excited and educated, and they naturally buy more."

Welcome as that new development was, it presented its own challenges in that retail shops did not have the space or financial means to stock the entire Paiste line. The company addressed the situation first by means of on-site display modules and helpful staff, and later by means of the Internet, with sound samples of every model.

Perhaps the most simultaneously enduring and transforming aspect of Paiste's cymbals was the sheer volume and variety of the offerings. Its sound development team in Switzerland constantly monitored new musical trends and initiated products in response. Vintage and classic sounds, such as the Giant Beat series originally launched in the 1960s, were also frequently reissued. Whether a percussionist needed tiny hand cymbals, a giant gong, or a ride cymbal with a punk-rock edge, Paiste's 400-some models presented both choice and consistency.

*Margaret L. Moser*

## PRINCIPAL DIVISIONS

Paiste America, Inc.; Paiste GmbH & Co. KG.

## PRINCIPAL COMPETITORS

Sabian Ltd.; Avedis Zildjian Company.

## FURTHER READING

Brookes, Robert, "Paiste Cymbals Come in for a Lot of Stick," SwissInfo, March 19, 2007, http://www.swissinfo.ch/eng/index/Paiste_cymbals_come_in_for_a_lot_of_stick.html?cid=5768448.

Long, Rick, "Paiste: Tradition, Innovation, and Family Values," *Drum Business*, November–December 2009.

"Paiste Alpha and PST Hand Cymbals," *Music Trades*, November 2009, p. 118.

"Paiste Gets in a RUDE mood," *MusicRadar*, March 25, 2008, http://www.musicradar.com/news/drums/paiste-gets-in-a-rude-mood-144769.

"Paiste's Attempt to 'De-accessorize' the Cymbal: Treating Cymbals as Serious Instruments Is the Key to Increased Sales," *Music Trades*, December 1989, p. 68.

Pinksterboer, Hugo, *The Cymbal Book*. Hal Leonard, 1993.

"The Paiste Cymbal Making Tradition: Although They Spent Much of the Past Century as Refugees, Fleeing War and Revolution, the Paiste Family Remained Committed in Their Quest to Build the Best Cymbals. Now Their Extensive Cymbal Line Is Being Offered by St. Louis Music," *Music Trades*, November 2009, p. 90.

"Yamaha: PAC Distributes Paiste to Independent Dealers," *Music Trades*, March 2006, p. 37.

# Pearle Vision, Inc.

———————■———————

**4000 Luxottica Place**
**Mason, Ohio 45040**
**U.S.A.**
**Telephone: (513) 765-3327**
**Toll Free: (800) 732-7531**
**Fax: (513) 765-6249**
**Web site: http://www.pearlevision.com**

*Private Company*
*Incorporated:* 1961
*Employees:* 3,700
*Sales:* $232 million (2009 est.)
*NAICS:* 339115 Ophthalmic Goods Manufacturing;
446130 Optical Goods Stores; 621320 Offices of
Optometrists

■ ■ ■

Pearle Vision, Inc., is one of several eyewear chains
owned by the Italian holding company Luxottica Group.
Other Luxottica holdings include LensCrafters and Sun-
glass Hut. In more than 800 locations in the United
States, Canada, the Caribbean, and Puerto Rico, Pearle
Vision outlets offer eye examinations, prescription
glasses, sunglasses, contact lenses, and other optical
goods. Some Pearle Vision outlets are company owned,
while others are franchises owned by eye doctors, opticians, and individual investors.

## ONE-STOP EYE CARE COMES TO
## SAVANNAH

Pearle's rapid rise to leadership in the optical retail
industry began in 1961, when Dr. Stanley Pearle opened

the first Pearle Vision Center in Savannah, Georgia.
Although the store was among many optical retail stores
competing at the time, Pearle's shop was different and
represented a major breakthrough in the eye-care
industry. The shop's distinguishing characteristic was
that it offered comprehensive, one-stop eye care: It
combined complete eye exams with an extensive selection of eyewear and convenient store hours. Thus, for
the first time, a person could go into a single store, get
an eye exam and prescription, select a pair of glasses,
and pick up the finished glasses there a few days later.
The consumer benefited from not having to visit both
an optometrist (eye doctor) and an optician (one that
makes and sells eyeglasses and contact lenses). Dr. Pearle
profited by providing both diagnostic and treatment
services.

## ROOTS OF SUCCESS

Pearle's innovative store was a hit, and he enjoyed immense growth and profits during the 1960s and 1970s.
But his was not an overnight success story. Pearle was
born in Pittsburgh in 1918 and graduated from high
school in 1936. Because of the severe recession at the
time, he was unable to attend college. Pearle was able to
find a job, though, and he later started optometry
school in Chicago. He graduated in 1940 and headed
back to Pennsylvania to take the optometry exam, but
he ended up in Texas. "I went back to Philadelphia to
take the Pennsylvania State Board of Optometry exam.
In those days, you had to wait two months before you
knew whether you passed—an eternity for a young man
waiting to start a career," Pearle recalled in company
annals. "A fellow optometrist suggested we both go to

## COMPANY PERSPECTIVES

■

We put people first and deliver a vision experience like no other, based not just on cutting-edge technology and retail selection, but on listening and respect. We establish the Pearle brand one neighborhood at a time by getting to know our customers, their families, and their vision needs.

Texas where they announce the test results the next day. So, I scrounged up $100 for expenses and a train ticket to Texas, took the state board exam, and passed. Although I found out that I had passed the Pennsylvania State Board, I just never left Texas."

Pearle started out in the optometry business, but his erratic career took several turns. He served a tour a duty with the U.S. Navy during World War II before returning to private practice in Corpus Christi, Texas. In 1948 he joined Lee Optical as a junior partner. He worked at Lee for 10 years before striking out on his own in 1958. Pearle was still living in Texas at the time he decided to open his own shop, but he was drawn to Savannah, Georgia, because he believed that the area offered greater opportunity. The move was profitable for Pearle, whose unique concept flourished. "My idea was to create modern-looking optical shops that combined top-quality service and products, convenient locations, expanded hours, competitive prices, and a better selection of eyewear styles," recalled Pearle. "Before that, eyeglass wearers had only a few styles to choose from, and all the dispensing was done out of a small area in the optometrist's office."

### GROWTH CONTINUES AND FRANCHISING BEGINS

Throughout the 1960s and 1970s Dr. Pearle added to his chain of Pearle Vision Centers at a rapid pace. In addition to building new outlets, he developed the company by purchasing other optical stores. Importantly, Pearle was joined by two other industry innovators in 1971, Robert Hillman and his partner Larry Kohan. Hillman, the son of an optician, had opened his first eyewear store in 1966 at the age of 23. Like Pearle Vision, the Hillman-Kohan chain expanded during the late 1960s by innovating. The partners are generally credited with inventing one-hour eyeglass services and with helping to pioneer the trend toward eye-care superstores. By 1971 the Hillman-Kohan chain had grown to 17 stores. Pearle became interested in both the

stores and their founders. He approached Hillman and Kohan, who agreed to sell their chain to Pearle Vision for $7 million. Hillman and Kohan both stayed on at Pearle Vision, and throughout the 1970s they helped to take the Pearle Vision chain national. Hillman and Kohan left the organization in 1980 and started Eyelab, the first true eyeglasses superstore.

Pearle Vision expanded its one-stop shop outlets across the United States during the 1970s and early 1980s. Throughout the period Pearle benefited from demographic, legal, and market trends that bolstered overall industry sales and profits. The federal government, for example, eased restrictions on advertising by optometrists. In addition, Pearle continued to innovate and create new opportunities. In 1981 Pearle began franchising its stores as opposed to owning all of them. Franchisees paid Pearle a fee to use the respected Pearle Vision name and proven business format, and Pearle trained them and helped with purchasing, marketing, lab processing, distribution, and other aspects of the business. Similarly, in 1984 Pearle introduced its successful Managed Vision Care unit, which offered a comprehensive vision benefit service to managed health care providers. The Managed Vision Care plan allowed managed care companies to provide benefits such as prepaid exams and optical materials for as little as $5 per member per year.

### GRAND METROPOLITAN ARRIVES FROM BRITAIN

After more than 20 years of steady growth, the Dallas-based Pearle Vision was among the largest optical retailers in the world, with stores throughout the United States. In September 1985 the company was purchased by Grand Metropolitan PLC. Based in the United Kingdom, Grand Metropolitan was a global leader in the food and beverage industry. Grand Metropolitan considered Pearle Vision a worthy diversification and it believed that it could use its own financial might to help Pearle dominate the increasingly consolidated retail optical industry. The 68-year-old Dr. Pearle remained active in the company as a consultant and as a representative in Pearle Vision's government relations.

Backed by Grand Metropolitan's massive capital base, Pearle Vision executives launched an aggressive expansion initiative during the late 1980s. They engineered the acquisition of a number of smaller chains in an effort to boost Pearle's market share and increase the company's economies of scale. By 1990 the Pearle chain had ballooned to more than 1,000 stores, including outlets in Japan and Europe. Unfortunately, an economic downturn from the late 1980s through the early 1990s hurt Pearle's sales, while competition from

**1961:** Dr. Stanley Pearle establishes first Pearle Vision office in Savannah, Georgia.
**1980:** Pearle Vision establishes its first franchise.
**1984:** Pearle Vision introduces its Managed Vision Care division.
**1985:** Grand Metropolitan PLC acquires Pearle Vision.
**1996:** Grand Metropolitan PLC sells its Pearle Vision division to Cole National Corporation.
**2004:** Luxottica Group acquires parent company Cole National Corporation.

both small and large rivals increased. Major chains like Precision LensCrafters and Cole Vision Corp. were aggressively competing with Pearle on a national scale, as were a growing number of giant warehouse and club chains. Likewise, a number of smaller regional operations were pressuring Pearle in local markets. For example, former Pearle executive Hillman was back in the eye-care game with his latest venture, Hillman Eyes, a growing chain of eye-care discount superstores.

### GETTING BACK ON TRACK

Pearle's financial performance deteriorated, which observers attributed not only to increased competition and the sluggish economy, but also to the fact that Pearle had expanded so rapidly. Sales increased to a record $670 million in 1991 as the number of stores grew to 1,054, but profits were elusive. The company's financial details were buried in statistics reported by its parent, Grand Metropolitan, but the *Dallas Business Journal* reported that former Pearle executives estimated that Pearle lost money in 1991. Recognizing the urgency of the situation, Grand Metropolitan took bold steps to turn the company around. The corporation effectively jettisoned Pearle's existing management team and brought in a new group. Bob Stetson was named president and chief executive officer and put in charge of the reorganization. Stetson had formerly served as an executive at Burger King, another Grand Metropolitan subsidiary.

Under Stetson's direction, Pearle slashed six of its nine layers of management as part of an effort to bring executives closer to customers. Furthermore, each division of the company was set up as a separate business unit, allowing each a greater degree of autonomy. Pearle laid off about 150 employees, including about 15 percent of the workers at its Dallas headquarters and 4 percent of its field force. Importantly, Stetson devised an ambitious franchising effort. He announced plans shortly after his arrival to begin selling franchises to people other than optometrists, opticians, and ophthalmologists. In theory, any entrepreneur would be considered a franchisee candidate. The strategy represented Pearle's response to the sweeping industry trend toward discounting. Stetson estimated that the plan could potentially double the number of Pearle outlets within five years and boost system-wide revenues into the $1.5 billion range. An important corollary of the tactic was that in the short term it would bring much needed cash into Pearle's coffers.

### MID-COURSE CORRECTIONS

Grand Metropolitan didn't like Stetson's strategy. After less than a year Stetson was replaced by David Nardle. "It was more of a philosophical difference," explained Ron Nykiel, senior vice president at Pearle, in the *Dallas Business Journal* on October 2, 1992. "Where Bob wanted quantity, David wanted quality." Nardle sustained Stetson's cost-cutting drive. He also pursued the franchising effort, although he tweaked it slightly. Rather than focusing on selling franchises to new store owners, Pearle would concentrate on making franchisees out of some of its existing store operators. By doing that, Pearle would enjoy an influx of up-front cash from the new store owners, albeit at the expense of long-term corporate revenue and earnings. The effort was also expected to improve the performance of formerly Pearle-owned stores because the new owner would have a greater incentive to run the business more efficiently.

Augmenting the franchise strategy was an ongoing program initiated by Pearle's human resource department in 1991. Roy J. Wilson, vice president for human resources, had spearheaded an effort to change the compensation system for the managers of Pearle-owned stores. He was given permission to implement his program after Pearle executives recognized that franchised stores consistently outperformed company-owned stores in profitability. To improve the performance of Pearle's store managers, Wilson and his subordinates devised a system that would empower the managers to make their own decisions and derive greater benefits from their successes. Part of the program entailed an unlimited bonus influenced by profit figures under the store manager's control. The initial results of the "Opti-preneur" program were impressive. In the first few months, the 14 stores tested increased their profits an average of 185 percent. Some store managers earned bonuses of more than $100,000 in just seven months, and the overall test resulted in hundreds of thousands of dollars in extra profits. Wilson began implementing the program system-wide in 1993.

## UPSWING AT CENTURY'S END

Grand Metropolitan shook up Pearle's management again early in 1994 when it hired Glenn E. Hammerle to take the helm. Hammerle left the CEO position at Crown Books to try his hand at improving Pearle's performance. Under Hammerle's hand, Pearle continued to restructure its management and incentive systems during the early 1990s. It also streamlined its organization by selling off stores. By late 1994, the Pearle Vision chain had been reduced to just over 900 down from a peak of about 1,100. The number of U.S. stores had fallen from 900 to 720. Remaining Pearle stores were located primarily in Canada, as well as in the Netherlands and Belgium. Although Pearle lost its status as the world's largest optical retailer to LensCrafters in 1994, its restructuring paid off. The company reported about $10 million in profit in 1994 from $601 million in sales, which was Pearle's first surplus since 1990.

Annual U.S. optical sales had surged from $8 billion in 1987 to $13 billion in 1994, and the retail optical business was becoming more competitive. Large chains such as Pearle increased their share of the market from less than 30 percent in the late 1980s to more than 35 percent in 1995. Pearle enjoyed a dominant market presence in 1995, controlling more than 5 percent of the U.S. optical market. It was one of only three chains with more than 500 stores and had just completed its reorganization.

## PURSUIT OF THE MANAGED CARE MARKET

A 1995 study on managed health-care plans commissioned by Pearle found that while 73 percent of respondents wanted vision care to be included in their health-care benefits, only 33 percent of respondents were entitled to an annual eye exam through their health plan. Realizing that demand for vision-care coverage would probably increase, resulting in more employers adding vision care to their health-care plans, Pearle continued to actively pursue the managed-care market. Between January and May of 1996 Pearle increased membership in its Pearle Managed Care division from 600,000 to 1.2 million individuals enrolled in health-care plans where Pearle Managed Care was the primary eye-care provider.

## GRAND METROPOLITAN GIVES WAY TO COLE NATIONAL

In 1996 Pearle Vision's British parent company, Grand Metropolitan PLC, announced plans to focus on its

leading international food and drink brands, which included Green Giant vegetables, Pillsbury baked goods, and Haagen-Dazs ice cream. In September GrandMet sold its Pearle Vision, Inc., division to Cleveland-based Cole National Corporation for $220 million in a sale finalized in November. Cole National financed the purchase through available cash and a private placement of up to $150 million in debt. Following its acquisition of the company, Cole announced plans to sell the 183 stores in Pearle's European division to a European investor group for $55 million, creating the now unrelated company Pearle Europe B.V. Cole retained a minority stake in the new company.

## CHALLENGES IN CALIFORNIA

In 2002 California's attorney general challenged Pearle Vision's practice of performing eye examinations and dispensing prescription eyewear from the same premises. The attorney general's office sued Pearle Vision for breaking a section of the state's business and professional code that prohibited an optician from directly or indirectly employing optometrists or maintaining them on the premises. "The focus should be on providing customers with quality eye care, not making cash registers ring from eyeglass sales," said Attorney General Bill Lockyer in a statement reported by the trade magazine *Optician* on September 6, 2002.

Immediately upon hearing of the suit, Pearle Vision issued a statement in which it claimed that optometrists and opticians working in Pearle outlets were employed by different companies. As reported by PR Newswire on February 16, 2002, the statement said: "Pearle Vision, Inc., does not employ optometrists in the state of California. Optometrists are employed by Pearle Vision-Care, Inc., a single-service HMO [health management organization], licensed by the state of California. We believe we are in compliance with California law and we look forward to quickly resolving this matter."

In 2003 consumer rights groups used the same section of the state code to sue LensCrafters, Inc., and National Vision, Inc., who also operated so-called one-stop shopping vision centers in California. Consumer rights attorney Matthew Davis discussed the intentions of the state code in an interview with Amanda Bronstad in the *Los Angeles Business Journal* in September 2003. "If you look at the legislative history of these laws," Davis said, "the reason they were enacted was to prevent businesses from influencing your doctor's decisions."

## TAKING CARE OF BUSINESS

In late 2003 Pearle Vision successfully sued one of its Dutch competitors, Specsavers Opticians, charging that the company falsely claimed in advertisements beginning in the early fall that its varifocal lenses were the least expensive available. Other Dutch optical retailers also sued Specsavers for the advertisements, which the company discontinued in November and replaced with an advertisement urging prospective customers to comparison shop.

Also in 2003 Pearle launched PearleNation, a new sub-brand targeted at teenage customers. Pearle believed that teenagers often have trouble finding eyewear that suits them, particularly as they transition from eyeglass frames intended for children to those meant for adults. The launch introduced special graphics and music intended for teens to Pearle Vision outlets.

## LUXOTTICA TAKES OVER

In 2004 the Milan-based Italian eyewear company Luxottica Group acquired Pearle Vision, Inc., in its $485 million purchase of Pearle's parent company, Cole National Corporation. Luxottica already owned Pearle's main competitor, LensCrafters, and marketing analysts quoted in *Crain's Cleveland Business* on August 9, 2004, speculated that the holding company would have to adjust its marketing strategies to allow the two former competitors to thrive and continue to prosper as separate retail chains. Analysts reflected that one chain might emerge as an upscale choice, offering brands such as Prada, Chanel, and Ray-Ban, while the other offered more modestly priced eyewear. An Italian analyst quoted by Eric Wahlgren in *Business Week Online* on August 11 predicted that the acquisition of Cole National could boost Luxottica's earnings by 15 percent in fiscal year 2006 if Pearle's performance could be boosted. At the time of acquisition by Luxottica Group, Pearle Vision was the second-largest U.S. retail vision chain.

Shortly after acquiring Cole National Corporation in 2004, Luxottica disbanded the company's Twinsburg, Ohio, headquarters and consolidated its operations in Cincinnati, already home to Luxottica's LensCrafters chain. The long-anticipated move eliminated some 800 jobs in northeastern Ohio.

## COURTS RULE IN BELGIUM AND CALIFORNIA

In the summer of 2005 a tribunal based in Leuven, Belgium, ordered Pearle Vision to stop using a European advertising campaign that claimed eyeglasses sold at Pearle outlets were 35 percent less expensive than those sold by independent optical practitioners. The Belgian Association of Independent Opticians and Optometrists had objected to the campaign, citing it as misleading and disparaging against independent opticians.

In 2006 a California court ruled that Pearle Vision violated California consumer law when it advertised that optometrists working near or in its retail outlets were independent of Pearle Vision, Inc., and were instead employed by a health management organization, Pearle VisionCare, Inc. The ruling allowed the case, originally brought by California attorney general Bill Lockyer in 2003, to proceed toward trial.

## A CLEAR VIEW FORWARD

In 2010 the Vision Council of America estimated that 86 percent of U.S. residents utilized some form of prescription or nonprescription eyewear. Demand for optical goods was expected to continue increasing as the U.S. population aged and the need for eye examinations and glasses grew. Optical retailers flourish when they can offer a wide range of product styles, competitive pricing, and keen attention to customer service. These business practices were well established at Pearle Vision and endured as the company transitioned from one parent company to another. Name recognition for Pearle remained high among U.S. consumers in 2010, and the company supported its franchisees with a marketing budget capable of maintaining and increasing recognition. Despite the tendency of eyewear sales to decrease in an economic downturn, such as the one that began in late 2007, Pearle's foundational strengths promised to sustain and enhance future prospects for success.

*Dave Mote*
*Updated, Joyce Helena Brusin*

## PRINCIPAL DIVISIONS

Pearle VisionCare, Inc.

## PRINCIPAL COMPETITORS

LensCrafters, Inc.; Emerging Vision, Inc.; Eye Care Centers of America, Inc.; National Vision, Inc.; U.S. Vision, Inc.

## FURTHER READING

Barton, Christopher, "Pearle Rebuilds with Focus on Managed Care Contracts," *Dallas Business Journal*, May 17, 1996.

Bronstad, Amanda, "Obscure Laws Trigger Suits That May Send Major Eye Care Outfits Packing," *Los Angeles Business Journal*, September 15, 2003.

"California Puts a Stop to the One-stop Shop," *Optician*, September 6, 2002.

"Eyeglass Retailers Merging: Cole National Corp Buys Pearle Vision," *The Record* (Bergen County, NJ), September 26, 1996, p. B1.

Ohr, Erica, "Independents Feel Squeezed as Chains Take Over Their Turf," *Baltimore Business Journal*, October 21, 1994, p. 28.

Oram, Roderick, "GrandMet Sells Pearle Vision," *Financial Times*, September 26, 1996.

Pearle, Stanley, *Dr. Stanley Pearle: A Man of Vision*, New York: Arbor Books, 2007.

Rouvalis, Cristina, "Pearle Vision Founder Fondly Recalls Early Years Here," *Pittsburgh Post-Gazette*, April 24, 2007.

Wahlgren, Eric, "Luxottica's Smart Style," *Business Week Online*, August 11, 2004.

*Yes, Virginia, There Really Is a Dr. Pearle*, Dallas: Pearle Vision, Inc., 1994.

# PGi

---■---

**Terminus Building**
**3280 Peachtree Road Northwest**
**Atlanta, Georgia 30305**
**U.S.A.**
**Telephone: (404) 262-8400**
**Toll Free: (866) 548-3203**
**Fax: (404) 262-8540**
**Web site: http://www.pgi.com/us/en**

*Public Company*
*Incorporated:* 1991 as Premiere Technologies, Inc.
*Employees:* 2,300
*Sales:* $601.52 million (2009)
*Stock Exchanges:* New York
*Ticker Symbol:* PGI
*NAICS:* 541990 All Other Professional, Scientific, and Technical Services; 517919 Other Telecommunications

■ ■ ■

PGi (formerly Premiere Global Services, Inc.) is a global provider of audio, video, and Web meeting solutions, including conferencing, electronic fax and document delivery, and digital notifications and reminders. Founded in 1991 as a long-distance calling-card provider, it has grown and evolved in tandem with the rise in interactive digital communications. It has shifted since then from a focus on individual users to business clients ranging from small companies to multinational corporations. Business took off in the new millennium, when globalization pushed companies and other large organizations to drastically reduce in-person meetings in favor of different forms of electronic conferencing. In 2009 PGi hosted 40 million meetings with 120 million people from 60 countries attending. By 2010 its clients included over 50,000 companies, among them almost 90 percent of the *Fortune* 500. Along the way PGi released a steady stream of new tools and solutions aimed at improving organizations' ability to connect their people and interact with their clients from any location.

## A HIGH-TECH START-UP

Kentucky-born entrepreneur Boland T. Jones founded Premiere Technologies, Inc., in 1991 as a long-distance calling-card company. Over the next five years the company evolved into a rapidly growing high-tech concern, offering software that allowed people to access computers, fax machines, and the Internet using virtually any telephone. That model enabled Premiere, which had moved its operations from Florida to Georgia, to post a $1.91 million profit in 1995 and, the following year, to conduct a successful initial public offering on the NASDAQ that raised $117 million.

With that, Jones, who had also become an "angel investor" in other high-tech start-ups, set about expanding the company, both as a direct supplier of services and through wholesale licensing agreements. Acquisitions were also part of the business plan, and Premiere bought a number of companies whose products either enhanced its current offerings or helped it to expand into new areas. An especially important move was the purchase in early 2008 of Xpedite, a leading maker of

## COMPANY PERSPECTIVES

▪

At PGi, we want to revolutionize the way people interact. Our mission is to craft immersive workplaces with our communication technologies where the world goes to collaborate. We like to use words like "dynamic" and "intuitive" to describe our technologies, because as your challenges evolve, so do our products and services. We enable over 50,000 businesses to conduct 12 million meetings a month by: Accelerating productivity in your business; Simplifying communications with customers, prospects and employees; Increasing sales and marketing effectiveness; Energizing your connections.

broadcast fax and electronic messaging systems, which could provide the simultaneous distribution of documents to multiple locations.

Xpedite offered an immediate boost to Premiere's business. Other acquisitions and new products, however, were not so successful even in the heady environment of the dot-com boom. Premiere invested heavily in Orchestrate, a universal messaging service that allowed customers to hear their e-mail over the phone using a proprietary text-to-speech technology and to retrieve voice-mail messages from the computer. After two relaunches, Orchestrate still failed to take off. In 1998 its shares were trading at around $1 apiece, and Premiere announced a $20 million restructuring that included a 10 percent workforce reduction.

Among Premiere's more successful investments was WebMD, where a 9 percent stake grew in value from $3.9 million to $195 million when Healtheon Corporation bought the Internet health-care portal operator in 1999. The new capital helped Jones to stabilize Premiere (now PTEK Holdings) by paying down its short-term debt. It then made a last, unsuccessful attempt to launch Orchestrate, and in March 2000 the company set up a venture-capital unit, PTEK Ventures. PTEK committed $125 million to the unit, which took two companies public. Then, however, the tech-stock boom evaporated.

By fall 2000 PTEK had posted losses for seven consecutive quarters. Although other companies with roots in that era collapsed (including one former Premiere strategic partner, WorldCom Inc.), PTEK hung on and soon enjoyed a resurgence. It sold its retail calling-card operation as well as its phone and voice-mail services for individual clients and refocused on its

core activities of conferencing, voice messaging, and broadcast faxing for businesses. As the economy slumped, many companies wanted to save money by cutting back on travel, replacing in-person meetings with virtual meetings over the phone and Internet. The terrorist attacks against the United States on September 11, 2001, helped accelerate the trend.

### HELPING BUSINESSES TO CONNECT

By the end of 2003 PTEK was reporting 12 percent yearly growth in sales generated from more than 32,000 corporate accounts, including the majority of the *Fortune* 500. "We learned during the [stock market] boom that we needed to focus on controlling expenses and leaning down the company," Randy Salisbury, executive vice president and chief marketing officer, told Patti Bond in the *Atlanta Journal-Constitution* in May 2004. "We did that, and now our profitability is increasing at a higher rate than revenue because our business model centers around a fixed-cost structure."

Cost-control measures enabled PTEK to nearly wipe out its debt and generate substantial cash, which topped $70 million in 2004. With that, the company was able to resume expanding and rolling out new services. In the same year its acquisitions included Resource Communications Inc. and ConferenceCallServices, both conferencing providers to small and midsized businesses; and I-Media SA, a French company carrying a diversified suite of electronic messaging services. By year's end PTEK's customer base topped 46,000 corporate accounts around the world.

PTEK's non-U.S. offerings were expanding. In 2003, responding to a 45 percent surge in its international conferencing revenue, it launched VisionCast to provide easy Web access for sharing documents and slides on desktop computers, and PremiereCall Auditorium, which offered operator assistance on audio conferences for large groups. Early in 2005, announcing its intention to keep growing the business, it stretched an existing credit line with Bank of America into a four-year, $180 million facility. Soon after, it used the credit line to purchase Netspoke, a company offering an integrated collaboration platform that would enable PTEK to expand into training, sales automation, and distance learning.

The company had in 2004 rebranded itself as Premiere Global Services, Inc., to emphasize the worldwide nature of its business. The company moved its listing from the NASDAQ to the New York Stock Exchange, and it went on to sign deals with strategic partners in China and India. It also extended its reach

## KEY DATES

**1991:** Premiere Technologies, Inc., is founded in Florida principally as a long-distance calling-card company.

**1996:** After a string of acquisitions and new-product launches, company goes public on the NASDAQ.

**2003:** Now PTEK Holdings, the company achieves 12 percent yearly growth in sales, reflecting a boom in the remote conferencing business.

**2004:** Company changes its name to Premiere Global Services and moves its listing to the New York Stock Exchange.

**2009:** After further expansion, company revises revenue projections downward, reflecting economic downturn.

**2010:** Company rebrands itself as PGi.

from office-based telecommunications solutions to mobile devices. In 2005 Premiere unveiled the Mobile Office Manager for the BlackBerry, enabling mobile subscribers to receive faxes electronically and print e-mails and attachments directly from their handheld devices using any fax machine in the world.

More rollouts followed, including Fund Manager Connect, a service tailored for investment managers needing to stay in regular and frequent contact with their clients, and the Learning Communications Center, which enables continuing education and eLearning providers to enroll, evaluate, accredit, and track participation in online education programs. In August 2008 Premiere added another service tailored to a particular industry when it purchased Soundpath Conferencing Services LLC, which provided conferencing services to the legal profession.

## ADAPTING TO NEW TECHNOLOGIES

By then, an economic downturn and crashing financial markets were taking a toll on Premiere's corporate clients. A month later the company announced it was restating its financial reports for 2007 to reflect a change in the fair value of interest rate swap agreements that were part of a revolving credit facility it entered into that year. "Our business momentum remains solid in the midst of continuing global economic uncertainty," Jones said in a press release dated November 9, 2009. "We continue to anticipate consolidated revenues in 2008 will increase at least 13 percent from 2007 totals

and that diluted EPS will increase at least 20 percent this year."

Premiere continued to augment its solutions package to keep up with trends in computing. In 2009 it launched PGiCOS e-mail, an Internet-based, "cloud computing" e-mail delivery platform for high-volume e-mail senders. Shortly thereafter, it unveiled PGi Mobile, a new application enabling users to host and manage virtual meetings directly from their iPhones. Nevertheless, the weakened economy, along with a weakening dollar, prompted the company in September to revise its financial outlook for the year, anticipating $595 million to $605 million in revenues, down from $620.4 million in 2008 (the final figure, released in the following February, was $601.52 million).

In November Premiere sold its e-mail marketing solution, Campaign Accelerator, as the company moved toward a tighter focus on its core customer audience. "Through our work to better understand Premiere Global customers, we recognize that our true strength lies in our focus on the IT buyer, IT challenges, and IT solutions," Jackie Yeaney, chief marketing officer, said in the November 9, 2009, press release.

The company's latest rebranding, as PGi, followed in January 2010, reflecting a marketing focus on responding to people's need to connect easily and affordably. That included regrouping its comprehensive package, Premiere Global Communications Operating Systems, into two enhanced solution sets: PGiMeet, which included conferencing and collaborations services, and PgiSend, its advanced messaging services.

The company's most important upcoming initiative was the launch of a new meeting platform, iMeet. In PGi's 2009 annual report, Jones said the platform combined Web, audio, and video conferencing in a single, browser-based application designed to aid any small business, enterprise customer, or individual. "iMeet is the culmination of our decades of experience and expertise in the collaboration space," Jones said, anticipating a release of the application in late 2010.

*Eric Laursen*

## PRINCIPAL SUBSIDIARIES

American Teleconferencing Services, Ltd.; Budget Conferencing Inc. (Canada); Clarinet, Inc.; Communications Network Enhancement Inc.; Enterprise Care Teleconferencing (Asia) Pty Ltd. (Australia); iMeet, Inc.; Intellivoice Communications, LLC; NetConnect Conferencing Inc. (Canada); NetConnect Systems Ltd. (UK); NetConnect Systems GmbH (Germany);

Netspoke, Inc.; Premiere Communications, Inc.; PCI Network Services, Inc.; Premiere Conferencing E.U.R.L. (France); Premiere Conferencing GmbH (Germany); Premiere Conferencing Limited (New Zealand); Premiere Conferencing Pte. Ltd. (Singapore); Premiere Conferencing Pty Limited (Australia); Premiere Conferencing (Canada) Limited; Premiere Conferencing (Hong Kong) Limited; Premiere Conferencing (Ireland) Limited; Premiere Conferencing (Japan), Inc.; Premiere Conferencing (UK) Limited; Premiere Conferencing Networks, Inc.; Premiere Global Services GmbH (Germany); Premiere Global Services Denmark ASP; Premiere Global Services Finland OY; Premiere Global Services International S.a.r.l. (Luxembourg); Premiere Global Services Norway AS; Premiere Global Services Sweden AB; Premiere Global Services (UK) Limited; Ptek, Inc.; Ptek Investors I LLC; PTEK Services, Inc.; Ptek Ventures I LLC; RCI Acquisition Corp.; Voice-Tel Enterprises, LLC; Voice-Tel Pty Ltd. (Australia); Xpedite, Inc. (Japan); Xpedite, Ltd. (Korea); Xpedite Network Services, Inc.; Xpedite Systems Limited (Hong Kong); Xpedite Systems Inc. (Malaysia) Sdn. Bhd.; Xpedite Systems AG (Switzerland); Xpedite Systems Holdings (UK) Limited; Xpedite Systems, LLC; Xpedite Systems Limited (New Zealand); Xpedite Systems Participation E.U.R.L. (France); Xpedite Systems Pte. Ltd. (Singapore); Xpedite Systems Pty Limited (Australia).

## PRINCIPAL COMPETITORS

ACT Teleconferencing, Inc.; Adobe Systems Inc.; Arkadin, Inc.; AT&T Inc.; BT Group plc; Cisco Systems, Inc.; Citrix Systems, Inc.; EasyLink Services International Corporation; Global Crossing Ltd.; International Business Machines Corporation; j2 Global Communications, Inc.; Microsoft Corporation; Oracle Corporation; Protus IP Solutions; Saba Software, Inc.; Varolii Corporation; Verizon Communications Inc.; West Corporation; Westell Technologies, Inc.

## FURTHER READING

Bond, Patti, "PTEK Holdings: Tough Choices in Past Set Stage for Stellar '03," *Atlanta Journal-Constitution*, May 23, 2004.

Hubbard, Caroline, "Maverick Head of Atlanta-Based Tech Company Remains Controversial," *Atlanta Journal-Constitution*, October 11, 2000.

PGi, "Mansell Group Acquires Campaign Accelerator Email Marketing Business from Premiere Global Services," press release, November 9, 2009.

PGi, "Premiere Global Enters Fast-Growing Chinese Market," press release, January 8, 2008.

PGi, "Premiere Global Services Launches New PGi Brand," press release, January 25, 2010.

PGi, "Premiere Global Services Provides Revised 2009 Financial Outlook Due to Continuing Impact of Global Economy and Higher Unemployment," press release, September 15, 2009.

PGi, "Tata Communications and Premiere Global Services Sign License Agreement to Launch New Services in India," press release, May 15, 2008.

"Premiere Global Services Introduces Mobile Document Management Solution for Blackberry," Business Wire, May 25, 2005.

"Premiere Global Services to Offer Fully Integrated Conferencing and Collaboration Solutions for Investor Relations and Crisis Management," M2 Presswire, July 6, 2005.

Van Dusen, Christine, and Caroline Wilbert, "The Show Must Go On: A Look at Atlanta's One-Time High-Tech Superstars, and What They're Up to Now," *Atlanta Journal-Constitution*, June 20, 2004.

# PHOENIX

*Where Excellence Grows®*

# The Phoenix Companies, Inc.

---

1 American Row
Hartford, Connecticut 06102-5056
U.S.A.
Telephone: (860) 403-5000
Toll Free: (800) 628-1936
Fax: (860) 403-5534
Web site: http://www.phoenixwm.com

*Public Company*
*Founded:* 1851
*Incorporated:* 2000
*Employees:* 1,100
*Sales:* $2.02 billion (2009)
*Total Assets:* $24.59 billion (2009)
*Stock Exchanges:* New York
*Ticker Symbol:* PNX
*NAICS:* 524113 Direct Life Insurance Carriers; 551112
Offices of Other Holding Companies

■ ■ ■

The Phoenix Companies, Inc., founded in 1851 and headquartered in Hartford, Connecticut, provides life insurance, annuities, and alternative retirement products that are primarily targeted at wealthy individuals and institutions. It markets its products through a nationwide network of banks, insurance companies, financial planners, and brokers and also offers underwriting, mortality management, distribution, and support services.

## FROM TWO BEGINNINGS: 19TH CENTURY

The current Phoenix Companies traces its origins to two 19th-century insurance companies, the American Temperance Life Insurance Company and Home Life Insurance Company. In 1851 the American Temperance Life Insurance Company was founded in Hartford, Connecticut, as a part-mutual, part-stock corporation. The organization, created by a group of business, civic, and religious leaders, provided insurance to members of temperance lodges. The company was based on the expectation that abstention from alcohol would lead to low mortality rates, and the insurers paid only three claims in the first two years and sold more than 900 policies. However, by 1861 the company realized that in order to continue in business it would have to stop restricting its client base to non-drinkers. The company name was changed to Phoenix Mutual Life Insurance Company (probably based on the mythological associations with renewal) and eliminated abstention as a requirement for purchasing insurance.

At about the same time, in 1860 in Brooklyn, New York, the Home Life Insurance Company, organized as a stock company, was founded to provide individual life insurance and annuities. With initial assets of $157,878, it was the first insurer authorized to do business in New York State by the fledgling New York Insurance Department.

After the Civil War numerous life insurance companies were formed to take advantage of the newly popular industry. However, an economic depression and increased competition led to almost 100 businesses closing between 1868 and 1877, including 32 that defaulted on their policyholders. Both Phoenix Mutual and Home Life were able to survive, although Home Life, threatened with a takeover, chose a unique way to retain its stockholder loyalty: it paid its dividends in gold. In 1889 Phoenix Mutual converted its corporate structure to become a fully mutual organization, which allowed policyholders unable to own stock to share in the company profits.

## INNOVATION AND EXCELLENCE: TURN OF THE 20TH CENTURY

Home Life, with steadily increasing sales and assets, had operated a branch office in Manhattan since 1866. In 1892 it held a competition for the plan of its new corporate headquarters to be located on lower Broadway. The resulting building, designed by Pierre LeBrun and completed in 1894, was an early steel-skeleton-framed skyscraper and, for a time, was the world's tallest building. It remains a designated New York City landmark.

Meanwhile, Phoenix Mutual was making its own innovative changes. In 1901 Phoenix Mutual introduced *The Field*, a pioneering instrument in corporate communications and among the first newsletters created for insurance agents. Shortly afterwards, in 1906, Phoenix Mutual published "A Prospectus and Ten Lessons upon Life Insurance," producing the first training course for insurance agents. Then, in 1912, the company launched a direct-mail advertising campaign. It was the first insurance organization to use this now widespread sales strategy.

During the 1920s Phoenix Mutual increased its advertising presence, using a promotion in *Literary Digest* to endorse the importance of having life insurance, followed by a magazine campaign to encourage retirement income planning. Its "smiling fisherman" print ad was featured in the book *The 100 Greatest Advertisements 1852–1958* by advertising industry historian Julian Lewis Watkins. The advertising copy, addressed "to men who want to quit work one day," touted the idea that these men, "by following a simple,

definite plan, can provide for themselves in later years *a guaranteed income they cannot outlive.*"

Home Life, which had reorganized in 1916 as a mutual company, also increased its marketing efforts. It created an innovative program that anticipated the now commonplace positioning of insurance agents as financial advisers. Its Planned Estates strategy helped the business achieve a 60 percent growth rate during the 1930s, despite the difficulties of the Great Depression.

## CONTINUED GROWTH THROUGH NEW PRODUCTS: MID-20TH CENTURY

Phoenix, like Home Life decades earlier, was also interested in architectural excellence. The company commissioned the renowned architect Max Abramovitz, known for such works as the United Nations Headquarters and Lincoln Center in New York City, to design its corporate headquarters in Hartford in the early 1960s. Known as the Boat Building, the Phoenix headquarters is a unique two-sided glass tower that was completed in 1963 and is considered a noteworthy example of mid-20th century modernist architecture. It was placed on the National Registry of Historic Places in 2005.

During this period Phoenix began offering discounted products to specific market segments. In 1955, recognizing the lower mortality rates for women in its underwriting calculations, Phoenix Mutual was the first insurance company to reduce the cost of life insurance premiums for women. In 1967, only three years after the Surgeon General of the United States reported that smoking could be hazardous to health, Phoenix Mutual became the first insurance company to offer discounted rates to nonsmokers.

In 1982 Phoenix Mutual introduced another product innovation with survivorship policies, a type of life insurance in which two or more lives (usually spouses or partners) are insured on one policy. Because the premiums are much lower for the combined policy than they would be for separate policies, survivorship policies soon became one of the company's premier offerings used in estate planning or to insure continuation of a business.

## MUTUAL MERGERS: MOVING INTO THE 21ST CENTURY

The U.S. insurance industry, marked by poor investments in real estate and junk bonds, and the regulatory seizure of several large insurance companies, experienced a troubled year in 1991. In December of that year, the Phoenix Mutual Life Insurance Company and Home

Life Insurance Company announced that they were proposing the first merger between two major carriers. The new organization would be called Phoenix Home Life Mutual Insurance Company. It would be the country's 13th largest mutual life insurance company with 700,000 policyholders.

Although the new company emphasized that the merger was not a response to financial problems, both companies had significant problematic real estate holdings, and the move was expected to save $70 million per year. The company planned a reduction of almost 1,000 employees and a consolidation of their computer centers. To get regulatory consent for this unique deal, the company agreed to make New York the company's legal home, while retaining most of its employee positions in Connecticut. The merger was approved in June 1992. Two of the top three executives of the new organization had been executive managers at Phoenix Mutual.

In 1995 Phoenix Home Life Mutual, with a small but successful investment management subsidiary called Phoenix Securities Group, decided to merge those operations with another profitable company, the Duff and Phelps Corporation. The new company, Phoenix Duff and Phelps (later Phoenix Investment Partners), transformed two small investment firms into one of the nation's 20 largest asset management firms, serving both individual and institutional accounts.

By the beginning of 1997, the new organization had filed a trademark for the Phoenix Duff and Phelps Affluent Investor Program, signaling Phoenix Home Life Mutual's growing emphasis on the high-end market. After a reinsurance debacle that involved Phoenix Home Life Mutual's participation in a reinsurance pool managed by the discredited Unicover, the company sold its reinsurance business (buying policies from other insurers

for a share of the premiums) to focus on its primary businesses: insurance, retirement programs, and investment management. By 2001 more than 50 percent of Phoenix Home Life Mutual's products concentrated on the high-net-worth segment of the insurance and investment business.

## REORGANIZING AS A PUBLIC COMPANY: 2001–08

In April 2001 Phoenix Home Life Mutual policyholders voted to convert the mutual insurance company to a publicly traded stock corporation. Policyholders were compensated through shares, cash, and policy benefits. On June 20 the re-named Phoenix Life Insurance Company was made a wholly owned subsidiary of The Phoenix Companies, Inc., which was listed on the New York Stock Exchange with an initial price of $17.50 per share. This restructuring was initiated to give the company greater access to cash through selling shares. Demutualization was also seen as a way for Phoenix to be a more aggressive competitor for an aging and affluent client base and to focus on increasing its share of the wealth management market.

Phoenix then launched a program with State Farm Insurance, a property and casualty insurer, marketing Phoenix wealth management services through State Farm agents. The alliance targeted those with assets of at least $1 million and aimed to increase the Phoenix distribution network for insurance, retirement, and estate planning services, while supporting State Farm's expansion into wealth management.

By 2008, however, despite its focused marketing efforts, increasing losses required Phoenix to restructure. In December 2008 Phoenix implemented a spin-off of its unprofitable asset management operations, Phoenix Investment Partners, now called Virtus Investment Partners. Phoenix stockholders received one share of Virtus stock (traded on the NASDAQ) for every 20 shares of Phoenix stock held. According to *Market Watch* (December 14, 2008), Dona Young, then Phoenix CEO, said that the move would clarify the valuation of both Phoenix and Virtus and enable each to focus on its own business and opportunities. Phoenix was once again primarily an insurance and annuity organization.

## FACING DIFFICULTIES: 2009–10

The company's troubles continued, however, and Phoenix posted quarterly losses throughout 2009. Phoenix had multiple rating downgrades from insurance analysts, and major distributors (including State Farm Insurance) suspended sales of Phoenix products.

Economies, including employee layoffs and reducing the size of the board of directors, helped to narrow the massive losses. A corporate leadership change was made in April, when James D. Wehr replaced Young as president and CEO. By the third quarter of 2009, the company had reduced its losses from $339.5 million in the third quarter of 2008 to $26.6 million in the third quarter of 2009.

Concentrating on increasing distribution for its core products, Phoenix introduced a new unit providing life insurance consultation services to financial advisers. Saybrus Partners (the name comes from a Gaelic word meaning wealth) began with an agreement with the brokerage firm Edward D. Jones & Co., and Phoenix planned on increasing its relationships with banks, brokerage firms and financial advisers.

In January 2010 Phoenix continued its restructuring through an agreement to sell PFG Holdings, a private placement insurance business specializing in custom policies for wealthy clients, to Tiptree Financial Partners. Phoenix had already sold off all its international interests, including an Argentine subsidiary and a British asset management firm. By the first quarter of 2010, Phoenix reported a net income of $13.7 million. At that time Wehr stated: "Our first quarter results demonstrate meaningful progress on the strategic goals we established a year ago," Relying on an expansion of its private label products, new retirement options, and improvement in its distribution channels, Phoenix planned to rise again.

*Grace Murphy*

## PRINCIPAL SUBSIDIARIES

PHL Variable Insurance Company; Phoenix Investment Management Company; Phoenix Investment Partners, Ltd.; Phoenix Life Insurance Company; PM Holdings, Inc.

## PRINCIPAL COMPETITORS

AEGON Americas; American International Group, Inc.; The Hartford Financial Services Group, Inc.; Massachusetts Mutual Life Insurance Company; Metropolitan Life Insurance Company; New York Life Insurance Company; The Northwestern Mutual Life Insurance Company; Prudential Financial. Inc..

## FURTHER READING

Block, Donna, "Phoenix Holders OK Demutualization," *Daily Deal (New York, NY)*, April 5, 2001.

"GE Capital to Buy Phoenix Home's Life Reinsurance Unit," *New York Times*, May 20, 1999.

Levick, Diane, "Phoenix Cos. Cuts 75 Hartford Jobs, They Won't Be the Last," *Hartford Courant*, April 22, 2009.

Lysiak, Fran, "State Farm Suspends Sales of Phoenix's Life Insurance, Annuities," *A.M. Best Newswire*, March 4, 2009.

Mercado, Darla, "After Sales Drought, Phoenix Creates Its Own Distributor; Firm Will Also Send Wealth Managers to Work with Edward Jones Reps," *Investment News*, November 9, 2009.

"New York Lets Insurers Join Forces," *New York Times*, June 18, 1992.

"Phoenix Cos. to Spin Off Asset-Management Unit, Phoenix Investment Partners," *Financial Wire*, February 8, 2008.

Reich-Hale, David, "Wealth Management? State Farm Is There Too Now," *American Banker*, April 9, 2001.

Thomas, Trevor, "Confidence Rising, the Affluent Are Warming to Advisors: Phoenix Finds Wealthy Clients' Optimism Is Breaking though Recession Blues," *National Underwriter Life & Health*, May 2010.

# PSS World Medical, Inc.

4345 Southpoint Boulevard
Jacksonville, Florida 32216
U.S.A.
Telephone: (904) 332-3000
Fax: (904) 332-3395
Web site: http://www.pssworldmedical.com

*Public Company*
*Incorporated:* 1983
*Employees:* 3,680
*Sales:* $1.95 billion (2009)
*Stock Exchanges:* NASDAQ
*Ticker Symbol:* PSSI
*NAICS:* 423450 Medical, Dental, and Hospital Equipment and Supplies Merchant Wholesalers

■ ■ ■

Based in Jacksonville, Florida, PSS World Medical, Inc., is the largest supplier of medical products to physician offices, long-term care and assisted living facilities, and home health and hospice providers in the United States. The company conducts business through two operating segments. Physician Sales and Service, Inc., serves the needs of physician offices. Gulf South Medical Supply, Inc., addresses the supply needs of long-term care, assisted living, and hospice facilities, as well as home health providers. Physician Sales and Service operates 28 service centers that distribute medical supplies to approximately 100,000 customers spread throughout all 50 states. Gulf South Medical operates 14 service centers and distributes over 20,000 products in all 50

states. Total sales for PSS World Medical reached $1.9 billion in 2009.

## PATRICK KELLY LEADS A TRIO OF FOUNDERS

Company founder Patrick Kelly grew up in a Richmond, Virginia, boys' home. His experience with both forgiving and strict guardians helped him to develop a penchant for risk taking, which he brought to PSS. "People here will never get in trouble for making a mistake," he told *Inc.* magazine in 1995. He also gained experience in the U.S. Army, where he issued weapons, and the practice of delegating decision making to young people impressed Kelly. These experiences became vital to his own training and recruiting methods.

With the help of an investor, Kelly, then in his mid-30s, founded PSS in the spring of 1983 in Jacksonville, Florida, with two partners, Bill Riddell, who served as executive vice president for sales and marketing, and Clyde Young. Kelly, Riddell, and Young had worked previously as sales representatives at another medical supply business. To facilitate decision making, Kelly received 31 percent ownership while Riddell, Young, and another owner each received 23 percent.

Physician offices and medical clinics have limited storage capacity and are prone to occasional shortages of critical supplies. To differentiate itself, PSS began to offer next-day delivery of most items instead of the usual wait of three to four days. This practice allowed PSS to charge premium prices, which financed technological improvements in its distribution and sales departments.

## COMPANY PERSPECTIVES

Our Purpose: Improving healthcare in America through innovative solutions.

Our Mission: Through our independence we will grow at twice the growth rate in new and existing markets. We will accomplish this by achieving superior customer satisfaction and profitability.

Our Unique Culture: From our humble beginnings in 1983 to the recent accolades garnered by the Company, the unique culture of PSS World Medical is the glue that holds us together. Not only do we take care of each other, we are active citizens in the communities in which we serve, logging thousands of hours each year in both company-organized and individual charitable involvement.

For example, competitors relied on commercial shipping companies but PSS bought its own trucks.

### MISSION AND INNOVATION

Kelly's initial goal was to make the same money at PSS as he had at his previous job. The company's growth in these years was encouraging but it did not become phenomenal until, in 1988, Kelly was inspired by a motivational speaker to set a bold goal for PSS. Its mission: to become the first national physician supply company in a field of regional players. The goal was heralded on banners and stationery and in conversation. The ambitious statement encouraged and emboldened the company's young staff. In 1987 PSS achieved sales of $13 million from its five Florida-based branches, but sales surged to $31 million in 1989 from 10 branches. In 1991 there were 32 branch offices.

The company was quick to use new information technology to improve service. In 1993 a new wireless data-transmission system supplied by RAM Mobile Data and Compaq Concerto laptop computers was implemented at a cost of $1.5 million. Nevertheless, noted the company's information technology vice president, Darlene Kelly (not related to Patrick Kelly), "the investment more than paid for itself in less than a year." Sales for the average representative increased roughly $10,000 each month, grossing $3,000 for the company. The system was first used to input orders from the field electronically, opening the possibility of same-day delivery for orders received by 11:00 a.m.

while increasing the time available for sales. Administrative work at the service center was also greatly reduced.

By 1995 PSS was boasting a same-day fill rate on 94 percent of items carried, or 16,000 products. The Instant Customer Order Network (ICON) enabled a decentralized approach at PSS, empowering sales representatives to make pricing decisions in the field. ICON was later upgraded to include instantly accessible pricing and usage histories, which allowed representatives to offer physicians timely, informed advice on budget and inventory management. Manufacturers' equipment catalogs and cost analyses were also immediately available.

### SALES REPS MAKE THE DIFFERENCE

Sales representatives, called "PSSers," were more than necessary to bring customers the benefits of this service and technology. Since the beginning Patrick Kelly had always practiced careful management of his staff. Experienced professionals had been difficult to acquire because of the company's short history. Nevertheless, the company developed a successful recruiting and training program for its young sales staff, who in 1995 averaged 27 years of age.

Kelly and his colleagues visited colleges, searching for candidates with ambition and drive rather than experience. Young team members brought many advantages to growth-oriented PSS. With fewer family connections, they could work longer hours and accept relocation to new facilities. They were also more amenable to performance-oriented compensation. True to his military background, Kelly promoted from within and not necessarily by seniority. A thinning of the top ranks through expansion created a considerable demand for new high-level managers, all either groomed from within or brought in through mergers. The wide-open possibilities for advancement in exchange for hard work seemed quite attractive to the type of individual Kelly sought. In return for the efforts laid out by his staff, Kelly, who disdained bureaucracy, promised to place no barriers on their potential for success.

### INVESTMENTS IN TRAINING

PSS trainees learned various areas of the company's operations: working in warehouses, making deliveries, studying sales techniques, and learning about the products. Eventually, the so-called PSS University was established in Jacksonville, Florida. After 16 weeks the trainees who made it through the first phase (about 90 percent of those who signed up) spent an intense week

## KEY DATES

**1983:** Patrick Kelly cofounds Physician Sales and Service, Inc. (PSS).
**1989:** Venture-capital firm Tullis-Dickerson & Co. purchases one-fifth of PSS.
**1993:** Network Plus buyer's club is established.
**1994:** PSS has its initial public stock offering.
**1995:** PSS acquires Taylor Medical.
**1996:** New subsidiary, WorldMed, Inc., is established.
**1997:** Diagnostic Imaging, Inc., becomes PSS subsidiary.
**1998:** Name of parent company is changed to PSS World Medical, Inc.
**2000:** Company founder and CEO Kelly resigns; David A. Smith is named president of PSS World Medical.
**2002:** Platinum Equity LLC purchases Diagnostic Imaging, Inc.; Smith is named CEO of PSS World Medical.
**2010:** President and CEO Smith resigns after 10 years and is replaced by former COO Gary Corless.

The job was demanding. In 1995 the average representative called on 200 clients. PSS salespeople were trained to keep clients informed of emerging developments in products and to develop consulting relationships that naturally would increase their persuasiveness in selling products. Incentives were impressive; every type of employee at PSS had the possibility of earning a bonus, which could be as much as several thousand dollars, based on branch profit rankings. To increase motivation, company numbers, including daily sales reports and monthly profit-and-loss statements, were kept highly visible. Kelly even took to passing out $20 bills during visits to branches, rewarding those who correctly answered a randomly chosen question from a book of 100 work-related questions. Similarly, surprise "Blue Ribbon" tours twice a year rated each branch on 100 standards for doing business.

The company needed a constant supply of leadership talent but found that promoting the best salespeople to management resulted in high turnover. Kelly's solution was to institute Creativity Week, a meeting aboard Kelly's boat during which prospective leaders read management texts such as Stephen Covey's *The Seven Habits of Highly Effective People* and discussed hypothetical cases. During the cruise, additional students were picked up each day, and the original three became mentors. Starting in 1987 all PSS managers went through the program.

studying the industry and PSS sales techniques. Full days in class (punctuated by written tests, role playing, and video critiques) were followed by dinner lectures emphasizing important points. PSS was eager to invest heavily in training, spending approximately $10,000 to $25,000 per salesperson, in order to foster phenomenal growth. The trainees reduced the need for full-time warehouse and customer-service employees.

Attrition in the training program reached 30 percent before the PSS Sales Interview Guide was drafted in 1989. Like the previous hiring strategy, it emphasized attitudes and behavior rather than experience. Qualities sought in salespeople were aggressiveness and energy. The sales-training dropout rate fell to 10 percent after the more highly selective interview guidelines were implemented; job offers were made to only 70 candidates out of 800 who applied in 1990. Cash incentives were a part of the process for those who did the hiring: Branch managers received $2,000 for each successfully trained candidate. Once hired and successfully trained, PSSers tended to remain loyal. In 1989 turnover was only 5 percent. Providing each employee a stake in the company's success was critical to this stability.

### SUSTAINED PERFORMANCE

PSS organized many recreational activities to motivate its troops and sustain an environment of expectancy. Regional annual picnics treated staff to two or three days at a distant resort. The interbranch volleyball tournament that began at these picnics culminated in playoffs at the national sales meeting, which also featured golf, and there were half-day trips for corporate staff. The company's focus on performance was enlivened by the PSS Challenge, which brought monthly performance meetings into recreational settings such as bowling alleys and ballparks. An integral part of the PSS Challenge was a game show-style contest in which teams tested their knowledge of a particular business subject. PSS also took care of advertising and promotion in-house, an approach that helped give its branch managers and sales representatives a feeling of ownership toward sales promotions.

Although the concentration on profits helped buffer the company against the potential drawbacks of rapid growth, it consistently ran into problems with nervous banks, which urged the company to build up more equity and to contain its sales growth. At least five banks dropped PSS until Kelly increased the company's equity. In 1983 his 21 employees invested $50,000 in PSS; the founding partners added $100,000. In 1995 an employee stock ownership plan (ESOP) owned one-fifth of the company's stock, valued at approximately $46 million, and offered pretax payroll deductions and matching company contributions. The ESOP was reportedly responsible for creating 40 millionaires. An employee stock-purchase plan intended for the after-tax sale of stock was added later, along with stock-option incentives. The venture-capital firm of Tullis-Dickerson & Co. bought one-fifth of PSS in 1989, and in 1994 its initial public offering at $11 per share raised almost $16 million, lowering its debt-to-equity ratio to around 1:1.

The PSS of the mid-1990s continued to boast a high level of customer responsiveness, featuring same-day service. PSS asked for no minimum order and provided simple statements free of hidden handling charges. Doctors in the United States became much more price-conscious after President Bill Clinton's health-care reform efforts in 1993. PSS responded by dropping prices on popular items and establishing a "comprehensive savings plan," Network Plus, a type of buyer's club that offered hassle-free credit and lower prices. Profits suffered with the new emphasis on lower costs but eventually market share increased, and lower expenses helped recover the difference.

The company also expanded its relationship with its clients, offering biomedical equipment repair and consulting services in the areas of space planning, laboratory design, federal safety regulation compliance, inventory management, financial services, and sterilization, sanitation, and infection control. Sales reached $169.7 million in 1994, an increase of more than 250 percent over 1990. Each sales representative wrote $468,000 in sales, an increase of nearly 40 percent since 1990. New branches typically became profitable within 18 months and eventually earned 8 percent profit on sales, which were increasing 22 percent per year at the average branch.

## ACQUISITIONS ADD TO VALUE

In 1995 sales reached $236.19 million before the acquisition of Taylor Medical, Inc., which PSS bought for $65 million. The privately owned company, based in Beaumont, Texas, was PSS's third-largest competitor, with 18,000 customers in 23 states and annual revenues of $122 million. At the time, PSS served 57,000 medical offices in 48 states with its existing 56 service centers. The deal also gave PSS 175 sales representatives, increasing its total to 620. PSS had previously acquired Lancet Medical Ltd. of St. Louis, where PSS had a service center. Lancet's 1994 sales were worth $1.5 million. PSS also signed an exclusive distribution agree-

ment with Abbott Laboratories to distribute its Physician Office Laboratory line of diagnostic equipment. This was projected to bring PSS $65 million the first year, and $100 million the next.

Around the same time as it acquired Taylor Medical, PSS also acquired two smaller physician distributors: Wasserott Medical Services, Inc., with two service centers in Pennsylvania, and Tolin Medical Supply Company, with a single service center in Utah. Financial terms of the acquisition were not released.

In 1996 PSS established a new subsidiary, WorldMed, Inc., to oversee foreign operations and to distribute medical supplies to nonphysician markets, such as hospitals, veterinarians, and dentists. In late 1996 the new subsidiary acquired the German medical distributor Franz GmbH, a supplier of products and services to physician offices, hospitals, and laboratories.

In a September 1996 interview for *Inc.* magazine, the company founder and CEO, Kelly, described how he founded the first national-level medical-supply company. "I didn't choose to become an entrepreneur," reported Kelly. "I got fired and started a company in order to earn a living. I had to learn to be a CEO." Kelly went on to recall how he encouraged his staff to ask questions and participate at staff meetings by paying them for each question, and how he reduced the bureaucracy of running a large company by limiting the number of memos employees were required to read each month.

## DIAGNOSTIC IMAGING ADDED

In early 1997 PSS completed an especially important transaction when it purchased Diagnostic Imaging, Inc., a distributor of radiological equipment and supplies. The company operated 13 sales locations in 5 southeastern states. Almost immediately the new PSS subsidiary began acquiring similar companies to expand its reach outside its home region. In July 1997 Diagnostic Imaging purchased General X-ray, Inc., a midwestern distributor of radiological supplies and equipment whose most recent annual sales totaled $76 million.

Other 1997 acquisitions swiftly followed, including an August purchase of S&W X-ray, Inc., of Rochester, New York, for an undisclosed amount. S&W had reported revenues of $73 million for its most recent fiscal year. Single acquisitions of a number of other companies followed in 1998. In March 1999 Diagnostic Imaging acquired four additional companies in one month, including two in California, one in New York, and another in Florida. In July of the same year, the PSS subsidiary expanded further when it acquired another four new companies, including ones in New York, Wisconsin, and Arizona.

In early 1998 PSS completed another important acquisition when it purchased the publicly held company Gulf South Medical Supply, Inc., in a stock deal estimated at $570.5 million. Gulf South Medical specialized in the delivery of services and products to the nursing-home and assisted-living industry. The increasing diversification of PSS and its expansion from an original focus on serving the needs of physicians in private practice was reflected in the March 1998 decision by PSS stockholders to approve a name change for the company. Physician Sales and Service became PSS World Medical, Inc. Physician Sales and Service; Gulf South Medical Supply, Inc.; and Diagnostic Imaging, Inc., all became subsidiaries of the parent company PSS World Medical.

In October 2000 Kelly resigned as chairman and CEO of PSS World Medical. His resignation followed significant decreases in the price of stock and the failure of Fisher Scientific International, Inc., to follow through on its planned acquisition of PSS. David A. Smith, executive vice president and chief financial officer, became the company president. Management of the company passed to Smith and the three heads of PSS World Medical's subsidiaries: Douglas J. Harper of Physician Sales and Service, Inc.; Kirk A. Zambetti of Diagnostic Imaging, Inc.; and Gary A. Corless of Gulf South Medical Supply, Inc.

In December 2000 Smith announced to stockholders that PSS would forgo any investigation of other merger opportunities and instead concentrate on building up its profits. According to a December 12, 2000, article in the *Florida Times-Union*, all three PSS subsidiaries had suffered financial setbacks during the previous fiscal year. Physician Sales and Service, Inc., lost $35 million in sales because of a product recall from its largest supplier, Abbott Laboratories. Diagnostic Imaging, Inc., lost $52 million in sales because of manufacturing problems at its largest supplier, Trex Medical Corporation. Finally, Gulf South Medical Supply, Inc., lost revenue because of changes in the nursing home industry.

## DIVESTITURES AND NEW PROFITS

PSS divested itself of one of its subsidiaries in November 2002 when Platinum Equity LLC, a Los Angeles-based global acquisitions firm, purchased Diagnostic Imaging, Inc., for $116 million. In its last fiscal year with PSS, the radiological supplier reported revenues of $712 million and employed 213 people in Jacksonville, Florida,

along with several hundred others around the country. During 2002 Smith, who was already president of PSS World Medical, was named chief executive officer of the company.

In August 2004 a *Business Week* article on PSS World Medical reported the company's total annual sales had reached $1.35 billion. Principal competitors McKesson Medical-Surgical, Inc., and Cardinal Health, Inc., were said to be interested in acquiring the company, whose stock price had reached $9.43 a share. President and CEO Smith stated in the article that although he had received informal acquisition offers, he would not seriously entertain any offers until he had built up the company's stock price.

In November 2004, through its subsidiary Gulf South Medical Supply, PSS acquired Associated Medical Products, an Indianapolis-based supplier of products and services to the elder-care industry.

In March 2006 the Physician Sales and Services subsidiary of PSS World Medical reached $1 billion in annual sales on its own. Chief Operating Officer Corless, a veteran of 16 years with the company, said in a press release published in *Business Wire* on March 10: "I remember celebrating our first $3 million month. Now we hit the $3 million mark daily between 8 a.m. and 2 p.m., which makes for a very different business to lead, manage and grow. However, the core principles of our success are the very same—know your customer better than everyone else and meet their needs before everyone else."

In August 2007 PSS paid $22.5 million to acquire 5 percent of Athenahealth, a Massachusetts-based provider of Internet-based business services and medical records technology to physician practices. The acquisition reflected increasing interest nationwide in electronic health records and Web-based technology that could speedily implement evolving industry requirements and government mandates. In March 2008 PSS sold a portion of the 1.5 million shares it had originally purchased in Athenahealth, but PSS reaffirmed its commitment to marketing Athenahealth's innovative products to the physician market.

PSS acquired the Washington-based company Cascade Medical Supply, Inc., a distributor of supplies covered by Medicare Part B and Medicaid to skilled-nursing and assisted-living facilities in the Pacific Northwest, in June 2008. The purchase offered opportunities for PSS to extend its Medicare billing services into an additional region and to offer equipment and supplies to an expanded elder-care market.

## RECOGNITION FOR ACHIEVEMENTS

In 2008 and 2009 PSS received significant recognition for its sustained growth and business achievements. The company was named to the *Forbes* Platinum 400, a list honoring the Best Big Companies in America, in 2008. The following year the same publication named PSS to its list of the Top 100 Most Trustworthy Companies. Also in 2009, for the third straight year, *Fortune* magazine named PSS World Medical to its list of Most Admired Companies.

PSS World Medical ended 2009 with its highest stock price ever, $22.89 a share. In March 2010 Smith stepped down after a decade as PSS World Medical president and CEO. Longtime company executive and former COO Corless succeeded him as president and CEO, and Delores P. Kesler succeeded Smith as chair of the PSS World Medical board of directors.

As it entered the second decade of the 21st century, PSS World Medical continued to do what had served it well since its founding as Physician Sales and Service in 1983. Its successful strategies included a focused and differentiated approach to serving both longtime and newly acquired customers, a well-prepared sales force responsive to customer needs, carefully maintained relationships with key manufacturers, receptivity to innovative ideas, and a company-wide culture of performance.

*Frederick C. Ingram*
*Updated, Joyce Helena Brusin*

## PRINCIPAL SUBSIDIARIES

Physician Sales and Service, Inc.; Gulf South Medical Supply, Inc.

## PRINCIPAL COMPETITORS

Cardinal Health, Inc.; Henry Schein, Inc.; McKesson Medical-Surgical, Inc.; Owens & Minor, Inc.

## FURTHER READING

Basch, Mark, "Buyer to Merge Medical Imaging Firms; Ex-PSS Subsidiary Is Part of New Deal," *Florida Times-Union*, November 22, 2002, p. D1.

"Focus Now on Profits, Not Merger, for PSS," *Florida Times-Union*, December 12, 2000, p. F1.

———, "Founder of Jacksonville, Florida Medical Supplies Company Resigns as CEO," *Florida Times-Union*, October 4, 2000.

"Best Performance by a Stand-Up CEO," *Inc.*, September 1996, p. 12.

Case, John, "The 10 Commandments of Hypergrowth," *Inc.*, October 1995, pp. 32–44.

Kelly, Patrick, *Faster Company: Building the World's Nuttiest, Turn-on-a-Dime, Home-Grown, Billion-Dollar Business*, Hoboken, NJ: Wiley, 1998.

Lynn, Jacquelyn, "Follow the Leaders: Imitation Is Fair Game When You're Building a Successful Company," *Entrepreneur*, November 1998.

Marcial, Gene G., "PSS Is Really Delivering the Goods," *Business Week*, August 30, 2004, p. 168.

"Physician Sales to Get Taylor Medical for $65 Million," *New York Times*, April 11, 1995.

Posner, Bruce G., "Growing Your Own: What to Do When You Can't Afford to Hire Experienced People," *Inc.*, June 1989, pp. 131–32.

"PSS Acquires Taylor Medical, Making It Nation's Largest Physician Supplier," *Health Industry Today*, May 1995, p. 16.

"PSS World Medical's Physician Business, Physician Sales & Service, Inc., Achieves Milestone of $1 Billion in Annual Net Sales," Business Wire, March 10, 2006.

Taylor, Thayer C., "Sales Automation Cuts the Cord," *Sales & Marketing Management*, July 1995, pp. 110–15.

# Quill Corporation

———■———

100 Schelter Road
Lincolnshire, Illinois 60069
U.S.A.
Telephone: (847) 634-6690
Toll Free: (800) 789-1331
Fax: (847) 821-2347
Web site: http://www.quill.com/

*Wholly Owned Subsidiary of Staples, Inc.*
*Founded:* 1956
*Employees:* 2,000 (est.)
*Sales:* $1 billion (2009 est.)
*NAICS:* 423420 Office Equipment Merchant Wholesalers; 424120 Stationery and Office Supplies Merchant Wholesalers; 454113 Mail-Order Houses

■ ■ ■

Quill Corporation is one of the largest and most successful business-to-business marketers of office products in the United States. As a wholly owned subsidiary of the office supply chain Staples, Inc., Quill markets and sells a wide range of office supplies, including items such as file folders, calendars, computers, copiers, tax forms, storage boxes, file cabinets, fax paper, office furniture, and classroom and janitorial supplies. Known across many industries for its discounted prices, the company's products are sold at significantly reduced costs to schools, businesses, professional associations, government institutions, and medical offices throughout the United States. Traditionally, Quill Corporation has sold its products through its extensive print catalog, which it

first launched in 1963. With the emergence of the Internet, however, much of the company's business has moved to its online clearinghouse, Quill.com. By 2009 its online sales accounted for roughly 75 percent of the company's total sales.

## ORIGINS AND EARLY GROWTH: 1956–63

Quill Corporation was the outgrowth of an idea by Jack Miller. Miller grew up on the north side of Chicago, Illinois, where his father sold live poultry and established a successful small business. Jack was pushed by his parents to attend college and, after graduating from the University of Illinois, he took a job as a door-to-door salesman of briefcases. By 1956 he had grown tired of peddling briefcases and founded Quill Corporation, his own office supply business. Working out of a room near his father's poultry business, Jack sold office supplies to small businesses and companies throughout Chicago's north side. Lacking retail experience, the young entrepreneur relied on his door-to-door selling technique, and when customers phoned, they could often hear chickens squawking in the background as their orders were being taken.

By the end of his first month in business, Jack had sold a mere $960 worth of office supplies. Over the next year the company grew steadily but slowly and by the time his brother Harvey joined him in the company, the two men were able to pay themselves a salary of $90 per week. As the company continued to grow, the two brothers divided Chicago into halves, with Jack making calls to firms on the north side of the city and Harvey

# COMPANY PERSPECTIVES

From the very beginning in Dad's chicken store, and each of the steps along the way, we're proud of the fact that we never lost sight of what it takes to make shopping for office products easier, more efficient and more economical.

That sense of pride is also shown in how we do things, in the ways we serve you.

Quill's exclusive everyday-low-pricing policy is just the start. Working hard to give you the very best customer service, like answering your calls quickly ... often before you even hear it ring, is also a matter of pride.

Our pride is also reflected in making ordering extremely easy and customer friendly ... in offering a wide variety of products ... and, most especially, in presenting the line of Quill national brand products with their high value and combination of performance, excellence and competitive prices. We are proud to be a supplier to you and we will continue to do everything possible to deserve your business.

making calls to firms located on the south side. In 1957 they moved out of their father's poultry store and into their uncle's basement, which served as their first office and warehouse.

In 1958 Quill moved into a more spacious 850-square-foot storefront, and then again in 1960 to an even larger warehouse and office space. The impetus behind the company's expansion was Jack and Harvey's original idea to send postcards and then fliers to current and potential customers notifying them of discounted office merchandise for sale. This method of selling office supplies, one of the first direct-mail efforts in the industry, worked so well that the two men were soon spending more time on the phone filling orders than selling their products door to door. The next step was a natural one. The Miller brothers glued together their first mail-order pamphlet complete with cut-out pictures from wholesale books, reduced their prices by 15 percent, offered to sell their supplies in bulk quantities direct from the manufacturer, and provided free delivery to all their customers. In 1963 the Miller brothers introduced Quill's first full-scale catalog, which transformed the company into being one of the first mail-order-only companies in the United States.

## RAPID EXPANSION: 1974–89

In 1974 Quill reported annual sales of $3.5 million. Two years later, in 1976, Arnold Miller, a certified public accountant, joined the family business as secretary. At first, the three brothers shared the responsibility of decision-making for the company. As the firm grew, however, the responsibility and duties of each brother needed to be clearly delineated. Jack chose marketing, Harvey decided on operations, and Arnold volunteered to supervise the company's finances. The triumvirate worked well, and the company grew rapidly.

During the early and mid-1980s the company's revenues skyrocketed, amounting to $180 million in 1986. Its mail-order business was the most successful within the office supplies market, with more than 40 million catalogs and flyers being sent to a customer base of approximately 600,000 businesses and organizations annually. With business booming, the company's number of employees rose to more than 850, providing some of the best customer service in the industry.

Meanwhile, a new and highly innovative breed of discount office supply warehouses arrived on the scene. The most successful and largest of the new deep-discount office supply firms was Office Depot, Inc., a company whose revenues had catapulted to over $300 million by the mid-1980s, surpassing Quill Corporation not only in sales but also in direct mail-order volume. With 80 stores in 15 states, Office Depot soon developed a reputation as one of the most aggressive discount price firms in the industry. Whereas Quill sold its own brand of copy paper for $37.90 per case, Office Depot sold its copy paper for a little over $20. Other deep-discount office supply stores, such as BizMart, Office Club, and Staples, followed Office Depot's lead, and by the late 1980s Quill Corporation's growth in certain geographical markets had ground to a complete halt.

The Miller brothers were determined not to lose ground without a fight. Jack directed the campaign to regain the markets Quill had lost, and he knew that it began with customer service. He focused on the training of pleasant customer service representatives, whom he recognized as the company's frontline sales force. He strategically increased the number of targeted mailings to prospective customers and introduced a new policy that guaranteed the delivery of all company products within three to five days. Most important, Jack focused on improving prices across the board. Under his direction the company not only slashed prices for all its office supplies but also streamlined and simplified its pricing strategy. By 1989 Quill Corporation was able to lower its prices for all products by nearly 15 percent, thereby reducing the firm's gross margins on average to a still healthy 30 percent. As a result, despite the

## KEY DATES

**1956:** Jack Miller founds Quill Corporation in Chicago, Illinois, operating out of his father's poultry store.

**1957:** Jack and his brother Harvey move Quill's operations into the basement of their uncle's house.

**1958:** Quill opens an 850-square-foot storefront.

**1963:** Quill introduces its first full-scale mail-order catalog.

**1976:** Arnold Miller, the brother of Jack and Harvey and a certified public accountant, joins the family business as secretary.

**1998:** The Miller brothers sell Quill to Staples, Inc.

**2001:** Quill enters into partnerships with a range of online business communities, among them Medsite, Inc., and Attorney Store.com.

**2002:** Quill implements Salesnet, an online tool aimed at improving sales efficiency.

**2006:** Quill launches Office Living, an online community for Quill customers.

competition from companies such as Office Depot and Staples, Quill continued to grow and prosper.

## BECOMING PART OF A LARGER BRAND: 1990–98

Confident of their ability to compete with the deep-discount office supply companies, the Miller brothers decided to make a foray into the retail store market. In 1990 they acquired the bankrupt chain of five Aaron's Office Furniture Warehouse stores in the Chicago metropolitan area. Jack managed to successfully expand the operations of the chain, which was renamed Quill's Office Furniture, and even opened another store by the end of 1994. The following year the company expanded its product line by carrying a wide range of school supplies, such as crayons, rulers, audiovisual equipment, erasers, and other items to meet the needs of primary, secondary, and vocational students.

Much of the company's growth during these years was due to an important case heard before the U.S. Supreme Court. The state of North Dakota had brought suit against Quill Corporation to force the out-of-state mail-order company to require that in-state customers pay taxes on their purchases. The litigation surrounding the case continued for a number of years before the Supreme Court ruled in 1992 in favor of Quill

Corporation. The majority opinion maintained that North Dakota could not require the firm to collect taxes from in-state customers because Quill Corporation did not have any employees or retail stores located in the state. Following this ruling, customers from around the country flocked to order from Quill because they did not have to pay taxes on their purchases.

In 1998, without much warning or notice, the Miller brothers announced that they were selling Quill Corporation to Staples, one of their traditional competitors. All the brothers were growing older, with Jack set to celebrate his 69th birthday during the year. Many of the company's employees were taken by surprise, as were industry analysts and other people working in the office supply products industry. According to Jack, the three brothers had wanted to keep the operation a family business. However, no one in their family was willing to assume the responsibilities and duties necessary to maintain the company's success. In addition, the Miller brothers could not find a suitable candidate from the outside that they thought could direct the firm into the future. Consequently, the three aging entrepreneurs sold Quill Corporation to Staples for $685 million in stock.

In 1998 Staples was operating 582 superstores throughout the United States, with a comprehensive line of office supply products that ranged from copy paper to office furniture. The acquisition of Quill, which the Staples management decided to run as an operating division under the Quill name and logo, gave Staples access not only to an extremely successful direct-mail catalog market but also to a new and burgeoning Internet market that Quill was just starting to expand. Quill's $8 million in sales over the Internet alone in 1997 was clearly an indication of a huge future market for office supplies.

Quill Corporation's future seemed assured under the auspices of Staples. The financial benefits of the acquisition became apparent almost immediately. During its first year under new ownership, Quill almost single-handedly tripled its parent company's mail-order revenues, from $270 million in 1997 to $825 million in 1998.

## INTERNAL IMPROVEMENTS AND STRATEGIC PARTNERSHIPS: 1999–2001

As it approached the new century, Quill Corporation remained focused on identifying new ways to expand its core business. The company took an important step toward broadening its geographical reach in early 1999, when it established a mail-order center in the United Kingdom. Quill also introduced a range of technological improvements aimed at improving the efficiency of its domestic ordering and distribution operations.

In response to the steady increase in online orders, the company implemented a new warehouse management system at its nine U.S. facilities, with the aim of reducing turnaround times on orders while simultaneously cutting inventory costs. Quill enhanced its Internet sales capability further in early 2001, when it launched a new database that was designed to consolidate all new and existing product information into a single integrated system. The database also enabled Quill to provide instant access to this information to vendors and customers via the company's Web site, Quill.com.

Over the course of 2001 Quill entered into a series of strategic partnerships, with the goal of expanding its customer base across a range of business sectors. In February the company partnered with Medsite, Inc., an Internet community that comprised more than 100,000 doctors, to create a link to Quill's online catalog on the Medsite home page. In June Quill forged a pact with Epylon Corporation, an online supply network for the education and government sectors, to become one of the company's preferred vendors. The deal gave the company access to more than 1,300 educational and government departments throughout the globe, accounting for a total revenue stream of roughly $900 billion annually. In July Quill entered into an agreement with eSchoolMall to become one of the network's preferred sellers. A month later the company became a preferred vendor for Attorney Store.com, the legal profession's largest office supply network.

## CONTINUED REVENUES GROWTH: 2002–10

In September 2002 Quill implemented Salesnet, an online sales tool that was designed to increase efficiencies in the selling process. The new system increased the company's monthly revenues by 10 percent over the course of an initial six-month period. By July 2003 Salesnet had spurred an overall sales growth of more than 30 percent. At around this time Quill also introduced a comprehensive price-reduction strategy aimed at maintaining heavy sales volume during a period of economic stagnation across diverse industries.

Meanwhile, online orders were becoming increasingly critical to the company's revenues, as Internet sales accounted for roughly 50 percent of Quill's total business by mid-decade. In general, the company's successful integration of its online store with its traditional mail-order catalog was having a profound effect on its bottom line. By 2005 Quill was posting annual revenues that exceeded $1 billion, compared with $700 million in annual sales at the beginning of the century.

In 2006 Quill Corporation celebrated the 50th anniversary of its founding. That same year the company introduced a new online community, Office Living, aimed at improving the company's relationship with its customers. Because the Internet was supplanting face-to-face interaction in many business segments, Quill executives began to seek ways to develop new forms of communication via the Internet. Through Office Living, the company encouraged customers to post information about their work experiences, including personal anecdotes, professional ambitions, and other stories from their life, and to make it available to other Quill clients. Quill hoped that the new community would add a personal touch to the e-commerce experience.

This strategy seemed increasingly vital to the company's long-term growth. By decade's end Quill was generating roughly three-quarters of its total business through online sales. With its proven commitment to innovation, Quill Corporation was clearly poised to remain a leader in the business-to-business office supply sector for years to come.

*Thomas Derdak*
*Updated, Stephen Meyer*

## PRINCIPAL COMPETITORS

Corporate Express US, Inc.; Office Depot, Inc.; Office-Max Incorporated.

## FURTHER READING

Barrier, Michael, "Brother Act," *Nation's Business*, January 1989, p. 41.

Bulkeley, William, "Staples, Moving beyond Superstores, Will Buy Quill for $685 Million in Stock," *Wall Street Journal*, April 8, 1999, p. B16.

Freeman, Laurie, "Frequent Mailings Keep Quill in Black Ink," *Advertising Age*, September 20, 1984, p. 9.

Harris, John, "The Battle of the Paper Clips," *Forbes*, May 14, 1990, p. 108.

Medill, Nicole Kuznia, "Quill Maintains a Family Feel," *Chicago Daily Herald*, June 6, 2006, p. 1.

Parr, Jan, "Quill's Miller Wields a Sharp Pencil," *Advertising Age*, October 17, 1998, p. S15.

"Quill Corporation Has Upgraded Its Corporate Web Site," *Purchasing*, February 11, 1999, p. 102.

"Quill Creates Online Forum for Busy Office Professionals," *PR Newswire*, November 15, 2006.

"The Rise of the Passionate Customer," *PR Newswire*, December 13, 2006.

Troy, Mike, "Quill Purchase Gives Staples e-Presence," *Discount Store News*, April 20, 1998, p. 3.

# ruukki

# Rautaruukki Oyj

Suolakivenkatu 1
Helsinki, FI-00810
Finland
Telephone: (+358) 20-5911
Fax: (+358) 20-5929-088
Web site: http://www.ruukki.com/

*Public Company*
*Incorporated:* 1960 as Rautaruuki Ltd.
*Employees:* 12,664
*Sales:* EUR 1.95 billion ($2.81 billion) (2009)
*Stock Exchanges:* NASDAQ OMX Helsinki
*Ticker Symbol:* RTRKS
*NAICS:* 331111 Iron and Steel Mills; 331221 Rolled Steel Shape Manufacturing

■ ■ ■

Rautaruukki Oyj (Ruukki) is a Finnish provider of metal-based components and systems to the construction and engineering industries. Active in 27 countries, the company operates in three business areas: construction, engineering, and metals. Ruukki Construction serves builders and developers of commercial, industrial, and office buildings in the Nordic countries, Baltic states, Eastern Europe, Ukraine, and Russia, with building frames, wall and roofing products as well as integrated systems. Other products and services include traffic noise barriers, construction highway guard rails, bridges, piles, retaining wall structures, and harbor construction foundations. Ruukki Engineering serves European companies involved in such industries as marine, offshore, and transportation equipment, paper and wood manufacturing, and energy production. Products and services include booms, masts, frames, windmill components, oil sumps, and medium and heavy welded structures. Ruukki Metals does business in the Nordic countries, Baltic states, Russia, and to a limited degree in Western Europe. Serving the transportation equipment, construction, engineering, and electronics industries, the unit offers special steel products, hot- and cold-rolled steel, metal- and color-coated steels and tubes, and prefabrication services. A public company listed on the NASDAQ; OMX; and Helsinki exchanges, Ruukki is 40-percent owned by the Finnish government, which is the company's largest shareholder.

## COMPANY FOUNDED: 1960

Ruukki was founded in 1960 as Rautaruuki Ltd., part of a post–World War II plan by the Finnish government to build an iron and steel works as a way to generate new jobs and ensure a supply of steel for the company's five corporate cofounders (Oy Fiskars AB, Outokumpu Oyj, Rauma-Repola Oy, Wärtsilä AB, and Valmet Oy) and other Finnish shipbuilding and metal industry companies. The government-owned Raahe Steel Works opened in 1964 and began producing pig iron, an intermediate product used in steelmaking. After some further investment in the facility, steel and hot-rolled plate production followed three years later. The Works was the first Western steelmaker to make use of the new continuous casting technique. Also of importance during its first decade in operation, Ruukki merged in 1968 with Otanmäki Ltd., a mining company.

Ruukki was well established by 1970 and expanded
its capabilities further in order to widen its range of
customers. A hot-strip mill was added to Raahe Steel
Works in 1971. A year later a cold-rolling mill opened
in Hämeenlinna, Finland, to produce cold-rolled and
galvanized steel, and in 1973 the facility launched tube
production as well. Tube production was bolstered
further by the 1975 acquisition of the Lappohja Works
and the building of tube works in Oulainen and Pulk-
kila, Finland, later in the decade. A second blast furnace
was also added at the Raahe Steel Works in 1975, and
in 1977 the Hämeenlinna plant began production of
color-coated sheets. In addition, Ruukki completed
several other important acquisitions during this period.
The Halikko Works and Ylivieska Works were acquired
in 1979. The company also completed its first foreign
acquisition when it bought Nordisk Simplex A/S's tube
works in Denmark in 1977. In that same year, Ruukki
opened a sales office in Norway.

## INTERNATIONAL EXPANSION: 1981–83

Ruukki now looked to expand further in and beyond
the Nordic countries. A sales company, Rautarukki UK
Ltd., was opened in the United Kingdom in 1981.
Similar operations followed in Germany in 1983 and
Sweden and the United States the following year. Several
significant acquisitions were also completed during the
1980s. The Toijala Works was added in 1983. A maker
of long steel products, Dalsbruk Oy Ab, was purchased
in 1987. A year later MetalColour S/S of Denmark, a
color-coating works, was acquired. In 1989 Norwegian
steel wholesaler CCB-Gruppen was added, as well as
Schmacke Rohr GmbH, a German tube mill.

In the midst of its aggressive acquisition program,
Ruukki did not forsake internal growth. A seven-year,
$446 million modernization program was initiated in
1983. The two blast furnaces at the Raahe mill were
automated, and bottom-blowing (a method of introducing inert gas such as nitrogen or argon into the bottom
of a furnace through a tube) was added to the three
basic oxygen furnaces to improve the production of low
alloy steel. In addition, improvements were made to the

mill's five continuous casters, and the first stage of a
coking plant was completed in 1987. Moreover, the
production of special rail transport cars began at the
company's Otanmäki facility in 1985, and at the end of
the decade a company was formed in Denmark, Stel-
form A/S, to produce cold-formed sections.

The 1980s brought additional changes to the
company's operations and structure. Ruukki exited the
mining business, closing its last working mine in Rau-
tavaara in 1988. Of greater importance, in 1989 the
Finnish government sold some of its stake in the
company in a stock offering to both Ruukki employees
and the general public. Ruukki shares were now publicly
traded and quoted on the Helsinki Stock Exchange.
State ownership was reduced further in 1994, when
Ruukki made a global share offering as part of Finland's
program to broaden ownership in state-owned
companies.

## PLANT MODERNIZATION BEGINS: 1995

Ruukki expanded on a number of fronts at the start of
the new decade. In 1990 the company completed several
acquisitions, including Star Tubes (UK) Ltd., a British
wholesaler of tubular products; Gavle Ahlsell AB, a
Swedish profiled-sheet manufacturer; and another Swedish firm, Wirsbo Stalror AB, a tube works. Additionally
Ruukki acquired minority positions in German, Swedish, and U.S. steel wholesalers. A year later, three Finnish profiled-sheet manufacturers were added to the fold:
Verho-Metalli Oy, Mäkelä Metals Oy, and Rannila Steel
Oy. Through Rannila, a steel roof manufacturer, Ruukki
expanded into the construction business. Ruukki bought
a 50-percent stake in a German tube works company,
Carl Froh Röhrenwerk GmbH & Co. in 1991 and three
years later acquired the rest of the business.
Furthermore, Ruukki's railcar production unit was
merged with Valmet to create a joint venture, Transtech
Ltd. in 1991, and it too became a wholly owned
subsidiary in 1995 when Ruukki bought out its partner.
A steel service center in Germany was acquired in 1994,
creating Rautaruukki Stahlservice GmbH. The early
1990s also saw the completion of the second stage of
the coking plant at the Raahe mill, and the beginning of
profiled-sheet manufacturing in Estonia. Sales
companies were also launched in Singapore in 1992 and
Poland and Dubai in 1993.

During the mid-1990s a five-year modernization
program was implemented. Costing about $500 million,
it was completed in the summer of 2000. It covered the
entire production technology system. Not only did steel
output grow by 2.8 million tons per year and hot-rolled
strip production increase 40 percent to 2.3 million tons

## KEY DATES

**1960:** Company is founded as Rautaruuki Ltd. by the Finnish State and a group of Finnish corporations.
**1964:** Raahe Steel Works opens.
**1989:** Company is taken public through shares offered on the Helsinki Stock Exchange.
**2000:** A five-year, $500 million modernization is program completed, improving technology and production throughout the company.
**2004:** The Ruukki name is adopted by all group companies.

per year, the Raahe Works and Hämeenlinna Works were now able to produce a greater range of steel grades and offer such new products as formable and corrosion-resistant steel and grades possessing excellent deep-drawing (shaping) properties. Additionally, a new galvanizing line was added to essentially double production capacity while allowing Ruukki to offer better surfaces and new types of coating for sheet products. Paint production capacity also increased 50 percent to 150,000 tons.

While the modernization effort was conducted, Ruukki continued to expand organically as well as through external means. Sales operations were opened in Latvia and Lithuania in 1995, and the production of profiled-sheet products began in Russia. Profiled sheets have applications in the construction industry, typically in roofing and siding. The following year Ruukki acquired a Finnish steel wholesaler, Keskometalli Oyj, and a steel service center was established to cover the Baltic area. In 1997 Ruukki began production of profiled sheet in the Czech Republic and did the same in Slovakia through a joint venture. The Rannila Steel subsidiary then began manufacturing profiled sheet in Ukraine and Lithuania in 1998. There were also some divestitures during this period. Transtech Taivalkoski Works was sold in 1998, and the following year Transtech Otanmäki Works was divested as well. Also of note in the late 1990s, the Finnish state reduced its holding in Ruukki through an international share offering in 1997. A year later the State reduced its holding further to 41.8 percent.

## NEW CENTURY SLUMP

Ruukki entered the new century on a downturn after posting a loss in 1999, which was a poor year for the entire European steel industry. Even Ruukki's business in Eastern Europe, which had been growing at an annual rate of 20 to 30 percent, slumped, due primarily to economic troubles in Russia. The modernization program completed in 2000 helped to revitalize Ruukki as the new century dawned. Business improved across the board in 2000 and the more efficient operation helped the company to generate net earnings of EUR 106 million.

Ruukki was now able to resume expansion. The Swedish stockholding company and service center Helens Stal AB was acquired in 2001 and renamed Asva AB. The same year, a production and service center was opened in St. Petersburg, Russia, and Rannila opened steel roofing factories in Poland and Ukraine. In 2002 a hard-chrome plating company, Fluid SpA, was acquired in Italy, a new rolling mill opened at Fundia Nedstaal in the Netherlands, and new steel structure plants opened in central Russia and Kazakhstan. The following year a metal product operation was launched in Norway.

The early 2000s also brought some changes to Ruukki's organization as the company adjusted its business model to accommodate changes in the marketplace, which saw a good deal of consolidation, specialization, and globalization in the steel industry as well as in the industries it served. As a result, Ruukki repositioned itself as a value-added metal solutions provider rather than a steel manufacturer, and the company divided its operations into three customer-oriented divisions: Construction Solutions, Mechanical Engineering Solutions, and Metal Fabrication Solutions. The goal was to develop products and systems to play a greater role in the value chain of Ruukki's customers. A fourth division, Metal Products, was responsible for prefabrication and the sale of steel and metal products. To further this new vision and improve branding, all of the companies in Rautaruukki Corporation began marketing themselves under the Ruukki name.

## VALUE-ADDED PRODUCTS EMPHASIZED: 2004–10

Under the leadership of a new chief executive officer, Sakari Tamminen, Ruukki moved away from what had been its core business for many years, rolled steel products, in favor of such value-added specialty structures and components as bridge and harbor fittings. The company also paid greater attention to the energy sector, for which it began producing window power components, oil rig structures, and components for power generation plants. The company hoped that by the end of the decade it would be able to strike a 50-50 balance between traditional steel and the new value-added products.

Ruukki adjusted its business mix over the next few years, completing acquisitions and launching operations that fit in with the new vision for the company while selling off assets that were no longer suitable. Sales offices were opened in Bulgaria in 2007, and Belarus and Kazakhstan in 2008. Plans were also laid to make the steel business more efficient, and steel products were merged with Ruukki Metals in 2009 to reduce the number of business areas to three. Although customer demand was greatly reduced because of a severe global recession that began in late 2008 and the company posted a net loss on the year, Ruukki remained well positioned to enjoy long-term success.

*Ed Dinger*

## PRINCIPAL OPERATING UNITS

Ruukki Construction; Ruukki Engineering; Ruukki Metals.

## PRINCIPAL COMPETITORS

Descours & Cabaud; Outokumpu Oyj; ThyssenKrupp Stainless International GmbH.

## FURTHER READING

Burgert, Philip, "Five-year, $503M Upgrade Completed by Rautaruukki," *American Metal Market*, August 16, 2000, p. 3.

——, "Rautaruukki Plans Galvanizing Growth," *American Metal Market*, January 9, 1998, p. 16.

Flaherty, Sharon, "Rautaruukki, Partners Selling Ovako Venture," *American Metal Market*, July 18, 2006, p. 6.

Kramer, David, "Finnish Steelmaker Plans $446M Modernization," *American Metal Market*, October 6, 1983, p. 4.

——, "More Finnish Steel Shares Go Private," *American Metal Market*, April 11, 1994, p. 1.

Saltmarsh, Matthew, "Finnish Steel Maker Hones a Specialty Niche," *International Herald Tribune*, November 17, 2007, p. 14.

Teaff, Rick, "Rautaruukki Knows Change Is Critical," *American Metal Market*, July 2, 1996, p. 5.

Zwick, Steve, "Boosting Output at Rautaruukki," *New Steel*, July 1998, p. 78.

# Rhodia S.A.

Immeuble Coeur Défense
Tour A, 110 Esplanade Charles de Gaulle
Courbevoie, 92400
France
Telephone: (+33-1) 53-56-64-64
Fax: (+33-1) 55-38-44-71
Web site: http://www.rhodia.com/

*Public Company*
*Incorporated:* 1998
*Employees:* 13,600
*Sales:* €4.03 billion ($5.48 billion) (2009)
*Stock Exchanges:* Paris
*Ticker Symbol:* RHA
*NAICS:* 325188 All Other Basic Inorganic Chemical Manufacturing; 325199 All Other Basic Organic Chemical Manufacturing; 325211 Plastics Material and Resin Manufacturing; 541380 Pollution Testing (except Automotive Emissions Testing) Services; 541690 Energy Consulting Services

■ ■ ■

Rhodia S.A. is one of the world's leading specialty chemicals companies. Headquartered in Courbevoie, France, the company oversees an extensive network of global operations, with manufacturing facilities in 25 countries. Rhodia is organized into six primary divisions that produce specialty chemicals for the automotive, electronics, personal care, and other industries. The company's principal products include acetate tow (a primary ingredient in cigarette filters), polyamide (used in plastics, paints, and food additives), silica, and sulfuric acid. During the first few years of the first decade of the 21st century, Rhodia nearly collapsed under the weight of massive debts, and it briefly became the subject of takeover rumors. After an exhaustive restructuring, however, the company was once again restored to profitability by 2006.

## THE FOUNDING OF THE FRENCH CHEMICALS EMPIRE

When Rhodia S.A. was created in 1998, it already boasted nearly 150 years of history. This history followed two threads that originated in the middle of the 19th century. The first of these was the founding of a small factory in 1856 that produced dyes, tanning agents, and other products for textile companies based in the Lyon region of France. The company's founders, Marc Gilliard and Jean Marie Cartier, later joined with Pierre Monnet of Switzerland, whose company, Pierre Monnet et Cie, specialized in synthetic dyes based on tar and other materials. The newly enlarged company became Gilliard, Monnet et Cartier.

Meanwhile, in 1858 Etienne Poulenc bought an apothecary in Paris and added his name to the billing to form the company Wittmann et Poulenc Jeune. Besides selling apothecary and pharmaceutical products, Poulenc eventually branched out to sell chemicals and supplies for the nascent photographic industry. When his brothers entered the firm, Poulenc's company was renamed Poulenc Frères. In 1900 the company went public and changed its again to Les Etablissements Poulenc Frères.

Rhodia's values are driven by our relationships with our stakeholders to our customers—we will always guarantee the integrity of our products and services. To our employees—we will always keep them safe, enter into dialogue with them, and improve their skills and employability. To our shareholders—we will be transparent in our corporate and financial dealings. To our suppliers—we will take a responsible approach to our purchasing policies. To our communities—we will work tirelessly to earn the respect of our neighbors. And to the environment—we will constantly strive to limit our impact on the world in which we live.

We take pride in these values, which govern the way in which we conduct business. They sit at the heart of everything we do and remind us of our responsibilities to both the worlds in which we operate—chemistry and commerce.

Both Poulenc Frères and Gilliard, Monnet et Cartier were at the forefront of developments in what was rapidly becoming the modern era of medicine and medical treatment. At the end of the 19th century Gilliard, Monnet et Cartier, which had begun investing in the research, development, and production of new chemical products, chose to emphasize its growing interest by changing its name to Société Chimique des Usines de Rhône in 1895. That same year the company also went public.

Among Poulenc Frères's accomplishments were a number of significant breakthroughs, such as its introduction of arsenobenzol, one of the earliest successful treatments of the hitherto incurable syphilis. Around this time Société Chimique des Usines de Rhône exited the textile dyes market to return to its focus on chemical and pharmaceutical products. In 1902 Société Chimique des Usines de Rhône also introduced the new trademark and brand name Rhodia to denote a number of its chemical products.

## DEVELOPMENT DURING AND AFTER THE WAR: 1914–30

World War I gave both companies a vast testing ground for their pharmaceutical products, as they developed new drugs and compounds to treat the wounds of the French war casualties. After the war Société Chimique des Usines de Rhône decided to enter perfume manufacturing. For this venture, the company used the Rhodia brand name. However, when it failed to make headway against its German competitors, which dominated the chemicals industry in Europe, Société Chimique des Usines de Rhône eventually decided to refocus its production entirely on specialty chemicals.

The end of the 1920s witnessed the birth of what was to become not only France's leading chemicals company but also the largest company in France. In 1928 Société Chimique des Usines de Rhône and Les Etablissements Poulenc Frères merged to form Société des Usines Chimiques Rhône Poulenc. Shortly after the merger, the company became the first French company to begin mass production of the drug penicillin, which had been discovered that same year.

## DOMESTIC AND INTERNATIONAL GROWTH: MID-FORTIES TO MID-EIGHTIES

The period following World War II marked an era of steady growth for Rhône Poulenc, as the company established not only its French dominance but also a worldwide reputation. The company's operations expanded throughout the world, including the United States, where it established the subsidiary Rhodia Inc. in 1948.

During this period Rhône Poulenc actively pursued a program of growth by making a number of significant purchases to help consolidate the French chemicals and pharmaceuticals industry, including the addition of the pharmaceutical company Theraplix in 1956. In 1961 the company changed its name to Rhône Poulenc S.A. During the 1960s the company acquired the pharmaceutical company Institut Mérieux. By the end of the decade Rhône Poulenc had solidified its leadership in the French market and eventually became the third-largest chemicals group in Europe.

During the 1970s both France and the world economy slipped into a prolonged recession. Feeling the effects of the recession, Rhône Poulenc watched its sales and revenues drop. The company also made a number of strategic errors, such as granting the United States marketing rights for Rhône Poulenc's highly successful drug Thorazine. Most important, Rhône Poulenc had long enjoyed a position of being protected by France's high tariff barriers, which effectively barred international competition. However, when the tariff barriers were taken away in the 1970s, Rhône Poulenc suddenly found itself in head-to-head competition with an array of foreign companies, including several U.S. and German chemicals and pharmaceuticals firms.

By the end of the 1970s Rhône Poulenc was struggling and, in the early 1980s, it posted losses of more

## KEY DATES

**1858:** Wittmann et Poulenc Jeune is founded.

**1895:** Gilliard, Monnet et Cartier is reformed as Société Chimique des Usines.

**1902:** The Rhodia trademark and brand name are first used.

**1928:** Poulenc and Société Chimique des Usines merge to form Société des Usines Chimiques Rhône Poulenc.

**1961:** The company changes its name to Rhône Poulenc S.A.

**1998:** Rhône Poulenc combines chemicals and polymers units to form Rhodia S.A., which is later spun off as a public company.

**2000:** Rhodia acquires the U.S.-based chemicals firm ChiRex.

**2006:** Rhodia posts its first annual profit since 2000.

than $500 million. Its troubles were compounded when it came under attack by a new adversary: François Mitterand. The rise to power of Mitterand's Socialist government had been won in part because of its promise to nationalize a number of key French industries. Mitterand made good on that promise in 1982, when Rhône Poulenc was taken over by the French government. Placed in charge of the newly nationalized company was Loïk Le Floch-Prigent, who was given the task of restructuring the ailing group. Le Floch downsized the number of employees, eliminated a number of the company's struggling business units and subsidiaries, and by the mid-1980s had succeeded in bringing Rhône Poulenc back into the black.

### INTERNATIONAL EXPANSION AND MERGERS: MID-EIGHTIES TO LATE NINETIES

In 1986 Le Floch turned over the leadership of the rejuvenated Rhône Poulenc to Jean-René Fourtou. Fourtou continued Le Floch's transformation of the company by slashing over 20 subsidiaries and by going on an international spending spree to add 30 new companies. Among the acquisitions were Union Carbide's agricultural chemicals division, Germany's Nattermann, and Stauffer's industrial chemicals business. Fourtou's attention had turned especially to the United States, where Rhône Poulenc had picked up some 18 acquisitions.

In 1990 the French government gave Rhône Poulenc 35 percent of Roussel-Uclaf, the country's number-three pharmaceuticals group. That same year Rhône Poulenc merged its own pharmaceuticals operations with that of the U.S.-based Rorer to form Rhône Poulenc Rorer, in which Rhône Poulenc held two-thirds of the shares. Meanwhile, Rhône Poulenc itself was teaming up with rival Merck & Co. to develop a series of children's vaccines in the early 1990s. The company was also pursuing its expansion in the booming Asian economies by building a series of new factories that served the plastics and chemicals industries.

In 1993 the French government returned Rhône Poulenc to the private sector. The company next began to expand into new areas of development, particularly the growing market for biotechnology products, techniques, and equipment. That same year Rhône Poulenc bought 37 percent of Applied Immune Sciences. In 1994 it acquired Fisons, a manufacturer of treatments for asthma and allergic reactions based in the United Kingdom.

After Rhône Poulenc and Merck joined to spin off their animal health care products operations into the new company Merial, the French chemicals and pharmaceuticals giants prepared to get even bigger. The increasing globalization of the world's marketplace caused Rhône Poulenc to seek out a partner with which to counter the expansion moves of its largest U.S. and European competitors. The company found that partner in the German company Hoechst AG, and in 1998 the two companies announced their intentions to merge to form Aventis.

### THE CREATION OF RHODIA S.A.: 1998

As part of the process leading to the Aventis merger, Rhône Poulenc decided to spin off its chemicals and polymers divisions to form a new separate company, Rhodia S.A., in 1998. The following year 30 percent of Rhodia's stock was sold on the Paris and New York stock exchanges. The new chief executive officer of Rhodia was Jean-Pierre Tirouflet, who led Rhodia on a restructuring of the assets inherited from Rhône Poulenc. Among the company's divestitures was its titanium dioxide operations. It also began to prepare for an exit from the polyester market by shutting down a number of its European polyester production facilities. Meanwhile, Rhodia unveiled an ambitious investment program to support its expansion drive in the Asia Pacific region. As Tirouflet told David Hunter of *Chemi-*

*cal Week*, the new company started business with "a business portfolio that's more balanced and able to withstand cycles."

In 1999 Rhône Poulenc sold its controlling shares in Rhodia, which set Rhodia free as an independent company. That same year Rhodia made a bold expansion move when it won a takeover battle for the United Kingdom's Albright & Wilson. As one of the world's largest producers of phosphates and other phosphorus-based products, the company reported annual sales of over €1.2 billion. Rhodia paid an estimated $850 million for the acquisition.

In July 2000 Rhodia once again made headlines when it reached an agreement to purchase ChiRex, a U.S.-based fine chemicals specialist. The acquisition, for a price of nearly $550 million, established Rhodia as a world leader in the specialties chemicals industry. However, the acquisition also increased the company's debt ratio, which topped 130 percent, and pushed down its stock price. As the specialties chemicals industry continued to consolidate at the beginning of the new century, industry observers began to question whether Rhodia's low stock price might not make it an attractive target for a takeover attempt.

## RESTRUCTURING IN THE FACE OF FINANCIAL PRESSURES: 2001–03

Rhodia's struggles worsened during the early part of 2001, as rising raw material costs, an overall slump in industry demand, and continually mounting debt all combined to cut into the company's net earnings. For the first quarter of the year, Rhodia's profits fell to €25.7 million ($22.6 million), a decline of 50 percent compared with the same period the previous year. By October of that year, Rhodia had become the subject of takeover rumors in the press, with rivals such as the Dutch chemical firm DSM N.V. and Switzerland's Clariant AG emerging as the most likely buyers. In December 2001 executives from DSM and Rhodia met to discuss a possible merger that was estimated to be worth €2.5 billion ($2.2 billion). The negotiations stalled, however, and Rhodia ultimately remained independent.

Still, the company's financial difficulties continued to mount. For 2001 Rhodia posted a loss of €225.3 million ($201.9 million). In an attempt to reverse this trend, the company began to sell a number of its business units. In April 2002 it divested its 50 percent stake in the hazardous waste subsidiary Teris S.A. for €100 million ($89 million). The following November Rhodia raised €150 million ($149.6 million) through the sale

of its European basic chemicals business to the U.S. private equity firm Bain Capital Inc. In February 2003 the company also announced plans to close 10 manufacturing plants in Europe and North America over the course of the next year, in the hope of further trimming costs. In spite of these efforts, revenues remained stagnant throughout 2003, as the company's debt swelled to €2.2 billion ($2.5 billion). In October 2003, in the face of continued quarterly losses, Tirouflet resigned from the post of CEO.

## NEW LEADERSHIP AND MORE RESTRUCTURING: 2004–10

After being selected to be the new CEO of Rhodia, Jean-Pierre Clamadieu announced a financial restructuring that was intended to reduce the company's massive debt. As part of the refinancing deal, Rhodia embarked on an aggressive sale of a number of its business assets, with the goal of raising €600 million ($707 million). In May 2004 the company unloaded its water treatment business to the Swedish firm Feralco AB for an undisclosed amount. A month later Rhodia sold its food ingredients unit to Danisco A/S for €320 million ($390 million). Less than two weeks later Bain Capital purchased Rhodia's North American phosphates operations for €457.3 million ($550 million). For 2004 the company posted a net loss of €633.6 million ($788.1 million). This figure actually represented a significant improvement over the company's 2003 performance, when losses topped €1.3 billion ($1.5 billion).

Even as Rhodia continued to trim its losses, 2005 proved another challenging year for the company, as it found itself the subject of a criminal investigation over its accounting practices, in a scandal so far-reaching that it eventually implicated the French finance minister. Rhodia's revenues also took a hit in September of that year, when Hurricane Katrina caused a general slowdown in the specialty chemicals sector in the Gulf Coast of the United States. By 2006 the company finally began to see positive results from its streamlining efforts. In 2006 Rhodia posted its first profit since 2000, with net earnings of €61.5 million ($77.3 million). In 2007 the company's profits more than doubled to €129 million ($176.8 million), on revenues of €5.1 billion ($7 billion). In 2008 the company's sales dropped slightly to €4.8 billion ($6.6 billion), and in 2009 its revenues fell to just over €4 billion ($5.8 billion). More significantly, the company posted a loss of €132 million ($190.2 million) for 2009, as the lingering effects of the global financial crisis that began in late 2007 continued to take a toll on the specialty chemicals industry. Nevertheless, in light of its brush with disaster at the beginning of the decade, Rhodia had every reason to believe that the worst was behind it.

*M. L. Cohen*
*Updated, Stephen Meyer*

## PRINCIPAL SUBSIDIARIES

Rhodia S.A. has 88 subsidiaries throughout Europe, North America, South America, Asia, and New Zealand. Rhodia's subsidiaries are principally engaged in various aspects of the company's chemical, energy, and emissions testing businesses.

## PRINCIPAL DIVISIONS

Acetow; Eco Services; Energy Services; Novecare; Polyamide; Silcea.

## PRINCIPAL COMPETITORS

Akzo Nobel N.V.; BASF SE; Bayer AG; Celanese Corporation; Clariant AG.

## FURTHER READING

David, Christian, "Jean-Pierre Tirouflet, génie de la finance monte en graine," *L'Expansion*, October 7, 1999, p. 22.

Duckers, John, "Low Demand Puts Rhodia under Cosh," *Birmingham Post* (England), April 8, 2003, p. 25.

Halpern, Nathalie, "Rhodia lance une OPA sur l'americain ChiRex pour 3.8 milliards de francs," *Les Echos* (France), July 25, 2000, p. 9.

Hunter, David, "Rhodia Works on Its Winners," *Chemical Week*, November 11, 1998, p. 96.

Jacobs, Caroline, "Rhodia Expects to Return to Profit this Year," *Birmingham Post* (England), March 2, 2006, p. 24.

Sedgwick, John, "Double Profits for Growing Rhodia," *Birmingham Post* (England), February 29, 2008, p. 24.

Tieman, Ross, "Bain Buying Rhodia Phosphates Unit," *Daily Deal*, June 14, 2004.

Tillier, Allan, and Jonathan Braude, "DSM Seen as Lead Bidder for Rhodia," *Daily Deal*, October 22, 2001.

Young, Andrew, "Rhodia Wins Battle for Albright," Reuters, May 13, 1999.

# S4C International

————————■————————

**Parc Ty Glas, Llanishen**
**Cardiff, CF14 5DU**
**Wales, United Kingdom**
**Telephone: (+44 29) 2074-7444**
**Fax: (+44 29) 2075-4444**
**Web site: http://www.s4c.co.uk**

*Private Company*
*Founded:* 1999
*Employees:* 154
*Sales:* £2.82 million ($4.1 million) (2008)
*NAICS:* 541512 Computer Systems Design Services;
541990 All Other Professional, Scientific and
Technical Services; 515120 Television Broadcasting

■ ■ ■

S4C International (S4CI) is the commercial arm of
S4C, the only bilingual television channel dedicated to
serving Wales and the Welsh-speaking population. Also
known as S4C *Rhyngwladol*, S4CI has as its main areas
of responsibility the distribution of S4CI's programs and
the generation of advertising and sponsorship revenues.
The S4CI animation catalog has won two Oscar nominations for *Famous Fred* and *The Canterbury Tales*, and it
also includes *SuperTed*, the first British animation series
to be broadcast by the Disney Channel. Other notable
titles in S4CI's animation catalog that are distributed
worldwide are *Sali Mali*, *Animated Tales of the World*,
and *Hana's Helpline*. S4CI is also internationally
recognized for its critically acclaimed documentaries,
such as *China Rises* and *Ancient Discoveries*, and for its

work with a variety of major broadcasters, including the
Discovery Channel, A&E, and New York Times Television, on a wide range of coproductions. In 2005 Barcud
Derwen, a television facilities group, and Parthenon
Entertainment, a wildlife producer and distributor,
formed a joint venture to run S4CI's operations. In addition to advertising and sponsorship revenues, S4C
receives funding from a fixed annual grant from the
U.K. Department for Culture, Media, and Sport.

## THE EVOLUTION OF S4C INTERNATIONAL

*Sianel Pedwar Cymru* is Welsh for "Channel Four
Wales," more commonly known as S4C. Before the
establishment of S4C in 1982, the availability of Welsh-
language programs was largely restricted to a few that
were scattered within the schedules of BBC1 and ITV,
two of the three channels in the United Kingdom at
that time. In the 1970s, recognizing the need for a
public service dedicated to speakers of Welsh as a first
language, activists campaigned for the creation of a new
channel. In the run-up to the United Kingdom's 1979
general election, both the Labour Party and the
Conservatives vowed to establish a fourth channel, but
after Margaret Thatcher's Conservative Party won,
Home Secretary William Whitelaw reneged on this
promise.

This led to public outrage, acts of civil disobedi-
ence, and mass demonstrations at U.K. studios. In 1980
Gwynfor Evans, former MP (Member of Parliament) for
Plaid Cymru (Party of Wales), threatened to go on a
hunger strike unless the new government followed

through on its campaign promise. Before the hunger strike was to begin, the government agreed to Evans's demands with the enactment of the 1980/81 Broadcasting Act, and S4C began broadcasting on November 1, 1982. The establishment of S4C boosted the economy throughout Wales. Barcud, a broadcast facilities company, was established in Caernarfon, Wales, to provide studios, editing suites, sound dubbing, and other services to the new channel. In 1988 Derwen, an editing facilities company, was founded in Cardiff.

In 1992, celebrating its 10-year anniversary, S4C introduced English subtitles to 75 percent of its programs to meet the needs of the country's non-Welsh speakers and to pave the way for expansion into new markets. In 1994 Huw Jones, a founding director of Barcud, became S4C's chief executive officer, a position he held until 2005. During his tenure the 1996 Broadcasting Act was enacted, addressing the development of digital terrestrial broadcasting. In 1997 Barcud and Derwen merged to form Barcud Derwen. The new company became a one-stop shop for S4C's broadcast needs. On November 15, 1998, S4C Digital was launched and provided over 80 hours per week of Welsh language programming.

The launch of the digital channel prompted S4C to establish a commercial arm that would source universal themes to be sold in the global marketplace. In March 1999 S4C International (S4CI) was formed. Having previously partnered with the Discovery channel on the *Egypt* documentary and with RTE (Ireland) and the History channel on *Saints and Sinners: The History of the Papacy*, S4C had already established its reputation as a viable coproducer. In addition, with only 25 percent of S4C's programs in the Welsh language, the company regularly produced programs in more than one language.

## S4C'S GLOBAL EXPANSION IN THE NEW MILLENNIUM

As the 1990s came to a close, S4C had a number of coproductions in the pipeline, including *The Celts* with Cardiff's Opus Television and *Parasites*, made in conjunction with the Discovery channel and Discovery

Networks International. In addition to distributing programs, S4CI's other mission was to raise revenue through advertising and sponsorship. In April 2001 S4CI launched an unconventional marketing campaign, offering advertisers the opportunity to have their ads dubbed into Welsh for free for a limited 12-month period. Less than four months later S4CI signed a lucrative four-year contract with Granada Enterprises to be the exclusive agent for the sale of the channel's advertising and sponsorship airtime.

In less than two years S4CI had closed five international documentary coproduction deals worth more than £4.0 million. In September 2001 S4CI signed a $700,000 deal with A&E Networks to produce a three-part documentary. S4CI was also making great strides with the company's animation catalog, with *Fireman Sam* showing in more than 40 countries. The *Sali Mali* series was sold to Nickoleon UK and other channels in Israel, Korea, and throughout the world, and in 2007 *Sali Mali* was broadcast in Arabic on Al Jazeera's children's channel.

In 2003 S4CI released the feature-length animated film *Otherworld*, based on the sixth-century Welsh Mabinogi legends, the inspiration for J. R. R. Tolkien's *The Lord of the Rings*. The film was produced in both Welsh and English by 200 animators and technicians in Wales and Russia for £6.6 million ($10 million).

Barcud Derwen was also raising its profile through acquisitions and organic growth. By April 2003 Barcud Derwen had companies throughout the British Isles, and it was the largest provider of broadcast facilities in the United Kingdom outside London. While S4C had begun to experience financial difficulties in 2003, Barcud Derwen's diverse range of resources, equipment, and skills assured the company's profitability.

One of the greatest factors effecting S4C's bottom line was the impending analog switch-off. After 2006 there would be more than 300 digital channels in competition with S4C. One of these, Channel 4, which accounted for a significant percentage of S4C's English-language output with shows such as *Friends* and *Sex and the City*, would have its own digital channel. Iona Jones, who left S4C as director of corporate affairs to move to ITV Wales in 2000, was brought back as director of programs to save the day. Jones immediately set her sights on improving the program schedules of the analog service while simultaneously revving up S4C Digital to be ready for the takeover after the analog switch-off. Looking forward in December 2003, Jones said to Rachell Murrell in *Televisual*, "If we can be there at the beginning, possibly by partnering with London companies, we can do something that might lead to suc-

## KEY DATES

**1982:** The S4C international catalogue is launched with "SuperTed," the first British animation series to be broadcast by Disney in the United States.

**1999:** S4C International, the commercial arm of channel S4C, is formed.

**2005:** Barcud Derwen Cyf. and Parthenon Entertainment Ltd. form a joint venture to operate S4C International.

**2005:** Iona Jones succeeds Huw Jones as chief executive officer of S4C.

**2007:** Random House Children's Books purchases the world rights of S4C's *Hana's Helpline* preschool series.

cess in a bigger market. Our commercial arm S4C International is always looking for projects."

## TRANSITIONING DURING THE DIGITAL AGE

By March 2004 S4C was broadcasting 33 hours of Welsh programming per week on analog television during peak hours. With the analog switch-off imminent, the channel needed to strengthen its off-peak programming. The digital switchover posed new challenges for the company that had created 2,000 jobs within Wales, and S4C made the unusual decision to be reviewed by the Department for Culture, Media, and Sport (DCMS). After a lengthy review, the S4C Authority appointed Iona Jones the channel's new CEO. Elan Closs Stephens, S4C chair, said in a May 2005 press release, "The S4C Authority has found in Iona the strategic and creative leader needed to take the channel forward into the digital age."

Within months Jones had made sweeping changes. In September 2005 Barcud Derwen partnered with Parthenon Entertainment to win the contract to run S4C International. Launched as a subsidiary of S4C at MIP-COM, the annual media event held in Cannes, France, S4CI would continue to do business under the same name despite the new management. In a December 2005 interview with Clive Jones of the BBC, Iona Jones said that her proudest achievement was "devising and implementing S4C's new program strategy, with its emphasis on landmark programming, which has led to an 11 percent year-on-year increase in peak time view-

ing, which runs counter to the current trend for terrestrial broadcasters."

In 2006 Jones appointed a new management team to undertake a rebranding strategy to reinforce the channel's Welsh identity in the global marketplace. The channel's rebrand, designed by Proud Creative under the direction of S4C's creative director, Dylan Griffith, was launched in January 2007 and won the Welsh Brand Category prize at the 2007 Bilingual Design Awards. The following month, S4CI sold the world rights to the preschool animation series *Hana's Helpline* to Random House Children's Books. The lucrative contract included translation rights and all English rights for a range of publications. In 2008, S4CI closed a deal with C&M Licensing to produce children's clothing based on the *Hana's Helpline* series. Although S4C directly employed fewer than 200 people, at the close of 2007 the channel was credited with creating 2,250 jobs within Wales and generating £87 million for the Welsh economy. Of an annual budget of £96 million, £90 million was funded by the DCMS, while the remainder was derived from S4CI's activities.

In S4C's Content Strategy report covering 2009 through 2013, the channel projected that the analog switch-off would be completed by the end of 2010. The channel was also planning to produce all programs in high definition by 2012. Although S4C Digital would contain only Welsh-speaking content, S4CI planned to continue its mission to source collaborative opportunities for documentaries and animations and to expand S4C's catalog with material that had worldwide appeal.

*Marie O'Sullivan*

## PRINCIPAL COMPETITORS

BBC Cymru Wales.

## FURTHER READING

"Barcud Derwen and Parthenon Take Reigns at S4C International," *Televisual*, September 8, 2005, p. 7.

Barry, Sion, "Thousands Feel the Benefits of S4C as the Country Cashes In on the Economic Boost Delivered by the Welsh Language Channel," *Western Mail* (Cardiff, Wales), October 10, 2007, p. 7.

"Hana Helps Dress Preschoolers with New Clothing Line," *License!* April 2008, p. 12.

Jones, Clive, "Iona Jones: My Life in Media," *The Independent* (United Kingdom), December 5, 2005.

Jones, David, "Publisher Buys World Rights to Pre-school Films," *Daily Post* (Liverpool, England), February 23, 2007, p. 31.

Murrell, Rachel, "S4C Goes Solo," *Televisual*, December 2003, p. 29.

"Proud Creative Gives S4C Identity an International Scope," *Design Week*, June 28, 2007, p. 6.

"Six Nominations for Welsh Arts Channel," *Western Mail* (Cardiff, Wales), October 25, 2008.

Wray, Richard, "Welsh-language Channel Invests in TV-on-PC Venture," *The Guardian* (London), June 5, 2008, p. 27.

Wynne Jones, Ivor, "Welsh TV Depends on Harsh Realities of Profit," *Daily Post* (Liverpool, England), October 22, 2002.

Savings Made Simple

# Sam's Club

———————■———————

608 SW Eighth Street
Bentonville, Arkansas 72716
U.S.A.
Telephone: (479) 277-7000
Toll Free: (888) 746-7726
Fax: (479) 273-4053
Web site: http://www.samsclub.com

*Division of Wal-Mart Stores, Inc.*
*Founded:* 1983 as Sam's Wholesale Club
*Employees:* 125,000 (est.)
*Sales:* $46.71 billion (2010)
*NAICS:* 45291 Warehouse Clubs and Superstores

■ ■ ■

Sam's Club, a division of discount merchandiser Wal-Mart Stores, Inc., is one of the nation's leading operators of members-only warehouse stores. It runs more than 600 stores across the United States and in Mexico, Puerto Rico, Brazil, and China. Sam's Club sells to some 47 million customers who pay an annual fee to become members. Members can shop at Sam's sprawling stores, which are typically 110,000 to 130,000 square feet and offer more than 4,000 items, from fresh groceries to auto supplies, clothing, and pharmaceuticals. The clubs also offer additional services such as a mail-order pharmacy, a travel club, Internet, long-distance phone services, car loans, and discount credit card processing. Markup on Sam's Club items is just over wholesale, so goods at these stores are deeply discounted over other vendors. Sam's Club sells to small

businesses such as restaurants, day-care centers, and offices, and also markets to individuals. Sam's Club entered the warehouse club market in the mid-1980s, after Wal-Mart founder Sam Walton studied the success of other similar ventures. After some consolidation in the industry, Sam's Club and its close competitor, Costco Wholesale Corporation, lead the market.

## CATCHING A TREND IN THE EIGHTIES

Sam's Club was created by Sam Walton, the remarkable retailer who brought the nation Wal-Mart stores. Walton had built a chain of Arkansas five-and-dimes in the 1960s and increased this to almost 300 stores in the South in the 1970s. Wal-Mart Stores, Inc., incorporated in 1971 and was a billion-dollar operation by 1980. Wal-Mart stores were located in small towns, usually in markets so small that other retailers avoided them. The stores offered deeply discounted goods, and rural people flocked to them. Wal-Mart continued to expand across the nation in the 1980s, mainly in small towns. Sam's debuted in 1983 as something of a corollary to the Wal-Mart small-town strategy. The warehouse stores were designed for an urban market, giving Wal-Mart Stores, Inc., access to customers it did not otherwise reach.

The warehouse club idea did not originate with Sam Walton. The designated father of the warehouse club industry was the aptly named Sol Price, who ran Price Club. Sol Price opened his first Price Club in San Diego in 1976. The chain spread across the West Coast in the 1980s. Price Club stores were huge, on average 108,000 square feet, and ran with no frills and a

## COMPANY PERSPECTIVES

Since our inception in 1983, our operating philosophy has remained the same—we work hard to be the buying agent for our Members and deliver upon this agreement by eliminating unnecessary costs and maintaining a simple shopping environment. We pass the savings on to the more than 47 million Members who shop our Clubs and samsclub.com, simplifying their shopping so that their everyday lives benefit, too.

minimum of employees. Sol Price guided Sam Walton through one of his stores in the early 1980s, and Walton acknowledged that his Sam's stores were patterned after the Price chain.

The first Sam's opened in Oklahoma City in 1983. It was called Sam's Wholesale Club, the name that stuck with the chain until 1990. By the end of 1983 there were two more stores, one in Kansas City, Missouri, and one in Dallas. Sales the first year were $40 million. In 1984 the chain added 8 stores, and these 11 stores brought in $225 million total that year. Sam's stores were located in leased warehouses, usually in rather desolate areas. They were huge, and bare of decoration. Goods were displayed on shipping pallets or on steel shelves that reached almost to the ceiling. "Displayed" might be putting it too strongly: The items were often simply set out stacked inside torn-open packing boxes. But the goods were brand-name, at prices much lower than elsewhere. Customers usually had to buy large sizes or multiple packs of things. Sam's took advantage of the distribution know-how of the Wal-Mart chain.

An analyst for Morgan Stanley, quoted in *Discount Store News* for December 9, 1985, described Wal-Mart's distribution network as using "some of the most sophisticated systems currently devised." The chain already knew how to hold down costs, and it amplified this skill at Sam's stores. Merchandise was moved mechanically whenever possible so that few human hands needed to touch it on its journey from factory to customer's car. In addition, Wal-Mart had studied the market carefully before plunging into the warehouse business. The urban market of the warehouse store was a great complement to the small-town market of the Wal-Mart chain. The two chains added to each other without competing. Another analyst, quoted in the *Discount Store News* article, claimed that Wal-Mart and Sam's together could "serve almost all the potential shoppers in a market." Serving everybody was quite a proposition, but it seemed possible. The Sam's chain grew rapidly and accounted for a larger portion of Wal-Mart's sales each year through the 1980s.

In 1986 warehouse club sales accounted for less than 1 percent of total U.S. retail sales. But what *Fortune* magazine dubbed a "mini-industry" was nevertheless worth about $4.4 billion annually at that time, and the level of profitability was enticing. The entrenched Price Co. was still the market leader in 1986, with sales of $1.9 billion and profits of $46 million. One key to the profitability of the warehouse concept was that goods turned over very quickly. Inventory at Sam's stores turned over on average 16 to 18 times per year. This high turnover meant that inventory was off the shelves and sold within 30 days, or before the store had to pay for it. Many retailers had jumped on the warehouse trend by the mid-1980s. Besides Sam's and Price Club, competitors in the industry included Costco, Pace Membership Warehouse, Warehouse Club Inc., Wholesale Club Inc., BJ's Wholesale Club, and Price Savers. Costco, Pace, Warehouse Club, and Wholesale Club all went public in 1986 to fund further expansion. BJ's also had expansion plans in the mid-1980s, and Price Savers got the backing of the large grocery chain Kroger when it was acquired in August 1985. The industry was getting crowded as chains competed for specific regional markets and then for membership within those markets.

Between its founding in 1983 and 1985, Sam's opened in urban markets in the South and Southwest. The chain entered the Midwest in 1986. By 1987 Sam's had 84 stores. This included stores it bought in 1987 when Sam's took over the warehouse chain Super Saver Wholesale. Super Saver had gone head-to-head with Sam's in ten southern cities, and had another 11 warehouse stores in the South. However, it was not profitable, and in 1987 Sam's took over the chain, closing some stores and reopening others under the Sam's banner. In 1989 Sam's began moving into the Northeast. This region had little exposure to the warehouse store concept, and was not a Wal-Mart stronghold either. Sam's opened its first store in the Northeast in Delran Township, New Jersey, and planned to open other stores in New York, Delaware, Maine, New Hampshire, and Pennsylvania. The other leading warehouse chains also targeted the Northeast at that time. The California-based Price Club chain had started Price Club East and had 11 stores in the Northeast by 1990. Costco also entered the Northeastern market in 1990, with a revamped store format that included a bakery.

By 1989 the Sam's Wholesale Club division brought in $4.8 billion in sales, rising more than 25

## KEY DATES

**1983:** The first Sam's Wholesale Club opens in Oklahoma City.
**1987:** Sam's acquires southern competitor Super Saver Wholesale chain.
**1990:** The chain changes its name to Sam's Club.
**1993:** The company acquires Pace Membership Club, a struggling chain owned by Kmart.
**1998:** The company undertakes a major renovation program.
**2000:** Sam's Club rolls out a Web site and "Click 'n Pull" shopping.
**2006:** Sam's Club begins accepting MasterCard at the register.
**2008:** The company celebrates its 25th anniversary.
**2009:** The company closes its Canadian stores.

percent over the previous year. The chain continued to account for a larger portion of Wal-Mart's total sales each year. By 1989 it was providing over 18 percent of Wal-Mart's total sales.

### CONSOLIDATION AND COMPETITION IN THE NINETIES

Sam's changed its name in 1990 from Sam's Wholesale Club to simply Sam's Club. A judge in North Carolina had ruled that the chain was not entitled to the word "wholesale" in its name, because in that state only from 11 to 15 percent of goods bought at the Sam's stores was actually intended for resale by others. State law required that at least 50 percent of goods sold be intended for resale in order to merit the "wholesale" appellation. Although the ruling only applied to North Carolina, the chain thought it would be confusing to have different names in different states, so it adopted the simpler Sam's Club name overall.

While the chain was taking "wholesale" out of its name, it coincidentally bought a rival chain called The Wholesale Club. Sam's paid about $175 million for the Indianapolis-based chain of 27 stores. The Wholesale Club was founded in 1982, the year before Sam's. It operated exclusively in the Midwest. The chain had experienced a slow start, then eventually took off, with sales climbing from $165 million in 1987 to approximately $700 million at the time of its acquisition by Sam's in 1990. It was poised to open three stores in the Chicago area when Sam's bought it. Sam's Club had been opening stores around Chicago, moving into

suburban locations and in smaller towns on the outskirts of the city such as Joliet and Rockford. Sam's acquisition of The Wholesale Club earned the company strength in the Midwest, just as other chains were also muscling into the area.

By 1990 competition between Sam's and the other leading chains was growing more intense as the big players moved out of their core markets. Where the different warehouse chains met head-on, they tried to differentiate. Some offered a brighter format, or emphasized fresh foods and baked goods. One advantage Sam's had was its relationship with Wal-Mart. Although Sam's had originally been designated for urban markets, where Wal-Marts opened in small towns, increasingly since the late 1980s Sam's opened alongside or nearby Wal-Marts. Because Sam's was for members only and appealed to small businesses, Wal-Mart's management claimed the two stores did not overlap. Half the new Sam's opened in 1990 were paired with a Wal-Mart. The size of the duo dwarfed other players in the same market.

The booming warehouse store market that the various players had struggled to divide since the mid-1980s began to cool in the early 1990s. The expanding warehouse chains could not keep up their momentum. The biggest players were still Sam's Club, Costco, Price, and Pace Membership Warehouse, which was run by the formidable retailer Kmart. A poor retail environment in the early 1990s, combined with the intensity of the competition among the chains as they reached out of their core geographical markets, caused several stumbles. Sam's apparently looked into acquiring Price or Costco, as did Kmart. Eventually Price and Costco merged, forming Price/Costco Inc. in 1993. (Within a few years the name reverted to Costco Companies Inc.) Kmart was unable to keep Pace Membership Warehouse going and sold 99 of its 113 stores to Sam's in 1993. At this juncture, Sam's was the biggest chain left, with about 400 stores and 1993 sales of $14.7 billion. Sam's also accounted for 22 percent of Wal-Mart's total sales by that year. Sam's, however, entered a period of doldrums. By the middle of 1994 same-store sales levels had fallen month by month for almost a solid year.

The company decided to refocus on its core of small business customers, targeting specific industries such as nursing homes, restaurants, hotel/motel operators, cleaning companies, and restaurants. It stocked items such as institutional quality sheets, heavy restaurant-grade cutlery, wheel chairs, and wrist splints. In targeting particular businesses, Sam's also moved to carry less of other items, such as housewares, that appealed more to consumers buying for themselves or their families. In 1994 Sam's also began stocking some unusual items, including juke boxes and grand pianos, that were meant to appeal to upscale consumers who enjoyed the thrill of bargain hunting.

Joseph Hardin Jr. became Sam's new president in late 1995, but he resigned in 1997 to take a job at the copy shop chain Kinko's. He was replaced by Mark Hansen. Sales remained slow at the chain, accounting for a shrinking percentage of Wal-Mart's total. Sam's had provided over 20 percent of Wal-Mart's sales in the early 1990s, but by 1997 this figure had dropped to 17.5 percent. In 1998 the company embarked on a major renovation program. It remodeled 70 stores, added bakeries or other new departments to 50 more stores, and expanded the fresh grocery departments of 120 stores. Some top buying personnel were replaced, and the chain announced it would build a new kind of store, a "Millennium Club," beginning with a model in San Diego. The Millennium Club stores offered more upscale items, such as wine, not found in other Sam's. Sam's Club stores also began offering a host of services, such as Airborne Express shipping service, discounted Internet access, a mail-order pharmacy, software training, and more. It introduced a new private label food line called Members Mark, and it assailed its members with direct mail claiming "the secret to living well" could be found at Sam's. All these moves seemed to have paid off, as 1998 was the best year the chain had had in a long time. Sales were close to $23 billion, and operating profits rose 15 percent over 1997.

However, there was more turnover at the top, with Tom Grimm becoming president of Sam's Club in October 1998. Grimm had formerly led the Pace Membership Club, which Sam's acquired from Kmart in 1993. Strong consumer spending in the late 1990s and through 2000 helped Sam's get back on its feet somewhat. Sales and earnings increased in 1999, and the company opened almost 20 new stores. By 2000 the warehouse club industry had shaken down to only three major players: Sam's, with over 450 stores; Costco, with close to 300; and BJ's Wholesale Club, with just over 100 units. Rivalry between Costco and Sam's continued unabated. Costco had subsumed the Price Club chain that Sam's was originally modeled after, and Sam's continued to take cues from Costco, offering similar goods and services. Sam's and Costco opened stores within the same city, and Sam's increasingly penetrated California, once a Costco stronghold. Also in 2000, Costco announced that it would open a new warehouse store in Arlington, Texas, only blocks from the site Sam's had picked for its new store.

Sam's hoped to prevail, enhancing its marketing through ventures such as catalogs geared toward specific groups of members, including day-care center operators. Sam's also began attaching gas stations to its stores, moving from a pilot of 7 in 1999 to a planned 100 or more by the end of the year. Sam's also enhanced its pharmacy operations, and it offered other services such as one-hour photo processing and prepared meals. Another innovation that came in 2000 was the Sam's Club Web site and online shopping option. Using a feature called Click 'n Pull, members can make their shopping selections online (or via Fax 'n Pull), then simply pick up their purchases at the store.

## COURTING BUSINESSES AND CONSUMERS IN THE TWENTIETH CENTURY

Although Sam's had recovered from its mid-1990s slump, Costco wrenched the market leadership from Sam's in 2001. Costco's more upscale clientele and inventory brought in stronger per-store sales, allowing the company to edge Sam's in total revenue despite a smaller number of locations. Some market analysts attributed Costco's advantage to superior customer service. Sam's and Wal-Mart employees are among the lowest paid in the retail industry, and the company has been dogged for years by complaints and class-action suits alleging unfair treatment of workers.

Sam's hired a new CEO, Kevin Turner, in 2002 and revamped its business model. The new emphasis came across in the slogan, "We're in business for small business." The company fashioned a list of specific business sectors it intended to serve, including restaurants and food service, convenience stores, offices, and motels. Turner's "1-2-3" program sought growth by concentrating on small business owners, going after those customers to use the clubs for their own families, and building the base of individual members from there. The strategy resulted in increased profits in 2003 and 2004.

In 2005 Turner was replaced by Doug McMillon. Within a year the company tweaked its image once again. Without abandoning its core small business market, the new leadership implemented changes to drive growth in the consumer sector. One significant change came at the checkout counter: In addition to cash, checks, debit cards, and Discover, Sam's began accepting MasterCard. The overwhelming response from members was that this form of payment was long overdue. Sam's also updated its merchandise selection to emphasize "affordable luxuries." Big-ticket consumer items such as high-end jewelry and flat-screen TVs were moved to the front of the center aisles. Sam's also began stocking more fresh food, including meat, produce, and baked goods, in an attempt to compete head-to-head with supermarkets.

Sam's Club announced several environmental initiatives in 2007. It opened a prototype store in Fayetteville, Arkansas, designed with sustainable features such as skylights, efficiencies in refrigeration and water conservation, and a composting facility. Wal-Mart also created a packaging scorecard for its suppliers, an attempt to persuade them to upgrade to sustainable packaging. Sam's also announced it was converting to Fair Trade–certified coffee for its in-house brand of ground Members Mark brew.

As Sam's approached its 25th anniversary in 2008, the company was in a strong position overall. Although it remained number two in the industry, behind Costco, the warehouse club market had become the fastest-growing sector in all of retail. With the economic downturn that began in early 2008, shoppers in all income strata were strapped for cash and flocking to discount retailers. These stores, however, faced a quandary: With the cost of food, fuel, and other goods rising steeply, Sam's was hesitant to slow down business by raising prices above the low levels customers expected. Some of the cost increases had to be absorbed before the company could pass them on to consumers. Nevertheless, Sam's finished 2008 with $46.8 billion in revenue, a 5.6 percent jump over the previous fiscal year. If Sam's Club were an independent company, this income would make it the seventh-largest U.S. retailer. As the steep recession continued, Sam's shuffled its merchandising mix again, cutting back on luxury goods in place of necessities, under the leadership of a new CEO, Brian Cornell.

Wal-Mart boasted more than 600 Sam's Club stores in 2009. The company's six outlets in Ontario, Canada,

were closed that year, to be replaced by Wal-Mart Supercenters. In early 2010 the parent company announced it was cutting more than 11,000 jobs from Sam's Club. Most of these were product demonstrator positions. The company had decided to outsource the task of conducting product demonstrations to another Arkansas-based firm, giving the laid-off workers an opportunity to retain their positions.

*A. Woodward*
*Updated, Roger K. Smith*

## PRINCIPAL COMPETITORS

Costco Wholesale Corporation; BJ's Wholesale Club, Inc.

## FURTHER READING

Orgel, David, "How Sam's Stands Out in the Shadows of Wal-Mart, Costco," *Supermarket News*, April 14, 2008.

Pinto, David, "Clubs Demonstrate Their Mettle," *MMR*, November 16, 2009, p. 8.

Rosenbloom, Stephanie, "Wal-Mart Tells Employees It Will Cut 11,200 Jobs," *New York Times*, January 24, 2010.

"Sam's Expansion Is Key to Wal-Mart's Success," *Discount Store News*, July 16, 1990, p. 85.

Saporito, Bill, "The Mad Rush to Join the Warehouse Club," *Fortune*, January 6, 1986, pp. 59–61.

"Top Two Raise Bar, Lift Sales," *DSN Retailing Today*, August 7, 2000, p. 43.

Troy, Mike, "Sam's Updates Market Strategies," *Discount Store News*, March 9, 1998, p. 5.

Vance, Sandra, and Roy V. Scott, *Wal-Mart: A History of Sam Walton's Retail Phenomenon*. New York: Twayne Publishers, 1994.

"Why Price Clubs Are Feeling the Pinch," *BusinessWeek*, August 14, 2008.

Zellner, Wendy, "Why Sam's Wants Businesses to Join the Club," *BusinessWeek*, June 27, 1994, pp. 48–50.

# Sheffield Forgemasters
# International Ltd.

———————■———————

P.O. Box 286, Brightside Lane
Sheffield, S9 2RW
United Kingdom
Telephone: (+44 114) 244 9071
Fax: (+44 114) 251 9013
Web site: http://www.sheffieldforgemasters.com/

*Private Company*
*Founded:* 1983
*Incorporated:* 2005
*Employees:* 742
*Sales:* €146.7 million ($179.70 million) (2008)
*NAICS:* 331513 Steel Foundries (except Investment);
   551112 Offices of Other Holding Companies

■ ■ ■

With a worldwide network of offices spanning three continents, Sheffield Forgemasters International Ltd. (SFIL) is the world's largest independently owned foundry, and one of only 14 large-scale open die companies in existence. SFIL's three major subsidiaries (Sheffield Forgemasters Steel Ltd., Sheffield Forgemasters Engineering Ltd., and Vulcan SFM) are engaged in the design, manufacture, and project management of high-quality engineered products, including steel forgings, castings, and components. Boasting the largest forging and foundry facilities in the United Kingdom, SFIL's products serve a diverse range of industries, including defense, nuclear, oil and gas exploration, power generation, marine, and construction. SFIL believes that this diversification, combined with an an-

nual investment of 5 percent to 10 percent of the company's profits in research and development, are the keys to securing a profitable future.

## SFIL'S ORIGINS

Even though the company's roots extend as far back as the 1750s, Edward Vickers, a miller with a watermill close to the center of Sheffield, and the Naylor family are credited with establishing the company in 1805. By the mid-19th century large-scale high-volume steel production had taken the world by storm, and Sheffield was one of the industry's major hubs. At the Great Exhibition of 1851, Vickers exhibited a steel ingot weighing more than 2,600 pounds, the largest of its time. In 1856 Henry Bessemer patented a bulk steel-making process capable of producing several tons of steel in less than an hour. The invention transformed Sheffield's steel industry and led to the development of several companies throughout the city. Among these companies was Tom Vickers's River Don Works, which was established in 1865.

Vickers's operation was impressive, and it even boasted a crucible melt shop that was capable of pouring a single 20-ton piece. Steel bells were in huge demand, and Vickers was exporting them around the world, including a 74-inch, 2.5-ton bell for a San Francisco fire station. Vickers's other achievements included developing the Mayer molding method for castings and installing a Siemens open hearth melting furnace for bulk steel production. This was followed in 1882 with the installation of the world's first heavy forging press.

# COMPANY PERSPECTIVES

■

As the world's largest independently-owned forgemaster, Sheffield Forgemasters International (SFIL) has a mission to combine investment in knowledge, experience and innovation to provide world class engineering services supplying the most demanding international markets. The ultimate aim is to be first choice for engineering excellence.

A large percentage of River Don Works's revenue was derived from the export of railroad equipment to the United States, but when the U.S. steel industry expanded, Vickers decided to diversify by moving into armaments. Vickers became a leading manufacturer of armor plate and was renowned for producing the Maxim machine gun. Vickers also established a shipyard in Barrow, where the first submarine was produced. By 1870 River Don Works was one of the world's largest steel companies, second only to Bochum in Germany. In 1897 River Don Works was merged with the Barrow Shipyard and Sir W. G. Armstrong Whitworth & Co. Ltd., which formed a leading steel production group that had subsidiaries and joint ventures in the Americas, Europe, and Asia.

## THE CREATION OF SHEFFIELD FORGEMASTERS IN THE TWENTIETH CENTURY

The demand for steel was at its height during World War I, but with much of the River Don workforce enlisting in the military, production levels were greatly reduced. In the late 1920s the Vickers group of companies was merged with Firth Brown and Cammell Laird, a leading shipbuilding firm, to form English Steel. To stay afloat during the Great Depression of the 1930s, Vickers established a reinvestment strategy, and with the onset of World War II in the 1940s steel was once again in great demand. As the only foundry capable of producing the crankshafts for the Spitfire and Lancaster aircraft, River Don Works was a highly valued facility and a prime target for enemy forces that failed to destroy the site during the Sheffield blitz in December 1940.

After the war, the company broadened its range of products to include turbine rotors and boiler drums for power stations and ships, railway equipment, rolling mill rolls, and components for the world's first nuclear power station at Calder Hall. In 1967 River Don Works

was renationalized into the British Steel Corporation, and the facility began producing castings for the offshore oil industry. British Steel invested an additional £4 million in River Don Works for the construction of a 10,000-ton world-class forge, and Firth Brown spent £12 million on a high-speed precision forge. These two specialist steel companies seemed poised for success, but by the early 1980s the UK engineering sector was in decline, steel was being overproduced, and the British pound was at an all time high. In 1982 Firth Brown and River Don Works reported losses, with the latter losing £33 million in the previous five years.

In 1983 River Don Works and Firth Brown merged to form the private company Sheffield Forgemasters Group Ltd. The following year the new company's shareholders wrote off their investments and replaced the entire board with new management. A survival plan, which included decentralization and a major reorganization, was also put into action. In 1985, after a four-month trade union strike, it was agreed that pay increases would be tied to increased productivity. It was during this period that River Don Castings and the OS-CAL offshore specialist subsidiaries were formed. In 1987, when British Steel was due for privatization, the management of Sheffield Forgemasters successfully completed a management buyout (MBO). By 1989 sales per employee had risen to £46,000 from £26,000 in 1985, and the company had sales of £115 million and pretax profits of £9 million. River Don Castings's achievements in the area of cast products for the offshore industry contributed significantly to these positive results and earned the company its first Queen's Award for Technology and Export.

## THE MAKING OF SHEFFIELD FORGEMASTERS INTERNATIONAL LTD.

In 1994 Sheffield Forgemasters was forced to combine its two subsidiaries, Forgemasters Steel and Forgemasters Engineering, due to poor market conditions and an 80 percent increase in scrap costs. Four years later, in 1998, Sheffield Forgemasters was sold to two U.S. companies, with the aerospace business going to Allegheny Teledyne Inc. and the remaining assets to the Atchison Casting Corp. for $51.5 million. For Atchison, the sale meant entry into the European market, whereas Sheffield hoped to expand its sales in the United States. In May 1998 Atchison consolidated Sheffield Forgemasters's four subsidiaries into two market-focused companies. British Rolls Corporation and Forged Rolls were combined to form Sheffield Forgemasters Rolls, and River Don Castings merged with Forgemasters Steel and Engineering to become Sheffield Forgemasters Engineering.

## KEY DATES

**1865:** Tom Vickers establishes River Don Works.

**1983:** River Don Works and Firth Brown merge to form Sheffield Forgemasters.

**1998:** The company is sold, with Allegheny Teledyne acquiring the aerospace business and Atchison Castings Corp. acquiring the River Don and Rolls businesses.

**2003:** Atchison files for Chapter 11 bankruptcy protection.

**2005:** Sheffield's management completes a management buyout, and the company is renamed Sheffield Forgemasters International Ltd.

The following year Sheffield Forgemasters Engineering signed an $8 million contract with the U.S. Navy to provide castings for its new generation of landing platform dock vessels. During the next two years the subsidiary secured major contracts to manufacture castings for UK submarines and for oil and gas projects in Norway, the Gulf of Mexico, and the Far East. The parent company and Sheffield Forgemasters Rolls did not fare as well. As a result, in August 2003 Atchison filed for Chapter 11 bankruptcy protection, and the Rolls subsidiary was placed into administration the following month.

In 2002 Graham Honeyman became the managing director of Sheffield Forgemasters Engineering. By 2005 the company was reporting operating profits of £2.5 million. That same year the company management completed an MBO and returned the company to British ownership. Renamed Sheffield Forgemasters International Ltd. (SFIL), the company was reorganized into three divisions: steel, engineering, and Vulcan SFM, a new design, manufacturing, and project specialist company. The entire workforce of 600 employees was based at SFIL's Brightside Lane facility in Sheffield. There were 41 skilled apprentices among the staff, and in 2005 SFIL received the Metals Industry Apprentice of the Year Award.

In July 2006 SFIL produced a 325-ton casting for Austria's Bohler press, an achievement that earned the company the Cast Component of the Year Award. That same year the company was awarded Yorkshire's Deal of the Year in "Best Deal under £10 million" for the 2005 MBO. By September 2006 SFIL had sales of £100 million and was exporting 80 percent of its products. In November 2006 Honeyman, who became SFIL's chief

executive officer following the MBO, told Peter Marsh of the *Financial Times* that he was positioning the company to be a specialist in the manufacture of complex components for the nuclear power market. Furthermore, he projected that 25 percent of the company's revenue would be derived from this sector by 2011.

### EXPANDING SFIL IN THE GLOBAL MARKETPLACE

In April 2007 Vulcan secured a lucrative contract with Bluewater, an offshore oil-processing specialist, to provide nine mooring-system components for its Aoka Mizu vessel. The following month SFIL signed the first part of a 10-year, £60 million contract with Germany to provide steel containers for its nuclear waste. The company suffered a minor setback in late June, when Sheffield's Don Valley was hit with floods and SFIL's entire 64-acre facility was deluged. Less than three weeks later and at an estimated cost of £15 million, SFIL was nearly back to full production capacity. In the two years following the MBO, SFIL had invested heavily in new technology and internal improvements and had expanded its portfolio through diversification. In December 2007 the company announced that it had secured its first major offshore contract in Brazil and that it was heading into a new year with an order book worth £120 million.

In February 2008 SFIL secured a lucrative contract with Italy's Ringmill to cast a 168-ton foundation base and another with Germany's SMS Meer GmbH that was worth £3.2 million. The following month the company reported that it planned to build a 15,000-ton press to meet the rising demand for nuclear power components. SFIL continued its international expansion with a £2 million contract to provide hydropower castings to India's Karcham Wangtoo Hydroelectric Project. That same year SFIL won its third Queen's Award in the international trade category, and Honeyman was awarded a Commander of the Order of the British Empire in recognition of his achievements in turning around a company that was facing collapse.

In March 2009 SFIL entered into a 10-year, £30 million joint venture with India's Bharat Heavy Electricals Ltd. to manufacture nuclear forgings. This was followed in June with new contracts in Argentina and South Korea to supply nuclear power components. In August 2009 the company marked its entrance into China when it produced a reactor coolant pump casing for the country's Westinghouse AP1000TM nuclear power plant. Wanting to play a pivotal role in the advancement of Britain's nuclear program, SFIL announced in December 2009 that it was a founding member of the Nuclear Advanced Manufacturing Research Centre.

SFIL entered 2010 with its biggest order book in the company's history, and it predicted that yearend sales would be the highest on record. The company planned to continue to cultivate a specialized workforce through its highly competitive award-winning apprentice scheme and to invest heavily in research and development to secure its competitive edge in the global marketplace.

*Marie O'Sullivan*

## PRINCIPAL SUBSIDIARIES

Sheffield Forgemasters Steel Ltd.; Sheffield Forgemasters Engineering Ltd.; Vulcan SFM.

## PRINCIPAL COMPETITORS

ArcelorMittal; Castings PLC; Chamerlin PLC; Corus Group; Eregli Iron and Steel Works Co.; ThyssenKrupp AG; United States Steel Corporation.

## FURTHER READING

Armitstead, Louise, "Sheffield Company Wins £80m to Become World Leader in Industry," *Daily Telegraph* (London), March 18, 2010, p. 2.

Ginns, Bernard, "Battle to Forge a Future in Nuclear Industry Depends on Government," *Yorkshire Post* (London), January 19, 2010.

Jameson, Angela, "Sheffield Steel Firm Presses ahead with Plans for Heavyweight Growth," *Times* (London), March 3, 2008, p. 44.

Marsh, Peter, "Sheffield Forgemasters Expects Power Bonanza," *Financial Times* (London), November 6, 2006, p. 21.

Marsh, Peter, and Jim Pickard, "Sheffield Manufacturer Hopes to Forge £30m Nuclear Future," *Financial Times* (London), November 24, 2008, p. 6.

Murphy, Lizzie, "A First for Sheffield as Firm Forges Link with China," *Yorkshire Post* (London), August 18, 2009.

Parkin, David, "Forgemasters Enters a New Era," *Yorkshire Post* (London), July 28, 2005.

"Forgemasters Back with 'Never Again' Warning: Sheffield Forgemasters Back to Work after the Floods," *Sheffield Telegraph* (London), July 19, 2007.

Van de Vliet, Anita, "Out of the Furnace," *Management Today*, January 1990, p. 50.

Webb, Tim, "Sheffield Edges Closer to Nuclear Deal," *Observer* (London), January 24, 2010, p. 2.

# Small World Toys

—— ∎ ——

1451 West Knox Street
Torrance, California 90501
U.S.A.
Toll Free: (800) 421-4153
Fax: (310) 410-9606
Web site: http://shop.smallworldtoys.com/

*Private Company*
*Founded:* 1962
*Employees:* 18
*Sales:* $15 million (2009)
*NAICS:* 339932 Game, Toy, and Children's Vehicle
Manufacturing

∎ ∎ ∎

Small World Toys has a reputation for producing high-quality, niche-market toys and games for preadolescent children of all ages. Sales categories include infant, preschool, early learning, imaginative, and active play. Small World Toys's products shun violence and focus on child development through education, the advancement of social skills, and the promotion of physical well-being. Award-winning brand names include Ryan's Room, Gertie Balls, Eric Carle, IQ Baby, and Neurosmith.

## EARLY BRAND LINES

In 1962 Edward Goldwasser cofounded Small World Toys (SWT), a privately held firm of which he was president. From the beginning, the company was a niche-market designer, manufacturer, and distributor of high-end specialty toys and games for children from 0 to 12 years old. Eschewing violence, its products were meant to support childhood development. By allowing the users to make choices among alternatives, SWT products helped children learn. They also promoted social and motor skills.

Gertie Balls was one of the firm's most popular early product lines. The inexpensive balls were bouncy, rubbery objects that could be inflated to different sizes for different ages while retaining their softness and flexibility. The balls could be safely thrown or kicked at things and people. They had a distinct, slightly sticky surface that made them easy for even the youngest users to grip, throw, and catch, which promoted social interaction and enhanced athletic ability. Furthermore, easy gripping made them suitable for special needs children.

Another early line of enduring popularity was Ryan's Room. Rooms could be assembled and placed in relationship to each other in any way the child fancied. The style of the house as a whole (a ranch house or a multistory structure) was up to the child. Various furnishings were provided, offering the users a multitude of additional choices. Eventually, families of various ethnicities were offered to populate the houses.

Old-fashioned, brightly colored wooden puzzles were persistent favorites. Besides being fun for younger children to play with, they promoted hand-to-eye coordination, visual discrimination, and critical thinking skills. SWT promoted its IQ Baby line, another favorite, as nurturing "mind, body, and spirit" through "vibrant, engaging toys." This line included musical toys and sets of multicolored, multishaped blocks. In 1988 SWT formulated, in conjunction with the Consumer Product Safety Commission, stringent twice-a-year testing procedures for toys aimed at children three and under.

## THRIVING AGAINST STRONG COMPETITION: 1990–2003

SWT's customers were primarily small specialty stores. Specialty stores and mass marketers operated in separate business universes. Goldwasser reported in 1996 that he had turned down a big order for Gertie Balls from the giant toy chain Toys "R" Us, even though the sale would have increased SWT's revenues for the year by 50 percent. Goldwasser explained his refusal to Joseph Pereira of the *Wall Street Journal*. "Once a specialty manufacturer does business with the mass market," Goldwasser said, "word spreads quickly like bad news" among the small stores because mass merchants could undersell them. It was important for SWT to secure the specialty store market, because specialty stores were particularly well-suited to sell the relatively sophisticated, high-end toys and games of SWT. These outlets hired moonlighting preschool and school teachers and other experts in childhood development to explain to parents the value of these products.

Goldwasser worked hard to win the favor of the specialty stores, especially since they were diminishing in numbers beginning in the 1970s as big companies bought them up or forced them out of business. In 1991, for example, the general manager of Hub Hobby Centers in Little Canada, Minnesota, praised SWT for its "dating program," which allowed him to receive $1,000 worth of goods in early autumn and not pay until Christmas, when the store had just rung up its biggest sales of the year. In 1997 Goldwasser wrote "Puzzles Get It All Together" for *Playthings*, an industry trade publication, in which he gave meticulously detailed advice on selling wooden puzzles, down to how to prevent puzzle boxes from falling off the shelf. He offered retailers racks and signage for creating the best possible displays and the free pamphlet "Value of Puzzle Play."

Consolidation affected toy manufacturers as well as retailers. In September 1993 Donna K. H. Walters of the *Los Angeles Times* stated that "the small players can stay only if they are clever and agile enough to keep out of the way" of the "big guys." SWT managed to thrive under these circumstances. Effective management and high-quality products, along with the decade's economic boom and a growing parental interest in educational toys, boosted sales to more than $50 million annually. Part of this success also stemmed from outsourcing manufacturing to China, which began in earnest around 1990.

During the 1990s SWT received substantial recognition for its products. In 1997 the nonprofit Parents' Choice Foundation gave a Gold Award for SWT's Creative Playhouse, a house in the Ryan's Room tradition that could be assembled in many different ways. In 1999 the American Specialty Toy Retail Association included SWT's Math Keyboard on a list of toys offering preschoolers enjoyable ways to learn important skills. A mathematical equation involving addition, subtraction, or multiplication was inscribed on each key. When the child pressed down on a key, the answer was revealed. That same year the Lion & Lamb Toy Project released its Top Twenty Toy List of creative and nonviolent toys, on which appeared SWT's Band in a Bag, a set of musical instruments.

During the 2001–03 recession toy sales in general were sluggish and SWT sales declined, totaling $26 million for 2003. The company, however, continued to make toys that were recognized for their merit in the toy and game industry. Taking advantage of the popularity of "junior cooking," for example, SWT introduced in August 2001 the Café Play line, which included child-sized but functional cookware such as whisks, sauté pans, pastry crumpers, and stockpots for making real food. Just three months later two products in this line, Café Play Boutique Bakery and Café Play Kitchenette, were recognized for their excellence. In its 2003 Toy Guide for Differently-abled Kids, Toys "R" Us included SWT's Rip Rolling Fun, a toddler's toy in which wooden triangles ran down a wooden track as designs on the triangles created optical illusions as they moved.

## NEW OWNERSHIP AND A NEW STRATEGY: 2004–05

In early 2004 an investment group headed by Debra Fine purchased Savon Team Sports, an unsuccessful online purveyor of sporting goods that had become a non-operating company. The group renamed the firm Small

## KEY DATES
∎

**1962:** Small World Toys is founded.
**1988:** Small World Toys develops stringent testing procedures in cooperation with the Consumer Product and Safety Commission.
**2004:** Small World Toys is acquired by Small World Kids and becomes a public company.
**2007:** Small World Toys is bought by Rivenrock Capital and again becomes a privately held company.
**2009:** Small World Toys is acquired by Vertex Capital.

World Kids (SWK), which became a publicly traded company. In May 2004 SWK spent $7.2 million to acquire SWT. SWK then functioned as a holding company with no significant operations or assets aside from SWT.

In June 2004 John Nelson, the chief operating officer (COO) of SWK, explained the purchase to *Home Accents Today*: "Small World Toys has a history of steady growth and the timing and opportunity for toy company acquisitions has never been better. After a period of slow growth, the toy industry is experiencing healthy growth." Fine, the chief executive officer (CEO) of SWK and SWT, articulated a new strategy of expansion through both internal growth and acquisitions. "We plan on getting very aggressive," Fine told Melinda Fulmer of the *Los Angeles Times*. In pursuit of this approach, SWK entered the $560 million electronic learning aid market with the acquisition of Neurosmith in September 2004. The following year SWK bought Imagiix, which had won awards for its infant, toddler, and preschool toys.

New product lines included Small World Living, including Japanese-, Italian-, and Chinese-influenced cooking products, and Everything Enchanted in Ryan's Room, an extension of the Ryan's Room brand centered around the world of fairies, both of which were introduced in 2005. Furthermore, new product lines were developed from licensing agreements with the popular children's book authors Eric Carle (2005), Dr. Seuss (2006), and Karen Katz (2006.) Seeking to expand its overseas sales, SWK announced in March 2005 international distribution agreements in six new markets: the United Kingdom, Spain, New Zealand, Hong Kong, Singapore, and the Philippines. At home, SWT began selling through mass market customers

COSTCO and Target, which was a deviation from earlier policy. Under Fine's leadership, sales reached $29.5 million in 2004, up 13.6 percent from 2003. SWT's sales grew another 14.5 percent to $33.8 billion in 2005.

## BANKRUPTCY AND NEW OWNERSHIP: 2006–10

In 2006, however, difficulties began to appear. In the first three quarters of the year, sales were $20.2 million, down from $22.8 million for the same period the preceding year. This was partly because of the late arrival of inventory. Speaking to Cliff Annicelli of *Playthings* in July 2006, Fine put her finger on a more fundamental problem for SWT: "Being public is difficult. We would be very, very profitable, except being public costs us about $1.5 million a year—and for a small-sized company that's extremely difficult unless you're doing $100 million in revenue.... Our goal has been to merge with or buy another company ... that gets us to the $100 million mark in sales."

To help reach this goal, SWT sought to enter the tween market for girls by a late 2005 bid to purchase the Bead Shop in Milwaukee, Wisconsin. SWT anticipated $17 million in sales for the year and $30 million in 2006. However, the deal fell through because SWT could only raise $10 million of the $15 million needed for the purchase. In mid-2006 Fine denied that the company was failing, but the inability to raise sufficient capital brought financial turmoil for the company. In August 2007 it filed for bankruptcy, and Fine resigned. Shortly thereafter, SWK went out of existence.

In October 2007 a group of former SWT managers under the name Rivenrock Capital purchased SWT and reestablished it as a private company. Nelson, a former COO, became the new CEO. Goldwasser, who had stayed with SWT under the Fine regime into 2005 and then left, rejoined the company as a consultant and member of the board of directors. In 2007 massive safety recalls throughout the toy industry drastically reduced the profits of several toy manufactures, and SWT was no exception. The deep recession that began in late 2007 and expanded in 2008 brought further losses.

In mid-2009 Vertex Capital, led by the turnaround specialist Larry Nusbaum, acquired SWT. *Business Wire* noted in July 2009 that the firm "will improve gross margins by sourcing more competitively in China while maintaining quality the brand is known for, rationalizing the overhead, creating impulse product lines with media support, and targeting the mass and discount channels for brand extensions to increase the revenue base." In sharp contrast to Fine's strategy, Nusbaum told Alexandra Frean of the *Times* of London that SWT would "shrink to profitability." Under the new leadership, SWT was profitable in the third and fourth quarters of 2009 following 26 straight quarters of loss. For 2010 Nusbaum's goal was $20 million in sales and $2 million in profit.

*Michael Levine*

## PRINCIPAL COMPETITORS

International Playthings LLC; LeapFrog Enterprises Inc.; Mattel Inc.

## FURTHER READING

Annicelli, Cliff, "A Valuable Lesson," *Playthings*, July 1, 2006, p. 6.

Filus, Sarah, "Toy Maker May Be at the End of Its Small World," *Los Angeles Business Journal*, August 13, 2007, p. 3.

Frean, Alexandra, "Anti-wrinkle Cream Is in the Bag, but Cuts Are Prescription for Fixing Sick Firms," *Times* (London), November 24, 2009, p. 60.

Fulmer, Melinda, "Small World Aims to Be Big in Learning Toys," *Los Angeles Times*, September 29, 2004, p. C2.

Goldwasser, Eddy, "Puzzles Get It All Together," *Playthings*, September 1997, p. 70.

Kellachan, Lauren, "Imagine That! The Role of a Lifetime," *Playthings*, May 2005, p. 45.

Pereira, Joseph, "A Small Toy Store Manages to Level Playing Field," *Wall Street Journal*, December 20, 1996, p. A1.

"Savon Team Sports Buys Small World Toys," *Home Accents Today*, June 2004, p. 22.

"Small World Toys Grows up Again: Receives New Ownership and Capital," *Business Wire*, July 21, 2009.

Walters, Donna K. H., "Masters of the Toy Universe," *Los Angeles Times*, September 2, 1993, p. D1.

# Special Broadcasting Service Corporation

———■———

14 Herbert Street
**Artarmon, New South Wales 2064**
**Australia**
**Telephone: (+61 02) 9430-2828**
**Toll Free: (800) 500-727**
**Fax: (+61 02) 9956-8130**
**Web site: http://www.sbs.com.au**

*Public Company*
*Founded:* 1978
*Incorporated:* 1991
*Employees:* 900 (est.)
*Sales:* $244 million (2009)
*NAICS:* 515111 Radio Networks; 515120 Television
   Broadcasting

■ ■ ■

Australia's Special Broadcasting Service (SBS) Corporation presents multilingual and multicultural television and radio programming. About 15 percent of Australians do not speak English at home, and the variety of ethnic groups increased after 1975, when Australia revised its immigration policy to end discrimination against nonwhites. To serve the ethnic groups, SBS TV presents about half of its programs in languages other than English, and most of SBS Radio's programs are in non-English languages. More than 60 languages are broadcast on television and 68 on radio. To promote multicultural harmony across ethnic lines, SBS TV subtitles its non-English-language programs and also presents English-language programs that feature information about the many ethnic cultures in Australia and around the world. Many of its offerings highlight interaction among members of different ethnic groups.

## THE EVOLUTION OF SBS SERVICES

In 1975 the government of Prime Minister Gough Whitlam introduced Medibank, a publicly funded universal health care system. Given the large number of Australians with weak English-language skills or none at all, the government decided that minority-language communities should be given the details of the new health plan in their own tongues. For this purpose, government-funded ethnic radio stations were established in 1975, one in Sydney, broadcasting in seven languages, and the other in Melbourne, broadcasting in eight languages. Legislation effective in 1978 established the Special Broadcasting Service, a government agency, to operate these radio stations on a permanent basis. Also, legislation established a government television service aimed at ethnic communities that began test transmissions in 1979 and the following year began broadcasting full time through stations in Sydney and Melbourne. In 1985 it was named SBS TV. The Special Broadcasting Service Act of 1991 established the combined television and radio services as a public corporation with a board of directors appointed by the government.

Originally, SBS TV broadcast on the VHF frequency band, but because of technical difficulties, it switched to UHF in 1986. During the 1980s and afterward, both SBS Radio and SBS TV expanded their

## COMPANY PERSPECTIVES

■

The multiple language programs available through SBS Television, Radio, and Online ensure that all Australians, including the estimated three million Australians who speak a language other than English in their homes, are able to share in the experiences of others, and participate in public life. The quality of our programs and the multiplicity of our viewpoints come from the freedom we have to draw on the best of all cultures for our programming.

broadcasting operations to cover most of the nation. From the beginning, both services continuously added or eliminated languages, or added or subtracted the number of hours devoted to a given language, based on the size of the respective ethnic communities and other factors, such as the percentage of new arrivals in an ethnic community. By the 1990s Arabic, Greek, Italian, Cantonese, Mandarin, and Vietnamese were, other than English, the major broadcast languages. SBS also carried programs with Aboriginal themes in various Aboriginal dialects.

In 1986 the government of Prime Minister Bob Hawke proposed legislation to merge SBS with Australia's other government-operated broadcaster, the English-language Australian Broadcasting Company (ABC). However, because ABC historically had showed little interest in ethnic broadcasting (one of the reasons SBS was established in the first place) and because ethnic broadcasting would only be a small part of the ABC organization, ethnic groups felt they would be ignored. Responding to their protests, Hawke reversed gears in 1987.

In 1994 Special Broadcasting Service Independent (SBSI) was founded to commission programs focusing on the regions of Australia, locally produced dramas and documentaries, low-budget features to maximize the range of affordable projects, and documentaries from outside the network. It also sought coproduction opportunities with non-Australian broadcasters. A major focus was finding programs produced by young Australians of a wide range of cultural backgrounds. Beginning in the 1990s, Web sites supplemented SBS's television and radio programming. Adding to its analog service, SBS TV in 2001 began digital broadcasting. SBS TV, working with Sun Microsystems, introduced interactive television on an experimental basis in December 2001. After a refining process, this became a

permanent service. In 2009 SBS TV was renamed SBS One simultaneously with the creation of a sister channel, SBS Two.

## MULTILINGUAL AND MULTICULTURAL PROGRAMS

SBS had two goals that were not entirely compatible. The SBS mandate required it to serve ethnic communities by running programs of particular interest to them in their own languages. The various ethnic groups tended to seek coverage for every significant event within their communities, said Malcolm Long, managing director of SBS from 1992 and 1997, upon his departure. Aside from being impractical, this would have left insufficient time for SBS to pursue its other goal: to promote multicultural understanding and harmony, which necessitated programming that cut across ethnic lines and appealed to Anglo Australians as well.

One way that consistency between these two purposes was promoted was by providing English subtitles for all non-English programs on SBS TV. Another way was to present English-language documentaries and series with multicultural themes. During 1996 SBS TV produced a series called *What Makes You Say That?*, which examined cultural diversity in the workplace. One episode showed how Australian companies could adjust policies to gain the most possible benefit from their work forces' cultural diversity. The weekly series *Global Village*, which began in 1998, examined cultures around the world. To build multicultural understanding, the 2005 documentary *Swapping Lives* featured a young Australian women and a young Indonesian woman who switched families for ten weeks. The year 2006 saw the premiere of the highly popular series *Food Safari*, which examined the cuisine of a different ethnic group in each program. The host revealed the basic ingredients of the cuisine being examined, told where they could be found in Australia, and demonstrated the preparation of basic ethnic dishes.

Starting in 2007 the romantic comedy *Kick*, set in Melbourne's suburbs, brought together characters of Croatian, Greek, Afghani, Maori, Vietnamese, and Lebanese backgrounds. *The Circuit*, a groundbreaking dramatic series, followed a city-educated Aboriginal legal services attorney who pursued his work in rural northwestern Australia. It was widely regarded, among Aborigines and others, as providing an unusually penetrating look at Aboriginal culture, capturing the deep social issues beleaguering Aborigines and their unique sense of humor. *First Australians*, a seven-part historical documentary series screened in 2008, traced modern Australian history from the point of view of Aborigines.

## NEWS, MOVIES, AND SPORTS

SBS made news broadcasts a major part of its schedule. While SBS Radio broadcast mostly in languages other than English, it also screened several English-language news programs: *World View*, a one-hour daily current affairs program; *Nightwatch*, a summary of the week's news, broadcast each Friday in Sydney and Melbourne; and a late-night program offering English news and current affairs from BBC World Service and Deutsche Welle. SBS TV ran several major, ongoing English-language offerings that emphasized international news. One was *World News Australia*, a half-hour, prime-time program enlarged to one hour in 2006. In keeping with SBS's multilingual broadcasting policy, beginning in 1997 foreign language material included in the newscast was broadcast in the original tongue with English subtitles. *Dateline*, another current-affairs program, pursued investigative journalism. Each episode of the program called *Insight* consisted of a discussion of a single issue in front of a studio audience.

SBS TV news sometimes aired major newsbreaking stories. In 2002 it released video footage of Zimbabwean opposition leader Morgan Tsvangirai and associates discussing the possibility of assassinating dictator Robert Mugabe. Three years later SBS TV aired video showing U.S. soldiers in Afghanistan desecrating and burning the bodies of dead Taliban soldiers. In 2006 SBS TV released new photos and videos of Iraqis being tortured at the Abu Ghraib prison in Baghdad, some more gruesome than those released by the United States two years earlier. The George W. Bush administration in the United States condemned their release.

Sports broadcasts, especially soccer matches, constituted a major source of programming, so much so that some jokingly said SBS stood for Soccer Broadcasting Service. SBS's rationale was that immigrants were more interested in the sport than other Australians, who favored Australian football, but the fact that soccer gained SBS TV its greatest viewership was undoubtedly another consideration. SBS TV also broadcast cycling, motorcycling, gymnastics, figure skating, skiing, and ice hockey events.

Another important part of SBS's television programming was film. By 2010 SBS TV had an international film library of more than 4,000 titles. It broadcast an average of 18 movies each week and up to 250 first-run movies each year. Many of the latter were recently released foreign, non-English-language, and sometimes risqué films with subtitles.

## RATINGS AND REVENUES

Public broadcaster ABC and the three commercial broadcast networks—the Seven Network, Nine Network, and Ten Network—all had higher viewership ratings than SBS. SBS managing director Malcolm Long told Amanda Meade in the September 17, 1997, issue of *The Australian*: "Everyone says about SBS: 'Great programs but nobody watches them.'" He went on, "If we wanted to have Channel Nine's [leading] share we have to be like Channel Nine. There's no secret to it. You have to have Nine's homogenous, very broadly targeted audience approach."

Still, SBS TV ratings have steadily grown. During the early 1980s, its share of the viewing audience was often below 2 percent. In the 1990s ratings were about 3 or 4 percent, and in the new century's first decade they increased to the range of 4 to 5 percent. Soccer broadcasts generated the highest ratings, with the 2002 World Soccer Cup broadcasts receiving ratings of up to 14 percent. In 1994 three million people watched SBS TV for at least one show per week. Three years later the figure was five million, and by 2010 the figure had surpassed seven million.

During the tenure of managing director Nigel Milan (1997–2006) in particular, many viewers and SBS staffers complained that the network was eroding its original multilingual, multicultural focus in an effort to increase its ratings. For example, protests were heard in 1999 when SBS TV hired a celebrity reporter and interviewer, Jana Wendt, who had worked at the Nine Network, to be the anchor of *Dateline*. Programs criticized for putting popularity above SBS's mission included the 2002 story of a pornography star who allegedly had sex with enough men to set a world record and a 2004 documentary called *Desperately Seeking Sheila*, in which lonely women competed to win the hearts of bachelors.

The great bulk of SBS funding came from the Australian government, but the corporation developed other sources of revenue as well. Originally commercial-free, SBS TV was permitted to introduce advertising in 1989 to address budget problems. The commercials, however, were limited. By law, they could account for no more than 5 minutes per hour, compared with 15 minutes for commercial television, and they could only run between programs. Because many viewers switched channels when commercials were stacked up, in-show advertising was allowed in 2006, with the five-minute hourly limit remaining in place. SBS Radio introduced advertising in 1997. SBS also found other ways to earn money. In 1995 it helped set up PAN TV, which was founded to produce The World Movies, a pay-TV channel. SBS owned a share of PAN TV, which proved profitable, and in 2009 SBS increased its holding from 40 percent to 100 percent. Also, using its staff of expert linguists, SBS leased subtitling and translating services.

*Michael Levine*

## PRINCIPAL DIVISIONS

New Media; SBS Independent; SBS Radio and Television Youth Orchestra; SBS Sport; SBS World News Australia.

## PRINCIPAL COMPETITORS

Australian Broadcasting Company.

## FURTHER READING

Alarcon, Camille, "Milan's out of Fashion at SBS," *B&T Weekly*, August 12, 2005, p. 6.

Appleton, Gillian, "Across the Multicultural Chasm," *Sydney Morning Herald*, September 15, 1986, p. 11.

"Broadcaster Breathes Diversity into Aussie TV," *Campaign*, September 5, 2008, p. 19.

Chai, Paul, "World Cup Runneth Over for Heady SBS," *Variety*, October 5, 2009, p. A1.

Hooks, Barbara, "Our SBS—All It Needs Is an Audience," *The Age*, March 23, 1995, p. 10.

Meade, Amanda, "Long Signs Off," *The Australian*, September 15, 1997, p. 12.

"Sydney-siders Value Sports Participation and Their Homes," *Market Asia Pacific*, December 1, 1993.

Thompson-Noel, Michael, "The Arts: Television—Australia Wastes a Multi-national Opportunity," *Financial Times*, August 18, 1982, p. 9.

# Takeda Pharmaceutical
# Company Limited

---■---

1-1, Doshomachi 4-chome, Chuo-ku
Osaka, 540-8645
Japan
Telephone: (+81-6) 6204-2111
Fax: (+81-6) 6204-2880
Web site: http://www.takeda.com/

*Public Company*
*Founded:* 1781
*Employees:* 19,362
*Sales:* ¥1.54 trillion ($15.69 billion) (2009)
*Stock Exchanges:* Tokyo
*Ticker Symbol:* 4502
*NAICS:* 325411 Medicinal and Botanical Manufacturing; 325412 Pharmaceutical Preparation Manufacturing

■ ■ ■

Takeda Pharmaceutical Company Limited is Japan's largest pharmaceutical company and is also one of the largest drug firms in the world. The company operates throughout the globe, with major offices and facilities in Europe, North America, and Southeast Asia. Until the late 1980s Takeda's name was virtually unrecognized outside the borders of its own nation. However, with the increasing presence of Japanese companies in the U.S. market during the 1990s, the company gained wider recognition. During this time, Takeda became known as the maker of the ulcer medication Prevacid and the diabetes drug Actos. In the first decade of the 21st century, Takeda embarked on an ambitious acquisi-

tion program, aimed both at boosting its share of the North American drug market and at developing a wider range of pipeline drugs. These efforts culminated with the company's 2008 acquisition of Millennium Pharmaceuticals for $8.8 billion. At the time, it was the largest merger in the history of the Japanese pharmaceuticals industry.

## EARLY HISTORY AND
## EXPANSION: 1781–1960

Takeda's corporate headquarters are located in Osaka, the same city of its origins. In the mid-18th century this urban center was the focus of the nation's drug business. Ohmiya Chobei, the company founder, established a small firm in 1781 to sell Japanese and Chinese medicines. During the late 1800s the firm's products expanded to include imported medicines from the West. After the company's first factory was completed in 1895, production began on manufactured pharmaceuticals. Fine chemicals were added to the production line in 1909, and four years later a modern factory was constructed to facilitate growth.

In 1925 the company's operations expanded significantly and transformed it from a local business to a major pharmaceutical concern. An important innovation during this period of growth was the successful synthesis of vitamin C in 1937 and vitamin B1 in 1938. Takeda marketed this product under the brand name Metabolin-Strong and became the manufacturer of Japan's first synthetic vitamin preparation. During the 1940s the company changed its name to Takeda Chemical Industries, Ltd., and absorbed two other firms, Kon-

We strive toward better health for individuals and progress in medicine by developing superior pharmaceutical products.

Working closely with the medical profession, the Takeda Group contributes to the health of individuals and to the progress of medicine by adhering to our mission of creating superior pharmaceutical products and offering top-quality services.

To more effectively achieve our goals and mission, we pledge to apply all our assets, both fiscal and intellectual, to realising even greater possibilities with new pharmaceutical products, concentrating on our pharmaceuticals business, and enhancing the lives and health of individuals.

ishi Pharmaceutical and Radium Pharmacy, into its operations.

The company's experience with vitamin production increased with the successful synthesis of a thiol derivative of thiamine, otherwise known as a long-acting vitamin Bl preparation. Alinamin, the brand name of this synthesized product, became one of Takeda's most popular items. During the postwar years Japanese citizens expressed a new health consciousness. A vigorous orientation toward health and hygiene found Takeda's products in great demand. By 1962, 30 percent of the nation's drug sales were generated from the sale of vitamin preparations. Takeda supplied nearly 50 percent of the total, earning the title "Takeda of Vitamin Fame."

Besides the manufacture of synthetic vitamins, Takeda's pharmaceutical products included tranquilizers, treatments for nervous disorders, and antibiotics. Takeda's formidable expansion allowed the company to invest unprecedented amounts of money into new equipment and facilities. Even more significant was Takeda's role in the inception of the drug export trade. By exporting manufacturing techniques for Alinamin, Takeda led the Japanese pharmaceuticals industry toward international expansion.

During the early 1960s the Japanese pharmaceuticals industry experienced an annual growth rate that exceeded 20 percent, making it one of the fastest-growing industries in the nation. In addition, sweeping changes in government regulation would soon make the industry one of the most profitable. Takeda was well positioned to capitalize on these changes because no one

single industry competitor came close to challenging its preeminence in sales and marketing.

## JAPANESE POLICY CHANGES AND MORE GROWTH: 1960–75

The 1961 implementation of the Japanese National Health Insurance system marked an important date for the pharmaceuticals industry. Under this system the patient's prescription costs were almost completely covered by the insurance program. In addition, the official drug pricing system allowed doctors full reimbursement for the cost of dispensing drugs. This structure, therefore, encouraged the generous prescription of drugs because doctors profited from the difference between the price at which they purchased drugs and the higher official price, set by the Ministry of Health and Welfare, at which they were reimbursed. For this reason the pharmaceuticals industry experienced unprecedented financial success.

Takeda's growth matched the expansion of the industry and the health insurance system. Under the leadership of Ohmiya Chobei Takeda VI, a descendant of the company founder, Takeda operated as a holding company for many subsidiaries, including Yoshitomi Pharmaceutical, Teikoku Hormone, and Biofermin Pharmaceutical. As profits increased the company established subsidiaries in Taiwan, Hong Kong, Thailand, the Philippines, Indonesia, West Germany, the United States, and Mexico. By 1970, 10 percent of the total national production of pharmaceuticals was traceable to Takeda operations. Moreover, even though Japan's industry share of drug exports remained only 2.9 percent of total sales, export figures increased 34.7 percent between 1968 and 1970, with Takeda's business accounting not only for 25 percent of total pharmaceutical exports but also for 25 percent of industrial chemicals exports.

Despite movement toward export expansion, the trade deficit in pharmaceuticals remained sizeable. As late as 1982, 80 percent of the drugs sold in Japan continued to be manufactured overseas or with technology developed abroad. It was precisely this trade deficit that compelled the Japanese government to implement changes. One cause for this imbalance was traceable to Japan's lack of strict patent laws in the pharmaceuticals industry that, in turn, made research and innovation unprofitable. To encourage the industry to be less reliant on foreign technology, the government passed stronger patent protection laws and altered the drug pricing system. By establishing high prices for innovative products, the development of new drugs suddenly became a highly lucrative business. Pharmaceutical companies immediately invested money in research and development and for the first time technology began moving from Japan to foreign markets. By 1977 Japan had received 1,700 drug and related product patents in the United States alone, ranking it second among all foreign recipients of U.S. drug patents.

## FOCUS ON RESEARCH AND DEVELOPMENT LICENSING AGREEMENTS: 1975-85

Takeda participated actively in this new orientation toward innovation. Between 1970 and 1974 research expenditures increased and a new plant in Kashima was built to strengthen these efforts. The number of patents received locally and abroad for products developed in Takeda laboratories surpassed 3,000. As leadership passed from Chobei Takeda to Shinbei Konishi, the new company president made the development of pharmaceuticals and the continued expansion into foreign markets the top priorities. Konishi's strategy proved successful. By the mid-1970s Takeda was instrumental in developing innovative antibiotics. By the early 1980s a majority of Takeda's $1.8 billion in sales was generated from the sale of vitamins and antibiotics. In fact, its cephalosporin antibiotics accounted for 24 percent of Japan's domestic drug sales by 1982.

The Japanese pharmaceuticals industry's increasing emphasis on research served not only to strengthen the domestic market but also to facilitate growth overseas. On the one hand, because large expenditures were now needed to support the industry-wide effort, drug companies initiated a concerted expansion into foreign markets as a means of recouping the millions of dollars necessary to develop one drug. On the other hand, Japan's innovation in antibiotics compelled foreign companies to solicit their expertise. Thus began the popular trend of securing foreign licensing agreements between Japanese drug companies and their foreign counterparts. Between 1970 and 1980 drug-licensing increased nearly four times. The enactment of the Pharmaceutical Affairs Act, effectively extending the time a Japanese company could market a drug under exclusive license, encouraged further agreements. Takeda, representing the largest of the Japanese pharmaceutical concerns, contributed largely to this increase. By 1983 the company was involved in agreements with over 20 companies, including the licensing of a cephalosporin antibiotic with Abbott Laboratories.

As industry analysts were keen to observe, licensing agreements with foreign companies were often just the first step in establishing independent foreign operations. Because agreements generally paid the licensee an initial fee and between 2 percent and 7 percent in royalties, a more lucrative endeavor was often pursued as a next step in securing overseas markets. Therefore, in 1985 Takeda initiated a joint venture with Abbott Laboratories where profits were split 50-50. Calling the venture Takeda Abbott Products (the named was eventually changed to TAP Pharmaceutical Products Inc.), the two partners worked to develop and market four new products, including a treatment for diabetes. Takeda's efforts to gain access to the U.S. market were not always easy. The U.S. Food and Drug Administration's (FDA) long approval process often frustrated company officials. Similarly, Takeda experienced difficulty securing a U.S. producer for Nicholin, a treatment for unconsciousness caused by brain damage.

## ADJUSTING TO MARKET CHANGES AND GOVERNMENT REGULATIONS: MID- TO LATE EIGHTIES

For the most part, however, Takeda's foreign expansion was successful, and the company received further impetus to pursue overseas partners when the Japanese National Health Insurance system was reformed during the 1980s. By 1982 the per capita drug bill for Japanese citizens reached $95, making the Japanese drug market the second-largest in the world. In an effort to halt escalating health care costs, the government reduced official drug prices by a total of nearly 50 percent and required elderly and insured workers to carry some of the costs of treatment. To maintain their respective market shares, companies reduced prices but continued to allot generous sums for research. Thus, foreign markets as a means of alleviating deteriorated domestic profit margins offered even greater appeal. In 1985, for example, Takeda opened a North Carolina plant to produce vitamin B1 in the United States.

While Takeda continued pursuing foreign ventures, its domestic sales were hurt drastically by the government reforms. Two of its best-selling antibiotics, Pansporin and Bestcall, were given between a 12 percent and 13 percent price reduction and total sales of antibiotics dropped from 18.4 percent to 16 percent. Similarly, vitamins, once accounting for close to 40 percent of sales, represented a mere 9 percent of the total. To ameliorate this trend, the company president Ikushiro Kurabayashi shifted Takeda's domestic market orientation toward the growing population of aged people.

According to a government-sponsored research study, one out of every four Japanese would be at least 65 years old by 2020. For this reason Takeda started to concentrate on drugs for geriatric diseases. One such drug, called Avan, treated senile dementia. Having entered the market in early 1987, Avan generated ¥1 billion a month. Following Avan, Takeda planned to release an antiosteoporosis drug aimed at treating the 4.3 million sufferers of this disease.

Takeda's research and development expenditures for 1985 reached ¥31.5 billion. This represented the highest budget allotment among all Japanese pharmaceutical companies. In 1988 the company opened its second research base, Tsukuba Research Laboratories. Aside from the drugs for geriatric diseases, the company began developing an antidiabetic agent and a high blood pressure treatment drug. Furthermore, Takeda's research made the company a world leader in biotechnology. Because Takeda also excelled in fermentation technology, foreign companies began to pursue this expertise as a means of manufacturing biotechnological products on a large scale.

## INTERNATIONAL EXPANSION AND LAWSUITS: 1990–2001

During the 1990s Takeda continued to expand its research and development efforts, secure strategic partnerships, and expand its presence in the United States. In 1991 the company launched Lansoprazole, which was used to treat ulcers. Developed with Abbott Laboratories, the drug was approved by the FDA in 1995. Selling under the names Prevacid, Ogast, and

Takepron, it quickly became the firm's best-selling product.

In 1995 the firm teamed up with SmithKline Beecham PLC to research, develop, and market pharmaceuticals in the genome field. The company then formed a joint venture with Human Genome Sciences (HGS) in which Takeda received sole rights to license certain HGS products in Japan. Takeda also joined with Novo Nordisk to research diabetes.

During the mid-1990s Japan's Ministry of Health and Welfare continued to cut pharmaceutical prices. Takeda responded to the cutbacks and increased foreign competition by restructuring its business operations and focusing on its international operations. In 1997 the company established the marketing subsidiary Takeda UK Ltd. and a manufacturing facility in Ireland. Takeda America Holdings Inc., a holding company for its U.S. business, was also created. The following year Takeda purchased a 100 percent interest in its marketing subsidiary in Italy and another in France. It also created a pharmaceutical marketing subsidiary in Switzerland and a development subsidiary in the United Kingdom.

As part of its strategic push into the U.S. market, the company created Takeda Pharmaceuticals America Inc. in 1998 as a marketing subsidiary. The move was seen by many as the beginning of its separation from Abbott Laboratories. Meera Somasundaram of *Crain's Chicago Business* claimed that "the bonds began to loosen in 1997 when Takeda decided not to renew a contract giving North Chicago-based Abbott a right of first refusal to distribute Takeda's new drugs." The TAP venture secured over $2 billion in 1998, however, and $3.5 billion in 2001. By that time, it was the one of the fastest-growing pharmaceutical firms in the world. Amid speculation, Takeda held strong to its 50 percent ownership.

The company's growth into international markets did not leave it unscathed. In 1999 Takeda and six other pharmaceutical concerns settled a $1.2 billion class-action suit brought against them by U.S. buyers. The companies had banded together to raise the prices of certain vitamins by 7 percent to 15 percent. Takeda pled guilty to the suit and apologized for its role in the vitamin price-fixing scandal. It came under public fire once again in 2001, when it settled a lawsuit that was filed under the Racketeer Influenced and Corrupt Organizations Act. The suit claimed that Takeda and its TAP subsidiary failed to act when finding out that certain physicians were billing or overbilling insurance companies for the drug Lupron, when they had received the drug for free or at drastically discounted prices. Takeda agreed to pay out $875 million to settle the case.

## DEVELOPMENT OF NEW DRUGS
## AND JOINT VENTURES: 2001–02

Despite its legal problems, Takeda continued to develop new drugs including Actos, an insulin sensitizer. It was sold in the United States in collaboration with Eli Lilly and Company. Takeda also launched the blood pressure drug Blopress. In 2001 it formed a joint venture with BASF AG in which the two companies merged their bulk vitamin business to form BASF Takeda Vitamins KK. Takeda then transferred control of its vitamin operations outside of Japan to BASF. The venture controlled nearly 30 percent of the global vitamin market. Takeda also partnered with Mitsui Chemicals Inc. to form Mitsui Takeda Chemicals Inc., a urethane chemicals and composite materials firm.

Takeda's ability to develop new drugs left it with substantial profit gains. In 2001 the company posted a record profit of $2.9 billion, which was a 32 percent increase over the previous year and marked the 10th straight year of pretax profit increases. The company continued to focus on its research and development efforts. It added a new genetics research facility at its Tsukuba Research Center and created Takeda Research Investment Inc., a subsidiary that invested in bioventure firms. Meanwhile, the company began focusing on developing a comprehensive global strategy to position itself as a leader in the emerging pharmaceutical markets in the United States and Europe. In mid-2002 the company announced a plan to build a new manufacturing plant in County Dublin, Ireland, that would produce the diabetes medicine Pioglitazone. With an estimated cost of €80 million ($69.7 million), the facility would be the company's first bulk pharmaceutical plant outside of Japan and was projected to become operational by 2004.

## REJUVENATING AN AGING DRUG
## PIPELINE: 2003–04

In 2003 Takeda continued to produce record earnings, posting net profits of ¥311 billion ($2.6 billion) for the fiscal year ending in March 2003. In spite of this robust financial performance, the company still faced many challenges moving forward. With patents on two of its best-selling drugs, Prevacid and Actos, due to expire by decade's end, Takeda needed to focus on developing new products to compensate for the projected losses in revenue. At the center of the company's strategy was its continued expansion into the rapidly growing North American drug business. The domestic Japanese pharmaceuticals industry was projected to have a growth rate of only 1 percent to 2 percent during this period, whereas the North American market was expected to increase 10 percent per year.

To capitalize on this trend, Takeda earmarked in July 2003 ¥308.3 billion ($2.6 billion) to building up its North American presence. In March 2004 the company entered into a strategic partnership with the U.S. biotechnology firm Array BioPharma Inc. The partnership was intended research new treatments for high blood pressure and diabetes. As part of the agreement, Takeda would assume ownership over any patents emerging from the two companies' efforts, while Array would receive financial compensation. In July of that year Takeda entered into a similar research venture with Lexicon Genetics Inc., spending an initial investment of $12 million. Both of these moves were intended to help the company get new drugs into the pipeline well ahead of the patent expirations for Prevacid and Actos.

Because it was devoting greater resources to increasing its share of the global drug market, Takeda decided to shed a number of its smaller businesses not related to its pharmaceutical operations. In August 2004 the company revealed that over the next three years it would sell its shares in a range of joint ventures, including holdings in the chemical, composite materials, and animal health sectors. The company planned to use the proceeds from these sales to seek out new acquisition opportunities in its core pharmaceutical business. In the wake of these announcements, the company formally changed its name to Takeda Pharmaceutical Company Limited. By this time Takeda had grown to become the 15th-largest drug company in the world, with roughly ¥1.3 trillion ($12.5 billion) available for investment. During the fiscal year ending in March 2004 the company's research and development budget grew to roughly ¥130 billion ($1.3 billion).

## ACQUISITIONS AND RESEARCH
## FUEL GROWTH: 2005–10

Heading into the second half of the decade, Takeda became increasingly committed to a growth strategy founded on aggressive acquisitions. In February 2005 the company purchased Syrrx Inc., a biotech company based in San Diego, California, for an estimated $270 million. With treatments for diabetes, cancer, and various metabolic disorders in development, Syrrx provided Takeda with a range of potential new drugs for its pipeline. In September of that year Takeda launched Rozerem, a new medication aimed at treating insomnia. Rozerem was the company's first new drug in six years. In 2007 Takeda increased its research and development budget to ¥200 billion ($1.8 billion), an increase of 20 percent over the previous year's spending, and the largest amount ever for a Japanese pharmaceutical company.

During this period the company also remained alert to new growth opportunities at home. In February 2008

Takeda acquired Amgen KK, the Japanese subsidiary of the U.S. pharmaceutical research firm Amgen Inc., for $1.2 billion. This acquisition enabled the company to obtain the Japanese rights to 13 potential drugs, including a promising new cancer medication. At the same time, Takeda continued to build its presence in North America. In March the company paid $5 billion to buy out Abbot Laboratories' 50 percent share in TAP Pharmaceutical Products. In April Takeda announced the acquisition of Millennium Pharmaceuticals, a U.S.-based biopharmaceutical firm known for its genomic research. The deal was worth an estimated $8.8 billion, making it the largest merger in history for a Japanese pharmaceutical company. To industry analysts, the move signified Takeda's intent to become more active in the field of cancer research, which was one of Millennium's areas of expertise. Indeed, this acquisition enabled Takeda to obtain the rights to Velcade, a drug used to treat the blood cancer myeloma.

As the decade drew to a close, Takeda had a host of new drugs in various stages of development. In February 2009 the company began selling Kapidex, an ulcer medication marketed as an upgrade over the company's best-selling Prevacid. Takeda also unveiled Uloric, a new drug designed to treat gout. Meanwhile, the company continued to increase its portfolio. In May it acquired IDM Pharma Inc., a cancer drug specialist based in California, for $175 million. In November Takeda purchased the U.S.-based Amylin Pharmaceuticals Inc. for $75 million, with the intention of developing drug treatments for obesity. Reporting revenues of ¥1.5 trillion ($15.6 billion) for the fiscal year ending in March 2009, it was clear that Takeda's aggressive global strategy was an integral part of its continued earnings growth.

*Christina M. Stansell*
*Updated, Stephen Meyer*

## PRINCIPAL SUBSIDIARIES

Amato Pharmaceutical Products, Ltd. (30%); Nihon Pharmaceutical Co., Ltd. (87.5%); P.T. Takeda Indonesia (70%); Takeda America Holdings, Inc.; Takeda Bio Development Center Limited; Takeda Clinical Research Singapore Private Limited; Takeda Europe Holdings B.V.; Takeda Healthcare Products Co., Ltd.; Takeda Ireland Limited; Takeda Pharmaceuticals Asia Private Limited; Takeda Pharmaceuticals Taiwan, Ltd.; Tianjin Takeda Pharmaceuticals Co., Ltd. (75%); Wako Pure Chemical Industries, Ltd. (70.3%).

## PRINCIPAL COMPETITORS

Astellas Pharma Inc.; Bayer AG; Daiichi Sankyo Company, Limited; Eli Lilly and Company; GlaxoSmithKline PLC; Merck & Co., Inc.; Novartis AG; Pfizer Inc.; Sanofi-Aventis; Shionogi & Co., Ltd.

## FURTHER READING

"British Authorities Approve BASF Deal," *Feedstuffs*, July 23, 2001, p. 18.

"Japan's Takeda Chemical Sees Record Pretax Profit for 10th Year," *AsiaPulse News* (Rhodes, Australia), November 7, 2001.

Klein, Sarah A., "Abott Joint Venture Faces More Lawsuits," *Crain's Chicago Business*, September 24, 2001, p. 62.

Mertens, Brian, "Healthy Player in a Vulnerable Industry," *Asian Business*, July 1996, p. 8.

Moore, Samuel K., "Vitamins Makers Settle U.S. Civil Suit for $1.17 Billion," *Chemical Week*, November 10, 1999, p. 15.

"Pharma Japan: Takeda Creates New U.S. Subsidiary to Invest in Bioventures," *Chemical Business Newsbase*, November 27, 2001.

Pollack, Andrew M., "Takeda to Purchase Drug Firm," *International Herald Tribune*, April 11, 2008, p. 16.

Somasundaram, Meera, "Hey, Abbott! Your Ally Goes It Alone: Takeda's U.S. Drive Starts Here," *Crain's Chicago Business*, March 1, 1999, p. 1.

"Takeda's Growth Plan Centers on U.S.," *Nikkei Weekly* (Tokyo), December 12, 2005.

"U.S. Scandal Cost Drug Giant Takeda 105 Bil. Yen," *Mainichi Daily News* (Osaka), October 5, 2001.

# Taylor Wimpey PLC

---

80 New Bond Street
London, W1S 1SB
United Kingdom
Telephone: (+44 20) 7355 8100
Fax: (+44 20) 7355 8197
Web site: http://www.taylorwimpeyplc.com/

*Public Company*
*Founded:* 1921
*Employees:* 4,708
*Sales:* £2.59 billion ($4.21 billion) (2009)
*Stock Exchanges:* London
*Ticker Symbol:* TW
*NAICS:* 236115 New Single-Family Housing Construction (except Operative Builders); 236116 New Multifamily Housing Construction (except Operative Builders); 236117 New Housing Operative Builders; 237210 Land Subdivision; 531110 Lessors of Residential Buildings and Dwellings; 531210 Offices of Real Estate Agents and Brokers

■ ■ ■

Taylor Wimpey PLC is one of the largest home building and general construction companies in the United Kingdom. It also has major property and construction operations in North America, Spain, and Gibraltar. The company's primary business is the development of sustainable communities of high-quality homes in these markets. In addition, it provides timber-frame solutions under Prestoplan and operates a supply-chain logistic business under Taylor Wimpey Logistics.

## THE EARLY YEARS

Frank Taylor, the founder of Taylor Woodrow, was a shopkeeper's son who became a tycoon and a peer of the realm. He grew up near Derbyshire, England, in a small house whose front room had been converted into a fruit shop. By the age of 11 Taylor was operating the business alone. While he was still a teenager the family moved to Blackpool, and his father established himself as a fruit wholesaler. In 1921 his father decided to buy a house, but he was unable to secure a loan. Sixteen-year-old Taylor offered the following arrangement: he would put up £30, his father £70, and the bank, with whom Taylor had negotiated, £400. Taylor proposed to build two houses with the money, including one for his uncle. In the end, Taylor sold the newly completed houses, realizing a handsome profit.

That same year Taylor founded his own company. Because he was a minor, his uncle Jack Woodrow lent his name for the company, and Taylor Woodrow came into existence. Taylor busied himself by building small developments of 20 to 30 houses. His plan was to make enough money to open a fruit wholesale business in California, but his early successes persuaded him to remain in the construction industry.

In 1930 Taylor moved his company to London, where he planned to build homes on the Grange Park Estate. By April 1931 he was completing four homes a day. During his first week of selling, he sold 50 houses at an average cost of £450 each. Over a span of three years, Taylor had built 1,200 homes on the estate. By 1934 Taylor Woodrow's profits were £54,000 and the firm was building estates throughout the home counties and southern England.

The company went public the following year with a capitalization of £400,000. Taylor, the managing director, then established a housing and apartment development company in Long Island, New York. Returning to London, he purchased 100 acres of land along the Grand Union Canal and built new company headquarters. The offices were designed so that they could be converted into houses if extra funds were needed.

In 1937 the company entered the construction and civil engineering field through the formation of Taylor Woodrow Construction Ltd. Even though civilian business for the new subsidiary got off to a slow start, Taylor Woodrow received contracts, shortly before World War II, from the war office to build military installations. After war was declared, the company constructed gunnery camps, land and sea defense works, hospitals, factories, and an aerodrome. When schedules were threatened because most of the workforce had been enlisted, Taylor hired laborers from Ireland, a technically neutral country. With workers and government contracts in plentiful supply, the company expanded dramatically. During the war the company acquired Greenham Plant Hire Co. and other firms that were involved in the supply of machinery and materials to the construction industry. These acquisitions formed the basis for subsidiaries that were later known as Greenham Trading and Greenham Construction Materials.

## POSTWAR OVERSEAS EXPANSION

After the war many buildings had to be replaced. Furthermore, the demobilization of troops created a massive demand for new homes. In concert with other builders, Taylor Woodrow funded the research and design of Arcon, a prefabricated housing system. The Ministry of Works ordered 43,000 of these units.

In spite of the amount of work available in the UK, Taylor Woodrow had grown so large that it needed to expand overseas. In a joint venture with Unilever, the company extended its operations into West Africa, where it erected Arcon tubular steel frames to which the walls of a variety of local materials could be added. In 1947 Taylor Woodrow (East Africa) was formed to build 127 miles of oil pipeline in Tanganyika. For three years company teams constructed a pipeline, erected a sawmill, and built prefabricated houses. However, dissatisfied with the project's central management, Taylor Woodrow eventually withdrew from the project.

The West and South African, U.S., and UK projects were more successful. In West and South Africa the company built entire towns, from housing to sewers to breweries. In the United States the firm continued its apartment complexes. In the UK Taylor Woodrow erected factories and added bridge and tunnel construction and opencast coal mining to its activities. In 1953 the company established Taylor Woodrow (Canada) Ltd. and purchased a controlling interest in Monarch Mortgage and Investments Ltd., a property development firm that owned land, apartment complexes, stores, and houses in Toronto, Canada. Monarch also had its own construction company.

Also during the postwar era Taylor Woodrow built several energy plants in the UK, including the Battersea Power Station and another near Castle Donington. It completed the world's first full-scale nuclear power station at Calder Hill in 1955. In conjunction with other companies, Taylor Woodrow also built the Hinkley, Sizewell, and Heysham nuclear power stations.

In 1964, having already entered the property investment field in Canada, Taylor Woodrow did the same in the UK with the formation of Taylor Woodrow Property Company Ltd. This firm was charged with purchasing land for development, with the developed property, such as office buildings and industrial parks, to be held in ownership as rental properties.

The company received the prestigious Queen's Award for Industry in 1966 for its development of a new pile driver, the Pilemaster. The firm also designed the first spherical prestressed concrete pressure vessels that were initially used for a power station at Wylfa. Among the major construction projects undertaken during the 1960s were the Miraflores earth-filled dam in Colombia and the Hong Kong Ocean Terminal, which opened in March 1966. The latter included what was at the time the largest shopping center in Asia.

```
┌─────────────────────────────────────────────┐
│                                               │
│              KEY DATES                        │
│                   ■                           │
│  ─────────────────────────────────────────    │
│                                               │
│  1921:  Frank Taylor founds Taylor Woodrow.   │
│  1937:  Taylor Woodrow establishes Taylor Woodrow │
│         Construction Ltd.                     │
│  1953:  Taylor Woodrow (Canada) Ltd. is established; │
│         Taylor Woodrow acquires a controlling inter- │
│         est in Monarch Mortgage and Investments │
│         Ltd.                                  │
│  1964:  Taylor Woodrow establishes Taylor Woodrow │
│         Property Company Ltd.                 │
│  2000:  Taylor Woodrow sells Greenham Trading and │
│         Greenham Construction Materials; it acquires │
│         the remaining shares of Monarch       │
│         Development.                          │
│  2001:  Taylor Woodrow acquires Bryant Group. │
│  2002:  Taylor Woodrow purchases Wilson Connolly. │
│  2007:  Taylor Woodrow merges with George     │
│         Wimpey, creating Taylor Wimpey PLC.   │
│                                               │
└─────────────────────────────────────────────┘
```

## SUCCESS OVERSEAS AND AT HOME: 1970–89

The building slump in the UK during the 1970s did not create any serious problems for Taylor Woodrow because it was operating successfully in developing countries, particularly in the Middle East. In Oman Taylor Woodrow built the first modern hospital, the first television studio, and Medinat Qaboos, a new township located near Muscat that included more than 1,000 homes. The company was also active in Dubai. There, Taylor Woodrow was involved in a massive development that included dry docks, ship repair shops, and harbor works. The new docks were opened in February 1979 by the Queen of England.

In England Taylor Woodrow's most prominent endeavor was the beginning of work on a massive redevelopment of London's crumbling Dockland, located near the Tower of London. Called St. Katharine Docks, the massive development was located on 25 acres, 10 of which were water, and was envisioned to include a multifunctional array of properties: a major hotel, restaurants, office buildings, residential housing, schools, and recreation facilities, including a yacht club and marina. Even though Taylor Woodrow Property was awarded a contract for developing St. Katharine Docks in 1969, the actual construction of what eventually became a world famous redevelopment complex continued, through several phases, into the 21st century.

Profits rose steadily throughout the 1970s, reaching £24 million by 1979. That same year Taylor resigned as managing director and became life president. Already knighted, he was elevated to the peerage in 1982 and assumed the title Baron Taylor of Hadfield.

Taylor Woodrow's three-pronged array of operations (property, housing, and construction) held it in good stead through the 1980s as profits peaked at £117 million in 1989. In the area of housing developments, the company was finding particular success in Canada and in Florida and California in the United States. Highlighting the construction sector was Taylor Woodrow's participation in the consortium that began building the Channel Tunnel in 1986. The engineering feat was completed in 1993. In 1988 Taylor Woodrow augmented its property portfolio through the purchase of 1.9 million square feet of commercial space and 58.5 acres of undeveloped land from the Warrington-Runcorn Development Corporation for £77.1 million. As the decade ended, Frank Gibb retired as chairman and chief executive officer (CEO) of the company. Peter Drew, who had led the development of St. Katharine Docks, became chairman and Tony Palmer took over as CEO.

## RESTRUCTURING: 1990–2000

The early 1990s brought a reversal of fortunes stemming from a severe downturn in the construction contracting sector, a deep recession in the UK housing market, and a collapse of UK commercial property prices. After the company posted losses in 1991, Drew retired as chairman in early 1992. Colin Parsons, who had headed the successful Canadian subsidiary Monarch Development, took over as chairman. Under the leadership of Parsons and Palmer, Taylor Woodrow managed a quick turnaround, returning to profitability by yearend 1992. Substantial restructuring efforts included the merger of the UK and international construction divisions and the withdrawal from unprofitable general building work in the UK. About 2,000 employees were cut from the company payroll. On the strength of a booming North American housing market and an improving UK commercial property market, Taylor Woodrow enjoyed steadily rising sales and profits through the mid-1990s, with sales reaching £1.3 billion and a net income hitting £56.2 million by 1997.

Executive turnover revisited the company in the late 1990s. In early 1997 John Castle became the first CEO to come from outside the group. He left, however, after just six months because of reported "incompatibilities." Parsons took over on an interim basis, until Keith Egerton was named CEO in November 1997, having previously headed Taylor Woodrow Property. The following summer Parsons retired from the company board and was replaced as chairman by Robert Hawley, a former CEO of British Energy PLC.

Egerton and Hawley initiated another round of restructuring of the company, having determined that the firm's future lay in housing and property. In 1999 the construction division was downsized into what the *PR Newswire* noted in December 2000 was a "focused provider of value added construction support." The construction workforce was reduced by about 250. A further contraction of the construction operations came the following year when the company announced plans to exit from foundation engineering, precast concrete products, and most other civil engineering work. In 2000 Taylor Woodrow divested itself of Greenham Trading and Greenham Construction Materials.

Meanwhile, in May 2000 the company spent £88.8 million to acquire the shares of Monarch Development that it did not already own. This move fit in with the company's strategy of building its core housing and property businesses worldwide. The purchase also enabled Taylor Woodrow to consolidate its North American operations into one management structure.

## ACQUISITION AND CONSOLIDATION: 2001–05

In January 2001 Taylor Woodrow acquired the Bryant Group, making it the fourth-largest home builder in the UK. Coming amid a flurry of consolidations in the UK housing market, the £556 million deal was funded in part by a £47.9 million profit from the sale of Greenham Trading and Greenham Construction Materials.

The company reorganized the following year when Iain Napier, a former head of Bass Brewers, replaced Egerton as CEO. Napier moved Taylor Woodrow's headquarters from Staines, Middlesex, to Solihull in the West Midlands. Soon after the move the company announced that it was shrinking its UK workforce by 180 jobs, which was expected to result in a savings of £21 million. In the United States the company continued to expand with the purchase of Jersey Homes in Arizona for £28.7 million.

Buoyed by a 15 percent rise in profits in 2002, for a record £233 million, Taylor Woodrow continued to expand through acquisition. In September, shortly after Norman Askew, a former head of East Midlands Electric, was picked to succeed Hawley as chairman, the company sealed a deal to purchase Wilson Connolly for £499 million. It was the largest transaction ever in the UK housing market, and it made Taylor Woodrow the country's second-largest home builder.

With the demand for homes soaring, the company needed to increase its supply of raw land for building.

In February 2004 it announced the purchase of a 209-acre site at Colchester, which was large enough to accommodate nearly one-fifth of the company's average annual output of houses. Taylor Woodrow expected to develop the property over the next five to six years at an undisclosed final cost.

Despite some weakening in the housing market as the year progressed, Taylor Woodrow was still looking for acquisitions. Higher profits in the United States spurred a 30 percent rise in the company's profits for 2004, and in July 2005 Napier said the company planned further expansion in North America, where, he told Michael Harrison of the London *Independent*, the outlook over the next six months was "absolutely fabulous" and would counterbalance any weakness in the UK. Taylor Woodrow's North American and Spanish operations posted record profits for 2005, accounting for half the company's profit overall. Departing in July after five years as CEO, Napier was succeeded by Ian Smith, a former CEO of General Healthcare Group.

## REORGANIZATION AND MERGER: 2006–07

Signs of weakness in the U.S. real estate market forced Taylor Woodrow to take a £20 million write-down against its North American properties. Regardless, it still posted a profit at the high end of analysts' expectations for 2006. While still looking for acquisitions in the United States, Smith put his mark on the UK business by reorganizing its sales grid into more manageable regional units. Smith told James Rossiter of the London *Times* that following the reorganization the company would be less "driven by cost consideration" and more focused on "listening to the market."

In February 2007 rumors began swirling of a possible deal involving Taylor Woodrow and George Wimpey, the third-largest home builder in the UK. A company with a similar mix of domestic and international business, George Wimpey had also been growing rapidly through acquisitions since 2000. Like Taylor Woodrow, George Wimpey had taken a write-down due to poor market conditions in the United States and posted a 15 percent drop in profits for 2006 after several years of strong earnings.

In March Taylor Woodrow and George Wimpey finalized a deal to merge, creating Taylor Wimpey PLC, the largest home builder in the UK. The all-stock deal was valued at £4.3 billion, with Taylor Woodrow shareholders ending up with 51 percent of the combined company and George Wimpey shareholders with 49 percent. Executives said the merger would result in some £50 million in annual cost reductions and that 700 jobs, or about 5 percent of the combined workforce, would be eliminated. Following the merger, Peter Redfern, who was the CEO of George Wimpey, became the CEO of Taylor Wimpey and Askew became the chairman.

## WEATHERING THE HOUSING COLLAPSE: 2007–10

The rapid deterioration of the U.S. real estate market swiftly challenged George Wimpey to adapt to a harsh new business environment. In May 2007 Taylor Wimpey announced that it was halting a housing development in Florida and cutting spending elsewhere in the country. In June it warned of a looming slowdown in the UK market. In January 2008 Taylor Wimpey told its suppliers that it would be paying 5 percent less as housing prices fell and credit became more scarce. In March it announced £283 million in write-downs in the United States.

Three months later Fitch Ratings downgraded Taylor Wimpey's £2 billion debt to junk status. In July the company reduced the value of its land and building sites in the UK, North America, and Spain by £660 million and confirmed that it was seeking an emergency £500 million cash injection from its main shareholders. The following month the company put its construction business up for sale. In November Taylor Wimpey reversed an earlier stand and agreed to sell to its creditors a 5 percent stake in the company in exchange for restructuring £2.5 billion of debt. The company's stock was valued at £46.4 million, just over 1 percent of its value after the merger less than a year and a half prior. At yearend 2008 the housing market collapse left Taylor Wimpey with a £1.5 billion loss that was driven by land and asset write-downs. Furthermore, its order book for new homes had fallen by nearly half from a year earlier.

The new year brought "encouraging signs of stability" in both the UK and the United States, Redfern told Graeme Wearden of the *Guardian*. Having shed 3,580 jobs, the company was much slimmer since the merger. It had taken another £527 million write-down, but its order book was beginning to grow again.

Early in 2010 Taylor Wimpey was considering selling Taylor Morrison, Inc. However, by the end of February the company had achieved 60 percent of its expected UK sales output for the year, marking what Redfern told John O'Doherty of the *Financial Times* was "a continuation of the better conditions of 2009." The company still posted a pretax loss in 2009, but at £700 million, it was 65 percent less than the previous year's and it included an operating profit in the second half.

In April, with selling prices up 9 percent, Ed Hammond of the *Financial Times* reported that Taylor

Wimpey's concerns turned in a different direction: a shortage of available land that could "artificially restrain" the housing market. By reducing its borrowings to £660 million from £750.9 million at the end of 2009, the company had clearly improved its ability to weather stormy markets.

*David E. Salamie*
*Updated, Eric Laursen*

### PRINCIPAL SUBSIDIARIES

Taylor Wimpey UK; Bryant Homes; Laing Homes Ltd.; George Wimpey; Taylor Morrison, Inc.; Monarch Corporation; Taylor Wimpey Spain; Taylor Woodrow (Gibraltar) Limited; Prestoplan; Taylor Wimpey Logistics; Wilson Connolly Logistics Ltd.

### PRINCIPAL DIVISIONS

UK Housing; North American Housing; Europe Housing; Prestoplan; Taylor Wimpey Logistics.

### PRINCIPAL COMPETITORS

Barratt Developments PLC; Berkeley Group Holdings PLC; Persimmon PLC; Redrow PLC; PulteGroup, Inc.

### FURTHER READING

Feltham, Cliff, "Write-Offs Push Taylor Wimpey to a Massive £1.5bn Loss," *Independent* (London), August 28, 2008.

Hammond, Ed, "Taylor Wimpey Warns on Land Shortage," *Financial Times* (London), April 29, 2010.

Harrison, Michael, "Taylor Woodrow Plans Expansion in North America," *Independent* (London), July 12, 2005, p. 56.

O'Doherty, John, "Taylor Wimpey Sees Signs of Recovery," *Financial Times* (London), March 3, 2010.

Rossiter, James, "New Chief Takes Fresh Approach at Taylor Woodrow," *Times* (London), February 21, 2007, p. 51.

Ruddick, Graham, "Taylor Wimpey Reveals Pounds 2bn Loss but Secures Its Future," *Daily Telegraph* (London), April 8, 2009.

"Taylor Woodrow PLC Preliminary Statement for the Year Ended 31 December 1999," *PR Newswire*, March 15, 2000.

Urquhart, Lisa, "Housebuilders Lay the Foundations for Growth," *Financial Times* (London), August 17, 2001.

Urry, Maggie "How Fear of Failure May Secure the Future for Taylor Woodrow," *Financial Times* (London), November 29, 2004.

Wearden, Graeme, "Construction: UK's Largest Housebuilder Sees 'Encouraging Signs of Stability,'" *Guardian* (London), August 6, 2009, p. 20.

# Tele2 AB

—■—

**Skeppsbron 18**
**PO Box 2094**
**Stockholm, SE-103 13**
**Sweden**
**Telephone: (+46 8) 5620-0060**
**Fax: (+46 8) 5620-0040**
**Web site: http://www.tele2.com**

*Public Company*
*Founded:* 1993 as NetCom Systems AB
*Incorporated:* 1996
*Employees:* 6,684
*Sales:* SEK 39.27 billion ($5.17 billion) (2009)
*Stock Exchanges:* NASDAQ OMX Stockholm
*Ticker Symbol:* TEL2
*NAICS:* 517110 Wired Telecommunications Carriers;
517210 Wireless Telecommunications Carriers
(Except Satellite); 515210 Cable and Other Sub-
scription Programming

■ ■ ■

Tele2 AB is one of Sweden's leading telecommunications providers. Originally known as NetCom Systems AB, the company traces its beginnings to 1993, when it was a subsidiary of the Swedish holding firm Industriförvaltnings AB Kinnevik; the firm went public in 1996 and changed its name to Tele2 in 2001. Tele2 offers a diverse portfolio of services, including mobile telecommunications, fixed telephony services, broadband Internet access, and network systems. In addition to its domestic operations, Tele2 has established a presence in key overseas regions over the years, notably in rapidly emerging markets in Russia and the Baltics. In addition, the company oversees operations in a number of highly competitive markets in Western Europe, with offices in Norway, the Netherlands, and Germany.

## ORIGINS OF A TELECOMMUNICATIONS PROVIDER

Although NetCom Systems was officially formed in 1993, the company's involvement in telecommunications actually began under former parent Kinnevik in the late 1970s. The pending deregulation of the Swedish and Scandinavian telecommunications markets encouraged Kinnevik to begin investing in the new technologies. With the government fixed telephony monopoly still very much in force, Kinnevik's first step was to enter the nascent mobile telecommunications market. In the late 1970s the company built its own analog mobile telephone network. Comviq AB began operations in 1981 and proved that there was a market for mobile telephones. Kinnevik's frequency allocations, however, remained limited to just 20,000 subscribers. Nonetheless, Comviq's analog system, if unable to expand, remained in operation until the mid-1990s.

While operating its analog network, Kinnevik also was investing in the emerging digital and satellite transmission technologies that would transform the telephone industry in the 1990s. Data transmission became technologically and commercially viable during the early 1980s, not only through traditional telephone lines, but also using satellite broadcasting technology. In

1986 Kinnevik inaugurated its own satellite link for data transmission, setting up subsidiary Comvik Skyport AB for its operations.

By the late 1980s, with Swedish telephone deregulation scheduled for 1993, Kinnevik began preparing to enter the voice transmission market as well. The company's first step was a 1989 joint investment agreement with Banverket, Sweden's national railway administration agency, to construct a fiber-optic network separate from the telephone monopoly's primarily copper wire-based network. Fiber-optic cables provided the additional advantage of far greater bandwidth than traditional cables, essential for the future boom in voice, data, and video transmission. Banverket's fiber-optic network would later reach more than 3,725 miles (6,000 kilometers), connecting all of Sweden's urban population. Kinnevik's telecommunications objectives received an additional boost in 1989 when it was awarded a nationwide license to operate a Global System for Mobile Communications (GSM) network. GSM was a European-wide collaboration to develop a digital network for voice and data transmission covering the entire continent, and beyond. During the 1980s Kinnevik added another important piece of what would later become the NetCom Systems puzzle, with the Kabelvision AB subsidiary and its cable television network. Despite competition, Kabelvision's subscriber base would grow to more than 300,000 by the 1990s.

## TELE2 NAME COMES INTO PLAY

After the agreement with Banverket, Kinnevik changed the name of its Comvik Skyport subsidiary to Tele2, not only to group its increasing fixed telephony interests, but also to emphasize its goal of challenging the nation's telephony services monopoly. Tele2 began operations of its data networking services in 1991, while continuing to build its network in preparation for the coming deregulation. Also in 1991 Tele2 received its license to offer telephony services. At the same time, Tele2 discovered a new market: the Internet. Although the

explosion of the Internet market would not occur until the mid-1990s (with the appearance of the graphically friendly World Wide Web), in 1991 Tele2 became the first to offer Internet access in Sweden, giving the company a long lead ahead of competitors, including the telephone monopoly.

Kinnevik's mobile telephone subsidiary changed its name to Comviq GSM and began offering services in September 1992. One of the first GSM operators in Europe, Comviq aimed at building an extensive network of transceivers (antennae), controllers, switches, and other equipment needed to provide full coverage in Sweden. The Swedish regulatory body, the National Post and Telecom Agency, was charged with enforcing a European-wide requirement that all highways and all urban centers with populations of 10,000 or more receive mobile telephone coverage.

At first, Comviq focused on the densest urban areas, then rolled out the service to the rest of the country. Initial operations, however, remained fairly modest. By the end of 1992 the company had enrolled 2,000 subscribers, a number that would grow to only 21,000 by the end of the following year. With Europe slipping deeper into an extended economic crisis during the first half of the 1990s, real growth in the mobile telephone market seemed to be on hold temporarily. Nevertheless, Comviq continued investing in building its network, using both its own network of radio transmission equipment and Banverket's fiber-optic network.

## DEREGULATION AND THE FORMATION OF NETCOM: 1993–95

The formal deregulation of the Swedish telecommunications market in 1993 led Kinnevik to regroup its telecommunications activities into a separate subsidiary. Called NetCom Systems AB, the new subsidiary began operations chiefly as a holding company for the former Kinnevik subsidiary Comviq. Tele2 and Kabelvision also were added to the NetCom Systems holding. With the deregulation of the Swedish market, Tele2 could at last begin offering its own telephone services. Tele2 began these operations in March 1993, with international calling services. Customers wishing to use Tele2 needed to dial 007; this requirement, viewed as giving the former government monopoly (later renamed Telia) an unfair advantage, was slated to be dropped in 1999. A service expected to be added in 1999 was telephone number portability, meaning that customers would be allowed to keep their telephone number regardless of the provider chosen. In 1994 Tele2 began offering domestic telephone services as well. By the end of that year the

## KEY DATES

**1991:** Tele2, a subsidiary of Kinnevik, becomes the first Internet provider in Sweden.

**1993:** Kinnevik reorganizes its telecom holdings into a new subsidiary, NetCom Systems AB.

**1996:** NetCom Systems becomes a public company.

**1997:** Company reorganizes its operations into a single subsidiary, Tele2 AB.

**2001:** NetCom Systems changes name to Tele2 AB.

**2004:** Tele2 establishes fixed-line operations in Ireland.

**2005:** Tele2 acquires Spanish telecommunications firm Comunitel Global SA.

**2007:** Tele2 divests holdings in the Netherlands, Belgium, Denmark, Portugal, and several other European markets.

**2009:** Tele2 assumes 100 percent ownership of Russian telecom Udmurtiya Cellular Communication.

**2010:** Tele2 acquires 100 percent stake in Rostov Cellular Communications.

company had established itself firmly as Sweden's number-two telephone company.

The year 1994 proved to be a breakthrough year for Comviq as well, as its subscriber base expanded to 136,000. By the end of 1995 Comviq's subscribers would surpass 450,000. In that year NetCom Systems began acting as an operating company, rather than a holding company. Tele2 and Kabelvision were grouped more directly under NetCom Systems. An early investor in Tele2, Britain's Cable and Wireless plc, which had controlled 39.9 percent of Tele2's shares, agreed to the restructuring, exchanging its Tele2 shares for a 9.2 percent stake in NetCom Systems. Both Tele2 and Comviq registered dramatic revenue growth from 1994 to 1995, boosting NetCom Systems' total sales to SEK 2 billion in 1995, compared with less than SEK 1 billion for 1994. Apart from the more than tripling of the number of Comviq subscribers, NetCom Systems was equally boosted by 1995's surge in Internet interest. Although Tele2 continued to seek the majority of its sales in telephone services, Internet access quickly became the subsidiary's second-largest revenue source.

As NetCom Systems expanded its activities in Sweden, it also was preparing to enter the markets of its Scandinavian neighbors. Already present in Norway through a 25 percent holding in NetCom ASA, formed with the deregulation of part of Norway's telecommunications market in 1993, NetCom ASA's chief activity became mobile GSM services, adding retail activities in the mid-1990s. NetCom Systems' direct participation in the Norwegian market remained limited to Internet and data transmission services, as the company awaited full deregulation of the Norwegian system, including its telephone system, slated for January 1998. In the meantime, NetCom Systems entered Denmark, with that country's deregulation in 1996, forming Tele2 A/S. The first company to break the 100-year-old government telephone monopoly, Tele2 A/S began building its infrastructure and client base, offering domestic and international telephone services, as well as Internet access and services.

### NETCOM GOES PUBLIC: 1996

In 1996 Kinnevik spun off NetCom Systems as an independent, publicly traded company. NetCom Systems shares were distributed among Kinnevik's shareholders, and NetCom Systems was listed on the Stockholm Stock Exchange. With the spin-off came new leadership: Anders Björkman, who had served as the company's vice president since 1995, was named president and CEO in 1996. Under Björkman, NetCom Systems completed the transition from holding company to active operating company. Grouped directly under the newly public company were Comviq GSM AB and Tele2 AB, while the company's Kabelvision operations continued to be listed as an associated company.

Both Comviq and Tele2 continued to post impressive gains into the second half of the decade. Comviq, after seeing its subscriber base stall somewhat in 1996 (hovering at 466,000), once again recorded a dramatic increase in 1997, building to more than 810,000 by the end of that year. By mid-1998 the company had recorded its one millionth customer. Aiding Comviq's growth were not only expanded GSM services, including data transmission and e-mail services, but also the successful launch of a prepaid, nonsubscription telephone credit card. The increasing popularity of GSM-based telephones in the rest of Europe also contributed to Comviq's fortunes at home, as customers moved to take advantage of a network that covered nearly the entire European continent.

Tele2 also achieved important growth in 1997, raising the number of customers to more than 310,000. In addition, Tele2 began marketing mobile telephone subscriptions based on the Comviq GSM network. At the same time, Tele2's Internet services were booming, more than doubling the number of subscribers to some 260,000, as the company maintained its position as Sweden's leading Internet service provider. Meanwhile,

Tele2 began eyeing the synergy possibilities available through Kabelvision, including not only Internet access but telephone applications as well. To strengthen these opportunities, NetCom Systems reorganized the company's operations in December 1997. All of the company's subsidiaries, including Kabelvision, now were grouped into a single subsidiary, Tele2 AB. The company's Danish and Norwegian subsidiaries, as well as its recently launched networking services subsidiary, NatTeknik, were placed under Tele2 AB. Each division would continue to operate under their well-established brand names.

## DEREGULATION IN NORWAY

The deregulation of the Norwegian telephone system occurred on January 1, 1998. NetCom Systems, through subsidiary Tele2 Norge AS, appeared to make strong gains into the new market, adding some 25,000 customers in just the first four weeks of operation. The company also boosted its network services position throughout Scandinavia by purchasing the Swedish, Danish, Norwegian, and Finnish Datametrix operations from Innova International Corporation. After announcing its one millionth Comviq GSM customer in mid-1998, NetCom Systems continued adding products, including an enhanced version of its prepaid GSM card, and testing of satellite telecommunications services. As in most Western European countries, the deregulation of long-held government telecommunications monopolies introduced enormous new opportunities. NetCom Systems' more than two decades of experience suggested that the company was prepared to meet the competition to conquer at least the Scandinavian region.

As the 1990s drew to a close, NetCom Systems began to identify new opportunities for expansion outside of the Scandinavian market. One area with enormous growth potential was in the Baltic region. In September 1998 the company acquired sizable shares in three cellular phone companies in Lithuania and Estonia. NetCom increased its foothold in the Estonian telecom industry the following January, purchasing a 90 percent stake in Levicom Cellular, as well as a 19.9 percent stake in Levicom Broadband. In October 2000 NetCom entered into an agreement to purchase Baltkom GSM, the second-largest cell-phone firm in Latvia, in a deal worth an estimated $277 million. With the completion of the merger, NetCom established a significant presence in all three Baltic countries.

During this period, NetCom continued to explore new business opportunities at home. In December 2000 the company's principal subsidiary, Tele2, acquired a highly coveted license from the Swedish government to develop third-generation (3G) mobile phone technology.

In January 2001, NetCom entered into a joint partnership with Telia AB, Sweden's largest telephone company, to develop a high-speed domestic phone network. Later that same month, NetCom officially changed its name to Tele2 AB. The change was primarily aimed to differentiate the company from its former Norwegian mobile phone business, NetCom ASA, which had become a subsidiary of Telia. As NetCom's strongest brand name, Tele2 seemed like the most logical replacement.

## EXPANSION TO OTHER MARKETS

Over the next several years, Tele2 continued its aggressive push into other markets. In May 2001, the company increased its stake in Estonia's Levicom Broadband from just under 20 percent to 60 percent. In October of that year, Tele2 created Tele2 Mobile, a new mobile virtual network operator, with the aim of extending cell-phone service to its existing 1.5 million fixed-line telephone customers in the Netherlands. Later that same month, the company entered into negotiations with Luxembourg-based Millicom International Cellular SA to acquire the firm's extensive telecom holdings in Russia. Meanwhile, the company's growth in the Baltic countries remained steady. By October 2002 Tele2's customer base in the region exceeded one million subscribers. Of these, 300,000 were in Lithuania, where Tele2 had emerged as the nation's third-largest mobile phone provider.

Over the course of the next year, Tele2's overseas holdings expanded rapidly. One notable area of growth was in Russia, where by September 2003 the company had seized controlling interests in 5 of the nation's 12 regional cell-phone operators. As the decade progressed, Tele2 became even more ambitious, as it shifted its focus to the more competitive telecom markets of Western Europe. In September 2004 the company established fixed-line operations in Ireland, while also launching an aggressive EUR 1 million ($1.22 million) marketing campaign promoting its new service. A month later, Tele2 agreed to terms on the acquisition of United Telekom Austria, in a deal worth EUR 213 million ($261.99 million). The merger was completed in December of that year.

In February 2005 Tele2 purchased Tiscali Denmark A/S for EUR 20.7 million ($26.91 million); the following July, the company established a vital foothold in Spain, with the acquisition of telecommunications carrier Comunitel Global SA. That same month, Tele2 made a EUR 1.33 billion ($1.6 billion) offer for the Dutch firm VersaTel Telecom International NV; the deal, however, was never completed.

## FOCUS ON DIVESTMENT AND EMERGING MARKETS

By this point, Tele2 began to recognize that its expansion strategy had left it vulnerable to increased competition in some of its core markets. In order to avoid becoming overextended, the company set out to divest several of its existing businesses. In August 2005 Tele2 shut down its operations in Finland, citing the nation's highly competitive telecom market, as well as its unfavorable regulatory climate. In December of that year, the company sold its fixed-line businesses in Ireland and the United Kingdom. After suffering significant losses in fiscal year 2006, the company intensified its streamlining efforts even further. In March 2007 Tele2 sold its telecom operations in Belgium and the Netherlands to Versatel; Tele2 divested its Danish subsidiary, Tele2 Denmark, two months later. By the end of the year, Tele2 had sold its businesses in Portugal and Hungary, as well as its fixed-line operations in Spain and Italy.

In the midst of this contraction, Tele2 renewed its focus on expanding into select growth areas, notably in the Baltic region and Russia. At the same time, the company bolstered its presence in the domestic telecom market, forging three crucial municipal service contracts in February 2008. By the end of that year, Tele2 had restored itself to financial health, posting a net profit of SEK 896 million ($115.45 million) for the fourth quarter, compared to a loss of SEK 31 million ($3.99 million) for the same period the previous year. With its more modest growth strategy in place, Tele2 continued to seek out new opportunities in core overseas markets. In July 2009 the company spent SEK 300 million ($38.9 million) to increase its stake in Russian telecom Udmurtiya Cellular Communications to 100 percent. In January 2010 Tele2 purchased all outstanding shares in Rostov Cellular Communications for SEK 350 million ($49.6 million). With its overseas acquisitions program now focused on emerging markets such as Russia, Tele2 had clearly built a business model designed to promote steady long-term growth.

*M. L. Cohen*
*Updated, Stephen Meyer*

## PRINCIPAL SUBSIDIARIES

Tele2 Europe SA (Luxembourg); Tele2 Norge Holding AB; Tele2 Russia Holding AB; Tele2 Russia Telecom BV (Netherlands); Tele2 Sverige AB; Tele2 Treasury AB.

## PRINCIPAL COMPETITORS

TDC A/S; Telenor ASA; TeliaSonera AB.

## FURTHER READING

Cattell, Brian, "Sweden's Tele2 Boosts Russian Holdings," *Daily Deal*, September 26, 2003.

Koza, Patricia, "Tele2 Shops Again," *Daily Deal*, July 19, 2005.

Lambert, Phineas, "Vodafone Snaps Up Tele2 Assets," *Daily Deal*, October 9, 2007.

"NetCom Systems Not Affected by Economic Fluctuations," *Dagens Industri*, January 15, 1997, p. 7.

"New NetCom Systems Head to Pursue Existing Strategy," *Dagens Industri*, October 2, 1996, p. 12.

O'Brien, Kevin J., "As Tele2 Owns More, Risks Rise," *International Herald Tribune*, October 31, 2005, p. 17.

O'Halloran, Barry, "Tele2 Puts Irish Arm Up for Sale," *Irish Times*, November 23, 2005, p. 19.

Pfalzer, Janina, "Retreat from Britain Leads to Loss for Tele2," *International Herald Tribune*, July 26, 2007, p. 16.

Wolfe, Elizabeth, "Sweden's Tele2 Dials into Russia," *Moscow Times*, November 2, 2001.

Zadvydas, Thomas, "Tele2 Increases Its Rostov Holding," *Daily Deal*, January 13, 2010.

# Telekom Austria AG

—— ■ ——

**Lassallestraße 9**
**Vienna, A-1020**
**Austria**
**Telephone:** (43) 59 0 59 10
**Web site:** http://www.telekomaustria.com

*Public Company*
*Founded:* 1887
*Incorporated:* 1996
*Employees:* 16,573
*Sales:* EUR 4.8 billion ($6.7 billion) (2009)
*Stock Exchanges:* Vienna
*Ticker Symbol:* TKA
*NAICS:* 517110 Wired Telecommunications Carriers;
517210 Wireless Telecommunications Carriers
(Except Satellite); 517410 Satellite Telecommuni-
cations

■ ■ ■

Telekom Austria AG is the largest telecommunications
company in Austria, operating fixed-line (Telekom
Austria TA) and mobile (mobilkom austria AG and
subsidiaries) telecommunications and telephony services
in one of the most competitive markets in Europe. Telekom Austria emerged in 1998 from the Post- und Telekom Austria. The latter evolved in 1996 from the state-
owned Post- und Telegraphenverwaltung (PTV), which
itself dates back to 1887's royal K.K. Post- und
Telegraphenverwaltung. Telekom Austria made its initial
public offering (IPO) in November 2000. Telekom
Austria operates nationally as well as internationally in

Belarus, Bulgaria, Croatia, Liechtenstein, Macedonia,
Serbia, and Slovenia. With more than 16,500
employees, Telekom Austria provides services and
products to over 2.3 million fixed-line customers and to
more than 18.9 million mobile customers, achieving
revenues of EUR 4.8 billion ($6.7 billion) in 2009.

## DEVELOPMENT OF POSTAL SYSTEM AND TELECOMMUNI-CATION IN EUROPE

Although three-quarters of its territory consists of
mountains and forests, Austria, like neighboring
Switzerland, has always been at the hub of Europe's
messenger routes. The history of Austria's postal communications have, in general, followed the usual
European pattern, but have also been affected by
Austria's eventful history and frequently altered identity.
An overall view shows a postal system of imperial
splendor and Byzantine complexity eventually replaced
by an efficient, logically organized industry, small by
international standards and tending to follow in areas
that it once led. Postal systems began in Europe before
the Common Era, in the form of an official Roman
messenger service, the *cursus publicus*, which disappeared
in the Dark Ages.

In the late 15th century, organized services, as
distinct from ad hoc personal arrangements, reemerged,
owned by rulers and institutions and gradually extended
to the carrying of passengers as well as of private mail.
State and commercial systems began to compete with
one another; by the late 18th century this fragmentation

---

## COMPANY PERSPECTIVES

Communication is the focus of our work. For people. From people.

---

had produced high charges and complicated, unstand-ardized procedures. With a marked increase in the political, social, and economic significance of postal and allied communications, as well as the size of the invest-ment required, postal services all over Europe fell under varying degrees of state control.

In the 19th century, the harnessing of electricity and the inventions of the telegraph and telephone, along with developments in road, rail, and water transport, changed the traditional notion of the message as an object transmitted bodily from sender to receiver without change of form, by a human intermediary, and telecommunications was born. With the electronic and aeronautics revolutions that followed the two world wars, post and telecommunications technology took off again and continued to gather momentum.

In the late 20th century and at the beginning of the 21st, telecommunications has become not only an es-sential part of every country's infrastructure, but in itself is an important sector of the economy it supports. The development of the high-speed Internet offers unprecedented access to knowledge, information, and ideas. Satellite communications offer unprecedented flexibility via mobile phones. The world has become a global village, and borders between nation-states have become virtually economically irrelevant. The inception of the European Union (EU) signaled (and at the same time sped up) the process of liberalization and privatiza-tion of the communications sector, breaking apart state monopolies all over Europe.

### EARLY HISTORY OF PTV

Telekom Austria's history dates back more than 275 years to the very beginnings of the country's royal com-munication system: In 1722 Emperor Charles VI put the postal service in state's hands, and his daughter, Empress Maria Theresa, and grandson, Emperor Joseph II, continued Charles's structural and organizational reforms. A central postal administration was set up in Vienna; the supervision of charges as well as a tighter timetable fell into state's hands. From 1749 new services were introduced, such as regular mail-coach and mounted-messenger links between the main cities of the empire, a parcel post in 1750, hand stamping of letters

with date of origin in 1751, and, from 1788, a registered post.

The system, however, was far from perfect. Some regional services continued to be handled by private operators, and the postal service did not extend to all of Austria-Hungary. Finally, between 1829 and 1848 under chief postal administrator, Maximilian Otto von Otten-feld, Austria's PTV coordinated its regional services and established an inspectorate. In 1839 printed guidelines were introduced, in 1847 the telegraph service came into being, and in 1850 Austria followed Great Britain's example and introduced the adhesive prepaid uniform-rate postage stamp, becoming the 16th nation in the world to do so. The modern postal service had emerged.

By 1866 the era of post and telecommunications supported by electricity, fast transport, and international cooperation was underway. The Austrian telegraph service was 19 years old and a series of bilateral treaties for postal cooperation with other European countries was preparing the ground for Austria's participation in the Universal Postal Union, between Austria and Germany, in 1850.

In 1881, five years after Alexander Graham Bell's first public demonstration of his invention, the telephone came to Vienna. The first telephone exchange was run by a private company, the Privat-Telegraphen-gesellschaft, under government license for a total of 154 subscribers, and the first public telephones appeared in 1882 at the Vienna Stock Exchange. Soon the new device was used in other Austrian cities, operated by various private companies. These companies, however, could not deliver adequate services, which proved expensive, ill-equipped, unreliable, and confined to cities. PTV moved to take over. In 1887 PTV inaugurated the first Austrian interurban telephone link, between Vienna and Brno (now in the Czech Republic). Others soon followed. The government started buying back the licenses it had granted, and in 1895 the telephone service was nationalized. The PTV did not change its name, as telephony was considered telegraphy through an acoustic apparatus.

Many of the developments that followed up to the end of World War I were necessary extensions of, or improvements to, existing postal, telegraph, and telephone services. In 1875 a pneumatic tube post started in Vienna; it lasted until 1956 when it was overtaken by high costs and competition from the telephone. In 1903 coin-operated telephones appeared. In 1907 General Director Friedrich Wagner von Jauregg embarked on the motorization of PTV with the inauguration of the post office's automobile passenger service, for which the lead had been assumed by Bavaria in 1905 and Switzerland in 1906. Another step forward

## KEY DATES

**1887:** K.K. Post- und Telegraphenverwaltung (PTV) inaugurates telephone link between Vienna and Brno.

**1996:** After over 100 years in state hands, PTV becomes the independent Post- und Telekom Austria AG; mobilkom austria operates independently.

**1998:** Telecommunications service is split off as independent company, Telekom Austria AG.

**2000:** Telekom Austria goes public on Vienna and New York stock exchanges.

**2001:** Mobilkom austria begins aggressive pursuit of international markets.

**2007:** Telekom Austria withdraws from New York Stock Exchange.

**2010:** Formation of Telekom A 1 Telekom Austria is announced.

was taken in 1910, when PTV began the long process of automating its telephone exchanges, which was completed in 1972 and eventually led to digitalization. Austria's digital network, which converts speech to electrical pulses, was initiated in the 1980s and completed by the end of the 20th century.

### THE PTV FROM 1918 TO 1980

World War I and its aftermath naturally set back the economics of the defeated powers, and progress at PTV was slow. After 1918, however, PTV was no longer a royal agency but the state-run service of a republic. In 1918 PTV operated the world's first civilian airmail service. Suspended almost at once by the end of the war, it was resumed in 1921. It began as an inland service but was extended overseas in 1928. In 1922 PTV introduced franking machines for automatic mail handling. A new field of activity opened in 1923 with the start of the ongoing partnership between PTV and Radio Austria A.G. Initially, PTV owned 30 percent of Radio Austria's shares but in 1956 the republic became the sole shareholder. In 1991 Radio Austria belonged effectively to PTV, was able to use the latter's cable and satellite installations, and was licensed by it to operate some international public telecommunications services.

The 1930s and 1940s brought a series of growth-inhibiting disasters for PTV, beginning with the years of the Great Depression, and, more significantly, the seven-year break in its identity that followed Germany's an-

nexation of Austria in 1938, when the Austrian postal services were absorbed into the Deutsche Reichspost until the end of World War II in 1945. Not only did the war almost eradicate Austria's postal and telecommunications infrastructure, but under the Allied occupation that followed, the country was divided into four administratively separate zones, in which the remnants of the mail, telegraph, and telephone systems had to reckon with control and censorship imposed by the occupiers.

Under Karl Dworschak, PTV's general director from 1945 until 1955, the resuscitated company began to recover. Postal operations covering the whole country were resumed in October 1945. The next objective was to begin catching up with the technological progress made in the outside world during Austria's troubles. The task was formidable but was undertaken against a new background of economic growth and political stability.

### PTV AND THE INFORMATION AGE

By 1957 Austria was making use of international satellites for radio, although it was not until 1971 that the country entered the expanding satellite communications field in its own right, deciding to build an earth station to connect with the existing international information satellite systems. PTV's Aflenz came into service on May 30, 1980, providing domestic and international links for telephone, radio, television, and data transmission. By the early 21st century more than 50 antennae with diameters of up to 32 meters would act as a gateway to the entire world.

Rapid technological developments in the text, image, and data services required a uniform system of data transmission. In 1992 PTV launched a local integrated services digital network (ISDN) pilot program in Vienna, originally providing 200 basic access lines. By the end of 1999, the Austrian fixed-line telephone network was fully digitalized. There were 247,000 access lines, a number that by 2002 had almost doubled to 438,000, offering ISDN data transmission, telephony, and virtual answering machine and fax transmissions to businesses and private customers.

Parallel to developments in the fixed-line service, PTV began the first mobile telephony service in Austria with the so-called A network in 1974 and added further networks in the following years, launching a mobile revolution in Austria that would eventually supersede fixed-net telephony services. Austria's PTV also invested in World Wide Web technology. In November 1995 Austria went online via the access platform Highway

194, which offered Internet access to business and private consumers.

## LIBERALIZATION AND PRIVATIZATION IN THE MID-NINETIES

In January 1995 the Republic of Austria became a full member of the EU. Following EU liberalization directives, the government passed the Austrian Post Restructuring Act, legislation to open the telecommunication and energy sectors to competition. More than 100 years of a telecommunications monopoly held by the state-owned PTV came to an end. On May 1, 1996, the PTV was separated from the federal administration and converted into a joint-stock company (AG) under the name Post- und Telekom Austria AG. At first the entire share capital was held solely by the Post- und Telekommunikationsbeteiligungsverwaltungsgesellschaft (PTBG), a state-owned holding company. PTBG comprised the postal service Österreichische Post AG and independently operating telecommunications companies, which had been extracted from the former PTV. Among them were mobilkom austria, which handled all former PTV mobile telephony services; Datakom GmbH, which handled corporate information technology services; and Highway 194 Internet Vertriebs GmbH, which served the World Wide Web. Preparations for privatization began immediately. As early as April 1997, 25 percent of its stock in mobilkom austria was sold to Telecom Italia.

When in 1998 the Austrian telecommunications market was fully deregulated, Post- und Telekom Austria AG was split into two companies, Telekom Austria AG and the postal service Österreichische Post AG. Unlike the Österreichische Post AG, which remained in state hands, Telekom Austria commenced privatization. That same year Telecom Italia purchased 25 percent of Telekom Austria AG. Two years later, in January 2000, PTBG merged with the Österreichische Industrieholding AG (ÖIAG), a fully state-owned industrial holding.

Following the Privatization Act 2000, ÖIAG held the state mandate to eventually fully privatize many of its companies, among them Telekom Austria AG. Hence, on November 21, 2000, Telekom Austria went public. In the to-date largest capital transaction in Austria, Telekom Austria stock was listed on the Vienna Stock Exchange and the New York Stock Exchange (NYSE). Telekom Austria was the first Austrian stock to ever trade on NYSE (it withdrew, however, in 2007 because of the subprime mortgage crisis). After the IPO, a little over 22 percent was free-floating private stock. Telecom Italia increased its share to a little over 29 percent, while almost 49 percent of the stock remained

in the hands of the state-owned ÖIAG. Over the next few years, free-floating private ownership of Telekom Austria increased steadily.

In 2002 Telekom Austria bought back Telecom Italia's shares in mobilkom austria. By 2004 Telecom Italia had sold its shares in Telekom Austria, increasing the free-float share percentage to 52.8 percent. At the end of that same year, ÖIAG reduced its stake from 48.2 percent to 31.2 percent, increasing the free-float stock share to 69.8 percent. By 2009 ÖIAG ownership of Telekom Austria had been further reduced to 28.4 percent, increasing the free-floating shares to almost 72 percent.

## FIERCE COMPETITION AND INTERNATIONAL EXPANSION AT THE DAWN OF THE 21ST CENTURY

Liberalization and privatization of the telecommunications industry led to fierce competition over the Austrian and other European markets. This in turn led to a race between telecommunications providers in Europe, offering the newest technological developments at competitive prices in both the mobile and fixed-line services, as well as Internet access.

In May 1996 a new online service, A-Online, was brought to the market. That same year, the company began to invest heavily in broadband, which, only three years later, counted 107,400 customers. By 2003 Telekom Austria was among the international leaders with over 200,000 asymmetrical digital subscriber line broadband customers. Also that year, Telekom Austria began offering customers telephony, Internet, and television services via broadband. In April 2010 the company reached a milestone: One million customers (97 percent of Austrian households) participated in the broadband network.

The same year, 1996, that A-online hit the market, Telekom Austria's mobile telephone division mobilkom austria was the first to offer mobile Internet access. Thus well-equipped to compete internationally, mobilkom austria founded a Croatian subsidiary, Vipnet d.o.o., in 1998. Two years later mobilkom austria began business in Liechtenstein through its subsidiary mobilkom liechtenstein AG. In 2001 mobilkom austria acquired stakes in the Slovenian provider Si.mobil d.d., thus expanding into southeastern Europe. In 2005 Mobiltel, a Bulgarian mobile phone provider, was also acquired; followed by etel in 2006, operating in central Europe; then Vip in 2007, a Serbian company.

## OUTLOOK

In the first decade of the 21st century, Austria was one of the most competitive mobile phone markets in Europe, forcing Telekom Austria to continuously offer increasingly competitive rates for mobile telephone and Internet services. Austrian consumers showed a relatively high preference rate for mobile telephone service over fixed-line services. In 2001 about two-thirds of total voice minutes moved over the fixed net. Eight years later this ratio had been reversed and approximately 80 percent of voice minutes moved over mobile nets. Despite higher subscription rates, Telekom Austria's mobile revenues decreased because of ever-dropping tariffs, and its fixed-line business decreased because customers favored cheaper mobile services. The company's annual report for 2009 showed a decrease of 8.8 percent in revenues of the fixed-net segment, as well as a 5.5 percent decrease in revenues of the mobile-communications segment.

In a forward-looking move in February 2010, the supervisory board of Telekom Austria approved a merger of the domestic fixed-net and mobile-communications operations of the company to better facilitate the market demand for integrated telecommunications solutions and convergent products. The merged company was to be called A 1 Telekom Austria. One resulting crossover product, A1 Network Professional, was announced in 2010: a voice telephony solution for companies that converged fixed-line and mobile services. Telekom Austria anticipated that merging fixed-net and mobile-communications operations in Austria would allow the company to respond to market developments and customer expectations, while reducing overhead and thus considerably boosting earning power in the coming years.

*Olive Classe*
*Updated, Helga Schier*

## PRINCIPAL SUBSIDIARIES

Telekom Austria TA AG; mobilkom austria; Mobiltel (Bulgaria), vip; mobilkom liechtenstein; Velcom (Belarus).

## PRINCIPAL DIVISIONS

Fixed Net; Mobile Communications.

## PRINCIPAL COMPETITORS

Hutchison 3G Austria GmbH; Orange Austria Telecommunication GmbH; T-Mobile Austria GmbH.

## FURTHER READING

Fokken, Ulrike, "It's No Longer a Question of Image: German Companies Are Leaving Wall Street," *Atlantic Times*, September 2007.

Groendahl, Boris, and Mark Heinrich, "Sistema Mulls Bid to Buy Telekom Austria," Reuters, March 27, 2010.

"Heisser Deal: Oligarch will die Telekom Austria kaufen," Krone.at, March 27, 2010.

Leberl, Eva, ed., *500 Jahre Europäische Postverbindungen 1490–1990. Aus Österreichs Postgeschichte- ein Kaleidoskop*, Vienna: Generaldirektion für die Post- und Telegraphenverwaltung, 1990.

"TA und Mobilkom fusionieren zu 'A1 Telekom Austria'," Krone.at, February 24, 2010.

"Telekom Austria Reaches 1 Million Broadband Customers," Rapid TV News, April 19, 2010.

# Torchmark Corporation

————————•————————

**3700 South Stonebridge Drive**
**McKinney, Texas 75070-8080**
**U.S.A.**
**Telephone: (972) 569-4000**
**Fax: (972) 569-3282**
**Web site: http://www.torchmarkcorp.com**

*Public Company*
*Founded:* 1900
*Incorporated:* 1929 as Liberty National Insurance
Company
*Employees:* 2,360
*Sales:* $3.27 billion (2009)
*Stock Exchanges:* New York
*Ticker Symbol:* TMK
*NAICS:* NAIC: 524113 Direct Life Insurance Carriers;
524114 Direct Health and Medical Insurance Car-
riers; 524126 Direct Property and Casualty Insur-
ance Carriers; 551112 Offices of Other Holding
Companies

■ ■ ■

Torchmark Corporation is an insurance and diversified
financial services holding company. Most of the
company's history involves a single corporate entity,
Liberty National Insurance Holding Co., but in the
1980s the company entered a period of aggressive
acquisition. By 1993 Torchmark controlled 10 principal
subsidiaries, branching out into individual life and
health insurance, as well as funeral, fire, and property
insurance, financial planning, mutual funds, and investment management services. After a period of consolida-

tion in the 1990s culminating in its decision to spin off
two of its subsidiaries in 1998, the company narrowed
its focus to the provision of life and health insurance
products, along with annuities, through its various
divisions. In 2010 Torchmark's clients resided in 51 million households representing 46 percent of all U.S.
households and were concentrated in the middle-income
niche with annual incomes of $25,000 to $75,000.

## IT BEGAN AS A SCAM IN THE EARLY 1900S

The company's roots extend back to the turn of the
20th century, when the Heralds of Liberty was
incorporated in Huntsville, Alabama. Although the
entity purported to be a fraternal benefit society, it was
actually a front for another company, headquartered in
Philadelphia. The fraternal charter limited the Alabama
Insurance Department's ability to oversee the Heralds of
Liberty, enabling the parent to circumvent state insurance regulations. The parent company's officers used a
variety of schemes to embezzle funds from the fraternity.
The officers sold it worthless bonds, borrowed money
on insufficient collateral, and had the Heralds make
"payments" to the parent. After 20 years of these illicit
practices resulted in a backlog of unpaid claims, the
Alabama Insurance Department took over the fraternity
in June 1921.

The state agency assigned deputy insurance commissioner Robert Park Davison to clean up the Heralds
of Liberty. He forced all of the fraternity's officers and
directors to resign and was made "Supreme Commander" of the group. Frank Park Samford, Davison's
colleague and cousin, was elected "Supreme Recorder."

# COMPANY PERSPECTIVES

Torchmark provides protection-oriented life and supplemental health insurance to middle-income Americans through its premier niche distribution organizations. We succeed in this market while many life insurers have moved upscale seeking the smaller high-income market focused on asset accumulation. We use our understanding of the middle-income market by segmenting our market efforts by various niche distribution methods. These include direct response and various types of agencies, as well as affinity groups within the broader market, for example, senior-age customers and labor union members. We market our products under the name of each subsidiary, rather than the Torchmark name, to take advantage of the strong market niche recognition that each of our subsidiaries already had developed before joining the Torchmark group. It would be difficult to overstate the value of the positive name recognition that our leading subsidiaries have as stable, high-quality organizations.

The unusual titles reflected the group's origins as a secret society. Davison and Samford went to the parent's headquarters in Philadelphia to begin reformation of the Heralds of Liberty. They found that the group was insolvent. Unpaid claims amounted to $80,000, but the firm held only $1,410 in cash. The Heralds had no reserves, and premiums on the policies that existed were insufficient to meet financial demands. Davison and Samford discovered that the only policy the Heralds had sold was a lottery-style plan, called a joint life distribution plan. The scheme divided policyholders into classes by age. When a policyholder died, his beneficiary and the holder of the lowest certificate number in each class were both paid. Although the Heralds had tried to eliminate these policies through exchanges and by introducing new insurance plans, the parent company was dependent on this business for financial support and was compelled by the nature of the plan to continue to place new policies in the existing classes. It took the new officers until the mid-1930s to rid the company of these policies.

## LIBERTY GOES LEGIT BY 1929

Davison and Samford worked during the 1920s to raise premiums, sell legal life insurance policies based on an

adequate reserve, pay past-due claims, and build up a team of trustworthy agents. In 1927, the year the headquarters of the reformed company moved to Birmingham, Alabama, it had 26 employees and one new officer, an assistant secretary. To build up a reserve fund, Davison and Samford made the company's first stock offering in 1929 under its new name, Liberty National Life Insurance Co. Many officers and agents borrowed money to purchase shares of the $325,000 offering. The stock offering was supplemented with an additional assessment on Heralds of Liberty policyholders. Liberty National's officers feared that many clients would cancel their policies, but by July 1929 the company appeared to have endured its transformation into a legitimate insurer.

Disaster struck again when the stock market crashed that year. Many of those who had borrowed to capitalize the new company were stuck with debts that exceeded the value of their collateral. To make matters worse, the cash generated by the initial stock issue had been deposited with the Southern Bank and Trust Company as trustee, and before Liberty National had a chance to invest, it became apparent that the money could not be withdrawn without breaking the bank. Unlike many other banks during this crisis, however, Southern managed to stay open, and Liberty National was able to withdraw its funds in small increments over the next few months.

Liberty National struggled over the next five years to endure the Great Depression. Income from premiums declined as customers were forced to cancel their policies, and losses were sustained when banks failed and debtors defaulted on their bonds. Cost-cutting helped the company survive losses during the Depression, and Liberty National even invested $95,000 to acquire the distribution system of a failing competitor. Circumstances compelled Liberty to use creative financing to remain solvent in the early years of the decade. In 1931 the company purchased a 70 percent interest in a headquarters building and claimed it as an asset to maintain an adequate surplus. Davison and Samford even offered to surrender some of their stock to the company in 1932 to subsidize Liberty National's surplus, but that drastic step was not necessary. In fact, Liberty National paid its first cash dividend the following year. The insurance company's officers perceived that its shareholders doubted the continued viability of Liberty National and felt that the $21,000 dividend would restore investor confidence. That first payment started a custom that was followed every year in the company's history.

When Davison died in 1934, Samford was elected president and chief executive officer, a more traditional

## KEY DATES

**1929:** Liberty National Insurance Company is founded.

**1981:** The company acquires United American Insurance Company and Waddell & Reed.

**1982:** Liberty National Insurance Holding Company is renamed Torchmark Corporation.

**1990:** Torchmark buys Family Life Insurance Company.

**1994:** American Income Life Insurance Company enters Torchmark fold.

**1998:** Family Life and Waddell & Reed are spun off.

**2005:** Waddell & Reed agrees to settle a longstanding legal dispute with Torchmark, paying its former parent $14.5 million.

**2006:** Torchmark is approved to sell Medicare Part D drug plans in all regions of United States except Alaska and Hawaii; the company moves its corporate headquarters from Birmingham, Alabama, to McKinney, Texas.

**2009:** Torchmark reports a decline in net operating income per share for 2008, attributed to exposure to troubled financial services companies in its investment portfolio.

pair of administrative titles than "Supreme Commander." Liberty National enjoyed a period of growth and prosperity after that year and worked to build a dependable base of financial strength. Innovative policies helped the company compete successfully with its older and larger rivals. Liberty National made its first acquisition in 1944 through an interesting series of events. Late in 1943 Rufus Lackey, the principal stockholder of the Brown-Service Insurance Company, offered to sell his share of the Alabama insurer to Liberty National for $5 million, provided the transaction was completed by the end of the year. Liberty National had the will but neither the cash nor the borrowing power to make the acquisition on such short notice. Samford and the company's general counsel secured personal loans with their Liberty National stock as collateral and purchased the stock themselves, and Brown-Service merged with Liberty National in 1944.

Brown-Service, a successful regional company, specialized in burial insurance plans. Liberty National utilized the subsidiary's large agency force to accomplish

the greatest market penetration ever achieved by a life insurance company. Although Liberty National later discontinued the sale of burial insurance policies, the plan provided substantial savings to many citizens of Alabama and helped Liberty National build a highly efficient and profitable operation. In the 1960s more than 80 percent of white Alabamans held Brown-Service policies. As late as the mid-1980s almost half of the people who died in Alabama each year were insured under a Brown-Service policy.

## EXPANSION AFTER WORLD WAR II

Liberty National progressed steadily after 1945. The company made several relatively minor acquisitions, expanded geographically, and introduced numerous new insurance products. In 1952 the company began recording consecutive annual increases in both earnings and dividends that went unmatched by any other member of the New York Stock Exchange.

In 1958 Liberty National altered Birmingham's skyline by placing a one-fifth-sized replica of the Statue of Liberty atop its Birmingham headquarters. During the 1950s and 1960s the insurer grew to become America's second-largest publicly owned provider of so-called industrial insurance. This type of policy was renewed weekly and had been discontinued by most other major insurers, but Liberty National was reluctant to abandon these policies, which were popular with the company's rural customers. By the end of the 1960s it ranked 18th in regular coverage and had expanded its geographic service area to include Georgia, Florida, Tennessee, and California. In 1968 Liberty National sold more than $1 billion in new policies for the first time.

Frank P. Samford Jr. replaced his father as president and chief executive officer of Liberty National in 1967. He served in that position until 1985. The younger Samford brought Liberty National's policyholders more modern coverage. In the late 1960s, for example, the company introduced an estate plan and a special program for college students. The company's agents continued to take a very personal approach to life insurance, however. In 1975 its 2,500 agents still sold monthly life insurance door to door. Other, more urban, companies had abandoned these low-premium policies, but Liberty National continued to earn profit margins of 15 percent on the old-style coverage.

## RESTRUCTURING AND ACQUISITION IN THE LATE SEVENTIES AND EIGHTIES

In 1979 Liberty National undertook an agenda of expansion and diversification through acquisition. Prior to that time most of the company's investments were concentrated in mortgages, bonds, and a limited number of stocks, but by the mid-1980s the company had grown from a regional life insurance firm into a diversified national insurance and financial services corporation. From 1980 to 1982 the company spent more than half a billion dollars to purchase several insurance and investment businesses. In 1980 the company bought Globe Life and Accident Insurance Company. Headquartered in Oklahoma City, Globe was founded in 1951 by John Singletary and Ralph Reese. Although the company was established with borrowed money, it had grown into a consistently profitable firm through the use of innovative marketing techniques such as direct mail. When Singletary died in 1977, Ronald K. Richey was elected president and CEO. In 1979 the company underwent a crisis when the executor of Singletary's estate sought to sell his 36 percent share. Liberty National purchased the company in a friendly takeover and made Richey a director of the parent. He succeeded Samford as president and CEO in 1986.

The year 1979 also saw the creation of the Liberty National Insurance Holding Company, which became the parent company of all of Liberty National's holdings following a corporate reorganization in 1980. The new entity made two major acquisitions in 1981: Continental Investment Corporation and United American Insurance Company of Dallas. Continental owned Waddell & Reed (W&R) and United Investors Life Insurance Company, two businesses that would become primary subsidiaries of Liberty National. W&R was created as a sales and distribution division for United Mutual Funds and was named for the fund's founders, Chauncey Waddell and Cameron Reed. United Mutual Funds became the first mutual fund group to be registered under the Investment Company Act of 1940, the legislation that brought funds under the jurisdiction of the Securities and Exchange Commission.

W&R hoped its group of mutual funds would make it easier for middle-income Americans to participate in the investing process. United Investors Life Insurance Company was created as an outgrowth of W&R in 1961. Its term insurance product soon accounted for a major part of Continental Investment Company's income. Problems in the national economy and the stock market, as well as difficulties stemming from Continental's ownership of W&R, combined to force W&R into bankruptcy reorganization in the 1970s. The firm emerged from the crisis with new leadership and new products: financial planning seminars and services. By the early 1980s W&R was a leading American financial planner. Liberty National

purchased W&R's parent, Continental Investment Corporation, for $155 million in 1981.

The United American Insurance Company of Dallas, Liberty National's other major acquisition of 1981, was founded in 1947 by Casey Dunlap and Russ Donovan. This company had pioneered the employment of independent health insurance agents in the mid-1950s. It parlayed this new sales system into a nationwide system that extended into Canada by the time it was acquired by Liberty National for $138 million.

Liberty National's expansion into mutual funds, health insurance, and financial services rendered its formal name, Liberty National Insurance Holding Co., too limiting. The company adopted the name Torchmark Corporation in 1982. Torchmark combined the Statue of Liberty's torch and the word "hallmark" to form a unique name that drew upon the company's long history and reflected its new components.

While many other insurance providers were lured into the high-return, high-risk junk bond and commercial real estate markets of the 1980s, Torchmark maintained three-fourths of its invested assets in reliable, government-guaranteed securities and short-term investments. When the bottom fell out of the junk bond and real estate markets in the late 1980s, Torchmark emerged unscathed. Torchmark's conservative investment strategies earned its primary subsidiaries the industry's highest ratings. The national scandals, however, did affect the company in the form of increased contributions to the federal guaranty fund to bail out insolvent insurers.

## THE NINETIES

The 1990s began promisingly for Torchmark, as 1992 marked the company's 41st consecutive year of growth. By then its stock price had shot up an astronomical 1,675 percent from its 1980 levels. In 1994, however, the company experienced some setbacks. Liberty National Life Insurance Company had become the target of several legal disputes in Alabama stemming from alleged misconduct by its agents. Some of thee cases involved age discrimination and punitive damages claims while others related to an exchange of Liberty's cancer policies. In large part as a result of fallout from these matters as well as some poorly performing investments, Torchmark's growth streak snapped. Revenues declined to $1.875 billion from 1993's $2.177 billion, and net income dropped $31 million from 1993's results, to $269 million.

The year 1994 also saw some alterations in the company's business balance. Noting that life insurance products tended to have higher operating margins, build better assets, and experience less year-to-year growth pressure, Torchmark made the strategic decision to focus more heavily on its life insurance operations at the expense of health insurance. Buoyed by the acquisition of American Family Life Insurance Company for $552 million in November of that year, Torchmark's life insurance revenues jumped 16 percent from 1993's levels, and the health insurance sector contracted by 31.2 percent over the same period.

The restructuring of 1994 helped stanch the decline in Torchmark's revenues as 1995 sales climbed to $2.067 billion, recouping nearly all of the 1993–94 drop. Net income, however, declined nearly 47 percent from 1994, to $143 million, as a result of poor growth in the Medicare supplemental insurance sector along with the company's litigation exposure, heavy debt burden from the American Family Life acquisition, and underperforming oil and gas investments. (The Medicare business had been slumping ever since federal legislation enacted in 1992 capped the commissions that vendors of such policies could charge.) To remedy this situation, Torchmark opted to divest itself of its holdings in the energy industry. It streamlined its operations and dedicated itself more closely to its core insurance, mutual fund, and asset management businesses. In 1995, therefore, Torchmark liquidated its investments in Torch Energy Advisors, Inc., and the Black Warrior coal mine venture and sold off its holdings in Nuevo Energy Co.

These maneuvers proved tremendously beneficial, and 1996 net income skyrocketed to $311 million on revenues of $2.071 billion. Life insurance operations remained the single largest growth engine, and the company's direct-response business was particularly profitable. (As the name suggests, direct response relies on marketing insurance directly to customers via post, television, and other media rather than by the traditional use of agents. Torchmark's Global Life and Accident Insurance Company spearheaded this portion of the company's business.)

Torchmark's success continued in 1997. Revenues increased to $2.282 billion and net income rose to $324 million. Every sector of the company except its Medicare supplement products showed strong growth while administrative efficiencies reduced operating expenses. In March 1998 Torchmark took more steps to reduce its indebtedness, placing an initial public stock offering of 34 percent of its ownership interest in W&R. In November Torchmark spun off the firm into a free-standing entity, though it continued to rely on its former subsidiary for some of its financial services operations. Torchmark also sold its Family Service Life subsidiary in June 1998 and used the proceeds to pay

down debt and buy back some of its outstanding shares. Revenues for the year climbed to $2.158 billion, though net income dropped to $244 million in light of the company's debt restructuring and discharge.

## NEW BUSINESS AND A SETTLEMENT WITH WADDELL & REED

Always looking for new ways to reach its target audience of middle-income households, Torchmark in September 1999 announced an alliance with Reader's Digest Association Inc. to market its health and life insurance products to the magazine's database of 100 million names in the United States and Canada. Initial results were not positive. Torchmark took a one-time after-tax charge of $13 million on the Reader's Digest deal for the fourth quarter of 1999, causing a drop in net earnings for the period. In a statement, Torchmark said its profit from the program was unlikely to exceed the amount it had agreed to pay Reader's Digest.

Geographically, however, Torchmark was still expanding. In December 2000 it received a license from the state of New York for a new unit, National Income Life Insurance Company of Syracuse, New York, a subsidiary of American Income Life Insurance. This rounded out Torchmark's coverage of the labor union market, which American Income Life already served in every other state.

Torchmark reported a 12 percent increase in net operating income for 2000 and a further 9 percent increase for 2001, despite losses it suffered on a portfolio of collateralized debt obligations and a decline in its sales of Medicare supplemental health policies. Profits grew steadily for Torchmark in the early years of the new century. Another 9 percent boost to net operating income followed in 2002, powered by higher total insurance sales and higher premium income that more than offset declining health insurance sales. Net operating income climbed again, by 5.4 percent in 2003 and by another 9 percent in 2004.

The following year saw the settlement of a legal dispute that had been dragging on since 2001 and that had its roots in Torchmark's period of ownership of Waddell & Reed. The initial lawsuit accused Torchmark and its former chief executive, Ronald K. Richey, of scheming to keep control over W&R after the 1998 spinoff, claiming damages of at least $58 million. Torchmark also sued, challenging the compensation that W&R had taken for selling variable annuities for United Investors.

The high-profile feud continued until April 2005, when W&R agreed to settle, paying Torchmark $14.5

million to end all outstanding litigation between the companies. A year later, in a separate dispute over taxes owed as well as tax refunds and reductions before the separation of the two companies, an arbitration panel ruled that the W&R owed Torchmark a further $7.4 million.

## MEDICARE PART D AND A NEW HOME IN TEXAS

Torchmark turned another page later in 2005 when C. B. Hudson, who had been chairman and CEO for seven years, stepped down and was succeeded by Mark S. McAndrew, who had been chairman of the company's insurance operations. Early in 2006 Hudson resigned as chairman as well, and he turned that position over to McAndrew. Cash flow from operations reached a nine-year high in 2005 of $767.1 million.

A gateway to potentially significant new business opened that same year when Torchmark's United American Insurance subsidiary received approval to sell Medicare Part D prescription drug plans in all regions of the United States except Alaska and Hawaii. United American Insurance, which to date had 300,000 Medicare supplement policyholders and other Medicare beneficiaries, would be providing the coverage through Medco Health Solutions, Inc., a leading pharmacy benefit manager.

Another long-simmering legal dispute was cleared out of the way in April 2006, when Liberty National Life Insurance agreed to pay $6 million to resolve a class-action lawsuit alleging racially discriminatory pricing in the sale of life insurance to African Americans prior to 1966. The suit dated from 1999 and was one of dozens filed against major U.S. insurance companies.

Torchmark, meanwhile, was literally on the move, as it announced the following month that after 75 years headquartered in Birmingham, Alabama, it was moving its corporate base of operations to McKinney, Texas, where United American Insurance was located. Liberty National Life Insurance would remain based in Birmingham. The Texas Enterprise Fund awarded Torchmark a $2 million grant to aid the move, which was expected to create 500 new jobs in the state. McAndrew unveiled plans for a $27 million, 150,000-square-foot headquarters facility that would help the company consolidate marketing and administrative functions for its subsidiaries, including a centralized computer processing and customer service center.

"We have found McKinney, the Dallas-Fort Worth area, and the state of Texas to be conducive to the growth and success of our businesses," McAndrew told *Texas Construction* magazine in an article published May

1, 2006. "With the business-friendly environment, easy transportation access, and a family-oriented community, it just makes good business sense to consolidate our administration here. The Texas Enterprise Fund, along with local incentives, was instrumental in our decision to relocate to Texas."

Medicare Part D business was proving its worth on the bottom line. By May 2006, when the first open-enrollment period ended for the federal government program, Torchmark had picked up more than 200,000 Medicare-confirmed enrollees, it announced in a press release. The new customers were instrumental in boosting fourth-quarter profit by nearly 13 percent. New operating income for the following year, 2007, rose 9 percent per share.

## THE ECONOMIC SLUMP

By mid-year 2008 the financial and economic slumps were starting to affect Torchmark's risk profile. Fitch Ratings cut its outlook for the company from stable to negative in June, citing declining statutory capital levels and competitive challenges in its individual life and supplemental health products. In September Torchmark revealed that it had investments in American International Group, Lehman Brothers, Fannie Mae, Freddie Mac, and Washington Mutual that could total $209 million, or 2 percent of its total invested assets.

Net operating income for the year was 6 percent per share, a decline from 2007. In April 2009 Fitch announced downgrades of debt issued by Torchmark and several of its subsidiaries, again citing its investment exposure to the financial sector. The company said in a statement that it was working to address concerns by cutting its outstanding commercial paper and that it had ample liquidity to do so, including $242 million of free cash flow.

Torchmark faced a new regulatory challenge in 2009 as well. In June 2009 Fran Matso Lysiak in *BestWeek* reported that the Florida Office of Insurance Regulation (OIR) was considering suspending or revoking Liberty National Life Insurance's sales license for alleged illegal discrimination against Haitians. Torchmark's vice president of investor relations, Mike Majors, said the OIR "has misinterpreted the facts in significant respects" and that the company "believes that its past and current practices were consistent with Florida law at the time, and is optimistic that a satisfactory resolution of this matter can be achieved through appropriate administrative procedures." Hearings were set in the matter for early 2010.

The poorly performing economy continued to erode Torchmark's financial results in 2009. A.M. Best

Co. revised its outlook for the company in June to negative from stable, although it affirmed its high ratings for Torchmark's major subsidiaries. The company still enjoyed "exceptional operating profitability" on strong earnings from its core products, Best said, while its large reserves should buffer any negative impact from its investment portfolio. Net operating income per share was down to 3 percent in 2009.

*April S. Dougal*
*Updated, Rebecca Stanfel; Eric Laursen*

## PRINCIPAL SUBSIDIARIES

American Income Life Insurance Company; First United Life Insurance Company; Globe Life and Accident Insurance Company; Liberty National Life Insurance Company; United American Insurance Company; United Investors Life Insurance Company.

## PRINCIPAL COMPETITORS

The Allstate Corporation; Citigroup Inc.; Conseco, Inc.; Liberty Mutual Insurance Companies; Metropolitan Life Insurance Company; Prudential Insurance Company of America; UNUMProvident; USAA.

## FURTHER READING

Frank, Robert, "Torchmark to Buy American Income for $563.5 Million," *Wall Street Journal*, September 16, 1994.

"Industrial Insurance Profitable Line for Liberty National Life," *Barron's*, July 29, 1968.

Lysiak, Fran, "Torchmark Says Liberty National Life Doesn't Discriminate," *BestWeek*, June 8, 2009.

Lysiak, Fran Matso, "Torchmark Unit Paying $6 Million to End Suit Alleging Racially Discriminating Pricing," *BestWeek*, April 7, 2006.

Samford, Frank P., Jr., *Torchmark Corporation: History of a New Company.* Princeton, NJ: Princeton University Press, 1985.

"Torchmark Corporation Discloses Investments in AIG, Lehman Brothers, Fannie Mae, Freddie Mac and Washington Mutual," PR Newswire, September 18, 2008.

"Torchmark Moves HQ to McKinney: Texas Secretary of State Roger Williams Announced That a $2 Million Grant from the Texas Enterprise Fund Will Lead to 500 New Jobs in North Texas," *Texas Construction*, May 1, 2006, p. 43.

"Torchmark to Spin Off Waddell & Reed United Sometime in Early 1998," *Wall Street Journal*, November 18, 1997.

"United American Gets Medicare Part D Prescription Drug Plan's Approval from CMS," *Drug Week*, October 7, 2005.

"Waddell & Reed Settles NASD, Torchmark Litigation," PR Newswire, April 29, 2005.

# United States Sugar Corporation

111 Ponce de Leon Avenue
Clewiston, Florida 33440
U.S.A.
Telephone: (863) 983-8121
Fax: (863) 983-9827
Web site: http://www.ussugar.com/

*Private Company*
*Incorporated:* 1931
*Employees:* 1,700
*Sales:* $398 million (2009 est.)
*NAICS:* 111930 Sugarcane Farming; 311311 Sugarcane
    Mills

■ ■ ■

Based in Clewiston, Florida, the United States Sugar Corporation is a major cane sugar and citrus grower. The privately held company operates on nearly 188,000 acres of farmland located in Glades, Hendry, and Palm Beach counties. U.S. Sugar produces 700,000 tons of raw sugar annually, about 10 percent of the sugar produced in the United States, making it the country's largest producer of cane sugar. When operating at full capacity during the harvest season between October and April, the company's raw sugar mill can process up to 40,000 tons of sugar a day. An adjacent sugar refinery is the only fully integrated operation in the country and is able to produce a full range of sugar products, from bulk sugar transported in railcars to individual packets to liquid sugar. All the Clewiston operations are powered by bagasse, which uses cane fiber that is leftover from the milling process to generate electricity. The company's refined sugar products are marketed to food retailers and food manufacturers by United Sugars, a joint venture with Minnesota and North Dakota beet sugar cooperatives. U.S. Sugar also produces more than 120 million gallons of orange juice each year on 30,000 acres of groves and is the largest supplier of not-from-concentrate orange juice in the United States.

## THE EARLY YEARS: 1930–50

U.S. Sugar was founded in 1931 by the U.S. industrialist Charles Steward Mott. Born in Newark, New Jersey, in 1875, Mott decided to study mechanical engineering rather than work in the family's cider and vinegar business, Genessee Fruit Company. More to his liking was a company that manufactured wire wheels for bicycles, which his father and uncle acquired and reorganized as the Weston-Mott Company. Mott was made the superintendent of the factory. He eventually became convinced that the emerging automobile industry offered greater opportunities, so with William Doolittle, a new part-owner, Weston-Mott was slowly shifted in that direction. The company forged a relationship with General Motors (GM), which eventually acquired Weston-Mott for stock, making Mott a wealthy man and one of GM's largest shareholders as well as a director. In 1920 he became an executive vice president of GM, a post he held for the next 17 years, but one that did not fully occupy his time. Like his family, he also remained interested in farming.

In 1931 Mott acquired a sugar mill built three years earlier in Clewiston, Florida, by the bankrupt Southern

Sugar Company and formed the United States Sugar Corporation. It was only in the late 1920s that Florida landowners had taken advantage of the rich black soil found south and east of Lake Okeechobee to grow sugar cane. During the wet season the lake also supplied overflow water to the Everglades further south, and the ecosystem would be adversely impacted by sugar cane production, a situation that would become of increasing importance to U.S. Sugar.

Dedicated to making a success out of U.S. Sugar, as he had with the other business ventures in his life, Mott brought in experts to solve the problems that had caused the failure of Southern Sugar. He took advantage of their experience in cane growing in Cuba, the West Indies, the Louisiana to determine the proper sugar cane variety to use and to solve drainage problems. Within 10 years Mott had turned U.S. Sugar into a profitable concern. Further keys to the company's success was the Clewiston Sugar House, which had been wisely built with future expansion in mind, and a 21-mile railroad that had been constructed to transport the sugar cane from the fields to the mill.

## COMPANY GROWTH: 1950–90

U.S. Sugar launched an expansion effort in the late 1950s, which led to the extension of the rail network in 1959 and the opening of a second mill, the Bryant Sugar House, in 1962. At the time, it was the most modern facility of its type in the world, and like the Clewiston mill, it was designed for future expansion. That extra capacity would be needed to support the Florida sugar industry that filled the void in the market created by the loss of sugar produced in Cuba, which underwent a Communist revolution in the late 1950s.

Over the next 20 years Florida emerged as the United States' largest sugar producer, and U.S. Sugar was the state's largest player. The company took advantage of its extensive land holdings to diversify into other crops as well as into cattle. In 1985 the company

elected to sell all of its cattle and shift to planting nearly 30,000 acres of orange groves. Also of note during the mid-1980s U.S. Sugar employees gained a majority ownership position in the company through an Employee Stock Ownership Plan. Charitable foundations established by Mott, who passed away in 1973, were other major stakeholders.

## GROWTH AND CONTROVERSY: EARLY TO MID-NINETIES

U.S. Sugar grew on a number of fronts during the 1990s. In January 1994 the Southern Gardens Citrus Processing plant was opened. This was the first new citrus processing plant to be built in Florida in over 20 years. Costing more than $100 million to construct, it was a state-of-the-industry facility. Like the Clewiston and Bryant mills, it was designed with the potential for expansion. Just two years later an addition was completed, allowing the plant to process 19 million boxes of fruit each season. The Southern Gardens plant was expected to eventually process 30 million boxes of fruit, which would produce 180 million gallons of juice.

U.S. Sugar also expanded its rail holdings. The link that connected Clewiston to the rest of the world had been long neglected. It became part of CSX in 1987 and three years later was acquired by South Central Florida Railroad. The poorly maintained branch suffered from regular derailments, and finally in September 1994 U.S. Sugar took charge and renamed the rail operation South Central Florida Express.

U.S. Sugar's core cane sugar business came under increasing fire during the 1990s, as did the entire industry in Florida, because of its impact on the 2 million-acre ecosystem of the Everglades National Park, the Big Cypress National Preserve, and the Loxahatchee National Wildlife Refuge. For decades sugar growers, as well as vegetable farmers, had been allowed to irrigate their fields with water from Lake Okeechobee and then pump their runoff, which was laden with fertilizer that was high in phosphorus, into the wetlands that fed the Everglades. Approximately 200 tons of phosphorus was pumped into the wetlands annually. The direct result was that several plants, including the cattail and the Brazilian pepper, thrived at the expense of the native vegetation on which fish and birdlife depended. In time, large dead zones in the ecosystem developed where little more than algae and microorganisms existed.

The sugar industry fought to continue it practices but faced stiff opposition, especially from the secretary of the interior Bruce Babbit, who proposed a plan to resurrect the ecosystem. He sued the Flo-Sun Corp., a major Florida sugar producer, and in 1994 a settlement

## KEY DATES

**1931:** The United States Sugar Corporation is founded.
**1962:** U.S. Sugar opens the Bryant Sugar House.
**1985:** U.S. Sugar coverts cattle lands to orange groves.
**1998:** U.S. Sugar opens a new sugar refinery.
**2008:** U.S. Sugar agrees to sell business to the state of Florida.

was reach in which Flo-Sun agreed to pay a penalty and reduce the phosphorous content of its discharge by about 80 percent. In return, the government promised to allow the company to operate until at least 2010. Also in 1994 the Florida governor Lawton Chiles signed water cleanup legislation brokered with sugar growers that established a $700 million, 20-year project to create marshes that would filter the polluted water before reaching the Everglades. Up to $320 million of the project was to be paid by the sugar growers. The growers also agreed to significantly reduce their use of phosphorus fertilizer, and the federal government pledged not to impose any new environmental taxes or cleanup regulations for the next decade.

### THE COMPANY AND THE ENVIRONMENT

With some certainty provided by the cleanup compromise, U.S. Sugar expanded its operations. In October 1998 a new cane sugar refinery was opened, the first refinery built in the United States in more than 25 years. Again, the company made sure the facility was designed with growth in mind. However, at the turn of the 21st century extra capacity was not needed as sugar prices plummeted and foreign sugar provided greater competition. In response, U.S. Sugar trimmed its payroll and reorganized its business, which was now split between two units: sugar and citrus.

As conditions improved, the new refinery's initial capacity of 540,000 tons per year was increased to more than 600,000 tons per year in an expansion that was completed in 2002. Moreover, $2.5 million was spent on a new liquid sugar production unit that opened in November of that year. Because of expansion and modernization in Clewiston, the Bryant mill was no longer necessary. It was shut down in 2005.

Environmental concerns continued for U.S. Sugar. In 2007 the company was not able to draw enough

water to irrigate its fields from Lake Okeechobee because of record low water levels. The company's proposal to use treated wastewater from its plants was denied. Company officials then met with the Florida governor Charlie Crist to complain, and Crist reportedly suggested that U.S. Sugar sell its land to the state of Florida. After months of negotiations, U.S Sugar and the state of Florida made a shocking announcement in June 2008: U.S. Sugar would sell all of its land, about 188,000 acres, for $1.8 billion, including its mill, citrus processing plant, and railroad line. The company would continue to farm the land and maintain its other operations for the next six years but would then go out of business and the state would use the land to construct a reservoir network to clear and store water that would then be released into the Everglades ecosystem to revitalize it.

### THE COURTS AND THE LAND SALE

The sweeping nature of the U.S. Sugar agreement garnered headlines, but the deal quickly unraveled. Just five months later the plan was cut back as the economy faltered and the state found itself strapped for cash. In November 2008 an amended deal called for the state of Florida to purchase about 180,000 acres but not the other U.S. Sugar assets for $1.3 billion. This amount also proved too expensive for the state and its troubled economy. In April 2009 the governor announced a further downsizing of the deal. Florida proposed to buy 72,800 acres from U.S. Sugar for $536 million and the rest of the land at some later date while the company remained in business.

The revised deal was met with opposition from environmentalists and others, who maintained that the land was overvalued by $400 million because the appraisals were based on values at the height of the real estate market. Opponents also maintained that even if Florida completed the purchase at this price, it would not have the money to actually build the reservoirs and treatment areas. As a result, the acquisition would do more to save the fortunes of U.S. Sugar, which was saddled with $500 million in debt, than it would the Everglades.

The Miccosukee Tribe of Native Americans, many of whom lived in the Everglades, had not been included in the deliberations and filed a lawsuit, claiming that the land sale would actually delay restoration of the Everglades. In March 2010 Don Van Natta Jr. and Damien Cave of the *New York Times* noted that Dexter Lehtinen, the tribe's attorney, called it a death sentence for the Everglades because "it sucks away all the money devoted to projects now in the pipeline." Critics also accused Governor Crist of making the deal as a way to further his political career. At the time of the announcement, he was on Senator John McCain's short list of potential running mates for the U.S. presidency.

The land sale became mired in litigation. In August 2009 a Palm Beach County Circuit Court judge allowed the $536 million plan to go forward but struck down a proposal to borrow as much as $2.2 billion to purchase additional acreage from U.S. Sugar and construct the reservoir network. This ruling was challenged, and the case eventually made its way to the Florida Supreme Court in April 2010. The land sale was further jeopardized by a federal court ruling that construction had to start on a $700 million reservoir in Palm Beach County. The cost of that project could very well make it impossible to complete the U.S. Sugar deal even if the Florida Supreme Court issued a favorable ruling. In any event, as of mid-2010 U.S. Sugar was likely to remain in business. However, how healthy a concern it would be going forward remained an unanswered question.

*Ed Dinger*

## PRINCIPAL OPERATING UNITS

Sugar; Citrus.

## PRINCIPAL COMPETITORS

Coca Cola Company; Florida Crystals Corporation; Imperial Sugar Company.

## FURTHER READING

"A Bitter Taste," *Economist*, February 19, 1994, p. A27.

Cave, Damien, "Court Ruling May Imperil Florida Deal," *New York Times*, April 1, 2010, p. A17.

Lewis, Robert G., "Railroad Cuts Costs for Sugar Cane Operation in Florida," *Railway Age*, January 1988, p. 53.

Mann, Joseph, "Clewiston, Fla.–Based Sugar Company Cuts Jobs," *Knight Ridder/Tribune Business News*, September 8, 2000.

"New Life for the 'Glades," *U.S. News & World Report*, May 16, 1994, p. 32.

"Sugar and Grass; The Everglades," *Economist*, December 13, 2008.

Van Natta, Don, Jr., and Damien Cave, "Deal to Save Everglades May Help Sugar Firm," *New York Times*, March 8, 2010, p. A1.

# Unitymedia GmbH

—————— ■ ——————

Aachener Strasse 746-750
Cologne, 50933
Germany
Telephone: (+49 221) 377 92 0
Fax: (+49 221) 377 92 871
Web site: http://www.unitymedia.de/

*Wholly Owned Subsidiary of Liberty Global Inc.*
*Founded:* 2005
*Employees:* 1,600
*Sales:* €1.04 billion ($1.29 billion) (2009)
*NAICS:* 517110 Cable Television Distribution Services

■ ■ ■

Unitymedia GmbH, a subsidiary of Liberty Global Inc., is Germany's second-largest cable operator after Kabel Deutschland GmbH. Located in Cologne, the media capital of Germany, Unitymedia covers the German federal states of North Rhine–Westphalia and Hesse, which are among the most prosperous and densely populated regions in both Germany and Europe. Unitymedia provides digital and analog cable television (TV), Internet, and telephony services. The company offers an Internet flat rate (1play), an Internet and telephone flat rate (2play), and an Internet, telephone, and TV flat rate (3play), in addition to separate basic digital-TV services and pay-TV. Unitymedia was the first company to offer 3play in Europe.

## THE EMERSION OF CABLE IN GERMANY: 1945–97

From 1945 to 1989 telecommunications in West Germany was overseen by the Deutsche Bundespost (DBP; German Postal Service), a state body under the control of a cabinet ministry. In 1984, under the leadership of Christian Schwarz-Schilling, the minister of post and communication, cable TV was introduced in West Germany. That same year commercial and private TV were broadcast for the first time, competing with ARD (established in 1950) and ZDF (established in 1963), the public service broadcasters in Germany that had monopolized radio and TV programming in West Germany.

In 1989 the DBP was divided into three distinct bodies: Deutsche Bundespost Postdienst (German Federal Postal Service), Deutsche Bundespost Postbank (German Federal Postal Bank), and Deutsche Bundespost Telekom (German Federal Telecommunications). However, the Ministry of Post and Communication still had ultimate supervisory and regulatory authority. The collapse of the Soviet Union in 1989 and the resulting reunification of Germany in 1991 started a development that ultimately led to the privatization of all telecommunications in Germany.

Surprisingly, cable had a rather slow start (as late as 1990 only about 8.1 million or 31.5 percent of West German households were connected to cable). Complicating matters, combining the East and West German communications systems required a major update of the infrastructure. By 1995 Deutsche Bundespost Telekom had doubled its cable network, connecting

15.8 million or 65.3 percent of all German households. The enormous costs of creating and implementing a cohesive satellite and cable network, mainly to facilitate an integrated telephone system in a reunified Germany, gave credence to parliamentary voices that favored the privatization of DBP. In 1994 the Posts and Telecommunications Reorganization Act was passed, and on January 1, 1995, Deutsche Bundespost Telekom was transformed into a public stock company and renamed Deutsche Telekom AG. However, the law required the German government to be the majority shareholder in the former Bundespost companies for at least five more years and extended the monopolies for postal and phone services until the end of 1997.

## FROM IESY AND ISH TO UNITY MEDIA: 1997–2005

The telecommunications law started the liberalization of the telecommunications sector and thus effectively ended the monopoly of Deutsche Telekom. Because of the increased competition in the wake of privatization and a few ill-fated partnerships, Deutsche Telekom suffered losses at the end of the 1990s. In addition, in 1998 the European Commission, which was overseeing the liberalization of the telecommunications market, called for the separation of telecommunication and cable TV networks. As a result, Deutsche Telekom had to sell its broadband cable networks to regional providers. To facilitate this sale, Deutsche Telekom founded in 1999 Kabel Deutschland GmbH, which proceeded to sell the cable networks of North Rhine–Westphalia to the U.S. investor Callahan Associates for $3 billion, and the cable networks of Hesse to the British investor Gary Klesch. ish, which took over the cable network in North Rhine–Westphalia, debuted in October 2001 as a subsidiary of

Callahan Kabel NRW. iesy, which covered Hesse, was founded in 2002.

To counteract initial financial difficulties, ish raised its fees in 2002. In 2004 ish introduced ish digital TV in North Rhine–Westphalia, which offered 30 additional TV programs. At the time, that was an unheard of number and variety of public, private, and international programming in Germany.

ish's financial troubles notwithstanding, the Federal Cartel Office thwarted a takeover bid by Kabel Deutschland, Germany's largest cable provider. Shortly thereafter, a consortium of German banks, led by the Deutsche Bank and CitiGroup, stepped in to buy ish. In June 2005 iesy, which was the smallest German cable provider operating in Hesse, took over. That same year, under the leadership of Parm Sandhu, the chief executive officer of ieasy, the cable providers ish and ieasy were merged to form Unity Media GmbH. Following the merger, Unity Media purchased Tele Columbus West, Germany's then-largest operator of in-house distribution networks. Thus, Unity Media became the second-largest cable provider in Germany, trailing behind Kabel Deutschland, and the third-largest cable provider in Europe.

## GROWTH WITH ARENA AND UNITY3PLAY: 2005–09

In 2005 Unity Media founded the pay-TV sports channel arena. In a surprising coup, arena purchased the rights to broadcast live all the games of the 2006–07 season of the Deutsche Bundesliga (the German national soccer league), outbidding the established pay-TV channel Premiere. Previously, the rights to broadcast soccer matches had been divided among the public TV channel ARD, the satellite channel Sat 1, the pay-TV channel Premiere, and RTL (owned by Bertelsmann AG). The coup brought a record number of new cable subscribers to Unity Media. In 2006, just in time for the soccer season, Unity Media introduced arenaSat, a nationwide satellite platform for sports broadcasting. This platform strengthened its hold on the German TV market beyond the borders of Hesse and North Rhine–Westphalia. After only one soccer season, Unity Media subleased the rights to the 2007–08 season of the Deutsche Bundesliga to Premiere, the very company it had previously outbid. Thus, Unity Media became a major stockholder of Premiere. In 2008 the company sold its 14 percent share of Premiere stock to Rupert Murdoch's NewsCorp at EUR 17.50 per share.

At the end of 2006 Unity Media began offering Unity3Play (Internet, telephone, and TV service over broadband) in select communities. Unity3Play made

## KEY DATES

**2001-02:** Deutsche Telekom AG divides and sells cable networks to regional providers; iesy (Hesse) and ish (North Rhine–Westphalia) emerge.

**2005:** The cable providers iesy and ish merge to form Unity Media GmbH; the new company launches the sports channel arena.

**2006:** Unity Media launches arenaSat as a nationwide satellite platform.

**2007:** The company changes its name to Unitymedia GmbH.

**2010:** Unitymedia is acquired by Liberty Global Inc.

Unity Media the first cable provider in Germany to offer a viable alternative to traditional DSL and telephone lines. In 2007 the company changed its name to Unitymedia GmbH.

Between 2007 and 2009 Unitymedia invested heavily in the expansion of its Unity3Play service, updating and modernizing the cable network of the former subsidiaries iesy and ish, as well as purchasing and updating the network of local cable operators throughout Hesse and North Rhine–Westphalia. In addition, Unitymedia began the initiative Jetzt Digital (Digital Now) and converted over 100,000 households to digital TV, adding to the success of Unity3Play.

In 2007 Unitymedia reported a 19 percent growth of revenue, and by June 2008 the company hit a major milestone: more than 1 million customers took advantage of the company's access to over 200 TV and audio programs. In 2008 the company opened customer service counters in electronic stores in select cities, among them Frankfurt and Cologne. The customer had a choice between flat rates for four distinct services: the basic flat rate for digital TV only; the 1play flat rate for Internet only; the 2play flat rate for Internet and telephone; and the 3play flat rate for Internet, telephone, and TV. That same year Unitymedia introduced niche content packages, such as children's programs and language programs, on digital cable to increase its share of subscribers. In addition, the company offered the first digital DVR recorder.

All these improvements and developments contributed to Unitymedia's continued growth. In 2009 the company offered Breitband Regional (Regional Broadband) to 99 rural communities in North Rhine–Westphalia and Hesse. This initiative eventually connected over 730,000 new households to Unitymedia's broadband infrastructure and contributed greatly to the 31 percent increase in new service subscription that year. The company reported a total of 4.5 million basic cable TV subscribers, of which almost 1 million were digital, 877,000 were Internet subscribers, 535,000 were telephone subscribers, and 470,000 were pay-TV subscribers.

## THE ACQUISITION OF UNITYMEDIA

The cartel restrictions placed on the German cable market prohibited a merger between the three German cable providers Kabel Deutschland, Unitymedia, and Kabel BW GmbH & Co. KG. As a result, competing with international telephone and Internet service providers such as the telecommunications giants Deutsche Telekom and Vodafone proved increasingly difficult. In 2010 the U.S.-based Liberty Global Inc., a leading international cable operator, purchased Unitymedia for $2.7 billion. Once the acquisition was completed, Liberty Global had access to a thriving German market and Unitymedia had access to a worldwide network of digital technology for on-demand programming and Internet access.

The future for Unitymedia appeared to promise more growth. According to Ragnhild Kjetland and Brett Pulley of *BusinessWeek Online*, European households subscribing to cable were expected double by 2014, and of those new customers about 41 percent would choose cable Internet access. Considering that North Rhine–Westphalia and Hesse were among the most affluent and densely populated areas in Europe, Unitymedia was strategically situated to grow with these new customers.

*Helga Schier*

### PRINCIPAL SUBSIDIARIES

arenaSAT.

### PRINCIPAL DIVISIONS

Unitymedia Cable arena.

### PRINCIPAL COMPETITORS

Kabel Deutschland GmbH; Kabel BW GmbH & Co. KG; Deutsche Telekom; Vodafone.

### FURTHER READING

Brockmeyer, Dieter, "Germany's Cable Revival," DigitalTVEurope.net, June 5, 2009, http://www.

digitaltveurope.net/feature/05_jun_09/germanys_cable_revival.

Cimilluca, Dana, and Jeffrey McCracken, "Liberty Global to Buy Germany," *Wall Street Journal*, November 13, 2009.

Engel, Christoph, *Kabelfernsehen*. Baden-Baden, Germany: Nomos, 1996.

Faul, Erwin, and Michael Jäckel, eds., *Kabelfernsehen in Deutschland. Pilotprojekte, Programmvermehrung, private Konkurrenz. Ergebnisse und Perspektiven*. Munich, Germany: R. Fischer, 1991.

Kjetland, Ragnhild, and Brett Pulley, "Cable King John Malone's New Run at the Old World," *BusinessWeek Online*, April 15, 2010, http://www.businessweek.com/magazine/content/10_17/b4175025762468.htm.

"Schlappe um Bundesliga-Rechte: Premiere verklagt Konkurrenten," FocusOnline.de, December 24, 2005, http://www.focus.de/finanzen/news/bundesliga-rechte_aid_102945.html.

"Unitymedia wächst mit Paketangebot," FocusOnline.de, November 12, 2009, http://www.focus.de/digital/computer/medien-unitymedia-waechst-mit-paketangebot_aid_453530.html.

"US-Medienmogul Malone übernimmt Unitymedia," FocusOnline.de, November 13, 2009, http://www.focus.de/digital/computer/medien-us-medienmogul-malone-uebernimmt-unitymedia_aid_453794.html.

# voestalpine
ONE STEP AHEAD.

# voestalpine AG

─────■─────

voestalpine-Straße 1
Linz, A-4020
Austria
Telephone: (43) 50304 15-0
Fax: (43) 50304 55-0
Web site: http://www.voestalpine.com

*Public Company*
*Incorporated:* 1945 as Vereinigte Österreichische Eisen-
und Stahlwerke AG
*Employees:* 41,200
*Sales:* EUR 11.6 billion ($16.6 billion) (2009)
*Stock Exchanges:* Vienna
*Ticker Symbol:* VAST
*NAICS:* 331111 Iron and Steel Mills; 331222 Steel
Wire Drawing; 331513 Steel Foundries (Except
Investment); 331210 Iron and Steel Pipe and Tube
Manufacturing from Purchased Steel; 321114
Wood Preservation

■ ■ ■

Voestalpine AG is a holding company for numerous
subsidiaries, whose activities include the manufacture,
processing, and sale of steel materials. Privatized in the
early 1990s and listed on the Vienna Stock Exchange in
1995, voestalpine is among the largest industrial
enterprises in Austria, with sales of EUR 11.6 billion
($16.6 billion) and a workforce of about 41,000
worldwide. Since the 1990s voestalpine has sought to
distance itself from its image as a steel producer and
increase its emphasis on steel-processing activities,

investing heavily in research and development for high-
quality, high-profit steel products.

The voestalpine Group comprises five principal
subsidiaries operating in five distinct divisions: voestalpine Stahl GmbH, a high-quality steel producer; Böhler-
Uddeholm AG, a producer and distributor of specialized
steel products and services; voestalpine Bahnsysteme
Gmbh & Co KG, which offers railway engineering and
infrastructure planning services, as well as high-tech rail
products; voestalpine Profilform GmbH, which
produces profiles (shaped tubes and hollow sections, as
well as other components); and voestalpine Automotive
GmbH, which develops and produces automotive
components.

## ORIGINS: 1938–48

The history of voestalpine AG goes back to 1938, when
the company was founded in Linz, Austria, as an affiliate of the state-owned Reichswerke Hermann Göring in
Berlin, Germany. Construction of a large steelworks
began in 1939 and continued throughout World War II.
The first two blast furnaces were completed in 1941,
and by 1944 the compound included open-hearth and
electric furnaces for steel conversion, as well as a
nitrogen plant. The company was a main supplier of
steel and iron for the German war industry. Because of
the acute labor shortage in Germany and Austria during
the war, forced laborers, prisoners of war, and concentration camp inmates played a major role in the production process, at times making up two-thirds of the
workforce. Allied bombing caused severe damage to the
works in 1944.

## COMPANY PERSPECTIVES

Where we want to go (Our vision)

We're the partner of choice worldwide for demanding product solutions involving steel and that allow our customers to stay that decisive step ahead.

Where we stand (Our positioning)

Voestalpine is a globally active group with a number of specialized and flexible companies that produce, process and further develop high-quality steel products. As a reliable partner to industry, voestalpine regards its customers' needs as its own.

What we stand for (Our mission)

Driven by our wide-ranging expertise and our conviction that there is always a better solution, we set ourselves the daily challenge of making the seemingly impossible happen.

In 1945 the U.S. military government confiscated the plants in Linz and renamed them as Vereinigte Österreichische Eisen- und Stahlwerke AG (Austrian Iron and Steelworks). "Vöest" is an acronym. Reconstruction of the works commenced, and production resumed in 1945. In the following year, the company was turned over to the Republic of Austria and nationalized as part of what would become the ÖIAG (Austrian Industries AG). Under the Marshall Plan, which was meant to support the rebuilding of Western Europe, Vöest pursued reconstruction and expansion. In 1946 over one million tons of crude steel were melted in the company's electric furnace. In 1947 the first blast furnace, the first open-hearth furnace, and the first coke ovens started production. The company commenced production of steel for highly stressed welded structures in 1948.

### REVOLUTIONARY INNOVATION IN 1949

In 1949 Vöest built the world's first steel mill with oxygen converters, and thus became a pioneer in the oxygen steelmaking process, which would eventually replace both open-hearth furnaces and Bessemer converters. Many steel industry experts consider the oxygen process to be the most important modern innovation in steelmaking, which clearly set the stage for the company's future growth. Vöest gained an advantage for its own steel production and created a downstream

business supplying other steelworks with steelmaking equipment.

Oxygen converters, which involve the blowing of oxygen at high velocity onto the surface of molten metal in a furnace, greatly reduce the cycle time for melts and thereby increase capacity and reduce the costs per ton of the steel produced. Although the advantages of using oxygen rather than air in steelmaking furnaces had long been recognized, the development of oxygen converters had been delayed owing to the lack of cheap supplies of oxygen. Because oxygen was a by-product at the Linz nitrogen plant, Vöest began to conduct a series of tests with oxygen conversion.

The engineers at the Linz plant, however, had trouble handling the increased heat generated by the accelerated conversion of iron to steel. Thus Vöest consulted with the Swiss engineer Robert Dürrer who, with Heinrich Hellbrügge, was conducting experiments using oxygen in a two-ton Bessemer converter and in an electric furnace. At first the Dürrer system failed as well, destroying parts of the equipment and failing to remove enough of the phosphorus impurity from the iron. Nevertheless, continued experiments and adjustments finally brought success. By 1949 Vöest had developed an oxygen converter that would produce high-quality steel without any damage to the equipment.

By late 1952 the Linz oxygen converter operated on a fully commercial scale with vessels of 35-ton capacity. In 1953 a second plant with oxygen converters began production at Donawitz, Austria. The oxygen converter system has since been called the LD process, from the initials of the Austrian towns Linz and Donawitz, where the first two plants were installed. By 1988 Vöest, a relatively small company, had installed 140 oxygen converters in steelworks around the world, by far surpassing the impact of larger U.S., German, Japanese, and British companies.

### EXPANSION AND DIVERSIFICATION IN THE FIFTIES AND SIXTIES

In the postwar years Vöest developed a broad range of downstream engineering businesses. In 1950 the engineering shops started production of lathes, and the development of water power plants began. The combination of electric steelmaking capacity, access to cheap electricity, and the oxygen converters made Vöest a leader in high-quality steel production while keeping costs relatively low, enabling the company to compete internationally. During the early 1950s, a new slabbing

## KEY DATES

**1938:** Reichswerke Hermann Göring is founded in Berlin, Germany.

**1945:** U.S. military government in Austria changes name of company to Vereinigte Österreichische Eisen- und Stahlwerke AG (Vöest; Austrian Iron and Steelworks).

**1949:** Vöest builds the world's first steel mill with oxygen converters, which later becomes the industry standard.

**1972:** Company becomes part of the state-owned holding company ÖIAG (Austrian Industries).

**1973:** Vöest merges with Österreichisch-Alpine Montangesellschaft.

**1988:** ÖIAG is reorganized into seven separate companies, one of which is Voest-Alpine Stahl AG (VA Stahl).

**1995:** VA Stahl makes its initial public offering on the Vienna Stock Exchange.

**2001:** VA Stahl becomes voestalpine AG.

**2007:** Company takes over Böhler-Uddeholm.

mill and cold-rolling stand were added to the works. At the same time, downstream expansion continued with the establishment of an industrial plant construction division.

The company expanded rapidly between 1955 and 1960. In 1955 a third oxygen converter was completed, and in 1959 a second LD steel mill with two 50-ton converters started production. In 1958 Vöest collaborated with the German company Krupp to build an LD steel mill at Rourkela, India. Blast furnace output passed one million tons for the first time in 1955. A new 4.2-meter plate mill was added in 1958 and a new coke oven battery in 1959.

In the first half of the 1960s, several state-owned businesses were transferred to Vöest in an attempt to increase administrative efficiency. At the same time, this extended the company's downstream activities. Notable LD developments were a Soviet order for an LD steel mill in 1963 and supplying a 300-ton oxygen converter to a steel mill at Taranto, Italy.

The latter half of the decade saw the spread of activities of the process plant contracting division. Examples showing the range of contracts obtained by the division were the construction of a fertilizer plant in Poland in 1965, a palletizing plant for iron ore in Brazil in 1966, and a fertilizer plant in France in 1969. An ethylene plant was also completed for ÖMV, another company in the Austrian public sector. Expansion of steel production continued, and in 1969 crude steel production capacity was increased from 2.3 million tons to 3.1 million tons a year. In 1966 production of special steels began and a sixth oxygen converter started up. The first continuous-casting machine started trials in the second LD steel mill in 1968, and in 1970 a multiroll stand was added, which made possible the production of very thin steel sheets.

## REORGANIZATION IN THE SEVENTIES

The 1970s began with major reorganization and technical development. In 1972 Vöest became part of the state-owned industrial holding company ÖIAG (Austrian Industries AG). Just one year later Vöest merged with the other leading Austrian steel producer, Österreichisch-Alpine Montangesellschaft, Vienna, which operated the Donawitz steelworks, to become Vöest-Alpine AG. In 1975 the Austrian special steels industry consolidated as Vereinigte Edelstahlwerke AG (VEW), which became the largest subsidiary of Vöest-Alpine AG. By the mid-1970s the parent company comprised over 100 companies.

By that time the first oil crisis had caused a serious downturn in the European steel industry. The cyclical fall in demand was reinforced by a move from steel toward other materials; by greater efficiency in the use of steel, involving the substitution of thinner gauges of steel; by a serious recession in some steel-using industries such as shipbuilding; and by the emergence of new low-cost steel-producing countries. The change in the industrial environment affected the Austrian steel industry. To counteract this downturn, a multidimensional business-segment structure was introduced in mid-1977. The Vöest-Alpine group was reorganized into separate business segments (steelworks, processing, finished products, and industrial plant construction), each of them responsible for its own profits and losses. In 1978 the umlaut was dropped from the company name and Vöest-Alpine AG became Voest-Alpine AG.

## THE VOEST DEBACLE IN THE EIGHTIES

The economic climate changed in the 1980s. The decade started with the second oil crisis and a recession. The steel industry had to brace against harsh winds that exposed the weaknesses of diversification into a wide range of engineering and other industries. Operating with a deficit since 1981, the Austrian government heavily subsidized the ÖIAG group, and the largest share of these subsidies went to the steel companies Voest-Alpine and VEW AG. In 1985 Voest-Alpine's trading losses reached ATS 12 billion, as a result of an unsuccessful microchip venture, participation in the unsuccessful Bayou Steel Corporation in the United States, and disastrous losses of Intertrading, a Voest-Alpine subsidiary involved in speculative oil deals. Voest-Alpine declared bankruptcy and the board resigned. The new management team, led by Chief Executive Dr. Herbert Lewinsky, created a restructuring plan, which involved dismantling 10,000 jobs.

In 1988, following the decision of the Austrian government to partially privatize ÖIAG, the holding company that had controlled Vöest since the end of 1972, ÖIAG was reorganized into seven separate companies. Voest-Alpine Stahl AG (VA Stahl) was one. The new company's activities included steelmaking at the Linz works; steel rolling at the Linz and Donawitz works; the manufacture of special steels (high-speed and tool steels) by the Böhler companies, which were subsidiaries of VA Stahl in Kapfenberg, Austria, and Düsseldorf, Germany; and steel stockholding and steel-scrap processing. The reorganization was designed to make the companies in the ÖIAG group more efficient, bring management decisions closer to the market, and expand internationally.

After the reorganization, VA Stahl specialized in making and shaping steel, while the downstream activities, which VA Stahl had developed or acquired, including the process plant activities, were split off into separate companies. In 1989 VA Stahl produced 3.35 million tons of crude steel and 2.76 million tons of flat rolled products at Linz. The company had a wide range of steel-finishing equipment. Apart from rolling mills, it had equipment for making tubes, rails, and wire; drop-forging facilities, which make shapes through the progressive forming of sheet metal in matched dies under repetitive blows of a hammer; and a steel foundry. The company's main investments in 1989 were designed to improve the quality of the products of the rolling mills; in addition, a second galvanizing plant was constructed.

The company then estimated that high-tech products accounted for about 10 percent of sales and it aimed to raise this share to 30 percent. The company's research and development program, which would play a part in achieving this target, included work on new steelmaking processes, improvements to existing processing technology, and applications. A long-term goal was to research and implement environmentally wise yet still time cost-effective processes. In 1987 an investment program motivated by environmental protection

concerns had been approved. One specialty was surface-treated products, including galvanized steel and plastic-coated strip steel. Evidence of the company's commitment to training was its employment of nearly 500 apprentices, equivalent to 4 percent of its workforce.

Because of the relatively small size of Austria, VA Stahl relied on exports to sell its output; 70 percent of its 1988 sales came from exports. Its principal export market was the European Economic Community, followed by Comecon; only 5 percent of sales were from overseas exports, outside Europe and Comecon. VA Stahl was well located to share in the demand for steel that would be generated by investment in the former East Germany and in Eastern European countries.

## PRIVATIZATION IN THE NINETIES

The 1990s were characterized by consolidation and international expansion into Eastern Europe. In 1990 VA Stahl acquired the Swedish Uddeholm Group, which merged with the companies of the Böhler Group to form Böhler-Uddeholm one year later. In 1992 VA Stahl acquired half-ownership and managerial control of the Dunaújváros plant in central Hungary, the country's largest cold-rolling mill. The investment gave VA Stahl a foothold to the Hungarian market and furthered its quest to become the primary steelmaker in east-central Europe.

In 1993 Austrian Industries (which comprised both ÖIAG and the companies it owned) began the privatization of some of its companies, among them VA Stahl and its sister company, Voest-Alpine Technologie AG (VA Technologie). VA Technologie, the engineering company, made its initial public offering on the Vienna Stock Exchange in 1994, and VA Stahl followed suit in 1995. That same year Böhler-Uddeholm shares were offered as well. The privatization of these two companies created the foundation for a renewed merger over a decade later, as privately held companies.

VA Stahl's initial issue of 11.2 million shares (8.2 million shares offered by ÖIAG, and 3 million new shares of a capital increase program) at EUR 20.71 ($26.30) per share represented one of the biggest privatizations in Austrian history.

The struggle to maintain autonomy remained paramount for VA Stahl, and the company continued its strategy of international expansion. In 1998 VA Stahl acquired the Birmingham, England-based engineering company Metsec. Also in 1998, VA Stahl entered a joint venture with the German company Vossloh AG to acquire more than 90 percent of the shares of VAE AG, the Austrian world leader in rail switching equipment manufacturing.

By expanding its operations into niche markets, both the Metsec and the VAE acquisitions helped to insulate VA Stahl from the dramatic cyclical downturn that hit the steel industry in the late 1990s. Indeed, in addition to the cyclical volatility of the company's core steel business, expansion opportunities in this area seemed limited, and VA Stahl was keen to broaden its activities to include higher value, more profitable products in complementary areas of business. This initiative became central to the company's strategy for the new century.

To this end, the VA Stahl subsidiary Voest Alpine Stahl Linz GmbH launched a concentrated effort to develop its interests in processing activities, particularly in the area of products for the automotive industry. In September 2000 it acquired Rotec Zug AG, a Swiss manufacturer of precision steel pipes. Part of Rotec's specialty involved its ability to deliver products ready for installation. As such, about 60 percent of Rotec's output went to the automotive industry. Voest Alpine Stahl Linz expected to realize significant synergies with Rotec, based on the companies' similar client structures.

## EFFECTING AN IMAGE CHANGE FOR THE 21ST CENTURY

A name change signaled a new start in the new century: In 2001 VA Stahl became voestalpine AG. Despite the persistent problem of overcapacity in the worldwide steel market, voestalpine AG was one of the few European steel companies to report consistently solid profits. Continuing its strategic move away from steel production and toward steel processing, voestalpine intensified its investment in the automotive supply industry. In June 2001 the company announced a restructuring plan whereby it would operate under four main divisions: automotive (voestalpine Automotive GmbH), railway systems (voestalpine Bahnsysteme GmbH & Co KG), profiles (voestalpine Profilform GmbH), and flat steel (voestalpine Stahl GmbH).

At the same time, voestalpine pursued further consolidation by acquiring majority shares of partner companies: In 2002 voestalpine acquired an additional 45.3 percent of VAE AG shares, which had been held by Vossloh. One year later, voestalpine purchased the remaining 9.4 percent shares still held by various holders and thus VAE became a fully owned subsidiary of voestalpine Bahnsysteme GmbH. This proved to be an ingenious move in the worldwide financial crisis toward the end of the new century's first decade.

In 2003 voestalpine bought back the last 15 percent of shares still owned by the national industrial holding company ÖIAG. The extremely successful privatization, which had begun almost a decade earlier, was complete.

The enormous success of the now private company led to the decision to purchase majority interests of Böhler-Uddeholm AG in 2007, which had been created in a merger of the Swedish steel company Uddeholm and the Böhler Group as a fully owned subsidiary of the ÖIAG, and like voestalpine, privatized in the 1990s. The EUR 4 billion acquisition was finalized following the acquisition of the remaining shares in 2008. Now a 100 percent subsidiary, Böhler-Uddeholm was integrated into voestalpine as the special steels division.

Now with five divisions (Steel, Special Steel, Railway Systems, Profiles, and Automotives), voestalpine had its most successful year in the history of the company in the fiscal year that ended March 31, 2008. Revenues surpassed the EUR 10 billion mark for the first time. The group was able to strengthen its national and international presence in Eastern Europe, India, China, Brazil, and the United Kingdom. India, in particular, as one of the fastest-growing rail markets in the world, promised future growth, helping to further defend voestalpine's position as the market leader in railway switching systems. By 2008 more than 50 percent of voestalpine employees worked outside of Austria.

## NAVIGATING THE ECONOMIC CRISIS AT THE END OF THE 21ST CENTURY'S FIRST DECADE

One year later the situation had changed drastically. The global credit crunch and the stock market crash in the wake of the disaster of the U.S. subprime market did not stop at the Austrian borders, and voestalpine was affected as well. Within only two years voestalpine stock plummeted from approximately EUR 54 in 2007 to EUR 9.85 in 2009.

The stellar rise of voestalpine came to a temporary halt. In part because of the ailing automobile industry (which was the industry most heavily hit by the economic crisis) and the ensuing lack of orders for the voestalpine automotive division, sales revenues decreased by 36 percent in the last quarter of the fiscal year that ended March 31, 2009.

Voestalpine reacted immediately and implemented far-reaching steps to ensure the company's long-term survival. Among the actions taken were staff reductions of almost 15 percent, achieved by a temporary regimen of reduced work hours and 3,500 layoffs. Synergies with the newly acquired Böhler-Uddeholm allowed a reduction of the company's overhead by 30 percent. Furthermore, a temporary halt of expansion projects, such as the construction of a new steel plant at the

Black Sea coast, curtailed investment by almost 50 percent. In addition, the acquisition of Böhler-Uddeholm made it possible to focus less on the company's economically vulnerable steel division and focus more instead on specialized steel products (which were attractive to a wide range of industries). In addition, the railways systems division, because of its customer base in governments and municipalities, proved traditionally less vulnerable to economic changes. Thus positioned as an industry leader in customized high-quality and high-tech steel products and solutions, voestalpine could look forward to long-term sustainability and growth.

*Cliff Pratten*
*Updated, Erin Brown; Helga Schier*

## PRINCIPAL SUBSIDIARIES

voestalpine Stahl GmbH; Böhler-Uddeholm AG; voestalpine Bahnsysteme GmbH & Co KG; voestalpine Profilform GmbH; voestalpine Automotive GmbH.

## PRINCIPAL DIVISIONS

Steel; Special Steel; Railway Systems; Profiles; Automotives.

## PRINCIPAL COMPETITORS

ArcelorMittal; Baosteel Group; Gerdau S.A.; Nippon Steel Corporation; Salzgitter AG; Sumitomo Metal Industries Ltd.; ThyssenKrupp AG; TSTG Schienen Technik GmbH & Co. KG; United States Steel Corporation.

## FURTHER READING

Blum, Patrick, "Austria Launches Privatizations," *Financial Times* (London), November 15, 1993, p. 23.

Cockerill, Anthony, *The Steel Industry*, New York: Cambridge University Press, 1974.

Hudson, Ray, and David Sadler, *The International Steel Industry*, New York: Routledge, 1989.

*The Making, Shaping, and Treating of Steel*, 11th ed., Pittsburgh, PA: AISE Steel Foundation, 1998.

Marsh, Peter, "Steelmakers Aim to Beat High-Tech Path to Profit: The Theme of This Year's Industry Gathering Was the Search for Ways to Overcome Global Overcapacity," *Financial Times* (London), October 16, 2002, p. 10.

"Metsec Agrees to £41m Austrian Bid," *Times* (London), May 30, 1998.

Pressberger, Thomas, "Voest knackt die 10 Milliarden," Wirtschaftsblatt.at, June 5, 2008.

Rodger, Ian, "Voest-Alpine Stahl Floated," *Financial Times* (London), October 6, 1995, p. 16.

"voestalpine bastelt Notfallplan fuer nachhaltige Krise," nachrichten.at, January 3, 2009.

"Voestalpine to Increase Investment in Research," *Austrian Times*, March 30, 2010.

# Watts Water Technologies, Inc.

**815 Chestnut Street**
**North Andover, Massachusetts 01845-6098**
**U.S.A.**
**Telephone: (978) 688-1811**
**Fax: (978) 688-1848**
**Web site: http://www.wattswater.com**

*Public Company*
*Founded:* 1874 as Watts Regulator Company
*Incorporated:* 1985 as Watts Industries, Inc.
*Employees:* 6,300
*Sales:* $1.23 billion (2009)
*Stock Exchanges:* New York
*Ticker Symbol:* WTS
*NAICS:* 332912 Fluid Power Valve and Hose Fitting Manufacturing; 332919 Other Metal Valve and Pipe Fitting Manufacturing; 334513 Instruments and Related Products Manufacturing for Measuring, Displaying, and Controlling Industrial Process Variables

■ ■ ■

Watts Water Technologies, Inc., is a leader in the design, manufacture, and supply of valves and other flow-control products for the global plumbing, heating, and water-quality industries. The company also produces water filtration and water-based heating, ventilation, and air conditioning (HVAC) systems for both residential and commercial use. As a producer of gas-flow system components, Watts supplies products for use in natural and propane gas systems. The company distributes its products through three main channels: do-it-yourself, wholesale, and original equipment manufacturing. Committed to continued growth through the acquisition of innovative product lines, Watts includes more than 40 wholly owned subsidiaries throughout North America, Europe, and China. In 2010 Watts had approximately 74 facilities in operation worldwide.

## A NEW FRONTIER

When Joseph Edwin Watts was 17 years old he emigrated from Cheshire, England, to the newly built town of Lawrence, Massachusetts. The town was founded in 1845 by a group of industrialists and entrepreneurs whose idea was to build the "Great Stone Dam" across the Merrimack River to harness the river's immense water power for industrial textile production.

The first records of Joseph Watts's employment were in 1867 as a machinist at the Pacific Mills in Lawrence. He worked there until 1874, when he left to go into business for himself. From his shop on Essex Street, he contracted work supplying parts and fittings for machinery at the nearby textile mills. He advertised himself in local trade publications as "Joseph E. Watts, Machinist and Brass Finisher, Manufacturer of Steam and Water Pressure Regulators." By 1893 Watts had constructed a block-long brick building on Lowell Street to house the Watts Regulator Company.

By that time Watts had become more than a machinist and manufacturer. He was also an inventor, and between 1881 and his death in 1894, he received 18 patents for valves that proved essential to almost

COMPANY PERSPECTIVES

Since 1874, the Watts Water Technologies family of companies has designed and manufactured valves and related products that promote the comfort and safety of people and the quality, conservation and control of water used in commercial, residential, industrial and municipal applications.

every manufacturing concern in the area. Soon manufacturers from all over the United States, Canada, and Europe were installing and using Watts valves.

After Watts's death the company was purchased by Robert E. Pickles and his partner, George W. Dodson. When Dodson left the company a few years later, Pickles brought in his brother Charles. Using advances in technology and improved materials, Robert Pickles was able to redesign many of Watts's valves so that they could be used not only for large industrial and municipal purposes but also for commercial household plumbing and heating.

## A FAMILY BUSINESS IS BORN:
### 1918–45

In 1918 Robert Pickles sold the Watts Regulator Company to a trio of investors who had each put up $25,000. They were Burchard Everett Horne, his uncle Herbert W. Horne, and their friend Norman Anderson. Within a year Burchard had bought out both his uncle's and Anderson's shares.

In the early 1860s the Horne family had moved from Lowell, Massachusetts, to Lawrence, where they had established the George W. Horne Roofing Company, which was eventually controlled by Burchard (better known as B.E.) Horne. By the time B.E. purchased the Watts Regulator Company, the textile industry, upon which the town of Lawrence had been founded, was in deep decline. The advent of steam power, with its advantages over water power, meant that textile mills could be set up anywhere that fuel was available. Other technical advances, plus high labor costs and taxes in the North, drove the textile industry farther and farther south.

Robert Pickles had begun the diversification of the Watts Regulator Company, and B.E. Horne quickly capitalized on his emphasis on plumbing and heating uses for Watts valves. In fact, they were so determined to accentuate their flexibility that, in their 1919 catalog,

the company stated, "We claim to be able to regulate and control any temperature or pressure of any fluid for any purpose and under any conditions."

A major development in Watts's expansion (and a major setback) came in the 1920s, when the company hired John G. Kelly, Inc., to handle its national distribution. Within a short period of time, Kelly landed the company a contract with Consolidated Gas of New York, manufacturers of mechanical refrigerators powered by gas. A Watts valve was installed in every Consolidated Gas refrigerator, which created a boom for the company. That boom lasted only a short time before Consolidated redesigned the refrigerator, eliminating the need for the Watts valve.

The company's breakthrough came in the late 1920s, when B.E. Horne and an inventor named Chetwood Smith developed and patented a combination temperature and pressure-relief valve, which came to be known as the T&P valve. The valve was an important development in the safety of hot-water supply tank systems. Overheated hot-water tanks had periodically exploded, causing extensive property damage and even fatalities. Although earlier valves had dealt with the problems of internal pressure building in the tanks, none had withstood the extremely high temperatures the water sometimes reached. The T&P valve was not perfect, but it provided a level of safety never before reached in hot-water tanks. This valve became the staple of Watts's business. The company even licensed other manufacturers to make the valve and received a royalty for every valve sold.

By 1936 B.E. Horne was becoming dissatisfied with the national sales effort of the John G. Kelly company. When his son George graduated from college, B.E. appointed him head of marketing for Watts. It was George Horne's job to educate the plumbing and heating industries about the dangers of overheating hot-water systems and the relief provided by the T&P valve. To that end he traveled the country setting up explosion demonstrations. He would mount a tank in a field, put it inside the shell of a house, and overheat the tank until it blew. This convinced people in the industry (who still thought that excess pressure was the only danger) of the necessity of the T&P valve. As the word spread, sales at the company began to rise dramatically, despite the sluggish economy of the Depression. As a result, George Horne finally convinced his father to give up the roofing business, which he continued to run, and to devote himself solely to Watts. By the time World War II broke out, U.S. Army engineers required T&P valves on all army hot-water supply tank installations.

## KEY DATES

**1874:** Joseph Watts founds Watts Regulator Company.
**1918:** Burchard Horne acquires company.
**1930s:** Watts introduces the temperature and pressure (T&P) relief valve.
**1961:** Watts opens first international manufacturing plant in Canada.
**1985:** Company incorporates as Watts Industries, Inc.
**1990s:** Watts creates Consumer Markets Division.
**1999:** Watts spins off industrial oil and gas sector.
**2003:** Watts Industries, Inc., becomes Watts Water Technologies, Inc.
**2006:** Annual sales top $1 billion.
**2009:** Watts launches lead-free product line.

### THE GREAT EXPANSION: 1945–72

After the war, the Watts patents on the T&P valve expired, and the company was forced to concentrate on developing and marketing new products. In 1951 B.E. Watts, always an avid sportsman, set off on a fishing expedition from which he never returned. He suffered a gallbladder attack while fishing, fell in the lake, and drowned. Control of the Watts Regulator Company was passed on to his son George. At the time, Watts sales totaled about $3.5 million a year.

Where B.E. Horne had been a conservative businessman, his son George was dedicated to progress and expansion. He expanded his sales force nationwide and often brought salespeople to Lawrence for training and new product education. He was constantly asking his sales force for ideas on new products. In the 1950s George Horne opened a fluid power division to make valves and control devices used on machine tools powered by air pressure.

In 1959 the company had outgrown its Lawrence premises, and George Horne opened a plant in Franklin, New Hampshire. The Lawrence plant continued to operate until 1970, but the workforce gradually shrank from 300 to 50. In addition to opening the Franklin plant, George Horne began to implement a professional management structure with two important hires. He brought in Robert Chaffee to take over the position of manager of sales, and he hired his son Tim as an all-around executive troubleshooter. In 1960 Watts, using an early-generation IBM punch-card-operated computer,

became one of the first companies to computerize its record keeping.

Robert Chaffee was in charge of revitalizing the sales force. He introduced regional company offices in Boston, Detroit, New York, San Francisco, Los Angeles, and Chicago. Another method Watts used for expansion in the 1960s was a "private label" program, which allowed companies to offer Watts products under their own names. One of the most successful aspects of the program was the relationship with Sears, Roebuck, in which valves that were manufactured by Watts were sold under the Sears name in their stores and catalogs.

By 1962 the company was expanding internationally, constructing a plant in Stroud, Gloucestershire, England, and another in Canada. In 1967 sales had risen to more than $17 million a year, and Tim Horne was promoted to vice president and assistant general manager. Five years later Robert Chaffee resigned, and Tim Horne was named executive vice president.

### NEW PRODUCTS, NEW MARKETS: 1972–84

In the early 1970s Colorado state sanitation inspectors approached George Horne to help them find a solution to backflow problems. Backflow is the reversal of the normal flow of water in a system. For example, opening one water source might create a vacuum in another water-supply line, which could be dangerous if the water-supply line is connected to a contaminated source. These potentially hazardous "cross connections" occur every day in such common areas as a garden hose connected to a tank of swimming-pool-treatment chemicals. Watts had been manufacturing two simple, inexpensive backflow prevention connections, but they did not protect against high-pressure backflow conditions.

Watts then began an intensive period of research and development to design a more effective, less expensive valve than the ones that were already on the market. Within a year the company was producing the Watts Model 900 Backflow Preventer. This marked the beginning of the company's move into the waterworks industry. Watts soon became a leader in the backflow prevention field, a position it would maintain into the 21st century.

In 1976 Tim Horne became president of the company, and in 1978, when George Horne retired, Tim became both president and chief executive officer. One of Tim Horne's first moves was to sell off the fluid power division and to develop a line of industrial ball valves, which allowed the company to move into the chemical-processing industry. Although sales rose from $39.5 million in 1978 to more than $100 million in 1984, inroads into the chemical-processing industry were difficult to navigate, and it took the company more than 10 years to establish itself in that field. That led Tim Horne to believe that the way of the future lay not only in new product development but in the acquisition of complementary companies.

## SOLUTIONS FOR GROWTH: INTO THE NINETIES

The year 1984 saw Watts's first acquisition: Spence Engineering, a manufacturer of steam regulators, which had $6.7 million in sales. Next came Hale Oilfield Products, a company that brought Watts into the oil and gas pipeline industry. Watts interrupted its acquisitions program in 1985 to prepare for its first public stock offering. In 1986 Tim Horne became chairman of the board and chief executive officer of Watts Industries, Inc., trading as WATTA on the NASDAQ with shares offered at $16.50 each.

Throughout the 1980s and into the 1990s, Watts continued its strategy of acquiring small niche companies to fill out its product line. In the early 1990s Watts began to acquire companies in Europe. These included the French plumbing and heating supplies manufacturer SFR, acquired in 1991, and the Austrian Intermes Group (1993). In the decade from 1985 to 1995 Watts Industries made 28 acquisitions.

The mid-1990s saw ups and downs for the company. According to a 1994 *Forbes* article, Watts suffered an economic downturn in 1993 mainly from a "sharp slump in aerospace and Navy contracts." By October 1994, however, *Money* magazine chose Watts Industries as one of "Eight Small Stocks for Big Gains." In 1995 Watts announced a joint venture with the Suzhou Valve Factory of the People's Republic of China, the company's second Chinese partnership after its initial 1994 joint venture with the Tianjin Tanggu Valve Plant. That same year, Watts began trading as WTS on the New York Stock Exchange.

One year later the company announced that Tyco International Ltd. had agreed to buy the waterworks valve business of Watts Industries. In 1997 Watts was back in an acquisitions mode, acquiring the Ames Company, a leader in the design, manufacture, and marketing of backflow prevention valves. That year Watts also consolidated two of its European holdings, SFR and Etablissements Trubert S.A., a French heating valve company, with the formation of Watts Eurotherm, later renamed Watts Industries France S.A.S. The 1999 purchase of Cazzaniga s.p.a., an Italian manufacturer of

plumbing and heating components, gave Watts additional manufacturing and sales capability and the opportunity to compete more effectively in European markets.

The 1990s were a time of rapid growth for Watts. The company actively sought to increase its retail sales presence with the creation of the Consumer Markets Division, set up to target customers in the home-improvement market through large retailers and catalog distributors. As part of its increased commitment to retail sales, Watts announced that it would spin off its industrial oil and gas businesses as a separate public company, CIRCOR International, Inc. Completed in 1999, the spin-off would allow Watts to focus on developing its water-based plumbing and heating product lines and water-quality systems. Watts also earned International Standards Organization (ISO) 9001 certification during this period, further bolstering the company's public image. Armed with renewed vision and sense of purpose, the company appeared on course for continued growth in the 21st century.

## A NEW CENTURY: THE FIRST DECADE

Watts began the new millennium focused on generating sales, streamlining operations, and continuing to make inroads into the retail home-improvement market. The company also made a series of strategic acquisitions designed to expand its line of specialized products, starting with the 2000 acquisition of Spacemaker Co., a leading manufacturer of water-heating components. That same year Watts Radiant (originally Heatway) joined Watts as its newest subsidiary, and it eventually became the largest U.S.-owned radiant floor heating company in North America. Radiant floor heating, an energy-efficient technology, delivers heat directly to a room through hot water tubing or electric cables lying below the floor surface.

From 2001 to 2003 the company made 10 more acquisitions on three continents. Dumser Metallbau GmbH, a leading German manufacturer of heating products and a 2001 acquisition of Watts Europe, added nearly $24 million in sales to the company's coffers in its first year alone. In 2003 company sales in the North American home-improvement market grew by 13 percent, and in spite of an economic downturn facing many European markets, sales in Europe continued to rise. In 2002 Watts's longtime leader, Tim Horne, retired, and Patrick S. O'Keefe joined the company as its new chief executive. To reflect the company's focus on water-based products and systems, the company changed its name to Watts Water Technologies, Inc., in 2003.

Watts experienced record increases in sales through 2007, breaking the $1 billion mark for the first time in 2006. The year 2006 also brought some unwelcome challenges, however, as the price of raw materials rose and the pace of new residential construction in North America and Europe slowed, a trend that would continue through 2009, a time of financial crisis for many of the world's markets. To meet these challenges, Watts began a restructuring of its global operations, including the transfer of several manufacturing operations to China, even as it continued to grow its core product lines through strategic acquisitions. In 2008 the company made its largest acquisition ever, buying Blücher Metals A/S, a Danish manufacturer of drainage products, for $170 million. That year sales to the European alternative energy market, as well as earnings from the Blücher purchase, helped Watts finish out the year with a 5.6 percent net increase in earnings. In 2009, in response to a growing U.S. demand for lead-free plumbing products, the company launched its first complete line of lead-free products.

Despite lingering economic uncertainty worldwide, Watts remained committed to growth through "selective acquisition," stating in its March 2010 10K filing with the Securities and Exchange Commission, "Our acquisition strategy focuses on businesses that manufacture preferred brand name products that address our themes of water quality, water conservation, water safety and water flow control." That focus, along with the ongoing search for innovative products and markets and the rising demand for clean water, should continue to serve Watts well in the years to come.

*Sharyn Kolberg*
*Updated, H. Schonthal*

## PRINCIPAL SUBSIDIARIES

Watts Asia (China); Watts Industries (Canada) Inc.; Watts Industries Deutschland GmbH (Germany); Watts Industries Europe B.V. (Netherlands); Watts Industries France S.A.S.; Watts Industries Italia s.r.l.; Watts Industries UK Ltd. (England); Watts Regulator Company.

## PRINCIPAL COMPETITORS

Flowserve Corporation; IMI plc; ITT Corporation; KSB AG; Parker Hannifin Corp.

## FURTHER READING

Douglas, Craig M., "Watts Water to Shed Another Business," *Boston Business Journal*, September 25, 2009, http://www.bizjournals.com/boston/stories/2009/09/21/daily66.html.

Lyon, David, *The Watts Way*. North Andover, MA: Watts Regulator Company, 1994.

Mader, Robert P., "Watts Creates Lead-free Plumbing Portal Site," *Contractor*, April 2, 2009, http://contractormag.com/green-contracting/watts-lead-free-plumbing-site-0309/.

Scherreik, Susan, "Eight Small Stocks for a Big Gain," *Money*, October 1994, p. 96.

"Watts Water Technologies Reports Preliminary Fourth Quarter 2009 Results," *Wall Street Journal*, February 16, 2009, http://online.wsj.com/article/PR-CO-20100216-908065.html.

# Welsh Rugby Union Limited

Westgate Terrace
**Millennium Stadium**
**Westgate Street**
**Cardiff, CF10 1NS**
**United Kingdom**
**Telephone: (+44 870) 013 8600**
**Fax: (+44 029) 2082 2474**
**Web site: http://www.wru.co.uk**

*Private Company*
*Founded:* 1881
*Employees:* 173
*Sales:* £49.4 million ($77 million) (2009)
*NAICS:* 711211 Sports Teams and Clubs

■ ■ ■

The Welsh Rugby Union Limited (WRU) is the governing body of professional and grassroots rugby in Wales. The WRU's revenue is derived from three key business segments: Elite Rugby, Community Rugby, and the Millennium Stadium. The 74,500-seat Millennium Stadium boasts the first fully retractable roof in the United Kingdom, and attracts more than 1.3 million visitors annually. This leading-edge, multifaceted event venue is credited with significantly contributing to the economic, sporting, social, and cultural enrichment in Wales.

The WRU's main subsidiaries are Millennium Stadium plc, WRU Supporters Club Limited, and the WRU National Centre of Excellence Limited. Opened in May 2009, the WRU National Centre of Excellence is a world-class international training and development facility for international players of all levels who are selected to represent Wales. The WRU's principal partners include Under Armour, Brains Beer, Invesco Perpetual, SWALEC, Carling, Powerade, and SEAT UK. In 2008 the WRU was voted the best governing body in world rugby by its peers at an inaugural awards ceremony at Rugby Expo.

## THE DEVELOPMENT OF THE WELSH RUGBY FOOTBALL UNION

Rugby was first played in Wales in the mid-19th century at Lampeter College. By 1875 the South Wales Football Union was formed, and matches were played against local clubs and teams from Western England. A pivotal year in the sport was 1881, when Richard Mullock selected the Welsh team that played against England on February 19 in Blackheath. England had been playing internationally for 10 years, while this was the first international outing for Wales. The inexperience of the Welsh team showed, with Wales losing 82-0 by current scoring methods. This humiliating loss prompted the formation of the Welsh Rugby Football Union (WRFU) the following month, which comprised 11 clubs from Swansea, Lampeter, Llandeilo, Cardiff, Newport, Llanelli, Merthyr Tydfil, Llandovery, Brecon, Pontypool, and Bangor. Swansea's Cyril Chambers was elected the first president of the WRFU, while Mullock, who was attached to the Newport club, was made honorary secretary and treasurer.

COMPANY PERSPECTIVES

COMPANY PERSPECTIVES

The purpose of the WRU is to promote, foster, encourage, control and improve rugby football in Wales. The Group's vision is three fold: Taking Wales to the world with our rugby; welcoming the world to Wales in our Stadium; defining Wales as a nation. The Group's mission continues to be based upon: leading Welsh rugby to the forefront of the global game in performance and reputation; maximizing participation and performance at all levels; developing grass roots rugby, supporting clubs, schools and colleges and bringing communities together; promoting the Millennium Stadium as a unique, must play, must visit venue. Our purpose, vision and mission are underpinned by values and beliefs which embrace integrity, excellence, success, courage, family and humour.

Wales finally defeated England in 1890. In 1893 Wales won the Triple Crown and became the dominant force in the world of rugby. Rugby became a game of global interest in 1905 when New Zealand's undefeated team, the All Blacks, lost to Wales by a score of 3-0. In the following years, rugby teams from Australia and South Africa were traveling to England and Wales to compete, with Wales defeating Australia in 1908. Between 1900 and 1911, Wales won six Triple Crowns and three Grand Slams, and went undefeated from March 1907 to January 1910.

The WRFU struggled throughout the 1920s and 1930s but did manage to defeat England at Twickenham in 1933, and the All Blacks in Cardiff in 1935. International sports were sidelined during World War II but by the 1950s the Welsh team was back in form, winning Grand Slams in 1950 and 1952. It would be 19 years before Wales would achieve its sixth Grand Slam. In 1969, with what was considered to be Wales' greatest team to date, the Welsh won the Triple Crown. This was followed by five more Triple Crowns and three Grand Slams during the 1970s. By now known as the Welsh Rugby Union (WRU), the group celebrated its 100th anniversary in 1981. The first Rugby World Cup took place in 1987, with the Welsh team taking third place after defeating Australia. The following year, Wales shared a joint championship with France but the team failed miserably on its New Zealand tour, resulting in the firing of the management team of Tony Gray and Derek Quinnell.

## A NEW ERA FOR RUGBY IN THE NINETIES

By 1990 rugby unions were recognized as viable business enterprises that contributed substantially to a nation's economic development. To keep its competitive edge, the WRU implemented a series of new marketing techniques under the direction of WRU Commercial Executive Jonathan Price. Price's marketing strategy, which included a single WRU logo, enhanced pregame features, and new outreach programs to recruit new talent, immediately boosted attendance at WRU matches. The WRU also decided to tear down the 62,000-seat Cardiff Arms Park, home to Welsh rugby since 1884, and replace it with a state-of-the-art multievent stadium. In 1999, in time for the Rugby World Cup, the 74,500-seat Millennium Stadium opened its doors, a venue that has played host to a diverse range of major sporting and musical events.

In 2001 sporting events throughout the United Kingdom were canceled in order to prevent the spread of foot-and-mouth disease. The WRU lost £1.4 million in ticket sales after its Six Nations match against Ireland was postponed. By February 2002 the WRU still had not recovered from the financial setbacks of the previous year, and the lackluster results of its teams paled in comparison to the glory days of the 1970s. Critics speculated that the WRU had mishandled the transition into the professional arena, allocating too much of its resources to Millennium Stadium and not enough on developing young talent.

In April 2002 it was clear that the best the Welsh national team could muster in the Six Nations was fourth place and, after a 20-year slump, the WRU called an extraordinary general meeting to discuss a restructuring of the domestic league. In December 2002 the WRU appointed David Moffett, former chief executive of the New Zealand Rugby Union, as the group's CEO. Other new positions in the restructuring included CEOs for the WRU and the Millennium Stadium divisions, and a group marketing chief. By the end of that month, Millennium Stadium posted pretax profits of £155,807 ($250,000), compared with a loss of £340,863 (nearly $500,000) the previous year. Events that contributed to the division's turnaround were the rescheduling of the Ireland-Wales Six Nations match in October and a series of rock concerts.

The group, however, was £60 million in debt, a figure attributed largely to the building and maintenance of Millennium Stadium. In March 2003 the WRU appointed Gwyn Thomas from Tesco Wales Group as the first general manager of commercial and marketing. This was the first of several new appoint-

## KEY DATES

**1881:** The Welsh Rugby Football Union is formed.

**1987:** Wales finishes third in the first Rugby World Cup.

**1999:** The Millennium Stadium opens its doors in time to host the Rugby World Cup.

**2005:** Wales becomes the first team to win the Grand Slam that played more games away than at home.

**2009:** The Welsh women's team wins their first Triple Crown in the Six Nations Tournament, qualifying the team for the Women's Rugby World Cup.

ments designed to modernize the governing body and implement strategies to increase revenues. The following month, the WRU received a much needed boost when it received planning permission for its training facility, the National Centre of Excellence at Island Farm, Bridgend. By March 2004 Moffett had a new management team and a focused business plan that promised to return the WRU to profitability.

## NEW SPONSORS

In June 2004 SA Brain & Company Ltd. (Brains), the largest producer of cask ale in Wales, was signed by Thomas as the sponsor of the national team's shirt. As part of the deal, Brains would also supply all of the beer at Millennium Stadium. In September 2004 the WRU seemed to be turning the corner on its financial woes. As it was looking forward, however, to the 2004–05 season, Thomas quit after a disagreement with Moffett over marketing strategy. With Tim Burton in place as head of strategy and funding, Moffett had no plans to replace Thomas.

Moffett and Thomas had focused on raising the WRU's professional image through investing additional resources in the areas of human resources, information technology, and commercial ventures. In October 2004 the land around Millennium Stadium was put on the market, the sale of which would generate multimillions in pounds for the WRU. The following month, Moffett announced that the group had reached a debt restructuring deal with Barclays Bank that would save the WRU £500,000 per year in interest payments.

In February 2005 the WRU issued 800 new Millennium Stadium debentures with the potential of rais-

ing more than £4 million. In that year, Wales won the Grand Slam and was attracting the attention of major sponsors. By October 2005 a number of companies had joined the WRU's commercial program, including Gilesports plc, which had more than 80 outlets throughout England and Wales and would serve as the WRU's official sports retailer until the end of the 2007 season. It was not enough, however, and one year later the WRU was £85.2 million in debt.

## RESTRUCTURING AND RECRUITMENT

In October 2006 Moffett was replaced by Roger Lewis, who immediately got to work on restructuring the executive board. In November Lewis implemented a recruitment campaign for a new finance director. This was followed six months later with a search for a new head of marketing, a position Lewis deemed vital for driving revenues, which was filled by Gwyn Dolphin. The fiscal year ending May 31, 2007, showed sales of £43.8 million, down from £46.1 million the previous year. The decline was partially attributed to playing only two home games during the Six Nations competition. By October 2007 the WRU's financial outlook had improved, with a five-year revenue cycle that included additional rugby events.

In February 2008 the group announced that it would be relocating all of its key departments to Millennium Stadium, a move that would save the WRU £100,000 per year in rent and increase the efficiency of its operations. In that same year, the Welsh team returned to form, winning the Grand Slam and the Triple Crown, and Brains renewed its sponsorship deal. By July 2008 the WRU had reduced its debt with Barclays Bank by £10 million, and had agreed on a new funding arrangement that would give the WRU the flexibility to make further investments at all team levels. In August 2008 the WRU announced an initiative that would allow the community clubs to apply for funding for club improvements. For the fiscal year ending May 2008, the group's sales had increased by 15 percent, with pretax profits of £2 million.

In 2009 the Welsh international women's rugby team won the Triple Crown in the Six Nations Tournament, and qualified for the Women's Rugby World Cup. After negotiating a number of major sponsorship contracts, including a new team uniform deal with Under Armour, Dolphin resigned his position in October 2009 citing family reasons. At the end of that month, the WRU's £4 million National Centre of Excellence was officially opened. In 2010 the WRU was gearing up for three Six Nations matches at its Millennium Stadium, with two more to follow in 2011, and each event was guaranteed to generate millions of pounds in revenue. In March 2010 it was announced that the Admiral Group plc would be replacing Brains as the new sponsor in November 2010. In April of that year, Craig Maxwell of Under Armour was named the WRU's new sales and marketing manager. In an interview with Graham Henry of Cardiff's *Western Mail*, Lewis said, "The brand of Welsh rugby is huge, not just in Wales but around the world, and we now have in place a team capable of exploiting our potential to the full."

*Marie O'Sullivan*

## PRINCIPAL SUBSIDIARIES

Millennium Stadium plc; WRU Supporters Club Limited; WRU National Centre of Excellence Limited; Six Nations Rugby Limited (Ireland; 17%); European Rugby Cup Limited (Ireland; 19%); Celtic Rugby Limited (Ireland; 33%); British Lions Limited (Ireland; 25%).

## PRINCIPAL DIVISIONS

Elite Rugby; Community Rugby; Millennium Stadium.

## PRINCIPAL COMPETITORS

Fédération Française de Rugby; Federazione Italiana Rugby; Irish Rugby Football Union; Rugby Football Union (England); Scottish Rugby Union plc.

## FURTHER READING

Barry, Sion, "An Excellent Year On and Off the Field for the WRU," *Western Mail* (Cardiff), September 3, 2008, p. 2.

———, "WRU Reduces Debt by Pounds 10m," *Western Mail* (Cardiff), July 23, 2008, p. 1.

Henry, Graham, "WRU's New Marketing Man Is Game for His Big Challenge," *Western Mail* (Cardiff), April 14, 2010, p. 6.

Rees, Paul, *Grand Slam!: Year of the Dragon*, Edinburgh: Mainstream, 2005, 224 p.

Richards, Huw, "Wales Fight for Fourth—and Then Their Future," *Financial Times*, April 5, 2002, p. 13.

———, "Welsh Game Sidestepped by Changing Society," *Financial Times*, April 9, 1999, p. 15.

Smith David, and Gareth Williams, *Fields of Praise: The Official History of the Welsh Rugby Union, 1881–1981*, Cardiff: University of Wales Press, 1980, 505 p.

Thomas, Richard, "Rugby at the Heart of Economy," *Western Mail* (Cardiff), February 24, 2010, p. 37.

Toor, Mat, "The Dragons Roar," *Marketing*, April 22, 1993, p. 22.

Williamson, David, "Welsh Rugby Out to Score across the World with Its Grand Slam Brand," *Western Mail* (Cardiff), June 10, 2005, p. 34.

# WestJet Airlines Ltd.

22 Aerial Place Northeast
Calgary, Alberta T2E 3J1
Canada
Telephone: (403) 444-2700
Toll Free: (888) 937-8538
Fax: (403) 444-2301
Web site: http://www.westjet.com

*Public Company*
*Founded:* 1996
*Incorporated:* 1996
*Employees:* 7,700
*Sales:* CAD 2.28 billion ($2.24 billion) (2009)
*Stock Exchanges:* Toronto
*Ticker Symbol:* WJA, WJA.A
*NAICS:* 481111 Scheduled Passenger Air Transportation; 481112 Scheduled Freight Air Transportation; 481211 Nonscheduled Chartered Passenger Air Transportation; 561599 All Other Travel Arrangement and Reservation Services

■ ■ ■

WestJet Airlines Ltd. brought the Southwest Airlines model of no-frills short hops to Canada. Following four years of success in the Canadian West, the airline brought low-cost flights to eastern Canada beginning in 2000 by establishing a new hub near Toronto. By 2009 the airline averaged 380 flights a day to 69 destinations in Canada, the United States, Mexico, and the Caribbean and was actively pursuing international partnership and code-sharing agreements. At the end of 2010 WestJet had more than 90 Boeing 737 jets in its fleet.

## A MID-NINETIES START-UP

Clive Beddoe was born in England in 1947. He emigrated from England to western Canada, and as president of the Hanover Group, Beddoe made a fortune developing commercial real estate in the Calgary area. He also owned a small private technical school called Career College.

According to *Canadian Business*, in 1994 Beddoe bought Western Concord Manufacturing Ltd., which brought him into the flying business. The company's executive air travel bills were totaling CAN 3,000 a week. He bought a twin engine Cessna 421 and flew it himself, saving thousands on fuel costs and pilot fees.

In addition, he leased the plane to other businesses through a local charter operation, Morgan Air Services Co. Ltd. Morgan Air president Tim Morgan and investors Don Bell and Mark Hill joined Beddoe in the idea of starting a discount airline. Hill wrote the original business plan and later became the director of strategic planning, while Morgan and Bell were named vice presidents in charge of operations and customer service, respectively. Beddoe would be chairman and CEO.

Much to its credit, the group consulted Morris Air founder David Neeleman for advice. He had sold his successful Salt Lake City–based airline to Southwest Airlines Co. in 1993. He had also developed a computer reservations system, One Skies, that he sold to Hewlett-Packard. Neeleman agreed to provide 5 percent of the

## COMPANY PERSPECTIVES
WestJet's strategic plan is built on four pillars for long-term success. First, we focus on people and culture by investing in and fostering the growth, development and commitment of our people. Next, we commit ourselves to consistently and continuously providing an amazing guest experience. Third, we address revenue and growth by achieving an average annual compound growth rate in available seat miles of 10 percent. Finally, we maintain low costs by achieving a targeted, sustainable profit margin that will be number one among North American airlines.

start-up capital himself and helped attract other investors. Ronald Greene of Renaissance Energy Ltd. joined them; Beddoe was also a major investor. By the spring of 1995 the group had more than $8.5 million in capital accumulated. The new company was named WestJet Airlines Ltd. in May 1995.

In January 1996 Research Capital Corp. helped place $20 million in stock with other private investors, the largest of which was the Ontario Teachers' Pension Plan Board. WestJet had become one of the most heavily capitalized airline start-ups in decades.

Still, the odds appeared stacked against the company. No scheduled airline had yet successfully competed against the market leaders, Air Canada and Canadian Airlines. (Canada 3000 Airlines Ltd. and Royal Airlines both were charter operations.) Fluctuations in the cost of fuel, an airline's largest expense, could devastate a small operation. In addition, Western Canada's lack of large population centers seemed to preclude the need for another airline.

However, WestJet's plan was to expand the market, much as Southwest had done in the United States, by lowering fares to the point that a new class of travelers could afford to fly. Beddoe called it the "VFR" market—"visiting friends and relatives." As such, West-Jet would compete with cars and buses as much as planes.

Controlling costs was critical to WestJet's plan. The airline started out with cheaper labor than that of the established, unionized carriers. In fact, the CEO drew no salary at all. *Canadian Business* noted that Beddoe paid for his office furnishings out of his own pocket. Stock-purchase and profit-sharing plans helped provide motivation, and the company fostered a casual and

upbeat working environment. Such a corporate culture was regarded as necessary for good customer service.

WestJet relied on energetic, motivated employees to perform fast turnarounds. As at Southwest, the flight crew and even executives were said to help tidy up the cabins between flights. WestJet also avoided carrying large amounts of debt, although it did buy its own well-used jets rather than lease new ones. The first had an average age of 23 years.

Commercial flight operations began with three planes on February 29, 1996. Vancouver, Kelowna, Calgary, Edmonton, and Winnipeg were the first cities served, and several were added in the first year. As might be expected, many of the perks of the big airlines were missing. WestJet offered no paper tickets, in-flight meals, frequent-flier program, or airport lounges. It had only one class of seating and was not a member of any of the computer reservation systems used by most airlines and travel agents. WestJet's fares were often more than 50 percent less than those of other airlines. The formula worked amazingly well. In its first six months, WestJet logged a profit of $2.5 million, surely one of the most successful airline launches ever.

### CRISIS IN 1996, FOLLOWED BY EXPANSION

In September 1996 Canadian transport officials found WestJet's maintenance record-keeping program inadequate and forced the carrier to suspend operations. The grounding cost the carrier CAN 300,000 a day and stranded many passengers. It was the kind of a blow that could easily bankrupt a fledgling airline, especially given the broad suspicion of budget carriers that followed the ValuJet crash in the Florida Everglades earlier that year. Beddoe later told *Canadian Business*, "I felt as if the company we had put so much toil and energy into was crashing down on top of me, and there was nothing I could do." The shutdown lasted 17 days.

In fact, WestJet did recover, and quickly. In its first fiscal year, which lasted 10 months, the airline managed a small profit on CAN 37.3 million in revenues. It carried 760,000 passengers in its first full year.

WestJet had already added another plane to its fleet, bringing the total to four. WestJet operated Boeing 737s, the small airliner Southwest Airlines used to pioneer its widely copied strategy for connecting underserved markets. The airline would not keep routes open if demand was insufficient. (It did offer "Limited Addition" temporary service to a few destinations in Manitoba and Alberta.) Often, though, the entrance of West-Jet doubled the existing traffic on a route. A typical fare was CAN 39 between Calgary and Edmonton.

## KEY DATES

**1994:** Clive Beddoe and partners discuss starting a budget airline.

**1995:** Calgary businessmen invest millions in venture.

**1996:** WestJet flies its first scheduled routes; the company survives a 17-day grounding, imposed by Canadian transport officials for inadequate record-keeping.

**1997:** Charter and cargo services are added to repertoire.

**1999:** WestJet goes public.

**2000:** WestJet expands into eastern Canada.

**2004:** WestJet begins regular service to the United States.

**2006:** WestJet launches WestJet Vacations.

**2009:** WestJet signs interline agreement with Air France/KLM; the airline opens a new operations complex in Calgary.

WestJet began operating charters in October 1997. Its first client was a major tour operator; soon the airline was regularly flying to Las Vegas on a chartered basis. The company also began carrying cargo in the fall of 1997. Early in 1998 WestJet explored the possibility of a marketing agreement with Air Canada. Pretax profits were CAN 12.4 million on revenues of CAN 125.9 million in 1998. The airline carried 1.7 million passengers and ended the year with more than 600 employees, or "WestJetters."

Steven Smith, formerly president of Air Ontario (a subsidiary of Air Canada), became WestJet president and CEO in March 1999. Beddoe remained chairman. (Neeleman had left to launch Jet Blue, another well-capitalized budget airline in New York City.) The fleet was up to 11 aircraft by the middle of 1999. By this time the company had paid out $3 million in profit-sharing disbursements. About 86 percent of employees owned stock in the company.

WestJet went public on the Toronto Stock Exchange in July 1999. *Canadian Business* noted that its IPO was such a success that the company's market capital was soon valued at $375 million, five times greater than that of Canadian Airlines. The company's simple profitability in a troubled industry made WestJet stock attractive. Proceeds from the IPO were earmarked toward buying new planes and building a new hangar and head-quarters.

In December 1999 Air Canada agreed to buy Canadian Airlines. The combined airline would be the world's tenth largest and would have an 80 percent share of the domestic market. Air Canada soon announced plans to reduce its domestic capacity by 15 percent.

### HEADING EAST IN 2000

By 2000 WestJet had 1,100 employees. In interviews, company executives stressed the importance of not expanding too quickly lest the vital relationship between employee and customer be strained. Nevertheless, Air Canada's takeover of Canadian Airlines and the prospect of other start-up airlines filling the void in the east prompted WestJet to accelerate its expansion plans. In the spring of 2000 the company announced plans to compete in the eastern half of Canada, Air Canada's home turf. At a time when WestJet's fleet contained 15 old Boeing 737s, the carrier ordered 20 new ones to provide capacity for the expansion.

In March 2000 WestJet opened a hub in Hamilton, about 40 miles from Toronto. Several eastern markets, including Ottawa, were added within several months. Fares were as little as one-sixth those charged by Air Canada.

A number of competitors, old and new, were also adding capacity to the market. According to *Canadian Business*, entrepreneur Ken Rowe had been planning to launch his own low-fare airline, dubbed CanJet Airlines, at Hamilton. Though he was reported to have changed his mind rather than challenge the more-established, better-funded WestJet, CanJet did in fact begin flying in September 2000. Air Canada was also planning to base its own discount airline (Air Canada Lite) at Hamilton. Some doubted the state carrier could succeed where Delta Air Lines, US Airways Inc., and Continental Airlines Inc. had failed. Even United Airlines, Inc., the largest airline in the world at the time, lost $200 million trying to create a low-cost unit to compete with Southwest. "The biggest risk for us," quipped Smith, "is that eastern Canadians won't like low fares."

Smith resigned in September 2000, purportedly due to differences in management style with Beddoe, who resumed the roles of president and CEO. Beddoe told the *National Post* that Smith did not fit in with West-Jet's corporate culture, and as a result, the company's energy and drive were threatened. Smith denied Beddoe's charges that he was "militaristic" and "dictatorial."

Just about all of the statistics that were used to measure an airline's financial performance (traffic counts, load factors, revenues, earnings) continued to rise for WestJet in 2000. Two years later the airline successfully added service to two new Ontario cities, London and Toronto, further putting the squeeze on its rival Air Canada. In 2003, acting on Beddoe's assertion of "continued commitment to expand our low-fare service to every major city in Canada," the airline began carrying passengers to Halifax and St. John's in Newfoundland and to Montreal, where it joined CanJet and Jetsgo Corp., another low-cost air carrier. By April the airline had become Canada's second-largest carrier. With reports of steady quarterly profits, WestJet looked toward an ambitious future.

## ACROSS THE BORDER IN 2004

In early 2004 WestJet announced plans to begin service to and from U.S. vacation spots in California, Florida, and Arizona, as well as New York's LaGuardia airport. The decision to go international was fueled in part by shrinking growth opportunities in Canada, as discount carriers operating along popular Canadian routes glutted the market. Service to the United States included scheduled flights from Calgary and Toronto. At the same time WestJet entered talks with China-based Cathay Pacific Airways Ltd. to provide "interline" services through the Vancouver and Toronto points of entry. Interlining is an agreement between airlines that allows passengers to fly on multiple carriers using a single ticket.

Expansion did not come without challenges, however. The airline faced a dip in net profits due to higher fuel prices and lower revenues as the competition for customers heated up. In addition, in 2004 Air Canada accused WestJet of corporate espionage and hit the airline with a $220 million lawsuit. In the suit Air Canada claimed that WestJet had hacked into Air Canada's reservations system to collect confidential data used to bolster WestJet's profits. WestJet eventually settled with Air Canada in 2006, admitting to "unethical and unacceptable" practices and agreeing to a fine of CAN 15.5 million.

The year 2005 saw an uptick in the airline's fortunes as Jetsgo Corp., WestJet's competitor in low-cost domestic air travel, shut down its operations in March. WestJet's shares soared 40 percent, to CAN 15.60, on the news of Jetsgo's demise. However, 2005 also marked the end of the airline's 31-month run of quarterly gains as WestJet's decision to retire 18 of its older, less fuel-efficient Boeing 737s cut into its profits. That year the airline broadened its cross-border presence to include flights from Canada to San Diego, Las Vegas, Honolulu, and Maui.

With an eye to continued growth, the company also exercised its options for 11 new 737s scheduled for delivery in 2006. In October 2005 WestJet won recognition as Canada's "most admired" corporate culture. The airline would be similarly recognized for four years running.

## BEYOND NORTH AMERICA IN 2006

In June 2006 WestJet launched WestJet Vacations Inc., a fully owned subsidiary offering discount travel packages to 33 destinations. The airline also inaugurated a new seasonal route from Toronto to Nassau, the Bahamas, marking the company's first destination outside of Canada and the United States. In September Clive Beddoe ceded the president's role to Sean Durfy, a former WestJet executive vice president. Beddoe would stay on as chairman and CEO.

Regular flights to other international travel destinations followed. In 2007 WestJet launched new routes to Mexico and the Caribbean islands of Jamaica and St. Lucia. The airline was forced to take a $30 million write-down when the new online reservations system in which it had invested was determined to be incapable of operating "code-sharing" partnerships with other airlines. Despite the setback, WestJet's revenues for 2007 topped CAN 2.1 billion. In 2008 WestJet signed a code-sharing agreement with Southwest, a cost-saving measure that allowed each airline to sell tickets for flights operated by the other. The pact between the two airlines lasted until 2010, when Southwest withdrew from the partnership.

The airline industry faced tough times in 2009, as much of the world's economy plunged into recession. WestJet continued to show net quarterly gains, however, as it focused on growing capacity, expanding flight routes, and keeping costs down. In July 2009 the airline announced an interline agreement with Air France/KLM, a profit-making move that seemed to lay the groundwork for future international code-sharing agreements. Later that year the rocky launch of the company's new SaberSonic reservations system, bogged down by computer glitches, compelled Sean Durfy to post an apology on the WestJet Web site. At the end of 2009 the number of employees exceeded 7,700. The company also opened the doors of its new Calgary campus, which it had begun in 2007.

In 2010 Sean Durfy resigned, paving the way for Craig Saretsky to assume the position of president and CEO. As outlined on the company Web site, WestJet's vision for the future appeared clear: "By 2016, WestJet will be one of the five most successful international airlines in the world providing our guests with a friendly and caring experience that will change air travel forever."

*Frederick C. Ingram*
*Updated, H. Schonthal*

## PRINCIPAL SUBSIDIARIES

WestJet Vacations, Inc.

## PRINCIPAL COMPETITORS

ACE Aviation Holdings Inc.; Air Transat Inc.; AMR Corporation; CanJet Airlines.

## FURTHER READING

Baglole, Joel, "Fledgling Is Taking on Air Canada—WestJet, a Southwest Clone, Plans Make-or-Break Bet on Nationwide Service," *Wall Street Journal*, April 24, 2000, p. A26.

Deveau, Scott, "New WestJet Chief Eyes Global Flight Path," *Financial Post*, March 26, 2010, http://www.financialpost.com/news-sectors/story.html?id=2731968.

Duvall, Mel, "Airline Reservation System Hits Turbulence," *Baseline*, July 25, 2007, http://www.baselinemag.com/c/a/Intelligence/Airline-Reservation-System-Hits-Turbulence/.

Flint, Perry, "WestJet Defies the Odds," *Air Transport World*, June 1999, pp. 82–83.

Jang, Brent, "WestJet Charts Bold New Path," *Globe and Mail*, March 26, 2010, http://www.theglobeandmail.com/globe-investor/westjet-charts-bold-new-path/article1514036/.

Karp, Aaron, "WestJet Agrees to Pay Fine, Admits Wrongdoing in Air Canada Dispute," *Air Transport World*, May 31, 2006, http://atwonline.com/it-distribution/news/westjet-agrees-pay-fine-admits-wrongdoing-air-canada-dispute-0309-0.

McMurdy, Deirdre, "Flying Around Air Canada," *Maclean's*, September 25, 2000.

Verburg, Peter, "Air Contrarian," *Canadian Business*, August 27, 1999, p. 24.

———, "Reach for the Bottom," *Canadian Business*, March 6, 2000, pp. 42–48.

———, "The Little Airline That Could," *Canadian Business*, April 1997, pp. 34–40.

# Woodstream Corporation

**69 North Locust Street**
**Lititz, Pennsylvania 17543-1714**
**U.S.A.**
**Telephone: (717) 626-2125**
**Toll Free: (800) 800-1819**
**Fax: (717) 626-1912**
**Web site: http://www.woodstream.com**

*Private Company*
*Incorporated:* 1881 as Oneida Community Ltd.
*Employees:* 450
*Sales:* $43 million (2007 est.)
*NAICS:* 325320 Pesticide and Other Agricultural
    Chemical Manufacturing; 332111 Iron and Steel
    Forging; 332510 Hardware Manufacturing; 339999
    All Other Miscellaneous Manufacturing

∎ ∎ ∎

A privately held company whose origins go back to the mid-19th century, Woodstream Corporation makes and merchandises goods in five product lines, which it calls rodent control products and solutions, caring control products for pets and wildlife, natural solutions for lawn and garden care, wild bird feeding products, and garden décor. Its most famous product is the Victor snap trap for killing rodents. Invented in the 1890s, the trap has since recorded more than one billion sales. Its customers are individual consumers and professional pest control experts. Woodstream's headquarters are in Lititz, Pennsylvania. The company has additional operations in Mechanicsburg, Pennsylvania; Denver, Colorado;

Knoxville, Tennessee; St. Joseph, Missouri; Brampton, Ontario, Canada; and Shenzhen, China. Woodstream is a financially successful firm whose sales have expanded rapidly since the start of the 21st century.

## THE FIRST 75 YEARS: 1850–1924

In 1848 John Humphrey Noyes established a utopian commune called the Oneida Community in Oneida, New York. It is remembered primarily for its system of Complex Marriage, in which each man in the commune was married to all the commune's women, and the other way around. Around 1850 Sewell Newhouse, a member of the community, began making wildlife traps, including traps for large fur-bearing animals such as bears, using scrap iron from his father's blacksmith shop. He bartered them for goods from Native Americans on the nearby Oneida Reservation. In 1881 the Oneida Community dissolved itself but at the same time its various business operations, including trap manufacture, were folded into a corporation called Oneida Community Ltd.

Meanwhile, in Lancaster, Pennsylvania, John Mast was manufacturing coleslaw, wooden fishing lures, and popcorn in his brick factory. Because his business attracted many mice, he began working on a mousetrap. During the 1890s he developed mouse killers, which he called "snap-shot" traps. When a mouse, attracted by bait, stepped onto the platform on which the bait was placed, strong spring action thrust a bar down, killing the animal instantly by breaking its neck. The descending bar's speed was later measured at 60 miles per hour.

## COMPANY PERSPECTIVES

With our proven brands, efficient manufacturing and sourcing, consolidated distribution, strong customer relationships, and innovative products, we have created a solid foundation for continued growth from which we can expand market share and build competitive advantages in all markets. Our strategies are straightforward—build brand awareness and acceptance of our superior products, continue to develop proprietary technologies, commercialize innovative new products, drive products through our diversified and growing distribution network, and maximize long-term profitability while increasing market share and revenues in key vertical markets.

Mast applied for a patent in 1899 and received it in 1903. Meanwhile, he had moved his operations to Lititz, Pennsylvania, in 1902. The trap sold well from the time Mast began marketing it in 1899 under the name Joker, with the accompanying slogan, "The joke is on the mouse that messes around the business end of this outfit." Because Mast's design required only a few moving parts stapled to a rectangular base made of pinewood, the traps sold for only five cents apiece in 1900. Their design changed only slightly over the next century, and they became the best-selling mouse catchers in the world. Mast also manufactured traps for rats and other fur-bearing animals.

In 1907 the Oneida Community Ltd. purchased J. M. Mast Co. and kept it in Lititz. Oneida by then had put silverware and cutlery manufacturing to the forefront of its product lines, but it operated the trap business as one of its many enterprises until 1924. At that time three of Oneida's executives, including Chester M. Woolworth, founder and president of the renowned Woolworth department-store chain, bought the firm's rodent-trap business, naming it the Animal Trap Company of America (ATC). It manufactured the traps under its Victor line of products.

## A LEADING MANUFACTURER: 1925–75

In the 1920s ATC was manufacturing 90 percent of the mouse, rat, and other rodent traps sold in the United States. Under Woolworth, who was the company's chairman of the board until his death in 1977, the company also became a leading manufacturer of products for outdoor sports. Beginning in 1918 the firm produced solid-wood duck decoys under the Victor brand line. This line was supplanted in 1939, when ATC purchased the Pratt Manufacturing Company of Joliet, Illinois. ATC inherited Pratt's hollowed, lighter duck decoys that included most duck species. In the 1940s ATC bought Poitevin Brothers, manufacturers of Singing River Decoys, and decoy manufacturer Cumbest Manufacturing Company. Both firms were located near the Pascagoula River in Mississippi. In the late 1950s and early 1960s, however, wooden decoys were replaced by plastic and papier-mâché models.

After World War II ATC greatly expanded its array and quantity of outdoor recreational equipment, so that in 1966 the company changed its name to Woodstream Corporation. The firm's output included fishing tackle, rods, and boots; ski glasses, goggles, and boots; and hunting equipment. During the 1970s Woodstream obtained the right to distribute the much-admired, high-performance Heschung leather ski boots, first produced in France in 1967. At around the same time, it established a joint venture with Hydron Technologies, Inc., for producing and distributing a coating for sunglasses and goggles than made them fog free. By the three-quarter mark of the 20th century, Woodstream was a major producer of sporting equipment.

Woodstream also continued to be the leading producer of animal-control equipment. Traditional traps for animal wildlife used legholds to ensnare their victims. People concerned with animal well-being disliked these traps because of the pain and maiming caused when the animals tried to escape. One of those people was fur trapper Frank Conibear, who in 1929 developed a quick-kill trap that he refined over the years. In the post-World War II period, it featured spring-powered steel jaws that, when activated by a baited trigger, snapped shut with such force that the animal's neck or chest was crushed, killing the animal immediately. Beginning in 1957 ATC (by arrangement with Conibear) was the first to produce the traps in large numbers, under the name Victor-Conibear trap. Woodstream also kept manufacturing its leghold traps.

## A BETTER MOUSETRAP: 1976–99

In the 1970s and afterward, Woodstream's Victor mousetrap continued to easily outsell its competitors. The firm's skillful marketing helped it to remain the leader in mousetrap sales and in the pest-control business generally. During the 1970s the company conducted the first survey of how people used their mousetraps. The survey surprised Woodstream management by finding that although men usually set the trap and disposed of it, the purchasers were mostly women,

# KEY DATES

**1881:** Oneida Community Ltd. is established.
**1903:** John Mast obtains a patent for his mousetrap.
**1957:** Woodstream begins manufacturing the Victor-Conibear trap.
**2000:** Purchased by the private-investment firm Fred Skoler & Co., Woodstream reverts to its earlier status as a private company.
**2007:** Large sales increases cause Woodstream to expand its distribution space.

probably because the hardware store was being replaced by the supermarket as the sales venue.

Woodstream reacted by "feminizing" the product. The male hand on the packaging became more refined, with a hint of pink polish on the nails. The traps' humane, quick-kill nature was stressed, so that slogans such as "No mouse will take the bait without losing its head!" were replaced with such expressions as "Mouse died peacefully" and "No mutilation." (Strangely, another slogan was "No Harm to Mouse.") It was estimated that in the last decades of the century, about 30 million Victor mousetraps were sold each year. By 2000 over one billion had been bought worldwide.

During the mid-1970s Woodstream began developing a product that, unlike the quick-kill Conibear trap and the Victor mousetrap, would not win applause from those promoting the humane treatment of animals. Sold starting in the early 1980s, it was a glue trap for mice, a rodent version of fly paper. It was perhaps the least humane way of catching mice, because they routinely maimed themselves trying to escape and then died slowly of starvation unless the trap's owner intervened to discard the trap and mouse. Nonetheless, it was a popular trap whose sales grew swiftly, to some extent at the expense of the Victor mousetrap.

Nonetheless, the growing strength of environmental, product safety, and animal rights groups in the late 20th and early 21st centuries pushed Woodstream in more caring directions. In 1999, for example, the company, noting that many children and pets were injured by household pesticides, introduced Victor Poison-Free Sprays, based on mint oil. The Victor sprays targeted insects, including ants, roaches, wasps, and hornets. Later in the year the firm launched the Victor Poison-Free PRO series for the professional pest control market. The sprays were harmless to people, plants, pets, and the environment, according to Woodstream. They

could be used in places such as aircraft, food-processing facilities, and poultry and meat plants.

In 1989 Woodstream was purchased by Ekco Group Inc., a public company that manufactured bakeware and kitchen tools. Ten years later it was sold to Corning Consumer Products Co., which made Woodstream part of a Corning affiliate. Less than a year later, Corning divested itself of Woodstream, selling it to the private-investment firm Fred Skoler & Co. of Saddle Brook, New Jersey, on undisclosed terms. After 10 years, Woodstream once again was a private firm.

## GROWTH THROUGH ACQUISITIONS: 2000–10

Woodstream grew quickly after its purchase by Skoler. In 2000 it acquired the segment of Verdant Brands that made environmentally safe insecticide, pest control, and fertilizer products sold at retail. That same year Woodstream introduced animal-repelling products under the Havahart line. With ingredients including capsaicin pepper and castor oil, the products fended off deer, rabbits, raccoons, squirrels, dogs, cats, moles, and other animals. Two years later Woodstream acquired two animal-repellent products from Deer-Off Inc. of Stamford, Connecticut. Other acquisitions by Woodstream in the first decade of the 21st century included the Safer low-toxic pest control line and K Feeder bird feeders. Thanks to its acquisitions and internal growth, Woodstream's sales doubled to nearly $80 million annually between 1999 and 2003.

In 2003 the Boca Raton, Florida-based private-equity firm Brockway Moran & Partners purchased Woodstream from Fred Skoler & Co. for $100 million. During the remainder of the decade, Woodstream's acquisitions included the 2005 purchase of FiShock, Inc., of Knoxville, Tennessee, a top producer of electric fencing and other animal containment products, which Woodstream sold under the FiShock name. Later that year Woodstream bought Colibri Holding Company, a manufacturer of wild bird feeders and plant care and garden accessories under names such as Perky-Pet, Yule-Hyde, and Gardener's Blue Ribbon. Early in 2010 Zareba Systems of Plymouth, Minnesota, a maker of electronic perimeter fence and access control systems, signed an agreement by which it would become a part of Woodstream.

New products designed within Woodstream included the humane Victor EMT (electronic mouse trap), which, using AA batteries, killed mice in five to ten seconds following a 7,500-volt shock. It was marketed in 2003. In 2004 Woodstream introduced Havahart Pet Doors, which made it possible for dogs to easily enter and exit a residence. That year the company also began marketing Critter Ridder, an all-natural granule repellent for small animals designed particularly for use in garages, attics, basements, and storage areas. In 2007 Woodstream obtained a patent for a new electronic animal trap. In 2009 Victor Multi-Kill Brand Blocks, a poison for killing rodents, was launched. Its chemical formulation, the firm said, made it twice as deadly for mice than previous rodenticides but four times safer for dogs.

In June 2005 Peter Brockway of Brockway Moran & Partners reviewed the record of Woodstream since its mid-2003 purchase by the equity firm. "Woodstream has performed exceptionally well … and has a strong track record of successfully acquiring and growing complementary businesses," reported Business Wire on August 24, 2005. Because of growing sales, the company found that its 150,000 square feet of distribution space in Lititz was inadequate. Therefore, in 2007 Woodstream leased a 204,000-square-foot building in Mechanicsburg, Pennsylvania. Woodstream was a world leader in most of its product lines, and as of 2010, more than 75 percent of its sales came from markets where it had the number-one or number-two market share.

*Michael Levine*

## PRINCIPAL DIVISIONS

FiShock; Havahart; Mosquito Magnet; Perky-Pet; Safer; Victor.

## PRINCIPAL COMPETITORS

Bowman Traps Ltd.; China Fenghua Technology Development Co., Ltd.; KB Manufacturing; Minnesota Trapline Products, Inc.

## FURTHER READING

Bass, Larisa, "Knoxville Fence Maker Sold to Penn. Company," *Knoxville (TN) News-Sentinel*, February 15, 2005.

"Brockway Moran Portfolio Company Acquires Colibri Holding Corporation," Business Wire, August 24, 2005.

Hinz, Christopher, "Business Is a Snap," *Reading (PA) Eagle*, July 10, 2006.

"Hot Melt Mixer Helps Company Build a Better Mousetrap," *Adhesives Age*, March 1993, p. 17.

Hudgens, David, "Public Outcry Prompts Rodent-Removal Research," *Knoxville (TN) News Sentinel*, September 29, 2004, p. WS9.

Mekeel, Tim, "Lititz, Pa.-Based Company Expands Animal-Repellent Business with Acquisition," *Lancaster (PA) New Era*, April 19, 2002.

Nathanson, Ari, "Brockway Catches an Add-On, Releases a Dividend," *Buyouts*, February 28, 2005.

"'Orphan' Companies Head for the Public Exits," *Minneapolis (MN) Star Tribune*, January 17, 2010, p. 2D.

# WorleyParsons Ltd.

Level 12, 141 Walker Street
North Sydney, New South Wales 2060
Australia
Telephone: (+61 2) 8923 6866
Fax: (+61 2) 8923 6877
Web site: http://www.worleyparsons.com/

*Public Company*
*Founded:* 1971 as Wholohan Grill and Partners
*Employees:* 28,800
*Sales:* AUD 6.23 billion ($5.07 billion) (2009)
*Stock Exchanges:* Sydney
*Ticker Symbol:* WOR
*NAICS:* 541330 Engineering Services; 541512 Computer Systems Design Services; 541620 Environmental Consulting Services; 236220 Commercial and Institutional Building Construction; 236210 Industrial Building Construction; 237990 Other Heavy and Civil Engineering Construction

■ ■ ■

WorleyParsons Ltd. is recognized around the world as being a provider of high-quality engineering, procurement, construction, and management (EPCM) services and specialties. Its Hydrocarbons, Infrastructure and Environment, Minerals and Metals, Power, and WorleyParsons Consulting Practices divisions reflect the company's industrial span. By assisting customers' three primary needs (selecting where and how to access raw material, delivering material to its next stage of production, and improving on existing production sites)

WorleyParsons has won recognition such as the 2006 Sir William Hudson Award, an award for excellence conferred by Engineers Australia. WorleyParsons has more than 28,000 employees in 37 countries.

## ENTREPRENEURIAL ENGINEERS: 1971–95

In 1971 John Grill joined Bill Paterson and others in founding Wholohan Grill and Partners, a small group of engineers whose office was located in Sydney, Australia. Grill had a background in civil engineering, with an emphasis in oil and gas, and Paterson's specialties were structural engineering in the public and urban spheres. The engineers' start-up involved an entrepreneurial synergy: together, they created an Australian-based firm that could do, locally, what other companies were coming to the country to undertake. As Andrew Heathcote of *BRW* noted, Grill's commitment to founding Wholohan Grill was such that he mortgaged his family's house to help finance the firm.

Initially, the company served as an engineering consultant on various projects. Discoveries and exploration in Australia of oil, gas, and nickel, which had been occurring since the post–World War II years, had the potential of shifting the country's dependence on importing these commodities. During the 1960s the development of oil wells and mines in the Queensland and New South Wales regions had revenue-attracting consequences for engineers. Grill, Paterson, and others assisted the flow by which investors brought resources from their raw state to product form for distribution and sale.

## COMPANY PERSPECTIVES

WorleyParsons Ltd. is an engineering, procurement, construction and management firm based in Australia whose mission is to be the preferred global provider of technical, project and operational support services to our customers, using WorleyParsons' distinctive culture to create value for our clients and prosperity for our people. We optimize our customer's investments across the entire asset life cycle, from detailed engineering, through vendor quality assurance, construction management to start-up and operations. We pride ourselves on a culture characterized by flexibility, capability and partnering.

During the mid-1980s Wholohan Grill began receiving greater attention, such as when it partnered with the structural engineer Robert Edwardes to improve some of Exxon Mobil's offshore oil platforms in Australia's Bass Straits. In 1987 Wholohan Grill acquired Worley Engineering Pty. Ltd. and changed its name to Worley Group Ltd. Having acquired Worley's interests in Australia and Southeast Asia, the company had many opportunities for growth.

For example, with Peter Meurs heading up the effort in Southeast Asia, the company received contracts in Thailand and Singapore. The company also established a number of long-term contracts in Brunei, Malaysia, and elsewhere. In 1995 Worley set up the subsidiary Worley Engineering (Malaysia) to establish joint ventures such as a 30 percent interest in Ranhill Worley International Sdn. Bhd. While focusing on offshore oil development, Ranhill Worley got other projects under way by buying Shapadu-ABB Global Engineering, obtaining its contracts and clients, and finishing or moving forward in the region with projects in Thailand, Pakistan, and Nigeria.

## OPPORTUNITIES AND EXPANSION: 1996–2004

In 1996 Worley celebrated its 25th anniversary. However, the celebrations were short lived because a number of challenges were beginning to emerge that affected not only Worley but also other EPCM companies. By the late 1990s investments in oil and gas projects declined and an economic crisis ensued in Southeast Asia. Engineering firms responded with a variety of strategies. Some firms relied on their project

backlogs, but this was an ineffective long-term solution because profitability needed to extend beyond the decline. Some EPCM companies instituted layoffs and office closings, whereas others conducted mergers and acquisitions to solidify ties and increase globalization. Another option, technological upgrades and licensing, had the potential of increasing a company's stability and instilling greater confidence in a company's clients. This was the option that Worley chose to exploit.

As other firms departed the Middle East, Worley seized the opportunity by gaining new clients and homing in with engineering and project management services. Another strategy involved alliances with established engineering firms. In March 2001 Tom Everett-Heath of *MEED: Middle East Economic Digest* observed, "Worley took over the US' Petrocon's position in its joint venture with Fahad Tamimi, and by doing so established a firm foothold in the Saudi market." Other achievements included a front-end engineering and design contract for an offshore gas recycling project as well as the friendly takeovers of Mannai Corporation's engineering division in Qatar and Stork Engineers & Contractors' offices and workers in Abu Dhabi, United Arab Emirates.

Worley also devoted some of its efforts to technological advances. For example, in 1999 the company debuted the software Database Assisted Design. The software's process instrumentation applications and specificity for brownfield efforts (where previous industrial sites required improvement for reuse) made it attractive among oil and gas clients. In 2000 the subsidiary Worley Qatar was created to oversee Worley's growth in the Middle East.

In 2002 Worley fueled its expansion with an initial public offering on the Australian Stock Exchange. Two years later, in 2004, Worley acquired Parsons E&C Corporation of Houston, Texas, for AUD 350 million ($255 million). The firm's engineering and construction specialties in oil and chemicals complemented Worley's portfolio and process background. Besides increasing its staff, Worley gained operations in 16 countries and strengthened its presence in the oil producing industry. Following the acquisition, Worley changed its name to WorleyParsons Ltd.

## NEW OUTLOOK: 2005–10

The acquisition increased WorleyParsons's ability to handle complex projects such as an oil sands contract in Alberta, Canada, where production contrasted distinctly with oil drilling elsewhere. WorleyParsons's alliances with Imperial Oil Ltd. and others involved gathering data, designing procedures and facilities, and pursuing

## KEY DATES

■

**1971:** John Grill and Bill Paterson help found Wholohan Grill and Partners.

**1987:** Wholohan Grill acquires Worley Engineering Pty. Ltd.; the company's name becomes Worley Group Ltd.

**1996:** Worley celebrates its 25th anniversary.

**2002:** Worley becomes a public company listed on the Australian Stock Exchange.

**2004:** Worley acquires Parsons E&C Corporation; the company is renamed WorleyParsons Ltd.

Out of all the company's divisions, the Hydrocarbons division remained its largest source of financial success. From 2007 to 2009 this division generated between 73 percent and 76 percent of WorleyParsons's total revenue, with AUD 4.8 billion in 2009 alone. Regardless, alternatives to the reliance on hydrocarbons were under way. In 2008 WorleyParsons funded a study of solar power plants for industrial production and for Australia's overall use. One conclusion from the study was that existing technology made 250-megawatt solar power plants feasible. Given the diversity of WorleyParsons's holdings and given that these holdings spanned the entire globe, the success and future growth of the company was guaranteed.

*Mary C. Lewis*

solutions to issues of water treatment, waste removal, and other aspects of production with environmental and profitability impact. Despite concern among environmentalists and others, production continued.

WorleyParsons's capabilities were reflected in other activities as well. For example, the company had an EPCM services contract in Western Australia with Fortescue Metals Group. Based on the needs to the project, WorleyParsons built an iron ore mine, temporary housing, an airstrip, a railway, and a shipping facility at the site. Beginning in 2006 deepwater and pipeline joint ventures with KBR, Inc., Fluor Corporation, and other firms were started in China, Nigeria, New Zealand, and elsewhere. The company's net profit grew from AUD 66.5 million in 2005 to AUD 139.1 million in 2006. In 2007 the acquisition of the Canadian-based Colt Group increased WorleyParsons's oil sands capability. That same year WorleyParsons established the EcoNomics initiative, which provided assistance with brownfield reclamation, waste treatment, greenhouse gas reduction practices, and other applications of environmentally appropriate efforts while maintaining profitability.

In 2008 the company acquired the Arctic specialist INTEC Engineering. The following year consulting services began on Egypt's first nuclear power plant and on a pipeline that was being constructed in Armenia. The company's 2009 annual report highlighted 57 contracts that were tagged as "mega-projects" because of their complexity and high revenues. From 2007 to 2009 the company's contract with BrightSource Industries focused on the feasibility of solar energy in California and Nevada. In 2010 WorleyParsons presented a new floating platform design that was notable for its improved stability.

## PRINCIPAL SUBSIDIARIES

WorleyParsons has over 75 subsidiaries worldwide in engineering, procurement, construction, and management services and specialties.

## PRINCIPAL DIVISIONS

Hydrocarbons; Infrastructure and Environment; Minerals and Metals; Power; WorleyParsons Consulting Practices.

## PRINCIPAL OPERATING UNITS

Advanced Analysis Group; Carbon Consulting Group; Eastern Operations; EcoNomics and Carbon EcoNomics; Mega-Projects; Refining and Petrochemicals; Sulphur Technology Group; Water Solutions Group; WorleyParsons Materials.

## PRINCIPAL COMPETITORS

Bechtel Group, Inc.; Fluor Corporation; Foster Wheeler AG; Halliburton Company; KBR, Inc.; McDermott International, Inc.

## FURTHER READING

Everett-Heath, Tom, "New Kid on the Block," *MEED: Middle East Economic Digest*, March 23, 2001, p. 34.

Heathcote, Andrew, "Cyclical Success," *BRW*, May 18–24, 2006, pp. 94–95.

Morgan, David, "Scaling the Pyrenees," OilOnline.com, April 20, 2006, http://www.oilonline.com/News/NewsArticles/Production/articleType/ArticleView/articleId/17889/Scaling-the-Pyrenees.aspx.

Orshal, Jody, Natasha Alperowicz, and Jarret Adams, "Rebuilding Profits: E&C Firms Get to Work," *Chemical Week*, May 26, 1999, p. 29.

Paganie, David, "DOT Presents New Floating Platform Designs," *Offshore*, March 2010, p. 22.

Puliyenthuruthel, Josey, "Worley Group Buys Parsons E&C," *Daily Deal*, October 8, 2004.

Singh, Paramjit, "Ranhill Bersekutu Sees RM85m Turnover in '96," *Business Times* (Kuala Lumpur), December 14, 1995, p. 5.

"Worley Slates Australia's Pilbara as Spot for Solar Power PJT," *AsiaPulse News*, August 12, 2008.

# Cumulative Index to Companies

FlightSafety International, Inc., 9
231–33; 29 189–92 (upd.)

Flint Ink Corporation, 13 227–29; 41
163–66 (upd.)

FLIR Systems, Inc., 69 170–73

Flo *see* Groupe Flo S.A.

Floc'h & Marchand, 80 119–21

Florida Crystals Inc., 35 176–78

Florida East Coast Industries, Inc., 59
184–86

Florida Gaming Corporation, 47
130–33

Florida Power & Light Company *see* FPL
Group, Inc.

Florida Progress Corp., V 621–22; 23
198–200 (upd.) *see also* Progress
Energy, Inc.

Florida Public Utilities Company, 69
174–76

Florida Rock Industries, Inc., 46
195–97 *see also* Patriot Transportation
Holding, Inc.

Florida's Natural Growers, 45 160–62

Florists' Transworld Delivery, Inc., 28
136–38 *see also* FTD Group, Inc.

Florsheim Shoe Group Inc., 9 234–36;
31 209–12 (upd.)

Flotek Industries Inc., 93 217–20

Flour City International, Inc., 44
181–83

Flow International Corporation, 56
132–34

Flowers Industries, Inc., 12 170–71; 35
179–82 (upd.) *see also* Keebler Foods
Co.

Flowserve Corporation, 33 165–68; 77
146–51 (upd.)

FLSmidth & Co. A/S, 72 138–40

Fluke Corporation, 15 173–75

Fluor Corporation, I 569–71; 8 190–93
(upd.); 34 164–69 (upd.); 112
176–82 (upd.)

Fluxys SA, 101 188–91

FlyBE *see* Jersey European Airways (UK)
Ltd.

Flying Boat, Inc. (Chalk's Ocean
Airways), 56 135–37

Flying J Inc., 19 158–60

Flying Pigeon Bicycle Co. *see* Tianjin
Flying Pigeon Bicycle Co., Ltd.

FMC Corp., I 442–44; 11 133–35
(upd.); 89 220–27 (upd.)

FMR Corp., 8 194–96; 32 195–200
(upd.)

FN Manufacturing LLC, 110 155–59

FNAC, 21 224–26

FNMA *see* Federal National Mortgage
Association.

Foamex International Inc., 17 182–85

Focus Features, 78 118–22

Fokker *see* N.V. Koninklijke Nederlandse
Vliegtuigenfabriek Fokker.

Foley & Lardner, 28 139–42

Follett Corporation, 12 172–74; 39
162–65 (upd.)

Foncière Euris, 111 136–40

Fonterra Co-Operative Group Ltd., 58
125–27

Food Circus Super Markets, Inc., 88
92–96

The Food Emporium, 64 125–27

Food For The Poor, Inc., 77 152–55

Food Lion LLC, II 626–27; 15 176–78
(upd.); 66 112–15 (upd.)

Foodarama Supermarkets, Inc., 28
143–45 *see also* Wakefern Food Corp.

FoodBrands America, Inc., 23 201–04
*see also* Doskocil Companies, Inc.;
Tyson Foods, Inc.

Foodmaker, Inc., 14 194–96 *see also* Jack
in the Box Inc.

Foot-Joy Inc., 113 146–49

Foot Locker, Inc., 68 157–62 (upd.)

Foot Petals L.L.C., 95 151–54

Foote, Cone & Belding Worldwide, I
12–15; 66 116–20 (upd.)

Footstar, Incorporated, 24 167–69 *see
also* Foot Locker, Inc.

Forbes Inc., 30 199–201; 82 115–20
(upd.)

Force Protection Inc., 95 155–58

The Ford Foundation, 34 170–72

Ford Gum & Machine Company, Inc.,
102 128–31

Ford Motor Company, I 164–68; 11
136–40 (upd.); 36 215–21 (upd.); 64
128–34 (upd.)

Ford Motor Company, S.A. de C.V., 20
219–21

FORE Systems, Inc., 25 161–63 *see also*
Telefonaktiebolaget LM Ericsson.

Foremost Farms USA Cooperative, 98
116–20

FöreningsSparbanken AB, 69 177–80

Forest City Enterprises, Inc., 16
209–11; 52 128–31 (upd.); 112
183–87 (upd.)

Forest Laboratories, Inc., 11 141–43; 52
132–36 (upd.); 114 195–200 (upd.)

Forest Oil Corporation, 19 161–63; 91
182–87 (upd.)

Forever 21, Inc., 84 127–129

Forever Living Products International
Inc., 17 186–88

FormFactor, Inc., 85 128–31

Formica Corporation, 13 230–32

Formosa Plastics Corporation, 14
197–99; 58 128–31 (upd.)

Forrester Research, Inc., 54 113–15

Forstmann Little & Co., 38 190–92

Fort Howard Corporation, 8 197–99 *see
also* Fort James Corp.

Fort James Corporation, 22 209–12
(upd.) *see also* Georgia-Pacific Corp.

Fortis, Inc., 15 179–82; 47 134–37
(upd.); 50 4–6

Fortum Corporation, 30 202–07 (upd.)
*see also* Neste Oil Corp.

Fortune Brands, Inc., 29 193–97 (upd.);
68 163–67 (upd.)

Fortunoff Fine Jewelry and Silverware
Inc., 26 144–46

Forward Air Corporation, 75 147–49

Forward Industries, Inc., 86 152–55

The Forzani Group Ltd., 79 172–76

The Foschini Group, 110 160–64

Fossil, Inc., 17 189–91; 112 188–93
(upd.)

Foster Poultry Farms, 32 201–04

Foster Wheeler Corporation, 6 145–47;
23 205–08 (upd.); 76 152–56 (upd.)

FosterGrant, Inc., 60 131–34

Foster's Group Limited, 7 182–84; 21
227–30 (upd.); 50 199–203 (upd.);
111 141–47 (upd.)

The Foundation for National Progress,
107 141–45

Foundation Health Corporation, 12
175–77

Fountain Powerboats Industries, Inc.,
28 146–48

Four Seasons Hotels Limited, 9 237–38;
29 198–200 (upd.); 106 191–95
(upd.)

Four Winns Boats LLC, 96 124–27

4imprint Group PLC, 105 187–91

4Kids Entertainment Inc., 59 187–89

Fourth Financial Corporation, 11
144–46

Fox Entertainment Group, Inc., 43
173–76

Fox Family Worldwide, Inc., 24 170–72
*see also* ABC Family Worldwide, Inc.

Fox, Inc. *see* Twentieth Century Fox Film
Corp.

Foxboro Company, 13 233–35

FoxHollow Technologies, Inc., 85
132–35

FoxMeyer Health Corporation, 16
212–14 *see also* McKesson Corp.

Fox's Pizza Den, Inc., 98 121–24

Foxworth-Galbraith Lumber Company,
91 188–91

FPL Group, Inc., V 623–25; 49 143–46
(upd.); 111 148–53 (upd.)

Framatome SA, 19 164–67 aee also
Alcatel S.A.; AREVA.

France Telecom S.A., V 291–93; 21
231–34 (upd.); 99 173–179 (upd.)

Francotyp-Postalia Holding AG, 92
123–27

Frank J. Zamboni & Co., Inc., 34
173–76

Frank Russell Company, 46 198–200

Franke Holding AG, 76 157–59

Frankel & Co., 39 166–69

Frankfurter Allgemeine Zeitung GmbH,
66 121–24

Franklin Covey Company, 11 147–49;
37 149–52 (upd.)

Franklin Electric Company, Inc., 43
177–80

Franklin Electronic Publishers, Inc., 23
209–13

The Franklin Mint, 69 181–84

Franklin Resources, Inc., 9 239–40

Frank's Nursery & Crafts, Inc., 12
178–79

Franz Haniel & Cie. GmbH, 109
250–55

Franz Inc., 80 122–25

Fraport AG Frankfurt Airport Services
Worldwide, 90 197–202

Fraser & Neave Ltd., 54 116–18

Gardner Denver, Inc., 49 158–60
Garmin Ltd., 60 135–37
Garst Seed Company, Inc., 86 156–59
Gart Sports Company, 24 173–75 *see also* Sports Authority, Inc.
Gartner, Inc., 21 235–37; 94 209–13 (upd.)
Garuda Indonesia, 6 90–91; 58 138–41 (upd.)
Gas Natural SDG S.A., 69 190–93
GASS *see* Grupo Ángeles Servicios de Salud, S.A. de C.V.
Gasunie *see* N.V. Nederlandse Gasunie.
Gate Gourmet International AG, 70 97–100
GateHouse Media, Inc., 91 196–99
The Gates Corporation, 9 241–43
Gateway Corporation Ltd., II 628–30 *see also* Somerfield plc.
Gateway, Inc., 10 307–09; 27 166–69 (upd.); 63 153–58 (upd.)
The Gatorade Company, 82 129–32
Gatti's Pizza, Inc. *see* Mr. Gatti's, LP.
GATX, 6 394–96; 25 168–71 (upd.)
Gaumont S.A., 25 172–75; 91 200–05 (upd.)
Gaylord Bros., Inc., 100 178–81
Gaylord Container Corporation, 8 203–05
Gaylord Entertainment Company, 11 152–54; 36 226–29 (upd.)
Gaz de France, V 626–28; 40 191–95 (upd.) *see also* GDF SUEZ.
Gazprom *see* OAO Gazprom.
GBC *see* General Binding Corp.
GC Companies, Inc., 25 176–78 *see also* AMC Entertainment Inc.
GDF SUEZ, 109 256–63 (upd.)
GE *see* General Electric Co.
GE Aircraft Engines, 9 244–46
GE Capital Aviation Services, 36 230–33
GEA AG, 27 170–74
GEAC Computer Corporation Ltd., 43 181–85
Geberit AG, 49 161–64
Gecina SA, 42 151–53
Gedney *see* M.A. Gedney Co.
Geek Squad Inc., 102 138–41
Geerlings & Wade, Inc., 45 166–68
Geest Plc, 38 200–02 *see also* Bakkavör Group hf.
Gefco SA, 54 126–28
Geffen Records Inc., 26 150–52
GEHE AG, 27 175–78
Gehl Company, 19 172–74
GEICO Corporation, 10 310–12; 40 196–99 (upd.)
Geiger Bros., 60 138–41
Gelita AG, 74 114–18
GEMA (Gesellschaft für musikalische Aufführungs- und mechanische Vervielfältigungsrechte), 70 101–05
Gemini Sound Products Corporation, 58 142–44
Gemplus International S.A., 64 144–47
Gen-Probe Incorporated, 79 185–88

Gencor Ltd., IV 90–93; 22 233–37 (upd.) *see also* Gold Fields Ltd.
GenCorp Inc., 9 247–49
Genentech, Inc., I 637–38; 8 209–11 (upd.); 32 211–15 (upd.); 75 154–58 (upd.)
General Accident plc, III 256–57 *see also* Aviva PLC.
General Atomics, 57 151–54; 112 194–98 (upd.)
General Bearing Corporation, 45 169–71
General Binding Corporation, 10 313–14; 73 159–62 (upd.)
General Cable Corporation, 40 200–03; 111 154–59 (upd.)
The General Chemical Group Inc., 37 157–60
General Cigar Holdings, Inc., 66 139–42 (upd.)
General Cinema Corporation, I 245–46 *see also* GC Companies, Inc.
General DataComm Industries, Inc., 14 200–02
General Dynamics Corporation, I 57–60; 10 315–18 (upd.); 40 204–10 (upd.); 88 105–13 (upd.)
General Electric Company, II 27–31; 12 193–97 (upd.); 34 183–90 (upd.); 63 159–68 (upd.)
General Electric Company, PLC, II 24–26 *see also* Marconi plc.
General Employment Enterprises, Inc., 87 172–175
General Growth Properties, Inc., 57 155–57
General Host Corporation, 12 198–200
General Housewares Corporation, 16 234–36
General Instrument Corporation, 10 319–21 *see also* Motorola, Inc.
General Maritime Corporation, 59 197–99
General Mills, Inc., II 501–03; 10 322–24 (upd.); 36 234–39 (upd.); 85 141–49 (upd.)
General Motors Corporation, I 171–73; 10 325–27 (upd.); 36 240–44 (upd.); 64 148–53 (upd.)
General Nutrition Companies, Inc., 11 155–57; 29 210–14 (upd.) *see also* GNC Corp.
General Public Utilities Corporation, V 629–31 *see also* GPU, Inc.
General Re Corporation, III 258–59; 24 176–78 (upd.)
General Sekiyu K.K., IV 431–33 *see also* TonenGeneral Sekiyu K.K.
General Signal Corporation, 9 250–52 *see also* SPX Corp.
General Tire, Inc., 8 212–14
Generale Bank, II 294–95 *see also* Fortis, Inc.
Générale des Eaux Group, V 632–34 *see also* Vivendi.
Generali *see* Assicurazioni Generali.
Genesco Inc., 17 202–06; 84 143–149 (upd.)

Genesee & Wyoming Inc., 27 179–81
Genesis Health Ventures, Inc., 18 195–97 *see also* NeighborCare,Inc.
Genesis Microchip Inc., 82 133–37
Genesys Telecommunications Laboratories Inc., 103 184–87
Genetics Institute, Inc., 8 215–18
Geneva Steel, 7 193–95
Genmar Holdings, Inc., 45 172–75
Genovese Drug Stores, Inc., 18 198–200
Genoyer *see* Groupe Genoyer.
GenRad, Inc., 24 179–83
Gentex Corporation, 26 153–57
Genting Bhd., 65 152–55
Gentiva Health Services, Inc., 79 189–92
Genuardi's Family Markets, Inc., 35 190–92
Genuine Parts Co., 9 253–55; 45 176–79 (upd.); 113 150–55 (upd.)
Genzyme Corporation, 13 239–42; 38 203–07 (upd.); 77 164–70 (upd.)
geobra Brandstätter GmbH & Co. KG, 48 183–86
Geodis S.A., 67 187–90
The Geon Company, 11 158–61
GeoResources, Inc., 101 196–99
Georg Fischer AG Schaffhausen, 61 106–09
Georg Jensen A/S, 110 173–77
George A. Hormel and Company, II 504–06 *see also* Hormel Foods Corp.
The George F. Cram Company, Inc., 55 158–60
George P. Johnson Company, 60 142–44
George S. May International Company, 55 161–63
George W. Park Seed Company, Inc., 98 145–48
George Weston Ltd., II 631–32; 36 245–48 (upd.); 88 114–19 (upd.)
George Wimpey plc, 12 201–03; 51 135–38 (upd.) *see also* Taylor Wimpey PLC.
Georgia Gulf Corporation, 9 256–58; 61 110–13 (upd.)
Georgia-Pacific LLC, IV 281–83; 9 259–62 (upd.); 47 145–51 (upd.); 101 200–09 (upd.)
Geotek Communications Inc., 21 238–40
Gerald Stevens, Inc., 37 161–63
Gerber Products Company, 7 196–98; 21 241–44 (upd)
Gerber Scientific, Inc., 12 204–06; 84 150–154 (upd.)
Gerdau S.A., 59 200–03
Gerhard D. Wempe KG, 88 120–25
Gericom AG, 47 152–54
Gerling-Konzern Versicherungs-Beteiligungs-Aktiengesellschaft, 51 139–43
German American Bancorp, 41 178–80
Gerresheimer Glas AG, 43 186–89
Gerry Weber International AG, 63 169–72

GWR Group plc, 39 198–200

Gymboree Corporation, 15 204–06; 69 198–201 (upd.)

# H

H&M Hennes & Mauritz AB, 98 181–84 (upd.)

H&R Block, Inc., 9 268–70; 29 224–28 (upd.); 82 162–69 (upd.)

H-P *see* Hewlett-Packard Co.

H.B. Fuller Company, 8 237–40; 32 254–58 (upd.); 75 179–84 (upd.)

H. Betti Industries Inc., 88 155–58

H.D. Vest, Inc., 46 217–19

H. E. Butt Grocery Company, 13 251–53; 32 259–62 (upd.); 85 164–70 (upd.)

H.F. Ahmanson & Company, II 181–82; 10 342–44 (upd.) *see also* Washington Mutual, Inc.

H. J. Heinz Company, II 507–09; 11 171–73 (upd.); 36 253–57 (upd.); 99 198–205 (upd.)

H.J. Russell & Company, 66 162–65

H. Lundbeck A/S, 44 208–11

H.M. Payson & Co., 69 202–04

H.O. Penn Machinery Company, Inc., 96 163–66

The H.W. Wilson Company, 66 166–68

Ha-Lo Industries, Inc., 27 193–95

The Haartz Corporation, 94 223–26

Habersham Bancorp, 25 185–87

The Habitat Company LLC, 106 213–17

Habitat for Humanity International, Inc., 36 258–61; 106 218–22 (upd.)

Hach Co., 18 218–21

Hachette Filipacchi Medias S.A., 21 265–67

Hachette S.A., IV 617–19 *see also* Matra-Hachette S.A.

Haci Omer Sabanci Holdings A.S., 55 186–89 *see also* Akbank TAS

Hackman Oyj Adp, 44 212–15

Hadco Corporation, 24 201–03

Haeger Industries Inc., 88 159–62

Haemonetics Corporation, 20 277–79

Haftpflichtverband der Deutschen Industrie Versicherung auf Gegenseitigkeit V.a.G. *see* HDI (Haftpflichtverband der Deutschen Industrie Versicherung auf Gegenseitigkeit V.a.G.).

Hagemeyer N.V., 39 201–04

Haggar Corporation, 19 194–96; 78 137–41 (upd.)

Haggen Inc., 38 221–23

Hagoromo Foods Corporation, 84 175–178

Hahn Automotive Warehouse, Inc., 24 204–06

Haier Group Corporation, 65 167–70

Haights Cross Communications, Inc., 84 179–182

The Hain Celestial Group, Inc., 27 196–98; 43 217–20 (upd.)

Hair Club For Men Ltd., 90 222–25

Hakuhodo, Inc., 6 29–31; 42 172–75 (upd.)

HAL Inc., 9 271–73 *see also* Hawaiian Airlines, Inc.

Hal Leonard Corporation, 96 167–71

Hale-Halsell Company, 60 157–60

Half Price Books, Records, Magazines Inc., 37 179–82

Halfords Group plc, 110 200–04

Hall, Kinion & Associates, Inc., 52 150–52

Halliburton Company, III 497–500; 25 188–92 (upd.); 55 190–95 (upd.)

Hallmark Cards, Inc., IV 620–21; 16 255–57 (upd.); 40 228–32 (upd.); 87 205–212 (upd.)

Halma plc, 104 179–83

Hamilton Beach/Proctor-Silex Inc., 17 213–15

Hammacher Schlemmer & Company Inc., 21 268–70; 72 160–62 (upd.)

Hammerson plc, IV 696–98; 40 233–35 (upd.)

Hammond Manufacturing Company Limited, 83 179–182

Hamon & Cie (International) S.A., 97 190–94

Hamot Health Foundation, 91 227–32

Hampshire Group Ltd., 82 170–73

Hampton Affiliates, Inc., 77 175–79

Hampton Industries, Inc., 20 280–82

Hancock Fabrics, Inc., 18 222–24

Hancock Holding Company, 15 207–09

Handleman Company, 15 210–12; 86 185–89 (upd.)

Handspring Inc., 49 183–86

Handy & Harman, 23 249–52

Hanesbrands Inc., 98 185–88

Hang Lung Group Ltd., 104 184–87

Hang Seng Bank Ltd., 60 161–63

Hanger Orthopedic Group, Inc., 41 192–95

Haniel *see* Franz Haniel & Cie. GmbH.

Hanjin Shipping Co., Ltd., 50 217–21

Hankook Tire Company Ltd., 105 200–03

Hankyu Corporation, V 454–56; 23 253–56 (upd.)

Hankyu Department Stores, Inc., V 70–71; 62 168–71 (upd.)

Hanmi Financial Corporation, 66 169–71

Hanna Andersson Corp., 49 187–90

Hanna-Barbera Cartoons Inc., 23 257–59, 387

Hannaford Bros. Co., 12 220–22; 103 211–17 (upd.)

Hanover Compressor Company, 59 215–17

Hanover Direct, Inc., 36 262–65

Hanover Foods Corporation, 35 211–14

Hansen Natural Corporation, 31 242–45; 76 171–74 (upd.)

Hansgrohe AG, 56 149–52

Hanson Building Materials America Inc., 60 164–66

Hanson PLC, III 501–03; 7 207–10 (upd.); 30 228–32 (upd.)

Hanwha Group, 62 172–75

Hapag-Lloyd AG, 6 397–99; 97 195–203 (upd.)

Happy Kids Inc., 30 233–35

Harbert Corporation, 14 222–23

Harbison-Walker Refractories Company, 24 207–09

Harbour Group Industries, Inc., 90 226–29

Harcourt Brace and Co., 12 223–26

Harcourt Brace Jovanovich, Inc., IV 622–24

Harcourt General, Inc., 20 283–87 (upd.)

Hard Rock Café International, Inc., 12 227–29; 32 241–45 (upd.); 105 204–09 (upd.)

Harding Lawson Associates Group, Inc., 16 258–60

Hardinge Inc., 25 193–95

HARIBO GmbH & Co. KG, 44 216–19

Harkins Amusement Enterprises, Inc., 94 227–31

Harland and Wolff Holdings plc, 19 197–200

Harland Clarke Holdings Corporation, 94 232–35 (upd.)

Harlem Globetrotters International, Inc., 61 122–24

Harlequin Enterprises Limited, 52 153–56

Harley-Davidson, Inc., 7 211–14; 25 196–200 (upd.); 106 223–28 (upd.)

Harley Ellis Devereaux Corporation, 101 229–32

Harleysville Group Inc., 37 183–86

Harman International Industries, Incorporated, 15 213–15; 101 233–39 (upd.)

Harmon Industries, Inc., 25 201–04 *see also* General Electric Co.

Harmonic Inc., 43 221–23; 109 285–88 (upd.)

Harmony Gold Mining Company Limited, 63 182–85

Harnischfeger Industries, Inc., 8 241–44; 38 224–28 (upd.) *see also* Joy Global Inc.

Harold's Stores, Inc., 22 248–50

Harper Group Inc., 17 216–19

HarperCollins Publishers, 15 216–18

Harpo Inc., 28 173–75; 66 172–75 (upd.)

Harps Food Stores, Inc., 99 206–209

Harrah's Entertainment, Inc., 16 261–63; 43 224–28 (upd.); 113 160–65 (upd.)

Harris Corporation, II 37–39; 20 288–92 (upd.); 78 142–48 (upd.)

Harris Interactive Inc., 41 196–99; 92 148–53 (upd.)

Harris Publishing *see* Bernard C. Harris Publishing Company, Inc.

The Harris Soup Company (Harry's Fresh Foods), 92 154–157

Harris Teeter Inc., 23 260–62; 72 163–66 (upd.)

Hero Group, 100 219–24

Héroux-Devtek Inc., 69 205–07

Herr Foods Inc., 84 188–191

Herradura *see* Grupo Industrial Herradura, S.A. de C.V.

Herschend Family Entertainment Corporation, 73 173–76

Hersha Hospitality Trust, 107 187–90

Hershey Company, II 510–12; 15 219–22 (upd.); 51 156–60 (upd.); 110 205–12 (upd.)

Herstal *see* Groupe Herstal S.A.

Hertie Waren- und Kaufhaus GmbH, V 72–74

The Hertz Corporation, 9 283–85; 33 190–93 (upd.); 101 240–45 (upd.)

Heska Corporation, 39 213–16

Heublein Inc., I 259–61

Heuer *see* TAG Heuer International SA.

Heuliez *see* Groupe Henri Heuliez S.A.

Hewitt Associates, Inc., 77 187–90

Hewlett-Packard Company, III 142–43; 6 237–39 (upd.); 28 189–92 (upd.); 50 222–30 (upd.); 111 198–204 (upd.)

Hexagon AB, 78 154–57

Hexal AG, 69 208–10

Hexcel Corporation, 28 193–95

HFF, Inc., 103 218–21

hhgregg Inc., 98 189–92

HI *see* Houston Industries Inc.

Hibbett Sporting Goods, Inc., 26 189–91; 70 120–23 (upd.)

Hibernia Corporation, 37 187–90

Hickory Farms, Inc., 17 230–32

HickoryTech Corporation, 92 168–71

High Falls Brewing Company LLC, 74 144–47

High Tech Computer Corporation, 81 178–81

Highland Gold Mining Limited, 95 184–87

Highlights for Children, Inc., 95 188–91

Highmark Inc., 27 208–11

Highsmith Inc., 60 167–70

Highveld Steel and Vanadium Corporation Limited, 59 224–27

Hikma Pharmaceuticals Ltd., 102 166–70

Hilb, Rogal & Hobbs Company, 77 191–94

Hildebrandt International, 29 235–38

Hilding Anders AB, 102 171–74

Hillenbrand Industries, Inc., 10 349–51; 75 188–92 (upd.)

Hillerich & Bradsby Company, Inc., 51 161–64

The Hillhaven Corporation, 14 241–43 *see also* Vencor, Inc.

Hills Industries Ltd., 104 200–04

Hill's Pet Nutrition, Inc., 27 212–14

Hills Stores Company, 13 260–61

Hillsdown Holdings, PLC, II 513–14; 24 218–21 (upd.)

Hillyard, Inc., 114 223–26

Hilmar Cheese Company, Inc., 98 193–96

Hilo Hattie *see* Pomare Ltd.

Hilti AG, 53 167–69

Hilton Group plc, III 91–93; 19 205–08 (upd.); 62 176–79 (upd.); 49 191–95 (upd.)

Hindustan Lever Limited, 79 198–201

Hines Horticulture, Inc., 49 196–98

Hino Motors, Ltd., 7 219–21; 21 271–74 (upd.)

HiPP GmbH & Co. Vertrieb KG, 88 183–88

Hiram Walker Resources Ltd., I 262–64

Hispanic Broadcasting Corporation, 35 219–22

HIT Entertainment PLC, 40 250–52

Hitachi, Ltd., I 454–55; 12 237–39 (upd.); 40 253–57 (upd.); 108 254–61 (upd.)

Hitachi Metals, Ltd., IV 101–02

Hitachi Zosen Corporation, III 513–14; 53 170–73 (upd.)

Hitchiner Manufacturing Co., Inc., 23 267–70

Hite Brewery Company Ltd., 97 204–07

Hittite Microwave Corporation, 106 229–32

HMI Industries, Inc., 17 233–35

HMV Group plc, 59 228–30

HNI Corporation, 74 148–52 (upd.)

Ho-Chunk Inc., 61 125–28

HOB Entertainment, Inc., 37 191–94

Hobby Lobby Stores Inc., 80 139–42

Hobie Cat Company, 94 236–39

Hochtief AG, 33 194–97; 88 189–94 (upd.)

The Hockey Company, 34 215–18; 70 124–26 (upd.)

Hodes *see* Bernard Hodes Group Inc.

Hodgson Mill, Inc., 88 195–98

Hoechst AG, I 346–48; 18 234–37 (upd.)

Hoechst Celanese Corporation, 13 262–65

Hoenig Group Inc., 41 207–09

Hoesch AG, IV 103–06

Hoffman Corporation, 78 158–12

Hoffmann-La Roche & Co *see* F. Hoffmann-La Roche & Co.

Hogan & Hartson L.L.P., 44 220–23

Hogg Robinson Group PLC, 105 216–20

Hohner *see* Matth. Hohner AG.

HOK Group, Inc., 59 231–33

Hokkaido Electric Power Company Inc. (HEPCO), V 635–37; 58 160–63 (upd.)

Hokuriku Electric Power Company, V 638–40

Holberg Industries, Inc., 36 266–69

Holden Ltd., 62 180–83

Holderbank Financière Glaris Ltd., III 701–02 *see also* Holnam Inc

N.V. Holdingmaatschappij De Telegraaf, 23 271–73 *see also* Telegraaf Media Groep N.V.

Holiday Inns, Inc., III 94–95 *see also* Promus Companies, Inc.

Holiday Retirement Corp., 87 221–223

Holiday RV Superstores, Incorporated, 26 192–95

Holidaybreak plc, 96 182–86

Holland & Knight LLP, 60 171–74

Holland America Line Inc., 108 262–65

Holland Burgerville USA, 44 224–26

Holland Casino, 107 191–94

The Holland Group, Inc., 82 174–77

Hollander Home Fashions Corp., 67 207–09

Holley Performance Products Inc., 52 157–60

Hollinger International Inc., 24 222–25; 62 184–88 (upd.)

Holly Corporation, 12 240–42; 111 205–10 (upd.)

Hollywood Casino Corporation, 21 275–77

Hollywood Entertainment Corporation, 25 208–10

Hollywood Media Corporation, 58 164–68

Hollywood Park, Inc., 20 297–300

Holme Roberts & Owen LLP, 28 196–99

Holmen AB, 52 161–65 (upd.); 111 211–17 (upd.)

Holnam Inc., 8 258–60; 39 217–20 (upd.)

Hologic, Inc., 106 233–36

Holophane Corporation, 19 209–12

Holson Burnes Group, Inc., 14 244–45

Holt and Bugbee Company, 66 189–91

Holt's Cigar Holdings, Inc., 42 176–78

Holtzbrinck *see* Verlagsgruppe Georg von Holtzbrinck.

Homasote Company, 72 178–81

Home Box Office Inc., 7 222–24; 23 274–77 (upd.); 76 178–82 (upd.)

Home City Ice Company, Inc., 111 218–22

The Home Depot, Inc., V 75–76; 18 238–40 (upd.); 97 208–13 (upd.)

Home Hardware Stores Ltd., 62 189–91

Home Inns & Hotels Management Inc., 95 195–95

Home Insurance Company, III 262–64

Home Interiors & Gifts, Inc., 55 202–04

Home Market Foods, Inc., 110 213–16

Home Product Center plc, 104 205–08

Home Products International, Inc., 55 205–07

Home Properties of New York, Inc., 42 179–81

Home Retail Group plc, 91 242–46

Home Shopping Network, Inc., V 77–78; 25 211–15 (upd.) *see also* HSN.

HomeBase, Inc., 33 198–201 (upd.)

Homestake Mining Company, 12 243–45; 38 229–32 (upd.)

Hometown Auto Retailers, Inc., 44 227–29

HomeVestors of America, Inc., 77 195–98

Quaker Foods North America, II 558–60; 12 409–12 (upd.); 34 363–67 (upd.); 73 268–73 (upd.)

Quaker State Corporation, 7 443–45; 21 419–22 (upd.) *see also* Pennzoil-Quaker State Co.

QUALCOMM Incorporated, 20 438–41; 47 317–21 (upd.); 114 337–43 (upd.)

Quality Chekd Dairies, Inc., 48 337–39

Quality Dining, Inc., 18 437–40

Quality Food Centers, Inc., 17 386–88 *see also* Kroger Co.

Quality King Distributors, Inc., 114 344–47

Quality Systems, Inc., 81 328–31

Quanex Corporation, 13 422–24; 62 286–89 (upd.)

Quanta Computer Inc., 47 322–24; 110 385–89 (upd.)

Quanta Services, Inc., 79 338–41

Quantum Chemical Corporation, 8 439–41

Quantum Corporation, 10 458–59; 62 290–93 (upd.)

Quark, Inc., 36 375–79

Québéc Hydro-Electric Commission *see* Hydro-Quebéc.

Quebecor Inc., 12 412–14; 47 325–28 (upd.)

Quelle Group, V 165–67 *see also* Karstadt Quelle AG.

Quest Diagnostics Inc., 26 390–92; 106 383–87 (upd.)

Questar Corporation, 6 568–70; 26 386–89 (upd.)

The Quick & Reilly Group, Inc., 20 442–44

Quick Restaurants S.A., 94 357–60

Quicken Loans, Inc., 93 363–67

Quidel Corporation, 80 300–03

The Quigley Corporation, 62 294–97

Quiksilver, Inc., 18 441–43; 79 342–47 (upd.)

QuikTrip Corporation, 36 380–83

Quill Corporation, 28 375–77; 115 403–06 (upd.)

Quilmes Industrial (QUINSA) S.A., 67 315–17

Quinn Emanuel Urquhart Oliver & Hedges, LLP, 99 350–353

Quintiles Transnational Corporation, 21 423–25; 68 308–12 (upd.)

Quixote Corporation, 15 378–80

The Quizno's Corporation, 42 295–98

Quovadx Inc., 70 243–46

QVC Inc., 9 428–29; 58 284–87 (upd.)

Qwest Communications International, Inc., 37 312–17

# R

R&B, Inc., 51 305–07

R&R Partners Inc., 108 407–10

R.B. Pamplin Corp., 45 350–52

R.C. Bigelow, Inc., 49 334–36

R.C. Willey Home Furnishings, 72 291–93

R.G. Barry Corp., 17 389–91; 44 364–67 (upd.)

R. Griggs Group Limited, 23 399–402; 31 413–14

R.H. Macy & Co., Inc., V 168–70; 8 442–45 (upd.); 30 379–83 (upd.) *see also* Macy's, Inc.

R.J. Reynolds Tobacco Holdings, Inc., 30 384–87 (upd.)

R. M. Palmer Co., 89 362–64

R.P. Scherer Corporation, I 678–80 *see also* Cardinal Health, Inc.

R.R. Bowker LLC, 100 362–66

R.R. Donnelley & Sons Company, IV 660–62; 38 368–71 (upd.); 113 316–21 (upd.)

Rabobank Group, 26 419; 33 356–58

RAC *see* Roy Anderson Corp.

Racal-Datacom Inc., 11 408–10

Racal Electronics PLC, II 83–84 *see also* Thales S.A.

RaceTrac Petroleum, Inc., 111 415–18

Racing Champions Corporation, 37 318–20

Rack Room Shoes, Inc., 84 314–317

Radeberger Gruppe AG, 75 332–35

Radian Group Inc., 42 299–301 *see also* Onex Corp.

Radiant Systems Inc., 104 383–87

Radiation Therapy Services, Inc., 85 344–47

@radical.media, 103 347–50

Radio Flyer Inc., 34 368–70

Radio One, Inc., 67 318–21

RadioShack Corporation, 36 384–88 (upd.); 101 416–23 (upd.)

Radius Inc., 16 417–19

RAE Systems Inc., 83 311–314

RAG AG, 35 364–67; 60 247–51 (upd.)

Rag Shops, Inc., 30 365–67

Ragdoll Productions Ltd., 51 308–11

Raha-automaattiyhdistys (RAY), 110 390–94

Raiffeisen Zentralbank Österreich AG, 85 348–52

RailTex, Inc., 20 445–47

Railtrack Group PLC, 50 369–72

Rain Bird Corporation, 84 318–321

Rainbow Media Holdings LLC, 109 457–60

Rainforest Café, Inc., 25 386–88; 88 312–16 (upd.)

Rainier Brewing Company, 23 403–05

Raisio PLC, 99 354–357

Raleigh UK Ltd., 65 295–97

Raley's Inc., 14 396–98; 58 288–91 (upd.)

Rallye SA, 54 306–09

Rally's, 25 389–91; 68 313–16 (upd.)

Ralph Lauren *see* Polo/Ralph Lauren Corportion.

Ralphs Grocery Company, 35 368–70

Ralston Purina Company, II 561–63; 13 425–27 (upd.) *see also* Ralcorp Holdings, Inc.; Nestlé S.A.

Ramsay Youth Services, Inc., 41 322–24

Ramtron International Corporation, 89 365–68

Ranbaxy Laboratories Ltd., 70 247–49

RAND Corporation, 112 307–10

Rand McNally & Company, 28 378–81; 53 122

Randall's Food Markets, Inc., 40 364–67 *see also* Safeway Inc.

Random House Inc., 13 428–30; 31 375–80 (upd.); 106 388–98 (upd.)

Randon S.A. Implementos e Participações, 79 348–52

Randstad Holding nv, 16 420–22; 43 307–10 (upd.); 113 322–26 (upd.)

Range Resources Corporation, 45 353–55

The Rank Group plc, II 157–59; 14 399–402 (upd.); 64 317–21 (upd.)

Ranks Hovis McDougall Limited, II 564–65; 28 382–85 (upd.)

RAO Unified Energy System of Russia, 45 356–60

Rapala-Normark Group, Ltd., 30 368–71

Rare Hospitality International Inc., 19 340–42

RAS *see* Riunione Adriatica di Sicurtà SpA.

Rascal House *see* Jerry's Famous Deli Inc.

Rasmussen Group *see* K.A. Rasmussen AS.

Rathbone Brothers plc, 70 250–53

RathGibson Inc., 90 348–51

ratiopharm Group, 84 322–326

Ratner Companies, 72 294–96

Rautakirja Oy, 104 388–92

Rautaruukki Oyj, 115 407–10

Raven Industries, Inc., 33 359–61

Ravensburger AG, 64 322–26

Raving Brands, Inc., 64 327–29

Rawlings Sporting Goods Company, 24 402–04; 107 368–72 (upd.)

Raychem Corporation, 8 446–47

Raycom Media, Inc., 106 399–402

Raymarine plc, 104 393–96

Raymond James Financial Inc., 69 308–10

Raymond Ltd., 77 351–54

Rayonier Inc., 24 405–07

Rayovac Corporation, 13 431–34; 39 336–40 (upd.) *see also* Spectrum Brands.

Raytech Corporation, 61 306–09

Raytheon Aircraft Holdings Inc., 46 354–57

Raytheon Company, II 85–87; 11 411–14 (upd.); 38 372–77 (upd.); 105 352–59 (upd.)

Razorfish, Inc., 37 321–24

RCA Corporation, II 88–90

RCM Technologies, Inc., 34 371–74

RCN Corporation, 70 254–57

RCS MediaGroup S.p.A., 96 343–46

RDO Equipment Company, 33 362–65

RE/MAX International, Inc., 59 344–46

Read-Rite Corp., 10 463–64

The Reader's Digest Association, Inc., IV 663–64; 17 392–95 (upd.); 71 295–99 (upd.)

Reading International Inc., 70 258–60

The Real Good Food Company plc, 99 358–361

Real Madrid C.F., 73 274–76

Sport Supply Group, Inc., 23 448–50; 106 440–45 (upd.)

Sportmart, Inc., 15 469–71 *see also* Gart Sports Co.

Sports & Recreation, Inc., 17 453–55

The Sports Authority, Inc., 16 457–59; 43 385–88 (upd.)

The Sports Club Company, 25 448–51

The Sportsman's Guide, Inc., 36 443–46

Springs Global US, Inc., V 378–79; 19 419–22 (upd.); 90 378–83 (upd.)

Sprint Nextel Corporation, 9 478–80; 46 373–76 (upd.); 110 427–33 (upd.)

SPS Technologies, Inc., 30 428–30

SPSS Inc., 64 360–63

SPX Corporation, 10 492–95; 47 374–79 (upd.); 103 401–09 (upd.)

Spyglass Entertainment Group, LLC, 91 441–44

SQM *see* Sociedad Química y Minera de Chile S.A.

Square D, 90 384–89

Square Enix Holdings Co., Ltd., 101 454–57

Squibb Corporation, I 695–97 *see also* Bristol-Myers Squibb Co.

SR Teleperformance S.A., 86 365–68

SRA International, Inc., 77 400–03

SRAM Corporation, 65 325–27

SRC Holdings Corporation, 67 358–60

SRI International, Inc., 57 333–36

SSA *see* Stevedoring Services of America Inc.

SSAB Svenskt Stål AB, 89 428–31

Ssangyong Cement Industrial Co., Ltd., III 747–50; 61 339–43 (upd.)

SSI (U.S.), Inc., 103 410–14 (upd.)

SSL International plc, 49 378–81

SSOE Inc., 76 333–35

St Ives plc, 34 393–95

St. *see under* Saint

St. James's Place Capital, plc, 71 324–26

The St. Joe Company, 31 422–25; 98 368–73 (upd.)

St. Joe Paper Company, 8 485–88

St. John Knits, Inc., 14 466–68

St. Jude Medical, Inc., 11 458–61; 43 347–52 (upd.); 97 350–58 (upd.)

St. Louis Music, Inc., 48 351–54

St. Luke's-Roosevelt Hospital Center *see* Continuum Health Partners, Inc.

St. Mary Land & Exploration Company, 63 345–47

St. Paul Bank for Cooperatives, 8 489–90

The St. Paul Travelers Companies, Inc., III 355–57; 22 492–95 (upd.); 79 362–69 (upd.)

STAAR Surgical Company, 57 337–39

The Stabler Companies Inc., 78 352–55

Stafford Group, 110 434–38

Stage Stores, Inc., 24 456–59; 82 348–52 (upd.)

Stagecoach Group plc, 30 431–33; 104 437–41 (upd.)

Stanadyne Automotive Corporation, 37 367–70

StanCorp Financial Group, Inc., 56 345–48

Standard Candy Company Inc., 86 369–72

Standard Chartered plc, II 357–59; 48 371–74 (upd.)

Standard Commercial Corporation, 13 490–92; 62 333–37 (upd.)

Standard Federal Bank, 9 481–83

Standard Life Assurance Company, III 358–61

Standard Microsystems Corporation, 11 462–64

Standard Motor Products, Inc., 40 414–17

Standard Pacific Corporation, 52 319–22

The Standard Register Company, 15 472–74; 93 419–25 (upd.)

Standex International Corporation, 17 456–59; 44 403–06 (upd.)

Stanhome Inc., 15 475–78

Stanley Furniture Company, Inc., 34 412–14

Stanley Leisure plc, 66 310–12

The Stanley Works, III 626–29; 20 476–80 (upd.); 79 383–91 (upd.)

Staple Cotton Cooperative Association (Staplcotn), 86 373–77

Staples, Inc., 10 496–98; 55 351–56 (upd.)

Star Banc Corporation, 11 465–67 *see also* Firstar Corp.

Star of the West Milling Co., 95 386–89

Starbucks Corporation, 13 493–94; 34 415–19 (upd.); 77 404–10 (upd.)

Starcraft Corporation, 30 434–36; 66 313–16 (upd.)

Starent Networks Corp., 106 446–50

StarHub Ltd., 77 411–14

Starkey Laboratories, Inc., 52 323–25

StarKist Company, 113 368–72

Starrett *see* L.S. Starrett Co.

Starrett Corporation, 21 471–74

StarTek, Inc., 79 392–95

Starter Corp., 12 457–458

Starwood Hotels & Resorts Worldwide, Inc., 54 345–48

Starz LLC, 91 445–50

The Stash Tea Company, 50 449–52

State Auto Financial Corporation, 77 415–19

State Bank of India, 63 354–57

State Farm Mutual Automobile Insurance Company, III 362–64; 51 341–45 (upd.)

State Financial Services Corporation, 51 346–48

State Grid Corporation of China, 108 470–74

State Street Corporation, 8 491–93; 57 340–44 (upd.)

Staten Island Bancorp, Inc., 39 380–82

Stater Bros. Holdings Inc., 64 364–67

Station Casinos, Inc., 25 452–54; 90 390–95 (upd.)

Statnett SF, 110 439–42

Statoil ASA, 61 344–48 (upd.)

The Staubach Company, 62 338–41

STC PLC, III 162–64 *see also* Nortel Networks Corp.

Ste. Michelle Wine Estates Ltd., 96 408–11

The Steak n Shake Company, 41 387–90; 96 412–17 (upd.)

Steamships Trading Company Ltd., 82 353–56

Stearns, Inc., 43 389–91

Steel Authority of India Ltd., IV 205–07; 66 317–21 (upd.)

Steel Dynamics, Inc., 52 326–28

Steel Technologies Inc., 63 358–60

Steelcase Inc., 7 493–95; 27 432–35 (upd.); 110 443–50 (upd.)

Stefanel SpA, 63 361–63

Steiff *see* Margarete Steiff GmbH.

Steilmann Group *see* Klaus Steilmann GmbH & Co. KG.

Stein Mart Inc., 19 423–25; 72 337–39 (upd.)

Steinberg Incorporated, II 662–65

Steiner Corporation (Alsco), 53 308–11

Steinway Musical Instruments, Inc., 19 426–29; 111 446–51 (upd.)

Stelco Inc., IV 208–10; 51 349–52 (upd.)

Stelmar Shipping Ltd., 52 329–31

Stemilt Growers Inc., 94 407–10

Stepan Company, 30 437–39; 105 438–42 (upd.)

The Stephan Company, 60 285–88

Stephens Inc., 92 344–48

Stephens Media, LLC, 91 451–54

Steria SA, 49 382–85

Stericycle, Inc., 33 380–82; 74 316–18 (upd.)

Sterilite Corporation, 97 382–85

STERIS Corporation, 29 449–52

Sterling Chemicals, Inc., 16 460–63; 78 356–61 (upd.)

Sterling Drug Inc., I 698–700

Sterling Electronics Corp., 18 496–98

Sterling European Airlines A/S, 70 300–02

Sterling Financial Corporation, 106 451–55

Sterling Software, Inc., 11 468–70 *see also* Computer Associates International, Inc.

STET *see* Società Finanziaria Telefonica per Azioni.

Steuben Glass *see* Corning Inc.

Steve & Barry's LLC, 88 377–80

Stevedoring Services of America Inc., 28 435–37

Steven Madden, Ltd., 37 371–73

Stew Leonard's, 56 349–51

Stewart & Stevenson Services Inc., 11 471–73

Stewart Enterprises, Inc., 20 481–83

Stewart Information Services Corporation, 78 362–65

Stewart's Beverages, 39 383–86

United Microelectronics Corporation, 98 421–24

United National Group, Ltd., 63 410–13

United Nations International Children's Emergency Fund (UNICEF), 58 349–52

United Natural Foods, Inc., 32 479–82; 76 360–63 (upd.)

United Negro College Fund, Inc., 79 447–50

United News & Media plc, 28 501–05 (upd.) *see also* United Business Media plc.

United Newspapers plc, IV 685–87 *see also* United Business Media plc.

United Online, Inc., 71 372–77 (upd.)

United Overseas Bank Ltd., 56 362–64

United Pan-Europe Communications NV, 47 414–17

United Paper Mills Ltd., IV 347–50 *see also* UPM-Kymmene Corp.

United Parcel Service, Inc., V 533–35; 17 503–06 (upd.); 63 414–19; 94 425–30 (upd.)

United Press International, Inc., 25 506–09; 73 354–57 (upd.)

United Rentals, Inc., 34 466–69

United Retail Group Inc., 33 426–28

United Road Services, Inc., 69 360–62

United Service Organizations, 60 308–11

United Services Automobile Association, 109 559–65 (upd.)

United States Cellular Corporation, 9 527–29 *see also* U.S. Cellular Corp.

United States Filter Corporation, 20 501–04 *see also* Siemens AG.

United States Health Care Systems, Inc. *see* U.S. Healthcare, Inc.

United States Pipe and Foundry Company, 62 377–80

United States Playing Card Company, 62 381–84

United States Postal Service, 14 517–20; 34 470–75 (upd.); 108 516–24 (upd.)

United States Shoe Corporation, V 207–08

United States Soccer Federation, 108 525–28

United States Steel Corporation, 50 500–04 (upd.); 114 494–500 (upd.)

United States Sugar Corporation, 115 465–68

United States Surgical Corporation, 10 533–35; 34 476–80 (upd.)

United States Tennis Association, 111 503–06

United Stationers Inc., 14 521–23

United Talent Agency, Inc., 80 392–96

United Technologies Automotive Inc., 15 513–15

United Technologies Corporation, I 84–86; 10 536–38 (upd.); 34 481–85 (upd.); 105 455–61 (upd.)

United Telecommunications, Inc., V 344–47 *see also* Sprint Corp.

United Utilities PLC, 52 372–75 (upd.)

United Video Satellite Group, 18 535–37 *see also* TV Guide, Inc.

United Water Resources, Inc., 40 447–50; 45 277

United Way Worldwide, 36 485–88; 112 451–56 (upd.)

UnitedHealth Group Incorporated, 103 476–84 (upd.)

Unitika Ltd., V 387–89; 53 341–44 (upd.)

Unitil Corporation, 37 403–06

Unitog Co., 19 457–60 *see also* Cintas Corp.

Unitrin Inc., 16 503–05; 78 427–31 (upd.)

Unitymedia GmbH, 115 469–72

Univar Corporation, 9 530–32

Universal American Corp., 111 507–10

Universal Compression, Inc., 59 402–04

Universal Corporation, V 417–18; 48 403–06 (upd.)

Universal Electronics Inc., 39 405–08

Universal Foods Corporation, 7 546–48 *see also* Sensient Technologies Corp.

Universal Forest Products, Inc., 10 539–40; 59 405–09 (upd.)

Universal Health Services, Inc., 6 191–93

Universal International, Inc., 25 510–11

Universal Manufacturing Company, 88 423–26

Universal Security Instruments, Inc., 96 434–37

Universal Stainless & Alloy Products, Inc., 75 386–88

Universal Studios, Inc., 33 429–33; 100 423–29 (upd.)

Universal Technical Institute, Inc., 81 396–99

Universal Truckload Services, Inc., 111 511–14

The University of Chicago Press, 79 451–55

University of Phoenix *see* Apollo Group, Inc.

Univision Communications Inc., 24 515–18; 83 434–439 (upd.)

UNM *see* United News & Media plc.

Uno Restaurant Holdings Corporation, 18 538–40; 70 334–37 (upd.)

Unocal Corporation, IV 569–71; 24 519–23 (upd.); 71 378–84 (upd.)

UNUM Corp., 13 538–40

UnumProvident Corporation, 52 376–83 (upd.)

Uny Co., Ltd., V 209–10; 49 425–28 (upd.)

UOB *see* United Overseas Bank Ltd.

UPC *see* United Pan-Europe Communications NV.

UPI *see* United Press International.

Upjohn Company, I 707–09; 8 547–49 (upd.) *see also* Pharmacia & Upjohn Inc.; Pfizer Inc.

UPM-Kymmene Corporation, 19 461–65; 50 505–11 (upd.)

The Upper Deck Company, LLC, 105 462–66

UPS *see* United Parcel Service, Inc.

Uralita S.A., 96 438–41

Uranium One Inc., 111 515–18

Urban Engineers, Inc., 102 435–38

Urban Outfitters, Inc., 14 524–26; 74 367–70 (upd.)

Urbi Desarrollos Urbanos, S.A. de C.V., 81 400–03

Urbium PLC, 75 389–91

URS Corporation, 45 420–23; 80 397–400 (upd.)

URSI *see* United Road Services, Inc.

US *see also* U.S.

US Airways Group, Inc., I 131–32; 6 131–32 (upd.); 28 506–09 (upd.); 52 384–88 (upd.); 110 472–78 (upd.)

US 1 Industries, Inc., 89 475–78

USA Interactive, Inc., 47 418–22 (upd.)

USA Mobility Inc., 97 437–40 (upd.)

USA Truck, Inc., 42 410–13

USAA, 10 541–43; 62 385–88 (upd.) *see also* United Services Automobile Association.

USANA, Inc., 29 491–93

USCC *see* United States Cellular Corp.

USF&G Corporation, III 395–98 *see also* The St. Paul Companies.

USG Corporation, III 762–64; 26 507–10 (upd.); 81 404–10 (upd.)

Ushio Inc., 91 496–99

Usinas Siderúrgicas de Minas Gerais S.A., 77 454–57

Usinger's Famous Sausage *see* Fred Usinger Inc.

Usinor SA, IV 226–28; 42 414–17 (upd.)

USO *see* United Service Organizations.

USPS *see* United States Postal Service.

USSC *see* United States Surgical Corp.

UST Inc., 9 533–35; 50 512–17 (upd.)

USTA *see* United States Tennis Association

USX Corporation, IV 572–74; 7 549–52 (upd.) *see also* United States Steel Corp.

Utah Medical Products, Inc., 36 496–99

Utah Power and Light Company, 27 483–86 *see also* PacifiCorp.

UTG Inc., 100 430–33

Utilicorp United Inc., 6 592–94 *see also* Aquilla, Inc.

UTStarcom, Inc., 77 458–61

UTV *see* Ulster Television PLC.

Utz Quality Foods, Inc., 72 358–60

UUNET, 38 468–72

Uwajimaya, Inc., 60 312–14

Uzbekistan Airways National Air Company, 99 470–473

# V

V&S Vin & Sprit AB, 91 504–11 (upd.)

VA TECH ELIN EBG GmbH, 49 429–31

Vail Resorts, Inc., 11 543–46; 43 435–39 (upd.)

Vaillant GmbH, 44 436–39

Vaisala Oyj, 104 459–63

Valassis Communications, Inc., 8 550–51; 37 407–10 (upd.); 76 364–67 (upd.)

Warner-Lambert Co., I 710–12; 10 549–52 (upd.) *see also* Pfizer Inc.

Warner Music Group Corporation, 90 432–37 (upd.)

Warners' Stellian Inc., 67 384–87

Warrantech Corporation, 53 357–59

Warrell Corporation, 68 396–98

Warsteiner Group, 113 460–64

Wärtsilä Corporation, 100 442–46

Warwick Valley Telephone Company, 55 382–84

Wascana Energy Inc., 13 556–58

The Washington Companies, 33 442–45

Washington Federal, Inc., 17 525–27

Washington Football, Inc., 35 462–65

Washington Gas Light Company, 19 485–88

Washington H. Soul Pattinson and Company Limited, 112 486–91

Washington Mutual, Inc., 17 528–31; 93 483–89 (upd.)

Washington National Corporation, 12 524–26

Washington Natural Gas Company, 9 539–41 *see also* Puget Sound Energy Inc.

The Washington Post Company, IV 688–90; 20 515–18 (upd.); 109 577–83 (upd.)

Washington Scientific Industries, Inc., 17 532–34

Washington Water Power Company, 6 595–98 *see also* Avista Corp.

Wassall Plc, 18 548–50

Waste Connections, Inc., 46 455–57

Waste Holdings, Inc., 41 413–15

Waste Management Inc., V 752–54; 109 584–90 (upd.)

Water Pik Technologies, Inc., 34 498–501; 83 450–453 (upd.)

Waterford Wedgwood plc, 12 527–29; 34 493–97 (upd.) *see also* WWRD Holdings Ltd.

Waterhouse Investor Services, Inc., 18 551–53

Waters Corporation, 43 453–57

Watkins-Johnson Company, 15 528–30

Watsco Inc., 52 397–400

Watson Pharmaceuticals Inc., 16 527–29; 56 373–76 (upd.)

Watson Wyatt Worldwide, 42 427–30

Wattie's Ltd., 7 576–78

Watts of Lydney Group Ltd., 71 391–93

Watts Water Technologies, Inc., 19 489–91; 115 479–83 (upd.)

Wausau-Mosinee Paper Corporation, 60 328–31 (upd.)

Waverly, Inc., 16 530–32

Wawa Inc., 17 535–37; 78 449–52 (upd.)

The Wawanesa Mutual Insurance Company, 68 399–401

WAXIE Sanitary Supply, 100 447–51

Waxman Industries, Inc., 9 542–44

WAZ Media Group, 82 419–24

WB *see* Warner Communications Inc.

WD-40 Company, 18 554–57; 87 455–460 (upd.)

We-No-Nah Canoe, Inc., 98 460–63

WE: Women's Entertainment LLC, 114 506–10

Weather Central Inc., 100 452–55

The Weather Channel Companies, 52 401–04 *see also* Landmark Communications, Inc.

Weather Shield Manufacturing, Inc., 102 444–47

Weatherford International, Inc., 39 416–18

Weaver Popcorn Company, Inc., 89 491–93

Webasto Roof Systems Inc., 97 449–52

Webber Oil Company, 61 384–86

Weber et Broutin France, 66 363–65

Weber-Stephen Products Co., 40 458–60

WebEx Communications, Inc., 81 419–23

WebMD Corporation, 65 357–60

Webster Financial Corporation, 106 486–89

Weeres Industries Corporation, 52 405–07

Weetabix Limited, 61 387–89

Weg S.A., 78 453–56

Wegener NV, 53 360–62

Wegmans Food Markets, Inc., 9 545–46; 41 416–18 (upd.); 105 488–92 (upd.)

Weider Nutrition International, Inc., 29 498–501

Weight Watchers International Inc., 12 530–32; 33 446–49 (upd.); 73 379–83 (upd.)

Weil, Gotshal & Manges LLP, 55 385–87

Weiner's Stores, Inc., 33 450–53

Weingarten Realty Investors, 95 442–45

The Weir Group PLC, 85 450–53

Weirton Steel Corporation, IV 236–38; 26 527–30 (upd.)

Weis Markets, Inc., 15 531–33; 84 422–426 (upd.)

The Weitz Company, Inc., 42 431–34

Welbilt Corp., 19 492–94; *see also* Enodis plc.

Welch Foods Inc., 104 470–73

Welcome Wagon International Inc., 82 425–28

Weleda AG, 78 457–61

The Welk Group, Inc., 78 462–66

Wella AG, III 68–70; 48 420–23 (upd.)

WellCare Health Plans, Inc., 101 487–90

WellChoice, Inc., 67 388–91 (upd.)

Wellco Enterprises, Inc., 84 427–430

Wellcome Foundation Ltd., I 713–15 *see also* GlaxoSmithKline plc.

Wellman, Inc., 8 561–62; 52 408–11 (upd.)

WellPoint, Inc., 25 525–29; 103 505–14 (upd.)

Wells' Dairy, Inc., 36 511–13

Wells Fargo & Company, II 380–84; 12 533–37 (upd.); 38 483–92 (upd.); 97 453–67

Wells-Gardner Electronics Corporation, 43 458–61

Wells Rich Greene BDDP, 6 50–52

Welsh Rugby Union Limited, 115 484–87

Wendell *see* Mark T. Wendell Tea Co.

Wendy's International, Inc., 8 563–65; 23 504–07 (upd.); 47 439–44 (upd.)

Wenner Bread Products Inc., 80 411–15

Wenner Media, Inc., 32 506–09

Werhahn *see* Wilh. Werhahn KG.

Werner Enterprises, Inc., 26 531–33

Weru Aktiengesellschaft, 18 558–61

Wesfarmers Limited, 109 591–95

Wessanen *see* Koninklijke Wessanen nv.

West Bend Co., 14 546–48

West Coast Entertainment Corporation, 29 502–04

West Corporation, 42 435–37

West Fraser Timber Co. Ltd., 17 538–40; 91 512–18 (upd.)

West Group, 34 502–06 (upd.)

West Linn Paper Company, 91 519–22

West Marine, Inc., 17 541–43; 90 438–42 (upd.)

West One Bancorp, 11 552–55 *see also* U.S. Bancorp.

West Pharmaceutical Services, Inc., 42 438–41

West Point-Pepperell, Inc., 8 566–69 *see also* WestPoint Stevens Inc.; JPS Textile Group, Inc.

West Publishing Co., 7 579–81

Westaff Inc., 33 454–57

Westamerica Bancorporation, 17 544–47

Westar Energy, Inc., 57 404–07 (upd.)

WestCoast Hospitality Corporation, 59 410–13

Westcon Group, Inc., 67 392–94

Westdeutsche Landesbank Girozentrale, II 385–87; 46 458–61 (upd.)

Westell Technologies, Inc., 57 408–10

Western Atlas Inc., 12 538–40

Western Beef, Inc., 22 548–50

Western Company of North America, 15 534–36

Western Digital Corporation, 25 530–32; 92 411–15 (upd.)

Western Gas Resources, Inc., 45 435–37

Western Oil Sands Inc., 85 454–57

Western Publishing Group, Inc., 13 559–61 *see also* Thomson Corp.

Western Refining Inc., 109 596–99

Western Resources, Inc., 12 541–43

The WesterN SizzliN Corporation, 60 335–37

Western Union Company, 54 413–16; 112 492–96 (upd.)

Western Wireless Corporation, 36 514–16

Westfield Group, 69 366–69

Westin Hotels and Resorts Worldwide, 9 547–49; 29 505–08 (upd.)

Westinghouse Electric Corporation, II 120–22; 12 544–47 (upd.) *see also* CBS Radio Group.

# Index to Industries

## Accounting

American Institute of Certified Public
  Accountants (AICPA), 44
Andersen, 29 (upd.); 68 (upd.)
Automatic Data Processing, Inc., III; 9
  (upd.); 47 (upd.)
BDO Seidman LLP, 96
BKD LLP, 96
CPP International, LLC, 103
CROSSMARK, 79
Deloitte Touche Tohmatsu International,
  9; 29 (upd.)
Ernst & Young Global Limited, 9; 29
  (upd.); 108 (upd.)
FTI Consulting, Inc., 77
Grant Thornton International, 57
Huron Consulting Group Inc., 87
JKH Holding Co. LLC, 105
KPMG International, 33 (upd.); 108
  (upd.)
L.S. Starrett Co., 13
McLane Company, Inc., 13
NCO Group, Inc., 42
Paychex, Inc., 15; 46 (upd.)
PKF International, 78
Plante & Moran, LLP, 71
PRG-Schultz International, Inc., 73
PricewaterhouseCoopers International
  Limited, 9; 29 (upd.); 111 (upd.)
Resources Connection, Inc., 81
Robert Wood Johnson Foundation, 35
RSM McGladrey Business Services Inc.,
  98
Saffery Champness, 80
Sanders\Wingo, 99
Schenck Business Solutions, 88
StarTek, Inc., 79
Travelzoo Inc., 79

Univision Communications Inc., 24; 83
  (upd.)

## Advertising & Business Services

ABM Industries Incorporated, 25 (upd.)
Abt Associates Inc., 95
Accenture Ltd., 108 (upd.)
AchieveGlobal Inc., 90
Ackerley Communications, Inc., 9
ACNielsen Corporation, 13; 38 (upd.)
Acosta Sales and Marketing Company,
  Inc., 77
Acsys, Inc., 44
Adecco S.A., 36 (upd.)
Adelman Travel Group, 105
Adia S.A., 6
Administaff, Inc., 52
Advertising Council, Inc., The, 76
Advisory Board Company, The, 80
Advo, Inc., 6; 53 (upd.)
Aegis Group plc, 6
Affiliated Computer Services, Inc., 61
AHL Services, Inc., 27
Allegis Group, Inc., 95
Alloy, Inc., 55
Amdocs Ltd., 47
American Building Maintenance
  Industries, Inc., 6
Amey Plc, 47
Analysts International Corporation, 36
aQuantive, Inc., 81
Arbitron Company, The, 38
Ariba, Inc., 57
Armor Holdings, Inc., 27
Asatsu-DK Inc., 82
Ashtead Group plc, 34
Associated Press, The, 13

Avalon Correctional Services, Inc., 75
Bain & Company, 55
Barrett Business Services, Inc., 16
Barton Protective Services Inc., 53
Bates Worldwide, Inc., 14; 33 (upd.)
Bearings, Inc., 13
Berlitz International, Inc., 13; 39 (upd.)
Bernard Hodes Group Inc., 86
Bernstein-Rein, 92
Big Flower Press Holdings, Inc., 21
Billing Concepts, Inc., 26; 72 (upd.)
Billing Services Group Ltd., 102
BISYS Group, Inc., The, 73
Booz Allen Hamilton Inc., 10; 101 (upd.)
Boron, LePore & Associates, Inc., 45
Boston Consulting Group, The, 58
Bozell Worldwide Inc., 25
BrandPartners Group, Inc., 58
Bright Horizons Family Solutions, Inc., 31
Brink's Company, The, 58 (upd.)
Broadcast Music Inc., 23; 90 (upd.)
Bronner Display & Sign Advertising, Inc.,
  82
Buck Consultants, Inc., 55
Bureau Veritas SA, 55
Burke, Inc., 88
Burns International Services Corporation,
  13; 41 (upd.)
Cambridge Technology Partners, Inc., 36
Campbell-Ewald Advertising, 86
Campbell-Mithun-Esty, Inc., 16
Cannon Design, 63
Capario, 104
Capita Group PLC, 69
Cardtronics, Inc., 93
Carmichael Lynch Inc., 28
Cash Systems, Inc., 93
Cazenove Group plc, 72
CCC Information Services Group Inc., 74

## Aerospace

## Agribusiness & Farming

## Airlines

Trico Products Corporation, 15
Triumph Motorcycles Ltd., 53
TRW Automotive Holdings Corp., 75 (upd.)
TRW Inc., 14 (upd.)
Ugly Duckling Corporation, 22
United Auto Group, Inc., 26; 68 (upd.)
United Technologies Automotive Inc., 15
Universal Technical Institute, Inc., 81
Valeo, 23; 66 (upd.)
Van Hool S.A./NV, 96
Vauxhall Motors Limited, 73
Visteon Corporation, 109
Volkswagen Aktiengesellschaft, I; 11 (upd.); 32 (upd.); 111 (upd.)
Wagon plc, 92
Walker Manufacturing Company, 19
Webasto Roof Systems Inc., 97
Wilhelm Karmann GmbH, 94
Winnebago Industries, Inc., 7; 27 (upd.); 96 (upd.)
Woodward Governor Company, 13; 49 (upd.); 105 (upd.)
Yokohama Rubber Company, Limited, The, V; 19 (upd.); 91 (upd.)
ZF Friedrichshafen AG, 48
Ziebart International Corporation, 30; 66 (upd.)

## Beverages

A & W Brands, Inc., 25
A. Smith Bowman Distillery, Inc., 104
Adolph Coors Company, I; 13 (upd.); 36 (upd.)
AG Barr plc, 64
Ajegroup S.A., 92
Allied Domecq PLC, 29
Allied-Lyons PLC, I
Anadolu Efes Biracilik ve Malt Sanayii A.S., 95
Anchor Brewing Company, 47
Andrew Peller Ltd., 101
Angostura Holdings Ltd., 114
Anheuser-Busch InBev, I; 10 (upd.); 34 (upd.); 100 (upd.)
Apple & Eve L.L.C., 92
Asahi Breweries, Ltd., I; 20 (upd.); 52 (upd.); 108 (upd.)
Asia Pacific Breweries Limited, 59
August Schell Brewing Company Inc., 59
Bacardi & Company Ltd., 18; 82 (upd.)
Baltika Brewery Joint Stock Company, 65
Banfi Products Corp., 36; 114 (upd.)
Baron de Ley S.A., 74
Baron Philippe de Rothschild S.A., 39
Bass PLC, I; 15 (upd.); 38 (upd.)
Bavaria S.A., 90
BBAG Osterreichische Brau-Beteiligungs-AG, 38
Belvedere S.A., 93
Ben Hill Griffin, Inc., 110
Berentzen-Gruppe AG, 113
Beringer Blass Wine Estates Ltd., 22; 66 (upd.)
Bernick Companies, The, 75
Bitburger Braugruppe GmbH, 110
Blue Ridge Beverage Company Inc., 82
Boizel Chanoine Champagne S.A., 94

Bols Distilleries NV, 74
Boston Beer Company, Inc., The, 18; 50 (upd.); 108 (upd.)
Brauerei Beck & Co., 9; 33 (upd.)
Britannia Soft Drinks Ltd. (Britvic), 71
Bronco Wine Company, 101
Brooklyn Brewery, The, 109
Brouwerijen Alken-Maes N.V., 86
Brown-Forman Corporation, I; 10 (upd.); 38 (upd.); 114 (upd.)
Budweiser Budvar, National Corporation, 59
Cadbury Schweppes PLC, 49 (upd.)
Cains Beer Company PLC, 99
California Dairies Inc., 111
Cameron Hughes Wine, 103
Canandaigua Brands, Inc., 13; 34 (upd.)
Cantine Giorgio Lungarotti S.R.L., 67
Caribou Coffee Company, Inc., 28; 97 (upd.)
Carlsberg A/S, 9; 29 (upd.); 98 (upd.)
Carlton and United Breweries Ltd., I
Casa Cuervo, S.A. de C.V., 31
Central European Distribution Corporation, 75
Cerveceria Polar, I
Chalone Wine Group, Ltd., The, 36
Champagne Bollinger S.A., 114
Charmer Sunbelt Group, The, 95
City Brewing Company LLC, 73
Clearly Canadian Beverage Corporation, 48
Clement Pappas & Company, Inc., 92
Click Wine Group, 68
Coca Cola Bottling Co. Consolidated, 10
Coca-Cola Company, The, I; 10 (upd.); 32 (upd.); 67 (upd.)
Coffee Holding Co., Inc., 95
Companhia de Bebidas das Américas, 57
Compania Cervecerias Unidas S.A., 70
Constellation Brands, Inc., 68 (upd.)
Corby Distilleries Limited, 14
Cott Corporation, 52
D.G. Yuengling & Son, Inc., 38
Dairylea Cooperative Inc., 111
Dallis Coffee, Inc., 86
Daniel Thwaites Plc, 95
Davide Campari-Milano S.p.A., 57
Dean Foods Company, 21 (upd.)
Delicato Vineyards, Inc., 50
Deschutes Brewery, Inc., 57
Desnoes and Geddes Limited, 79
Diageo plc, 79 (upd.)
Direct Wines Ltd., 84
Distillers Company PLC, I
Double-Cola Co.-USA, 70
Dr Pepper/Seven Up, Inc., 9; 32 (upd.)
Drie Mollen Holding B.V., 99
Drinks Americas Holdings, LTD., 105
E. & J. Gallo Winery, I; 7 (upd.); 28 (upd.); 104 (upd.)
Eckes AG, 56
Edrington Group Ltd., The, 88
Embotelladora Andina S.A., 71
Empresas Polar SA, 55 (upd.)
Energy Brands Inc., 88
F. Korbel & Bros. Inc., 68
Faygo Beverages Inc., 55

Federico Paternina S.A., 69
Ferolito, Vultaggio & Sons, 27; 100 (upd.)
Fiji Water LLC, 74
Florida's Natural Growers, 45
Foster's Group Limited, 7; 21 (upd.); 50 (upd.); 111 (upd.)
Freixenet S.A., 71
Frucor Beverages Group Ltd., 96
Fuller Smith & Turner P.L.C., 38
G. Heileman Brewing Company Inc., I
Gambrinus Company, The, 40
Gano Excel Enterprise Sdn. Bhd., 89
Gatorade Company, The, 82
Geerlings & Wade, Inc., 45
General Cinema Corporation, I
Glazer's Wholesale Drug Company, Inc., 82
Gluek Brewing Company, 75
Golden State Vintners, Inc., 33
Gosling Brothers Ltd., 82
Grand Metropolitan PLC, I
Grands Vins Jean-Claude Boisset S.A., 98
Green Mountain Coffee Roasters, Inc., 31; 107 (upd.)
Greenalls Group PLC, The, 21
Greene King plc, 31
Groupe Danone, 32 (upd.); 93 (upd.)
Grupo Industrial Herradura, S.A. de C.V., 83
Grupo Modelo, S.A. de C.V., 29
Gruppo Italiano Vini, 111
Guinness/UDV, I; 43 (upd.)
Hain Celestial Group, Inc., The, 43 (upd.)
Hansen Natural Corporation, 31; 76 (upd.)
Heineken N.V, I; 13 (upd.); 34 (upd.); 90 (upd.)
Heublein, Inc., I
High Falls Brewing Company LLC, 74
Hindustan Lever Limited, 79
Hiram Walker Resources, Ltd., I
Hite Brewery Company Ltd., 97
illycaffè S.p.A., 50; 110 (upd.)
Imagine Foods, Inc., 50
Interbrew S.A., 17; 50 (upd.)
Irish Distillers Group, 96
Ito En Ltd., 101
J.J. Darboven GmbH & Co. KG, 96
J. Lohr Winery Corporation, 99
Jacob Leinenkugel Brewing Company, 28
JD Wetherspoon plc, 30
Jim Beam Brands Worldwide, Inc., 58 (upd.)
John Dewar & Sons, Ltd., 82
Jones Soda Co., 69
Jugos del Valle, S.A. de C.V., 85
Karlsberg Brauerei GmbH & Co KG, 41
Kemps LLC, 103
Kendall-Jackson Winery, Ltd., 28
Kikkoman Corporation, 14
Kirin Brewery Company, Limited, I; 21 (upd.); 63 (upd.)
Kobrand Corporation, 82
König Brauerei GmbH & Co. KG, 35 (upd.)

## Bio-Technology

Invitrogen Corporation, 52
Judge Group, Inc., The, 51
Kendle International Inc., 87
Landec Corporation, 95
Life Technologies, Inc., 17
LifeCell Corporation, 77
Lonza Group Ltd., 73
Martek Biosciences Corporation, 65
Medarex, Inc., 85
Medtronic, Inc., 8; 30 (upd.); 67 (upd.)
Meridian Bioscience, Inc., 115
Millipore Corporation, 25; 84 (upd.)
Minntech Corporation, 22
Mycogen Corporation, 21
Nektar Therapeutics, 91
New Brunswick Scientific Co., Inc., 45
Omrix Biopharmaceuticals, Inc., 95
Pacific Ethanol, Inc., 81
Pharmion Corporation, 91
Qiagen N.V., 39
Quintiles Transnational Corporation, 21
RTI Biologics, Inc., 96
Seminis, Inc., 29
Senomyx, Inc., 83
Serologicals Corporation, 63
Sigma-Aldrich Corporation, I; 36 (upd.);
   93 (upd.)
Starkey Laboratories, Inc., 52
STERIS Corporation, 29
Stratagene Corporation, 70
Talecris Biotherapeutics Holdings Corp.,
   114
Tanox, Inc., 77
TECHNE Corporation, 52
TriPath Imaging, Inc., 77
Viterra Inc., 105
Waters Corporation, 43
Whatman plc, 46
Wilmar International Ltd., 108
Wisconsin Alumni Research Foundation,
   65
Wyeth, 50 (upd.)

## Chemicals

A. Schulman, Inc., 8; 49 (upd.)
Aceto Corp., 38
Air Products and Chemicals, Inc., I; 10
   (upd.); 74 (upd.)
Airgas, Inc., 54
Akzo Nobel N.V., 13; 41 (upd.); 112
   (upd.)
Albaugh, Inc., 105
Albemarle Corporation, 59
AlliedSignal Inc., 9; 22 (upd.)
ALTANA AG, 87
American Cyanamid, I; 8 (upd.)
American Vanguard Corporation, 47
Arab Potash Company, 85
Arch Chemicals Inc., 78
ARCO Chemical Company, 10
Arkema S.A., 100
Asahi Denka Kogyo KK, 64
Atanor S.A., 62
Atochem S.A., I
Avantium Technologies BV, 79
Avecia Group PLC, 63
Azelis Group, 100

Baker Hughes Incorporated, III; 22
   (upd.); 57 (upd.)
Balchem Corporation, 42
BASF SE, I; 18 (upd.); 50 (upd.); 108
   (upd.)
Bayer A.G., I; 13 (upd.); 41 (upd.)
Betz Laboratories, Inc., I; 10 (upd.)
BFGoodrich Company, The, 19 (upd.)
BOC Group plc, I; 25 (upd.); 78 (upd.)
BorsodChem Zrt., 113
Braskem S.A., 108
Brenntag Holding GmbH & Co. KG, 8;
   23 (upd.); 101 (upd.)
Burmah Castrol PLC, 30 (upd.)
Cabot Corporation, 8; 29 (upd.); 91
   (upd.)
Calgon Carbon Corporation, 73
Caliper Life Sciences, Inc., 70
Calumet Specialty Products Partners, L.P.,
   106
Cambrex Corporation, 16
Campbell Brothers Limited, 115
Catalytica Energy Systems, Inc., 44
Celanese Corporation, I; 109 (upd.)
Celanese Mexicana, S.A. de C.V., 54
CF Industries Holdings, Inc., 99
Chemcentral Corporation, 8
Chemi-Trol Chemical Co., 16
Chemtura Corporation, 91 (upd.)
China Petroleum & Chemical
   Corporation (Sinopec Corp.), 109
Church & Dwight Co., Inc., 29
Ciba-Geigy Ltd., I; 8 (upd.)
Clorox Company, The, III; 22 (upd.); 81
   (upd.)
Croda International Plc, 45
Crompton Corporation, 9; 36 (upd.)
Cytec Industries Inc., 27
Degussa-Hüls AG, 32 (upd.)
DeKalb Genetics Corporation, 17
Dexter Corporation, The, I; 12 (upd.)
Dionex Corporation, 46
Dow Chemical Company, The, I; 8
   (upd.); 50 (upd.); 114 (upd.)
DSM N.V., I; 56 (upd.)
Dynaction S.A., 67
E.I. du Pont de Nemours & Company, I;
   8 (upd.); 26 (upd.); 73 (upd.)
Eastman Chemical Company, 14; 38
   (upd.)
Ecolab Inc., I; 13 (upd.); 34 (upd.); 85
   (upd.)
Eka Chemicals AB, 92
Elementis plc, 40 (upd.)
Engelhard Corporation, 72 (upd.)
English China Clays Ltd., 15 (upd.); 40
   (upd.)
Enterprise Rent-A-Car Company, 69
   (upd.)
Equistar Chemicals, LP, 71
Ercros S.A., 80
ERLY Industries Inc., 17
Ethyl Corporation, I; 10 (upd.)
Evonik Industries AG, 111 (upd.)
Ferro Corporation, 8; 56 (upd.)
Firmenich International S.A., 60
First Mississippi Corporation, 8
FMC Corporation, 89 (upd.)

Formosa Plastics Corporation, 14; 58
   (upd.)
Fort James Corporation, 22 (upd.)
Fuchs Petrolub AG, 102
G.A.F., I
General Chemical Group Inc., The, 37
Georgia Gulf Corporation, 9; 61 (upd.)
Givaudan SA, 43
Great Lakes Chemical Corporation, I; 14
   (upd.)
GROWMARK, Inc., 88
Grupo Comex, 115
Guerbet Group, 46
H.B. Fuller Company, 8; 32 (upd.); 75
   (upd.)
Hauser, Inc., 46
Hawkins Chemical, Inc., 16
Henkel KGaA, III; 34 (upd.); 95 (upd.)
Hercules Inc., I; 22 (upd.); 66 (upd.)
Hillyard, Inc., 114
Hoechst A.G., I; 18 (upd.)
Hoechst Celanese Corporation, 13
Huls A.G., I
Huntsman Corporation, 8; 98 (upd.)
Ikonics Corporation, 99
IMC Fertilizer Group, Inc., 8
Imperial Chemical Industries PLC, I; 50
   (upd.)
Inergy L.P., 110
International Flavors & Fragrances Inc., 9;
   38 (upd.)
Israel Chemicals Ltd., 55
KBR Inc., 106 (upd.)
Kemira Oyj, 70
KMG Chemicals, Inc., 101
Koppers Industries, Inc., I; 26 (upd.)
Kwizda Holding GmbH, 102 (upd.)
L'Air Liquide SA, I; 47 (upd.)
Lawter International Inc., 14
LeaRonal, Inc., 23
Loctite Corporation, 30 (upd.)
Lonza Group Ltd., 73
Loos & Dilworth, Inc., 100
Lubrizol Corporation, The, I; 30 (upd.);
   83 (upd.)
LyondellBasell Industries Holdings N.V.,
   45 (upd.); 109 (upd.)
M.A. Hanna Company, 8
MacDermid Incorporated, 32
Makhteshim-Agan Industries Ltd., 85
Mallinckrodt Group Inc., 19
MBC Holding Company, 40
Melamine Chemicals, Inc., 27
Methanex Corporation, 40
Mexichem, S.A.B. de C.V., 99
Minerals Technologies Inc., 52 (upd.)
Mississippi Chemical Corporation, 39
Mitsubishi Chemical Corporation, I; 56
   (upd.)
Mitsui Petrochemical Industries, Ltd., 9
Monsanto Company, I; 9 (upd.); 29
   (upd.)
Montedison SpA, I
Morton International Inc., I; 9 (upd.); 80
   (upd.)
Mosaic Company, The, 91
Nagase & Company, Ltd., 8

## Conglomerates

## Construction

Ledcor Industries Limited, 46
Lennar Corporation, 11
L'Entreprise Jean Lefebvre, 23
Lincoln Property Company, 8
Lindal Cedar Homes, Inc., 29
Linde A.G., I
M. A. Mortenson Company, 115
Manitowoc Company, Inc., The, 18; 59 (upd.)
MasTec, Inc., 55
Matrix Service Company, 65
May Gurney Integrated Services PLC, 95
McCarthy Building Companies, Inc., 48
MDU Resources Group, Inc., 114 (upd.)
Mellon-Stuart Company, I
Michael Baker Corp., 14
Modtech Holdings, Inc., 77
Morrison Knudsen Corporation, 7; 28 (upd.)
Morrow Equipment Co. L.L.C., 87
Mota-Engil, SGPS, S.A., 97
New Holland N.V., 22
Newpark Resources, Inc., 63
Nortek, Inc., 34
NVR Inc., 8; 70 (upd.)
Obayashi Corporation, 78
Obrascon Huarte Lain S.A., 76
O'Connell Companies Inc., The, 100
Ohbayashi Corporation, I
Opus Corporation, 34; 101 (upd.)
Orascom Construction Industries S.A.E., 87
Orleans Homebuilders, Inc., 62
Panattoni Development Company, Inc., 99
Parsons Brinckerhoff Inc., 34; 104 (upd.)
Parsons Corporation, The, 8; 56 (upd.)
PCL Construction Group Inc., 50
Peninsular & Oriental Steam Navigation Company (Bovis Division), The, I
Pepper Construction Group, LLC, The, 111
Perini Corporation, 8; 82 (upd.)
Peter Kiewit Sons' Inc., 8
Philipp Holzmann AG, 17
Pinguely-Haulotte SA, 51
Post Properties, Inc., 26
Pulte Homes, Inc., 8; 42 (upd.); 113 (upd.)
Pyramid Companies, 54
Redrow Group plc, 31
Rinker Group Ltd., 65
RMC Group p.l.c., III; 34 (upd.)
Robertson-Ceco Corporation, 19
Rooney Brothers Co., 25
Rottlund Company, Inc., The, 28
Roy Anderson Corporation, 75
Ryan Companies US, Inc., 99
Ryland Group, Inc., The, 8; 37 (upd.); 107 (upd.)
Sandvik AB, IV; 32 (upd.); 77 (upd.)
Schuff Steel Company, 26
Seddon Group Ltd., 67
Servidyne Inc., 100 (upd.)
Shimizu Corporation, 109
Shorewood Packaging Corporation, 28
Simon Property Group Inc., 27; 84 (upd.)
Skanska AB, 38; 110 (upd.)

Skidmore, Owings & Merrill LLP, 69 (upd.)
SNC-Lavalin Group Inc., 72
Speedy Hire plc, 84
Stabler Companies Inc., 78
Standard Pacific Corporation, 52
Stone & Webster, Inc., 64 (upd.)
Strabag SE, 113
Structure Tone Organization, The, 99
Suffolk Construction Company, Inc., 114
Sundt Corp., 24
Swinerton Inc., 43
Tarmac Limited, III; 28 (upd.); 95 (upd.)
Taylor Wimpey PLC, I; 38 (upd.); 115 (upd.)
Technical Olympic USA, Inc., 75
Terex Corporation, 7; 40 (upd.); 91 (upd.)
ThyssenKrupp AG, IV; 28 (upd.); 87 (upd.)
TIC Holdings Inc., 92
Tishman Construction Company, 112
Toll Brothers Inc., 15; 70 (upd.)
Trammell Crow Company, 8
Tridel Enterprises Inc., 9
Tully Construction Co. Inc., 114
Turner Construction Company, 66
Turner Corporation, The, 8; 23 (upd.)
U.S. Aggregates, Inc., 42
U.S. Home Corporation, 8; 78 (upd.)
Urban Engineers, Inc., 102
Urbi Desarrollos Urbanos, S.A. de C.V., 81
VA TECH ELIN EBG GmbH, 49
Vecellio Group, Inc., 113
Veidekke ASA, 98
Veit Companies, 43; 92 (upd.)
Vinci S.A., 113 (upd.)
Wacker Construction Equipment AG, 95
Walbridge Aldinger Co., 38
Walter Industries, Inc., III; 22 (upd.); 72 (upd.)
Weitz Company, Inc., The, 42
Whiting-Turner Contracting Company, 95
Willbros Group, Inc., 56
William Lyon Homes, 59
Wilson Bowden Plc, 45
Wood Hall Trust PLC, I
WorleyParsons Ltd., 115
Yates Companies, Inc., The, 62
Zachry Group, Inc., 95

## Containers

Ball Corporation, I; 10 (upd.); 78 (upd.)
BWAY Corporation, 24
Chesapeake Corporation, 8; 30 (upd.); 93 (upd.)
CLARCOR Inc., 17; 61 (upd.)
Constar International Inc., 64
Continental Can Co., Inc., 15
Continental Group Company, I
Crown Cork & Seal Company, Inc., I; 13 (upd.); 32 (upd.)
Crown Holdings, Inc., 83 (upd.)
DIC Corporation, 115
Gaylord Container Corporation, 8
Golden Belt Manufacturing Co., 16

Graham Packaging Holdings Company, 87
Greif Inc., 15; 66 (upd.)
Grupo Industrial Durango, S.A. de C.V., 37
Hanjin Shipping Co., Ltd., 50
Heekin Can Inc., 13
Inland Container Corporation, 8
Interpool, Inc., 92
Kerr Group Inc., 24
Keyes Fibre Company, 9
Libbey Inc., 49
Liqui-Box Corporation, 16
Longaberger Company, The, 12
Longview Fibre Company, 8
Mead Corporation, The, 19 (upd.)
Metal Box PLC, I
Mobile Mini, Inc., 58
Molins plc, 51
National Can Corporation, I
Owens-Illinois, Inc., I; 26 (upd.); 85 (upd.)
Packaging Corporation of America, 51 (upd.)
Pochet SA, 55
Primerica Corporation, I
Printpack, Inc., 68
PVC Container Corporation, 67
Rexam PLC, 32 (upd.); 85 (upd.)
Reynolds Metals Company, 19 (upd.)
Royal Packaging Industries Van Leer N.V., 30
RPC Group PLC, 81
Sealright Co., Inc., 17
Shurgard Storage Centers, Inc., 52
Smurfit Kappa Group plc, 112 (upd.)
Smurfit-Stone Container Corporation, 26 (upd.); 83 (upd.)
Sonoco Products Company, 8; 89 (upd.)
Thermos Company, 16
Tim-Bar Corporation, 110
Toyo Seikan Kaisha, Ltd., I
U.S. Can Corporation, 30
Ultra Pac, Inc., 24
Viatech Continental Can Company, Inc., 25 (upd.)
Vidrala S.A., 67
Vitro Corporativo S.A. de C.V., 34

## Drugs & Pharmaceuticals

A.L. Pharma Inc., 12
A. Nelson & Co. Ltd., 75
Abbott Laboratories, I; 11 (upd.); 40 (upd.); 93 (upd.)
Aché Laboratórios Farmacêuticas S.A., 105
Actavis Group hf., 103
Actelion Ltd., 83
Adolor Corporation, 101
Akorn, Inc., 32
Albany Molecular Research, Inc., 77
Alfresa Holdings Corporation, 108
Allergan, Inc., 77 (upd.)
Alpharma Inc., 35 (upd.)
ALZA Corporation, 10; 36 (upd.)
American Home Products, I; 10 (upd.)
American Oriental Bioengineering Inc., 93
American Pharmaceutical Partners, Inc., 69

## Education & Training

DeVry Inc., 29; 82 (upd.)
ECC International Corp., 42
Edison Schools Inc., 37
Educate Inc., 86 (upd.)
Education Management Corporation, 35
Educational Testing Service, 12; 62 (upd.)
GP Strategies Corporation, 64 (upd.)
Green Dot Public Schools, 99
Grupo Positivo, 105
Huntington Learning Centers, Inc., 55
ITT Educational Services, Inc., 39; 76 (upd.)
Jones Knowledge Group, Inc., 97
Kaplan, Inc., 42; 90 (upd.)
KinderCare Learning Centers, Inc., 13
Knowledge Learning Corporation, 51; 115 (upd.)
Kumon Institute of Education Co., Ltd., 72
LeapFrog Enterprises, Inc., 54
Learning Care Group, Inc., 76 (upd.)
Learning Company Inc., The, 24
Learning Tree International Inc., 24
Lincoln Educational Services Corporation, 111
LPA Holding Corporation, 81
Management and Training Corporation, 28
Mount Sinai Medical Center, 112
National Heritage Academies, Inc., 60
New School, The, 103
Noah Education Holdings Ltd., 97
Nobel Learning Communities, Inc., 37; 76 (upd.)
Plato Learning, Inc., 44
Renaissance Learning, Inc., 39; 100 (upd.)
Rosetta Stone Inc., 93
Scientific Learning Corporation, 95
Strayer Education, Inc., 53
Sylvan Learning Systems, Inc., 35
Whitman Education Group, Inc., 41
Youth Services International, Inc., 21

## Electrical & Electronics

ABB ASEA Brown Boveri Ltd., II; 22 (upd.)
ABB Ltd., 65 (upd.)
Acer Incorporated, 16; 73 (upd.)
Acuson Corporation, 10; 36 (upd.)
ADC Telecommunications, Inc., 30 (upd.)
Adtran Inc., 22
Advanced Circuits Inc., 67
Advanced Micro Devices, Inc., 6; 30 (upd.); 99 (upd.)
Advanced Technology Laboratories, Inc., 9
Agere Systems Inc., 61
Agilent Technologies Inc., 38; 93 (upd.)
Agilysys Inc., 76 (upd.)
Aiwa Co., Ltd., 30
AKG Acoustics GmbH, 62
Akzo Nobel N.V., 13; 41 (upd.)
Alienware Corporation, 81
Alliant Techsystems Inc., 30 (upd.); 77 (upd.)
AlliedSignal Inc., 9; 22 (upd.)
Alpine Electronics, Inc., 13
Alps Electric Co., Ltd., II; 44 (upd.)

Altera Corporation, 18; 43 (upd.); 115 (upd.)
Altron Incorporated, 20
Amdahl Corporation, 40 (upd.)
American Power Conversion Corporation, 24; 67 (upd.)
American Superconductor Corporation, 97
American Technical Ceramics Corp., 67
American Technology Corporation, 103
Amerigon Incorporated, 97
Amkor Technology, Inc., 69
AMP Incorporated, II; 14 (upd.)
Amphenol Corporation, 40
Amstrad plc, 48 (upd.)
Analog Devices, Inc., 10
Analogic Corporation, 23
Anam Group, 23
Anaren Microwave, Inc., 33
Andrew Corporation, 10; 32 (upd.)
Anixter International Inc., 88
Anritsu Corporation, 68
Anthem Electronics, Inc., 13
Apex Digital, Inc., 63
Apple Computer, Inc., 36 (upd.); 77 (upd.)
Applied Materials, Inc., 114 (upd.)
Applied Micro Circuits Corporation, 38
Applied Power Inc., 9; 32 (upd.)
Applied Signal Technology, Inc., 87
Argon ST, Inc., 81
Arotech Corporation, 93
ARRIS Group, Inc., 89
Arrow Electronics, Inc., 10; 50 (upd.); 110 (upd.)
Artesyn Technologies Inc., 46 (upd.)
Ascend Communications, Inc., 24
Astronics Corporation, 35
ASUSTeK Computer Inc., 107
Atari Corporation, 9; 23 (upd.); 66 (upd.)
ATI Technologies Inc., 79
Atmel Corporation, 17
ATMI, Inc., 93
AU Optronics Corporation, 67
Audiovox Corporation, 34; 90 (upd.)
Ault Incorporated, 34
Autodesk, Inc., 10; 89 (upd.)
Avnet Inc., 9; 111 (upd.)
AVX Corporation, 67
Axcelis Technologies, Inc., 95
Axsys Technologies, Inc., 93
Ballard Power Systems Inc., 73
Bang & Olufsen Holding A/S, 37; 86 (upd.)
Barco NV, 44
Bel Fuse, Inc., 53
Belden CDT Inc., 19; 76 (upd.)
Bell Microproducts Inc., 69
Benchmark Electronics, Inc., 40
Bharat Electronics Limited, 113
Bicoastal Corporation, II
Black Box Corporation, 20; 96 (upd.)
Blonder Tongue Laboratories, Inc., 48
Blue Coat Systems, Inc., 83
BMC Industries, Inc., 17; 59 (upd.)
Bogen Communications International, Inc., 62
Borrego Solar Systems, Inc., 111

Bose Corporation, 13; 36 (upd.)
Boston Acoustics, Inc., 22
Bowthorpe plc, 33
Braun GmbH, 51; 109 (upd.)
Bridgelux, Inc., 112
Brightpoint Inc., 18; 106 (upd.)
Brightstar Corp., 114
Broadcom Corporation, 34; 90 (upd.)
Bull S.A., 43 (upd.)
Burr-Brown Corporation, 19
BVR Systems (1998) Ltd., 93
Cabletron Systems, Inc., 10
Cadence Design Systems, Inc., 48 (upd.)
Cambridge SoundWorks, Inc., 48
Campbell Hausfeld, 115
Canadian Solar Inc., 105
Canon Inc., III; 18 (upd.); 79 (upd.)
Carbone Lorraine S.A., 33
Cardtronics, Inc., 93
Carl Zeiss AG, III; 34 (upd.); 91 (upd.)
Cash Systems, Inc., 93
CASIO Computer Co., Ltd., III; 16 (upd.); 40 (upd.)
C-COR.net Corp., 38
CDW Computer Centers, Inc., 52 (upd.)
Celestica Inc., 80
Checkpoint Systems, Inc., 39
Chi Mei Optoelectronics Corporation, 75
Christie Digital Systems, Inc., 103
Chubb, PLC, 50
Chunghwa Picture Tubes, Ltd., 75
Cirrus Logic, Inc., 48 (upd.)
Cisco Systems, Inc., 34 (upd.); 77 (upd.)
Citizen Watch Co., Ltd., III; 21 (upd.); 81 (upd.)
Clarion Company Ltd., 64
Cobham plc, 30
Cobra Electronics Corporation, 14
Coherent, Inc., 31
Cohu, Inc., 32
Color Kinetics Incorporated, 85
Comfort Systems USA, Inc., 101
Compagnie Générale d'Électricité, II
Concurrent Computer Corporation, 75
Conexant Systems Inc., 36; 106 (upd.)
Continental Graphics Corporation, 110
Cooper Industries, Inc., II; 44 (upd.)
Cray Inc., 75 (upd.)
Cray Research, Inc., 16 (upd.)
Creative Technology Ltd., 57
Cree Inc., 53
CTS Corporation, 39
Cubic Corporation, 19; 98 (upd.)
Cypress Semiconductor Corporation, 20; 48 (upd.)
D&H Distributing Co., 95
Dai Nippon Printing Co., Ltd., 57 (upd.)
Daiichikosho Company Ltd., 86
Daktronics, Inc., 32; 107 (upd.)
Dallas Semiconductor Corporation, 13; 31 (upd.)
DDi Corp., 97
De La Rue plc, 34 (upd.)
Dell Inc., 9; 31 (upd.); 63 (upd.)
DH Technology, Inc., 18
Dictaphone Healthcare Solutions, 78
Diehl Stiftung & Co. KG, 79
Digi International Inc., 9

Nexans SA, 54
Nintendo Company, Ltd., III; 7 (upd.);
  28 (upd.); 67 (upd.)
Nokia Corporation, II; 17 (upd.); 38
  (upd.); 77 (upd.)
Nortel Networks Corporation, 36 (upd.)
Northrop Grumman Corporation, 45
  (upd.); 111 (upd.)
Oak Technology, Inc., 22
Océ N.V., 24; 91 (upd.)
Oki Electric Industry Company, Limited,
  II
Omnicell, Inc., 89
OMRON Corporation, II; 28 (upd.); 115
  (upd.)
Oplink Communications, Inc., 106
OPTEK Technology Inc., 98
Orbit International Corp., 105
Orbotech Ltd., 75
Otari Inc., 89
Otter Tail Power Company, 18
Palm, Inc., 36; 75 (upd.)
Palomar Medical Technologies, Inc., 22
Parlex Corporation, 61
Peak Technologies Group, Inc., The, 14
Peavey Electronics Corporation, 16
Philips Electronics N.V., II; 13 (upd.)
Philips Electronics North America Corp.,
  13
Pioneer Electronic Corporation, III; 28
  (upd.)
Pioneer-Standard Electronics Inc., 19
Pitney Bowes Inc., III; 19 (upd.); 47
  (upd.)
Pittway Corporation, 9; 33 (upd.)
Pixelworks, Inc., 69
Planar Systems, Inc., 61
Plantronics, Inc., 106
Plessey Company, PLC, The, II
Plexus Corporation, 35; 80 (upd.)
Polaroid Corporation, III; 7 (upd.); 28
  (upd.); 93 (upd.)
Polk Audio, Inc., 34
Potter & Brumfield Inc., 11
Premier Industrial Corporation, 9
Protection One, Inc., 32
QUALCOMM Incorporated, 114 (upd.)
Quanta Computer Inc., 47; 79 (upd.);
  110 (upd.)
Racal Electronics PLC, II
RadioShack Corporation, 36 (upd.); 101
  (upd.)
Radius Inc., 16
RAE Systems Inc., 83
Ramtron International Corporation, 89
Raychem Corporation, 8
Raymarine plc, 104
Rayovac Corporation, 13; 39 (upd.)
Raytheon Company, II; 11 (upd.); 38
  (upd.); 105 (upd.)
RCA Corporation, II
Read-Rite Corp., 10
Redback Networks, Inc., 92
Reliance Electric Company, 9
Research in Motion Ltd., 54
Rexel, Inc., 15
Richardson Electronics, Ltd., 17

Ricoh Company, Ltd., III; 36 (upd.); 108
  (upd.)
Rimage Corp., 89
Rival Company, The, 19
Rockford Corporation, 43
Rogers Corporation, 61; 80 (upd.)
S&C Electric Company, 15
SAGEM S.A., 37
St. Louis Music, Inc., 48
Sam Ash Music Corporation, 30
Samsung Electronics Co., Ltd., 14; 41
  (upd.); 108 (upd.)
Sanmina-SCI Corporation, 109 (upd.)
SANYO Electric Co., Ltd., II; 36 (upd.);
  95 (upd.)
Sarnoff Corporation, 57
ScanSource, Inc., 29; 74 (upd.)
Schneider Electric SA, II; 18 (upd.); 108
  (upd.)
SCI Systems, Inc., 9
Scientific-Atlanta, Inc., 45 (upd.)
Scitex Corporation Ltd., 24
Seagate Technology, 8; 34 (upd.); 105
  (upd.)
SEGA Corporation, 73
Semitool, Inc., 79 (upd.)
Semtech Corporation, 32
Sennheiser Electronic GmbH & Co. KG,
  66
Sensormatic Electronics Corp., 11
Sensory Science Corporation, 37
SGI, 29 (upd.)
Sharp Corporation, II; 12 (upd.); 40
  (upd.); 114 (upd.)
Sheldahl Inc., 23
Shure Inc., 60
Siemens AG, II; 14 (upd.); 57 (upd.)
Sierra Nevada Corporation, 108
Silicon Graphics Incorporated, 9
Siltronic AG, 90
SL Industries, Inc., 77
Sling Media, Inc., 112
SMART Modular Technologies, Inc., 86
Smiths Industries PLC, 25
Solectron Corporation, 12; 48 (upd.)
Sony Corporation, II; 12 (upd.); 40
  (upd.); 108 (upd.)
Spansion Inc., 80
Spectrum Control, Inc., 67
SPX Corporation, 10; 47 (upd.); 103
  (upd.)
Square D, 90
Sterling Electronics Corp., 18
STMicroelectronics NV, 52
Strix Ltd., 51
Stuart C. Irby Company, 58
Sumitomo Electric Industries, Ltd., II
Sun Microsystems, Inc., 7; 30 (upd.); 91
  (upd.)
Sunbeam-Oster Co., Inc., 9
SunPower Corporation, 91
Suntech Power Holdings Company Ltd.,
  89
Suntron Corporation, 107
SunWize Technologies, Inc., 114
Synaptics Incorporated, 95
Syneron Medical Ltd., 91
SYNNEX Corporation, 73

Synopsys, Inc., 11; 69 (upd.)
Syntax-Brillian Corporation, 102
Sypris Solutions, Inc., 85
SyQuest Technology, Inc., 18
Taiwan Semiconductor Manufacturing
  Company Ltd., 47
Tandy Corporation, II; 12 (upd.)
Tatung Co., 23
TDK Corporation, II; 17 (upd.); 49
  (upd.); 114 (upd.)
TEAC Corporation, 78
Technitrol, Inc., 29
Tech-Sym Corporation, 18
Tektronix, Inc., 8
Teledyne Technologies Inc., 62 (upd.)
Telxon Corporation, 10
Teradyne, Inc., 11; 98 (upd.)
Texas Instruments Inc., II; 11 (upd.); 46
  (upd.)
Thales S.A., 42
Thomas & Betts Corporation, 11; 54
  (upd.); 114 (upd.)
THOMSON multimedia S.A., II; 42
  (upd.)
THQ, Inc., 92 (upd.)
Titan Corporation, The, 36
TiVo Inc., 75
TomTom N.V., 81
Tops Appliance City, Inc., 17
Toromont Industries, Ltd., 21
Trans-Lux Corporation, 51
Trimble Navigation Limited, 40
TriQuint Semiconductor, Inc., 63
TT electronics plc, 111
Tweeter Home Entertainment Group,
  Inc., 30
Ultimate Electronics, Inc., 69 (upd.)
Ultrak Inc., 24
Uniden Corporation, 98
Unisys Corporation, 112 (upd.)
United Microelectronics Corporation, 98
Universal Electronics Inc., 39
Universal Security Instruments, Inc., 96
Varian, Inc., 12; 48 (upd.)
Veeco Instruments Inc., 32
VIASYS Healthcare, Inc., 52
Viasystems Group, Inc., 67
Vicon Industries, Inc., 44
Victor Company of Japan, Limited, II; 26
  (upd.); 83 (upd.)
Vishay Intertechnology, Inc., 21; 80
  (upd.)
Vitesse Semiconductor Corporation, 32
Vitro Corp., 10
Vizio, Inc., 100
VLSI Technology, Inc., 16
Vorwerk & Co. KG, 112 (upd.)
VTech Holdings Ltd., 77
Wells-Gardner Electronics Corporation,
  43
Westinghouse Electric Corporation, II; 12
  (upd.)
Winbond Electronics Corporation, 74
Wincor Nixdorf Holding GmbH, 69
  (upd.)
WuXi AppTec Company Ltd., 103
Wyle Electronics, 14
Xantrex Technology Inc., 97

## Engineering & Management Services

## Entertainment & Leisure

## Financial Services: Banks

## Financial Services: Excluding Banks

## Food Products

## Food Services, Retailers, & Restaurants

## Health Care Services

## Health, Personal & Medical Care Products

## Hotels

## Information Technology

## Insurance

## Legal Services

# Manufacturing

# Nonprofit & Philanthropic Organizations

## Paper & Forestry

## Personal Services

## Petroleum

## Publishing & Printing

## Retail & Wholesale

## Textiles & Apparel

## Tobacco

## Transport Services

## Utilities

## Waste Services

# Geographic Index

## Cayman Islands

## Chile

## China

# Germany

## United States

CompuAdd Computer Corporation, 11
CompuCom Systems, Inc., 10
CompuDyne Corporation, 51
CompUSA, Inc., 10; 35 (upd.)
CompuServe Interactive Services, Inc., 10; 27 (upd.)
Computer Associates International, Inc., 6; 49 (upd.)
Computer Data Systems, Inc., 14
Computer Learning Centers, Inc., 26
Computer Sciences Corporation, 6
Computerland Corp., 13
Computervision Corporation, 10
Compuware Corporation, 10; 30 (upd.); 66 (upd.)
Comsat Corporation, 23
Comshare Inc., 23
Comstock Resources, Inc., 47
Comtech Telecommunications Corp., 75
Comverse Technology, Inc., 15; 43 (upd.)
ConAgra Foods, Inc., II; 12 (upd.); 42 (upd.); 85 (upd.)
Conair Corporation, 17; 69 (upd.)
Concentra Inc., 71
Concepts Direct, Inc., 39
Concord Camera Corporation, 41
Concord EFS, Inc., 52
Concord Fabrics, Inc., 16
Concur Technologies, Inc., 106
Concurrent Computer Corporation, 75
Condé Nast Publications, Inc., 13; 59 (upd.); 109 (upd.)
Cone Mills LLC, 8; 67 (upd.)
Conexant Systems Inc., 36; 106 (upd.)
Confluence Holdings Corporation, 76
Congoleum Corporation, 18; 98 (upd.)
CONMED Corporation, 87
Connecticut Light and Power Co., 13
Connecticut Mutual Life Insurance Company, III
Connell Company, The, 29; 104 (upd.)
Conner Peripherals, Inc., 6
Connetics Corporation, 70
Conn's, Inc., 67
Conn-Selmer, Inc., 55
ConocoPhillips, IV; 16 (upd.); 63 (upd.)
Conrad Industries, Inc., 58
Conseco, Inc., 10; 33 (upd.); 112 (upd.)
Conso International Corporation, 29
CONSOL Energy Inc., 59
Consolidated Delivery & Logistics, Inc., 24
Consolidated Edison, Inc., V; 45 (upd.); 112 (upd.)
Consolidated Freightways Corporation, V; 21 (upd.); 48 (upd.)
Consolidated Graphics, Inc., 70
Consolidated Natural Gas Company, V; 19 (upd.)
Consolidated Papers, Inc., 8; 36 (upd.)
Consolidated Products Inc., 14
Consolidated Rail Corporation, V
Constar International Inc., 64
Constellation Brands, Inc., 68 (upd.)
Consumers Power Co., 14
Consumers Union, 26
Consumers Water Company, 14
Container Store, The, 36

ContiGroup Companies, Inc., 43 (upd.)
Continental Airlines, Inc., I; 21 (upd.); 52 (upd.); 110 (upd.)
Continental Bank Corporation, II
Continental Cablevision, Inc., 7
Continental Can Co., Inc., 15
Continental Corporation, The, III
Continental General Tire Corp., 23
Continental Grain Company, 10; 13 (upd.)
Continental Graphics Corporation, 110
Continental Group Company, I
Continental Medical Systems, Inc., 10
Continental Resources, Inc., 89
Continucare Corporation, 101
Continuum Health Partners, Inc., 60
Control Data Corporation, III
Control Data Systems, Inc., 10
Converse Inc., 9; 31 (upd.)
Con-way Inc., 101
Cook Group Inc., 102
Cooker Restaurant Corporation, 20; 51 (upd.)
CoolSavings, Inc., 77
Cooper Cameron Corporation, 20 (upd.); 58 (upd.)
Cooper Companies, Inc., The, 39
Cooper Industries, Inc., II; 44 (upd.)
Cooper Tire & Rubber Company, 8; 23 (upd.)
Coopers & Lybrand, 9
Copart Inc., 23
Copley Press, Inc., The, 23
Copps Corporation, The, 32
Corbis Corporation, 31
Corcoran Group, Inc., The, 58
Cordis Corporation, 19; 46 (upd.); 112 (upd.)
CoreStates Financial Corp, 17
Corinthian Colleges, Inc., 39; 92 (upd.)
Corky McMillin Companies, The, 98
Cornell Companies, Inc., 112
Corning Inc., III; 44 (upd.); 90 (upd.)
Corporate Executive Board Company, The, 89
Corporate Express, Inc., 22; 47 (upd.)
Corporate Software Inc., 9
Corporation for Public Broadcasting, 14; 89 (upd.)
Correctional Services Corporation, 30
Corrections Corporation of America, 23
Corrpro Companies, Inc., 20
CORT Business Services Corporation, 26
Corus Bankshares, Inc., 75
Cosi, Inc., 53
Cosmair, Inc., 8
Cosmetic Center, Inc., The, 22
Cosmolab Inc., 96
Cost Plus, Inc., 27; 107 (upd.)
CoStar Group, Inc., 73
Costco Wholesale Corporation, V; 43 (upd.); 105 (upd.)
Cost-U-Less, Inc., 51
Cotter & Company, V
Cotton Incorporated, 46
Coty Inc., 36; 115 (upd.)
Coudert Brothers, 30

Council on International Educational Exchange Inc., 81
Country Kitchen International, Inc., 76
Countrywide Financial, 16; 100 (upd.)
County Seat Stores Inc., 9
Courier Corporation, 41
Cousins Properties Incorporated, 65
Covance Inc., 30; 98 (upd.)
Covanta Energy Corporation, 64 (upd.)
Coventry Health Care, Inc., 59
Covington & Burling, 40
Cowen Group, Inc., 92
Cowles Media Company, 23
Cox Enterprises, Inc., IV; 22 (upd.); 67 (upd.)
Cox Radio, Inc., 89
CPAC, Inc., 86
CPC International Inc., II
CPI Aerostructures, Inc., 75
CPI Corp., 38
CPP International, LLC, 103
CR England, Inc., 63
CRA International, Inc., 93
Cracker Barrel Old Country Store, Inc., 10
Craftmade International, Inc., 44
Craig Hospital, 99
craigslist, inc., 89
Crain Communications, Inc., 12; 35 (upd.)
Cramer, Berkowitz & Co., 34
Cramer-Krasselt Company, 104
Crane & Co., Inc., 26; 103 (upd.)
Crane Co., 8; 30 (upd.); 101 (upd.)
Cranium, Inc., 69
Crate and Barrel, 9
Cravath, Swaine & Moore, 43
Crawford & Company, 87
Cray Inc., 75 (upd.)
Cray Research, Inc., III; 16 (upd.)
Crayola LLC, 115 (upd.)
Creative Artists Agency LLC, 38
Credence Systems Corporation, 90
Credit Acceptance Corporation, 18
Cree Inc., 53
Crete Carrier Corporation, 95
Crispin Porter + Bogusky, 83
Crocs, Inc., 80
Crompton Corporation, 9; 36 (upd.)
Croscill, Inc., 42
Crosman Corporation, 62
Cross Country Healthcare, Inc., 105
CROSSMARK 79
Crosstex Energy Inc., 107
Crowley Maritime Corporation, 6; 28 (upd.)
Crowley, Milner & Company, 19
Crown Books Corporation, 21
Crown Central Petroleum Corporation, 7
Crown Crafts, Inc., 16
Crown Equipment Corporation, 15; 93 (upd.)
Crown Holdings, Inc., 83 (upd.)
Crown Media Holdings, Inc., 45
Crown Vantage Inc., 29
Crown, Cork & Seal Company, Inc., I; 13; 32 (upd.)
CRSS Inc., 6